Lecture Notes in Computer Science 8465

Valentina Presutti Claudia d'Amato
Fabien Gandon Mathieu d'Aquin
Steffen Staab Anna Tordai (Eds.)

The Semantic Web: Trends and Challenges

11th International Conference, ESWC 2014
Anissaras, Crete, Greece, May 25-29, 2014
Proceedings

Springer

Volume Editors

Valentina Presutti
Institute of Cognitive Sciences and Technologies, Rome, Italy
E-mail: valentina.presutti@cnr.it

Claudia d'Amato
University of Bari, Italy
E-mail: claudia.damato@uniba.it

Fabien Gandon
University of Nice - Sophia Antipolis, France
E-mail: fabien.gandon@inria.fr

Mathieu d'Aquin
The Open University, Milton Keynes, UK
E-mail: m.daquin@open.ac.uk

Steffen Staab
University of Koblenz-Landau, Koblenz, Germany
E-mail: staab@uni-koblenz.de

Anna Tordai
Elsevier B.V., Amsterdam, The Netherlands
E-mail: atordai@elsevier.com

ISSN 0302-9743 e-ISSN 1611-3349
ISBN 978-3-319-07442-9 e-ISBN 978-3-319-07443-6
DOI 10.1007/978-3-319-07443-6
Springer Cham Heidelberg New York Dordrecht London

Library of Congress Control Number: 2014939148

LNCS Sublibrary: SL 3 – Information Systems and Application, incl. Internet/Web and HCI

Typesetting: Camera-ready by author, data conversion by Scientific Publishing Services, Chennai, India

Printed on acid-free paper

Springer is part of Springer Science+Business Media (www.springer.com)

Preface

The 11th edition of ESWC took place in Crete (Greece), during May 25–29, 2014. Its exciting program included three keynotes by: Steffen Staab (Universität Koblenz-Landau), Luciano Floridi (University of Oxford), and Lise Getoor (University of Maryland).

The main scientific program of the conference comprised 50 papers: 41 research and nine in-use, selected out of 204 submissions, which corresponds to an acceptance rate of 23% for research papers, and of 34.6% for in-use papers. The program was completed by a demonstration and poster session, in which researchers had the chance to present their latest results and advances in the form of live demos. In addition, the conference program included 13 workshops, eight tutorials, as well as a PhD Symposium, the AI Mashup Challenge, the LinkedUp Challenge, the Semantic Web Evaluation Track (featuring three challenges), the EU Project Networking session and a panel on "data protection and security on the Web." The PhD Symposium program included 11 contributions, selected out of 15 submissions.

This year's edition can be described with the following keywords: visionary, advancing, pioneering, trendy.

Visionary, as we had three keynote speakers that brought three very different and inspiring views on the future of the Semantic Web. Steffen Staab, advocating the need for new programming paradigms for dealing with the nature of the Semantic Web; Luciano Floridi, who challenged our community with a vision of a Semantic Web as a means for predicting and manipulating autonomous choices; and Lise Getoor, who showed us how optimization methods can support turning large-scale data into knowledge.

Advancing, as we extended an already excellent scientific program with a new track named "Semantic Web Evaluation" (SemWebEval). The aim of this track is to provide a clear reference to the state of the art on specific Semantic Web tasks, and favor the spreading of proper empirical approaches for their future advancement. SemWebEval features three challenges, each of which rigorously defines a number of Semantic Web tasks and accompanies them with their evaluation datasets and criteria. This year we had a total of ten tasks addressing three main topics: Semantic Publishing, Concept-Level Sentiment Analysis, and Linked Open Data-enabled Recommender Systems. The description of tasks, datasets, and evaluation criteria together with their best results will be published as part of a journal special issue that will follow the publication of these conference proceedings.

Pioneering, as we decided to support workshops that address promising although not yet established topics such as "Semantic Web and Sentiment Analysis" and "Human-Semantic Web Interaction"; as well as emerging topics such as "Finance and Economics on the Semantic Web," and "Semantic Publishing."

We also introduced a unique social identifier for each paper: The reader will notice that each paper in these proceedings includes an official hashtag; it can be used when discussing the paper on social networks and is handy if one wants to retrieve all past and current discussions about it.

Trendy, as we did not overlook to properly address the latest Tim Berners-Lee call for an Internet users' bill of rights. In fact, the ESWC 2014 program included a panel dedicated to "data protection and security on the Web."

As General and Program Committee chairs, we would like to thank everybody that was involved in the organization of ESWC 2014.

First of all, our thanks go to track chairs and all reviewers for their great work, which supported us in building an excellent scientific program. Special thanks go to the PhD symposium chairs, Mathieu d'Aquin and Steffen Staab, who realized an innovative format aimed at ensuring proper mentoring to our promising students. We had a great selection of workshops and tutorials thanks to the excellent work of our workshop chair Harald Sack and our tutorial chair Nathalie Aussenac-Gilles. Thanks to our EU Project Networking session chairs and to our great keynote speakers.

This year we broke the record of poster and demo paper submissions, and we had an extremely high-quality selection of papers (43 demos and 20 posters) thanks to the excellent work of our Poster and Demo Chairs Eva Blomqvist and Raphaël Troncy.

We would like to dedicate a special thanks to Milan Stankovic and all the challenges chairs, who accepted and successfully achieved the organization of the new challenging "Semantic Web Evaluation" track. We were also very happy to host the AI Mashup challenge and the LinkedUp challenge, which contributed to bringing new ideas and exciting application demos.

Thanks to STI International for supporting the conference organization, to Ioan Toma (from STI) for taking care of the budget, and thanks also to our local organizer Irini Fundulaki. YouVivo GmbH deserves a special acknowledgment, in particular Martina Hartl, for the great professional support of the conference organization.

We are very grateful to Silvio Peroni, who spread news about ESWC news timely and effectively, to Serge Tymaniuk, who administered the website, and to our sponsor chairs Axel Ngonga and Achim Rattinger for their precious help in collecting sponsorships for the conference.

We want to point out the remarkable job of the Semantic Technologies coordinators, Luca Costabello, Maribel Acosta Deibe, Anna Lisa Gentile, Alessio Ianbichella, and Andrea Giovanni Nuzzolese, who developed our great "ESWC Conference Live" mobile app.

A special thanks also to our proceedings chair Anna Tordai, who did a remarkable job in preparing this volume with the kind support of Springer.

Last but not least, thanks to all our sponsors listed in the next pages, for their trust in ESWC.

April 2014

Valentina Presutti
Claudia d'Amato
Fabien Gandon

Organization

Organizing Committee

General Chair

Valentina Presutti	STLab ISTC-CNR, Italy

Program Chairs

Fabien Gandon	Wimmics, Inria, I3S, CNRS, University of Nice Sophia Antipolis, France
Claudia d'Amato	University of Bari, Italy

Local Chair

Irini Fundulaki	Institute of Computer Science - FORTH, Greece

Poster and Demo Chairs

Raphaël Troncy	EURECOM, France
Eva Blomqvist	Linköping University, Sweden

Workshop Chair

Harald Sack	Hasso Plattner Institute for IT Systems Engineering, University of Potsdam, Germany

Tutorial Chair

Nathalie Aussenac-Gilles	MELODI, IRIT - CNRS, Université de Toulouse, France

PhD Symposium Chairs

Steffen Staab	Institute for Web Science and Technologies - WeST, Universität Koblenz-Landau, Germany
Mathieu d'Aquin	Knowledge Media Institute, The Open University, UK

Semantic Web Evaluation Challenges Coordinator

Milan Stankovic	Université Paris-Sorbonne, STIH and Sépage, France

Semantic Technologies Coordinators

Andrea Giovanni Nuzzolese	University of Bologna/STLab ISTC-CNR, Italy
Anna Lisa Gentile	University of Sheffield, UK
Maribel Acosta Deibe	Karlsruhe Institute of Technology, Germany
Luca Costabello	Inria, France

EU Project Networking Session Chairs

Mari Carmen Suárez-Figueroa	Universidad Politécnica de Madrid, Spain
Alessio Iabichella	STLab ISTC-CNR, Italy
Sergio Consoli	STLab ISTC-CNR, Italy

Publicity Chair

Silvio Peroni	University of Bologna / STLab ISTC-CNR, Italy

Proceedings Chair

Anna Tordai	Elsevier B.V., Amsterdam, The Netherlands

Sponsorship Chairs

Axel-Cyrille Ngonga Ngomo	University of Leipzig, Germany
Achim Rettinger	Karlsruhe Institute of Technology, Germany

Treasurer

Ioan Toma	STI International, Austria

Local Organization and Conference Administration

Martina Hartl	youvivo GmbH, Germany
Edith Leitner	youvivo GmbH, Germany

Website Administrator

Serge Tymaniuk	STI International, Austria

Program Committee

Program Chairs

Fabien Gandon	Wimmics, Inria, I3S, CNRS, University of Nice Sophia Antipolis, France
Claudia d'Amato	University of Bari, Italy

Track Chairs

Maria Keet	University of KwaZulu-Natal, South Africa
Jérôme Euzenat	Inria and LIG, France
Thomas Lukasiewicz	University of Oxford, UK
Sebastian Rudolph	Technische Universität Dresden, Germany
Laura Hollink	VU University Amsterdam, The Netherlands
Vojtěch Svátek	University of Economics, Prague, Czech Republic
Matthew Rowe	Lancaster University, UK
Maria-Esthel Vidal	Universidad Simón Bolívar, Venezuela
Jacopo Urbani	VU University Amsterdam, The Netherlands
Elena Montiel-Ponsoda	Universidad Politécnica de Madrid, Spain
Diana Maynard	University of Sheffield, UK
Nicola Fanizzi	Università degli studi di Bari Aldo Moro, Italy
Agnieszka Lawrynowicz	Poznan University of Technology, Poland
Payam Barnaghi	CCSR, University of Surrey, UK
Kerry Taylor	CSIRO, Australian National University and University of Melbourne, Australia
Matthias Klusch	German Research Center for Artificial Intelligence, DFKI, Germany
Freddy Lécué	IBM Research, Ireland
Aldo Gangemi	Université Paris 13 - Sorbonne Paris Cité - CNRS, France / ISTC-CNR Rome, Italy
Krzysztof Janowicz	University of California, Santa Barbara, USA
Renato Iannella	Semantic Identity, Australia
Pompeu Casanovas	Universitat Autònoma de Barcelona, Spain
Massimo Romanelli	Attensity Europe GmbH, Germany
Stefan Rüger	Knowledge Media Institute, The Open University, UK
Evelyne Viegas	Microsoft Research, USA
Milan Stankovic	Université Paris-Sorbonne, STIH and Sépage, France
Erik Cambria	National University of Singapore, Singapore
Diego Reforgiato	STLab ISTC-CNR, Italy
Ivan Cantador	Universidad Autónoma de Madrid, Spain
Tommaso Di Noia	Polytechnic University of Bari, Italy
Angelo Di Iorio	University of Bologna, Italy
Christoph Lange	University of Birmingham, UK

Reviewers (All Tracks)

Sven Abels
Benjamin Adams
Eneko Agirre
Guadalupe Aguado-De-Cea

Harith Alani
José Luis Ambite
Sofia Angeletou
Kemafor Anyanwu
Marcelo Arenas
Lora Aroyo
Ioannis N. Athanasiadis
Nathalie Aussenac-Gilles
Jean-François Baget
Claudio Baldassarre
Jie Bao
Pierpaolo Basile
Zohra Bellahsene
Paolo Bellavista
Bettina Berendt
Michael K. Bergman
Elisa Bertino
Isabelle Bichindaritz
Antonis Bikakis
Christian Bizer
Fernando Bobillo
Alexander Boer
Uldis Bojars
Piero Bonatti
Stefano Borgo
Gosse Bouma
Paolo Bouquet
Charalampos Bratsas
John Breslin
Christopher Brewster
Michel Buffa
Christoph Bussler
Elena Cabrio
Jean-Paul Calbimonte
Andrea Cali
Amparo E. Cano
David Carral
Gerard Casamayor
Nuria Casellas
Pierre-Antoine Champin
Jean Charlet
Vinay Chaudhri
Gong Cheng
Philipp Cimiano
Michael Compton
Mariano Consens
Bonaventura Coppola
Olivier Corby
Oscar Corcho
Fabio Gagliardi Cozman
Isabel Cruz
Philippe Cudré-Mauroux
Olivier Curé Carlos Damasio
Danica Damljanovic
Florian Daniel
Jérôme David
John Davies
Brian Davis
Ernesto William De Luca
Stefan Decker
Jaime Delgado
Emanuele Della Valle
Gianluca Demartini
Leon Derczynski
Ian Dickinson
Stefan Dietze
Leigh Dodds
Wlodek Drabent
David Duce
Michel Dumontier
Guillaume Ereteo
Vadim Ermolayev
Sebastian Ewert
James Fan
Catherine Faron Zucker
Miriam Fernandez
Alberto Fernandez Gil
Tim Finin
Sergio Flesca
Kenneth Forbus
Enrico Francesconi
Flavius Frasincar
Fred Freitas
Roberto Garcia
Andrs Garca-Silva
Anna Lisa Gentile
Manolis Gergatsoulis
Chiara Ghidini
Alain Giboin
Claudio Giuliano

François Goasdoué
José Manuel Gómez-Pérez
Jorge González-Conejero
John Goodwin
Guido Governatori
Jorge Gracia
Tom Grahame
Michael Granitzer
Alasdair J.G. Gray
Gregory Grefenstette
Ruediger Grimm
Gunnar Aastrand Grimnes
Paul Groth
Tudor Groza
Michael Gruninger
Gerd Gröner
Giancarlo Guizzardi
Cathal Gurrin
Christophe Guéret
Peter Haase
Harry Halpin
Siegfried Handschuh
Andreas Harth
Olaf Hartig
Oktie Hassanzadeh
Tom Heath
Johannes Heinecke
Sebastian Hellmann
Martin Hepp
Stijn Heymans
Pascal Hitzler
Rinke Hoekstra
Aidan Hogan
Matthew Horridge
Andreas Hotho
Dirk Hovy
Eero Hyvönen
Giovambattista Ianni
Antoine Isaac
Robert Isele
Pramod Jamkhedkar
Anja Jentzsch
Robert Jäschke
Lalana Kagal
Pavan Kapanipathi
Kristian Kersting
Hak Kim
Ross King
Pavel Klinov
Roman Kontchakov
Spyros Kotoulas
Manolis Koubarakis
Udo Kruschwitz
Markus Krötzsch
Birgitta König-Ries
Patrick Lambrix
Ulrich Lampe
Christoph Lange
Arnaud Le Hors
Danh Le Phuoc
Michel Leclère
Jens Lehmann
Domenico Lembo
Wenwen Li
Jean Lieber
Thorsten Liebig
Dong Liu
Yong Liu
Vanessa Lopez
Heiko Ludwig
Joao Magalhaes
Frederick Maier
Ioana Manolescu
Mercedes Martinez-Gonzalez
Wolfgang May
John P. Mccrae
Alexander Mehler
Roger Menday
Pablo Mendes
Peter Mika
Alessandra Mileo
Riichiro Mizoguchi
Dunja Mladenic
Pascal Molli
Alexandre Monnin
Mikolaj Morzy
Ralf Möller
Roberto Navigli
Adeline Nazarenko
Matteo Negri

Axel-Cyrille Ngonga Ngomo
Matthias Nickles
Nadeschda Nikitina
Andriy Nikolov
Malvina Nissim
Andrea Giovanni Nuzzolese
Alessandro Oltramari
Ugo Pagallo
Matteo Palmonari
Jeff Pan
Heiko Paulheim
Terry Payne
Carlos Pedrinaci
Tassilo Pellegrini
Silvio Peroni
Rafael Peñaloza
H. Sofia Pinto
Marta Poblet
Axel Polleres
Guilin Qi
Yuzhong Qu
Jorge-Arnulfo Quiané-Ruiz
Yves Raimond
Dnyanesh Rajpathak
Chantal Reynaud
German Rigau
Giuseppe Rizzo
Vctor Rodríguez Doncel
Riccardo Rosati
Marie-Christine Rousset
Catherine Roussey
Edna Ruckhaus
Carlos Ruiz
Marta Sabou
Harald Sack
Kurt Sandkuhl
Giovanni Sartor
Felix Sasaki
Kai-Uwe Sattler
Uli Sattler
Sebastian Schaffert
Bernhard Schandl
Francois Scharffe
Thomas Scharrenbach
Simon Scheider
Ansgar Scherp
Christoph Schlieder
Stefan Schlobach
Ute Schmid
Thomas Schneider
Stefan Schulte
Frederique Segond
Juan F. Sequeda
Luciano Serafini
Bariş Sertkaya
Amit Sheth
Pavel Shvaiko
Kiril Simov
Elena Simperl
Sergios Soursos
Biplav Srivastava
Steffen Staab
Milan Stankovic
Yannis Stavrakas
Thomas Steiner
Armando Stellato
Giorgos Stoilos
Umberto Straccia
Markus Strohmaier
Heiner Stuckenschmidt
Fabian M. Suchanek
Mari Carmen Suárez-Figueroa
Ondřej Šváb-Zamazal
Marcin Sydow
Jeni Tennison
Matthias Thimm
Andreas Thor
Thanassis Tiropanis
Ioan Toma
Sara Tonelli
Alessandra Toninelli
Farouk Toumani
Thanh Tran
Raphaël Troncy
Anni-Yasmin Turhan
Joerg Unbehauen
Christina Unger
Alejandro A. Vaisman
Herbert Van De Sompel
Willem Robert Van Hage

Frank Van Harmelen
Pierre-Yves Vandenbussche
Joaquin Vanschoren
Daniel Vila-Suero
Serena Villata
Boris Villazon-Terrazas
Johanna Voelker
Piek Vossen
Kewen Wang
Shenghui Wang
Wei Wang
Rigo Wenning
Erik Wilde
Cord Wiljes
Gregory Todd Williams
René Witte
Adam Wyner
Josiane Xavier Parreira
Fouad Zablith
John Zeleznikow
Ziqi Zhang
Jun Zhao
Antoine Zimmermann

Additional Reviewers

Zahid Abul-Basher
Mario Alviano
Pramod Anantharam
Patrick Arnold
Ghislain Auguste Atemezing
Judie Attard
Konstantina Bereta
David Berry
Camila Bezerra
Stefano Bortoli
Alessander Botti Benevides
Martin Brümmer
Janez Brank
Carlos Buil Aranda
Claudio Caletti
Delroy Cameron
Stephane Campinas
Annalina Caputo
Michelle Cheatham
Michel Chein
Jules Chevalier
Anna Corazza
Matthew Damigos
Prajit Das
Maxim Davidovsky
Brian Davis
André de Oliveira Melo
Steven De Rooij
Jeremy Debattista
Auriol Degbelo
Renaud Delbru
Djellel Eddine Difallah
Zlatan Dragisic
Fabien Duchateau
Alistair Duke
Lorena Etcheverry
Javier D. Fernández
Daniel Fleischhacker
Giorgos Flouris
Andre Freitas
Riccardo Frosini
Mouzhi Ge
Leticia Gomez
Thomas Gottron
Anika Groß
Martin Grund
Konrad Höffner
Alice Hermann
Luis Daniel Ibáñez
Armen Inants
Valentina Ivanova
Nophadol Jekjantuk
Amit Joshi
Fabrice Jouanot
Natalya Keberle
Sabrina Kirrane
Bettina Klimek
Matthias Knorr

Magnus Knuth
George Konstantinidis
Dimitris Kontokostas
Seifeddine Kramdi
Adila A. Krisnadhi
Sarasi Lalithsena
Daniel Lamprecht
Chang Liu
Esther Lozano
Andy Luecking
Marco Manna
Flavio Martins
Christian Meilicke
Robert Meusel
Gabriela Montoya
Vinh Nguyen
Christos Nomikos
Blaž Novak
Özgür Lütfü Özçep
Tope Omitola
Filipa Peleja
Giulio Petrucci
Christoph Pinkel
Simone Paolo Ponzetto
Riccardo Porrini
Freddy Priyatna
Roman Prokofyev
Behrang Qasemizadeh
Venkat Raghavan Ganesh
Padmashree Ravindra
Yuan Ren
Laurens Rietveld
Bene Rodriguez-Castro
Anisa Rula
Hassan Saif
Reza Samavi
Brahmananda Sapkota
Victor Saquicela
Bahar Sateli
Luigi Sauro
Christin Seifert
Oshani Seneviratne
Philipp Singer
Hala Skaf-Molli
Panayiotis Smeros
Tadej Štajner
Nadine Steinmetz
Kurt Uwe Stoll
Jeni Tennison
Konstantin Todorov
Alberto Tonon
Jürgen Umbrich
Tim Vor der Brück
Joerg Waitelonis
Simon Walk
Xin Wang
Zhe Wang
Honghan Wu
Marcin Wylot
Roberto Yus
Stamatis Zampetakis
Lei Zhang
Yuting Zhao

PhD Symposium Program Committee

Chairs

Steffen Staab — Institute for Web Science and Technologies - WeST, Universität Koblenz-Landau, Germany
Mathieu d'Aquin — Knowledge Media Institute, The Open University, UK

PhD Symposium Reviewers

Alessandro Adamou
Ehsan Asgarian
Nathalie Aussenac-Gilles
Kai Barkschat
Behshid Behkamal
Rathachai Chawuthai
Pieter Colpaert
Oscar Corcho
Philippe Cudré-Mauroux
Aldo Gangemi
Chiara Ghidini
Rakebul Hasan
Sumera Hayat
Cheikh Kacfah Emani
Robin Keskisärkkä
Ananthi M.
Mohamed Mouhoub
Tamer Omar
Sergio Oramas
Guillermo Palma
Jeff Z. Pan
Dimitris Plexousakis
Sebastian Rudolph
John Samuel
Ansgar Scherp
Stefan Schlobach
Heiner Stuckenschmidt
Vojtěch Svátek
Ricardo Usbeck
Frank van Harmelen

Additional Reviewers

Mauro Dragoni
Giorgos Flouris
Kyriakos Kritikos

Steering Committee

Chair

John Domingue	KMI, The Open University, UK and STI International, Austria

Members

Grigoris Antoniou	Forth, Greece
Lora Aroyo	VU University of Amsterdam, The Netherlands
Phillipp Cimiano	Bielefeld University, Germany
Oscar Corcho	UPM, Spain
Marko Grobelnik	JSI, Slovenia
Eero Hyvönen	Aalto University, Finland
Axel Polleres	Siemens AG, Austria
Elena Simperl	University of Southampton, UK

Sponsoring Institutions

Keynotes

Programming the Semantic Web

Steffen Staab

Institute for Web Science and Technologies,
University of Koblenz-Landau, Germany

Abstract. The Semantic Web changes the way we deal with data, because assumptions about the nature of the data that we deal with differ substantially from the ones in established database approaches. Semantic Web data is (i) provided by different people in an ad-hoc manner, (ii) distributed, (iii) semi-structured, (iv) (more or less) typed, (v) supposed to be used serendipitously. In fact, these are highly relevant assumptions and challenges, since they are frequently encountered in all kind of data-centric challenges also in cases where Semantic Web standards are not in use. However, they are only partially accounted for in existing programming approaches for Semantic Web data including (i) semantic search, (ii) graph programming, and (iii) traditional database programming approaches. The main hypothesis of this talk is that we have not yet developed the right kind of programming paradigms to deal with the proper nature of Semantic Web data, because none of the mentioned approaches fully considers its characteristics. Thus, we want to outline empirical investigations of Semantic Web data and recent developments towards Semantic Web programming that target the reduction of the impedance mismatches between data engineering and programming approaches.

Keywords: #eswc2014Staab.

Coordination, Semantics, and Autonomy

Luciano Floridi

Oxford Internet Institute, University of Oxford, UK

Abstract. The lecture is divided into four parts. In the first part, I offer a brief and simple introduction to four well-known senses in which different scientific fields speak of complexity, namely state complexity, Kolmogorov complexity, computational complexity, and programming complexity. I then suggest an intuitive way in which they can all be linked in a conceptual, unified view. Against this background, in the second part, I outline a new concept of complexity, which I shall call coordination complexity. This completes the unified view. I then argue, in the third part, that the semantic web helps us dealing with problems with increasingly high degree of coordination complexity, which require the mobilisation of whole systems to be tackled. In the last and concluding part, I highlight one of the consequences of the resolution of problems with high degree of coordination complexity: the predictability and manipulability of autonomous choices.

Keywords: #eswc2014Floridi.

Combining Statistics and Semantics to Turn Data into Knowledge

Lise Getoor

University of Maryland, USA

Abstract. Addressing inherent uncertainty and exploiting structure are fundamental to turning data into knowledge. Statistical relational learning (SRL) builds on principles from probability theory and statistics to address uncertainty while incorporating tools from logic to represent structure. In this talk I will overview our recent work on probabilistic soft logic (PSL), a SRL framework for collective, probabilistic reasoning in relational domains. PSL is able to reason holistically about both entity attributes and relationships among the entities, along with ontological constraints. The underlying mathematical framework supports extremely efficient inference. Our recent results show that by building on state-of-the-art optimization methods in a distributed implementation, we can solve large-scale knowledge graph extraction problems with millions of random variables orders of magnitude faster than existing approaches.

Keywords: #eswc2014Getoor.

Machine Learning with Knowledge Graphs

Volker Tresp

Siemens and Ludwig Maximilian University of Munich, Germany

Abstract. Most successful applications of statistical machine learning focus on response learning or signal-reaction learning where an output is produced as a direct response to an input. An important feature is a quick response time, the basis for, e.g., real-time ad-placement on the Web, real-time address reading in postal automation, or a fast reaction to threats for a biological being. One might argue that knowledge about specific world entities and their relationships is necessary if the complexity of an agent's world increases, for example if an agent needs to function in a complex social community. As one is quite aware in the Semantic Web community, a natural representation of knowledge about entities and their relationships is a directed labeled graph where nodes represent entities and where a labeled link stands for a true fact. A number of successful graph-based knowledge representations, such as DBpedia, YAGO, or the Google Knowledge Graph, have recently been developed and are the basis of applications ranging from the support of search to the realization of question answering systems. Statistical machine learning can play an important role in knowledge graphs as well. By exploiting statistical relational patterns one can predict the likelihood of new facts, find entity clusters and determine if two entities refer to the same real world object. Furthermore, one can analyze new entities and map them to existing entities (recognition) and predict likely relations for the new entity. These learning tasks can elegantly be approached by first transforming the knowledge graph into a 3-way tensor where two of the modes represent the entities in the domain and the third mode represents the relation type. Generalization is achieved by tensor factorization using, e.g., the RESCAL approach. A particular feature of RESCAL is that it exhibits collective learning where information can propagate in the knowledge graph to support a learning task. In the presentation the RESCAL approach will be introduced and applications of RESCAL to different learning and decision tasks will be presented.

The presentation builds to a large degree on the dissertation of Maximilian Nickel, now MIT.

Keywords: #eswc2014Tresp.

Table of Contents

Invited Paper

Mobile, Sensor and Semantic Streams

Services, Processes and Cloud Computing

Social Web and Web Science

Data Management

Natural Language Processing

Reasoning

Machine Learning

Linked Open Data

Cognition and Semantic Web

In-Use and Industrial Track

Vocabularies, Schemas, Ontologies

PhD Symposium

Erratum

Programming the Semantic Web

Steffen Staab, Stefan Scheglmann, Martin Leinberger, and Thomas Gottron

Institute for Web Science and Technologies, University of Koblenz-Landau, Germany

Abstract. The Semantic Web changes the way we deal with data, because assumptions about the nature of the data that we deal with differ substantially from the ones in established database approaches. Semantic Web data is (i) provided by different people in an ad-hoc manner, (ii) distributed, (iii) semi-structured, (iv) (more or less) typed, (v) supposed to be used serendipitously. In fact, these are highly relevant assumptions and challenges, since they are frequently encountered in all kind of data-centric challenges also in cases where Semantic Web standards are not in use. However, they are only partially accounted for in existing programming approaches for Semantic Web data including (i) semantic search, (ii) graph programming, and (iii) traditional database programming approaches.

The main hypothesis of this talk is that we have not yet developed the right kind of programming paradigms to deal with the proper nature of Semantic Web data, because none of the mentioned approaches fully considers its characteristics. Thus, we want to outline empirical investigations of Semantic Web data and recent developments towards Semantic Web programming that target the reduction of the impedance mismatches between data engineering and programming approaches.

1 Introduction

The way data is published on the Semantic Web poses a challenge when making use of this data—in particular in the context of programming with Semantic Web data. The flexibility of distributed data providers to freely choose an individual schema layout and to use an appropriate mix of vocabularies causes the nature of the data to be substantially different from data obtained, e.g., from relational databases. For instance, data consumers and programmers do not know apriori how semantic vocabularies are actually used to describe data, which schematic layout underlies the data and where the data resides on the Web. This lack of knowledge affects three levels of interaction with data on the Semantic Web: (1) how programmers *select* the data they are interested in, (2) how they *fetch* and retrieve the data they incorporate in their own programs and (3) which concepts of programming methods they use for an *idiosyncratic programming* with the obtained data.

The *selection* of data is different from classical settings of programming against a known backend data store. Programmers cannot rely on a pre-defined and given schema of the data nor on any global convention of how data is modelled and published. Schematic patterns in the data are rather emerging properties of the Semantic Web. These patterns are a hybrid phenomenon which is caused by recommendations and best practices (e.g. Linked Data guidelines), social processes (e.g. reusing popular

V. Presutti et al. (Eds.): ESWC 2014, LNCS 8465, pp. 1–5, 2014.

vocabularies) and technical factors (e.g. common data conversion tools using similar approaches for representing relational data). Thus, the challenge in selecting the appropriate data pertains to the problem of how to describe the data which is needed in a particular application context.

Fetching data from the Semantic Web is also a non standardised process. A multitude of options is available on the Web, they range from browsing Linked Data over querying SPARQL endpoints to downloading bulk data files, using semantic search engines or even accessing proprietary programmable interfaces. These options do not only affect the way data is requested, but also the granularity, precision and volume of data which is retrieved and needs to be handled and managed.

The question of *idiosyncratic processing* of Semantic Web data is probably the least addressed so far. The issue here is that for selecting and fetching of data, one may consider generic approaches, but for arbitrary processing of data, one needs a paradigm that allows for ideosyncractic code to handle Semantic Web data. And this code should be easy to write, easy to maintain and deal with the characteristics that are common to Semantic Web data described above. For instance, programming Semantic Web data as triples is possible, but it does not ensure *any* consistency with regard to data types by the programming paradigm itself.

In this keynote we postulate, that we will need to challenge existing views of how to program the Semantic Web. Rather than a one-solution-fits all approach, we might actually need to look into a toolbox of methods which fit the programmer's need of how to select, fetch and program with semantic data. We will need to identify patterns of how to combine paradigms from the three levels in a suitable way. To underline our statement we will motivate and explain the challenges on each level, provide an overview of different processes and give examples for generic methods which could be assets in this toolbox and can be combined for supporting programmers in their specific application scenarios.

2 Selecting Data

The challenge in selecting data is twofold. On the one hand, it implies the choice of how to find and address the data. The range of possible choices comprises approaches for finding and selecting data via *structured query languages*, *semantic search* or *browsing* the data graph on the Web. Once the method for finding data has been chosen there is, on the other hand, still a challenge in identifying a suitable, concise and appropriate description. In analogy to the approaches for finding data, the description can be a declarative description, a key word based query or a traversal path in a graph of linked data items.

The choice of the paradigm for finding data might be influenced or even dictated by the use case setting or application requirements. However, the choice of the approach has an impact of how flexible and suitable it is to address certain characteristics of Semantic Web data. This impact is outlined in Table 1. Structured query languages are prone to difficulties in selecting data from distributed data sources. Approaches for query federation require information about the data sources as well as end points capable of answering the structured queries themselves. This does not fit well the ad-hoc manner provision of semi-structured data. Also semantic search has to cope with

Table 1. Approaches for selecting data from the Semantic Web

	Structured Query Languages	Semantic Search	Browsing
(i) ad-hoc manner	(√)	(√)	–
(ii) distributed sources	–	(√)	√
(iii) semi-structured	(√)	√	√
(iv) (more or less) typed	√	√	√
(v) used serendipitously	–	√	√

similar problems. The reason, however, is that semantic search needs to build index structures over semantic web data, which need to be maintained and updated. Finally, identifying a browsing path to a data source is less suitable for the ad-hoc provision of the data as novel data sources might not be well connected and are difficult to come across.

The challenge of finding a suitable, concise and appropriate description is mainly related to structured query languages and semantic search. The reasons for this challenge is that it does not only involve the program's need for data but also the way the data providers have published their data. This means, we need to enable the programmers to create a match between their need and the description of available data. A common approach for enabling this match is to analyze data on the Semantic Web for the purpose of detecting patterns and agreements on how data is modeled and published. One such observable pattern is the schema of Semantic Web data. It is not predefined but emerges on the basis of how data appears on the Web. In this context, we think of schema information in two forms. On the one hand, the schema is given by RDF types associated with the modeled entities. On the other hand, the schema is also described by the properties of entities, i.e. the RDF predicates used to interlink entities. To render an emerging schema into an explicit form, it needs to be induced from the data. Various approaches have been investigated in this direction: statistical schema induction [5], explicit description [1] and structural analysis [4]. Questions such as "Which RDF types are commonly appearing together?", "Which properties are typically used in the context of given types?" and "Which kind of entities can I expect to find when looking at the objects in the range of certain predicates?" can directly be answered on a schema level. Recently, automated methods have been developed to help and support a programmer in this explorative process [2,3].

3 Fetching Data

Ways to handle and manage the data are just as many as to access the data. Approaches range from downloading readily packaged *bulk data* over *querying* an index to *dereferencing URIs* and referring to the data providers for the original data.

A bulk download of data is hardly possible if many distributed data sources are addressed. The problem is that this option might simply not be available. Furthermore, adhoc updates and modifications of the data need to be tracked and might not be reflected

Table 2. Approaches for fetching data from the Semantic Web

	Bulk Download	**Querying**	**Dereferencing**
(i) ad-hoc manner	(√)	(√)	√
(ii) distributed sources	–	–	√
(iii) semi-structured	√	√	√
(iv) (more or less) typed	√	√	√
(v) used serendipitously	√	–	(√)

Table 3. Approaches for programming with data from the Semantic Web

	Graph-Centric	**Triple-Centric**	**Schema-Centric**
(i) ad-hoc manner	√	√	–
(ii) distributed sources	(√)	(√)	–
(iii) semi structured	√	√	–
(iv) (more or less) typed	√	√	–
(v) used serendipitously	√	√	√

in a bulk download. The challenge of federating queries has already been mentioned before and obviously extends also to fetching data from distributed data sources. Moreover, the need to precisely describe the requested data when querying a SPARQL endpoint does not suit the idea of serendipitous use. Finally, also endpoints for querying are not omnipresent in the Semantic Web. Thus, also this option is not available for all data sources. Dereferencing URIs and fetching live data from the Semantic Web, instead, is less susceptible to these problems. Looking up live data from online sources does not pose challenges with outdated information and is by definition capable of dealing with distributed data sources. This mode of fetching data is also entirely independent of the structure or typing of the data. However, the serendipitous use of data is limited as the URIs of data sources need to be known a-priori.

4 Idiosyncratic Programming

While we discussed the selection and fetching of data so far, programming against such data also means to manipulate it. This involves changing of existing properties or even the creation of completely new instances. There are several different approaches to an APIs that allows such a manipulation identifiable. Tables 3 tries to give an overview over these.

Low level RDF APIs mostly use a **graph-centric** or **triple-centric** data access model. In a graph-centric approach, the data is provided as nodes (subjects, objects) and edges (predicates). The slightly more specific triple-centric approach provides the data as subject-predicate-object triples (or n-tuples). Both approaches have the advantage that they can cope with the whole flexibility of the RDF data model, such as semi-structured data the ad-hoc manner. Since they build on the atomic entities of the RDF model, they are also robust against changes in the data as well as source and type independent. Tackling the distribution of data sources needs to be implemented in the according API, but it is generally feasible.

However, for more sophisticated applications it is tenacious to deal with data on such a low level. On top of low-level APIs several object persistence APIs exist. Most of them apply mappings similar to object-relational mappings. Such a **schema-centric** manner allows us to access data on type/entity-level, but the object-triple mapping is dependent on schematic information. Due to its reliance on a schema it is challenging to facilitate the ad-hoc manner, the semi-structuredness and the inconsistent use of types in Linked Data. Also, the handling of distributed data is only possible if a global schema exists.

5 Conclusion

The Semantic Web may change the way we deal with data, but we still don't have an approach that fully considers its characteristics. While there are techniques that deal with the three aspects - selecting, fetching and programming - individually, we haven't yet found a perfect pattern to combine the three. All of the existing approaches fall short in some areas. However, before the Semantic Web can reach its full potential, we need to deal with this impedance mismatch.

Acknowledgements. This work has been supported by Microsoft. The research leading to these results has received funding from the European Community's Seventh Framework Programme (FP7/2007-2013), REVEAL (Grant agree number 610928).

References

1. Alexander, K., Cyganiak, R., Hausenblas, M., Zhao, J.: Describing linked datasets with the void vocabulary, `http://www.w3.org/TR/void/` (last visited August 30, 2011)
2. Gottron, T., Scherp, A., Krayer, B., Peters, A.: LODatio: Using a Schema-Based Index to Support Users in Finding Relevant Sources of Linked Data. In: K-CAP 2013: Proceedings of the Conference on Knowledge Capture, pp. 105–108 (2013)
3. Gottron, T., Scherp, A., Scheglmann, S.: Providing alternative declarative descriptions for entity sets using parallel concept lattices. In: Presutti, V., d'Amato, C., Gandon, F. (eds.) ESWC 2014. LNCS, vol. 8465, pp. 362–376. Springer, Heidelberg (2014)
4. Konrath, M., Gottron, T., Staab, S., Scherp, A.: SchemEX—Efficient Construction of a Data Catalogue by Stream-based Indexing of Linked Data. Web Semantics: Science, Services and Agents on the World Wide Web 16(5), 52–58 (2011)
5. Völker, J., Niepert, M.: Statistical schema induction. In: Antoniou, G., Grobelnik, M., Simperl, E., Parsia, B., Plexousakis, D., De Leenheer, P., Pan, J. (eds.) ESWC 2011, Part I. LNCS, vol. 6643, pp. 124–138. Springer, Heidelberg (2011)

The CLOCK Data-Aware Eviction Approach: Towards Processing Linked Data Streams with Limited Resources*

Shen Gao, Thomas Scharrenbach, and Abraham Bernstein

University of Zurich, Department of Informatics, Zurich, Switzerland
{shengao,scharrenbach,bernstein}@ifi.uzh.ch

Abstract. Processing streams rather than static files of Linked Data has gained increasing importance in the web of data. When processing data-streams system builders are faced with the conundrum of guaranteeing a constant maximum response time with limited resources and, possibly, no prior information on the data arrival frequency. One approach to address this issue is to delete data from a cache during processing – a process we call *eviction*. The goal of this paper is to show that data-driven eviction outperforms today's dominant data-agnostic approaches such as first-in-first-out or random deletion.

Specifically, we first introduce a method called CLOCK that evicts data from a join cache based on the likelihood estimate of contributing to a join in the future. Second, using the well-established SR-Bench benchmark as well as a data set from the IPTV domain, we show that CLOCK outperforms data-agnostic approaches indicating its usefulness for resource-limited linked data stream processing.

Keywords: #eswc2014Gao.

1 Introduction

Streams of Data have become increasingly common in the Web of Data (WoD). Constant streams of weather data, stock ticker information, tweets, bids on an auction site, and TV viewers switching channels are all examples of such streams. When processing such streams, one typically attempts to answer queries or evaluate some functions as data comes along. To that end, SPARQL-like [1] languages such as SPARQLStream [2], C-SPARQL [3], CQELS [4], TEF-SPARQL [5], and EP-SPARQL [6] were proposed to allow joining elements of the stream with each other or some rich background data set.

In contrast to static data processing systems, *stream processing systems need to be reactive*: they must process continuously arriving new data within a given set of Quality of Service (QoS) constraints. Given that latency (or the delay by which newly incoming data impacts results) is usually among these constraints,

* The research leading to these results has received funding from the European Union Seventh Framework Program FP7/2007-2011 under grant agreement No.296126.

V. Presutti et al. (Eds.): ESWC 2014, LNCS 8465, pp. 6–20, 2014.

Little's law [7] 'commands' that we change from all-time semantics to one-time-semantics: data arriving after the accepted latency will not influence an answer produced by the system. Consequently, stream processing systems have to implement measures to cope with situations where the incoming data-rate overwhelms the systems' processing capabilities – a situation we call a *stressed* system. Stress, in turn, occurs either because the constant data rate is overwhelming, hence the environment is *overloaded*, or *bursts* in the data-rate inundates the system.

Current systems typically try to avoid stress by limiting the scope of the query using a time-window – a language feature many systems support to define the *context* of a query. This solution is, however, limited to situations in which the window that is semantically relevant according to the application domain limits the arriving data to volumes that can be handled by the system. Hence, even in the light of query contexts it is easy to imagine a use case with a data rate that will overwhelm the system.

In order to deal with stress, stream processing systems can sample the incoming data, an operation called *load shedding* [8–10]. In this paper, we propose *to delete data from the caches of the operators*, as this operation can exploit the state of the operators in addition to data statistics to reduce stress. We refer to this as *eviction*, as it expels data items from the cache of operators. Both load-shedding and eviction allow maintaining the QoS constraints of a stream processing system in the light of limited resources. They do so at the cost of possibly introducing *errors*: mistakenly evicting data-items from intermediate caches that would lead to results can lower recall and even precision (when using the 'non-open world assumption' operators such as average).

This paper proposes the computationally efficient data-aware eviction strategy CLOCK that evicts data from a join cache based on an estimate of contributing to a join in the future. Specifically, we show that our method outperforms data-agnostic strategies such as random or First-In-First-Out (*FIFO*) using both SRBench, a standard benchmark for evaluating the performance of Linked Data stream processing systems [11], and a real-world IPTV data set. As such, the paper extends a preliminary study that showed that an omniscient eviction strategy (i.e., a strategy that could look into the future) could outperform data-agnostic scheduling strategies [12] and makes it practical due to removal of the reliance on future knowledge.

Consequently, we address the following Research Questions (RQ):

RQ 1: Real-world datasets, such as the ones in our study, can induce stress even when context limitations are present.

RQ 2: Eviction can curb memory consumption at the cost of lower recall.

RQ 3: Our CLOCK data-aware eviction strategy outperforms data-agnostic eviction strategies in terms of recall.

RQ 4: CLOCK outperforms the Least Recently Used (*LRU*) strategy, which are often used in cache management, in terms of recall.

Outline: After a conceptualization of load shedding and eviction for processing streams of data (cf. Section 2), Section 3 presents our CLOCK method, followed by a thorough evaluation of our research questions on two real-world data sets (cf. Section 4). After a discussion of limitations (cf. Section 5) and related work (cf. Section 6) we close with a summary of our findings (cf. Section 7).

2 System Model: A Conceptualization of Load Shedding and Eviction

A data stream processing system can be conceptualized as Processor P that continuously consumes one or more input data streams IS_i and transforms them through a series of operators O into one or more internal flows IF_j, some of which are emitted as output data streams OS_j. Hence, $P = (IS \cup OS \cup IF, O)$ can be seen as a directed graph, where the data flows along directional edges $(IS \cup OS \cup IF)$ that connect the operators $o_i \in O$, which are the nodes. All internal flows $if \in IF$ connect two operators, whilst the input streams IS_i and output streams OS_j are only connected to one operator.

In the context of the WoD the input streams IS_i typically consist of sequentially arriving data tuples of the format $< s, p, o > [t_{start}, t_{end}]$, where $< s, p, o >$ is a triple representing a fact and t_{start} / t_{end} denotes the start/end time of the triple's validity. Alternatively, when $t_{start} = t_{end}$ (i.e., the triple describes an event at time t rather than a fact) the incoming tuples can be abbreviated as $< s, p, o > t$ or, when only relative temporal order is implied by arrival time, t can be dropped. The output streams OS_j contain a continuous sequence of tuples either in the same format as the ones in the input stream or denoting bindings to a query. Note that all our considerations do not take the format of the input and output into account. Hence, our findings generalize to all stream processing systems.

System Stress. This conceptualization indicates that a system can be stressed either by overwhelming the load on the operators or by inundating the bandwidth and latency constraints on the edges. This paper will focus uniquely on the former problem: It will assume that the bandwidth/latency constraints of the edges are adequate for tasks at hand. Note that operators can be overwhelemed either by time complexity (e.g., an operator that computes the factorial of large numbers) or by space complexity (e.g., a join that has to maintain a cache).

A context can curtail stress, as it allows the system ignoring nonsensical data-items and concentrating on data relevant for answering a query. A context is defined for an operator and defines which data is valid for evaluating the operator. One oftentimes used context is a time-window. Consider we want to count the audience for a certain TV channel based on a stream of events indicating which viewer switches to what TV channel. We need to know the set of data items the count is based on, i.e., the context of the operation. Prudent choices are, for example, time-based windows such as the last second (referring to the current TV ratings) or the past hour (referring to past ratings). For a detailed overview over windows and operators, we refer to [13].

Dealing with Stress. We know of two approaches for dealing with stress: load shedding and eviction.

In *load shedding* the stream processing system samples the input streams and only considers part of the data. Formally, it is a sample operation $s : IS_i \mapsto \widehat{IS_i}$, where $\widehat{IS_i} \subset IS_i$. Figure 1 illustrates this for a join between stream IS_x and stream IS_y. Here stream IS_x sheds its data item x^5 at $t = 3$ by deleting it from the considered input stream. Load shedding strategies range from deleting data at random (e.g., useful for dealing with high-frequency sensor reporting averages per time unit), via a scheduling strategy such as *FIFO*, to estimating statistics of which data to delete and which not [8–10].

In *eviction* the stream processing system removes data from the internal memory of the operators to preserve computational resources. Formally, eviction is the extension of the operators $o_i \in O$ with one or more eviction strategies $es : memory \mapsto \overline{memory}$, where $\overline{memory} \subset memory$. Figure 1 illustrates two eviction strategies: First, it 'garbage collects' items that exit the context windows win_{now} of streams IS_x and IS_y. At time $t = 2$ for both streams these are all data items, which we observed at $t = 1$, i.e., x^2 and y^2. Second, *due to the limited size of its join cache*, it decides to remove data item y^3 of stream IS_y. Note that this second strategy removes a data item which we observed at $t = 3$, i.e., a data item which would be still valid with respect to the context of stream IS_y.

This paper focuses on the impact of eviction strategies on the potential error in the resulting data. Specifically, the next section will introduce two traditional, data-agnostic evictions strategies (e.g., random eviction and *FIFO*), one

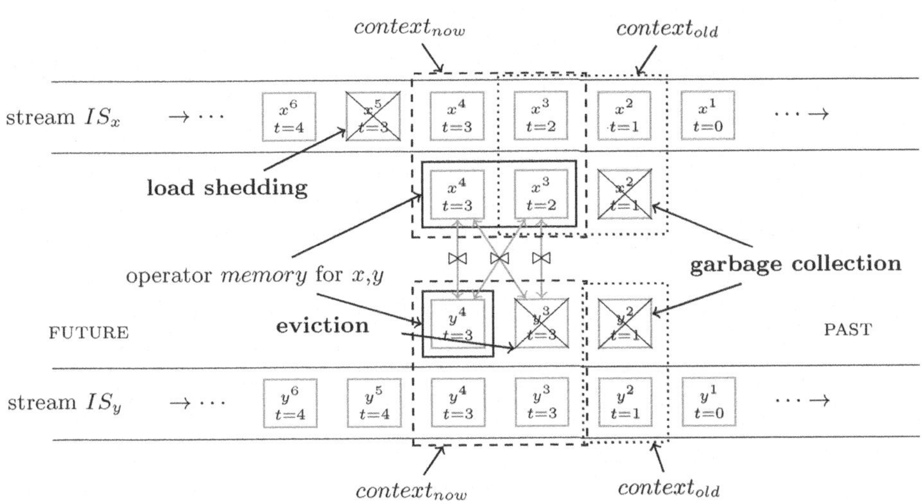

Fig. 1. Depiction of stress handling approaches in a join of two input streams. Load shedding on input stream IS_y, garbage collection on both join caches, and other (unspecified) eviction on join cache of stream IS_x. Context is shown as windows (dashed: now, dotted: past) and cache memory sizes are two items for the upper and one item for the lower stream.

based on the nature of the data (e.g., garbage collection) as well as our own CLOCK strategy, which relies on the likelihood of future joins.

3 Eviction Strategies

Eviction removes items from the internal memory (or cache) of an operator to save space. Most WoD stream processing systems extend the SPARQL algebra in order to allow evaluation of SPARQL operators on streams. As a consequence, the operators' caches typically hold candidate variable bindings. Hence, the role of the eviction strategy is to choose variable bindings to delete from the cache.

Formally, an operator's cache (or short cache) C_{op} with *limit* M and *size* N is a finite set of variable bindings $\mu_1, \ldots, \mu_N$, where $N \leq M$. We say there exists an overflow for C, if and only if $N > M$, i.e. in case the number of items in the cache exceeds the cache's limit. An eviction strategy es removes data items from a cache C such that $C' = es(C, M)$ is a cache of limit M and $|C'| \leq M$, i.e. it has no overflow. In the sequel we define different eviction strategies.

Note that in this study we consider eviction for caches of two-way-joins, i.e., joins with two join partners sharing one common join variable. We discuss possibilities for extensions to other operators in Section 5.

3.1 Baseline Eviction Strategies

In this section we succinctly introduce the four baseline or traditional eviction strategies: random, *FIFO*, *LRU*, and garbage collection.

Random eviction deletes variable bindings from a cache according to a uniform distribution $U(0, N)$ over all cache entries. To deal with cache overflow, it requires to compute $O(N - M)$ random indices to delete from the cache.

First-In-First-Out (FIFO) maintains a queue of items, where the head of the queue is deleted whenever an overflow occurs. It requires $O(N - M)$ calls to the queue. Together with random eviction *FIFO* has been adopted by today's conventional systems [10].

Least-Recently-Used (LRU), a strategy widely adopted in cache management including the SASE+ stream management system [14], extends *FIFO* by moving items to the back of the deletion queue whenever they are accessed. As with *FIFO*, handling an overflow requires $O(N - M)$ operations on the *LRU* queue.

Garbage Collection removes irrelevant data items from the operator cache. Relevancy may be determined via the context of a query. When processing TV viewership data, e.g., current viewers of a program are determined by joining the most recent program changes and user channel switches. Older channel switches by a user can, therefore, safely be garbage collected, as they are irrelevant to the query. Pure garbage collection is an incomplete eviction strategy, as it may not be able to remove enough items from the cache, when the context is not sufficiently restrictive.

Following the example of Section 2, random eviction would delete user sessions at random while *FIFO* would delete the oldest sessions – both while the session would be still valid. In a data agnostic way they 'blindly' follow their eviction strategies independent of possible future results. Garbage collection would delete all invalid sessions. It relies on data context but ignores the performance of the item in contributing to the operation. As a metric of past performance *LRU* deletes valid sessions with no recent activity. It favors temporal recency but ignores the magnitude of a binding's past performance. In the next subsection we introduce our CLOCK approach that estimates the future likelihood of usefulness based on past performance. It extends *LRU* by considering both recency and magnitude of usefulness.

3.2 The Clock Strategy

CLOCK is a data-aware eviction strategy that considers both recency and magnitude of past usefulness of a binding to estimate the likelihood of future usefulness, which it employs as a criteria for eviction. CLOCK associates each binding with a score. Whenever an item is matched, it increases that score. When it looks for items to evict, it first depreciates the bindings' scores, and then evicts those with lower scores. Thus, the score combines a measure of recency with a measure of magnitude.

Specifically, CLOCK maintains a circular buffer cache of M slots containing the bindings μ with their associated scores w_μ and a pointer to a position p in the circle.[1] When a new data item arrives, it gets assigned an initial score $w_\mu = w^0$. If there are empty slots, it is added to one. Else the pointer depreciates the score of the item at position p using the depreciation function *dep*(). If the item's new score is lower than some threshold τ, then it gets evicted and the newly arrived binding takes its place. Otherwise, the pointer moves to the next position and repeats this procedure. Whenever a binding contributes to a join, its score gets increased by one (i.e., $w_\mu := w_\mu + 1$).

Following the example of Section 2, CLOCK increases the count whenever we observe a session activity, i.e. a user switches channels. At each point in time we decrease the count whenever we observed no activity.

Practically, we propose two different depreciation functions. The linear depreciation function $dep_{lin}(w) = w - 1$ just decreases the value of a score by one. It is associated with the threshold $\tau = 0$. Alternatively, we can depreciate exponentially with a depreciation rate ρ resulting in $dep_{exp}(w) = w * \rho$ $(0 < \rho \leq 1)$. In this case w_μ will never reach 0. Hence, we picked $\tau = 0.01$ as a threshold. We call this extended version CLOCK$_{exp}$.

In its baseline description without any extensions, CLOCK may have to circle around the cache a number of times before finding a suitable candidate for eviction. With an extension containing the currently smallest score in the cache CLOCK needs at most $O(M)$ (limit of the cache) depreciation steps to find a

[1] Using a circular cache allows us to efficiently find eviction candidates by circular iterations over the buffer.

victim for eviction. CLOCK also requires a constant amount of additional memory (in particular M) for storing the scores w_μ of the bindings.

Observations: First, as mentioned, CLOCK can be seen as an extension of *LRU* that considers both temporal recency and past join history. The weight between these two factors can by set by adjusting ρ.

Second, the initial score w^0 reflects the degree to which we give a binding μ an initial chance to find a join partner. It should be sufficiently high, such that it has a chance to survive initially. It should be sufficiently low to ensure the timely eviction of less useful bindings. In CLOCK$_{exp}$ it determines together with ρ how dynamic the eviction strategy is.

Third, CLOCK could be easily extended to multi-way joins by using different-sized increments for partial vs. full join results.

Fourth, the CLOCK eviction strategy is founded on the following assumptions: in burst streams, eviction only takes place eventually. As a result, cache entries for which we observed no join partners could remain in the cache for a long time until eviction takes place. In an overloaded environment, there is only little chance that such items stay in the cache for long periods.

4 Evaluation

This paper argues that real-world and, hence, resource-limited WoD stream processing systems will be subject to stress even when using a use-case motivated context to limit the data that needs to be taken into consideration. To deal with stress it proposes to employ eviction – an approach that removes data from the caches of the operators of the stream processor. Specifically, it suggests to employ a data-aware eviction strategy over (more traditional) data-agnostic eviction strategies and introduces the CLOCK approach that is based on a likelihood estimate of future usefulness of an item.

To support this argumentation this section will provide empirical evidence for the research questions (RQ) we defined in Section 1:

RQ 1: Real-world datasets, such as the ones in our study, can induce stress even when context limitations are present.
RQ 2: Eviction can curb memory consumption at the cost of lower recall.
RQ 3: Our CLOCK data-aware eviction strategy outperforms data-agnostic eviction strategies in terms of recall.
RQ 4: CLOCK outperforms the Least Recently Used (*LRU*) strategy, which are often used in cache management, in terms of recall.

As a consequence, this section will first lay out the experimental setup (Section 4.1) and then proceed to discuss each of these research questions in turn. We first show that our data sets can be used to evaluate RQ2 and RQ3 (Section 4.2). We then evaluate these with two different experiments: first, we show the general performance of CLOCK versus other strategies (Section 4.3), then we show that we can optimize CLOCK with regards to learning its parameters (Section 4.4).

4.1 Evaluation Setup

To evaluate our research questions we built a *stream processing simulator* that allows to precisely measure, curb, and manipulate the memory consumption of the involved operators via pluggable load shedding and eviction strategies. Whilst the system does correctly identify the bindings, we call the system a simulator rather than a full-fledged stream processing systems as it was built for experimentation rather than efficient processing and lacks elements such as a query parser/optimizer.

Given our research questions, the *Key Performance Indicator (KPI) of our evaluation is recall*, which is defined as the ratio between the number of results with a given cache size to that with unlimited cache size. We disregarded the time complexity of the eviction strategy as we found that all the strategies were faster than 40 ms ($\mu = 9.45ms, var = 15.03ms$) per data item – a performance we deem sufficient for most applications.

To ensure realistic data we employ *two real-world data sets*: SRBench and ViSTA-TV. *SRBench* [11] is a well-established benchmark for assessing the semantic streaming processing engines. It comprises the LinkedSensorData, GeoNames and DBpedia.[2] Our test query focuses on the wind speed data set, because it is reported by most of the sensor stations. To simplify our experiments, we pre-processed the SRBench dataset and extracted all of the 603'642 windspeed data entries, where each triple has the format: $< sensorID, \mathsf{reports}, windSpeed >$ $time$. Since the queries of *SRBench* were designed to benchmark the functionality of different engines, we designed a new query focused on establishing the performance of eviction strategies. The query (cf. Listing 1), defined using the TEF-SPARQL [5] semantics, aims to find sensors with similar wind speeds using a self-join on the *windSpeed* entry – an operation, where recall depends greatly on the size of join-cache employed.

```
SELECT ?sensor1, ?sensor2 FROM STREAM windSpeed
WHERE {
      ?sensor1  reports  ?windSpeed ?T1 .
      ?sensor2  reports  ?windSpeed ?T2 .
      FILTER (?sensor1 != ?sensor2) .
      FILTER(?windSpeed >= 10^^xsd:int) .
}
CONTEXT((?T1 - ?T2) <= 200^^xsd:millisecond) .
```

Listing 1. A self-join query inspired by SRBench

ViSTA-TV[3] is a FP7 financed EU project that investigates the real-time processing of TV viewership information. The data set we employed for evaluation contains anonymous IPTV viewership logs (Log) in the format $< userID$, $\mathsf{watches}, channelID > [t_{start_{viewer}}, t_{end_{viewer}}]$ and Electronic Program Guide

[2] http://wiki.knoesis.org/index.php/LinkedSensorData, http://geonames.org, http://dbpedia.org

[3] http://vista-tv.eu/

(EPG) data $< channelID$, plays, $programID > [t_{start_{EPG}}, t_{end_{EPG}}]$. Each data entry is annotated by a starting time stamp and an ending time stamp. A data entry is consider to be expired when the system time has passed its ending time. We used three-day's Log and EPG data, which contains 1'887'256 viewership events and 31'960 EPG entries. As defined in TEF-SPARQL [5], the query (cf. Listing 2) is a two-way join operation, which represents the use case to find all users that are currently watching a specific TV-program. To ensure that all caches were in steady state, first one third amount of data in each data set are used to 'warm up' the system and the rest are reported here.

All experiments were conducted on a MacBookPro with a 2.7 GHz Intel Core i7, 16GB of RAM, and 256 GB of SSD disk space running Mac OX 10.9.1.

```
SLECT ?user, ?program FROM STREAM Log, EPG
WHERE{
      ?userID      watches ?channelID   ?Tstart_viewer ?Tend_viewer .
      ?channelID plays     ?programID   ?Tstart_EPG    ?Tend_EPG .
}
CONTEXT((!?Tend_viewer < ?Tstart_EPG) && (!?Tend_EPG < ?Tstart_viewer)).
```

Listing 2. ViSTA-TV query

4.2 RQ1: Real-World Systems Are Subject to Stress

To elucidate if real-world systems are likely to be subject to stress, we graphed the cache sizes necessary to fully answer our queries for the two data sets. In other words, we assumed a system without any memory limitations and elaborated how much memory (i.e., number of triples inside cache) it needed to provide correct answers (i.e., 100% precision and recall) to our queries. Figure 2a/2b graphs 8 minutes/72 hours worth of data measured every 10 seconds/1 hour for SRBench/ViSTA-TV.

We can observe significant fluctuations in the memory size needed irrespective of the context limitations provided by the queries (e.g., the limitation on a $200ms$

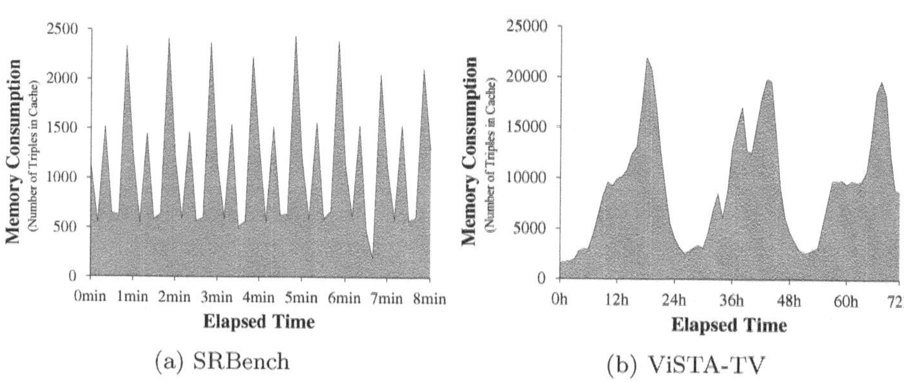

Fig. 2. Fluctuations in memory consumption per time unit

window in the SRBench case). In SRBench, this is because some sensors cluster their reporting. In ViSTA-TV, the start/end times of major shows may lead to fluctuations in load.

Whilst these findings do not provide proof that systems will undergo stress conditions, they strongly indicate that real-world systems are subject to massive changes in load (hence stress). Consequently, we can argue that for any real-world system there would be a real-world data set that would overwhelm the available resources either by overloading or by burst. This, in turn, would argue for systems that are resilient against stress supporting the premise of this paper and answering *RQ1*.

4.3 RQ2-4 Eviction Results: Memory Consumption and Recall

The fact that eviction can curb memory consumption is almost self-evident. Obviously, randomly deleting data items whenever a cache-size limit is met will curb cache size. The more interesting question is what the cost of the memory limitations would be in terms of recall for a given eviction strategy.

We measured the recall gained with different cache sizes for four eviction strategies: Random, *FIFO*, *LRU*, as well as CLOCK using the linear depreciation function $dep_{lin}()$ with $\tau = 0$. Note that we did not include our prior approach [12], as it can only be used offline due to its reliance on the whole dataset; including items not yet encountered in the stream.

The results are reported in Figures 3a and 3b. All strategies were combined with garbage collection to give them the advantage of logically evicting data items that would not be used anymore.[4] We can make the following observations:

First, all strategies perform similarly with large cache sizes: systems with sufficient memory are unlikely to be stressed. Hence, eviction does not impact recall significantly.

Second, with decreasing cache size, the data-aware strategies strongly outperform Random and *FIFO* by up to 78% and 81% in ViSTA-TV and 12 and 50 times in SRBench. These results show that a *stressed* system with limited memory resources dramatically benefit from data-aware eviction strategies.

Refinement under Stress. To further highlight these results, Figures 4a and 4b plot the performance results under *stressed* conditions. Hence, recalls are computed only during the number of data items per second surpassed the respective average input rate of SRBench and ViSTA-TV. The results further reinforce the above findings: CLOCK outperforms the traditionally employed *LRU* by up to 147% for SRbench and 162% for ViSTA-TV.

These results provide evidence to answer *RQ2*, *RQ3*, and *RQ4*. We can clearly conclude that for the given data sets data-aware methods outperform data-agnostic methods in the light of resource constraint. Further, we established that our CLOCK strategy outperforms the traditional *LRU* approach. What remains open is how robust CLOCK is towards varying depreciation functions.

[4] Note that we cannot measure garbage collection alone, as it does not guarantee limited cache size usage.

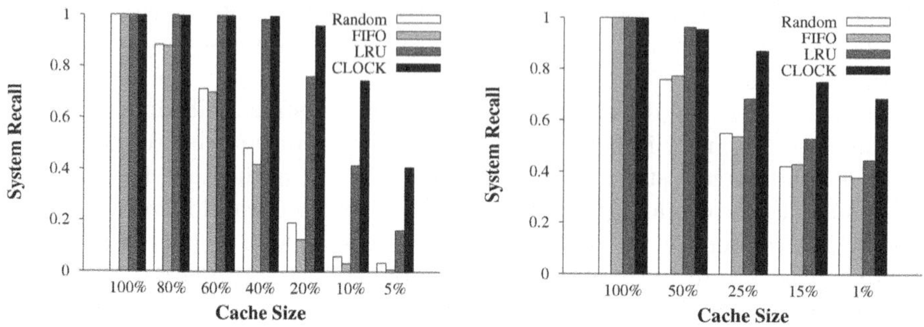

(a) SR-Bench (b) ViSTA-TV

Fig. 3. System recall with varying cache size

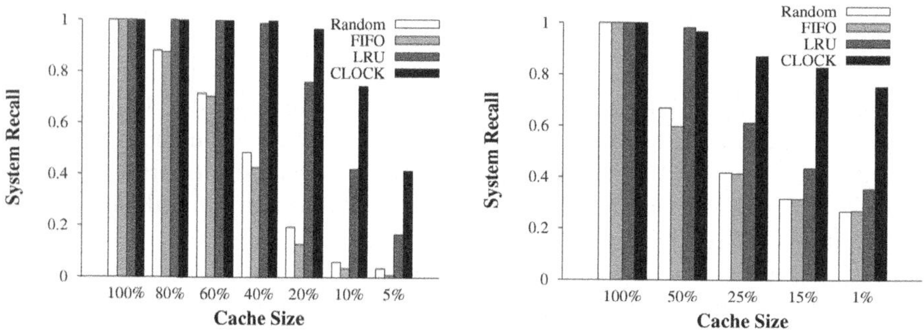

(a) SR-Bench (b) ViSTA-TV

Fig. 4. Results of a *stressed* system

Specifically, how does CLOCK compare to CLOCK_{exp} with different depreciation weights ρ that we discussed in Section 3.2 – a topic we will investigate in the next subsection.

4.4 Tuning Clock via Varying Depreciation Weights ρ

Different data sets may exhibit varying degrees of 'decay' in the applicability of their data items. We, hence, investigated if CLOCK could be better tuned to a data set using the depreciation functions *dep*. Specifically, we ran both CLOCK and CLOCK_{exp} on our two data sets. For CLOCK_{exp} we varied ρ between the following values: $\rho \in \{0.95, 0.57, 0.5.0.25\}$.

Figure 5 shows heat-maps depicting the recall for both SRBench (on the left) and ViSTA-TV (on the right). The heat-maps clearly show that the depreciation rate ρ has a profound influence in recall. For example, in SRBench, the best performance is obtained when $\rho = 0.95$. In the ViSTA-TV data set, $\rho = 0.5$ seems to provide the best performance for smaller cache sizes. Hence, in the ViSTA-TV data set it appears to better emphasize more on recent items and depreciate results faster than in SRBench. Consequently, CLOCK can be tuned according

	SRBench					ViSTA-TV			
	60%	*40%*	*20%*	*10%*	*5%*	*50%*	*25%*	*15%*	*1%*
LRU	0.972	0.919	0.786	0.571	0.266	0.964	0.635	0.529	0.446
CLOCK_exp 0.25	0.991	0.966	0.875	0.654	0.291	0.964	0.865	0.740	0.526
CLOCK_exp 0.5	0.998	0.989	0.936	0.770	0.413	0.932	0.818	0.762	0.683
CLOCK_exp 0.75	0.999	0.997	0.965	0.852	0.545	0.965	0.789	0.753	0.683
CLOCK_exp 0.95	0.999	0.998	0.979	0.896	0.650	0.961	0.761	0.694	0.622
CLOCK	0.997	0.992	0.967	0.875	0.567	0.956	0.799	0.751	0.685

Fig. 5. Parameter tuning for CLOCK and CLOCK_{exp} (with $\rho \in \{0.95, 0.57, 0.5.0.25\}$) on SRBench and ViSTA-TV

to the idiosyncrasies of a data set by choosing an appropriate depreciation rate. We hope to investigate automated tuning in the future.

5 Limitations

First, our current evaluation is limited to one operator: the join. We believe that focusing on joins for a first study made sense, as it is both the most used operator and one of the most intricate. As mentioned in Section 3, our CLOCK method could be easily extended to multi-way joins. Projections can be supported without any cache. Aggregation functions have constant memory implementations or approximations requiring investigations similar to ours. Filters are interesting, as their implementation will greatly depend on the definition of context.

Second, not neglecting the importance of throughput and latency, we deliberately focused on the very KPI that eviction will impact negatively, i.e. , recall. Other metrics will be evaluated when we implement CLOCK in real stream processing systems. Despite this limitation we believe that CLOCK's performance regarding throughput is comparable with other methods, given its low computational overhead (cf. Section 3).

A disadvantage of CLOCK is that it has to invest additional memory for storing the scores w_μ. With the same amount of memory, methods like *FIFO* and *LRU* may, hence, cache more bindings than CLOCK. However, this overhead could be minimized by implementing the score as a bitmap. Moreover, as CLOCK only needs to adjust the score for each binding, its implementation is orthogonal to other internal memory structures (e.g., a B-tree) and will not impose extra overhead on them. A next study will have to investigate the trade-off between using some memory for eviction-bookkeeping and using it only for storing bindings.

Last but not least, we will need to consider additional datasets. Whilst the two data sets considered come from two vastly different real-world applications we believe that many more data characteristics. The compilation of more good data sets for WoD stream processing seems to be a challenge for the whole community.

6 Related Work

We discuss related work in the followings. We will first introduce different Semantic Flow Processing (SEP) systems and then discuss query processing in memory-constrained environments. Finally, we review related load shedding strategies for data stream processing.

Semantic Flow Processing Systems. C-SPARQL [3] performs query matching on subsets of the information flow, which are defined by windows. The decidability of SPARQL query processing on such windows of RDF triples causes the number of variable bindings produced to be finite. However, the size of variable bindings may still become prohibitively large, e.g., when using non-shrinking semantics for aggregates [15]. For a cache of a given window size, our eviction strategies could be directly applied.

EP-SPARQL [6] and TEF-SPARQL [5] are both complex event processing systems for semantic data flows. EP-SPARQL extends the ETALIS system with a flow-ready extension of SPARQL. TEF-SPARQL distinguishes between *Events* that happen at a specific time point and *Facts* that remain valid until some events alter them. Both systems incorporate a garbage collection facility that can "prune outdated events". Since garbage collection is orthogonal to our strategies (cf Section 4.3), our findings are directly applicable to these systems.

CQELS [4] "implements the required query operators natively to avoid the overhead and limitations of closed system regimes". It optimizes the execution by dynamically re-ordering operators because "the earlier we prune the triples that will not make it to the final output, the better, since operators will then process fewer triples". This pruning does, however, not make any guarantees about the number of variable bindings created by the processors. Our methods should be directly applicable to CQELS as it provides a native implementation of the operators which contain lists of active variable bindings.

Query Processing in Memory-Constrained Environments. In memory-constrained environments various techniques have been proposed to reduce the memory footprint of query planners and the number of intermediate results.

Targeting SPARQL queries Stocker et al.[16] investigated the selectivity estimates to optimize query execution. To efficiently generate alternative query plans, [17] proposed a branch-and-bound to enumerate join plans for left-deep processing trees. This method requires less memory as it prunes the search space during enumeration. Our eviction strategies are designed for caches and assume a given query execution plan.

Regarding multiple aggregate queries over stream data Naindu et al. [18] proposed a new hash model for estimating the cost for intermediate aggregates. This method groups common attributes of related queries and reduces overall memory usage. Based on this new model, they also proposed a greedy heuristic to generate the execution plan. Our eviction strategies are designed for general semantic streaming systems that perform not only aggregate query, but also other kinds of queries.

In a XML processing system the memory consumption for XML processing can greatly exceed the actual file size. Therefore, an entire XML document may not fit into main memory. In [19] the authors proposed a method that analyses XQuery to identify and extract only useful attributes form XML documents during compilation to reduce the file size. Our eviction strategies deal with semantic data, where it is straightforward to identify useful attributes from input stream. Meanwhile our strategies are also applicable to projected variable bindings.

Load Shedding. Load shedding has been applied to information flow processing. Approaches like [8–10] perform load shedding by dropping tuples from the stream, i.e., dropping data instead of variable bindings.

In [10] the authors proposed to insert a "drop operator" into the query execution plan, which automatically decides where, when and how to perform load shedding. Regarding how to perform load shedding they proposed a random method as a baseline and a "semantic method" which decides whether to retain a data entry based on estimating its impact on QoS. In addition to their approach, our strategies also take into account the time a data entry has resided in memory. Similar to [10], [9] also proposed a special operator that decides where and when to drop unprocessed data by using statistical methods. However, [9] only focuses on aggregate queries.

SASE+ [14] employs an automata-based matching approach. Similar to our case of caching variable bindings, SASE+ stores automata states. The authors do apply some eviction strategy. However, their strategy is based on a deterministic approach that is similar to *FIFO* and *LRU* in our baseline approaches.

Finally, Das et al. [8] propose a simple equi-join on two incoming streams and to evict tuples that are unlikely to find a join partner. However, this method works only with a sliding window and with a single equi-join of two streams. Our approaches could be applied on caches for any kind of join.

7 Conclusion and Outlook

In this paper, we presented our data-aware eviction strategy Clock, which addresses stress in WoD stream processing systems. We found that stress in terms of overloading and bursts occurred in our two real-world datasets. In addition, Clock and its variant Clock_{exp} outperform the often-used *LRU* strategy by factors between 1.5 and almost 3 and *FIFO* strategy by even higher factors.

The next step in our investigation will be to implement these strategies in a real stream processing system to study the trade-off between recall and other KPIs such as latency and throughput with different data sets. Whilst our work is only a first step in investigating resource-limited stream processing, we believe it pursues an important direction that sets the expectation for the real-world usage of such systems.

Acknowledgments. We would like to thank Khoa Nguyen for all his earlier work on this topic and Daniel Spicar for his constructive advice.

References

1. Harris, S., Seaborne, A.: SPARQL 1.1 Query Language. Technical report, The World Wide Web Consortium (W3C) (2011)

2. Calbimonte, J.-P., Corcho, O., Gray, A.J.G.: Enabling ontology-based access to streaming data sources. In: Patel-Schneider, P.F., Pan, Y., Hitzler, P., Mika, P., Zhang, L., Pan, J.Z., Horrocks, I., Glimm, B. (eds.) ISWC 2010, Part I. LNCS, vol. 6496, pp. 96–111. Springer, Heidelberg (2010)
3. Barbieri, D.F., Braga, D., Ceri, S., Della Valle, E., Grossniklaus, M.: C-SPARQL: A Continuous Query Language for RDF Data Streams. International Journal of Semantic Computing (1), 3–25 (2010)
4. Le-Phuoc, D., Dao-Tran, M., Xavier Parreira, J., Hauswirth, M.: A Native and Adaptive Approach for Unified Processing of Linked Streams and Linked Data. In: Aroyo, L., Welty, C., Alani, H., Taylor, J., Bernstein, A., Kagal, L., Noy, N., Blomqvist, E. (eds.) ISWC 2011, Part I. LNCS, vol. 7031, pp. 370–388. Springer, Heidelberg (2011)
5. Kietz, J.U., Scharrenbach, T., Fischer, L., Bernstein, A., Nguyen, K.: TEF-SPARQL: The DDIS query-language for time annotated event and fact Triple-Streams. Technical report, University of Zurich, Department of Informatics (2013)
6. Anicic, D., Fodor, P., Rudolph, S., Stojanovic, N.: EP-SPARQL: a unified language for event processing and stream reasoning. In: Proc. WWW, pp. 635–644 (2011)
7. Little, J.D.C.: A proof for the queuing formula: L= λ w. Operations Research 9(3), 383–387 (1961)
8. Das, A., Gehrke, J., Riedewald, M.: Approximate join processing over data streams. In: Proc. SIGMOD, New York, USA, pp. 40–51 (2003)
9. Babcock, B., Datar, M., Motwani, R.: Load shedding for aggregation queries over data streams. In: Proc. ICDE, pp. 350–361 (2004)
10. Tatbul, N., Çetintemel, U., Zdonik, S., Cherniack, M., Stonebraker, M.: Load Shedding in a Data Stream Manager. In: 29th International Conference VLDB, pp. 309–320 (2003)
11. Zhang, Y., Duc, P.M., Corcho, O., Calbimonte, J.-P.: SRBench: A Streaming RDF/SPARQL Benchmark. In: Cudré-Mauroux, P., Heflin, J., Sirin, E., Tudorache, T., Euzenat, J., Hauswirth, M., Parreira, J.X., Hendler, J., Schreiber, G., Bernstein, A., Blomqvist, E. (eds.) ISWC 2012, Part I. LNCS, vol. 7649, pp. 641–657. Springer, Heidelberg (2012)
12. Nguyen, K., Scharrenbach, T., Bernstein, A.: Eviction Strategies for Semantic Flow Processing Systems. In: Proc. SSWS (2013)
13. Cugola, G., Margara, A.: Processing flows of information. ACM Computing Surveys 44(3), 1–62 (2012)
14. Diao, Y., Immerman, N., Gyllstrom, D.: Sase+: An agile language for kleene closure over event streams. Technical report, University of Massachusetts Amherst, Department of Computer Science (2008)
15. Barbieri, D.F., Braga, D., Ceri, S., Della Valle, E., Grossniklaus, M.: Incremental reasoning on streams and rich background knowledge. In: Aroyo, L., Antoniou, G., Hyvönen, E., ten Teije, A., Stuckenschmidt, H., Cabral, L., Tudorache, T. (eds.) ESWC 2010, Part I. LNCS, vol. 6088, pp. 1–15. Springer, Heidelberg (2010)
16. Stocker, M., Seaborne, A., Bernstein, A., Kiefer, C., Reynolds, D.: Sparql basic graph pattern optimization using selectivity estimation. In: Proc. WWW, pp. 595–604 (2008)
17. Bowman, I., Paulley, G.: Join enumeration in a memory-constrained environment. In: Proc. ICDE, pp. 645–654 (2000)
18. Naidu, K., Rastogi, R., Satkin, S., Srinivasan, A.: Memory-constrained aggregate computation over data streams. In: Proc. ICDE, pp. 852–863 (2011)
19. Marian, A., Siméon, J.: Projecting XML documents. In: Proc. VLDB, pp. 213–224 (2003)

Plan-Based Semantic Enrichment of Event Streams

Kia Teymourian and Adrian Paschke

Freie Universität Berlin, Institute for Computer Science, AG Corporate Semantic Web
Berlin, Germany
{kia,paschke}@inf.fu-berlin.de

Abstract. Background knowledge about the application domain can be used in event processing in order to improve processing quality. The idea of semantic enrichment is to incorporate background knowledge into events, thereby generating enriched events which, in the next processing step, can be better understood by event processing engines. In this paper, we present an efficient technique for event stream enrichment by planning multi-step event enrichment and processing. Our optimization goal is to minimize event enrichment costs while meeting application-specific service expectations. The event enrichment is optimized to avoid unnecessary event stream enrichment without missing any complex events of interest. Our experimental results shows that by using this approach it is possible to reduce the knowledge acquisition costs.[1]

Keywords: #eswc2014Teymourian.

1 Motivation

The fusion of background knowledge with data from an event stream can help the event processing engines to know more about incoming events and their relationships to other related resources. The usage of background knowledge in event processing requires reasoning on domain knowledge in order to be able to detect complex events based on the domain background information.

Typically there is a trade-off between the high expressiveness of the used background knowledge, which leads to higher levels of computational complexity, and the efficiency and scalability needed in real-time event processing. In this paper, we address the problem of a hybrid approach - expressive reasoning on external background knowledge for usage in high-performance real-time event processing. We propose an approach for knowledge-based event processing using semantic enrichment of event streams (section 2). The main optimization goal of our approach is the detection of events based on reasoning on huge amounts of domain background knowledge. We present a method for planning the event enrichment process[2] in order to optimize the load on the external knowledge base for knowledge acquisition (section 3).

We describe our approach in the context of the use case scenario of a high level stock market monitoring system. In today's world economy, companies are highly interconnected and depending on each other. They require, for example, raw materials,

[1] This work has been partially supported by the "InnoProfile-Transfer Corporate Smart Content" project funded by the German Federal Ministry of Education and Research (BMBF) and the BMBF Innovation Initiative for the New German Länder-Entrepreneurial Regions.

[2] See [7] for an overview on different event processing functions.

V. Presutti et al. (Eds.): ESWC 2014, LNCS 8465, pp. 21–35, 2014.

share distribution channels and markets, have affiliations or simply reside in the same areas. Such information yields a valuable source for knowledge-based complex event processing and can be leveraged in order to empower event processing with semantic technologies in order to grasp underlying relationships and utilize them in the course of the event processing.

Let's consider the case that a company X produces products and requires the raw materials which are procured by another company Y. The company Y is on the other hand financed by company Z. The relation between these companies defines the complex event pattern which can only be extracted from the background knowledge. An example of a pattern for complex events is the case that three stock ticks, respectively the associated companies, exhibit a specific relation in the background knowledge, and the relation spans a connection between some resources in the background knowledge. The complex event can be specified based on the company business relations and the event correlations of the stock market events. Another example of a pattern for complex events is the case that a market broker might define a detection pattern like: *select stocks when the stock price of the three companies decrease in sequence within 10 min where the first company demands for its products special computer chips and the second company produces these chips using raw materials which is supplied by the third company.* For this kind of event detection, it is required to have background knowledge about the application domain while monitoring the real-time event stream and integrating the knowledge to the real-time data stream.

2 Semantic Enrichment of Event Streams

Previously, we have proposed a new approach for semantic enabled complex event processing (SCEP) [11,12]. We proposed that the usage of background knowledge about events and other related concepts can improve the quality of event processing. We proposed to use an external *Knowledge Base (KB)* which provides background knowledge (conceptual and assertional, T-Box and A-Box of an ontology) about the events and other non-event resources. We also include a DL-reasoner on the top of the external knowledge base so that we can reason on the externally stored knowledge.

Our event model is adopted from the event models in the state of the art event processing approaches like DistCED [8]. *An Event is a tuple of* $\langle \bar{a}, t_s, t_e \rangle$ *where* $\bar{a}$ *is a multiset of fields* $\bar{a} = (a_1, ..., a_n)$*, and is defined by the schema* $\mathbb{S}$. The t 's are temporal values representing the different happening times of the event, the start t_s and end timestamps t_e of the event (timestamps can also be defined as a sequence of timestamps). For example an event in stock market applications has the fields *(name, price, volume, timestamps)*, e.g., *(IBM, 80, 2400, 10:15, 10:15)*, where the start and end time of this event are the same, because it is an instantaneous event. An *Event* can also be considered as a set of attribute values $\langle \bar{av}, t_s, t_e \rangle$ where $\bar{av}$ is a multiset of attribute value tuples $\bar{av} = ((a_1, v_1), \ldots, (a_n, v_n))$. For the above example we have:
(((name,IBM), (price,80), (volume,2400)) , 10:15, 10:15)

We assume that one or more attributes of events are in relation to resources in the KB (such as individuals, concepts, roles and sentences). It is possible to ask the KB and retrieve background knowledge about the attributes of events. For example the stock market symbol is linked to the company resource in the background knowledge so that knowledge about the company can be extracted.

An event detection query is a declarative rule which defines a detection pattern for complex events and can include one or more sets of triple patterns (SPARQL basic triple patterns BGPs) to query external KBs. With the term *sQuery*, we refer to the whole event detection rule which includes sets of triple patterns and is combined with event algebra operations. We define the operational semantics for the four main event detection operations, SEQ, AND, OR and NOT from the window w (a time or count window) as follows:

$$\mathsf{SEQ}(e_1,e_2)[w] = \forall(t_s^1,t_s^2)(e_1(\bar{t^1}) \wedge e_2(\bar{t^2}) \wedge t_s^1 \leq t_s^2 \wedge (e_1,e_2) \in w)$$
$$\mathsf{AND}(e_1,e_2)[w] = \forall(t_s^1,t_s^2)(e_1(\bar{t^1}) \wedge e_2(\bar{t^2}) \wedge (e_1,e_2) \in w)$$
$$\mathsf{OR}(e_1,e_2)[w] = \forall(t_s^1,t_s^2)((e_1(\bar{t^1}) \vee e_2(\bar{t^2})) \wedge (e_1,e_2) \in w)$$
$$\mathsf{NOT}(e_1)[w] = e_1(\bar{t^1}) \notin w$$

A possible approach for the processing of events based on background knowledge is to enrich the event stream prior to the complex event detection with new derived event attributes. The Semantic Enrichment of Event Streams (SEES) is the enrichment of events with background information about them and about other possibly related concepts from the knowledge base.

The process of semantic enrichment of an event stream is illustrated in Fig. 1. A knowledge base is used by Event Mapping Agents (EMAs) to generate derived events by performing reasoning and interacting with the knowledge base. The EMAs can be replicated and deployed in parallel to achieve efficient scalability with respect to throughput. In the next step, the enriched event stream is monitored by several Event Processing Agents (EPAs). The EPAs process the enriched event stream in order to detect complex events matching the event query. The main disadvantage of semantic enrichment of events is the huge amounts of derived event data which is produced by each incoming event that needs to be processed by the final EPA to match complex queries. The raw event stream is enriched by one or many EMAs resulting in an enriched outbound event stream which is processed by a set of EPAs in order to detect complex events which can require derived events for being triggered.

An example of a complex event pattern is visualized in Fig. 2. A pattern is defined over three event instances. The query given at the top defines a connecting path between the nodes associated with the event instances e_1, e_2, and e_3. The order of occurrence of the three arbitrary event instances e_1, e_2, and e_3 is defined using the event algebra operators SEQ and AND. Thus, the sequence of e_1 followed by e_2 and e_3 is matched in case the resources referenced by e_1, e_2, and e_3 can be connected by a path corresponding to the triple statements from the query. The event detection pattern is a combination of event algebra operators for the specification of temporal relations of events and basic triple patterns for the specification of a knowledge pattern.

A specific type of event detection queries is, if it specifies a complex event containing only one single event. We call it *star-shaped event pattern*, because of the form of attributes (triple pattern predicates) around a single event instance. This kind of event pattern detects only one single event instance from an event stream.

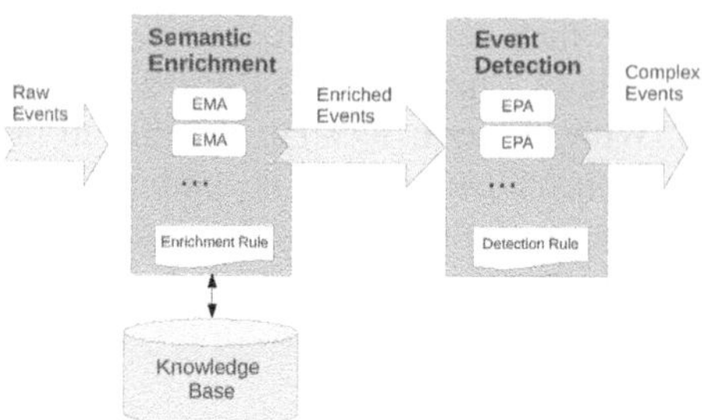

Fig. 1. Semantic Enrichment of Event Stream (SEES)

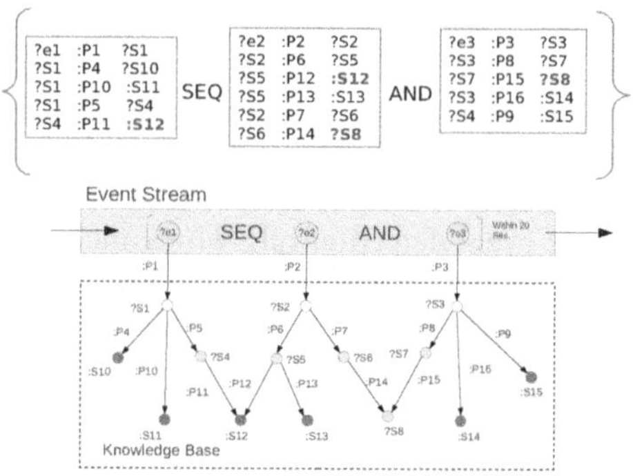

Fig. 2. Relations between Events

3 Plan-Based Semantic Enrichment

The process of semantic enrichment can be optimized to reduce the cost of event enrichment and increase the throughput of event processing by reducing the amount of raw event enrichment tasks. We propose an approach for optimization of knowledge-based event detection by using a technique for multi-step and greedy knowledge acquisition and event detection. In our approach, we define several steps for sequential enrichment and event detection. In each step the events are enriched with knowledge. The event detection engine can filter out some of the raw events based on the enriched knowledge so that only the relevant raw events are forwarded to the next step. By using this approach we can avoid the unnecessary full enrichment of all raw event instances.

The trade-off between knowledge acquisition costs (computation load on external KB and result transmission) and event processing latency are important factors for planning the execution of event enrichment and detection. Our aim is to discover a low-cost event detection plan while we meet the user-specified latency expectations so that we can reduce the polling load on the external knowledge base. One of the important constrains for generating plans is the user-specified latency expectation. We are looking for a plan which can meet this expectation and causes an acceptable load on the triplestore side.

The user query can be preprocessed and separated into several subqueries. We generate a plan for stepwise processing of the generated subqueries so that we can pre-filter the raw event stream to reduce the cost of event enrichment. In each step, we check only a part of the user query. If any of the subqueries cannot be matched, the whole query is not matched and the EPA sends the event to the event sink.

The input for the optimization problem are the user query *sQuery*, the raw event stream (including event types) and some heuristics about the external KB. We are looking for an optimized execution plan of the user query with acceptable latency and costs (computation, materialization and network transmission costs).

The user-given query *sQuery* includes a graph G_{user} (the given triple pattern combined with event algebra operations) which can be pre-processed and rewritten to several subgraphs G_{SUBs} so that we have $G_{user} = \{G_{SUB1} \cup \ldots \cup G_{SUBn}\}$. The G_{user} is matched if and only if all of its subgraphs G_{SUBs} are matched.

The first step of our approach is to split the G_{user} into several main subgraphs G_{Events} based on nodes which represent the raw events and are separated by the event algebra operations (e.g., AND, SEQ). For each event we have a tree structured graph (a cycle-free directed graph) which has one of the raw events as its root. We also mark the nodes which are in the intersection of G_{Events}.

In the second step, we divide the G_{Events} based on its tree structure. By starting from its roots (the events) we traverse the tree to its leafs and divide the tree to its branches so that we generate several sub-graphs G_{SUBs}. A sub-graph is generated for each path branch from the root to one of the leafs. For each raw event type we also generate all of the joint possibilities of subgraphs (based on the event operator). At the end of this step we have a multi-set of graphs MS_{GSUBs}.

For example for event pattern e_1 shown in Fig. 2, we will generate the subgraph set like { {(?e1, :p1, ?s1)}, {(?s1, :p4, :s10)}, {(?e1,:p1,?s1), (?s1, :p10, :s11)}, {(?e1, :p5, ?s4), (?s4,:p11,:s12)}, {(?e2, :p2, ?s2), (?s2, :p6, ?s5), (?s5, :p12, :s12)}, {(?e2, :p2, ?s2), (?s2 , :p7, ?s6), (?s6, :p14, ?s8)}, ... }.

We expand the subgraphs to their semantically similar patterns. For example, if the leaf nodes of subgraphs are bounded resources, we check them against the knowledge in KB to find if they are connected to other resources through the *sameAS* predicate (The *sameAS* predicate gives two resources exact the same semantic meaning). If we can find new resources through the *sameAS* predicate, we generate a new sub-graph G_{SUB} with the new resource and add it to the multi source. We also follow up the type hierarchy of resources (e.g., rdf:type) and add new upper resources in the type hierarchy. We also check the properties of the graph, whether we can find any subProperties of them, and add the new graphs to the multi-set. In this way, it is possible to take the semantics of resources (and their relations) into account for the calculation of sub-graphs.

Planning of Event Processing in Multi-Steps: In each processing step the required knowledge for one of the attributes is enriched to the raw event stream. If an event instance can be matched to one of the attributes it is forwarded to the following step, until all of the attributes can be matched.

For the planning of subqueries, we need to estimate the matching probability of subgraphs. We expect that queries with a high number of results are more likely to be matched. We assume that we can have some statistics about the external knowledge bases, so that we can estimate the enrichment cost based on the collected heuristic data about external KBs. We consider the following statistics about the KB: the total number of existing triples in the KB for each of the predicates (N_p) and the total number of triples stored in the KB ($N_{Triples}$) are known . These statistics are used to optimize the search process for an acceptable plan because the search space is exponential to the number of subgraphs and number of processing steps.

Furthermore, we do the following assumptions: all of the subgraphs with only a single triple pattern have a bounded predicate and all of the other subgraphs have at least one triple pattern with a bounded predicate. Any updates on the knowledge base can only minimally change the above statistics about the KB, and the statistics can be recalculated in the future time-intervals.

We expect that queries with a high number of results are more selective (materialization costs) and cause high load. For the subqueries with two or more triple patterns, the computation of joins will cause more computation load than the subgraphs with a single triple pattern.

The calculation of the reasoning costs on the KB is highly complex and depends on the complexity of the reasoning algorithm and the reasoning rules. As we need only an estimation of the costs for each subgraph, we define an estimation factor for each of the predicates. Based on the reasoning rules, each of the predicates can activate a different set of rules which will cause different computation costs. For example, based on the reasoning level, and complexity of the used rules the predicates like *"rdf:type"* or *"owl:sameAs"* can activate different reasoning rules than the other predicates like *"owl:intersectionOf"*. We call this factor the reasoning factor $F_{reasoning}$ and assume that we can define for each of the predicates a reasoning factor, a number between 0 and 1. For example, the predicates like *"rdf:type"* or *"owl:sameAs"* have the highest factors. We assume that we can define this factor manually, by looking at the chains in the reasoning rules. We consider the reasoning factor for object properties that are not explicitly defined in the reasoning rules as zero and the data predicates have also a reasoning factor of zero. The *estimated matching probability factor of predicates* F_p^{EM} is calculated by the following function: $F_p^{EM} = 2/(F_{reasoning} * N_p/(N_{Triples} - N_P) + N_p/N_{Triples})$

Filter Functionality Estimation of Subgraphs: In the multi-step SCEP the throughput of an event stream in each step is highly depending on the rate of events matched in the previous step. Subgraphs with less results are good filters for event detection, because they are less likely to be matched. In the case that they are used at the beginning of multi-step event enrichment and detection, the rate of the events in the following step can be highly reduced. A *filter functionality factor* is introduced for each of the subgraphs. This factor is calculated based on the *estimated matching probability factor of the predicate* (F_p^{EM}) and the graph structure properties of the user query. The subgraph marks a specific part of the graph pattern of a user query which can have different properties, e.g., if the subgraph is positioned in the leaf of a tree structure, or if it is in the intersection of subgraphs (see Figure 2). The intersection nodes are nodes on the graph where event operations divide the graph. We define two factors for the graph properties of the subgraph, F_{Leaf} is 2 if final leaf of G_{SUB} is bounded and 1 if not. F_{Inter} is 2 if G_{SUB} includes intersection nodes and 1 if not.

Sometimes in a user query a subgraph is repeated in several places on the graph pattern. In this case this subgraph might have a better filtering functionality for the event detection than the other subgraphs. We consider this effect with the factor for repetition of subgraphs: $F_{Repetition} = N_{Repetition}/N_{total}$

$N_{repetition}$ is the repetition count number of the G_{SUB} in the multi-set MS_{GSUBs} (how many times a subgraphs appears in the whole graph pattern).

We estimate the cost of different subgraphs included in the query based on some heuristics of the stored data on KB (like shown example data in Table 1) so that we can compare the subgraphs and organize the sequence order of processing in multi-step SCEP. Based on the estimated cost we can calculate the saving cost by changing the order of subgraphs. The filter functionality of each subgraphs is calculated by the following equation: $F_{Filter} = (F_{Leaf} * F_{Inter} * F_{Repetition} * max(F_p^{EM}))/AvgNumberOfResults$

One of the heuristics about the used predicates in BGPs is how many answer triples have the triple pattern in average ($AvgNumberOfResults$), e.g., a triple with *dbpedia-owl:location* has how many triple results in average.

Transmission Cost: If the query to the external KB has several results, the EMA can retrieve them and transmit them to the enrichment base node. In the case that the user query includes BGPs with RDF data properties, the result of such triple pattern has only one single literal as result. If the BGP includes an object property it can have several result resources as results (URIs). For our cost estimation we can count the number of result items (resources or literals).

Based on the order of subgraphs in an execution plan and number of processing steps, different latencies and loads can be generated. The total load of a plan is estimated with the total number of queries sent to the external KB, and the total number of transmitted results within a time window (for a user query).

Algorithm 1. Algorithm for Selecting of Execution Plan for Subgraphs

```
Data: MS_GSUBs a multiset of subgraphs
Data: latency_expected user specified latency expectation
Result: plan: an execution Plan for enrichment and detection
FirstStepGraphs = selectFirstStepGraphs(MS_GSUBs);
SelectedGraph = getFirstElement(sort(FirstStepGraphs,F_Filter));
while hasNextPlan do
    NextStepGraph = MS_GSUBs \ SelectedGraph;
    plan = (SelectedGraph,NextStepGraph);
    (latency_current, load_current) = execute(plan,Time_t);
    if (latency_current ≤ latency_expected ∧ load_current ≥ load_previous) then
        SelectedGraph = getFirstElement(sort(NextStepGraph,F_Filter));
        MS_GSUBs = MS_GSUBs \ (SelectedGraph ∪ FollowingStep);
        Add a new processing step, if all plans for the number of steps are searched ;
        load_previous = load_current;
    else
        return PLAN;
    end
end
```

Our approach for searching an acceptable plan is presented in Algorithm 1. We sort the list of subgraphs based on their estimated filter functionality factor F_{Filter}. For the generation of an execution plan, we use this list as initial execution plan. Our algorithm is a greedy algorithm which starts with an initial plan. To avoid the exponential search effort for testing the costs of all possible plans, we start with an estimated plan (a plan that might have an acceptable cost and latency) and then run several iterations with other plans which might improve the latency and load, until we find an acceptable plan for the user query.

Our algorithm starts by using a two-step processing plan. If the average latency is acceptable and the subgraph set has more elements, then a new processing step is added.

This process is continued until the latency of the overall system is greater than the user expected latency.

We monitor the latency and the total result transmission for a time period, if the requirements can not be satisfied, then we change the execution plan until we have one of the acceptable plans. If the latency is under the threshold of the user expectation, we change the plan to check if we can reduce the caused load on the external KB. In the case that the load is acceptable for the external KB, we can accept the current plan as our execution plan.

4 Evaluation

We have implemented a prototype of our multi-step approach and its algorithms in Java. We use the OpenRDF framework[3] to process the triple patterns and send them as SPARQL queries to an external triplestore. For the event detection steps, we used the Esper[4] event processing engine. In our experiments, we forwarded the output stream of event enrichment to the event detection step so that they can build up the multi-step processing steps. To cleanly separate the impact of our approach from the underlying implementation and configuration choices, we compared the evaluation metrics with each other on the same implementation setup and used abstract performance metrics. We compared different transmission costs of different approaches on the same implementation and data setups. To separate the impact of specific data on our experimental results, we executed the experiments on different event streams, knowledge bases and queries.

For our experiments we needed two kind of test datasets; the event data stream (dynamic data part) and the background knowledge base. We used in our experiments both synthetic and real-world data sets.

Event Stream Dataset: We have used an event stream which simulates the event stream of a stock market exchange. We use a list of 500 companies (S&P500), each event is the price change of a company in stock market. The event stream is generated by randomly selecting one of the companies in the list and sending the event object to the stream. Each event instance includes a string for stock symbol, a string for stock name, an integer for stock latest price, an integer for stock last volume and a string for the link URL (the URL links the event instances to the relevant resources in the KB, e.g. a stock event to the appropriate company). We use the synthetically generated stream to be able to conduct performance and cost experiments.

Background Knowledge Dataset: As background knowledge we have used a complete mirror of DBpedia (version 3.4). Each of the event instances includes a URL which maps to a DBpedia resource. By using this link, the SCEP system can extract background knowledge. To each event instance a payload is added which is a key-value set of the enriched attributes and the extracted value for the attribute.

---

[3] OpenRDF `http://www.openrdf.org/`

[4] `http://esper.codehaus.org`, version 4.6.0

Experiment Setup: As our evaluation metrics do not depend on the run-time environment, the hardware setup[5] and configurations used in the experimentation do not impact our evaluation results, due to the reason that we compare the different approaches to each other. However, we mention some of the results of event processing in some of the experiments, like the performance of the event processing or the latency of detection complex events.

4.1 Evaluation of Multi-Step Processing

We conducted several experiments with different types of event detection queries to investigate the effect of multi-step event enrichment and detection. The main effects that we investigated are the overall performance, the detection delay time (the total transit time of events identified as complex event) and the overall load on the external knowledge base (number of queries to the KB, number of transmitted results).

Star-Shaped Event Patterns: One of the pattern types used for event enrichment and detection is the simple star-shaped event patterns. We conducted several experiments and changed the number of BGPs in the event enrichment queries and measured the average processing performance, the latencies of detection of complex events and the transmission costs. Our experiments have been done on queries which include 2 up to 7 BGPs. The number of BGPs specified also the number of processing steps, i.e., a query with 3 BGPs is processed in maximal 3 steps. A complete list of our queries is listed on this URL.[6] The SPARQL queries which we used in our experiments on star-shaped patterns are sQ2 to sQ7 for event enrichment (including 2 to 7 BGPs) and the Esper queries eQs2 to eQs7 for event detection. Table 1 shows the relevant statistics about the predicates. The column *"Result"* is the average number of results for a BGP with this predicate.

Table 1. Distribution of RDF Predicates used in our Queries in DBpedia Dataset

No.	Predicate	Numbers	% of KB	Results
1	*dbpedia-owl:location*	219880	0.076%	2
2	*dbpedia-owl:industry*	31047	0.011%	2
3	*dbpedia-owl:numberOfEmployees*	12425	0.004%	1
4	*dbpprop:products*	11899	0.004%	2
5	*dbpedia-owl:subsidiary*	2663	0.001%	1
6	*rdf:type*	11085199	3.849%	3
7	*dcterms:subject*	13606126	4.724%	4
Others Predicates		263044482		
No. Triples in the KB		288013721		

[5] In our experiments we use one single instance of the Virtuoso triple store, version 06.01.3127. It is installed on a host (Intel Xeon CPU E31245 @ 3.30GHz) with 8 GB RAM and Ubuntu Linux 12.04. The event mapping agents and the event processing agents (EPAs) are installed on a separated host (i7-2600 CPU @ 3.40GHz) with 16 GB RAM. Each of the processing agents are different java threads on the same host.

[6] List of our queries `http://download.teymourian.de/scep-queries.html`

The comparison of processing performance of single-step processing with two-step and multi-step approaches for different star-shaped patterns are presented in Fig. 3. We conducted different experiments with queries including 2 BGPs up to 7 BGPs. In single-step processing we enriched each event instance with the results of the complete query, i.e., sending the query as a whole to the KB and enrich the results to the event stream. In two-step processing we used the first BGP (with predicate *dbpedia-owl:location*) for the first processing step and the rest of query in the following second step, e.g., for a query with 7 BGPs, 1 BGP in first step and 6 in the following step. In multi-step processing, we extended the processing steps to the number of existing BGPs in the user query, i.e., for a query with 7 BGPs we have 7 processing steps. The performance of the single-step processing approach is continuously reduced with the number of BGPs as illustrated in Fig. 3. We observed that the performance of two step processing and multi-step processing are very close to each other and they significantly differ from the performance of single step processing.

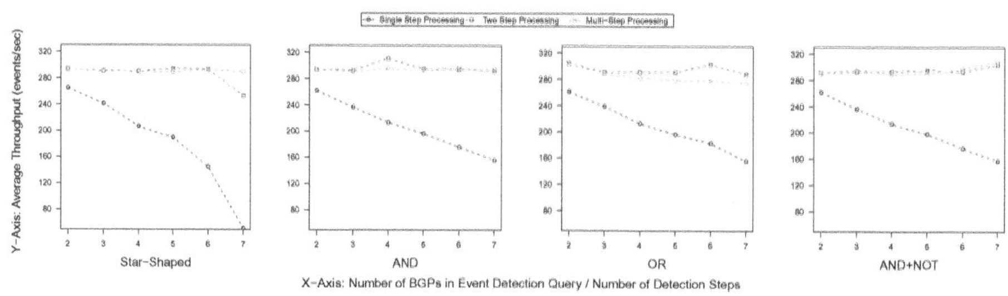

Fig. 3. Performance Comparison of Multi-Step Processing

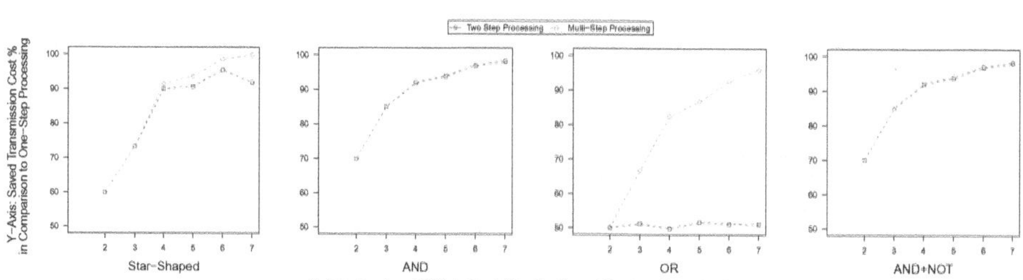

Fig. 4. Saved Transmission Costs in Comparison to Single-Step Processing

We sent 50000 raw events (50k events) through the system and counted the total number of transmitted results (No. of transmitted RDF resource or literals) from the knowledge bases to the event detection point. The saved transmission cost in comparison to the single-step processing is shown in Fig. 4. As it is shown, we can significantly save costs if we do two-step or multi-step processing. For a query with two BGPs we can save up to 60% of transmission costs and for a query with 6 or 7 BGPs up to 90% of costs. One interesting observation is that the difference of transmission cost saving between two-step processing and multi-step processing (in our case up to 7-steps) are

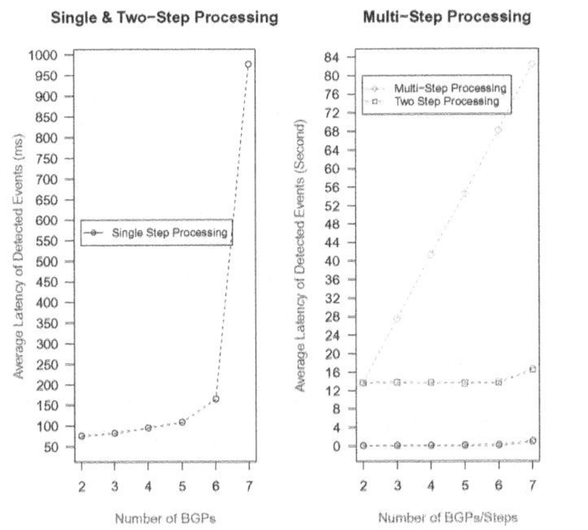

Fig. 5. Average Latency of Detected Complex Events in Multi-Step Processing (Star-Shaped Query)

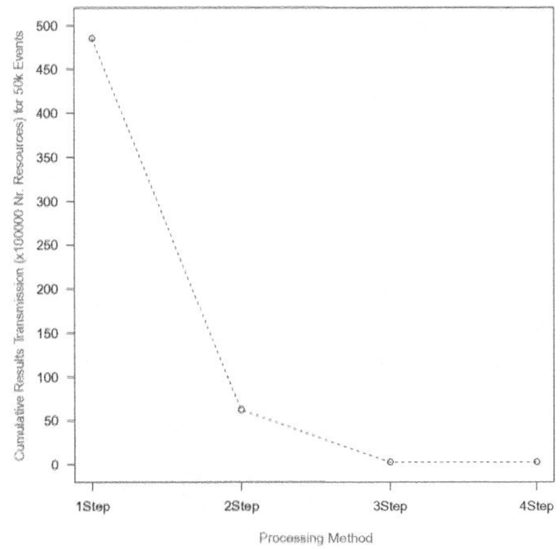

Fig. 6. Cumulative Transmission Cost for Different Steps using AND OP

very close to each other. When we add more steps beyond the second step we do not save much more of processing costs. However, the existing small difference of cost reduction between two-step and multi-step is depending on the query used for the first step. In each of the processing steps based on the filter functionality factor of queries, a large amount of events are filtered out and only a subset of them are forwarded. As expected, the forwarding of events to the next step causes a delay for the detection of complex events. Fig. 5 shows the comparison of latencies of different approaches (single, two and multi-step), it only shows the latency of detected of complex events (not the latency of the dropped events), i.e., the time difference between event generation and detection of complex event in the final stage. The single step processing has the lowest latency due to the fact that the events are processed in single step.

With the comparison of two Figures 3 and 4 we can argue that the two-step processing has a good balance between the performance, latency and the generated transmission costs. The single step processing might not be suitable for use cases with a high throughput event stream, and causes a high load on the KB, but has an acceptable latency when the complex events are detected and the time between event capturing and event detection is very low. The two-step processing has high performance and saves transmission costs, but the event detection latency should be in the expected range for an specific use case.

Different Effects of Event Operators. We conducted experiments for analysing the effects of event algebra operators on multi-step event processing. We made different experiments for OR, AND, SEQ, and NOT operators.[7]

[7] The queries `http://download.teymourian.de/scep-queries.html` for the event enrichment are the same SPARQL queries sQ2 to sQ7 and sQorm2 to sQorm7. For the event detection based we used eQopm1 to eQopm7 and eQorm1 to eQorm7 (changed based on event operators).

Star-Shaped Event Patterns: For the evaluation of execution plans for the star-shaped event pattern, we use the same event enrichment and detection queries as used for previous experiments. In our experiment we consider a multi-step event enrichment and detection for a query with 7 different subgraphs (7 BGPs) which are processed in 7 processing steps. The cumulative KB result transmission for four different execution plans is presented in Fig. 7a. Our experiments shows that the Plan-3 (7,6,1,2,4,3,5) has the maximum of the KB results transmitted and the Plan-2* (5,3,4,2,1,6,7) has the minimum result transmission (selected by our algorithm).

AND and SEQ Operators: As previously described, the processing of AND and SEQ can be handled in a sequential process, and every single event instance can be checked for the possible matching in sub-graphs/sub-events. The performance and cost reduction is very similar to star-shaped event patters. The cost reduction differs from the cost reduction effect of the OR operator. The cost reduction can only be compared with the single step processing and not with the OR operator.

OR Event Algebra Operation: The OR operation has an impact on the topology of the multi-step event processing, due to the nature of the OR operator. As we can see the performance is significantly higher than the single-step processing and very close to multi-step processing. The transmission cost reduction shows that the cost reduction for two-step processing is mostly around 50% in comparison to the single-step processing and it significantly increases with the multi-step approach. However, the average latency for detection of complex events is increased with the usage of the multi-step approach.

NOT Operator: We used the NOT operator together with an AND operator due to the fact that only a single NOT operator can only change the detection topography in the multi-step processing. The result of our experiments shows that the performance and cost reduction of the (AND+NOT) operator is very similar to the AND operator.

Multi-Step Planning: We compare the performance, enrichment and transmission costs of different plans provided by our algorithm (marked with *) with some of the randomly selected plans. We evaluate the proposed planning algorithm for different SCEP query types, Star-Shaped and combination with different event operators. The optimization of execution plans also has its effects on the performance of the overall system. The Throughput performance for the Plan-2 is about 270 events/s and for the Plan-3 (the worst plan) is 310 events/sec. One acceptable plan is the two-step processing plan in which the first step filters the high rate of raw events and in the following step the rest of the extracted query subgraphs are matched. Thereby, we can improve the throughput and latency of event processing, and reduce the processing and transmission costs.

Effect of Operators on Planning: We consider a query which includes two event component parts which are combined with an event operator. In our first experiment we use the AND operator and setup 4 different processing steps. The table 2 shows the different predicates used in the 4 processing steps for event enrichment and detection, in step 4 the AND operator is applied.

The Figure 7b shows the cumulative transmission of results with different plans. Plan-4 shows one of the maximum cost plans and plan-1 one of the optimal plans, any other plans may have a cost in this range. The Figure 6 shows the comparison of

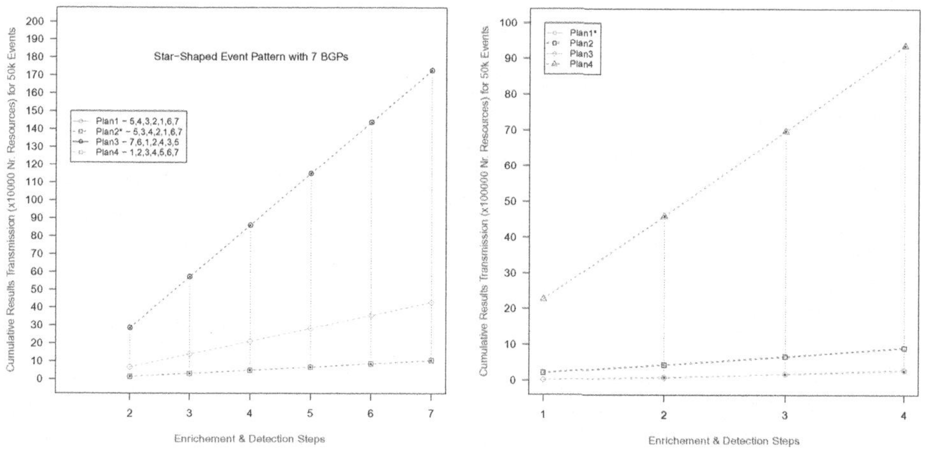

(a) Plans for Star-Shaped Pattern (b) Plans for AND Operator

Fig. 7. Cumulative Transmission Costs for different Plans

Table 2. Execution Plan-1

Steps	Enrichment Predicates	Matching Predicates
Step-1	5,3	(5 OR 3)
Step-2	4,2	(4 OR 2)
Step-3	1,6	(1 OR 6)
Step-4*	7	((5,4,1,6) AND (3,2,6,7))

Table 3. Four Enrichment Plans

Plans	Step-1	Step-2	Step-3	Step-4
Plan-1	5,4	3,2	1,6	7
Plan-2*	5,3	4,2	1,6	7
Plan-3	7,6	1,2	4,3	5
Plan-4	1,2	3,4	5,6	7

commutative transmission costs in the case that we apply a different number of processing steps. We observe a high cost reduction from single step processing to 4 step processing. The Table 3 shows the Plan-2* (generated by our algorithm) and 3 randomly selected processing plans.

The effect of the *SEQ Operator* is very similar to the AND operator with the small difference that first event component of the complex event should happen before the other event components. And the effect of the OR operator is very similar to the shown star-shaped pattern. Since a major assumption in our approach for the semantic enrichment of events is that the knowledge bases in the use case is huge, the experiment with the proposed framework with respect to the different sizes and complexity of KBs can only effect the performance of the CEP system but it does not effect our greedy algorithm for the planning of event enrichment and detection.

5 Related Work

Margara et al. [6] provide a survey on event processing and data stream processing systems. The event processing approaches can be categorized in rule-based and non-rule-based approaches. Our plan-based event processing approach extends the research results from the previous work on plan-based event processing [1,9]. These systems deal with planning the event acquisition to reduce the network transmission costs. In our approach, we have to optimized the load and transmission costs of knowledge acquisition.

Several stream reasoning languages [4] and processing approaches [2,10] haven been proposed. Bolles et. al. propose StreamSPARQL [4] for extending SPARQL for the propose querying RDF streams. It enables window-based and event-based windowing on RDF streams. Barbieri et al. propose Continuous SPARQL (C-SPARQL) [3] as a language for continuous query processing and Stream Reasoning. Stream reasoning approaches like [13] are proposed for reasoning on RDF streams, and are not designed for fusion of background KBs and event streams.

CQELS [10] is a query processor for unified query processing over both Linked Stream Data and Linked Data. ETALIS [2] is a rule-based stream reasoning and complex event processing (CEP) system. ETALIS is implemented in Prolog and uses a Prolog inference engine for event processing. ETALIS provides EP-SPARQL as a language for complex events and stream reasoning.

The differences of our approach with the RDF streaming approach are: 1. Some of the RDF stream reasoning systems may also use 'static' reference knowledge along with RDF streams, but the amounts of static reference knowledge is limited to the main memory of the reasoner, because they have to include the knowledge into the reasoner memory. In our approach the reasoning is delegated to a highly optimized external reasoner. We assume that the external KB is a highly scalable triple store with a scalable reasoner (a distributed triple store and reasoner). The event mapping engine can query the external knowledge base and activate the reasoner for the external knowledge. The result of the reasoning is then enriched to the event stream and forwarded for the event pattern matching in the following event detection phase. 2. In our approach the event stream is not mapped to an RDF stream. The event stream is based on an event model, e.g., a name/value pair stream, as it is usual in most of the event processing use cases.

6 Discussion

We have shown that our approach for planning of multi-step event enrichment and detection can be optimized so that we can avoid as much as possible the full stream enrichment to optimize the knowledge acquisition costs. One main conclusion of our work is that within the user event processing latency expectation it is possible to plan the enrichment and detection steps so that the knowledge acquisition costs can be reduced. One future optimization of our work would be to optimize the query planning algorithms by considering the intermediate joins of event detection graphs.

References

1. Akdere, M., Çetintemel, U., Tatbul, N.: Plan-based complex event detection across distributed sources. Proc. VLDB Endow. 1, 66–77 (2008)
2. Anicic, D., Fodor, P., Rudolph, S., Stühmer, R., Stojanovic, N., Studer, R.: ETALIS: Rule-Based Reasoning in Event Processing. In: Helmer, S., Poulovassilis, A., Xhafa, F. (eds.) Reasoning in Event-Based Distributed Systems. SCI, vol. 347, pp. 99–124. Springer, Heidelberg (2011)

3. Barbieri, D.F., Braga, D., Ceri, S., Grossniklaus, M.: An execution environment for c-sparql queries. In: Proceedings of the 13th International Conference on Extending Database Technology, EDBT 2010, pp. 441–452. ACM, New York (2010)
4. Bolles, A., Grawunder, M., Jacobi, J.: Streaming SPARQL extending SPARQL to process data streams. In: Bechhofer, S., Hauswirth, M., Hoffmann, J., Koubarakis, M. (eds.) ESWC 2008. LNCS, vol. 5021, pp. 448–462. Springer, Heidelberg (2008)
5. Bry, F., Paschke, A., Eugster, P.T., Fetzer, C., Behrend, A. (eds.): Proceedings of the Sixth ACM International Conference on Distributed Event-Based Systems, DEBS 2012, Berlin, Germany, July 16-20. ACM (2012)
6. Margara, A., Cugola, G.: Processing flows of information: from data stream to complex event processing. In: Proceedings of the 5th ACM International Conference on Distributed Event-Based System, DEBS 2011, pp. 359–360. ACM, New York (2011)
7. Paschke, A., Vincent, P., Alves, A., Moxey, C.: Tutorial on advanced design patterns in event processing. In: Bry, et al. (eds.) [5], pp. 324–334.
8. Pietzuch, P.R., Shand, B., Bacon, J.: A framework for event composition in distributed systems. In: Endler, M., Schmidt, D.C. (eds.) Middleware 2003. LNCS, vol. 2672, pp. 62–82. Springer, Heidelberg (2003)
9. Schultz-Møller, N.P., Migliavacca, M., Pietzuch, P.: Distributed complex event processing with query rewriting. In: Proceedings of the Third ACM International Conference on Distributed Event-Based Systems, DEBS 2009, pp. 4:1–4:12. ACM, New York (2009)
10. Serrano, M., Le-Phuoc, D., Zaremba, M., Galis, A., Bhiri, S., Hauswirth, M.: Resource optimisation in iot cloud systems by using matchmaking and self-management principles. In: Galis, A., Gavras, A. (eds.) FIA 2013. LNCS, vol. 7858, pp. 127–140. Springer, Heidelberg (2013)
11. Teymourian, K., Paschke, A.: Semantic rule-based complex event processing. In: Governatori, G., Hall, J., Paschke, A. (eds.) RuleML 2009. LNCS, vol. 5858, pp. 82–92. Springer, Heidelberg (2009)
12. Teymourian, K., Rohde, M., Paschke, A.: Fusion of background knowledge and streams of events. In: Bry, et al. (eds.) [5], pp. 302–313.
13. Walavalkar, O., Joshi, A., Finin, T., Yesha, Y.: Streaming Knowledge Bases. In: Proceedings of the Fourth International Workshop on Scalable Semantic Web knowledge Base Systems (October 2008)

Error-Tolerant RDF Subgraph Matching for Adaptive Presentation of Linked Data on Mobile

Luca Costabello

Inria, Sophia Antipolis, France
luca.costabello@inria.fr

Abstract. We present PRISSMA, a context-aware presentation layer for Linked Data. PRISSMA extends the Fresnel vocabulary with the notion of mobile context. Besides, it includes an algorithm that determines whether the sensed context is compatible with some context declarations. The algorithm finds optimal error-tolerant subgraph isomorphisms between RDF graphs using the notion of graph edit distance and is sublinear in the number of context declarations in the system.

Keywords: #eswc2014Costabello.

1 Introduction

Semantic Web mobile applications might not have built-in assumptions about the schemas of the data they consume, as data models could be unknown a-priori, and provided by heterogeneous sources: users might consume any type of data, as long as it is relevant to their context [17]. To improve the effectiveness of Linked Data consumption, content adaptation must be adopted, i.e. the process of selecting, generating, or modifying content units in response to a requested URI[1]. Essential in the mobile Web, such process is driven by the multifaceted notion of *client context* [9]. Content adaptation reduces the fan-out of RDF entities, and provides coherent information by using context as a dynamic filter. Furthermore, it orders, groups, and formats triples, thus creating "optimized" content units ready for user consumption.

This paper addresses the question of *how to enable context-aware adaptation for Linked Data consumption.* We split up the problem in two sub-questions: i) *how to model context for Linked Data presentation* and ii) *how to deal with context imprecision to select proper presentation metadata at runtime.* Modelling context-aware presentation concepts for Linked Data needs a proper ontology that fills the gap between traditional context ontologies and the Web of Data (e.g. support for future extensions, adoption of a lightweight vocabulary instead of a vast, monolithic context ontology, etc). The selection of presentation metadata is complicated by a series of constraints: first, the intrinsic imprecision of context data determines the need for an error-tolerant strategy that takes into account possible discrepancies between context descriptions and actual context.

[1] See *Adaptation* definition: `http://www.w3.org/TR/di-gloss/#sec-glossary`

V. Presutti et al. (Eds.): ESWC 2014, LNCS 8465, pp. 36–51, 2014.

Second, this error-tolerant mechanism must support heterogeneous context dimensions (e.g. location, time, strings). Third, since the procedure must run on the client-side - to avoid disclosing sensitive context data - we must design a mobile-friendly algorithm, with acceptable time and space complexity. Finally, the adopted strategy must support runtime updates of RDF graphs, as context descriptions might be fetched from remote repositories and added to the selection process at runtime, and the sensed context may change at any time.

Our contribution is PRISSMA, a context-aware presentation framework for Linked Data. PRISSMA answers our two-fold research question with the following contributions: i) a vocabulary for describing context conditions, compatible with Fresnel [19], and ii) an error-tolerant subgraph matching algorithm that determines whether the sensed context is compatible with context declarations.

In Section 2 we present the state-of-the-art presentation-level frameworks for the Semantic Web, along with an overview of error-tolerant matching techniques. Section 3 describes the PRISSMA vocabulary and explains the error-tolerant presentation metadata selection algorithm. The algorithm experimental evaluation results are described in Section 4.

2 Related Work

As shown in Table 1a, none of the existing presentation frameworks for Linked Data [1,4,8,11,12,15,20] completely supports context awareness. One of these works is Fresnel [19], a rendering engine for RDF. Fresnel is built on the assumption that data and its related schema do not carry sufficient information for representing triples, hence it provides additional presentation-level knowledge. Developers create Fresnel declarations for RDF instances or classes that will be displayed by their applications using the Fresnel vocabulary, an ontology built on the separation between *data selection* and *formatting*. Data selection and filtering is implemented by Fresnel *Lenses*, while *Formats* define how to present data.

Castano et al. [3] provide an overview of matching techniques for RDF instances; most of these works stem from ontology matching strategies [10]. Figure 1b compares error-tolerant works closer to our requirements: iSPARQL [16] is designed for error-tolerant matching, but it neither supports heterogeneous dimensions (such as location), nor is it designed for computationally-constrained mobile platforms. The Silk framework [24] includes geographical and time distances but such metrics do not consider data imprecision. Furthermore, Silk is not designed to run on mobile devices. RDF semantics states that two RDF graphs are semantically equivalent if they entail one another[2], and, as underlined by Carrol [2], the important concept for entailment between RDF graphs is *subgraph isomorphism*, known to be NP-complete. Subgraph isomorphism is at the heart of a recent pattern matching engine for SPARQL by Zou et al. [25]. Unfortunately, the authors do not provide an *error-tolerant* version of their algorithm. It has been proved [6] that finding the optimal error-tolerant subgraph

[2] `http://www.w3.org/TR/rdf-concepts/`

Table 1. A comparison of presentation layers for the Semantic Web (a) and of error-tolerant matching techniques for RDF (b). Full support is identified by •, partial support by ○, no support by the empty cell.

	Haystack Ozone[15]	Noadster[22]	Surrogates[12]	Fresnel[19]	Xenon[20]	Tal4Rdf[4]	LESS[1]	Hide the Stack[8]	LDVM[11]	PRISSMA
Declarative approach	•		•	•	•	•	•	•	•	•
Domain Independence	•	•	•	•	•	•			•	•
Standard Languages	•		•	•	•			•	•	•
Context Awareness			○							•
Automatic stylesheets			○							
Evaluation								•		•
Distribution							•			○
Multimodality			•	•		○	○			•

(a)

	iSPARQL[16]	Silk[24]	Zou et al.[25]	Messmer and Bunke[18]	PRISSMA
RDF-specific	•	•	•		•
Data Heterogeneity		○		○	•
Client-side Execution				○	•
Incremental index updates	•			•	•
Selective matching cache				○	○

(b)

isomorphism between two graphs can be reduced to the computation of *graph edit distance*: the idea is that differences between graphs can be modelled in terms of operations to apply to graphs, such as adding a node or modifying an arc. Graph edit distance provides the required flexibility for building an error-tolerant subgraph matching algorithm, and supports customized and heterogeneous cost functions (comparing contexts means dealing with data such as location, time, string literals, URIs). Nevertheless, computational complexity is exponential in the number of graph nodes, since graph edit distance algorithms assume that every node can be mapped on every node of another graph. Although context descriptions are rather small graphs, computing graph edit distance remains a computationally expensive task, in particular on mobile devices. Traditional approaches to compute graph edit distance between an input graph and a set of reference graphs apply a pairwise comparison, but such methods do not scale well and badly perform with runtime updates [13]. Messmer and Bunke [18] adopt a different strategy: they fragment directed, labelled graphs into smaller subgraphs, and store them into a single data structure, to avoid duplicates. Given an input graph, an online search algorithm searches for the error-tolerant subgraph isomorphisms with the lowest edit costs.

3 Prism Selection Algorithm

We extend the Fresnel presentation-level ontology with context awareness. The PRISSMA vocabulary[3] (Figure 1) broadens the semantics of `fresnel:Purpose`

[3] `http://ns.inria.fr/prissma`

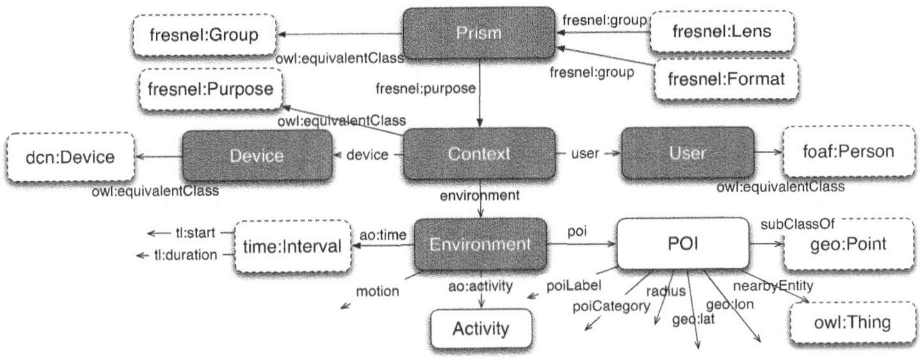

Fig. 1. The PRISSMA vocabulary

to delegate the selection of Lenses and Formats to a broader and more expressive definition of mobile context, modelled by the `prissma:Context` class. PRISSMA is not meant to provide yet another mobile context model, as that is out of the scope of our work. Instead, we reuse and combine well-known vocabularies: we are based on the widely-accepted formalization of context proposed by Dey [9] and we extend the W3C Model-Based User Interface Incubator Group[4] proposal, that models mobile context as the sum of the *User* model, the *Device* features, and the *Environment* in which the action is performed (we have described the PRISSMA vocabulary in further detail in [7]). To wrap up each context-aware presentation-level unit of information, the concept of *Prism* is introduced (a Prism is `owl:equivalentClass` to a `fresnel:Group`):

Definition 1 (Prism). *A Prism P is an RDF graph that describes the context conditions under which a given RDF presentation must be activated.*

Fig. 2 shows the sample Prism `:museumPrism`. The Prism styles `dbpedia:Museum` instances when requested by art-loving users walking in Paris. Fresnel lenses and formats (8-27) are coupled to the PRISSMA context description of lines 29-43.

Before rendering an RDF resource with Fresnel, PRISSMA-equipped applications search the available Prisms and select the better match for the context in which the desired resource is accessed, thus our second research question: *how to select the proper context description at runtime?* The most relevant challenge of this task is the imprecise and incomplete nature of context data, that complicates the matching procedure between declared and sensed contexts, and requires an error-tolerant approach. Context data is riddled by the following issues:

Ambiguity. Some RDF Entities and literals used in PRISSMA declarations might not match with the actual context entities. Nevertheless, in some cases entities and literals might be *similar*.

Incompleteness. The authors of PRISSMA context declarations might omit or forget certain properties, when describing a context. Nevertheless, in

[4] `http://www.w3.org/2005/Incubator/model-based-ui/XGR-mbui/`

```
# Styles a Museum when walking in Paris
:museumPrism a prissma:Prism ;
             a fresnel:Group ;
 fresnel:purpose :
       walkingInParisArtLover ;
 fresnel:stylesheetLink <style.css>.

# Fresnel presentation-level triples
:museumlens a fresnel:Lens;
   fresnel:group :museumPrism;
   fresnel:classLensDomain dbpedia:
         Museum;
   fresnel:showProperties (
                     dbpprop:location
                     dbpprop:
                            publictransit
                     ex:telephone
                     ex:openingHours
                     ex:ticketPrice ) .

:addressFormat a fresnel:Format ;
   fresnel:group :museumPrism ;
   fresnel:propertyFormatDomain
                     dbpprop:location ;
   fresnel:label "Address" ;
   fresnel:labelStyle
          "css-class1"^^fresnel:styleClass
                     ;
   fresnel:valueStyle
          "css-class2"^^fresnel:styleClass
                     .

# [...]

# PRISSMA context description
:walkingInParisArtLover a prissma:
        Context ;
   prissma:user :artLover ;
   prissma:environment :parisWalking .

:artLover a prissma:User ;
   foaf:interest "art".

:parisWalking a prissma:Environment ;
   prissma:poi :paris ;
   prissma:motion "walking" .

:paris geo:lat "48.8567" ;
   geo:long "2.3508" ;
   prissma:radius "5000" .
```

Fig. 2. A sample Prism (prefixes are omitted)

certain cases the context graph, although topologically different, should still be considered as a valid candidate by the selection algorithm.

Sensor Noise. Onboard sensors might provide erroneous information that will be part of the actual context graph [14]. This is a well-known problem when determining geographic location (e.g. weak GPS signal, indoor location, etc).

To overcome such issues, we extended and adapted to RDF the Messmer and Bunke error-tolerant algorithm for finding *optimal* subgraph isomorphisms for labelled, directed graphs [18].

3.1 Definitions

Before describing the adapted algorithm, we remind some useful definitions provided in Messmer [18], adjusting them to our scenario:

Definition 2 (RDF Graph). *An RDF graph is a set of RDF triples* $G = \{(s_1, p_1, o_1) \dots (s_n, p_n, o_n)\} = (V, E)$ *where* s_t *is the subject,* p_t *the property and* o_t *the object of each triple* t*.* V *is the set of labelled vertices and contains the elements* s_t *and* o_t*, that are entities or literals.* E *is the set of directed edges and contains all the triple properties* p_t*.*

Definition 3 (Graph Edit Operation). *Given an RDF graph* $G = (V, E)$*, a graph edit operation* $\delta(G)$ *is one of the following:*

- $v \rightarrow v'$, $v \in V, v' \in V$ *(substituting an RDF entity or literal)*
- $e \rightarrow e'$, $e \in E$ *(substituting an RDF property)*
- $v \rightarrow \epsilon$, $v \in V$ *(deleting an RDF instance or literal)*
- $e \rightarrow \epsilon$, $e \in E$ *(deleting an RDF property)*

- *$\epsilon \rightarrow e$ (adding an RDF property between existing nodes)*
where ϵ is an empty RDF entity, literal, or property.

These five edit operations are sufficient to transform any graph G into a subgraph of any graph G'. Note that the algorithm searches for subgraph isomorphisms from a model graph to the input graph, hence there is no need to consider exterior RDF instances or literals in the input graph, i.e. there is no need for a $\epsilon \rightarrow v,\ v \in V$ operation.

Definition 4 (Edited Graph). *Given an RDF graph G and a sequence* $\Delta = (\delta_1, \delta_2, \ldots, \delta_n)$ *of edit operations, the edited graph* $\Delta(G) = (\Delta(V), \Delta(E))$ *is the graph* $\Delta(G) = \delta_n(\ldots\delta_1(G))$.

Definition 5 (Error-Tolerant RDF Subgraph Isomorphism). *Given two RDF graphs* $G = (V, E)$ *and* $G' = (V', E')$, *an error-tolerant RDF subgraph isomorphism f from G to G′ is a two-tuple* $f = (\Delta, f_\Delta)$ *where:*
- *Δ is a sequence of graph edit operations that transforms G in $\Delta(G)$.*
- *f_Δ is an injective function $f_\Delta : \Delta(V) \rightarrow V'$ such that $\exists$ a graph isomorphism[5] from $\Delta(G)$ to a subgraph $S \subseteq G'$.*

We now introduce the definition of *cost of error-tolerant subgraph isomorphism*, preceded by the *cost* of an edit operation:

Definition 6 (Cost of Edit Operation). *Given an edit operation δ_i, the cost of δ_i is a value $C(\delta_i) \in [0, 1]$.*

The cost $C(\delta_i)$ of an edit operation δ_i varies according to the type of edit operation (e.g. instance substitution, property deletion, etc.) and the nature of the involved RDF element. We cover in more details $C(\delta_i)$ in Section 3.4.

Definition 7 (Cost of Error-Tolerant RDF Subgraph Isomorphism). *Given an error-tolerant RDF subgraph isomorphism $f = (\Delta, f_\Delta)$, its cost $C(f)$ is defined as the normalized cost of the sequence of edit operations $\Delta = (\delta_1, \ldots \delta_n)$,* $C(f) = \frac{C(\Delta)}{n} = \frac{\sum_{i=1}^{n} C(\delta_i)}{n}$.

The cost of error-tolerant subgraph isomorphism described in Definition 7 adopts the arithmetic mean to normalize the cost of the sequence of edit operations. Other strategies might be adopted, such as using a weighted mean or the maximum cost in the sequence.

It is evident that there might exist multiple sequences Δ of edit operations from graph G to graph G', each with a different cost: we are interested in finding the *optimal error-tolerant subgraph isomorphism*, i.e. the error-tolerant subgraph isomorphism with the least expensive sequence of edit operations. In other words, we want to find the minimum amount of distortion needed to transform a Prism into the actual mobile context, thus computing their graph edit distance [21]:

Definition 8 (Optimal Error-Tolerant RDF Subgraph Isomorphism). *Given the set of error-tolerant subgraph isomorphisms $F = f_1 \ldots f_n$ between two graphs, the optimal error-tolerant subgraph isomorphism f_{opt} is the element of F with cost $C(f_{opt}) = \min_{f_i \in F} C(f_i)$.*

[5] Definition of graph isomorphism provided in [18].

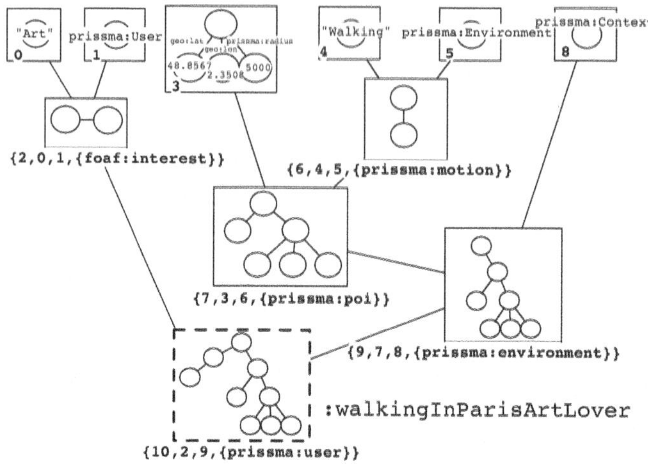

Fig. 3. A decomposition of context data of :museumPrism showed in Figure 1

3.2 Decomposition

The context-related triples included in each Prism are split in subgraphs and saved in a structure called *decomposition*, a recursive partitioning of a set of RDF models (Prisms). The decomposition algorithm works on the set of Prisms pre-loaded by the PRISSMA-equipped mobile application. The idea is building the decomposition by detecting and merging common subgraphs: in the decomposition, subgraphs duplicated in different Prisms are collapsed and represented only once, thus providing a compact representation of possible contexts. As remarked by Messmer and Bunke, there exists more than one decomposition for a set of graphs: the adopted strategy does not provide an optimal decomposition (e.g. in the number of elements), but it is computationally inexpensive compared to other strategies [18].

The elements of a decomposition are tuples that include graph patterns sharing the same topology and whose RDF elements have the same classes. Among the decomposition elements, some consist in groups of non-decomposable, atomic graph patterns called *context units*:

Definition 9 (Context Unit). *A context unit is an RDF graph $U = (V_U, E_U)$ representing atomic context information. A context unit U consists in either a single class, or a single RDF entity, or a single literal, or in a graph that describes an atomic context information.*

In the original proposition, Messmer and Bunke deal with graphs with a limited range of discrete values, thus they decompose graphs up to single nodes. We compare more complex structures, hence the need to preserve context units (e.g. we cannot split latitude, longitude, and radius when comparing locations). Thus, different types of context units have been defined, according to the type of context information: *Class* context units consist in core PRISSMA classes (e.g. `prissma:Context`, `prissma:User`, `prissma:Environment`, and `prissma:Device`). *Class* context units are created by a preliminary step, where instances of core PRISSMA classes are substituted by their class. This operation decreases the size of the decomposition without losing information, since the URIs of such core instances are not important for matching purposes. *Entity* context units are RDF entities, whose classes are not among PRISSMA core classes. Entity context units may be blank nodes. *Geo* context units represent geographic locations, while *Time* elements include temporal information. Both Geo and Time context units may be blank nodes. *String* and *Numeric* context units are associated to string and numeric literals. The decomposition is formally defined as follows:

Definition 10 (Decomposition). *Given a set of Prisms $P = \{P_1, \ldots, P_n\}$, the decomposition $D(P)$ is a set of 4-tuple (G, G', G'', E) where:*

1. *G, G', G'' are RDF graphs, with $G', G'' \subset G$*
2. *E is a set of RDF properties such that $G = G^{'} \cup_E G''$, where $\cup_E$ is the union of G' and G'' properties.*
3. *for each P_i there exists a 4-tuple $(P_i, G', G'', E) \in D(P)$*
4. *for each 4-tuple (G, G', G'', E) there exists no other 4-tuple $(G_1, G'_1, G''_1, E) \in D(P)$ with $G = G_1$*
5. *for each 4-tuple $(G, G', G'', E) \in D(P)$*
   (a) *if G' is not a context unit, there exists a 4-tuple $(G_1, G_1^{'}, G_1^{''}, E) \in D(P)$ such that $G' = G_1$*
   (b) *if G'' is not a context unit, there exists a 4-tuple $(G_2, G_2^{'}, G_2^{''}, E) \in D(P)$ such that $G'' = G_2$*
   (c) *if G' is a context unit, there exists no 4-tuple $(G_3, G_3^{'}, G_3^{''}, E) \in D(P)$ such that $G' = G_3$*
   (d) *if G'' is a context unit, there exists no 4-tuple $(G_4, G_4^{'}, G_4^{''}, E) \in D(P)$ such that $G'' = G_4$*

Figure 3 shows the decomposition of `:walkingInParisArtLover`, the Prism in Figure 2. Uppermost elements are context units: 0 and 4 are "String" context units, 1, 5, and 8 are "Class" context units, and 3 is a "Geo" context unit. Each decomposition elements contains the IDs of the ancestors (G', G'') and the set of connecting RDF properties E. Element 10 represents the complete `prissma:Context` graph.

The recursive function *decompose*() (Algorithm 1) is executed on each Prism G in the decomposition D. The function searches in the decomposition for S_{max}, the biggest subgraph of G (lines 3-5): the goal is to determine if there exists a graph pattern in common with the decomposition[6]. If S_{max} is isomorphic[6] to G, then G is already represented in D and the algorithm stops (lines 6-7). If no subgraph is found, and G can be further decomposed (i.e. it is not a context unit), the procedure chooses S_{max} (line 9) and recursively decomposes it

[6] The graph isomorphism and the exact subgraph isomorphism operations are delegated to off-the-shelf algorithms, such as [23] whose description is out of the scope of this work.

Alg. 1. decompose(G,D)

```
  Data: a Prism G, the decomposition D
  Result: The updated decomposition D
1 S_max = ∅
2 if G not context unit then
3     foreach (G_i, G'_i, G''_i, E_i) do
4         if G_i is a subgraph of G and S_max smaller than G_i then
5             S_max = G_i
6     if S_max is isomorphic to G then
7         exit
8     if (S_max = ∅) then
9         choose subgraph S_max, priority to PRISSMA properties
10        decompose(S_max)
11    decompose(G − S_max)
12    add (G, S_max, G − S_max, E) to D
```

(line 10). The choice of S_{max} is determined by a list of ordered RDF properties, with a priority for PRISSMA background ontology core properties (e.g. `prissma:user`, `prissma:environment`, `prissma:device`, etc). This enhances the chances of merging decomposition elements, thus resulting in a more compact structure. The procedure is invoked recursively on $G - S_{max}$, the part of G not yet decomposed (line 11). Finally, $(G, S_{max}, G - S_{max}, E)$ is added to D.

3.3 Search Algorithm

Every significant context change[7] detected by the device triggers the search for Prisms that fit the updated context requirements. PRISSMA carries out this operation with an adapted version of Messmer and Bunke online search algorithm [18]. The algorithm detects *optimal* error-tolerant subgraph isomorphisms between the graph of the sensed context and the Prisms stored in the decomposition. The algorithm first computes edit operations between context units in the decomposition D and context units of the input graph. Second, it combines such edit operations to obtain optimal error-tolerant subgraph isomorphisms for larger patterns, up to complete Prisms (Algorithm 3). To avoid combinatorial explosion, the concatenation of error-tolerant subgraph isomorphisms includes only the cheapest error-tolerant graph isomorphisms: this guarantees to find optimal error-tolerant subgraph isomorphisms.

Algorithm 2 presents the *search* procedure: first, it finds the error-tolerant subgraph isomorphisms from each context unit S of the decomposition D to the input context graph G_I and stores them in the list *candidates*(S) (lines 1-2). This operation is performed by the *context_unit_matching()* function. From line 3 to 12 such error-tolerant subgraph isomorphisms are concatenated to find error-tolerant subgraph isomorphisms for larger graphs, up to Prisms:

[7] The notion of *significant* context change is scenario-dependent, and it is not investigated in this paper.

Alg. 2. *search*(G_I, D)

Data: a Decomposition D, a context graph G_I
Result: the result set R containing selectable Prisms
1 **foreach** S *context unit in* D **do**
2 $\quad$ $candidates(S) = context\_unit\_matching(S, G_I)$
3 **while** *choose* $S_1 \mid \exists\ f_1 \in candidates(S_1)$ *with* $C(f_1)$ *minimal in* D *and* $C(f_1) \leq T$ **do**
4 $\quad$ $winners(S_1) = winners(S_1) \cup \{f_1\}$
5 $\quad$ $candidates(S_1) = candidates(S_1) - \{f_1\}$
6 $\quad$ **if** S_1 *is a Prism* **then**
7 $\quad\quad$ $R = R \cup \{S_1\}$
8 $\quad$ **foreach** $(S, S_1, S_2, E) \in D \mid\mid (S, S_2, S_1, E) \in D$ **do**
9 $\quad\quad$ **foreach** $f_2 \in winners(S_2)$ **do**
10 $\quad\quad\quad$ $f = combine(S_1, S_2, E, G_I, f_1, f_2)$
11 $\quad\quad\quad$ **if** $f \neq \emptyset$ **then**
12 $\quad\quad\quad\quad$ $candidates(S) = candidates(S) \cup \{f\}$
13 return R

Alg. 3. *combine()*

Data: $S_1, S_2, E, G_I, f_1 = (\Delta_1, f_{\Delta_1}), f_2 = (\Delta_2, f_{\Delta_2}), \Delta_1 = (\Delta_{V_1}, \Delta_{E_1}), \Delta_2 = (\Delta_{V_2}, \Delta_{E_2})$
Result: f
1 **if** $f_{\Delta_1}(\Delta_{V_1}) \cap f_{\Delta_2}(\Delta_{V_2}) \neq \emptyset$ **then**
2 $\quad$ exit
3 **foreach** $v \in (\Delta_{V_1} \cup \Delta_{V_2})$ **do**
4 $\quad$ **if** $v \in V_{\Delta_1}$ **then**
5 $\quad\quad$ $f_\Delta(v) = f_{\Delta_1}(v)$
6 $\quad$ **else if** $v \in V_{\Delta_2}$ **then**
7 $\quad\quad$ $f_\Delta(v) = f_{\Delta_2}(v)$
8 $\Delta = \Delta_1 + \Delta_2 + \Delta_E$
9 return $f = (\Delta, f_\Delta)$

Alg. 4. *context_unit_matching*(U, G_I)

Data: context unit U, input context graph $G_I = (V_I, E_I)$
Result: the list of error-tolerant subgraph isomorphisms F
1 $F = \emptyset$
2 **foreach** *context unit* $U_I \in G_I$ **do**
3 $\quad$ generate an error-tolerant subgraph isomorphism f between U and U_I
4 $\quad$ $F = F \cup \{f\}$
5 $f' = (\Delta', f'_\Delta)$ with $\Delta' = (v \rightarrow \epsilon)$ and $f'_\Delta = \emptyset$
6 $F = F \cup \{f'\}$
7 return F

in line 3 we select the subgraph S_1 whose error-tolerant subgraph isomorphism f_1 has the minimum cost in D. Note that $C(f_1)$ must be lower than a threshold $T \in [0, 1]$. The error-tolerant subgraph isomorphism f_1 is removed from $candidates(S_1)$ in line 5 and added to the list $winners(S_1)$, the container of error-tolerant subgraph isomorphism chosen to be combined. If S_1 is a Prism, the algorithm has found a result (lines 6-7). Otherwise, we generate error-tolerant subgraph isomorphisms for each subgraph S having S_1 as ancestor (lines 8-12). Such generation is done with the *combine()* function that concatenates f_1 to each $f_2 \in winners(S_2)$, where S_2 is the other ancestor of S. If a combination is feasible, the resulting error-tolerant subgraph isomorphism is added to $candidates(S)$ (line 12).

Algorithm 3 details the *combine()* procedure: first (line 1), the function tests if f_1 and f_2 do not contain mappings to the same node in G_I (this is necessary because subgraph isomorphisms are injective functions [18]). If this condition is satisfied, an error-tolerant subgraph isomorphism is constructed as a concatenation of the edit operations of f_1 and f_2 and of the edit operations on the edge between S_1 and S_2, Δ_E (line 8). Mappings are chosen among the mappings of f_1 and f_2 (lines 3-7).

We now discuss in further detail *context_unit_matching()*, the function used by the search algorithm to compute error-tolerant subgraph isomorphisms for context units (Algorithm 4). Given a context unit U and an input context graph G_I, the procedure finds the edit operations from U to each context unit of G_I (line 2-3) and stores them as error-tolerant subgraph isomorphisms. Moreover, the deletion of U is considered (line 5).

Worst case computational complexity analysis shows that the complexity of the search procedure varies from $O(Lm^n n^2)$ when Prisms in the decomposition are completely different, to $O(m^n n^2)$ when Prisms are highly similar (L is the number of Prisms in the decompositions, m the number of vertices of the input context graph and n the number of vertices of each Prism included in a decomposition D made of Prisms with same number of nodes). Hence, the search algorithm is sublinear in the number L of Prisms included in the decomposition (for a detailed theoretical analysis of the computational complexity of the search algorithm, see [18]). This is an important property of the algorithm, since the number of Prisms in the system can be potentially high and unknown a priori.

3.4 Cost of Edit Operations

Each graph edit operation δ computed by the Prism selection algorithm is associated to a cost $C(\delta) \in [0, 1]$. Unlike Messmer and Bunke that only consider topological differences and limit to graphs with discrete node values, in our scenario cost functions are influenced by the presence of heterogeneous context dimensions.

Topology. The algorithm assigns the highest cost $C(\delta) = 1$ to the substitution of "Class" context units, core PRISSMA vocabulary properties (such as `prissma:environment`), and to the deletion of "Class", "Geo" or "Time" context units. Hence, whenever an input context graph needs such edit operations, the cost of the resulting error-tolerant subgraph isomorphism will be higher than the threshold T. The algorithm assigns lower costs for edit operations on non-core properties, and on "Entity" context units (e.g. a missing `foaf:interest` property in the user dimension may not prevent a Prism match). Such cost is determined by the $C_{topology} \in [0, 1]$ parameter. Note that the presence of additional properties between two context units is not considered to affect global cost, and is therefore assigned cost 0.

Location. A "Geo" context unit is a subgraph composed by `geo:lat`, `geo:long` and a `prissma:radius` (e.g. context unit 3 in Fig. 3). The cost of the substitution of a location context unit depends on the geographic distance. We first compute the distance d of the two points using the Haversine formula. If d is within the declared radius, the edit operation has cost $C(\delta) = 0$. Otherwise, PRISSMA features an exponential decay function to smooth the transition between a perfect match and a mismatch[8]:

[8] More refined geospatial matching techniques are out of the scope of this work, e.g. `http://linkedgeodata.org/`

$$C_{geo}(d) = \begin{cases} 0 & \text{if } d < d_{radius} \\ e^{\frac{-d}{\lambda_{geo}}} & \text{if } d > d_{radius} \end{cases}$$

Time. Temporal context units include a start timestamp t_{start} and a duration Δ_t (Figure 1). The cost of the substitution of a temporal pattern is computed to an exponential decay function:

$$C_{time}(t) = \begin{cases} e^{\frac{t-t_{start}}{\lambda_{time}}} & \text{if } t < t_{start} \\ 0 & \text{if } t_{start} < t < t_{start} + \Delta_t \\ e^{\frac{-t+t_{start}+\Delta_t}{\lambda_{time}}} & \text{if } t > t_{start} + \Delta_t \end{cases}$$

Strings. The cost C_{string} of substituting a string literal is computed with an approximate string matching strategy, to overcome problems such as spelling variants (to date, the Prism selection algorithm focus only on this string similarity problem). The algorithm adopts the Monge-Elkan distance function (according to Cohen et al. [5] such function outperforms other approaches when dealing with spelling variants).

Precision-recall analysis[9] has been carried out to assess the validity of the Prism selection algorithm with different cost functions parameters, and with different similarity thresholds T. Future work will include a thorough campaign evaluation to assess the algorithm performance on a wider scale, and will involve PRISSMA-enabled applications users in the loop.

4 Evaluation

The PRISSMA decomposition and selection algorithms have been implemented as an Android library[9]. The library is showcased by the PRISSMA Browser[9], a mobile Linked Data browser enhanced with PRISSMA context-aware adaptation (Figure 5).

The first test analyses the decomposition memory consumption (Figure 4a). The test measured the decomposition size of groups of Prisms with a variable number of identical context units. Groups included 20 Prisms, each containing 10 context units. Overall, test Prisms accounted for 340 triples. The percentage of identical context units in each group of Prisms is progressively increased, ranging from 10% to 100% (where the latter means that all Prisms in the group are represented by the same decomposition item).

We assigned an arbitrary size of 30 Bytes to context units (we consider UTF-8 strings with an average length of 30 characters), and 42 Bytes to intermediate decomposition elements (one integer ID, two integer ancestors IDs, and a list of connecting edges. Each edge includes a triple of estimated size 90 characters). The size of PRISSMA decompositions are compared with the retained size of a group of Jena Model[10], each containing a test Prism. As expected, with higher

[9] Binaries, code, and evaluation results available at:
`http://wimmics.inria.fr/projects/prissma`

[10] `http://jena.apache.org/documentation/notes/model-factory.html`

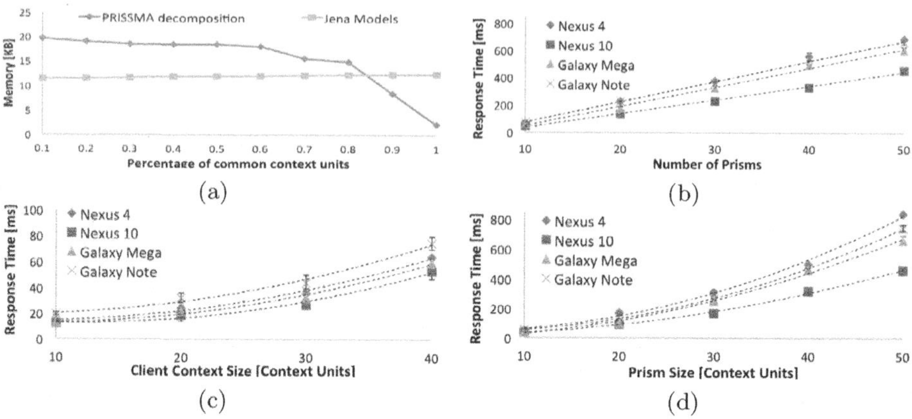

Fig. 4. Memory consumption (a) and Response time (b,c,d) of Prism selection algorithm

common context units percentages, we have lower decomposition memory footprints. Nevertheless, the memory size of PRISSMA decomposition is in the same order of magnitude as the Jena models size.

A series of tests have been run to prove the computational complexity analysis of the search algorithm. The algorithm response time has been tested with the proof-of-concept PRISSMA Browser on a group of Android mobile devices (Google Nexus 4, Google Nexus 10, Samsung Galaxy Mega, and Samsung Galaxy Note). All phones were running Android 4.2.2. Figure 4b shows the relationship between L, the number of Prisms in the decomposition, and response time. Prisms in each group are all different (thus testing the worst case decomposition configuration). Prisms contain $n = 10$ context units and the test context to be matched is made of $m = 10$ context units. Five independent runs have been executed for each group of Prisms, thus computing average response time measurements. Results prove a linear dependency, thus confirming the worst case complexity analysis of the search algorithm for what concerns the number of Prisms $O(L)$. Figure 4c shows how the size of the incoming context graph impacts on response time. In this case, each run varied the size m of input context (ranging from 10 to 50 context units) using a fixed group of $L = 5$ Prisms each made of $n = 2$ context units. Results match computational complexity analysis, thus giving a $O(m^n)$ relationship (experimental setup shown in Figure 4c has $n = 2$, thus giving a $O(m^2)$ relationship). Unlike the number of Prisms, the growth associated to the size of the incoming context graph suggests that the size of the latter must be kept as small as possible, to consistently reduce response time. Finally, in Figure 4d the size n of each Prism has been tested. Five independent test runs assessed response time using an incoming context graph of $m = 50$ context units and a decomposition made of $L = 5$ Prisms.

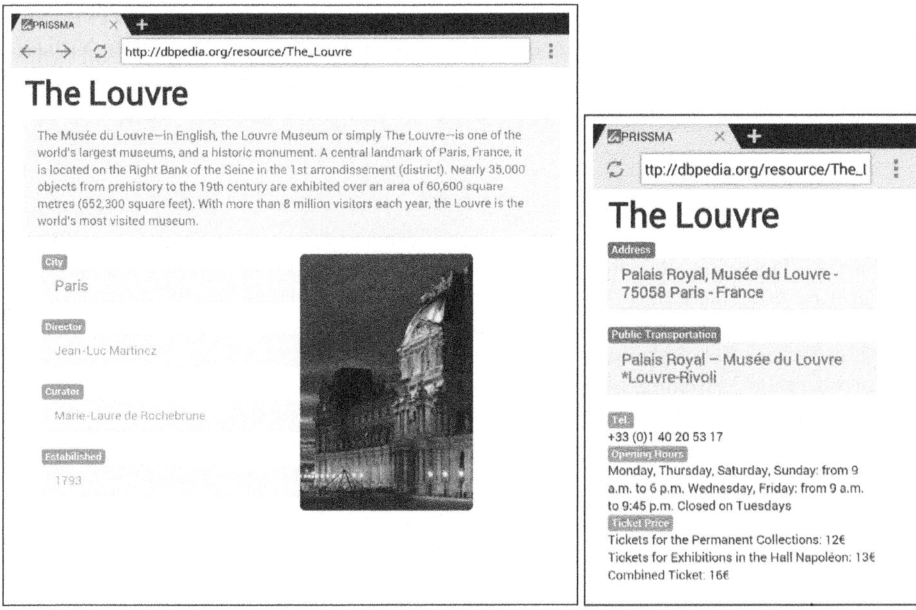

(a) (b)

Fig. 5. Two screenshots of the PRISSMA Browser Android application. Content and layout in (a) are optimized for tablets, while (b) is optimized for users walking in Paris (see the Prism in Figure 2).

Results confirm the complexity analysis $O(n^2)$. As for the case of incoming context graph, the size of Prisms impacts with a quadratic growth on response time, thus it is important to avoid defining useless context conditions in Prisms to lower response time.

5 Conclusions

Extending Fresnel with context awareness favours the sharing and reuse of prisms across applications, does not introduce new formalisms, and is extensible to domain-specific context data. Operating on the client side guarantees privacy preservation, because context data does not have to be disclosed to third-party adaptation servers. Moreover, the decomposition structure supports incremental updates. Memory consumption tests show that the decomposition structure reduces memory usage when Prisms contain repeated subgraphs. Response time test campaign shows the sublinear dependence on the number of Prisms in the system. The main limitation of PRISSMA is the need for a proper parametrization of the selection algorithm. This is a well-known issue of strategies based on graph edit distance, that will be addressed in future work with machine learning techniques. Additional cost functions will be added (e.g. semantic distance between URIs). Response time comparison with cited state-of-the-art solutions is envisaged, although experimental conditions vary, making the task tricky. Future work will also include deal user acceptability evaluation campaigns. Prisms distribution has not been examined yet: PRISSMA might support multiple strategies for discovery, retrieve, and consume Prisms published as Linked Data.

References

1. Auer, S., Doehring, R., Dietzold, S.: LESS - Template-Based Syndication and Presentation of Linked Data. In: Aroyo, L., Antoniou, G., Hyvönen, E., ten Teije, A., Stuckenschmidt, H., Cabral, L., Tudorache, T. (eds.) ESWC 2010, Part II. LNCS, vol. 6089, pp. 211–224. Springer, Heidelberg (2010)
2. Carroll, J.J.: Matching RDF Graphs. In: Horrocks, I., Hendler, J. (eds.) ISWC 2002. LNCS, vol. 2342, pp. 5–15. Springer, Heidelberg (2002)
3. Castano, S., Ferrara, A., Montanelli, S., Varese, G.: Ontology and instance matching. In: Paliouras, G., Spyropoulos, C.D., Tsatsaronis, G. (eds.) Multimedia Information Extraction. LNCS, vol. 6050, pp. 167–195. Springer, Heidelberg (2011)
4. Champin, P.-A.: T4R: Lightweight presentation for the Semantic Web. In: Scripting for the Semantic Web, workshop at ESWC (2009)
5. Cohen, W.W., Ravikumar, P.D., Fienberg, S.E.: A comparison of string distance metrics for name-matching tasks. In: IIWeb, pp. 73–78 (2003)
6. Conte, D., Foggia, P., Sansone, C., Vento, M.: Thirty years of graph matching in pattern recognition. In: IJPRAI, pp. 265–298 (2004)
7. Costabello, L.: DC proposal: PRISSMA, towards mobile adaptive presentation of the web of data. In: Aroyo, L., Welty, C., Alani, H., Taylor, J., Bernstein, A., Kagal, L., Noy, N., Blomqvist, E. (eds.) ISWC 2011, Part II. LNCS, vol. 7032, pp. 269–276. Springer, Heidelberg (2011)
8. Dadzie, A.-S., Rowe, M., Petrelli, D.: Hide the Stack: Toward Usable Linked Data. In: Antoniou, G., Grobelnik, M., Simperl, E., Parsia, B., Plexousakis, D., De Leenheer, P., Pan, J. (eds.) ESWC 2011, Part I. LNCS, vol. 6643, pp. 93–107. Springer, Heidelberg (2011)
9. Dey, A.K.: Understanding and using context. Personal Ubiquitous Comput. 5(1), 4–7 (2001)
10. Euzenat, J., Shvaiko, P.: Ontology matching. Springer (2007)
11. Fernéandez, J.M.B., Auer, S., Garcia, R.: The linked data visualization model. In: ISWC (Posters & Demos) (2012)
12. Gandon, F.L.: Generating surrogates to make the semantic web intelligible to end-users. In: Web Intelligence, pp. 352–358 (2005)
13. Gao, X., Xiao, B., Tao, D., Li, X.: A survey of graph edit distance. Pattern Analysis & Applications 13(1), 113–129 (2010)
14. Henricksen, K., Indulska, J.: Modelling and using imperfect context information. In: PerCom Workshops, pp. 33–37 (2004)
15. Huynh, D., Karger, D.R., Haystack, D.Q.: A platform for creating, organizing and visualizing information using rdf. In: Semantic Web Workshop (2002)
16. Kiefer, C., Bernstein, A., Stocker, M.: The fundamentals of iSPARQL: A virtual triple approach for similarity-based semantic web tasks. In: Aberer, K., Choi, K.-S., Noy, N., Allemang, D., Lee, K.-I., Nixon, L.J.B., Golbeck, J., Mika, P., Maynard, D., Mizoguchi, R., Schreiber, G., Cudré-Mauroux, P. (eds.) ASWC 2007 and ISWC 2007. LNCS, vol. 4825, pp. 295–309. Springer, Heidelberg (2007)

17. Schraefel, M.C., Rutledge, L.: User interaction in semantic web research. J. Web Sem. 8(4), 375–376 (2010)
18. Messmer, B., Bunke, H.: A new algorithm for error-tolerant subgraph isomorphism detection. IEEE Transactions on Pattern Analysis and Machine Intelligence (1998)
19. Pietriga, E., Bizer, C., Karger, D.R., Lee, R.: Fresnel: A browser-independent presentation vocabulary for RDF. In: Cruz, I., Decker, S., Allemang, D., Preist, C., Schwabe, D., Mika, P., Uschold, M., Aroyo, L.M. (eds.) ISWC 2006. LNCS, vol. 4273, pp. 158–171. Springer, Heidelberg (2006)
20. Quan, D., Karger, D.R.: Xenon: An RDF stylesheet ontology. In: Procs of WWW (2005)
21. Riesen, K., Jiang, X., Bunke, H.: Exact and inexact graph matching: Methodology and applications. In: Managing and Mining Graph Data, pp. 217–247 (2010)
22. Rutledge, L., van Ossenbruggen, J., Hardman, L.: Making RDF presentable: integrated global and local semantic web browsing. In: WWW (2005)
23. Ullmann, J.R.: An algorithm for subgraph isomorphism. J. ACM 23(1) (1976)
24. Volz, J., Bizer, C., Gaedke, M., Kobilarov, G.: Discovering and maintaining links on the web of data. In: Bernstein, A., Karger, D.R., Heath, T., Feigenbaum, L., Maynard, D., Motta, E., Thirunarayan, K. (eds.) ISWC 2009. LNCS, vol. 5823, pp. 650–665. Springer, Heidelberg (2009)
25. Zou, L., Chen, L., Özsu, M.T., Zhao, D.: Answering pattern match queries in large graph databases via graph embedding. VLDB J. 21(1), 97–120 (2012)

RDSZ: An Approach for Lossless RDF Stream Compression

Norberto Fernández[1], Jesús Arias[1], Luis Sánchez[1], Damaris Fuentes-Lorenzo[1], and Óscar Corcho[2]

[1] Dpto. Ing. Telemática, Universidad Carlos III de Madrid, Spain
{berto,jaf,luiss,dfuentes}@it.uc3m.es

[2] Ontology Engineering Group, Universidad Politécnica de Madrid, Spain
ocorcho@fi.upm.es

Abstract. In many applications (like social or sensor networks) the information generated can be represented as a continuous stream of RDF items, where each item describes an application event (social network post, sensor measurement, etc). In this paper we focus on compressing RDF streams. In particular, we propose an approach for lossless RDF stream compression, named RDSZ (RDF Differential Stream compressor based on Zlib). This approach takes advantage of the structural similarities among items in a stream by combining a differential item encoding mechanism with the general purpose stream compressor Zlib. Empirical evaluation using several RDF stream datasets shows that this combination produces gains in compression ratios with respect to using Zlib alone.

Keywords: #eswc2014Fernandez.

1 Introduction

The popularization of streaming data on the Web has fostered the interest of the Semantic Web community on this kind of data. Some evidences of this interest are, for instance, proposals like C-SPARQL [4] or SPARQL$_{\text{Stream}}$ [5], which aim to define query languages for RDF streams, work like [13], centered on stream reasoning, CQELS Cloud [9], which addresses the problem of scalable stream processing, or Ztreamy [2], which presents a scalable middleware for stream publishing. As a result of this interest, a W3C community group on RDF Stream Processing[1] has recently started. It is focused on defining a common model for producing, transmitting and continuously querying RDF Streams.

Recent work, particularly CQELS Cloud [9] and Ztreamy [2] has pointed out the importance of compression to reduce communication overheads when transmitting RDF streams. Though the problem of RDF compression has been previously addressed, notably by [1, 6–8, 12], these approaches are mostly centered on compressing static RDF files and datasets. As streams cannot normally be

[1] http://www.w3.org/community/rsp/ (January 13th, 2014)

V. Presutti et al. (Eds.): ESWC 2014, LNCS 8465, pp. 52–67, 2014.

```
class RDSZCompressor {
  CONSTRUCTOR(cacheSize)
  COMPRESS(RDFgraph)
  data FLUSH()
}
```

```
class RDSZDecompressor {
  CONSTRUCTOR(cacheSize)
  RDFgraph[] DECOMPRESS(data)
}
```

Fig. 1. RDSZCompressor (left) and RDSZDecompressor (right) APIs

stored in their entirety, compressing streaming data requires different techniques than compressing files. In particular, it requires keeping state information about past data in order to compress future items in the stream, an aspect not covered by the aforementioned approaches.

Taking this into account, in this paper we present an algorithm for lossless RDF stream compression, named RDSZ (RDF Differential Stream compressor based on Zlib). Our approach takes advantage of the fact that, in many cases, RDF streams are constituted by items built automatically by software components according to a single RDF schema (or a small set of them). Due to this, these items have structural similarities that can be exploited by a differential item encoding mechanism, so that new items in the stream can be represented on the basis of the previously processed items. To take advantage of additional redundancies, the results of this differential encoding process are later on compressed using a general-purpose streaming compressor. In particular, due to its popularity, we selected Zlib [10], which implements DEFLATE [11].

Empirical evaluation using several heterogeneous datasets shows that the combination of differential item encoding with Zlib outperforms the usage of Zlib alone. Despite its simplicity, our approach achieves significant improvements, with gains around 9%-31% on the compressed size of some datasets.

The rest of this paper is organized as follows: Section 2 describes the RDSZ algorithm. The empirical evaluation of the algorithm is reported in Section 3. Section 4 offers a discussion on related work. Finally, Section 5 presents some conclusions and future lines of development of this work.

2 The RDSZ Algorithm

This section describes the RDSZ algorithm. Section 2.1 introduces its programming interface and intended usage by applications, whereas sections 2.2 and 2.3 describe the algorithm compression and decompression stages.

2.1 Programming Interface and Usage

The RDSZ API, shown in Figure 1, is based on the Zlib API. When an application needs to compress an RDF stream, it instantiates an RDSZCompressor object. Then, it calls the other two methods in the interface. The method *compress* is called to provide the compressor with a new RDF item in the stream to be compressed. This item may have been obtained, for instance, from a continuous *CONSTRUCT* query in an RDF stream processing engine. The method

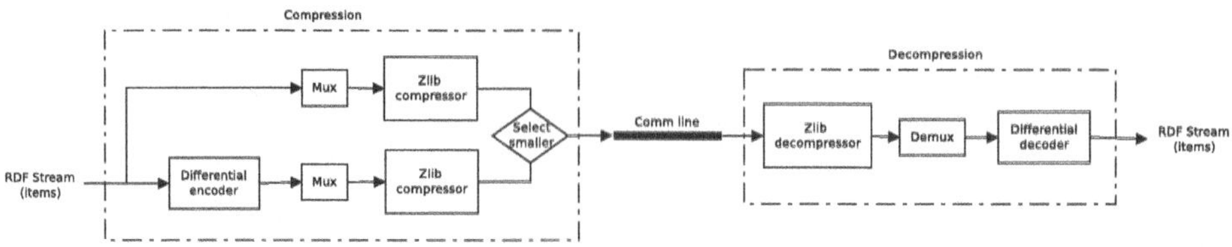

Fig. 2. Processing blocks of RDSZ

receives as input a memory data structure that represents the RDF graph of the item[2], containing one or several triples. This RDF graph is buffered by the RDSZ compressor. When a certain number of items have been buffered or after a certain period of time, the application calls *flush*. Then, the compressor flushes its internal buffer, processing the buffered RDF graphs and producing a binary output ready to be sent to an output stream (for instance, a network socket).

The decompression process takes as input a buffer of binary data read from an input stream. To decompress this data, applications should instantiate an RDSZDecompressor object. Later on, they call the *decompress* method, providing the binary data as input and obtaining as result a list of RDF graphs, each of them representing an item in the RDF stream.

The RDSZ compressor and decompressor and all their methods are described with more detail in the following sections.

2.2 Compression

The pseudocode of the RDSZ compressor is provided in Algorithm 1. The main processing blocks of this compressor (shown in Figure 2) are:

- **Differential encoder** (*DiffEncoder* in Algorithm 1): it carries out the differential encoding of each stream item at the input, on the basis of previously processed items. For each input item, it produces as output an encoded item, in a text-based format.
- **Multiplexer** (*Mux* in Figure 2): it takes as input a sequence of items (encoded or not) and converts it into a single string by concatenating the text serialization of the items. A special delimiter is used to mark the limits of each item, so that the decompressor can separate them again.
- **Zlib compressor:** it takes as input the string generated by the multiplexer and compresses that string using Zlib to exploit additional redundancies.

As shown in Algorithm 1, RDSZ compresses the items in the RDF stream in two different ways: (1) using only Zlib, and (2) using the differential encoder followed by Zlib. Later on, when the results of both mechanisms are obtained, the smaller option is selected. Note that, in principle, it is possible to run in parallel both alternative mechanisms (to take advantage of multi-core processors). However, our current implementation does not exploit this possibility.

[2] In our Python implementation, this RDF graph is an *rdflib.Graph* object.

Algorithm 1. RDSZ compressor

```
/* Build a RDSZ compressor object */
function CONSTRUCTOR(cacheSize)
    compressor ← ZlibCompressor()
    mux ← Multiplexer()
    encoder ← DiffEncoder(cacheSize)
    items ← []
end function

/* Append an RDF item to the compressor buffer */
function COMPRESS(RDFgraph)
    items.append(RDFgraph)
end function

/* Flush the buffer and compress the RDF items */
function FLUSH
    compressorCopy ← compressor /* Clone the state of the Zlib compressor */

    /* Compress the items (serialized in Turtle) only with Zlib */
    turtleItems ← serializeInTurtle(items)
    string ← mux.multiplex(turtleItems)
    outZlib ← compressorCopy.compress(string)

    /* Compress the items with differential encoding plus Zlib */
    encodedItems ← encoder.encode(items)
    string ← mux.multiplex(encodedItems)
    outDiffZlib ← compressor.compress(string)

    /* Clean the buffer */
    items ← []

    /* Select the best strategy (that with smaller results) */
    if size(outZlib) ≤ size(outDiffZlib) then
        compressor ← compressorCopy
        return outZlib
    else
        return outDiffZlib
    end if
end function
```

Of the three main processing blocks that constitute the RDSZ compressor, the multiplexer and the Zlib compressor carry out well-known tasks: data concatenation (multiplexer) and standard compression using Zlib. Thus, we will focus the rest of this section in the analysis of the differential encoder.

Algorithm 2 details the pseudocode of the differential encoder. The input received by this encoder (line 4 in Algorithm 2) consists of a sequence of items in an RDF stream. We will use an example to illustrate the process carried out by this component. For instance, let us assume that the input is composed by the items represented in Turtle in figures 3 (first item in the sequence), and 4 (second item).

The RDF items in the input are processed sequentially and separately by the encoder. The first processing carried out with an item is to decompose it into a triple pattern and a set of variable bindings. This process is represented by the call to the method *buildPattern* in Algorithm 2 (line 9).

For the sake of brevity, we will not include here the full pseudocode of the *buildPattern* method. It works in a two stage process:

Algorithm 2. Differential encoder

```
/* Build a differential encoder object */
function CONSTRUCTOR(cacheSize)
    cache ← LRUCache(cacheSize)
end function

/* Encode a sequence of RDF items in the stream */
function ENCODE(items)
    encodedItems ← [] /* Initialize to empty list */
    for item in items do

        /* Decompose the item into a triple pattern and variable bindings */
        (pattern, bindings) ← BUILDPATTERN(item)

        /* Use differential encoding if possible (pattern previously processed) */
        if pattern in cache then
            (patternId, prevBindingsPattern) ← cache.get(pattern)
            encodedItem ← SERIALIZE(bindings, patternId, prevBindingsPattern)
        else
            patternId ← GENID(cache)
            encodedItem ← serializeInTurtle(item)
        end if

        encodedItems.append(encodedItem) /* Append encoded item to results */
        cache.put(pattern, (patternId, bindings)) /* Update the cache */

    end for
    return encodedItems
end function
```

```
@prefix dc: <http://purl.org/dc/elements/1.1/> .
@prefix wtl: <http://webtlab.it.uc3m.es/> .

wtl:_556103084 dc:date "2013-02-20T16:58:32Z";
    dc:author "Wonderboy";
    wtl:pageid 6227038;
    wtl:title "Villeroy & Boch" .
```

Fig. 3. Differential encoder example: 1st input item

```
@prefix dc: <http://purl.org/dc/elements/1.1/> .
@prefix wtl: <http://webtlab.it.uc3m.es/> .

wtl:_556103110 dc:date "2013-02-20T16:58:40Z";
    dc:author "Wonderboy";
    wtl:pageid 31317733;
    wtl:title "2013 Women's Cricket World Cup" .
```

Fig. 4. Differential encoder examples: 2nd input item

1. It orders the triples in the RDF graph of the item. The triples are first ordered taking into account the Turtle serialization of the subject. Those with the same subject are ordered on the basis of the Turtle serialization of the property. Finally, those sharing subject and property are ordered taking into account the Turtle serialization of the object.
2. It iterates over the ordered list of triples in the input RDF item and, for each of these triples, replaces the subject and object by variables. It returns as result a string, which represents the *pattern* obtained as an output of the replacement process, plus a table of variable *bindings*, which map each variable to its particular value in the input.

For instance, given the input RDF item shown in Figure 3, the output of the *buildPattern* method consists of: (1) a string with the pattern represented

```
?x0 <http://purl.org/dc/elements/1.1/author> ?x1 .
?x0 <http://purl.org/dc/elements/1.1/date> ?x2 .
?x0 <http://webtlab.it.uc3m.es/pageid> ?x3 .
?x0 <http://webtlab.it.uc3m.es/title> ?x4 .
```

Fig. 5. Triple pattern for RDF items in figures 3 and 4

Table 1. Variable bindings for RDF item in Figure 3

variable	value
?x0	<http://webtlab.it.uc3m.es/_556103084>
?x1	"Wonderboy"
?x2	"2013-02-20T16:58:32Z"
?x3	6227038
?x4	"Villeroy & Boch"

Table 2. Variable bindings for RDF item in Figure 4

variable	value
?x0	<http://webtlab.it.uc3m.es/_556103110>
?x1	"Wonderboy"
?x2	"2013-02-20T16:58:40Z"
?x3	31317733
?x4	"2013 Women's Cricket World Cup"

in Figure 5; and, (2) the variable bindings represented in Table 1. Note that, in case of the RDF item shown in Figure 4, the pattern would be the same, whereas the bindings would be those indicated in Table 2.

Once the decomposition into pattern and bindings of the input RDF item has been obtained, the encoder needs to determine whether this item can be represented on the basis of a previously processed item in the stream or not.

To take this decision, the encoder uses information about previously processed items that is stored within a Least Recently Used (LRU) cache of size *cacheSize* (defined in line 2 of Algorithm 2). This cache stores patterns of recently processed items. For each pattern, the associated bindings and a unique pattern identifier (an integer $idx \in [0, cacheSize - 1])$ are also stored.

Using the cache information, the encoder takes one of the following options:

(I) If the pattern of the RDF item being processed is already within the cache, this means that another item with the same pattern has been recently processed. Thus, the current item is encoded on the basis of the preceding one. As both items have the same pattern, there is no need to explicitly send all the pattern information to the decompressor again. Only the pattern identifier will be included in the encoded item. Regarding the bindings, the variables may have the same value both in the current and preceding RDF item or not. If the value is the same, there is no need to send it again. Otherwise, the value is included within the encoded item. The result of the encoding process in this case is a string that contains a line for the pattern identifier plus a line for each variable in the bindings. We adopt the following conventions to serialize variable values:

- The variables are included in the order of their number. The value for variable $?x0$ will be the first, then the value for $?x1$, etc. Due to this, there is no need to include the variable name in the encoded item.
- The variable values are represented in Turtle format (URIs between <>, string literals between quotes, etc.). Blank nodes are represented

```
1
<http://webtlab.it.uc3m.es/_556103110>

"2013-02-20T16:58:40Z"
31317733
"2013 Women's Cricket World Cup"
```

Fig. 6. Differential encoder example: results of the *serialize* method

with a single underscore (note that when several blank nodes are present, each of them will be a different, unambiguous variable).

- When a variable has the same value both in the current and preceding items, an empty line is included in the encoded item.

The process of representing the current item on the basis of a preceding one is denoted by a call to method *serialize* in Algorithm 2 (line 14). As it can be seen, this method receives as input all the required information: the bindings of both the current item (*bindings*) and the preceding item (*prevBindingsPattern*), and the pattern identifier (*patternId*).

In our particular example, the encoder uses differential encoding when processing the second RDF item, because it has the same pattern as the first item (see Figure 5). The result of the *serialize* method in this case is shown in Figure 6, where it has been assumed, without loss of generality, that the *patternId* in the cache for the pattern of this item is $idx = 1$. It can also be seen the empty line used to represent that the value of $?x1$ is the same for both RDF items (compare Table 1 and Table 2). Note also that some redundancies are present in the results of *serialize* (for instance, two variables share the prefix *"2013*). These redundancies are later exploited by the Zlib compressor included in RDSZ.

(II) In case the pattern of the RDF item being processed is not included within the cache, the *encodedItem* variable is assigned the string serialization in Turtle of the RDF item, without any change (line 17 in Algorithm 2).

In any case, the *encodedItem* is added (line 20 of Algorithm 2) to the list of encoded items to be returned as output.

Finally, the differential encoder updates the cache, storing the information about the RDF item just processed (line 21 of Algorithm 2). In particular, the cache maps the pattern of the item to the associated bindings plus a pattern identifier. The value of this identifier depends on whether the pattern was already in the cache or not. In case the pattern was already in the cache, its previous identifier is reused. In case the pattern was not previously in the cache, a new identifier is generated (call to method *genId* on line 16 of Algorithm 2). This method returns the index of the cache where the new entry is going to be stored.

Once all the input RDF items are processed, the result of the encoding process (list *encodedItems* in Algorithm 2) is returned as output to be processed by the next element in the compressor pipeline: the multiplexer (see Figure 2).

Algorithm 3. RDSZ decompressor

```
/* Build a RDSZ decompressor object */
function Constructor(cacheSize)
    decompressor ← ZlibCompressor()
    demux ← Demultiplexer()
    decoder ← DiffDecoder(cacheSize)
end function

/* Decompress a buffer with binary data */
function Decompress(buffer)
    string ← decompressor.decompress(buffer)
    tokens ← demux.demultiplex(string)
    decodedItems ← decoder.decode(tokens)
    return decodedItems
end function
```

2.3 Decompression

The pseudocode of the RDSZ decompressor is provided in Algorithm 3. It consists of a set of blocks (see Figure 2) that carry out the inverse processes of their compressor counterparts:

- **Zlib decompressor:** it takes as input binary data in a buffer and decompresses it using Zlib, obtaining a string.
- **Demultiplexer** (*Demux* in Figure 2): it splits the string generated by the decompressor into a sequence of tokens (each of them representing an RDF item, encoded or not). To do so, it uses the same delimiter defined in the compressor multiplexer.
- **Differential decoder** (*DiffDecoder* in Algorithm 3): gets the tokens from the demultiplexer and decodes the items that have been encoded at compression time, returning as result a list of RDF graphs, each of them representing an item in the stream.

The rest of this section will be focused on the RDSZ differential decoder, as the processes of the other two components are well-known. The pseudocode of this decoder is shown in Algorithm 4. It processes the tokens provided by the demultiplexer one by one. For each token it carries out the following tasks:

(I) The tokens at the input can represent an encoded item (like the one depicted in Figure 6) or an unencoded one (that is, a Turtle serialization of the RDF item as shown for instance in Figure 3). The decoder differentiates between these cases by checking the first line of the token, which can be an integer (the *patternId* of an encoded item) or not (unencoded item).

   (a) In case the token represents an encoded item, it is decoded. To do so:

      i. The decoder reads the *patternId* from the first line of the input token (line 10 in Algorithm 4).

      ii. It uses its internal state (a LRU cache with the same information as the encoder cache at the compressor) to obtain the pattern and bindings associated to the *patternId* (line 11 in Algorithm 4).

Algorithm 4. Differential decoder

```
   /* Build a differential decoder object */
1: function CONSTRUCTOR(cacheSize)
2:     cache ← LRUCache(cacheSize)
3: end function

   /* Decode a sequence of tokens from the demultiplexer */
4: function DECODE(tokens)
5:     decodedItems ← [] /* Initialize to empty list */
6:     for token in tokens do
7:
8:         /* Check if the token is really encoded or not */
9:         if token is encoded then
10:            patternId ← token.readFirstLine()
11:            (pattern, prevBindingsPattern) ← cache.searchID(patternId)
12:            decodedItem ← DESERIALIZE(pattern, token, prevBindingsPattern)
13:        else
14:            decodedItem ← deserializeFromTurtle(token)
15:        end if
16:
17:        decodedItems.append(decodedItem) /* Append decoded item to results */
18:
19:        /* Update the cache to keep it in sync with the compressor */
20:        (pattern, bindings) ← BUILDPATTERN(decodedItem)
21:        if pattern in cache then
22:            patternId ← cache.get(pattern)
23:        else
24:            patternId ← GENID(cache)
25:        end if
26:        cache.put(pattern, (patternId, bindings))
27:
28:    end for
29:    return decodedItems
30: end function
```

iii. It reconstructs the original set of triples in the RDF item (call to *deserialize* in line 12 of Algorithm 4) and stores the results in the *decodedItem* variable. Note that using the differential encoding process does not introduce any RDF information loss, as the original item triples are reconstructed at the receiver.

In our particular example, if the token contains the encoded representation of the second input item, shown in Figure 6, the decoder:

i. Reads the pattern identifier ($idx = 1$) from the first line.
ii. Obtains from the cache the pattern for that identifier (pattern in Figure 5) as well as the associated bindings (that will be those of the preceding item with the same pattern, that is, the bindings of the first item, shown in Table 1).
iii. With the bindings of the first item and the contents of the token, the bindings of the second item (Table 2) can be obtained. Then, a variable replacement process over the pattern serves to obtain the triples of the second item and, from them, its RDF graph.

(b) If the token represents an unencoded item, the *decodedItem* variable is assigned the RDF graph obtained by deserializing the Turtle representation of the RDF item (line 14 in Algorithm 4). Obviously, as the original item is received in this case, no information loss has been introduced by RDSZ.

(II) Once the *decodedItem* has been obtained, it is added to a list of *decodedItems* to be returned as result (line 17 in Algorithm 4).

(III) The decoder cache is updated (lines 20 to 26 in Algorithm 4), to keep it in sync with its counterpart at the encoder. In order to do so, the decoder carries out the same processing as is done in the encoder.

Once all the input tokens are processed, the result of the decoding process (*decodedItems* in Algorithm 4) is returned as output of the decompression process.

3 Evaluation

We implemented a first prototype of the RDSZ algorithm using Python 2.7.3 and RDFLib 4.0.1[3]. We used this prototype to validate empirically our approach, centering our evaluation in two aspects: compression performance, and processing time.

Next sections describe the datasets used in our experiments (Section 3.1), as well as the results of our analysis regarding both the compression performance (Section 3.2) and processing time (Section 3.3).

3.1 Datasets

RDSZ uses differential item encoding, which depends on the item structure. Hence we are interested in evaluating the algorithm using several different datasets with different item schemas. Table 3 describes the datasets used in the experimental evaluation[4], including name, size in bytes, number of RDF items it contains, size in triples, and average size of an item in triples (*Avg.*). We also include in the last column the number of different structural patterns found in the dataset when running RDSZ, which is related with the possibility (or not) of using differential encoding when compressing the dataset. Note that this should be a number between one (every item has the same pattern) and the total number of items in the dataset (every item has a unique pattern).

The datasets *AEMET1* and *AEMET2* represent, using different schemas, information taken from wheather stations in Spain [3]. They were obtained from the Spanish Meteorological Office (AEMET). The dataset *Identica* represents in RDF the messages in the public streamline of the microblogging site Identica[5] on a several day time frame. The dataset *Wikipedia* was obtained by monitoring every 30 seconds for a period of several hours the edits carried out on the English Wikipedia, and representing in RDF information about these edits (page,

[3] `https://github.com/RDFLib` (January 13th, 2014)
[4] Available for download at: `http://www.it.uc3m.es/berto/RDSZ/`
[5] `http://identi.ca/` (January 13th, 2014)

Table 3. Description of the experimental datasets

Name	Size (bytes)	#Items	#Triples	Avg.	#Patterns
AEMET1	34,344,498	33,095	1,018,815	30.78	1,459
AEMET2	263,640,938	398,347	2,788,429	7	2
Identica	17,559,385	25,749	256,699	9.97	104
Wikipedia	14,994,109	2,004	359,028	179.16	2,004
Petrol	324,265,505	419,577	3,356,616	8	1
LOD	27,621,020	25,906	258,533	9.98	5
Mix	5,327,406	5,000	93,048	18.61	371

timestamp, etc). The *Petrol* dataset was provided by the Spanish start-up Localidata[6], and provides metadata about credit card transactions in petrol stations. The *LOD* dataset represents sensor observations of different wheather parameters. It was extracted from the *Linked Observation Data*[7] dataset. Finally, the *Mix* dataset was generated by randomly combining items from the other datasets, so that each dataset has the same probability to contribute an item.

3.2 Compression Performance

The compression performance of RDSZ depends on several parameters. First, the structure of the items in the stream, that is, the dataset schema, has an impact on the differential encoding process. Second, the results of RDSZ depend on the size of the pattern cache (*cacheSize*). Third, the performance depends also on how items in the stream are grouped to be processed by the compressor, that is, in how many calls to *compress* are made between two successive calls to *flush*, according to the interface shown in Section 2.1. We name this parameter as *batchSize*. The reason for this dependency is that each time the Zlib compressor processes a batch of items, it inserts specific information (in particular, related to Huffman coding) to be sent to the decompressor. Increasing the *batchSize* (that is, compressing larger groups) reduces the total number of item batches to be processed and, thus, reduces the Zlib (and hence RDSZ) overhead.

We first analyze the impact of the dataset on the compression performance. To do so, we run RDSZ in the different datasets assuming a fixed *batchSize* of 5 items and a *cacheSize* of 100 entries. For comparison purposes, we use as baseline the results achieved when the differential encoding process is not used, that is when the items are just serialized (using either RDF/XML, Turtle, NTriples or JSON-LD), multiplexed and compressed with Zlib. Table 4 shows the compressed size in bytes for each approach. The last column indicates the percentage of gain provided by RDSZ with respect to the best performing reference.

According to the results in Table 4, the best performing reference in all the datasets is that where Turtle serialization is used. RDSZ outperforms this reference in all but one of the datasets (*Wikipedia*). Note that, taking into account

[6] `http://www.localidata.com/` (January 13th, 2014)

[7] `http://wiki.knoesis.org/index.php/LinkedSensorData` (January 13th, 2014)

Table 4. Analysis of the compression performance of RDSZ on the different datasets

Dataset	Zlib baseline (No differential encoding)				RDSZ	RDSZ
	XML size (bytes)	Turtle size (bytes)	N-Triples size (bytes)	JSON-LD size (bytes)	size (bytes)	Gain
AEMET1	4,325,202	2,299,308	5,552,972	3,051,049	**1,876,624**	18.38%
AEMET2	12,854,321	8,120,614	16,930,673	9,432,218	**5,633,763**	30.62%
Identica	3,335,047	2,604,441	3,569,338	3,078,349	**2,266,868**	12.96%
Wikipedia	3,017,381	**2,466,633**	3,450,287	2,821,515	**2,466,633**	0%
Petrol	29,370,624	23,594,420	34,368,532	25,689,604	**19,806,835**	16.05%
LOD	1,230,708	784,298	1,652,188	1,056,188	**537,646**	31.45%
Mix	889,410	665,786	1,019,060	804,721	**599,775**	9.91%

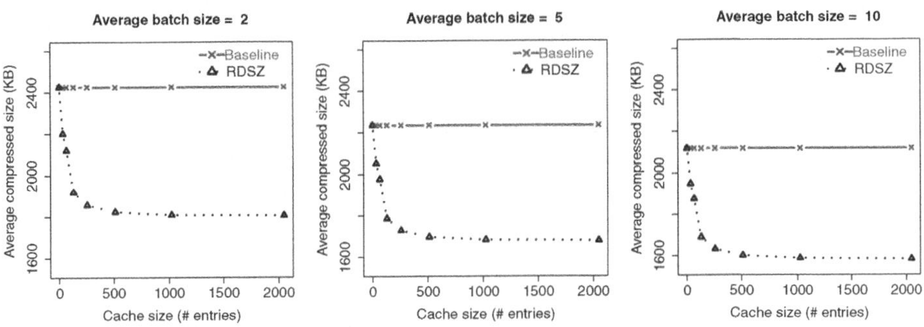

Fig. 7. Evaluating the impact of the *cacheSize* and *batchSize* parameters on the compression performance

the information shown in Table 3, this is an expected result, because in the *Wikipedia* dataset all the items have a different pattern and, thus, RDSZ does not take any advantage from using differential encoding.

To evaluate the impact of the *batchSize* and *cacheSize* we ran several experiments on the AEMET1 dataset with the following setup: (1) the *cacheSize* parameter varied from 32 to 2048 on a power of two basis; and (2) the *batchSize* was modelled using a Poisson random process, to simulate the scenario of an application that produces stream items (and calls *compress*) according to a Poisson traffic model and calls *flush* periodically. Figure 7 reports the results for the Turtle baseline and RDSZ when the average of the *batchSize* process was set to 2, 5 and 10 items. Due to the random nature of the Poisson process, the experiment was repeated for each pair {*cacheSize*, *batchSize*} to compute the average of the compressed size and its 95% confidence interval. The average values (in Kilobytes) are reported in Figure 7. The confidence intervals were found to be very small (with a maximum error of less than 3KB) and, thus, were not represented to ease visualization. Note that we have also included as reference in Figure 7 the results when the *cacheSize* is 0, where RDSZ matches the baseline.

Table 5. Analysis of the processing time of RDSZ

Dataset	No differential encoding (Turtle)		RDSZ		Ratio
	Compre. time per item (ms)	Decompre. time per item (ms)	Compre. time per item (ms)	Decompre. time per item (ms)	
AEMET1	5.58	5.30	9.81	17.08	2.47
AEMET2	1.75	1.87	2.33	5.57	2.18
Identica	2.27	2.02	3.07	6.57	2.25
Wikipedia	38.05	33.48	101.48	92.29	2.71
Petrol	2.09	2.05	2.77	6.00	2.12
LOD	2.69	2.70	3.51	7.82	2.10
Mix	3.71	3.48	6.72	10.03	2.37

As shown in Figure 7, increasing the *cacheSize* benefits performance. Furthermore, as expected, increasing the *batchSize* has a positive impact for both RDSZ and the baseline (as both of them use Zlib). Thus, it may seem that a possibility to improve compression performace is simply to increase the *batchSize* arbitrarily. However, this affects the delay perceived when transmiting the stream over a communication line, since larger batches require waiting for more items to be available at the compressor. Thus, the tradeoff *batchSize* versus delay needs to be considered for each particular application. For instance, applications with no real-time restrictions may wait to buffer a large number of items (large *batchSize*) before calling *flush*, whereas applications with real-time restrictions may prefer to call *flush* periodically with a small period to limit the delay, even if the *batchSize* to be processed at each period is small.

3.3 Processing Time

We are interested in measuring the average processing time per item of our current implementation of RDSZ, as this time has an impact in the throughput that can be achieved with our stream compressor. Furthermore, as in Section 3.2, we are also interested in analyzing the influence of the dataset, the *batchSize* and the *cacheSize* into this processing time. To do so, we run our experiments in an Ubuntu 12.04 laptop with an Intel Core2 Duo, 2.53GHz CPU and 8GB RAM.

First, we measure the average compression and decompression time per item in the different datasets, assuming a constant *batchSize* of 5 items and *cacheSize* of 100 entries. The results for RDSZ and the baseline that uses Turtle serialization (the best according to results in Table 4) are reported in Table 5 (measured in milliseconds). The last column in this table shows the ratio obtained by dividing the total (compression plus decompression) average processing time per item of RDSZ by that of the baseline. As indicated in Table 5, the processing time of RDSZ is worse than that of the baseline, as expected, due to the extra processing introduced by RDSZ, and the fact that we are evaluating an unoptimized prototype.

Second, we are also interested in analyzing how the total average processing time per item of our RDSZ prototype depends on the average number of triples per item. To do so, we fitted a linear model between these two variables as measured in all the datasets. This resulted in a line with slope $\alpha = 1.08604$ and $Intercept = -1.55013$. The high $R^2 = 0.9984$ and low $p-value = 2.372e-08$ of the fitted linear model indicate that it explains adequately the relation between the variables, which suggests that the processing time per item is proportional to the number of triples per item for the datasets considered.

Finally, we followed the same experimental setup as in Section 3.2 to evaluate the impact of the *batchSize* and *cacheSize* parameters in the processing time. However, in this case we have not found any significant dependency with these parameters. In particular, running the experiments with different *batchSize* and *cacheSize* values, the maximum difference between the total average processing time per item measured between any two runs was less than 1 millisecond.

4 Related Work

RDF compression has been only widely addressed recently. One early reference on this topic is [6], where different compression approaches are tested, including: (1) use of general purpose algorithms and (2) definition of compact RDF representations that are later compressed. The conclusions of this work suggest that RDF is highly compressible, especially with compact RDF representations.

In [7] the authors present a compact binary RDF representation, named HDT, that consists of three elements: a header, a dictionary of symbols and the triples encoded according to the dictionary. This structure can be later compressed using Huffman coding and predictive high-order compression techniques, and the result, according to the authors, outperforms universal compressors.

Another relevant work is [1], which describes a compact RDF structure (k2-triples) that allows SPARQL queries to be performed on the compressed representation and, thus, can be used to implement in-memory RDF indexes.

A logical approach to lossless RDF dataset compression is presented in [8]. It consists on automatically building a set of inference rules from the dataset to be compressed and removing all the triples that can be inferred using these rules. The remaining triples plus the inference rules constitute the compressed representation of the original dataset.

The topic of scalable compression of large RDF datasets is addressed in [12], where the authors present a parallel RDF data compression approach based on dictionary encoding techniques and MapReduce.

All of the aforementioned approaches are centered on the compression of large, static, RDF datasets. Compared to that work, the main contribution of this paper is the definition of a lossless compression algorithm for RDF streams.

The topic of RDF stream compression has been indirectly covered in CQELS Cloud [9] and Ztreamy [2]. These references stress the importance of compression for scalable transmission of RDF streams over the network. They also suggest potential approaches to deal with this issue: dictionary encoding in [9], and Zlib in [2]. However, compression is not the central topic of these papers, and they do not provide an exhaustive analysis of these approaches.

5 Conclusions and Future Lines

In this paper we presented the RDSZ algorithm for lossless RDF stream compression. It allows to reduce the communication overheads when transmitting RDF streams. The algorithm is based on the combination of a differential item encoding mechanism, which takes advantage of the structural similarities between items in the stream, with the general purpose stream compressor Zlib, to take advantage of additional redundancies. The approach was implemented and evaluated using several heterogeneous RDF stream datasets. The results of this evaluation indicate that the combination in RDSZ of differential item encoding and Zlib produces gains in compression ratios with respect to using Zlib alone.

The current version of RDSZ is not designed to allow querying the compressed RDF stream without decompressing it beforehand. Addressing this issue and integrating our approach into an RDF stream processing engine could represent potential future lines of development of the work presented in this paper.

References

1. Álvarez-García, S., Brisaboa, N.R., Fernández, J.D., Martínez-Prieto, M.A.: Compressed k2-Triples for Full-In-Memory RDF Engines. In: AMCIS (2011)
2. Arias, J., Fernández, N., Sánchez, L., Fuentes-Lorenzo, D.: Ztreamy: A middleware for publishing semantic streams on the web. Web Semantics: Science, Services and Agents on the World Wide Web (in print)
3. Atemezing, G., Corcho, O., Garijo, D., Mora, J., Poveda-Villalón, M., Rozas, P., Vila-Suero, D., Villazón-Terrazas, B.: Transforming Meteorological Data into Linked Data. Semantic Web Journal (2012)
4. Barbieri, D.F., Braga, D., Ceri, S., Grossniklaus, M.: An execution environment for C-SPARQL queries. In: Proceedings of the 13th International Conference on Extending Database Technology, EDBT 2010, pp. 441–452 (2010)
5. Calbimonte, J.-P., Corcho, O., Gray, A.J.G.: Enabling ontology-based access to streaming data sources. In: Patel-Schneider, P.F., Pan, Y., Hitzler, P., Mika, P., Zhang, L., Pan, J.Z., Horrocks, I., Glimm, B. (eds.) ISWC 2010, Part I. LNCS, vol. 6496, pp. 96–111. Springer, Heidelberg (2010)
6. Fernández, J.D., Gutierrez, C., Martínez-Prieto, M.A.: RDF compression: basic approaches. In: Proceedings of the 19th International Conference on World Wide Web, WWW 2010, pp. 1091–1092 (2010)
7. Fernández, J.D., Martínez-Prieto, M.A., Gutiérrez, C., Polleres, A., Arias, M.: Binary RDF representation for publication and exchange (HDT). Web Semantics: Science, Services and Agents on the World Wide Web 19, 22–41 (2013)
8. Joshi, A., Hitzler, P., Dong, G.: Logical linked data compression. In: Cimiano, P., Corcho, O., Presutti, V., Hollink, L., Rudolph, S. (eds.) ESWC 2013. LNCS, vol. 7882, pp. 170–184. Springer, Heidelberg (2013)

9. Le-Phuoc, D., Nguyen Mau Quoc, H., Le Van, C., Hauswirth, M.: Elastic and scalable processing of linked stream data in the cloud. In: Alani, H., Kagal, L., Fokoue, A., Groth, P., Biemann, C., Parreira, J.X., Aroyo, L., Noy, N., Welty, C., Janowicz, K. (eds.) ISWC 2013, Part I. LNCS, vol. 8218, pp. 280–297. Springer, Heidelberg (2013)
10. Deutsch, P., Gailly, J.-L. (eds.): ZLIB Compressed Data Format Specification version 3.3. Internet RFC 1950 (May 1996)
11. Deutsch, P. (ed.): DEFLATE Compressed Data Format Specification version 1.3. Internet RFC 1951 (May 1996)
12. Urbani, J., Maassen, J., Drost, N., Seinstra, F., Bal, H.: Scalable RDF data compression with MapReduce. Concurrency and Computation: Practice and Experience 25(1), 24–39 (2013)
13. Valle, E.D., Ceri, S., Harmelen, F.V., Fensel, D.: It's a streaming world! reasoning upon rapidly changing information. IEEE Intelligent Systems 24(6), 83–89 (2009)

Linked USDL: A Vocabulary for Web-Scale Service Trading

Carlos Pedrinaci[1], Jorge Cardoso[2,3], and Torsten Leidig[4]

[1] Knowledge Media Institute, The Open University, Milton Keynes, United Kingdom
carlos.pedrinaci@open.ac.uk
[2] CISUC/Dept. Informatics Engineering, University of Coimbra, Coimbra, Portugal
[3] Technical University of Dresden, Dresden, Germany
jcardoso@dei.uc.pt
[4] SAP Research Karlsruhe, Germany
torsten.leidig@sap.com

Abstract. Real-world services ranging from cloud solutions to consulting currently dominate economic activity. Yet, despite the increasing number of service marketplaces online, service trading on the Web remains highly restricted. Services are at best traded within closed silos that offer mainly manual search and comparison capabilities through a Web storefront. Thus, it is seldom possible to automate the customisation, bundling, and trading of services, which would foster a more efficient and effective service sector. In this paper we present Linked USDL, a comprehensive vocabulary for capturing and sharing rich service descriptions, which aims to support the trading of services over the Web in an open, scalable, and highly automated manner. The vocabulary adopts and exploits Linked Data as a means to efficiently support communication over the Web, to promote and simplify its adoption by reusing vocabularies and datasets, and to enable the opportunistic engagement of multiple cross-domain providers.

Keywords: #eswc2014Pedrinaci, Services, Vocabulary, Linked Data, USDL, eCommerce.

1 Introduction

The importance of real-world services, that is business activities of a mostly intangible nature (e.g., life insurance, consulting), has grown over the last 50 years to dominate economic activity [1]. Because of their intangible nature, services can often be bundled, adapted, and traded in an automated manner. In an attempt to exploit the Web as a service trading platform a number of service marketplaces have emerged, ranging from purely technical registries like UDDI [2], to business-oriented marketplaces such as Google Helpouts. Technical registries have for the most part focussed on the computer science aspects of services which is limiting as it ignores fundamental characteristics of services including the economic, social, and business contexts [3]. Business-oriented marketplaces on the other hand have focussed on providing silos that offer limited search and

V. Presutti et al. (Eds.): ESWC 2014, LNCS 8465, pp. 68–82, 2014.

comparison capabilities through an essentially human-oriented storefront [4]. As a result, common and essential economic activities in the service sector such as the generation of customised offerings, the creation and trading of possibly cross-domain and multi-provider service bundles, or simply the communication between customer and provider remain largely manual activities [4].

Supporting the trading of services over the Web in an open, scalable, and automated manner enabling the opportunistic engagement of multiple cross-domain providers requires a shared means for capturing and reasoning upon the economic, social, and technical aspects governing service exchanges [1,3,4]. The Unified Service Description Language (USDL) is the most comprehensive attempt in this direction but it has received limited adoption due to its complexity, while it also exhibited limitations with respect to the level of extensibility and automation supported. In this paper we present Linked USDL[1], a new vocabulary which builds upon the results and experience gained with USDL combined with prior research on Semantic Web Services, business ontologies, and Linked Data to better support Web-scale automated service trading. We present the methodology and main decisions adopted for transforming the complex USDL specification into a network of vocabularies that is anchored on simplicity as well as on vocabulary and data reuse. The resulting vocabulary is thoroughly evaluated in terms of domain coverage, suitability for purpose, and its current level of adoption.

2 Related Work

Service Science aims to reach a better understanding of services, service networks, value co-creation and service innovation, to name a few of the main research topics [1]. These efforts, which encompass several disciplines, are geared towards establishing solid foundations for advancing our ability to design, create, and analyse service systems with both business and societal purposes in mind.

Relevant work in Computer Science includes service-oriented systems, which approach the development of complex applications by integrating networked software components called Web services [2]. This area has been prolific in terms of both tooling and specifications including a number of approaches for describing technical services semantically, e.g., OWL-S, SAWSDL, and WSMO [5,6]. Although (semantic) Web services work provides advanced support for discovering or composing technical services, it disregards the fundamental socio-economic context of real-world services (e.g., value chains and offerings), and does not cover the widespread manual services (e.g., consulting) [3]. Complementary work on Workflow and Business Process Management has focussed on the operationalisation of the processes within enterprises [2,3,5], which has more recently also incorporated human activities [7]. This work is, however, centred on a procedural view on how activities are carried out within an organisation which is orthogonal to the business characteristics of the services offered (e.g., speed of internet connection offered) which are essential to service trading.

[1] See `http://linked-usdl.org/`

The most notable effort able to represent and reason about business models, services, and value networks is the e^3 family of ontologies which includes the e^3service and e^3value ontologies [3,8]. This research has, however, not been much concerned with the computational and operational perspectives covering for instance the actual interaction with services. Likewise, the technical issues related to enabling a Web-scale deployment and adoption of these solutions were not core to this work. GoodRelations [9] (GR) on the contrary is a popular vocabulary for describing semantically products and offerings. Although GR originally aimed to support both services and products, it is mostly centred on products to the detriment of its coverage for modelling services, leaving aside for instance the coverage of modes of interaction, or the support for value chains.

USDL [4,10] is, to date, the most comprehensive approach to supporting the description of services for automated processing. USDL consists of 9 modules modelled in eCore capturing services, interaction interfaces, pricing models, service level agreements, and related legal issues[2]. Despite its comprehensive support, this effort underestimated the need for such an all encompassing model to be widely open, highly flexible and extensible, and yet simple in nature [11]. On the one hand, the rather centralised and controlled nature of the approach led to an overly complex model hard to grasp and apply. On the other hand, eCore exhibited technical limitations towards its extensibility and its use as a lingua franca on the Web where Linked Data and light semantics are currently considered a more adequate technology.

3 Requirements Analysis

Informed by research carried out on services, including the related work covered earlier, we have elicited a number of requirements that Linked USDL and any other language or vocabulary with such an ambitious purpose should address. This includes notably coverage requirements, which we shall cover first. We also present additional criteria that we identified during the standardisation activities of USDL as potential issues and limitations for its Web-scale adoption [11].

3.1 Description Requirements

One of the essential difficulties when dealing with services beyond mere technical interfaces, is the fact that they are at the intersection of many diverse disciplines that range from technical aspects, to operational ones, socio-economic concerns, or even legal issues. Being able to move across each of these domains is essential to support the trading of services online. We detail the main dimensions next.

Functionality. Services are business activities that normally take place through (possibly technology mediated) interactions between stakeholders, resulting

[2] See the full specification at `http://www.internet-of-services.com/fileadmin/IOS/user_upload/pdf/USDL-3.0-M5-Archive.zip`

in benefits to the actors involved. Fundamental to the notion of service is therefore its functionality in terms of what it does, requires, and provides. Given the highly diverse nature of services this should cover the entire spectrum from fully automated provisioning (e.g., Spotify) to those essentially manual (e.g., car repair service). Depending on the stakeholder, the level of abstraction could vary from a detailed operational view (provider), to a high-level one for customers.

Agents and Networks. Services delivery engages several stakeholders in (possibly ephemeral) ad-hoc business networks, e.g., banks often engage in partnerships with insurances to provide accounts with integrated travel insurance. The modelling of services should seamlessly support both the emergence and analysis of such networks in order to enable the dynamic co-creation of value through Web-wide service trading. Important aspects to be covered are thus the agents involved in a certain network and the role(s) they play.

Service Relationships. Thanks to their intangible nature, services can be combined, repurposed, and adapted to better fulfil customer needs. Services are often related to other services and products. For instance, services can often be *enhanced* with others, or there can be *variations* over established types. Services are often *bundled*, i.e., aggregated and offered jointly in packages like broadband and TV services. And in the case of automated services, services may be *composed* according to specific data and control flow to achieve a complex objective out of simpler components.

Operational and Delivery. The delivery of services is often subject to restrictions or conditions. These may range from geographical concerns (e.g., the insured individual should live in the UK), temporal availability, legal issues, variable pricing, and so on. From a service provider operational perspective, there may well be limitations due to the resources required, e.g., staffing, that need to be tracked as they determine the costs and the capacity for providing a service.

Consumption. Services are most often accessed or "consumed" through interactions by means of designated *communication channels*. For example, making an insurance claim may require the customer to phone the insurance company, or fill up a form online. These communication channels may vary during the service delivery process (e.g., initially claim by phone and check the progress online), and there may exist restrictions on how interactions should take place. For instance a car repair service may require you to bring the car to the garage whereas in other cases the service may take care of sending a mechanic within some geographical boundaries.

3.2 Language Requirements

In addition to the aforementioned coverage requirements, research in the area has highlighted further requirements that the language should meet. First and foremost given the complexity of the domain and the fact that the aim is to maximise to the extent possible the level of automation that can be achieved during the life-cycle of services, the modelling of services needs to rely on a conceptual model with formal foundations that can enable automated processing [3,10]. Nonetheless the language should be modular and extensible in order to be able to accommodate different domains and the many facets of services while minimising the complexity for users and tool developers.

Our subsequent work on standardisation highlighted that although necessary, these requirements did not appear to be sufficient for Web-scale adoption:

An Open Solution. To support the engagement of any business entity across any domain the technological approach should be open. It should be open so as to allow anybody to engage and trade services online, as well as towards its evolution in order to cater for new requirements, accommodate new ways of doing business, or support new domains.

A Web-Based Solution. A scenario like the one envisaged requires an approach that can support the engagement of millions of service providers and consumers in exposing, locating, interpreting, and contracting services. This necessarily calls for highly interoperable and scalable solutions in terms of data sharing, data processing, and communication protocols.

Promoting Take Up. While providing an open solution is likely to have a positive impact on technology take up, adoption will largely be determined by the simplicity with which any business entity could adopt a solution based on these technologies and the compatibility with existing legacy systems.

4 Linked USDL Vocabulary

Driven by the aforementioned requirements and informed by the drawbacks exhibited by USDL we worked on Linked USDL focussing essentially on reducing the complexity underlying USDL and fostering its wider adoption through the use of Web-centric technologies that are more amenable to extension, modification, and automation at large scale.

4.1 Design Decisions

First, due to the success, scale, growth, and current adoption of the Web for world-wide telecommunication and electronic commerce we believe that any technology hoping to enable service trading online should necessarily embrace and build upon the Web principles and technologies [12]. Notably Linked USDL should also embrace principles like i) the establishment of global identifiers, e.g., by using URIs to identify services and providers; ii) the use of links to other resources on the Web to enrich a particular datum with reusable and externally provided information, e.g., pointing to complementary services; iii) the use of HTTP as a simple uniform protocol for supporting interactions; and iv) the decoupling between resources and their representation. Doing so brings a technology stack that has proven to support large scale, efficient, multi-party interactions, as well as it directly provides an integration point with open, standard technologies that are already widely used and supported.

Second, to enable effective interactions at the business level, we need to provide standards that go beyond data transportation and syntactic representation [1]. To this end, Linked USDL embraces the use of formal ontology representation languages to capture the semantics of services such that they are amenable to automated reasoning. Linked USDL goes one step forward in the adoption of Web technologies to embrace the emerging standard approach for data sharing online, namely Linked Data [13]. Adopting these principles enables Linked USDL to capture, share, and interlink data about services of highly heterogeneous nature and domains, in an open, scalable, and uniform manner. Linked Data principles promote and support reuse which in turn helps to reduce the data modelling overhead (e.g., by reusing conceptual models and existing data sets), and maximise the compatibility with existing tooling. Both aspects are major challenges earlier versions of USDL faced which this work aims to alleviate.

4.2 Design Methodology

Following common Knowledge Engineering best practices [14], we aimed at creating a modular solution based on well-designed, widely adopted vocabularies that did not introduce substantial ontological commitments away from the core topics of interest. Thus, considerable effort was devoted to identifying and evaluating reusable ontologies.

First, we identified the main topics to be covered given the original USDL specification and determined some core terms characterising each of these topics. Informed by the topics and terms identified, we carried out both a manual and semi-automated search to determine potentially relevant reusable ontologies. On the one hand, we performed a state of the art analysis to identify ontologies that were relevant for the modelling of services, see [11] and Section 2. On the other hand, we used Swoogle [15], Watson [16], LOD Stats [17], and the Linked Open Vocabularies (LOV)[3] engines to search for ontologies covering the main terms identified. For each of the queries asked, we kept the top 10 results. The resulting list was eventually enriched with widely-used general purpose vocabularies such as Dublin Core (DC) and Simple Knowledge Organisation Scheme (SKOS).

Second, for each of the vocabularies identified, we used both LOD Stats and LOV to figure out the number of datasets using these terms, the number of instances of the main concepts of interest present in datasets on the Web, and the number of times the vocabulary is reused elsewhere. The search for reusable ontologies provided us pointers to existing vocabularies of potential interest together with indications regarding their use and popularity. Table 1 shows the results obtained for the vocabularies for which there was at least one instance found on the Web[4]. Indeed, the statistics should not be taken as an exact value of the overall use of these vocabularies (e.g., GR is used more frequently than what is reflected by this analysis), but rather as a relative indication. Indeed we also took into account the properties defined by these vocabularies which are in some cases (e.g., DC Terms) the main constructs reused.

[3] `http://lov.okfn.org`

[4] These statistics were last retrieved in November 2013.

Table 1. Top Vocabularies per Topic

Topic	Vocabulary	# Datasets		# Instances		LOV Reuse
		LOD	LOV	LOD	LOV	
Service	GR	6	45	146	0	6
	MSM	2	0	41,368	0	0
	OSLC	2	0	2	0	0
	COGS	N/A	5	N/A	0	3
Offering	GR	6	8	824	656	4
Location	vCard (v3 & v4)	5	0 + 2	3,684	3,686 + 3	0 + 2
	WGS84	11	1	3,204	1,7651	1
	AKT Signage	18	0	11,789	0	0
	DC Terms	1	9	39	39	6
	Schema.org	-	1	-	5	1
Business Entities	Schema.org	2	4	1,570,778	1,570,778	3
	FOAF	60	135	14,613	14,557	29
	GR	1	N/A	3,918	N/A	N/A
	W3C Org.	1,050	11	2	1,050	2
Time	W3C Time	9	N/A	236,433	N/A	N/A

The design of Linked USDL was driven by these statistics, and a manual assessment of the quality, coverage, and potential alignments of the vocabularies.

4.3 Model

Informed by the aforementioned analysis, Linked USDL, which is publicly available together with further examples in GitHub[5], builds upon a family of complementary networked vocabularies that provide good coverage of necessary aspects and are widely used on the Web for capturing their particular domains. In particular Linked USDL builds upon:

- DC Terms[6] to cover general purpose metadata such as the creator of a certain description, its date of creation or modification, etc.
- SKOS providing low-cost support for capturing knowledge organisation systems (e.g., classifications and thesauri) in RDF.
- Time Ontology (Time)[7] for covering basic temporal relations. The ontology allows us to capture temporal relationships such as *before* and *during*.
- vCard vocabulary[8] a vCard 4 compatible vocabulary to support providing location and contact information for people and organisations.
- Minimal Service Model[9] (MSM) [18] to provide coverage for automated service-based interactions including Remote Procedure Call solutions (e.g., WSDL services) and RESTful services.
- GR[10] [9] to provide core coverage for services, business entities, offerings, and products.

[5] `https://github.com/linked-usdl/usdl-core`
[6] `http://purl.org/dc/terms/`
[7] `http://www.w3.org/TR/owl-time`
[8] `http://www.w3.org/TR/vcard-rdf/`
[9] `http://iserve.kmi.open.ac.uk/ns/msm`
[10] `http://purl.org/goodrelations/`

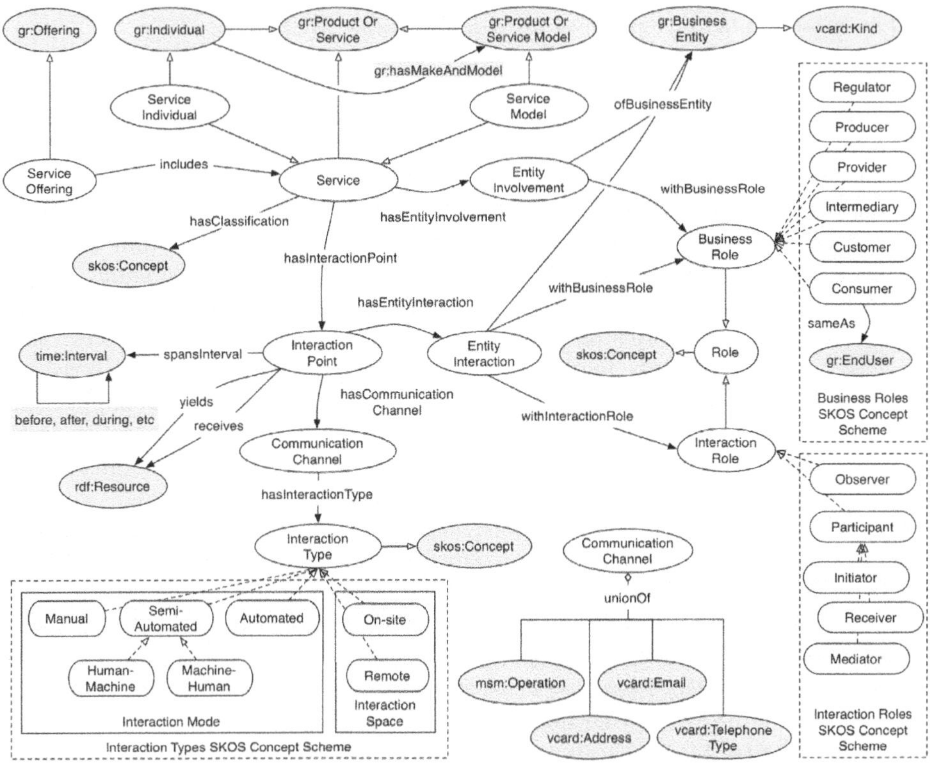

Fig. 1. Linked USDL Core

The vocabulary has been modelled mostly using RDF/RDFS constructs and we have limited the inclusion of abstract foundational concepts, so as to attain a model that is simple enough for its adoption online. The reader is referred to [19] for indications on how this model could be mapped to a foundational ontology.

As the core and initial module of a set of vocabularies for supporting service trading online Linked USDL Core, see Figure 1, aims to cover four essential aspects: offerings, services, the business entities involved in the delivery chain, and the actual interaction points allowing consumers to contract or trigger the benefits of contracted services.

Linked USDL extends GR which is nowadays the de-facto standard vocabulary for publishing semantic descriptions for products. It is worth noting that although services are accommodated within GR, their coverage is rather basic at this stage. Extending GR enables linking services and products descriptions which is particularly useful since many products are often sold in combination with a service, e.g., a repair or replace service. Additionally, it also ensures that an initial alignment with the increasingly popular vocabulary Schema.org is in place, for GR is already largely aligned to it.

The most important concepts provided by Linked USDL are:

Service is a refinement of *gr:ProductOrService* and subsumes all classes describing service types. Examples of subclasses of *Service* could be "internet provisioning service" and "insurance service". Instances of *Service* may define i) prototypical services part of a portfolio, e.g., "BT unlimited broadband service", as covered by *ServiceModel*, ii) one-of services custom tailored for a potential customer, or iii) actually contracted services, e.g., "your concrete life insurance provided by AXA", as covered by *gr:ServiceIndividual*.

ServiceModel is a refinement of *gr:ProductOrServiceModel* which specifies common characteristics (e.g., download speed) of a family of services. *ServiceModel* thus defines families of *Services* sharing common characteristics, e.g., "*BT unlimited broadband services* share the characteristic of supporting unlimited download". An actual service instance shares the properties of its service model. This is a feature that requires non-standard reasoning which specific implementations should take care of.

ServiceIndividual is a subclass of *gr:Individual* and *Service*. Instances of *ServiceIndividual* are actual services that are creating value to a network of business entities. For instance, "your concrete life insurance provided by AXA" is a *ServiceIndividual* which is providing value to yourself and AXA.

ServiceOffering is a subclass of *gr:Offering* and represents essentially offerings by a business entity *including* at least one *Service*. *ServiceOffering* may have limited validity over geographical regions or time.

EntityInvolvement is introduced in Linked USDL in order to enable capturing service value networks. In a nutshell, Entity Involvement allows capturing a ternary relationship expressing that a business entity, e.g., "AXA", is involved in a service, e.g., "basic life insurance" playing a business role, e.g., "provider". Linked USDL provides a reference SKOS taxonomy of basic business roles that covers the most typical ones encountered such as regulator and intermediary.

InteractionPoint link services to interactions that may be possible or required between the members of a service value network and the service during its life cycle. This allows answering questions such as "*what is the sequence of interactions I may expect if I want to make an insurance claim and what communication channels are available to that end?*".

CommunicationChannel is the class of all different communication channels that business entities could use for communication. Linked USDL covers the most widely used channels by means of 2 vocabularies: vCard (e.g., email, phone), and MSM (e.g., Web services, and RESTful services). Communication channels are additionally characterised by their interaction type. Linked USDL provides 2 reference SKOS taxonomies covering the main modes (e.g., automated) and the interaction space (e.g., on-site).

EntityInteraction links interaction points to business entities or types (e.g., provider), and the role they play within the interaction (e.g., initiator). *EntityInteraction* allows expressing things like "to *make a claim*, the *consumer* should first *contact* the insurance *provider* and provide the *policy number*".

Classifications. Classifications or taxonomies of entities are most often used when describing services to capture, for instance, service types, business entity roles, e.g., "provider", as well as interaction related issues, e.g., "manual vs automated". We also expect that classifications will be needed in forthcoming modules addressing strategic issues or the internals of delivery chains.

This could be approached directly using subclassing which is directly supported by RDFS. However, the use of a hierarchy of classes establishes strict relationships which may not adequately match existing organisation schemes. For this reason, in Linked USDL we have accommodated the use of SKOS, which enables capturing classification schemes and taxonomies. Indeed, this mechanism does not prevent users from providing their own domain-specific categorisations through subsumption if they wish to. This approach thus enriches Linked USDL with a powerful, yet flexible and extensible means for creating categorisations.

The current version of Linked USDL includes three SKOS schemes with reference categorisations for *BusinessRoles*, *InteractionRoles*, and *InteractionTypes*, see Figure 1. These schemes have been, however, kept as separate modules so that different schemes can be used if necessary.

5 Evaluation

We have evaluated Linked USDL using three well-known and recommended techniques [20] including domain coverage, suitability for an application or task, and vocabulary adoption.

5.1 Coverage Evaluation

Ontologies are often evaluated by comparing them to a gold standard ontology [20]. In our case, we have done such an evaluation by comparing the resulting model to USDL, the most comprehensive model available for describing services. Doing so allows us to get a clear indication of the overall coverage of the domain, and to identify as well the main deviations from USDL.

A fundamental goal of this work is providing a conceptual model that would be easy to grasp, populate, process, and ultimately be adopted for Web-scale use. Thus, out of the 9 modules of USDL we have essentially deferred covering the following modules: Service[11], Legal, Service Level, and Pricing. Nonetheless, for every module we have checked the coverage of the main concepts defined in order to get an indication of both module-specific and the overall coverage of Linked USDL. The results of this analysis are summarised in Table 2.

This analysis shows that thanks to integrating an reusing existing vocabularies we have managed to cover the vast majority of USDL, by providing a vocabulary consisting of 12 concepts and 3 complementary SKOS categorisations. In particular, from an original specification with 125 concepts we cover 74%, if we limit ourselves to the specific modules we targeted, and 60% overall, which shall contribute towards reducing the overhead related to understanding

[11] The Service module covers the internal details of a service which are often private.

Table 2. Evaluation of Linked USDL coverage of USDL (version M5)

USDL Module	Topic	Vocabulary	Comments	Classes	Covered	Ratio
Foundation	Time	Time	Advanced temporal reasoning provided	46	35	76%
	Contact Details	GR & vCard				
	Agents	GR & vCard				
	Conditions	±	Deferred to modules, e.g., Technical			
	Resources	X				
Technical	Interfaces	MSM	Higher automation through semantics	10	8	80%
	Protocols	HTTP & MSM	HTTP & SOAP/WSDL			
	Access Profile	X				
Interaction	Simple Protocols	Linked USDL		6	3	50%
	Complex Protocols	Linked USDL	Partial. Conditions at the operations level.			
Participants	Roles	Linked USDL	Business Roles SKOS	7	6	86%
	Target Consumers	X				
Functional	Parameters & Faults	MSM		4	2	50%
	Functions	GR	Basic coverage			
Approximate Coverage of Main Addressed Modules of USDL M5				73	54	74%
Service	Single Services	Linked USDL		11	5	45%
	Service Variants	Linked USDL & GR	Partial with Service Model			
	Service Types	Linked USDL	Interaction Types SKOS			
	Composite Services	X	Offering bundles supported			
Pricing	Basic Pricing	GR	Payment types, taxes, cost	19	7	37%
	Variable Pricing	X				
Service Level	Metrics & Conditions	GR & MSM		9	4	44%
	Guarantees	X				
Legal	Basic Legal	GR	License, Validity, etc	13	5	38%
	Rights, Requirements	X				
Approximate Total Coverage of USDL M5				125	75	60%

and adopting Linked USDL. It is worth noting that out of the concepts not explicitly covered several are sometimes redundant (e.g., Condition is subclassed in many modules), or were seldom properly understood and used (e.g., Functions, Phases of interactions, Service Level Agreements).

5.2 Suitability for Tasks and Applications

Given that Linked USDL does not cover all concepts present in USDL it is worth assessing the impact of such decisions. Table 2 shows the main aspects and their current coverage. In qualitative terms, the decisions adopted are such that Linked USDL does not currently provide support for capturing how providers deliver services in terms of resources needed, complex internal workflows, or strategic decisions (e.g., targeted markets). The reason for this is two-fold. First, such aspects are often not automated and when they are, providers already have mechanisms in place to this end. Second, these are private concerns that are orthogonal to the trading of services. Similarly, Linked USDL does not currently include support for conceptualising complex agreements including legal requirements and guarantees as these were barely used or understood by users. Finally, we have opted for a simple mechanism for capturing prices and have deferred to a separate module the modelling of more complex dynamic pricing that are less often used and usually remain private to the provider.

Despite these changes, Linked USDL provides advanced support for modelling, comparing, discovering, and trading services and service bundles. It provides means for tracking and reasoning about the involvement of entities within delivery chains which informs the trading and comparison of services as well as it enables the tracing and analysis of service value networks. It provides advanced support for automating the interactions between actors during the life-cycle of services. Additionally it includes support for capturing service offerings, for combining services and products (e.g., a car often comes with a warranty), and for applying temporal reasoning, which were not previously available. Finally, and most importantly, these activities can be achieved with a greater level of automation benefitting from automated reasoning and they can be performed on a Web-scale across Web-sites and service providers thanks to capturing and sharing the semantics of services as Linked Data.

Empirically, the suitability of the language for supporting the automation of key tasks has been evaluated by two main means. On the one hand, we have reused and developed tools that provide support for these tasks, and, on the other hand, we are continuously applying Linked USDL in a number of domains. In terms of reuse, thanks to the adoption of existing Linked Data vocabularies, Linked USDL benefits from general purpose tooling, e.g., SPARQL engines and RDF stores, but also from vocabulary-specific solutions. This notably concerns existing advanced machinery for discovering, composing, and invoking technical services (i.e., RESTful and WSDL services) described in terms of MSM [18].

Additionally, general purpose infrastructure has been developed specifically for Linked USDL. A Web-based Linked USDL editor is currently available to help providers to easily generate Linked USDL descriptions[12]. There is also an advanced multi-party dynamic and open service marketplace[13] developed in the context of the FI-WARE project[14], able to gather, combine, and exploit rich service descriptions from distributed providers to help match offer and demand. Notably the marketplace supports consumers in searching for service offerings, comparing them, and contracting them.

Finally, from the perspective of its suitability for supporting service trading across domains, Linked USDL is currently being applied in a variety of domains. For instance, in the field of Software as a Service we have explored the use of Linked USDL in conjunction with TOSCA[21]. Linked USDL was used to formalise, structure, and simplify the discovery and selection of services of the Web-based customer relationship management (CRM) platform SugarCRM, while TOSCA supported the automated deployment and management of the services. Additionally this work helped us evaluate the extensibility of Linked USDL by integrating it with complementary third party specifications such as TOSCA. In the FI-WARE project Linked USDL is used to support a service infrastructure supporting service ecosystems in the cloud covering both

[12] See `https://github.com/linked-usdl` for existing tooling and model extensions.

[13] `http://store.testbed.fi-ware.org/`

[14] `http://www.fi-ware.eu/`

the technical and business perspectives. The FINEST[15] project aims to support the transport and logistics (T&L) ecosystem, in which many service providers collaborate in order to transport goods over what is referred to as a "chain of legs". Therein Linked USDL is being exploited in the planning of chains of legs to support searching and matching transport service offerings in a transparent, distributed, and multi-party manner.

Across the diverse domains where Linked USDL is being applied (see list of projects next), it has proven to be a valuable resource as a means to provide shared and globally accessible service descriptions integrating both technical and business aspects. The genericity, modularity, and extensibility of the approach has enabled extending the vocabulary with dedicated domain-specific vocabularies in the areas of SaaS and T&L, while generic software infrastructure was easily reused across domains.

5.3 Vocabulary Adoption and Use

When evaluating ontologies and vocabularies, one aspect that is often taken into account is their adoption and use. This evaluation may be carried over the ontology itself and/or over the different ontologies that are imported. The former gives an indication of the acceptance and adoption of the ontology in its entirety whereas the latter provides a more granular assessment over the reused ontologies. In this section we mainly address the latter but also provide preliminary indications of the overall adoption of Linked USDL.

The methodology that was followed, see Section 4.2, was centred on the reuse of widely adopted vocabularies. Table 1 presented earlier shows the main vocabularies that were identified through search engines, together with core indicators of their use on the Web. These figures highlight that Linked USDL is based on vocabularies that are the most used in their respective domains of interest. Only two exceptions exist, AKT Signage which was not adopted for it was not dereferenceable, and Schema.org which is indirectly aligned via GR. This approach in turn reduces the potential overhead one would incur when using Linked USDL: frequently reused vocabularies are likely to have greater acceptance and support by people and existing systems.

Additionally, the availability of datasets with instances in terms of the vocabularies reused guarantees that new descriptions could reuse and link to existing resources, e.g., allowing the reuse of descriptions of companies. Doing so provides clear benefits from the perspective of data acquisition which was one of the main concerns Linked USDL was trying to address. Additionally, by linking to existing instances the data provided is enriched which may in turn enable further advanced processing as well as it may increase the discoverability of services.

Providing a substantial account of the adoption of Linked USDL would require a reasonable wait from its first release, which coincides with this publication. Nonetheless, Linked USDL is currently already in use within more than 10 research projects, namely FI-WARE, FINEST, Value4Cloud, Deutsche

[15] `http://www.finest-ppp.eu/`

Digitale Bibliothek, MSEE, FIspace, FITMAN, FI-CONTENT, ENVIROFI, OUTSMART, SMARTAGRIFOOD, IoT-A, Broker@Cloud, and GEYSERS. These projects are using Linked USDL as the core vocabulary for describing services, contributing to validate the suitability, genericity, and extensibility of Linked USDL for different domains. This also highlights that despite its youth, Linked USDL is already witnessing a promising adoption.

6 Conclusion

Despite the importance of services in developed economies, the widespread adoption of world-wide electronic commerce over the Web, most service trading is still essentially carried out via traditional and often manual communication means. A fundamental reason for this is the difficulty for capturing the abundant information and knowledge governing services and their related transactions in a way amenable to computer automation. Out of the wealth of work around services, USDL is the most comprehensive solution proposed thus far for enabling (semi)automated service trading. Yet, work on its standardisation highlighted a number of limitations for Web-scale service trading.

We have presented Linked USDL, the next evolution of USDL centred on fostering its wider adoption and better automation support through the (re)use of Linked Data. Linked USDL has been developed following a methodology centred on maximising the reuse of existing vocabularies and datasets and minimising the complexity. The resulting vocabulary has been evaluated in terms of domain coverage, suitability for purpose, and vocabulary adoption.

Despite the good evaluation results obtained, Linked USDL is to be regarded as one step towards enabling Web-scale service trading, albeit a fundamental one. Further work is required for covering aspects such as complex dynamic pricing models and agreements which are common in certain domains such as Cloud services. Additionally, from the tooling perspective, developing advanced mechanisms able to support steps such as the negotiation between service providers and consumers, or the bundling of services would also be necessary. We expect in this last regard to take inspiration and adapt solutions developed for the e^3 family of ontologies.

Acknowledgment. This work was partially funded by DFG under project agreements SFB 912/1 2011, and by the COMPOSE (FP7-ICT-317862) and FI-WARE (FI-PPP-285248) EU projects. We also thank all the members of the W3C USDL Incubator Group.

References

1. Chesbrough, H., Spohrer, J.: A research manifesto for services science. Communications of the ACM 49(7), 35 (2006)
2. Papazoglou, M.P., Traverso, P., Dustdar, S., Leymann, F.: Service-Oriented Computing: State of the Art and Research Challenges. Computer 40(11), 38–45 (2007)

3. Akkermans, H., Baida, Z., Gordijn, J., Peña, N., Altuna, A., Laresgoiti, I.: Value Webs: Ontology-Based Bundling of Real-World Services. IEEE Intelligent Systems 19(4), 57–66 (2004)
4. Cardoso, J., Barros, A., May, N., Kylau, U.: Towards a Unified Service Description Language for the Internet of Services: Requirements and First Developments. In: IEEE International Conference on Services Computing (SCC), pp. 602–609 (2010)
5. Cardoso, J., Sheth, A.: Semantic e-workflow composition. Journal of Intelligent Information Systems (JIIS) 21(3), 191–225 (2003)
6. Pedrinaci, C., Domingue, J., Sheth, A.: Semantic Web Services. In: Handbook on Semantic Web Technologies. Volume Semantic Web Applications. Springer (2010)
7. Oppenheim, D.V., Varshney, L.R., Chee, Y.-M.: Work as a service. In: Kappel, G., Maamar, Z., Motahari-Nezhad, H.R. (eds.) ICSOC 2011. LNCS, vol. 7084, pp. 669–678. Springer, Heidelberg (2011)
8. Gordijn, J., Yu, E., van der Raadt, B.: e-service design using i* and e3value modeling. IEEE Software 23, 26–33 (2006)
9. Hepp, M.: GoodRelations: An Ontology for Describing Products and Services Offers on the Web. In: Gangemi, A., Euzenat, J. (eds.) EKAW 2008. LNCS (LNAI), vol. 5268, pp. 329–346. Springer, Heidelberg (2008)
10. Oberle, D., Barros, A., Kylau, U., Heinzl, S.: A unified description language for human to automated services. Information Systems (2012)
11. Kadner, K., Oberle, D., Schaeffler, M., Horch, A., Kintz, M., Barton, L., Leidig, T., Pedrinaci, C., Domingue, J., Romanelli, M., Trapero, R., Kutsikos, K.: Unified Service Description Language XG Final Report. Technical report (2011)
12. Jacobs, I., Walsh, N.: Architecture of the World Wide Web, Volume One. W3C Recommendation (2004)
13. Bizer, C., Heath, T., Berners-Lee, T.: Linked Data - The Story So Far. International Journal on Semantic Web and Information Systems (IJSWIS) (2009)
14. Suárez-Figueroa, M.C., Gómez-Pérez, A., Motta, E., Gangemi, A. (eds.): Ontology Engineering in a Networked World. Springer (2011)
15. Ding, L., Finin, T., Joshi, A., Pan, R., Cost, R.S., Peng, Y., Reddivari, P., Doshi, V.C., Sachs, J.: Swoogle: A Search and Metadata Engine for the Semantic Web. In: CIKM 2004: Thirteenth ACM International Conference on Information and Knowledge Management (2004)
16. d'Aquin, M., Motta, E.: Watson, more than a Semantic Web search engine. Semantic Web 2(1), 55–63 (2011)
17. Auer, S., Demter, J., Martin, M., Lehmann, J.: LODStats – an extensible framework for high-performance dataset analytics. In: ten Teije, A., Völker, J., Handschuh, S., Stuckenschmidt, H., d'Acquin, M., Nikolov, A., Aussenac-Gilles, N., Hernandez, N. (eds.) EKAW 2012. LNCS, vol. 7603, pp. 353–362. Springer, Heidelberg (2012)
18. Pedrinaci, C., Domingue, J.: Toward the Next Wave of Services: Linked Services for the Web of Data. Journal of Universal Computer Science 16(13), 1694–1719 (2010)
19. Ferrario, R., Guarino, N., Janiesch, C., Kiemes, T., Oberle, D., Probst, F.: Towards an ontological foundation of services science: The general service model. Wirtschaftsinformatik, 16–18 (February 2011)
20. Sabou, M., Fernandez, M.: Ontology (network) evaluation. In: Suárez-Figueroa, M.C., Gómez-Pérez, A., Motta, E., Gangemi, A. (eds.) Ontology Engineering in a Networked World, pp. 193–212. Springer (2012)
21. Cardoso, J., Binz, T., Breitenbücher, U., Kopp, O., Leymann, F.: Cloud Computing Automation: Integrating USDL and TOSCA. In: Salinesi, C., Norrie, M.C., Pastor, Ó. (eds.) CAiSE 2013. LNCS, vol. 7908, pp. 1–16. Springer, Heidelberg (2013)

SentiCircles for Contextual and Conceptual Semantic Sentiment Analysis of Twitter

Hassan Saif[1], Miriam Fernandez[1], Yulan He[2], and Harith Alani[1]

[1] Knowledge Media Institute, The Open University, UK
{h.saif,m.fernandez,h.alani}@open.ac.uk
[2] School of Engineering and Applied Science, Aston University, UK
y.he@cantab.net

Abstract. Lexicon-based approaches to Twitter sentiment analysis are gaining much popularity due to their simplicity, domain independence, and relatively good performance. These approaches rely on sentiment lexicons, where a collection of words are marked with fixed sentiment polarities. However, words' sentiment orientation (positive, neural, negative) and/or sentiment strengths could change depending on context and targeted entities. In this paper we present SentiCircle; a novel lexicon-based approach that takes into account the contextual and conceptual semantics of words when calculating their sentiment orientation and strength in Twitter. We evaluate our approach on three Twitter datasets using three different sentiment lexicons. Results show that our approach significantly outperforms two lexicon baselines. Results are competitive but inconclusive when comparing to state-of-art SentiStrength, and vary from one dataset to another. SentiCircle outperforms SentiStrength in accuracy on average, but falls marginally behind in F-measure.

Keywords: #eswc2014Saif, Sentiment analysis, Semantics, Twitter.

1 Introduction

With over 500 million users and 400 million tweets daily, Twitter has now become a goldmine for monitoring the sentiment of the crowd. Most current approaches for identifying the sentiment of tweets can be categorised into one of two main groups: *supervised approaches* [15,4,12], which use a wide range of features and labelled data for training sentiment classifiers, and *lexicon-based approaches* [22,14,6], which make use of pre-built lexicons of words weighted with their sentiment orientations to determine the overall sentiment of a given text. Some of these methods tend to achieve good and consistent level of accuracy when applied to well known domains and datasets, where labelled data is available for training, or when the analysed text is well covered by the used sentiment lexicon.

Popularity of lexicon-based approaches is rapidly increasing since they require no training data, and hence are more suited to a wider range of domains than supervised approaches [22]. Nevertheless, lexicon-based approaches have two main limitations. Firstly, the number of words in the lexicons is finite, which may constitute a problem when extracting sentiment from very dynamic environments such as Twitter, where new terms, abbreviations and malformed words constantly emerge. Secondly and more

V. Presutti et al. (Eds.): ESWC 2014, LNCS 8465, pp. 83–98, 2014.

importantly, sentiment lexicons tend to assign a fixed sentiment orientation and score to words, irrespective of how these words are used in the text. Words could express a different sentiment in different contexts. For example, the word "`great`" should be negative in the context of a "`problem`", and positive in the context of a "`smile`".

In this paper we propose an approach called SentiCircles, which builds a dynamic representation of context to tune the pre-assigned strength and polarity of words in the lexicon. This approach incorporates two types of semantics; *contextual semantics*, i.e., semantics inferred from the co-occurrence of words [27], and *conceptual semantics*, i.e., semantics extracted from background ontologies such as DBpedia.

Contextual semantics (aka statistical semantics) [27] has been traditionally used in diverse areas of computer science including Natural Language Processing and Information Retrieval [25]. The main principle behind the notion of contextual semantics comes from the dictum-"You shall know a word by the company it keeps!" [10]. This suggests that words that co-occur in a given context tend to have certain relation or semantic influence, which we try to capture with our SentiCircle approach.

We evaluate our approach using three different sentiment lexicons and with three different datasets, and compare its performance against various lexicon baseline methods. Our results show that our SentiCircle approach outperforms the other lexicon methods by nearly 20% in accuracy and 30-40% in F-measure. We also compare our approach against SentiStrength [22], which, to our knowledge, is the leading lexicon-based sentiment detection approach for social media. Our approach outperformed SentiStrength in accuracy in 2 datasets, and in F-measure in one dataset only (detailed later).

The main contributions of this paper can be summarised as follows:

- Introduce a novel lexicon-based approach using a contextual representation of words, called SentiCircles, which is able to capture the implicit semantics of words from their concurrence [27], and to update their sentiment orientation accordingly.
- Conduct several experiments and test the effectiveness of our proposed approach for sentiment detection of tweets against several state-of-the-art baselines.
- Propose two different methods of employing SentiCircles for sentiment detection of tweets and evaluate their effectiveness against other baselines.
- Incorporate conceptual semantics into SentiCircle and study their impact on sentiment detection performance.

In the rest of this paper, related work is discussed in Section 2, and SentiCircle approach and deployment is presented in Sections 3 and 4. Experiments and results are presented in Sections 5 and 6 respectively. Discussion and future work are covered in Section 7. Finally, we conclude our work in Section 8.

2 Related Work

Most existing approaches to Twitter sentiment analysis focus on classifying the individual tweets into subjective (positive or negative) or objective (neutral). They can be categorised as *supervised approaches* and *lexicon-based approaches*.

Supervised approaches are based on training classifiers from various combinations of features such as word n-grams [15,5], Part-Of-Speech (POS) tags [4,1], and tweets syntax features (e.g., hashtags, retweets, punctuations, etc.) [12]. These methods can achieve 80%-84% in accuracy [17]. However, training data is usually expensive to obtain [13] especially for continuously evolving subject domains as in Twitter. Furthermore, classifiers trained on data on a specific domain (e.g., movie reviews) may produce low performance when applied to a different domain (e.g., camera reviews) [2].

Lexicon-based methods use the sentiment orientation of opinionated words (e.g., `great, sad, excellent`) found in a given text to calculate its overall sentiment [14,6]. Instead of using training data to learn sentiment, lexicon-based methods rely on pre-built dictionaries of words with associated sentiment orientations [20], such as SentiWordNet [3] or the MPQA subjectivity lexicon [26]. Thelwall et al. [23,22] proposed SentiStrength; a lexicon-based method for sentiment detection on the social web. This method overcomes the common problem of ill-formed language on Twitter and the like, by applying several lexical rules, such as the existence of emoticons, intensifiers, negation and booster words (e.g., absolutely, extremely).

Lexicon-based methods not only provide sentiment polarity (positive/negative), but also *strength*. For example, SentiStrength computes the positive sentiment strength in the range from 1 (not positive) to 5 (extremely positive). One limitation of lexicons is their static sentiment values of terms, regardless of their contexts. Although authors in [23] proposed an algorithm to update the sentiment strength assigned to terms in a lexicon, this algorithm required training from manually annotated corpora.

Another common problem with the above approaches is their full dependence on the presence of words or syntactical features that explicitly reflect sentiment. In many cases however, the sentiment of a word is implicitly associated with the semantics of its context [7]. Several methods have been proposed for exploring semantics for sentiment analysis, which can be categorised into *contextual semantic approaches*, and *conceptual semantic approaches*.

Contextual semantic approaches determined semantics from the co-occurrence patterns of words, which is also known as *statistical semantics* [25,27], and have often been used for sentiment analysis [24,21].

Conceptual semantic approaches use external semantic knowledge bases (e.g., ontologies and semantic networks) with NLP techniques to capture the conceptual representations of words that implicitly convey sentiment. In our previous work we showed that incorporating general conceptual semantics (e.g., "`president`", "`company`") into supervised classifiers improved sentiment accuracy [18]. SenticNet [8],[1] is a concept-based lexicon for sentiment analysis. It contains 14k fine-grained concepts collected from the Open Mind corpus and coupled with their sentiment orientations. SenticNet was proved valuable for sentiment detection in conventional text (e.g., product reviews) [11]. Unlike SentiStrength [23], SenticNet is not tailored for Twitter and the like. Although conceptual semantic approaches have been shown to outperform purely syntactical approaches [7], they are usually limited by the scope of their underlying knowledge bases, which is especially problematic when processing general Twitter streams, with their rapid semiotic evolution and language deformations.

To address the limitations above, we developed SentiCircle, which (1) is based on a lexicon and hence can be applied to data of different domains, (2) captures the

[1] `http://sentic.net/`

contextual semantics of words to update their sentiment orientation and strength, and (3) allows for conceptual semantics to be added to enrich the sentiment analysis task.

3 Capturing and Representing Semantics for Sentiment Analysis

In the following we explain the SentiCircle approach and its use of contextual and conceptual semantics. The main idea behind our SentiCircle approach is that the sentiment of a term is not static, as in traditional lexicon-based approaches, but rather depends on the context in which the term is used, i.e., it depends on its contextual semantics. We define context as a textual corpus or a set of tweets.

To capture the contextual semantics of a term we consider its co-occurrence patterns with other terms, as inspired by [27]. Following this principle, we compute the semantics of a term m by considering the relations of m with all its context words (i.e., words that occur with m in the same context). To compute the individual relation between the term m and a context term c_i we propose the use of the *Term Degree of Correlation (TDOC)* metric. Inspired by the TF-IDF weighting scheme this metric is computed as:

$$TDOC(m, c_i) = f(c_i, m) \times \log \frac{N}{N_{c_i}} \tag{1}$$

where $f(c_i, m)$ is the number of times c_i occurs with m in tweets, N is the total number of terms, and N_{c_i} is the total number of terms that occur with c_i. In addition to each TDOC computed between m and each context term c_i, we also consider the *Prior Sentiment* of c_i, extracted from a sentiment lexicon. As with common practice, if this term c_i appears in the vicinity of a negation, its prior sentiment score is negated. The negation words are collected from the General Inquirer under the NOTLW category.[2]

3.1 Representing Semantics with SentiCircles

Contextual semantics of a term m are represented as a geometric circle; *SentiCircle*, where the term is situated in the centre of the circle, and each point around it represents a context term c_i. The position of c_i is defined jointly by its prior sentiment and its degree of correlation (TDOC). The rational behind using this circular representation shape, which will become clearer later, is to benefit from the trigonometric properties it offers for estimating the sentiment orientation, and strength, of terms. It also enables us to calculate the impact of context words on the sentiment orientation and on the sentiment strength of a target-word separately, which is difficult to do with traditional vector representations. Formally, a SentiCircle in a polar coordinate system can be represented with the following equation:

$$r^2 - 2rr_0cos(\theta - \phi) + r_0^2 = a^2 \tag{2}$$

where a is the radius of the circle, (r_0, ϕ) is the polar coordinate of the centre of the circle, and (r, θ) is the polar coordinate of a co-occurring term on the circle. For simplicity, we assume that our SentiCircles are centred at the origin (i.e., $r_0 = 0$).

[2] `http://www.wjh.harvard.edu/~inquirer/NotLw.html`

Hence, to build a SentiCircle for a term m, we only need to calculate, for each context term c_i a radius r_i and an angle θ_i. To do that, we use the prior sentiment score and the TDOC value of the term c_i as:

$$\begin{aligned} r_i &= \text{TDOC}(m, c_i) \\ \theta_i &= \text{Prior\_Sentiment}(c_i) * \pi \end{aligned} \tag{3}$$

We normalise the radii of all terms in a SentiCircle to a scale between 0 and 1. Hence, the radius a of any SentiCircle is equal to 1. Also, all angles' values are in radian.

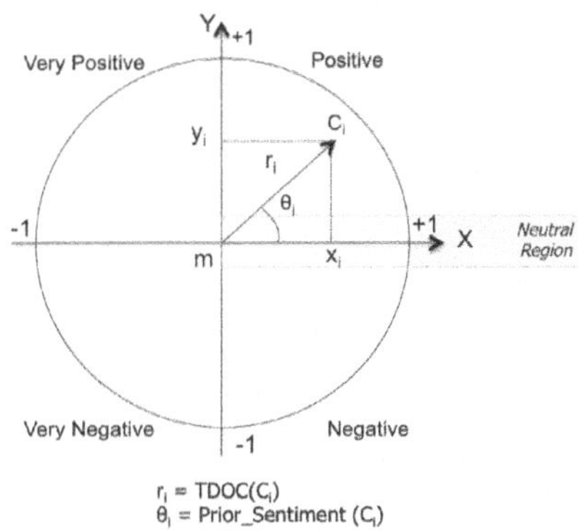

Fig. 1. SentiCircle of a term m

The SentiCircle in the *polar coordinate system* can be divided into four sentiment quadrants as shown in Figure 1. Terms in the two upper quadrants have a positive sentiment ($\sin\theta > 0$), with upper left quadrant representing stronger positive sentiment since it has larger angle values than those in the top right quadrant. Similarly, terms in the two lower quadrants have negative sentiment values ($\sin\theta < 0$). Although the radius of the SentiCircle of any term m equals to 1, points representing context terms of m in the circle have different radii ($0 \leq r_i \leq 1$), which reflect how important a context term is to m. The larger the radius, the more important the context term to m.

We can move from the *polar coordinate system* to the *Cartesian coordinate system* by simply using the trigonometric functions `sine` and `cosine` as:

$$x_i = r_i \cos\theta_i \qquad\qquad y_i = r_i \sin\theta_i \tag{4}$$

Moving to the *Cartesian coordinate system* allows us to use the trigonometric properties of the circle to encode the contextual semantics of a term in the circle as sentiment orientation and sentiment strength. Y-axis in the Cartesian coordinate system defines the sentiment of the term, i.e., a positive y value denotes a positive sentiment and vice versa. The X-axis defines the sentiment strength of the term. The smaller the x value, the stronger the sentiment.[3] Moreover, a small region called the "*Neutral Region*" can

[3] This is because $\cos\theta < 0$ for large angles.

be defined. This region, as shown in Figure 1, is located very close to X-axis in the "*Positive*" and the "*Negative*" quadrants only, where terms lie in this region have very weak sentiment (i.e., $|\theta| \approx 0$). The "*Neutral Region*" has a crucial role in measuring the overall sentiment of a given SentiCircle as will be shown in the subsequent sections.

Note that in the extreme case, where $r_i = 1$ and $\theta_i = \pi$ we position the context term c_i in the "*Very Positive*" or the "*Very Negative*" quadrants based on the sign of its prior sentiment score.

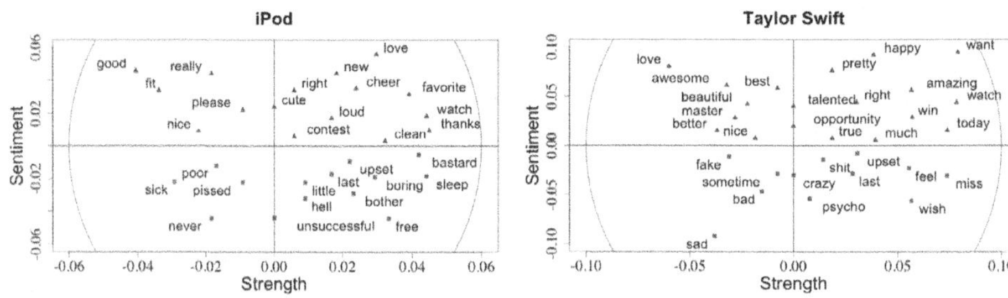

(a) iPod. (b) Taylor Swift.

Fig. 2. Example SentiCircles for "`iPod`" and "`Taylor Swift`". We removed points near the origin to ease visualisation. Dots in the upper half of the circle (triangles) represent terms bearing a positive sentiment while dots in the lower half (squares) are terms with a negative sentiment.

Figure 2 shows the SentiCircles of the entities "`iPod`" and "`Taylor Swift`". Terms (i.e., points) inside each circle are positioned in a way that represents their sentiment scores and their importance (degree of correlation) to the entity. For example, "`Awesome`" in the SentiCircle of "`Taylor Swift`" has a positive sentiment and a high importance score, hence it is positioned in the "*Very Positive*" quadrant (See Figure 2(b)). The word "`Pretty`", in the same circle, also has positive sentiment, but it has lower importance score than the word "`Awesome`", hence it is positioned in the "*Positive*" quadrant. We also notice that there are some words that appear in both circles, but in different positions. For example, the word "`Love`" has a stronger positive sentiment strength with "`Taylor Swift`" compared to "`iPod`", although it has a positive sentiment (similar y-value) in both circles.

As described earlier, the contribution of both quantities (prior sentiment and degree of correlation) is calculated and represented in the SentiCircle separately by means of the projection of the context term along X-axe (sentiment strength) and Y-axe (sentiment orientation). Such level of granularity is crucial when we need, for example, to filter those context words that have low contribution towards the sentiment orientations or strength of the target word.

3.2 Using SentiCircles to Measure Sentiment

The above examples show that, although we use external lexicons to assign initial sentiment scores to terms, our SentiCircle representation is able to amend these scores according to the context in which each term is used. To compute the new sentiment of the term based on its SentiCircle we use the *Senti-Median* metric. We now have the SentiCircle of a term m which is composed by the set of (x, y) Cartesian coordinates of all the context terms of m, where the y value represents the sentiment and the x value represents the sentiment strength. An effective way to approximate the overall sentiment of a given SentiCircle is by calculating the geometric median of all its points. Formally, for a given set of n points $(p_1, p_2, ..., p_n)$ in a SentiCircle Ω, the 2D geometric median g is defined as:

$$g = \arg\min_{g \in \mathbb{R}^2} \sum_{i=1}^{n} |||p_i - g||_2, \quad (5)$$

where the geometric median is a point $g = (x_k, y_k)$ in which its Euclidean distances to all the points p_i is minimum. We call the geometric median g the Senti-Median as it captures the sentiment (y-coordinate) and the sentiment strength (x-coordinate) of the SentiCircle of a given term m.

Following the representation provided in Figure 1, the sentiment of the term m is dependent on whether the Senti-Median g lies inside the neutral region, the positive quadrants, or the negative quadrants. Formally, given a Senti-Median g_m of a term m, the term-sentiment function $\mathcal{L}$ works as:

$$\mathcal{L}(g_m) = \begin{cases} \text{negative} & \text{if } y_g < -\lambda \\ \text{positive} & \text{if } y_g > +\lambda \\ \text{neutral} & \text{if } |y_g| \leq \lambda \ \& \ x_g \leq 0 \end{cases} \quad (6)$$

where λ is the threshold that defines the Y-axis boundary of the neutral region. Section 5 illustrates how this threshold is computed.

3.3 Enriching SentiCircles with Conceptual Semantics

We take conceptual semantics to refer to the semantic concepts (e.g., "`person`", "`company`", "`city`") that represent entities (e.g., "`Steve Jobs`", "`Vodafone`", "`London`") appearing in tweets. In this section we describe the addition of conceptual semantics into the SentiCircle representation.

As in our previous work [18], AlchemyAPI[4] came first amongst the set of entity extractors we tested on Twitter. Here we use AlchemyAPI again to extract all named entities in tweets with their associated concepts. We add the concepts into the SentiCircle representation using the **Semantic Augmentation** method [18], where we add the semantic concepts to the original tweet before applying our representation model (e.g., "`headache`" and its concept "`Health Condition`" will appear together in the SentiCircle). Also note that each extracted concept will be represented by a SentiCircle in order to compute its overall sentiment.

The rational behind adding these concepts is that certain entities and concepts tend to have a more consistent correlation to terms of positive or negative sentiment. This can help determining the sentiment of semantically relevant or similar entities which do not explicitly express sentiment. In the example in Figure 4, "`Wind`" and

[4] `www.alchemyapi.com`

"Humidity" have negative SentiCircles as they tend to appear with negative terms in tweets. Hence their concept "Weather Condition" will have a negative sentiment. The tweet "Cycling under a heavy rain.. What a #luck!" is likely to have a negative sentiment due to the presence of the word "rain" which is mapped to the negative concept "Weather Condition". Moreover, the word heavy in this context is more likely to have a negative sentiment due to its correlation with "rain" and "Weather Condition".

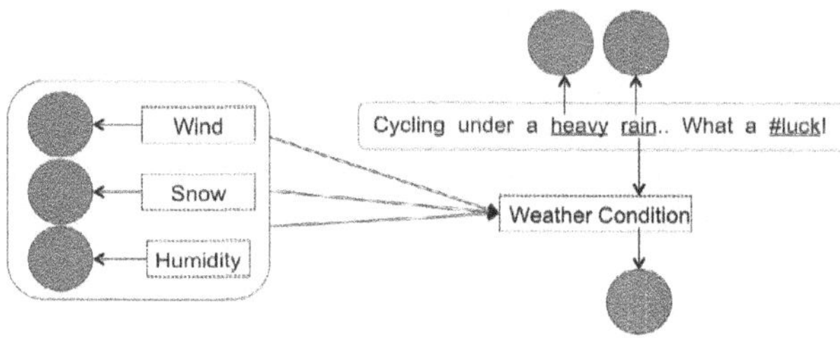

Fig. 3. Mapping semantic concepts to detect sentiment

4 Using SentiCircles for Tweet-level Sentiment Analysis

There are several ways in which the SentiCircle representations of the terms in a tweet can be used to determine the tweet's overall sentiment. For example, the tweet "iPhone and iPad are amazing" contains five terms. Each of these terms has an associated SentiCircle representation, which can be combined in different ways to extract the tweet's sentiment. We experiment with two ways for using SentiCircle representations for tweet-level sentiment detection:

Median Method: This method takes the median of all Senti-Medians, and this assumes all tweet terms to be equal. Each tweet $t_i \in \mathcal{T}$ is turned into a vector of Senti-Medians $\boldsymbol{g} = (g_1, g_2, ..., g_n)$ of size n, where n is the number of terms that compose the tweet and g_j is the Senti-Median of the SentiCircle associated with term m_j. Equation 5 is used to calculate the median point q of $\boldsymbol{g}$, which we use to determine the overall sentiment of tweet t_i using Function 6.

Pivot Method: This method favours some terms in a tweet over others, based on the assumption that sentiment is often expressed towards one or more specific targets, which we refer to as "Pivot" terms. In the tweet example above, there are two pivot terms, "iPhone" and "iPad" since the sentiment word "amazing" is used to describe both of them. Hence, the method works by (1) extracting all pivot terms in a tweet and; (2) accumulating, for each sentiment label, the sentiment impact that each pivot term receives from other terms. The overall sentiment of a tweet corresponds to the sentiment label with the highest sentiment impact. Opinion target identification is a challenging task and is beyond the scope of our current study. For simplicity, we assume that the pivot terms are those having the POS tags: $\{Common\ Noun, Proper\ Noun, Pronoun\}$ in a tweet. For each candidate pivot term, we build a SentiCircle from which the sentiment impact that a pivot term receives from all the other terms in a tweet can be computed. Formally, the Pivot-Method seeks to find the sentiment $\hat{s}$ that receives the maximum sentiment impact within a tweet as:

$$\hat{s} = \arg\max_{s \in \mathcal{S}} \mathcal{H}_s(\boldsymbol{p}) = \arg\max_{s \in \mathcal{S}} \sum_{i}^{N_p} \sum_{j}^{N_w} \mathcal{H}_s(p_i, w_j) \tag{7}$$

where $s \in \mathcal{S} = \{Positive, Negative, Neutral\}$ is the sentiment label, $\boldsymbol{p}$ is a vector of all pivot terms in a tweet, $N_{\boldsymbol{p}}$ and $N_{\boldsymbol{w}}$ are the sets of the pivot terms and the remaining terms in a tweet respectively. $\mathcal{H}_s(p_i, w_j)$ is the sentiment impact function, which returns the sentiment impact of a term w_j in the SentiCircle of a pivot term p_i. The sentiment impact of a term within a SentiCircle of a pivot term is the term's Euclidean distance from the origin (i.e., the term's radius). Note that the impact value is doubled for all terms located either in the "*Very Positive*" or in the "*Very Negative*" quadrants.

If the Pivot method fails to detect a pivot term (e.g., if tweet is too short or has many ill-formed words), or finds a zero sentiment impact for all pivot terms (e.g., $N_{\boldsymbol{w}}$ terms are positioned at the origin (0,0)), then the method will revert back to the Median method.

5 Experimental Setup

As mentioned in Section 4 the contextual semantics captured by the SentiCircle representation are based on terms co-occurrence from the corpus and an initial set of sentiment weights from a sentiment lexicon. We propose an evaluation set up that uses three different corpora (collections of tweets) and three different generic sentiment lexicons.

Datasets: We use three Twitter datasets which have been used in other sentiment analysis literature. Numbers of positive and negative tweets within these datasets are summarised in Table 1, and detailed in the references added in the table.

Table 1. Twitter datasets used for the evaluation

Dataset	Tweets	Positive	Negative
Obama McCain Debate (OMD)[9]	1081	393	688
Health Care Reform (HCR)[19]	1354	397	957
Standford Sentiment Gold Standard (STS-Gold)[16]	2034	632	1402

Sentiment Lexicons: As describe in Section 4, initial sentiments of terms in SentiCircle are extracted from a sentiment lexicon (prior sentiment). We evaluate our approach using three external sentiment lexicons in order to study how the different prior sentiment scores of terms influence the performance of the SentiCircle representation for sentiment analysis. The aim is to investigate the ability of SentiCircles in updating these *context-free* prior sentiment scores based on the contextual semantics extracted from different tweets corpora. We selected three state-of-art lexicons for this study: (i) the

SentiWordNet lexicon [3], (ii) the MPQA subjectivity lexicon [26] and, (iii) Thelwall-Lexicon [23,22].

Baselines: We compare the performance of SentiCircle in sentiment polarity detection of tweets (positive vs. negative) against the following baselines:

- *Lexicon labelling:* Use the MPQA (hereafter *MPQA-Method*) and the SentiWordNet (hereafter *SentiWordNet-Method*) lexicons to extract sentiment. If a tweet contains more positive words than negative ones, it is labelled as positive, and vice versa.
- *SentiStrength* [23,22]: is a state-of-the-art approach, which assigns to each tweet two sentiment strengths: a negative strength between -1 (not negative) to -5 (extremely negative) and a positive strength between +1 (not positive) to +5 (extremely positive). A tweet is considered positive if its positive sentiment strength is 1.5 times higher than the negative one, and negative otherwise.[5] Note that SentiStrength come with manually-defined lexical rules, such as the existence of emoticons, intensifiers, negation and booster words (e.g., absolutely, extremely), to compute the average sentiment strength of a tweet.

Thresholds and Parameters Tuning: When computing sentiment in a SentiCircle (Function 6) it is necessary to set the geometric boundaries of the neutral region where neutral terms reside. While the boundaries of the neutral region are fixed for the X-axis $[0, 1]$ (see Section 4), the boundaries of the Y-axis need to be determined. Neutral areas tend to have a high density of terms, since the number of neutral terms is usually larger than the number of positive and negative terms.

The limits of the neutral region vary from one SentiCircle to another. For simplicity, we assume the same neutral region boundary for all SentiCircles emerging from the same corpus and sentiment lexicon. To compute these thresholds we first build the SentiCircle of the complete corpus by merging all SentiCircles of each individual term and then we plot the density distribution of the terms within the constructed SentiCircle. The boundaries of the neutral are delimited by an increase/decrease in the density of terms.

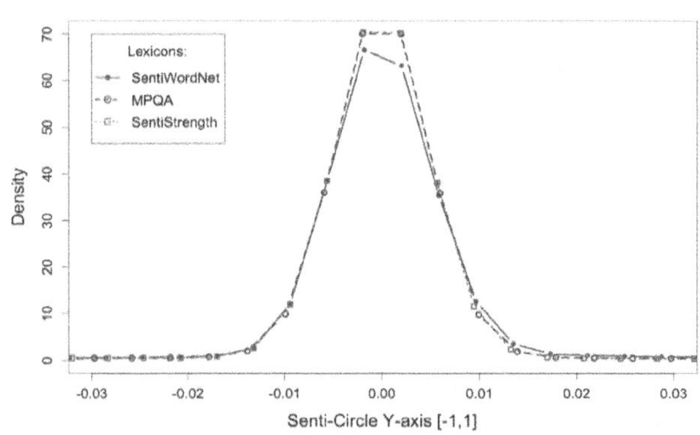

Fig. 4. Density geometric distribution of terms on the OMD dataset

[5] `http://sentistrength.wlv.ac.uk/documentation/SentiStrengthJavaManual.doc`

Table 2. Neutral region boundaries for Y-axis

	SentiWordNet	MPQA	Thelwall-Lexicon
OMD	[-0.01, 0.01]	[-0.01, 0.01]	[-0.01, 0.01]
HCR	[-0.1, 0.1]	[-0.05, 0.05]	[-0.05, 0.05]
STS-Gold	[-0.1, 0.1]	[-0.05, 0.05]	[-0.001, 0.001]

Figure 4 shows the three density distribution plots for the OMD dataset with SentiWordNet, MPQA and Thelwall lexicons. The boundaries of the neutral area are delimited by the density increase, falling in the $[-0.01, 0.01]$ range. Note that the generated SentiCircles vary depending on corpus and sentiment lexicon. For evaluation, we computed nine neutral regions, one for each corpus and sentiment lexicon used (see Table 2).

6 Evaluation Results

In this section we report the results from using SentiCircle to identify tweet sentiment, with all three methods described in Section 4, using SentiWordNet, MPQA and Thelwall lexicons on OMD, HCR and STS-Gold datasets. We compare our results with those obtained from the baselines described in Section 5. Later we report on the impact of adding conceptual semantics to the analysis (Section 3.3).

We report these results in two different settings. In the first setting, only contextual semantics are considered when constructing the SentiCircle representation. In our second setting, conceptual semantics are added to the SentiCircle representation. Our aim is to study up to which level the introduction of more fine-grained conceptual semantics can help to enrich the contextual semantics for sentiment analysis.

6.1 Results of Sentiment Detection with Contextual Semantics

Figure 5 shows the results in accuracy (left column) and average F-measure (F1-score) (right column) of all the methods and across all three datasets. The significantly worst performing baselines are the ones based solely on lexicons: the MPQA and SentiWordNet lexicons. Remember that SentiStrength adds a wide range of rules on top of the lexicon.

SentiCircle consistently achieved better results when using the MPQA or Thelwall lexicons than SentiWordNet. We also notice generally better results of SentiCircle when favouring target terms in tweets (Pivot method - Section 4), demonstrating good potential of such an approach.

The results show a close competition between our SentiCircle method and the SentiStrength method. For the OMD dataset, SentiCircle outperforms SentiStrength by 5.6% in accuracy (70.58 / 66.79 = 1.056) and 9% in F-measure (66.94 / 61.4 = 1.09) when using MPQA lexicon. For HCR, SentiCircle achieves 5.5% higher accuracy, whereas SentiStrength provides a 1.2% better F-measure. As for STS-Gold, SentiStrength gives around a 1.2% win in both accuracy and F-measure. The average accuracy of SentiCircle and SentiStrength across all three datasets is 72.39 and 71.7 respectively, and for F-measure it is 65.98 and 66.52. Also, the average precision and recall for SentiCircle are %66.82 and %66.12 and for SentiStrength are %67.07 %66.56 respectively.

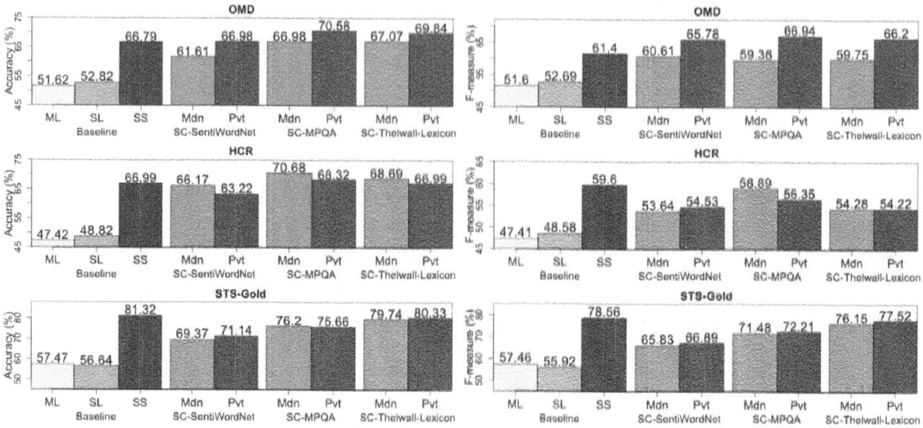

Fig. 5. Sentiment detection results (Accuracy and F-measure). ML: MPQA lexicon, SL: SentiWordNet lexicon, SS: SentiStrength, SC is SentiCircle approach, SC-SentiWordNet: SC with SentiWordNet lexicon, Mdn: SentiCircle with Median method, Pvt: SentiCircle with Pivot method.

Although the potential is evident, clearly there is a need for more research to determine the specific conditions under which SentiCircle performs better or worse. One likely factor that influences the performance of SentiCircle is the balance of positive to negative tweets in the dataset. For example, we notice that SentiCircle produces, on average, 2.5% lower recall than SentiStrength on positive tweet detection. This is perhaps not surprising since our tweet data contain more negative tweets than positive ones with the number of the former more than double the number of the latter (see Table 1).

Remember that the motivation behind SentiCircle is that sentiment of words may vary with context. By capturing the contextual semantics of these words, using the SentiCircle representation, we aim to adapt the strength and polarity of words. We show here the average percentage of words in our three datasets for which SentiCircle changed their prior sentiment orientation or strength.

Table 3 shows that on average 27.1% of the unique words in our datasets were covered by the sentiment lexicons and were assigned prior sentiments accordingly. Using the SentiCircle representation, however, resulted in 59.9% of these words flipping their sentiment orientations (e.g., from positive to negative, or to neutral) and 37.43% changing their sentiment strength while keeping their prior sentiment orientation. Hence only 2.67% of the words were left with their prior sentiment orientation and strength unchanged. It is also worth noting that our model was able to assign sentiment to 38.93% of the *hidden* words that were not covered by the sentiment lexicons. In future work we plan to investigate these results further to understand the influence of these type of changes individually on the overall sentiment analysis performance.

Our evaluation results showed that our SentiCircle representation coupled with the MPQA or Thelwall lexicons gives the highest performance amongst the other three lexicons. However, Table 3 shows that only 9.61% of the words in the three datasets were covered by the Thelwall-Lexicon, and 16.81% by MPQA. Nevertheless, SentiCircle

Table 3. Average percentage of words in three datasets, which their sentiment orientation or strength were updated by their SentiCircles

	SentiWordNet	MPQA	Thelwall-Lexicon	Average
Words found in the lexicon	54.86	16.81	9.61	27.10
Hidden words	45.14	83.19	90.39	72.90
Words flipped their sentiment orientation	65.35	61.29	53.05	59.90
Words changed their sentiment strength	29.30	36.03	46.95	37.43
New opinionated words	49.03	32.89	34.88	38.93

performed best with these two lexicons, which suggests that it was able to cope with this low coverage by assigning sentiment to a large proportion of the *hidden* words.

6.2 Incorporating Conceptual Semantics in Sentiment Detection

In this section we report the results when enriching the SentiCircle representation with conceptual semantics by using the augmentation method (see Section 3.3). As explained earlier, we used AlchemyAPI to extract the semantic concepts for the three evaluation datasets. Table 4 lists the total number of entities and concepts extracted for each dataset.

Table 4. Entity/concept extraction statistics of OMD, HCR and STS-Gold using AlchemyAPI

	HCR	OMD	STS-Gold
No. of Entities	1194	1392	2735
No. of Concepts	14	19	23

Figure 6 depicts the win/loss in accuracy and F-measure when adding the conceptual semantics to the SentiCircle model across all datasets. Note that here we used the Thelwall-Lexicon to obtain the word prior sentiments in our three sentiment detection methods.

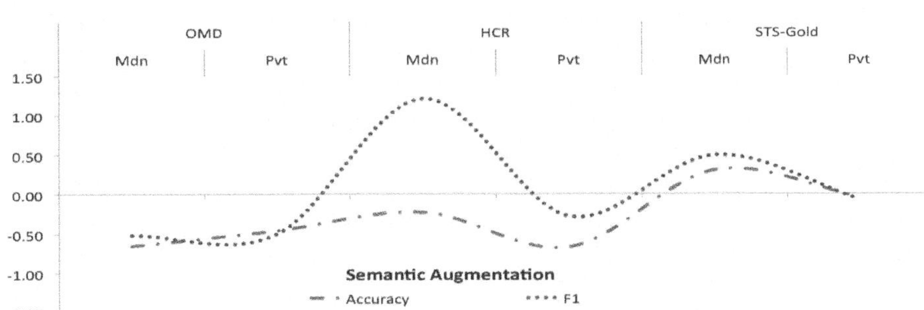

Fig. 6. Win/Loss in Accuracy and F-measure of incorporating conceptual semantics into SentiCircles, where Mdn: SentiCircle with Median method, Pvt: SentiCircle with Pivot method

The results show that the impact of conceptual semantics on the performance of SentiCircles varies across datasets. On the HCR dataset, a 1.21% gain in F-measure is obtained using the Median method. Also the Median method is more affected by semantic incorporation than the Pivot method, where a much clearer shift in performance can be observed across datasets. This can be explained as the Median method considers all the incorporated concepts in the SentiCircle, whereas the Pivot method focus more on concepts that are associated to target terms in tweets (See Section 4).

As shown in Table 4, the number of entities extracted for the STS-Gold dataset is almost twice as for HCR or OMD. Nonetheless, the results show that semantic incorporation seems to have a lower impact on the STS-Gold dataset than on the OMD and HCR datasets. This might be due to the topical-focus of each dataset. While OMD and HCR are both composed of a smaller number of tweets about specific topics (the US Health Care Reform bill and the Obama-McCain debate), the STS-Gold dataset contains a larger number of tweets with no particular topical focus.

7 Discussion and Future Work

We showed the potential of using SentiCircle for sentiment detection of tweets. The evaluation was performed on three Twitter datasets and using three different sentiment lexicons. Compared to SentiStrength, the results were not as conclusive, since SentiStrength slightly outperformed SentiCircle on the STS-Gold dataset, and also yielded marginally better F-measure for the HCR dataset. This might be due to the different topic distribution in the datasets. STS-Gold dataset contains random tweets, with no particular topic focus, whereas OMD and HCR consist of tweets that discuss specific topics, and thus the contextual semantics extracted by SentiCircle are probably more representative in these datasets than in STS-Gold. Other important characteristics could be the sparseness degree of data and the positive and negative distribution of tweets. In future work, we plan to further investigate these issues and their individual influence on the performance of our approach.

SentiCircle updates the sentiment of terms to match their context. Part of our future work is to study which type of terms change their sentiment, and which are more stable. This can help improving performance by filtering out stable terms. Another evaluation dimension is how SentiCircle performs in monitoring sentiment around a subject over time, to further demonstrate its power and value of updating terms' sentiment with time.

Since all the baselines used in our evaluation are purely syntactical methods, we aim in the future to compare our approach to other, which take word semantics into account for sentiment detection, such as SenticNet.

In this work, the context, in which the semantics of words were extracted and used for sentiment, is defined at the corpus level, that is, by taking into account the occurrence patterns of terms in the whole tweet corpus. We are currently investigating defining the context of terms at more fine-grained levels including tweet- and sentence levels.

We proposed and tested methods that assign positive, negative or neutral sentiment to terms and tweets based on their corresponding SentiCircle representations. However, there could be a need for cases where terms with "`Mixed`" sentiment emerge, when their SentiCircle representations consist of positive and negative terms only.

We extracted opinion targets (Pivot terms) in the Pivot-Method simply by looking at their POS-tags assuming that all pivot terms in a given tweet receive similar sentiment. We aim next to evaluate this process and to consider cases, where the tweet contains several pivot terms of different sentiment orientations.

We investigated adding conceptual semantics to SentiCircles and studied their impact on the overall sentiment detection performance. In general, a marginal loss in performance (especially in accuracy) was observed comparing to only using contextual semantics. This might be due to the generality of some of the extracted concepts (e.g., "`person`", "`company`"), which were applied to many terms of opposite sentiment. These concepts were regarded as normal terms in tweets, and had their own SentiCircles, which might have had a negative impact on the extraction of sentiment. A fix might be to extract more specific concepts, using other concept extractors (e.g., SenticNet).

8 Conclusions

In this paper we proposed a novel semantic sentiment approach called SentiCircle, which captures the semantics of words from their context and update their sentiment orientations and strengths accordingly. We described the use of SentiCircle for lexicon-based sentiment identification of tweets using different methods. We showed that our approach outperformed other lexicon labelling methods and overtake the state-of-the-art SentiStrength approach in accuracy, with a marginal drop in F-measure. Unlike most other lexicon-based approaches, SentiCircle was able to update the sentiment strength of many terms dynamically based on their contextual semantics.

We enriched the SentiCircle representation with conceptual semantics extracted using AlchemyAPI. Results showed that adding concepts to SentiCircle has a good potential, and indicated that the use of conceptual semantics with SentiCircle might be more appropriate when the datasets being analysed are large and cover a wide range of topics.

Acknowledgment. This work was supported by the EU-FP7 project SENSE4US (grant no. 611242).

References

1. Agarwal, A., Xie, B., Vovsha, I., Rambow, O., Passonneau, R.: Sentiment analysis of twitter data. In: Proc. ACL 2011 Workshop on Languages in Social Media, Portland, Oregon (2011)
2. Aue, A., Gamon, M.: Customizing sentiment classifiers to new domains: A case study. In: Proc. Recent Advances in Natural Language Processing (RANLP), Borovets, Bulgaria (2005)
3. Baccianella, S., Esuli, A., Sebastiani, F.: Sentiwordnet 3.0: An enhanced lexical resource for sentiment analysis and opinion mining. In: Seventh Conference on International Language Resources and Evaluation, Valletta, Malta (May 2010) (retrieved)
4. Barbosa, L., Feng, J.: Robust sentiment detection on twitter from biased and noisy data. In: Proceedings of COLING, Beijing, China (2010)

5. Bifet, A., Frank, E.: Sentiment knowledge discovery in twitter streaming data. In: Pfahringer, B., Holmes, G., Hoffmann, A. (eds.) DS 2010. LNCS, vol. 6332, pp. 1–15. Springer, Heidelberg (2010)
6. Bollen, J., Mao, H., Zeng, X.: Twitter mood predicts the stock market. Journal of Computational Science 2(1), 1–8 (2011)
7. Cambria, E.: An introduction to concept-level sentiment analysis. In: Castro, F., Gelbukh, A., González, M. (eds.) MICAI 2013, Part II. LNCS, vol. 8266, pp. 478–483. Springer, Heidelberg (2013)
8. Cambria, E., Havasi, C., Hussain, A.: Senticnet 2: A semantic and affective resource for opinion mining and sentiment analysis. In: FLAIRS Conference, pp. 202–207 (2012)
9. Diakopoulos, N., Shamma, D.: Characterizing debate performance via aggregated twitter sentiment. In: Proc. 28th Int. Conf. on Human Factors in Computing Systems. ACM (2010)
10. Firth, J.R.: A synopsis of linguistic theory. Studies in Linguistic Analysis (1930-1955)
11. Garcia-Moya, L., Anaya-Sanchez, H., Berlanga-Llavori, R.: Retrieving product features and opinions from customer reviews. IEEE Intelligent Systems 28(3), 19–27 (2013)
12. Kouloumpis, E., Wilson, T., Moore, J.: Twitter sentiment analysis: The good the bad and the omg? In: Proceedings of the ICWSM, Barcelona, Spain (2011)
13. Liu, B.: Sentiment analysis and subjectivity. Taylor and Francis Group (2010)
14. O'Connor, B., Balasubramanyan, R., Routledge, B.R., Smith, N.A.: From tweets to polls: Linking text sentiment to public opinion time series. ICWSM 11, 122–129 (2010)
15. Pak, A., Paroubek, P.: Twitter as a corpus for sentiment analysis and opinion mining. In: Proceedings of LREC 2010, Valletta, Malta (2010)
16. Saif, H., Fernandez, M., He, Y., Alani, H.: Evaluation datasets for twitter sentiment analysis. In: Proceedings, 1st Workshop on Emotion and Sentiment in Social and Expressive Media (ESSEM) in Conjunction with AI*IA Conference, Turin, Italy (2013)
17. Saif, H., He, Y., Alani, H.: Alleviating data sparsity for twitter sentiment analysis. In: Proc. Workshop on Making Sense of Microposts (#MSM2012) in WWW 2012, Lyon, France (2012)
18. Saif, H., He, Y., Alani, H.: Semantic sentiment analysis of twitter. In: Cudré-Mauroux, P., Heflin, J., Sirin, E., Tudorache, T., Euzenat, J., Hauswirth, M., Parreira, J.X., Hendler, J., Schreiber, G., Bernstein, A., Blomqvist, E. (eds.) ISWC 2012, Part I. LNCS, vol. 7649, pp. 508–524. Springer, Heidelberg (2012)
19. Speriosu, M., Sudan, N., Upadhyay, S., Baldridge, J.: Twitter polarity classification with label propagation over lexical links and the follower graph. In: Proceedings of the EMNLP First Workshop on Unsupervised Learning in NLP, Edinburgh, Scotland (2011)
20. Taboada, M., Brooke, J., Tofiloski, M., Voll, K., Stede, M.: Lexicon-based methods for sentiment analysis. Computational Linguistics 37(2), 267–307 (2011)
21. Takamura, H., Inui, T., Okumura, M.: Extracting semantic orientations of words using spin model. In: Proc. 43rd Annual Meeting on Association for Computational Linguistics (2005)
22. Thelwall, M., Buckley, K., Paltoglou, G.: Sentiment strength detection for the social web. J. American Society for Information Science and Technology 63(1), 163–173 (2012)
23. Thelwall, M., Buckley, K., Paltoglou, G., Cai, D., Kappas, A.: Sentiment strength detection in short informal text. J. American Society for Info. Science and Technology 61(12) (2010)
24. Turney, P., Littman, M.: Measuring praise and criticism: Inference of semantic orientation from association. ACM Transactions on Information Systems 21, 315–346 (2003)
25. Turney, P.D., Pantel, P., et al.: From frequency to meaning: Vector space models of semantics. Journal of Artificial Intelligence Research 37(1), 141–188 (2010)
26. Wilson, T., Wiebe, J., Hoffmann, P.: Recognizing contextual polarity in phrase-level sentiment analysis. In: Proceedings of the conference on Human Language Technology and Empirical Methods in Natural Language Processing, Vancouver, British Columbia, Canada (2005)
27. Wittgenstein, L.: Philosophical Investigations. Blackwell, London (1953, 2001)

User Interests Identification on Twitter Using a Hierarchical Knowledge Base*

Pavan Kapanipathi[1], Prateek Jain[2], Chitra Venkataramani[2], and Amit Sheth[1]

[1] Kno.e.sis Center, Wright State University
{pavan,amit}@knoesis.org
[2] IBM TJ Watson Research Center
{jainpr,chitrav}@us.ibm.com

Abstract. Twitter, due to its massive growth as a social networking platform, has been in focus for the analysis of its user generated content for personalization and recommendation tasks. A common challenge across these tasks is identifying user interests from tweets. Semantic enrichment of Twitter posts, to determine user interests, has been an active area of research in the recent past. These approaches typically use available public knowledge-bases (such as Wikipedia) to spot entities and create entity-based user profiles. However, exploitation of such knowledge-bases to create richer user profiles is yet to be explored. In this work, we leverage hierarchical relationships present in knowledge-bases to infer user interests expressed as a *Hierarchical Interest Graph*. We argue that the hierarchical semantics of concepts can enhance existing systems to personalize or recommend items based on a varied level of conceptual abstractness. We demonstrate the effectiveness of our approach through a user study which shows an average of approximately eight of the top ten weighted hierarchical interests in the graph being relevant to a user's interests.

Keywords: #eswc2014Kapanipathi, User Profiles, Personalization, Social Web, Semantics, Twitter, Wikipedia, Hierarchical Interest Graph.

1 Introduction

A squirrel dying in your front yard may be more relevant to your interests right now than people dying in Africa. - Mark Zuckerberg, Facebooks CEO[1].

* This material is based on the first author's work at IBM Research, complemented in part based upon work supported by the National Science Foundation SoCS program under Grant No.(IIS-1111182, 09/01/2011-08/31/2014). Any opinions, findings, and conclusions or recommendations expressed in this material are those of the author(s) and do not necessarily reflect the views of the employer or funding organization. We would like to thank: (1) Zemanta for their support; (2) Participants of the user study; (3) T K Prasad, Delroy Cameron, Sarasi Lalithasena, Sanjaya Wijeyaratne and Revathy Krishnamurthy for their invaluable feedback.

[1] `http://www.nytimes.com/2011/05/23/opinion/23pariser.html`

V. Presutti et al. (Eds.): ESWC 2014, LNCS 8465, pp. 99–113, 2014.

Content personalization based on social activities (clicks, posts) is gaining increasing traction with web companies day by day. A variety of services and platforms on the digital web, right from movies on Netflix to navigation routes on GPS (Waze) are personalized based on what you like and what you did. The personalized content for each individual is determined using various metrics such as click behavior, collaborative filtering and cookies. A common element across these techniques is the focus on using current browsing session for providing personalization and therefore a lack of identification of the broader interests.[2]

In this work, we try to address this shortcoming of content personalization by providing a framework for identification of broader user interests based on the content generated by them on Twitter. Specifically, given a tweet *"Now the sensible thing to do would be to conserve the money I have. But I want a new pair of trainers"*[3], our work provides a framework to identify that a person expressing an interest in buying a pair of *"training shoes"* is potentially interested in *"running"*. Once *"running"* is identified as an interest, a recommendation engine can utilize it in conjunction with other metrics to personalize user experience and recommend content. We utilize Twitter due to (1) higher degree of openness, and (2) in [2,17], tweets have been demonstrated to be a good indicator for determining user interests. For identification of hierarchical categories, we exploit Wikipedia (specifically the category graph) as the knowledge source. The inferred interests are represented in the form of a *Hierarchical Interest Graph (HIG)*. This representation will provide a personalization and recommendation engine with the flexibility to filter content based on abstract interests of users.

The key contributions of our work are as follows: (1) We propose a novel approach that extends the entity-based representation of user interests to a hierarchical representation. (2) We determine the interest scores for the categories in the *Hierarchical Interest Graph* by adapting the spreading activation algorithm [4] for the Wikipedia Category Graph (WCG). (3) We demonstrate a simple but efficient approach to transform the Wikipedia Category Graph into a hierarchy. This hierarchy is used as the base hierarchy for the Interest Graphs. Our evaluation shows an overlap of 87% hierarchical links between mapped categories with a manually created taxonomy - DMoz. (4) We present a user study of 37 participants with a comprehensive evaluation of our approach. The results show that our approach is practically useful with *top-10* ranked interests evaluating a mean average precision of 88%.

Example and Terminology. Consider the following tweets from a user:
- *Great day for Chicago sports as well as Cubs beat the Reds, Sox beat the Mariners with Humber's perfect game, Bulls win and Hawks stay alive*
- *Not sure who the Reds will look too replace Dusty.some very interesting jobs open (Cubs, Mariners, Reds, poss Yanks) Girardi the domino*

Preponderance posting of such tweets, we can determine that the user might be interested in Baseball teams such as *Cincinnati Reds, Chicago Cubs, Boston Red Sox.* We term the entities that can be directly spotted from user's tweets

[2] Netflix and Pandora get explicit input from users to generate broader interests.

[3] `http://bit.ly/sectorRoadMapGigaom`

as ***Primitive Interests***. Further, our approach exploits the knowledge linked to *Primitive Interests* (Baseball teams) in Wikipedia to determine that the user might be also interested in broader categories such as *Category: Major League Baseball, Category: Baseball.* These categories are termed as ***Hierarchical Interests***. Our goal is to determine the most relevant *Hierarchical Interests* by using *Primitive Interests* extracted from tweets.

Most Wikipedia entities have categories with the same label (*ex: Cincinnati Reds and Category: Cincinnati Reds*). The categories *(Hierarchical Interests)* that syntactically do not match entities (*Primitive Interests*) are termed as ***Implicit Interests***, also because they are not explicitly mentioned in tweets by the user. Formally, *Implicit Interests* $\subseteq$ *Hierarchical Interests.*

Spreading Activation. In this work, the Spreading Activation theory is used to assign appropriate scores for the categories in the Wikipedia hierarchy. Spreading activation theory builds on the assumption that the information in the human memory is represented either through association [10] or via semantic networks [20]. This theory has been utilized for various domains ranging from cognitive, neural sciences to Information Retrieval [5] and Semantic Web. The Spreading Activation theory in its pure form consists of a simple processing technique on a network data structure. A network data structure consists of nodes connected by means of links or edges.

Given a set of initially activated nodes, the processing technique consists of a series of iterations. An iteration can consist of one or more pulses or a termination check. A pulse can consist of three different phases (1) Pre-adjustment phase (2) Spreading (3) Post-adjustment phase. Of the three, pre-adjustment and post-adjustment phases are optional and consist of applying some form of an activation decay to the active nodes. The spreading phase consists of sending activation waves from one node to all the other directly connected nodes. The activation is however, controlled by an application dependent *activation function.* These iterations continue until a stopping condition is reached or the processing is halted by the user. More details on Spreading Activation is presented in [4].

In the next Section (Section 2) we present the approach followed by evaluation in Section 3. Section 4 details the related work whereas the last Section 5 concludes with future work.

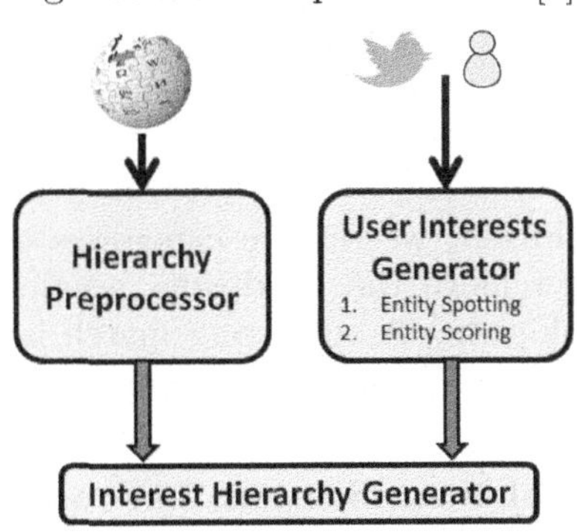

Fig. 1. Architecture

2 Approach

The goal of our approach is to construct a *Hierarchical Interest Graph (HIG)* for a Twitter user. To accomplish this our system as illustrated in Fig. 1, performs the following steps: (1) **Hierarchy Preprocessor** transforms the *Wikipedia Category Graph* (WCG) into a hierarchy that is needed to generate all the *HIG*s. This pre-processing step is necessary because of the challenges introduced by Wikipedia (detailed in Section 2.1). (2) **User Interests Generator** generates the *Primitive Interests* (defined in Section 1-Terminology) from the tweets of a user. The module (Section 2.2) first spots entities that are Wikipedia articles *(Primitive Interests)* and then scores them to reflect users' interests. (3) **Interest Hierarchy Generator** maps the *Primitive Interests* to *Wikipedia Hierarchy* and uses an adaptation of the spreading activation algorithm to infer a weighted *HIG* for the user (Section 2.3). Step 1 is updated periodically to keep abreast with the changes in Wikipedia whereas Step 2, 3 are performed for each user.

2.1 Hierarchy Preprocessor

We utilize Wikipedia as the knowledge-base for inferring *Hierarchical Interests.* Although, there are other free ontologies such as OpenCyc[4], and the ODP taxonomy[5], we opted for Wikipedia because of its vast domain coverage. However, a major challenge faced in utilizing Wikipedia as a hierarchy is that, its category graph (*WCG*) comprises of cycles and hence it is neither a taxonomy nor a hierarchy. These cycles make it non trivial to determine the hierarchical relationships between categories. For example, determining that *Category:Baseball* is conceptually more abstract than *Category:Major League Baseball* is difficult if there exists cycles in the graph. Therefore we transform *WCG* to a hierarchy by assigning levels of abstraction for each category.

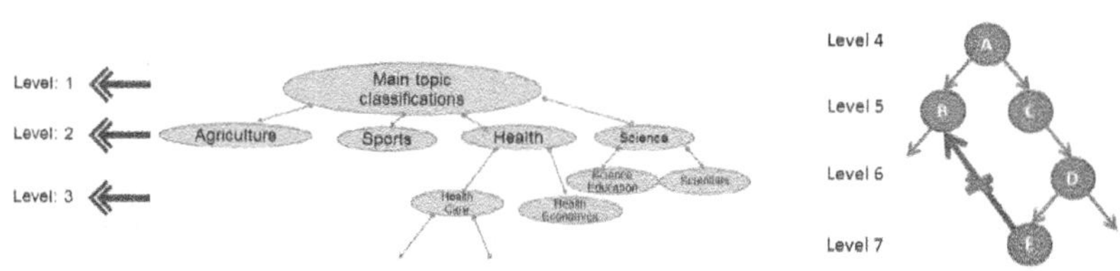

(a) Hierarchy Level Assignments

(b) Non Hierarchical Links

Fig. 2. Hierarchy Preprocessing

Firstly, we remove categories that are irrelevant for our work. Specifically, we remove the Wikipedia admin categories[6] that are used only to manage Wikipedia. A sub-string match is employed for the categories with the set of labels used in [18]. Consequently, around 64K categories with 150K links are removed from *WCG* as shown in Table 1.

Level Identification. The root category (node) of *WCG* is *Category: Main Topic Classifications*, which subsumes 98% of the categories (Table 1, 0.80M

[4] `http://www.opencyc.org/`
[5] `http://www.dmoz.org/`
[6] `http://en.wikipedia.org/wiki/Category:Wikipedia_administration`

out of 0.82M categories). Selecting this root node as the most abstract category, we determine the relative hierarchical levels of other categories. We assign the shortest distance to the category from the root as its hierarchical level (level of abstractness) as shown in Fig. 2(a).

Non Hierarchical Links Removal. Once the hierarchical levels are assigned we remove the edges that do not conform to a hierarchical structure, i.e. all the directed edges from a category of larger hierarchical level (specific) to a smaller hierarchical level (conceptually abstract) are removed. Considering Fig. 2(b), the link such as those from node $\boldsymbol{E}$ to node $\boldsymbol{B}$ are removed, since node $\boldsymbol{E}$ has been determined as a more specific node (Level 7) in the hierarchy than node $\boldsymbol{B}$ (Level 5). Performing this task reduced *WCG* from 1.9M links to 1.2M links (Table 1), also leading to the removal of cycles in WCG.

The output of this process is a hierarchy with $height = 15$, rooted at the node *Category: Main Topic Classifications.* The nodes in the hierarchy have many to many relationships and hence it is still not a taxonomy. This refined graph with directed edges that conform to a hierarchy is referred to as *Wikipedia Hierarchy* (*WH*).

Table 1. Wikipedia Categories and Links. WA: Without Admin, WH: Hierarchy Preprocessed.

	Categories	Links
Wiki	884,838	2,074,173
Wiki(WA)	820,476	1,922,441
Wiki(WH)	802,194	1,177,558

2.2 User Interests Generator

This module identifies *Primitive Interests* from a user's tweets by *Entity Recognition*, and scores them based on their frequency.

Entity Recognition. The first step towards identification of *Primitive Interests* is Entity Recognition[7] in tweets. Entity recognition in tweets is non trivial due to the informal nature and ungrammatical language [23] of tweets. Since the focus of our work is on hierarchical interests identification and not entity recognition, we used an existing solution.

In [6] authors have compared three different state of the art systems namely Dbpedia Spotlight [14], Zemanta[8] and TextRazor[9] for entity recognition in tweets. These results have been summarized in Table 2. We opted to use Zemanta for our work because of the following reasons: (1) Zemanta links the entities spotted in tweets to their corresponding Wikipedia articles (*Primitive*

Table 2. Evaluation of Web Services for Entity Resolution and Linking from [6]. Pr: Precision, Re: Recall, F-M: F-Measure.

Extractors	Pr	Re	F-M	Limit
Spotlight	20.1	47.5	28.3	N/A
TextRazor	**64.6**	26.9	38.0	500/day
Zemanta	57.7	31.8	**41.0**	**10,000/day**

[7] Details on different techniques for Entity Recognition in tweets is presented in [6]

[8] `http://developer.zemanta.com/`

[9] `http://www.textrazor.com/technology`

Interests); (2) Zemanta has relatively superior performance to other services as shown in Table 2; and (3) Zemanta increased the rate limit of their API[10] to 10,000 per day, on request for research purposes.

Scoring User Interests. Once the *Primitive Interests* are identified, the next task is to score them to find the degree of user's interests across different entities. This is important as the scores of *Primitive Interests* are utilized in scoring the appropriate *Hierarchical Interests* (Section 2.3) for the user. We employ a frequency based scoring mechanism similar to those used in [2,27]. The score for an entity is determined using the equation: $nf_i = frequency(e_i)/frequency(e_{max})$. The score ranges between 0-1, as in the formula the frequency of mentions of an entity in tweets ($frequency(e_i)$) is normalized by the frequency of the entity that is mentioned the most by the user ($frequency(e_{max})$). To summarize, the results of this module are a set of weighted *Primitive Interests* with weights reflecting the user's degree of interest.

2.3 Interest Hierarchy Generator

For each user, the Interest Hierarchy Generator takes a set of scored *Primitive Interests* and the *WH* as input to generate a weighted *HIG*. The *Primitive Interests* are added as leaf nodes to the *WH* by linking to their appropriate categories. Then, the scores of *Primitive Interests* are propagated up the hierarchy as far as the root using Spreading Activation theory to determine the interest categories and their appropriate weights. The propagation of scores to the categories is performed using an activation function (see Section 1 - Spreading Activation). A basic activation function is shown in Equation 1.

$$A_i = A_i + A_j \times W_{ij} \times D \tag{1}$$

where i is the node to be activated (Parent Category) and A_i is its activation value; j is the activated child node of i (*Primitive Interests*/Child Category); W_{ij} is the weight of the edge connecting node i and j; D is the decay factor. We utilized different variations of *Activation functions* as follows:

1. We experimented with a *no-weight no-decay* option on the basic spreading activation function (Equation 1 with $W_{ij} = 1$, $D = 1$). The resulting *HIG* had higher scores for interest categories that are higher (conceptually abstract) in the hierarchy. This is intuitive, because the activation values were propagated up the hierarchy without any constraints. Further, we experimented with empirically decided, decay factors ($D = 0.4, 0.6, 0.8$) as constraints up the hierarchy. Although there were slight variations, there were no significant improvements with the results. This motivated us to analyze the distribution of nodes in the hierarchy for better normalization.

2. The distribution of categories across the hierarchy follows a bell curve as shown in Fig. 3(a). This uneven distribution impacts the propagated scores by increasing the scores of categories with more child nodes. Therefore, we normalized the activation value of each of the *Hierarchical Interests* based on the

[10] `http://developer.zemanta.com/docs/suggest/`

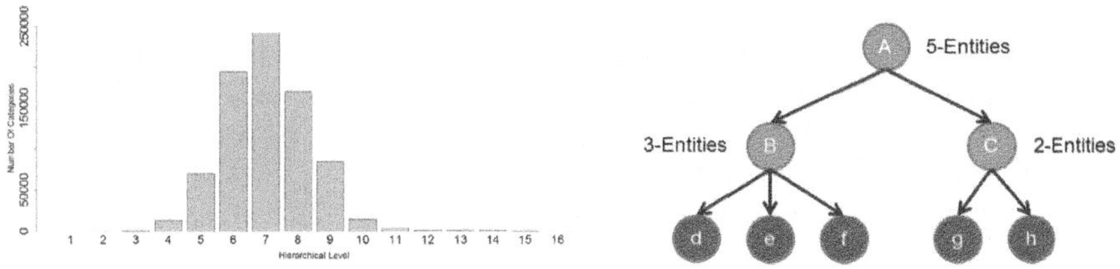

(a) Nodes Distribution (b) Intersect Booster

Fig. 3. Interest Hierarchy Generator

number of sub-categories at its child level. This was experimented with the raw count of the node frequency (Equation 2). As shown in Fig. 3(a), the peak of the bell curve is at level 7 with about 250k nodes. if Equation 2 is used, these large values have a heavier penalty on the interest scores. Therefore, we also experimented with log scale of the raw numbers (Equation 3).

$$F_i = \frac{1}{nodes_{(h_i+1)}} \quad (2) \qquad FL_i = \frac{1}{\log_{10} nodes_{(h_i+1)}} \quad (3)$$

where h_i is the hierarchical level of node i; $nodes_h$ is number of nodes at hierarchical level h.

3. *Preferential Path Constraint*: The nodes in *WH* have many categories associated with them. Considering our example in Section 1, (Dated-Jan 9th 2014) *Cincinnati Reds* has categories starting with *Major League Baseball teams, Sports in Cincinnati, Ohio, Sports clubs established in 1882, etc.* One of the problems we noticed is that all these categories were given equal priority and hence equal weights were being propagated. Therefore, we introduced the *preferential path constraint* to prioritize the categories for a node. The motivation is drawn from the Wikipedia category structure where for any article or category, on their Wikipedia page, the parent categories are ordered from left to right in decreasing order of significance. Having the categories of *Cincinnati Reds* in the same order as mentioned above implies that *Category:Major League Baseball teams* is more suitable as a category of *Cincinnati Reds* than the rest. We utilize this heuristic as preferential path constraint in the activation function. This is similar to adding weights to the edges in *WH* and is accomplished using the Equation 4.

$$P_{ij} = \frac{1}{priority_{ji}} \quad (4)$$

where $priority_{ji}$ is the priority of category i for subcategory j. $priority_{ji}$ increases linearly $(1, 2, ..)$ reflecting the order of categories from left to right.

4. *Intersect Booster*: We utilize this variation to boost the categories (nodes) in the hierarchy that forms the intersecting point of multiple *Primitive Interests* for a given user. For example, consider the hierarchy in Fig. 3(b), where *d, e, f, g, h* are entities and *A, B, C* are categories. If only *d, e, f* are considered as user's *Primitive Interests*, the most appropriate *Hierarchical Interests* would be *Category:B*. On the other hand, if entities *g, f* are also user's interests then

Category:A would be the more appropriate due to the intersection of maximum *Primitive Interests* at *Category:A*. Therefore, to formalize this aspect and boost the score of intersecting nodes, we introduced Equation 5.

$$B_i = \frac{N_{e_i}}{N_{e_{cmax}}} \tag{5}$$

where N_{e_i} is the total number of entities activating node i; $cmax$ is the subcategory of i that has been activated with max number of entities.

In Fig. 3(b), if *d, e, f* are *Primitive Interests* then for *Category A*, $B_A = \frac{3}{3}$. If *g, h* are *Primitive Interests*, then $B_A = \frac{5}{3}$ (increases).

Activation Functions. Using the variations explained above, we created different activation functions which are as follows:

–*Bell*: The Bell function is as shown in Equation 6. This function spreads the activation value up the hierarchy with a raw normalization (Equation 2).

$$A_i = A_i + A_j \times F_i \tag{6}$$

–*Bell Log*: This function (Equation 7) uses the log normalization (Equation 3) to reduce the impact of the raw count.

$$A_i = A_i + A_j \times FL_i \tag{7}$$

–*Priority Intersect*: The final activation function that we experimented with builds on the *Bell Log* function (Equation 3). This function rewards the categories on the left (Equation 4) and boosts the interesting nodes (Equation 5). Formally, the function is represented by the Equation 8.

$$A_i = A_i + A_j \times FL_i \times P_{ij} \times B_i \tag{8}$$

3 Evaluation

The input to our system is a set of tweets for a given user and the *WCG*, whereas the output is a weighted *HIG* for each user. We evaluate the following two aspects of the system: (1) We perform a user study to evaluate the *Hierarchical Interests* generated for each user using the activation functions explained in Section 2.3. (2) Since the Wikipedia Hierarchy plays an important role in generating *HIG*s, we evaluate the hierarchy against a manually constructed taxonomy - DMoz.

3.1 Hierarchical Interests Evaluation

Evaluation of personalization and/or recommendation systems typically involves a user study as performed in various works [1,17,19]. The user studies involve a set of users participating in evaluating the results generated by the system.

User Study. 37 users agreed to participate in our user study by giving us access to their tweets and agreeing to evaluate the results. Our system analyzed their tweets and generated results using the following activation functions: (1) *Bell*, (2) *Bell Log*, (3) *Priority Intersect.*

Each activation function when employed generated corresponding weighted *HIGs* for users. The *top-50* scored *Hierarchical Interests* from each *HIG* were selected for user evaluation. The evaluation requested the users to mark the *Hierarchical Interests* as *Yes/No/Maybe* to indicate their interest or lack of. To ensure unbiased results from the users, the *Hierarchical Interests* when presented to the user neither had any order (based on score) nor contained any associated information such as the tweets or the associated activation functions.

The guidelines provided to users included: (1) The interests provided were categories (conceptually abstract) not entities; (2) The interest generation did not involve a temporal aspect. If the user at any point of time was interested in an event or a topic (*Category:Super Bowl, Category:United States presidential election, 2012*) then they have to be considered as their interests; (3) It is unlikely that users tweet about everything which is of interest to them. Therefore, the users were asked to mark for relevance based on the topics they tweet or had tweeted in the past. For instance, if a user has never tweeted about *Category:Pets* and the system marks it as an interest then such interests should be marked as irrelevant; (4) The *Maybe* option in evaluation is introduced due to the abstractness of the interests. For example, for users who are only interested in *Baseball, American Football*, an interest such as *Category:Sports* inferred might be too broad/abstract to mark *Yes.*

Fig. 4. Users Tweets Distribution

Data. The survey was conducted with 37 Twitter users having varying number of tweets. The "users to tweets" distribution is shown in Fig. 4. Table 3 shows the user statistics, the volume of tweets and number of entities identified in the tweets. Approximately 32K tweets were obtained using the Twitter API[11]. Due to the restriction enforced by Twitter Search API, for seven users who have more tweets, we could retrieve only 3200 per user. From 32k tweets, 29k entities were extracted, out of which approximately 45% are distinct. Further, the users found 58% of the interest categories identified by our system to match with their interests (Yes), limited confidence in 12% (Maybe) and 30% were marked irrelevant (No).

Results. In order to compare the three activation functions and evaluate their results, we answered the below questions and accordingly selected the evaluation metrics. The selected evaluation metrics are standard metrics in Information Retrieval and more details can be found in [13].

[11] `https://dev.twitter.com/docs/api/1.1/get/search/tweets`

Table 3. User Study Data

	Users	Tweets	Entities	Distinct Entities	Tweets with Entities	Categories in HIG
Total	37	31927	29146	13150	16464	111535
Average		864	787	355	445	3014

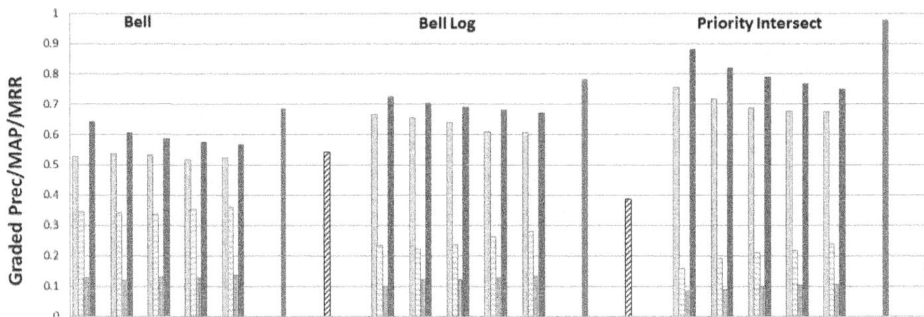

	Bell @10	Bell @20	Bell @30	Bell @40	Bell @50	Bell MRR Y	Bell MRR N	Bell Log @10	Bell Log @20	Bell Log @30	Bell Log @40	Bell Log @50	Bell Log MRR Y	Bell Log MRR N	Priority Intersect @10	Priority Intersect @20	Priority Intersect @30	Priority Intersect @40	Priority Intersect @50	Priority Intersect MRR Y	Priority Intersect MRR N
yes	0.53	0.54	0.53	0.52	0.52			0.67	0.66	0.64	0.61	0.61			0.76	0.72	0.69	0.68	0.67		
no	0.34	0.34	0.34	0.35	0.36			0.23	0.22	0.24	0.26	0.28			0.16	0.19	0.21	0.22	0.24		
maybe	0.13	0.12	0.13	0.13	0.14			0.1	0.12	0.12	0.13	0.13			0.08	0.09	0.1	0.11	0.11		
MAP	0.64	0.61	0.59	0.58	0.57			0.72	0.7	0.69	0.68	0.67			0.88	0.82	0.79	0.77	0.75		
MRRY						0.69							0.78							0.98	
MRRN							0.54							0.39							0.18

Fig. 5. Evaluation Results – MAP: Mean Average Precision; MRR-Y/N: Mean Reciprocal Recall-Relevant/Irrelevant Results

How many relevant/irrelevant Hierarchical Interests are retrieved at top-k ranks?: To assess this question, we adapt the *Precision@k* metric to deal with the graded (*Yes/No/Maybe*) results from our user study. We term the metric as *GradedPrecision* and is as shown in Equation 9

$$GradedPrecision_{res}@k = \frac{1}{|Q|}\sum_{i=1}^{|Q|}\frac{HI_{res}@k}{k} \tag{9}$$

where k is the rank; Q is the set of users in the user study; res is the one of the options evaluated by the user *Yes/No/Maybe*; $HI_{res}@k$ is the total number of *Hierarchical Interests* marked res at rank k.

The equation for graded *Hierarchical Interests* results in the distribution of each grade between the range 0-1. We employed *GradedPrecision* for every rank interval of 10 for *top-50 Hierarchical Interests* for each activation function. Fig. 5 shows that, on an average the *Bell* is able to retrieve 53% relevant *Hierarchical Interests* from the *top-10* interests, whereas the *Priority Intersect* is able to retrieve 76% of relevant results. This is accompanied with lesser retrieval of irrelevant results by *Priority Intersect* compared to *Bell Log* and *Bell.* We need to note that, although the number of *maybe's* are low, they hold a potential of being interesting to the users. Thus to summarize, the *Priority Intersect* retrieves more (23% more than the baseline *Bell* at *top-10*) relevant *Hierarchical Interests* than the other two activation functions.

How well are the retrieved relevant Hierarchical Interests ranked at top-k?: This question is answered by employing the standard ranking evaluation metric *Mean Average Precision (MAP)*. *MAP* is used with binary results and hence, we considered the *Hierarchical Interests* marked *Yes* as relevant and *No/Maybe* as irrelevant for further variations of this evaluation. Formally *MAP* is as follows:

$$MAP(Q) = \frac{1}{|Q|}\sum_{j=1}^{|Q|}\frac{1}{m_j}\sum_{k=1}^{m_j} Precision(R_{jk}) \tag{10}$$

where Q is the set of users in the user study; m_j is the total number of relevant *Hierarchical Interests*; $Precision(R_{jk})$ is the *Precision@k* of user j.

Similar to *GradedPrecision*, we calculated *MAP* for every interval of 10 ranked *Hierarchical Interests.* Higher the *MAP*, better are the relevant *Hierarchical Interests* ranked. As shown in Fig. 5, *Priority Intersect* does convincingly better in ranking the *top-10* relevant *Hierarchical Interests* with *MAP* of 88% compared to 72% of *Bell Log* and 64% of *Bell.* If *Hierarchical Interests* marked *Maybe* by users are considered relevant then *MAP* at *top-10* increases to 92% for *Priority Intersect*, 82% for *Bell Log* and 71% for *Bell.*[12]

How early in the ranked Hierarchical Interests can we find a relevant result?: The Mean Reciprocal Rank (MRR) metric captures the answer to the above question. Formally, the metric is as shown in Equation 11.

$$MRR_{res} = \frac{1}{|Q|}\sum_{i=1}^{|Q|}\frac{1}{rank_i} \tag{11}$$

where Q is the set of users in the user study; $rank_i$ is the rank at which the first yes/no result is found for user i; res is either relevant or irrelevant result (yes/no).

We have employed *MRR* for both relevant (MRR_Y in Fig. 5) and irrelevant results (MRR_N in Fig. 5). If the system finds a relevant *Hierarchical Interests* sooner in the ranked list for the users then MRR_Y is higher. On the other hand, if an irrelevant interest is ranked higher then MRR_N is higher. Therefore, a system is better if MRR_Y is higher and MRR_N is lower. Fig. 5 shows that, *Priority Intersect* was able to rank a relevant *Hierarchical Interests* at the top for all users but one ($MRR_Y = 0.98$). The *Bell Log* does fairly good with an MRR_Y of 0.78 for relevant result.

How many of the categories, inferred by the system, were not explicitly mentioned by the user in his/her tweets?: By answering this question, we will be able to evaluate the *Hierarchical Interests* that had no syntactic mentions in the tweets of users and hence are inferred by exploiting the knowledge-base. In other words, we evaluate the *Implicit Interests* (see Section 1 for definition and example) detected by our system. Although *Primitive Interests* and *Hierarchical Interests (Implicit Interests)* are semantically different, we intended to signify the value added by the knowledge-bases.

[12] Please visit the project page
`http://wiki.knoesis.org/index.php/Hierarchical_Interest_Graph`

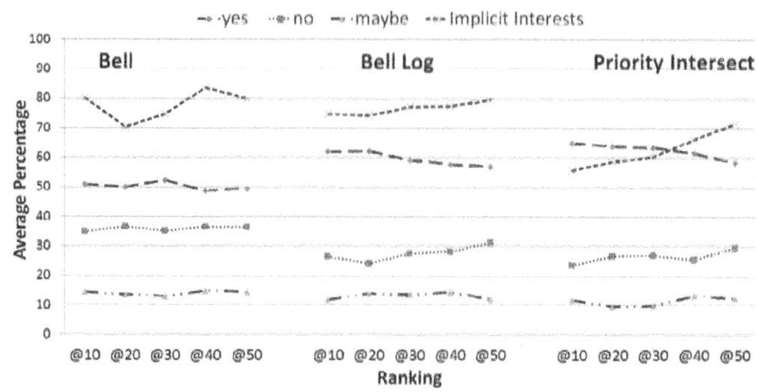

Fig. 6. Evaluation of Implicit Categories. Primary Y-Axis for Graded Precision (yes,no,maybe). Secondary Y-Axis for Average Percentage (*Implicit Interests*).

Fig. 6 shows the average percentage of *Implicit Interests* by each activation function to be 81% for *Bell*, 78% for *Bell Log* to 71% for *Priority Intersect* for the *top-50* ranked *Hierarchical Interests.* We then calculated *GradedPrecision* for *Implicit Interests* (*Yes/No/Maybe*) detected by the activation functions. Fig. 6 shows that *Priority Intersect* achieves the best results (65% of the *top-10 Implicit Interests* were relevant to the users). From this evaluation we can conclude that our approach is able to detect implicit *Hierarchical Interests* that have no explicit mention in users' tweets.

Overall, Fig. 5 and Fig. 6 illustrates all our evaluations on the quality of *Hierarchical Interests* generated by our approach. We can hence conclude that our approach with *Priority Intersect* activation function performs the best in determining *Hierarchical Interests* of a user that is represented as *HIG*.

Comparative Evaluation. The closest work to our approach that has been published in its initial stages is a system called Twopics [15]. Twopics generates a ranked list of Wikipedia categories as user interests from tweets. Twopics extracts entities from user's tweets and then for each of these entities infer the categories upto five levels from WCG. The scoring of these categories is based on the frequency of it being inferred for a user. The paper has a very initial evaluation and does not provide any gold standard dataset to compare against. Therefore, we implemented their approach. Although their approach did not result in a hierarchical representation of interests, we found that the ranked interest categories were similar to our *no-weight no-decay* activation function where the more abstract categories were ranked higher. We compared Twopics to our baseline –*Bell*, using a small scale user study with 6 users. The evaluation of *top-50* results showed that *Bell* activation function with 52% relevant results performed better than Twopics with 38% relevant results. Confirming our intuition of similarity with *no-weight no-decay* results, the analysis of the small scale evaluation ranked abstract categories higher in the interest list.

3.2 Wikipedia Hierarchy Evaluation

In order to evaluate the quality of the automatically generated hierarchy by our approach, we followed a similar methodology used by [18]. In [18] the authors have constructed a taxonomy from *WCG* and have evaluated it by comparing it with Research Cyc. We would have preferred to use their implementation, however we did not receive any response for our request.

We evaluated the *WH* with the category system of manually constructed taxonomy DMoz. The information on DMoz category hierarchy is available on DMoz download page.[13] The methodology is as follows:(1) We mapped categories from the *WH* to DMoz categorization. We performed a simple string match between the category labels of Wikipedia and DMoz. 141,506 categories matched. (2) Next, we traversed through the *WH* to find category-subcategory relationships of all distances (transitively related sub-categories) between the mapped categories. We found 46,226 category-subcategory relationships. Our Next step was to check the quality of these links by its presence in DMoz (Gold Standard). (3) In order to verify the Wikipedia category-subcategory relationships from Step 2, we traversed through DMoz category hierarchy to check the existence of directed paths between the same categories and subcategories. **87.62%** of the *WH* relationships were found in DMoz. Therefore, we concluded that our automatic hierarchy generation approach has high overlap of category-subcategory relationships for the mapped categories with manually created DMoz. This is a good indication about the quality of links in the *WH*, which in-turn evaluates the quality of links present in the *HIG*s generated by our approach.

NOTE: More analysis, evaluations and datasets is available on *project page*[14].

4 Related Work

Personalization on the web started by analyzing web documents that users visit in order to generate user's interests [8,22]. Recently, the increasing adoption of social networks such as Twitter, has shifted the personalization systems to analyze user activities on these platforms. Each of these work either uses Bag of Words [16], Topic Models [9,21] or Bag of Concepts [1,2,17] approach. In our work we started with the Bag of Concepts approach due to the availability of knowledge-bases linked to the concepts that are leveraged to infer *Hierarchical Interests*. On the other hand, Bag of Words and Topic Models (shallow inferencing) lack this advantage of utilizing explicit semantics. Furthermore, it has been argued that these techniques may not perform so well on tweets as the tweet content is short and informal [26].

In the area of web personalization and recommendation, generating hierarchical interests for a user involves analyzing web documents. In [8,29], the authors have realized top-down techniques to hierarchically cluster web documents the user is interested in. Both the techniques are built upon Bag Of Words approach and the hierarchical clusters of terms form the user profiles. On the other hand, work in [22,25] analyze web documents and leverage ontologies to create contextual user profiles. The former [22] use Bag Of Words approach to map web documents to Wikipedia concepts. Sieg et al. [25] used DMoz with an adaptation of spreading activation to map web documents to DMoz articles.

[13] `http://www.dmoz.org/rdf.html`

[14] `http://wiki.knoesis.org/index.php/Hierarchical_Interest_Graph`

User interests extracted from social messages have been represented as Bag Of Concepts in various works [2,12,17,27]. One of the main aspects of these works is the weighting schemes used to reflect user's interests towards the concepts. Abel et al. in their work [2] compare hashtag-based, entity-based and topic-based user models generated from tweets, for news recommendation. The approach scores the concepts/interests based on simple term frequency technique. The same technique is employed by TUMS system developed by Tao et al. [27] to generate semantic user profiles from tweets. However, the focus of TUMS is on the semantic representation of the user profiles. The weighting scheme used by Orlandi et al. [17] to generate semantic user profiles, provides an aggregated score for concepts from multiple social networks (Facebook and Twitter) with a temporal decay. Other techniques such as tf-idf, temporal scoring [3,17] have also been used to score interests. Although, it will be interesting to evaluate the impact of these scoring mechanisms (specifically the temporal factor) on the weights of interest categories in *HIG* (see future work in Section 5), in this work we have focused on including the most relevant categories in the *HIG*.

Wikipedia Graph has been leveraged as the base for generating *HIG* in our approach. Other approaches have utilized it for tasks such as ontology alignment [11], and clustering [28], classification of tweets [7]. Further, Spreading Activation theory used in our approach to assign interest scores has also been adapted to tasks such as document categorization [24] and search results personalization [25].

5 Conclusion and Future Work

In this paper, we have presented an approach that generates *Hierarchical Interest Graph* for Twitter users by leveraging *Wikipedia Category Graph*. We showed that the approach is practically useful in determining *Hierarchical Interests* with an extensive user study involving Twitter users with mean average precision close to approximately 90% for the *top-10 Hierarchical Interests*. We also showed the advantage of utilizing background knowledge (automatically created Wikipedia Hierarchy) for user interest identification. In future, we intend to utilize the *Hierarchical Interest Graphs* for personalizing and recommending Tweets/News articles. Further, we want to include temporal aspect to score interests where recently mentioned interests are scored higher.

References

1. Abel, F., Gao, Q., Houben, G.-J., Tao, K.: Analyzing User Modeling on Twitter for Personalized News Recommendations. In: Konstan, J.A., Conejo, R., Marzo, J.L., Oliver, N. (eds.) UMAP 2011. LNCS, vol. 6787, pp. 1–12. Springer, Heidelberg (2011)
2. Abel, F., Gao, Q., Houben, G.-J., Tao, K.: Semantic Enrichment of Twitter Posts for User Profile Construction on the Social Web. In: Antoniou, G., Grobelnik, M., Simperl, E., Parsia, B., Plexousakis, D., De Leenheer, P., Pan, J. (eds.) ESWC 2011, Part II. LNCS, vol. 6644, pp. 375–389. Springer, Heidelberg (2011)
3. Albakour, M.-D., Macdonald, C., Ounis, I.: On Sparsity and Drift for Effective Real-time Filtering in Microblogs. In: CIKM 2013 (2013)
4. Collins, A.M., Loftus, E.F.: A spreading-activation theory of semantic processing. Psychological Review 82(6), 407–428 (1975)

5. Crestani, F.: Application of Spreading Activation Techniques in InformationRetrieval. Artificial Intellence Review
6. Derczynski, L., Maynard, D., Aswani, N., Bontcheva, K.: Microblog-genre Noise and Impact on Semantic Annotation Accuracy. In: HT 2013 (2013)
7. Genc, Y., Sakamoto, Y., Nickerson, J.V.: Discovering Context: Classifying Tweets Through a Semantic Transform Based on Wikipedia. In: Schmorrow, D.D., Fidopiastis, C.M. (eds.) FAC 2011. LNCS, vol. 6780, pp. 484–492. Springer, Heidelberg (2011)
8. Godoy, D., Amandi, A.: Modeling User Interests by Conceptual Clustering. Inf. Syst. (2006)
9. Harvey, M., Crestani, F., Carman, M.J.: Building User Profiles from Topic Models for Personalised Search. In: CIKM 2013 (2013)
10. Hinton, G.E.: Parallel Models of Associative Memory (1989)
11. Jain, P., Hitzler, P., Sheth, A.P., Verma, K., Yeh, P.Z.: Ontology Alignment for Linked Open Data. In: Patel-Schneider, P.F., Pan, Y., Hitzler, P., Mika, P., Zhang, L., Pan, J.Z., Horrocks, I., Glimm, B. (eds.) ISWC 2010, Part I. LNCS, vol. 6496, pp. 402–417. Springer, Heidelberg (2010)
12. Kapanipathi, P., Orlandi, F., Sheth, A.P., Passant, A.: Personalized Filtering of the Twitter Stream. In: SPIM Workshop at ISWC 2011 (2011)
13. Manning, C.D., Raghavan, P., Schütze, H.: Introduction to Information Retrieval (2008)
14. Mendes, P.N., Jakob, M., García-Silva, A., Bizer, C.: DBpedia Spotlight: Shedding Light on the Web of Documents. In: I-Semantics 2011 (2011)
15. Michelson, M., Macskassy, S.A.: Discovering Users' Topics of Interest on Twitter: A First Look. In: AND 2010 (2010)
16. Mislove, A., Viswanath, B., Gummadi, K.P., Druschel, P.: You Are Who You Know: Inferring User Profiles in Online Social Networks. In: WSDM 2010 (2010)
17. Orlandi, F., Breslin, J., Passant, A.: Aggregated, Interoperable and Multi-domain User Profiles for the Social Web. In: I-SEMANTICS 2012 (2012)
18. Ponzetto, S.P., Strube, M.: Deriving a Large Scale Taxonomy from Wikipedia. In: AAAI 2007 (2007)
19. Qiu, F., Cho, J.: Automatic Identification of User Interest for Personalized Search. In: WWW 2006 (2006)
20. Quilian, M.R.: Semantic Memory. In: M. Minski (ed.). Semantic Information Processing. MIT Press, Cambridge (1968)
21. Ramage, D., Dumais, S.T., Liebling, D.J.: Characterizing Microblogs with Topic Models. In: ICWSM 2010 (2010)
22. Ramanathan, K., Kapoor, K.: Creating User Profiles Using Wikipedia. In: Laender, A.H.F., Castano, S., Dayal, U., Casati, F., de Oliveira, J.P.M. (eds.) ER 2009. LNCS, vol. 5829, pp. 415–427. Springer, Heidelberg (2009)
23. Ritter, A., Clark, S., Mausam, Etzioni, O.: Named entity recognition in tweets: An experimental study. In: EMNLP 2011 (2011)
24. Schonhofen, P.: Identifying Document Topics Using the Wikipedia Category Network. In: WI 2006 (2006)
25. Sieg, A., Mobasher, B., Burke, R.: Web Search Personalization with Ontological User Profiles. In: CIKM 2007 (2007)
26. Sriram, B., Fuhry, D., Demir, E., Ferhatosmanoglu, H., Demirbas, M.: Short Text Classification in Twitter to Improve Information Filtering. In: SIGIR 2010 (2010)
27. Tao, K., Abel, F., Gao, Q., Houben, G.-J.: TUMS: Twitter-Based User Modeling Service. In: García-Castro, R., Fensel, D., Antoniou, G. (eds.) ESWC 2011. LNCS, vol. 7117, pp. 269–283. Springer, Heidelberg (2012)
28. Xu, T., Oard, D.W.: Wikipedia-based Topic Clustering for Microblogs. In: Proceedings of the American Society for Information Science and Technology (2011)
29. Xu, Y., Wang, K., Zhang, B., Chen, Z.: Privacy-enhancing Personalized Web Search. In: WWW 2007 (2007)

Identifying Diachronic Topic-Based Research Communities by Clustering Shared Research Trajectories

Francesco Osborne, Giuseppe Scavo, and Enrico Motta

Knowledge Media Institute, The Open University, MK7 6AA, Milton Keynes, UK
{f.osborne,g.scavo,e.motta}@open.ac.uk

Abstract. Communities of academic authors are usually identified by means of standard community detection algorithms, which exploit 'static' relations, such as co-authorship or citation networks. In contrast with these approaches, here we focus on *diachronic topic-based communities* –i.e., communities of people who appear to work on semantically related topics at the same time. These communities are interesting because their analysis allows us to make sense of the dynamics of the research world –e.g., migration of researchers from one topic to another, new communities being spawn by older ones, communities splitting, merging, ceasing to exist, etc. To this purpose, we are interested in developing clustering methods that are able to handle correctly the dynamic aspects of topic-based community formation, prioritizing the relationship between researchers who appear to follow the same *research trajectories*. We thus present a novel approach called *Temporal Semantic Topic-Based Clustering (TST)*, which exploits a novel metric for clustering researchers according to their research trajectories, defined as distributions of *semantic topics* over time. The approach has been evaluated through an empirical study involving 25 experts from the Semantic Web and Human-Computer Interaction areas. The evaluation shows that TST exhibits a performance comparable to the one achieved by human experts.

Keywords: #eswc2014Osborne, Community Detection, Scholarly Data, Scholarly Ontologies, Semantic Technologies, Clustering, Similarity Metrics, Fuzzy C-Means.

1 Introduction

Communities of academic authors are usually identified by using standard community detection algorithms, which typically exploit co-authorship or citation graphs [1]. However, an interesting type of community, which has received much less attention in the literature [2], is formed by the set of researchers who, at a given time, are working on the same topic. Obviously, this type of *topic-based community* has a degree of overlap with co-authorship and citation communities; nonetheless it provides a distinct way of identifying groups of related researchers. Co-authorship communities can certainly be seen as examples of topic-based communities, however one does not need to co-author with another researcher in order to be part of the same

V. Presutti et al. (Eds.): ESWC 2014, LNCS 8465, pp. 114–129, 2014.

topic-based community. Hence, co-authorship networks only provide an incomplete view of a topic-based community. In addition co-authorship relations can span different topics, hence providing a noisy mechanism to identify a topic-based community. An analogous argument applies to the use of citation networks to identify topic-based communities: on the one hand citations may cut across different topics and on the other hand there is no guarantee that people working on the same topic actually cite each other. Hence, citation networks also define poor approximations of topic-based communities.

Topic-based communities are interesting because their analysis allows us to make sense of the dynamics of the research world –e.g., migration of researchers from one topic to another, new communities being spawn by older ones, communities (and therefore associated topics) splitting, merging, ceasing to exist, etc. More precisely, the formal identification and characterization over time of topic-based communities allows us to give an extensional computational treatment of a topic (or set of topics), say T, in terms of all the researchers and publications related to T at a given time. Thus, we can then measure precisely the size of the topic, its scientific impact (in terms of a variety of academic impact measures), its evolution, relations between topics in terms of overlap of researchers, migrations across topics, etc. In the rest of the paper we will use the term *temporal topic-based community* to refer to this type of communities.

In this paper we propose a novel approach to identifying temporal topic-based communities, called *Temporal Semantic Topic-Based Clustering (TST).* TST exploits a novel metric, called *ATTS* (*Adjusted Temporal Topic Similarity*), which measures the similarity between *research trajectories.* These are in turn defined as distributions of *semantically-characterized topics* over time –i.e., topics structured in terms of semantic relationships, such as *skos:broaderGeneric* or *relatedEquivalent* [3]. Thus, TST is able to detect *diachronic* groups of authors with similar behavior over a period of time.

An important aspect of TST is that, in contrast with methods which rely on co-authorship or citation networks, it does not require a complete graph of relations between community members. Hence, it can also be used in non-academic contexts, where such relations are typically not available. In addition, we characterize temporal topic-based communities as fuzzy clusters and as a result each author is then associated with a set of membership values, which express the degree of work done for different communities. Hence, this model naturally handles both the common situation in which an author contributes to more than one community and also the situation in which a community is defined in terms of multiple dynamic topics over time –e.g., the community of all researchers who worked in Knowledge Acquisition during the 90s and then worked primarily on the Semantic Web during the 00s.

Our approach increases the granularity of the representation of the research environment and makes it possible to discover interesting dynamics. For example, we can highlight the behaviour of groups of researchers reacting to a mutation in the scientific environment, such as the introduction of a new technology (e.g., Mobile Devices), a new vision (e.g., Semantic Web), or a grant on a particular theme (e.g., Smart Cities). We can also get interesting insights into the 'DNA' of specific communities. For example, a topic-centred analysis of Semantic Web (SW) researchers over time reveals that the authors with a World-Wide-Web (WWW) background, who joined the SW research area in the first years of this century, were by and large the ones who progressed the Linked Data topic at the end of the decade.

A similar analysis in the Human-Computer Interaction (HCI) area shows that authors in the HCI community who had a background in User Modeling and Ubiquitous Computing were the ones at the forefront of research on Mobile Devices, once the smartphone became a reality.

TST is integrated within Rexplore [4], a system that combines statistical analysis, semantic technologies and visual analytics to provide support for exploring and making sense of scholarly data. To evaluate our approach we performed an empirical study involving 25 experts from the SW and HCI areas, who were asked to aggregate a set of selected topics to generate the main topic-based communities in their field. The results indicate a high degree of agreement among the experts, confirming that topic-based communities are indeed objective entities that can be recognized by experts. In addition, TST performed at expert level – i.e., its results are statistically consistent with those of the experts.

2 State of the Art

Current approaches to community detection are usually classified according to the strategy they use [1], as either *optimization-based* or *heuristic* methods. The former use either *local search* [4] or *spectral methods* [6], whereas the latter exploit domain-specific assumptions to direct the clustering [7]. Unfortunately these methods tend to rely on topological structures, such as the ones defined by citation or co-authorship networks, and as a result they are not applicable to our scenario, where, as explained in the previous section, we do not have topological structures that completely and correctly define our space. As discussed by Ding et al. [2], it is therefore important to develop novel approaches to community detection, which are able to focus on the relationship between communities and topics and can correctly model their dynamics over time. A first step in this direction is provided by the work of Upham et al. [8], who define an algorithm for identifying topic-based communities which, in addition to the citation graph, also exploits language-level similarities between papers to identify communities. Hence, they are able to group together authors who work on the same topic but are not necessarily related through explicit co-authorship or citation relationships. However, while this approach provides an improvement over purely topological analyses, it seems to us that the focus on publications (rather than authors) and the reliance on language similarities provide too weak a method to detect temporal topic-based communities. In particular, it is not possible in this approach to express explicitly which authors belong to a particular community (or set of communities) at a particular time.

Racherla and Hu [9] identify topic communities by exploiting a topic similarity matrix and assigning a predefined research topic to each document and author. However, this approach is much too limited, as they assume a rigid 1-1 relationship between researchers and topics. In contrast with this work, TST is more flexible and can correctly handle both the situation where a researcher belongs to multiple communities and also that where a community is characterised by a distribution of topics over time.

Semantic technologies have been shown to improve the quality of clusters of different kinds of entities, such as images [10] and tags [11]. Some approaches rely on the detection of latent topics for capturing semantic relationships between keywords, using methods such as *Probabilistic Latent Semantic Indexing* (pLSI) [12] or *Latent Dirichlet Allocation* [13]. For example, the *Author-Conference-Topic* model (ACT) [14] treats authors and venues as probability distributions over topics extracted by means of an unsupervised learning technique. Mei et al. [15] propose a framework to model topics by regularizing a statistical topic model through a harmonic regularizer, which is based on a graph structure. Differently from these methods, we exploit an automatically generated knowledge base [3] to characterize research topics semantically and we use this as the basis for associating a diachronic semantic topic distribution with each author. The knowledge base is extracted from publication metadata by means of *Klink* [3], an algorithm that combines machine-learning methods and background knowledge to identify research topics and to generate semantic relations between them. Adopting a similar perspective, Erétéo et al. [16] proposed SemTagP, an algorithm which uses existing ontologies to detect communities from the directed typed graph formed by RDF descriptions of social networks and folksonomies. However, their approach is based on label propagation and, in contrast with TST, does not take in account the temporal dimension, which is important for gaining an understanding of community evolution over time and is also being investigated in the emergent field of temporal networks [17].

TST relies on the *Fuzzy C-Means* [18] algorithm, which is a popular unsupervised clustering algorithm that has been applied successfully to a number of real life problems. Clustering techniques (e.g., modularity-based clustering [19] or the k-means algorithm [20]) have also been used by other authors to detect research communities. However, these approaches exploit the similarity between topic vectors associated to publications and, as a result, exhibit limitations when compared to our method. In particular, their topic vectors lack a semantic characterization and, in addition, by focusing on publications rather than authors, they fail to take into account the diachronic dimension. As we will show in Section 4, in contrast with the aforementioned approaches, the use of semantic topics and the adoption a diachronic approach yields a dramatic increase in the quality of the detected communities.

3 Detecting Temporal Topic-Based Communities

We will now discuss the TST approach to identifying clusters of researchers who share common research trajectories – i.e., researchers who appear to work on the same topics at the same time. We refer to these clusters as *temporal topic-based communities (TTCs)*.

The TST approach for automatically computing TTCs in a given research area, say R, follows three steps:

1. **Semantic topic enrichment**, during which the topic distributions associated with each author are semantically enhanced by taking into account the semantic relationships between research topics.
2. **Topic vector weighing**, during which each component of a topic vector, say T, is given a bonus proportional to the degree of similarity between T and R.
3. **Temporal topic-based clustering**, during which the authors are clustered by means of a Fuzzy C-Means algorithm, using the aforementioned *ATTS* metric.

These steps are discussed in the following sub-sections.

3.1 Semantic Topic Enrichment

The authors to be clustered are characterized as a collection of topic vectors, one for each year over the examined timeframe, where each value represents the number of publications in a topic during a certain year.

A naive approach here would be to use as topics the keywords associated to the publications. However this method may yield poor results, since, as discussed in [3], the keywords associated to academic publications lack structure and are often noisy. Analogously, the keywords extracted by natural language techniques may also be noisy and may include terms that do not define research areas.

To address this issue we use the Klink algorithm [3], which is able i) to identify keywords that refer to a research area and distinguish them from those which do not and ii) to detect three types of semantic relationships. Specifically, Klink can detect: *skos:broaderGeneric* (topic T_1 is a sub-topic of topic T_2), *relatedEquivalent* (two topics are alternative names for the same research area) and *contributesTo* (research in topic T_1 is an important contribution to research in topic T_2, however T_1 is not a sub-topic of T_2). Hence, the output of an application of Klink to a corpus of publications tagged with keywords is a knowledge base comprising semantic topics structured according to three relations and linked to the relevant publications (and therefore with the relevant authors and organizations).

Taking advantage of this knowledge base, we label with topic T_1 any publication tagged with topic T_2, if T_2 is a sub-topic of T_1 or it is *relatedEquivalent* to T_2. This simple step can yield a dramatic increase in the quality and quantity of data about a certain topic. For example, as a result of applying Klink to a corpus of about 15 million publications in Computer Science, we were able to identify 18 sub-topics of Semantic Web (e.g., "Linked Data", "Semantic Wiki" and "OWL") and 11 *contributesTo* relationships (e.g., "Description Logic"), thus increasing the number of publications in the Semantic Web from 11998 to 20751. In the same way we were able to detect 22 sub-topics of HCI (e.g., "Affective Computing" and "User Interface") and 7 *contributesTo* relationships (e.g., "Task Analysis"), thus increasing the number of publications tagged as "HCI" from 9850 to 93583.

We then build the topic distribution for each author in year t as a vector in which each topic is associated with the number of publications in the same year. Finally, for each couple of topics, $<T_1,T_2>$, sharing a *contributesTo*(T_1,T_2) relationship, we assign to T_2 a fraction of the publications in T_1 according to the formula:

$$CT(T) = \sum_{i=1}^{n} P\big(T\big|ct(i,T)\big)^{\varphi}$$

where $ct(i,T)$ indicates the set of topics associated with the *i-th* publication that is in a *contributesTo* relationship with T. $P(T|ct(i,T))$ is the probability for a paper with such a set of topics to be also explicitly associated with topic T (or with a topic having a *broaderGeneric* or *relatedEquivalent* relationship with T) at the time of publication of the *i-th* paper. The summation is carried out over the number n of publications that are not already associated with T but have at least one topic in a *contributesTo* relationship with T. The exponent φ serves to modulate the *contributesTo* relationship and was empirically set to 0.5. The outputs are semantic topic vectors that include only semantically characterized research areas, whose associated values are weighed according to the semantic relationships between research areas.

3.2 Topic Vector Weighing

In most cases it is useful to detect the communities within a certain *main topic* (e.g., Semantic Web), to allow a user to make sense of elements of the research dynamics within the topic. For this reason we take as input only the authors with a significant amount of publications in the main topic. For example in the evaluation we will take in consideration only the authors who have published at least 10 papers in the Semantic Web area in the 2005-2010 interval. Moreover, to highlight the communities strongly related to the main topic, we weigh each topic according to its relationship with the main topic. Given a semantic topic *T*, the weight *W(T)* is calculated as follows:

$$W(T) = 1 + k\frac{C(T)}{S(T)}$$

where *C(T)* is the number of co-occurrences of topic *T* with the main topic in the selected time interval; *S(T)* is the number of total occurrences of the topic *T* in the selected time interval, and *k* is an arbitrary constant (empirically set to 2 in the evaluation) that can be tuned to amplify the effect of the weight on the system. Here it is important to emphasise that, as a result of the semantic topic enrichment carried out in the previous step, the co-occurrences used in this formula are actually applied on semantic topics rather than defining standard keyword co-occurrences.

This step can be skipped if the main topic is not defined.

3.3 Temporal Topic-Based Clustering

In the final step of TST, a Fuzzy C-means (FCM) algorithm is applied to the weighted topic vectors to compute a set of fuzzy clusters of authors associated with their distribution of topics over the years. Here, we have adopted a fuzzy clustering technique since most researchers tend to work in more than one community, and a clustering algorithm that forced them to be members of only one would be unfeasible. Moreover, associating authors with a degree of memberships to each community allows for a more granular characterization of their research interests.

FCM is one of the main unsupervised clustering algorithms and has been applied successfully to a number of scenarios. It classifies entities by minimizing the following objective function:

$$J_m = \sum_{i=1}^{N}\sum_{j=1}^{C} u_{ij}^m \left\|x_i - c_j\right\|^2 , \quad 1 \leq m < \infty$$

where N is the number of entities (in this case authors), C the number of the chosen centroids, u_{ij} is the degree of membership of x_i in the cluster j, m is a number ≥ 1, x_i is the ith entity, c_j is the centroid of the cluster, and ||*|| is a norm expressing the similarity between any entity and the centroid.

We will not elaborate here on the details of the algorithm since it is well known – see [18] for an in-depth description.

In our case, we need a norm that takes into account the topic vectors over the years. To this end we have introduced a novel similarity measure called *adjusted temporal topic similarity* (*ATTS*).

We first define the *topic similarity* (*TS*) between two authors *A* and *B* in a time interval t_1-t_2 as:

$$TS(A,B,t_1,t_2) = \cos(\textstyle\sum_{i=t_1}^{t_2} \hat{a}_i , \sum_{i=t_1}^{t_2} \hat{b}_i)$$

where $\hat{a}_i$ and $\hat{b}_i$ are the topic vectors of the two authors in the i-th year and *cos(s,t)* is the cosine similarity.

This metric however does not take into account possible common shifts of interests of the authors. In fact, if author *A* worked on topic T_1 and then shifted to topic T_2, he/she will be considered similar to author *B* who was originally in T_2 and then moved to T_1. To avoid this problem, we need a metric that pays attention to the period of time in which an author addresses a specific topic, rewarding common trajectories. Hence, in order to strengthen the importance of the time factor we compute TS recursively on increasingly shorter time intervals and then average the results. More formally, we define the *temporal topic similarity* TTS between author *A* and author *B* in the interval t_1-t_2 as:

$$TTS(A,B,t_1,t_2) = \frac{\sum_{i=0}^{m}\left[\left(\sum_{j=0}^{2^i-1}\mathrm{TS}\left(A,B,t_1+\left\lceil\frac{j\cdot(t_2-t_1)}{2^i}\right\rceil,t_1+\left\lfloor\frac{(j+1)\cdot(t_2-t_1)}{2^i}\right\rfloor\right)\right)/2^i\right]}{(m+1)},$$

$$m = \lfloor log_2(t_2 - t_1)\rfloor$$

The temporal topic similarity covers well the case in which both authors are present in the same time interval. However an author may start publishing after the beginning of the interval or suspend his/her career before the end of it. These cases may be accounted for by introducing a penalty for authors who do not share the entire timeframe. We quantified the penalty *P* as the average TS of *n* authors randomly extracted from the input (*n=500* in the prototype).

Finally, we define the *adjusted temporal topic similarity*, ATTS, as:

$$ATTS(A,B,t_1,t_2) = TTS(A,B,t_1,t_2)K_s + PK_{ns} \quad ,$$

$$K_s = \frac{I_s^{\gamma}}{I_s^{\gamma}+I_{ns}^{\gamma}}, \quad K_{ns} = \frac{I_{ns}^{\gamma}}{I_s^{\gamma}+I_{ns}^{\gamma}}$$

where I_s is the number of years in which both authors were active, I_{ns} is the remaining number of years, and $\gamma>1$ a parameter for weighing their relationship ($\gamma = 2$ in the present evaluation). If γ is high, an author active in a good portion of the interval is barely penalized, thus allowing for latecomers to be assigned to the cluster if their topic trajectory is similar enough to the community centroid. Since ATTS is a similarity measure that varies in the interval [0,1], while a FCM needs a distance in the interval [0, ∞], we use as norm the inverse of the ATTS minus 1.

The output of FCM depends on the initial guess on the number of clusters and the candidate centroids. In this scenario there is no absolutely correct initial number of centroids, since even different user experts will suggest a different number of communities. However, we suggest two techniques to select the initial number of centroids. The first, and most conservative one, is to compute the set of clusters for different numbers of centroids and for different random initializations and then select the one with the highest compactness (see Section 5). In this paper we used the PCAES [21] *(Partition Coefficient and Exponential Separation)* as measure for compactness. This is a cautious approach that will produce very compact communities, but may also miss some of the minor ones. The second approach is the *subtractive clustering method* [22]. This technique estimates the initial centroids by assigning a "potential" to each individual in the dataset, so that an individual with many neighbours will have a high potential. While this approach may build less compact communities, it nevertheless appears to produce results that are very similar to the ones generated by the domain experts (see Section 4).

FCM returns a list of cluster centroids and a partition matrix where each element is associated with its degree of membership to each cluster.

The centroids of the clusters detected by the FCM algorithm are characterized by the topic vectors of the communities for each year in the interval, which can be used to study the community evolution. In fact, by studying the change in the distribution of topics in subsequent years it is possible to detect trends (e.g., a topic is growing considerably and thus may continue to grow in the future) and shifts (e.g., a marginal topic is becoming dominant, such as "Augmented Reality" becoming a more important component of the Virtual Reality community after the introduction of mobile devices). This possibility opens up very interesting scenarios and it is one of the main assets of TST.

By summing the vectors over the years and selecting the topics with the highest values it is possible to label communities according to their most significant topics. For example, a key community, which emerges when analysing the Semantic Web area, has the highest values associated to the topics "Artificial Intelligence", "Knowledge Base" and "Ontology", and therefore we can refer to it as the "AI, KB, Ontology" community.

4 Evaluation

We conducted an empirical study with 25 human experts, 13 from the Semantic Web and 12 from the Human Computer Interaction field. These were chosen among experienced researchers in the two fields. Specifically, we wanted to verify i) if the experts could agree on the main topic-based communities in a field - i.e., if the concept of topic-basic community is clear and well defined enough for human users, and ii) if the proposed method could perform similarly to the experts and thus be considered reliable in detecting this kind of communities.

For setting up the study we first built a dataset covering the SW and HCI areas, by exploiting the Microsoft Academic Search (MAS) API[1], a service that makes it possible to access metadata about authors, publications and keywords. We retrieved authors and papers labelled with HCI or SW or with their first 50 co-occurring topics and we then ran Klink on this dataset to obtain a populated ontology of these two research areas for the semantic topic enrichment phase (see Section 3.1). We then selected as "basic topics" the 35 semantic topics[2] that were most often used as tags for SW or HCI papers in the years 2005-2010 –as a result, some topics that have grown in importance since 2010 may be missing from this sample. We then removed from this

[1] `http://academic.research.microsoft.com/`

[2] See `http://rexplore.kmi.open.ac.uk/data/tce.rtf` for a list of the topics used in the experiment.

set highly generic topics (e.g., Artificial Intelligence) to simplify the task for the experts. In fact, these topics tended to be associated with pretty much every single one of the 35 topics used in the experiment and therefore held no discriminatory power. Here, it is important to emphasise that keeping such highly generic topics would have not affected the algorithm, which would have simply assigned them to more than one community with different degrees, while of course it would have complicated significantly the task for the experts.

We used WebSort[3], a card sorting online service, to assist the experts in building the clusters. We allowed for each topic to be associated with only one community at a time, since it would have been cumbersome to ask experts to create overlapping communities or communities characterized by potentially different topics for each year, as our algorithm is able to do. We thus modified the output of the algorithm to follow the same limitations by merging the topic vectors of the different years and assigning each topic only with the community with which it had the highest score. Hence, we gave the experts a collection of "basic topics" related to their field and asked them to aggregate the topics together to shape what they considered to be the main communities in their field. For example an expert in HCI could decide to group together topics such as "Ubiquitous Computing", "Mobile Device" and "Context Aware" and label them as "Mobile Interaction" community.

The SW experts suggested an average of 7.9 ± 2.3 communities, whereas HCI experts suggested an average of 6.7 ± 1.9. We then examined the degree of agreement among experts and with our algorithm. To compute the agreement between two sets of clusters we used the pairwise F-Measure, the harmonic means of the pairwise precision and recall.

We tested four algorithms on the same dataset: 1) FCM using cosine similarity on regular keywords (labelled *F*), 2) FCM using cosine similarity on semantic topics (*FC*), 3) FCM using ATTS on semantic topics (*FT*) and 4) FCM using ATTS on *weighted semantic topics* (*TST*). We selected as input the set of authors with at least 10 publications about SW/HCI in the 2005-2010 interval. The total amounted to 431 authors for SW, and 458 authors for HCI. The initial centroids were estimated by means of the subtractive clustering method [22].

Figure 1 and Figure 2 show the average degree of agreement of each expert with all the others. For SW, the ANOVA version of the variance test over all experts evidenced statistically significant differences (visible also in the graph), yielding p=0.02. Only seven experts exhibited agreement among themselves (p=0.18) and they also agreed with the final version of the algorithm, TST (p=0.12). Actually there is a fair degree of agreement between the SW experts and our algorithm: the average F-Measure is 0.48±0.04 for the former and 0.44±0.07 for the latter. For HCI, the ANOVA test on experts yielded p=0.45. Including as a 'special expert' the final version of our algorithm (TST) yielded p=0.14. Since in both cases p >> 0.05, we can conclude that there are no statistically significant differences among the experts and between experts and the final version of the algorithm.

The results of the three most basic versions of our algorithm are significantly different, both from the TST version and also from the experts (in all comparisons

[3] http://uxpunk.com/websort

p <0.0001 with Friedman test for correlated samples). In particular, the version without semantics (F) performed disastrously. The FC and FT version yielded increasingly better results both in SW and HCI, showing how the use of a semantic characterization of topics and the ATTS metric crucially ensures that our method is able to perform consistently with the experts.

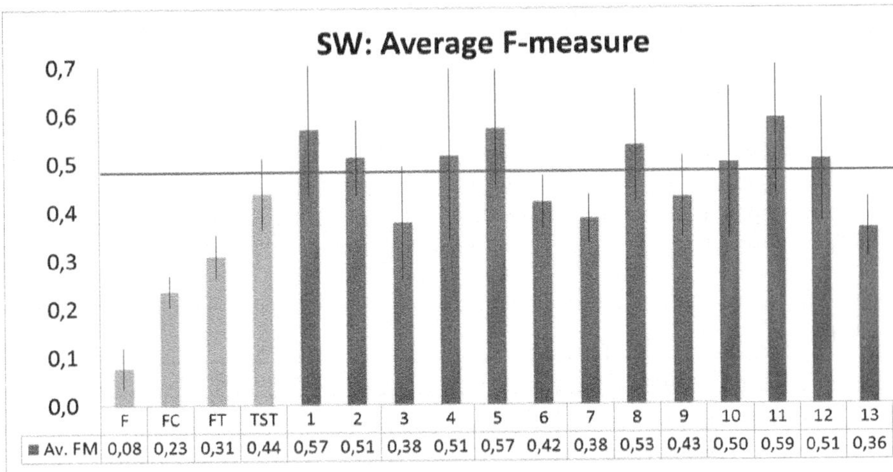

Fig. 1. Average F-measure between each expert/algorithm and all the other experts for the SW topic. The red line represents the average F-measure of the experts.

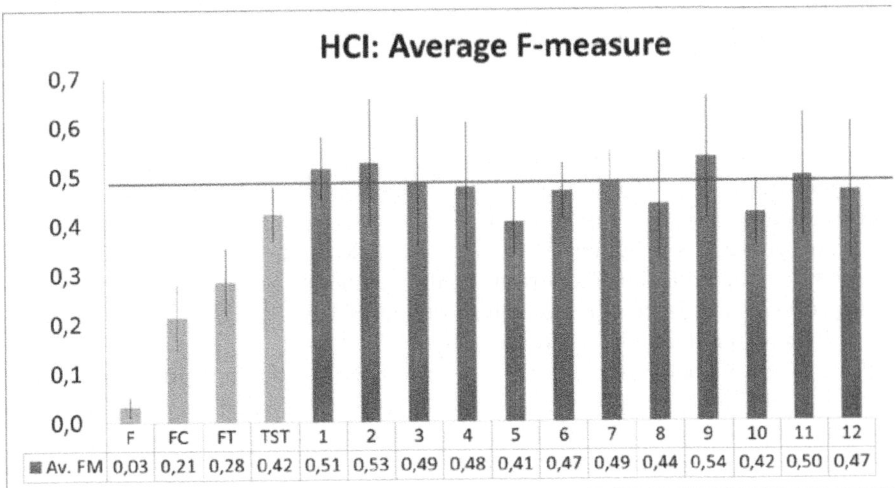

Fig. 2. Average F-measure between each expert/algorithm and all other experts for HCI

A careful look at the crafted communities evidences that most experts actually agreed on the general picture (the macro-communities) of their field, but sometimes disagreed on how to split some macro-groups, creating sub-groups according to different perspectives. For example in SW the topics “Ontology Engineering” and

"Ontology Mapping" are aggregated by some experts within the "Formal Ontology" community, while, according to other experts, they should instead be in two different communities.

Table 1 shows the macro-communities on which most experts agree. We composed it by analysing the labels of the experts and the usual topic components. Thus, for example, an area such as "Ubiquitous Computing/Mobile Device" may either include or not include "Context Aware" according to different experts, but it is usually associated with the same topics and yields similar labels to "Mobile interaction" or "Mobile HCI". SW enjoys 4 size macro-communities on which more than 70% of experts agree, while HCI has 6 of them. Some macro-communities, such as Description Logic in SW and Virtual Reality in HCI, are so well defined that they get almost full agreement. We can say that the skeleton or general frame of the communities appears to be well defined, whereas the details, such as the position of individual fine-grained topics, may vary according to individual experts.

Table 1. The macro-communities (with more than 40% agreement) in SW and HCI according to the experts

SW Communities	%	HCI Communities	%
Knowledge Base/Des. Logic	100	Virtual Reality	92
Linked Data/Sem. Annotation	100	Information retrieval/WWW	92
Semantic Web Service	77%	Ubiquitous Computing/Mobile Device	83
Ontology Mapping/O. Matching	77%	Interaction Design/Usability Testing	83
Intelligent Agents	69%	Pattern Rec./Gesture Rec./Speech Rec.	75
Ontology Engineering	61%	System Design/Software Engineering	75
WWW/Information Retrieval	61%	AI /Machine Learning/Neural Network	55
Social Semantic Web	46%	Human Robot Inter. /Affective Comp.	42

To study the similarities and differences between the results obtained by our approach and those generated by the experts, we ran TST over an increasing number of clusters (from 4 to 10) to highlight the macro-areas and how they split as the number of clusters grows. Figure 3 and Figure 4 show the result. In most cases the algorithm behaved as a human expert, for example splitting the macro-community "Ontology" in its main sub components as the number of required clusters increased. Our approach found 5 macro communities in both SW and HCI, which can be further split in 10 sub-communities for SW and 9 for HCI.

While here we label each community with the name of the most frequent topics for the sake of simplicity, actually the TTCs are described by a rich distribution of topics over time, which can reveal interesting insights on the dynamics of the research communities. For example, the "Linked Data" community includes a variety of equally represented topics up to 2007, such as "Query Language", "Semantic Annotation" and "Information Retrieval", while from 2008 we see the strong onset of the actual "Linked Data" topic. This reflects an interesting dynamics, where the different research areas that were addressing alternative challenges associated with research on Semantic Web eventually converged on "Linked Data" once a number of underlying technologies became sufficiently mature. In the same way, by analysing the topic distribution of the "Virtual Reality" community, we can see the onset of topics such as "Mobile Device" and "Augmented Reality" after 2007, which help to analyse the impact of the introduction of smartphones (the first iPhone was realized in 2007) and anticipate the vast amount of work that will be done on these topics in the following years.

All macro-communities in Table 1 are detected by our algorithm, except for "Social Semantic Web" for SW and the "AI-Reasoning" for HCI. "Social Semantic Web" is usually composed by topics such as "Social Networks" and "Semantic Wiki". The experts found it natural to aggregate these research areas into one category that today is becoming more and more important. The algorithm did not, because according to the dataset this area did not have enough authors and publications to be considered as a main community during the time frame in question. In sum, this was an unfortunate consequence of not being able to run the experiment on the most recent data (the MAS API did not provide us with much data after 2010).

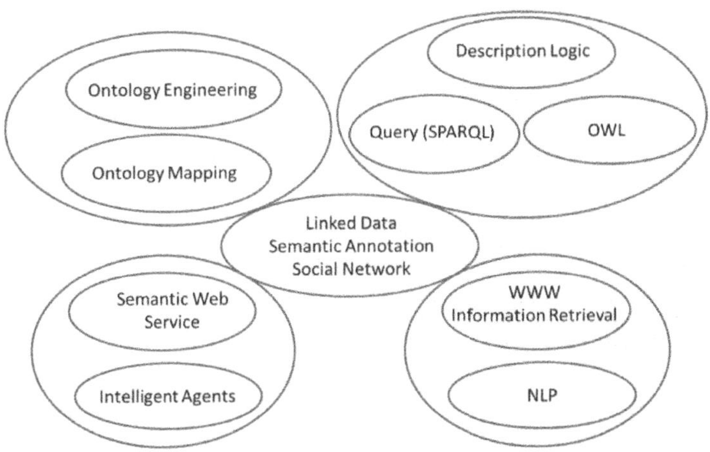

Fig. 3. The SW main communities and how they are split in sub-communities by our algorithm. To increase the readability of the image, only the most important topics are shown.

The "AI-Reasoning" macro-community is a particularly interesting case, since it is an abstract category where different human experts placed AI techniques, such as Machine Learning, Neural Networks, User Model and Data Mining. To a human in fact it makes sense to have this kind of abstract categorization of techniques that can be applied in different fields. The algorithm instead is designed to assign each one of these topics to the communities who mostly use them. For example, Machine Learning was associated in most years with the Pattern Recognition and the Information Retrieval/World-Wide-Web communities; Data Mining and Mobile Device with IR /WWW and User Model mostly with Recommender Systems.

In conclusion, human experts are able to create abstract categories, when appropriate, while TST cannot do this (unless an abstract category emerges from the clustering process). TST detects categories on the basis of the trends and practical use in a research area. We believe that these two perspectives are actually complementary: we need the abstract classification provided by experts in order to identify groups of generically applicable techniques/tools relevant to different communities, but we also need the data-driven perspective, to understand by which communities and in which context these are used.

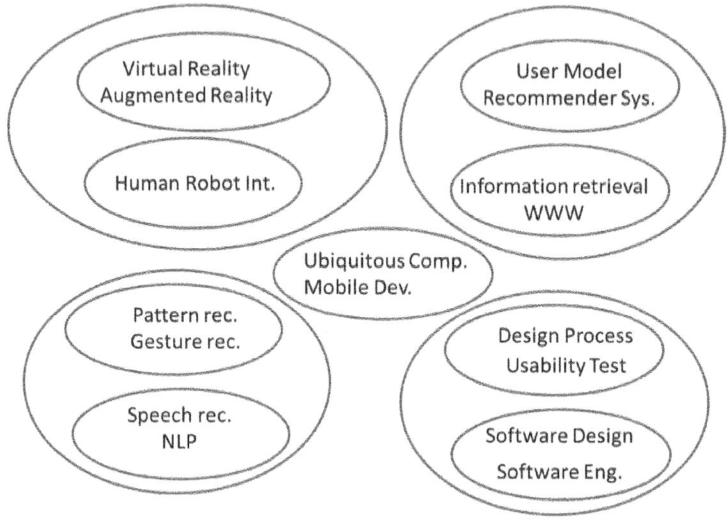

Fig. 4. The main communities in HCI and how they are split in sub-communities by our algorithm. To increase the readability of the image, only the most important topics are shown.

5 Evaluation of Cluster Compactness

In this section we briefly present an evaluation of the *compactness* within each community cluster. We do so by using a standard validity index for fuzzy clustering, *PCAES* [21]. PCAES varies between $-n$ and n, where n is the number of clusters. A large PCAES value means that each cluster is compact and well separated from the others. We ran the different versions of the algorithm to find n communities under SW/HCI, with $4<n<10$. Figure 5 shows the average *PCAES* for SW and HCI over 20 runs: the best performance for all three techniques is reached for HCI in correspondence of n=4, whereas for SW the best overall performance corresponds to the use of TST with n=5. FC and FT obtain the best result with n=4. These values are slightly inferior (but still within two standard deviations) to the values of 7.9 ± 2.3 for SW and 6.7 ± 1.9 for HCI indicated by the experts, possibly because they tend to favor a more articulate classification, even at the cost of some less well-defined communities.

We have thus chosen n=4 and n=5 as the number of clusters on which to run a statistical evaluation of the performance of the three techniques, and in particular of TST relative to the other two, based on the Wilcoxon non-parametric test for correlated pairs. In the SW case, for n=5 we obtain p=0.005 for both TST vs. FT and for TST vs. FC. For n=4, the difference gets less marked, with p reaching the threshold of 0.05 in both comparisons. FT and FC have essentially similar behaviours for both values of n (p=0.35). In the HCI case, using *n*=4 (best value for all three techniques), the comparison of TST relative to FT and to FC evidences in both cases statistically significant differences, respectively with p= 0.01 and 0.005. Using *n*=5, TST still dominates over FC (p=0.02) but no longer over FT (p=0.23).

This confirms that TST is able to produce significantly more compact clusters, in particular when using the optimal value for *n*, mainly due to the use of topic vector weighing (see Section 3.3). We obtained similar results by selecting the maximum *PCAES* over 20 runs. In the SW case, given 4 clusters we obtained PCAES=2.09 for TST, 1.42 for FT, and 1.17 for FC (with 5 clusters the values were 2.89, 1.19 and 1.16). In HCI, given 4 clusters, we obtained *PCAES*=0.79 for TST, -0.32 for FT, and -0.28 for FC.

Interestingly, the cluster sets in SW seems to be more compact than the HCI ones. The results seem to contradict the human experts, who actually showed a higher degree of agreement when composing HCI communities. However, what is considered the best clustering according to these metrics is not always perceived as such by human experts. The reasons why HCI clusters have a lower PCEAS may in fact simply lie in the fact that HCI authors tend to address more heterogeneous themes and work across different communities. On the contrary a number of people working in the Semantic Web tend to publish most of their work within a particular community. We thus may need novel evaluation metrics to be able to take in account the peculiarities associated with different topic-based research communities.

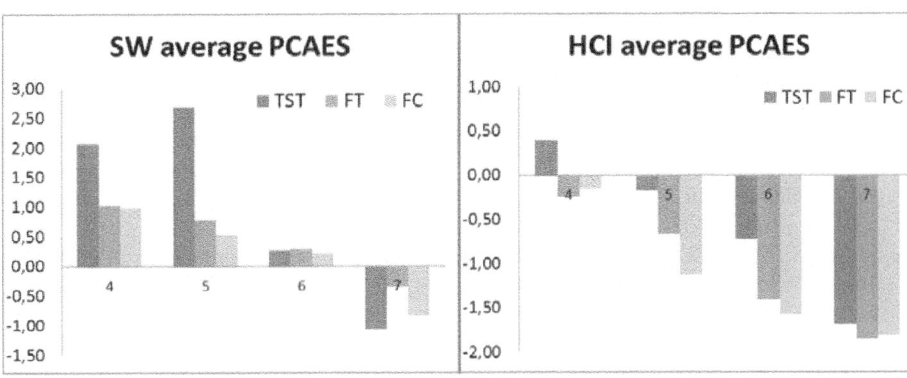

Fig. 5. Average PCAES for Semantic Web and HCI

6 Conclusions

In this paper we have presented TST, a novel approach to automatically detect diachronic topic-based communities –i.e., communities of researchers who work on semantically related topics at the same time.

The user study presented in this paper shows that our approach yields results that are statistically consistent with those obtained from domain experts. The study also shows that the adoption of i) a semantic characterization of the research topics (see Section 3.1), ii) the topic vector weighing (see Section 3.2) and iii) the ATTS metric (see Section 3.3) dramatically increases the quality of the detected communities. Moreover, according to the PCAES index, the use of topic vector weighing also increases significantly the degree of compactness of the detected communities.

Our approach opens up many interesting directions of work. Currently we are working on a novel method to automatically detect different kinds of patterns in the research flow, such as the merging/splitting of different communities or the occurrence of topic shifts within a community. In addition, we also plan to build on this approach to develop effective methods to measure the impact of specific events on the research environment, such as the introduction of a new technology or the award of a new grant. Such functionality is of particular importance to research managers and funding bodies, who need better tools to measure the impact of policy decisions. Finally, we plan to work on a predictive technique, aimed at forecasting the behaviour that a community is likely to exhibit in the short and medium term.

References

1. Zhao, Z., Feng, S., Wang, Q., Huang, J.Z., Williams, G.J., Fan, J.: Topic oriented community detection through social objects and link analysis in social networks. Knowledge-Based Systems 26, 164–173 (2012)
2. Ding, Y.: Community detection: topological vs. topical. Journal of Infometrics 5(4) (2011)
3. Osborne, F., Motta, E.: Mining Semantic Relations between Research Areas. In: Cudré-Mauroux, P., et al. (eds.) ISWC 2012, Part I. LNCS, vol. 7649, pp. 410–426. Springer, Heidelberg (2012)
4. Osborne, F., Motta, E., Mulholland, P.: Exploring Scholarly Data with Rexplore. In: Alani, H., Kagal, L., Fokoue, A., Groth, P., Biemann, C., Parreira, J.X., Aroyo, L., Noy, N., Welty, C., Janowicz, K. (eds.) ISWC 2013, Part I. LNCS, vol. 8218, pp. 460–477. Springer, Heidelberg (2013)
5. Smyth Guimera, R., Amaral, L.A.N.: Functional cartography of complex metabolic networks. Nature 433(7028), 895–900 (2005)
6. Smyth, S., White, S.: A spectral clustering approach to finding communities in graphs. In: 5th SIAM International Conference on Data Mining, pp. 76–84 (2005)
7. Flake, G.W., Lawrence, S., Giles, C.L., Coetzee, F.M.: Self-organization and identification of web communities. Computer 35(3), 66–70 (2002)
8. Upham, S.P., Rosenkopf, L., Ungar, L.H.: Innovating knowledge communities. Scientometrics 83(2), 525–554 (2010)
9. Racherla, P., Hu, C.: A social network perspective of tourism research collaborations. Annals of Tourism Research 37(4), 1012–1034 (2010)
10. Wang, S., Jing, F., He, J., Du, Q., Zhang, L.: Igroup: presenting web image search results in semantic clusters. In: Proceedings of the SIGCHI Conference on Human Factors in Computing Systems, pp. 587–596. ACM (2007)
11. Schrammel, J., Leitner, M., Tscheligi, M.: Semantically structured tag clouds: an empirical evaluation of clustered presentation approaches. In: Proceedings of the SIGCHI Conference on Human Factors in Computing Systems, pp. 2037–2040. ACM (2009)
12. Hofmann, T.: Probabilistic latent semantic indexing. In: 22nd ACM SIGIR Conference on Research and Development in Information Retrieval, Berkeley, CA, pp. 50–57 (1999)
13. Blei, D.M., Ng, A.Y., Jordan, M.I.: Latent Dirichlet allocation. Journal of Machine Learning Research 3, 993–1033 (2003)

14. Tang, J., Zhang, J., Yao, L., Li, J., Zhang, L., Su, Z.: ArnetMiner: extraction and mining of academic social networks. In: 14th Int. Conference on Knowledge Discovery and Data Mining, pp. 990–998 (2008)
15. Mei, Q., Cai, D., Zhang, D., Zhai, C.: Topic modeling with network regularization. In: 17th International Conference on World Wide Web, pp. 101–110. ACM (2008)
16. Erétéo, G., Gandon, F., Buffa, M.: Semtagp: semantic community detection in folksonomies. In: IEEE/WIC/ACM International Conference on Web Intelligence and Intelligent Agent Technology (WI-IAT), vol. 1, pp. 324–331. IEEE (2011)
17. Holme, P., Saramäki, J.: Temporal networks. Physics Reports 519(3), 97–125 (2012)
18. Bezdek, J.C., Ehrlich, R., Full, W.: FCM: The fuzzy c-means clustering algorithm. Computers and Geosciences 10(2), 191–203 (1984)
19. Van Eck, N.J., Waltman, L.: Software survey: VOSviewer, a computer program for bibliometric mapping. Scientometrics 84(2), 523–538 (2010)
20. Yan, E., Ding, Y., Jacob, E.: Overlaying communities and topics. Scientometrics 90(2), 499–513 (2012)
21. Wu, K.L., Yang, M.S.: A cluster validity index for fuzzy clustering. Pattern Recognition Letters 26(9), 1275–1291 (2005)
22. Chiu, S.L.: Fuzzy model identification based on cluster estimation. Journal of Intelligent and Fuzzy Systems 2(3), 267–278 (1994)

Pay-as-you-go Approximate Join Top-k Processing for the Web of Data

Andreas Wagner[1], Veli Bicer[2], and Thanh Tran[1]

[1] Karlsruhe Institute of Technology, Germany
[2] IBM Research Centre Dublin, Ireland
{a.wagner,thanh.tran}@kit.edu, velibice@ie.ibm.com

Abstract. For effectively searching the Web of data, ranking of results is a crucial. *Top-k processing* strategies have been proposed to allow an efficient processing of such ranked queries. Top-k strategies aim at computing k top-ranked results *without complete result materialization.* However, for many applications result computation time is much more important than result accuracy and completeness. Thus, there is a strong need for *approximated ranked results.* Unfortunately, previous work on approximate top-k processing is not well-suited for the Web of data. In this paper, we propose the *first approximate top-k join framework for Web data and queries.* Our approach is very lightweight – *necessary statistics are learned at runtime in a pay-as-you-go manner.* We conducted extensive experiments on state-of-art SPARQL benchmarks. Our results are very promising: we could achieve up to 65% time savings, while maintaining a high precision/recall.

Keywords: #eswc2014Wagner.

1 Introduction

With the proliferation of the Web of data, RDF has become an accepted standard for publishing data on the Web. RDF data comprises a set of *triples* $\{\langle s, p, o\rangle\}$, which forms a data graph, cf. Fig. 1-a.

User-/Query-Dependent Ranking. For web-scale data, queries often produce a large number of results (*bindings*). Given large result sets, *result ranking* becomes a key factor for an effective search. However, ranking functions often need to *incorporate query or user characteristics* [1,4,19]:

Example 1. *Find movies with highest ratings, featuring an actress "Audrey Hepburn", and playing close to Rome, cf. Fig. 1.*

Exp. 1 would require a ranking function to incorporate the movie rating, quality of keyword matches for "Audrey Hepburn", and distance of the movie's location to Rome. While one may assume that a higher `rating` value is preferred by any user and query, *scores for keyword and location constraint dependent on query and user characteristics.* For instance, in order to rank a binding for "Audrey Hepburn", a function may measure the edit distance between that keyword and the binding's attribute value, Fig. 1-c. Notice, given another keyword

V. Presutti et al. (Eds.): ESWC 2014, LNCS 8465, pp. 130–145, 2014.

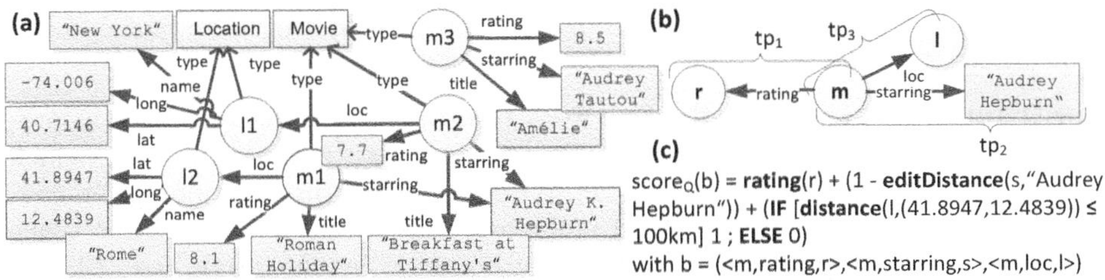

Fig. 1. (a) RDF data graph about the movies "Roman Holiday", "Breakfast at Tiffany's", and "Amélie". (b) Query graph asking for a movie `starring` "Audrey Hepburn". (c) Scoring function that aggregates scores for triple pattern bindings (bold): movie ratings, edit distance w.r.t. "Audrey Hepburn", and distance of the movie's location to Rome (lat: 41.8947, long: 12.4839) $\leq$ 100 km.

(e.g., only "Audrey"), the very same attribute value would yield a different score. Further, depending on the user's geographic knowledge of Italy, she may have different notions of "closeness" to Rome, e.g., distance $\leq$ 100 km, cf. Fig. 1-c.

Join Top-k Processing. *Top-k processing* aims at computing k top-ranked bindings without full result materialization [7,8]. That is, after computing some bindings, the algorithm can terminate early, because it knows that no binding with higher ranking score exists. For efficiently processing ranked queries over Web data, two recent works employed top-k processing techniques [9,22].

However, many applications do not require a high result accuracy or completeness. In fact, result computation time is often the key factor. Thus, there is a strong need for *approximated ranked results.* That is, a system should be able to trade off result accuracy and completeness for computation time.

Approximate Join Top-k Processing. Unfortunately, existing approaches for top-k processing over RDF data compute *only exact and complete results* [9,22]. Moreover, previous works for approximate top-k processing over relational databases [2,3,12,18,20] are not suitable for Web queries/data. This is because these works *assume complete ranking score statistics at offline time:*

(P.1) *Web Queries.* Query-/user-dependent ranking functions are employed for many important Web queries, e.g., keyword, spatial or temporal queries [1,4,19]. However, such *ranking scores are only known at runtime.* Consider tp_2 and tp_3 in Fig. 1-b: binding scores are decided by query (i.e., edit distance to query keyword "Audrey Hepburn") or user characteristics (i.e., the user-defined distance to Rome). So, no offline score statistics can be computed for tp_2 or tp_3.

(P.2) *Web Data.* Web data is commonly *highly distributed and frequently updated.* For instance, movie `ratings` for pattern tp_1 (Fig. 1-b) may be spread across multiple data sources – some of them even "hidden" behind SPARQL endpoints. Moreover, these sources may feature constantly updated `rating` scores. Thus, while constructing an offline statistic for `rating` scores is feasible, it comes with great costs in terms of maintenance. This problem is exacerbated by the fact that RDF allows for very *heterogeneous data.* For example, the `rating` predicate in tp_1

could be used to specify the rating of movies as well as products, restaurants etc. Thus, score statistics may grow quickly and become complex.

Contributions. (1) This is the first work towards approximate top-k join processing for the Web of data. That is, we propose a lightweight approach, which addresses problem P.1 and P.2: (P.1) We learn score distributions in a pay-as-you-go manner at runtime. (P.2) Our score statistics have a constant space complexity and a computation complexity bounded by the result size. (2) We conducted experiments on two SPARQL benchmarks: we could achieve time savings of up to 65%, while still allowing for a high precision/recall.

Outline. We outline preliminaries in Sect. 2 and present the approximate top-k join in Sect. 3. In Sect. 4, we discuss evaluation results. Last, we give an overview over related works in Sect. 5 and conclude with Sect. 6.

2 Preliminaries

Data and Query Model. We use RDF as data model:

Definition 1 (RDF Graph). *Given a set of edge labels* ℓ*, a RDF graph is a directed labeled graph* $\mathcal{G} = (\mathcal{V}, \mathcal{E}, \ell)$*, where* $\mathcal{V} = \mathcal{V}_E \uplus \mathcal{V}_A$ *with entity nodes as* $\mathcal{V}_E$ *and attribute nodes as* $\mathcal{V}_A$*. Edges* $\mathcal{E} = \{\langle s, p, o\rangle\}$ *are called triples, with* $s \in \mathcal{V}_E$ *as subject,* $p \in \ell$ *as predicate, and* $o \in \mathcal{V}_E \uplus \mathcal{V}_A$ *as object.*

An example is depicted in Fig. 1-a. Further, we employ basic graph patterns (BGPs) as query model:

Definition 2 (BGP Query). *A BGP query* $\mathcal{Q}$ *is a directed labeled graph* $\mathcal{Q} = (\mathcal{V}^{\mathcal{Q}}, \mathcal{E}^{\mathcal{Q}})$*, with* $\mathcal{V}^{\mathcal{Q}} = \mathcal{V}_V^{\mathcal{Q}} \uplus \mathcal{V}_C^{\mathcal{Q}}$ *as union of variables* $\mathcal{V}_V^{\mathcal{Q}}$ *and constants* $\mathcal{V}_C^{\mathcal{Q}}$*. Edges* $\mathcal{E}^{\mathcal{Q}}$ *are called triple patterns. Triple pattern* $tp = \langle s, p, o\rangle$ *with* $s \in \mathcal{V}_V^{\mathcal{Q}} \uplus \mathcal{V}_C^{\mathcal{Q}}$*,* $p \in \ell \uplus \mathcal{V}_V^{\mathcal{Q}}$*, and* $o \in \mathcal{V}_V^{\mathcal{Q}} \uplus \mathcal{V}_C^{\mathcal{Q}}$*. We write* $\mathcal{Q}$ *as set of its triple patterns:* $\mathcal{Q} = \{tp_i\}$*.*

Example 2. In Fig. 1-b, pattern $\langle m,$ `starring`*, "Audrey Hepburn"*$\rangle$ *has* m *as variable, constant "Audrey Hepburn" as object, and* `starring` *as predicate.*

Given a query $\mathcal{Q}$, a *binding* b is a vector $(t_1, \ldots, t_n)$ of triples such that: each triple t_i *matches* exactly one pattern $\mathrm{tp_i}$ in $\mathcal{Q}$ and triples in b form a subgraph of the data graph, $\mathcal{G}$. We say b *binds* variables to nodes in the data via the matching of patterns in $\mathcal{Q}$. Formally, for binding b there is a function $\mu_b : \mathcal{V}_V^{\mathcal{Q}} \mapsto \mathcal{V}$ that maps every variable in $\mathcal{Q}$ to an entity/attribute node in the data.

Partial bindings (featuring some patterns with no matching triple) occur during query processing. For a partial binding b, we refer to a pattern $\mathrm{tp_i}$ with no matching triple as *unevaluated* and write $*$ in b's i-th position: $(t_1, \ldots, t_{i-1}, *, t_{i+1}, \ldots, t_n)$. We denote the set of unevaluated patterns for partial binding b as $\mathcal{Q}^u(b) \subseteq \mathcal{Q}$. A binding b *comprises* a binding b', if all triples in b' are also contained in b. If b comprises b', we say binding b' *contributes* to b.

Example 3. Given Fig. 1-b, a partial binding $b_{31} = (*, *, t_{31} = \langle m_1,$ `loc`*,* $l_2\rangle)$ *in Fig. 2-a matches pattern* tp_3*, while* $\mathcal{Q}^u(b_{31}) = \{tp_1, tp_2\}$ *are unevaluated.* b_{31} *binds variable* m *and* l *to entity* m_1 *and* l_1*. Further, the complete binding* $b = (t_{12}, t_{21}, t_{31})$ *comprises partial binding* $b_{31} = (*, *, t_{31})$*.* b_{31} *contributes to* b*.*

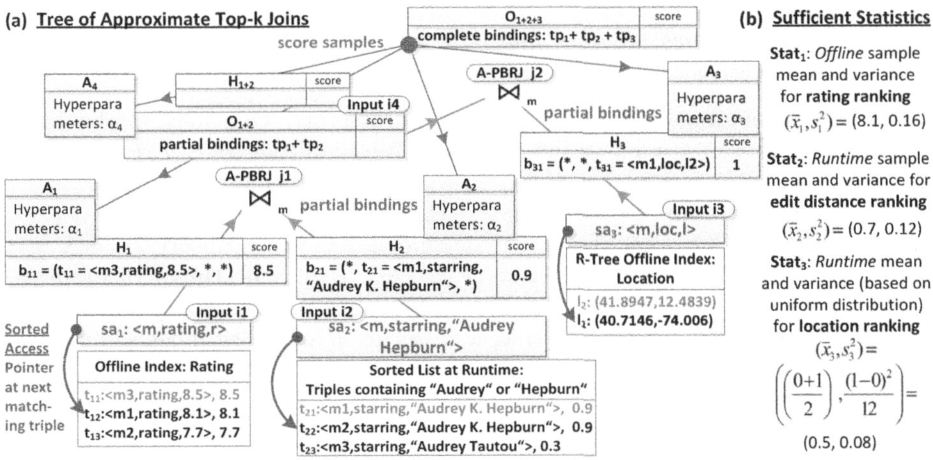

Fig. 2. (a) A-PBRJ tree for Fig. 1-b. Two information flows occur in the tree: partial bindings (green) and score samples (blue). (b) Sufficient statistics based on scores observed at indexing time (stat_1) and runtime (stat_2 and stat_3).

Ranking Function. To quantify the relevance of a binding b w.r.t. a query/user, we employ a *ranking function*: $score_{\mathcal{Q}} : \mathcal{B}^{\mathcal{Q}} \mapsto \mathbb{R}$, with $\mathcal{B}^{\mathcal{Q}}$ as set of all partial/-complete bindings for $\mathcal{Q}$. That is, $score_{\mathcal{Q}}(b)$ is defined as aggregation over b's triples: $score_{\mathcal{Q}}(b) = \bigoplus_{t \in b} score_{\mathcal{Q}}(t)$, with $\oplus$ as monotonic aggregation function. A ranking function for our example is in Fig. 1-c. Note, $score_{\mathcal{Q}}$ could be defined as part of the query, e.g., by means of the `ORDER BY` clause in SPARQL.

Sorted Access. For every pattern tp_i in query $\mathcal{Q}$, a *sorted access* sa_i *retrieves matching triples in descending score order*. Previous works on join top-k processing over Web data introduced efficient sorted access implementations for RDF stores [9,22]. Let us present simple approaches for our example (Fig. 2-a):

Example 4. Given the keyword pattern $tp_2 = \langle m,$ `starring`, *"Audrey Hepburn"*$\rangle$, *a sorted access must materialize all triples, which have a value that contains "Audrey" or "Hepburn". After materialization, these triples are sorted with descending similarity w.r.t. that keyword (e.g., measured via edit distance). On the other hand, for pattern* $\langle m,$ `loc`, $l\rangle$, *an R-tree on the attribute pair (*`lat`, `long`*) may be used. This offline computed index yields two hits:* l_1 *and* l_2. *While* l_2 *is an exact match (thus, triple* t_{31} *has max. score 1),* l_1 *is more distant from Rome. Last, an index for attribute* `rating` *can be constructed offline: triples are stored with descending rating value. Then, sorted access* sa_1 *can iterate over this list.*

Partial bindings retrieved from sorted accesses are combined via joins. That is, an equi-join combines two (or more) inputs. This way, multiple joins form a tree. For instance, three sorted accesses are combined via two joins in Fig. 2-a.

Problem. Our goal is to compute k high-ranked query bindings that may differ from the true top-k results in terms of false positives/negatives. These approximations aim at saving computation time. For this, we use a top-k test: *given* *a partial binding, we estimate its probability for contributing to the final top-k results and discard such bindings that have only a small a probability.*

We exploit *conjugate priors* for learning necessary probability distributions.

Bayesian Inference. Let Θ be a set of parameters. One may model *prior beliefs* about these parameters in the form of probabilities: $\Theta \sim P(\Theta \mid \alpha)$ with $\Theta \in \boldsymbol{\Theta}$ [6]. Here, α is a vector of *hyperparameters* allowing to parametrize the prior distribution. Suppose we observe relevant data $\mathbf{x} = \{x_1, \ldots, x_n\}$ w.r.t. Θ, where each $x_i \sim P(x_i \mid \Theta)$. Then, the dependency between observations $\mathbf{x}$ and prior parameters Θ can be written as $P(\mathbf{x} \mid \Theta)$. Using the Bayes theorem we can estimate a *posterior* probability, which captures parameters Θ conditioned on observed events $\mathbf{x}$. In simple terms, *a posterior distribution models how likely parameters Θ are, in light of the seen data $\mathbf{x}$ and the prior beliefs* [6]:

$$P(\Theta \mid \mathbf{x}, \alpha) \propto P(\mathbf{x} \mid \Theta) \cdot P(\Theta \mid \alpha) = \frac{P(\mathbf{x} \mid \Theta) \cdot P(\Theta \mid \alpha)}{\sum_{\boldsymbol{\Theta}} P(\mathbf{x} \mid \Theta) P(\Theta)} \tag{1}$$

Example 5. For pattern tp_1 in Fig-2-a, scores are based on rating values. So, we can compute sufficient statistics (mean $\bar{x}_1 = 8.1$ and variance $s_1^2 = 0.16$) for these scores at offline time, cf. $stat_1$ in Fig-2-b. Such statistics represent prior beliefs about the "true" distribution, which is capturing only those scores for bindings of tp_1 that are part of a complete binding. Only triple t_{12} and t_{13} contribute to complete bindings. Thus, only their scores should be modeled via a distribution. We update the prior beliefs using scores samples $\mathbf{x}$ observed during query processing, thereby learning the true (posterior) distribution as we go.

As we are interested in *unobserved* events x^*, we need the *posterior predictive distribution*, i.e., the distribution of new events given observed data $\mathbf{x}$:

$$P(x^* \mid \mathbf{x}, \alpha) = \sum_{\boldsymbol{\Theta}} P(x^* \mid \Theta) P(\Theta \mid \mathbf{x}, \alpha) \tag{2}$$

An important kind of Bayesian priors are the *conjugate priors*. Intuitively, conjugate priors require the posterior and prior distribution to belong to the same distribution family. In other words, these priors provide a "computational convenience", because they give a closed-form of the posterior distribution [6]. Thus, posterior computation is easy and efficient for conjugate priors.

3 Approximate Top-k Join

We now present an *approximate* top-*k* processing for the Web of data. In contrast to existing works [2,3,12,18,20], we follow a *lightweight* approach: (1) We *learn all necessary score statistics at runtime*, cf. Algo. 2 (P.1, Sect. 1). (2) We show our score distribution learning to have a *constant space complexity* and a *runtime complexity bounded by the result size*, cf. Thm. 1 (P.2, Sect. 1).

3.1 Approximate Rank Join Framework

We follow [17] and define an approximate Pull/Bound Rank Join (A-PBRJ) framework that comprises three parts: a pulling strategy $\mathcal{PS}$, a bounding strategy $\mathcal{BS}$, and a probabilistic component $\mathcal{PC}$. $\mathcal{PS}$ determines the next join input to pull from [17]. The bounding strategy $\mathcal{BS}$ gives an upper bound, β, for the maximal possible score of unseen join results [17]. Last, we use $\mathcal{PC}$ to estimate a probability for a partial binding to contribute to the final top-k result.

Approximate Pull/Bound Rank Join. The A-PBRJ is depicted in Algo. 1. Following [17], on line 4 we check whether output buffer $\mathbf{O}$ comprises k complete bindings and if there are unseen bindings with higher scores (measured via bound β). If both conditions hold, the A-PBRJ terminates and reports $\mathbf{O}$. Otherwise, $\mathcal{PS}$ selects an input i to pull from (line 5) and produces a new partial binding b from the sorted access on input i, line 6. After materialization, we update β using bounding strategy $\mathcal{BS}$.

Example 6. In Fig. 2-a, join j_2 decides (via strategy $\mathcal{PS}$) to first pull on sa_3 and load partial binding t_{31}. Then, join j_2 pulls on input i_4 (join j_1), which in turn pulls on its input i_1 (sa_1) loading binding t_{11} and afterwards on input i_2 (sa_2) loading t_{21}. The join attempt $t_{11} \bowtie t_{21}$ in join j_1 fails, because entity $m_3 \neq m_1$.

Algorithm 1. Approx. Pull/Bound Rank Join (A-PBRJ).

```
   Param.: Pulling strategy $\mathcal{PS}$, bounding strategy $\mathcal{BS}$, probabilistic comp. $\mathcal{PC}$.
   Index : Sorted access $sa_i$ and $sa_j$ for input $i$ and $j$, respectively.
   Buffer : Output buffer $\mathbf{O}$. $\mathbf{H}_i$ and $\mathbf{H}_j$ for "seen" bindings from $sa_i$ and $sa_j$.
   Input : Query $\mathcal{Q}$, result size $k$, and top-$k$ test threshold $\tau$.
   Output: Approximated top-$k$ result.
1  begin
2      $\beta \leftarrow \infty, \quad \kappa \leftarrow -\infty$
3      $\mathcal{PC}$.initialize()
4      while $|\mathbf{O}| < k$ or $\min_{b' \in \mathbf{O}} score_{\mathcal{Q}}(b') < \beta$ do
5          $i \leftarrow \mathcal{PS}$.input() // choose next input via pulling strategy $\mathcal{PS}$
6          $b \leftarrow$ next partial binding from sorted access $sa_i$
7          $\beta \leftarrow \mathcal{BS}$.update($b$) // update $\beta$ via bounding strategy $\mathcal{BS}$
           // top-$k$ test, cf. Algo. 3
8          if $\mathcal{PC}$.probabilityTopK($b,\kappa$) $> \tau$ then
9              $\mathbf{O} \leftarrow \mathbf{H}_j \bowtie \{b\}$
10             $b \cup \mathbf{H}_i$ // add $b$ to buffer $\mathbf{H}_i$
11             if #new bindings $\mathbf{b}$ in $\mathbf{O} \geq$ training threshold then
                   // score distribution learning, cf. Algo. 2
12                 $\mathcal{PC}$.train($\mathbf{b}$)
13                 Retain only $k$ top-ranked bindings in $\mathbf{O}$
14             if $|\mathbf{O}| \geq k$ then $\kappa \leftarrow \min_{b' \in \mathbf{O}} score_{\mathcal{Q}}(b')$
       // return approximated top-$k$ results
15     return $\mathbf{O}$
```

In line 8, $\mathcal{PC}$ estimates the probability for partial binding b leading to a complete top-k binding: *the top-k test.* If b fails this test, it will be *pruned.* That is, we do not attempt to join it and do not insert it in $\mathbf{H}_i$. $\mathbf{H}_i$ is a buffer that holds "seen" bindings from input i. Otherwise, if the top-k test holds, b is further processed (lines 9 - 14). That is, we join b with seen bindings from the other input j and add results to $\mathbf{O}$. Further, b is inserted into buffer $\mathbf{H}_i$, line 10. For learning the necessary probability distributions, $\mathcal{PC}$ trains on seen bindings/-scores in $\mathbf{O}$, line 12. Notice, we continuously train $\mathcal{PC}$ throughout the query processing – every time "enough" new bindings are in $\mathbf{O}$, line 11. $\mathcal{PC}$ requires parameter κ for its pruning decision. κ holds the the smallest currently known top-k score (line 14). On line 2, κ is initialized as $-\infty$.

Choices for $\mathcal{BS}$ and $\mathcal{PS}$. Multiple works proposed bounding strategies, e.g., [5,7,10,17] as well as pulling strategies, e.g., [7,11]. Commonly, the *corner bound* [7] is employed as bounding strategy $\mathcal{BS}$:

Definition 3 (Corner Bound). *For a join operator, we maintain u_i and l_i for each input i. u_i is the highest score observed from i, while l_i is the lowest observed score on i. If input i is exhausted, l_i is set to $-\infty$. The bound for scores of unseen join results is* $\beta := \max\{u_1 \oplus l_2, u_2 \oplus l_1\}$.

In example Fig. 2-a, join j_1 currently has $\beta = \max\{8.5 + 0.9, 0.9 + 8.5\}$, with $u_1 = l_1 = 8.5$ and $u_2 = l_2 = 0.9$. On the other hand, the *corner-bound-adaptive strategy* [7] is frequently used as pulling strategy $\mathcal{PS}$:

Definition 4 (Corner-Bound-Adaptive Pulling). *The corner-bound-adaptive pulling strategy chooses the input i such that: $i = 1$ iff $u_1 \oplus l_2 > u_2 \oplus l_1$ and $i = 2$ otherwise. In case of a tie, the input with less unseen bindings is chosen.*

For instance, in join j_1 (Fig. 2-a) either input may be selected, because $8.5+0.9 = 0.9 + 8.5$ and both inputs have two unseen partial bindings.

3.2 Probabilistic Component $\mathcal{PC}$

Given a partial binding b, we wish to know how likely b will contribute to the final top-k results. For this, the top-k test exploits two probabilities: (1) The probability that b contributes to a complete binding (*binding probability*). (2) The probability that complete bindings comprising b have higher scores than the current top-k bindings (*score probability*).

Binding Probability. To address the former probability, we use a selectivity estimation function *sel*. Simply put, given a query $\mathcal{Q}$, $sel(\mathcal{Q})$ estimates the probability that there is at least one binding for $\mathcal{Q}$ [14,15]. For example, selectivity of pattern $tp_3 = \langle m, \texttt{loc}, l\rangle$ is $sel(tp_3) = \frac{2}{3}$, because out of the three movie entities only two have a `loc` predicate, cf. Fig. 1-a.

Further, we define a *complete binding indicator* for a partial binding b:

$$\mathbf{1}\{\mathcal{Q}^u(b) \mid b\} := \begin{cases} 1 & \text{if } sel(\mathcal{Q}^u(b) \mid b) > 0 \\ 0 & \text{otherwise} \end{cases} \tag{3}$$

Intuitively, for a partial binding b, $\mathbf{1}\{\mathcal{Q}^u(b) \mid b\}$ models *whether matching triples for b's remaining unevaluated patterns can exist, given variable assignments dictated by b*. That is, $\mathcal{Q}^u(b) \mid b$ is a set of patterns $\{\overline{\text{tp}}_i\}$, such that pattern $\text{tp}_i \in \mathcal{Q}^u(b)$ and each variable v in tp_i that is bound by b is replaced with its assignment in b, $\mu_b(v)$, which results in a new pattern $\overline{\text{tp}}_i$.

	(a) Predictive Dist.	(b) Priors
Input i_1	$P(X^s_{i_1})$ $\mathcal{Q}^u = \{tp_2, tp_3\}$	stat$_2 \oplus$ stat$_3$: $(0.7+0.5, 0.12+0.08)$
Input i_2	$P(X^s_{i_2})$ $\mathcal{Q}^u = \{tp_1, tp_3\}$	stat$_1 \oplus$ stat$_3$: $(8.1+0.5, 0.16+0.08)$
Input i_3	$P(X^s_{i_3})$ $\mathcal{Q}^u = \{tp_1, tp_2\}$	stat$_1 \oplus$ stat$_2$: $(8.1+0.7, 0.16+0.12)$
Input i_4	$P(X^s_{i_4})$ $\mathcal{Q}^u = \{tp_3\}$	stat$_3$: $(0.5, 0.08)$

Fig. 3. (a) Given joins in Fig. 2-a, we train four predictive score distributions (one for each input). For instance, $X^s_{i_1}$ models scores for bindings of tp$_2 \bowtie$ tp$_3$. (b) Priors are based on sufficient statistics in Fig. 2-b. The aggregation function $\oplus$ is a summation in Fig. 1-c. Thus, e.g., stat$_1 \oplus$ stat$_3$ $= (8.1 + 0.5, 0.16 + 0.08) = (8.6, 0.24)$.

Example 7. *Consider partial binding* $b_{11} = (t_{11} = \langle m_3,$ `rating`, $8.5\rangle, *, *)$ *in Fig. 2-a.* $\mathcal{Q}^u(b_{11}) \mid b_{11} = \{\langle m_3,$ `starring`, *"Audrey Hepburn"*$\rangle, \langle m_3,$ `loc`, $l\rangle\}$, *because variable* m *in pattern* tp_2 *and* tp_3 *is replaced with its assignment in* b_{11}, $\mu_{b11}(m) = m_3$. $\mathbb{1}\{\mathcal{Q}^u(b_{11}) \mid b_{11}\} = 0$, *as selectivity for both patterns is* 0.

Notice, *any selectivity estimation implementation* may be used for the complete binding indicator. We employed [14,15] for our experiments.

Score Probability. For a partial binding b, let *scores for bindings of b's unevaluated patterns,* $\mathcal{Q}^u(b)$, be captured via a random variable $X^s_{\mathcal{Q}^u(b)}$.

Example 8. *In Fig. 2-a, partial binding* b_{31} *currently has a score of* 1. *However, scores for bindings to* tp_1 *and* tp_2 *are unknown and modeled via* $X^s_{\mathcal{Q}^u(b_{31})}$.

Then, we can obtain the probability for b contributing to a complete binding that has a score $\geq x$ as:

$$P\left(X^s_{\mathcal{Q}^u(b)} \geq \delta(x, b)\right) \tag{4}$$

where $\delta(x, b) := x - score_{\mathcal{Q}}(b)$. Note, partial binding b has a current score, $score_{\mathcal{Q}}(b)$, and only the score for its unevaluated patterns is unknown. So, $\delta(x, b)$ is the "delta" between b's current score and a desired score x.

Top-k Test. Finally, we use (1) the complete binding indicator to determine whether b might contribute to any complete binding. Further, (2) the score probability to estimate how likely a complete binding comprising b has a score that is larger than the smallest known top-k score, κ (cf. Algo. 1 line 14):

$$\underbrace{\mathbb{1}(\mathcal{Q}^u(b) \mid b)}_{(1)} \cdot \underbrace{P(X^s_{\mathcal{Q}^u(b)} \geq \delta(\kappa, b))}_{(2)} > \tau \tag{5}$$

with $\tau \in [0, 1]$ as top-k test threshold.

3.3 Score Distribution Learning

Distributions for random variables $X^s_{\mathcal{Q}^u(b)}$ may be obtained by learning a score distribution $P(X^s_i)$ for each join input i. Note, partial bindings, which come from the same input, have the same set of unevaluated triple patterns. Thus, X^s_i *captures scores of the unevaluated patterns from its partial bindings.*

Example 9. *In Fig. 2-a, all partial bindings from input* i_1 *have* $\mathcal{Q}^u = \{tp_2, tp_3\}$ *as unevaluated patterns. Thus,* $P(X^s_{\mathcal{Q}^u(b_{11})}) = P(X^s_{i_1})$, *as binding* b_{11} *is produced* *by input i_1. In fact, all bindings from i_1 follow the same distribution, $P(X^s_{i_1})$, which captures scores of $tp_2 \bowtie tp_3$. Overall, we learn four distributions, cf. Fig. 3.*

We do not know the true distribution for X^s_i. In such a case, a common assumption is to use a *Gaussian distribution* for X^s_i, cf. Eq. 6a. We employ a conjugate prior to train its unknown mean and variance, respectively.

As shown in [6], the mean of X^s_i follows a Gaussian distribution (Eq. 6b) and the variance of X^s_i follows an inverse-Gamma distribution (Eq. 6c). Hyperparameters $\alpha_0 = (\mu_0, \eta_0, \sigma_0^2, \nu_0)$ parameterize both distributions, where μ_0 is prior mean with quality η_0, and σ_0^2 is prior variance with quality ν_0 [6]:

$$X^s_i \sim \text{normal}\left(\mu, \sigma^2\right) \tag{6a}$$

$$\mu \mid \sigma^2 \sim \text{normal}\left(\mu_0, \frac{\sigma^2}{\eta_0}\right) \tag{6b}$$

$$\sigma^2 \sim \text{inverse-gamma}\left(0.5 \cdot \nu_0, 0.5 \cdot \nu_0 \sigma_0^2\right) \tag{6c}$$

Algorithm 2. $\mathcal{PC}$.train()

Params: Weight $w \geq 1$ for score sample $\mathbf{x}$.
Buffer : Buffer $\mathbf{A}$ storing hyperparameters α.
Input : Complete bindings $\mathbf{B} \subseteq \mathbf{O}$ and join j.

begin
  foreach *input i in join j* **do**
    `// load prior hyperparameters for input` i
    $\alpha_n = (\mu_n, \eta_n, \sigma_n^2, \nu_n) \leftarrow \mathbf{A}_i$
    `// get scores of bindings for input` i`'s unevaluated patterns`
    foreach *complete binding $b \in \mathbf{B}$* **do**
      get binding b' *comprised in* b, which matches unevaluated patterns
      add $score_Q(b')$ to score sample $\mathbf{x}$
    `// compute sample mean and variance`
    $\bar{x} \leftarrow \text{mean}(\mathbf{x}) = \frac{1}{n}\sum x_i$
    $s^2 \leftarrow \text{var}(\mathbf{x}) = \frac{1}{(n-1)}\sum (x_i - \bar{x})^2$
    `// compute posterior hyperparameters`
    $\nu_{n+1} \leftarrow \nu_n + w, \quad \eta_{n+1} \leftarrow \eta_n + w$
    $\mu_{n+1} \leftarrow \frac{1}{\eta_{n+1}} \cdot (\eta_n \mu_n + w\bar{x})$
    $\sigma_{n+1}^2 \leftarrow \frac{1}{\nu_{n+1}} \cdot \left(\nu_n \sigma_n^2 + (w-1)s^2 + \frac{\eta_n w}{\eta_{n+1}} \cdot (\bar{x} - \mu_n)^2\right)$
    `// store new (posterior) hyperparameters for input` i
    $\mathbf{A}_i \leftarrow \alpha_{n+1} = (\mu_{n+1}, \eta_{n+1}, \sigma_{n+1}^2, \nu_{n+1})$

Prior Distribution. Prior initialization is called on line 3 in Algo. 1. For each input i we specify a prior distribution for X^s_i via prior hyperparameters α_0. For α_0 we require sufficient score statistics in the form of a sample mean, $\bar{x} = \frac{1}{n}\sum_{x_i \in \mathbf{x}} x_i$, and a sample variance $s^2 = \frac{1}{(n-1)}\sum_{x_i \in \mathbf{x}} (x_i - \bar{x})^2$, with $\mathbf{x}$ as sample. There are multiple ways to obtain the necessary score samples:

Example 10. *Fig. 2-b depicts three sufficient statistics based on information from the sorted accesses: (1) Offline information in the case of* sa_1. *That is, scores are known before runtime, thus,* $\bar{x}_1 = 8.1$ *and* $s_1^2 = 0.16$ *can be computed offline. (2) Online information for access* sa_2. *Recall, the list of matching triples for keywords "Audrey" and "Hepburn" must be fully materialized. So,* $\bar{x}_2 = 0.7$ *and* $s_2^2 = 0.12$ *may be computed from runtime score samples. (3) Last, given access* sa_3, *we have neither offline scores, nor a fully materialized list of triples (*sa_3 *loads a triple solely upon a pull request). In lack of more information, we assume each score to be equal likely, i.e., a uniform distribution. With min. score as* 0 *and max. score as* 1*:* $\bar{x}_3 = 0.5$ *and* $s_3^2 = 0.08$.

We initialize hyperparameters α_0 with μ_0 as sample mean, σ_0^2 as sample variance, and $\eta_0 = \nu_0$ as sample quality. For every input, we aggregate necessary sample means/variances for μ_0/σ_0^2. For example, given input i_1 with unevaluated pattern $\{\text{tp}_2, \text{tp}_3\}$, we sum up (aggregate) statistics stat_2 and stat_3: $\bar{x}_2 + \bar{x}_3$ for μ_0 and $s_2^2 + s_3^2$ for σ_0^2, cf. Fig. 3. Note, η_0 and ν_0 are used to quantify the prior quality. For instance, stat_1 and stat_2 are exact statistics, while stat_3 relies on a uniform distribution. So, weighting reflects the prior's trustworthiness.

Posterior Distribution. Having estimated a prior distribution, *we continuously update the distribution with scores seen during query processing.*

Intuitively, each time new complete bindings are produced, all prior distributions could be trained, cf. Algo. 1 line 11 and Algo. 2. That is, complete binding scores are used to update hyperparameters from the previous n-th training iteration, α_n, resulting in new posterior hyperparameters, α_{n+1}. For this, we use standard training on lines 10-11 (Algo. 2) [6]. In simple terms, the prior mean μ_n is updated with the new sample mean $\bar{x}$, line 10, and the prior variance σ_n^2 is updated with the sample variance s^2, line 11. Note, each input computes its "own" score sample $\mathbf{x}$ (Algo. 2, lines 5-6).

Prior hyperparameters are weighted via η_n and ν_n. Further, for each hyperparameter update, a parameter w is used as weight (indicating the quality of samples $\mathbf{x}$). Finally, new hyperparameters α_{n+1} are stored on line 12, Algo. 2.

Example 11. *Given input* i_1 *and* $\eta_0 = \nu_0 = 1$ *in Fig. 3. Then, its prior is* $\alpha_0 = (1.2, 1, 0.2, 1)$. *We observe scores* $\mathbf{x} = \{x_1, x_2\}$ *from* $\mathbf{B} = \{(t_{12}, t_{21}, t_{31}), (t_{13}, t_{22}, t_{32})\}$, *with* $w = |\mathbf{x}| = 2$, $x_1 = 1.9 = score_Q(t_{21}) + score_Q(t_{31})$, *and* $x_2 = 0.9 = score_Q(t_{22}) + score_Q(t_{32})$. *So,* $s^2 = 0.5$, $\bar{x} = 1.4$, *which leads to posterior hyperparameters:* $\eta_1 = \nu_1 = 1 + 2 = 3$ *and*

$$\sigma_1^2 = \frac{1}{3} \cdot \left(0.2 + (2-1) \cdot 0.5 + \frac{(1.4 - 1.2)^2}{3}\right) = 0.71$$

$$\mu_1 = \frac{(1.2 + 2 \cdot 1.4)}{3} = 1.33$$

After each such update only posterior hyperparameters are stored, thereby making the learning highly time and space efficient:

Theorem 1 (Score Distribution Learning Time/Space Complexity). *Given an A-PRBJ operator* j, *at any time during query processing, we require* $O(1)$ *of space for score distribution learning. Further, given* $\mathbf{B}$ *complete bindings, score learning time complexity is bounded by* $O(|\mathbf{B}|)$.

Proof. A proof can be found in our report [21].

Algorithm 3. $\mathcal{PC}$.probabilityTopK()

Buffer : Buffer **A** storing hyperparameters.
Input : Partial bindings b, input i, and join j.
Output: Probability that b will result in one (or more) final top-k bindings.

1 **begin**
  // load hyperparameters α_n for input i
2   $\alpha_n = (\mu_n, \eta_n, \sigma_n^2, \nu_n) \leftarrow \mathbf{A}_i$
  // posterior predictive distribution based on hyperparam. α_n
  // in closed-form as Student's t-distribution
3   $X_i^s \sim t_{(\nu_n)}\left(x \mid \mu_n, \frac{\sigma_n^2(\eta_n+1)}{\eta_n}\right)$
  // compute score probability
4   $p_{\mathcal{S}} \leftarrow P\left(X^s_{\mathcal{Q}^u(b)} \geq \delta(\kappa, b)\right) = P\left(X_i^s \geq \delta(\kappa, b)\right)$
  // compute binding probability
5   $p_{\mathcal{B}} \leftarrow \mathbf{1}\{\mathcal{Q}^u(b) \mid b\}$
  // probability that b contributes to top-k results
6   **return** $p_{\mathcal{S}} \cdot p_{\mathcal{B}}$

Predictive Distribution. In Algo. 3, we provide an implementation of the top-k test. At any point during query processing, one may need to perform this test, Algo. 1 line 8. Thus, our approach allows to always give a distribution for X_i^s based on the currently known hyperparameters α_n (Algo. 3, line 2). Since hyperparameters are continuously trained, the distributions improve over time.

More specifically, we use the posterior predictive distribution. This distribution estimates probabilities for *new* scores, based on observed scores and the prior distribution. For a Gaussian conjugate prior, this distribution can be easily obtained in a closed form as non-standardized Student's t-distribution with ν_n degrees of freedom [6], cf. Algo. 3, line 3. Then, we compute $P(X^s_{\mathcal{Q}^u(b)}) = P(X_i^s)$ by means of the posterior predictive distribution on line 4. Last, we compute the binding probability via a selectivity estimation function (Eq. 3) on line 5 and return b's top-k test probability, cf. line 6.

4 Evaluation

Benchmarks. We used two SPARQL benchmarks: (1) The SP^2 benchmark featuring synthetic DBLP data [16]. (2) The DBpedia SPARQL benchmark (DBPSB), which holds real-world DBpedia data and queries [13]. For both benchmarks we generated datasets with 10M triples. We translated the SPARQL benchmark queries to our query model (BGPs). Queries featuring no BGPs were discarded, i.e., we omitted 12 and 4 queries in DBPSB and SP^2. We generated DBPSB queries as proposed in [13]: Overall, used 8 seed queries with 15 random bindings, which led to a total of 120 DBPSB queries. For SP^2 we employed 13 queries. In total, we had a comprehensive load of 133 queries. Query statistics and a complete query listing is given in [21].

Systems. We randomly generated bushy query plans. For a given query, all systems rely on the same plan. We implemented three systems that solely differ in their join operator: (1) A system with *join-sort* operator, JS, which *does not employ top-k processing*, but instead produces all results and then sorts them. (2) An *exact* and complete top-k join operator, PBRJ, featuring the corner-bound in Def. 3 and the corner-bound-adaptive pulling strategy in Def. 4. PBRJ is identical to Algo. 1, however, no top-k test is applied. Note, PBRJ resembles previous approaches for top-k processing over RDF data [9,22]. (3) Last, we implemented our *approximate* operator, A-PBRJ, see Algo 1 in Sect. 3.

Score learning and top-k test implementation for the A-PBRJ operator follows Algo. 2 and Algo. 3, cf. Sect. 3.3. Further, we used sufficient statistics based on a uniform distribution over $[0, 1]$, as discussed in Exp. 10 for sorted access sa_3. Prior weights ν_0 and η_0 are both 1, Algo. 2. Weight w in Algo. 2 is the sample size, $|\mathbf{x}|$. We reused the selectivity estimation implementation from [14,15] for our binding probabilities.

Hypothesis (H.1): We expect that JS is outperformed by PBRJ, as it computes all results for a query. Further, we expect A-PBRJ to outperform JS and PBRJ. A-PBRJ's savings come at the cost of effectiveness.

We implemented all systems in Java 6. Experiments were run on a Linux server with two Intel Xeon 5140 CPUs at 2.33GHz, 48GB memory (16GB assigned to the JVM), and a RAID10 with IBM SAS 148GB 10K rpm disks. Before each query execution, all operating system caches were cleared. The presented values are averages collected over five runs.

Ranking Function. We chose triple pattern binding scores, $score_{\mathcal{Q}}(t)$, at random with distribution $d \in \{u, n, e\}$ (uniform, normal, and exponential distribution). We employed a summation as aggregation function, $\oplus$. By means of varying distributions, we aim at an abstraction from a particular ranking function and examine performance for different "classes" of functions. We employed standard parameters for all distributions and normalized scores to be in $[0, 1]$. *Hypothesis (H.2): A-PBRJ's efficiency and effectiveness is not influenced by the score distribution.*

Parameters. We vary the number of results $k \in \{1, 5, 10, 20\}$. *Hypothesis (H.3): We predict efficiency to decrease in parameter k for A-PBRJ and PBRJ.* Further, we used top-k test thresholds $\tau \in [0, 0.8]$ for inspecting the trade-off between efficiency and effectiveness.

Metrics. We measure efficiency via: (1) #Inputs processed. (2) Time needed for result computation. As effectiveness metrics we use: (1) Precision: fraction of approximated top-k results that are exact top-k results. (2) Recall: fraction of exact top-k results, which are reported as approximate results. Notice, precision and recall have identical values, as both share the same denominator k. We therefore discuss only precision results in the following. Further, precision is given as average over our query load (so-called macro-precision). (3) Score error: approximate vs. exact top-k score: $\frac{1}{k}\sum_{b=1,\ldots,k} |score^*_{\mathcal{Q}}(b) - score_{\mathcal{Q}}(b)|$, with $score^*_{\mathcal{Q}}(b)$ and $score_{\mathcal{Q}}(b)$ as approximated and exact score for binding b [20].

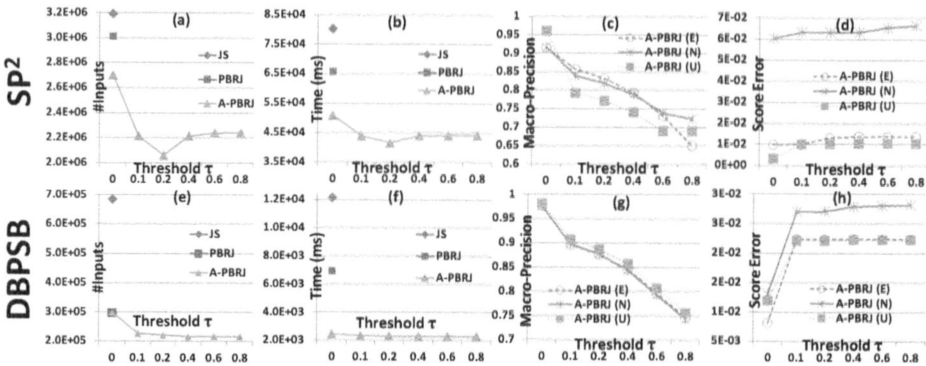

Fig. 4. Evaluation results for SP²/DBPSB: (a)/(e) Efficiency: #inputs vs. threshold τ. (b)/(f) Efficiency: time vs. threshold τ. (c)/(g) Effectiveness: macro-precision vs. threshold τ. (d)/(h) Effectiveness: score error vs. threshold τ.

Efficiency Results. Efficiency results are depicted in Fig. 4-a/e (b/f) for SP² (DBPSB). *As expected in hypothesis H.1, we observed* `A-PBRJ` *to save #inputs and computation time.* For SP² (DBPSB), `A-PBRJ` needed up to 25% (23%) less inputs vs. baseline `PBRJ` and 30% (67%) vs. `JS`. We explain these gains with pruning of partial bindings via our top-k test, thereby omitting "unnecessary" joins and join attempts. In fact, we were able to prune up to 40% (90%) of the inputs, given SP² (DBPSB). Fewer #inputs translated to time savings of 35% (65%) vs. `PBRJ` and 47% (80%) vs. `JS`, given SP² (DBPSB).

Interestingly, we saw an increase in #inputs for $\tau \in [0.2, 0.4]$ in SP² and $\tau \in [0.4, 0.8]$ in DBPSB, cf. Fig. 4-a/e. For instance, comparing $\tau = 0.2$ and $\tau = 0.4$ in SP², `A-PBRJ` read 8% more inputs. DBPSB was less affected: we noticed a marginal increase of 2% for $\tau = 0.4$ vs. $\tau = 0.6$. We explain the increase in both benchmarks with a too "aggressive" pruning – too many partial bindings were pruned wrongfully. That is, many pruned bindings would have led to a larger or even a complete binding. In turn, this led to more inputs being read, in order to produce the desired k results. In fact, $\tau \in [0.6, 0.8]$ was even more aggressive. However, the ratio between pruned bindings and read inputs was high enough to compensate for the extra inputs. Overall, we saw a "sweet spot" at $\tau \approx 0.2$ for SP² and DBPSB. Here, we noted pruning to be fairly accurate, i.e., only few partial bindings were wrongfully pruned. In fact, we observed high precision (recall) values for both benchmarks given $\tau \approx 0.2$: 88% (95%) in SP² (DBPSB) – as discussed below. With regard to computation time for SP² and DBPSB queries, we noticed similar effects as for the #inputs, cf. Fig. 4-b/f. In particular, the "sweet spot" at $\tau \approx 0.2$ is also reflected here.

As expressed by hypothesis H.3, we observed #inputs and time to increase in k for `A-PBRJ` *and* `PBRJ`. For instance, comparing $k = 1$ and $k = 20$, `A-PBRJ` needed a factor of 1.2 (5.7) more time, given SP² (DBPSB). Similarly, 1.2 (6.8) times more inputs were consumed by `A-PBRJ` for SP² (DBPSB). We explain this behavior with more inputs/join attempts being required to produce a larger result. `PBRJ` leads to a similar performance decrease. For instance given $k = 1$

vs. $k = 20$ in SP[2], PBRJ needed a factor of 1.3 (1.2) more inputs (time). Note, as baseline JS simply computed all results, this system was not affected by k.

Furthermore, we can confirm our hypothesis H.2 with regard to system efficiency: *we cloud not find a correlation between system performance and score distributions.* In other words, score distributions (ranking functions) had no impact on A-PBRJ's performance. For instance given DBPSB queries, A-PBRJ resulted in the following gains vs. PBRJ w.r.t. #inputs (time): 27% (65%) for e distribution, 23% (64%) given u distribution, and 21% (64%) for n distribution.

Last, with regard to parameter τ, we noted A-PBRJ's efficiency to increase with $\tau \in [0, 0.2]$, given SP[2] and DBPSB. However, as outlined above, too aggressive pruning let to "inverse" effects. An important observation is, however, that our approach was already able to achieve performance gains with a very small $\tau < 0.1$. Here, partial bindings were pruned primarily due to their low binding probability. In fact, A-PBRJ could even save time for $\tau = 0$: 26% (60%) with SP[2] (DBPSB). We inspected queries leading to such saving and saw that many of their partial bindings had a binding probability ≈ 0. We argue that this a strong advantage of A-PBRJ: *even for low error thresholds (leading to a minor effectiveness decrease), we could achieve efficiency gains.*

Effectiveness Results. Next, we analyze A-PBRJ in terms of its accuracy. Baselines PBRJ and JS *always compute exact and complete results.* So, we restrict our attention to the A-PBRJ system and different score distributions $d \in \{u, n, e\}$.

Fig. 4-c/g (d/h) depicts the macro-precision (score error) for varying score distributions. We observed high precision values of up to 0.98 for both benchmarks, see Fig. 4-c/g. More precisely, we saw best results for a small $\tau < 0.1$ and the exponential distribution. However, differences are only marginal. That is, given $\tau < 0.1$, all distributions led to very similar precision results $\in [0.8, 0.95]$ and $[0.90, 0.98]$ for SP[2] and DBPSB, respectively. In other words, A-PBRJ's effectiveness is not affected by a particular score distribution. We explain these good approximations with accurate score/binding probabilities.

Moreover, even for large $\tau \in [0.6, 0.8]$ A-PBRJ achieved a high macro-precision in $[0.75, 0.8]$ on DBPSB queries. This is because DBPSB queries featured selective patterns and had only a small result cardinality ≤ 10. Thus, "chances" of pruning a final top-k binding were quite small – even for a large τ. Moreover, A-PBRJ let to a very effective pruning via binding probabilities, as many partial bindings had a binding probability ≈ 0 (due to the high query selectivity). This way, A-PBRJ pruned up to 97% of the total inputs for some DBPSB queries.

In order to quantify "how bad" false positive/negative results are, we employed the score error metric, see Fig. 4-d/h. For both benchmarks, we observed that score error was $\in [0.07, 0.11]$ for a small $\tau < 0.1$. We explain this with our high precision (recall). That is, A-PBRJ led to only few false positive/negative top-k results given $\tau < 0.1$. As expected, score error increased in τ, due to more false positives/negatives top-k results. Overall, however, score error results were very promising: we saw an average score error of 0.03 (0.02), given SP[2] (DBPSB).

With regard to parameter k, we observed that k does not impact A-PBRJ's effectiveness. Given SP[2], we saw A-PBRJ to be fairly stable in different values for parameter k. For instance, macro-precision was in $[0.8, 0.85]$ as average over all k

and $\tau = 0.1$. Also for the DBPSB benchmark, we noted only minor effectiveness fluctuations: macro-precision varied around 7% with regard to different k.

We noticed `A-PBRJ`'s effectiveness to not be influenced by varying score distributions, see Fig. 4-c/g/d/h. Given SP^2, we saw a macro-precision of: 0.79 for u distribution, 0.79 for e distribution, and 0.80 for n distribution. Also for the DBPSB benchmark, we observed only minor changes in macro-precision: 0.87 for u distribution, 0.85 for e as well as n distribution.

With regard to the effectiveness of `A-PBRJ` versus parameter τ, we noticed that metrics over both benchmarks decreased with increasing τ. For instance, macro-precision decreased for $\tau = 0$ versus $\tau = 0.8$ with 27% (23%), given SP^2 (DBPSB). Such a behavior can be expected, since chances of pruning "the wrong" bindings increase with higher τ values. *Overall, this confirms H.1: A-PBRJ trades off effectiveness for efficiency, as dictated by threshold τ.*

5 Related Work

There is a large body of work on top-k query processing for relational databases [8]. Most recently, such approaches have been adopted to RDF data and SPARQL queries [9,22]. These works *aim at exact and complete top-k results.* However, for many applications result accuracy and completeness is not important. Instead, result computation time is the key factor.

To foster an efficient result computation, *approximate top-k* techniques have been proposed [2,3,12,18,20]. Most notably, [20] used score statistics to predict the highest possible complete score of a partial binding. Partial results are discarded, if they are not likely to contribute to a top-k result. Focusing on distributed top-k queries, [12] employed histograms to predict aggregated score values over a space of data sources. Anytime measures for top-k processing have been introduced by [2,3]. For this, the authors used offline score information, e.g., histograms, to predict complete binding scores at runtime. In [18], approximate top-k processing under budgetary has been addressed.

Unfortunately, all such approximate top-k approaches heavily rely on *score statistics at offline time.* That is, scores must be known at indexing time for computing statistics, e.g., histograms. However, offline statistics lead to major drawbacks in a Web setting – as outlined in problem (P.1) and (P.2), cf. Sect. 1. In contrast, we propose a lightweight system: *we learn our score distributions in a pay-as-you-go manner at runtime.* In fact, our statistics cause only *minor overhead in terms of space and time*, cf. Thm. 1.

6 Conclusion

In this paper, we introduced an approximate join top-k algorithm, `A-PBRJ`, well-suited for the Web of data (P.1+P.2, Sect. 1). For this, we extended the well-known PBRJ framework [17] with a novel probabilistic component. This component allows to prune partial bindings, which are not likely to contribute to the final top-k result. We evaluated our `A-PBRJ` system by means of two SPARQL benchmarks: we could achieve times savings of up to 65%, while maintaining a high precision/recall.

References

1. Agrawal, R., Rantzau, R., Terzi, E.: Context-sensitive ranking. In: SIGMOD (2006)
2. Arai, B., Das, G., Gunopulos, D., Koudas, N.: Anytime measures for top-k algorithms. In: VLDB (2007)
3. Arai, B., Das, G., Gunopulos, D., Koudas, N.: Anytime measures for top-k algorithms on exact and fuzzy data sets. VLDB Journal (2009)
4. Chaudhuri, S., Das, G., Hristidis, V., Weikum, G.: Probabilistic information retrieval approach for ranking of database query results. In: TODS (2006)
5. Finger, J., Polyzotis, N.: Robust and efficient algorithms for rank join evaluation. In: SIGMOD (2009)
6. Hoff, P.D.: A First Course in Bayesian Statistical Methods. Springer (2009)
7. Ilyas, I.F., Aref, W.G., Elmagarmid, A.K.: Supporting top-k join queries in relational databases. VLDB Journal (2004)
8. Ilyas, I.F., Beskales, G., Soliman, M.A.: A survey of top-k query processing techniques in relational database systems. ACM Comput. Surv. (2008)
9. Magliacane, S., Bozzon, A., Della Valle, E.: Efficient execution of top-K SPARQL queries. In: Cudré-Mauroux, P., Heflin, J., Sirin, E., Tudorache, T., Euzenat, J., Hauswirth, M., Parreira, J.X., Hendler, J., Schreiber, G., Bernstein, A., Blomqvist, E. (eds.) ISWC 2012, Part I. LNCS, vol. 7649, pp. 344–360. Springer, Heidelberg (2012)
10. Mamoulis, N., Yiu, M.L., Cheng, K.H., Cheung, D.W.: Efficient top-k aggregation of ranked inputs. In: TODS (2007)
11. Martinenghi, D., Tagliasacchi, M.: Cost-Aware Rank Join with Random and Sorted Access. In: TKDE (2012)
12. Michel, S., Triantafillou, P., Weikum, G.: KLEE: a framework for distributed top-k query algorithms. In: VLDB (2005)
13. Morsey, M., Lehmann, J., Auer, S., Ngonga Ngomo, A.-C.: DBpedia SPARQL Benchmark – Performance Assessment with Real Queries on Real Data. In: Aroyo, L., Welty, C., Alani, H., Taylor, J., Bernstein, A., Kagal, L., Noy, N., Blomqvist, E. (eds.) ISWC 2011, Part I. LNCS, vol. 7031, pp. 454–469. Springer, Heidelberg (2011)
14. Neumann, T., Moerkotte, G.: Characteristic sets: Accurate cardinality estimation for RDF queries with multiple joins. In: ICDE (2011)
15. Neumann, T., Weikum, G.: Scalable join processing on very large RDF graphs. In: SIGMOD (2009)
16. Schmidt, M., Hornung, T., Lausen, G., Pinkel, C.: SP^2Bench: A SPARQL Performance Benchmark. In: ICDE (2009)
17. Schnaitter, K., Polyzotis, N.: Evaluating rank joins with optimal cost. In: PODS (2008)
18. Shmueli-Scheuer, M., Li, C., Mass, Y., Roitman, H., Schenkel, R., Weikum, G.: Best-Effort Top-k Query Processing Under Budgetary Constraints. In: ICDE (2009)
19. Telang, A., Li, C., Chakravarthy, S.: One Size Does Not Fit All: Toward User- and Query-Dependent Ranking for Web Databases. In: TKDE (2012)
20. Theobald, M., Weikum, G., Schenkel, R.: Top-k query evaluation with probabilistic guarantees. In: VLDB (2004)
21. Wagner, A., Bicer, V., Tran, D.T.: Pay-as-you-go Approximate Join Top-k Processing for the Web of Data (2013), `http://www.aifb.kit.edu/web/Techreport3040`
22. Wagner, A., Duc, T.T., Ladwig, G., Harth, A., Studer, R.: Top-k linked data query processing. In: Simperl, E., Cimiano, P., Polleres, A., Corcho, O., Presutti, V. (eds.) ESWC 2012. LNCS, vol. 7295, pp. 56–71. Springer, Heidelberg (2012)

A Framework for Iterative Signing of Graph Data on the Web

Andreas Kasten[1], Ansgar Scherp[2], and Peter Schauß[1]

[1] University of Koblenz-Landau, Koblenz, Germany
{andreas.kasten,schauss}@uni-koblenz.de
[2] Kiel University and Leibniz Information Centre for Economics, Kiel, Germany
asc@informatik.uni-kiel.de

Abstract. Existing algorithms for signing graph data typically do not cover the whole signing process. In addition, they lack distinctive features such as signing graph data at different levels of granularity, iterative signing of graph data, and signing multiple graphs. In this paper, we introduce a novel framework for signing arbitrary graph data provided, e g., as RDF(S), Named Graphs, or OWL. We conduct an extensive theoretical and empirical analysis of the runtime and space complexity of different framework configurations. The experiments are performed on synthetic and real-world graph data of different size and different number of blank nodes. We investigate security issues, present a trust model, and discuss practical considerations for using our signing framework.

Keywords: #eswc2014Kasten.

1 Introduction

Trusted exchange of graph data on the Semantic Web requires to verify the authenticity and integrity of the graph data through digital signatures. It ensures that graph data is actually created by the party who claims to be its creator and modifications on the data are only carried out by authorized parties [29]. Existing algorithms cover only a specific part of the whole graph signing process. Tummarello et al. [32] is—to the best of our knowledge—the only solution addressing the whole signing process. However, it has severe limitations as its graph signing function can only be applied on simple graphs, so-called minimum self-contained graphs (MSGs). An MSG is the smallest subgraph of a complete RDF graph that contains a specific statement d and the statements of all blank nodes associated directly or indirectly with d. Thus, in the worst case a RDF graph consists of as many MSGs as the number of statements it contains. As each statement needs to be signed separately, the approach by Tummarello et al. results in a high signature overhead in terms of time required to sign the graph as well as statements needed to represent the MSGs' signatures.

There is no solution available today that supports signing graphs at different levels of granularity (e. g., single MSGs, ontology design patterns, and entire graphs). In addition, there is no support for signing multiple graphs or iteratively signing graphs. The latter is important as it allows to build chains of signatures for provenance tracking and building a network of trust on the Semantic Web.

V. Presutti et al. (Eds.): ESWC 2014, LNCS 8465, pp. 146–160, 2014.

We address these shortcomings by a generic approach for signing graphs such as RDF(S) graphs, Named Graphs, and OWL graphs. We introduce a framework that divides the process of signing and verifying graph data into different steps as depicted in Fig. 1. These steps follow the XML standard [2]. First, a *canonicalization function* is applied to normalize the data. Thus, given two graphs that differ only in the blank node identifiers, the canonicalization function ensures that their representation is the same. This is important for the subsequent *serialization function* that transforms the canonicalized data into a sequential representation before applying a *hash function* [27] to compute a cryptographic hash value on the serialized data. Finally, the *signature function* combines the graph's hash value with a signature key [27]. The results of these four functions constitute the graph signing step. Subsequently, the *assembly function* creates a signature graph containing all data for *verifying* the graph's integrity and authenticity including the signature value and an identifier of the signature verification key. The actual verification is conducted in the last step.

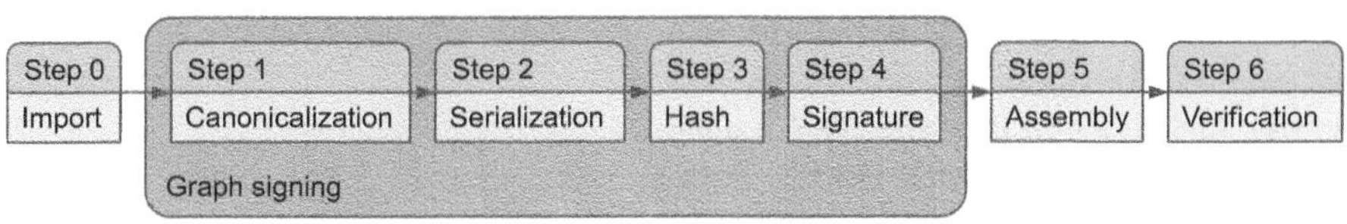

Fig. 1. The general process of signing and verifying graph data (cf. [2])

Our approach can be considered a framework, as each of these steps can be implemented in different, independent software components [31]. Due to the formal specification of the framework's interfaces, the concrete algorithms used to implement the components can be arbitrarily combined. This enables a better comparison of different algorithms and allows to configure the framework such that it is optimized towards efficiency of the signing process or minimizing the signature overhead. In summary, the contributions and novel features of our graph signing framework are:

(i) Support for signing graphs on different levels of granularity such as minimum self-contained graphs (MSGs), set of MSGs, and entire graphs.
(ii) Support for signing multiple graphs at once.
(iii) Iterative signing of graph data for provenance tracking.

The need for our signing framework and its novel features is presented along a concrete use case in the subsequent section. Related work and implementations of concrete functions used in the graph signing process are presented in Sections 3 and 4, respectively. A formal definition of our framework is given in Section 5. Four example configurations are presented in Section 6 and their performance is empirically evaluated in Section 7. A threat model and security analysis of the example configurations is presented in Section 8. Finally, we discuss the key management and trust model in Section 9, before we conclude.

2 Scenario: Trust Network for Web Content

We consider building a trust network for Internet regulation in Germany. The information about what kind of content is to be regulated is provided as graph data by different authorities as shown in Fig. 2. In the trust network, an authority receives signed graph data from another authority, adds its own graph data, digitally signs the result again and publishes it on the web.

In the scenario, the German Federal Criminal Police Office (Bundeskriminalamt, BKA) provides a blacklist of web sites to be blocked. For example, until today the access to neo-Nazi material on the Internet is prohibited by German law (Criminal Code, §86 [8]). According to §86, the BKA digitally signs the blacklist graph along with its legal background and sends it to Internet service providers (ISPs) such as the German Telecom. By verifying its authenticity and integrity, the ISPs can trust the BKA's data. This data only describes what is to be regulated and not how it is regulated. Thus, ISPs like the German Telecom add concrete details such as proxy servers used for blocking illegal web sites. The technical details comprise graph data of different granularity such as ontology design patterns modeling the regulation meta-information as well as concrete IP addresses of the German Telecom's hardware (see graphs of different granularity (i)). The ISP adds its technical regulation details to the BKA's original blacklist graph. Subsequently, the German Telecom signs its own data together with the already signed BKA data to model its provenance relation (see iterative signing (iii) in the introduction). Customers of the Germany Telecom such as the primary school depicted in Fig. 2 are able to verify the authenticity and integrity of the regulating information. The school has to ensure that its students cannot access illegal content. The iterative signing of the regulation data allows the school to check which party is responsible for which parts of the data, i. e., it can track the provenance of the regulation data. Furthermore, the school has to ensure that adult content cannot be accessed by the students, too. To this end, it receives regulation information for adult content from private authorities such as ContentWatch. The company offers regulation data as Named Graphs to protect children from Internet pornography and the like. Thus, different regulation information from multiple sources is incorporated by the school and digitally signed, before it is deployed to the school's computers (see signing multiple graphs (ii)). This ensures that the students using these computers can access the Internet only after passing the predefined protection mechanisms.

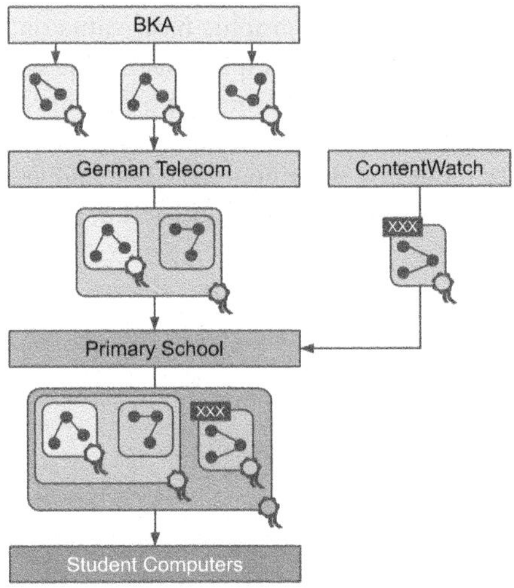

Fig. 2. Trust Network of Web Content

3 Approaches for Signing and Verifying Graphs

First, we discuss different graph signing functions as depicted in Figure 1. Subsequently, we discuss existing assembly functions. Verification functions operate similarly to graph signing functions and use the same sub-functions or their inverse. Thus, they are not discussed in more detail.

Graph Signing Functions. Tummarello et al. [32] present a graph signing function for fragments of RDF graphs. These fragments are so-called minimum self-contained graphs (MSGs) and are defined over RDF statements. An MSG of a statement d is the smallest subgraph of the entire RDF graph which contains this statement d and the statements of all blank nodes associated with it. Consequently, statements without blank nodes are an MSG on their own. The approach of Tummarello et al. is based on signing one MSG at a time. Thus, signing a full graph with multiple MSGs requires multiple signatures which creates a high overhead of signature statements for the whole graph. The signature of an MSG is stored as six statements, which are linked to the signed MSG via RDF Statement reification of one of its statements. This RDF reification is used for identifying the signed MSG. Due to the RDF Statement reification mechanism, if the original MSG contains blank nodes, the signature statements become part of the signed MSG as well. Signing this MSG again creates additional signature statements which also become part of the signed MSG. Thus, signature statements created in the ith signing iteration are referring to the signed MSG in the same way as the signature statements created in $i + 1$st iteration. Thus, it is impossible to distinguish between different signing iterations.

Signing a graph can also be accomplished by signing a document containing a serialization of the graph [26]. For example, a graph can be serialized using an XML-based format such as RDF/XML [4] or OWL/XML [17] and signed using the XML signature standard [2]. If the graph is serialized using a plain text-based format such as the statement-based serializations N-Triples [3] or N3 [6], also standard text document signing approaches may be used [27]. However, this means that the created signature can only be verified with the very single concrete encoding of the graph [26]. For example, if the serialized graph data changed the order of its statements (e. g., when being transferred to a triple store and retrieved back) it may not be possible anymore to verify the authenticity and integrity of the graph with the signature.

Assembly Function. Tummarello et al. [32] present a simple assembly function which adds statements to the signed MSG containing the signature value and a URL to the signature verification key used for the signature's verification. Information about the graph signing function and its sub-functions is not provided. Once the URL to the verification key is broken, i. e., the key is not available anymore at this URL, the signature can no longer be verified. Even if a copy of the verification key is still available at a different location, the verifier cannot check the true authenticity of the key as the issuer is only implicitly encoded in the key itself. Finally, the XML signature standard [2] defines a schema for describing details of the assembly function like the canonicalization function, hash function, and signature function used for computing the signature value.

4 Theoretical Analysis of Graph Signing Sub-functions

As outlined in the introduction, a graph signing function consists of four different sub-functions, namely the canonicalization function, serialization function, hash function for graphs, and signing function. We describe different implementations of the sub-functions and discuss their runtime complexity and space complexity. A formal definition of all sub-functions is provided in Section 5. Table 1 summarizes the complexity of different implementations of the four sub-functions. In the table, n refers to the number of statements to be signed and b corresponds to the number of blank nodes in the graph.

A *canonicalization function* assures that the in principle arbitrary identifiers of a graph's blank nodes do not affect the graph's signature. Carroll [9] presents a canonicalization function for RDF graphs that replaces all blank node identifiers with uniform place holders, sorts all statements of the graph based on their N-Triples [3] representation, and renames the blank nodes according to the order of their statements. If this results in two blank nodes having the same identifier, additional statements are added for these blank nodes. Carroll's canonicalization function uses a sorting algorithm with a runtime complexity of $\mathcal{O}(n \log n)$ and a space complexity of $\mathcal{O}(n)$ with n being the number of statements in the graph [9]. Fisteus et al. [12] perform a canonicalization of blank node identifiers based on the hash values of a graph's statements. First, all blank nodes are associated with the same identifier. Second, a statement's hash value is computed by multiplying the hash values of its subject, predicate, and object with corresponding constants and combining all results with XOR modulo a large prime. If two statements have the same hash value, new identifiers of the blank nodes are computed by combining the hash values of the statements in which they occur. This process is repeated until there are no collisions left. Colliding hash values are detected by sorting them. Using a sorting algorithm such as merge sort leads to a runtime complexity of $\mathcal{O}(n \log n)$ and a space complexity of $\mathcal{O}(n)$. Finally, Sayers and Karp [25] provide a canonicalization function for RDF graphs, which stores the identifier of each blank node in an additional statement. If the identifier is changed, the original one can be recreated using this statement. Since this does not require sorting the statements, the runtime complexity of the function is $\mathcal{O}(n)$. In order to detect already processed blank nodes, the function maintains a list of additional statements created so far. This list contains at most b entries with b being the total number of additional blank node statements. Thus, the space complexity of the function is $\mathcal{O}(b)$.

Table 1. Complexity of the functions used by the graph signing function σ_N. n is the number of statements and b is the number of blank nodes in the statements

Function	Example	Runtime	Space
Canonicalization κ_N	Carroll [9], Fisteus et al. [12]	$\mathcal{O}(n \log n)$	$\mathcal{O}(n)$
	Sayers and Karp [25]	$\mathcal{O}(n)$	$\mathcal{O}(b)$
Serialization ν_N	N-Triples [3], N3 [6], TriG [7], and others	$\mathcal{O}(n)$	$\mathcal{O}(1)$
Hash λ_N	Melnik [16], Carroll [9]	$\mathcal{O}(n \log n)$	$\mathcal{O}(n)$
	Fisteus et al. [12], Sayers and Karp [25]	$\mathcal{O}(n)$	$\mathcal{O}(1)$
Signature ϵ	RSA [24], Elliptic Curve DSA [21]	$\mathcal{O}(1)$	$\mathcal{O}(1)$

A *serialization function* transforms an RDF graph into a sequential representation such as a set of bit strings. This representation is encoded in a specific format such as statement-based N-Triples [3] and N3 [6] or XML-based RDF/XML [4] and OWL/XML [17]. TriG [7] is a statement-based format built upon N3, which allows for expressing Named Graphs. When signing RDF graphs, statement-based formats are often preferred to XML-based notations due to their simpler structure. If a serialization function processes each statement in the graph individually, it can be implemented with a runtime complexity of $\mathcal{O}(n)$ and a space complexity of $\mathcal{O}(1)$. Some canonicalization functions like [9,25] also include a serialization function and provide a canonicalized, serialized graph as output.

Applying a *hash function* on a graph is often based on computing the hash values of its statements and combining them into a single value. Computing a statement's hash value can be done by hash functions such as SHA-2 [20]. Melnik [16] uses a simple hash function for RDF graphs. A statement's hash value is computed by concatenating the hash value of its subject, predicate, and object and hashing the result. The hash values of all statements are sorted, concatenated, and hashed again to form the hash value of the entire RDF graph. Using a sorting algorithm like merge sort, the function's runtime complexity is $\mathcal{O}(n \log n)$ and its space complexity is $\mathcal{O}(n)$. Carroll [9] uses a graph-hashing function which sorts all statements, concatenates the result, and hashes the resulting bit string using a simple hash function such as SHA-2 [20]. As the function uses a sorting algorithm with a runtime complexity of $\mathcal{O}(n \log n)$ and a space complexity of $\mathcal{O}(n)$, the runtime complexity and the space complexity of the function are the same. Fisteus et al. [12] suggest a hash function for N3 [6] datasets. The statements' hash values are computed with the canonicalization function of the same authors described above. The hash value of a graph is computed by incrementally multiplying the hash values of its statements modulo a large prime. Since this operation is commutative, sorting the statements' hash values is not required. Thus, the runtime complexity of the hash function is $\mathcal{O}(n)$. Due to the incremental multiplication, the space complexity is $\mathcal{O}(1)$. Finally, Sayers and Karp [25] compute a hash value of an RDF graph similar to the approach of Fisteus et al. First, the statements are serialized as single bit string and then hashed. Second, the incremental multiplication is conducted. Thus, the runtime complexity of this approach is $\mathcal{O}(n)$ and the space complexity is $\mathcal{O}(1)$.

A *signature function* computes the actual graph signature by combining the graph's hash value with a secret key. Existing signature functions are Elliptic Curve DSA [21] and RSA [24]. Since the graph's hash value is independent from the number of statements, the signature is as well. Thus, the runtime complexity and the space complexity of all signature functions are $\mathcal{O}(1)$.

5 Formalization of Graph Signing Framework

Based on the related work and existing graph signing sub-functions, we formally define our graph signing framework. The formalization is required for the analysis of the complexity classes of the different combinations of the sub-functions in the graph signing process. However, the reader may also directly continue with the different configurations of our graph signing framework in Section 6. By design, our framework supports signing at different levels of granularity (requirement (i) in the introduction), iterative signing ((iii) in the introduction), and signing multiple graphs at once (requirement (ii)). These requirements are fulfilled by different functions of the framework as explained in more detail in this section.

Definition of Graphs. An RDF graph G is a finite set of RDF triples t. The set of all RDF triples is defined as $\mathbb{T} = (\mathbb{R} \cup \mathbb{B}) \times \mathbb{P} \times (\mathbb{R} \cup \mathbb{B} \cup \mathbb{L})$ with the pairwise disjoint sets of resources $\mathbb{R}$, blank nodes $\mathbb{B}$, predicates $\mathbb{P}$, and literals $\mathbb{L}$. Thus, it is $t = (s, p, o)$ with $s \in \mathbb{R} \cup \mathbb{B}$ being the subject of the triple, $p \in \mathbb{P}$ being the predicate, and $o \in \mathbb{R} \cup \mathbb{B} \cup \mathbb{L}$ being the object [1]. An OWL graph can be mapped to an RDF graph [22]. Thus, in the following we will only denote RDF graphs and include OWL graphs mapped to RDF graphs. The set of all possible RDF graphs is $\mathbb{G} = 2^{\mathbb{T}}$. A Named Graph extends the notion of RDF graphs and associates a unique name in form of a URI to a single RDF graph [10] or set of RDF graphs. This URI can be described by further statements, which form the so-called *annotation graph*. Consequently, the original RDF graph is also called the *content graph*. A Named Graph $NG \in \mathbb{G}_N$ is defined as $NG = (a, A, \{C_1, C_2, \ldots, C_l\})$ with $a \in \mathbb{R} \cup \{\varepsilon\}$ being the name of the graph, $A \in \mathbb{G}$ being the annotation graph, and $C_i \in \mathbb{G}_N$ being content graphs with $i = 1 \ldots l$. If a Named Graph does not explicitly specify an identifier, ε is used as its name. This corresponds to associating a blank node with the graph. In this case, the annotation graph A is empty, i. e., $A = \emptyset$. Any RDF graph $G \in \mathbb{G}$ can be defined as Named Graph C using the notation above as $C = (\varepsilon, \emptyset, G)$. The set of all Named Graphs $\mathbb{G}_N$ is defined as $\mathbb{G}_N = ((\mathbb{R} \cup \mathbb{B}) \times \mathbb{G} \times 2^{\mathbb{G}_N}) \cup \{(\varepsilon, \emptyset, G)\}$ with $G \in \mathbb{G}$.

Graph Signing Function. Our graph signing function σ_N is built upon the functions described in the introduction. Input is a secret key k_s and a set of m Named Graphs NG_i with $NG_i = (a_i, A_i, \{C_{1_i}, \ldots, C_{l_i}\})$ and $i = 1, \ldots, m$. The resulting signature s is a bit string of length $d' \in \mathbb{N}$, i. e. $s \in \{0, 1\}^{d'}$. The design of the graph signing function supports signing of multiple graphs at once (ii). Singing different levels of granularity (i) is achieved by interpreting all triples to be signed as graph $G \in \mathbb{G}$ and mapping G to Named Graph $C = (\varepsilon, \emptyset, G)$. C can then be signed with the graph signing function σ_N.

$$\sigma_N : \mathbb{K}_s \times 2^{\mathbb{G}_N} \rightarrow \{0, 1\}^{d'}, \quad \sigma_N(k_s, \{NG_1, \ldots, NG_m\}) := s \tag{1}$$

$$\sigma_N(k_s, \{NG_1, \ldots, NG_m\}) := \epsilon(k_s, \lambda(\nu_N(\kappa_N(NG_1)) \cdot \ldots \cdot \nu_N(\kappa_N(NG_m))))$$

The different sub-functions of the graph signing function are defined below: The *canonicalization function* κ transforms a graph $G \in \mathbb{G}$ into its unique canonical form $\hat{G} \in \hat{\mathbb{G}}$ with $\hat{\mathbb{G}} \subset \mathbb{G}$ being the set of all canonical graphs. If two graphs $G_1, G_2 \in \mathbb{G}$ only differ in their blank node identifiers, it is $\kappa(G_1) = \kappa(G_2)$.

$$\kappa : \mathbb{G} \rightarrow \hat{\mathbb{G}}, \quad \kappa(G) := \hat{G} \tag{2}$$

For Named Graphs, the canonicalization function κ_N is recursively defined. It computes a canonical representation of a Named Graph $NG = (a, A, \{C_1, \ldots, C_l\})$ by computing the canonical representations $\hat{A}$ and $\hat{C}_i$ of its annotation graph A and its content graphs C_i. The result is a canonical representation $\hat{NG} \in \hat{\mathbb{G}}_N$ with $\hat{\mathbb{G}}_N \subset \mathbb{G}_N$ being the set of all canonical Named Graphs.

$$\kappa_N : \mathbb{G}_N \rightarrow \hat{\mathbb{G}}_N, \quad \kappa_N(NG) := \hat{NG} \tag{3}$$

$$\kappa_N(NG) := \begin{cases} (\varepsilon, \emptyset, \hat{G}) & \text{if } NG = (\varepsilon, \emptyset, G),\ G \in \mathbb{G} \\ (a, \hat{A}, \{\hat{C}_1, \ldots, \hat{C}_l\}) & \text{if } NG = (a, A, \{C_1, \ldots, C_l\}) \end{cases}$$

The *serialization function* ν transforms a graph $G \in \mathbb{G}$ into a set of bit strings $\overline{G} \in 2^{\{0,1\}^*}$. A single bit string represents a statement in the graph G. The concrete characteristics of the bit strings in $\overline{G}$ depend on the used serialization format.

$$\nu : \mathbb{G} \to 2^{\{0,1\}^*}, \quad \nu(G) := \overline{G} \tag{4}$$

The serialization function ν can be extended to the function ν_N for Named Graphs $NG \in \mathbb{G}_N$. The result of ν_N is a set of o bit strings $\overline{NG} \in 2^{\{0,1\}^*}$ with $\overline{NG} = \{b_1, b_2, \ldots, b_o\}$. The function is recursively defined as follows:

$$\nu_N : \mathbb{G}_N \to 2^{\{0,1\}^*}, \quad \nu_N(NG) := \overline{NG} \tag{5}$$

$$\nu_N(NG) := \begin{cases} \overline{G} & \text{if } NG = (\varepsilon, \emptyset, G),\ G \in \mathbb{G} \\ \{a\} \cup \overline{A} \cup \overline{C}_1 \cup \ldots \cup \overline{C}_l & \text{if } NG = (a, A, \{C_1, \ldots, C_l\}) \end{cases}$$

The *hash function* λ computes a hash value h of arbitrary bit strings $b \in \{0,1\}^*$. The resulting hash value h has a fixed length $d \in \mathbb{N}$, i. e., $h \in \{0,1\}^d$.

$$\lambda : \{0,1\}^* \to \{0,1\}^d, \quad \lambda(b) := h \tag{6}$$

The hash function λ_N computes a hash value h_N of a serialized Named Graph $\overline{NG} = \{b_1, b_2, \ldots, b_o\}$ and is built upon the function λ. The function λ_N computes a hash value of each bit string $b_i \in \overline{NG}$ with $b = 1, \ldots, o$ and combines the results into a new bit string $h_N \in \{0,1\}^d$ using a combining function ϱ. Example combining functions ϱ are discussed in [25]. The function ϱ is defined as follows:

$$\varrho : 2^{\{0,1\}^d} \to \{0,1\}^d, \quad \varrho(\{h_1, h_2, \ldots, h_o\}) := h_N \tag{7}$$

Using λ and ϱ, the hash function λ_N for Named Graphs is defined as follows:

$$\lambda_N : 2^{\{0,1\}^*} \to \{0,1\}^d, \quad \lambda_N(\overline{NG}) := h_N = \varrho(\{\lambda(b_1), \lambda(b_2), \ldots, \lambda(b_o)\}) \tag{8}$$

A *signature function* ϵ computes the signature value of a graph based on the graph's hash value $h_N \in \{0,1\}^d$ and a cryptographic key. The keyspace, i. e., the set of all asymmetric, cryptographic keys is defined as $\mathbb{K} = \mathbb{K}_p \times \mathbb{K}_s$ with $\mathbb{K}_p$ as the set of public keys and $\mathbb{K}_s$ as the set of secret keys. For computing signatures, a secret key $k_s \in \mathbb{K}_s$ is used. Using $s \in \{0,1\}^{d'}$ as identifier for the resulting bit string, the signature function is defined as follows:

$$\epsilon : \mathbb{K}_s \times \{0,1\}^d \to \{0,1\}^{d'}, \quad \epsilon(k_s, b) := s \tag{9}$$

Assembly Function. An assembly function ς_N creates the signature graph $S \in \mathbb{G}$ and includes it in a Named Graph NG_S. The content and structure of S depend on the implementation of the function ς_N. The graph provides information about how to verify a graph's signature. This includes all sub-functions of the graph signing function σ_N, the public key k_p of the used secret key k_s, the identifiers a_i of the signed Named Graphs, and the signature value s. A possible structure of a signature graph is shown in the examples in [14]. The Named Graph NG_S contains the signature graph S as its annotation graph and the signed graphs NG_i as its content graphs. In order to support iterative signing of Named Graphs (iii), the result of the assembly function ς_N is also a Named Graph which can be signed again using the graph signing function σ_N.

$$\varsigma_N : \mathbb{K}_s \times 2^{\mathbb{G}_N} \rightarrow \mathbb{G}_N \tag{10}$$

$$\varsigma_N(k_s, \{NG_1, \ldots, NG_m\}) := (a_S, S, \{NG_1, \ldots, NG_m\})$$

Verification Function. The verification of a signature is similar to its creation. A verification function γ_N requires a canonicalization function κ_N, a serialization function ν_N, and a hash function λ_N. It also requires a signature verification function δ as inverse of the signature function ϵ. The function δ requires a bit string $s \in \{0,1\}^{d'}$ and a public key $k_p \in \mathbb{K}_p$ as input. It is defined as follows with $b \in \{0,1\}^d$ being the resulting bit string. It holds $\delta(k_p, \epsilon(k_s, b)) = b$ with the secret key k_s.

$$\delta : \mathbb{K}_p \times \{0,1\}^{d'} \rightarrow \{0,1\}^d, \quad \delta(k_p, s) := b \tag{11}$$

The verification function γ_N checks whether or not a given signature is a valid signature of a set of Named Graphs. The function requires a public key k_p, a signature value s, and set of signed Named Graphs $\{NG_1, \ldots, NG_m\}$. All values can be taken from the signature graph S. The function γ_N combines the signature value s with the public key k_p and computes the hash value h' of the Named Graphs NG_i. The signature is valid iff both computed values are equal. It is $h' = \lambda_N(\nu_N(\kappa_N(NG_1)) \cup \ldots \cup \nu_N(\kappa_N(NG_m)))$.

$$\gamma_N : \mathbb{K}_p \times 2^{\mathbb{G}_N} \times \{0,1\}^* \rightarrow \{TRUE, FALSE\} \tag{12}$$

$$\gamma_N(k_p, \{NG_1, \ldots, NG_m\}, s) := \begin{cases} TRUE & \text{if } \delta(k_p, s) = h' \\ FALSE & \text{otherwise} \end{cases}$$

6 Four Configurations of the Graph Signing Framework

The runtime complexity and space complexity when signing a graph depends on the characteristics of the graph as well as on the graph signing function σ_N and its sub-functions. The signature overhead depends on the additional statements created by these functions and on the size of the signature graph created by the assembly function ς_N. Table 2 summarizes four possible configurations A, B, C, and D of the signing framework as well as their complexity and signature overhead for signing a single graph. The example configurations correspond to the related work described in Sections 3 and 4 and are referred to by the names of their authors. Also new configurations can be created by combining different algorithms from different authors. To ease comparability, each configuration uses N-Triples for serialization and RSA as signature function ϵ. Except for B, the configurations differ only in the canonicalization function κ_N and hash function λ_N. Configuration B implements the approach by Tummarello et al. and needs an additional preparation function to split a graph into MSGs. This is required as otherwise configuration B would not be able to sign entire graphs.

A) Carroll. The canonicalization function and hash function of Carroll [9] both have a runtime complexity of $\mathcal{O}(n \log n)$ and a space complexity of $\mathcal{O}(n)$ (see detailed discussion in Section 4). A graph signing function built upon these functions shares the same complexity. The canonicalization function creates b_h additional statements with $b_h \leq b$ being the number of blank nodes sharing the same identifier (see Section 4). Thus, the canonicalized graph contains b_h more statements than the original graph. A signature graph as it is used in [14] consists of 19 statements and results in a signature overhead of $b_h + 19$ statements.

B) Tummarello et al. The approach by Tummarello et al. [32] is based on the canonicalization function and hash function of Carroll [9], i. e., on configuration A. However, Tummarello et al. only allows for signing individual MSGs. In order to sign a complete graph, it has to be split into r disjoint MSGs first. Splitting the graph can be done with a runtime complexity of $\mathcal{O}(n)$ and a space complexity of $\mathcal{O}(n)$ by using an implementation based on bucket sort [15] where each MSG corresponds to one bucket. Each MSG is then signed individually using Carroll's functions. Signing a complete graph results in a runtime complexity of $O\left(\sum_{i=1}^{r} n_i \log n_i\right)$ and a space complexity of $O\left(\sum_{i=1}^{r} n_i\right)$ with n_i being the number of statements in MSG i. Since all MSGs are disjoint, it is $\sum_{i=1}^{r} n_i = n$. Thus, the total runtime complexity is $\mathcal{O}(n \log n)$ and the space complexity is $\mathcal{O}(n)$. The signature of each MSG is stored using six additional statements. Signing a graph requires r different signatures. The overhead created by the assembly function of Tummarello et al. is six statements. Thus, the overhead for r MSGs is $6r$ statements. Combined with the b_h statements from Carroll's canonicalization function results in a total overhead of $b_h + 6r$ statements.

Table 2. Configurations A–D of a signing function σ_N with runtime complexity, space complexity, and signature overhead. n is the number of statements, b is the number of blank nodes, and b_h is the number of blank nodes which require special treatment.

Configuration	**Complexity of σ_N** runtime	space	**Signature overhead of σ_N and ς_N**
A) Carroll [9]	$\mathcal{O}(n \log n)$	$\mathcal{O}(n)$	$b_h + 19$ statements, $b_h \leq b$
B) Tummarello et al. [32]	$\mathcal{O}(n \log n)$	$\mathcal{O}(n)$	$b_h + 6r$ statements, $b_h \leq b, r \leq n$
C) Fisteus et al. [12]	$\mathcal{O}(n \log n)$	$\mathcal{O}(n)$	$0 + 19$ statements
D) Sayers and Karp [25]	$\mathcal{O}(n)$	$\mathcal{O}(n)$	$b + 19$ statements

C) Fisteus et al. The approach by Fisteus et al. [12] results in a configuration with minimum signature overhead. The canonicalization function has a runtime complexity of $\mathcal{O}(n \log n)$ and the hash function has a runtime complexity of $\mathcal{O}(n)$. Since these functions have a space complexity of $\mathcal{O}(n)$ and $\mathcal{O}(1)$, respectively, the runtime complexity of the signing function σ_N is $\mathcal{O}(n \log n)$ and the space complexity is $\mathcal{O}(n)$. As the functions of Fisteus et al. do not create any additional statements, the signature overhead is independent of the signed graph and only depends on the signature graph S.

Using a signature graph S consisting of 19 statements results in a signature overhead of 19 statements.

D) Sayers and Karp. The approach by Sayers and Karp [25] leads to a minimum runtime complexity of $\mathcal{O}(n)$. In order to detect already handled blank nodes, the canonicalization function maintains a list of additional statements created so far. This list contains at most b entries with b being the total number of additional statements. Assuming that each statement of a graph can contain no, one, or two blank nodes and that a blank node is part of at least one statement, the graph can contain at most twice as many blank nodes as statements, i. e., $b \leq 2n$. This results in a space complexity of $\mathcal{O}(n)$ of the graph signing function. The signing overhead is b statements added by the blank node labeling algorithm and 19 statements created by the assembly function.

7 Empirical Evaluation

We evaluate the four example configurations of our graph signing framework and their sub-functions and compare the experimental findings with our theoretical analysis in Section 6. In the experiments, we measure the runtime and the space required for singing a whole graph as well as the number of additional statements created by the graph signing function and the assembly function. As data sets, we use synthetically created RDF graphs and real graph data ranging from 10,000 to 250,000 statements. In order to measure the influence of blank nodes in the graph on the graph signing function and the assembly function, we generate different percentages of blank nodes for the graph with 250,000 statements.

The results of our evaluation confirm our theoretical analysis concerning the runtime and required memory of the algorithms as well as the signature overhead. As described in Section 4, some canonicalization functions and hash functions sort the statements in a graph. Our evaluation shows that the sorting operation performed by a hash function profits from sorting operations that are performed by a preceding canonicalization function. This results in less runtime of the hash function. The overall runtime of configurations A, C, and D is mainly influenced by the runtime of the configurations' canonicalization functions and hash functions. On the other hand, the main part of the overall runtime of configuration B is the signature function. This is due the fact that configuration B signs each MSG in the graph separately whereas all other configurations compute only one signature for the whole graph.

In our evaluation, we used RSA with a key length of 2048 bit as signature function. This corresponds to a cryptographic security of 112 bit [19]. Using a key length of 3072 bit, which corresponds to a cryptographic security of 128 bit, takes about three times longer than using a key length of 2048 bit. This does hardly affect configurations A, C, and D as they only compute a single signature. However, it highly increases the overall runtime of configuration B that needs to sign each MSG separately. As alternative, one could use Elliptic Curve DSA [21] with a key length of 256 bits. It has the same security as RSA with 3072 bit keys but is about 76 times faster (measured using a single CPU with 2.53GHz and 4G RAM).

As practical implications from the results of the empirical investigation, we can suggest that one should use the approach by Sayers and Karp (configuration D) to sign graph data that contains few blank nodes. The approach by Fisteus et al. (configuration C) might be used for graphs with many blank nodes. If indeed the approach by Tummarello et al. (configuration B) shall be used, e. g., when no iterative signing is needed, we suggest applying the faster Elliptic Curve DSA as signature function.

8 Threat Model and Security Analysis

Essential security requirements for signing graph data are to ensure the integrity and authenticity of the data. Authenticity means that the party who claims to have signed the data is really the signature's creator. This requirement is achieved with trust models which are further described in Section 9. Integrity means that the signed data was not modified after the signature was created. Achieving this security requirement depends on the used cryptographic functions that are applied on the RDF graph and its statements. Thus, we can derive the following *threat model* which covers possible actions of an attacker:

- Removing existing statements from the signed graph.
- Inserting additional statements into the signed graph.
- Replacing existing statements of the signed graph with different statements. This also covers modifying statements in the graph.

A *comprehensive security analysis* of a graph signing function σ_N must cover all possible algorithms used for its sub-functions. However, only those functions have to be analyzed which perform cryptographic operations such as the basic hash function λ, hash function λ_N for graphs, and signature function ϵ. Functions that do not perform any cryptographic operations such as sorting functions or serialization functions ν_N do not influence the security of the graph signing function. The basic hash function λ and the signature function ϵ are used in any example configuration of our graph signing framework. Thus, we conduct a security analysis of these functions first, before we discuss the particular security aspects of the four concrete configurations.

The cryptographic strength of the basic hash function λ determines the difficulty of modifying the signed graph data without being noticed by the verification mechanism. The more collision-resistant the chosen hash function is, the less likely are unauthorized modifications on the graph data such as removing statements, adding new statements, or replacing statements with other statements. A cryptographic strength of 112 bit can be achieved using SHA-2 [20] with an output length of 224 bits, whereas 128 bit security requires an output length of at least 256 bit [19]. The signature function ϵ determines the difficulty for an attacker masquerading as another party. A cryptographically strong signature function prohibits such attacks. 112 bit security can be achieved using RSA [24] with a key length of 2048 bits or Elliptic Curve DSA [21] with a key length of 224 bit. In order to achieve 128 bit security, an RSA key must be at least 3072 bits long and an Elliptic Curve DSA key must have at least 256 bits [19].

Configuration A uses the canonicalization function of Carroll [9], which does not perform any cryptographic operations. However, Carroll's graph hash function sorts all serialized statements, concatenates them, and computes a hash value of the result using a basic hash function λ. The resulting hash value is directly signed with the signature function ϵ. Thus, the security of configuration A solely depends on λ as well as ϵ. If an attacker removes a statement from the signed graph, its hash value changes and results in an invalid signature. Similarly, adding new statements to the graph or replacing statements with other statements changes the graph's hash value and thus invalidates the signature as well. *Configuration B* differs from configuration A only by using an additional split function. However, this split function does not require any cryptographic operations. Thus, the security analysis of configuration B is basically the same.

Regarding *configuration C*, both the canonicalization function and the hash function for graphs of Fisteus et al. [12] are computed based on the hash values of the statements in the graph using a hash function λ_S. The function λ_S uses a basic hash function λ for computing the hash value of a statement's subject, predicate, and object and combines the three results with a prime p. The size of p determines the bit length of the resulting hash value and thus the security of the hash function. The hash value of an entire graph is computed by applying the function λ_S on all statements in the graph. The results of single hash operations are combined using *MuHASH* [5], which is further discussed below.

Finally, *configuration D* uses the hash function for graphs by Sayers and Karp, which computes the hash values of each statement and combines the results using a combining function like *AdHASH* or *MuHASH* [5]. AdHASH adds all hash values to be combined modulo a large number m. MuHASH multiplies the hash values modulo a large prime p. In order to ensure 80 bit security, m must be chosen such that $m \gg 2^{1600}$ [33]. However, this would reduce the performance of the combining function. On the other hand, the security of MuHASH is based on the discrete logarithm problem which is proven to be hard to solve [5]. The size of p generally depends on the application in which the combining function is used. For signing graph data, one can choose a prime p with a length of at least 1024 bits as recommended in the literature [30].

9 Key Management and Trust Model

Digitally signing data is a mechanism for achieving integrity and authenticity of the data. Implementing these security requirements not only depends on the algorithms used for creating the signature but also on the organizational management of the used key material [28] and the trust model that is applied. This section briefly explains the necessity of key management and trust models as two main aspects in safely using digital signatures for graphs. Please note that our signing framework is independent from any particular key management system and trust model and can be used in any particular implementation.

Key management covers different organizational mechanisms for protecting a key pair from being compromised and misused by unauthorized parties. It ensures that a private signature key is only known to and used by its actual owner and that a public signature verification key can be related to the owner of the key pair. In order to achieve this, key management covers different tasks which have to be met when digitally signing graph data. These tasks cover secure creation and storing of keys as well as destroying old keys and revoking compromised keys [28]. Creating a key pair and storing the private key in a secure environment such as a dedicated cryptographic hardware module ensures that only authorized parties can access the private key. Destroying old keys is necessary to prohibit a usage beyond their intended lifetime. Keys which are too old may not be secure anymore due to new attacks or greater computational power available to break the keys. Compromised keys must be revoked to prevent that they are further used. Finally, the particular implementation of a key management depends also on the application in which signed graph data is used, e. g., professional environments have in general higher security requirements than private uses. Detailed guidelines for key management in professional environments are given, e.g., in [18,19].

A *trust model* defines under which conditions a management of a public key is considered trustworthy. Public key certificates establish such trust by providing some information about the key owner together with the public key. A public key certificate is signed by a trusted party known as the *certificate authority* (CA) [28]. By signing a public key certificate, a CA states that the public key in the certificate is really owned by the party described in the certificate. Thus, the trustworthiness of a public key and its owner depends on the trustworthiness of the CA, which signed the corresponding certificate. Two widely used models for managing public key certificates are PGP [34] and X.509 [11]. X.509 follows a strict hierarchical model with a few trusted root CAs, which are often pre-configured as trust-worthy in most operating systems. An example application for X.509 certificates is SSL [13]. On the other hand, PGP has no hierarchy and allows participants to be both end users and CAs at the same time. Applying a particular trust model depends on the intended application. While X.509 may be used in professional environments, PGP is mostly sufficient for private use. For an overview of other trust models and their characteristics, please refer to [23].

10 Conclusion

Our framework allows for signing RDF(S) graphs, OWL graphs, and Named Graphs. As described in Section 5, the framework provides supports for signing graph data at different levels of granularity (i), signing multiple graphs at once (ii), as well as iteratively signing graph data (iii). We have discussed four different example configurations of our framework and conducted a detailed theoretical analysis as well as empirical evaluation on graph data of different size and characteristics.

References

1. Arenas, M., Gutierrez, C., Pérez, J.: Foundations of RDF databases. In: Tessaris, S., Franconi, E., Eiter, T., Gutierrez, C., Handschuh, S., Rousset, M.-C., Schmidt, R.A. (eds.) Reasoning Web. LNCS, vol. 5689, pp. 158–204. Springer, Heidelberg (2009)
2. Bartel, M., Boyer, J., Fox, B., LaMacchia, B., Simon, E.: XML signature syntax and processing. W3C (2008), http://www.w3.org/TR/xmldsig-core/
3. Beckett, D.: N-Triples. W3C (2001), http://www.w3.org/2001/sw/RDFCore/ntriples/
4. Beckett, D.: RDF/XML syntax specification. W3C (2004), http://www.w3.org/TR/rdf-syntax-grammar/
5. Bellare, M., Micciancio, D.: A new paradigm for collision-free hashing: Incrementality at reduced cost. In: Fumy, W. (ed.) EUROCRYPT 1997. LNCS, vol. 1233, pp. 163–192. Springer, Heidelberg (1997)
6. Berners-Lee, T., Connolly, D.: Notation3 (N3). W3C (2011), http://www.w3.org/TeamSubmission/n3/

7. Bizer, C., Cyganiak, R.: TriG: RDF Dataset Language. W3C (2013), http://www.w3.org/TR/trig/
8. Bundesrepublik Deutschland. §86 StGB (1975), http://www.gesetze-im-internet.de/stgb/__86.html
9. Carroll, J.J.: Signing RDF graphs. In: Fensel, D., Sycara, K., Mylopoulos, J. (eds.) ISWC 2003. LNCS, vol. 2870, pp. 369–384. Springer, Heidelberg (2003)
10. Carroll, J.J., Bizer, C., Hayes, P., Stickler, P.: Named graphs, provenance and trust. In: WWW, pp. 613–622. ACM (2005)
11. Cooper, D., Santesson, S., Farrell, S., Boeyen, S., Housley, R., Polk, T.: Internet X.509 public key infrastructure. RFC 5280, IETF (May 2008)
12. Fisteus, J.A., García, N.F., Fernández, L.S., Kloos, C.D.: Hashing and canonicalizing Notation 3 graphs. JCSS 76(7), 663–685 (2010)
13. Freier, A.O., Karlton, P., Kocher, P.C.: The secure sockets layer (SSL) protocol version 3.0. RFC 6101, IETF (2011)
14. Kasten, A., Scherp, A.: Towards a configurable framework for iterative signing of distributed graph data. In: PrivOn (2013)
15. Knuth, D.E.: Sorting and searching, 2nd edn. Art of Computer Programming, vol. 3. Addison-Wesley (1998)
16. Melnik, S.: RDF API draft (2001), http://infolab.stanford.edu/~melnik/rdf/
17. Motik, B., Parsia, B., Patel-Schneider, P.F.: OWL 2 web ontology language XML serialization. W3C (2009), http://www.w3.org/TR/owl2-xml-serialization/
18. NIST. Recommendation for cryptographic key generation. SP 800-133 (2012), http://dx.doi.org/10.6028/NIST.SP.800-133
19. NIST. Recommendation for key management pt. 1. SP 800-57 (2012), http://csrc.nist.gov/publications/nistpubs/800-57/sp800-57_part1_rev3_general.pdf
20. NIST. Secure hash standard. FIPS PUB 180-4 (March 2012), http://csrc.nist.gov/publications/fips/fips180-4/fips-180-4.pdf
21. NIST. Digital signature standard (DSS). FIPS PUB 186-4 (June 2013), http://nvlpubs.nist.gov/nistpubs/FIPS/NIST.FIPS.186-4.pdf
22. Patel-Schneider, P.F., Motik, B.: OWL 2 web ontology language mapping to RDF graphs. W3C (2012), http://www.w3.org/TR/owl2-mapping-to-rdf/
23. Perlman, R.: An overview of pki trust models. IEEE Network 13(6), 38–43 (1999)
24. Rivest, R., Shamir, A., Adleman, L.: A method for obtaining digital signatures and public-key cryptosystems. CACM 21(2), 120–126 (1978)
25. Sayers, C., Karp, A.H.: Computing the digest of an RDF graph. Technical report, HP Laboratories (2004)
26. Sayers, C., Karp, A.H.: RDF graph digest techniques and potential applications. Technical report, HP Laboratories (2004)
27. Schneier, B.: Protocol Building Blocks. In: Applied Cryptography. Wiley (1996)
28. Schneier, B.: Key Management. In: Applied Cryptography. Wiley (1996)
29. Schneier, B.: Security Needs. In: Secrets and Lies. Wiley (2004)
30. Stanton, P.T., McKeown, B., Burns, R., Ateniese, G.: FastAD: An authenticated directory for billions of objects. ACM SIGOPS 44(1), 45–49 (2010)
31. Szyperski, C.: Component Software: Beyond Object-Oriented Programming. Addison-Wesley (2002)
32. Tummarello, G., Morbidoni, C., Puliti, P., Piazza, F.: Signing individual fragments of an RDF graph. In: WWW, pp. 1020–1021. ACM (2005)
33. Wagner, D.: A generalized birthday problem. In: Yung, M. (ed.) CRYPTO 2002. LNCS, vol. 2442, p. 288. Springer, Heidelberg (2002)
34. Zimmermann, P.R.: The official PGP user's guide. MIT Press (1995)

Perplexity of Index Models over Evolving Linked Data

Thomas Gottron[1] and Christian Gottron[2]

[1] Institute for Web Science and Technologies, University of Koblenz-Landau, Germany
gottron@uni-koblenz.de

[2] Multimedia Communications Lab, Technische Universitä Darmstadt, Germany
Christian.Gottron@kom.tu-darmstadt.de

Abstract. In this paper we analyse the sensitivity of twelve prototypical Linked Data index models towards evolving data. Thus, we consider the reliability and accuracy of results obtained from an index in scenarios where the original data has changed after having been indexed. Our analysis is based on empirical observations over real world data covering a time span of more than one year. The quality of the index models is evaluated w.r.t. their ability to give reliable estimations of the distribution of the indexed data. To this end we use metrics such as perplexity, cross-entropy and Kullback-Leibler divergence. Our experiments show that all considered index models are affected by the evolution of data, but to different degrees and in different ways. We also make the interesting observation that index models based on schema information seem to be relatively stable for estimating densities even if the schema elements diverge a lot.

Keywords: #eswc2014GottronTC.

1 Introduction

Thanks to the Linked Data movement, the Web of Data has reached a point where billions and billions of RDF statements are publicly available. Many applications leverage this valuable resource of information and consume, analyse, present, interlink or produce new data on the Web. The fact that Linked Open Data (LOD) is provided in a distributed fashion across many different data sources motivates the need for approaches to index and cache data on the Web. These indices are used, for instance, to facilitate a fast lookup of data sources on the Web, which provide data with certain characteristics, to federate distributed queries, to estimate result set sizes or for caching data locally for faster access.

Along with the lively growth of the Web of Data comes a certain degree of development, maintenance and, thus, dynamics of the data. Data is not anymore just published in a static fashion, but more often and more frequently, data is updated, extended, revised and refactored. Recent investigations in this direction revealed substantial fluctuations and dynamics of LOD under various aspects and for various data sources [9,1].

These changes in evolving Linked Data are a challenge to index structures. Indices become outdated and—as a consequence—might provide incomplete or wrong information. So far, the sensitivity of index models towards evolving data has not been analysed. Therefore, in this paper we will take a first step in this direction, propose an application independent evaluation approach and perform an empirical survey of twelve

V. Presutti et al. (Eds.): ESWC 2014, LNCS 8465, pp. 161–175, 2014.

different prototypical indexing models and how they behave over evolving Linked Data. The index models are taken from related work and cover a substantial part of different application scenarios, methods and index granularities.

Our analysis is based on an empirical evaluation using real world data of weekly snapshots of Linked Data over a period of more than one year. We use implementations of index models to estimate densities for the distribution of the data. Density estimates are central to several applications, e.g. result set size estimation [12], query optimisation for federated querying [2], information theoretic analysis of LOD [4] or statistical schema induction [16]. Furthermore, densities have the advantage of being application and domain independent. As such they are suitable for a generic evaluation of index models and their sensitivity towards evolving data. For measuring the divergence between a distribution estimated over an index and the distribution estimated from data which has evolved since the creation of the index, we use metrics like perplexity, cross entropy and Kullback-Leibler divergence as well as the Jaccard-similarity over the set of index key elements. Based on these metrics we can see how stable the index models are over evolving data. While all index models are affected by changes in the data, we also make the interesting observation that index structures based on schema information seem to be relatively stable for estimating densities. This is surprising given that the underlying schema information is diverging a lot.

The rest of the paper is structured as follows. We start with a survey and unified formalisation of index models in Section 2. Subsequently we describe how we estimate densities of data distributions from these indices. In Section 4 we present our evaluation: the experimental setup, the applied metrics as well as an overview and discussion of the results. Thereafter, we survey research that is related to our work before we conclude the paper in Section 6.

2 Index Models for Linked Data

In recent years, various index models over LOD have been proposed. Many of them focus on specific aspects of the data or are dedicated to support application specific tasks. The index models in this paper have been selected on the basis of covering a wide range of methods and different levels of granularity. Before going into the details of the models we will briefly introduce a formalisation framework that helps us to describe index models in a unified, application and implementation independent way.

In the context of LOD, we assume data to be available in the form of RDF triples and to be spread across different data sources. Thus, we can assume the atomic data items to be in the form of quads (s, p, o, c) where s, p, and o correspond to the subject, predicate and object of the RDF triple statement and c provides the context, i.e. the data source on the Web where this statement was published. Formally, we consider the sets of all possible URIs U, blank nodes B and literals L. Then in a quad (s, p, o, c) the subject $s \in U \cup B$ can be a URI or a blank node, the predicate $p \in U$ a URI, the object $o \in U \cup B \cup L$ a URI, a blank node or a literal and the context $c \in U$ a URI.

Thus, we assume an index model for LOD to operate on a data set R of (s, p, o, c) quads. Depending on the application scenario, the index model will typically not serve to store all information of the quads. Rather it will define a derived set D of managed data items which typically constitutes a constraint of the quads to smaller tuples. In this paper we consider two different types of data item sets: (1) the set $D_{SPO} := \{(s,p,o) \mid \exists c : (s,p,o,c) \in R\}$ of full RDF triples and (2) the set $D_{USU} := \{s \mid \exists p,o,c : (s,p,o,c) \in R\}$ of all unique subject URIs (USUs). The data items in D_{SPO} are typically used in a context where an index is based on using a part of the quad information (e.g. the object) to look up matching triple statements (e.g. the subject or the predicate). D_{USU}, instead is typically used in index models where information from several statements (e.g. a set of several RDF types) is used to look up a specific entity URI.

Furthermore, an index model has to define a set $\mathcal{K}$ of key elements which are used to lookup and retrieve data items. These key elements are used as domain for a selection function $\sigma : \mathcal{K} \to \mathcal{P}(D)$ to select a subset of the data items in the index. In the context of this paper we consider only data structures for which the selection function σ is operating solely on information provided by the Linked Data set R and does not make use of external information or additional meta data (e.g. provenance information).

Accordingly we define an abstract index model as a tuple $(D, \mathcal{K}, \sigma)$ of the stored data items D, the key elements $\mathcal{K}$ used for the lookup index and the selection function σ to retrieve data from the index.

2.1 Triple Based Indexing

A very common approach for indexing RDF data is to use the three entries in the triples, i.e. the URIs filling the subject, predicate and object positions in the RDF statements. Such indices can be used to retrieve all statements affecting an entity in a subject or object position as well as all statements expressing a certain relation. Implementations of this index model can be found in RDF data stores as well as in a combined fashion such as the QTree index [8]. As data items we assume the full triple to be of interest, thus, we use D_{SPO}.

Subject Index: $I_S := (D_{SPO}, \mathcal{K}_S, \sigma_S)$, where:
- Key elements: $\mathcal{K}_S := \{s \in U \mid \exists p,o,c : (s,p,o,c) \in R\}$
- Selection function: $\sigma_S(k) := \{(s,p,o) \mid s = k\}$

Predicate Index: $I_P := (D_{SPO}, \mathcal{K}_P, \sigma_P)$, where:
- Key elements: $\mathcal{K}_P := \{p \in U \mid \exists s,o,c : (s,p,o,c) \in R\}$
- Selection function: $\sigma_P(k) := \{(s,p,o) \mid p = k\}$

Object Index: $I_O := (D_{SPO}, \mathcal{K}_O, \sigma_O)$, where:
- Key elements: $\mathcal{K}_O := \{o \in U \mid \exists s,p,c : (s,p,o,c) \in R\}$
- Selection function: $\sigma_O(k) := \{(s,p,o) \mid o = k\}$

2.2 Index Models Based on Meta Data (Keywords, Source)

Another common type of index makes use of meta data, e.g. the context or textual descriptions and labels used in triple statements. The textual descriptions for entities provide easy to understand descriptions which help human users to interpret the data. Accordingly, index models based on this information are of particular interest for HCI scenarios. Index structures in this context hardly use a full literal as key elements for indexing, but rather apply term based relevance scores and retrieval methods. Thus, the key elements are terms w taken from a vocabulary V_R of observed words in the literal values of RDF statements in R. To obtain realistic indices we apply common techniques from the field of Information Retrieval, such as case folding and stemming. As queries we assume single term queries, which form the basis for more complex and combined queries in a typical Information Retrieval setting.

Keyword Index: $I_{keyword} := (D_{SPO}, \mathcal{K}_{keyword}, \sigma_{keyword})$, where:
- Key elements: $\mathcal{K}_{keyword} := \{w \mid w \in V_R\}$
- Selection function: $\sigma_{keyword}(k) := \{(s,p,o) \mid o \in L \wedge k \text{ contained in } o\}$

Index models focusing on the context in the quads, i.e. the source providing the information on the Web, are geared more towards settings where the provenance of a statement is of importance (e.g. for evaluating the credibility of information or to be able to consult the original publisher).

Context Index: $I_C := (D_{SPO}, \mathcal{K}_C, \sigma_C)$, where:
- Key elements: $\mathcal{K}_C := \{c \mid \exists s,p,o : (s,p,o,c) \in R\}$
- Selection function: $\sigma_C(k) := \{(s,p,o) \mid (s,p,o,k) \in R\}$

In this setting, rather than considering a concrete context URI, data is sometimes aggregated per pay level domain (PLD)[1] to better reflect the authorities behind the published data. Such an aggregation of data is used in various contexts, among which Linked Data analysis, e.g. in [9]. Defining the function *pubSuffix* to provide the PLD for a given URI, a PLD level index can be defined as follows:

PLD Index: $I_{PLD} := (D_{SPO}, \mathcal{K}_{PLD}, \sigma_{PLD})$, where:
- Key elements: $\mathcal{K}_{PLD} := \{pubSuffix(c) \mid \exists s,p,o : (s,p,o,c) \in R\}$
- Selection function: $\sigma_{PLD}(k) := \{(s,p,o) \mid (s,p,o,c) \in R \wedge pubSuffix(c) = k\}$

2.3 Schema Level Indexing

Several index models use schema level information to organise RDF data. Most of these models use joint information from several triple statements to provide a schema level description for entities. These descriptions then serve as key elements. Thus, we will use the set of USUs D_{USU} as data elements for these index models.

The assignment of classes to entities is of relevance in many contexts. It allows for specifying a categorial identification of entities and is used in various applications. As key elements both of the following is considered: URIs used as objects in statements with an rdf:type predicate as well as URIs which are specifically modelled to be a class themselves.

---

[1] The pay level domain consist of the public suffix (e.g. `.org`, `.co.uk`) and the preceding domain name. It represents the level at which Internet users can directly register names and is thus a good estimate for an authority responsible for Linked Data. We obtained the list of public suffixes from `http://publicsuffix.org/list/`

RDF Type Index: $I_T := (D_{USU}, \mathcal{K}_T, \sigma_T)$, where:

- Key elements: $\mathcal{K}_T := \{o \mid \exists s, c : (s, \textsf{rdf:type}, o, c) \in R\} \cup \{s \mid \exists c : (s, \textsf{rdf:type}, \textsf{rdfs:Class}, c) \in R\}$
- Selection function: $\sigma_T(k) := \{s \mid \exists c : (s, \textsf{rdf:type}, k, c) \in R\}$

A variation to this index model is to form groups of types which jointly describe an entity [11]. These *type sets* characterise an entity more specific and precise.

RDF Type Set (TS) Index: $I_{TS} := (D_{USU}, \mathcal{K}_{TS}, \sigma_{TS})$, where:

- Key elements: $\mathcal{K}_{TS} := \mathcal{P}(\mathcal{K}_T)$
- Selection function: $\sigma_{TS}(k) := \{s \mid (\forall t \in k : (\exists c : (s, \textsf{rdf:type}, t, c) \in R)) \land \forall (s, \textsf{rdf:type}, o, c) \in R : (o \in k)\}$

An analogous extension to indexing individual predicates is to consider the set of predicates used to describe the properties of a specific entity. This *property set* (sometimes also referred to as *characteristic set*) provides a more specific description of the entity. Such index models are used for accurate result set size estimations when querying distributed RDF data stores [12] or for generating SPARQL queries to feed into federated querying testbeds [3].

Property Set (PS) Index: $I_{PS} := (D_{USU}, \mathcal{K}_{PS}, \sigma_{PS})$, where:

- Key elements: $\mathcal{K}_{PS} := \mathcal{P}(\mathcal{K}_p)$
- Selection function: $\sigma_{PS}(k) := \{s \mid (\forall p \in k : (\exists o, c : (s, p, o, c) \in R)) \land \forall (s, p, o, c) \in R : (p \in k)\}$

In the context of statistic schema induction [16] also the set of incoming properties is considered. This corresponds to the set of predicates which all affect the same object in RDF triple statements.

Incoming Property Set (IPS) Index: $I_{IPS} := (D_{USU}, \mathcal{K}_{IPS}, \sigma_{IPS})$, where:

- Key elements: $\mathcal{K}_{IPS} := \mathcal{P}(\mathcal{K}_P)$
- Selection function: $\sigma_{IPS}(k) := \{o \mid (\forall p \in k : (\exists s, c : (s, p, o, c) \in R)) \land \forall (s, p, o, c) \in R : (p \in k)\}$

The combination of property sets and type sets leads to the definition of *extended characteristic sets* (ECS). ECS based index models constitute a more extensive approach to schema level indexing as they combine both type and property information. Such index models have been used for measuring redundancy in schema information on the LOD cloud [4,5] and for measuring dynamics of LOD on a schema level [1].

Extended Characteristic Set (ECS) Index: $I_{ECS} := (D_{USU}, \mathcal{K}_{ECS}, \sigma_{ECS})$, where:

- Key elements: $\mathcal{K}_{ECS} := \mathcal{P}(\mathcal{K}_P \cup \mathcal{K}_T)$
- Selection function: $\sigma_{ECS}(k) := \{s \mid (\forall p \in k \cap \mathcal{K}_P : (s \in \sigma_{PS}(p))) \land (\forall t \in k \cap \mathcal{K}_T : (s \in \sigma_{TS}(t)))\}$

While ECS based index models already address a lot of the schema information encoded in LOD, there exist models which make use of yet more complex and more fine grained structures to capture schema information. SchemEX as a schema level index for querying distributed Linked Data falls into this category [11,7].

SchemEX Index: $I_{SchemEX} := (D_{USU}, \mathcal{K}_{SchemEX}, \sigma_{SchemEX})$, where:

- Key elements: $\mathcal{K}_{SchemEX} := \mathcal{P}(\mathcal{K}_{TS} \times \mathcal{P}(\mathcal{K}_{PS} \times \mathcal{K}_{TS}))$
- Selection function: $\sigma_{SchemEX}(k = (ts, E)) := \{s \mid s \in \sigma_{TS}(ts) \wedge \forall (ps, ts_2) \in E : (s \in \sigma_{PS}(ps) \wedge \exists o \in \sigma_{TS}(ts_2) : (\forall p \in ps : (\exists c : (s, p, o, c) \in R))\}$

3 Index Based Estimates for the Distribution of Data Elements

We implemented[2] the index models presented in Section 2 to estimate density functions over key elements. This means, we estimate how probable it is for an element to belong to one specific index key k and—conversely—the amount of data obtained when querying the index for this key element k.

Depending on the type of index model, we look up the distribution of triples or USUs over the index structure. If we consider the distribution over an index $I = (D, \mathcal{K}, \sigma)$, this effectively corresponds to modelling a random variable X taking values of the key elements $\mathcal{K}$. The density we estimate is the distribution of this random variable X. This means we need to determine the probability $P(X = k)$ for each entry $k \in \mathcal{K}$ to be associated with a data item. To estimate the densities we use the count information of data elements associated with the key elements in an index. This corresponds to using a maximum likelihood estimation to derive a distribution, i.e.

$$P(X = k) = \frac{|\sigma(k)|}{\sum_{k' \in \mathcal{K}} |\sigma(k')|} \tag{1}$$

where $\sigma(k)$ indicates the result set obtained from an index when querying for a specific key element k.

As we are considering evolving data it is highly likely that the set of key elements is not stable but evolving itself. Thus, it can happen that certain key elements will disappear as the data evolves (i.e. there are no more data items for that index entry) or might come up as novel, previously unseen key elements. For instance we might encounter new combinations of properties which spawn new property sets in an I_{PS} implementation. As we are interested in comparing densities over our indices we need to consider the effect of such zero-size entries. Using a maximum likelihood estimation for the densities would lead to zero probabilities for certain events which renders comparisons of densities impractical. We apply smoothing to overcoming zero probabilities. We make use of Laplace smoothing which adds a small constant value of λ to all counts obtained for the number of results $|\sigma(k)|$. The parameter λ was set to 0.5 in our experiments.

[2] The implementation of the index models has been released under an open source license at `https://github.com/gottron/lod-index-models`

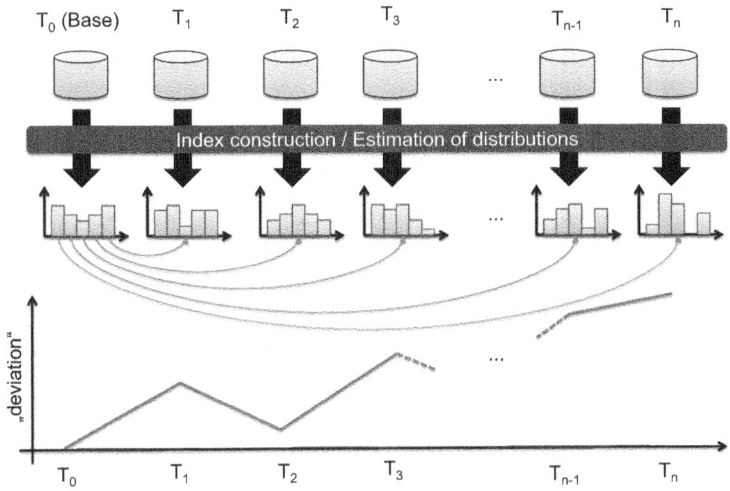

Fig. 1. Evaluation of index stability: we built indices at different points in time over an evolving data set. The deviation in the distribution is measured by comparing the initial distribution to the distributions of the evolved data.

4 Experiments: Measuring Deviation of Index Models over Evolving Data

In our experiments, we empirically evaluate how accurate are density estimates obtained from implementations of index models over evolving data. To this end we build an index over the data at an initial point in time and obtain its distribution from the index. Then we compare this distribution to densities estimated over the same data at later points in time, when the data has potentially undergone changes. Figure 1 illustrates this process.

4.1 Metrics

We are comparing estimates of the density function for distributions of Linked Data items in an index structure. Common metrics to compare density functions are cross entropy, Kullback-Leibler divergence and perplexity. We briefly review the definitions of these metrics and explain their interpretation.

Assume we have estimated two probability distributions $P_1(X)$ and $P_2(X)$ at different points in time over an evolving data set. Then the cross entropy is defined as:

$$H(P_1, P_2) = -\sum_{k \in \mathcal{K}} P_1(X = k) \log(P_2(X = k)) \qquad (2)$$

In the context of compression theory, cross entropy can be interpreted as the average number of bits needed to encode events following the distribution P_1 based on an optimal encoding scheme derived from P_2. If the two distributions are equivalent, then cross entropy corresponds to the normal entropy $H(P_1)$. The entropy of P_1 also provides a lower bound for cross entropy. Based on this interpretation, the Kullback-Leibler divergence gives the deviation in entropy (or overhead in encoding) relative to the entropy for P_1 and is defined as:

$$D_{KL}(P_1, P_2) = H(P_1, P_2) - H(P_1) \tag{3}$$

Therefore, if two distributions are equivalent, they have a Kullback-Leibler divergence of zero. This is a desirable feature for our evaluation as it renders the comparison of distributions of evolving data independent from the different levels of the entropy observed for different index structures.

Perplexity, instead, provides an evaluation of a distribution by giving the number of events which under a uniform distribution would have the same entropy value. As such it is considered to be more easily interpretable by humans than the somewhat abstract entropy values. Perplexity itself is defined over entropy values, though. Here we formulate it directly on the basis of cross entropy:

$$PP(P_1, P_2) = 2^{H(P_1, P_2)} \tag{4}$$

Perplexity is a standard metric for evaluating probabilistic models. The lower the perplexity is, the better a model explains observed data and the more truthful are its estimates of the probabilities. When looking at perplexity over the cross entropy $H(P_1, P_2)$ in particular, there is also another interesting interpretation of the values. If perplexity is higher than the number of events considered, then using a simple uniform distribution instead of P_2 would correspond to a better approximation of the distribution P_1. Furthermore, the interpretation of perplexity relative to the event space allows for a normalisation. The normalised perplexity PP_{norm} is defined as $\frac{PP}{|X|}$, where $|X|$ denotes the size of the event space.

In addition to the metrics for comparing the density estimates, we use the Jaccard-similarity over the set of key elements. Let $\mathcal{K}_1$ and $\mathcal{K}_2$ be the sets of key elements derived at two points in time. Then the Jaccard-similarity is defined as:

$$Jaccard(\mathcal{K}_1, \mathcal{K}_2) = \frac{|\mathcal{K}_1 \cap \mathcal{K}_2|}{|\mathcal{K}_1 \cup \mathcal{K}_2|} \tag{5}$$

A higher similarity value indicates a larger overlap between the sets of key elements while a low value indicates a stronger deviation. In this way we can get an impression of how stable the set of elements used for indexing is in the different indexing approaches.

To summarise: cross entropy provides an impression of the evolution of the absolute density, Kullback-Leibler divergence the deviation from the initial density, perplexity gives a more human interpretable view on the changes in the entropy values and the Jaccard-similarity allows for an assessment of the stability of the set of key elements used for indexing.

4.2 Data Set

We use the Dynamic Linked Data Observatory [10,9] data set. The data set provides weekly crawls of LOD data sources starting from always the same set of seed URIs. The initial snapshot from the 6th of May 2012 contains 16,376,867 RDF triples and covers a wide range of data sources. The data is provided in the form of quads containing the RDF statement as well as the source URI, where the triple was crawled from. Thus, it suits our formal requirements for the index models. Details on the design considerations, implementation and crawling strategy for the data set can be found in the original publications.

We used 77 data snapshots from the 6th of May 2012 up to the 8th of December 2013 for our experiments. The data was fed as raw input to implementations of all the twelve indexing models, without any further pre-processing[3].

4.3 Results

We will now look at the performance of the different indexing models w.r.t. to the metrics measuring the ability to truthfully estimate density functions over evolving data.

We start to look at the development of cross entropy over time. The plots in Figure 2 show the result for the triple (Figure 2(a)), metadata (Figure 2(b)) and schema based index models. For the schema level index models we differentiate between the simpler models in Figure 2(c) and the ECS and SchemEX models making use of more extensive schema information in Figure 2(d). We can see nicely the different entropy levels for the individual indices. The explanation for this are more skewed distributions of the data in the index structures as well as different sizes of the key element sets. We can also observe some impacts of the evolving data on the entropy levels. The increase is not monotone, but shows some fluctuations over time. This can be attributed, on the one hand, to the data not shifting away homogeneously from its original distribution. On the other hand, such a behaviour can also be explained with the limited availability of certain data sources over time. As seen in previous analysis of the same data set, some data sources were not always available at all moments in time, causing a shift in the distribution due to the lack of the corresponding data and to peaks in the observed plots. Note, that this is not a flaw in the data set as it reflects a realistic scenario on the Web.

When looking at the Kullback-Leibler divergence in Figure 3, it can be seen how the deviations from the initial values develop. For most indices the development is behaving comparable in the sense that deviations appear approximately at the same points in time with the same direction of the deviations (this can be seen quite nicely for the triple and metadata based indices in Figure 3(a) and 3(b)). Two exceptions are the keyword based index, which has a much more stable behaviour in general, and the context based index, which exhibits an increase in Kullback-Leibler divergence around week 60. The stability of density estimates obtained from the keyword index are conceptual. As the

[3] Please note that SchemEX [11] is typically computed using an approximative, highly efficient stream-based approach. While in general the results of this approach are of high quality [6] we want to make sure it does not introduce a bias in the analysed index structures. Thus, we decided to compute precise, truthful and lossless SchemEX indices.

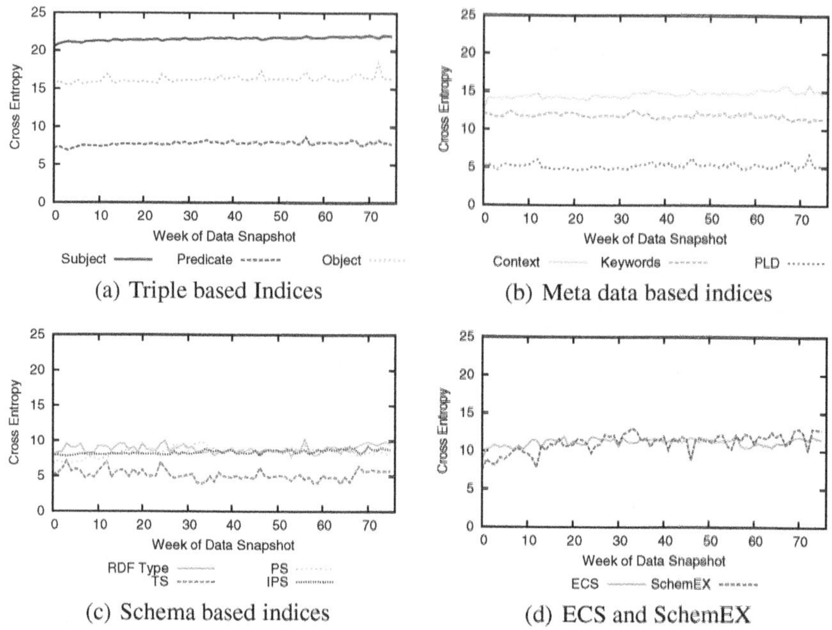

(a) Triple based Indices (b) Meta data based indices

(c) Schema based indices (d) ECS and SchemEX

Fig. 2. Evolution of cross entropy for densities estimated over index structures

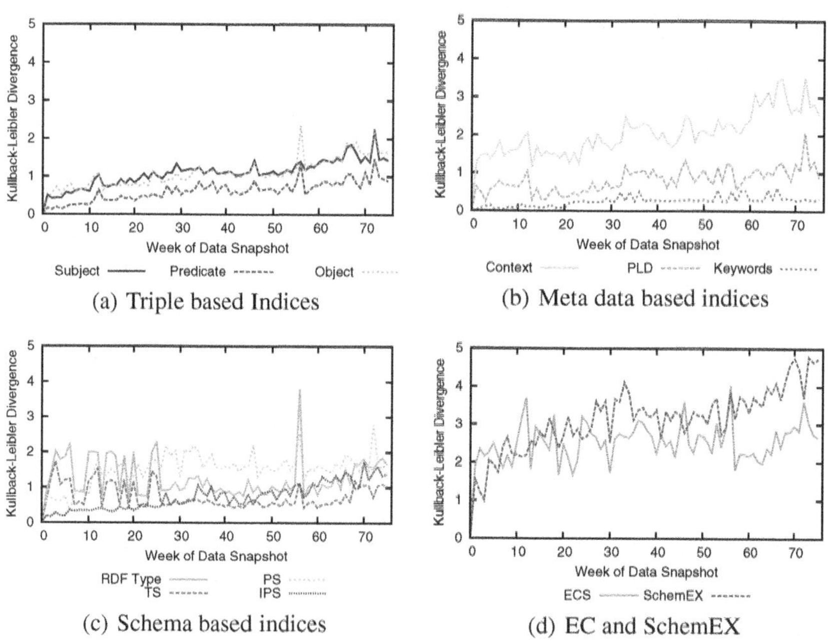

(a) Triple based Indices (b) Meta data based indices

(c) Schema based indices (d) EC and SchemEX

Fig. 3. Evolution of Kullback-Leibler divergence for densities estimated over index structures

Table 1. Average and maximal perplexity of indices over evolving data

Index	S	P	O	C	PLD	Keyword	T	TS	PS	IPS	ECS	SchemEX
Size Key Set	3,665,267	11,554	2,887,357	68,665	746	1,057,790	11,154	25,727	35,985	12,555	89,252	118,473
Max. PP	4,237,601	421	368,459	59,888	107	5,837	1,201	140	919	611	4,699	8,632
Max. PP_{norm}	1.156	0.036	0.128	0.872	0.143	0.006	0.108	0.005	0.026	0.048	0.053	0.073
Avg. PP	3,148,052	230	83,438	25,758	38	3,660	506	42	380	342	2,430	2957
Avg. PP_{norm}	0.860	0.020	0.029	0.375	0.051	0.003	0.045	0.002	0.011	0.027	0.027	0.025

index effectively operates over single words as key elements, the density corresponds to a unigram language model. Given that the domain of the data did not change, we can hypothesise that the language style and domain remained relatively stable. The explanation for the increase in divergence of the context index around week 60, instead, lies in the data set. Investigating the data closer, revealed that at this point in time one particular data source (`taxonconcept.org`) started to contribute a significantly higher amount of triples than before. Thus, the strong impact on the context index.

The quality and stability of the density estimations can best be seen in the plots of the perplexity values in Figure 4. Again, we can observe a big difference in the absolute values. The overall highest values are observed for the subject based index. We can see in Figure 4(a), that the perplexity of this index increases relatively homogeneously and reaches it maximal value around week 70. Also several other indices show a more or less steady increase in perplexity. The simpler schema level indices in Figure 4(c), however, are relatively stable—with the exception of a few high peeks. The peeks align again with the unavailability of some data sources. In Figure 4(d) it is interesting to observe, that the perplexity of SchemEX is comparable to the one of the ECS index. This is surprising as SchemEX conceptually is more complex than the ECS and uses more extensive schema patterns. However, it seems with the more fine-grained schema level model it can better distinguish between the parts which have evolved and those which have remained stable. Therefore, also the density estimation is more reliable.

Table 1 provides an aggregated view on perplexity. The table lists information about the maximal and average perplexity values as well as normalised perplexity. There, we can see, for instance, that the maximal value of the subject based index corresponds to a perplexity value of 4,237,601. Given the initial size of the key element set of 3,665,267, the normalised entropy at this point in time reaches a values of 1.156. Thus, assuming a simple uniform distribution of the key elements would provide a more accurate estimation of the distribution. It remains to be said, though, that the distribution of the subject key elements in the analysed data set is in fact relatively close to a uniform distribution.

More interesting is the insight which can be obtained from the average normalised perplexity values in Table 1. Here, the single peeks of perplexity due to unavailable data sources have a lower impact. Furthermore, the normalisation renders the values comparable over all indices. We observe, that all schema level indices have very low values. This underlines the stability of these indices. Also, we can see again the keyword based index to have a low average normalised perplexity. Both observations align with the impression we obtained from the analysis of the Kullback-Leibler divergence.

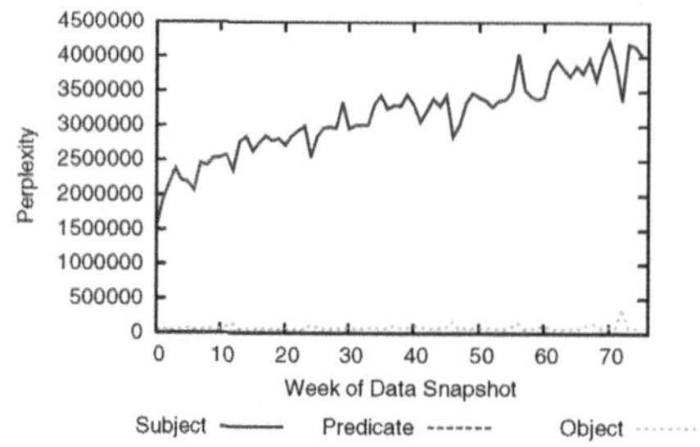

(a) Triple based Indices

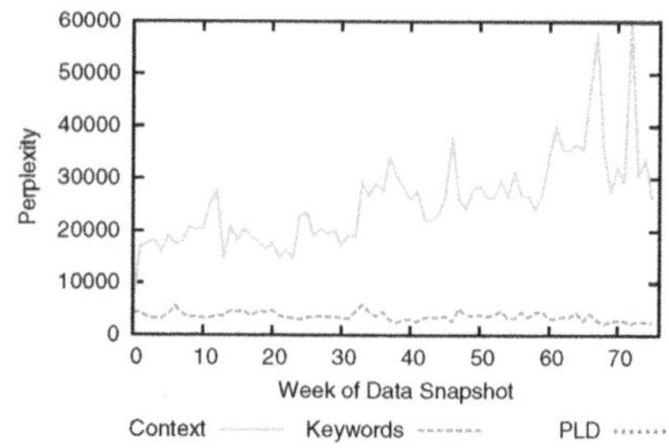

(b) Meta data based indices

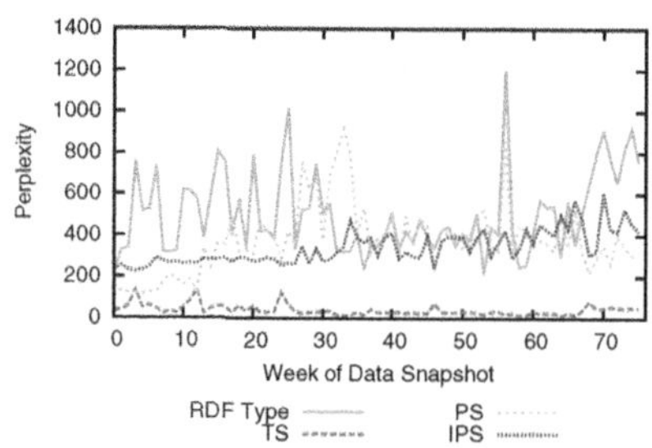

(c) Schema based indices

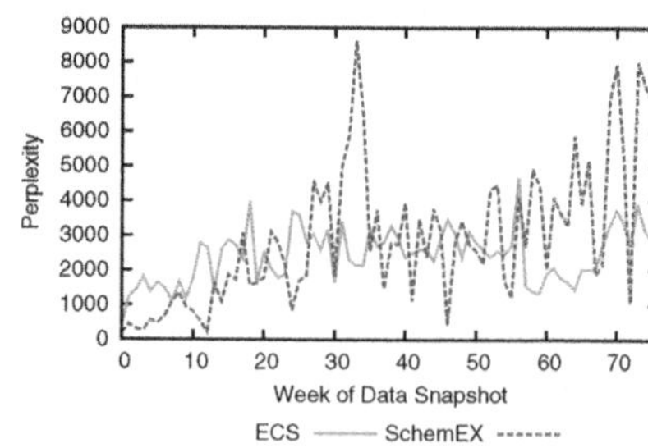

(d) ECS and SchemEX

Fig. 4. Evolution of Perplexity for densities estimated over index structures

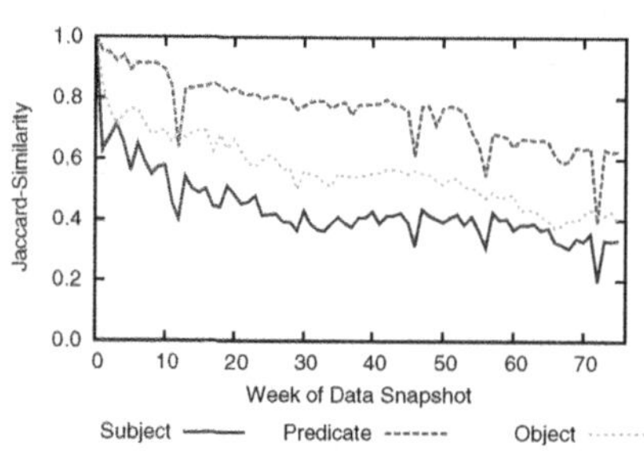

(a) Triple based Indices

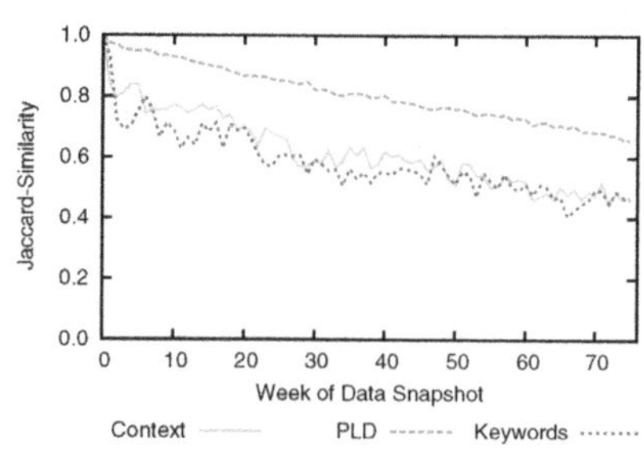

(b) Meta data based indices

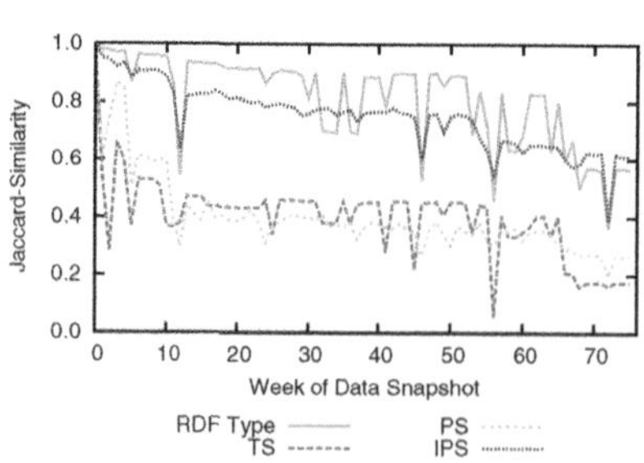

(c) Schema based indices

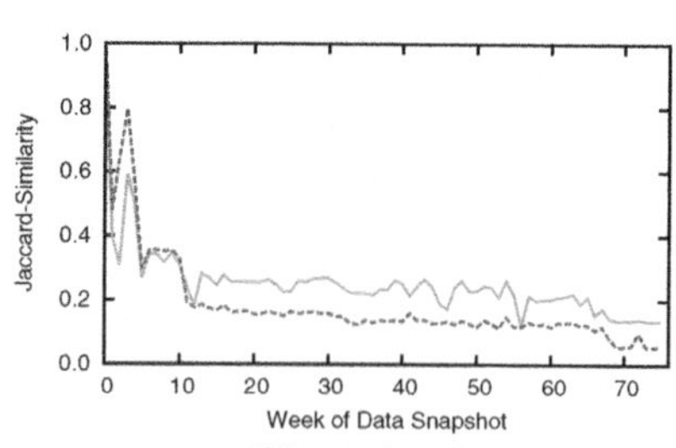

(d) ECS and SchemEX

Fig. 5. Evolution of the Jaccard-similarity over the index element sets

Finally, when looking at the evolution of the set of key elements over time in Figure 5, we can get some additional insights. While the similarity between the sets of key elements decreases more or less steadily for the triple and meta data based index models, it drops to relatively low values for several schema based models quite immediately. Most models drop to a Jaccard-similarity of 0.5 and below already after 10 weeks. The SchemEX index even drops to values of approximately 0.2. However, from a low overlap in the set of key elements we can not judge the overall quality of the index, as it is not clear how many data items are affected by the changed key elements. As we have seen before when looking at perplexity, SchemEX seems to cope very well in capturing and distinguishing patterns that are more or less stable. Thus, even if some of the key elements with very few associated data entries disappear, the effect on the estimates of densities is relatively low.

Quite interesting is also the observation that the deviations in the key elements set in IPS index seem much lower than for the IP index. This, however is an artefact of the data set and how it is generated. Given that the data set essentially corresponds to a crawl of a fixed set of seed URIs, we naturally get a change of all the modelled subject entities and their properties. For the objects, instead, we can only observe changes in the incoming relations from the considered subjects in the seed set. We cannot observe changes for those objects on the rest of the LOD cloud. On an unbiased data set, we would expect the two types of indices to behave comparable. This, however, remains to be verified.

5 Related Work

The changes and dynamics of Linked Data have been investigated in several publications. Umbrich et al. [15] give a good survey and provide a distinction between dynamics on the document and entity level. The Dynamic Linked Data Observatory data set has been introduced in [9]. It was analysed for changes in the data regarding triples, USUs, volume per data source, availability of the data on the Web (i.e. reachability of URIs) etc. The analysis showed a varying degree of changes in the data depending on the features considered. An extension of the analysis towards the schema level of LOD was presented by Dividino et al. [1]. A more detailed analysis of schema information revealed that also the schema level is heavily affected by the change in the data. The notion of schema elements in [1] is based on an ECS index model. However, all analytics focus on changes and dynamics on the side of the data. To the best of our knowledge, the impact of the changes on the accuracy of index models has not been analysed so far.

Index models and index structures for Linked Data or RDF in general are discussed in various contexts. Driven by the obvious need to index, cache and query distributed data, a wide range of solutions and applications have been proposed. We covered relevant publications in Section 2 when introducing the index models. However, when analysing index models most work considers mainly the efficiency of index structures for retrieving data or their effectiveness in a specific application context [13,14]. In these scenarios it is usually considered normal, that the index is aware of all changes in the data and is updated accordingly. Few publications consider index structures that are not always accurate. The motivation is either a more efficient computation of the index over large scale data [11] or a distributed scenario where not all data is under the control of the authority managing the index, e.g. when federating SPARQL queries [2]. However, also in these cases the loss of accuracy has so far only been analysed for static data sets [11,6].

6 Conclusions and Future Work

In this paper we addressed the impact of evolving Linked Data on the accuracy of index models in providing reliable density estimations. Answering this question plays an important role given that, on the one hand, density estimations are central to several applications and that, on the other hand, Linked Open Data has been shown to be quite dynamic and evolving under several aspects. We formalised and implemented twelve prototypical index models from related work and evaluated their accuracy in estimating the density over evolving data. Employing metrics for comparing probability distributions we empirically analysed how far the densities obtained from an index diverged from the actual distributions in the evolving data. We observed that all densities estimated from implementations of the index models diverge from the densities of the evolving data. The divergence increases over time and particular events in the data caused stronger deviations for specific index models. For instance, models based on the data source were affected stronger by a burst and increase in the data volume provided by one specific data source. Finally, we also observed that models based on schema information seem to provide relatively stable estimations.

As future work we will investigate index specific strategies for performing evaluations of their own accuracy and corresponding update plans. This will include sampling strategies to identify the degree of data changes without considering the full data set. Furthermore, we will investigate more detailed methods for analysing the accuracy of index models when it comes to responding to concrete queries. The challenge in this case will be to provide representative queries, which cover all aspects of the data and how to deduce the overall change rate of the data from the divergence of query results.

Acknowledgements. The research leading to these results has received funding from the European Community's Seventh Framework Programme (FP7/2007-2013), REVEAL (Grant agree number 610928). The authors would like to thank Julius Gottron for a fruitful and lively discussion on indexing strategies.

References

1. Dividino, R., Scherp, A., Gröner, G., Gottron, T.: Change-a-LOD: Does the Schema on the Linked Data Cloud Change or Not? In: COLD 2013: International Workshop on Consuming Linked Data (2013)
2. Görlitz, O., Staab, S.: Splendid: Sparql endpoint federation exploiting void descriptions. In: Proceedings of the 2nd International Workshop on Consuming Linked Data, Bonn, Germany (2011)
3. Görlitz, O., Thimm, M., Staab, S.: Splodge: Systematic generation of sparql benchmark queries for linked open data. In: Cudré-Mauroux, P., et al. (eds.) ISWC 2012, Part I. LNCS, vol. 7649, pp. 116–132. Springer, Heidelberg (2012)

4. Gottron, T., Knauf, M., Scheglmann, S., Scherp, A.: A systematic investigation of explicit and implicit schema information on the linked open data cloud. In: Cimiano, P., Corcho, O., Presutti, V., Hollink, L., Rudolph, S. (eds.) ESWC 2013. LNCS, vol. 7882, pp. 228–242. Springer, Heidelberg (2013)
5. Gottron, T., Knauf, M., Scherp, A.: Analysis of schema structures in the linked open data graph based on unique subject uris, pay-level domains, and vocabulary usage. In: Distributed and Parallel Databases, pp. 1–39 (2014)
6. Gottron, T., Pickhardt, R.: A detailed analysis of the quality of stream-based schema construction on linked open data. In: Li, J., Qi, G., Zhao, D., Nejdl, W., Zheng, H.T. (eds.) Semantic Web and Web Science. Springer Proceedings in Complexity, pp. 89–102. Springer, New York (2013)
7. Gottron, T., Scherp, A., Krayer, B., Peters, A.: LODatio: Using a Schema-Based Index to Support Users in Finding Relevant Sources of Linked Data. In: K-CAP 2013: Proceedings of the Conference on Knowledge Capture, pp. 105–108 (2013)
8. Harth, A., Hose, K., Karnstedt, M., Polleres, A., Sattler, K.U., Umbrich, J.: Data summaries for on-demand queries over linked data. In: Int. Conf. on World wide web, pp. 411–420. ACM (2010)
9. Käfer, T., Abdelrahman, A., Umbrich, J., O'Byrne, P., Hogan, A.: Observing linked data dynamics. In: Cimiano, P., Corcho, O., Presutti, V., Hollink, L., Rudolph, S. (eds.) ESWC 2013. LNCS, vol. 7882, pp. 213–227. Springer, Heidelberg (2013)
10. Käfer, T., Umbrich, J., Hogan, A., Polleres, A.: DyLDO: Towards a Dynamic Linked Data Observatory. In: Workshop on Linked Data on the Web (LDOW) (2012)
11. Konrath, M., Gottron, T., Staab, S., Scherp, A.: Schemex—efficient construction of a data catalogue by stream-based indexing of linked data. Web Semantics: Science, Services and Agents on the World Wide Web 16(0), 52–58 (2012), The Semantic Web Challenge 2011
12. Neumann, T., Moerkotte, G.: Characteristic sets: Accurate cardinality estimation for rdf queries with multiple joins. In: Proceedings of the 27th International Conference on Data Engineering, ICDE 2011, Hannover, Germany, April 11-16, pp. 984–994 (2011)
13. Neumann, T., Weikum, G.: Scalable join processing on very large rdf graphs. In: Proceedings of the 2009 ACM SIGMOD International Conference on Management of Data, pp. 627–640. ACM (2009)
14. Stocker, M., Seaborne, A., Bernstein, A., Kiefer, C., Reynolds, D.: Sparql basic graph pattern optimization using selectivity estimation. In: Proceedings of the 17th International Conference on World Wide Web, pp. 595–604. ACM (2008)
15. Umbrich, J., Hausenblas, M., Hogan, A., Polleres, A., Decker, S.: Towards Dataset Dynamics: Change Frequency of Linked Open Data Sources. In: LDOW (2010)
16. Völker, J., Niepert, M.: Statistical schema induction. In: Antoniou, G., Grobelnik, M., Simperl, E., Parsia, B., Plexousakis, D., De Leenheer, P., Pan, J. (eds.) ESWC 2011, Part I. LNCS, vol. 6643, pp. 124–138. Springer, Heidelberg (2011)

HiBISCuS: Hypergraph-Based Source Selection for SPARQL Endpoint Federation

Muhammad Saleem and Axel-Cyrille Ngonga Ngomo

Universität Leipzig, IFI/AKSW, P.O. 100920, 04009 Leipzig, Germany
{lastname}informatik.uni-leipzig.de

Abstract. Efficient federated query processing is of significant importance to tame the large amount of data available on the Web of Data. Previous works have focused on generating optimized query execution plans for fast result retrieval. However, devising source selection approaches beyond triple pattern-wise source selection has not received much attention. This work presents HiBISCuS, a novel hypergraph-based source selection approach to federated SPARQL querying. Our approach can be directly combined with existing SPARQL query federation engines to achieve the same recall while querying fewer data sources. We extend three well-known SPARQL query federation engines with HiBISCus and compare our extensions with the original approaches on FedBench. Our evaluation shows that HiBISCuS can efficiently reduce the total number of sources selected without losing recall. Moreover, our approach significantly reduces the execution time of the selected engines on most of the benchmark queries.

Keywords: #eswc2014Saleem.

1 Introduction

The Web of Data is now a large compendium of interlinked data sets from multiple domains with large datasets [12] being added frequently [3]. Given the complexity of information needs on the Web, certain queries can only be answered by retrieving results contained across different data sources (short: sources). Thus, the optimization of engines that support this type of queries, called *federated query engines*, is of central importance to ensure the usability of the Web of Data in real-world applications. One of the important optimization steps in federated SPARQL query processing is the efficient selection of relevant sources for a query. To ensure that a recall of 100% is achieved, most SPARQL query federation approaches [4,8,10,14,15,11] perform *triple pattern-wise source selection* (TPWSS). The goal of the TPWSS is to identify the set of relevant (also called capable, formally defined in section 3) sources against individual triple patterns of a query [11]. However, it is possible that a relevant source does not *contribute* to the final result set of the complete query. This is because the results from a particular data source can be excluded after performing *joins* with the results of other triple patterns contained in the same query. An overestimation of such sources increases the network traffic and can significantly affect the overall query processing time.

An example for such a query is SSQ1 in Figure 1. A TPWSS that retrieves all relevant sources for each individual triple pattern would lead to all sources in the example being queried. Yet, the complete result set of SSQ1 can be computed without querying

V. Presutti et al. (Eds.): ESWC 2014, LNCS 8465, pp. 176–191, 2014.

```
@prefix ns1:<http://auth1/scma/>.
@prefix ns2:<http://auth2/scma/>.
@prefix ns1_2:<http://auth12/scma/>.
@prefix ns1_3:<http://auth13/scma/>.
@prefix cp:<http://common/scma/>.
ns1_3:s1 cp:p1 ns1_3:o11.
ns1:s2 cp:p3 ''o12''.
ns1_2:s3 cp:p4 cp:o13.
ns1_2:s3 cp:p5 "o14".
ns2:o21 cp:p2 "o15".
ns1:p3 cp:p6 cp:p8 .
```

(a) Dataset d_1

```
@prefix ns2:<http://auth2/scma/>.
@prefix ns3:<http://auth3/scma/>.
@prefix ns1_3:<http://auth13/scma/>.
@prefix ns1_2:<http://auth12/scma/>.
@prefix cp:<http://common/scma/>.
ns1_2:s1 cp:p1 ns2:o21 .
ns1_2:s3 cp:p3 "o22".
ns2:s4 cp:p5 "o23".
cp:p2 cp:p6 cp:p7 .
ns1_2:s1 cp:p0 ns1_3:o25 .
ns3:s3 cp:p9 ns3:o26.
```

(b) Dataset d_2

```
@prefix ns2:<http://auth2/scma/>.
@prefix ns3:<http://auth3/scma/>.
@prefix ns1_3:<http://auth13/scma/>.
@prefix cp:<http://common/scma/>.
ns1_3:s1 cp:p2 "o31".
ns3:s1 cp:p3 "o32".
ns3:s2 cp:p4 cp:o13 .
ns1_3:s5 cp:p5 "o34".
ns2:o21 cp:p3 "o35".
ns3:s3 cp:p9 ns1_3:o25 .
ns3:s4 cp:p0 ns2:o25 .
```

(c) Dataset d_3

```
PREFIX cp: <http://common/schema/>
SELECT * WHERE {
?s cp:p1 ?v1.          d1 d2
?s cp:p2 ?v2.}         d1 d3
# TP. sources = 4
# Optimal TP. sources = 2
# Results = 1
```

(d) Star-shaped query SSQ1

```
PREFIX cp: <http://common/schema/>
SELECT * WHERE {
?s cp:p1 ?v1 .         d1 d2
?v1 cp:p3 ?v2 .}       d1 d2 d3
# TP. sources = 5
# Optimal TP. sources = 2
# Results = 1
```

(e) Path-shaped query PSQ2

```
PREFIX cp: <http://common/schema/>
PREFIX ns3:<http://auth3/schema/>
SELECT * WHERE {
ns3:s3 cp:p9 ?v0.      d2 d3
?s1 cp:p0 ?v0.         d2 d3
?s1 cp:p1 ?v1 .        d1 d2
?v1 cp:p2 ?v2 .        d1 d3
?v1 cp:p3 "o35"}       d3
# TP. sources = 9
# Optimal TP. sources = 5
# Results = 1
```

(f) Hybrid query HSQ3

Fig. 1. Motivating Examples. #TP is the total number of triple pattern-wise sources selected. The relevant sources for each are shown next to each triple pattern. The sources marked in red contribute to the final query result set.

d_2 due to the type of join used in the query. We thus propose a *novel join-aware approach to TPWSS* dubbed HiBISCuS. Our approach goes beyond the state of the art by aiming to compute the sources that actually contribute to the final result set of an input query and that for each triple pattern. To the best of our knowledge, this join-aware approach to TPWSS has only been tackled by an extension of the ANAPSID framework presented in [9]. Yet, this extension is based on evaluating namespaces and sending ASK queries to data sources at runtime. In contrast, HiBISCuS relies on an index that stores the authorities of the resource URIs[1] contained in the data sources at hand. Our approach proves to be more time-efficient than the ANAPSID extension as shown by our evaluation in Section 5.

HiBISCuS addresses the problem of source selection by several innovations. Our first innovation consists of modelling SPARQL queries as a sets of *directed labelled hypergraphs* (DLH). Moreover, we rely on a *novel type of summaries* which exploits the fact that the resources in SPARQL endpoints are Uniform Resource Identifiers (URIs). Our *source selection algorithm is also novel* and consists of two steps. In a first step, our approach *labels the hyperedges* of the DLH representation of an input SPARQL query q with relevant data sources. In the second step, the summaries and the type of joins in q are used to *prune the edge labels*. By these means, HiBISCuS can discard sources (without losing recall) that are not pertinent to the computation of the final result set of the query. Overall, our contributions are thus as follows:

1. We present a formal framework for modelling SPARQL queries as directed labelled hypergraphs.
2. We present a novel type of data summaries for SPARQL endpoints which relies on the authority fragment of URIs.

[1] http://tools.ietf.org/html/rfc3986

3. We devise a pruning algorithm for edge labels that enables us to discard irrelevant sources based on the types of joins used in a query.
4. We evaluate our approach by extending three state-of-the-art federate query engines (FedX, SPLENDID and DARQ) with HiBISCuS and comparing these extensions to the original systems. In addition, we compare our most time-efficient extension with the extension of ANAPSID presented in [9]. Our results show that we can reduce the number of source selected, the source selection time as well as the overall query runtime of each of these systems.

The structure of the rest of this paper is as follows: we first give a brief overview of federated query engines. Then, we present our formalization of SPARQL queries as directed labelled hypergraphs. The algorithms underlying HiBISCuS are then explained in detail. Finally, we evaluate HiBISCuS against the state-of-the-art and show that we achieve both better source selection and runtimes on the FedBench [13] SPARQL query federation benchmark.

2 Related Work

The approaches related to query federation over the Web of Data can be divided into three main categories (see Table 1 obtained from our public survey results[2]).

(1) *Query federation approaches over multiple SPARQL endpoints* make use of the SPARQL endpoints due to which they provide a time-efficient solution to SPARQL query federation. However, the RDF data needs to be exposed as SPARQL endpoints. Due to which they are unable to deal with whole LOD. (2) *Query federation over Linked Data* do not require the data to be exposed via SPARQL endpoints. The only requirement is that it should follow the Linked Data principles.[3] Due to URI lookups at runtime, these type of approaches are commonly slower than the previous type of approaches. (3) *Query federation approaches on top of Distributed Hash Tables* store the RDF data on top of Distributed Hash Tables (DHTs). This is a space-efficient solution and can reduce the network cost as well. However, an important fraction of the LOD datasets is not stored using DHTs.

The source selection approaches used in each of the categories can further divided into three sub-categories(see Table 1). (1)*Catalog/index-assisted source selection* only makes use of an index/data catalog (also called data summaries) to perform TPWSS. The result completeness (100% recall) must be ensured by keeping the index up-to-date. (2)*Catalog/index-free source selection* approaches do not make use of any pre-stored index and can thus always compute complete and up-to-date records. However, they commonly have a longer query execution time due to the extra processing required for collecting on-the-fly statistics (e.g. SPARQL ASK operations). (3) *Hybrid source selection* approaches are a combination of the previous approaches.

In this paper, we propose a novel hybrid source selection approach for SPARQL endpoint federation systems dubbed HiBISCuS. In contrast to the state of the art, HiBISCuS uses hypergraphs to detect sources that will not generate any relevant results

[2] Survey: `http://goo.gl/iXvKVT`, Results: `http://goo.gl/CNW5UC`

[3] `http://www.w3.org/DesignIssues/LinkedData.html`

Table 1. Classification of SPARQL federation engines. (**SEF** = SPARQL Endpoints Federation, **DHT** = DHT Federation, **LDF** = Linked Data Federation, **Ctg.** = Federation Type, **FdX** = FedX, **SPL** =SPLENDID, **ADE** = ADERIS, **I.F** = Index-free, **I.O** = Index-only, **HB** = Hybrid, **C.A.** = Code Availability, **S.S.T.** = Source Selection Type, **I.U.** = Index Update, **NA** = Not Applicable, **(A+I)** = SPARQL ASK and Index, **(C+L)** = Catalog and online discovery via Link-traversal, *only source selection approaches.).

	FedX [14]	LHD [15]	SPL [4]	DAW* [11]	ANAPSID [1]	ADE [8]	DARQ [10]	LDQP [7]	WoDQA [2]	Atlas [6]	QTree* [5]	HiBISCus*
Ctg.	SEF	SEF	SEF	-	SEF	SEF	SEF	LDF	LDF	DHT	-	-
C.A	✓	✓	✓	✗	✓	✓	✓	✗	✓	✓	✗	✓
S.S.T	I.F	HB(A+I)	HB(A+I)	HB(A+I)	HB(A+I)	I.O	I.O	HB(C+L)	HB(A+I)	I.O	I.O	HB(A+I)
Cache	✓	✗	✗	✓	✗	✗	✗	✗	✓	✗	✗	✓
I.U	NA	✗	✗	✗	✓	✗	✗	✗	✓	✗	✓	✓

both at triple-pattern level and at query level. By these means, HiBISCuS can generate better approximations of the sources that should be queried to return complete results for a given query.

3 Preliminaries

In the following, we present some of the concepts and notation that are used throughout this paper. RDF resources are identified by using a Unified Resource Identifier (URI). Each URI has a generic syntax consists of a hierarchical sequence of components namely the *scheme*, *authority*, *path*, *query*, and *fragment*[4]. For example, the prefix $ns1 = <http://auth1/scma/>$ used in Figure 1 consist of scheme $http$, authority $auth1$, and path $scma$. The details of the remaining two components are out of the scope of this paper. In the rest of the paper, we jointly refer to the first two components (path, authority) as *authority* of a URI.

The standard for querying RDF is SPARQL.[5] The result of a SPARQL query is called its *result set*. Each element of the result set of a query is a set of *variable bindings*. *Federated SPARQL queries* are defined as queries that are carried out over a set of sources D = $\{d_1, \ldots, d_n\}$. Given a SPARQL query q, a source $d \in D$ is said to *contribute* to q if at least one of the variable bindings belonging to an element of q's result set can be found in d.

Definition 1 (Relevant source Set). *A source $d \in D$ is* relevant *(also called* capable*) for a triple pattern $tp_i \in TP$ if at least one triple contained in d matches tp_i.*[6] *The relevant source set $R_i \subseteq D$ for tp_i is the set that contains all sources that are relevant for that particular triple pattern.*

For example, the set of relevant sources for the triple pattern $<?s, \texttt{cp:p1}, ?v1>$ of SSQ1 is $\{d_1, d_2\}$. It is possible that a relevant source for a triple pattern does not *con-*

[4] URI syntax: `http://tools.ietf.org/html/rfc3986`

[5] `http://www.w3.org/TR/rdf-sparql-query/`

[6] The concept of matching a triple pattern is defined formally in the SPARQL specification found at `http://www.w3.org/TR/rdf-sparql-query/`

tribute to the final result set of the complete query q. This is because the results computed from a particular source d for a triple pattern tp_i might excluded while performing *joins* with the results of other triple patterns contained in the query q. For example, consider SSQ1. The results from d_2 for <?s, cp:p1, ?v1> and d_3 for <?s, cp:p2, ?v1> are excluded after performing the *join* between the results of the two triple patterns.

Definition 2 (Optimal source Set). *The optimal source set $O_i \subseteq R_i$ for a triple pattern $tp_i \in TP$ contains the relevant sources $d \in R_i$ that actually contribute to computing the complete result set of the query.*

For example, the set of optimal sources for the triple pattern <?s, cp:p2, ?v2> of SSQ1 is $\{d_3\}$, while the set of relevant sources for the same triple pattern is $\{d_1, d_3\}$. Formally, the problem of TPWSS can then be defined as follows:

Definition 3 (Problem Statement). *Given a set D of sources and a query q, find the optimal set of sources $O_i \subseteq D$ for each triple pattern tp_i of q.*

Most of the source selection approaches [4,8,10,14,15] used in SPARQL endpoint federation systems only perform TPWSS, i.e., they find the set of relevant sources R_i for individual triple patterns of a query and do not consider computing the optimal source sets O_i. In this paper, we present an index-assisted approach for (1) the time-efficient computation of relevant source set R_i for individual triple patterns of the query and (2) the approximation of O_i out of R_i. HiBISCuS approximates O_i by determining and removing irrelevant sources from each of the R_i. We denote our approximation of O_i by RS_i. HiBISCuS relies on directed labelled hypergraphs (DLH) to achieve this goal. In the following, we present our formalization of SPARQL queries as DLH. Subsequently, we show how we make use of this formalization to approximate O_i for each tp_i.

4 HiBISCuS

In this section we present our approach to the source selection problem in details. We begin by presenting our approach to representing BGPs[7] of a SPARQL query as DLHs. Then, we present our approach to computing *lightweight data summaries*. Finally, we explain our approach to source selection.

4.1 Queries as Directed Labelled Hypergraphs

An important intuition behind our approach is that each of the BGP in a query can be executed separately. Thus, in the following, we will mainly focus on how the execution of a single BGP can be optimized. The representation of a query as DLH is the union of the representations of its BGPs. Note that the representations of BGPs are kept disjoint even if they contain the same nodes to ensure that the BGPs are processed independently. The DLH representation of a BGP is formally defined as follows:

Definition 4. *Each basic graph patterns BGP_i of a SPARQL query can be represented as a DLH $HG_i = (V, E, \lambda_e, \lambda_{vt})$, where*

[7] http://www.w3.org/TR/sparql11-query/#BasicGraphPatterns

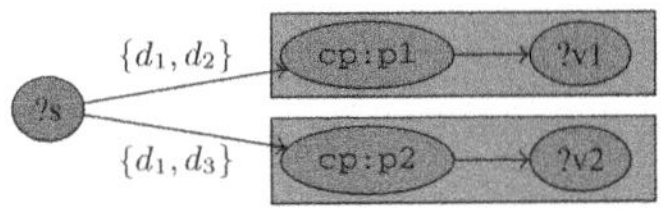

$V_s = \{?s\}, V_p = \{\texttt{cp:p1}, \texttt{cp:p2}\}, V_o = \{?v1, ?v2\},$
$V = V_s \cup V_p \cup V_o = \{?s, \texttt{cp:p1}, \texttt{cp:p2}, ?v1, ?v2\},$
$E = \{e_1, e_2\}, e_1 = (?s, \texttt{cp:p1}, ?v1), e2 = (?s, \texttt{cp:p2}, ?v2),$
$\lambda_e(e_1) = \{d_1, d_2\}, \lambda_e(e_2) = \{d_1, d_3\}.$

(a) SSQ1

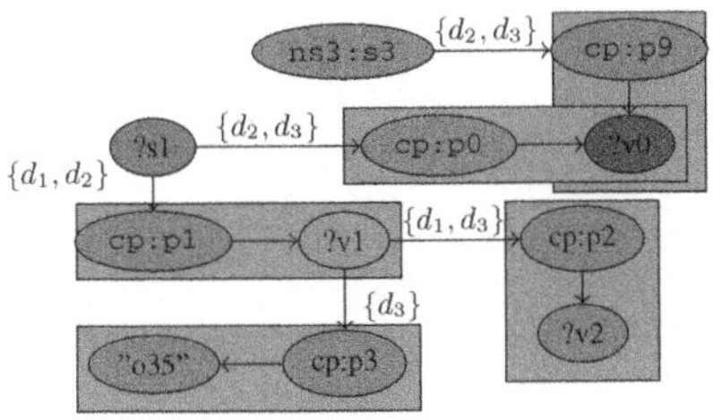

$V_s = \{\texttt{ns3:n3}, ?s1, ?v1\}, V_o = \{?v0, ?v1, ?v2, "o35"\}$
$V_p = \{\texttt{cp:p9}, \texttt{cp:po}, \texttt{cp:p1}, \texttt{cp:p2}, \texttt{cp:p3}\}$
$V = V_s \cup V_p \cup V_o\} = \{\texttt{ns3:n3}, ?s1, ?v1, \texttt{cp:p9}, \texttt{cp:po}, \texttt{cp:p1}, \texttt{cp:p2}, \texttt{cp:p3}, ?v0, v2, "o35"\}$
$E = \{e_1, e_2, e_3, e_4, e_5\}$
$e_1 = (\texttt{ns3:s3}, \texttt{cp:p9}, ?v0), e_2 = (?s1, \texttt{cp:p0}, ?v0),$
$e_3 = (?s1, \texttt{cp:p1}, ?v1), e_4 = (?v1, \texttt{cp:p2}, ?v2)$
$e_5 = (?v1, \texttt{cp:p3}, "o35"), \lambda_e(e_1) = \{d_2, d_3\}, \lambda_e(e_2) =$
$\{d_2, d_3\}, \lambda_e(e_3) = \{d_1, d_2\}, \lambda_e(e_4) = \{d_1, d_3\}, \lambda_e(e_5) = \{d_3\}$

(b) HSQ3

Fig. 2. Labelled hypergraph of query SSQ1 and query HSQ3 of Figure 1

1. $V = V_s \cup V_p \cup V_o$ *is the set of vertices of* HG_i, V_s *is the set of all subjects in* HG_i, V_p *the set of all predicates in* HG_i *and* V_o *the set of all objects in* HG_i*;*
2. $E = \{e_1, \ldots, e_t\} \subseteq V^3$ *is a set of directed hyperedges (short: edge). Each edge* $e = (v_s, v_p, v_o)$ *emanates from the triple pattern* $<v_s, v_p, v_o>$ *in* BGP_i*. We represent these edges by connecting the head vertex* v_s *with the tail hypervertex* (v_p, v_o)*. In addition, we use* $E_{in}(v) \subseteq E$ *and* $E_{out}(v) \subseteq E$ *to denote the set of incoming and outgoing edges of a vertex* v*;*
3. $\lambda_e : E \mapsto 2^D$ *is a hyperedge-labelling function. Given a hyperedge* $e \in E$*, its edge label is a set of sources* $R_i \subseteq D$*. We use this label to the sources that should be queried to retrieve the answer set for the triple pattern represented by the hyperedge* e*;*
4. λ_{vt} *is a vertex-type-assignment function. Given an vertex* $v \in V$*, its vertex type can be 'star', 'path', 'hybrid', or 'sink' if this vertex participates in at least one join. A 'star' vertex has more than one outgoing edge and no incoming edge. 'path' vertex has exactly one incoming and one outgoing edge. A 'hybrid' vertex has either more than one incoming and at least one outgoing edge or more than one outgoing and at least one incoming edge. A 'sink' vertex has more than one incoming edge and no outgoing edge. A vertex that does not participate in any join is of type 'simple'.*

Figure 2a shows the hypergraph of SSQ1 and Figure 2b represents the hypergraph of HSQ3 of motivating example given in Figure 1. We can now reformulate our problem statement as follows:

Definition 5 (Problem Reformulation). *Given a query* q *represented as a set of hypergraphs* $\{HG_1, \ldots, HG_x\}$*, find the labelling of the hyperedges of each hypergraph* HG_i *that leads to an optimal source selection.*

Listing 1.1. HiBISCuS example. Prefixes are ignored for simplicity

```
[] a ds:Service ;
  ds:endpointUrl <http://dbpedia.org/sparql> ;
 ds:capability
   [ ds:predicate  dbpedia:kingdom ;
     ds:sbjAuthority  <http://dbpedia.org/> ;
     ds:objAuthority  <http://dbpedia.org/> ;
     ] ;
 ds:capability
   [ ds:predicate  rdf:type ;
     ds:sbjAuthority  <http://dbpedia.org/> ;
     ds:objAuthority  owl:Thing, dbpedia:Station; #we store all distinct classes
     ] ;
 ds:capability
   [ds:predicate  dbpedia:postalCode ;
    ds:sbjAuthority  <http://dbpedia.org/> ;
    #No objAuthority as the object value for dbpedia:postalCode is string
    ] ;
```

4.2 Data Summaries

HiBISCuS relies on *capabilities* to compute data summaries. Given a source d, we define a capability as a triple $(p, SA(d,p), OA(d,p))$ which contains (1) a predicate p in d, (2) the set $SA(d,p)$ of all distinct *subject authorities* (ref. section 3) of p in d and (3) the set $OA(d,p)$ of all distinct *object authorities* of p in d. In HiBISCuS, a *data summary* for a source $d \in D$ is the set $CA(d)$ of all *capabilities* of that source. Consequently, the total number of capabilities of a source is equal to the number of distinct predicates in it.

The predicate `rdf:type` is given a special treatment: Instead of storing the set of all distinct object authorities for a capability having this predicate, we store the *set of all distinct class URIs* in d, i.e., the set of all resources that match $?x$ in the query $?y$ `rdf:type` $?x$. The reason behind this choice is that the set of distinct *classes* used in a source d is usually a small fraction of the set of all resources in d. Moreover, triple patterns with predicate `rdf:type` are commonly used in SPARQL queries. Thus, by storing the complete class URI instead of the object authorities, we might perform more accurate source selection. Listing 1.1 shows an example of a data summary. In the next section, we will make use of these data summaries to optimize the *TPWSS*.

4.3 Source Selection Algorithm

Our source selection comprise two steps: given a query q, we first *label all hyperedges* in each of the hypergraphs which results from the BGPs of q, i.e., we compute $\lambda_e(e_i)$ for each $e_i \in E_i$ in all $HG_i \in DHG$. We present two variations of this step and compare them in the evaluation section. In a second step, we *prune the labels of the hyperedges* assigned in the first step and compute $RS_i \subseteq R_i$ for each e_i. The pseudo-code of our approaches is shown in Algorithms 1, 2 (labelling) as well as 3 (pruning).

Labelling Approaches. We devised two versions of our approach to the hyperedge labelling problem, i.e., an ASK-dominant and an index-dominant version. Both take the set of all sources D, the set of all disjunctive hypergraphs DHG of the input query q and the data summaries $HiBISCuS_D$ of all sources in D as input (see Algorithms 1,2).

Algorithm 1. ASK-dominant hybrid algorithm for labelling all hyperedges of each disjunctive hypergraph of a SPARQL query

---

```
Require: D= {d_1, ..., d_n}; DHG = {HG_1, ..., HG_x}; HiBISCuS_D //sources, disjunctive
    hypergraphs of a query, HiBISCuSmaries of sources
 1: for each HG_i ∈ DHG do
 2:    E = hyperedges (HG_i)
 3:    for each e_i ∈ E do
 4:       s = subjvertex(e_i); p = predvertex(e_i); o = objvertex(e_i);
 5:       sa = subjauth(s); oa = objauth(o); //can be null i.e. for unbound s, o
 6:       if !bound(s) ∧ !bound(p) ∧ !bound(o) then
 7:          λ_e(e_i) = D
 8:       else if bound(p) then
 9:          if p = rdf : type ∧ bound(o) then
10:             λ_e(e_i) = HiBISCuS_Dlookup(p, o)
11:          else if !commonpredicate(p) ∨ (!bound(s) ∧ !bound(o)) then
12:             λ_e(e_i) = HiBISCuS_Dlookup(sa, p, oa)
13:          else
14:             if cachehit(s, p, o) then
15:                λ_e(e_i) = cachelookup(s, p, o)
16:             else
17:                λ_e(e_i) = ASK(s, p, o, D)
18:             end if
19:          end if
20:       else
21:          Repeat Lines 14-18
22:       end if
23:    end for
24: end for
25: return DHG //Set of labelled disjunctive hypergraphs
```

They return a set of *labelled* disjunctive hypergraphs as output. For each hypergraph and each hyperedge, the subject, predicate, object, subject authority, and object authority are collected (Lines 2-5 of Algorithms 1,2). Edges with unbound subject, predicate, and object vertices (e.g e = (?s, ?p, ?o)) are labelled with the set of all possible sources D (Lines 6-7 of Algorithms 1,2). A data summary lookup is performed for edges with the predicate vertex `rdf:type` that have a bound object vertex. All sources with matching capabilities are selected as label of the hyperedge (Lines 9-10 of Algorithms 1,2).

The *ASK-dominant version* of our approach (see Algorithm 1, Line 11) makes use of the notion of *common predicates*. A common predicate is a predicate that is used in a number of sources above a specific threshold value θ specified by the user. A predicate is then considered a common predicate if it occurs in at least $\theta|D|$ sources. We make use of the ASK queries for triple patterns with common predicates. Here, an ASK query is sent to all of the available sources to check whether they contain the common predicate *cp*. Those sources which return `true` are selected as elements of the set of sources used to label that triple pattern. The results of the ASK operations are stored in a cache. Therefore, every time we perform a cache lookup before SPARQL ASK operations (Lines 14-18). In contrast, in the *index-dominant* version of our algorithm, an index lookup is performed if any of the subject or predicate is bound in a triple pattern.We will see later that the index-dominant approach requires less ASK queries than the ASK-dominant algorithm. However, this can lead to an overestimation of the set of relevant sources (see section 5.2).

Algorithm 2. Index-dominant hybrid algorithm for labelling all hyperedges of each disjunctive hypergraph of a SPARQL query

```
Require: D= {d1,...,dn}; DHG = {HG1,...,HGx}; HiBISCuS_D //sources, disjunctive
    hypergraphs of a query, HiBISCuSmaries of sources
for each HGi ∈ DHG do
    E = hyperedges (HGi)
    for each ei ∈ E do
        s = subjvertex(ei); p = predvertex(ei); o = objvertex(ei);
        sa = subjauth(s); oa = objauth(o); //can be null i.e. for unbound s, o
        if !bound(s) ∧ !bound(p) ∧ !bound(o) then
            λe(ei) = D
        else if bound(s) ∨ bound(p) then
            if bound(p) ∧ p = rdf : type ∧ bound(o) then
                λe(ei) = HiBISCuS_D lookup(p, o)
            else
                λe(ei) = HiBISCuS_D lookup(sa, p, oa)
            end if
        else
            if cachehit(s, p, o) then
                λe(ei) = cachelookup(s, p, o)
            else
                λe(ei) = ASK(s, p, o, D)
            end if
        end if
    end for
end for
return DHG //Set of labelled disjunctive hypergraphs
```

4.4 Pruning Approach

The intuition behind our pruning approach is that knowing which authorities are relevant to answer a query can be used to discard triple pattern-wise (TPW) selected sources that will not contribute to the final result set of the query. Our source pruning algorithm (ref. Algorithm 3) takes the set of all labelled disjunctive hypergraphs as input and prune labels of all hyperedges which either incoming or outgoing edges of a 'star','hybrid', 'path', or 'sink' node. Note that our approach deals with each BGP of the query separately (Line 1 of Algorithm 3).

For each node v of a DLH that is not of type 'simple', we first retrieve the sets (1) $SAuth$ of the subject authorities contained in the elements of the label of each outgoing edge of v (Lines 5-7 of Algorithm 3) and (2) $OAuth$ of the object authorities contained in the elements of the label of each ingoing edge of v (Lines 8-10 of Algorithm 3). Note that these are sets of sets of authorities. For the node $?v1$ of HSQ3 in our running example (see Figure 3), we get $SAuth = \{\texttt{auth13, auth2}\}$ for the ingoing edge and $OAuth = \{\{\texttt{auth13, auth2}\}, \{\texttt{auth2}\}\}$ for the outgoing edges. Now we merge these two sets to the set A of all authorities. For node $?v1$ in HSQ3, $A = \{\{\texttt{auth13, auth2}\}, \{\texttt{auth13, auth2}\}, \{\texttt{auth2}\}\}$. The intersection $I = \left(\bigcap_{a_i \in A} a_i \right)$ of these elements sets is then computed. In our example, this results in $I = \{\texttt{auth2}\}$. Finally, we recompute the label of each hyperedge e that is connected to v. To this end, we compute the subset of the previous label

Algorithm 3. Hyperedge label pruning algorithm for removing irrelevant sources

Require: DHG //disjunctive hypergraphs
1: **for** each $HG_i \in DHG$ **do**
2:     **for** each v $\in$ vertices(HG_i) **do**
3:         **if** $\lambda_{vt}(v) \neq$ 'simple' **then**
4:             $SAuth = \emptyset$; $OAuth = \emptyset$;
5:             **for** each $e \in E_{out}(v)$ **do**
6:                 $SAuth = SAuth \cup \{$subjectauthories(e)$\}$
7:             **end for**
8:             **for** each $e \in E_{in}(v)$ **do**
9:                 $OAuth = OAuth \cup \{$objectauthories(e)$\}$
10:             **end for**
11:             $A = SAuth \cup OAuth$ // set of all authorities
12:             I = A.get(1) //get first element of authorities
13:             **for** each $a \in A$ **do**
14:                 $I = I \cap a$ //intersection of all elements of A
15:             **end for**
16:             **for** each $e \in E_{in}(v) \cup E_{out}(v)$ **do**
17:                 $label = \emptyset$ //variable for final label of e
18:                 **for** $d_i \in \lambda_e(e)$ **do**
19:                     **if** authorities(d_i) $\cap I \neq \emptyset$ **then**
20:                         $label = label \cup d_i$
21:                     **end if**
22:                 **end for**
23:                 $\lambda_e(e) = label$
24:             **end for**
25:         **end if**
26:     **end for**
27: **end for**

of e which is such that the set of authorities of each of its elements is not disjoint with I (see Lines 16-23 of Algorithm 3). These are the only sources that will really contribute to the final result set of the query.

We are sure not to lose any recall by this operation because joins act in a conjunctive manner. Consequently, if the results of a data source d_i used to label a hyperedge cannot be joined to the results of at least one source of each of the other hyperedges, it is guaranteed that d_i will not contribute to the final result set of the query. In our example, this leads to d_1 being discarded from the label of the ingoing edge, while d_3 is discarded from the label of one outgoing hyperedge of node $?v1$ as shown in Figure 3. This step concludes our source selection.

5 Evaluation

In this section we describe the experimental evaluation of our approach. We first describe our experimental setup in detail. Then, we present our evaluation results. All data used in this evaluation is either publicly available or can be found at the project web page.[8]

[8] `https://code.google.com/p/hibiscusfederation/`

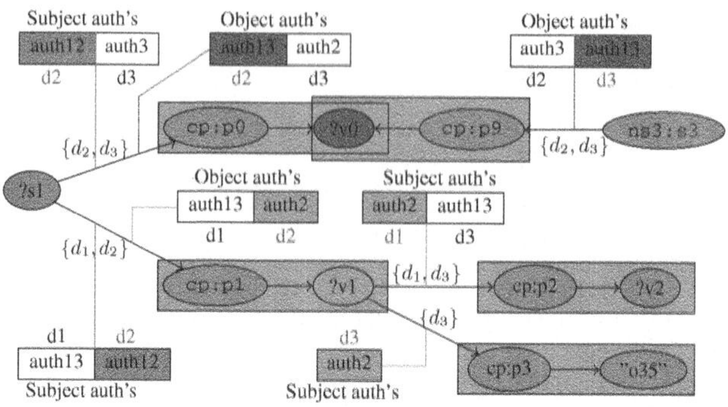

Fig. 3. Source pruning of Labeled hypergraph HSQ3 of Figure 1. All the sources highlighted in red are finally selected.

5.1 Experimental Setup

Benchmarking Environment: We used FedBench [13] for our evaluation. It is the only (to the best of our knowledge) benchmark that encompasses real-world datasets and commonly used queries within a distributed data environment. Furthermore, it is commonly used in the evaluation of SPARQL query federation systems [14,4,9,11]. Each of FedBench's nine datasets was loaded into a separate physical virtuoso server. The exact specifications of the servers can be found on the project website. All experiments were ran on a machine with a 2.70GHz i5 processor, 8 GB RAM and 300 GB hard disk. The experiments were carried out in a local network, so the network costs were negligible. Each query was executed 10 times and results were averaged. The query timeout was set to 30min (1800s). The threshold for the ASK-dominant approach was best selected to 0.33 after analysing results of different threshold values.

Federated Query Engines: We extended three SPARQL endpoint federation engines with HiBISCuS: DARQ [10] (index-only), FedX [14] (index-free), and SPLENDID [4] (hybrid). In each of the extensions, we only replaced the source selection with HiBISCuS. The query execution mechanisms remained unchanged. We compared our best extension (i.e., SPLENDID+HiBISCuS) with ANAPSID as this engine showed competitive results w.r.t. its index compression and number of TPW sources selected.

Metrics: We compared the three engines against their HiBISCuS extension. For each query we measured (1) the total number of TPW sources selected, (2) the total number of SPARQL ASK requests submitted during the source selection, (3) the average source selection time and (4) the average query execution time. We also compare the source index/data summaries generation time and index compression ratio of various state-of-the art source selection approaches.

5.2 Experimental Results

Index Construction Time and Compression Ratio. Table 2 shows a comparison of the index/data summaries construction time and the compression ratio[9] of various state-

[9] The compression ratio is given by (1 - index size/total data dump size).

Table 2. Comparison of index construction time and compression ratio. QTree's compression ratio is taken from [5]. (NA = Not Applicable).

	FedX	SPLENDID	LHD	DARQ	ANAPSID	Qtree	HiBISCuS
Index Generation Time (min)	NA	75	75	102	6	-	36
Compression Ratio (%)	NA	99.998	99.998	99.997	99.999	96	99.997

of-the art approaches. A high compression ratio is essential for fast index lookup during source selection. HiBISCuS has an index size of 458KB for the complete FedBench data dump (19.7 GB), leading to a high compression ratio of 99.99%. The other approaches achieve similar compression ratios. HiBISCuS's index construction time is second only to ANAPSID's. This is due to ANAPSID storing only the distinct predicates in its index. Our results yet suggest that our index containing more information is beneficial to the query execution time on FedBench.

Efficient Source Selection. We define efficient source selection in terms of: (1) the total number of TPW sources selected, (2) total number of SPARQL ASK requests used to obtain (1), and (3) the TPW source selection time. Table 3 shows a comparison of the source selection approaches of FedX, SPLENDID, ANAPSID and HiBISCuS based on these three metrics. Note that FedX (100% cached) means that we gave FedX enough memory to use only its cache to perform the complete source selection. This is the best-case scenario for FedX. Overall, HiBISCuS (ASK-dominant) is the most efficient approach in terms of total TPW sources selected, HiBISCuS (Index-dominant) is the most efficient *hybrid* approach in terms of total number of ASK request used, and FedX (100% cached) is most efficient in terms of source selection time. However, FedX (100% cached) clearly overestimates the set of sources that actually contributes to the final result set of query. In the next section, we will see that this overestimation of sources greatly leads to a slightly higher overall query runtime. For ANAPSID, the results are based on Star-Shaped Group Multiple endpoint selection (SSGM) heuristics presented in its extension [9]. Further, the source selection time represents the query decomposition time as both of these steps are intermingled.

Query Execution Time. The most important criterion when optimizing federated query execution engines is the query execution time. Figures 4, 5, and 6 show the results of our query execution time experiments. Our main results can be summarized as follows:

(1) Overall, *the ASK-dominant (AD) version of our approach performs best.* AD is on average (over all 25 queries and 3 extensions) 27.82% faster than the index-dominant (ID) version. The reason for this improvement is due to ID overestimating sources in some queries. For example, in CD1, AD selects the optimal number of sources (i.e., 4) while ID selects 12 sources. In some cases, the overestimation of sources by ID also slows down the source pruning (e.g. CD2),

(2) A comparison of our extensions with AD shows that *all extensions are more time-efficient than the original systems.* In particular, FedX's (100% cached) runtime is

Table 3. Comparison of the source selection in terms of total TPW sources selected **#T**, total number of SPARQL ASK requests **#A**, and source selection time **ST** in msec. **ST*** represents the source selection time for FedX(100% cached i.e. #A =0 for all queries) which is very rare in practical. **ST**** represents the source selection time for HiBISCuS (AD,warm) with #A =0 for all queries. (**AD** = ASK-dominant, **ID** = index-dominant, **ZR** = Zero results, **NS** = Not supported, **T/A** = Total/Avg., where Total is for #T, #A, and Avg. is ST, ST*, and ST**).

	FedX				SPLENDID			DARQ			ANAPSID			HiBISCuS(AD)				HiBISCuS(ID)		
Qry	#T	#A	ST	ST*	#T	#A	ST	#T	#A	ST	#T	#A	ST	#T	#A	ST	ST**	#T	#A	ST
CD1	11	27	285	6	11	27	392	NS	NS	NS	3	20	667	4	18	215	36	12	0	363
CD2	3	27	200	6	3	18	294	10	0	6	3	1	42	3	9	4	3	3	0	57
CD3	12	45	367	8	12	18	304	20	0	12	5	2	73	5	0	77	41	5	0	91
CD4	19	45	359	8	19	9	310	20	0	12	5	3	128	5	0	54	52	5	0	179
CD5	11	36	374	7	11	9	313	11	0	4	4	1	66	4	0	25	23	4	0	58
CD6	9	36	316	8	9	9	298	10	0	11	10	11	140	8	0	36	23	8	0	54
CD7	13	36	324	9	13	9	335	13	0	6	6	5	ZR	6	0	30	35	6	0	55
LS1	1	18	248	9	1	0	217	1	0	4	1	0	35	1	0	5	6	1	0	9
LS2	11	27	264	8	11	27	390	NS	NS	NS	12	30	548	7	18	118	60	7	0	118
LS3	12	45	413	8	12	9	310	20	0	9	5	13	808	5	0	31	27	5	0	200
LS4	7	63	445	7	7	18	287	15	0	15	7	1	314	7	0	8	9	7	0	15
LS5	10	54	440	8	10	9	308	18	0	13	7	4	885	8	0	20	21	8	0	44
LS6	9	45	430	8	9	18	347	17	0	7	5	13	559	7	0	23	22	7	0	42
LS7	6	45	389	8	6	9	292	6	0	5	7	2	193	6	0	18	17	6	0	24
LD1	8	27	297	8	8	9	295	11	0	7	3	1	428	3	0	24	19	3	0	21
LD2	3	27	320	7	3	9	268	3	0	9	3	0	34	3	0	3	5	3	0	6
LD3	16	36	330	9	16	9	324	16	0	11	4	2	130	4	0	31	29	4	0	48
LD4	5	45	326	7	5	18	290	5	0	17	5	0	33	5	0	6	7	5	0	10
LD5	5	27	280	8	5	18	236	13	0	4	3	2	210	3	0	9	9	3	0	19
LD6	14	45	385	8	14	9	331	14	0	8	14	12	589	7	0	32	30	7	0	136
LD7	3	18	258	7	3	9	235	4	0	4	2	4	223	4	0	7	7	4	0	11
LD8	15	45	337	8	15	9	333	15	0	7	9	7	1226	5	0	23	25	5	0	41
LD9	3	27	228	12	3	18	188	6	0	3	3	3	1052	3	9	50	3	3	0	17
LD10	10	27	274	8	10	9	309	11	0	6	3	4	2010	3	0	19	18	3	0	27
LD11	15	45	351	7	15	9	260	15	0	9	5	2	2904	7	0	23	24	7	0	42
T/A	**231**	**918**	**330**	**8**	**231**	**315**	**299**	**274**	**0**	**8**	**134**	**143**	**554**	**123**	**54**	**36**	**22**	**131**	**0**	**67**

improved in 20/25 queries (net query runtime improvement of 24.61%), FedX's (cold) is improved in 25/25 queries (net improvement: 53.05%), SPLENDID 's is improved in 25/25 queries (net improvement: 82.72%) and DARQ's is improved in 23/23 (2 queries are not supported) queries (net improvement: 92.22%). Note that these values were computed only on those queries that did not time-out. Thus, the net improvement brought about by AD is actually even better than the reported values. The reason for our slight (less than 5 msec) greater runtime for 5/25 queries in FedX (100% cached) is due to FedX (100% cached) already selecting the optimal sources for these queries. Thus, the overhead due to our pruning of the already optimal list of sources affects the overall query runtime.

(3) *Our extensions allow some queries that timed out to be carried out before the time-out.* This is especially the case for our DARQ extension, where LD6 and LD10 are

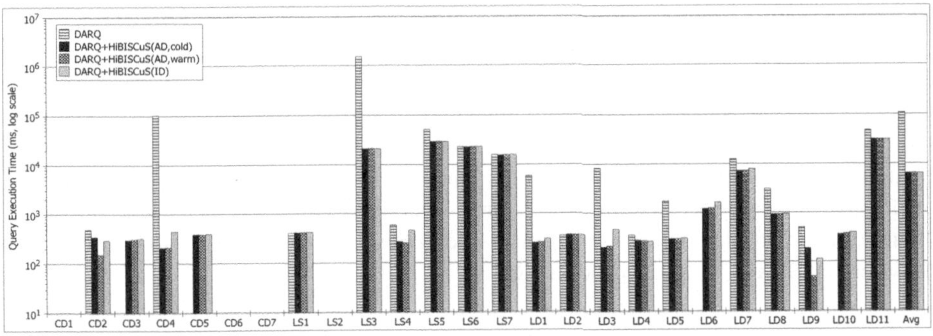

Fig. 4. Query runtime of DARQ and its HiBISCuS extensions. CD1, LS2 not supported, CD6 runtime error, CD7 time out for both. LD6, LD10 timeout and CD3 runtime error for DARQ.

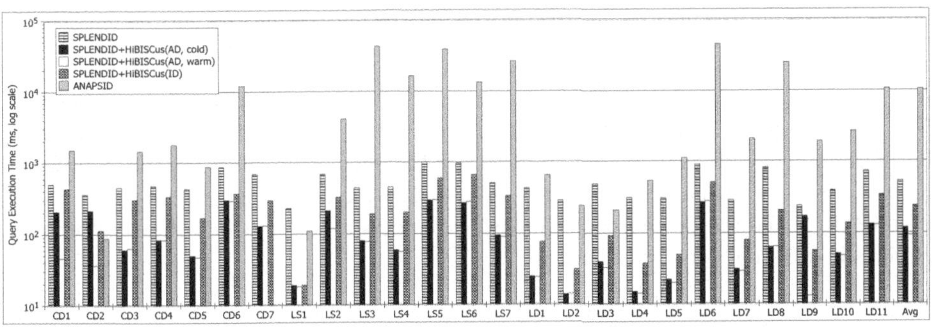

Fig. 5. Query runtime of ANAPSID, SPLENDID and its HiBISCuS extensions. We have zero results for ANAPSID CD7.

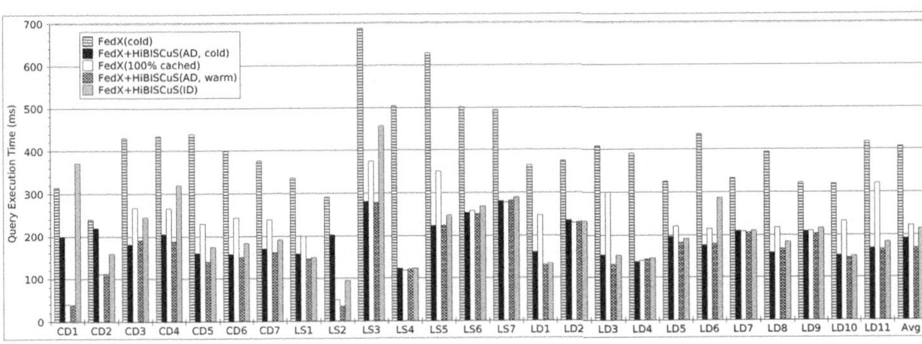

Fig. 6. Query runtime of FedX and its HiBISCuS extensions

carried out in 1123 msec and 377 msec respectively by DARD+AD, while they did not terminate within the time-out limit of 30 minutes on the original system.

(4) Our SPLENDID (AD) extension is 98.91% faster than ANAPSID on 24 of the 25 queries. For CD7, ANAPSID returned zero results.

An interesting observation is that FedX(100%) is better than SPLENDID in 25/25 queries and 58.17% faster on average query runtime. However, our AD extension of SPLENDID is better than AD extension of FedX(100%) in 20/25 queries and 45.20% faster on average query runtime. This means that SPLENDID is better than FedX in term of pure query execution time (excluding source selection time). A deeper investigation of the runtimes of both systems shows that SPLENDID spends on average 56.10% of total query execution on source selection. Thus, our extension showcase clearly that an efficient source selection is one of key factors in the overall optimization of federated SPARQL query processing.

6 Conclusion and Future Work

In this paper we presented HiBISCus, a labelled hypergraph based approach for efficient source selection for SPARQL endpoint federation. We evaluated our approach against DARQ, SPLENDID, FedX and ANAPSID. The evaluation shows that the query runtime of the first three systems is improved significantly on average.

In future, we will investigate the impact of the threshold θ on our approach. We will also study the effect of our source pruning algorithm on SPARQL 1.1 queries with SPARQL *service clause*, where the TPW sources are already specified by the user. Furthermore, we will evaluate our approach on big data as the query execution time for majority of the FedBench queries is less than 1s, which make it difficult to select the best SPARQL federation engine and have have a deeper look into the behaviour of these engines in different data environments.

Acknowledgments. This work was partially financed by the FP7 project GeoKnow (GA no. 318159).

References

1. Acosta, M., Vidal, M.-E., Lampo, T., Castillo, J., Ruckhaus, E.: ANAPSID: An adaptive query processing engine for SPARQL endpoints. In: Aroyo, L., Welty, C., Alani, H., Taylor, J., Bernstein, A., Kagal, L., Noy, N., Blomqvist, E. (eds.) ISWC 2011, Part I. LNCS, vol. 7031, pp. 18–34. Springer, Heidelberg (2011)
2. Akar, Z., Halaç, T.G., Ekinci, E.E., Dikenelli, O.: Querying the web of interlinked datasets using void descriptions. In: LDOW at WWW (2012)
3. Auer, S., Lehmann, J., Ngonga Ngomo, A.-C.: Introduction to linked data and its lifecycle on the web. In: Polleres, A., d'Amato, C., Arenas, M., Handschuh, S., Kroner, P., Ossowski, S., Patel-Schneider, P. (eds.) Reasoning Web 2011. LNCS, vol. 6848, pp. 1–75. Springer, Heidelberg (2011)
4. Görlitz, O., Staab, S.: Splendid: Sparql endpoint federation exploiting void descriptions. In: COLD at ISWC (2011)
5. Harth, A., Hose, K., Karnstedt, M., Polleres, A., Sattler, K.-U., Umbrich, J.: Data summaries for on-demand queries over linked data. In: WWW (2010)
6. Kaoudi, Z., Koubarakis, M., Kyzirakos, K.: Atlas: Storing, updating and querying rdf(s) data on top of dhts. JWS 8(4) (2010)

7. Ladwig, G., Tran, T.: Linked data query processing strategies. In: Patel-Schneider, P.F., Pan, Y., Hitzler, P., Mika, P., Zhang, L., Pan, J.Z., Horrocks, I., Glimm, B. (eds.) ISWC 2010, Part I. LNCS, vol. 6496, pp. 453–469. Springer, Heidelberg (2010)
8. Lynden, S., Kojima, I., Matono, A., Tanimura, Y.: ADERIS: An adaptive query processor for joining federated SPARQL endpoints. In: Meersman, R., et al. (eds.) OTM 2011, Part II. LNCS, vol. 7045, pp. 808–817. Springer, Heidelberg (2011)
9. Montoya, G., Vidal, M.-E., Acosta, M.: A heuristic-based approach for planning federated sparql queries. In: COLD (2012)
10. Quilitz, B., Leser, U.: Querying distributed RDF data sources with SPARQL. In: Bechhofer, S., Hauswirth, M., Hoffmann, J., Koubarakis, M. (eds.) ESWC 2008. LNCS, vol. 5021, pp. 524–538. Springer, Heidelberg (2008)
11. Saleem, M., Ngonga Ngomo, A.-C., Xavier Parreira, J., Deus, H.F., Hauswirth, M.: DAW: Duplicate-aWare federated query processing over the web of data. In: Alani, H., et al. (eds.) ISWC 2013, Part I. LNCS, vol. 8218, pp. 574–590. Springer, Heidelberg (2013)
12. Saleem, M., Shanmukha, S., Ngonga, A.-C., Almeida, J.S., Decker, S., Deus, H.F.: Linked cancer genome atlas database. In: I-Semantics (2013)
13. Schmidt, M., Görlitz, O., Haase, P., Ladwig, G., Schwarte, A., Tran, T.: FedBench: A benchmark suite for federated semantic data query processing. In: Aroyo, L., Welty, C., Alani, H., Taylor, J., Bernstein, A., Kagal, L., Noy, N., Blomqvist, E. (eds.) ISWC 2011, Part I. LNCS, vol. 7031, pp. 585–600. Springer, Heidelberg (2011)
14. Schwarte, A., Haase, P., Hose, K., Schenkel, R., Schmidt, M.: FedX: Optimization techniques for federated query processing on linked data. In: Aroyo, L., Welty, C., Alani, H., Taylor, J., Bernstein, A., Kagal, L., Noy, N., Blomqvist, E. (eds.) ISWC 2011, Part I. LNCS, vol. 7031, pp. 601–616. Springer, Heidelberg (2011)
15. Wang, X., Tiropanis, T., Davis, H.C.: Lhd: Optimising linked data query processing using parallelisation. In: LDOW at WWW (2013)

Generating Synthetic RDF Data with Connected Blank Nodes for Benchmarking

Christina Lantzaki, Thanos Yannakis, Yannis Tzitzikas, and Anastasia Analyti

Computer Science Department, University of Crete,
Institute of Computer Science, FORTH-ICS, Greece
{kristi,yannakis,tzitzik,analyti}@ics.forth.gr

Abstract. Generators for synthetic RDF datasets are very important for testing and benchmarking various semantic data management tasks (e.g. querying, storage, update, compare, integrate). However, the current generators do not support sufficiently (or totally ignore) blank node connectivity issues. Blank nodes are used for various purposes (e.g. for describing complex attributes), and a significant percentage of resources is currently represented with blank nodes. Moreover, several semantic data management tasks, like isomorphism checking (useful for checking equivalence), and blank node matching (useful in comparison, versioning, synchronization, and in semantic similarity functions), not only have to deal with blank nodes, but their complexity and optimality depends on the connectivity of blank nodes. To enable the comparative evaluation of the various techniques for carrying out these tasks, in this paper we present the design and implementation of a generator, called BGen, which allows building datasets containing blank nodes with the desired complexity, controllable through various features (morphology, size, diameter, density and clustering coefficient). Finally, the paper reports experimental results concerning the efficiency of the generator, as well as results from using the generated datasets, that demonstrate the value of the generator.

Keywords: #eswc2014Lantzaki.

1 Introduction

Several works (e.g. [10]) have demonstrated the usefulness of blank nodes for the representation of the Semantic Web data. In a nutshell, from a theoretical perspective blank nodes play the role of the existential variables and from a technical perspective, as gathered in [2], they give the capability to (a) describe multi-component structures, like the RDF containers, (b) apply reification (i.e. provenance information), (c) represent complex attributes without having to name explicitly the auxiliary node (e.g. the address of a person consisting of the street, the number, the postal code and the city) and (d) offer protection of the inner information (e.g. protecting the sensitive information of the customers from the browsers). In [10] the authors survey the treatment of blank nodes in RDF data and prove the relatively high percentages of their usage. Indicatively,

V. Presutti et al. (Eds.): ESWC 2014, LNCS 8465, pp. 192–207, 2014.

and according to their results, the data fetched from the 'rdfabout.com' domain and the 'opencalais.com' domain, both of them parts of the LOD (Linked Open Data) cloud, consist of 41.7% and 44.9% of blank nodes, respectively.

However, their existence requires special treatment in various tasks. For instance, [10] states that the inability to match blank nodes increases the delta size (the number of triples that need to be deleted and added in order to transform one graph to another) and does not assist in detecting the changes between subsequent versions of a Knowledge Base, while [15] proves that building a mapping between the blank nodes of two compared Knowledge Bases that minimizes the delta size is NP-Hard in the general case. In [6] it is proved that (a) deciding simple or RDF/S entailment of RDF graphs is NP-Complete, and (b) deciding equivalence of simple RDF graphs is Isomorphism-Complete. In [8], a tutorial on how to publish Linked Data, the authors state that it becomes much more difficult to merge data from different sources when blank nodes are used, as there is no URI to serve as a common key. However we should note that the above tasks become tractable for the cases of non-directly connected blank nodes. Still, more complex blank node structures (i.e. cyclic) occur in practice. Indicatively, in [10] 1.6% of the structures are cyclic, while when querying the LOD Cloud Cache endpoint[1] we found out that it contains around 19 millions of blank nodes and almost 30 thousands of them participate in cyclic blank node structures.

In the face of strong identification needs, skolemization[2] is suggested, that replaces (some or all of) the anonymous resources with globally unique URIs. However, we will never "escape" from blank nodes. Even if we assign to all blank nodes URIs, we are obliged to treat them as *unnamed elements* when comparing or integrating data. For example, suppose that we want to integrate personal data from two or more sources where URIs are used for addresses (an address groups a street, a number, a city, etc). If we do not treat addresses as blank nodes, then we will treat all addresses as different, and thus we will end up with very poor information integration. We should also note that blank nodes is not an idiosyncratic feature of RDF. They occur everywhere; consider for instance the world of relational databases, and suppose that the same information is stored in two different relational databases, each supporting two different policies for *autokeys*. If we compare these databases then we would like to conclude that they are identical, but without treating the autokeys as blank nodes this is obviously impossible.

As regards the tasks in which blank nodes require special treatment, studies are oriented towards either finding special cases where the problems become tractable, or constructing algorithms that approximate the optimal solutions. Indicatively, [15] elaborates on a special case (i.e. RDF graphs with no directly connected blank nodes) where the problem of finding the optimal blank nodes mapping is solved in polynomial time, and provides two polynomial algorithms that approximate this mapping and can be used in the general case. One of them can map 150 thousands of bnodes in around 10 seconds. Another notable instance

[1] `http://lod.openlinksw.com/sparql/`

[2] `http://www.w3.org/TR/rdf11-concepts/#section-skolemization`

is [14], where the authors introduce the concept of bounded treewidth to prove that entailment checking can be efficient for RDF blank node structures that have bounded treewidth. Other works avoid matching blank nodes and instead make some quite simplistic assumptions (e.g. [9] for studying the dynamics of Linked Data).

In any of the above cases, an integrated benchmark would be really useful in order to create a common way to evaluate and compare these (and forthcoming) works. To fill this gap, in this paper we present the design and implementation of a generator, called BGen, which allows building big datasets containing blank nodes satisfying particular connectivity requirements. BGen is not the first RDF generator; there are several examples of RDF generators (described in Section 2). However, none of them deals sufficiently with the issue of benchmarking methods that become hard in the presence of blank nodes. The main objective of this generator is to create datasets with blank nodes of variable complexity. Key element for controlling the complexity of blank nodes is the notion of *BComponent* which is essentially a maximal sub-graph of blank nodes that is part of the whole graph. Having isolated this component we can control its complexity, through features like the size, the diameter, the density and the clustering coefficient.

The key contribution of this work is that we provide a method to produce variable in size and in complexity blank node components supporting a plethora of configuration parameters; including diameter, density, clustering coefficient, as well as a parameter for controlling the similarity of the named resources connected to the blank nodes. With the introduced method we can produce big graphs in size under a plausible time and without main memory problems. We also provide evidence that the selected features succeed in capturing the complexity that is crucial for the intended tasks, by reporting experimental results of blank node matching over the produced datasets.

The rest of this paper is organized as follows. Section 2 describes related generators and introduces the basic requirements of BGen. Section 3 describes the generator, i.e. its schema, parameters and phases. Section 4 reports experimental results regarding time and space, as the generated datasets are scaled up, and uses the generated datasets to evaluate an approximation task. Finally, Section 5 concludes the paper and identifies issues for further research. More information is available in the Web[3].

2 Related Work

Benchmarking in RDF is focused on the performance evaluation of the Semantic Web repositories. Some notable benchmark tools and works follow. The Lehigh University Benchmark (LUBM) [5,4] aims at benchmarking systems with respect to use in OWL applications with large repositories. For data generation, they have built the UBA (Univ-Bench Artificial) data generator, that features random and repeatable data generation. The minimum unit of data generation is the

[3] `http://www.ics.forth.gr/isl/bnodeland`

university and for each university a set of OWL files describing its departments (e.g. courses, students, professors) are generated.

The BSBM benchmark [1] is built around an e-commerce use case, and its data generator supports the creation of arbitrarily large datasets using the number of products as scale factor.

The Social Intelligence BenchMark (SIB) [11] is an RDF benchmark that introduces the S3G2 (Scalable Structure-correlated Social Graph Generator) for generating social graphs that contain certain structural correlations. Regarding qualitative evaluation, they evaluate the ability to have some plausible correlation in the data, while regarding quantitative evaluation, they evaluate scalability in terms of various parameters like clustering coefficient, average path length and number of the users. Even though S3G2 offers correlation between the graph structure and the generated data, it does not handle blank nodes and their connectivity issues.

A slightly adjusted version of the UBA generator was used to generate synthetic data with blank nodes in [15]. However, that version supports a limited set of control parameters (e.g. it does not support control over cycles, clustering coefficient etc); consequently it is not convenient for benchmarking.

To the best of our knowledge there is no generator in the literature that deals with the generation of blank nodes adequately. Although there is not any particular difficulty in adjusting an already existing generator to produce blank nodes, the difficulty arises when the blank nodes should be connected under particular connectivity patterns. These patterns differentiate from the previous, as the performance criteria of the evaluated functions are different, too. To fill this gap in this paper we focus on connectivity issues between the blank nodes of the instance layer.

3 The BGen Generator

At first we describe the requirements of the generator (§3.1), the RDF/S schema that we have defined (§3.2), and provide a simple instantiation example of that schema which also introduces the notion of *BComponent* (§3.3). Then, we analyze how we control the structural complexity of a *BComponent* (§3.4), and finally we present the main algorithm and its phases (§3.5 - §3.7).

3.1 Requirements

Here we list the main requirements, while in Section 3.5 we describe how BGen meets these requirements.

A. Correlation of data. The generator should produce resources that are not randomly correlated in order to control the structure of the generated data set and gain realism. A sensible method to implement such a correlation is to produce data over a specific real-world-like schema that supports various kinds of relationships (i.e. one-to-one, one-to-many, many-to-many).

B. Scaling of data. The generator should be able to generate big datasets suitable for evaluating how the tasks/applications (or the RDF systems upon which they are built) scale.

C. Generation of anonymous data. The generator should support the creation of blank nodes as a percentage of the totally generated resources.

D. Connectivity in anonymous data. The generator should allow controlling the way blank nodes are connected using various features like diameter, density, clustering coefficient. The connectivity between the anonymous and the named data should also be controlled (through the schema and a similarity mode).

3.2 The Social Network Schema

Analogously to the UBA generator [5], we have created a schema that describes some basic classes and relations inside a social network. It is illustrated as a UML class diagram in Figure 1. A *social network* is the minimum unit of data generation. The primitive building block of this network is the class *Person* representing the members of this network. Each *person* has its *personal info*, described through its *name* (first name and last name), its *address* (street, zipcode, number and *city*), its gender and its birth date. Additionally, it has one or more *public messages* (where each *public message* is characterized by its content and its date). The instance *personal info* has its own *security mode*, which can get one of the following values: FriendsOnly, Public, Private.

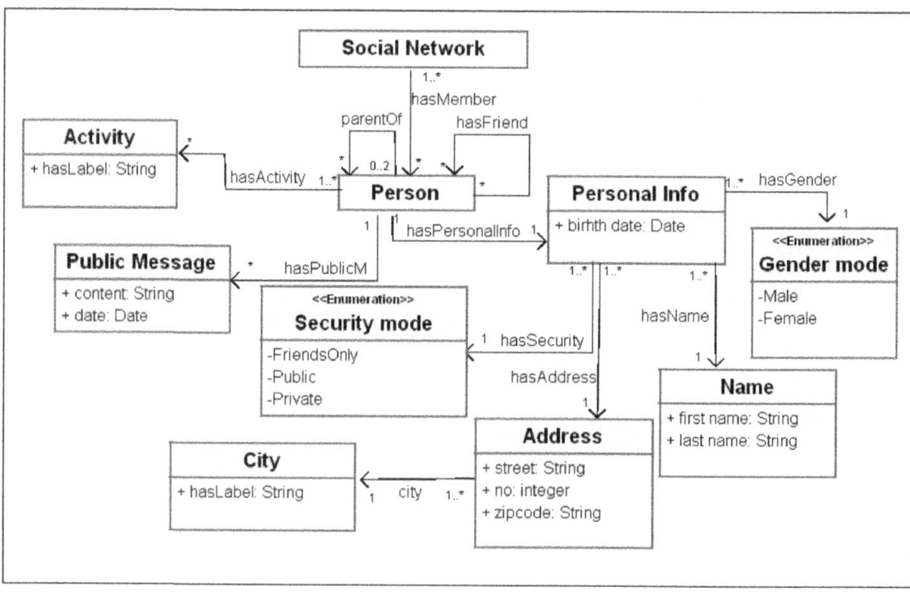

Fig. 1. The Social Network Schema of BGen

Each *person* is also connected with other *persons* through the `hasFriend` property indicating who is friend of whom. Apart from the friendship connections, other relationships (`parentOf`, `siblingOf`) can be created, too.

The class diagram of Figure 1 is represented in RDF/S and all classes are represented as instances of the `rdfs:Class`, while the ranges of their attributes are represented as subclasses of the `rdfs:Literal`. The enumeration classes (Gender mode, Security mode) are represented through the `owl:DataOneOf`. To make the schema as realistic as possible, some restrictions were applied based on common sense and domain investigation: they are denoted in Figure 1 by the multiplicities of the depicted associations, e.g. each *person* has one *personal info*, while it can have more than one *public messages* and friends.

3.3 Instantiating the Social Network Schema: Example

Here we provide an example showing how the schema is instantiated. Figure 2 shows a *person* (always represented as a blank node instance) accompanied with its *personal info*, its *messages* etc. inside a *social network*, named `sn:socialNet1` (always represented as a URI instance). We shall call this a *BPerson instantiation.*

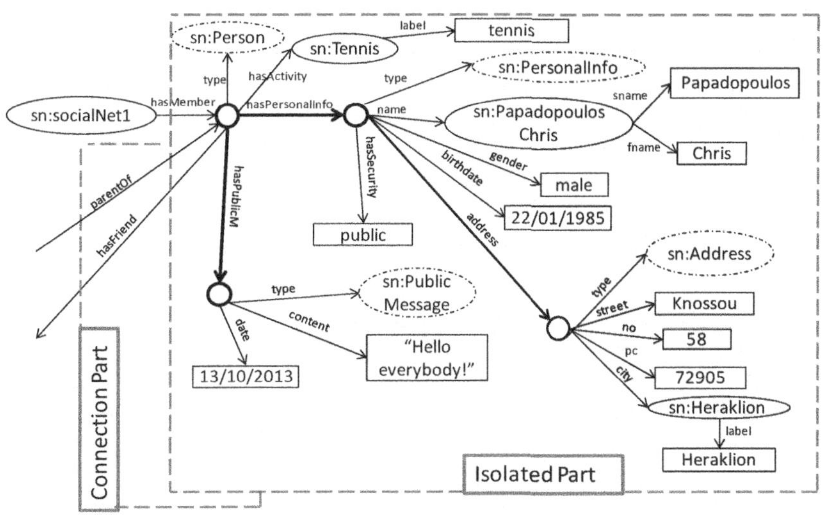

Fig. 2. A simple instantiation paradigm

The decision on how many of the generated instances inside a *BPerson instantiation* will be presented as blank nodes is based on a parameter named $|bPer|$, where $|bPer| \geq 1$ (i.e. a *person* is always instantiated as blank node), while $|uPer|$ controls how many will be presented as URIs. For the *BPerson instantiation* of Figure 2 we can see that $|bPer| = 4$ and $|uPer| = 3$ (3 URI instances). Although all classes of the social network schema can potentially acquire blank nodes as instances, the classes *City* and *Activity* are instantiated only by URIs because these resources need to be identified and indicated locally and even globally in real-world-like datasets.

Notice that each *BPerson instantiation* produces exactly one maximal tree of blank nodes, that is called *bTree* (nodes and edges in bold in Figure 2). More complex structures of blank nodes (e.g. cycles) require more than one *BPerson instantiations* to be connected and will be analyzed later. For the case where $|bPer| = 1$ the *bTree* is actually a single node and its height is 0, while as $|bPer|$ increases it becomes wider and its height can come up to 2 (the schema itself poses this upper bound, as the longest paths that can be created for a *BPerson instantiation* is `hasPersonalInfo-address` and `hasPersonalInfo-name`).

For comprehension reasons we further separate a *BPerson instantiation* into two parts: (a) the *isolated part* that contains the personal information, the activities, and the public message(s) (upper right part of Figure 2), and (b) the *connection part* that contains all the connections of the *person* with other *persons* (lower left part). These connections are achieved through the properties `hasFriend` and `parentOf` (or `siblingOf`).

Let us now focus on the way a *person* is connected with other *persons*. To make the example as simple as possible, we shall consider the whole *isolated part* instantiation of a *person* as *one* instance that we will illustrate as a *single node* for visualization convenience. In Figure 3 (left) we have three *BPerson instantiations* which are connected through two friendship properties. Essentially three *bTrees* are connected and merged under a common tree, which will be called *BComponent*. However, this component is not always that simple. Figure 3 (right) shows a more complex connection between seven *BPerson instantiations* through six friendship properties, two parent relations and four sibling relations. We can now formalize the notion of *BComponent*.

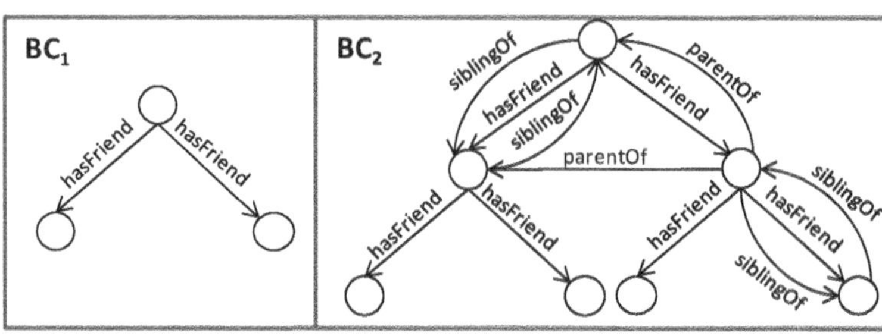

Fig. 3. The construction of two *BComponents*

Definition 1. We call a triple *btriple* if it contains only one blank node, and *bbtriple* if it contains two. Each maximal set of connected *bbtriples* of an RDF graph G forms a sub-graph, called *BComponent* of G. $\diamond$

It follows that Figure 3 illustrates two *BComponents*. These components and their features are crucial for controlling the blank nodes connectivity (analyzed shortly). In the context of the social network schema of BGen, a *BComponent* actually forms a community of connected *persons*.

3.4 Controlling the Complexity of *BComponents*

The problems, whose tasks are under evaluation (e.g. isomorphism checking, optimal bnode matching), become hard or even intractable for cases where the *BComponents* contain blank nodes that are connected with properties of the same label and where their directly connected named parts are similar enough (i.e. blank nodes of the same `rdf:type`). In such cases, each blank node cannot easily be distinguished from the others and the evaluated functions either become more time consuming, or their output deviates significantly from the optimal one. Therefore, the following parameters are critical for controlling the *BComponents* and generating the desired datasets.

Intra-*BComponent* Complexity. (*morphology, clustering coefficient, density*) The generator's parameter *morphology* controls how the blank nodes of a *BComponent* are connected through `hasFriend` properties, and can take four values: 1) *'Single'* corresponding to a *BComponent* with only one *person* (i.e. 'anti-social' community), 2) *'Tree'* corresponding to a *BComponent* whose *persons* form a directed *tree* structure (i.e. 'pyramid' community), 3) *'DAG'* corresponding to a *BComponent* whose *persons* form a *directed acyclic graph* (i.e. 'semi-sociable' community), and 4) *'Graph'* corresponding to a *BComponent* whose *persons* form a graph with directed *cycles*, like that in Figure 4 (i.e. 'sociable' community). Note that the `hasFriend` property is not symmetric and both directions should be defined explicitly in order two *persons* to be friends of each other.

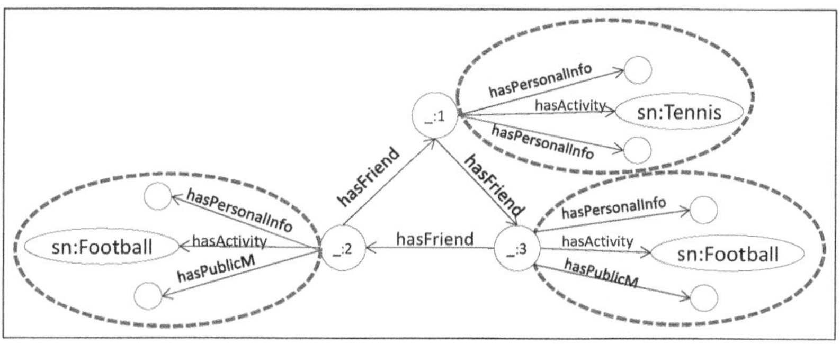

Fig. 4. A BComponent with similarly structured blank nodes

As a refinement parameter (over the *morphology*) we propose the parameter *average clustering coefficient*, $\bar{C}$ (formulated in equation 1) [16], that gives an average of the *local clustering coefficients*, C_k (formulated in equation 2), that quantifies the degree to which the friends of each *person* (incoming and outgoing) in the *BComponent BC* are friends between them (i.e. how strongly connected the community is). In the following equations assume that n is the number of blank node instances of the class *Person* inside the *BC*.

$$\bar{C} = \frac{1}{n}\sum_{k=1}^{n} C_k, \tag{1}$$

$$C_k = \frac{|\{(s, \texttt{hasFriend}, o) \in BC \mid s, o \in DFG(k)\}|}{|DFG(k)|(|DFG(k)| - 1)}, where \tag{2}$$

$$DFG(k) = \{s \mid (s, \texttt{hasFriend}, k) \in BC\} \cup \{o \mid (k, \texttt{hasFriend}, o) \in BC\}$$

Note that only the `hasFriend` property and the instances of the class *Person* are taken into account. For the *Single* and *Tree* morphologies $\bar{C} = 0$, while for the *DAG* and *Graph* morphologies $\bar{C} \in (0, 1]$. For example, for the *Graph BComponent* of Figure 4 the average clustering coefficient is $\bar{C} = 1/2$.

For making the dataset more realistic we allow other relations (apart from `hasFriend`) to exist between two *persons* (i.e. the relations `parentOf` and `siblingOf` for our schema). The number of these properties inside a *BComponent* is computed by the parameter *density* [3], D (formulated in equation 3).

$$D = \frac{|\{(s, \texttt{parentOf}, o) \in BC\} \cup \{(s, \texttt{siblingOf}, o) \in BC)\}|}{n(n-1)} \tag{3}$$

Density actually counts the number of `parentOf` and `siblingOf` relations that are going to be added between the *persons* of the *BComponent.* Even though the theoretical upper bound of *density* is 1, it will rarely have high values (i.e. it is very rare all the *persons* of the *BComponent* to be parents or siblings between them).

***BComponent* Similarity.** It is not hard to see that the named parts of the RDF graphs assist the matching algorithms to identify and match their blank nodes. In our schema the named information (URIs or literals) that is connected directly with the *person* (i.e. *activity, personal info, public messages*) gives to this blank node a higher discrimination ability. For instance, in Figure 4 *person* _ : 1 differentiates from *person* _ : 2 through its different *activity.* On the other hand, *persons* _ : 2 and _ : 3 have exactly the same named parts (i.e. both of them have Football as their activity). The *similarityMode* of the generator provides the ability to make the adjacent named structure of the blank nodes as similar as possible by (i) turning more URIs to blank node instances (increasing the $|bPer|$ parameter), (ii) making more URIs and literals same (i.e. more *persons* with same *activity,* street or *city*). In particular, the generator supports three scales of similarity: *easy*, *medium*, and *hard.* As it scales up, the similarity becomes higher and thus the bnode matching (as well as other tasks like *blocking* [13]) becomes more difficult.

3.5 The Generation Algorithm (Parameters and Phases)

The main algorithm of BGen takes the following seven input parameters[4] that express the desired features of the data set to be created:

1. N: the number of *resources* of the graph
2. P: the number of *persons*

[4] In case the combination of the values produces non-valid states, the user is urged to adjust them appropriately.

3. $|BC|$: the number of *BComponents* (i.e. the number of communities of the social network)
4. $[minDmtr, maxDmtr]$: the range of the *diameter*[5] between the *persons* of the *BComponents*. Diameters will be distributed uniformly to the *BComponents*.
5. *morphologies*: a subset of $\{Single, Tree, DAG, Graph\}$ that controls how the *persons* of the *BComponents* are connected (as described earlier)
6. $mode_1$: its range is $\{realistic,\ uniform,\ powerlaw\}$ and controls the distribution of the *BComponents* to the *morphologies*. The *realistic* mode distributes them according to the results of an analyzed corpus of real data in [10], the *uniform* mode distributes them equally, while the *powerlaw* mode approximates the 80 - 20 rule [12].
7. $mode_2$: its range is $\{random,\ uniform,\ powerlaw\}$ and controls the distribution of the *persons* to the *BComponents*. The *random* mode distributes the *persons* randomly, the *uniform* equally, and the *powerlaw* according to the Zipfian distribution [12].

In order to give the user the ability to evaluate the approximation functions to a greater extent, the following three parameters are also configurable (their values are auto-configured in case they are not given as input):

1. $[min\bar{C},\ max\bar{C}]$: the range for the *average clustering coefficient* between the *persons* of the *BComponents*.
2. $[minD,\ maxD]$: the range of the *density* between the *persons* of the *BComponents*.
3. $similarityMode$: its range is $\{easy, medium, hard\}$ and controls the similarity of the named resources connected to the *BComponents*.

Note that for the ranges ($[min\bar{C},\ max\bar{C}]$,$[minD,\ maxD]$) their values are distributed uniformly to the *BComponents*. Recall that both *morphology* and *average clustering coefficient* are computed in terms of the `hasFriend` properties of a *BComponent*, while the *density* is computed in terms of the `parentOf` and `siblingOf` properties. Let us now see the production process. Initially, the generator enters the *Preparation* phase (described in §3.6) that aims at computing all the necessary parameters for the internal steps of the algorithms (i.e. it computes the features of *each BComponent* that will be created). Then, it enters the *Instance Generation* phase (described in §3.7) that produces all the *BComponents*, as well as the named resources that are connected with them. The last phase is the *Connection* phase, that connects all the generated *BComponents* under the finally generated graph. Below we present analytically these three phases.

3.6 Phase I: The Preparation Phase

The *Preparation Phase* takes as input the parameters of the main algorithm and outputs a set of arrays; one array with $|BC|$ elements for each feature of the

[5] The diameter is the greatest distance between any pair of vertices [7].

BComponents to be created. Thus, each *BComponent* BC_i of the final graph is described through the values of the i-th elements of the exported arrays.

At first, the algorithm computes the number of blank nodes (B) and the number of URIs (U) taking N, P and $similarityMode$ into account. The rest of the algorithm computes the following features of each *BComponent* BC_i: (a) $|bPer_i|$: the number of blank nodes inside each one of the *BPerson instantiations* of BC_i, (b) $|uPer_i|$: the number of URIs inside each one of the *BPerson instantiations* of BC_i, (c) $|per_i|$: the number of *persons* in BC_i, (d) mor_i: the *morphology* of BC_i, (e) $dmtr_i$: the diameter of BC_i, (f) $|friends_i|$: the number of friends that each *person* of BC_i has, when $\bar{C}_i = 0$, (g) $\bar{C}_i$: the *average clustering coefficient* of the *persons* in BC_i and (h) D_i: the density of *persons* in BC_i.

Specifically, in order to compute the $|uPer_i|$, the U URIs are shared to the P *persons* uniformly. The $|BC|$ *BComponents* are split to the available *morphologies* ($\subseteq$ {*Single*, *Tree*, *DAG*, *Graph*}) based on the parameter $mode_1$.

The $|Single|$ *BComponents* can be easily initialized, since all their features are fixed. For the rest $|BC| - |Single|$ *BComponents*, $|per_i|$ is decided according to $mode_2$.

It follows the computation of the parameters $dmtr_i$, $\bar{C}_i$ and D_i which applies the uniform distribution to the ranges $[minDmtr, maxDmtr]$, $[min\bar{C}, max\bar{C}]$ and $[minD, maxD]$, respectively. Finally, the parameter $|friends_i|$ is computed for each *BComponent* separately by solving the following equation:

$$dmtr_i = \left\lceil \log_{|friends_i|}(|friends_i| - 1) + \log_{|friends_i|} |per_i| - 1 \right\rceil$$

As regards $dmtr_i$, the main structure of each *BComponent* forms a non-perfect k-ary tree of size N, where $k = |friends_i|$ and $N = |per_i|$ (recall the connection of *bTrees* into a common tree). The *diameter* of the *BComponent*, $dmtr_i$, is actually given as the height of this tree[6]. Afterwards, this tree is enriched with more `hasFriend` properties according to the value of $\bar{C}_i$.

3.7 Phase II: Instance Generation and Connection phase

At this phase BGen has a table with all the values that are needed to describe the *BComponents*. For each tuple i of this table it produces the triples of the *BComponent* BC_i. Having explained the features of a *BComponent*, let us show how the parameters determine the generated sub-graph through the examples of Figure 3. Recall that each *isolated part* instantiation (illustrated as a super node in Figure 3) is actually a set of instances of a *BPerson instantiation*. For this example, suppose that the $similarityMode$ is set to *easy* for both *BComponents*; each instantiation contains only one blank node, so $|bper_1| = |bper_2| = 1$.

For the first *BComponent*, say BC_1, we get that there are three *BPerson instantiations*, so $|per_1| = 3$ and $dmtr_1 = 1$. From these values, we get that each *person* (apart from the leaf nodes) should be connected with two outgoing *hasFriend* relations, so $|friends_1| = 2$. Finally, $mor_1 = Tree$, $\bar{C}_1 = 0$, as no

[6] `http://xlinux.nist.gov/dads/HTML/perfectKaryTree.html`

cycles or DAGs are formed between them through the *hasFriend* relations, and $D_1 = 0$, as no other relations (i.e.`parentOf, siblingOf`) exist.

For the second *BComponent*, say BC_2, there are seven *BPerson instantiations*, so $|per_2| = 7$. As, $dmtr_2 = 2$ each one of the *persons* is connected with two outgoing `hasFriend` relations; so $|friends_2| = 2$. Moreover, there are four `siblingOf` relations and two `parentOf` relations, as $D_2 = 0.07$. Again, since $mor_2 = Tree$, $\bar{C}_2 = 0$ (i.e. there are no cycles or DAGs between them through friendship relations).

Phase III: Connection Phase. Finally, all the created *BComponents* with their connected information (URIs and literals) are connected into the same graph. This is implemented by connecting each *person* with a common instance of the *Social Network*.

4 Usage and Experimental Evaluation

The experimental evaluation[7] has two main objectives: (a) to investigate the time efficiency of the generator and how that depends on the input parameters (§4.1), and (b) to provide evidence that the selected features succeed in capturing the complexity that is crucial for the intended tasks (§4.2).

4.1 Evaluating Efficiency

In brief, for creating a data set of 5 millions triples the required time ranges from 3.5 to 8 minutes depending on the complexity of blank nodes. These timings do not include the time required for saving in disk the output which depends on the technology of the storage media, rather than the problem at hand. Most of the time is spent in the instance generation phase, so the algorithm does not have any forbidding complexity, memory requirements or overhead.

Increasing the Number of Resources. We generated datasets having *BComponents* of moderate complexity, where their resources (N, P, $|BC|$) gradually scale up ceteris paribus (i.e. keeping the complexity of the *BComponents* stable).

Figure 5(left) shows how this scaling impacts the total time, as well as the partial times for (i) the *preparation* phase, (ii) the construction of blank nodes in the *BComponents*, (iii) the generation of the rest of the graph (URIs and literals) (i.e. population time), and (iv) writing triples to the repository. It is evident that the times increase linearly to the number of resources. Just indicatively, for the given main memory space, BGen can generate a data set of up to 15 million resources (53 million triples) in less than 10 minutes.

[7] All experiments were conducted using the Sesame SailRepository over Main Memory Store (`http://openrdf.callimachus.net/sesame/2.7/apidocs/org/openrdf/repository/sail/SailRepository.html`) using a PC with Intel i5-2500 3.3 GHz, 8 GB Ram, running Windows 7 (64-bit).

Increasing the Complexity of Resources. Regarding the rest of the parameters, we produce datasets with a stable number of resources ($N = 5$ million) scaling up the complexity of the *BComponents*, by gradually scaling the complexity parameters.

Figure 5(right) shows four different groups of datasets and how the total time is affected when increasing the complexity of the *BComponents*. Inside each group the aforementioned parameters are scaled up in three complexity levels. *Clustering coefficient* gets $[0.2, 0.4]$,$[0.6, 0.8]$ and $[0.6, 0.8]$, *density* gets $[0, 0.1]$, $[0, 0.2]$ and $[0, 0.4]$, while the *similarityMode* gets *easy*, *medium* and *hard*, for each complexity level, low, medium, high, respectively. From one group to the other, $|BC|$ is scaled down creating *BComponents* with more *persons* (as shown in the X-axis). As the complexity of *BComponents* increases we can see a linear increase in the total generation time; thus BGen remains time efficient.

The only restriction factor for BGen is the data structure that temporarily stores the `hasFriend` properties of a current *BComponent*. On the worst case scenario, where $|BC| = 1$ and $\bar{C} = 1$, the space complexity comes to P^2. Indicatively, for the given memory space, in the extreme case where $N = 10^7$, $P = 10^7$, and $|BC| = 1$ we get an out of memory exception for $\bar{C} = 0.8$.

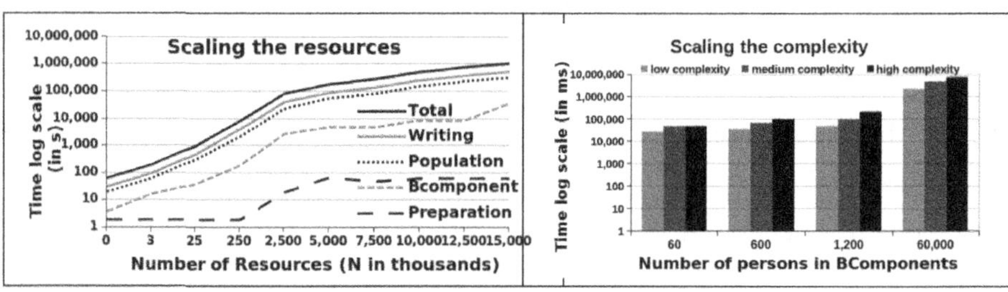

Fig. 5. Generation times scaling up the resources and their complexity

4.2 Using the Generated Datasets for Benchmarking

For checking that the selected features succeed in capturing the complexity that is crucial for tasks like blank node matching, we generated one group of eight datasets scaling up the values of the *average clustering coefficient* for each *similarityMode*, *easy*, *medium* and *hard*, respectively. Each generated dataset has $N = 25{,}000$, $P = 3{,}000$, $|BC| = 10$, $[minDmtr, maxDmtr] = [1, 3]$, contains *graph morphologies*, $[minD, maxD] = 0$, and $mode1 = mode2 = uniform$. The range $[min\bar{C}, max\bar{C}]$ is [0, 0.2] for the dataset KB_1, [0,0.4] for KB_2, [0.2, 0.4] for KB_3, [0.3,0.5] for KB_4, [0.4, 0.6] for KB_5, [0.5, 0.7] for KB_6, [0.6, 0.8] for KB_7, and [0.7, 0.8] for KB_8. Each dataset is compared to itself. Because of space limitations, the datasets were only tested using the `signature`-based blank node matching method introduced in [15][8]. This method returns a mapping between

[8] The datasets are also tested using other blank node matching methods in `http://www.ics.forth.gr/isl/bgen/results`

the blank nodes of two graphs, aiming at minimizing the delta size when comparing these graphs. However, note that this method only approximates the optimal solution. The following experiments will allow us to consider which factors and in what way make this method deviate from the optimal. Figure 6 (left) shows the delta size, when each one of these datasets is compared to itself and Figure 6 (right) shows the time needed for this matching. It is evident that both the *average clustering coefficient* and the *similarityMode*, affect the deviation from the optimal delta size, that is zero, as the dataset is compared to itself. They also affect the time efficiency of the `signature` method. Recall that according to [15] the method can map 153,600 bnodes in 11 seconds. The current experiments show that for the non-*easy similarityMode* the method loses its capability to detect the optimal solutions even for low values of the *average clustering coefficient*. As these values increase the deviation is increased gradually. Notice that the delta size comes up to $234,676$ triples for the last pair of datasets, where each dataset contains $291,000$ triples, has $[min\bar{C}, max\bar{C}]$ in $[0.6, 0.8]$ and the *similarityMode* is *hard*. As regards time, the `signature`-based method has time complexity linear to the number of blank nodes (i.e. $P * |bPer|$); therefore the increase of the clustering coefficient does not impact significantly on time. The small increases are explained because of the increase of the `hasFriend` properties that means bigger signatures. As the *similarityMode* increases we observe bigger increases in time because of the increase of the number of blank nodes (through the increase of $bPer$).

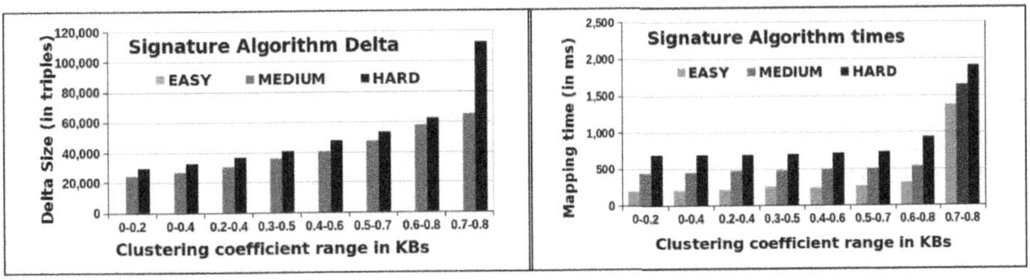

Fig. 6. Using the generated datasets to evaluate the `signature` method

In conclusion, we can say the generated datasets succeed in making clear how approximate solutions deviate from the optimal solution, and thus such datasets are suitable for comparatively evaluating such methods, e.g. for rapidly evaluating the potential and limits of various heuristics. All datasets used in this paper, as well as the current version of the generator are accessible for use[9].

5 Concluding Remarks

BGen is the first Semantic Web synthetic data generator able to create datasets with blank nodes appropriate for comparing and benchmarking various semantic data management tasks, e.g. equivalence and comparison.

[9] `http://www.ics.forth.gr/isl/bgen/results`

Since the complexity of solving optimally such problems depends on the connectivity of blank nodes, the datasets produced by BGen can aid the assessment and the comparative evaluation of the various techniques that have been (or will be) proposed for carrying out such tasks.

The proposed method can produce variable in size and in complexity structures of blank nodes controlled through a plethora of configuration parameters, e.g. morphology (tree, DAG, cycle), diameter, density, clustering coefficient, similarity of the named resources connected to the blank nodes.

The construction algorithm has linear time and space requirements with respect to the number of resources. We also provided evidence that the selected features succeed in capturing the complexity that is crucial for the intended tasks, by reporting experimental results of bnode matching over the produced datasets. The results make evident how approximate solutions deviate from the optimal ones.

In the future we will use BGen for evaluating (and devising new) bnode matching techniques. We also plan to make this generator publicly available and associate it with LDBC[10]. Moreover one could easily extend the generator, e.g. by adding parameters controlling the lexical similarity of URIs and literals, for using it also for entity matching.

References

1. Bizer, C., Schultz, A.: The berlin SPARQL benchmark. International Journal on Semantic Web and Information Systems (2009)
2. Chen, L., Zhang, H., Chen, Y., Guo, W.: Blank Nodes in RDF. Journal of Software (2012)
3. Coleman, T.F., More, J.J.: Estimation of Sparse Jacobian Matrices and Graph Coloring Problems. SIAM Journal on Numerical Analysis (1983)
4. Guo, Y., Pan, Z., Heflin, J.: An evaluation of knowledge base systems for large OWL datasets. In: McIlraith, S.A., Plexousakis, D., van Harmelen, F. (eds.) ISWC 2004. LNCS, vol. 3298, pp. 274–288. Springer, Heidelberg (2004)
5. Guo, Y., Pan, Z., Heflin, J.: LUBM: A benchmark for OWL knowledge base systems. In: Selected Papers from the Intern. Semantic Web Conf. ISWC (2004)
6. Gutierrez, C., Hurtado, C., Mendelzon, A.: Foundations of Semantic Web Databases. In: Proceedings of the Twenty-Third Symposium on Principles of Database Systems (PODS), Paris, France (2004)
7. Harary, F.: Graph Theory. Addison-Wesley, Reading (1969)
8. Heath, T., Bizer, C.: Linked Data: Evolving the Web into a Global Data Space. Morgan & Claypool (2011)
9. Käfer, T., Abdelrahman, A., Umbrich, J., O'Byrne, P., Hogan, A.: Observing Linked Data Dynamics. In: Cimiano, P., Corcho, O., Presutti, V., Hollink, L., Rudolph, S. (eds.) ESWC 2013. LNCS, vol. 7882, pp. 213–227. Springer, Heidelberg (2013)
10. Mallea, A., Arenas, M., Hogan, A., Polleres, A.: On Blank Nodes. In: Aroyo, L., Welty, C., Alani, H., Taylor, J., Bernstein, A., Kagal, L., Noy, N., Blomqvist, E. (eds.) ISWC 2011, Part I. LNCS, vol. 7031, pp. 421–437. Springer, Heidelberg (2011)

[10] http://www.ldbc.eu/

11. Pham, M.-D., Boncz, P., Erling, O.: S3G2: A Scalable Structure-Correlated Social Graph Generator. In: Nambiar, R., Poess, M. (eds.) TPCTC 2012. LNCS, vol. 7755, pp. 156–172. Springer, Heidelberg (2013)
12. Newman, M.E.J.: Power laws, pareto distributions and zipf's law. Contemporary Physics (2005)
13. Papadakis, G., Ioannou, E., Palpanasa, T., Niederee, C., Nejdl, W.: A blocking framework for entity resolution in highly heterogeneous information spaces. IEEE Knowledge and Data Engineering (2012)
14. Pichler, R., Polleres, A., Wei, F., Woltran, S.: dRDF: Entailment for Domain-Restricted RDF. In: Bechhofer, S., Hauswirth, M., Hoffmann, J., Koubarakis, M. (eds.) ESWC 2008. LNCS, vol. 5021, pp. 200–214. Springer, Heidelberg (2008)
15. Tzitzikas, Y., Lantzaki, C., Zeginis, D.: Blank Node Matching and RDF/S Comparison Functions. In: Cudré-Mauroux, P., et al. (eds.) ISWC 2012, Part I. LNCS, vol. 7649, pp. 591–607. Springer, Heidelberg (2012)
16. Watts, D.J., Strogatz, S.H.: Collective dynamics of small-world networks. Nature (1998)

Distributed Keyword Search over RDF via MapReduce

Roberto De Virgilio and Antonio Maccioni

Dipartimento di Ingegneria
Universitá Roma Tre, Rome, Italy
{dvr,maccioni}@dia.uniroma3.it

Abstract. Non expert users need support to access linked data available on the Web. To this aim, keyword-based search is considered an essential feature of database systems. The distributed nature of the Semantic Web demands query processing techniques to evolve towards a scenario where data is scattered on distributed data stores. Existing approaches to keyword search cannot guarantee scalability in a distributed environment, because, at runtime, they are unaware of the location of the relevant data to the query and thus, they cannot optimize join tasks. In this paper, we illustrate a novel distributed approach to keyword search over RDF data that exploits the MapReduce paradigm by switching the problem from graph-parallel to data-parallel processing. Moreover, our framework is able to consider ranking during the building phase to return directly the best (top-k) answers in the first (k) generated results, reducing greatly the overall computational load and complexity. Finally, a comprehensive evaluation demonstrates that our approach exhibits very good efficiency guaranteeing high level of accuracy, especially with respect to state-of-the-art competitors.

Keywords: #eswc2014Virgilio.

1 Introduction

The size of the Semantic Web is rapidly increasing due to numerous organizations that are opening up their databases on the Web following the linked data principles. This causes that, often, RDF datasets do not fit on a single machine. Moreover, data are linked only in a logical way, whereas, frequently, they are physically distributed over different locations. Obviously, RDF data management systems should be able to process distributed data [16]. There exists approaches to query distributed RDF data with SPARQL-like queries [8,13,17]. Usually, they exploit optimizations based on structural information (i.e. graph partitioning), but unfortunately, they cannot adapt to answer structure-free queries, such as keyword search-based queries. Keyword search is gathering the attention of Semantic Web practitioners, who want to support users in accessing linked (open) data. In fact, these users: (i) are usually unaware of the way in which data is organized, (ii) do not know how to interpret a Web ontology (if present) and (iii) do

V. Presutti et al. (Eds.): ESWC 2014, LNCS 8465, pp. 208–223, 2014.

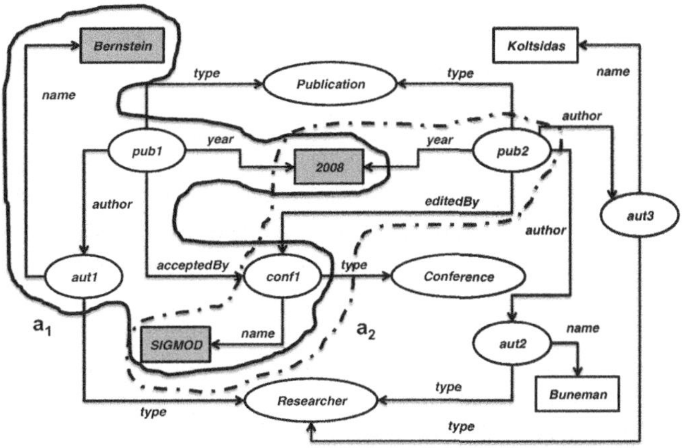

Fig. 1. An RDF graph G_1 from DBLP

not know the syntax of a specific query language (e.g., SPARQL). Clearly, there is an imminent necessity to process efficiently keyword queries over distributed RDF data stores. Unfortunately, approaches for keyword search over RDF data are all centralized (e.g., [6,15,18]). This is due to the fact that the keywords in the query do not help to identify how the RDF dataset has to be explored. Consequently, they are compelled to compute many expensive join operations over data distributed over different locations. Recently, MapReduce [5] has become a "de-facto" standard for distributed and parallel massive data processing on a cluster of commodity machines. MapReduce offers a high-level abstraction for solving problems through *rounds* of two independent and subsequent functions, i.e. *map* and *reduce*. MapReduce is an effective paradigm to compute algorithms that require to read the data just once and for this reason, it is not efficient to perform joins and graph algorithms [14].

Problem. Let us show with the example of G_1 in Fig. 1 how the RDF keyword queries are solved in order to point out why existing centralized approaches (i.e. [15]) are not feasible in this context. G_1 is a sample RDF version of the DBLP dataset (a database about scientific publications). Vertices in ovals represent entities, such as *aut1* and *aut2*, or concepts, such as *Conference* and *Publication*. Vertices in rectangles are literal values, such as *Bernstein* and *Buneman*. Edges describe connections between vertices. For instance, entity *aut1* is a *Researcher* whose name is *Bernstein*.

Given a keyword search query over RDF, a generic approach would: ① identify the vertices of the RDF graph holding the data matching the input keywords, ② traverse the edges to discover the connections between them to build n candidate answers (with $n > k$), and ③ rank answers according to a relevance criteria to return the top relevant k. While ① can be easily solved considering an indexing method over the content of the RDF graph, the task in ② requires to compute lot of joins over the distributed data, which are disk and network intensive.

Moreover, the task in ② intrinsically computes more answers (an overset of the most relevant answers) than required and the task in ③ cannot be computed by independent parallel processes. It would be ideal to avoid ③ by generating exactly the best k answers in ②. Considering our running example with the query Q_1 = {`Bernstein, SIGMOD, 2008`}, a_1 (i.e. articles of *Bernstein* published in *SIGMOD 2008*) is intuitively more relevant than a_2 (i.e. articles of *Buneman* published in *SIGMOD 2008*) because it includes more keywords and it should be retrieved as the first answer. Note that ranking functions consider more elaborate criteria to evaluate the relevance of an answer. Ideally, if one is interested in the top-2 answers, only a_1 and a_2 shall be computed, hence avoiding a ranking procedure. In this way, at each step the answer generated is the best possible in the sense that the answers generated next cannot have a higher relevance. This property is called *monotonicity* and a process satisfying such property is a *monotonic* process. A monotonic process allows to reduce the *time-to-result* because the user can get an answer before the computation of the following one is completed. Hence, a monotonic processing is particularly desirable in the context of MapReduce to mitigate the latency of the execution.

Contribution. In this paper, we present a novel distributed keyword-based search technique over RDF data that builds the best k results in the first k generated answers. We exploit the MapReduce [5] paradigm in order to benefit from the features (i.e. load balancing, fault tolerance, job scheduling, etc.) that current implementations (e.g., Hadoop or variants thereof) give to developers. Nevertheless, MapReduce is a data-parallel paradigm that is not very efficient for the processing of RDF data, which usually requires join-intensive tasks. By exploiting a path-store for RDF, we reverse the distributed keyword search over RDF from a graph-parallel problem to a data-parallel problem. This store is an implementation of the work in [1] on Hadoop/HBase and it is not a contribution for this paper. Intuitively, in this store, the connections among elements (i.e. adjacencies and intersections) of the RDF graph are explicitly stored in *paths*, allowing us to avoid, in this way, the computation of joins. In general, while existing approaches explore the dataset to find sub-graphs holding relevant information to the query, we only combine the RDF paths according to their precomputed intersections. In addition, since the relevance of answers is highly dependent on both the construction of candidates and on their ranking, our query answering combines search and ranking. In our approach the RDF paths that are relevant to the query are retrieved from the store and then grouped (i.e. clustered) with respect to a criteria that captures the type of information in the path. Then, we compute, at each step, the most relevant answer by picking and combining the most relevant paths from each group. The relevance is given by a scoring function. Note that, however, our approach is scoring functions agnostic. Note that this approach is inspired by the theoretical results in [4], but it proposes different algorithms. To validate our approach, we have developed a distributed system for keyword-based search over RDF data that implements the techniques described in this paper. Experiments over widely used benchmarks have shown very good results with respect to other approaches, in terms of both effectiveness and efficiency.

Outline. The rest of the paper is organized as follows. Section 2 introduces some preliminary issues. Section 3 overviews the proposed approach to keyword search, while Section 4 illustrates the distributed algorithms in detail. In Section 5, we discuss related research and in Section 6, we present the experimental results. Finally, in Section 7, we draw our conclusions and sketch future research.

2 Basic Concepts

This section introduces some preliminary notions and the problem we address.

Data Structures. RDF datasets are naturally represented as labeled directed graphs.

Definition 1 (RDF Data Graph). *An RDF data graph is a labeled directed graph* $G = \{V, E, \Sigma_V, \Sigma_E, L_G\}$ *where* V *is a set of vertices and* $E \subseteq V \times V$ *is a set of ordered pairs of vertices, called edges.* Σ_V *and* Σ_E *are the sets of vertices and edge labels, respectively. The labeling function* L_G *associates an element of* V *to an element of* Σ_V *and an element of* E *to an element of* Σ_E.

We call *start* vertex, the vertices of G with no in-going edges, and *end* vertices, the vertices of G with no out-going edges. Basically, a *path* in a graph G is a sequence of labels from a start vertex to an end vertex of G. In the case of cycles, a path ends, intuitively, just before the repetition of a vertex label. Moreover, if there is no start vertex in G, a path starts from vertices whose difference between the number of outgoing edges and the number of the incoming edges is maximal in G. We call these vertices *hubs.*

Definition 2 (Path). *Given a graph* $G = \{V, E, \Sigma_V, \Sigma_E, L_G\}$, *a path is a sequence* $p = l_{v_1} - l_{e_1} - l_{v_2} - l_{e_2} - \ldots - l_{e_{v-1}} - l_{v_j}$ *where: (i)* $l_{v_i} = L_G(v_i)$, $l_{e_i} = L_G(e_i)$, *and* $v_i \in V$, $e_i = (v_i, v_{i+1}) \in E$, *(ii)* v_1 *is either a start vertex or, if G has no start vertices, a hub, and (iii)* v_j *is either an end vertex or a vertex such that there is no edge* (v_j, v_{j+1}) *such that* $L_G(v_{j+1})$ *(the label of* v_j*) already occurs in* p.

In the following, we will call v_1 and v_j the *source* and the *sink* of a p, respectively. The *length* of a path is the number of vertices occurring in the path, while the *position* of a vertex corresponds to its position among the vertices in the path. For instance, the graph in Fig. 1 has two sources: *pub1* and *pub2*. An example of path is p_2 = pub1-author-aut1-name-Bernstein, whose length is 3 and the vertex aut1 has position 2. In our approach we exploit a path-store inspired by [1] that indexes all paths starting from a source and ending with a sink. Obviously, at running time we are interested in the paths relevant to the query, that is, the paths whose sinks match at least one keyword of the query. As in [15], we assume that users enter keywords corresponding to attribute values, that are necessarily within the sink's labels. This is not a limitation because vertices labeled by URIs are usually linked to literals, which represent verbose descriptions of such URIs. In our implementation, the operation of *matching* is executed with standard libraries based on full text search techniques (such as stemming). Since this aspect is outside the scope of the paper, we will simply assume, hereinafter, that the operation of matching provides a support for imprecise matching between labels and we will use the term matching between values in this sense, without discussing this aspect further. In a path, the sequence of edge labels describes the corresponding structure. To some extent, such a structure describes a schema for the values on vertices that share the same connection type. While we cannot advocate the presence of a schema, we can say that such a sequence is a *template* for the path. Therefore, given a path p, its template t_p results from the path where each vertex label is replaced with the wild-card #. In the example of Fig. 1, the template t_{p_2} associated to $p_2 =$ publ-author-aut1-name-Bernstein is #-author-#-name-#. We say that p_2 *satisfies* t_{p_2}, denoted with $p_2 \approx t_{p_2}$. Multiple paths that share the same template can be considered as homogeneous.

When two paths p_i and p_j share a common vertex, we say that there is an intersection between p_i and p_j and we indicate it with $p_i \leftrightarrow p_j$. Finally, an answer a to Q over G is a set of paths forming a connected components, i.e. a directed labeled sub-graph of G where the paths present pairwise intersections as defined below.

Definition 3 (Answer). *An answer a is a set of paths $p_1, p_2, \ldots, p_n$ where $\forall p_a, p_b \in a$ there exists a sequence $[p_a, p_{w_1}, \ldots, p_{w_m}, p_b]$, with $m < n$, such that $p_{w_i} \in a$, $p_a \leftrightarrow p_{w_1}$, $p_b \leftrightarrow p_{w_m}$, and $\forall i \in [1, m\text{-}1] : p_{w_i} \leftrightarrow p_{w_{i+1}}$.*

Note that, since the paths form a connected component, our notion of answer basically corresponds to the notion of RDF sub-graph answer used by other approaches.

Ranking and Monotonicity. To assess the relevance of an answer a for a query Q, a scoring function $score(a, Q)$ is adopted. It returns a number that is greater when the answer is more relevant. Then, the ranking is given by ordering the answers according to their relevance. A query answering process is monotonic if the i-th generated answer is always more relevant than the $(i+1)$-th. It follows that, if a query answering is monotonic, a ranking task is needless. Since a single path can be an answer, it is reasonable to consider the same scoring function to evaluate both paths and answers. In the following sections, we will use the notation $score(p, Q)$ and $score(a, Q)$ to evaluate the relevance of a path p and of an answer a with respect to the query Q, respectively. We remark that, unlike all current approaches, we are independent from the scoring function: we do not impose a monotonic, aggregative nor an "ad-hoc for the case" scoring function.

Problem Definition. Given a labeled directed graph G and a keyword search based query $Q = \{q_1, q_2, \ldots, q_n\}$, where each q_i is a keyword, we aim at finding the top-k ranked answers $a_1, a_2, \ldots, a_k$ to Q.

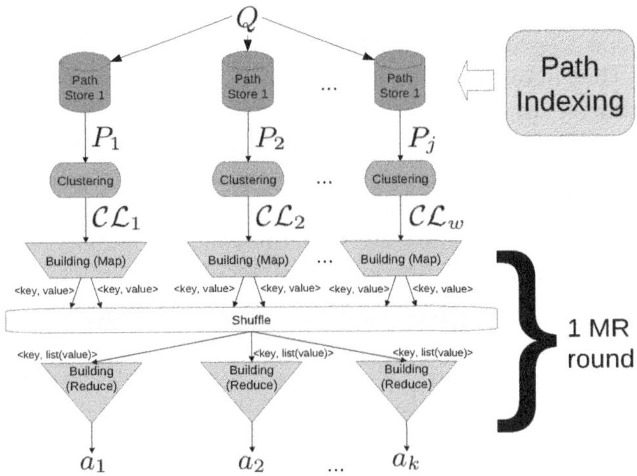

Fig. 2. The flow of execution

3 Monotonic Keyword Search

This section overviews our distributed approach to keyword search over RDF and discusses the conditions under which the answer generation process exhibits a monotonic behaviour. The flow of execution is shown in Fig. 2, but the algorithms of each block will be detailed in the next Section 4.

Let G be an RDF data graph and Q a keyword query over it. Our approach provides two main phases: the *indexing* (done off-line), in which all the paths of G are indexed in the store (the orange part of Fig. 2), and the *query processing* (done on-the-fly), where the query evaluation takes place. The first task will be described in more detail in Section 6. Intuitively, let us consider a distributed environment composed by two machines. For example, the paths of G can be stored within the two independent path stores in Fig. 3. Note that the replication of data is transparent to the developer in MapReduce, so we assume the content of the two path stores to be disjoint.

PATH STORE 1 :

p_1 : pub1-year-2008
p_2 : pub1-author-aut1-name-Bernstein
p_4 : pub2-year-2008
...

PATH STORE 2 :

p_3 : pub1-acceptedBy-conf1-name-SIGMOD
p_5 : pub2-editedBy-conf1-name-SIGMOD
...

Fig. 3. Distributed Path-Store

In the second phase, all paths P relevant for Q (i.e. all paths whose sinks match at least one keyword of Q) are retrieved by exploiting the store. Then, the best answers are generated from P (blue part of Fig. 2). An important feature of this phase is the use of the scoring function while computing the answers. This phase is performed by the following two main tasks:

Clustering. In this task (the green part of Fig. 2) we group the paths of P into clusters according to their template. Every distributed node manages a set of clusters, that in our running example with Q_1 over G_1 are $\mathcal{CL}_1$ and $\mathcal{CL}_2$ as showed in Fig. 4. In this case clusters cl_1, cl_2, cl_3 and cl_4 correspond to the different templates extracted from P. Before the insertion of a path p in the cluster, we evaluate its score. The paths in a clusters are ordered according to their score with the greater coming first, i.e. $score(p_1, Q_1) \geq score(p_4, Q_1)$. It is straightforward to demonstrate that the time complexity of the clustering is $O(|P|)$: it executes $|P|$ insertions into the clusters.

$$\mathcal{CL}_1 : \begin{pmatrix} cl_1[\#\text{-year-}\#] : & p_1, p_4 \\ cl_2[\#\text{-author-}\#\text{-name-}\#] : & p_2 \end{pmatrix} \qquad \mathcal{CL}_2 : \begin{pmatrix} cl_3[\#\text{-acceptedBy-}\#\text{-name-}\#] : & p_3 \\ cl_4[\#\text{-editedBy-}\#\text{-name-}\#] : & p_5 \end{pmatrix}$$

Fig. 4. Clustering of paths

Building. The last task aims at generating the most relevant answers by combining the paths in the clusters (yellow part of Fig. 2). This is done by picking and combining the paths with greatest score from each cluster, i.e. the most promising paths. Note that we diversify the answer content by not including homogeneous data, that is paths from the same cluster.

The combination of paths is led by a strategy that decides whether a path has to be inserted in a final answer or not. Two different strategies are defined:

1. *linear strategy*: it guarantees a linear time complexity with respect to the size of the input in a single round of MapReduce. Basically, the final answers are the connected components of the most relevant paths of the clusters.
2. *monotonic strategy*: it generates the answers in order according to their relevance in a quadratic time complexity with respect to the size of the input. It completes in $2 \times k$ rounds of MapReduce, at most. As the linear strategy, it computes the connected components from the most relevant paths in the clusters, but differently, the path interconnection is not the only criterion to form an answer. At this point every connected components is analysed to check if it fulfils the monotonicity, that is to check if the answer we are generating is optimum. This check is supported by the so called τ-*test*, which is explained in [4].

4 MapReduce Building Strategies

Given the query Q and the set P of paths matching the query Q, retrieved from the path-store, we compose those paths to generate the final top-k answers. In the following we discuss separately the two strategies implemented in MapReduce.

Algorithm 1. LinearBuilding (Map)

Input : The map $\mathcal{CL}$.
Output: A list of pairs $< key, value >$.

```
1 iteration ← 1;
2 while CL is not empty do
3     foreach cl ∈ CL do
4         first_cl ← cl.DequeueTop() ;
5         foreach p ∈ first_cl do
6             output(<iteration, p >) ;
7     iteration ← iteration + 1;
```

4.1 The Linear Strategy

Given the set of clusters $\mathcal{CL}$, the building of answers is performed by generating the connected components CC from the most promising paths in $\mathcal{CL}$. The linear strategy requires only one round of MapReduce. Every machine executes a *map* job (Algorithm 1), while the total number of *reduce* jobs is the maximum number of different scores present in the clusters. Algorithm 1 iterates over the local clusters (lines [3-6]) to extract the top paths from `cl` (line [4]), i.e. all paths having the same (top) score. The iterations continue until the clusters are empty (line [2]). At each iteration, the top paths are inserted in `first_cl` and each of them is returned as *value* in a pair with the number of the iteration as *key* (line [6]).

Algorithm 2. LinearBuilding (Reduce)

Input : A pair $< key, value >$.
Output: A list of answers.

```
1 CC ← FindCC(value);
2 ans ← ∅;
3 foreach cc ∈ CC do
4     ans.Enqueue(cc);
5 return ans ;
```

A reduce function (Algorithm 2) receives a list *value* of paths extracted during the same iteration and an integer *key* (that is not used). Out of *value*, we compute the connected components CC (line [1]), each of which represents an answer. Referring again to our example, the mappers produce the pairs $< 1, p_1 >$, $< 1, p_2 >$, $< 1, p_3 >$, $< 1, p_5 >$ and $< 2, p_4 >$. After the shuffle phase, we have the pairs $< 1, (p_1, p_2, p_3, p_5) >$ and $< 2, (p_4) >$ which are assigned to different reducers. The first reducer produces $cc_1 = \{p_1, p_2, p_3, p_5\}$, while the other produces $cc_2 = \{p_4\}$. All the answers are returned in output (line [5]). Note that, if we retrieve k answers, we stop the launch of more reducers.

Computational Complexity. Algorithm 1 and Algorithm 2 produce the answers in linear time with respect to the number I of paths matching the input query Q. The Algorithm 1 is in $O(I)$ because it makes I extractions and I insertions of pairs. Algorithm 2 is in $O(I)$ in the worst case, which happens when only one reducer is called (the case is similar to a sequential version of the algorithm). Therefore, the computation is given by the call of `FindCC` that has a complexity of $O(I)$ (it iterates over I paths once, see pseudo-code in [4]) followed by I insertions at most. We can state that the overall linear strategy is in $O(I)$.

Ranking. This strategy produces good answers efficiently; in our example, we have $a_1 = \{p_1, p_2, p_3, p_5\}$ and $a_2 = \{p_4\}$. Observing the answers with respect to Q_1, a_1 contains the unnecessary p_5, while a_2 is partially incomplete (i.e. it should include p_5). Such strategy tends to produce *exhaustive* answers but not optimally *specific*, that is to include all relevant information matching the query but not optimally limiting the irrelevant ones. The answer generated at each step may not be the optimum answer: it may happen to generate a sequence of two answers, a_i and a_{i+1}, where $score(a_{i+1}, Q) > score(a_i, Q)$. Moreover, since we output the answers as soon as they are built, we do not control if a_{i+1} is completed before a_i. The ranking of this strategy cannot guarantee monotonicity.

4.2 The Monotonic Strategy

In this section, we provide a second strategy that implements the *τ-test* (see Theorem in [4]) while building the answers. In this case the iterations are dependent on each other because discarded paths have to be used in the next iterations.

Algorithm 3. MonotonicBuilding (Map Round 1)

Input : The map $\mathcal{CL}$.
Output: A list of pairs < *key*, *value* >.

```
1 first ← ∅;
2 foreach cl ∈ CL do
3     first ← first ∪ cl.DequeueTop() ;
4 CC ← FindCC(first );
5 foreach cc ∈ CC do
6     output(<1, cc>) ;
```

To produce an answer we launch two rounds of MapReduce. The first round (Algorithm 3 and Algorithm 4) produces the connected components among the most relevant distributed paths; the second round (Algorithm 5 and Algorithm 6) analyses the connected components in parallel, producing the final answers. After the clustering of paths in $\mathcal{CL}$, the mappers (Algorithm 3) compute the local connected components (line [4]) of the most relevant paths (lines [2-3]). Then, each connected component *cc* is sent to the same reducer (lines [5-6]). The reducer of the first round is in Algorithm 4. It takes all the locally computed connected components and produce the global connected components. It calls the function `FindCC` (line [1]) taking advantage from partially computed connected components of the input.

Algorithm 4. MonotonicBuilding (Reduce Round 1)

Input : A pair $< key, value >$.
Output: a list of global connected components.

```
1 CC ← FindCC(value);
2 return CC ;
```

The map function of the second round (Algorithm 5) dispatches every global connected component *cc* to a different reducer (lines [2-4]).

Every reducer of the second round (Algorithm 6) receives a connected component as *value* and launches a local analysis procedure, i.e. `MonotonicityAnalysis` (line [1]), to apply the *τ-test*. For the purpose, the reducer uses as input the more relevant path p_s in $\mathcal{CL}$. This path is kept as a global variable within the distributed environment[1] . At the end of the analysis, an optimal answer *a* is returned (line [3]) and the discarded paths of the connected components *value* are inserted back into the clusters (line [2]). Note that, since there are more reducers returning an optimum answer, we only output one of them to the user and the others are reinserted into the clusters.

Algorithm 5. MonotonicBuilding (Map Round 2)

Input : The list of connected components CC.
Output: A list of pairs $< key, value >$.

```
1 i ← 0;
2 foreach cc ∈ CC do
3 |   i ← i + 1;
4 |   output(<i, cc>) ;
```

Monotonicity Analysis. Algorithm 7 checks if the answer we are generating is (still) optimum, thus, it preserves the monotonicity. It is a recursive function that generates the set `OptAns` of all answers (candidate to be optimum) by combining the paths in a connected component *cc*. At the end, it returns an answer `optA` given by the maximal and optimum subset of paths in *cc*. It takes as input the connected component *cc*, the current optimum answer `optA` and the top path p_s contained in $\mathcal{CL}$. If *cc* is empty, we return `optA` as it is (lines [1-2]). Otherwise, we analyze all paths $p_x \in cc$ that present an intersection with a path

[1] The global variable is implemented by means of the Hadoop's Distributed Cache functionality.

Algorithm 6. MonotonicBuilding (Reduce Round 2)

```
Input  : A pair < key, value >, a path p_s.
Output: an answer.
a ← MonotonicityAnalysis(value, ∅, p_s );
InsertPathsInClusters(value, CL );
return a;
```

p_i of `optA` ($p_x \leftrightarrow p_i$). If there is no intersection, then `optA` is the final optimum answer (lines [6-7]). Otherwise, for each p_x, we calculate τ (line [10]), through the function `getTau`, and then execute the τ-*test* on each new answer `optA'`, that is `optA` $\cup \{p_x\}$. If `optA'` satisfies the τ-*test* (line [11]), then it represents the new optimum answer: we insert it into `OptAns` and we invoke the recursion on `optA'` (line [12]). Otherwise, we keep `optA` as optimum answer and skip p_x (line [14]). At the finish, we want an optimal answer that is not a subset of any other. This is done by selecting the maximal `optA` from `OptAns` by using `TakeMaximal` (line [15]).

Let us consider our running example. In the first round we produce the connected components. The mappers produce the local connected components through the pairs $< 1, \{p_1, p_2\} >$ and $1, \{p_3, p_5\} >$, the reducer produces one global connected component $cc_1 = \{p_1, p_2, p_3, p_5\}$, whose paths have, by using the scoring function implemented in [4], score 2.05, 1.63, 1.6 and 1.49, respectively. In the reduce phase of the second round, we analyse all possible combinations of the paths in cc_1 to find the optimum answer(s). Therefore, at the beginning we have `optA` $= \{p_1\}$, since p_1 has the highest score, and p_s is p_4 (i.e. it is the only path in the clusters). The value of τ is 1.86. Then, the algorithm retrieves the following admissible optima answers: $a'_1 = \{p_1, p_2, p_3\}$, $a'_2 = \{p_1, p_3\}$, and $a'_3 = \{p_1, p_2, p_5\}$. These answers are admissible because they satisfy the τ-*test* and their paths present pairwise intersections. During computation, the analysis skips answers $a'_4 = \{p_1, p_2, p_3, p_5\}$ and $a'_5 = \{p_1, p_3, p_5\}$ because they do not satisfy the τ-*test*: they have scores 1.55 and 1.26, respectively. Finally, the function `TakeMaximal` selects a'_1 as the final first optimum answer a_1 since it has more paths and the highest score. Following a similar process, at the second round, the algorithm returns $a_2 = \{p_4, p_5\}$ with a lesser score than a_1.

Computational Complexity. Following the discussion illustrated in [4], although this analysis achieves our goal, the computational complexity of the generation process is in $O(I^2)$, where I is the number of paths matching the input query Q. The execution of the first round functions is in $O(I)$ because: in the mapper we have that lines [2-3] are in $O(|\mathcal{CL}|) \in O(I)$, line [4] (it iterates over I paths once, see pseudo-code in [4]) and lines [5-6] are also in $O(I)$; line [1] of the reducer is in $O(I)$. Then, the connected components $cc \in$ `CC` are parallelly analysed in the second round. Algorithm 5 iterates over `CC` and therefore it is in $O(I)$. Algorithm 6 computes at most I insertions (through `InsertPathsInClusters`) and launches the function `MonotonicityAnalysis` that is in $O(I^2)$. This is a re-

Algorithm 7. Monotonicity Analysis

Input : A set of paths cc, an answer optA, a path p_s.
Output: The new (in case) optimum answer optA.

```
1  if cc is empty then
2      return optA;
3  else
4      OptAns ← ∅;
5      foreach p_x ∈ cc do
6          if (∄p_i ∈ optA : p_x ↔ p_i) and optA is not empty then
7              OptAns ← OptAns ∪ optA ;
8          else
9              optA' ← optA ∪ {p_x};
10             τ ← getTau(cc - {p_x }, p_s );
11             if score(optA', Q) ≥ τ then
12                 OptAns ← OptAns ∪ MonotonicityAnalysis(cc - {p_x }, optA',
                   p_s);
13             else
14                 OptAns ← OptAns ∪ optA ;
15     optA ← TakeMaximal(OptAns ) ;
16     return optA;
```

cursive function where the main executions are in lines [9-12] and line [15]. Both the executions are in $O(I)$, since we have I elements to analyse at the most. The recursion is called at most I times and therefore `MonotonicityAnalysis` is in $O(I^2)$, which is also the computational time complexity of the overall monotonic strategy. In the worst case, the computation is computed in $2 \times k$ rounds, two for each generated answer. A comprehensive discussion about the quality and accuracy of the answers according to measures of *exhaustivity* ($\mathcal{EX}$) and *specificity* ($\mathcal{SP}$) can be found in [4].

5 Related Work

We consider two different categories of related work that we discuss separately in the following.

RDF Keyword Search. Ad-hoc approaches for RDF have been proposed [6,15,18]. The work in [15] proposes a semi-automatic system to interpret the query into a set of candidate conjunctive queries. Users can refine the search by selecting the computed candidate queries to submit that represent their information need. Candidate queries are computed exploring the top-k sub-graphs matching the keywords. The approach in [18] relies on a RDFS domain knowledge to convert keywords in query-guides, which help users to incrementally build the desired semantic query. While unnecessary queries are not built (thus not executed), there is a strict dependency on user feedback. The work in [6] employs a ranking model based on IR and statistical methods.

Distributed RDF Processing. The distributed nature of the Semantic Web infrastructure arises the necessity to compute RDF data in a parallel and distributed fashion. Most of the works in this context [10,7,9,8,11,13,17] employ a distributed environment of RDF data-stores and compute SPARQL queries over them. In particular, the works in [10,8,9,11] make use of Hadoop or Hadoop/HBase to compute joins and manage the distribution of the query. DARQ [13] implements a framework to solve federated SPARQL queries. The work in [16] proposes a scalable P2P system for computing reasoning on RDF(S), while the work in [12] solves RDF path queries in MapReduce. All of these approaches exploit the structural information of the RDF data graph and are not applicable for solving keyword search queries, which miss such specifications. For this reason, all existing RDF keyword search approaches are centralized. TrinityRDF [17] considerably differs from the other approaches. It is an in-memory store where data is natively modelled as a graph. TrinityRDF is able to expedite the query processing by optimizing graph random accesses. Unfortunately, it requires a huge amount of memory and it is more suitable for a cloud infrastructure rather than a cluster of commodity machines.

6 Experimental Evaluation

We implemented our approach in YAANIIMR, a Java system for keyword search over RDF graphs, that is a MapReduce implementation of YAANII discussed in [4]. In our experiments, we used the benchmark provided by Coffman et al. [2] that employs two well-know datasets, IMDB and WIKIPEDIA, and an ideal counterpart due to its smaller size, MONDIAL. In our context, we used the RDF versions of three datasets: DBPEDIA (i.e. 266M triples) including *Linked IMDb*[2] for the benchmark related to IMDB, BILLION (i.e. 1000M triples) that is the *Billion Triple Challenge Dataset 2008*[3] including *Wikipedia3*[4] for WIKIPEDIA, while for MONDIAL we converted the SQL dump into RDF ourselves (i.e. 15000 triples). For each dataset, we run the set of 50 queries provided by [2] (see the paper for details and statistics). Since the results, and therefore the effectiveness, of YAANIIMR is the same of YAANII [4], in this section we focus exclusively on the performance.

Benchmark Environment. We deployed YAANIIMR on EC2 clusters. In particular, to fully understand the scale-up properties of YAANIIMR, we consider three EC2 *clusters quadruple* (i.e. *cc1.4xlarge* configuration as detailed by Amazon Web Service): 10, 50 and 100 nodes. YAANIIMR is provided with the Hadoop file system (HDFS) version 1.1.1 and the HBase data store version 0.94.3, and

[2] Available at `http://linkedmdb.org/`
[3] Available at `http://challenge.semanticweb.org/`
[4] Available at `http://stats.lod2.eu/rdfdocs/228`

compiled and run using Java 7. The performance of our systems has been measured with respect to data loading, memory footprint, and query execution.

Data Loading. We employ a path-based store on RDF for a distributed environment that is the evolution of the index in [1]. This is stored in HBase and supported by the distributed file system HDFS. The RDF dataset is indexed off-line. In particular, we index all the shortest paths starting from a source and ending with a sink. This task is efficiently performed by an optimized implementation of the *Breadth-first search* (BFS) strategy through MapReduce [3]. At running time we use the index to retrieve the paths whose sink node matches a keyword.

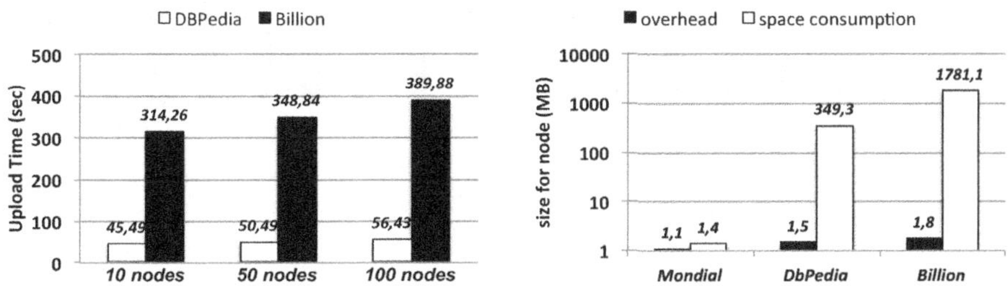

(a) (b)

Fig. 5. (a) Data loading times in seconds and (b) Data Space consumption expressed in MB in 10-nodes EC2 cluster

We used the three EC2 clusters to evaluate the upload time (the time to build all paths and to import them into our index) as showed in Fig. 5.(a). In particular the figure illustrates times only for DBPEDIA and BILLION, since MONDIAL spends only few seconds for starting up all jobs. Both DBPEDIA and BILLION achieve roughly the same upload times in any configuration, providing a linear trend: overall, these results show the efficiency of data loading in our system when scaling-out. Another significant advantage of our system relies in memory and space consumption. Let us consider the 10-nodes EC2 cluster. The overall memory overhead needed to maintain our index remains almost constant, and amounts to circa 1 MB of RAM for node. The total distributed space consumption for node scales perfectly with the size of the dataset. As illustrated in Fig. 5.(b), we have 1.4 MB, 349.3 MB and 1781.1 MB for node to store MONDIAL, DBPEDIA and BILLION in our cluster. Proportionally, we have the same behaviour for 50 and 100 nodes.

MapReduce Job Execution. The second evaluation analyses the performance of YAANIIMR when running MapReduce jobs. To this aim we measure the *end-to-end* job run-times, which is the time a given job takes to run completely. In this case, we perform three runs for each of the 50-queries (over the three datasets) to retrieve the top-10 answers: at the end we evaluate the geometric mean of all the runs of the 50 queries for dataset in the three EC2 clusters configurations (i.e. 10, 50 and 100 nodes), as shown in Fig. 6. In the figure, the job runtime is made by the *ideal time* (T_{ideal}) and the *overhead* ($T_{overhead}$) that are the effective time to run the query and the time to startup all necessary jobs, respectively. For each dataset we evaluate the average response time (i.e. computed by the geometric mean of times) of all queries executed by using both the linear, i.e. **L**, and the monotonic, i.e. **M**, strategy. Finally we replicated this experiment in 10-nodes, 50-nodes and 100-nodes cluster.

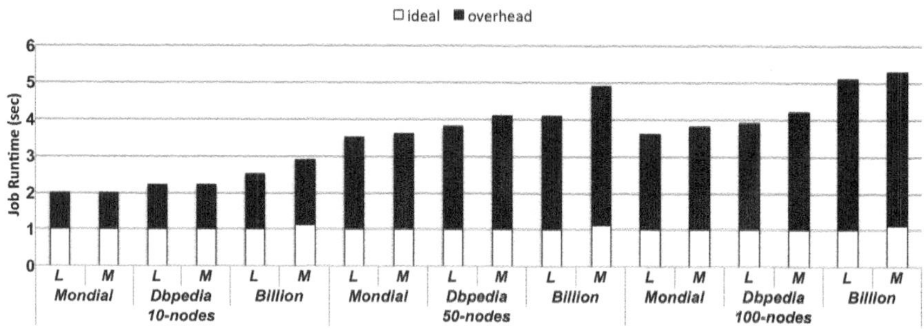

Fig. 6. End-to-end job runtimes

As we can see, $T_{overhead}$ dominates the total job runtime. To schedule a single job, Hadoop spends 1 or 2 seconds even though the actual task (query execution) just runs in a few ms. Therefore, it is comparable to YAANII [4]. Our implementation in MapReduce scales perfectly with respect to both the number of machines (i.e. 10, 50 and 100) and the dataset size (i.e. MONDIAL, DBPEDIA and BILLION).

7 Conclusions and Future Work

In this paper, we presented a novel approach to distributed keyword search query over large RDF datasets. It relies on a MapReduce environment and comprise two strategies for top-k query answering. The linear strategy enables the search to scale seamlessly with the size of the input, while the monotonic strategy guarantees the monotonicity of the output. Experimental results confirmed our algorithms and the advantage over other approaches. This work now opens several directions of further research. From a practical point of view, we are widening a more synthetic catalogue to store information and optimization techniques to speed-up the index creation and update.

References

1. Cappellari, P., De Virgilio, R., Maccioni, A., Roantree, M.: A path-oriented RDF index for keyword search query processing. In: Hameurlain, A., Liddle, S.W., Schewe, K.-D., Zhou, X. (eds.) DEXA 2011, Part II. LNCS, vol. 6861, pp. 366–380. Springer, Heidelberg (2011)

2. Coffman, J., Weaver, A.: An empirical performance evaluation of relational keyword search techniques. TKDE 99(PrePrints), 1 (2012)
3. Cosulschi, M., Cuzzocrea, A., De Virgilio, R.: Implementing bfs-based traversals of rdf graphs over mapreduce efficiently. In: CCGRID, pp. 569–574 (2013)
4. De Virgilio, R., Maccioni, A., Cappellari, P.: A linear and monotonic strategy to keyword search over RDF data. In: Daniel, F., Dolog, P., Li, Q. (eds.) ICWE 2013. LNCS, vol. 7977, pp. 338–353. Springer, Heidelberg (2013)
5. Dean, J., Ghemawat, S.: Mapreduce: Simplified data processing on large clusters. In: OSDI, pp. 137–150 (2004)
6. Elbassuoni, S., Blanco, R.: Keyword search over rdf graphs. In: CIKM (2011)
7. Harris, S., Lamb, N., Shadbolt, N.: 4store: The design and implementation of a clustered rdf store. In: SSWS (2009)
8. Huang, J., Abadi, D.J., Ren, K.: Scalable sparql querying of large rdf graphs. PVLDB 4(11), 1123–1134 (2011)
9. Husain, M.F.: Heuristics-based query processing for large rdf graphs using cloud computing. TKDE 23(9), 1312–1327 (2011)
10. Farhan Husain, M., Doshi, P., Khan, L., Thuraisingham, B.: Storage and retrieval of large RDF graph using hadoop and mapReduce. In: Jaatun, M.G., Zhao, G., Rong, C. (eds.) Cloud Computing. LNCS, vol. 5931, pp. 680–686. Springer, Heidelberg (2009)
11. Papailiou, N., Konstantinou, I., Tsoumakos, D., Koziris, N.: H2rdf: adaptive query processing on rdf data in the cloud. In: WWW, pp. 397–400 (2012)
12. Przyjaciel-Zablocki, M., Schätzle, A., Hornung, T., Lausen, G.: RDFPath: Path query processing on large RDF graphs with mapReduce. In: García-Castro, R., Fensel, D., Antoniou, G. (eds.) ESWC 2011. LNCS, vol. 7117, pp. 50–64. Springer, Heidelberg (2012)
13. Quilitz, B., Leser, U.: Querying distributed RDF data sources with SPARQL. In: Bechhofer, S., Hauswirth, M., Hoffmann, J., Koubarakis, M. (eds.) ESWC 2008. LNCS, vol. 5021, pp. 524–538. Springer, Heidelberg (2008)
14. Ravindra, P., Hong, S., Kim, H., Anyanwu, K.: Efficient processing of rdf graph pattern matching on mapreduce platforms. In: DataCloud-SC 2011, pp. 13–20 (2011)
15. Tran, T., Wang, H., Rudolph, S., Cimiano, P.: Top-k exploration of query candidates for efficient keyword search on graph-shaped (rdf) data. In: ICDE, pp. 405–416 (2009)
16. Tsatsanifos, G., Sacharidis, D., Sellis, T.K.: On enhancing scalability for distributed rdf/s stores. In: EDBT, pp. 141–152 (2011)
17. Zeng, K., Yang, J., Wang, H., Shao, B., Wang, Z.: A distributed graph engine for web scale rdf data. PVLDB 6(4), 265–276 (2013)
18. Zenz, G., Zhou, X., Minack, E., Siberski, W., Nejdl, W.: From keywords to semantic queries - incremental query construction on the semantic web. Journal of Web Semantics 7(3), 166–176 (2009)

NLP Data Cleansing Based on Linguistic Ontology Constraints

Dimitris Kontokostas[1], Martin Brümmer[1], Sebastian Hellmann[1], Jens Lehmann[1], and Lazaros Ioannidis[2]

[1] Universität Leipzig, Institut für Informatik, AKSW, Germany
{lastname}@informatik.uni-leipzig.de
http://aksw.org

[2] Aristotle University of Thessaloniki, Medical Physics Laboratory, Greece
lioannid@math.auth.gr

Abstract. Linked Data comprises of an unprecedented volume of structured data on the Web and is adopted from an increasing number of domains. However, the varying quality of published data forms a barrier for further adoption, especially for Linked Data consumers. In this paper, we extend a previously developed methodology of Linked Data quality assessment, which is inspired by test-driven software development. Specifically, we enrich it with ontological support and different levels of result reporting and describe how the method is applied in the Natural Language Processing (NLP) area. NLP is – compared to other domains, such as biology – a late Linked Data adopter. However, it has seen a steep rise of activity in the creation of data and ontologies. NLP data quality assessment has become an important need for NLP datasets. In our study, we analysed 11 datasets using the *lemon* and *NIF* vocabularies in 277 test cases and point out common quality issues.

Keywords: #eswc2014Kontokostas, Linked Data, NLP, data quality.

1 Introduction

Linked Data (LD) comprises of an unprecedented volume of structured data on the Web and is adopted from an increasing number of domains. However, the varying quality of the published data forms a barrier in further adoption, especially for Linked Data consumers.

Natural Language Processing (NLP) is – compared to other domains, such as Biology – a late LD adopter with a steep rise of activity in the creation of vocabularies, ontologies and data publishing. A plethora of workshops and conferences such as LDL `http://ldl2014.org/`, WoLE `http://wole2013.eurecom.fr`, LREC `http://lrec2014.lrec-conf.org`, MLODE `http://sabre2012.infai.org/mlode`, NLP&DBpedia `http://nlp-dbpedia2013.blogs.aksw.org/program/`) motivate researchers to adopt Linked Data and RDF/OWL and convert traditional data formats such as XML and relational databases. Although guidelines and best practices for this conversion exist, developers from NLP are

V. Presutti et al. (Eds.): ESWC 2014, LNCS 8465, pp. 224–239, 2014.

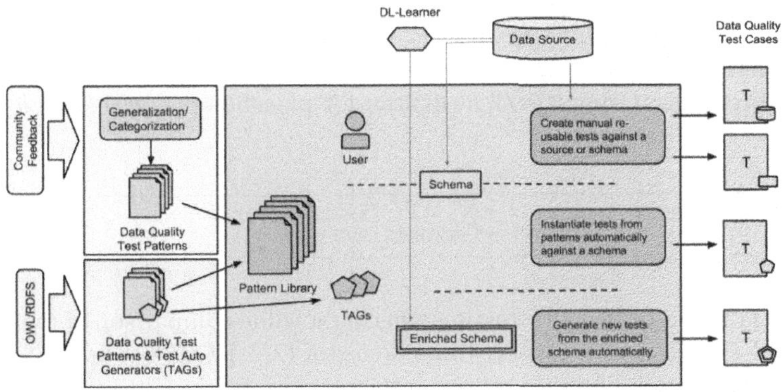

Fig. 1. Flowchart showing the test-driven data quality methodology. The left part displays the input sources of our pattern library. In the middle part the different ways of pattern instantiation are shown which lead to the Data Quality Test Cases on the right.

often unfamiliar with them, resulting in low quality and inoperable data. In this paper, we address the subsequently arising need for data quality assessment of those NLP datasets.

We extended a recently introduced test-driven data quality methodology [12] inspired by tests in software engineering. In its introduction, the methodology in [12] focused on two approaches: (1) automatically-generated test cases which were derived from the OWL/RDFS schema of the ontologies and (2) test cases adhering to patterns from a pattern library. These two approaches were evaluated on popular ontologies and data sets such as FOAF or the DBpedia Ontology and it was shown that the methodology is well suited for horizontal, multi-domain data quality assessment, i.e. massive detection of errors for five large-scale LOD data sets as well as on 291 vocabularies, independent of their domain or their purpose. In this paper, we will briefly introduce the methodology in Section 2 including a comparison of our methodology to `OWL` reasoning. The *Test Driven Data Engineering Ontology* is described in Section 3. Using the ontology, we can annotate test cases and provide support for different levels of result reporting allowing to give feedback to developers when running these tests and ultimately improving data quality.

Additionally, we show progress in implementing domain-specific validation by quickly improving existing validation provided by ontology maintainers. We specifically analysed datasets for two emerging domain ontologies, the *lemon model* [13] and the *NIF 2.0 Core Ontology* [10] in Section 4 and evaluated 11 datasets in Section 5.

2 Overview of Test-Driven Data Assessment Methodology

In this section we introduce basic notions of our methodology. A thorough description of test-driven quality assessment methodology can be found in [12].

Data Quality Test Pattern (DQTP). A data quality test pattern is a SPARQL query template with variable placeholders. Possible types of the pattern variables are IRIs, literals, operators, datatype values (e.g. integers) and regular expressions. Using %%v%% as syntax for placeholders, an example DQTP is:

```
SELECT ?s WHERE { ?s %%P1%% ?v1. ?s  %%P2%%   ?v2 .
                  FILTER ( ?v1 %%OP%% ?v2 ) }
```

This DQTP can be used for testing whether a value comparison of two properties $P1$ and $P2$ holds with respect to an operator OP. DQTPs represent abstract patterns, which can be further refined into concrete data quality test cases using test pattern bindings.

Test Pattern Binding. Test pattern bindings are valid DQTP variable replacements.

Data Quality Test Case. Applying a pattern binding to a DQTP results in an executable SPARQL query. Each result of the query is considered to be a violation of a test case. A test case may have four different results: success (empty result), violation (results are returned), timeout (test is marked for further inspection) and error (something prevented the query execution). An example test pattern binding and resulting data quality test case is[1]:

```
P1  =>  dbo:birthDate |   SELECT ?s WHERE {
P2  =>  dbo:deathDate |    ?s  dbo:birthDate  ?v1.
OP  =>  >             |    ?s  dbo:deathDate  ?v2.
                      |    FILTER ( ?v1 > ?v2 ) }
```

Test Auto Generator (TAG). A Test Auto Generator reuses the RDFS and OWL modelling of a knowledge base to verify data quality. In particular, a TAG, based on a DQTP, takes a schema as input and returns test cases. TAGs consist of a detection and an execution part. The detection part is a query against a schema and for every result of a detection query, a test case is instantiated from the respective pattern, for instance:

```
# TAG                                 | # TQDP
SELECT DISTINCT ?P1 ?P2               | SELECT DISTINCT
WHERE {                               | ?s WHERE {
?P1 owl:propertyDisjointWith ?P2.     | ?s %%P1%% ?v.
}                                     | ?s %%P2%% ?v.}
```

Additionally, we devise the notion of RDF test case coverage based on a combination of six individual coverage metrics [12].

[1] We use `http://prefix.cc` to resolve all name spaces and prefixes. A full list can be found at `http://prefix.cc/popular/all`

The test-driven data quality methodology is illustrated in Figure 1. As shown in the figure, there are two major sources for the creation of tests. One source is stakeholder feedback from everyone involved in the usage of a dataset and the other source is the already existing `RDFS/OWL` schema of a dataset. Based on this, there are several ways to create tests:

1. *Manually create test cases:* Test cases specific to a certain dataset or schema can be written manually. This can be guided choosing suitable DQTPs of our pattern library. Tests that refer to the schema of a common vocabulary can become part of a central library to facilitate later reuse.
2. *Reusing tests based on common vocabularies:* Naturally, a major goal in the Semantic Web is to reuse existing vocabularies instead of creating new ones. We detect the used vocabularies in a dataset, which allows to re-use tests from a test pattern library.
3. *Using `RDFS/OWL` constraints directly:* As previously explained, tests can be automatically created via TAGs in this case.
4. *Enriching the `RDFS/OWL` constraints:* Since many datasets provide only limited schema information, we perform automatic schema enrichment as recently researched in [4]. Those schema enrichment methods can take an `RDF` dataset or a SPARQL endpoint as input and automatically suggest schema axioms with a certain confidence value by analysing the dataset. In our methodology, this is used to create further tests via TAGs.

The *RDFUnit* Suite [2] [3] implements the test driven data assessment methodology The methodology is implemented in a Java component and released as open source under the Apache licence.

Relation between SPARQL Test Cases and OWL Reasoning. SPARQL test cases can detect a subset of common validation errors detectable by a sound and complete `OWL` reasoner. However, this is limited by a) the reasoning support offered by the used SPARQL endpoint and b) the limitations of the OWL-to-SPARQL translation. On the other hand, SPARQL test cases can find validation errors that are not expressible in `OWL`, but within the expressivity of SPARQL (see [1] for more details and a proof that SPARQL 1.0 has the same expressive power as relational algebra under bag semantics). This includes aggregates, property paths, filter expressions etc. Please note that for scalability reasons full `OWL` reasoning is often not feasible on large datasets. Furthermore, many datasets are already deployed and easy to access via SPARQL endpoints. Additionally, the *Data Quality Test Pattern* (DQTP) library may arguably provide a more user friendly approach for building validation rules compared to modelling `OWL` axioms. However, the predefined DQTP library has some limitations as well, in particular a) it requires familiarity with the library in order to choose the correct DQTP and 2) custom validations cannot always correspond to an existing DQTP and manual SPARQL test cases are required.

[2] `https://github.com/AKSW/RDFUnit`

[3] `http://RDFUnit.aksw.org`

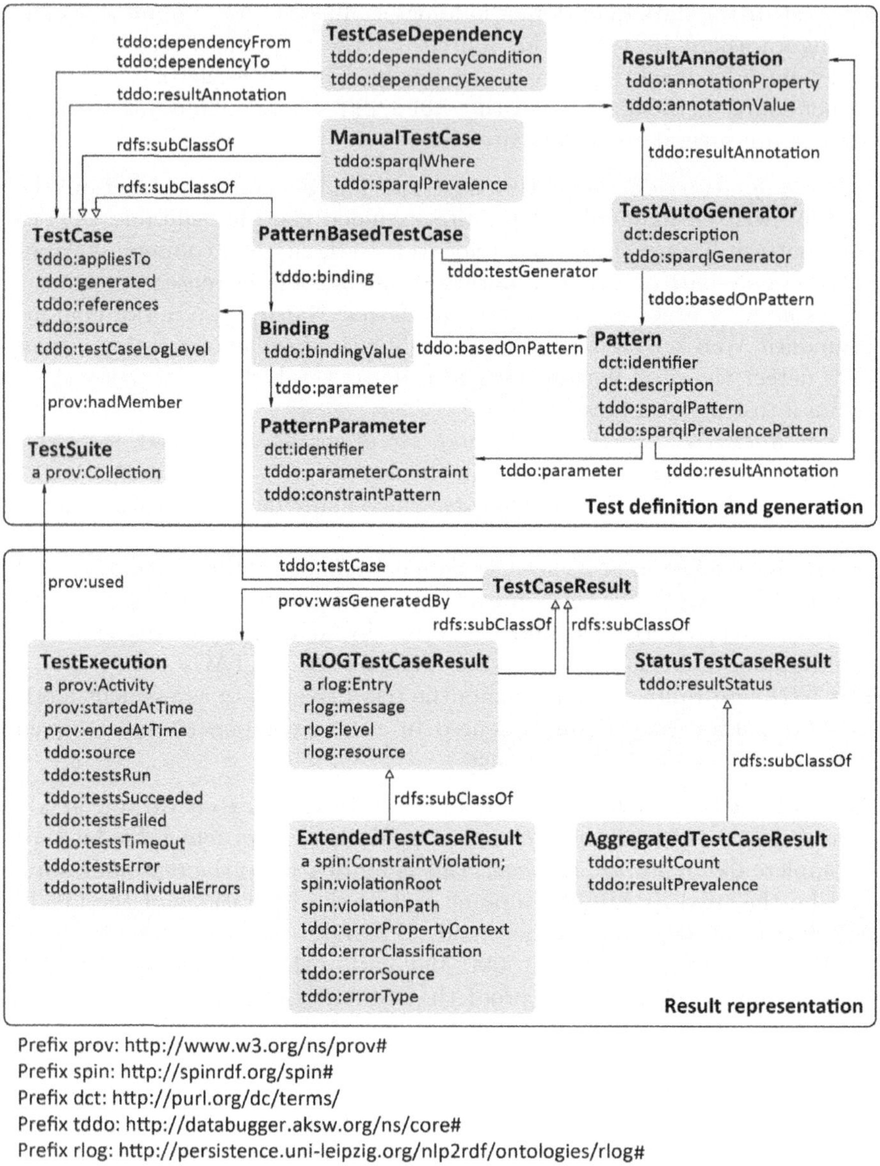

Fig. 2. Class dependencies for the test driven data engineering ontology

3 Test Driven Data Engineering Ontology

The Test Driven Data Assessment methodology is implemented using RDF as input and output and complies with our accompanied ontology.[4] The ontology

[4] `http://RDFUnit.aksw.org/ns/core#`

additionally serves as a self-validation layer for the application input (test-cases, DQTPs and TAGs) and output (validation results). The ontology consists of 20 classes and 36 properties and reuses the PROV [2], RLOG[5] and spin[6] ontologies. As depicted in Figure 2, the ontology is centered around two concepts, the test case definition and generation and the result representation.

Test Case Definition and Generation. We encapsulate a list of test cases in a *TestSuite*, a subclass of `prov:Collection` that enumerates the contained test cases with `prov:hadMember`. The class *TestCase* describes an abstract test case. For each test case, we provide provenance with the following properties:

- `:appliesTo` to denote whether the test case applies to a schema, a dataset or an application.
- `:source`, the URI of the schema, dataset or application.
- `:generated` on how the test case was created (automatic or manually).
- `:references` a list of URIs a test case uses for validation.
- `:testCaseLogLevel` an `rlog:Level` this test case is associated with. In accordance to software development, the available log levels are: TRACE, DEBUG, INFO, WARN, ERROR and FATAL.

Additionally, each *TestCase* is associated with two SPARQL queries, a query for the constraint violations and a query for the prevalence of the violations. The prevalence query is optional because it cannot be computed in all cases.

```
# Violation Query                | # Prevalence Query
SELECT DISTINCT ?s WHERE {       | select count(distinct ?s) WHERE {
  ?s  dbo:birthDate  ?v1.        |    ?s dbo:birthDate ?v1 .
  ?s  dbo:deathDate  ?v2.        |    ?s dbo:deathDate ?v2 . }
  FILTER ( ?v1 > ?v2 ) }         |
```

Concrete instantiations of a *TestCase* are the *ManualTestCase* and the *PatternBasedTestCase* classes. In the former, the tester defines the SPARQL queries manually while the in the latter she provides *Bindings* for a *Pattern*. Additionally, the ontology allows the definition of dependencies between test cases. For example *if test case A fails, do not execute test case B*. This is achieved with the *TestCaseDependency* class where `:dependencyFrom` and `:dependencyTo` define the dependent test cases, `:dependencyCondition` is the status result that triggers an execute or don't execute (`:dependencyExecute`) for the dependant test case.

A *Pattern* is identified and described with the `dct:identifier` and `dct:description` properties. The `:sparqlPattern` and `:sparqlPrevalencePattern` properties hold the respective SPARQL queries with placeholder for replacement. For each placeholder a *PatternParameter* is defined and connected to the pattern with the `:parameter` property.

PatternParameters are described with a `dct:identifier` and two restriction properties: the `:parameterConstraint` to restrict the type of a parameter to

[5] `http://persistence.uni-leipzig.org/nlp2rdf/ontologies/rlog#`

[6] `http://spinrdf.org`

Operator, Resource, Property or Class and the optional `:constraintPattern` for a regular expression constraint on the parameter values.

Bindings link to a *PatternParameter* and a value through the `:parameter` and `:bindingValue` properties respectively. *PatternBasedTestCases* are associated with *Bindings* through the `:binding` property.

```
[] a tddo:PatternBasedTestCase ;
   tddo:binding [ a        tddo:Binding ;
       tddo:bindingValue lemon:Node ;
       tddo:parameter tddp:OWLDISJC-T1 ] ;
```

A *PatternBasedTestCase* can be automatically instantiated through a *TestAutoGenerator*. Generators hold a `dct:description`, a sparql query (`:generatorSparql`) and a link to a pattern (`:basedOnPattern`).

Result Representation. For the result representation we reuse the PROV Ontology. The *TestExecution* class is a subclass of `prov:Activity` that executes a *TestSuite* (`prov:used`) against a `:source` and generates a number of *TestCaseResults*. Additional properties of the *TestExecution* class are `prov:startedAtTime` and `prov:endedAtTime` as well as aggregated execution statistics like: `:testsRun`, `:testsSucceeded`, `:testsFailed`, `:testsTimeout`, `:testsError` and `:totalIndividualErrors`.

The ontology supports four levels or result reporting, two for report on the test case level and two for individual error reporting. All result types are subclasses of the *TestCaseResult* class and for provenance we link to a *TestCase* with `:testCase` and a *TestExecution* with `prov:wasGeneratedBy` properties. The *StatusTestCaseResult* class contains a single `:resultStatus` that can be one of *Success*, *Fail*, *Timeout* and *Error*. The *AggregatedTestCaseResult* class adds up to the *StatusTestCaseResult* class by providing an aggregated view on the individual errors of a test case with the properties `:resultCount` and `:resultPrevalence`.

For the individual error reporting the *RLOGTestCaseResult* generates logging messages through the RLog ontology. For every violation, we report the erroneous resource (`rlog:resource`), a message (`rlog:message`) and a logging level (`rlog:level`). The logging level is retrieved from the *TestCase*.

The *ExtendedTestCaseResult* class extends *RLOGTestCaseResult* by providing additional properties for error debugging by reusing the spin ontology. In detail, an *ExtendedTestCaseResult* is a subclass of `spin:ConstraintViolation` and may have the following properties:

- `spin:violationRoot`: the erroneous resource.
- `spin:violationPath`: the property of the resource that the error occurs.
- `:errorPropertyContext`: lists additional properties that may provide a better context for fixing the error. For example, in the `dbo:birthDate` before a `dbo:deathDate` case, `dbo:birthDate` can be the `spin:violationPath` and `dbo:deathDate` the `:errorPropertyContext`.
- `:errorClassification`: is a sub-property of `dct:subject` that points to a SKOS error classification category.

Table 1. Number of automatically generated test cases per ontology. We provide the total number of test cases as well as separated per `rdfs domain` and `range`, literal datatype, `OWL` cardinality (min, max, exact), property & class disjointness, functional and inverse functional constraints.

	Total	Domain	Range	Datatype	Card.	Disj.	Func.	I. Func.
Lemon	172	40	34	1	29	64	3	1
NIF	86	42	24	4		6	10	

- `:errorSource`: is a sub-property of `dct:subject` that points to a SKOS error source category. Example values can be data parsing, data publishing, mapping, pre processing, post processing, etc.
- `:errorType`: is a sub-property of `dct:subject` and that points to a SKOS error type category on the triple level. Example values can be: missing property, redundant property, inaccurate property.

The extended error annotation is generated through the *ResultAnnotation* class that is attached to a *TestCase* through the `:resultAnnotation` property. A ResultAnnotation must contain an `:annotationProperty` linking to one of the allowed *ExtendedTestCaseResult* properties and an appropriate value for `:annotationValue`. For the schema-based automatic test case generation some of the annotation may be known only on the *Pattern* level and other on the *TestAutoGenerator* level. Thus, *ResultAnnotations* are allowed in both classes and the error annotation are added up on the test case generation.

Finally, we provide `:testSuite`, an ontology annotation property, that links an ontology to an appropriate *TestSuite* for data validation purposes.

```
<http://example.com/ontology#>
    a owl:Ontology ;
    tddo:testCase <http://example.com/testCase> .
```

4 Test Case Implementation for Linguistic Ontologies

In this section, we will discuss the employment of RDFUnit for *lemon* and *NIF*, especially with regard to these questions: (1) What is the coverage of the automatically generated tests, what are their limitations. (2) Where is it feasible to use the predefined patterns from the pattern library [12]? Are there test cases that are too complex and need manual creation by an expert? (3) Which test cases can not be expressed at all as they are not expressible via SPARQL?

By running the existing RDFUnit Test Auto Generators (TAG) on the *lemon* and *NIF* ontologies we automatically generated 172 test cases for *lemon* and 86 test cases for *NIF* (cf. Table 1). Both ontologies are of similar size: *NIF* contains 19 classes and 46 properties while *lemon* 23 classes and 55 properties. The number of increased test cases in *lemon* results from the higher amount of defined cardinality and disjointness restrictions. The RDFUnit Suite, at the time of writing, does not provide full OWL coverage and thus, complex `owl:Restrictions` cannot be handled yet. In the frame of the examined ontologies, RDFUnit did not produce test cases for unions of (`owl:unionOf`) restrictions such as multiple cardinalities for `lemon:LexicalSense` and `lemon:LemonElement` or restrictions with `owl:allValuesFrom`, `owl:someValuesFrom` and `owl:hasSelf` for *NIF*.

Both *NIF* and *lemon* have defined semantic constraints that can not be captured in OWL and are too complex for the above-mentioned pattern library. In particular, *NIF* and *lemon* use natural language text in the `rdfs:comment` properties as well as their documentations and specification documents.

For *lemon*, the maintainers implemented a Python validator[7], which enables us to directly compare our efforts to a software validator. For *NIF* there was an early prototype of RDFUnit that used only manual SPARQL test cases.

4.1 Lemon

According to Table 1, test cases for `rdfs:domain` and `rdfs:range` restrictions are the largest group, at 43.8%, followed by tests for disjointness (37.4%) and cardinality restrictions (18.8%). The existing *lemon* validator contains 24 test cases for some structural criteria of the *lemon* ontology. 14 of these tests are natively covered by the existing RDFUnit TAGs. Out of the 10 remaining cases, four where on warning and info level, based on recommendations from the ontology's guidelines. They are thus not explicitly stated in OWL, because they don't constitute logical errors and can not be covered by automatic test generation. Of the six remaining errors, two where expressed via `owl:unionOf` and two could not be expressed by the ontology's author because OWL is not able to express them. Additionally, the *lemon* validator reported undeclared properties under the *lemon* namespace. Although this test case can be expressed in SPARQL, it was not implemented at the time of writing.

The last error case not covered was due to an error in the ontology itself. *Lemon* defines that every instance of `lemon:LexicalEntry` may have a maximum of one `lemon:canonicalForm` property. Yet, the validator fails if the instance has no `lemon:canonicalForm`, thus suggesting that instead of the `owl:maxCardinality`, a `owl:cardinality` restriction was intended in this case. These kind of semantic subtleties are usually very hard to detect in the complex domain of ontology engineering. It shows that the intensive engagement necessary to write the test cases already serves to debug the ontologies underlying the datasets. This extends the test-driven approach to the ontology development, apart from the quality assessment.

These test cases could directly be translated into SPARQL queries for testing with RDFUnit. For example, it is suggested that a `lemon:LexicalEntry` should contain an `rdfs:label`. As there is no possibility to express these optional constraints in OWL, this test case was added manually to log matching resources as an info-level notice.

[7] `https://github.com/jmccrae/lemon-model.net/blob/master/validator/lemon-validator.py`

Beyond the implementation of the *lemon* validator as test cases, some additional test cases were added to test for semantic correctness or properties that could be added. For example, the `lemon:narrower` relation, which denotes that one sense of a word is narrower than the other, must never be symmetric or contain cycles.

```
SELECT DISTINCT ?s WHERE {
  ?s lemon:narrower+ ?narrower .
  ?narrower lemon:narrower+ ?s . }
```

Similarly, if one resource is `lemon:narrower` to another resource, the inverse relationship (`lemon:broader`) should exist in the database.

From the total of ten manual test cases that were defined for *lemon*, five were described as *PatternBasedTestCases*, using the existing pattern library, and five as *ManualTestCases* using custom SPARQL queries. However, for brevity we described the test case with the final SPARQL queries.

4.2 NIF

Almost 50% of automated *NIF* test cases were for `rdfs:domain` constraints, 27% for `rdfs:range`, 11% for `owl:FunctionalPropery` restrictions, 7% for disjointness and 5% for proper datatype usage. The early prototype of RDFUnit that is used as the *NIF* validator did not cover any schema constraints and consists of 10 test cases. There exists one test case on the warning level that reports classes of the old namespace.

Other manual test cases include the following restrictions:

- An occurrence of `nif:beginIndex` inside a `nif:Context` must be equal to zero (0).
- The length of `nif:isString` inside a `nif:Context` must be equal to `nif:endIndex`.
- A `nif:anchorOf` string must match the substring of the `nif:isString` from `nif:beginIndex` to `nif:endIndex`. For example:

```
SELECT DISTINCT ?s WHERE  {
  ?s  nif:anchorOf ?anchorOf ;  nif:beginIndex ?beginIndex ;
      nif:endIndex ?endIndex  ;
      nif:referenceContext [ nif:isString ?referenceString ]  .
  BIND (SUBSTR(?referenceString ,
               ?beginIndex , (?endIndex - ?beginIndex) ) AS ?test ) .
  FILTER (str(?test) != str(?anchorOf )) . }
```

- `nif:CString` is an abstract class and thus a subclass such as `nif:CStringImpl` or `nif:RFC5147String` must be used.
- All instances of `nif:CString` that are not `nif:Context` must have a `nif:referenceContext` property.
- All instances of `nif:Context` must also be instances of a `nif:CString` subclass.
- Misspelled `rdf:type` declarations for class names, for example `nif:RFC5147String`.

- All instances of `nif:CString` must have the properties `nif:beginIndex` and `nif:endIndex`.
- all `nif:Context` must have an explicit `nif:isString`, `nif:isString` can only occur with `nif:Context`.

5 Evaluation

For evaluation purposes we gathered a representative sample of *lemon* and *NIF* datasets in Table 2. We loaded all the datasets in an open-source edition of Virtuoso server (version 7.0)[8] and ran RDFUnit for each one of them. The results of the dataset evaluation are provided in Table 3.

Looking at the results of Table 3 we observe that manual test cases can be of equal importance to the schema restrictions. Additionally we notice that the *lemon*-based datasets were more erroneous than the *NIF*-based datasets. This may be attributed to the following reasons:

- the *NIF* datasets were smaller in size and, thus, better curated.
- the DBpedia Wiktionary datasets is derived from a crowd-sourced source, which makes it more prone to errors.
- the *lemon* ontology is stricter than the *NIF* ontology.
- [16] already used the early prototype of RDFUnit and fixed all data errors found by manual test cases.

All *lemon* datasets failed the info level test case that required at least one and unique `lemon:language` in a `lemon:LexicalEntry`. The existence of a `lemon:subsense` or exactly one `lemon:reference` also failed in all datasets with a high number of violations, except Wordnet that had only 33. Additionally, all datasets had a high number of violation on the `owl:minCardinality` of 1 constraint of `lemon:lexicalForm` on the `lemon:LexicalEntry` class. However, all datasets had the appropriate number of `lemon:canonicalForm` properties, which is a sub-property of `lemon:lexicalForm` and invalidates these errors. This constraint of RDFUnit, stems from the fact that transitive sub-property checking is not implemented at the time of writing. Except from the DBpedia Wiktionary dataset, all other *lemon* datasets had many reports of a `lemon:LemonEntry` without a label.

The DBpedia Wiktionary dataset had only five failed test cases. With an addition to the previous three, the dataset returned 163K violations due to the disjointness of the `lemon:LexicalEntry` class with the `lemon:LexicalSense` class constraint and 3.5M violations of missing a required `lemon:lexicalForm` property in a `lemon:LexicalEntry`. The same query returned 270K errors in the QHL dataset.

The Uby Wiktionaries had many failed test cases with a very low (less than 10) number of violations except from `owl:minCardinality` of one in `lemon:Form` class for the `lemon:representation` property. This test case returned 430K errors on the English version and 200K errors on the German. Wordnet also failed this test case with 130K violations. Finally, other high in number of violation

[8] `http://virtuoso.openlinksw.com`

Table 2. Tested datasets

Name	Description	Ontology	Type
lemon datasets			
LemonUby Wiktionary EN [9] [5]	Conversion of the English Wiktionary into UBY-LMF model	lemon, UBY-LMF	Dictionary
LemonUby Wiktionary DE [10] [5]	Conversion of the German Wiktionary into UBY-LMF model	lemon, UBY-LMF	Dictionary
LemonUby Wordnet [11] [5]	Conversion of the Princeton WordNet 3.0 into UBY-LMF model	lemon, UBY-LMF	WordNet
DBpedia Wiktionary [12] [9]	Conversion of the English Wiktionary into lemon	lemon	Dictionary
QHL [13] [15]	Multilingual translation graph from more than 50 lexicons	lemon	Dictionary
NIF datasets			
Wikilinks[14] [10]	sample of 60976 randomly selected phrases linked to Wikipedia articles	NIF	NER
DBpedia Spotlight dataset[15] [18]	58 manually NE annotated natural language sentences	NIF	NER
KORE 50 evaluation dataset[16] [18]	50 NE annotated natural language sentences from the AIDA corpus	NIF	NER
News-100[17] [16]	100 manually annotated German news articles	NIF	NER
RSS-500[18] [16]	500 manually annotated sentences from 1,457 RSS feeds	NIF	NER
Reuters-128[19] [16]	128 news articles manually curated	NIF	NER

[9] http://lemon-model.net/lexica/uby/WktDE/WktEN.nt.gz
[10] http://lemon-model.net/lexica/uby/WktDE/WktDE.nt.gz
[11] http://lemon-model.net/lexica/uby/wn/wn.nt.gz
[12] http://downloads.dbpedia.org/wiktionary/dumps/en/wiktionary_en_2013-09-17_dump-20130726.ttl.bz2
[13] http://linked-data.org/datasets/qhl.ttl.zip
[14] http://mlode.nlp2rdf.org/datasets/wikilinks-sample.ttl.tar.gz
[15] http://www.yovisto.com/labs/ner-benchmarks/data/dbpedia-spotlight-nif.ttl
[16] http://www.yovisto.com/labs/ner-benchmarks/data/kore50-nif.ttl
[17] https://raw.github.com/AKSW/n3-collection/master/News-100.ttl
[18] https://raw.github.com/AKSW/n3-collection/master/RSS-500.ttl
[19] https://raw.github.com/AKSW/n3-collection/master/Reuters-128.ttl

Table 3. Overview of the NLP datasets test execution. For every dataset, we provide the size in triples count, the number of test cases that were successful, failed, timed-out and did not complete due to an error. Additionally, we mention the total the number of the individual violations from automated test cases along with errors, warnings and infos from manual test cases.

	Size	SC	FL	TO	ER	AErrors	MErrors	MWarn	MInfo
WiktDBp	60M	177	5	-	-	3.746.103	7.521.791	-	3.582.837
WktEN	8M	168	14	-	-	752.018	394.766	-	633.270
WktDE	2M	170	12	-	-	273.109	66.268	-	155.598
Wordnet	4M	166	16	-	-	257.228	36	-	257.204
QHL	3M	170	11	-	1	433.118	538.933	-	538.016
Wikilinks	0.6M	91	4	-	1	141.528	21.246	-	-
News-100	13K	91	2	-	3	3.510	-	-	-
RSS-500	10K	91	2	-	3	3.000	-	-	-
Reuters-128	7K	91	2	-	3	2.016	-	-	-
Spotlight	3K	92	3	-	1	662	68	-	-
KORE50	2K	89	6	-	1	301	55	-	-

test cases are found in the QHL dataset and regard incorrect domain (30K) and range (68K) of `lemon:entry` and wrong range of `lemon:sense` (67K).

The most common test case that failed in all *NIF* datasets is the incorrect datatype of `nif:beginIndex` and `nif:endIndex`. Both properties are defined as `xsd:nonNegativeInteger` but were used as string Literals. This is due to a recent change of the *NIF* specification but also showcases the usefulness of our methodology for data evolution. The correct datatype of `nif:beginIndex` and `nif:endIndex` are also the reason for the *NIF* test cases that returned an error. In these cases, substrings based on these properties were calculated on the query (cf. Section 4.2) and non-numeric values did not allow a proper SPARQL query evaluation. This case also expresses the need for chained test cases execution (*TestCaseDependency* in cf. Section 3). The existence of a `nif:beginIndex` and `nif:endIndex` in a `nif:CString` also return violation in spotlight (68) kore50 (51) and Wikilinks (21K) datasets. Finally 21K objects in a `nif:wasConvertedFrom` relation did not have `nif:String` as range.

A direct comparison or our results with the results of the implemented validators cannot be provided in a consistent way. The *NIF* validator contained only 10 test cases while our approach had a total of 96 test cases. The *lemon* validator on the other hand could not finish after 48 hours for the DBpedia Wiktionay dataset and resulted in a multitude of non-RDF logging messages that were hard to filter and aggregate.

6 Related Work

There exist several approaches for assessing the quality of Linked Data. They can be broadly classified into (i) automated (e.g. [8]), (ii) semi-automated (e.g. [6]) or (iii) manual (e.g. [3,14]) methodologies. These approaches are useful at the process level wherein they introduce systematic methodologies to assess the quality of a dataset. However, the drawbacks include a considerable amount of user involvement, inability to produce interpretable results, or not allowing a user the freedom to choose the input dataset. In [11] errors occurring while publishing RDF data along were detected with a description of effects and means to improve the quality of structured data on the web. In a recent study, 4 million RDF/XML documents were analysed which provided insights into the level of conformance these documents had in accordance to the Linked Data guidelines. On the one hand, these efforts contributed towards assessing a vast amount of Web or RDF/XML data, however, most of the analysis was performed automatically, therefore overlooking the problems arising due to contextual discrepancies.

The approach described in [7] advocates the use of SPARQL and SPIN for RDF data quality assessment and shares some similarity with our methodology. However, a domain expert is required for the instantiation of test patterns. *SPARQL Inferencing Notation* (SPIN) [20] is a W3C submission aiming at representing rules and constraints on Semantic Web models. SPIN also allows users to define SPARQL functions and reuse SPARQL queries. The difference between SPIN and our pattern syntax, is that SPIN functions would not fully support our *Pattern Bindings*. SPIN function arguments must have specific constraints on the argument datatype or argument class and do not support operators, e.g. '=', '>', '!', '+', '*', or property paths.[21] However, our approach is still compatible with SPIN when allowing to initialise templates with specific sets of applicable operators. In that case, however, the number of templates increases. Due to this restrictions, with SPIN we can define fewer but more general constraints. One of the advantages of converting our templates to SPIN is that the structure of the SPARQL query itself can be stored directly in RDF, which is, however, very complex and difficult to manage. From the efforts related to SPIN, we re-used their existing data quality patterns and ontologies for error types.

Pellet Integrity Constraint Validator [17](ICV)[22] translates OWL integrity constraints into SPARQL queries. Similar to our approach, the execution of those SPARQL queries indicates violations. An implication of the integrity constraint semantics of Pellet ICV is that a partial unique names assumption (all resources are considered to be different unless equality is explicitly stated) and a closed world assumption is in effect. We use the same strategy as part of our methodology, but go beyond it by allowing users to directly (re-)use DQTPs not necessarily encoded in OWL.

7 Conclusion and Future Work

In this article, we extended a previously introduced methodology for test-driven quality assessment. In particular, a data engineering ontology was described in detail. We applied the RDFUnit Suite implementing this methodology to the

[20] `http://www.w3.org/Submission/spin-overview/`
[21] `http://www.w3.org/TR/2010/WD-sparql11-property-paths-20100126/`
[22] `http://clarkparsia.com/pellet/icv/`

NLP domain, an area in which RDF usage is currently rising and there is a need for quality assessment. In particular, we devised 277 test cases for NLP datasets using the Lemon and *NIF* vocabularies.

In future work, we aim to extend the test cases to more NLP ontologies, such as MARL, NERD and ITSRDF. We also plan to further increase the scope of the framework, e.g. for the recently changed namespaces of *NIF* and *lemon* deprecation warnings should be produced. Another extension is the modeling of dependencies between test cases, which is currently done manually and could be automated. Furthermore, we also want to apply our methods on services: Usually, semantically enriched NLP services use text as input and return annotations in RDF, which could then be verified by RDFUnit to validate their output.

Acknowledgments. We would like to thank John McCrae for his support regarding lemon. This work was supported by grants from the EU's 7th Framework Programme provided for the projects LIDER (GA no. 610782), LOD2 (GA no. 257943) and GeoKnow (GA no. 318159).

References

1. Angles, R., Gutierrez, C.: The expressive power of SPARQL. In: Sheth, A.P., Staab, S., Dean, M., Paolucci, M., Maynard, D., Finin, T., Thirunarayan, K. (eds.) ISWC 2008. LNCS, vol. 5318, pp. 114–129. Springer, Heidelberg (2008)
2. Belhajjame, K., Cheney, J., Corsar, D., Garijo, D., Soiland-Reyes, S., Zednik, S., Zhao, J.: Prov-o: The prov ontology. Technical report (2013)
3. Bizer, C., Cyganiak, R.: Quality-driven information filtering using the WIQA policy framework. Web Semantics 7(1), 1–10 (2009)
4. Bühmann, L., Lehmann, J.: Pattern based knowledge base enrichment. In: Alani, H., et al. (eds.) ISWC 2013, Part I. LNCS, vol. 8218, pp. 33–48. Springer, Heidelberg (2013)
5. Eckle-Kohler, J., McCrae, J.P., Chiarcos, C.: lemonuby - a large, interlinked, syntactically-rich resource for ontologies. Submitted to the Semantic Web Journal
6. Flemming, A.: Quality characteristics of linked data publishing datasources. Master's thesis, Humboldt-Universität of Berlin (2010)
7. Fürber, C., Hepp, M.: Using SPARQL and SPIN for data quality management on the semantic web. In: Abramowicz, W., Tolksdorf, R. (eds.) BIS 2010. LNBIP, vol. 47, pp. 35–46. Springer, Heidelberg (2010)
8. Guéret, C., Groth, P., Stadler, C., Lehmann, J.: Assessing linked data mappings using network measures. In: Simperl, E., Cimiano, P., Polleres, A., Corcho, O., Presutti, V. (eds.) ESWC 2012. LNCS, vol. 7295, pp. 87–102. Springer, Heidelberg (2012)
9. Hellmann, S., Brekle, J., Auer, S.: Leveraging the crowdsourcing of lexical resources for bootstrapping a linguistic data cloud. In: Takeda, H., Qu, Y., Mizoguchi, R., Kitamura, Y. (eds.) JIST 2012. LNCS, vol. 7774, pp. 191–206. Springer, Heidelberg (2013)
10. Hellmann, S., Lehmann, J., Auer, S., Brümmer, M.: Integrating NLP using linked data. In: Alani, H., Kagal, L., Fokoue, A., Groth, P., Biemann, C., Parreira, J.X., Aroyo, L., Noy, N., Welty, C., Janowicz, K. (eds.) ISWC 2013, Part II. LNCS, vol. 8219, pp. 98–113. Springer, Heidelberg (2013)

11. Hogan, A., Harth, A., Passant, A., Decker, S., Polleres, A.: Weaving the pedantic web. In: LDOW (2010)
12. Kontokostas, D., Westphal, P., Auer, S., Hellmann, S., Lehmann, J., Cornelissen, R.: Test-driven evaluation of linked data quality. In: WWW (to appear, 2014)
13. McCrae, J., Aguado-de Cea, G., Buitelaar, P., Cimiano, P., Declerck, T., Gmez-Prez, A., Gracia, J., Hollink, L., Montiel-Ponsoda, E., Spohr, D., Wunner, T.: Interchanging lexical resources on the semantic web. LRE 46(4), 701–719 (2012)
14. Mendes, P.N., Mühleisen, H., Bizer, C.: Sieve: linked data quality assessment and fusion. In: EDBT/ICDT Workshops, pp. 116–123. ACM (2012)
15. Moran, S., Brümmer, M.: Lemon-aid: using lemon to aid quantitative historical linguistic analysis. In: LDL (2013)
16. Röder, M., Usbeck, R., Hellmann, S., Gerber, D., Both, A.: N3 - a collection of datasets for named entity recognition and disambiguation in the nlp interchange format. In: LREC (2014)
17. Sirin, E., Tao, J.: Towards integrity constraints in owl. In: Proceedings of the Workshop on OWL: Experiences and Directions, OWLED (2009)
18. Steinmetz, N., Knuth, M., Sack, H.: Statistical Analyses of Named Entity Disambiguation Benchmarks. In: NLP and DBpedia WS @ ISWC (2013)

Using Semantic and Domain-Based Information in CLIR Systems

Alessio Bosca[1], Matteo Casu[1], Mauro Dragoni[2], and Chiara Di Francescomarino[2]

[1] Celi s.r.l., via S.Quintino 31, 10131, Torino, Italy
[2] FBK–IRST, Trento, Italy
{alessio.bosca,casu}@celi.it, {dragoni,dfmchiara}@fbk.eu

Abstract. Cross-Language Information Retrieval (CLIR) systems extend classic information retrieval mechanisms for allowing users to query across languages, i.e., to retrieve documents written in languages different from the language used for query formulation. In this paper, we present a CLIR system exploiting multilingual ontologies for enriching documents representation with multilingual semantic information during the indexing phase and for mapping query fragments to concepts during the retrieval phase. This system has been applied on a domain-specific document collection and the contribution of the ontologies to the CLIR system has been evaluated in conjunction with the use of both Microsoft Bing and Google Translate translation services. Results demonstrate that the use of domain-specific resources leads to a significant improvement of CLIR system performance.

Keywords: #eswc2014Bosca.

1 Introduction

Cross-Language Information Retrieval (CLIR) deals with the problem of finding documents written in a language different from the one used for query formulation. If attempts to model multilinguality in information retrieval date back to the early Seventies [1], a renewed interest was brought to the field by the rise of the Web in the mid-Nineties, when pages written in different languages started to become suddenly available to geographically distributed users of the Web. International organizations, governments of multi-lingual countries, to name the most important ones, have been traditional users of CLIR systems. In the last decade, however, with the growth in the number of Web users, the need of facing the problem of the language barriers for exchanging information has notably increased and the need for CLIR systems in everyday life has become more and more clear (the recent book by J.-Y. Nie [2] exposes in detail the need for cross-language and multilingual IR).

There are several ways to cross the language barriers in CLIR systems. All of them, however, have to deal with the problem of the language mismatch between the queries and, at least, part of the document content. We can group the possible CLIR scenarios into the following three main settings:

1. the document collection is monolingual, but users can formulate queries in more than one language.

V. Presutti et al. (Eds.): ESWC 2014, LNCS 8465, pp. 240–254, 2014.

2. the document collection contains documents in multiple languages and users can query the entire collection in one or more languages.
3. the document collection contains documents with mixed-language content and users can query the entire collection in one or more languages.

In this paper, we present an approach facing the third scenario. The proposed CLIR system manages a collection of documents containing multilingual information as well as user queries that may be performed in any language supported by the system. The discussed approach uses domain-specific ontologies for increasing the effectiveness of already-available machine translation services (like Microsoft Bing[1] and Google Translate[2]) by expanding the queries with concepts coming from the ontologies.

The originality of the implemented system consists of the combination of two crucial aspects: (i) domain-specific multilingual ontologies are used for performing query expansion operations; and (ii) these ontologies are exploited also for enriching the representation of documents within the index. This way, the gained benefit expected by the proposed approach is twofold: an improvement of the effectiveness of the ranks produced by the CLIR systems; and the evidence that multilingual ontologies help to have an accurate enrichment of document representation.

The remainder of the paper is structured as follows. Section 2 presents an overview of the works carried out in the field of CLIR systems. Section 3 describes the implemented system and the algorithms used for indexing documents and for computing the IR relevance score. In Section 4 we show how the evaluation has been set up; while, in Section 5 we discuss the obtained results. Finally, Section 6 concludes.

2 Related Work

The problem of multilingual text retrieval has a long history. First experiments on multilingual text retrieval systems, based on the use of bilingual thesaurus, were performed by Salton [1]. Although the proposed approaches are no more feasible in modern systems, their underlying rationale is the basis of modern approaches that use Machine-Readable Dictionaries (MRD). Such approaches use controlled vocabularies for translating terms at query or indexing time. Examples of these approaches are presented in [3] and [4] where frequency statistics are used for selecting the translation of a term; contrariwise, in [5] and [6] more sophisticated techniques exploiting term co-occurrence statistics are described.

MRD-based approaches demonstrated to be effective for addressing the CLIR problem; however, when CLIR systems are applied to specific domains, they suffer of the "Out-Of-Vocabulary" (OOV) issue [7]. OOV problem consists of having a dictionary that is not able to completely cover all terms of a language or, more generally, of a domain. Several studies recognized that the problem of translating OOV has a significant impact on the performance of CLIR systems [8,9]. This problem has been addressed in two different ways in the literature. A first group of approaches [10,11] relies on augmenting the translation lexicon by mining comparable corpora. A second set of

[1] `http://www.bing.com/translator`

[2] `translate.google.com`

approaches, instead, employs Machine Transliteration systems to transliterate proper nouns. Discussions about this strategy are presented in [12] and [13].

Contrarily to the OOV approaches, CLIR domain-based approaches aim at providing systems that, by adapting themselves to a particular domain, are able to obtain higher effectiveness values due to their higher coverage of domain specific terms. For example, in [14], the authors present an approach in which they exploit domains, coming from Web directories, for providing better translations of queries. In [15] a cross-language medical information retrieval system has been implemented by exploiting for translations, a thesaurus enriched with medical information. In both works, the results demonstrated that the idea of using domain specific resources for CLIR is promising.

Recently, approaches exploiting the use of semantics have been explored. Such approaches enrich the document representation by injecting in the index of each document, a set of concepts coming from thesauri and/or ontologies in order to facilitate the cross-language retrieval of the document itself [16].

This work falls in both the last two streams of works, borrowing from the former the advantages deriving from the usage of domain-specific terms in the query translation and from the latter the capability to exploit semantic knowledge for retrieving information.

Other specific works on CLIR within the multilingual semantic web may be found in [17] and [18], while a complete overview of the ongoing research on CLIR is available at the Cross-Language Evaluation Forum (CLEF[3]), one of the major references concerning the evaluation of multilingual information access systems.

3 Approach and Implemented System

In this section, we describe the approach we have adopted for addressing the CLIR problem. Since the main goal of the presented work consists of exploring the impact of domain-specific semantic resources on the effectiveness of CLIR systems, in our investigations we will focus on the strategies for matching textual inputs to ontological concepts (applied to both the query and the documents in the target collection) rather than on the translation of the textual query.

The system described in this work has been developed in the context of the Organic.Lingua[4] EU-funded project that aims at providing automated multilingual services and tools facilitating the discovery, retrieval, exploitation and extension of digital educational contents related to the domain of Organic Agriculture and AgroEcology. The proposed approach supports two terminology resources: the multilingual ontology from the Organic.Edunet portal[5] (specifically developed in the context of the project for annotating documents) and a more generic resource, but domain-specific, namely Agrovoc that is a multilingual theasurus from FAO[6]. Both resources are expressed with SKOS format.

[3] http://www.clef-initiative.eu

[4] http://www.organic-lingua.eu

[5] http://organic-edunet.eu/

[6] http://aims.fao.org/standards/agrovoc/about

The system presented in this paper follows the Model-independent approach and treats translation and retrieval as two separate processes. The queries are first translated into the document language and monolingual IR models are then directly applied. A typical and also broadly used approach of this type is the machine translation (MT) approach (e.g.[19]) which employs MT systems to translate queries or documents before applying the monolingual retrieval process. In our implementation we followed such an approach for query translation and exploited Google Translate[7] and Bing Translator[8] as MT services.

In the subsections below, we describe how the proposed system performs the document indexing and their retrieval.

3.1 From Query Terms to Concepts

The component for matching a textual input with elements from domain terminologies is based on the Search Engines technology and exploits its built-in textual search capabilities. In our implementation, we exploited the open source Lucene search engine[9] and created a search index for each of the supported languages, containing the textual labels of the terminology elements (both SKOS preferred labels and alternative ones) along with their URI. The terms labels are indexed in their original form as well as in their stemmed form by means of the default stemming resources available in the Lucene framework.

In order to find the terminological entries within a textual input expressed in a given language a two steps procedure is applied:

- At first, the text is used as a query and is searched over the index in order to find a list of all the terminology elements containing a textual fragment present in the text.
- As a second step, in order to retain only the domain terms with a complete match (no partial matches) and locate them in the text, a new search index is built in memory, containing a single document: the original textual input. Then the candidate terminology elements found in the first step are used as queries over the in-memory index and a Highlighter component of the Search Engine is exploited to locate them in the text. A longest match criterion is used when the found terminology elements refer to overlapping spans of text.

This procedure is applied at indexing time in order to find references to ontological concepts within the textual fields of the documents and at query time in order to locate domain concepts in the query submitted by users. In the retrieval phase, the conceptual references found in the query are matched against the concepts annotated in the indexed documents.

3.2 Indexing

In order to compute the document index, each field with textual contents is extracted from the documents. Stop-word removal and stemming algorithms suited for each spe-

[7] `http://translate.google.com`
[8] `http://www.bing.com/translator`
[9] `https://lucene.apache.org`

cific language are applied to the fields before indexing them. The procedure for textual match described in the previous section allows for the enrichment of documents with annotations referencing ontology concepts.

Besides the annotations computed automatically, the original collection of documents exploited in our experimental evaluation already includes manual annotation with respect to the Organic.Lingua domain ontology (described in Section 4).

Moreover, in order to store into the index the information related to the context of each conceptual annotation, each concept used for annotating the document is expanded by considering its ontological parents and by indexing them according to a decreasing weight that depends on their semantic distance from the concept [20]. Therefore, the final representation of each document in the index is given by textual fields (exploited for the textual search) and annotations fields (exploited for the conceptual search). All fields are indexed by using the Lucene variation of the TF-IDF model.

Table 1 presents a statistic of the manual and automatic semantic annotations created at indexing time.

Table 1. Statistics of Manual and Automatic Conceptual Annotations performed at indexing time

Domain Ontology	Number of Concepts	Manual Annotations	Automatic Annotations
Agrovoc	32061	0	133596 annotations about 5834 distinct concepts
Organic.Lingua	291	27871 about 264 distinct concepts	16434 annotations about 208 distinct concepts

3.3 Retrieval

The proposed CLIR system provides two different components for transforming the queries formulated by users into the final ones performed on the index. These components interact, respectively, with the MT services and with the domain-specific ontology deployed on the CLIR system. At query time, the CLIR system may perform the construction of three types of queries, starting from the ones formulated by users, based on the system configuration:

1. Only Translations: query terms are translated into the reference language used for retrieving documents.
2. Only Semantic: for each query term, the CLIR system looks for a match into the ontology. If a match is found, the concept is put into the semantic transformation of the original query, together with its parent concepts extracted from the ontology; otherwise, the term is discarded from the final query. This way, the final query will be composed only by the list of the terms for which an ontological match is found, plus the list of concepts representing their contexts.
3. Translation + Semantic: the final query is the combination of the two approaches described above. Therefore, given a list of query terms, they are both translated in the reference language, and matched with ontology concepts. The result is a query composed of three parts: the translation of the original query, the set of concepts matching the terms contained in the original query, and their semantic context.

4 Experiments Setup

In this section, we describe the concrete exploitation of multilingual ontologies in a cross-language resource retrieval use-case in the context of the Organic.Lingua project. The evaluation of the proposed approach has been inspired by the activities of the CLEF, one of the major references concerning the evaluation of multilingual information access systems. Based on this methodology, the resources used for such an evaluation include[10]:

1. A set of queries that express information needs in a given language identified with a unique ID. The approach adopted for selecting the queries consisted of choosing the most popular searches performed by real users on the Organic.Lingua portal filtered by domain experts. This way, we are able to cover as many topics as possible, while avoiding similar queries. The number of queries used for these experiments is 48. Each query has been originally provided in the English language and it has been manually translated in the set of the other languages and verified by both Domain and Language experts.
2. A collection of documents that satisfies the information needs expressed in the queries. In the Organic.Lingua test environment this corpus is composed of a multilingual collection of about 13000 documents.
3. A gold standard that, for each query, provides the list of the relevant documents used to evaluate the results provided by the CLIR system. In the provided evaluation, the gold standard was manually created by the domain experts. It contains only results that are related to queries expressed or translated in English and that have at least one field (either a textual or an annotation one) in English.

4.1 Evaluation Metrics

For evaluating the effectiveness of the CLIR system, different standard metrics have been adopted. Besides the well-known Precision and Recall measure, other metrics are widely used in the IR community. By keeping as reference the CLEF evaluation campaigns, the metrics used in recent years include R-Precision, Precision@X (representing the Precision obtained after X retrieved documents, i.e. Prec@10 is the precision after 10 docs) and the Mean Average Precision (MAP). Since the evaluation of the Organic.Lingua CLIR system is based on the methodology introduced by CLEF [21,22], the same metrics will be used for evaluating the described system.

5 Evaluation and Discussion

The set of topics considered in the experiment is composed of queries in 8 different languages: French, Italian, Spanish, German, Polish, Portuguese, Hungarian, Turkish. The queries have been translated in English by using the external machine translation

[10] All the evaluation resources are freely available online for reproducing the experiments: `http://www.organic-lingua.eu/deliverables/OrganicLingua_CLIR_Evaluation.zip`

services connected with the CLIR system and then, they have been enriched with concepts coming from the ontologies that match query terms. Finally, queries are performed on the Organic.Lingua document collections. The CLIR system has been evaluated by adopting three different configurations and the results have been compared with the gold standard, according to the metrics described above.

1. *Query Translation configuration*: each query is translated in English by using the Microsoft Bing Translator or the Google Translate service, and the retrieval is performed on the textual fields (i.e., title, abstract and content; while, fields containing media data that are present in some documents have not been considered in our work) of the indexed documents. This configuration permitted to define the baseline of our experiments (Table 2).
2. *Semantic Expansion by exploiting the domain ontology*: this configuration combines the previous ones with the term match approach described in Section 3. Each query is translated and its terms are mapped to the Domain Ontology (Sections 5.1, 5.2, and 5.3). Retrieval is performed both on the textual fields and on the ontological annotation fields (manual, automatic, or both depending on the configuration) of the indexed documents.
3. *Ontology Matching Only configuration*: each query term is mapped to one or more concepts of the Domain Ontology by using the approach described in Section 3 and only queries containing at least one match to the Domain Ontology are performed on the index. Retrieval is performed both on the textual fields and on the ontological annotation fields of the indexed documents (Section 5.4).

Moreover, for the second and third configurations, different variants, described in more detail in the following subsections, have been applied.

Tables from 2 to 12 report the results of the performed evaluation split in different subsections based on the configuration type. Table 2 reports only data referring to the baseline that we adopted for comparing the proposed approach. The columns of each table show the Mean Average Precision, the Precisions at 5, 10, 20, and 30, the Average Recall, the Average R-Precision, and the number of queries that have been performed.

In the following subsections, we will present the results obtained with the different configurations adopter for evaluating the proposed CLIR system.

5.1 Semantic Expansion with Automatic Annotations Only

In this experiment, queries are performed only on document fields containing automatic annotations. In particular, we have explored three variants; queries have been expanded by exploiting (i) only the Agrovoc ontology (Table 3), (ii) only the Organic.Lingua ontology (Table 4) ,or (iii) both ontologies (Table 5).

The results obtained by performing the annotation of documents and the expansion of queries by using only automatic annotations highlight that the use of the ontologies leads to an improvement of the system effectiveness. A first important aspect to observe, is that the sole use of the Agrovoc ontology gives a higher contribution with respect to the sole use of the Organic.Lingua one as it may be inferred from the δ values. The reason is given by the highest coverage of the Agrovoc ontology with respect to the Organic.Lingua one.

Table 2. Baseline results obtained by translating the queries using public available machine translations services like Microsoft Bing and Google Translate without using semantic expansion techniques

Lang	MAP		Prec@5		Prec@10		Prec@20		Avg. Recall		Avg. R-Prec.		Query Num.
	BING	GOOG	BING	GOOG	BING	GOOG	BING	GOOG	BING	GOOG	BING	GOOG	
en	0.681	0.681	0.742	0.742	0.644	0.644	0.553	0.553	0.970	0.970	0.653	0.653	48
el	0.519	0.555	0.604	0.592	0.517	0.523	0.431	0.463	0.923	0.933	0.514	0.551	48
lv	0.581	0.551	0.629	0.613	0.560	0.542	0.465	0.445	0.960	0.958	0.563	0.537	48
pl	0.540	0.540	0.617	0.617	0.550	0.550	0.468	0.468	0.921	0.921	0.533	0.533	48
it	0.605	0.613	0.675	0.675	0.579	0.594	0.481	0.509	0.942	0.903	0.599	0.597	48
fr	0.513	0.475	0.567	0.517	0.513	0.477	0.441	0.398	0.917	0.863	0.494	0.470	48
tr	0.477	0.456	0.550	0.508	0.494	0.471	0.447	0.413	0.898	0.885	0.466	0.445	48
hu	0.482	0.531	0.563	0.583	0.521	0.542	0.457	0.465	0.895	0.910	0.475	0.515	48
et	0.462	0.495	0.546	0.554	0.471	0.469	0.397	0.407	0.871	0.866	0.451	0.490	48
de	0.564	0.527	0.613	0.588	0.540	0.513	0.449	0.438	0.904	0.886	0.538	0.510	48
es	0.598	0.623	0.671	0.688	0.596	0.598	0.508	0.514	0.936	0.959	0.591	0.613	48
pt	0.616	0.614	0.704	0.671	0.608	0.579	0.496	0.483	0.951	0.942	0.607	0.605	48
AVG.	0.553	0.555	0.623	0.612	0.549	0.542	0.466	0.463	0.924	0.916	0.540	0.543	

Table 3. Results obtained by performing queries using the machine translation service enriched with the matched URIs coming from Agrovoc ontology

Lang	MAP		Prec@5		Prec@10		Prec@20		Avg. Recall		Avg. R-Prec.		Query Num.
	BING	GOOG	BING	GOOG	BING	GOOG	BING	GOOG	BING	GOOG	BING	GOOG	
en	0.692	0.692	0.746	0.746	0.671	0.671	0.566	0.566	0.972	0.972	0.663	0.663	48
el	0.535	0.568	0.617	0.608	0.540	0.540	0.457	0.484	0.933	0.957	0.524	0.556	48
lv	0.593	0.572	0.638	0.633	0.585	0.567	0.482	0.462	0.965	0.965	0.578	0.563	48
pl	0.561	0.561	0.654	0.654	0.588	0.588	0.488	0.488	0.941	0.941	0.545	0.545	48
it	0.627	0.623	0.708	0.688	0.608	0.613	0.497	0.519	0.944	0.938	0.615	0.605	48
fr	0.532	0.510	0.583	0.533	0.554	0.492	0.463	0.419	0.946	0.929	0.508	0.497	48
tr	0.491	0.478	0.563	0.533	0.519	0.502	0.457	0.433	0.914	0.923	0.481	0.470	48
hu	0.500	0.552	0.588	0.613	0.552	0.575	0.475	0.484	0.923	0.933	0.494	0.533	48
et	0.494	0.517	0.579	0.588	0.513	0.504	0.429	0.437	0.924	0.921	0.481	0.521	48
de	0.582	0.549	0.642	0.613	0.563	0.548	0.463	0.456	0.924	0.935	0.569	0.546	48
es	0.610	0.634	0.679	0.700	0.619	0.617	0.522	0.522	0.951	0.965	0.595	0.613	48
pt	0.631	0.627	0.704	0.671	0.629	0.598	0.510	0.495	0.960	0.964	0.623	0.612	48
AVG.	0.571	0.573	0.642	0.632	0.578	0.568	0.484	0.480	0.941	0.945	0.556	0.560	48
δ w.r.t. Baseline (%)	3.161	3.316	2.952	3.173	5.283	4.808	3.857	3.772	1.899	3.156	2.979	3.142	

Since manual annotations have not been performed on the Agrovoc ontology, the results shown in Table 3 are the same for all running configuration (except the one using only ontological concepts for performing queries). Therefore, they will not be reported in the next two subsections.

5.2 Semantic Expansion with Automatic and Manual Annotations (Same Weights)

In this experiment, we have performed queries on both the fields containing automatic and those containing manual annotations. In this case, we have explored only two variants; queries are expanded by exploiting (i) only the Organic.Lingua ontology (Table 6) or (ii) both ontologies (Table 7).

Indeed, the evaluation adopting only the Agrovoc ontology is not available because this ontology has not been exploited for annotating documents manually.

Table 4. Results obtained by performing queries using the machine translation service enriched with the matched URIs coming from Organic.Lingua ontology.

Lang	MAP		Prec@5		Prec@10		Prec@20		Avg. Recall		Avg. R-Prec.		Query Num.
	BING	GOOG	BING	GOOG	BING	GOOG	BING	GOOG	BING	GOOG	BING	GOOG	
en	0.683	0.683	0.733	0.733	0.652	0.652	0.559	0.559	0.970	0.970	0.653	0.653	48
el	0.527	0.560	0.608	0.588	0.525	0.535	0.442	0.468	0.924	0.933	0.511	0.550	48
lv	0.594	0.569	0.638	0.625	0.588	0.567	0.482	0.462	0.965	0.961	0.574	0.556	48
pl	0.554	0.554	0.633	0.633	0.565	0.565	0.491	0.491	0.931	0.931	0.545	0.545	48
it	0.611	0.617	0.683	0.671	0.596	0.608	0.497	0.518	0.944	0.908	0.602	0.599	48
fr	0.539	0.504	0.596	0.529	0.546	0.477	0.466	0.407	0.930	0.907	0.526	0.503	48
tr	0.489	0.480	0.563	0.546	0.504	0.500	0.453	0.442	0.905	0.909	0.487	0.470	48
hu	0.500	0.540	0.600	0.588	0.546	0.552	0.467	0.473	0.889	0.908	0.488	0.519	48
et	0.487	0.509	0.579	0.579	0.500	0.485	0.428	0.424	0.883	0.871	0.476	0.504	48
de	0.576	0.542	0.638	0.608	0.554	0.533	0.460	0.450	0.910	0.893	0.556	0.524	48
es	0.607	0.632	0.675	0.692	0.604	0.608	0.517	0.524	0.938	0.962	0.594	0.619	48
pt	0.625	0.622	0.700	0.671	0.621	0.585	0.509	0.492	0.954	0.954	0.613	0.609	48
AVG.	0.566	0.568	0.637	0.622	0.567	0.556	0.481	0.476	0.929	0.926	0.552	0.554	48
δ w.r.t. Baseline (%)	2.341	2.288	2.225	1.586	3.163	2.594	3.186	2.780	0.522	1.024	2.223	2.031	

Table 5. Results obtained by performing queries using the machine translation service enriched with the matched URIs coming from both Agrovoc and Organic.Lingua ontologies.

Lang	MAP		Prec@5		Prec@10		Prec@20		Avg. Recall		Avg. R-Prec.		Query Num.
	BING	GOOG	BING	GOOG	BING	GOOG	BING	GOOG	BING	GOOG	BING	GOOG	
en	0.691	0.691	0.746	0.746	0.669	0.669	0.567	0.567	0.972	0.972	0.661	0.661	48
el	0.535	0.567	0.617	0.608	0.538	0.538	0.458	0.485	0.933	0.957	0.522	0.554	48
lv	0.592	0.572	0.638	0.633	0.583	0.565	0.482	0.462	0.965	0.965	0.576	0.562	48
pl	0.560	0.560	0.654	0.654	0.585	0.585	0.488	0.488	0.941	0.941	0.543	0.543	48
it	0.626	0.622	0.708	0.688	0.606	0.610	0.497	0.519	0.944	0.938	0.613	0.604	48
fr	0.532	0.510	0.583	0.533	0.554	0.492	0.463	0.419	0.946	0.929	0.508	0.497	48
tr	0.490	0.477	0.563	0.533	0.517	0.500	0.457	0.433	0.914	0.923	0.480	0.469	48
hu	0.497	0.550	0.583	0.608	0.546	0.569	0.474	0.483	0.923	0.933	0.488	0.527	48
et	0.494	0.517	0.579	0.588	0.508	0.500	0.431	0.438	0.924	0.921	0.478	0.518	48
de	0.582	0.549	0.638	0.608	0.563	0.548	0.463	0.456	0.924	0.935	0.569	0.546	48
es	0.610	0.633	0.679	0.700	0.617	0.615	0.522	0.522	0.951	0.965	0.594	0.612	48
pt	0.630	0.626	0.704	0.671	0.627	0.596	0.510	0.495	0.960	0.964	0.622	0.611	48
AVG.	0.570	0.573	0.641	0.631	0.576	0.565	0.484	0.480	0.941	0.945	0.555	0.559	48
δ w.r.t. Baseline (%)	3.055	3.210	2.840	3.059	4.871	4.391	3.914	3.808	1.899	3.156	2.669	2.829	

The introduction of manual annotations done with the concepts defined in the Organic.Lingua ontology boosted the effectiveness of CLIR system. Indeed, if we compare the δ values obtained by running this configuration, with respect to the ones obtained with the previous configuration, we observe that the gain registered with the use of the sole Organic.Lingua ontology significantly improved. This positive improvement affects also the combined use of the two ontologies for both annotating documents and querying the repository. As for the previous configuration, the highest gain with respect to the baseline is observed for the Prec@10 values, but, in general, there are significant improvements also for the other Prec@X values.

5.3 Semantic Expansion with Automatic and Manual Annotations (Different Weights)

Also in this experiment, we have performed queries on both the fields containing automatic and those containing manual annotations and we have explored two variants

Table 6. Results obtained by performing queries using the machine translation service enriched with the matched URIs coming from Organic.Lingua ontology.

Lang	MAP		Prec@5		Prec@10		Prec@20		Avg. Recall		Avg. R-Prec.		Query Num.
	BING	GOOG	BING	GOOG	BING	GOOG	BING	GOOG	BING	GOOG	BING	GOOG	
en	0.676	0.676	0.742	0.742	0.650	0.650	0.562	0.562	0.972	0.972	0.646	0.646	48
el	0.545	0.565	0.642	0.608	0.550	0.544	0.463	0.472	0.928	0.935	0.528	0.552	48
lv	0.601	0.571	0.654	0.633	0.594	0.573	0.496	0.472	0.968	0.966	0.579	0.552	48
pl	0.542	0.542	0.642	0.642	0.579	0.579	0.500	0.500	0.934	0.934	0.529	0.529	48
it	0.590	0.609	0.675	0.679	0.581	0.600	0.497	0.520	0.954	0.914	0.574	0.587	48
fr	0.520	0.501	0.596	0.567	0.533	0.508	0.459	0.424	0.934	0.925	0.502	0.494	48
tr	0.457	0.460	0.525	0.533	0.496	0.490	0.450	0.433	0.907	0.912	0.435	0.441	48
hu	0.487	0.531	0.592	0.596	0.535	0.550	0.469	0.477	0.897	0.928	0.476	0.514	48
et	0.493	0.516	0.588	0.596	0.515	0.506	0.440	0.433	0.890	0.877	0.480	0.502	48
de	0.570	0.535	0.638	0.604	0.556	0.535	0.470	0.460	0.914	0.897	0.549	0.519	48
es	0.622	0.645	0.692	0.708	0.615	0.621	0.524	0.528	0.945	0.968	0.602	0.625	48
pt	0.628	0.637	0.721	0.717	0.627	0.621	0.520	0.517	0.957	0.957	0.614	0.622	48
AVG.	0.561	0.566	0.642	0.635	0.569	0.565	0.487	0.483	0.933	0.932	0.543	0.549	48
δ w.r.t. Baseline (%)	1.407	1.905	3.008	3.799	3.640	4.261	4.567	4.391	1.027	1.720	0.511	0.986	

Table 7. Results obtained by performing queries using the machine translation service enriched with the matched URIs coming from both Agrovoc and Organic.Lingua ontologies.

Lang	MAP		Prec@5		Prec@10		Prec@20		Avg. Recall		Avg. R-Prec.		Query Num.
	BING	GOOG	BING	GOOG	BING	GOOG	BING	GOOG	BING	GOOG	BING	GOOG	
en	0.691	0.691	0.754	0.754	0.671	0.671	0.570	0.570	0.973	0.973	0.659	0.659	48
el	0.554	0.574	0.654	0.625	0.560	0.548	0.475	0.484	0.936	0.958	0.539	0.560	48
lv	0.609	0.579	0.667	0.646	0.606	0.588	0.500	0.477	0.970	0.969	0.589	0.564	48
pl	0.557	0.557	0.675	0.675	0.606	0.606	0.502	0.502	0.943	0.943	0.537	0.537	48
it	0.617	0.620	0.708	0.696	0.608	0.617	0.501	0.525	0.952	0.942	0.601	0.601	48
fr	0.538	0.525	0.608	0.579	0.556	0.521	0.466	0.437	0.949	0.938	0.512	0.515	48
tr	0.481	0.481	0.550	0.550	0.515	0.508	0.457	0.441	0.917	0.926	0.465	0.459	48
hu	0.506	0.562	0.600	0.629	0.565	0.573	0.480	0.492	0.931	0.952	0.495	0.535	48
et	0.512	0.532	0.613	0.613	0.527	0.525	0.448	0.453	0.928	0.924	0.485	0.519	48
de	0.580	0.547	0.642	0.617	0.571	0.554	0.476	0.471	0.926	0.937	0.564	0.541	48
es	0.627	0.649	0.700	0.717	0.629	0.633	0.530	0.531	0.955	0.969	0.604	0.626	48
pt	0.642	0.648	0.721	0.717	0.640	0.633	0.521	0.516	0.962	0.966	0.634	0.634	48
AVG.	0.576	0.580	0.658	0.651	0.588	0.581	0.494	0.491	0.945	0.950	0.557	0.562	48
δ w.r.t. Baseline (%)	4.172	4.582	5.514	6.410	7.021	7.337	5.958	6.190	2.298	3.642	3.124	3.553	

too, due to the same reason explained in the previous section. Therefore, queries are expanded by exploiting (i) only the Organic.Lingua ontology (Table 8); or (ii) both ontologies (Table 9). In both cases, the query result considers the field containing manual annotations (that refer only to Organic.Lingua concepts) with a double weight.

By considering the improvements obtained with the usage of the manual annotations, we performed experiments by boosting the fields containing the manual annotations in order to verify if further improvements are obtained. Unfortunately, it seems that boosting these fields does not lead to any improvement. Indeed, except for the Prec@5 and the Prec@10 values, we registered a general decrease of the improvements with respect to the results obtained by running the previous configuration. Moreover, we may observe the only negative value with respect to the baseline of the entire evaluation, that

Table 8. Results obtained by performing queries using the machine translation service enriched with the matched URIs coming from Organic.Lingua ontology. The fields containing manual annotations have been weighted double.

Lang	MAP		Prec@5		Prec@10		Prec@20		Avg. Recall		Avg. R-Prec.		Query Num.
	BING	GOOG	BING	GOOG	BING	GOOG	BING	GOOG	BING	GOOG	BING	GOOG	
en	0.670	0.670	0.742	0.742	0.648	0.648	0.554	0.554	0.972	0.972	0.635	0.635	48
el	0.542	0.562	0.642	0.608	0.552	0.544	0.457	0.470	0.928	0.935	0.522	0.545	48
lv	0.597	0.575	0.654	0.646	0.592	0.583	0.490	0.466	0.968	0.966	0.573	0.545	48
pl	0.536	0.536	0.633	0.633	0.579	0.579	0.493	0.493	0.934	0.934	0.524	0.524	48
it	0.584	0.601	0.675	0.675	0.583	0.600	0.490	0.513	0.954	0.914	0.562	0.575	48
fr	0.519	0.499	0.592	0.567	0.533	0.506	0.458	0.424	0.934	0.925	0.503	0.496	48
tr	0.458	0.463	0.533	0.542	0.492	0.492	0.449	0.434	0.907	0.912	0.443	0.448	48
hu	0.480	0.525	0.596	0.588	0.529	0.552	0.458	0.469	0.897	0.928	0.467	0.509	48
et	0.488	0.511	0.583	0.596	0.517	0.510	0.434	0.424	0.890	0.877	0.473	0.492	48
de	0.570	0.536	0.633	0.604	0.558	0.538	0.469	0.459	0.914	0.897	0.547	0.517	48
es	0.618	0.639	0.688	0.708	0.615	0.617	0.516	0.519	0.945	0.968	0.595	0.613	48
pt	0.622	0.631	0.721	0.717	0.631	0.623	0.513	0.508	0.957	0.957	0.606	0.611	48
AVG.	0.557	0.562	0.641	0.636	0.569	0.566	0.482	0.478	0.933	0.932	0.538	0.543	48
δ w.r.t. Baseline (%)	0.693	1.306	2.820	3.783	3.580	4.460	3.361	3.186	1.010	1.719	-0.524	-0.138	

is the Avg. R-Precision. However, in spite of lower performance values of the sole application of the Organic.Lingua ontology, the improvements obtained by combining the two ontologies still remain in line with the ones obtained without boosting the manual annotations fields.

5.4 Use of Ontology Concepts Only

Here, queries are performed only on document fields containing ontological annotations. For this experiment, we have explored all three variants; queries have been performed (i) on fields containing Agrovoc annotations (Table 10); (ii) on fields containing Organic.Lingua annotations (both automatic and manual annotations) (Table 11); and (iii) on fields containing Agrovoc or Organic.Lingua annotations (Table 12). In this case, only queries containing at least one term matching the Domain Ontology have been performed.

From an initial glance, we may notice that in the results obtained with this configuration not all queries were able to be performed because, for some of them, no matches have been found in the respective ontologies. For instance, if we consider the Estonian language (that, by the way, is available only in the Organic.Lingua ontology) only for 6 queries there were found matches between query terms and ontology concepts. Moreover, not all languages are available for all ontologies. Indeed, Agrovoc ontology covers 9 out 12 languages; while, Organic.Lingua ontology covers 10 out of 12 languages. These two aspects confirm what we have already described previously in the paper where we stated that one of the main problems in using semantics and multilinguality for indexing and retrieving purposes is the non-complete coverage of the language terms and, sometimes, the unavailability of all languages in the semantic resources.

Besides this, it is anyway interesting to observe the results obtained by performing queries using only the ontological concepts that match query terms. As we expected, the results obtained by using the sole Organic.Lingua ontology outperforms both other

Table 9. Results obtained by performing queries using the machine translation service enriched with the matched URIs coming from both Agrovoc and Organic.Lingua ontologies. The fields containing manual annotations have been weighted double.

Lang	MAP		Prec@5		Prec@10		Prec@20		Avg. Recall		Avg. R-Prec.		Query Num.
	BING	GOOG	BING	GOOG	BING	GOOG	BING	GOOG	BING	GOOG	BING	GOOG	
en	0.688	0.688	0.750	0.750	0.671	0.671	0.570	0.570	0.973	0.973	0.659	0.659	48
el	0.553	0.573	0.646	0.621	0.563	0.548	0.475	0.484	0.936	0.958	0.538	0.558	48
lv	0.606	0.577	0.663	0.642	0.602	0.588	0.499	0.478	0.970	0.969	0.587	0.564	48
pl	0.552	0.552	0.667	0.667	0.602	0.602	0.503	0.503	0.943	0.943	0.535	0.535	48
it	0.609	0.616	0.700	0.692	0.600	0.613	0.501	0.524	0.952	0.942	0.593	0.598	48
fr	0.522	0.511	0.596	0.579	0.552	0.523	0.463	0.440	0.949	0.938	0.498	0.502	48
tr	0.462	0.463	0.529	0.533	0.506	0.500	0.451	0.434	0.917	0.926	0.444	0.439	48
hu	0.496	0.548	0.596	0.625	0.560	0.571	0.479	0.492	0.931	0.952	0.485	0.521	48
et	0.510	0.529	0.604	0.604	0.533	0.525	0.449	0.454	0.928	0.924	0.483	0.517	48
de	0.578	0.546	0.638	0.613	0.569	0.552	0.476	0.471	0.926	0.937	0.564	0.541	48
es	0.625	0.648	0.696	0.713	0.629	0.633	0.530	0.531	0.955	0.969	0.604	0.626	48
pt	0.639	0.646	0.713	0.713	0.635	0.629	0.524	0.520	0.962	0.966	0.631	0.631	48
AVG.	0.570	0.575	0.650	0.646	0.585	0.580	0.493	0.492	0.945	0.950	0.552	0.558	48
δ w.r.t. Baseline (%)	3.043	3.543	4.237	5.498	6.507	6.967	5.847	6.210	2.291	3.647	2.113	2.638	

Table 10. Results obtained by performing queries using only the terms matching concepts defined in the Agrovoc ontology

Lang	MAP	Prec@5	Prec@10	Prec@20	Avg. Recall	Avg. R-Prec.	Query Numbers
en	0.139	0.156	0.180	0.177	0.681	0.146	45
pl	0.115	0.171	0.183	0.159	0.509	0.139	35
it	0.140	0.195	0.195	0.191	0.546	0.168	38
fr	0.110	0.145	0.145	0.155	0.506	0.131	40
tr	0.122	0.171	0.181	0.164	0.531	0.145	42
hu	0.160	0.216	0.214	0.196	0.578	0.177	37
de	0.150	0.231	0.213	0.209	0.461	0.181	32
es	0.145	0.214	0.202	0.186	0.612	0.166	42
pt	0.153	0.200	0.205	0.178	0.544	0.174	43
AVG.	0.137	0.189	0.191	0.179	0.552	0.159	

configurations. Indeed, while the Agrovoc ontology is used only for the automatic annotation of documents, the Organic.Lingua one is exploited also for performing manual annotations. This further enrichment of the documents representation permits to increase the effectiveness of the CLIR system.

However, the combined use of the two ontologies is destructive with respect to the use of the sole Organic.Lingua one. We may notice that the number of queries matched by the two ontologies is different, and, from a more in depth analysis, we observed that some of the queries contains only partial matches with the Agrovoc concepts; while, by considering the Organic.Lingua one, no matches are found. This fact, even if it permits to handle more queries, it introduces in the evaluation results that reduce the overall effectiveness of the system.

5.5 General Remarks

Summarizing what we observed in our experiments, we may state that the use of domain-specific multilingual resources for enriching basic CLIR systems leads to

Table 11. Results obtained by performing queries using only the terms matching concepts defined in the Organic.Lingua ontology

Lang	MAP	Prec@5	Prec@10	Prec@20	Avg. Recall	Avg. R-Prec.	Query Numbers
en	0.267	0.381	0.343	0.338	0.683	0.283	21
el	0.288	0.381	0.367	0.345	0.640	0.302	21
lv	0.079	0.100	0.100	0.100	0.513	0.095	14
it	0.242	0.300	0.325	0.317	0.663	0.267	12
fr	0.218	0.300	0.236	0.214	0.598	0.240	14
tr	0.261	0.427	0.368	0.336	0.552	0.285	22
hu	0.350	0.471	0.421	0.454	0.677	0.373	14
et	0.243	0.333	0.233	0.308	0.741	0.263	6
de	0.333	0.491	0.436	0.473	0.679	0.381	11
es	0.324	0.427	0.382	0.348	0.654	0.341	22
AVG.	0.260	0.359	0.319	0.322	0.635	0.283	

Table 12. Results obtained by performing queries using only the terms matching concepts defined in the Agrovoc or in the Organic.Lingua ontologies

Lang	MAP	Prec@5	Prec@10	Prec@20	Avg. Recall	Avg. R-Prec.	Query Numbers
en	0.176	0.236	0.242	0.232	0.700	0.179	45
el	0.288	0.381	0.367	0.345	0.640	0.302	21
lv	0.079	0.100	0.100	0.100	0.513	0.095	14
pl	0.115	0.171	0.183	0.159	0.509	0.139	35
it	0.143	0.200	0.197	0.194	0.561	0.173	39
fr	0.126	0.181	0.171	0.167	0.528	0.143	41
tr	0.166	0.262	0.248	0.216	0.561	0.179	42
hu	0.193	0.268	0.242	0.241	0.610	0.201	38
et	0.243	0.333	0.233	0.308	0.741	0.263	6
de	0.202	0.303	0.279	0.280	0.545	0.234	33
es	0.215	0.307	0.274	0.249	0.672	0.223	43
pt	0.153	0.200	0.205	0.178	0.544	0.174	43
AVG.	0.173	0.247	0.226	0.221	0.586	0.192	

effective results. Indeed, in all experiments performed on our document collection, the usage (sole or combined) of the two described ontologies outperformed our baseline.

It is important to highlight also that the used baselines represent two of the most important and effective translation systems currently available. With respect to what we discussed previously in the paper, these baselines systems have been built by using dictionaries that almost completely cover each language. By comparing the proposed approach with them, it presents at least two important benefits: (i) the problem of building an effective machine translation system is demanded to external services and (ii) different ontologies, based on the domain/s that the system has to cover, may be plugged in order to improve its effectiveness.

By analyzing the results, we may observe that the major improvements are visible for the Prec@5 and Prec@10 values. This result demonstrates the feasibility of the approach that is able to improve the rank of the traditional first page results of information retrieval systems.

Concerning recall values, we may notice that the baselines already obtain significant recall values and the improvements obtained by adopting the ontologies are quite limited. This is an interesting point because it demonstrates that, even if we use a domain-specific scenario, the adopted baselines performed well during translation operations because relevant documents are not lost during the retrieval phase. Therefore, we have a further evidence that the use of the ontologies for supporting general purpose machine translation services boosted the quality of the produced ranks.

However, we have also seen that the use of manual annotation significantly improves the results: around 7% versus around 4% for the automatic annotations. Moreover, if we observe the results obtained by performing queries containing only the ontology concepts, the use of the Organic.Lingua ontology (for which manual annotations are provided) leaded to significant better results (Table 11). Obviously, on the one hand it is almost well-known that the use of manual annotations improves the effectiveness of retrieval systems, but on the other hand, it requests a significant effort for keeping the system updated and, in complex real-world applications where thousands or million of documents are managed, it is not feasible.

6 Future Work and Concluding Remarks

In this work, we have presented a CLIR system based on the combination of the usage of domain-specific multilingual ontologies (i) for expanding queries and (ii) for enriching document representation with the index in a multilingual environment. The goal of the presented study was the investigation on the effectiveness of integrating semantic domain-specific resources, like ontologies, into a CLIR context. The implemented approach has been applied to a document collection built in the context of the Organic.Lingua EU-funded project where documents are domain-specific and where they have been annotated with concepts coming from domain-specific ontologies. The results have shown that the use of domain-specific resources for enriching the document representation and for performing a semantic expansion of queries is a suitable approach for improving the effectiveness of CLIR systems.

References

1. Salton, G.: Automatic processing of foreign language documents. In: COLING (1969)
2. Nie, J.Y.: Cross-Language Information Retrieval. Synthesis Lectures on Human Language Technologies. Morgan & Claypool Publishers (2010)
3. Ballesteros, L., Croft, W.B.: Resolving ambiguity for cross-language retrieval. In: SIGIR, pp. 64–71. ACM (1998)
4. Aljlayl, M., Frieder, O.: Effective arabic-english cross-language information retrieval via machine-readable dictionaries and machine translation. In: CIKM, pp. 295–302. ACM (2001)
5. Liu, Y., Jin, R., Chai, J.Y.: A maximum coherence model for dictionary-based cross-language information retrieval. In: Baeza-Yates, R.A., Ziviani, N., Marchionini, G., Moffat, A., Tait, J. (eds.) SIGIR, pp. 536–543. ACM (2005)
6. Gao, J., Nie, J.Y.: A study of statistical models for query translation: finding a good unit of translation. In: Efthimiadis, E.N., Dumais, S.T., Hawking, D., Järvelin, K. (eds.) SIGIR, pp. 194–201. ACM (2006)
7. Fung, P., Lo, Y.Y.: An ir approach for translating new words from nonparallel, comparable texts. In: Boitet, C., Whitelock, P. (eds.) COLING-ACL, pp. 414–420. Morgan Kaufmann Publishers/ACL (1998)

8. Pirkola, A., Toivonen, J., Keskustalo, H., Järvelin, K.: Fite-trt: a high quality translation technique for oov words. In: Haddad, H. (ed.) SAC, pp. 1043–1049. ACM (2006)
9. Mandl, T., Womser-Hacker, C.: How do named entities contribute to retrieval effectiveness? In: Peters, C., Clough, P., Gonzalo, J., Jones, G.J.F., Kluck, M., Magnini, B. (eds.) CLEF 2004. LNCS, vol. 3491, pp. 833–842. Springer, Heidelberg (2005)
10. Munteanu, D.S., Marcu, D.: Extracting parallel sub-sentential fragments from non-parallel corpora. In: Calzolari, N., Cardie, C., Isabelle, P. (eds.) ACL. The Association for Computer Linguistics (2006)
11. Al-Onaizan, Y., Knight, K.: Translating named entities using monolingual and bilingual resources. In: ACL, pp. 400–408. ACL (2002)
12. Jaleel, N.A., Larkey, L.S.: Statistical transliteration for english-arabic cross language information retrieval. In: CIKM, pp. 139–146. ACM (2003)
13. Li, H., Sim, K.C., Kuo, J.S., Dong, M.: Semantic transliteration of personal names. In: Carroll, J.A., van den Bosch, A., Zaenen, A. (eds.) ACL. The Association for Computational Linguistics (2007)
14. Kimura, F., Maeda, A., Hatano, K., Miyazaki, J., Uemura, S.: Cross-language information retrieval by domain restriction using web directory structure. In: HICSS, p. 135. IEEE Computer Society (2008)
15. Lu, W.H., Lin, R.S., Chan, Y.C., Chen, K.H.: Using web resources to construct multilingual medical thesaurus for cross-language medical information retrieval. Decision Support Systems 45(3), 585–595 (2008)
16. Sacaleanu, B., Buitelaar, P., Volk, M.: A cross language document retrieval system based on semantic annotation. In: EACL, pp. 231–234 (2003)
17. Sorg, P., Cimiano, P.: Exploiting wikipedia for cross-lingual and multilingual information retrieval. Data Knowl. Eng. 74, 26–45 (2012)
18. Aggarwal, N.: Cross lingual semantic search by improving semantic similarity and relatedness measures. In: Cudré-Mauroux, P., et al. (eds.) ISWC 2012, Part II. LNCS, vol. 7650, pp. 375–382. Springer, Heidelberg (2012)
19. Braschler, M.: Combination approaches for multilingual text retrieval. Inf. Retr. 7(1-2), 183–204 (2004)
20. Dragoni, M., da Costa Pereira, C., Tettamanzi, A.: A conceptual representation of documents and queries for information retrieval systems by using light ontologies. Expert Syst. Appl. 39(12), 10376–10388 (2012)
21. Braschler, M., Peters, C.: Clef 2002 methodology and metrics. In: Peters, C., Braschler, M., Gonzalo, J. (eds.) CLEF 2002. LNCS, vol. 2785, pp. 512–525. Springer, Heidelberg (2003)
22. Agosti, M., Di Nunzio, G.M., Ferro, N.: Scientific data of an evaluation campaign: Do we properly deal with them? In: Peters, C., Clough, P., Gey, F.C., Karlgren, J., Magnini, B., Oard, D.W., de Rijke, M., Stempfhuber, M. (eds.) CLEF 2006. LNCS, vol. 4730, pp. 11–20. Springer, Heidelberg (2007)

These Are Your Rights

A Natural Language Processing Approach to Automated RDF Licenses Generation

Elena Cabrio[1,2], Alessio Palmero Aprosio[3], and Serena Villata[1]

[1] INRIA Sophia Antipolis, France
{firstname.lastname}@inria.fr
[2] EURECOM, France
[3] Machine Linking Srl, Italy
alessio@machinelinking.com

Abstract. In the latest years, the Web has seen an increasing interest in legal issues, concerning the use and re-use of online published material. In particular, several open issues affect the terms and conditions under which the data published on the Web is released to the users, and the users rights over such data. Though the number of licensed material on the Web is considerably increasing, the problem of generating machine readable licenses information is still unsolved. In this paper, we propose to adopt Natural Language Processing techniques to extract in an automated way the rights and conditions granted by a license, and we return the license in a machine readable format using RDF and adopting two well known vocabularies to model licenses. Experiments over a set of widely adopted licenses show the feasibility of the proposed approach.

Keywords: #eswc2014Cabrio, RDF-based licenses specifications, Natural Language Processing.

1 Introduction

The material published on the Web is usually associated to its terms of use and re-use, which provide the legal permissions and requirements the user has to comply with when dealing with such material. In the Web of Data, the majority of the published datasets are associated to specific licenses: as it has been shown in [9,17], about 75% of all Linked Data datasets listed in the CKAN archive[1] (Comprehensive Knowledge Archive Network) is associated to a license. Specifying the terms of re-use of the data is particularly important to foster the use and re-use of the data itself, as underlined in [11]. However, apart from the problem of specifying the license under which a certain dataset is released, other problems arise in the actual licenses and copyright specification in the Web of Data scenario, and in the Web in general. In particular, despite the Linked Data principles [2], only few datasets are associated to the machine readable version of the adopted license. As discussed by Rodriguez-Doncel et al. [17], specific

[1] `http://datahub.io/`

V. Presutti et al. (Eds.): ESWC 2014, LNCS 8465, pp. 255–269, 2014.

licensing terms are still referenced in natural language (NL) text, and there is the need to provide tools for supporting users in producing rights expressions in a machine readable format, such that more datasets could be easily associated to licenses. The lack of machine readable licenses specifications affects also the development and adoption of frameworks dealing with the licensing terms in an automated way, like for instance the licenses compatibility and composition framework proposed by Governatori et al. [9].

In this paper, we answer the following research question:

- How to support the creation of machine readable licensing information, starting from the natural language specification of the licenses?

The first point to be addressed consists in deciding the language to adopt to specify the licenses in a machine readable format. We choose to rely on the RDF language[2], since it is a standard model for data interchange on the Web. Moreover, it is the language adopted by the Creative Commons Rights Expression Language (CC REL)[3], that explains how license information may be described in a machine readable format using RDF. We aim at supporting both human users and automated systems to generate, starting from the natural language specification of the licenses, their RDF counterpart. Our scenario is as follows. On the one side, we have a human user publishing a dataset on the Web of Data; she wants to release its dataset for instance under the Open Government License[4] and, to be compliant with the Linked Data principles [2], she wants to specify in RDF such license. This means she has to know the possible vocabularies able to express licensing terms, and she has to go through the license text "translating" natural language terms into RDF. On the other side, an automated tool, like those presented in [19,9], retrieves a number of datasets on the Web of Data, and it needs the licensing information about such data. The problem is that each dataset only provides, e.g., in its VoID description[5], only the link to the natural language text of the license. In order to retrieve processable licensing information, it has to crawl the natural language text and automatically build its RDF description. Therefore, our research question breaks down into the following sub-questions: *i)* Which vocabularies have to be adopted to express licenses in RDF?, and *ii)* How to develop an automated framework to support the generation of RDF licenses specifications from their natural language texts?

First, we analyze existing vocabularies to represent licensing information, and we choose two of them, namely the Creative Commons Rights Expression Language Ontology[6], and the Open Digital Rights Language (ODRL) Ontology[7]. In particular, we adopt the former to represent in RDF Creative Commons (CC) licenses, and the latter to model all other licenses, given its broader scope. Our

[2] `http://www.w3.org/2011/rdf-wg/wiki/Main_Page`
[3] `http://wiki.creativecommons.org/CC_REL`
[4] `http://www.nationalarchives.gov.uk/doc/open-government-licence/`
[5] `http://www.w3.org/TR/void/`
[6] `http://creativecommons.org/ns`
[7] `http://www.w3.org/ns/odrl/2/`

RDF-based representation of licenses represents the specific rights (i.e., permissions, prohibitions and duties) granted by the licenses in the NL text.

Second, we adopt Natural Language Processing (NLP) techniques to develop an automated online framework called *NLL2RDF* (*Natural Language License to RDF*) able to "translate" natural language licenses specifications into their RDF definition using either the ODRL or the CC REL vocabulary. More precisely, NLL2RDF relies on machine learning techniques: the task is treated as a classification problem in supervised learning, and the adopted learning algorithm is Support Vector Machines (SVM) [4]. The algorithm is then trained over a set of manually annotated licenses.

The proposed approach is a first attempt to provide an automated framework able to output the RDF representation of the natural language description of a license. NLL2RDF is intended to support the diffusion of RDF-based licensing information attached to the datasets published on the Web of Data. Moreover, our approach is not limited to the Web of Data scenario, but it can be used to provide machine readable representation of licensing information not only for datasets but also for documents or software products, e.g., the Apache License[8]. Note that, given the complexity of the task, the current version of NLL2RDF provides an RDF representation of licenses considering their basic deontic components only, i.e., we model *permissions*, *prohibitions*, and *duties* only, and we do not consider at the present stage further constraints expressed by the licenses, e.g., about time, payment information, and sub-licensing. The automated treatment of such information is left as future work.

The remainder of the paper is as follows. Section 2 describes the vocabularies, and details the architecture of the proposed RDF licenses generation framework. Section 3 presents the experimental setting, and the evaluation of NLL2RDF. Section 4 compares the proposed approach with the related work in the literature.

2 Licenses: From Terms and Conditions to Triples

In this section, we first motivate our choice of the ODRL and CC REL vocabularies, and we then describe the classes and properties we adopt from such vocabularies (Section 2.1). Finally, we present the proposed framework to translate NL licenses into their RDF representation (Section 2.2).

2.1 CC REL and ODRL Vocabularies

Several vocabularies have been proposed in the last years to model licensing information. In particular, the following interconnected vocabularies provide high level descriptions of licenses, with a particular attention to the Web of Data scenario: LiMO[9], L4LOD[10], and ODRS[11]. More complex licenses information can

[8] `http://www.apache.org/licenses/LICENSE-2.0`

[9] `http://data.opendataday.it/LiMo`

[10] `http://ns.inria.fr/l4lod/`

[11] `http://schema.theodi.org/odrs/`

be defined with one of the digital Rights Expression Languages like ODRL[12] or MPEG-21, a machine-readable language that allows to declare rights and permissions using the terms as defined in the Rights Data Dictionary.[13] These vocabularies, ODRL in particular, have not been specifically conceived for the Web of Data scenario, but they intend to provide flexible mechanisms to support transparent and innovative use of digital content in publishing, distribution and consumption of digital media across all sectors. So far only the CC REL [1], the standard recommended by CC for the machine-readable expression of licensing terms, has been used by the Linked Data community.

We choose ODRL and CC REL vocabularies for our purposes. The reasons are the following: *i)* CC REL is the vocabulary to be used for all CC licenses, and it is the mostly adopted vocabulary in the Linked Data community for licenses specification; and *ii)* ODRL allows the specification of fine grained licensing terms both for data (thus satisfying the Web of Data scenario), and for all other digital media, allowing a broader application of NLL2RDF.

CC REL specifies for each `cc:License` a set of `cc:Permissions` (an action that may or may not be allowed), `cc:Requirements` (an action that may or may not be requested to the user), and `cc:Prohibitions` (something the user is asked not to do). The vocabulary specifies the following permissions (`cc:Reproduction`, `cc:Distribution`, `cc:DerivativeWork`, `cc:Sharing`), requirements (`cc:Notice`, `cc:Attribution`, `cc:ShareAlike`, `cc:SourceCode`, `cc:Copyleft`, `cc:LesserCopyleft`), and prohibitions (`cc:CommercialUse`, and `cc:HighIncomeNationUse`). For more details on the CC REL vocabulary, see [1]. Let us consider a license, like CC Attribution-NonCommercial License[14], where permissions are Reproduction, Distribution and Derivative Works, requirements are Notice and Attribution, and Commercial Use is prohibited. The license is represented in RDF (Turtle syntax[15]) using the CC REL vocabulary as follows:[16]

```
:licCC-BY-NC a cc:License;
         cc:legalcode <http://creativecommons.org/licenses/by-nc/4.0/>;
             cc:permits cc:Reproduction;
             cc:permits cc:Distribution;
             cc:permits cc:DerivativeWorks;
             cc:requires cc:Notice;
             cc:requires cc:Attribution;
             cc:prohibits cc:CommercialUse.
```

ODRL specifies, instead, different kinds of Policies (i.e., Agreement, Offer, Privacy, Request, Set and Ticket). In NLL2RDF we adopt `Set`, a policy expression that consists in entities from the complete model. Permissions, prohibitions and duties (i.e., the requirements specified in CC REL) are specified in terms of

[12] `http://www.w3.org/community/odrl/`
[13] `http://iso21000-6.net/`
[14] `http://creativecommons.org/licenses/by-nc/4.0/`
[15] `http://www.w3.org/TeamSubmission/turtle/`
[16] Prefixes are omitted for clarity reasons.

an `action`. For instance, we may have the action of attributing an `asset` (anything which can be subject to a policy), i.e., `odrl: action odrl: attribute`. For more details about the ODRL vocabulary, refer to the ODRL Community group.[17] The following example shows a Set policy expression, stating that the licensed asset is the target of the permission to reproduce, distribute, derive, the duty to attribute and attach the policy and, the prohibition to commercialize. It expresses the same rights as the CC license reported above.

```
:licCC-BY-NC a odrl:Set;
        odrl:permission [
            a odrl:Permission;
            odrl:action odrl:reprodice;
            odrl:action odrl:distribute;
            odrl:action odrl:derive
        ] ;
        odrl:prohibition [
            a odrl:Prohibition;
            odrl:action odrl:commercialize
        ] ;
        odrl:duty [
            a odrl:Duty;
            odrl:action odrl:attribute;
            odrl:action odrl:attachPolicy
       ] .
```

The NLL2RDF framework will adopt CC REL vocabulary to specify CC licenses, and the ODRL vocabulary to specify all other licenses.

2.2 The NLL2RDF Framework

After choosing the vocabularies to be used to express licenses in RDF, we can now describe our framework for RDF-based licenses specifications automatically extracted from natural language texts. The architecture of NLL2RDF is visualized in Figure 1. NLL2RDF can be accessed both by humans through the web interface[18] and by automated tools through the API of the system.

NLL2RDF input is the natural language definition of the licensing terms to be "translated" into RDF. NLL2RDF access such NL text T and applies some preprocessing steps: tokenization, lemmatization, part-of-speech tagging. After that, a classification step is performed, using kernel methods. We first embed the input data in a suitable feature space, and then use a linear algorithm to discover nonlinear patterns in the input space. Typically, the mapping is performed implicitly by a so-called *kernel function*.

Formally, the kernel is a function $k : X \times X \rightarrow \mathbb{R}$ that takes as input two data objects (e.g., vectors, texts, parse trees) and outputs a real number characterizing

[17] `http://w3.org/ns/odrl/2/`

[18] A demo of NLL2RDF is available at `www.airpedia.org/NLL2RDF`

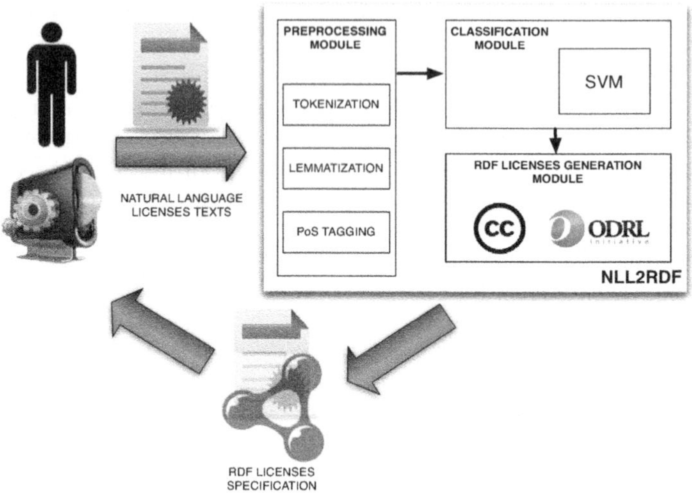

Fig. 1. The architecture of NLL2RDF

their similarity, with the property that the function is symmetric and positive semi-definite. That is, for all x_1, $x_2 \in X$, it satisfies

$$k(x_1, x_2) = \langle \phi(x_1), \phi(x_2) \rangle,$$

where ϕ is an explicit mapping from X to an (inner product) feature space $\mathcal{F}$. For our task, we work at sentence level, meaning that each sentence is considered as a vector. We define and combine two different kernel functions that calculate the pairwise similarity between sentences (*bag-of-words* and *verb*). Many classifiers can be used with kernels, we use Support Vector Machine. In particular, we used libSVM 3.12[19], a freely available tool.

The simplest method to calculate the similarity between two sentences is to compute the inner product of their vector representation in the vector space model (VSM). Formally, we define a space of dimensionality N in which each dimension is associated with one feature, and the sentence s is represented by a row vector

$$\phi_j(s) = (w(f_1, s), w(f_2, s), \ldots, w(f_N, s)), \tag{1}$$

where the function $w(f_k, s)$ records whether a particular feature f_k is active in the sentence s. Using this representation, we define the *bag-of-features kernel* between sentences as

$$K_F(s_1, s_2) = \langle \phi_j(s_1), \phi_j(s_2) \rangle, \tag{2}$$

Bag-of-words **Kernel.** The *bag-of-words kernel* (K_W) is defined as in Equation (2) where the function $w(f_k, s)$ in Equation (1) is the standard *term frequency-inverse document frequency* (tf $\times$ idf) of the word f_k in the sentence s.

[19] `http://www.csie.ntu.edu.tw/~cjlin/libsvm/`

***Verb* Kernel.** The *verb kernel* (K_V) is defined as in Equation (2) where the f_k in Equation (1) are elements of the set including the union of all the verb tokens (part-of-speech tags starting with "V") and the same tokens preceded by the token "not" in the sentence. Each verb token t is associated to two different features, depending on whether it is preceded by "not". In particular, if s contains that token, the corresponding feature is activated (that is $w(f_k, s) = 1$).

Composite Kernel. Having defined the two basic kernels representing different characteristics of entity descriptions, we finally define the composite kernel as

$$K_{\text{COMBO}}(s_1, s_2) = K_W(s_1, s_2) + K_V(s_1, s_2) \tag{3}$$

The individual kernels are normalized. This plays an important role in allowing us to integrate information from heterogeneous feature spaces. It follows directly from the explicit construction of the feature space and from closure properties of kernels that the composite kernel is a valid kernel.

NLL2RDF returns to the querying agent the RDF description of the licensing terms provided in natural language. Note that NLL2RDF does not provide any triple about the licensed work/asset. This means that, in case the generated RDF license has to be used to license a specific asset `asset841`, then a triple concerning the connection between the license and the asset has to be added by the agent (human or automated) who uses NLL2RDF.

3 Experimental Setting

To experiment our framework NLL2RDF, we selected a set of licenses (i.e. all the licenses adopted to certify data in the Linked Data cloud, plus additional software and online published material licenses) to create our reference dataset (described in Section 3.1). We then run NLL2RDF to generate the machine readable version of these licenses. More details on the experiments, and a discussion of the results we have obtained are reported in Section 3.2.

3.1 Dataset Creation

In order to evaluate NLL2RDF, as a first step we selected a set of licenses to build our reference dataset. More specifically, our reference dataset is composed by 37 licenses, comprising all the licenses adopted to certify data in the Linked Data cloud (as all the Creative Commons licenses[20]), software licenses (as Mozilla Public License[21] and Microsoft License[22]), and additional licenses for other material on the Web (as the UK Open Government license, and the New Free Documentation License[23]).

---

[20] `http://creativecommons.org/licenses/`

[21] `http://www.mozilla.org/MPL/2.0/`

[22] `http://referencesource.microsoft.com/referencesourcelicensing.aspx`

[23] `http://www.gnu.org/copyleft/fdl.html`

As a second step, we manually "translated" the textual version of each license into RDF, adopting the vocabularies described in Section 2.1 (i.e. CC REL for Creative Commons and ODRL for all the other licenses). Given for instance a textual fragment of the ODC Open Database License (ODbL)[24]:

You are free: To Share: To copy, distribute and use the database. To Create: To produce works from the database. To Adapt: To modify, transform and build upon the database. As long as you: Attribute: You must attribute any public use of the database, or works produced from the database, in the manner specified in the ODbL. For any use or redistribution of the database, or works produced from it, you must make clear to others the license of the database and keep intact any notices on the original database. Share-Alike: If you publicly use any adapted version of this database, or works produced from an adapted database, you must also offer that adapted database under the ODbL. [...]

we manually built the machine readable version of the license as follows:

```
@prefix odrl:  http://www.w3.org/ns/odrl/2/.
@prefix : http://example/licenses.

:licODBL a odrl:Set;
         odrl:permission [
           a odrl:Permission;
           odrl:action odrl:derive;
           odrl:action odrl:share
       ] ;
       odrl:duty [
           a odrl:Duty;
           odrl:action odrl:attribute;
           odrl:action odrl:shareAlike
       ] .
```

We use this machine readable version of the licenses as a goldstandard, i.e., to be compared with NLL2RDF's output in order to evaluate its ability in generating a correct RDF from the licenses texts.

As a third step in the creation of the reference dataset, we annotated in the textual version of the license the sentences containing the lexicalization of the ontological relations (i.e., the sentences whose meaning correspond to the ontological relations), to train our system. For instance, in the example of the ODbL license above, we annotated the sentence *You are free: To Share the database* with the ODRL relation `odrl:Permission` and the value `odrl:share`; the sentence *You are free: To produce works from the database* with the ODRL relation `odrl:Permission` and the value `odrl:derive`; the sentence *As long as you: Attribute: You must attribute any public use of the database, or works produced from the database, in the manner specified in the ODbL* with the ODRL relation `odrl:Duty` and the value `odrl:attribute`; and the sentence *As long*

[24] http://opendatacommons.org/licenses/odbl/summary/

as you: Share-Alike: If you publicly use any adapted version of this database, or works produced from an adapted database, you must also offer that adapted database under the ODbL with the ODRL relation `odrl:Duty` and the value `odrl:shareAlike`.

The same annotation task has been carried out on Creative Common licenses adopting CC REL ontology. For instance, given a textual fragment of the Attribution 4.0 International (CC BY 4.0) license[25]:

You are free to: Share - copy and redistribute the material in any medium or format. Adapt - remix, transform, and build upon the material for any purpose, even commercially. The licensor cannot revoke these freedoms as long as you follow the license terms. Under the following terms: Attribution - You must give appropriate credit, provide a link to the license, and indicate if changes were made. You may do so in any reasonable manner, but not in any way that suggests the licensor endorses you or your use. No additional restrictions You may not apply legal terms or technological measures that legally restrict others from doing anything the license permits.

we manually built the machine readable version of the license as follows:[26]

```
@prefix cc: http://creativecommons.org/ns.
@prefix : http://example/licenses.

:licCC-BY a cc:License;
            cc:legalcode <http://creativecommons.org/
                                                licenses/by/4.0/legalcode>;
            cc:requires cc:Notice;
            cc:requires cc:Attribution;
            cc:permits cc:Reproduction;
            cc:permits cc:Distribution;
            cc:permits cc:DerivativeWorks.
```

We then annotate in the textual version of the license the sentences whose meaning correspond to the ontological relations: the sentence *You are free to: copy the material in any medium or format* with the CC REL relation `cc:permits` and the value `cc:Reproduction`; the sentence *You are free to: redistribute the material in any medium or format* with the CC REL relation `cc:permits` and the value `cc:Distribution`; the sentence *You are free to: remix, transform, and build upon the material for any purpose* with the CC REL relation `cc:permits` and the value `cc:DerivativeWorks`; the sentence *You must provide a link to the license* with the CC REL relation `cc:requires` and the value `cc:Notice`; the sentence *You must give appropriate credit* with the CC REL relation `cc:requires` and the value `cc:Attribution`.

---

[25] `http://creativecommons.org/licenses/by/4.0/`

[26] CC licenses are also available in XML/RDF format on the CC website. CC-BY in particular is available at `http://creativecommons.org/licenses/by/4.0/rdf`

For the dataset annotation we adopted the CONLL IOB format[27], usually used in the NLP community for Natural Language Learning shared tasks. We first tokenized the sentences using Stanford Parser [18], and we then added two columns, the first one for the annotation of the relation, and the second one for the value, as follows[28]:

```
#id-004
1   You        PRP    B-PERMISSION       DERIVE
2   are        VBP    I-PERMISSION
3   free       JJ     I-PERMISSION
4   :          :      O
[...]               O
5   To         TO     I-PERMISSION
6   produce    VB     I-PERMISSION
6   works      VBZ    I-PERMISSION
7   from       IN     I-PERMISSION
8   the        DT     I-PERMISSION
15  database  NN    I-PERMISSION
16  .          .    O
```

The dataset has been annotated and independently verified by two annotators, with a complete agreement on the annotations (as introduced before, at this stage NLL2RDF considers licenses' basic deontic components only, for which human agreement is complete on almost all of them).

3.2 Evaluation

In our experiments, we use a linear SVM classifier for each possible relation-value present in all the licenses. In addition, we mapped the CC REL vocabulary labels on the ODRL labels, to increase the number of examples to train and test NLL2RDF (we apply then the mapping in the reverse order to generate the correct RDF for CC REL licenses). Only the couples relation-values with more than 5 occurrences in the data are reported.[29] Table 1 describes the NLL2RDF performances in the relation assignment over the licenses included in our dataset.

[27] In this scheme, each token is tagged with one of three special chunk tags, I (inside), O (outside), or B (begin). A token is tagged as B if it marks the beginning of a chunk. Subsequent tokens within the chunk are tagged I. All other tokens are tagged O. The B and I tags are suffixed with the chunk type according to our annotation task, e.g. B-PERMISSION, I-PERMISSION. Of course, it is not necessary to specify a chunk type for tokens that appear outside a chunk, so these are just labeled O.

[28] The annotated dataset is available at `www.airpedia.org/NLL2RDF/dataset-licenses`. Each couple relation-value has been annotated in a separate file, contained in a folder with the license name.

[29] The following couples relation-values with less than 5 occurrences in the data are: `Permission:read` (1 occurrence), `Permission:commercialize` (3), `Permission:share` (4), `Duty:attachSource` (1), `Prohibition:distribute` (3), and `Prohibition:modify` (1).

Given a sentence, we test it against every classifiers, so that we can intercept those sentences containing more than one relation (see Section 3.1 for an example). Performances are calculated using the n-fold cross-validation ($n = 3$). The annotated data set is randomly split into 3 parts containing the same number of examples (1/3 of the total, around 560 sentences). A single subset is retained as test set, while the remaining 2 subsets are used as training data. The process is executed 3 times, each time with a different subset used for validation, giving 3 different pairs of precision/recall values. These values are then averaged to obtain the final results.

Table 1. Performances of NLL2RDF on the correct assignment of each triple

relation-value	# occurr.	precision	recall	f-measure
`Permission:distribute`	28	0.74	0.59	0.65
`Permission:derive`	15	0.66	0.51	0.56
`Permission:reproduce`	14	0.55	0.51	0.46
`Permission:modify`	13	0.66	0.2	0.3
`Permission:copy`	11	0.77	0.22	0.34
`Permission:sell`	6	0.83	0.38	0.53
`Duty:shareAlike`	17	0.72	0.3	0.36
`Duty:attachPolicy`	16	0.76	0.63	0.68
`Duty:attribute`	15	1	0.66	0.78
`Prohibition:commercialize`	7	1	0.33	0.49

NLL2RDF reaches quite interesting results for some relation-value assignment, mainly for the ones with a high number of occurrences in the training data (e.g. `Permission:distribute`, `Duty:attachPolicy`, `Duty:attribute`). For some other relations, SVM performances are far from being optimal, due to *i)* the sparsity of some relations in the data (i.e. for some couples relation-value only few examples are present in the data, e.g. `Prohibition:commercialize`), *ii)* the fact that the lexicalizations of relations such as `Permission:modify` involve a lot of language variability, each one not supported by a sufficient number of occurrences in the text (e.g. *you are free to modify*; *assure everyone the effective freedom [...] with modification*), and *iii)* very similar surface forms can refer to different relations-values (for instance for `Duty:shareAlike` and `Duty:attachPolicy`, we have the textual representations *Redistributions must reproduce the above copyright notice* for the former, and *Redistributions must retain the copyright notice* for the latter). We are aware that the current version of NLL2RDF is not yet fully reliable, but at the present stage our system is not yet intended to completely substitute users: it is intended as a tool to support them in specifying the machine readable version of licensing information. As a short improvement, we are planning to collect and annotate other licenses, to increase our training dataset in size and variability. Moreover, since certain structures in licenses appear over and over, we are envisaging to add manually written rules to capture recurrent patterns. In general, more efforts would also be required from the community, to encourage data providers to publish machine readable licenses, semi-automatically and with the support of the NLL2RDF system.

4 Related Work

Heath and Bizer [11] underline that "the absence of clarity for data consumers about the terms under which they can reuse a particular dataset, and the absence of common guidelines for data licensing, are likely to hinder use and reuse of data". Therefore, all Linked Data on the Web should include explicit licenses, or waiver statements, as discussed by [13], who propose the Open Data Commons licenses that try to fully license any rights that cover databases and data.

Beside the vocabularies mentioned in Section 2.1, other few vocabularies have been proposed in the literature to model, to different extent, licensing information. The Waiver vocabulary[30], for instance, defines properties to use when describing waivers of rights over data and content, where a waiver is defined as a voluntary relinquishment or surrender of some known right or privilege. As underlined by [9,17], licenses are usually connected to the data through the VoID description. In particular, the Dublin Core vocabulary[31] is usually adopted to associate licenses to resources through the property `dc:license`, and the class `dc:LicenseDocument` provides the legal document giving official permission to do something with the resource. Two further vocabularies which may be adopted to define the licensing terms associated to the data on the Web are the Description of a Project vocabulary (DOAP)[32], and the Ontology Metadata vocabulary (OMV)[33]. More precisely, DOAP specifies a property `doap:license` referring to the URI of an RDF description of the license the software is distributed under; OMV defines the property `omv:hasLicense`, which provides the underlying license model, and a class `omv:LicenseModel`, which describes the usage conditions of an ontology. The attachment of additional information like rights or licenses to RDF triplets may be done also by adopting named graphs [3]. Carroll et al. [3] introduce them to allow publishers to communicate assertional intent and to sign their assertions. Moreover, the W3C Provenance WG [10] defines the kind of information to be used to form assessments about data quality, reliability or trustworthiness.

The different licenses, e.g., Creative Commons, Open Data Commons, have common features, but also differ from each others. The requirement to mention the author (attribution) seems to be one of the best shared features. Most legal frameworks allow commercial use: that is, they make it possible for re-users to sell public data without transforming or enriching them. The Web NDL Authority license[34] is an exception, and prohibits reuse as is of its data for commercial

[30] `http://vocab.org/waive/terms/`
[31] `http://dublincore.org/documents/dcmi-terms/`
[32] `http://usefulinc.com/ns/doap`
[33] `http://omv2.sourceforge.net/index.html`
[34] `http://iss.ndl.go.jp/ndla/use/`

purposes: a further individual examination by the licensor is necessary. For a further discussion about rights declaration in Linked Data, see [17].

In the Web scenario, a number of works address the problem of representing and/or reasoning over licensing information. Iannella [35] presents the Open Digital Rights Language (ODRL) for expressing rights information over content, and Gangadharan et al. [5] further extend ODRL developing the ODRL-S language to implement the clauses of service licensing. Gangadharan et al. [6] address the issue of service license composition and compatibility analysis basing on ODRL-S. They specify a matchmaking algorithm which verifies whether two service licenses are compatible. If so, the services can be composed and the framework determines the license of the composite service. Truong et al. [19] address the issue of analyzing data contracts, based again on ODRL-S. Contract analysis leads to the definition of a contract composition where first the comparable contractual terms from the different data contracts are retrieved, and second an evaluation of the new contractual terms for the data mash-up is addressed. Krotzsch and Speiser [12] present a semantic framework for evaluating ShareAlike recursive statements. In particular, they develop a general policy modelling language, then instantiated with OWL DL and Datalog, for supporting self-referential policies as expressed by CC. Finally, Gordon [8] presents a legal prototype for analyzing open source licenses compatibility using the Carneades argumentation system. All these works assume licensing information to be expressed in some kind of machine readable format or formal syntax. Given that licenses are always expressed first in natural language, these frameworks could rely on NLL2RDF to have a first machine readable version of the license in RDF. Then, the "translation" from RDF to the specific formal syntax they need to reason over licensing terms has to be performed. However, this step is usually less demanding than a direct translation form NL to a specific syntax, given the high complexity and variability of natural language texts.

Closer to the general purpose of our work of supporting users in defining machine readable descriptions of licenses, Nadah et al. [14] propose to assist licensors' work by providing a generic way to instantiate licenses, independent from specific formats. Then they translate such license into more specific terms compliant with the specific standards used by distribution systems, i.e., ODRL and MPEG Rights Data Dictionaries. They do not address the problem of providing an automated tool to move from NL licenses to their RDF representation, but they propose a model to move from a license description through a particular ontology to the description of the same license using another ontology.

Rodriguez-Doncel et al. [16,15] discuss licenses patterns for Linked Data. They first analyze and discuss six rights expression languages, abstracting their commonalities and outlining their underlying pattern. Second, they propose the License Linked Data Resources pattern which provides a solution to describe existing licenses and rights expressions both for open and not open scenarios. Even if our final goal is different from theirs, the LLDR pattern is useful for an overall structured representation of the different rights expression languages.

[35] `http://odrl.net/1.1/ODRL-11.pdf`

5 Conclusions

In this paper, we presented NLL2RDF, an automated framework to support RDF-based licenses specifications starting from natural language texts. The goal of NLL2RDF is to provide both human users, and automated systems with a support to generate machine readable representations of licensing terms. We adopt the CC REL and the ODRL vocabularies to specify the licenses in RDF. Our framework relies on NLP techniques to generate in an automated way such RDF based licenses descriptions. In particular, the framework exploits SVM to classify the couples relation-value present in the licenses, and then the RDF version of the license is generated filling a pre-defined RDF template. In order to train the system, two annotators independently marked up a set of 37 licenses, selected among the set of widely adopted licenses in the Web of Data in particular, and in the Web in general. The experimental evaluation shows the feasibility of the proposed framework and fosters to pursue with this research direction. Both the dataset and the system, as web service, are available online.

NLL2RDF provides a first step towards the automatic analysis of natural language licenses texts to return their machine readable description. However, several open challenges still remain to be addressed. For instance, user evaluation is the first step of future works, even if we have already started to gather feedback about the systems' results from legal experts in the Web area. Second, we will extend the dataset to train our system by adding other licenses in order to improve the performances of our system, particularly with respect to those deontic components which do not appear frequently nowadays in the dataset. We are planning to collect and annotate other licenses, to increase our training dataset (so that to capture enough language variability to improve the system robustness). Third, we will improve the precision of RDF licenses description. As we previously motivated, at the present time we model licenses using only the basic deontic components they express without taking into account any further constraint or exception stated in the NL license text. Moreover, we plan to couple machine learning algorithms with pattern-based approaches for information extraction (following [7]). Finally, the system can be extended to a multilingual scenario (as far as a NLP tool to process the language at issue is available), to provide machine readable versions of licenses published by national institutions, or licenses published in different languages.

Acknowledgements. The work of Elena Cabrio was funded by the French Government (National Research Agency, ANR) through the "Investments for the Future" Program reference # ANR-11-LABX-0031-01.

References

1. Abelson, H., Adida, B., Linksvayer, M., Yergler, N.: ccREL: The creative commons rights expression language. Technical report, Creative Commons (2008)
2. Bizer, C., Heath, T., Berners-lee, T.: Linked Data - The Story So Far. International Journal on Semantic Web and Information Systems 5, 1–22 (2009)

3. Carroll, J., Bizer, C., Hayes, P., Stickler, P.: Named graphs. J. Web Sem. 3(4), 247–267 (2005)
4. Cristianini, N., Shawe-Taylor, J.: An Introduction to Support Vector Machines and Other Kernel-based Learning Methods. Cambridge University Press (2010)
5. Gangadharan, G.R., D'Andrea, V., Iannella, R., Weiss, M.: Odrl service licensing profile (ODRL-S). In: Proceedings of Virtual Goods (2007)
6. Gangadharan, G.R., Weiss, M., D'Andrea, V., Iannella, R.: Service license composition and compatibility analysis. In: Krämer, B.J., Lin, K.-J., Narasimhan, P. (eds.) ICSOC 2007. LNCS, vol. 4749, pp. 257–269. Springer, Heidelberg (2007)
7. Gerber, D., Ngomo, A.-C.N.: Extracting multilingual natural-language patterns for RDF predicates. In: ten Teije, A., Völker, J., Handschuh, S., Stuckenschmidt, H., d'Acquin, M., Nikolov, A., Aussenac-Gilles, N., Hernandez, N. (eds.) EKAW 2012. LNCS, vol. 7603, pp. 87–96. Springer, Heidelberg (2012)
8. Gordon, T.F.: Analyzing open source license compatibility issues with Carneades. In: Proceedings of ICAIL, pp. 51–55. ACM (2011)
9. Governatori, G., Rotolo, A., Villata, S., Gandon, F.: One license to compose them all - a deontic logic approach to data licensing on the web of data. In: Alani, H., et al. (eds.) ISWC 2013, Part I. LNCS, vol. 8218, pp. 151–166. Springer, Heidelberg (2013)
10. Groth, P.T., Gil, Y., Cheney, J., Miles, S.: Requirements for provenance on the web. IJDC 7(1), 39–56 (2012)
11. Heath, T., Bizer, C.: Linked Data: Evolving the Web into a Global Data Space. Morgan & Claypool (2011)
12. Krötzsch, M., Speiser, S.: ShareAlike Your Data: Self-referential Usage Policies for the Semantic Web. In: Aroyo, L., Welty, C., Alani, H., Taylor, J., Bernstein, A., Kagal, L., Noy, N., Blomqvist, E. (eds.) ISWC 2011, Part I. LNCS, vol. 7031, pp. 354–369. Springer, Heidelberg (2011)
13. Miller, P., Styles, R., Heath, T.: Open data commons, a license for open data. In: Proceedings of LDOW (2008)
14. Nadah, N., de Rosnay, M.D., Bachimont, B.: Licensing digital content with a generic ontology: escaping from the jungle of rights expression languages. In: Proceedings of ICAIL, pp. 65–69. ACM (2007)
15. Rodriguez-Doncel, V., Figueroa, M.S., Gomez-Perez, A., Villalon, M.P.: License linked data resources pattern. In: Proc. of the 4th International Workshop on Ontology Patterns (2013)
16. Rodriguez-Doncel, V., Figueroa, M.S., Gomez-Perez, A., Villalon, M.P.: Licensing patterns for linked data. In: Proc. of the 4th International Workshop on Ontology Patterns (2013)
17. Rodríguez-Doncel, V., Gómez-Pérez, A., Mihindukulasooriya, N.: Rights declaration in linked data. In: Hartig, O., Sequeda, J., Hogan, A., Matsutsuka, T. (eds.) COLD. CEUR Workshop Proceedings, vol. 1034. CEUR-WS.org (2013)
18. Socher, R., Bauer, J., Manning, C.D., Ng, A.Y.: Parsing with compositional vector grammars. ACL (1), 455–465 (2013)
19. Truong, H.L., Gangadharan, G.R., Comerio, M., Dustdar, S., Paoli, F.D.: On analyzing and developing data contracts in cloud-based data marketplaces. In: IEEE Proceedings of APSCC, pp. 174–181 (2011)

Scaling Parallel Rule-Based Reasoning

Martin Peters[1], Christopher Brink[1], Sabine Sachweh[1], and Albert Zündorf[2]

[1] University of Applied Sciences Dortmund,
Department of Computer Science, Germany
{martin.peters,christopher.brink,sabine.sachweh}@fh-dortmund.de
[2] University of Kassel, Germany, Software Engineering Research Group,
Department of Computer Science and Electrical Engineering, Germany
zuendorf@cs.uni-kassel.de

Abstract. Using semantic technologies the materialization of implicit given facts that can be derived from a dataset is an important task performed by a reasoner. With respect to the answering time for queries and the growing amount of available data, scaleable solutions that are able to process large datasets are needed. In previous work we described a rule-based reasoner implementation that uses massively parallel hardware to derive new facts based on a given set of rules. This implementation was limited by the size of processable input data as well as on the number of used parallel hardware devices. In this paper we introduce further concepts for a workload partitioning and distribution to overcome this limitations. Based on the introduced concepts, additional levels of parallelization can be proposed that benefit from the use of multiple parallel devices. Furthermore, we introduce a concept to reduce the amount of invalid triple derivations like duplicates. We evaluate our concepts by applying different rulesets to the real-world DBPedia dataset as well as to the synthetic Lehigh University benchmark ontology (LUBM) with up to 1.1 billion triples. The evaluation shows that our implementation scales in a linear way and outperforms current state of the art reasoner with respect to the throughput achieved on a single computing node.

Keywords: #eswc2014Peters, scaleable reasoning, rule-based reasoning, GPU, parallel, RETE algorithm.

1 Introduction

In order to enable the semantic web and other semantic applications, the derivation of new facts based on a given dataset is one key feature that is provided by the use of reasoners. Query answering and the provision of a complete set of information often is a performance critical task. This gets even more important with respect to the growing amount of available information, that often needs to be processed. Thus, fast and scaleable reasoning is essential for the success of many semantic applications. In [1] we described first results of a rule-based and highly parallel reasoner running on massively parallel hardware like GPUs. Unlike many other parallel reasoner implementations (e.g. [2], [3], [4]), our approach is based on the RETE algorithm [5] and does not rely on a cluster-based

V. Presutti et al. (Eds.): ESWC 2014, LNCS 8465, pp. 270–285, 2014.

approach like MapReduce implementations. The use of RETE allows us to easily load different rulesets and apply them to input data. Thus, our forward chaining reasoner is not dependent on a specific ruleset like RDFS or pD* [6] and can be used for inference based on any application specific semantics that can be expressed using rules.

In this paper we introduce new concepts of workload partitioning as well as new levels of parallelization. Both aspects allow us to perform a scaleable and efficient reasoning using parallel hardware even on large ontologies that do not fit into the on-board memory of a GPU. In particular, we introduce a workload partitioning for each of the different steps of the RETE algorithm. This workload partitioning on the one hand allows us to introduce a further parallelization on the host side (that part of the application, that does not run on massively parallel hardware), and on the other hand easily allows to distribute the workload over multiple GPUs and thus to scale the hardware in a horizontal way.

In the next section we start with an introduction to the parallel implementation of the RETE algorithm for semantic reasoning before we introduce the workload partitioning schemes. Based on the partitioning schemes new levels of parallelization are proposed (new levels because they can be applied in addition to the already introduced parallel matching algorithm described in [1]). Furthermore, a strategy for reducing the derivation of invalid triples like duplicates is presented in section 3. Section 4 will evaluate our approach and show different aspects of scaleability, effectiveness of parallelization and performance of the reasoner. For this purpose we reason about datasets with up to 1.1 billion triples using different rulesets. Finally we discuss our findings with respect to related work and conclude the paper.

2 Using RETE for a Rule-Based Reasoner Implementation

The RETE algorithm is a pattern matching algorithm and was introduced by Charles L. Forgy [5]. The algorithm is based on a network of nodes, which are derived by the given set of rules. The network consists of alpha and beta nodes, where an alpha node has no parents and represents exactly one rule-term. Thus, for each unique rule-term of a given ruleset an alpha node is created. A beta node in turn always has two parents which may be alpha or beta nodes. Thus, a beta node always represents at least two rule patterns and links two or more single rule-terms of one rule. Assuming the rules R1 and R2 from the pD* rules (also known as OWL-Horst) the resulting network is shown in figure 1.

$$(?v \text{ owl:hasValue } ?w)\ (?v \text{ owl:onProperty } ?p)\ (?u\ ?p\ ?w) \rightarrow (?u \text{ rdf:type } ?v) \tag{R1}$$

$$(?v \text{ owl:hasValue } ?w)\ (?v \text{ owl:onProperty } ?p)\ (?u \text{ rdf:type } ?v) \rightarrow (?u\ ?p\ ?w) \tag{R2}$$

Finally, the node $\beta 2$ represents the complete rule R1 and the node $\beta 3$ the rule R2. To apply the ruleset to a set of input triples (each consisting of a subject, predicate and object (s, p, o)), basically three steps are necessary. The first one

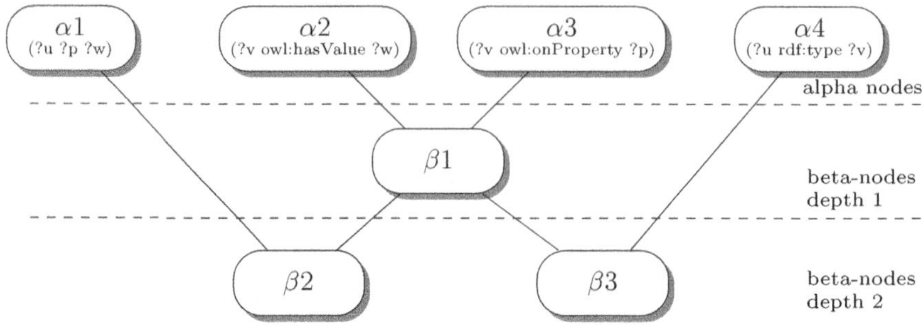

Fig. 1. RETE network for rules R1 and R2

is the alpha-matching and means to match every input triple against every alpha node. Because $\alpha1$ is completely unbound (all of the three rule-term elements are variables) every triple will match. To match the condition of $\alpha2$, the predicate of a triple needs to be *owl:hasValue*. Other alpha nodes are treated accordingly. For each node a list of matching triples (working memory) is created. Basically this list consists of references to the corresponding triples. The working memories of the alpha-nodes are the starting point for the second step of the RETE algorithm, the beta-matching.

During beta-matching, each match of the first parent node is combined with each match of the second parent node to see, if both matches together satisfy the conditions of the beta node. For example for $\beta1$ the matches of $\alpha2$ and $\alpha3$ need to share the subject (?*v*) to be a match of $\beta1$. After the matches of the beta nodes of the depth 1 (see figure 1) are computed, the matches of the next level of beta-nodes can be computed, too. Once the matches of all beta nodes are determined, the working memories of the final nodes of a rule can be used to fire the rules and derive new facts, which is the third step of the RETE algorithm. The final node of a rule is that node, that represents the complete rule body like mentioned before. Thus, the working memory of $\beta2$ is used to fire R1 and the working memory of $\beta3$ is used to fire R2. The new derived triples then need to be propagated through the network until no new triples are derived.

2.1 Parallelizing the RETE algorithm

Addressing massively parallel hardware like GPUs the main challenge is to partition the workload in a way that it can be computed by millions of threads in parallel. Looking at the RETE algorithm we have to consider the three different steps of alpha-matching, beta-matching and rule-firing that need to be parallelized. The concepts for a parallel alpha- and beta-matching were already introduced in [1]. The main idea for an efficient alpha-matching is to match every triple against all of the alpha nodes and not the other way round. This means that the number of threads that are submitted to the parallel hardware is equal to the number of input triples. The resulting list then is transformed to the working memories of the individual alpha-nodes.

The beta-matching is based on a similar concept. To compute the matches of one beta-node, the amount of threads is created on a parallel hardware that corresponds to the number of matches of one of the parent nodes. Each of the created threads holds a reference to exactly one match of the corresponding parent node and iterates through all of the matches of the second parent node. Assuming that $\alpha 2$ in figure 1 has 500 matches and $\alpha 3$ has 300 matches, a total of 500 threads is created where each thread iterates through all of the 300 matches of $\alpha 3$. For more details regarding the alpha- and beta-matching as well as an efficient matching implementation on the GPU we refer to [1].

Rule firing in [1] was performed in a serial way, which means that a single thread iterated through all matches of the final node of a rule and created the resulting triples. However, this easily can be performed in parallel, too, by submitting a thread for each match of a final node to the parallel hardware and derive the triples. Note that a thread on massively parallel hardware is much more lightweight than for example in a Java application and thus the overhead is accordingly small. The resulting triples finally need to be checked against duplicates and can be propagated through the RETE network, too.

2.2 Introducing Workload Partitioning

Like the evaluation in [1] showed, the introduced concept for a parallel RETE implementation running on massively parallel hardware performed very well regarding the performance. Nevertheless, the concept was limited by the size of the input data that could be processed. To address this issue for the alpha-matching, the workload can easily be partitioned into smaller chunks that can be processed independently and thus can be sized to an adequate size with respect to the target device. Note that in parallel programming the *device* always refers to the parallel hardware like a GPU. Figure 2 illustrates the partitioning in preparation of an alpha step for n input triples that need to be matched against p alpha nodes.

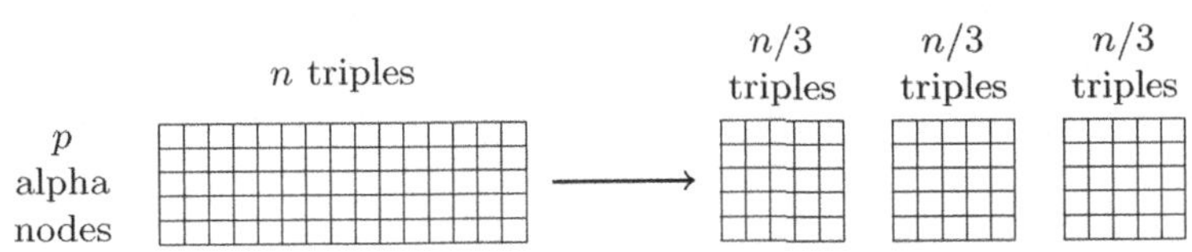

Fig. 2. Workload partitioning for alpha-matching

For beta-matching and rule-firing this partitioning is not applicable because the working memories of the nodes in the RETE network, that are used for both steps, consist of references to triples of the internal triple store. To perform the matching or rule-firing, these references need to be resolved because the corresponding triples are needed for further processing (like the matching). Thus, the complete set of available triples needs to be loaded to the main memory of the GPU. Accordingly the maximum size of the processable input data depends on the memory size of the device. To overcome this issue, we introduce a *triple-match* with the following definition:

Definition 1. *A triple-match* $m = (s, p, o, r)$ *is a quadruple with s=subject, p=predicate, o=object of a triple and r=triple reference (unique number, that is used for identification in the internal triple store).*

According to this definition, a triple-match not only holds the reference r to the corresponding triple, but also the triple itself. By using this data structure for computations on parallel devices instead of the pure working memory of a node we eliminate the need to transfer the complete set of available triples to the device. However, working memories that are needed for example for a beta-match processing need to be transferred to a list of triple-matches before execution. Because the triple-match holds the triple itself as well as the reference, the resulting data of an alpha- or beta-matching can still consists only of the triple references.

Another benefit on using triple-matches during a beta-match is that it allows us to perform a similar workload partitioning like for the alpha-matching. Because during beta-matching all matches of one parent node (n_{parent_1} matches) are matched against all matches of the other parent node (m_{parent_2} matches), n and m (see figure 3) both might become very large. Thus, not only a partition in one dimension is desirable, but also in two dimensions.

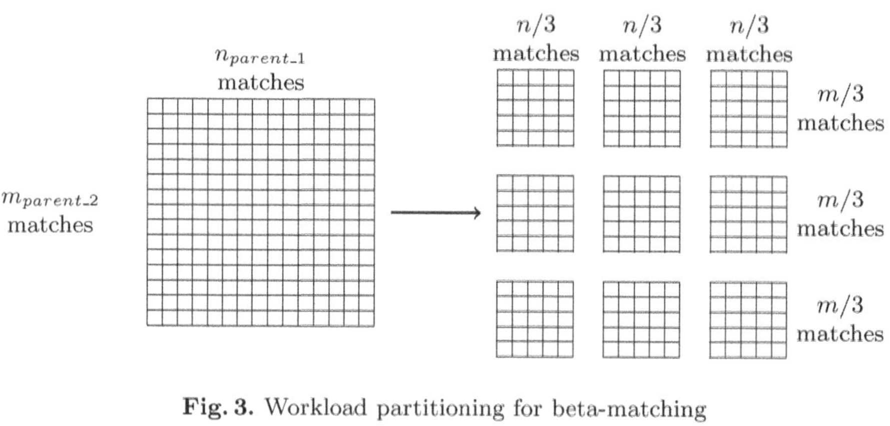

Fig. 3. Workload partitioning for beta-matching

As illustrated in figure 3 the complete workload can be divided into smaller chunks, where the size of the chunks can be chosen with respect to the used device considering for example the amount of available memory. This allows to separately submit each chunk for processing to the device and reading back the results.

For rule-firing the use of triple-matches also allows to partition the workload. Therefore, the matches of a final node can be split up into chunks of an adequate size, transferred into triple-matches and being processed on the device. The resulting triples that are transferred back from the device to the host finally can be submitted to the triple-store of the reasoner where they need to be checked against duplicates.

2.3 Workload Distribution

The introduced workload partitioning not only allows to process large datasets in small chunks, it also enables us to introduce new levels of parallelization and finally to distribute the workload over multiple devices. Considering the example from figure 1, it can be seen that the beta-matching of all beta nodes of one depth can be performed independently and thus simultaneously. That is because a beta-matching in a depth of d always relies on the results of nodes with a depth $< d$. Based on this understanding the first level of additional parallelization can be introduced by computing beta-matches of all beta-nodes of one depth in parallel. A further level of parallelization is possible through the workload partitioning, where each single partition of one beta-node can be processed in parallel, too.

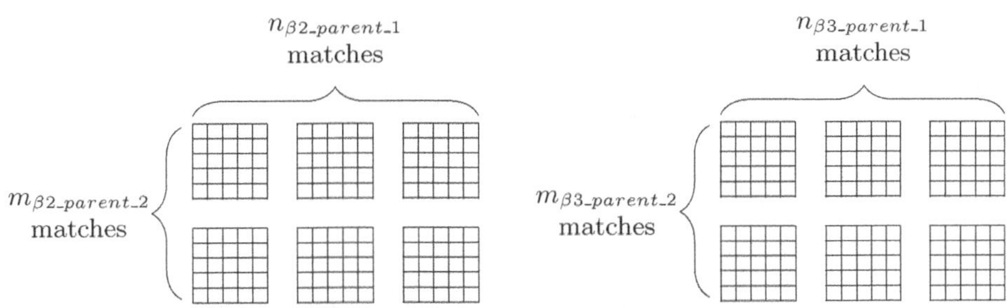

Fig. 4. Further levels of parallelization for beta-matching

Figure 4 illustrates the two levels of parallelization by showing the partitioned workload for $\beta 2$ and $\beta 3$ from the example RETE-network. Besides the fact that both nodes can compute their matches independently of one another, the created chunks can be computed in parallel, too. Finally this leads to the following number of possible parallel computations of one depth:

$$\sum_{i=1}^{B} \frac{n_i}{chunkwidth_i} * \frac{m_i}{chunkheight_i} \tag{1}$$

Note that B denotes to the number of beta-nodes in one depth and *chunkwidth* and *chunkheight* are constants defining the size of a chunk, which can be chosen with respect to the target device and size of n_i and m_i. We further assume that n_i always divides by *chunkwidth* and m_i by *chunkheight*.

Applying this additional parallelization allows to easily use multiple massively parallel devices like GPUs. While one GPU can only perform one task (for example process one chunk) at a time, the total workload can be distributed over multiple devices. This way the reasoner can be parallelized on the host side (the host defines the execution environment like a java application from where a parallel device is accessed) as well as on the device side. This concept can also be applied to the rule-firing, where each rule can be processed independently of one another and thus can be processed in parallel, too. A further level of parallelization is achieved by the workload partitioning, which has been mentioned before.

3 Reduction of Invalid Triples

As already stated out in [1], rule-firing can be the most time consuming task during the reasoning process, depending on the used rules and dataset. One reason for this is the huge amount of duplicates as well as triples holding a literal as a subject, that get inferred during rule-firing. Such triples need to be identified and rejected by the triple store of the reasoner before the new triples are stored. While the check of a literal-subject can for example be performed by a direct lookup using an array holding a boolean value for every unique triple element (s, p, o), the identification of duplicates is often performed using a HashMap. Nevertheless, both methods of triple validation have the drawback that they are performed after the triples have been created. Thus, the triples first need to be derived before they can be validated.

The issue of a high rate of invalid triples is particularly noticeable computing the complete RDFS closure, where most of the triples are derived by the following rules:

$$(?x\ ?p\ ?y) \rightarrow (?p\ \text{rdf:type rdf:Property}) \tag{R3}$$

$$(?x\ ?p\ ?y) \rightarrow (?x\ \text{rdf:type rdfs:Resource}) \tag{R4}$$

$$(?x\ ?p\ ?y) \rightarrow (?y\ \text{rdf:type rdfs:Resource}) \tag{R5}$$

What can be seen on looking at these rules is, that all existing triples will match the condition of the rules. That means that the number of output triples that finally need to be validated is equal to the number of input triples for the rule-firing of these rules. However, many of the derived triples will be duplicates because for R4 for example, all triples which share one subject will produce the same output triple. The same applies to R3 and R5 except that the output triple only depends on the predicate or object of the input triples.

With the proposed concept of triple-matches, which are also used for rule-firing on parallel hardware, we can use these findings to introduce a simple reduction of duplicates by an evaluation during the triple-match creation. When preparing the triple-matches for rule-firing of a specific rule, the rule header is also known and can be evaluated to the condition that there is only one variable term like $?x$ in the header. On the other side it is known, which triple element (subject, predicate or object) of the input triples will be placed to the variable of the rule header. For R4 for example the subject of the input triple would be placed to the subject of the resulting triple, too. Thus, a HashMap can be created which stores all occurrences of subjects during triple-match creation. Based on this HashMap a check can reveal if the subject already exists in the Map and thus the triple-match would result in a duplicate. If so, the triple-match can be rejected.

This does not only reduce the amount of triples that need to be validated before they are stored to the triple store, it also reduces the amount of triple-matches that need to be created and processed on the device. A similar concept can be applied to rules where the subject of the rule-header is a variable. In this case, the element that would be placed to the subject of the resulting triple can be checked if it is a literal or not. Only in the later case, the triple-match needs to be created. Nevertheless, these concepts provide a cheap way in terms of computation time to reduce the amount of invalid triples. They do not completely avoid the derivation of invalid triples and thus a final check before storing is still necessary.

4 Evaluation

Our evaluation has three goals: First of all we want to show the impact of the introduced concepts to avoid invalid triple derivations. Secondly we want to analyze the effect of the new levels of parallelization as well as workload distribution by using multiple GPUs. Finally we want to test the scaleability of our approach for datasets with up to one billion triples.

4.1 Implementation

For evaluation purpose of the proposed concepts we extended our implementation of the reasoner presented in [1]. The reasoner is written in Java and uses OpenCL[1] to perform highly parallel processing tasks on heterogenous devices like multicore CPUs or GPUs. The jocl-Library[2] is used for OpenCL Java bindings. The internal triple store is implemented as a singleton and manages the parsed triples as well as derived triples. Lists and HashMaps are used to store the data and to allow a fast lookup, for example to check against duplicates. The new levels of parallelization that were introduced in section 2 are implemented using multithreading in Java. Each thread that is responsible to compute one chunk, for example during beta-matching, prepares all needed data like the triple-matches and submits a task to a synchronous queue. For every available GPU in the execution environment of the reasoner a worker-thread is created, that polls for

[1] OpenCL: open standard for parallel programming of heterogeneous systems, `http://www.khronos.org/opencl/`

[2] `http://www.jocl.org/`

new tasks on the queue and executes it on the corresponding parallel device. This way it can be guaranteed that each processing task has exclusive rights to the device during execution. We also optimize the idle time of the devices by ensuring that each task that is submitted to the queue has already prepared all needed data. By using the concept of worker-threads that are responsible to access the available devices, the application dynamically adapts to the number of existing parallel devices and thus fully exploits the hardware.

4.2 Test Environment and Datasets

To evaluate the proposed concepts, we use three different rulesets with varying complexity that are often implemented by other reasoners, too. The ρdf [7] ruleset is a simplified version of the RDFS vocabulary and consists of all RDFS rules with at least two rule terms. This ruleset is often used for a time efficient reasoning, because the results of the omitted rules could be provided by the reasoner on the fly if required. The second ruleset is the complete RDFS ruleset like it is defined by the W3C[3]. Finally we use the pD* [6] ruleset (also know as OWL-Horst) which incorporates RDFS and D entailment and has some basic support for OWL. For the complete set of pD* rules we refer to [2].

The used datasets are the DBPedia Ontology 3.9 [8], including the mapping-based types and mapping-based properties, as well as the Lehigh University benchmark (LUBM) ontology [9]. The DBPedia ontology is a lightweight ontology containing extracted information from Wikipedia and thus is a real world dataset. The complete datasets consists of more than 41 million triples. Nevertheless, we scaled this dataset to different sizes by using only every n'th instance triple to get $1/2^{th}$, $1/4^{th}$, $1/8^{th}$, $1/16^{th}$, and $1/32^{nd}$ of the dataset. The LUBM ontology is designed for benchmarks and is a de-facto standard for performance evaluations and comparison for RDF reasoner. A generator can be used to create datasets representing a university scenario, where the number of generated universities is used to size the resulting dataset. Thus, it can be used to create artificial datasets of an arbitrary size. The LUBM datasets used for evaluation are annotated with the corresponding number of universities that are included, such that for example LUBM250 refers to 250 universities. Figure 5 gives an detailed overview of the used datasets.

We perform our tests on two different machines. The first one that is used for all tests except the scaleability test is equipped with two mid range AMD 7970 gaming GPUs, each having 3 GB of on-board memory, a 2.0 GHz Intel Xeon processor with 6 cores and 64 GB of system memory. For the scaleability test more system memory is needed to process the large LUBM datasets, which is why we use a cloud server with a total of 192 GB of memory, two Tesla M2090 GPUs each having 6GB of on-board memory and a 2.4 GHz Intel Xeon processor with 12 cores. Every test is executed five times and the average time, excluding dictionary encoding, is given.

---

[3] `http://www.w3.org/TR/rdf-mt/#RDFSRules`

Dataset	Scale	Triples
DBPedia	1/32	1,322,055
	1/16	2,627,952
	1/8	5,238,518
	1/4	10,453,153
	1/2	20,807,047
	full	41,447,376

Dataset	Scale	Triples
LUBM	125	17,607,267
	250	35,150,241
	500	72,090,481
	1000	144,121,737
	2000	289,967,483
	4000	581,452,623
	8000	1,164,702,737

Fig. 5. Used datasets

4.3 Invalid triples

First of all we want to analyze the impact of the proposed concepts for reducing invalid triples during triple-match creation. Therefore, we use two different datasets with a similar size (LUBM250 ≈ 35M triple, DBPedia ≈ 41M triple) and apply the RDFS ruleset. We chose the DBPedia as well as the LUBM dataset because LUBM has a very high number of instance triples (ABox) while the TBox is proportionally small. The DBPedia dataset in turn also has a larger TBox and should provide more reliable results for a real world scenario. We compare the use of a non-parallel implementation of rule-firing with a parallel implementation using the GPU as well as a parallel implementation using the proposed concepts for reducing invalid triple derivations.

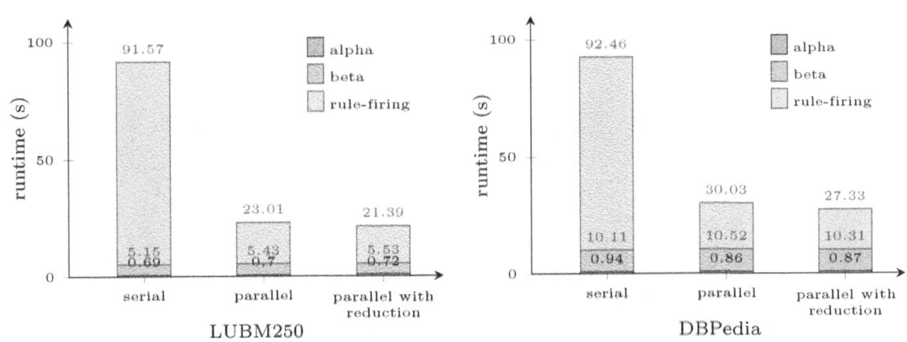

Fig. 6. Detailed reasoning time for LUBM250 and DBPedia using serial rule-firing, parallel rule-firing and parallel rule-firing with reduction of invalid triples

Figure 6 illustrates the processing time for the different phases of the RETE algorithm for each of the different rule-firing strategies. First of all it can be noted that the parallel implementation of rule-firing is about four times faster than the serial one. This speedup is achieved only by building the resulting triples including their hash-code on the GPU. The triples still need to be added to the internal triple-store where they are validated against duplicates before they get stored. By applying the concept of invalid triple reduction the triples that were submitted to be stored could be reduced for the LUBM dataset from about 227M to 130M which corresponds to a reduction of about 43%. For the DBPedia dataset a reduction of 35% could be achieved (202M triple creations instead of 312M). Nevertheless, the speedup that is accomplished for rule-firing is only 12.75% for DBPedia and 9.76% for LUBM. This is on the one hand because the application of the reduction strategy introduces an overhead during triple-match creation, too. On the other hand the deduplication based on a hash-lookup, where the hash is already computed together with the triple on the GPU, is very effective.

4.4 Parallelization

Furthermore we want to evaluate the impact of the new introduced levels of parallelization as well as the impact on using multiple GPUs to distribute the workload. Therefore, we use the RDFS as well as the pD* ruleset. We chose these two because they differ in complexity and thus can benefit in different ways from the introduced concepts.

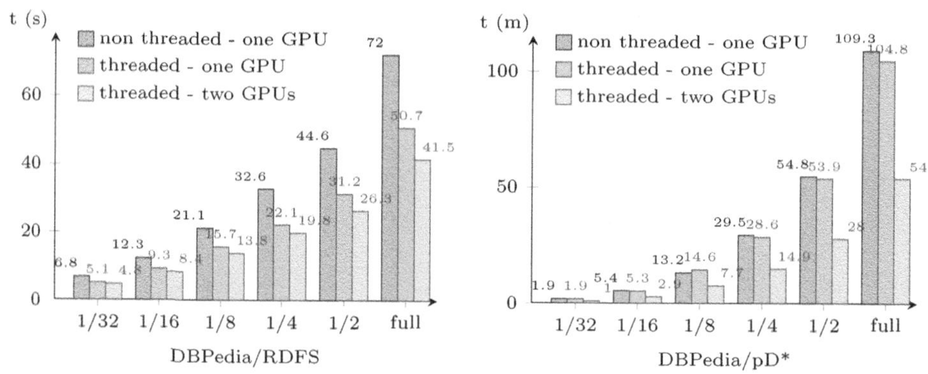

Fig. 7. Using RDFS (left) and pD* (right) on the DBPedia datasets

Because the computation of RDFS does not rely too much on work that needs to be performed on the GPU (all submitted tasks are of an adequate size), figure 7 shows that RDFS benefits primarily from the new introduced level of parallelization. This kind of parallelization allows the reasoner to perform much more work on the host at the same time while the time that a process is waiting to be executed on the GPU is relatively moderate. Thus, the speedup achieved by using a second GPU is of moderate size, too. On the other side the pD* ruleset relies much more on a high number of matches that need to be computed and thus executed on the GPU. Accordingly, the use of a second GPU drastically speeds up the execution time such that a doubling of the number of GPUs nearly results in a half of the processing time. It also can be expected that additional GPUs would further speedup the execution time as the use of additional hardware does not introduce an overhead. Both results show, that the workload partitioning and the concepts of further parallelization build on the partitioning are very efficient.

4.5 Scaleability

Finally we want to examine the execution time for the full materialization for datasets with a growing number of triples. For this tests we use the ρdf ruleset as well as the RDFS ruleset because both are widely used for performance and scaleability tests on LUBM datasets [10] [4] [11] [12] [13] and thus offer a good comparability. Figure 8 shows the results for both rulesets applied to the LUBM datasets from 17.6M triples to more than 1.1 billion triples.

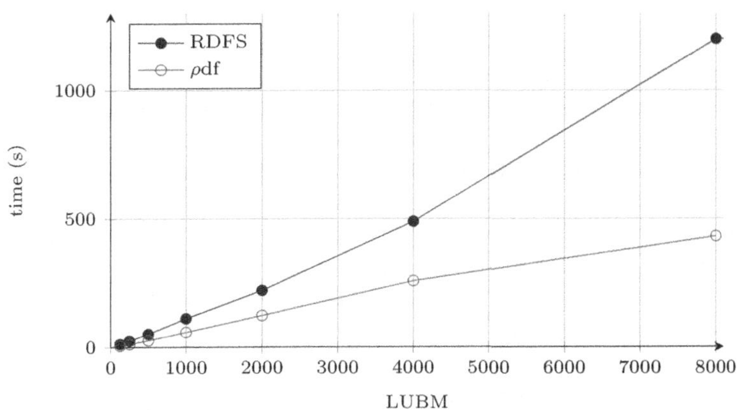

Fig. 8. Complete materialization time for LUBM datasets with up to 1.1 billion triples

As can be seen our implementation has a good scaleability since the execution time grows almost in a linear way with respect to the number of input triples for both rulesets. For the LUBM8000 dataset using the RDFS ruleset a further overhead is caused by the fact, that the size of the working memories for some beta-nodes exceeds 2 billion matches and we have to swap the matches to the hard-disk. By appending all matches to a file and accessing them in a partitioned way using a random access, we overcome the issue of the max array size in Java.

We further observe that the computation of ρdf is much faster than RDFS, which among other things can be explained by the number of inferred triples (for example on LUBM4000 143.7M inferred triples for ρdf and 238.2M for RDFS) and the findings of figure 6 that show, that the rule-firing is still the most computation intensive task for RDFS. This also illustrates the bottleneck of our implementation for these two rulesets. While the pD* ruleset could benefit from additional GPUs, the less computation intensive rulesets are thwarted by the internal triple-store which only allows to write new triples for a single process at a time. Nevertheless, we reach a throughput of up to 2.7M triples/sec. for ρdf and 1.4M triples/sec. for RDFS, which to our knowledge is the highest throughput for a single machine ever published.

5 Related Work and Discussion

While many reasoner, whether they use one computing node or a cluster of nodes, programmatically implement a specific set of rules, our implementation is based on the RETE algorithm and thus independent of a specific ruleset. In [13] an inference system that is able to support user-defined rules is proposed. The implementation is based on an Oracle database and is evaluated against LUBM datasets, too. Nevertheless, to apply RDFS to a LUBM1000 dataset a processing time of 6:34 hours is reported, while our approach performs the same computation in 269 seconds. Another single-node implementation, but with the limitation of a predefined set of rules, is shown in [12]. The DynamiTE reasoner is capable to perform stream reasoning and thus focuses on incrementally maintaining large datasets. While our approach is not able to process RDF streams, the pure materialization of ρdf in [12] achieves a throughput of 227 triples/sec. which is about 12 times slower than our results. In [14] an approach for reasoning on massively parallel hardware is presented that, in contrast to our approach which implements a generic rule engine, implements only the ρdf ruleset based on methods that are executed in a given order to produce the results. Another limitation of the reasoner in [14] is that only datasets, that fit into the device memory of a single GPU (multiple GPUs are not supported) can be processed. Both approaches were already used in [1] for a performance comparison. Further implementations of reasoners that allow a scaleable processing of large datasets often rely on the MapReduce framework. WebPIE [2][15] for example uses the MapReduce implementation Hadoop and is able to perform RDFS as well as pD* reasoning. WebPIE was evaluated against LUBM datasets with up to 100 billion triples and reached a maximum throughput of 2.1M triples/sec [15] on 64 computing nodes for ρdf. The same ruleset was applied by our implementation to the LUBM dataset with a throughput of 2.7M triples/sec. on a single machine. Nevertheless, our implementation is limited regarding the size of the dataset by the availability of main memory on the used computing node and is not able to handle such large datasets. Other MapReduce implementations differ for example in the implemented semantics [3][16].

In [4] an embarrassingly parallel algorithm is introduced, that computes the complete RDFS closure. The evaluation is performed on a cluster with up to 128 parallel processes. The largest dataset used is a LUBM10k/4 (LUBM10000 where only every fourth instance triple was used), which is comparable to a LUBM 2500 dataset. While [4] report a computation time of 291.46 seconds without a global deduplication, our approach performs the complete materialization on a similar dataset using only a single node in 270 seconds and infers only unique triples.

The evaluation showed that our implementation reaches a high throughput and offers a good scaleability for different rulesets with a limited complexity (RDFS and ρdf) on different datasets. Nevertheless, especially for ρdf and RDFS the rule-firing is still a bottleneck and consumes up to 70% of the processing time. The introduced concept to reduce the amount of invalid triple derivation only showed a small increase in speed. In [14] further concepts for deduplication (and thus for reducing invalid triples) are introduced. While the *global strategy* relies on the order of rules and thus is not applicable for our approach, the *local strategy* performs a reduction of duplicates on the GPU. To do so, the inferred triples are sorted such that a comparison with the neighbour-triple can reveal if the triple is already derived during the current processing step. Finally, only the non duplicate triples are transferred back to the host and added to the triple-store. However, to sort and rearrange the triples on the GPU was much slower for our implementation than to derive the triples and validate them using a fast hash-lookup. Rather than focusing on a reduction schema on the GPU we think that a parallel, non blocking triple-store that can be accessed by multiple threads at the same time would be much more efficient. This is particularly the case when using the new levels of parallelization which also allow the use of multiple GPUs.

A further limitation of our approach exists in the need to hold all triples for a fast access during triple-match creation in the main memory. While our implementation may be improvable with respect to memory consumption, the available main memory does limit the size of processable datasets. To overcome this issue, on the one side a distributed approach using multiple nodes equipped with massively parallel hardware might be interesting. On the other side a stream reasoning approach could also be implemented based on the proposed concepts of fast matching.

6 Conclusion

In this paper we introduced new concepts for a further parallelization and workload distribution on top of the results presented in [1], where a rule-based reasoner using massively parallel hardware is presented. The additional host-side parallelization is achieved by taking advantage of the fact, that matches of nodes of one depth in the RETE network can be computed independently. We further introduced the concept of triple-matches, which allow to perform a partitioning of the workload that needs to be computed for a single node. By using triple-matches we also overcome the issue that the maximum size of datasets that can be processed is limited by the onboard-memory of a GPU. Aside from that the partitioning allows a simple way for workload distribution over multiple parallel devices and thus for an additional parallelization. Furthermore, a strategy to reduce the amount of invalid triple derivations was introduces that is able to reduce the number of derived triples by more than 40%.

Future work will focus on different aspects. On the one side we are going to investigate how our approach can benefit from a cluster-based approach to distribute the workload not only to multiple devices, but to multiple computing nodes. This will include the need to reduce the memory usage on a single node. On the other side a faster and possibly parallel triple-store should be part of further developments to achieve a faster rule-firing.

To conclude the paper, we have shown how to scale a rule-based reasoner based on different concepts of workload partitioning and distribution. The proposed concepts where evaluated for datasets with up to 1.1 billion triples and we achieved a throughput of up to 2.7M triples/sec., which is significantly higher than provided by other state of the art reasoners for a single computing node. Thus, our system not only provides a dynamic and flexible way to apply application specific rules to a set of input data, but also a scaleable and fast way with respect to the current state of the art.

References

1. Peters, M., Brink, C., Sachweh, S., Zündorf, A.: Rule-based reasoning on massively parallel hardware. In: 9th International Workshop on Scalable Semantic Web Knowledge Base Systems, pp. 33–49 (2013)
2. Urbani, J., Kotoulas, S., Maassen, J., van Harmelen, F., Bal, H.: OWL reasoning with webPIE: Calculating the closure of 100 billion triples. In: Aroyo, L., Antoniou, G., Hyvönen, E., ten Teije, A., Stuckenschmidt, H., Cabral, L., Tudorache, T. (eds.) ESWC 2010, Part I. LNCS, vol. 6088, pp. 213–227. Springer, Heidelberg (2010)
3. Liu, C., Qi, G., Wang, H., Yu, Y.: Reasoning with large scale ontologies in fuzzy pD* using MapReduce. IEEE Computational Intelligence Magazine 7(2) (2012)
4. Weaver, J., Hendler, J.A.: Parallel materialization of the finite RDFS closure for hundreds of millions of triples. In: Bernstein, A., Karger, D.R., Heath, T., Feigenbaum, L., Maynard, D., Motta, E., Thirunarayan, K. (eds.) ISWC 2009. LNCS, vol. 5823, pp. 682–697. Springer, Heidelberg (2009)
5. Forgy, C.L.: Rete: a fast algorithm for the many pattern/many object pattern match problem. In: Raeth, P.G. (ed.) Expert Systems, pp. 324–341 (1990)
6. ter Horst, H.J.: Completeness, decidability and complexity of entailment for RDF Schema and a semantic extension involving the OWL vocabulary. Web Semantics: Science, Services and Agents on the World Wide Web 3(2-3), 79–115 (2005)
7. Muñoz, S., Pérez, J., Gutierrez, C.: Minimal deductive systems for RDF. In: Franconi, E., Kifer, M., May, W. (eds.) ESWC 2007. LNCS, vol. 4519, pp. 53–67. Springer, Heidelberg (2007)
8. DBPedia, `http://wiki.dbpedia.org/`
9. Guo, Y., Pan, Z., Heflin, J.: Lubm: A benchmark for OWL knowledge base systems. Web Semant., 158–182 (October 2005)
10. Soma, R., Prasanna, V.: Parallel inferencing for OWL knowledge bases. In: 37th International Conference on Parallel Processing, ICPP 2008, pp. 75–82 (2008)
11. Urbani, J., Kotoulas, S., Oren, E., van Harmelen, F.: Scalable distributed reasoning using mapReduce. In: Bernstein, A., Karger, D.R., Heath, T., Feigenbaum, L., Maynard, D., Motta, E., Thirunarayan, K. (eds.) ISWC 2009. LNCS, vol. 5823, pp. 634–649. Springer, Heidelberg (2009)
12. Urbani, J., Margara, A., Jacobs, C., van Harmelen, F., Bal, H.: DynamiTE: Parallel materialization of dynamic RDF data. In: Alani, H., et al. (eds.) ISWC 2013, Part I. LNCS, vol. 8218, pp. 657–672. Springer, Heidelberg (2013)

13. Wu, Z., Eadon, G., Das, S., Chong, E.I., Kolovski, V., Annamalai, M., Srinivasan, J.: Implementing an inference engine for RDFS/OWL constructs and user-defined rules in Oracle. In: IEEE 24th International Conference on Data Engineering, ICDE 2008, pp. 1239–1248 (2008)
14. Heino, N., Pan, J.Z.: RDFS reasoning on massively parallel hardware. In: Cudré-Mauroux, P., et al. (eds.) ISWC 2012, Part I. LNCS, vol. 7649, pp. 133–148. Springer, Heidelberg (2012)
15. Urbani, J., Kotoulas, S., Massen, J., van Harmelen, F., Bal, H.: WebPIE: A web-scale parallel inference engine using MapReduce. Web Semantics: Science, Services and Agents on the World Wide Web (2012)
16. Maier, F., Mutharaju, R., Hitzler, P.: Distributed reasoning with EL++ using MapReduce. Technical report, Kno.e.sis Center, Wright State University, Dayton, Ohio (2010)

A Probabilistic Approach for Integrating Heterogeneous Knowledge Sources

Arnab Dutta, Christian Meilicke, and Simone Paolo Ponzetto

Research Data and Web Science, University of Mannheim, Germany
{arnab,christian,simone}@informatik.uni-mannheim.de

Abstract. Open Information Extraction (OIE) systems like NELL and ReVERB have achieved impressive results by harvesting massive amounts of machine-readable knowledge with minimal supervision. However, the knowledge bases they produce still lack a clean, explicit semantic data model. This, on the other hand, could be provided by full-fledged semantic networks like DBPEDIA or YAGO, which, in turn, could benefit from the additional coverage provided by Web-scale IE. In this paper, we bring these two strains of research together, and present a method to align terms from NELL with instances in DBPEDIA. Our approach is unsupervised in nature and relies on two key components. First, we automatically acquire probabilistic type information for NELL terms given a set of matching hypotheses. Second, we view the mapping task as the statistical inference problem of finding the most likely coherent mapping – i.e., the maximum a posteriori (MAP) mapping – based on the outcome of the first component used as soft constraint. These two steps are highly intertwined: accordingly, we propose an approach that iteratively refines type acquisition based on the output of the mapping generator, and vice versa. Experimental results on gold-standard data indicate that our approach outperforms a strong baseline, and is able to produce ever-improving mappings consistently across iterations.

Keywords: #eswc2014Dutta.

1 Introduction

The last few years have witnessed much work in information extraction (IE). Although Wikipedia-based IE projects such as DBPEDIA [3] and YAGO [24] have been in development for several years, systems like NELL [6] and REVERB [12] have gained importance more lately. State-of-the art IE systems work on very large, i.e., Web-scale text corpora and are based on the general paradigm of *Open* Information Extraction (OIE) [2], which identifies IE systems that are not constrained by the boundaries of encyclopedic knowledge or a corresponding fixed schemata, unlike, for instance, those used by YAGO or DBPEDIA.

The data maintained by OIE systems is important for analyzing, reasoning about, and discovering novel facts on the web and has the potential to result in a new generation of web search engines [10]. However, while OIE systems have

V. Presutti et al. (Eds.): ESWC 2014, LNCS 8465, pp. 286–301, 2014.

very large coverage, they lack a full-fledged, clean ontological structure which, on the other hand, is essential in order to be able to exploit their output for Semantic Web applications. Often, the facts extracted by these systems are hard to decipher, and terms occurring in these very same facts can be highly ambiguous. For instance, let us consider a typical NELL extraction in the form of a *property(subject, object)* triple such as `agentcollaborateswithagent`(*knight, indiana*). While we might have an intuitive understanding of the property, it is difficult to determine the correct references of the terms in the triple. Actually, our example refers to 'Bob Knight', the head coach of the basketball team 'Indiana Hoosiers'. In contrast, an ontological resource, like DBPEDIA, uses a URI to uniquely identify each entity that appears within a triple. In our case, any DBPEDIA triple that talks about Bob Knight uses an unique URI to refer to that specific person. Thus, the meaning of a triple is precisely and uniquely specified.

In general, OIE systems trade-off large coverage for a weak, e.g., schema-less or schema-poor, semantic representation. In this work, we address this problem by bringing together information from a state-of-the-art OIE system and DBPEDIA. We achieve this by mapping the subject and object terms from NELL to DBPEDIA entities. Specifically, we propose a method to automatically determine the correct references of terms from OIE systems using probabilistic reasoning. We embed our probabilistic model that exploits the type hierarchy from DBPEDIA within a bootstrapping approach. As a result of this, we are able to provide via linking a clear semantic representation for both subject and object terms that occur within triples generated by a OIE system. Our hunch here is to provide a framework that makes it possible for different OIE projects to take advantage of the schema information provided by structured ontological resources like YAGO and DBPEDIA. This way the output of OIE is fully semantified within structured resources with an ontological model: by converse, the reference ontologies can benefit from the broader coverage of OIE projects.

2 Problem Statement

We present a methodology to map the output of OIE systems to an ontological resource like any of DBPEDIA, YAGO or FREEBASE. Key to our method is the synergistic integration of (i) information about the entity types the OIE terms can refer to and (ii) a method to find a global, optimal solution to the mapping problem across multiple extractions on the basis of statistical reasoning techniques. These two phases are highly intertwined, thus, we alternate between them by means of an iterative approach.

Given an OIE triple, there can be multiple plausible mappings to a set of highly related entities in the target ontology. For instance, the term *tom sawyer* occurring within the NELL triple `bookwriter`(*tom sawyer, twain*) can be mapped to a set of DBPEDIA entities: the fictional character Tom Sawyer (*Tom_Sawyer*), the actual book written by Mark Twain (*The_Adventures_of_Tom_Sawyer*), or the many screen adaptions of the book (e.g., *Tom_ Sawyer_(1973_film)*). While all these entities provide plausible meanings for the occurrence of *tom sawyer*, knowing (or estimating) their types would allow us to further filter out meanings which are incompatible with the types of entities that occur as arguments of the property `bookwriter`. For instance, knowing that `bookwriter` relates books and authors would allow us to conclude that the correct mapping for *tom sawyer* in DBPEDIA is probably not a film or a fictional character, but rather an instance of a book. However, domain or range restriction in terms of DBPEDIA concepts are not defined for the extraction results of OIE systems. When including entity type information in the mapping problem, we are faced with two challenges, namely: (i) to estimate weights for the domain and range type of a NELL property term using the terminology of DBPEDIA; (ii) to effectively exploit this information in the actual mapping task.

With respect to the range of `bookwriter`, a good weight distribution would, for example, entail that the type `Writer` is more probable than `Politician` and `Politician` is more probable than `Location`. Note that its not sufficient to determine `Writer` as range of `bookwriter`, because many entities writing books are not explicitly typed as `Writer` but are of different types (e.g. `Athletes` can also write books). Given a weight distribution for domain and range types of entities, we want to exploit this information in a way as to automatically identify the correct mappings. Using a statistical approach, we can start with some prior probabilities for each of the mapping candidates, and combine these priors with weighted type information such that we produce the best set of matches as output.

We show in the following that, for the resource mapping task at hand, acquiring type information and producing high-quality mappings are two highly intertwined problems. Our method starts with a set of mapping hypotheses between OIE terms and DBPEDIA instances. We combine these potential mappings with automatically learned entity type information (Section 3.1), and define a joint inference task within Markov Logic Network (Section 3.2). Furthermore, we propose a bootstrapping algorithm (Section 3.3) that generates better mapping hypotheses and refines the weight distribution for the learned types over a repeated number of iterations. In Section 4 we report about the experimental results. In Section 5 we provide an overview of related work and, finally, we conclude in Section 6 with scopes of possible extension.

3 Methodology

Our approach consists of three main phases. We first derive a distribution of weights over the possible domains and ranges of a given set of matching hypotheses for those triples that share the same property (Section 3.1). Next, we formalize the task of choosing a set of mappings from a set of candidates using Markov Logic Networks (Section 3.2). Finally, we use the previously explained components within a bootstrapping architecture in order to iteratively improve the final outcome (Section 3.3).

Our algorithm requires a set of matching hypotheses, also referred to as mappings, as input. In the rest of the paper, we use the notation $n{:}x \rightarrow d{:}y$ to refer to such mappings, where *n:x* refers to a term that occurs within a NELL triple, and *d:y* to a DBPEDIA instance. x and y can refer to the s(ubject), p(redicate) and o(bject) of an arbitrary triple. We require mappings to be annotated with weights, which quantify the likelihood of an OIE term referring to a DBPEDIA instance. Intuitively, the higher the weight, the more likely it is that the mapping is true. An example of three different candidate mappings for the NELL term *n:hemingway* are the following ones.

$$+1.34 : \textit{n:hemingway} \rightarrow \textit{d:Ernest\_Hemingway}$$
$$-2.22 : \textit{n:hemingway} \rightarrow \textit{d:Hemingway,\_South\_Carolina}$$
$$-2.58 : \textit{n:hemingway} \rightarrow \textit{d:Hemingway\_(comics)}$$

The framework we propose in this paper is independent of the specific method of generating the initial mappings. However, the method should generate meaningful weights that can be interpreted in a probabilistic context. An example for such a method is presented in our previous work [9] where, we extract the *top-k* most frequent senses of OIE terms from the Wikipedia corpus.

3.1 Probabilistic Type Generation

Let us in the following consider NELL triples of the format *n:p*(*n:s*, *n:o*), namely consisting of a *n:s*(ubject) and *n:o*(bject) that share the same property *n:p*. For each triple we create the matching hypotheses both for *n:s* and *n:o* by applying an arbitrary matching method that generates mappings annotated with weights. We refer to this set of mappings as $\mathcal{H}$. We next select a subset of $\mathcal{H}$ that consists of only the *best* (*top-1*) candidate for each NELL term. The resulting set of matching hypotheses contains two mappings for each triple, namely *n:s* → *d:s'* and *n:o* → *d:o'*. In the rest of the paper, we denote this set of functional mapping hypotheses as $\mathcal{M}$, which is essentially a subset of $\mathcal{H}$.

In the next step, the types of *d:s'* and *d:o'* are used as markers for the domain and range restrictions of *n:p*. We distinguish between the direct and indirect type of an instance. Class C is a direct type of instance a, denoted by $C(a)$, if there exists no sub class D of C, denoted by $D \sqsubseteq C$, such that $D(a)$ exists. We count the direct type of each mapped DBPEDIA instance in $\mathcal{M}$. Finally, we obtain a distribution over the direct type counts for the possible concepts, both for the domain and range of *n:p*. Figure 1 depicts a snippet of the concept hierarchy for the range of the property `bookwriter`, where the nodes represent the concepts and the numbers (in non-bold) denote their direct type counts. The sum of the counts at a particular level do not add up to their parent node's count, since we are only counting the direct types of each instance.

Key to our method is the observation that an appropriate weight distribution helps us establish whether a certain candidate mapping is correct or not, according to the type of *d:s'* or *d:o'*. Considering the most frequent class as a hard domain/range restriction could potentially perform well, but this would fail to consider other instances writing books, e.g. philosophers, researchers or even athletes. On the other extreme, it seems rational to also count the indirect

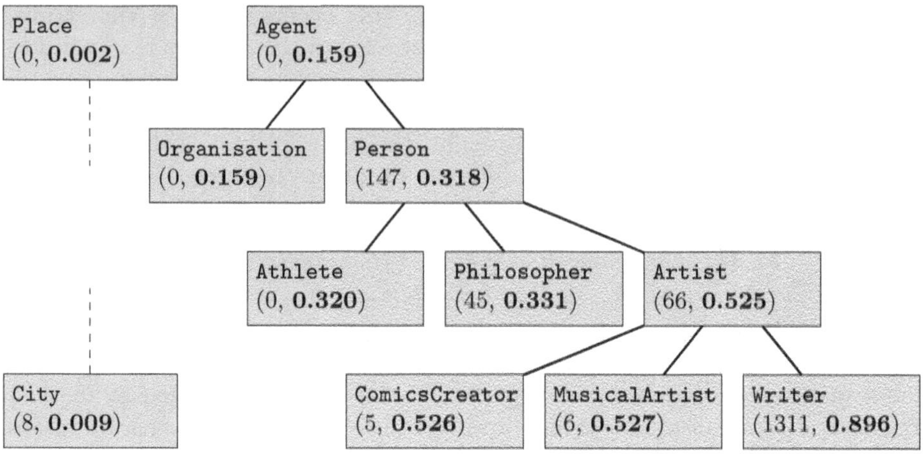

Fig. 1. Counting and weighing the range types of the `bookwriter` property. Each concept is accompanied by the counts of the direct types and the normalized S_d score for $\alpha = 0.5$ (shown in bold).

types or to propagate the count for a direct type recursively up to the parent nodes. However, this would result in a type restriction that takes only top-level concepts into account and completely disregards the finer differences expressed in the lower levels of the hierarchy. For example, a writer is more likely to write a book compared to an athlete. Accordingly, we opt for a hierarchical scaling of weights along the levels, such that the most likely class in the hierarchy is determined by the instance distribution of both its children and parent.

Hence, we propose a simple formulation to compute an appropriate score for each concept n. First, we introduce the *up-score*, S_u which is defined as

$$S_u(n) = S_o(n) + \alpha \sum_{c \in child(n)} S_u(c)$$

where $child(n)$ denotes the children of n, $S_o(n)$ refers to the direct type count and α is a constant, which works as a *propagation factor* with $\alpha \in [0, 1]$. The computation of this score starts from the leaf nodes, which are initialized with their direct count $S_o(n)$. S_u is defined recursively and, accordingly, the S_u score for n is computed based on the S_u score for the children of n. Furthermore, we also define a *down-score* S_d as

$$S_d(n) = \begin{cases} S_d(parent(n)) + (1-\alpha)S_u(n) & ; n \neq \textit{top-concept} \\ S_u(n) & ; n = \textit{top-concept} \end{cases}$$

where $parent(n)$ denotes the parent node of n. We refer to the concept hierarchy annotated with the S_d scores as the so-called *α-tree* in the rest of the paper.

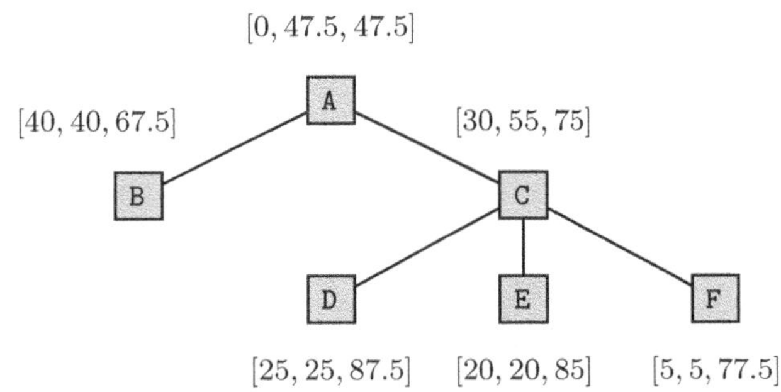

Fig. 2. Propagating direct counts in the alpha tree. Shown scores are $[S_o, S_u, S_d]$

We present in Figure 2 an example illustrating a simple hierarchy consisting of six concepts.The relevant scores for $\alpha = 0.5$ are shown adjacent to the nodes as $[S_o, S_u, S_d]$. This example illustrates that the sibling classes D, E and F, eventually, have the highest S_d scores, while the order among them, as defined by S_o, is still preserved in the order defined by S_d. As a final step, the down-scores are normalized by dividing them by the sum of the direct counts S_o for each node. With respect to Figure 2, the sum of S_o is $40+30+25+20+5 = 120$ and so the normalized S_d for node D, say, is estimated as a probability of $87.5/120 = 0.73$.

Obviously, the choice of the constant α is critical in achieving the desired result. Setting $\alpha = 0$, neutralizes the effect of child nodes on parent nodes. In this case we have $S_d(n) = S_o(n)$, which means that the type hierarchy is completely ignored. On the other extreme, setting $\alpha = 1$ propagates the scores to the full degree, but always creates the same scores for all concepts in the same branch. With respect to the example shown in Figure 1, we would learn that all concepts in the `Agent` branch have the same weight, while there are no differences between the concepts `Organisation` and `Writer`. In Section 4 we discuss the choice of the optimal α and report about experimental results related to different α values.

3.2 Modeling with Markov Logic Network

Markov Logic Networks (MLN) [23] are a framework for combining probability theory and first-order logic. Probabilities allow to quantify the uncertainty associated with complex processes and tasks, while first-order logic helps to capture the logical aspects of the problems. Formally, an MLN is a set of weighted first-order logic formulae. Under a set of constants, it instantiates into a ground Markov network where every node is a binary random variable and called a *ground atom*. In our task, we use three atoms to build the formulae of the MLN. We use `map` for mapping NELL terms to DBPEDIA instances, `isOfType` for specifying the types of the DBPEDIA instances, and `propAsst` for representing the NELL triples. Our set of constants is the set of NELL terms and the set of DBPEDIA instances that are the potential mapping candidates.

We can have several ($\approx 2^{\#groundings}$) network states for different boolean assignments of the ground atoms. Every such state is also called a *world.* In those worlds different formulae hold true and if some do not, then the world is penalized according to the weights attached with the violating formulae. As a result, that world becomes less likely to hold (note that unweighted formulae can instead never be violated). According to [23], the probability of a world x is defined as $P(X = x) = \frac{1}{Z}exp(\sum_i w_i n_i(x))$ where w_i is the weight attached to the first-order logic formula F_i, $n_i(x)$ is the number of true groundings of F_i in x and Z is the normalizing factor (also called *partition function*) given as $\sum_{x\in\mathcal{X}}\prod_k \phi_k(x_{\{k\}})$, where, $\phi_k(x_k)$ is the feature function (usually binary) defined over the kth clique in the ground network.

In our task, we employ both hard and soft formulae. The hard formula (one which cannot be violated) for our model is a restriction on the maximum number of mappings a particular NELL term can have. This is formally stated as

$$|\texttt{map}(n{:}t,\ \ d{:}t)| <= \ \ 1$$

which denotes, for all possible instantiations of the map atom, that every NELL term *n:t* can have at most one mapping to a DBPEDIA instance *d:t*, i.e. we force the mapping to be functional. For each mapping candidate in $\mathcal{H}$, we add a weighted formula of the form

$$w : \texttt{map}(n{:}t,\ \ d{:}t)$$

where w is computed by applying the logit function[1] to the original probability awarded by the method that was used for generating $\mathcal{H}$. This adapts the weights to the underlying log-linear model of MLN.

To additionally take type information into account, we extend our model with two soft formulae for each possible combination of NELL property P and DBPEDIA type C. The first formula reflects a weighted domain restriction and the second formula reflects a weighted range restriction.

$$w_d(P,C) : \texttt{isOfType}(C,\ \ d{:}s) \wedge \texttt{propAsst}(P, n{:}s, n{:}o) \wedge \texttt{map}(n{:}s, d{:}s)$$
$$w_r(P,C) : \texttt{isOfType}(C,\ \ d{:}o) \wedge \texttt{propAsst}(P, n{:}s, n{:}o) \wedge \texttt{map}(n{:}o, d{:}o)$$

Note that P and C are replaced by constant values, while *n:s*, *n:o*, *d:s*, and *d:o* are quantified variables. $w_d(P,C)$ and $w_r(P,C)$ are the weights for type C with respect to property P computed with the α-tree as discussed in Section 3.1. If the type weight $w_d(P,C)$ is high, it makes the mapping $n{:}s \rightarrow d{:}s$ more likely in case that *n:s* appears in subject position of P and *d:s* is of type C.

Based on our model, we compute the MAP state, i.e., the most probable world which coincides in our scenario with the most probable mapping. As a result we select a subset $\mathcal{M}$ from the set of all mapping hypotheses $\mathcal{H}$. In particular, we want to select a better subset than just choosing the top-1 candidate for each

[1] The logit function is the inverse of the sigmoidal logistic function. For a probability P, the logit function is defined as $\log \frac{P}{1-P}$.

Algorithm 1. Bootstrapping algorithm

procedure BOOTSTRAP
    $\mathcal{H} \leftarrow$ set of mapping hypotheses
    $\mathcal{M}_0 \leftarrow$ *top-1*$(\mathcal{H})$
    $i \leftarrow 0$
    while $\mathcal{M}_i \neq \mathcal{M}_{i-1}$ **do**
        $i \leftarrow i + 1$
        $\mathcal{T}_i \leftarrow alphaTree(\mathcal{M}_{i-1})$
        $\mathcal{M}_i \leftarrow computeMAPState(\mathcal{H}, \mathcal{T}_i)$
    end while
    return $\mathcal{M}_i$ ▷ filtered output
end procedure

NELL term. Note also that our model can easily be extended by adding more complex rules. The MAP inference is conducted with the RockIt system [20]. RockIt computes the most probable world by formulating the task as an Integer Linear Program. The solution of the resulting optimization is the MAP state of the Markov Logic Network.

3.3 Bootstrapping

So far, we used a subset of $\mathcal{H}$, namely the top-1 candidates, as input for computing the α-tree. Obviously, the quality of the chosen set of mappings directly impacts the quality of the resulting α-tree. At the same time, a better α-tree, represented as soft constraints in the MLN, can be expected to result in a better MAP state. Thus, we explore how to use the mapping that corresponds to the MAP state as input for constructing the α-tree and to use the resulting α-tree as input to recompute the MAP state.

We present our bootstrapping approach in Algorithm 1. The algorithm starts with the set of matching hypotheses $\mathcal{H}$. In the first iteration, we initialize $\mathcal{M}_0 \subset \mathcal{H}$ by selecting the top-1 candidates in $\mathcal{H}$. $\mathcal{M}_0$ is used as input to create the α-tree $\mathcal{T}_1$, which is then used together with $\mathcal{H}$ to generate the set of mappings for the next iteration, namely $\mathcal{M}_1$. Next, the algorithm checks if there is any difference between $\mathcal{M}_1$ and $\mathcal{M}_0$. If this is the case, the algorithm continues and repeats the same procedure, this time based on $\mathcal{M}_1$. With every iteration, each mapping going additionally into the hypothesis set, creates a refined α-tree, makes the added mapping more probable and so it stays in. Now, it cannot happen that it is added and then removed in subsequent iterations since it defies the reason for which it was added the first place. But, removal and then subsequent addition can happen. But once added, it stays. This continues as long as there are differences between $\mathcal{M}_i$ and $\mathcal{M}_{i-1}$ and terminates eventually. Finally, the last mapping set $\mathcal{M}_i$ that was generated in the i-th iteration is returned. Note that the functions *alphaTree* and *computeMAPState* refer to the modules described in Section 3.1 and Section 3.2 respectively.

4 Experiments

4.1 Metrics and Datasets

We apply the frequency based method as proposed in [9] to generate the set of input mappings $\mathcal{H}$ for our experiments. In the paper, we reported a micro-average precision of 82.78% and a recall of 81.31% for the subset defined by selecting the best candidate from $\mathcal{H}$. By choosing this subset as $\mathcal{M}_0$ in Algorithm 1, we are able to start with a set of input mappings that is already highly precise, thus ensuring high-quality information as seed for the bootstrapping method. We will use $\mathcal{M}_0$ as baseline and report about the improvements gained by each iteration of our algorithm.

The performance of our proposed approach is measured in terms of precision and recall. Let $\mathcal{M}$ refer to the set of mappings generated by our algorithm, and $\mathcal{G}$ refer to the set of mappings in the gold standard. Precision is defined as $|\mathcal{M} \cap \mathcal{G}|/|\mathcal{M}|$ and recall as $|\mathcal{M} \cap \mathcal{G}|/|\mathcal{G}|$. The F_1-measure is the equally weighted harmonic mean of both values. In particular, we compute these values for $\mathcal{M}_i$ after every i^{th} iteration (including the baseline $\mathcal{M}_0$).

We compare the results of our method with the gold standard $\mathcal{G}$, presented in [9].[2] This dataset has been created by randomly choosing twelve NELL properties. For each of these properties 100 triples have been sampled from the NELL dataset resulting in a rich set of 1200 triples for which subject and object mappings to DBPEDIA have been specified by human annotators.

4.2 Learning α

Our method relies on the choice of a proper value for the parameter α. In a first set of experiments, we analyze how to learn an appropriate α score. With respect to these experiments we report about results of our algorithm related to the final outcome of its last iteration. Experiments that focus on the impact of the different iterations are presented in Section 4.3.

Parameter Search: In the following we report about repeatedly performing a 2-fold cross validation on different samples of the whole dataset. For that purpose we restrict the possible values of α to a be multiples of 1/8 in the interval $[0, 1]$, which allows us to repeat the overall process over a large number of sampling steps ($\approx$ 100000). At each sampling step, we first randomly pick half of the properties. This choice defines two datasets consisting of 6 properties (the chosen properties and the residual properties). We call one the training set D_{train} and the other the testing set, D_{test}. For every D_{train} we find the α giving the maximum averaged F_1 score over D_{train}. Then we apply our algorithm with that α on D_{test} and compute the resulting F_1. For 35% of the samples we learned α=0.5, for 30% we learned α=0.375, and for 18% we learned α=0.625. Approximately 85% of all samples yield an α in the interval $[0.375, 0.625]$, signifying that learning produces a stable outcome. Applying the learned α on D_{test} results in

[2] The dataset is publicly available at `https://madata.bib.uni-mannheim.de/65/`

Table 1. Effect of α on the overall performance compared to the baseline

α	$prec$ (Δ_{prec})	rec (Δ_{rec})	F_1 (Δ_{F_1})
0.0	95.1 (+12.30)	76.1 (-5.20)	84.1 (+2.26)
0.125	94.8 (+12.04)	77.6 (-3.70)	84.9 (+3.08)
0.25	94.7 (+11.96)	78.5 (-2.80)	85.4 (+3.66)
0.375	94.4 (+11.58)	79.0 (-2.26)	85.6 (+3.84)
0.5	93.1 (**+10.34**)	79.9 (**-1.39**)	85.7 (**+3.94**)
0.625	92.3 (+9.48)	80.2 (-1.08)	85.6 (+3.76)
0.75	91.4 (+8.63)	80.4 (-0.96)	85.3 (+3.46)
0.875	90.3 (+7.53)	80.6 (-0.67)	85.0 (+3.15)
1.0	87.6 (+4.80)	81.0 (-0.35)	84.0 (+2.17)
Baseline	82.78	81.31	81.8

an increased average F_1 score of 85.74% (+3.94%) compared to the baseline with an average F_1 score of 81.8%. Thus, it is possible to learn α based on a small training set (600 triples) that results in a significant improvement of the mapping quality.

Parameter Effect: Finally we compute recall, precision and F_1 values on the entire dataset for all values of α in the $[0, 1]$ range with step sizes of 0.125. This helps us to better understand the impact of α on precision and recall. In Table 1 we report the absolute scores along with the differences (Δ) in scores over the most frequent baseline of [9] ($\mathcal{M}_0$ in Algorithm 1), and the output of the final iteration of the bootstrapped approach. Our results corroborate the findings from our cross-validation runs in that we achieve the best performance on the full dataset for $\alpha = 0.5$, which yields an improvement of +3.94% in terms of F_1 with respect to the baseline. Low values of α increase the precision by up to +12.3% ($\alpha = 0.0$), thus resulting in an overall precision of 95.1%, with a loss of 5.2% of recall as trade-off. While low values of α increase precision by aggressively eliminating many incorrect mappings, increasingly higher values lead to a drop in precision, indicating an ever increasing number of incorrect mappings being produced. This illustrates nicely that we can use α to adapt our approach to the needs of a certain application scenario, where precision or recall might be more important.

4.3 Algorithm Performance

In Table 2 we report the performance figures of our approach for each of the properties in the evaluation dataset. As baseline and inital starting point $\mathcal{M}_0$ we use the most frequent mapping presented in [9]. The following columns ($\mathcal{M}_i$, $i \neq 0$) report the F_1 scores of our proposed approach. For all experiments we set α=0.5. This choice is supported by the results of the previously-described cross-validation approach as well as by the theoretical considerations presented above. The results highlight that, thanks to our iterative approach, we are able to beat the baseline, and improve our results in average across iterations.

In our experiments, we found no improvements beyond the third iterations $\mathcal{M}_3$, thus indicating that our method quickly converges after few iterations.

Table 2. F_1 scores of the baseline ($\mathcal{M}_o$) and our bootstrapping approach, α=0.5

Nell Property	$\mathcal{M}_0$	$\mathcal{M}_1$	$\mathcal{M}_2$	$\mathcal{M}_3$
actorstarredinmovie	81.3	87.7	94.5	-
agentcollaborateswithagent	83.7	76.4	82.0	-
animalistypeofanimal	85.9	86.0	86.7	-
athleteledsportsteam	87.0	92.6	93.2	-
bankbankincountry	79.6	86.4	83.4	82.8
citylocatedinstate	80.7	83.2	83.2	83.0
bookwriter	82.6	86.7	86.7	89.0
companyalsoknownas	64.1	64.6	67.1	-
personleadsorganization	76.7	78.1	77.2	77.6
teamplaysagainstteam	81.3	89.6	90.9	-
weaponmadeincountry	87.0	87.0	-	-
lakeinstate	91.4	94.4	94.7	-
Cumulative Gain (%)	-	2.62	3.89	3.94

Performance figures indicate the gradual saturation in the scores after each iteration. As expected, with each iteration the output gets more refined until a plateau in the results is reached, and no further improvement is gained with our method. In some cases our approach does not modify the original baseline (e.g. `weaponmadeincountry`). This is mostly attributed to missing type information in DBpedia. Note that results get slightly worse for some properties in some of the iterations. In the following section we analyze the behavior of our algorithm in details by looking at some concrete examples. These examples help to understand why some cases deviate from the general positive trend.

4.4 Analysis

First, we focus on the object of the Nell triple `actorstarredinmovie`(*al pacino, scarface*). The object term *scarface* has three possible mapping candidates, which are shown in the first column of Table 3 together with the case in which no candidate is chosen (identified by `None` in the table). In the table, we identify the candidate chosen in each iteration with a grey cell. `None` is chosen if the sum of all weights is less than 0, which means that all mapping candidates have a probability of less than 50%. For the column baseline, the only relevant weight corresponds to the most frequently-linked mapping candidate. No type-related weights are available, and accordingly the wrong entity *Scarface_(rapper)* is chosen. In the first iteration, the weights for the types are added to those of the mapping hypothesis. These type weights are obtained by applying the α-tree computation to the baseline. With respect to our example, this results in rejecting all of the candidates, because each has a probability of less than 50%. Specifically, we observe that the weight attached to the range type `Film` is not yet high enough to increase the overall score for the two movies up to a score greater than 0. The second iteration uses the type weights computed on the refined α-tree, which is created on the basis of the outcome from the previous iteration. The weights attached to `Film` have now increased significantly, and consequently one of the two movies is chosen. In this case, the algorithm chooses the right

Table 3. Weight refinements across iterations for the object of the triple `actorstarredinmovie`(*al pacino, scarface*) and for the subject of the triple `bookwriter`(*death of a salesman, arthur miller*). Grey cells refer to the mappings generated at each iteration.

Candidate	Type	Baseline	1st Iteration	2nd Iteration
Scarface_(rapper)	`MusicalArtist`	0.06	0.06 − 3.04=−2.98	0.06 − 13.81=−13.75
Scarface_(1983)	`Film`	−0.58	−0.58 + 0.36=−0.22	−0.58 + 3.37=2.79
Scarface_(1932)	`Film`	−2.22	−2.22 + 0.36=−1.86	−2.22 + 3.37=1.15
`None`	`[-]`	0.0	0.0 + 0.0=0.0	0.0 + 0.0=0.0
Salesman	`Play`	1.59	1.59 + 0.08=1.67	1.59 + 0.83=2.42
Salesman_(1951)	`Film`	−2.50	−2.50 − 0.05=−2.55	−2.50 + 0.57=−1.93

candidate. However, this example also reveals the limits of our approach, namely the fact that our method solely relies on type-level information. For this reason, the final choice between the movie from 1983 and the movie from 1932 is only based the fact that the movie from 1983 has a higher mapping weight, namely it is more often referred to by the surface form *Scarface*. That is, all things being equal (i.e., given the same type-level information), our approach will still choose the most popular entity, which might be a wrong choice.

The second example is the mapping of the subject term in `bookwriter`(*death of a salesman, arthur miller*). In this example, the candidate chosen by the baseline is also that chosen in each subsequent iterations. Contrary to the first example, the type of the chosen candidate is not the highest scoring type according to the α-tree, namely `Book`. While for the second iteration the weight for `Book` is +1.62, the weight for `Play` is +0.83, based on the fact that `Play` is a sibling of `Book`. Thus, its weight is not only supported by all matched plays, but also indirectly by all matched books. This example illustrates the benefits of the α-tree and the differences of our approach compared to an approach that simply uses the majority type as a hard restriction.

5 Related Work

Information Extraction: Key contributions in Information Extraction from the past years have concentrated on minimizing the amount of human supervision required in the knowledge harvesting process. To this end, much work has explored unsupervised bootstrapping for a variety of tasks, including the acquisition of binary relations [4], facts [11] and instances [21]. Open Information Extraction further focused on approaches that do not need any manually-labeled data [12] however, the output of these systems still needs to be disambiguated to entities and relations from a knowledge base. Recent work has extensively explored the usage of distant supervision for IE, namely by harvesting sentences containing concepts whose relation is known, and using them as training data for supervised extractors [27]. High-quality data can then be ensured by means of heuristics based on syntactic constraints [27] or encyclopedic content [14].

Matching Candidates: For over quite some time, researchers have made considerable efforts in solving the tasks of Entity Linking (EL) [15] and Word Sense Disambiguation (WSD) [17]. Seminal work in EL includes contributions by Bunescu and Paşca [5] and Cucerzan [7], who focused on the usage of Wikipedia categories and global contexts, respectively. The Silk framework [26] discovers missing links between entities across linked data sources by employing similarity metrics between pairs of instances. Dredze et al. [8] achieved remarkable results using supervised approaches, in which they were able to link entities with missing knowledge base entries. Similarly for WSD, supervised systems have been shown to achieve the highest performance, although questions remain on whether these approaches perform well when applied to domain-specific data [1]. Besides, recent work indicates that knowledge-based methods can perform equally well when fed with high-quality and wide-coverage knowledge [22,18]. In contrast to all these approaches, our method employs the most frequent sense of a term from Wikipedia. This consists of a simple, yet high-performing baseline that provides us with high-quality seeds for our bootstrapping approach.

Weighing Domain and Range: The task of learning domain and range weights closely matches with the ontology learning task. In this regard, association rule mining techniques have been employed to learn the axioms of an ontology by Völker er. al. [25]. Our way to generate weighted domain and range restrictions can be considered as a special case of ontology learning where we also assign a probabilistic rank to each of the concepts. However, our algorithm computes the weighted domain and range restrictions not as an end in itself, but as a means for improving the mapping quality between terms and instances.

Reasoning and Optimization Techniques: Niepert et.al. [19] focused in previous work on probabilistic alignment of ontologies: in our work, we focus instead on refining instance mappings by exploiting an ontological backbone. Recently, Galárraga et. al. [13] tackled the task of integrating knowledge bases (KB) by aligning instances across different KBs. Their approach involves the combination of multiple KBs into one, and learning logical rules using rule mining techniques. We have a minor overlap with their work in aligning instances across KBs. Our work of finding inconsistencies in a KB is more closely related to that of Jian et al. [16], who also use Markov Logic Networks to refine a knowledge base. Jian et al. also rely on data from NELL. However, in their work they manually assign weights to first order logic rules, whereas we use only a single parameter α, which can be learned in an automated way. Wang et. al [28] have employed (ProbKB) MLN for the task of automated KB creation through deduction and using parallel Gibbs sampling, which sets it different from our task of refinement.

6 Conclusions and Future Work

We presented a probabilistic approach to link terms from an OIE system to instances of a semantic resource in order to unambiguously determine the meaning of terms occurring within triples generated by an OIE system. In particular, we introduced a way to learn and assign weights to the possible domain and range types, defined in the terminology of the semantic resource, of a property from the OIE system. We formalized the task as a Markov Logic Network and solve the resulting optimization problem as a MAP inference task. As a result, we are able to achieve highly refined mappings in terms of both precision and recall. Moreover, we have shown how to extend this approach in an iterative way to improve the results across iterations. Our method does not use any specific parameter settings apart from the propagation factor α, which is automatically learned from our data. Based on our iterative approach, we are able to increase the F_1-measure from 81.8% to 85.74%.

In the future, we plan to extend our method to exploit more than just the type hierarchy, where alternatives are typed with the same or a similarly weighted concept. In particular, we plan to jointly reason combinations of candidates for object and subject terms of a given triple by exploiting their attached properties. For instance, two instances in a `bookwriter` relation cannot have a negative difference between the book's publishing year and the writer's birth year. To this end, we will explore kernel density estimation techniques to learn the typical relation between the relevant data values. Note that this component can easily be integrated in the iterative framework, working as a booster for the type acquisition component and vice versa.

We will apply the overall framework on other OIE datasets, ReVerb [12] in particular. While NELL has a fixed number of cleaned properties, this is not the case for ReVerb. A property like `bookwriter` might be expressed by terms like `written by`, `has author`, or by an inverse term like `is author of`. The challenging task herein is to cluster corresponding property terms and apply the proposed mechanism. Finally, we plan to run more comprehensive evaluations with the aim to re-build a significant part of, e.g., DBpedia using the triple sets generated by different OIE systems. Ultimately, our vision is to extend knowledge bases like DBpedia with a rich set of highly precise novel RDF triples that fully exploit the potential of OIE systems. Our current results are promising in that they indicate that this could lead to a highly beneficial solution to synergistically exploit IE and OIE systems together.

Acknowledgments. We thank Mathias Niepert for his contributions and valuable feedback on this work. The authors gratefully acknowledge the support of a Google Faculty Research Award (see `http://dws.informatik.uni-mannheim.de/en/projects/current-projects/` for details).

References

1. Agirre, E., de Lacalle, O.L., Soroa, A.: Knowledge-based WSD on specific domains: performing better than generic supervised WSD. In: Proc. of IJCAI (2009)
2. Banko, M., Cafarella, M.J., Soderland, S., Broadhead, M., Etzioni, O.: Open information extraction from the Web. In: Proc. of IJCAI 2007 (2007)

3. Bizer, C., Lehmann, J., Kobilarov, G., Auer, S., Becker, C., Cyganiak, R., Hellmann, S.: DBpedia – A crystallization point for the web of data. Journal of Web Semantics 7(3) (2009)
4. Brin, S.: Extracting patterns and relations from the World Wide Web. In: Proc. of WebDB Workshop at EDBT 1998 (1998)
5. Bunescu, R., Paşca, M.: Using encyclopedic knowledge for named entity disambiguation. In: Proc. of EACL 2006 (2006)
6. Carlson, A., Betteridge, J., Kisiel, B., Settles, B., Hruschka, E.R., Mitchell, T.M.: Toward an architecture for never-ending language learning. In: Proc. of AAAI (2010)
7. Cucerzan, S.: Large-scale named entity disambiguation based on Wikipedia data. In: Proc. of EMNLP-CoNLL 2007 (2007)
8. Dredze, M., McNamee, P., Rao, D., Gerber, A., Finin, T.: Entity disambiguation for knowledge base population. In: Proc. of COLING 2010 (2010)
9. Dutta, A., Niepert, M., Meilicke, C., Ponzetto, S.P.: Integrating open and closed information extraction: Challenges and first steps. In: Proc. of the ISWC 2013 NLP and DBpedia workshop (2013)
10. Etzioni, O.: Search needs a shake-up.. Nature 476(7358), 25–26 (2011)
11. Etzioni, O., Cafarella, M., Downey, D., Kok, S., Popescu, A.-M., Shaked, T., Soderland, S., Weld, D.S., Yates, A.: Web-scale information extraction in KnowItAll (Preliminary results). In: Proc. of WWW (2004)
12. Fader, A., Soderland, S., Etzioni, O.: Identifying relations for open information extraction. In: Proc. of EMNLP (2011)
13. Galárraga, L.A., Preda, N., Suchanek, F.M.: Mining rules to align knowledge bases. In: Proc. of AKBC 2013 (2013)
14. Hoffmann, R., Zhang, C., Weld, D.S.: Learning 5000 relational extractors. In: Proc. of ACL 2010 (2010)
15. Ji, H., Grishman, R.: Knowledge base population: Successful approaches and challenges. In: Proc. of ACL 2011(2011)
16. Jiang, S., Lowd, D., Dou, D.: Learning to refine an automatically extracted knowledge base using markov logic. In: Proc. of ICDM 2012 (2012)
17. Navigli, R.: Word Sense Disambiguation: A survey. ACM Computing Surveys 41(2), 1–69 (2009)
18. Navigli, R., Ponzetto, S.P.: Babelnet: The automatic construction, evaluation and application of a wide-coverage multilingual semantic network. Artificial Intelligence 193, 217–250 (2012)
19. Niepert, M., Meilicke, C., Stuckenschmidt, H.: A probabilistic-logical framework for ontology matching. In: Proc. of AAAI (2010)
20. Noessner, J., Niepert, M., Stuckenschmidt, H.: RockIt: Exploiting parallelism and symmetry for map inference in statistical relational models. In: Proc. of AAAI (2013)
21. Paşca, M., Van Durme, B.: Weakly-supervised acquisition of open-domain classes and class attributes from Web documents and query logs. In: Proc. of ACL 2008 (2008)
22. Ponzetto, S.P., Navigli, R.: Knowledge-rich Word Sense Disambiguation rivaling supervised systems. In: Proc. of ACL 2010 (2010)
23. Richardson, M., Domingos, P.: Markov logic networks. Machine Learning 62(1-2) (2006)

24. Suchanek, F.M., Kasneci, G., Weikum, G.: Yago: A Core of Semantic Knowledge. In: Proc. of WWW 2007. ACM Press (2007)
25. Völker, J., Niepert, M.: Statistical schema induction. In: Proc. of ESWC 2011 (2011)
26. Volz, J., Bizer, C., Gaedke, M., Kobilarov, G.: Silk - A Link Discovery Framework for the Web of Data. In: Proc. of LDOW 2009 (2009)
27. Wu, F., Weld, D.: Open information extraction using Wikipedia. In: Proc. of ACL 2010 (2010)
28. Yang Chen, D.Z.W.: Web-scale knowledge inference using markov logic networks. In: ICML workshop on Structured Learning: Inferring Graphs from Structured and Unstructured Inputs (2013)

WaterFowl: A Compact, Self-indexed and Inference-Enabled Immutable RDF Store

Olivier Curé[1], Guillaume Blin[1], Dominique Revuz[1], and David Célestin Faye[2]

[1] Université Paris-Est, LIGM - UMR CNRS 8049, France
{ocure,gblin,drevuz}@univ-mlv.fr
[2] Université Gaston Berger de Saint-Louis, LANI, Sénégal
dfaye@igm.univ-mlv.fr

Abstract. In this paper we present WaterFowl, a novel approach for the storage of RDF triples that addresses scalability issues through compression. The architecture of our prototype, largely based on the use of succinct data structures, enables the representation of triples in a self-indexed, compact manner without requiring decompression at query answering time. Moreover, it is adapted to efficiently support RDF and RDFS entailment regimes thanks to an optimized encoding of ontology concepts and properties that does not require a complete inference materialization or query reformulation. This approach implies to make a distinction between the terminological and the assertional components of the knowledge base early in the process of data preparation, *i.e.*, preprocessing the data before storing it in our structures. The paper describes our system's architecture and presents some preliminary results obtained from evaluations on different datasets.

Keywords: #eswc2014Cure.

1 Introduction

The emergence of big data imposes to face important data management issues: the most predominant ones being scalability, distribution, fault tolerance and low latency query answering. The current trends in handling large data volumes focus on parallel processing, *e.g.*, with MapReduce [3] like frameworks. We consider that, for at least cost efficiency reasons, this approach may soon not be satisfactory anymore and should be combined with local data compression.

Due to the production of an increasing number of voluminous datasets, RDF (Resource Description Framework) is concerned with this phenomenon. In this data model, a triple is made up of a subject, a property and an object and is generally represented as a graph. To foster interoperability among applications manipulating RDF data, vocabularies such as RDFS (RDF Schema) and OWL (Web Ontology Language) have been defined in the context of the W3C's Semantic Web Activity. They support further means to describe the structure and semantics of RDF graphs and are themselves expressed as RDF triples. When considered together, RDF data and its vocabulary represent a knowledge base

V. Presutti et al. (Eds.): ESWC 2014, LNCS 8465, pp. 302–316, 2014.

which presents the main advantage of consistently managing the data and metadata within the same data model. In the context of a Semantic Web knowledge base, handling inferences adds to the list of standard query processing database management issues, *i.e.*, parsing, optimizing and executing a query.

In this paper, we design a new architecture for immutable RDF database systems that addresses compression and inference-enabled query answering and evaluate it using a proof of concept prototype (see Section 5). This framework will serve as the cornerstone for upcoming features that will include data partitioning and supporting data updates and thus becoming mutable. The foundation of our system consists of a high compression, self-indexed storage structure supporting data retrieving decompression-free operations. By self-indexed, we mean that one can seek and retrieve any portion of the data without accessing the original data itself. Succinct Data Structures (henceforth SDS – see Section 2) provide such properties and are extensively used in our architecture (especially wavelet trees). The high rate compression obtained from SDS enables the system to keep a large portion of the data in-memory. Moreover, efficient SDS serialization/deserialization operations support fast disk-oriented IOs, *e.g.*, data loading. Based on a preliminary work of Fernández *et al.* called HDT (Header Dictionary Triples) [4] – considered as a first attempt in this direction – we propose to push its inner concept further to its logical conclusion by relying exclusively on bit maps and wavelet trees at all levels of our architecture (Section 4). Moreover, the used data structures motivate the design of an original query processing solution that integrates efficient optimization and RDFS inferences which were not considered in [4] nor in [9]. The basic idea is to use an encoding of the data that will capture the subsumption relationships of both concepts and properties. Therefore, the encoded data will enclose – without extra cost – both raw data and ontology hierarchies. Our approach differs from existing ones, such as in [13], since our encoding, which is prefix-based, will allow us to further restrict the number of SDS operations needed to answer a query implying inference. To do so, the system will need to adapt standard *rank* and *select* wavelet tree operations into ones that consider prefix of binary encoded identifiers [7]. This solution will spare the use of an expensive query rewriting approach or complete inference materialization (via a forward-chaining approach) when requesting a given ontology element, *i.e.*, concept or property, and all its sub-elements. In order to complete RDFS entailment regime, we address *rdfs:domain* and *rdfs:range* through a minimalist materialization of subject, respectively object, *rdf:type* properties.

2 Succinct Data Structures

The family of SDS uses a compression rate close to theoretical optimum, but simultaneously allows efficient decompression-free query operations on the compressed data. This property is obtained using a small amount of extra bits to store additional information. Bit vectors (*a.k.a.* bit maps) are useful to represent data while minimizing its memory footprint. In its classical shape, a bit vector allows, in constant time, to access and modify a value of the vector. Munro [10] designed an asymptotic optimal version where, in constant time, one can (i) count the number of 1 (or 0) appearing in the first x elements of a bit vector (denoted $rank_b(x)$ with b $\in$ {0,1}), (ii) find the position of the xth occurrence of a bit (denoted $select_b(x)$, b $\in$ {0,1}) and (iii) retrieve the bit at position x (denoted $access(x)$). In the remainder of this paper, we do not precise the bit b anymore for these operations and simply write *rank* and *select*. Naturally, these operations on bit vectors would be of great interest for a wider alphabet. The original solution was provided by Grossi *et al.* [6] and roughly consists in using a balanced binary tree – so-called wavelet tree. The alphabet is split into two equal parts. One attributes a 0 to each character of the first part and a 1 to the other. The original sequence is written, at the root of the tree, using this encoding. The process is repeated, in the left subtree, for the subsequence of the original sequence only using characters of the first part of the alphabet and, in the right subtree, for the second part. The process iterates until ending up on singleton alphabet. Roughly, one has provided an encoding of each character of the alphabet. Using *rank* and *select* operations on the bit vectors stored in the nodes of the tree, one is able to compute *rank* and *select* operations on the original sequence in O(log |alphabet|) by deep traversals of the tree. These operations can be easily adapted to only traverse until a given depth – referred as *rank_prefix* and *select_prefix* operations (that will be of great interest for us along with our encoding of ontology concepts and properties). Wavelet trees have been well studied since then and both space and time efficient implementations are now available, *e.g.*, the libcds library[1] which we have extended with rank and select prefix operations.

3 Related Work

Abadi *et al*'s paper [1] reinvigorated the development of novel approaches to design RDF engines. In particular, performance of query processing started to get more attention. Solutions such as RDF-3X [11] were designed using multiple indexes to address this issue but index proliferation also came at the cost of high memory footprint. Matrix Bit loaded [2] is another multiple indexes solution which stores compressed data into bit matrices. Comparatively, our approach proposes a single structure that enables indexed access on all triple elements.

Our approach is inspired by the HDT [4] system which mainly focuses on data exchange (and thus on data compression). Its former motivation was to support the exchange of large datasets highly compressed using SDS. Later, [9] presented HDT FoQ, an extension of the structure of HDT that enables some simple data retrieving operations. Nevertheless, this last contribution was not allowing any form of reasoning nor was detailing query processing mechanisms. In fact, WaterFowl brings the HDT FoQ approach further to its logical conclusion by using a pair of wavelet trees in the object layer (HDT FoQ uses an adjacency list for this layer) and by integrating a complete query processing solution with complete RDFS reasoning (*i.e.*, handling any inference using RDFS

[1] `https://code.google.com/p/libcds/`

expressiveness). This is made possible by an adaptation of both the dictionary and the triple structures. Note that this adaptation enables to retain the nice compression properties of HDT FoQ (see Section 5).

Concerning query processing in the presence of inferences, several approaches have been proposed. Among them, the materialization of all inferences within the data storage solution is a popular one, which is generally performed using an off-line forward chaining approach. This avoids query reformulation at run-time but is associated with an expansion of the memory footprint and difficulties to handle update operations. To address this last issue, [5] proposes to qualify each triple with a boolean value that states whether a triple is the result of a previous inference and a count on the triple appearance in the data set. One advantage of this approach is to consider updates at both the ABox and TBox levels but it requires a larger memory footprint. Another approach consists in performing query rewriting at run-time. It guarantees a light memory footprint but it is associated with a significant increase of queries generated. Presto [14] and Requiem [12] are systems adopting this approach with different algorithms. By adopting a rewriting approach into non recursive datalog, Presto achieves to perform this operation in non exponential time. The encoding of ontology elements, *i.e.*, concepts and properties, used in our system is related to a third approach which consists in encoding elements in a clever way that retains the subsumption hierarchy. This is the approach presented in [13] and implemented in the Quest system (a relational database management system). The work of Rodriguez-Muro *et al.* [13] relies on integer identifiers modeling the subsumption relationships which are being used to rewrite SQL queries ranging over identifiers intervals, *i.e.*, specifying boundaries over indexed fields in the WHERE clause of a SQL query. In comparison, our work tackles the encoding at the bit level and focuses on the sharing of common prefixes in the encoding of the identifiers. The main benefit of this approach compared to [13] is that the queries may be rewritten in terms of *rank_prefix* and *select_prefix* operations which will not require a full deep traversal of the wavelet trees (*i.e.*, inducing less operations on the SDS). Furthermore, it allows high rate compression and does not require extra specific indexing processes. Finally, our solution focuses on query processing of SPARQL queries. It aims to minimize the memory footprint required during query execution and to perform optimizations in terms of SDS operations complexities: *access*, *rank*, *rank_prefix*, *select* and *select_prefix*. Moreover, our query optimizer also takes into account triple pattern heuristics adapted from [15] as well as some simple statistics computed when generating the dictionaries.

4 System Components

4.1 Dictionary Component

In WaterFowl, dictionaries (see Figure 1) are used to: (i) transform the triple patterns, called Basic Graph Pattern (BGP), of SPARQL queries into their encoded version, (ii) transform the encoded result of a query back to their original verbose values and (iii) support various inference-related operations such as a

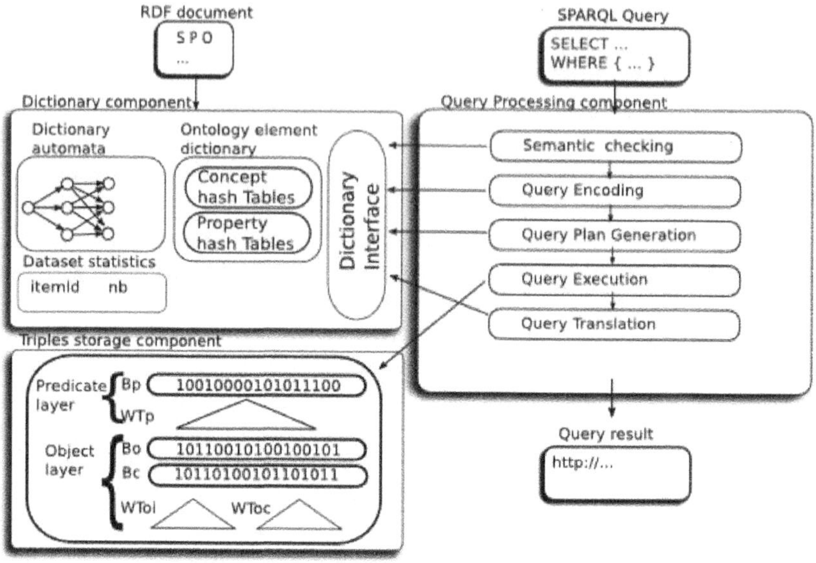

Fig. 1. WaterFowl's architecture

form of query transformation and semantic checking. Our dictionary structures are responsible for storing some simple data statistics. They are used for query optimization and are much simpler than histograms found in RDBMS due to the prohibitive size and time that would be required to respectively store and compute them. The stored statistics correspond to the total number of subjects, predicates and objects in the dataset as well as the number of occurrences of distinct subjects, predicates and objects. These statistics mainly help in discovering the most cost-efficient physical plan of a given query. We will provide more details in Section 4.3. The dictionary interface supports the communication between the query processing and the dictionary components.

In the remainder of this section, we focus on the ontology dictionaries, *i.e.*, concepts and properties (one for each), which is performed off-line. Details on the instance dictionary, which is based on common dictionary practices, are omitted due to space limitation. The ontology encoding is characterized by integer identifiers attributed to each ontology element entry. These integer values are possibly shared with entries of our other dictionaries, *i.e.*, an integer can identify both an instance, a property and a concept, without ambiguities since they are contextualized. That is, we know that each value appearing in the second position of a triple or of a SPARQL triple pattern is necessarily a property. Similarly for concept identifiers, we know that in the dataset their appearances as an object are associated with an *rdf:type* property. Since our method to handle SPARQL BGP is based on navigating through our two-layered structure, we always get the information required to consider the context. This identifier sharing char-

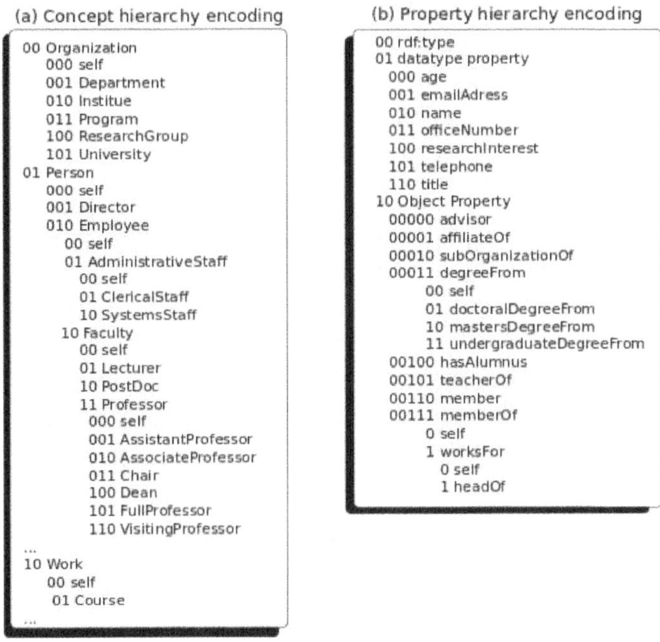

Fig. 2. Encoding for an extract of LUBM's ontology hierarchies

acteristic among our different dictionaries opens up the encoding of large set of identifiers, regardless of the structure of concept and property hierarchies. We will see that the distribution of identifiers generated for the ontology dictionaries is qualified by a possibly high sparsity. Hence, enabling an encoding over large sets of identifiers ensures to support large datasets and ontologies. The overall objective is to encode the data itself and the ontology hierarchies (that is the subsumption relations) in a compact way.

Prior to encoding, we are using a Description Logic reasoner, *e.g.*, Pellet[2], to perform the classification of concepts. Note that this approach enables to consider ontologies more expressive than RDFS, *e.g.*, OWL2DL. Then, we navigate in a breadth-first search manner through this classification. This enables to compute the representation of all concepts such that any pair of concepts sharing a common ancestor in the concept hierarchy will share a common prefix in their representation (corresponding to this common ancestor). To do so, starting from the *owl:Thing* and an empty prefix, we compute the number of direct subconcepts of *owl:Thing*. We encode each of these last with a minimum number of bits. The encoding of each such concept will be a common prefix to the encoding of any concept belonging to its sub-hierarchy (based on the subsumption relation). Figure 2(a) represents an extract of the Lehigh University Benchmark (LUBM) ontology. It emphasizes that `owl:Thing`'s direct subsumption hierarchy

[2] `http://clarkparsia.com/pellet/`

is encoded on 2 bits and that any subconcept of *Organization* (resp. *Person*, *Work*) is encoded with prefix 00 (resp. 01, 10). We will now act in a similar way for each direct subconcepts of *owl:Thing*. The only difference being the assumption that any concept (except *owl:Thing*) has a direct subconcept named *self*. This is needed to differentiate, in query processing, a query targeting a given concept (referred as *self*) or its set of subconcepts. For ease of treatment, we will always attribute the 0 value to *self*. Hence the encoding associated to *self* will correspond to a given concept (as if it was a subconcept of itself) while the identifier of the concept corresponds to its set of subconcepts. For example, querying any concept encoded with the prefix 00 will correspond to seeking for any kind of *Organization* while querying any concept encoded with the prefix 00 000 will seek specifically for *Organization* excluding its subconcepts. Indeed, the prefix 00 000 excludes *Department* which is encoded by the prefix 00 001 while the prefix 00 includes all kind of *Organization*. Recall that we use $rank\_prefix$ and $select\_prefix$ operations which differentiate 00 and 00 000. By recursively processing the hierarchy of concepts, one will end up with a prefix encoding (as illustrated in Figure 2). This *self* mechanism is not required for *owl:Thing* since it is handled natively within our framework. Provided with this encoding one can easily query any entry regarding a given concept and its subconcepts by the use of *rank_prefix* and *select_prefix* operations. Considering the properties, we first distinguish between the *rdf:type*, datatype and object properties encountered in the datasets and assign specific prefixes of 2 bits to each of them (resp. 00, 01 and 10). For both the sets of object and datatype properties, we apply a similar process as for the concepts in order to achieve a prefix encoding. Figure 2(b) displays the property encodings for an extract of the LUBM's ontology.

The corresponding encodings are stored in two types of hash tables: (i) one with an identifier as key and URI as value, denoted H_1, and (ii) one with URI as key and a tuple consisting of (a) an identifier, (b) the number of bits required to encode the direct sub-elements of this element, (c) some additional parameters such as number of occurrences, finally (d) range and domain information, denoted H_2. This additional information are necessary to allow for the completeness of the RDFS entailment regime and to detect unsatisfiable queries, *e.g.*, when a SPARQL variable is bound to a concept C that is not instantiated in the dataset, which may require inferences, *i.e.*, modifying the query such that the variable ranges over the subconcepts of C. It is also useful for reordering graph patterns in order to minimize the memory footprint of the executed query. For example, considering datasets generated from the LUBM, there is no instance for the *Professor* concept and LUBM's query #4 is unsatisfiable. Nevertheless, this query returns some results if the system seeks for all subconcepts of *Professor*.

Our approach is adapted to tree-like hierarchies. Nevertheless, we can support multiple inheritance of ontology entities in several ways. First of all, in order to capture all the knowledge, one would have to use different prefixes for the same ontology entity. For example, let us consider a concept A having X and Y as super-concepts respectively identified by the prefixes 00 and 01. Our solution relies on providing a single prefix to any concept – even the ones with multiple super-concepts. Arbitrarily, we decide to assign the prefix corresponding to the first super-concept encountered in the data. Hence, all occurrences of a concept in the dataset will share a single common prefix. There will be no expansion of the dataset. In order to be able to derive all the knowledge induced by the multiple inheritance, we introduce an `equivalence` data structure that provides all encodings for a given concept. Considering our previous example, concept A appears in the data as 01 10 as well as 00 01. Our solution, will thus use some query rewriting techniques to retrieve all information induced by the multiple inheritance. For example, if one wants to retrieve all information regarding any sub-concept of X, this request should require any concept encoded using the prefix 00. Queries requiring to access the content of the `equivalence` structure contain `UNION` clauses to address all its (sub-) concepts. Let the encoding of A be 00 01, in order to retrieve any information of Y or of one of its sub-concepts, one will ask for the union of any concept with prefix 01 or 00 01 since in the equivalence data structure, 01 01 is equivalent to 00 01. Even if this approach has some drawbacks (possibly heavy query rewriting), one only needs to efficiently know which subsumption relation are not directly expressed in the data and to store multiple inheritance for the direct common sub-concept only (which clearly are rare). On the whole, this solution seems more acceptable for our purpose than heavy materialization.

4.2 Triples Storage Component

Once the dictionaries have been defined, the triples can be encoded in a structure that makes intensive use of SDS. To illustrate the structure, we will encode the following simple RDF triples: {`(Uni0, rdf:type, ub:University), (Uni0, ub:name, "University0"), (Dpt0, rdf:type, ub:Department), (Dpt0, ub:name, "Department0"), (Dpt0, ub:subOrganizationOf, Uni0), (AP0, rdf:type, ub:AssociateProfessor), (AP0, ub:name, "Cure"), (AP0, ub:teacherOf, C15), (AP0, ub:teacherOf, C16), (AP0, ub:worksFor, Dpt0), (C15, rdf:type, ub:Course), (C15, ub:name, "Course15"), (C16, rdf:type, ub:Course)`} .

The triples are first ordered by subjects, predicates and then objects. The ordered forest of Figure 3(a) will serve to demonstrate the creation of our two-layered structure where each layer is composed of bitmaps and wavelet trees.

The first layer encodes the relation between the subjects and the predicates; that is the edges between the root of each tree and its children. The bitmap B_p is defined as follows. For each root of the trees in Figure 3(a) – that is each subject – the leftmost child is encoded as a 1, and the others as a 0. On the whole, B_p contains as many 1's as subjects in the dataset and is of length equal to the number of predicates in the dataset. In Figure 3(c), one obtains 101001000101 since there are 5 subjects with the last subject having 1 predicate, the first and fourth subjects having 2 predicates, the second one having 3 while the third one has 4. The wavelet tree WT_p encodes the sequence of predicates obtained from a pre-order traversal in the forest (*i.e.*, second row in Figure 3(a)). The construction of the wavelet tree follows the method described in Section 2.

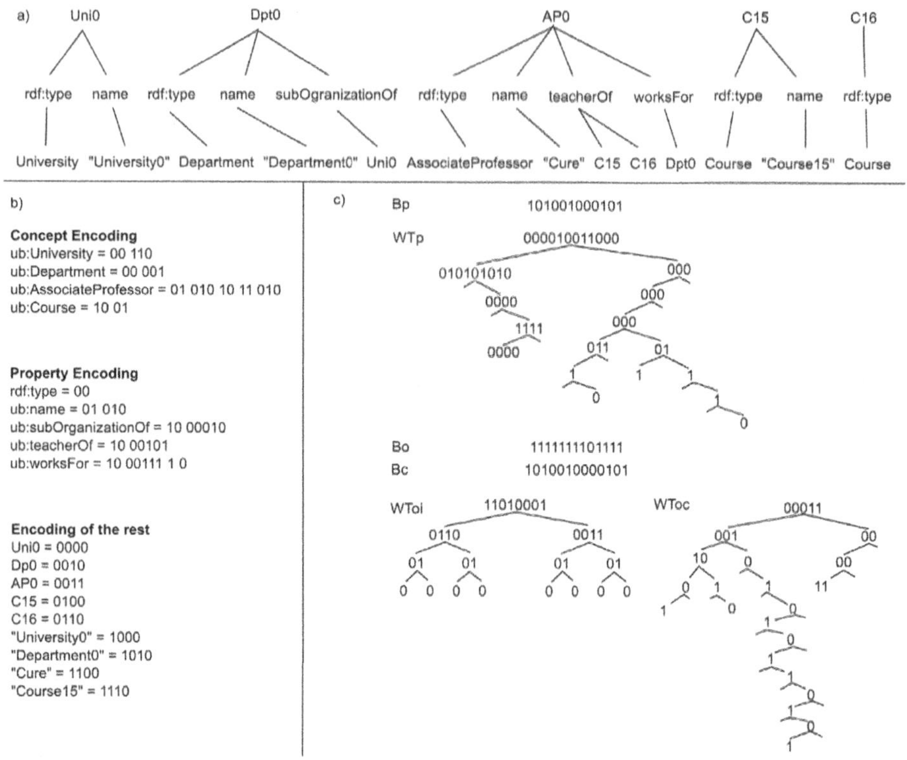

Fig. 3. Two-layered structure. For ease of presentation, URIs have been shorten. a) Tree-like representation of some RDF triples. b) Encodings. c) Corresponding storage.

Unlike the first layer, the second one has two bitmaps and two wavelet trees. B_o encodes the relation between the predicates and the objects; that is the edges between the leaves and their parents in the tree representation. Whereas, the bitmap B_c encodes the positions of ontology concepts in the sequence of objects obtained from a pre-order traversal in the forest (*i.e.*, third row in Figure 3(a)). The bitmap B_o is defined as B_p considering the forest obtained by removing the first layer of the tree representation (that is the subjects). In Figure 3(a), one obtains 1111111101111. The bitmap B_c stores a 1 at each position of an object which is a concept; a 0 otherwise. This is processed using a predicate contextualization, *i.e.*, in the dataset whenever a *rdf:type* appears, we know that the object corresponds to an ontology concept. In Figure 3(a), considering that the predicate *rdf:type* is encoded by 00, one obtains 1010010000101. Finally, the sequence of objects obtained from a pre-order traversal in the forest (*i.e.*, third row in Figure 3(a)) is split into two disjoint subsequences; one for the concepts and one for the rest. Each of these sequences is encoded in a wavelet tree (resp. WT_{oc} and WT_{oi}). This architecture reduces sparsity of identifiers and enables the management of very large datasets and ontologies while allowing time and space efficiency.

4.3 Query Processing Component

The query processing component contains the modules displayed on the right part of Figure 1. It coincides with the classical modules found in standard relational database management systems. Nevertheless, these modules are adapted to optimize performances of query answering in the context of an RDF data model and SDS operations. Due to space limitations, this section details the aspects related to query processing involving inferences and only provides general information on the aspects not requiring any form of reasoning, *i.e.*, we do not provide a complete presentation of our query optimization strategy. In the remainder of this section, we will illustrate several aspects in the context of the LUBM [8] ontology with the following SPARQL query (henceforth denoted $QR1$) which seeks for pairs of *Professor/Department* satisfying the fact that the *Professor* works for that *Department*: `SELECT ?x ?y WHERE {?y rdf:type ub:Department. ?x rdf:type ub:Professor. ?x ub:worksFor ?y.}`

A first step consists in parsing the SPARQL query and checking for its well-formedness. For each valid query, a semantic checking step is performed. It first involves to communicate with the dictionary component to make sure that each element of a SPARQL graph pattern is present in the dictionaries. This is performed with both the instance and ontology dictionaries through the use of a dictionary interface (Figure 1) which receives a set of triples of the BGP. Given a triple context, the system seeks in the appropriate dictionary (*e.g.*, search the object in the concept dictionary if the predicate is *rdf:type*). The system detects two cases of unsatisfiability: (i) one of the graph pattern's element (excluding variables) is not present in any of the dictionaries, (ii) a graph pattern element has no occurrences in the datasets and, in the case of a concept or property, has no instantiated sub-elements occurrences neither. Otherwise, the BGP is satisfiable and the module obtains identifiers and statistics associated to each non variable graph pattern element. Note that in the case of a concept or property element with sub-elements, it is the identifier associated to its *self* counterpart that is returned. In the case of $QR1$, the identifier and statistic associated to *Professor* are respectively 01 010 10 11 000, *i.e.*, *Professor*'s *self* entry, and 0 since LUBM's datasets do not instantiate directly this concept. This approach enables to detect unsatisfiable queries rapidly since it detects that the query's result set is empty without executing any other steps of the query processing component. A query is considered unsatisfiable if at least one triple of the BGP is unsatisfiable otherwise, the whole query is satisfiable.

A satisfiable query is then encoded in terms of identifiers retrieved from the set of dictionaries. It results in a query containing integer-based graph patterns and variables. In this step, the statistics associated to concepts and properties encountered in the BGP may imply some form of reasoning. For instance, consider that a concept C or property P has no instances, then since the query is satisfiable, it means that C or P has some sub-elements. Hence, some of its direct or indirect sub-elements may be instantiated and are expected in the result set of the query. The solution we are proposing is to replace the identifier of C or P's *self* entry with C or P's own identifier, *i.e.*, removing *self*'s local identifier in the query. In the context of $QR1$, it implies removing 000, *self*'s local identifier, from 01 010 10 11 000 which yields to 01 010 10 11. It corresponds to the *Professor* concept and is a common prefix to all its subconcepts.

To complete the support for RDFS entailment regime, we have implemented a materialization-based approach for the *rdfs:domain* and *rdfs:range* properties. Intuitively, we provide, if one is not available, or refine, if one is available, a type to the subject (resp. object) of a triple whose property has some domain (resp. range) information. The refinement aspect corresponds to typing a subject (or object) with the most specific concept among a set of valid ones. This enables to limit the size of our materialization by preventing over typing. Our typing mechanism is based on the following RDFS entailment rules (denoted rdfs2 and rdfs3 in the RDF Semantics W3C Recommendation[3]): (i) if *aaa rdfs:domain xxx. uuu aaa yyy.* then add *uuu rdf:type xxx.* and (ii) if *aaa rdfs:range xxx . uuu aaa vvv.* then add *vvv rdf:type xxx.*

Let us demonstrate this aspect with an example. In the LUBM ontology, the axioms $\top \sqsubseteq \forall\ advisor^{-}.Person$ and $\top \sqsubseteq \forall\ advisor.Professor$ resp. define that the *advisor* property has the concept *Person* as domain and *Professor* as range. Let also consider a dataset with the {`(ex:smith, ub:advisor, ex:gblin)`, `(ex:gblin, ub:worksFor, ex:esipe)`} triples. We now present two cases where, according to the RDFS entailment regime, the `(ex:gblin, ex:esipe)` tuple should be part of the $QR1$ answer set. In a first case, we assume that neither `gblin` nor `smith` are typed. Then our materialization strategy adds the triples {`(ex:smith, rdf:type, Person)`, `(ex:gblin, rdf:type, Professor)`} and ensures the completeness of the answer set. In a second case, the triple {`(ex:gblin, rdf:type, Person)`} was part of the dataset and will be replaced by {`(ex:gblin, rdf:type, Professor)`} since `Professor` is more specific than `Person`. In cases of multiple incomparable classes for which no "most specific" class exists then several types are stored for the considered instance. These materializations are part of our data preprocessing and make an intensive use of the H_2 structure. In Section 4.1, we emphasized that the H_2 structure stores in its value the concepts associated to the *rdfs:domain* and *rdfs:range* of each property. Finally, note that this solution does not come at the cost of expanding our two-layered structure and it does not imply any query reformulation.

We now sketch the main aspects of our query execution and optimization process. A best effort query plan is searched using a set of heuristics. A first one is especially designed to reduce the cost of navigating in the two-layered structure, in terms of *rank*, *select* and *access* SDS operations. That is, we try as much as possible to favor *rank* operations against *select* ones since most implementations guarantee constant time *rank* operations on bitmap but not for *select* ones which either need lot of extra space or logarithmic time. Two other heuristics are provided to take advantage of state of the art RDF access pattern [15], and statistics stored in the dictionary structures. Again, these heuristics have been adapted to reorder some access patterns which is a major source of optimizations for SPARQL queries containing many graph patterns. This results

[3] `http://www.w3.org/TR/rdf-mt/#rdf_entail`

in the generation of query plans taking the form of left-deep join trees which is being translated and executed in terms of compositions of *rank*, *select* and *access* SDS operations (and their prefix forms). In order to support `DISTINCT`, `LIMIT`, `OFFSET` and `ORDER BY` SPARQL operators, we provide a k-partite graph based storing system for the candidate tuples that allow us to store and filter them in an efficient way avoiding as much as possible unnecessary Cartesian product. Finally, the identifiers of the result are translated in terms of their associated values in the dictionaries. The supported SPARQL operators needed the development of optimization techniques in the query execution module: the `UNION` of graph patterns requires a lazy approach of common patterns, `FILTER` accesses the dictionary and `OPTIONAL` prevents the creation of bindings in the absence of a matching for the optional graph patterns.

5 Experimental Evaluation

5.1 System and Datasets

All experiments have been conducted on a HP Z800 workstation with 2 Quad-Core Intel Xeon Processors with 12Mbytes L2 cache, 8Gbytes of memory and running Gentoo 2.6.37 generic x86-64. It contains two 500GB SATA disks running at 7200 rpm. We used gcc version 4.5.2 running on 64 bits with glibc 2.13. We modified the libcds v1.0.13 in order to obtain *rank_prefix* and *select_prefix* operations on the proposed SDS. We have compared our system with RDF-3X version 0.3.7, BigOWLIM version 3.5 and Jena 2.6.4 together with its TDB 0.8.10. We do not propose a comparison with Hexastore since it was not possible to load the datasets we are working with. This is due to its in-memory approach and the large number of set indexes, *i.e.*, 6, it requires to process queries efficiently. Note that this aspect was confirmed in [9] which essentially focuses on data loading, compression rates and times required for indexes creation. Our current WaterFowl framework uses pointer-free wavelet trees (which were giving best results compared to pointer based wavelet trees and wavelet matrices).

In this section, we present the results of our evaluation performed on a set of synthetic and a real world datasets. The synthetic datasets correspond to instances of the LUBM [8]. The main characteristics of LUBM are to feature an OWL ontology for the university domain, to enable scaling of datasets to an arbitrary size and to provide a set of 14 SPARQL queries of varying complexities. Out of these queries, 10 require a form of inference, namely dealing with concept and property hierarchies as well as inverse and transitive roles which we are not testing since they require OWL entailments. We are testing our system on datasets for 100 and 1000 universities, resp. 13.4 (1.12Gb) and 133.5 (11.3Gb) million triples The real-world dataset is Yago (37.5 million triples and 5.32Gb) and is mainly used on the first aspect of our evaluation.

5.2 Results

The results concern three aspects of our system: (i) memory footprint and time required to prepare a dataset, (ii) query processing not requiring inferences and

(iii) query answering requiring RDFS entailment regime. The first one aims to demonstrate that a system designed on SDS possesses interesting properties in terms of data compression rate, time to prepare a dataset, *i.e.*, total duration required to create the dictionary, index the data, compute some statistics and serialize the database structure. It is presented in Table 1 and confirms the results contained in [9]. We can see that most compressed versions of WaterFowl, *i.e.*,mode 2 and 3 relying respectively on pointer-free wavelet tree and wavelet matrix (while mode 1 uses pointers) require between 5 and 9% of the space required by RDF-3X and this is even more important compared to BigOWLIM and Jena TDB. This is due to the high compression rate of the SDS we are using and the single, opposed to 15 for RDF-3X, index we are generating. The sizes required for BigOWLIM and Jena TDB are explained by their approach which require full materialization. Moreover, times to prepare a dataset are about half of the duration taken by RDF-3X. This is easily explained by the number of indexes RDF-3X is building. Obviously, due to the materialization, the times needed to process and store the datasets are even more important for BigOWLIM and Jena TDB. Finally, our mode 2 (pointer-free Wavelet), based on a pointer-free wavelet tree implementation seems to be an interesting trade-off between size of the generated dataset and generation time.

The two next aspects of our evaluation concerns query processing. First, we consider queries that are not requiring reasoning. Then, we study some queries requiring the RDFS entailment regime. We consider that by investigating both aspects of query answering, we are able to highlight the pros and cons of our complete query processing component. Our evaluation methodology includes a warm-up phase before measuring the execution time of the queries. This is required for the 3 compared systems but not for WaterFowl since its data reside in main-memory. All the queries are first ran in sequence once to warm-up the systems, and then the process is repeated 5 times. The following tables (Table 2) report the mean values for each query and each system.

In the first context, we compare our approach with the 3 other systems on a subset of LUBM queries (#1, #2 and #14). Table 2 emphasizes that the performances with the RDF-3X system are comparable. Unsurprisingly, the two other systems are slower than RDF-3X on Queries #1 and #3. A fact which has been highlighted on many other evaluations. Note that these queries have different characteristics since they respectively correspond to large input with

Table 1. Size of database serialization (MB) and Time to prepare datasets

	Size in MB			Time in sec		
	univ100	univ1000	Yago	univ100	univ1000	Yago
RDF-3X	831,717	7,795,458	2,189,735	240	3050	1090
BigOWLIM	2,411,260	22,600,088	6,348,338	838	10640	3708
Jena TDB	1,492,057	13,984,467	3,928,271	1285	16332	5837
WaterFowl Mode 1	91,539	922,106	271,616	168	2134	768
WaterFowl Mode 2	71,064	720,396	210,556	119	1515	545
WaterFowl Mode 3	77,351	798,829	203,728	107	1488	513

Table 2. Query answering times (sec) on univ1000

	LUBM QR#1	LUBM QR#2	LUBM QR#14
RDF-3X	1.65	14.88	1640
BigOWLIM	138	5.7	3320
Jena TDB	3.52	2.18	2998
WaterFowl Mode 2	1.80	10.18	1710
WaterFowl Mode 3	1.75	10.13	1680

high selectivity, complex 'triangle' query pattern and large input with low selectivity. Query #2 is performed more rapidly by Jena TDB and BigOWLIM but WaterFowl is faster than RDF-3X. We consider that this is due to a better consideration of this query particular pattern. It highlights that our query optimization has room for improvement.

Table 3. Inference-based query answering times (sec) on univ100

	QR#4	QR#5	QR#6	QR#7	QR#10
RDF-3X	4.2	2.5	15.3	1.4	1.6
OWLIM-SE	705	16771	72	1708	3.65
Jena TDB	4.85	6.3	30.7	207	1.55
WaterFowl Mode 2	3.66	2.3	13.4	1.2	1.4

In the context of queries requiring RDFS entailment, we are testing RDF-3X with query rewriting performed using a DL reasoner against our system. That is, we have implemented a simple RDFS query rewriting on top of RDF-3X which generates SPARQL queries with `UNION` clauses. The RDF-3X approach enables to perform query rewriting in the context of the considered fastest RDF Store. Note that the two other systems do not require this machinery since they rely on a materialization approach. Table 3 highlights that our system slightly outperforms the inference-enable RDF-3X on a set of five distinct LUBM queries, requiring different forms of reasoning, *i.e.*, based on concept and property subsumption relationships. It has already been emphasized that due to its large number of indexes, RDF-3X is very competitive or even faster than some materialization-based systems. Due to our ontology elements encoding with prefix enabled navigation and minimalist materialization of *rdfs:domain* and *rdfs:range* information, we outperform all systems on these five queries.

6 Conclusion

We have designed and implemented a novel type of immutable RDF store that addresses a set of issues of big data and of the semantic web. Each database instance regroups a set of dictionaries and a dataset represented in a compact, self-indexed manner using some succinct data structures. The evaluation we have conducted emphasize that our system is clearly very efficient in terms of data compression and can thus be considered as an interesting alternative when one is concerned with data exchange. Moreover, on our query processing experimentations, our system presents performances that are comparable to the domain's reference, *i.e.*, RDF-3X. We consider that this is quite a strong encouragement toward pursuing our work on WaterFowl. We consider that this is due to the advantage of our highly compressed data and implementing all data retrieving operations on SDS functions, *i.e.*, *access*, *rank*, *select* and their prefix counterparts. We also believe that adapting all our query optimization heuristics on state of the art solutions is part of the good performances our system provides. Nevertheless, we are convinced that there is plenty of room for more optimizations in all modules of WaterFowl, *e.g.*, pipelined parallelism in query execution.

Our future investigations will include the distribution of triples over a cluster of machines and the support for updates in both the TBox and the ABox, which is not trivial since actual wavelet trees do not support efficient updates.

References

1. Abadi, D.J., Marcus, A., Madden, S., Hollenbach, K.J.: Scalable semantic web data management using vertical partitioning. In: VLDB, pp. 411–422 (2007)
2. Atre, M., Chaoji, V., Zaki, M.J., Hendler, J.A.: Matrix "bit" loaded: a scalable lightweight join query processor for rdf data. In: WWW, pp. 41–50 (2010)
3. Dean, J., Ghemawat, S.: Mapreduce: Simplified data processing on large clusters. In: OSDI, pp. 137–150 (2004)
4. Fernández, J.D., Martínez-Prieto, M.A., Gutierrez, C.: Compact representation of large RDF data sets for publishing and exchange. In: Patel-Schneider, P.F., Pan, Y., Hitzler, P., Mika, P., Zhang, L., Pan, J.Z., Horrocks, I., Glimm, B. (eds.) ISWC 2010, Part I. LNCS, vol. 6496, pp. 193–208. Springer, Heidelberg (2010)
5. Goasdoué, F., Manolescu, I., Roatis, A.: Efficient query answering against dynamic RDF databases. In: EDBT, pp. 299–310 (2013)
6. Grossi, R., Gupta, A., Vitter, J.S.: High-order entropy-compressed text indexes. In: SODA, pp. 841–850 (2003)
7. Grossi, R., Ottaviano, G.: The wavelet trie: maintaining an indexed sequence of strings in compressed space. In: PODS, pp. 203–214 (2012)
8. Guo, Y., Pan, Z., Heflin, J.: Lubm: A benchmark for OWL knowledge base systems. J. Web Sem. 3(2-3), 158–182 (2005)
9. Martínez-Prieto, M.A., Gallego, M.A., Fernández, J.D.: Exchange and consumption of huge RDF data. In: ESWC, pp. 437–452 (2012)
10. Munro, J.I.: Tables. In: FSTTCS, pp. 37–42 (1996)
11. Neumann, T., Weikum, G.: The RDF-3X engine for scalable management of RDF data. VLDB J. 19(1), 91–113 (2010)
12. Pérez-Urbina, H., Horrocks, I., Motik, B.: Efficient query answering for OWL2. In: ISWC, pp. 489–504 (2009)
13. Rodriguez-Muro, M., Calvanese, D.: High performance query answering over DL-lite ontologies. In: KR (2012)
14. Rosati, R., Almatelli, A.: Improving query answering over DL-lite ontologies. In: KR (2010)
15. Tsialiamanis, P., Sidirourgos, L., Fundulaki, I., Christophides, V., Boncz, P.A.: Heuristics-based query optimisation for SPARQL. In: EDBT, pp. 324–335 (2012)

Ontology-Based Data Access Using Rewriting, OWL 2 RL Systems and Repairing

Giorgos Stoilos

School of Electrical and Computer Engineering
National Technical University of Athens, Greece

Abstract. In previous work it has been shown how an OWL 2 DL ontology $\mathcal{O}$ can be 'repaired' for an OWL 2 RL system ans—that is, how we can compute a set of axioms $\mathcal{R}$ that is independent from the data and such that ans that is generally incomplete for $\mathcal{O}$ becomes complete for all SPARQL queries when used with $\mathcal{O} \cup \mathcal{R}$. However, the initial implementation and experiments were very preliminary and hence it is currently unclear whether the approach can be applied to large and complex ontologies. Moreover, the approach so far can only support instance queries. In the current paper we thoroughly investigate repairing as an approach to scalable (and complete) ontology-based data access. First, we present several non-trivial optimisations to the first prototype. Second, we show how (arbitrary) conjunctive queries can be supported by integrating well-known query rewriting techniques with OWL 2 RL systems via repairing. Third, we perform an extensive experimental evaluation obtaining encouraging results. In more detail, our results show that we can compute repairs even for very large real-world ontologies in a reasonable amount of time, that the performance overhead introduced by repairing is negligible in small to medium sized ontologies and noticeable but manageable in large and complex one, and that the hybrid reasoning approach can very efficiently compute the correct answers for real-world challenging scenarios.

Keywords: #eswc2014Stoilos.

1 Introduction

The use of OWL ontologies to provide a formal and semantically rich conceptualisation of the underlying data sources is becoming the basis in many modern applications [7,10]. However, the expressive power of OWL 2 DL comes at a price of high computational complexity [12], hence, even after intense implementation work and the design of modern optimisations, fully-fledged OWL 2 DL reasoners are still not able to cope with large datasets containing billions of triples.

As a consequence, in real-world applications, developers often employ efficient and provably scalable query answering systems which usually support only the OWL 2 RL fragment of OWL 2 DL. Prominent examples include OWLim [7], Oracle's Semantic Graph [19], Apache Jena,[1] and many more. Such systems can

[1] `http://jena.apache.org/`

V. Presutti et al. (Eds.): ESWC 2014, LNCS 8465, pp. 317–332, 2014.

load any OWL ontology but they will ignore all its parts that do not fall within the fragment they support. As a result they are *incomplete*—that is, for some ontology, query and dataset they will fail to compute all certain answers.

Although scalability is very attractive, incomplete query answering may, on the one hand, not be acceptable in several critical applications like healthcare or defense and, on the other hand, improving completeness by computing as many 'missed' answers as possible without affecting performance would be beneficial for many applications. Hence, approaches for improving the completeness of incomplete reasoners have recently been investigated [20,13,8]. A common technique in most of these works is to use a fully-fledged OWL 2 DL reasoner to 'materialise' certain kinds of axioms which, when taken together with the input ontology and the data, will 'help' the system compute more answers than it would normally do. However, in all previous approaches there are still combinations of inputs for which the systems would miss answers even after materialisation.

Stoilos et al. [17] investigated whether it is possible to compute *all* query answers by using the materialisation approach. They introduced the notion of a *repair* of an ontology $\mathcal{O}$ for an incomplete system ans which, roughly speaking, is an ontology $\mathcal{R}$ such that ans that is generally incomplete for $\mathcal{O}$ becomes complete for *all* SPARQL queries *and* datasets when used with $\mathcal{O} \cup \mathcal{R}$. Interestingly, by recent results [4,3] it follows that repairs always exists for Horn fragments of OWL 2 DL and in many cases even for arbitrary OWL 2 DL ontologies. Moreover, since repairs are independent from the data and the query, they only need to be computed once at a pre-processing step. Hence, repairing is a promising approach to scalable and complete query answering and ontology-based data access.

However, despite initial encouraging results there are still several open issues and questions. First, computing a repair is a computationally very expensive process and the original implementation was using arguably obsolete systems and featured no optimisations. Second, the experimental evaluation was very preliminary and it used two rather small and simple ontologies, namely LUBM and a (very small) fragment of Galen. Hence, the practicality of the approach when it comes to large and complex ontologies is unclear. Third, although instance (SPARQL) queries are highly important the approach still does not support arbitrary queries which are needed in several real-world applications.

In the current paper we extensively study repairing as an approach to scalable (and complete) query answering. First, we investigate on how to efficiently compute repairs by providing several optimisations to the first prototype. Second, we show how general queries can be supported by integrating well-known query rewriting techniques [2] with OWL 2 RL systems, hence, providing a hybrid approach to query answering. Third, we perform an extensive experimental evaluation using both synthetic and real-world benchmarks. More precisely, first, we apply our tool over a large number of well-known ontologies to see how efficiently repairs can be computed in practice. Interestingly, our results show that computing repairs is practically feasible even for large and complex ontologies mostly due to the new optimisations. Second, we investigate how much repairing affects the performance of the OWL 2 RL reasoner in practice. Our results show that in medium sized ontologies the overhead is negligible, while in very large ones it can become noticeable. Still, however, this overhead regards only a pre-processing (loading) step and, in return, after repairing the system is indistinguishable from two OWL 2 DL reasoners over a well-known benchmark (UOBM). Third, we evaluate our hybrid query answering approach obtaining encouraging results. In more detail, the system computed all correct answers over a real-world highly expressive ontology almost instantaneously. Our current repair tool supports the DL language $\mathcal{ELHI}$, hence, given the proven scalability of the used OWL 2 RL system it is safe to conclude that this is currently one of the most scalable approaches to answering arbitrary queries over an important fragment of OWL 2.

2 Preliminaries

We use standard notions from first-order logic, like variable, predicate, atom, constant, satisfiability, and entailment (denoted by $\models$).

Description Logics and OWL 2. We assume that the reader is familiar with the basics of the OWL 2 DL language[2] and its relation to Description Logics (DLs) [1]. As usual, we make a distinction between the *schema* of an ontology, called TBox $\mathcal{T}$, which consists of all class and property axioms, and the *data*, called ABox $\mathcal{A}$, which consists of all class and property assertions (we assume only simple assertions). Then, an ontology is a set of the form $\mathcal{O} = \mathcal{T} \cup \mathcal{A}$.

Due to the high computational complexity of query answering over OWL 2 DL ontologies [12] a number of profiles have been defined. A prominent example is the OWL 2 RL language[3] for which many empirically scalable systems have been implemented and deployed in real-world applications.

Datalog and Conjunctive Queries. A *datalog rule* r is an expression of the form $H \leftarrow B_1 \wedge \ldots \wedge B_n$ where H, called *head*, is a function-free atom, $\{B_1, \ldots, B_n\}$, called *body*, is a set of function-free atoms, and each variable in the head also occurs in the body. A *datalog program* $\mathcal{P}$ is a finite set of datalog rules. A *union of conjunctive queries* (UCQ) $\mathcal{Q}$ is a set of datalog rules such that their head atoms share the same predicate, called *query predicate*, which does not appear anywhere in the body. A *conjunctive query* (CQ) is a UCQ with exactly one rule. Variables that appear in the body and not the head are called *non-distinguished* variables. CQs with no non-distinguished variables form the basis of SPARQL hence. in the following, we call them *SPARQL queries*.

We often abuse notation and identify a CQ with the only rule it contains instead of a singleton set. For a query $\mathcal{Q}$ with query predicate Q, a tuple of constants $\vec{a}$ is an answer of $\mathcal{Q}$ w.r.t. a TBox $\mathcal{T}$ and an ABox $\mathcal{A}$ if the arity of $\vec{a}$ agrees with the arity of Q and $\mathcal{T} \cup \mathcal{A} \cup \mathcal{Q} \models Q(\vec{a})$. We denote with $\mathsf{cert}(\mathcal{Q}, \mathcal{T} \cup \mathcal{A})$ the answers to $\mathcal{Q}$ w.r.t. $\mathcal{T} \cup \mathcal{A}$.

[2] `http://www.w3.org/TR/owl2-syntax/`

[3] `http://www.w3.org/TR/owl2-profiles/`

Ontology and Query Rewriting. Rewriting is a prominent approach to query answering over ontologies. In such an approach the input TBox $\mathcal{T}$ (and query $\mathcal{Q}$) is transformed into a new set of sentences that capture all the information that is relevant from $\mathcal{T}$ for answering any SPARQL CQ (resp. answering $\mathcal{Q}$) over an arbitrary ABox $\mathcal{A}$ [9,2]. The typical target language for computing rewritings is datalog in an effort to exploit mature (deductive) database technologies to compute the answers over the original TBox.

Definition 1. *Let $\mathcal{T}$ be a TBox. A $\mathcal{T}$-*rewriting *is a datalog program* Rew_D *such that for each $\mathcal{A}$ consistent with $\mathcal{T}$ and each SPARQL CQ $\mathcal{Q}_g$ we have:*

$$\mathsf{cert}(\mathcal{Q}_g, \mathcal{T} \cup \mathcal{A}) = \mathsf{cert}(\mathcal{Q}_g, \mathsf{Rew}_D \cup \mathcal{A})$$

*Let in addition $\mathcal{Q}$ be a CQ with query predicate Q. A $(\mathcal{Q},\mathcal{T})$-*rewriting *is a set of the form* $\mathsf{Rew}_D \uplus \mathsf{Rew}_Q$ *with* Rew_D *a set of datalog rules not mentioning Q and* Rew_Q *a UCQ with query predicate Q, and where for each ABox $\mathcal{A}$ consistent with $\mathcal{T}$ we have:*

$$\mathsf{cert}(\mathcal{Q}, \mathcal{T} \cup \mathcal{A}) = \mathsf{cert}(\mathsf{Rew}_Q, \mathsf{Rew}_D \cup \mathcal{A})$$

Note that a $\mathcal{T}$-rewriting is only complete for all SPARQL queries.

Example 1. Consider the TBox $\mathcal{T}$ consisting of the following axioms:

$$\mathsf{PhDSt} \sqsubseteq \mathsf{GradSt} \qquad \mathsf{GradSt} \sqsubseteq \exists \mathsf{takes}.\mathsf{Course}$$
$$\exists \mathsf{takes}.\mathsf{Course} \sqsubseteq \mathsf{Student} \qquad \mathsf{Student} \sqsubseteq \mathsf{Person}$$

and consider also the CQ $\mathcal{Q} = Q(x) \leftarrow \mathsf{takes}(x,y) \wedge \mathsf{Course}(y)$.

The set $\mathsf{Rew}_1 = \{\mathcal{Q}, \mathcal{Q}_1, \mathcal{Q}_2\}$, where $\mathcal{Q}_1, \mathcal{Q}_2$ are presented next, is a $(\mathcal{Q},\mathcal{T})$-rewriting while the set $\mathsf{Rew}_2 = \{r_1, r_2, r_3, r_4\}$ is a $\mathcal{T}$-rewriting.

$$\mathcal{Q}_1 = Q(x) \leftarrow \mathsf{GradSt}(x) \qquad \mathcal{Q}_2 = Q(x) \leftarrow \mathsf{PhDSt}(x)$$

$$r_1 = \mathsf{Person}(x) \leftarrow \mathsf{Student}(x) \qquad r_2 = \mathsf{Student}(x) \leftarrow \mathsf{takes}(x,y) \wedge \mathsf{Course}(y)$$
$$r_3 = \mathsf{Student}(x) \leftarrow \mathsf{GradSt}(x) \qquad r_4 = \mathsf{GradSt}(x) \leftarrow \mathsf{PhDSt}(x)$$

It can be seen that Rew_1 (Rew_2) captures all information that is relevant for answering $\mathcal{Q}$ (any SPARQL CQ) over $\mathcal{T}$. For example, $\mathcal{Q}_1$ captures the fact that according to $\mathcal{T}$ graduate students take some course, hence, in any ABox that contains an assertion of the form $\mathsf{GradSt}(a)$, a is a certain answer. Similarly, r_3 captures the fact that graduate students are also students.

Abstract Query Answering Systems. In the following, in order to abstract away from concrete systems we recall the notion of a query answering system [17].

Definition 2. *A* (query answering) system ans *is a procedure that takes as input an OWL 2 DL TBox $\mathcal{T}$, an ABox $\mathcal{A}$, and a CQ $\mathcal{Q}$ and returns a set of tuples* $\mathsf{ans}(\mathcal{Q}, \mathcal{T} \cup \mathcal{A})$ *that have the same arity as the query predicate of $\mathcal{Q}$. Let $\mathcal{L}$ be a fragment of OWL 2 DL and let $\mathcal{T}|_{\mathcal{L}}$ denote all $\mathcal{L}$-axioms of a TBox $\mathcal{T}$. Then,* ans *is called* complete *for $\mathcal{L}$ if for each CQ $\mathcal{Q}$ and ABox $\mathcal{A}$ we have* $\mathsf{cert}(\mathcal{Q}, \mathcal{T}|_{\mathcal{L}} \cup \mathcal{A}) \subseteq \mathsf{ans}(\mathcal{Q}, \mathcal{T} \cup \mathcal{A})$.

Most OWL 2 RL reasoners known to us can be captured by the above definition. More precisely, for $\mathcal{T}|_{\mathsf{rl}}$ all the OWL 2 RL-axioms of a TBox $\mathcal{T}$, these systems essentially return $\mathsf{cert}(\mathcal{Q}, \mathcal{T}|_{\mathsf{rl}} \cup \mathcal{A})$. Note that ans need not be sound.

3 Repairing Incompleteness in a Nutshell

Stoilos et al. [17] provided the first systematic approach to improving the completeness of (incomplete) OWL 2 RL systems via ABox independent materialisation. They have introduced the notion of a *repair* of a TBox $\mathcal{T}$ for a system ans which, roughly speaking, is a set of axioms $\mathcal{R}$ such that i) $\mathcal{T} \models \mathcal{R}$ and ii) for each SPARQL CQ $\mathcal{Q}$ and ABox $\mathcal{A}$ we have $\mathsf{cert}(\mathcal{Q}, \mathcal{T} \cup \mathcal{A}) \subseteq \mathsf{ans}(\mathcal{Q}, \mathcal{T} \cup \mathcal{R} \cup \mathcal{A})$. For example, the set $\mathcal{R} = \{\mathsf{GradSt} \sqsubseteq \mathsf{Student}\}$ is a repair of the TBox $\mathcal{T}$ of Example 1 for an OWL 2 RL system ans.

It was additionally shown that for systems complete for OWL 2 RL a repair exists if a $\mathcal{T}$-rewriting for the input TBox exists. Interestingly, by recent results such rewritings always exist for TBoxes expressed in Horn-$\mathcal{SHIQ}$ [4] (a fairly expressive fragment of OWL 2) and they might also exist even for arbitrary OWL 2 TBoxes [3]. Hence, repairing is a promising approach to scalable (and complete) ontology-based data access. Finally, it was shown how to minimise a repair (cf. steps 2. and 3. next). Overall the procedure of computing a repair $\mathcal{R}$ of a TBox $\mathcal{T}$ for an OWL 2 RL system ans, denoted by Repair($\mathcal{T}$), is summarised by the following three steps:

1. Compute an initial repair $\mathcal{R}^1$ using a $\mathcal{T}$-rewriting Rew.
2. Remove from $\mathcal{R}^1$ all axioms α such that $\mathcal{T}|_{\mathsf{rl}} \models \alpha$. Moreover, for each pair of distinct axioms α_1, α_2 remove α_2 if $\mathcal{T}|_{\mathsf{rl}} \cup \{\alpha_1\} \models \alpha_2$. Let $\mathcal{R}^2$ be the resulting set of this step.
3. Finally, perform again a similar procedure like that in step 2 but this time using ans. For example, roughly speaking, remove from $\mathcal{R}^2$ all elements α such that $\mathcal{T}|_{\mathsf{rl}} \models_{\mathsf{ans}} \alpha$ and remove all α_2 such that for some α_1 we have $\mathcal{T}|_{\mathsf{rl}} \cup \{\alpha_1\} \models_{\mathsf{ans}} \alpha_2$.[4] The result of this step is the desired repair.

4 Computing Repairs in Practice

In previous work it was argued that computing a repair can be done easily by using any state-of-the-art (query) rewriting system, OWL 2 DL reasoner, and OWL 2 RL system in order to implement steps 1, 2, and 3 of procedure Repair, respectively [17]. However, this is far from being true for at least two reasons that are related to the efficiency of steps 1 and 2.

Regarding step 1 the issue is that, before computing a $\mathcal{T}$-rewriting, many state-of-the-art systems would normalise an input TBox $\mathcal{T}$ by replacing complex classes with *fresh* atomic ones. For example, if $\mathcal{T}$ contains $\exists R.(E \sqcap F) \sqsubseteq A$ then this axiom would be transformed into the pair $\exists R.A_0 \sqsubseteq A$ and $E \sqcap F \sqsubseteq A_0$, where

[4] The reader is referred to [17] for details about how $\models_{\mathsf{ans}}$ can be checked in practice.

A_0 is a new class. Hence, the computed rewriting, call it Rew'_D in the following, would also mention such fresh predicates, e.g., in this case it would contain the rules $A(x) \leftarrow R(x,y) \wedge A_0(y)$ and $A_0(x) \leftarrow E(x) \wedge F(x)$ (we informally call such rewritings *normalised*). As a consequence, Rew'_D cannot be used as a basis for computing a repair—that is, if $\mathcal{R}$ is the output of procedure $\textsc{Repair}(\mathcal{T})$ when computing Rew'_D at step 1, then we will generally have $\mathsf{cert}(\mathcal{Q},\mathcal{T}\cup\mathcal{A}) \not\subseteq \mathsf{ans}(\mathcal{Q},\mathcal{T}\cup\mathcal{R}\cup\mathcal{A})$ for some ABox $\mathcal{A}$.

The obvious solution to the above problem is to eliminate the fresh symbols in Rew'_D by 'unfolding' their definitions creating new rules which contain only symbols from $\mathcal{T}$ (we informally call such rewritings *unfolded*). In the previous example by unfolding the rule containing $A_0(x)$ into the one containing $A_0(y)$ we can compute the new rewriting Rew_D that instead contains the rule $A(x) \leftarrow R(x,y) \wedge E(y) \wedge F(y)$. Clearly, $\mathcal{T} \models \mathsf{Rew}_D$ and hence Rew_D can be used to compute an initial repair. However, first, it is well known that this unfolding transformation can cause an exponential blow-up in the size of the rewriting [16,6] (and hence of the repair) and, second, experimental evaluation has shown that it is very time consuming or even impossible to complete within a reasonable amount of time in large and complex TBoxes.

Although normalised rewritings would generally not lead to repairs of the input TBox, as shown next, they do lead to repairs of the *normalised* input TBox, which provides a way to apply repairing even on large and complex TBoxes.

Proposition 1. *Let $\mathcal{T}$ be an OWL 2 DL TBox, let* ans *be an OWL 2 RL system, let* $\mathsf{Rew}' = \mathsf{Rew}'_D \uplus \mathsf{Rew}'_Q$ *be a $\mathcal{T}$-rewriting computed by some query rewriting system, and let $\mathcal{T}'$ be the version of $\mathcal{T}$ that it used to compute* Rew'*, i.e., let $\mathcal{T}'$ be such that for each $\mathcal{A}$ and SPARQL CQ $\mathcal{Q}$* $\mathsf{cert}(\mathcal{Q},\mathcal{T}\cup\mathcal{A}) = \mathsf{cert}(\mathcal{Q},\mathcal{T}'\cup\mathcal{A})$ *and* $\mathsf{cert}(\mathcal{Q},\mathcal{T}'\cup\mathcal{A}) = \mathsf{cert}(\mathsf{Rew}'_Q,\mathsf{Rew}'_D\cup\mathcal{A})$*. Finally, let $\mathcal{R}'$ be the output of* $\textsc{Repair}(\mathcal{T})$ *when* Rew' *is computed at step 1. Then, for every $\mathcal{Q}$ and $\mathcal{A}$ we have* $\mathsf{cert}(\mathcal{Q},\mathcal{T}\cup\mathcal{A}) \subseteq \mathsf{ans}(\mathcal{Q},\mathcal{T}'\cup\mathcal{R}'\cup\mathcal{A})$.

Besides computational efficiency, as shown next, normalised repairs also tend to be smaller in size.

Example 2. Consider the following TBox $\mathcal{T}$ and CQ $\mathcal{Q}$:

$$\mathcal{T} = \{A \sqsubseteq B \sqcap \exists R.(\{o\} \sqcup D), B \sqsubseteq C\} \qquad \mathcal{Q} = Q(x) \leftarrow C(x)$$

Since the first axiom is not in OWL 2 RL we have $\mathcal{T}|_{\mathsf{rl}} = \{B \sqsubseteq C\}$ and hence any OWL 2 RL system ans would be in general incomplete; e.g., for $\mathcal{A} = \{A(a)\}$ we have $\mathsf{cert}(\mathcal{Q},\mathcal{T}|_{\mathsf{rl}}\cup\mathcal{A}) = \emptyset$ while $\mathsf{cert}(\mathcal{Q},\mathcal{T}\cup\mathcal{A}) = \{a\}$. Hence, any repair $\mathcal{R}$ of $\mathcal{T}$ for ans must contain the axiom $A \sqsubseteq C$; then, $\mathsf{cert}(\mathcal{Q},\mathcal{T}|_{\mathsf{rl}}\cup\mathcal{R}\cup\mathcal{A}) = \{a\}$.

However, after normalisation we have $\mathcal{T}' = \{A \sqsubseteq B, A \sqsubseteq \exists R.(\{o\} \sqcup D), B \sqsubseteq C\}$, hence also $\mathcal{T}'|_{\mathsf{lr}} = \{A \sqsubseteq B, B \sqsubseteq C\}$ and thus $\mathsf{ans}(\mathcal{Q},\mathcal{T}'|_{\mathsf{lr}}\cup\mathcal{A}) = \{a\}$. Consequently, the empty set is a repair of $\mathcal{T}'$ for ans. ♢

Unfortunately, the normalised TBox can be quadratically larger than the input TBox. Hence, reasoning over the former and the respective repair might be more time consuming compared to reasoning over the input TBox and the standard repair. Indeed, as our evaluation will show, such repairs should be used only in cases where an unfolded rewriting for a (complex) TBox cannot be computed.

Regarding the efficiency of step 2, as can be seen, this step consists of two loops (the second one of which is quadratic) over the set $\mathcal{R}^1$, in which a number of entailment checks using a fully-fledged OWL 2 DL reasoner are performed. Since the computation of $\mathcal{R}^1$ is based on a $\mathcal{T}$-rewriting Rew, then $\mathcal{R}^1$ can be exponentially larger than $\mathcal{T}$. Hence, despite how optimised an OWL 2 DL reasoner is, the number of entailment checks in large and complex TBoxes would simply be too much for this step to behave well in practice.

Fortunately, its performance can be significantly improved by observing that most parameters in these entailment checks are fixed or rarely changing. More precisely, in both entailment checks the TBox ($\mathcal{T}|_{\mathsf{rl}}$) is always fixed and in the quadratic loop, the axiom α_1 changes only when all entailments $\mathcal{T}|_{\mathsf{rl}} \cup \{\alpha_1\} \models \alpha_2$ for each $\alpha_2 \in \mathcal{R}^1$ have been checked. This can be exploited as follows. First, we can exhaustively apply the calculus of the OWL 2 DL reasoner over $\mathcal{T}|_{\mathsf{rl}}$ and mark the completion of the execution. Then, in the first case, we can check $\mathcal{T}|_{\mathsf{rl}} \models \alpha$ by resuming the execution from the previous point while, in the second case, the same strategy can be followed for $\mathcal{T}|_{\mathsf{rl}} \cup \{\alpha_1\}$ and each check $\mathcal{T}|_{\mathsf{rl}} \cup \{\alpha_1\} \models \alpha_2$. As we will see, this strategy leads to significant time savings.

Finally, we note that similar observations can also be made for the for-loops in step 3. However, due to the minimisations performed in step 2 we expect that the size of the repair at this point is quite small and hence this step should behave well in practice.

5 Supporting Queries With Non-distinguished Variables

Despite the fact that, after repairing, the OWL 2 RL system can answer correctly all SPARQL queries, there are still certain applications where answering queries containing non-distinguished variables is of great importance. For these cases the straightforward approach would be to compute a $(\mathcal{Q}, \mathcal{T})$-rewriting Rew and then use a datalog engine to evaluate Rew over the given dataset $\mathcal{A}$. However, in many cases Rew can be large and complex and hence this process might not scale well in practice, requiring the integration of techniques for minimising and/or simplifying the structure of Rew [14,15]. Although to a great extent successful, these techniques usually depend on the data assuming also additional conditions on them which in some cases might not hold, they so far have been designed to work only over ontologies expressed in rather inexpressive languages (e.g., OWL 2 QL), and they require manual effort to implement and integrate.

Interestingly, repairing can potentially provide the basis for a practical approach to efficiently answer arbitrary CQs. It suffices to observe that $\mathcal{R}$ together with $\mathcal{T}$ capture all ground entailments—that is, for any $(\mathcal{Q}, \mathcal{T})$-rewriting $\mathsf{Rew}_D \uplus \mathsf{Rew}_Q$, any ABox $\mathcal{A}$, and any assertion α such that $\mathcal{T} \cup \mathcal{A} \models \alpha$, we have $\mathsf{Rew}_D \cup \mathcal{A} \models \alpha$ if and only if $\mathcal{T} \cup \mathcal{R} \cup \mathcal{A} \models \alpha$. Hence, we have the following result.

Proposition 2. *Let $\mathcal{T}$ be an OWL 2 DL TBox, let $\mathcal{Q}$ be a CQ, and let* ans *be a query answering system complete for OWL 2 RL. Let also* $\mathsf{Rew}_D \uplus \mathsf{Rew}_Q$ *be a*

$(\mathcal{Q},\mathcal{T})$-rewriting and let $\mathcal{R}$ be a repair of $\mathcal{T}$ for ans. *Then, for every ABox $\mathcal{A}$ we have* $\mathsf{cert}(\mathcal{Q},\mathcal{T}\cup\mathcal{A})\subseteq\mathsf{ans}(\mathsf{Rew}_Q,\mathcal{T}\cup\mathcal{R}\cup\mathcal{A})$.

The previous proposition suggests the following approach to answering queries with non-distinguished:

1. Compute a repair $\mathcal{R}$ of $\mathcal{T}$ for ans using procedure REPAIR.
2. Load the dataset $\mathcal{A}$, the input TBox $\mathcal{T}$, and the repair $\mathcal{R}$ to ans.
3. For a CQ $\mathcal{Q}$ with non-distinguished variables, compute a $(\mathcal{Q},\mathcal{T})$-rewriting $\mathsf{Rew}_D\uplus\mathsf{Rew}_Q$ using any rewriting system and then evaluate Rew_Q using ans.

The above approach has at least three advantages: first, for a TBox $\mathcal{T}$ steps 1 and 2 need to be done *only once* as a pre-processing step; second, Rew_Q is usually expected to be small and simple in structure, hence, step 3 would potentially behave well in practice; and third, the approach is very easy to implement and it can easily exploit any existing and future development in query rewriting and OWL 2 RL systems without requiring to adapt or modify them.

6 Implementation and Evaluation

We have implemented a prototype ontology repair and query answering tool called Hydrowl.[5] The tool uses Rapid [18], a highly-optimised query rewriting system,[6] the OWL 2 DL reasoner HermiT [11], and the OWL 2 RL reasoner OWLim [7].

Regarding whether an unfolded or a normalised rewriting was used at step 1 of REPAIR, our system supports three modes, namely *no-normalisation*, where the rewriting is unfolded as much as possible, *lite-normalisation*, where only some parts are unfolded, and *full-normalisation*, where no unfolding occurs. Furthermore, to implement our incremental optimisation for step 2 we have modified HermiT internally to mark the completion of the application of the calculus and to be able to backtrack to such points after each entailment check.

Regarding experimental evaluation we performed three experiments which we will present next. First, we evaluated how efficiently repairs can be computed in practice by applying our tool over a large ontology corpus containing many challenging ontologies. Second, we loaded some of the repaired ontologies into OWLim to see how much loading is affected by repairing. Since most OWL 2 RL systems perform reasoning during loading then, w.r.t. SPARQL CQs, this reflects the total performance overhead introduced by repairing. Finally, we used the approach illustrated in the previous section to answer queries with non-distinguished variables over a real-world large and complex ontology.

Our test dataset contains 145 ontologies from the Gardiner corpus, a well-known library [5] that consists of many real-world ontologies containing more

[5] `http://www.image.ece.ntua.gr/~gstoil/hydrowl/`

[6] Since Rapid currently supports the DL $\mathcal{ELHI}$, our tool is guaranteed to repair only the $\mathcal{ELHI}$ fragment of an ontology. However, as mentioned, repairing larger fragments is theoretically possible and work towards practical algorithms is ongoing.

than 1000 axioms (we discarded all ontologies for which we either encountered a parsing error or they are expressed in OWL full) and the well-known ontologies FoodWine, UOBM, Propreo, CIDOC-CRM, nci 3.09d, Galen-doctored, and Fly; hence we have a total of 152 ontologies.

All experiments were conducted on an average speed machine (Intel© Core™ 2 Duo E8400 3.00GHz) with 2GB of memory assigned to the JVM.

6.1 Repairing a Large Ontology Corpus

From our 152 ontologies, we managed to compute a repair using no-normalisation for 146 of them, while for the remaining 6 we had to use some of the two normalisation modes (no-normalisation either threw an out of memory exception or after 45 minutes it was still at a very early stage of step 1, hence we aborted). This also verifies in practice that there are ontologies for which completing step 1 of Repair is not trivial and using normalisation is a necessity.

Regarding computation time, all aforementioned 146 ontologies were processed in about 13 minutes with only four requiring more than a minute. More precisely, nci required 251 seconds (the longest time), GO 179 seconds, propreo 155 seconds, and Family 116 seconds. Moreover, only two required more than 10 seconds, namely UOBM which required 16.1 seconds and MadCows which required 10.6 seconds. All other ontologies required less than a couple of seconds and in most cases just a few milliseconds. Hence, we see that for many real-world ontologies repairs can be computed very efficiently in practice.

Regarding the size of the repairs, interestingly for 134 out of the 146 ontologies we computed an empty repair. For the remaining 12 we ran Hydrowl using all normalisation modes in order to investigate on the differences and properties of the different modes. The results are summarised in Table 1 where $|\mathcal{T}|$ denotes the number of axioms of the $\mathcal{ELHI}$ fragment of the input ontology (recall that Hydrowl currently supports $\mathcal{ELHI}$), $|\mathcal{T}'|$ the number of axioms of the normalised ontology, t the computation time in seconds, $|\mathcal{R}|$ the number of axioms of the repair, the columns denoted by $\sqsubseteq$, $\sqcap$, and $\exists$, denote how many axioms of the form $A \sqsubseteq B$, $A \sqcap B \sqsubseteq C$, and $\exists R.C \sqsubseteq B$, respectively the repair has, 'd' the maximum depth encountered in axioms of the form $\exists R.C \sqsubseteq B$, and Inv the number of inverse object properties in $\mathcal{R}$. The results for each ontology are split into three lines which correspond to no-, light-, and full-normalisation, respectively; we do not present results for full-normalisation over Koala, FoodWine, mindswappers, and Family since lite-normalisation computed an empty repair.

From the table we can observe that in general repairs are rather small and simple and usually contain axioms of the first two forms, however, only half of them contain only axioms of the form $A \sqsubseteq B$; hence, previous approaches [20,13,8] that mainly classify the input are indeed going to miss answers in many practical cases. The most complex repair was computed for propreo using no-normalisation which was the only ontology where a depth of 2 in axioms of the form $\exists R.C \sqsubseteq B$ was observed. Moreover, we note that normalisation usually doubles the size of the ontology which is better than a quadratic increase, however, it is noticeable.

Table 1. Results for the 12 ontologies with non-empty repairs

$\mathcal{T}$	$\vert\mathcal{T}\vert$	$\vert\mathcal{T}'\vert$	t	$\vert\mathcal{R}\vert$	$\sqsubseteq$	$\sqcap$	$\exists$	Inv	d	$\mathcal{T}$	$\vert\mathcal{T}\vert$	$\vert\mathcal{T}'\vert$	t	$\vert\mathcal{R}\vert$	$\sqsubseteq$	$\sqcap$	$\exists$	Inv	d
			1.7										0.9						
mged-1	449	456	1.4	2	2	0	0	0	0	CopyRight	193	266	1.2	3	3	0	0	0	0
			0.8										0.6						
			0.8										3.2	1	1	0	0	0	0
mged-2	407	415	0.9	1	1	0	0	0	0	PeoplePets	53	130	1.3	19	16	0	3	0	1
			0.6										0.7	18	18	0	0	0	0
			3.1	4	0	1	3	1	1				10.6	13	12	0	1	1	1
Travel	48	68	0.2	3	0	3	0	0	0	MadCows	48	129	0.3	15	12	0	3	0	1
			0.2	2	2	0	0	0	0				0.5	15	15	0	0	0	0
Koala	22	31	2.2	2	0	0	2	1	1	FoodWine	166	212	5.6	1	1	0	0	0	0
			0.1	0	-	-	-	-	-				2.6	0	-	-	-	-	-
			155.1	15	0	0	15	18	2				16.1	9	5	1	3	1	1
Propreo	450	715	4.3	2	2	0	0	0	0	UOBM	118	161	0.5	6	6	0	0	0	0
			1.4	2	2	0	0	0	0				0.3	6	6	0	0	0	0
Mindsw.	101	125	0.5	1	0	0	1	1	2	Family	48	95	116.4	13	13	0	0	0	0
			0.2	0	-	-	-	-	-				1.4	0	-	-	-	-	-

Finally, repairs computed using normalisation are usually smaller and simpler as they rarely contain axioms of the form $\exists R.C \sqsubseteq B$.

For the cases where using different modes of our tool has yielded differences in the repairs (e.g., differences with respect to size) we have performed a further analysis. More precisely, for each of the axioms of each repair, we extracted a justification—that is, a minimal subset $\mathcal{J} \subseteq \mathcal{T}$ such that $\mathcal{J} \models \alpha$, and we have manually examined them to get an insight about their differences. In the following we present our conclusions for some interesting cases.

Interestingly, in FoodWine the no-normalisation mode computed a repair containing a single axiom while the two normalisation modes computed an empty repair. The additional axiom computed was $\alpha = \mathsf{WhiteNonSweetWine} \sqsubseteq \mathsf{PotableLiquid}$ and its justification consisted of the following axioms:

$$\begin{aligned}\mathsf{WhiteNonSweetWine} &\equiv \mathsf{WhiteWine} \sqcap \exists \mathsf{hasSugar}.\{dry, offDry\}\\ \mathsf{WhiteWine} &\equiv \mathsf{Wine} \sqcap \exists \mathsf{hasColor}.\{white\}\\ \mathsf{Wine} &\sqsubseteq \mathsf{PotableLiquid}\end{aligned}$$

Consequently, the reasons for the observed differences are similar to those highlighted in Example 2—that is, since concept $\{dry, offDry\}$ is outside OWL 2 RL, then the TBox $\mathcal{T}|_{\mathsf{rl}}$ will not contain the first axiom which is important for deducing α. In contrast, in the normalised TBox $\mathcal{T}'$ the former axiom is transformed (amongst others) to $\mathsf{WhiteNonSweetWine} \sqsubseteq \mathsf{WhiteWine}$ which is in OWL 2 RL and hence for the OWL 2 RL fragment of $\mathcal{T}'$ we have $\mathcal{T}'|_{\mathsf{rl}} \models \alpha$. Consequently, in the first case the repair contains α while in the latter it doesn't. Similar observations can also be made for Koala, mindswapper, Family, for the

Table 2. Results for the ontologies that can only be processed using normalisation.

$\mathcal{T}$	$\lvert\mathcal{T}\rvert$	$\lvert\mathcal{T}'\rvert$	mode	t'	t	$\lvert\mathcal{R}\rvert$	$\sqsubseteq$	$\sqcap$	$\exists$	d
DOLCE-lt	260	350	lite		9.0	0	-	-	-	-
xobjects	264	1087	lite		13.1	0	-	-	-	-
Not-Galen	5471	10967	full	1706	298(42)	3015(4153)	3015	0	0	0
Galen	4229	8559	full	1157	257(24)	3012(3062)	2667	345	0	0
Galen-doc	4229	8763	full	3427	1152(28)	6051(6176)	3743	1412	896	1
Fly	19845	24594	full	13758	2884(178)	10361(12368)	10361	0	0	0

13 additional axioms computed for propreo, and for the 3 additional axioms computed for UOBM by the no-normalisation mode.

Another noteworthy case is observed in PeoplePets where the repair computed using no-normalisation contains a single axiom while the repairs in both normalisation modes many more. One extra axiom in the two normalisation modes is $\mathsf{OldLady} \sqsubseteq \mathsf{CatOwner}$ and its justification is the following:

$$\mathsf{OldLady} \sqsubseteq \exists \mathsf{hasPet.Animal} \sqcap \forall \mathsf{hasPet.Cat}$$
$$\mathsf{CatOwner} \equiv \exists \mathsf{hasPet.Cat}$$

Although, the first axiom contains an existential restriction and hence is outside OWL 2 RL, we concluded that when there is a pair of axioms of the form $A \sqsubseteq \exists R.C \sqcap \forall R.D$ and $\exists R.D \sqsubseteq B$, OWLim is able to deduce that $A \sqsubseteq B$. In contrast, in the normalised ontology the first axiom in the justification is split into $\mathsf{OldLady} \sqsubseteq \exists \mathsf{hasPet.Animal}$ and $\mathsf{OldLady} \sqsubseteq \forall \mathsf{hasPet.Animal}$, then the former is discarded and hence the interaction is not identified. Indeed, we have verified our speculations using two small tests. Similar observations also apply to the discrepancies observed in the MadCows ontology. Consequently, besides increasing the completeness of an OWL 2 RL reasoner normalisation can in some rare cases also decrease it and hence force repairs to be larger.

Finally, Table 2 presents the results for the 6 challenging ontologies, where all columns are like in Table 1 with the addition of column 'mode', which denotes which normalisation mode was used, and column 't'', which denotes the time to compute a repair without our optimisations for step 2. As can be seen, even for these very challenging ontologies we were able to compute a repair in a fairly reasonable amount of time given the size and complexity of each ontology. This is mostly due to normalisation and our optimisation for step 2 which as shown by contrasting columns 't'' and 't' makes a large difference in practice. Moreover, due to the size and complexity of these ontologies the computed repairs are quite large (about half the size of the input ontology), however, they are usually simple in structure (an exception being Galen-doc) and are never exponentially large.

It is also interesting to note that most of the computation time was spent in the second part of step 2 (the quadratic loop). In columns 't' and $|\mathcal{R}|$ in parenthesis we give the computation time and the size of the repair after executing only step 1 and the first part of step 2, discarding its second phase. As can be seen these steps are completed in a matter of seconds and the respective repairs are not much larger than the optimal one. As we will see next, using these non-optimal repairs does not seem to have a huge difference in practice.

6.2 Loading Under the Presence of Repairs

From our ontology dataset we selected the Fly ontology which comes with an ABox containing more than 6,000 assertions and UOBM for which there exists a data generator[7] that can be used to generate ABoxes of arbitrary size. For these ontologies we load the TBox with and without the repair together with ABoxes of varying size and measure the time that OWLim requires to load the data.

We used the UOBM data generator to generate ABoxes for 1, 2, 5, 10, and 20 universities. Then, we loaded them to OWLim using the original ontology and two repaired versions of UOBM, one computed using no-normalisation and one computed using lite-normalisation. Table 3(a) presents the results where UOBM$'\cup\mathcal{R}'$ denotes the normalised ontology and the repair computed using lite-normalisation. As we can see, repairing does introduce some additional overhead, however, this is relatively small (loading UOBM$\cup\mathcal{R}$ was at most 50% slower than without the repair). The penalty when using UOBM$'\cup\mathcal{R}'$ was much larger, which suggests that normalisation should be used mainly when unfolded rewritings cannot be computed. Moreover, we have tested the completeness of OWLim for the 13 test queries of UOBM.[8] When using the original ontology OWLim was found incomplete for three of them, while when we also loaded the repairs it computed the same answers as HermiT and Pellet for all of them.

Regarding Fly, we have replicated the original ABox up to 5 times.[9] Table 3(b) shows the loading time for each ABox using the original ontology and two repairs, the minimal one ($\mathcal{R}$) computed after completing all steps of Repair and a non-minimal one ($\mathcal{R}^-$) computed discarding the second phase of step 2. As can be seen, in contrast to UOBM, there is a relatively significant increase in loading time which reflects the size and complexity of Fly. However, since loading is performed only once and, as we will see in the next section, despite the high expressivity of this ontology afterwards we are able to compute all answers to user queries in a matter of milliseconds, we feel that this penalty is worth it. Moreover, interestingly, using the non-minimal instead of the minimal repair does not seem to make a large difference in practice. Hence, this suggests that one could perhaps completely dispense with the second phase of step 2 if this takes a considerable amount of time in the computation of a repair.

6.3 Evaluating Hybrid Query Answering

The Fly ontology comes with five real-world queries, four of which contain non-distinguished variables. As illustrated in Section 5, to compute answers for them,

[7] `http://www.cs.ox.ac.uk/isg/tools/UOBMGenerator/`

[8] The UOBM benchmark has two more test queries but computing answers for them requires reasoning over constructors which Hydrowl does not support yet.

[9] To the best of our knowledge, no better method to 'scale-up' an ABox exists.

Table 3. Loading times for Fly and UOBM for the various ABoxes

	1	2	5	10	20
UOBM	4.1	6.8	16.2	31.9	73.2
UOBM$\cup\mathcal{R}$	4.4	8.3	24.3	44.9	108.1
UOBM$'\cup\mathcal{R}'$	5.6	13.0	40.0	98.9	276.9

(a) UOBM

	$\mathcal{A}_1$	$\mathcal{A}_2$	$\mathcal{A}_3$	$\mathcal{A}_4$	$\mathcal{A}_5$
Fly	14.0	21.9	22.7	27.9	31.5
Fly$\cup\mathcal{R}$	31.9	55.1	68.5	93.0	119.3
Fly$\cup\mathcal{R}^-$	33.2	62.1	70.1	100.6	118.2

(b) Fly

Table 4. Results for Answering the Fly Queries

$\mathcal{Q}_1$			$\mathcal{Q}_2$			$\mathcal{Q}_3$			$\mathcal{Q}_4$			$\mathcal{Q}_5$		
$\lvert\mathsf{R}_Q\rvert$	t_{rew}	t_{ans}	$\lvert\mathsf{R}_Q\rvert$	t_{rew}	t_{ans}	$\lvert\mathsf{R}_Q\rvert$	t_{rew}	t_{ans}	$\lvert\mathsf{R}_Q\rvert$	t_{rew}	t_{ans}	$\lvert\mathsf{R}_Q\rvert$	t_{rew}	t_{ans}
64	0.31	0.31	2880	0.90	1.28	1	0.00	0.00	91	0.07	0.04	6	0.05	0.02

we first loaded Fly together with its repair and the ABox to OWLim and then for each query we computed a $(\mathcal{Q},\mathcal{T})$-rewriting Rew using Rapid and evaluated only its UCQ part over the initialised OWLim. Table 4 presents the size of the UCQ part of the rewriting (R_Q), the time Rapid required to compute it (t_{rew}), and the time OWLim required to evaluate it over the loaded ontology, repair, and data (t_{ans}).

As we can see the results are highly promising. In most cases we can compute and evaluate a rewriting almost instantaneously with the exception of query $\mathcal{Q}_2$ where, due to the large size of R_Q, it required around two seconds; still a small number though. Furthermore, our system computed the *same* answers as the ones reported in [21] (i.e., all the correct answers) even though, interestingly, the Fly ontology is expressed in the highly expressive DL $\mathcal{SRI}$. All in all, computing a non-optimal repair, loading it into OWLim together with the original Fly TBox and ABox, loading Fly on Rapid and, finally, computing the answers for all 5 queries required a total of 233.2 seconds (computing the repair required 178 seconds, loading into OWLim and Rapid around 48.2 seconds and computing and evaluating all rewritings over OWLim around 7 seconds). In contrast, as mentioned in [21,22], over a much faster machine than the one used here, HermiT requires several hours to compute the answers, while the approach proposed in [21,22] requires 657 seconds to pre-process the Fly ontology and an average of 117 seconds *per* query to compute the answers.

7 Conclusions

In this paper we investigate on ontology repairing for OWL 2 RL reasoners as a practical approach to scalable (and complete) ontology-based data access. First, we revisit our previous implementation and propose novel optimisations for its two complex and time consuming steps, namely steps 1 and 2, in order to be able to cope with large and complex ontologies. More precisely, for step 1 we show how datalog rewritings (which can be computed efficiently by state-of-the-art rewriting systems) can be used to compute repairs, while, for step 2 we show how the internals of an OWL 2 DL reasoner can be changed in order to avoid repeating much of the necessary work. Second, we push the envelope of ontology repairing by showing how we can also support queries containing non-distinguished variables by integrating query rewriting with (repaired) OWL 2 RL systems. Our techniques have many advantages as they delegate most of the hard work to a pre-processing step (i.e., computing the repairs and loading everything to the OWL 2 RL system) that can be performed only once and leave for on-line processing either the task of simply matching the query to the data (case of SPARQL CQs) or computing the UCQ part of a rewriting and matching that over the data (case of non-distinguished variables). Moreover, our approach is easy to implement and reuses existing technology without any internal modifications (only HermiT was modified for the goal of further optimising it).

Finally, our experimental evaluation has provided with very promising results. First, we were able to compute repairs very efficiently (in a matter of milliseconds) for the vast majority of ontologies and even able to process large and complex ones in a reasonable amount of time (in less than 1 hour). Since for a fixed or rarely changing ontology computing repairs is performed mostly once as a pre-processing step we feel that this is a tolerable time. Even more, our results suggest that the most expensive step of the repair computation procedure can possibly be discarded, in which case repairs even for large ontologies can be computed in a matter of seconds. Second, our experiments also showed that loading the repair in addition to the standard input provides with an additional overhead only in very large ontologies (e.g., Fly) while in UOBM the penalty was fairly unimportant. Still, even in large ontologies, if we take into account that loading is performed mostly once and that, after repairing, the OWL 2 RL system is indistinguishable from OWL 2 DL reasoners w.r.t. SPARQL queries we feel that this extra overhead is worth paying for. Finally, with respect to queries containing non-distinguished variables, we were able to compute all the correct answers to the queries of the Fly ontology almost instantaneously although Fly is expressed in the highly expressive DL $\mathcal{SRI}$. To the best of our knowledge, no other system can match these times.

Regarding directions for future work we plan to extend our implementation to support more expressive fragments of OWL like Horn-$\mathcal{SHIQ}$ [4] or even non-Horn fragments of OWL [3] and conduct further experiments. This is far from trivial as, to the best of our knowledge, algorithms for computing rewritings in such languages either do not exist or have not shown to scale over large and complex ontologies.

Acknowledgements. The work was funded by a Marie Curie FP7-Reintegration-Grant within EU's 7th Framework Programme (2007-2013) under REA grant agreement 303914 and by project Europeana Fashion within EU's Competitiveness and Innovation Framework Programme under grant agreement 297167. We would also like to thank Yujiao Zhou for providing fly_anatomy and its queries.

References

1. Baader, F., McGuinness, D., Nardi, D., Patel-Schneider, P.F.: The Description Logic Handbook: Theory, implementation and applications. Cambridge University Press (2002)
2. Calvanese, D., De Giacomo, G., Lembo, D., Lenzerini, M., Rosati, R.: Tractable reasoning and efficient query answering in description logics: The DL-Lite family. J. of Autom Reas 39(3), 385–429 (2007)
3. Grau, B.C., Motik, B., Stoilos, G., Horrocks, I.: Computing datalog rewritings beyond horn ontologies. In: Proceedings of the Twenty-Third International Joint Conference on Artificial Intelligence, IJCAI 2013 (2013)
4. Eiter, T., Ortiz, M., Simkus, M., Tran, T.-K., Xiao, G.: Query rewriting for Horn-$\mathcal{SHIQ}$ plus rules. In: Proc. of AAAI (2012)
5. Gardiner, T., Tsarkov, D., Horrocks, I.: Framework for an automated comparison of description logic reasoners. In: Cruz, I., Decker, S., Allemang, D., Preist, C., Schwabe, D., Mika, P., Uschold, M., Aroyo, L.M. (eds.) ISWC 2006. LNCS, vol. 4273, pp. 654–667. Springer, Heidelberg (2006)
6. Kikot, S., Kontchakov, R., Podolskii, V.V., Zakharyaschev, M.: Long rewritings, short rewritings. In: Proc. of DL (2012)
7. Kiryakov, A., Bishoa, B., Ognyanoff, D., Peikov, I., Tashev, Z., Velkov, R.: The Features of BigOWLIM that Enabled the BBCs World Cup Website. In: Workshop on Semantic Data Management, SemData (2010)
8. Meditskos, G., Bassiliades, N.: Combining a DL reasoner and a rule engine for improving entailment-based OWL reasoning. In: Sheth, A.P., Staab, S., Dean, M., Paolucci, M., Maynard, D., Finin, T., Thirunarayan, K. (eds.) ISWC 2008. LNCS, vol. 5318, pp. 277–292. Springer, Heidelberg (2008)
9. Motik, B.: Description Logics and Disjunctive Datalog—More Than just a Fleeting Resemblance?. In: Proc. of M4M-4, vol. 194, pp. 246–265 (2005)
10. Motik, B., Horrocks, I., Kim, S.M.: Delta-Reasoner: A Semantic Web Reasoner for an Intelligent Mobile Platform. In: Proceedings of the 21st International World Wide Web Conference (WWW 2012), pp. 63–72 (2012)
11. Motik, B., Shearer, R., Horrocks, I.: Hypertableau Reasoning for Description Logics. Journal of Artificial Intelligence Research 36, 165–228 (2009)
12. Ortiz, M., Calvanese, D., Eiter, T.: Data complexity of query answering in expressive description logics via tableaux. Journal of Automated Reasoning 41(1), 61–98 (2008)
13. Pan, Z., Zhang, X., Heflin, J.: DLDB2: A scalable multi-perspective semantic web repository. In: Proc. International Conference on Web Intelligence and Intelligent Agent Technology, WI-IAT 2008, pp. 489–495 (2008)
14. Rodriguez-Muro, M., Calvanese, D.: Dependencies: Making ontology based data access work. In: Proc. of AMW 2011 (2011)
15. Rosati, R.: Prexto: Query Rewriting under Extensional Constraints in $DL - Lite$. In: Simperl, E., Cimiano, P., Polleres, A., Corcho, O., Presutti, V. (eds.) ESWC 2012. LNCS, vol. 7295, pp. 360–374. Springer, Heidelberg (2012)
16. Rosati, R., Almatelli, A.: Improving query answering over DL-Lite ontologies. In: Proc. of KR 2010 (2010)
17. Stoilos, G., Cuenca Grau, B., Motik, B., Horrocks, I.: Repairing ontologies for incomplete reasoners. In: Aroyo, L., Welty, C., Alani, H., Taylor, J., Bernstein, A., Kagal, L., Noy, N., Blomqvist, E. (eds.) ISWC 2011, Part I. LNCS, vol. 7031, pp. 681–696. Springer, Heidelberg (2011)

18. Trivela, D., Stoilos, G., Chortaras, A., Stamou, G.: Optimising resolution-based rewriting algorithms for DL ontologies. In: Proceedings of the 26th Workshop on Description Logics, DL 2013 (2013)
19. Wu, Z., Eadon, G., Das, S., Chong, E.I., Kolovski, V., Annamalai, M., Srinivasan, J.: Implementing an inference engine for RDFS/OWL constructs and user-defined rules in oracle. In: Proc. of ICDE, pp. 1239–1248. IEEE (2008)
20. Zhou, J., Ma, L., Liu, Q., Zhang, L., Yu, Y., Pan, Y.: Minerva: A scalable OWL ontology storage and inference system. In: Mizoguchi, R., Shi, Z.-Z., Giunchiglia, F. (eds.) ASWC 2006. LNCS, vol. 4185, pp. 429–443. Springer, Heidelberg (2006)
21. Zhou, Y., Grau, B.C., Horrocks, I., Wu, Z., Banerjee, J.: Making the most of your triple store: Query answering in owl 2 using an rl reasoner. In: Proc. WWW 2013, pp. 1569–1580 (2013)
22. Zhou, Y., Nenov, Y., Cuenca Grau, B., Horrocks, I.: Complete query answering over horn ontologies using a triple store. In: Alani, H., et al. (eds.) ISWC 2013, Part I. LNCS, vol. 8218, pp. 720–736. Springer, Heidelberg (2013)

Dedalo: Looking for Clusters Explanations in a Labyrinth of Linked Data

Ilaria Tiddi, Mathieu d'Aquin, and Enrico Motta

Knowledge Media Institute
The Open University, United Kingdom
{ilaria.tiddi,mathieu.daquin,enrico.motta}@open.ac.uk

Abstract. We present Dedalo, a framework which is able to exploit Linked Data to generate explanations for clusters. In general, any result of a Knowledge Discovery process, including clusters, is interpreted by human experts who use their background knowledge to explain them. However, for someone without such expert knowledge, those results may be difficult to understand. Obtaining a complete and satisfactory explanation becomes a laborious and time-consuming process, involving expertise in possibly different domains. Having said so, not only does the Web of Data contain vast amounts of such background knowledge, but it also natively connects those domains. While the efforts put in the interpretation process can be reduced with the support of Linked Data, how to automatically access the right piece of knowledge in such a big space remains an issue. Dedalo is a framework that dynamically traverses Linked Data to find commonalities that form explanations for items of a cluster. We have developed different strategies (or heuristics) to guide this traversal, reducing the time to get the best explanation. In our experiments, we compare those strategies and demonstrate that Dedalo finds relevant and sophisticated Linked Data explanations from different areas.

Keywords: #eswc2014Tiddi, Linked Data, Hypothesis Generation, Knowledge Discovery.

1 Introduction

When running a Knowledge Discovery (KD) process, the last step usually consists in interpreting the results (sometimes called "patterns") that have been extracted from data during the data mining step. In most real-world scenarios, those results are given to experts that, with their background knowledge, analyse and give them their own interpretation. However, if given to someone without such expertise, the results would hardly be understandable. Also, additional knowledge from domains that the expert might not be aware of could affect the quality of the interpretation. This makes the interpretation process laborious, manual and time-consuming.

With that said, the Web of Data links datasets of different areas using RDF standards, making sources of knowledge accessible (and interpretable) by machines. With the amount of information shared through Linked Data, it should

V. Presutti et al. (Eds.): ESWC 2014, LNCS 8465, pp. 333–348, 2014.

therefore be possible to find common characteristics (properties) of the items of a cluster that significantly distinguish them from others, therefore forming hypotheses for the explanation of their grouping. In this scenario, it is clear that the major issue consists of deciding which is the correct piece of knowledge to look at first, in order to quickly find a plausible explanation and not get lost in the Linked Data web.

One of our use-cases consists of coherent clusters obtained through applying Network Partitioning to the co-authorship graph of academic researchers of the same department. While someone familiar with such a department, given those clusters, would explain them saying that each cluster corresponds to a group working on similar topics, someone without such knowledge would find the clusters meaningless. One might require even more background knowledge to state that researchers of the same cluster have worked on projects led by the same person. Our assumption is that, Linked Data can be used to give such explanations. In this scenario, the major issue is to access the right information (research topics of academics, project memberships, etc.) in the Linked Data cloud, assuming of course that such knowledge is herein represented, to find relevant explanations in a short time.

In this paper, we present Dedalo, a framework that, based on a subfield of Machine Learning (Inductive Logic Programming [15]), automatically provides explanations for clusters using Linked Data. When given a set of clusters, Dedalo traverses Linked Data in order to find the best explanation. We used different strategies (or heuristic scoring measures of the properties to inspect) to guide this traversal and in the experiments section we present an evaluation of their performance.

2 Foundations and Related Work

Hypothesis Generation. Hypothesis generation is defined as "*the pre-decisional process by which it is possible to formulate explanations and beliefs regarding the occurrences observed in a specific environment*" [20]. Systems presented in the literature can be classified according to different dimensions: (i) manual or automatic, (ii) domain-specific or domain-independent and (iii) ontology- or Linked Data-driven. In the past, ontologies revealed their usefulness for automatically generating hypotheses; however, this has been mostly shown in specific contexts, e.g. medical computer science or biology, where systems such as Adam, Eira or HyBrow [7,12,19] have used OWL reasoning and first-order logic to automatically derive explanations. Hypothesis generation is also the last step of the KD process (sometimes called "data post-processing"), where results obtained from the data mining step are interpreted and refined to start a new iteration on the data. Attempts at using ontologies to produce explanations for KD results (clusters or association rules) can be found in [1,8,11]. While [1] describes a domain-specific but automatic process, [8,11] are domain-independent but require the experts to manually validate the generated hypotheses.

In this context, our first challenge is to produce an automatic, domain-independent process to generate hypotheses.

Assumption 1. *Given a set of clusters* $\mathcal{C}=\{\mathcal{C}_0, \mathcal{C}_1, \ldots, \mathcal{C}_n\}$ *extracted from a set of items* $\mathcal{R}=\{r_0, ..., r_m\}$ *(where* $\mathcal{C}_i \subseteq \mathcal{R}$*), there exists a set of explanations* $\mathcal{H}_i = \{h_0, ..., h_j\}$ *coming from some background knowledge* $\mathcal{B}$ *for each* $\mathcal{C}_i \in \mathcal{C}$.

Linked Data for Hypothesis Generation. The potential of Linked Data for accessing cross-disciplinary linked knowledge is shown in research which uses them to generate hypotheses starting from semi-structured data (such as web tables or statistics) [16,17,24]. The importance of selecting the correct background knowledge in order to reduce the computational efforts required by the process emerges from that research line. In the KD field, frameworks for analysing data mining results still select the background knowledge from Linked Data manually, such as in [2,3,18,23]. Following this research line, our second challenge is to automatically select the background knowledge from Linked Data to produce explanations.

Assumption 2. *Given a cluster* $\mathcal{C}_i \in \mathcal{C}$*, Linked Data contains enough connected knowledge to produce a set of explanations* $\mathcal{H}_i$ *for each* $\mathcal{C}_i \in \mathcal{C}$.

Automatic Hypothesis Generation. The automatic generation of hypotheses has been investigated in a field at the intersection of Machine Learning and Logic Programming, called Inductive Logic Programming (ILP, which first appeared in [15]). ILP constructs first-order logic clausal theories (as in Logic Programming) starting from a set of positive and negative examples (as in Machine Learning). To derive those theories, or hypotheses, ILP applies reasoning upon some background knowledge about the examples (both positive and negative).

For example, imagine we want to automatically learn "why someone attends ESWC": `attendsESWC(X)`. In Table 1, the examples show who is participating in ESWC (e^+), and who is not (e^-). In the background knowledge, some more information about those examples is given. While one can see that all the examples submitted a paper to ESWC, only two of them had their paper accepted. So, in order to go to ESWC, a person will have to have submitted a paper but also have it accepted:

Table 1. An example of the ILP framework

	Examples	Background Knowledge
e^+	`attendsESWC(MathieuDAquin).`	`submitted(MathieuDAquin).` `submitted(EnricoMotta).`
e^+	`attendsESWC(VanessaLopez).`	`submitted(VanessaLopez).`
e^-	`attendsESWC(EnricoMotta).`	`acceptedPaper(MathieuDAquin,'ESWC').` `acceptedPaper(VanessaLopez,'ESWC').`

```
goesToESWC(X) <- submitted(X)∧paperAccepted(X,'ESWC')
```

Lately, ontologies have attracted the interests of several researchers in this area, as they see the formalised knowledge of ontologies as a possible support to build the background knowledge for ILP. A survey of systems exploiting ontologies in ILP is presented in [10]. Similarly, other works have combined Logic Programming and ontologies in the field of Description Logic Programming [6,13] and Onto-Relational Learning [9].

While no work (other than our first attempt reported in [22]) in the ILP field seems so far to have taken into consideration the Linked Data potential, we consider Linked Data a promising set of resources to help the automatic building of the ILP background knowledge. Given our second assumption, our third challenge is to automatically build the background knowledge of an ILP process using Linked Data.

Assumption 3. *Given a set $\mathcal{C}^+$ of positive examples (where $\mathcal{C}^+ \subseteq \mathcal{R}$ and $\mathcal{C}^+ \in \mathcal{C}$) which we want to find explanations for, a set of negative examples (the remaining clusters of $\mathcal{C}$: $\mathcal{C}^- = \mathcal{R} \setminus \mathcal{C}^+$), we can use Linked Data as background knowledge $\mathcal{B}$ to find explanations about $\mathcal{C}^+$.*

However, using the full Linked Data graph as background knowledge in an ILP process is obviously unfeasible because of the time and computational costs it would imply, while most of this knowledge would certainly be irrelevant. It is then necessary to detect and select only the salient information for our background knowledge. Hence, in our ILP-based framework, we have to focus on finding a clever heuristic to guide the traversal of Linked Data and select relevant background knowledge for generating explanations of the cluster in hand.

3 Dedalo's Framework

Dedalo is conceived as a graph-search process. Here, Linked Data are considered a graph of resources and properties (respectively nodes and edges) and traversed to collect candidate hypotheses about the items $r_i \in \mathcal{R}$, that are used as roots of the graph. Our intuition is that, given a subset of items $r_i \in \mathcal{R}$, there are *paths* (i.e. chains of property assertions) and an end value they have in common: this is how we define a *hypothesis*. We can then assume that when items in the same cluster $\mathcal{C}_i$ share a hypothesis more commonly than items outside the cluster, then that hypothesis constitutes an explanation for $\mathcal{C}_i$.

Path. *A chain of RDF properties defined as* $\mathfrak{p}=\langle p_0 \rightarrow p_1 \rightarrow ... \rightarrow p_n \rangle$.
Hypothesis. *A path* $\mathfrak{p}$ *and an end value* v_i, *defined as* $h_i = \langle \mathfrak{p}.v_i \rangle$.

As our objective is to find the best hypotheses, the graph needs to be iteratively traversed. A complete iteration consists of (see Fig. 1 for an overview):

1. URI Expansion, to resolve a Linked Data entity;
2. Path Extraction, to know which path of the graph leads to a given entity;
3. Path Ranking, to choose the best path to use in the following iteration;
4. Path Values Selection, to select the values of a path that will be further explored;
5. Hypotheses Evaluation, to extract and rank the hypotheses found at the current iteration.

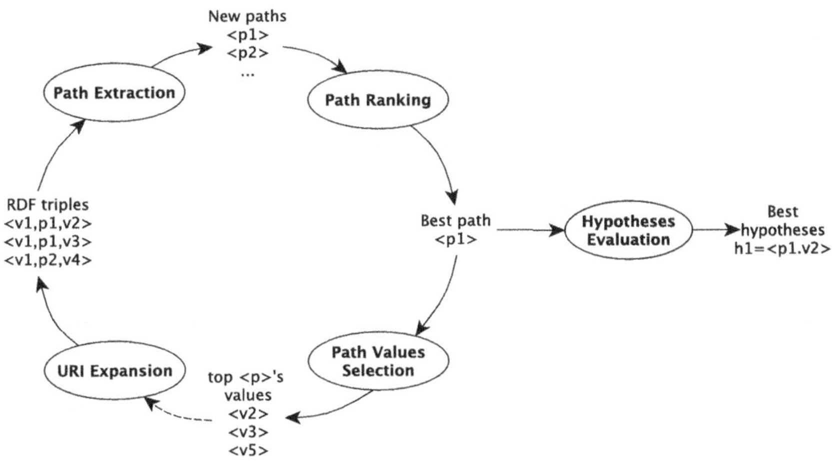

Fig. 1. Overview of Dedalo's structure

Within a new iteration, two scenarios are possible: (i) we find a better hypothesis, which explains more items $r_i \in \mathcal{C}^+$ than the previous one, or (ii) no better hypotheses are found, and therefore we still consider the current hypothesis as the best one. In other words, by augmenting the time of the traversal, results can only increase in quality. Therefore, Dedalo can be considered an **anytime process**.

As already introduced in the previous section, it becomes clear that, being limited in time and computational resources, a complete graph traversal is not conceivable. Moreover, in an ample space such as Linked Data connected through the `<owl:sameAs>` predicates, the number of paths to follow increases exponentially. This is why we developed several heuristics in order to find the one that was able to predict the most promising path to follow, optimising the process of quickly finding the best hypotheses.

3.1 Algorithm

This section presents the components of Dedalo. For a better understanding of our framework, we will use the graph given in Fig. 2 as an example.

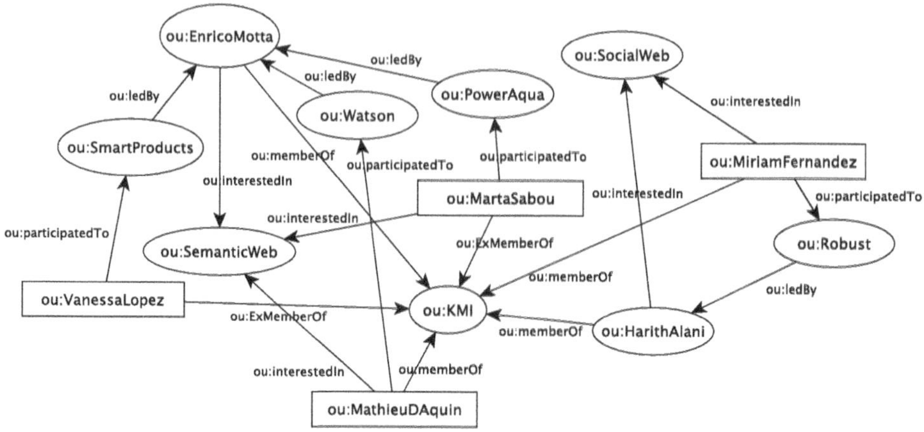

Fig. 2. Graph example using a group of academic researchers. Items in rectangles are the roots of the graph: $r_i \in \mathcal{R}$.

1 – URI Expansion. Given a resource, we resolve its URIs and collect all the property-value pairs $<p_i.v_i>$ from the RDF entity description. For instance, we resolve the resource `<ou:MathieuDAquin>` and extract the couples `<ou:memberOf.ou:KMI>` and `<ou:participatedTo.ou:Watson>`.

2 – Path Extraction. We detect which is the path that has led us to a given resource (which means, detecting which depth of the graph we have reached). As we already defined a path as a sequence of properties, $\mathfrak{p}=\langle p_0 \rightarrow p_1 \rightarrow ... \rightarrow p_n \rangle$, in the case we reached the resource `<ou:EnricoMotta>`, $\mathfrak{p}$=⟨ou:participatedIn → ou:ledBy⟩. A path $\mathfrak{p}$ has also the following properties:

$||\mathfrak{p}||$ – the number of properties composing it, showing how deep we descended in the graph. In the current example, $||\mathfrak{p}||=2$.

roots$(\mathfrak{p})$ – the set of roots that share this same path. As the three root items `<ou:MathieuDAquin>`, `<ou:MartaSabou>` and `<ou:VanessaLopez>` are all followed by $\mathfrak{p}$, $|roots(\mathfrak{p})|=3$.

vals$(\mathfrak{p})$ – the set of ending values the path can have. In the current example, $|vals(\mathfrak{p})|=2$ because both `<ou:EnricoMotta>` and `<ou:HarithAlani>` are ending values of $\mathfrak{p}$.

Each detected $\mathfrak{p}$ is added to the list of paths to be ranked further ($add(\mathfrak{p}, paths)$).

3 – Path Ranking. To deepen the graph exploration to collect new hypotheses, we need to choose the best path to follow before starting a new iteration. The set of paths discovered at that moment are therefore ranked according to one of the strategies we have defined (presented in the next subsection). In our example, we will have to establish whether we want to follow $\mathfrak{p}_1$=⟨ou:memberOf⟩ or $\mathfrak{p}_2$ = ⟨ou:participatedIn→ou:ledBy⟩.

4 – Paths Values Selection. Once the best path is chosen, its values $vals(\mathfrak{p})$ are expanded (as in step 1), and new (longer) paths are collected (as in step 2). If we chose to follow $\mathfrak{p}_2$, the next values to expand will be `<ou:EnricoMotta>` and `<ou:HarithAlani>`. By iteratively expanding those values and collecting new paths, we deepen the search in the Linked Data graph: this process is defined as "the Linked Data traversal", and it is detailed in the function in Algorithm 1.

Algorithm 1. Linked Data traversal

```
function TRAVERSELINKEDDATA(uris)
    for uri in uris do
        newValues ← expandURI(uri)                    ▷ step 1
    end for
    for value in newValues do
        newPath ← extractPath(value)                  ▷ step 2
        if newPath not in paths then
            add(newPath, paths)
        end if
    end for
end function
```

5 – Hypotheses Evaluation. This step is composed of two parts. At a first stage (called $hypos(\mathfrak{p})$), given the best $\mathfrak{p}$, we extract the hypotheses we can derive from it, by chaining it to its end values $vals(\mathfrak{p})$. In a second phase ($evaluate(h_i)$), each hypothesis in $hypos(\mathfrak{p})$ is evaluated and associated to a score. The score is based on the number of root items $r_i \in \mathcal{C}^+$ sharing the given hypothesis h_i (i.e., the path $\mathfrak{p}$ chained to one of its end values v_i, or $\langle \mathfrak{p}.v_i \rangle$). The best scored will be the best hypothesis $top(\mathcal{H})$ of the current iteration.

The score is calculated according to the hypothesis evaluation measure. The literature includes a wide range of rule evaluation measures [5]. Since the scope of our work is to find the best strategy to traverse Linked Data and get the best hypotheses, we briefly explored them and decided to use the Weighted Relative Accuracy (WR_{acc}). A more complete assessment of evaluation measures is planned for future work. WR_{acc} is part of the probability-based rules classification measures, commonly used to establish the statistical significance of an explanation. It takes into account both the generality (i.e. how big is the portion of $\mathcal{C}^+$ that the hypothesis is matching, compared to the whole dataset) and the reliability (how frequent is the hypothesis in the whole dataset) of a rule. The generality of a hypothesis h_i is defined by the number of roots $r_i \in \mathcal{R}$ matched by h_i, while its reliability is defined in terms of how much h_i matches elements from the cluster $\mathcal{C}^+$ compared to the size of $\mathcal{R}$. WR_{acc} is therefore defined as follows:

$$WR_{acc}(h_i) = \frac{|roots(h_i)|}{|\mathcal{R}|} \left(\frac{|roots(h_i) \cap \mathcal{C}^+|}{|roots(h_i)|} - \frac{|\mathcal{C}^+|}{|\mathcal{R}|} \right) \quad (1)$$

The detailed algorithm is shown in Algorithm 2.

Algorithm 2. Dedalo's complete algorithm

```
cycle = 0
R ← getRoots(R)                                  ▷ R = {r_0, ... ,r_i}
paths ← list()                                   ▷ empty list of 𝔭
traverseLinkedData(R)                            ▷ steps 1-2 on roots
while (time < limit) do
    rank(paths)                                  ▷ step 3
    topPath ← top(paths)
    for hypo in hypos(topPath) do                ▷ step 5
        evaluate(hypo)
        add(hypo, hypos)
    end for
    topValues ← vals(topPath)                    ▷ step 4
    traverseLinkedData(topValues)                ▷ step 1-2 on the path values
    remove(topPath, paths)                       ▷ new iteration
    cycle++
end while
```

3.2 Driving the Linked Data Search: Heuristics

With a limited time and computational resources, choosing the best strategy becomes the most important factor to obtain the hypotheses. We adapted some existing measures, in order to define the most effective one, where effective means a measure giving the best hypotheses score in the shortest number of cycles.

1 – Path Length. Our baseline to compare the other measures is the length of $\mathfrak{p}$. This measure assumes that the best paths are the closest to a root item r_i. $\mathcal{L}en$ counts the number of properties p_i composing a $\mathfrak{p}$, and favours the shortest ones.

$$\mathcal{L}en(\mathfrak{p}) = \frac{1}{||\mathfrak{p}||} \tag{2}$$

Ex. If $\mathfrak{p}_1$=⟨ou:MemberOf⟩ and $\mathfrak{p}_2$=⟨ou:participatedIn→ou:ledBy⟩, then $\mathcal{L}en(\mathfrak{p}_1) > \mathcal{L}en(\mathfrak{p}_2)$.

2 – Path Frequency. $\mathcal{F}q$ estimates the frequency of a path $\mathfrak{p}$ among the dataset $\mathcal{R}$ by counting how many roots r_i share $\mathfrak{p}$. It assumes that the most important paths are the most frequent.

$$\mathcal{F}q(\mathfrak{p}) = \frac{|roots(\mathfrak{p})|}{|\mathcal{R}|} \tag{3}$$

Ex. In Fig. 2, if $\mathfrak{p}_1$=⟨ou:MemberOf⟩ and $\mathfrak{p}_2$=⟨ou:exMemberOf⟩, then $\mathcal{F}q(\mathfrak{p}_1) > \mathcal{F}q(\mathfrak{p}_2)$.

3 – Pointwise Mutual Information. $\mathcal{PMI}$ is used in Information Theory and Statistics to measure the discrepancy of a pair of random variables x and y given their joint distribution $p(x|y)$ and individual distributions $p(x)$ and $p(y)$. In our scenario, we measure the probability that $\mathfrak{p}$ is shared by the root items of the considered cluster $\mathcal{C}^+$.

$$\mathcal{PMI}(\mathfrak{p}) = log \frac{|roots(\mathfrak{p}) \cap \mathcal{C}^+|}{|\mathcal{R}| \times |roots(\mathfrak{p})|} \tag{4}$$

Ex. If `<ou:MathieuDAquin>` and `<ou:MiriamFernandez>` are roots of $\mathcal{C}^+$, while `<ou:MartaSabou>` and `<ou:VanessaLopez>` are not, by comparing $\mathfrak{p}_1$=⟨ou:MemberOf⟩ with $\mathfrak{p}_2$=⟨ou:exMemberOf⟩, then $\mathcal{PMI}(\mathfrak{p}_1) > \mathcal{PMI}(\mathfrak{p}_2)$ because $\mathfrak{p}_1$ is only shared by the items of $\mathcal{C}^+$.

4 – Adapted TFIDF. We adapted the very well known TFIDF measure to evaluate the relevancy of a path $\mathfrak{p}$ (the *term*) in a given cluster $\mathcal{C}^+$, compared to its frequency across $\mathcal{C}$ (the set of *documents*).

$$TFIDF(\mathfrak{p}) = \frac{|roots(\mathfrak{p}) \cap \mathcal{C}^+|}{|\mathcal{C}^+|} \times log \frac{|\mathcal{C}|}{|\{\mathcal{C}_i \in \mathcal{C} | roots(\mathfrak{p}) \cap \mathcal{C}_i \neq \emptyset\}|} \tag{5}$$

Ex. If $\mathfrak{p}_1$=⟨ou:MemberOf⟩ and $\mathfrak{p}_2$ = ⟨ou:exMemberOf⟩ and `<ou:MathieuDAquin>` and `<ou:MiriamFernandez>` are in $\mathcal{C}^+$, then TFIDF($\mathfrak{p}_1$)>TFIDF($\mathfrak{p}_2$) as $\mathfrak{p}_1$ is only shared by roots belonging to $\mathcal{C}^+$.

5 – Delta Function. We developed a function comparing the number of values of a $\mathfrak{p}$ and the number of clusters in the dataset. Δ assumes that the best $\mathfrak{p}$ is the one having a different end value v_i for each cluster $\mathcal{C}_i \in \mathcal{C}$, so $|vals(\mathfrak{p})| = |\mathcal{C}|$. The closer the cardinality of $vals(\mathfrak{p})$ is to that of $\mathcal{C}$, the better the score is.

$$\Delta(\mathfrak{p}) = \frac{1}{1 + ||vals(\mathfrak{p})| - |\mathcal{C}||} \tag{6}$$

Ex. Given $|\mathcal{C}| = 2$ and $\mathfrak{p}$=⟨ou:participatedIn→ou:ledBy⟩, if $|vals(\mathfrak{p})|$=2 means that there is a different value for each cluster in $\mathcal{C}$ and therefore $\Delta(\mathfrak{p})$ is 1. On the other hand, with $\mathfrak{p}$=⟨ou:MemberOf⟩, $\Delta(\mathfrak{p})$ would be low as the only value of $\mathfrak{p}$ is `<ou:KMi>`. Similarly, if the values of $\mathfrak{p}$ were too sparse (i.e. $|vals(\mathfrak{p})|$>2)), $\Delta(\mathfrak{p})$ would also be very low.

6 – Entropy. Starting with Shannon's theory [21], a broad variety of works have applied the notion of entropy to graphs a networks in different disciplines (see [4,14]for detailed surveys). Entropy (H, the Greek letter "eta") is a measure analysing the performance of communication channels. According to [14], given a random process $\mathcal{X}=\{x_0, x_1, ..., x_n\}$ with n possible outcomes, the amount of uncertainty removed by equiprobable messages increases monotonically with the number of existing messages, meaning that the bigger is n, the less information is gained (and the more $\mathcal{X}$ is uncertain). Considering this, we used a naïve adaptation of Shannon's Entropy, in which the random process $\mathcal{X}$ corresponds to $\mathfrak{p}$, while its n possible outcomes are the values $v_i \in vals(\mathfrak{p})$.

$$\mathsf{H}(\mathfrak{p}) = \sum_{i=1}^{|vals(\mathfrak{p})|} \frac{|roots(\langle \mathfrak{p}.v_i \rangle)|}{|\mathcal{R}|} log \frac{|roots(\langle \mathfrak{p}.v_i \rangle)|}{|\mathcal{R}|} \tag{7}$$

Ex. $\mathfrak{p}_1$=⟨ou:MemberOf⟩ and $\mathfrak{p}_2$= ⟨ou:interestedIn⟩. $\mathfrak{p}_1$ has only one possible outcome, so there is no information gain (also defined as "surprise") when finding it in the graph. The gain of information is much higher with $\mathfrak{p}_2$, as it has more uncertain values and therefore $\mathsf{H}(\mathfrak{p}_2) > \mathsf{H}(\mathfrak{p}_1)$.

7 – Conditional Entropy. Similarly, Conditional Entropy measures the information gain of a random variable $\mathcal{X}$ given the knowledge of a random variable $\mathcal{Y}$. In this scenario, $\mathsf{H}(\mathfrak{p}|\mathcal{C}^+)$ measures how much information gain $\mathfrak{p}$ brings, if we know which items belong to $\mathcal{C}^+$ (i.e. how specific $\mathfrak{p}$ and its values are in $\mathcal{C}^+$).

$$\mathsf{H}(\mathfrak{p}|\mathcal{C}^+) = \sum_{i=1}^{|vals(\mathfrak{p})|} \frac{|root(\langle p.v_i \rangle) \cap \mathcal{C}^+|}{|\mathcal{R}|} log \frac{|root(\langle p.v_i \rangle) \cap \mathcal{C}^+|)}{|root(\langle p.v_i \rangle)|} \tag{8}$$

Ex. If `<ou:MathieuDAquin>`, `<ou:VanessaLopez>` and `<ou:MartaSabou>` are $r_i \in \mathcal{C}^+$, and $\mathfrak{p}_1$=⟨ou:MemberOf⟩ and $\mathfrak{p}_2$= ⟨ou:interestedIn⟩ then $\mathsf{H}(\mathfrak{p}_2) > \mathsf{H}(\mathfrak{p}_1)$ because Semantic Web is specific to $\mathcal{C}^+$ only.

4 Experiments

This section presents the different experiments we ran to evaluate the paths ranking measures, in order to find the best one. The datasets, resulting hypotheses, and evaluations here presented are also available online[1].

4.1 Datasets

As an input for Dedalo's Linked Data traversal, we used three datasets, differing in topic (authors, papers and books), size and clustering methods (see Table 2). While the two first can be seen as test examples in a restricted and well understood area, the third represents a realistically large use case (close to 7,000 root items, leading to the traversal of millions of triples distributed in several datasets). This demonstrates the feasibility of the approach at different scales and using clusters that can be easily understood and evaluated. Future work will focus on increasing the complexity of the use cases.

KMiA – *The Knowledge Media Institute co-authorship.* A set of researchers have been clustered according to the papers they have written together. We

[1] `http://linkedu.eu/dedalo/`

Table 2. Detailed description of the datasets used for the experiments

Dataset	Size	$\lvert\mathcal{R}\rvert$	$\lvert\mathcal{C}\rvert$	Clustering method
KMiA	small	92	6	Network partitioning clustering
KMiP	medium	865	6	X-KMeans clustering
Huds	large	6969	11	KMeans clustering

obtained 6 clusters that an expert validated as consisting of people working on the same topics.

KMiP – *The Knowledge Media Institute publications.* Research papers from the department have been clustered according to the words that have been used in the abstract (TFIDF-weighted keywords). In this case, the expert explained that papers about the same topic have been clustered together.

Huds – *The books borrowing observations.* Books borrowed by university students have been clustered according to the Faculty the students belong to. The expert explained that books of the same topics have been clustered together.

4.2 Best Hypotheses

Dedalo was run to find the best hypotheses for clusters of each dataset. Some examples of the best hypothesis $top(\mathcal{H})$ automatically found at different iterations are presented in Table 3. For the purpose of the reader's understanding, the second column shows the explanation the experts have given.

In KMiA–1, the explanation for h_2 is that people who worked on Semantic Web have been clustered together because they have all been part of a project whose director was someone working himself on the SmartProducts project[2] (with a WR_{acc} score of 12.8%), which is much deeper in the graph than h_1 (those people are associated to the Semantic Web topic, WR_{acc} 7.6%). Also, this kind of explanations could only be given by someone knowing the department well enough to affirm that those people worked in projects under the same director. Typically, this is an example in which explanations are hidden and only an expert with the right background knowledge could provide it.

Those results also demonstrate that Dedalo is agnostic to the process used to obtain the cluster, as well as the topic of the dataset, as by changing them, we obtained satisfactory hypotheses.

Finally, we also remark how, by using the connections between datasets in the Linked Data cloud, we can also get better explanations. In Huds–1, while first we get explanations from the British Library dataset[3] ("books borrowed by students of the Music Technology faculty are about sound recording", WR_{acc} 0.2%), when descending the graph we reach the Library Of Congress dataset[4] and find a better explanation that "those borrowed books are about a topic

[2] `http://www.smartproducts-project.eu/`

[3] `http://bnb.data.bl.uk/`

[4] `http://id.loc.gov/authorities/subjects.html`

Table 3. Examples of *top*($\mathcal{H}$) in our experiments. The full URIs are indicated in the online results.

	$\mathcal{C}^+$	$\lvert\mathcal{C}^+\rvert$	*top*($\mathcal{H}$)	WR_{acc}
KMiA	(1) Semantic Web people	22	h_1=⟨tag:taggedWithTag.ou:SemanticWeb⟩	7.6%
			h_2=⟨org:hasMembership→ox:hasPrincipalInvestigator→ org:hasMembership.ou:SmartProducts⟩	12.8%
	(2) Learning Technology people	23	h_1=⟨org:hasMembership.ou:open-sensemaking-communities⟩	7.3%
			h_2=⟨org:hasMembership→ox:hasPrincipalInvestigator→ org:hasMembership.ou:SocialLearn⟩	12.7%
KMiP	(1) "*learning data, user, technology*" papers	601	h_1=⟨dc:creator→org:hasMembership.ou:StoryMakingProject⟩	3.8%
			h_2=⟨dc:creator→org:hasMembership→ox:hasPrincipal-Investigator→ntag:isRelatedTo.ou:LearningAnalytics⟩	4.2%
	(2) "*ontology, knowledge, system*" papers	220	h_1=⟨dc:creator.ou:EnricoMotta⟩	6.1%
			h_2=⟨dc:creator→ntag:isRelatedTo.ou:SemanticWeb⟩	7.3%
Huds	(1) borrowings of Music Technology students	335	h_1=⟨dc:subject.bl:SoundsRecording⟩	0.2%
			h_2=⟨dc:creator→bl:hasCreated→dc:subject.bl:SoundsRecording⟩	0.4%
			h_3=⟨dc:creator→owl:sameAs→skos:broader skos:broader→skos:broader.lcsh:PhysicalScience⟩	0.5%
	(2) borrowings of Theatre students	919	h_1=⟨dc:subject.bl:EnglishDrama⟩	0.4%
			h_2=⟨dc:creator→owl:sameAs→skos:narrower.lcsh:EnsembleTheatre⟩	0.7%
			h_3=⟨dc:creator→bl:hasCreated→dc:subject.bl:EnglishDrama⟩	1.3%

referenced in the LCSH dataset as a narrower topic of Physical Science" (WR_{acc} 0.5%). Although it is an intuitively easier explanation to make, it shows that more accurate explanations can be found using Linked Data connections among datasets and domains.

4.3 Results and Discussion

We compared the measures presented in section 3 on our examples, to see which was the fastest at reaching the best hypotheses given a fixed number of iterations. In Fig. 3–5, the X axis represents the cycles the process has gone through, and the Y axis represents the WR_{acc} score (in %) of the *top*($\mathcal{H}$) found at that given iteration. As we explained, each improvement of the WR_{acc} score means that new *top*($\mathcal{H}$) have been found by Dedalo.

Our experiments show that Entropy outperforms the other measures. The Entropy method reduces redundancy (i.e. following wrongs paths) and allows Dedalo to directly detect the most promising paths to follow. The Conditional Entropy measure, showing a very good performance as well, is the second best performing in 5 of out 6 experiments. In Fig. 5b, Conditional Entropy even finds better explanations of the cluster. The reason is that items of that cluster had hypotheses specific enough when compared to the rest of the dataset.

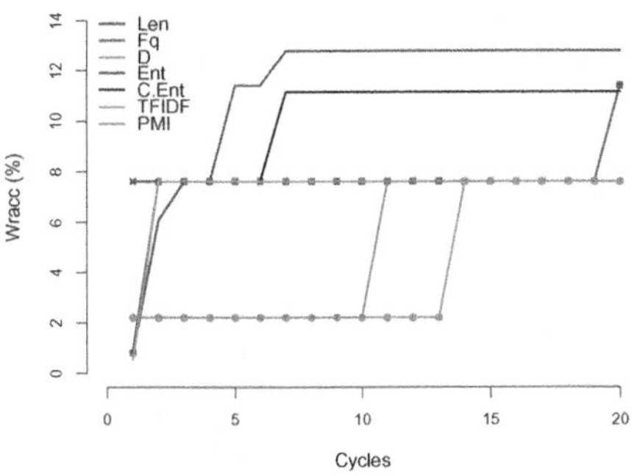

(a) KMiA–1. Semantic Web people.

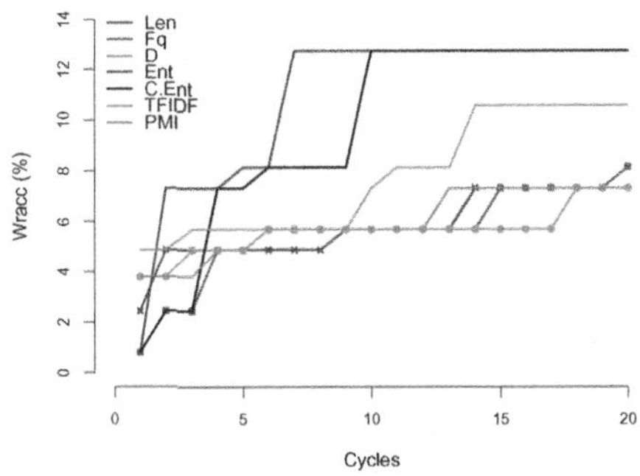

(b) KMiA–2. Learning Analytics people.

Fig. 3. KMiA results. Dedalo ran 20 iterations.

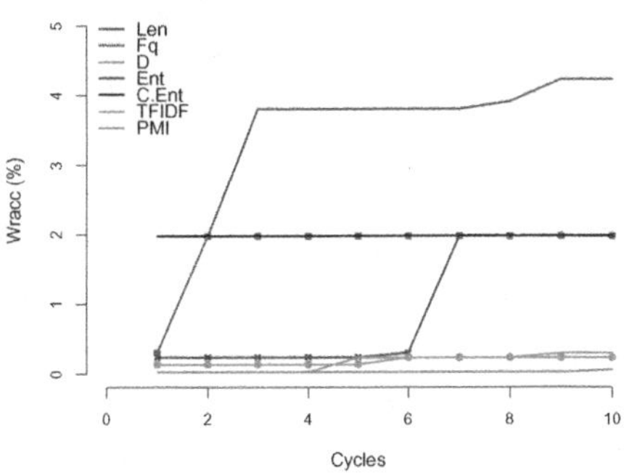

(a) KMiP–1. Learning analytics topic.

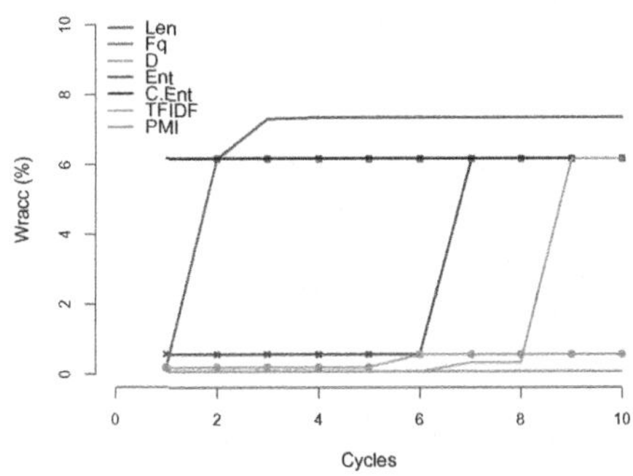

(b) KMiP–2. Semantic Web topic.

Fig. 4. KMiP results. Dedalo ran 10 iterations.

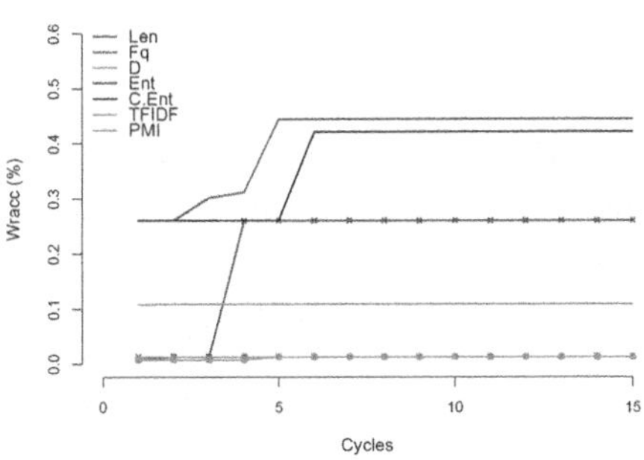

(a) Huds–1. Music Technology.

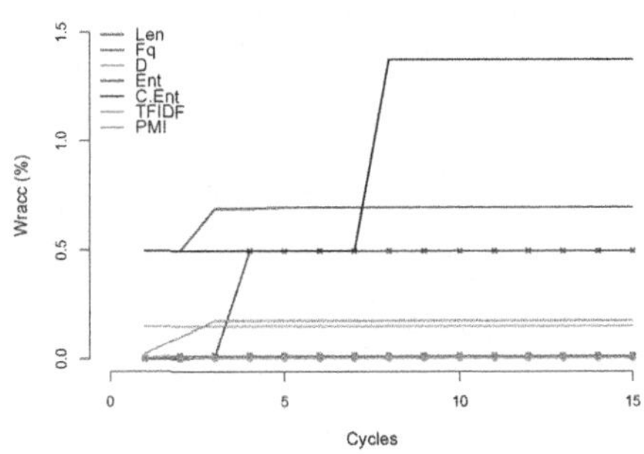

(b) Huds–2. Theatre.

Fig. 5. Huds results. Dedalo ran 15 iterations.

The $\mathcal{PMI}$, TFIDF and Δ measures have the worst performances, possibly because our use-cases were homogeneously composed and each entity, regardless which cluster it belonged to, had approximately the same properties. For instance, TFIDF works relatively well in the case illustrated in Fig. 3b. In that case, the experts explained that we were dealing with a more heterogeneous cluster of data. $\mathcal{L}en$ and $\mathcal{F}q$ are good in finding an explanation in the first cycles, but then they plateau and take time before getting any improvement. They are not able to follow the correct path, until it finally shows up in the queue of paths to further analyse. $\mathcal{L}en$ seems to have a better performance on big clusters with smaller numbers of properties, as shown in Fig. 5a and 5b.

The experiments also showed an apparent phenomenon that the bigger the dataset, the lower is WR_{acc}. This can probably be explained by the fact that it is harder to find strong explanations in a larger population.

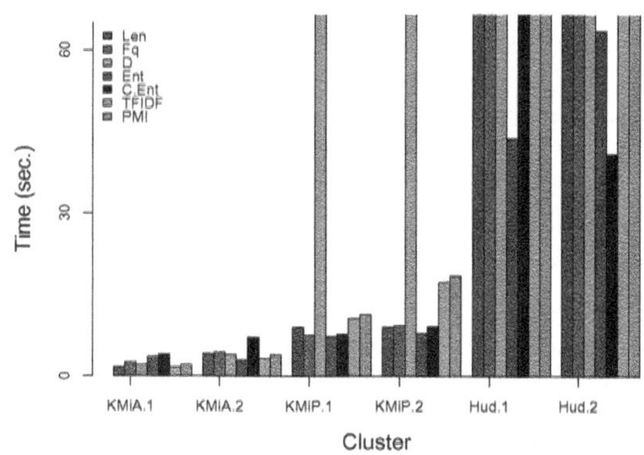

Fig. 6. Time (in seconds) the measures needed to reach $top(\mathcal{H})$. The process assumes that the data have been cached locally, as the times to retrieve entities from different datasets are not comparable.

In Fig. 6, we compared the time the measures need to reach the same hypothesis. We choose as $top(\mathcal{H})$ the last and most common hypothesis after a fixed number of iterations (20th, 10th and 15th). In most of the examples, relatively to the scale of the dataset, Entropy is among the fastest measures also in time, while Conditional Entropy appears slightly slower.

5 Conclusions and Future Work

In this work we presented Dedalo, an ILP-inspired approach that automatically produces explanations for clusters using Linked Data as background knowledge. We have shown not only that hidden explanations for clusters can be extracted from Linked Data, and that this can come from the different domains connected in the Linked Data cloud, but also that it is important to correctly choose the direction in the graph in order to save computational effort and time. We developed and evaluated different measures to traverse Linked Data to access the explanation in the shortest time. The Entropy and Conditional Entropy measures performed best in all test cases.

In our future work, we intend to pursue three main lines: (i) exploring different hypothesis evaluation measures, other than WR_{acc}, to detect if the best explanation or the heuristic are affected by changing the measure; (ii) refining the discovery of paths, using inverse properties, and of hypotheses, combining the best hypotheses to obtain a better score; and finally (iii) deal with the issue of the lack of connections between datasets. In fact, we are aware that Dedalo works as far as Linked Data sources (and therefore, domains) are interconnected. In another example, in which students have been clustered according to the region they come from, it turned out that in certain regions, some faculties attract more students than others (for instance, a lot of students have enrolled in the Health&Social Care Faculty in the East-Midlands, while the Law&Business Faculty attracts students from regions around London). While we know that there is a possibly eco-demographic explanation to this, and that Linked Data contain datasets to give us such information, at the current stage we cannot obtain it because of the lack of connections between these datasets. Our future work will be focused on this issue.

References

1. Brisson, L., Collard, M., Pasquier, N.: Improving the knowledge discovery process using ontologies. In: Proceedings of the IEEE MCD International Workshop on Mining Complex Data, pp. 25–32 (November 2005)
2. Brisson, L., Collard, M.: How to Semantically Enhance a Data Mining Process? In: Filipe, J., Cordeiro, J. (eds.) Enterprise Information Systems. LNBIP, vol. 19, pp. 103–116. Springer, Heidelberg (2009)
3. d'Aquin, M., Jay, N.: Interpreting Data Mining Results with Linked Data for Learning Analytics: Motivation, Case Study and Direction. In: LAK 2013 (2013)
4. Dehmer, M., Mowshowitz, A.: Generalized graph entropies. Complexity 17(2), 45–50 (2011)
5. Geng, L., Hamilton, H.J.: Interestingness measures for data mining: A survey. ACM Computing Surveys (CSUR) 38(3), 9 (2006)
6. Grosof, B.N., Horrocks, I., Volz, R., Decker, S.: Description logic programs: Combining logic programs with description logic. In: Proceedings of the 12th International Conference on World Wide Web, pp. 48–57. ACM (May 2003)
7. King, R.D., Rowland, J., Oliver, S.G., Young, M., Aubrey, W., Byrne, E., Clare, A.: The automation of science. Science 324(5923), 85–89 (2009)
8. Lavrač, N., Vavpetič, A., Soldatova, L., Trajkovski, I., Novak, P.K.: Using ontologies in semantic data mining with SEGS and g-SEGS. In: Elomaa, T., Hollmén, J., Mannila, H. (eds.) DS 2011. LNCS, vol. 6926, pp. 165–178. Springer, Heidelberg (2011)
9. Lisi, F.A.: Inductive Logic Programming in Databases: From Datalog to DL+log. Theory and Practice of Logic Programming 10(3), 331–359 (2010)
10. Lisi, F.A., Esposito, F.: On ontologies as prior conceptual knowledge in inductive logic programming. In: Berendt, B., Mladenič, D., de Gemmis, M., Semeraro, G., Spiliopoulou, M., Stumme, G., Svátek, V., Železný, F. (eds.) Knowledge Discovery Enhanced with Semantic and Social Information. SCI, vol. 220, pp. 3–17. Springer, Heidelberg (2009)
11. Marinica, C., Guillet, F.: Knowledge-based interactive postmining of association rules using ontologies. IEEE Transactions on Knowledge and Data Engineering 22(6), 784–797 (2010)
12. Moss, L., Sleeman, D., Sim, M., Booth, M., Daniel, M., Donaldson, L., Kinsella, J.: Ontology-driven hypothesis generation to explain anomalous patient responses to treatment. Knowledge-Based Systems 23(4), 309–315 (2010)
13. Motik, B., Rosati, R.: Closing semantic web ontologies. Technical report, University of Manchester, UK (2006)

14. Mowshowitz, A., Dehmer, M.: Entropy and the complexity of graphs revisited. Entropy 14(3), 559–570 (2012)
15. Muggleton, S., De Raedt, L.: Inductive logic programming: Theory and methods. The Journal of Logic Programming 19, 629–679 (1994)
16. Mulwad, V., Finin, T., Syed, Z., Joshi, A.: Using Linked Data to Interpret Tables. In: COLD 2010 (2010)
17. Paulheim, H.: Generating Possible Interpretations for Statistics from Linked Open Data. In: Simperl, E., Cimiano, P., Polleres, A., Corcho, O., Presutti, V. (eds.) ESWC 2012. LNCS, vol. 7295, pp. 560–574. Springer, Heidelberg (2012)
18. Paulheim, H.: Exploiting Linked Open Data as Background Knowledge in Data Mining. In: CEUR Workshop Proceedings DMoLD 2013 Collocated with ECMLP-KDD 2013, pp. 1–10. RWTH, Aachen (2013)
19. Racunas, S.A., Shah, N.H., Albert, I., Fedoroff, N.V.: HyBrow: a prototype system for computer-aided hypothesis evaluation. Bioinformatics 20(suppl. 1), i257–i264 (2004)
20. Roos, M., Marshall, M.S., Gibson, A., Schuemie, M., Meij, E., Katrenko, S., Adriaans, P.: Structuring and extracting knowledge for the support of hypothesis generation in molecular biology. BMC Bioinformatics 10(suppl. 10), S9 (2009)
21. Shannon, C.: A Mathematical Theory of Communication. Bell System Technical Journal 27(3), 379–423 (1948)
22. Tiddi, I., d'Aquin, M., Motta, E.: Explaining Clusters with Inductive Logic Programming and Linked Data. In: 12th International Semantic Web Conference (2013)
23. Tiddi, I.: Explaining data patterns using background knowledge from Linked Data. In: ISWC 2013 Doctoral Consortium, Sydney, Australia (2013)
24. Zapilko, B., Harth, A., Mathiak, B.: Enriching and analysing statistics with Linked Open Data. In: Eurostat (ed.) NTTS - Conference on New Techniques and Technologies for Statistics. S8 Paper 1, Brüssel (2011)

A Knowledge Based Approach for Tackling Mislabeled Multi-class Big Social Data

Minyi Guo[1], Yi Liu[1], Jie Li[1], Huakang Li[2], and Bei Xu[2]

[1] Department of Computer Science and Engineering,
Shanghai Jiao Tong University, China
guo-my@cs.sjtu.edu.cn

[2] School of Computer Science & School of Software,
Nanjing University of Posts and Telecommunications, China
huakanglee@njupt.edu.cn

Abstract. The performance of classification models extremely relies on the quality of training data. However, label imperfection is an inherent fault of training data, which is impossible manually handled in big data environment. Various methods have been proposed to remove label noises in order to improve classification quality, with the side effect of cutting down data bulk. In this paper, we propose a knowledge based approach for tackling mislabeled multi-class big data, in which knowledge graph technique is combined with other data correction method to perceive and correct the error labels in big data. The knowledge graph is built with the medical concepts extracted from online health consulting and medical guidance. Experimental results show our knowledge graph based approach can effectively improve data quality and classification accuracy. Furthermore, this approach can be applied in other data mining tasks requiring deep understanding.

Keywords: #eswc2014Guo, label imperfection, knowledge graph, label correction, classification.

1 Introduction

For machine learning research, many researchers focus on improving learning algorithms with least learning bias, thus the data quality has become the crucial issue when it is given to a certain machine learning algorithm. Unfortunately, real world data inevitably contains unexpected noises (i.e. label errors) which can disturb the performance of classification in multiple aspects like accuracy, modeling time and computing complexity. It proves that classification accuracies almost decline linearly with the increase of noise level [1].

Most label errors in training data come from data entry errors, transmit errors and subjectivity of taggers and so on. Data entry errors in large dataset are severe and common. The noise level is usually around 5% or more [1]. Furthermore, it seems difficult to avoid or even to cut down on the errors because there are no standards or specifications dealing with data entry errors. Transmission errors

V. Presutti et al. (Eds.): ESWC 2014, LNCS 8465, pp. 349–363, 2014.

take place in communication breakdown. Therefore, in order to increase the accuracy, most of training data are labeled manually even if the people are very subjective because of the knowledge limitation in specific domains. Even experts and professionals are not absolutely confident about their labeling. Therefore, the necessity of developing methods to remove or correct label errors is self-evident.

Many learning algorithms made label noised treatment mechanisms. For example, pruning in decision tree algorithm can avoid over-fitting caused by noises [2]. Still, when noise level is high, learning algorithms are not able to effectively. Other methods try to handle the noises in data before classification, including filtering noises and correcting noises.

This paper proposed an approach based on knowledge graph technique to perceive and correct label errors in big data environment. Knowledge graph is a concept proposed by Google[1] for its search engine and other applications, whose kernel is utilizing ontology to simulate entities and relationships in the real world to help machine understand the world intelligently. The usage of knowledge graph enable machines to better understand text documents [3]. Therefore we introduce this concept in noise correction to better perceive the nature conditions. We use big social data collected from medical Q&A web sites to validate our approach for tackling label imperfection. Medical Q&A system serves for online health consulting and medical guidance. A study reports 83% of Internet users in the U.S. seek health information online [4] and health care system are playing a much more essential role in the recent life [5].

Our approach implements the knowledge graph on a label correction method raised by Teng et al. [6]. Concretely, Naive Bayes classifier is utilized to recognize and modify the error labels of training data. After label modification, the noise level has proven to decline dramatically than before. Then we use the modified data to construct classifier for classification rather than correction, and the accuracy has improved than before. The main contributions of this paper are outlined as follows:

- We build a knowledge graph base containing medical entities such as diseases entities, symptom entities, medicine entities and their relationships from large scale of Q&A healthcare web sites, using several knowledge extraction techniques.
- We validate the effect of knowledge graph in tackling label imperfection problem comparing with other approaches. Our approach is more effective than other ways on improving classification quality and data quality.
- Our approach can be used for a relatively high noise level and still achieve satisfying performance.

This paper is organized as follows. Section 2 reviews the most related works in respects of label errors handling. Section 3 presents our approach to construct knowledge graph base. Section 4 describes polishing and our knowledge graph based combined approach. Section 5 describes the experimental performance and measures the affection of depth of knowledge as well. Finally, we conclude and discuss the possible directions of future works in Section 6.

[1] `http://www.google.com/insidesearch/features/search/knowledge.html`

2 Related Work

Over the course of the past 20 years, solving the problem of noises in the data has been the considerable attention in the field of machine learning and data mining. Most of learning algorithms developed mechanisms to diminish the impact that noises bring to the classification performance. Pruning in a decision tree is used to avoid overfitting caused by noise. Wilson et al. [7,8] applied several instance-pruning techniques which can remove noise from the training set and reduce the storage consumption. However, the performance of these learning algorithms becomes very bad when the noise level is too high, and classification accuracy declines almost linearly with the rise of the noise level [1].

As long as the noise exists in training data, the classification quality will be affected severely. Thus, some approaches use filtering mechanisms to identify and filter the noise examples before feeding them to the classifier. Wilson et al. [9] attempted to filter the noise examples by using a 3-NN classifier and apply 1-NN classifier on the filtered data. Aha et al. [10] proposed IB3(a version of instance-based learning algorithm) to remove noise with lower updating costs and lower storage requirements. Brodley et al. [11,12] used a set of learning algorithms to construct classifiers as filters to dataset before feeding it to classifier and achieved to significantly improvement for noise level up to 30%.

However, filtering noises enhances data quality at the cost of decreasing the amount of data retained for training. It also seems petty and inappropriate to discard error label data especially when the training data is difficult to re-collect such as historical data [13]. Correcting the label error instead of simply filtering them is a better approach that accomplishes both data quality and data amount. Zeng et al. [6] proposed a method called ADE (automatic data enhancement), which can correct label errors through numbers of iterations using multi-layer neural networks trained by back propagation in the basic framework. Teng et al. [13, 14] introduced a noise correction mechanism called polishing and correct noises both in classes and attributes. Teng also compared polishing with filtering and traditional approach of avoiding overfitting, and proved noise correction recovers information not available with the other two approaches [14, 15]. Since we apply polishing as our basic method, more detailed description about polishing will be presented in Section 4.1.

The approaches discussed above contain the following limitations: (i) Some use filtering which may decrease the bulk of data. (ii) Most of these approaches have no significant performance at a high noise level. (iii) Most of these works only measured the promotion that their approaches bring to classification performance, yet haven't measured the exact values of data quality promotion. Therefore, we propose an approach based on knowledge graph to tackle these limitations.

3 Knowledge Graph Building

3.1 Data Source

We use a big dataset over 1000GB collected from a Chinese medical social Q&A website[2] and Chinese Encyclopedia website Baidu Encyclopedia (BE)[3] to build a medical knowledge base. Figure 1 shows a glimpse of a few entities and relationships in the graph. The edge between a disease entity and a symptom entity implies the disease seems to have a lot of symptoms. For example, *gastritis* has *diarrhea* and *vomit* symptoms, and *fatigue* can be explained by *anemia* or *Parkinson*. There are 3 types of entities in the knowledge graph, and two entities of the same type cannot be connected directly. This assumption is justifiable. Because in the real world, two diseases are related since they share several common symptoms. Two medicines are related since they can be both employed to treat one disease. Their relationship is linked by other entities, not themselves directly.

Besides, the Q&A archives are used to establish training data sets applied for label correction. The Q&A archives contain nearly 20 million Q&A pairs in which every pair contains the question put forward by patients and the answer given by doctors and medical experts. The pair also contains departmental information about which hospital department the patient should seek help for. It's appropriate to use these data to validate our approach. We extract a training example from each Q&A pair. Features are extracted from patients' descriptions in questions, and departments are used as labels in the correction phase.

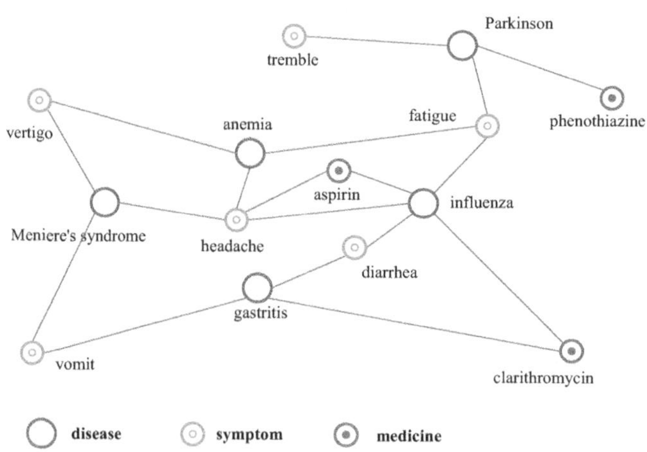

Fig. 1. A local structure of the medical knowledge graph

[2] http://www.120ask.com

[3] http://baike.baidu.com

3.2 Entities Extraction

To build the knowledge graph base, we extract disease entities, symptom entities and medicine entities. These are done by following steps:

- In the first phase, we use web crawling technique to acquire disease entities, medicine entities from BE. As BE pages are well structured and tagged, we adopt Maximum Entropy algorithm to classify these entities to broad categories. After sorting out these entities and their categories, we obtain a known entity set.
- In the second phase, we conclude linguistic patterns of entities and use these patterns to find more entities in the Q&A archives. Bootstrapping on syntactic patterns are frequently used to extract knowledge [3]. Chinese words are composed of characters, and affixes (prefixes and suffixes, contains one or more characters) usually have specific meaning about the type of words. For example, medicine words 'mizolastine', 'clemastine' and 'levocabastine' all share the same suffix 'stine', because they are similar in chemical composition. So we use prefixes and suffixes concluded from the known entities set to find more and more entities. After acquiring these new entities, we conduct artificial selection to discard entities which do not belong to the medical domain. Hence, we get a bigger set of entities than the first phase.
- Then we perform several iteration of the second phase and finally get a set of nearly 30,000 disease entities and 30,000 medicine entities.

Since most patients describe their symptoms orally and informally, symptoms cannot be extracted from encyclopedia web sites. We firstly use TFIDF [16] and IG(information gain) techniques [17] to find words and phrases that are more informative in the Q&A archives, and artificially select some symptom entities. Then we use bootstrapping to seek more and more symptom entities. Finally we obtain a set of nearly 4,000 symptom entities.

3.3 Relationship Extraction

In most of the existed knowledge bases such as Wikipedia[4], Freebase[5], YAGO[6], Wordnet[7], the relationships between entities or relationships between entities and their attributes are established manually by experts in related field. Our knowledge base contains a relatively big amount of entities and we don't have professional knowledge in medical taxonomy. Therefore we adopt a method to automatically extract relationships between entities from big data, whose details will be discussed in Section 4.2.

In our opinion, the entity that occurs simultaneously in one Q&A pair that has some relationships. We make an assumption that the more frequently entities

[4] http://www.wikipedia.org

[5] http://www.freebase.com

[6] http://www.mpi-inf.mpg.de/yago-naga/yago

[7] http://wordnet.princeton.edu

occur simultaneously in Q&A pair, the stronger relationships they have. Hence, we extract relationships between entities based on the $co - occurrencerate$ of entities. Details on $co - occurrencerate$ are discussed in Section 4.2.

4 Mislabel Correction

As we mentioned above, polishing proposed by Teng et al. [13, 14] proves to be quite well in mislabeled correction. The kernel of our approach is to adopt polishing as the basic method and use information from the established knowledge graph to adjust the weight of entity features in label correction phase. Since knowledge graph represents the relationships of entity features, it can be utilized to strengthen the more informative entity features and weaken the less informative entity features. We assume that the entity with more connection to other entities and greater co-occurrence rates with others plays the more important role in mislabeled correction. Thus, they should be endowed with more weight.

4.1 Polishing

The basic polishing algorithm comprises two phases: prediction and adjustment [14]. The prediction phase aims at finding candidate training examples that are suspected to control error labels, while the adjustment phase decides the final changes into the candidates. The polishing algorithm can predict and correct both attributes errors and label errors(i.e. class errors). In this paper, we use it to correct label errors.

In the prediction phase, a chosen learning algorithm performs K-fold cross validation. Teng et al. set K to be 10. The K-fold cross validation divides all the examples in K groups called folds, and constructs K classifiers each using K-1 folds as training set and the folding left out as the test set. If the K-fold cross validation algorithm predicts a label inconsistent with the original label, this sample will be added to suspected candidates.

In the adjustment phase, for each example of candidates set, K classifiers constructed in the prediction phase are used to predict labels of this example. If the predicted labels of K classifiers are identical and different from the original label, polishing judges the new label to be the right one and modifies the example using the new label.

4.2 Knowledge Graph

We define our knowledge graph to be a set of vertices $(v_1, v_2, \ldots, v_m)$ and edges $(e_1, e_2, \ldots, e_m)$. Each vertex represents an entity and each edge represents a direct relationship between two entities. Direct relationship means a strong connection between two entity vertices. For instance, a brief example of relationships of several entities have been shown in Fig. 1, *gastritis* has symptoms of *vomit* and *diarrhea*, so they are connected directly. And the relationship between $Meniere's\ syndrome$ and *gastritis* cannot be described, we only know they share some common symptoms, so their relationship is indirect.

We define *distance* as the shortest path length between two vertices. *distance* between any two vertices can be computed once the *length* of any edges is known. The *length* of edge is computed using the formula:

$$length(v_i, v_j) = \frac{1}{co - occurrence\ rate(v_i, v_j))} \tag{1}$$

$co - occurrence\ rate$ can measure closeness of two entity vertices if they have direct relationship. The smaller *length* is, the larger $co - occurrence\ rate$ is, meaning the relationship between two entity vertices is closer. The $co - occurrence\ rate$ is computed from the Q&A data according to the formula:

$$co - occurrence\ rate(v_i, v_j) = \frac{2 * n_{ij}}{n_i + n_j} \tag{2}$$

Here v_i, v_j represents any two entity vertices. n_{ij} represents the number of Q&A pairs in which v_i and v_j occur simultaneously, n_i defines the account of pairs in which v_i occurs, and n_j defines the number of pairs in which v_j occurs. Apparently the $co - occurrence\ rate$ is maximum value 1 if two entities always occur simultaneously in Q&A pair. If $co - occurrence\ rate$ is below a threshold M, we assume the two entity vertices have no direct relationship, thus no edge existing between them.

Also, we define *related degree* to measure relationship closeness between two vertices even when they are not directly connected in the knowledge graph (namely no edge between them).

$$related\ degree(v_i, v_j) = \frac{1}{distance(v_i, v_j)} \tag{3}$$

Obviously *related degree* is equivalent to $co - occurrence\ rate$ when there is an edge directly connecting two entity vertices. *distance* is computed using Dijkstra Shortest Path algorithm [18]. And we define $step(v_i, v_j)$ as the edge num of the shortest path between v_i and v_j. *step* measures the depth of knowledge we dig in the graph.

One advantage of knowledge graph is that we can extend or modify the graph once we grasp new knowledge through science researches. When we discover a new disease, we add it into the graph and connect it to other symptoms or medicines based on the information we know about it. And if the latest medical research shows some kind of medicine can help treat a disease, which hasn't been applied before, we can connect them and endow them some kind of relationship.

4.3 Weight Adjustment

Numerous feature weighting methods have been applied to classification and prove to have a promotive effect on classification accuracy. These methods include information gain (IG), term frequency-inverse document frequency (TFIDF), mutual information (MI), χ^2 statistic (CHI) [17]. Most of them depend on statistical analysis on training data to select and strengthen the informative features. When applying these methods in label correction, the noise part of training data probably interferences the outcome when the noise level is relatively high. Therefore we use knowledge graph to adjust weights of entity features, because knowledge graph has several advantages as below:

- Knowledge graph technique is able to mine deep relationships among features, while traditional statistical methods simply analyze shallow relationships among features.
- Knowledge graph is similar to a real world model. It is more reasonable and precise to simulate relationships.
- The knowledge cannot only be extracted from corpora but also come from scientific knowledge and latest research, which makes the graph to be extensible and renewable.

Specifically, we compute the weights of entity features according to the formula:

$$\begin{aligned} weight(v_i) =& initial\ weight + \alpha \sum_{v_j \in V, v_j \neq v_i} related\ degree(v_i, v_j), \\ & \forall step(v_i, v_j) < MAXSTEP \end{aligned} \tag{4}$$

V is the vertices set in the graph and $MAXSTEP$ is defined as the depth of relationships we mine. We define *initial weight* to be 1, and α is the adjustment factor to control the impact of knowledge graph to feature weights. $MAXSTEP$ sets a limit to which vertices to be considered when computing the weight of a vertex, namely the analysis depth of knowledge graph. We believe the weight is more specific if the depth goes deeper. However, there is a tradeoff between analysis depth and computational complexity because the related vertices number is quite large when we analyze graph quite deeply. We will conduct experiments about the effect of knowledge depth on correction labels in the Section 4.2.

4.4 Combined Algorithm

Our approach combines polishing and weight adjustment by knowledge graph to correct noise labels in training examples. We use Multinomial Naive Bayes (MNB) classifier as the basic classifier in K-fold cross validation. We choose MNB because it proves to be both efficient and accurate for text classification tasks [19]. Still, MNB makes a poor assumption that features of examples are independent of others, which are clearly unreasonable in most real-world tasks. We adjust feature weights in MNB classifier according to knowledge graph to compensate for this assumption. Weights of entity features are calculated according to formula (4) and weights of other features are defined as 1. When corrupt training data is prepared, we adjust the weight of features in the training examples, and get the adjusted training data. Then we utilize this data to follow the same procedures for polishing in Section 4.1. We also set K to be 10 in the K-fold cross validation. Afterwards we can obtain data corrected by our combined approach. Experiments of our combined approach to medical Q&A

data will be revealed in the following section. We will evaluate the effect of our approach on both classification accuracy and data quality promotion.

5 Experiment and Evaluation

This section provides empirical evidence that our knowledge graph based approach is effective in improving data quality and classification scores.

5.1 Data Sets

Table 1. the format of Q&A pairs

description	answer	department
I'm 23 and my hands always shake...and it gets worse when I'm nervous...	There are many reasons for your shaky hands. It's hard to guess it...	neurology
I play badminton and when I use backhand serve, my hand tremble. My brachioradialis hurts too...	It may be caused by overexercise, I suggest you see a bone surgery doctor to ...	surgery

As we mentioned above, our data is extracted from a huge set of nearly 20 million medical Q&A pairs. The format of data is specified in Table 1, each example has a description text which patients depict about their circumstances and symptoms, and each example has a department label showing the department where this patient should be treated. The description text of Q&A pair is usually short, less than 200 characters. The whole data sets contain more than 10 departments, Table 2 shows the department names and their probability distribution. We use our approach to obtain and correct the error department labels in training examples. Since the corpus is in Chinese, we use several NLP methods specialized in handling Chinese text: tokenizing Chinese text and transfer traditional Chinese characters to Chinese simplified characters. Afterwards, we extracted approximately 200,000 features from the raw data. Finally, we get nearly 9,725,000 training instances.

In order to obtain the corrupt data, we artificially corrupt the data with random label noises. In the following subsections we will conduct our approach with different noise levels.

5.2 Evaluation Measures

As Teng et al. points out, there are two kinds of measurement methods to evaluation label correction [13]. One method aims at finding out to what degree the label correction improves classification score, including accuracy, F1 score, F2 score etc. We choose accuracy as the measure metric to evaluate the classification quality improvement after label correction. The other method measures

Table 2. department labels and their distribution

department	distribution
obstetrics and gynaecology	26.6%
internal medicine	20.4%
surgery	11.3%
pediatrics	9.9%
dermatology	7.9%
ophthalmology and otorhinolaryngology	5.8%
neurology	5.5%
psychology	5.1%
traditional Chinese Medicine	3.1%
infectious diseases	1.9%
oncology	1.9%
plastic surgery	1.0%

the data quality in a classification-independent way, considering we may want to put the corrected data in additional uses other than building classifiers. Unlike the Net Reduction and Correct Adjustment used by Teng [13] to measure reduction in attribute noises, we use different metrics to evaluate the data quality promotion. These metrics are *noise reduction rate*, *precision* and *recall*. As our approach and in polishing correct labels by the judgement of 10 classifier voters, the changes made to the examples are not always right. So these metrics are used to evaluate these changes. *noise reduction rate*(NRR) is defined in (5) and measures the noise level decrease after label correction. *precision* measures the percentage of right changes in the whole changes made by label correction approaches. *recall* measures the percentage of error labels which is actually corrected. It's obvious that *noise reduction rate* most intuitively reflects the data quality promotion.

$$NRR = noise\ level\ in\ origin\ data - noise\ level\ in\ corrected\ data \tag{5}$$

We use three methods: *Unpolishing*, *Polishing* and *Polishing* + KG in classification accuracy comparison. *Unpolishing* approach uses the unmodified corrupt data to build classifier. *Polishing* approach uses the data corrected by polishing method to build classifier. And *Polishing*+KG approach uses the data corrected by our approach to build classifier. All the three approaches are applied in accuracy comparison, and the latter two are applied in mislabeled reduction rate comparison. In addition, we set $MAXSTEP$ to 1 in *Polishing*+KG when compared with other two approaches.

5.3 Classification Accuracy

We compare the classification accuracy on training data produced by three approaches mentioned above. For each approach, 10-fold cross validation is performed on data to obtain classification accuracy. In each trial, nine folds are

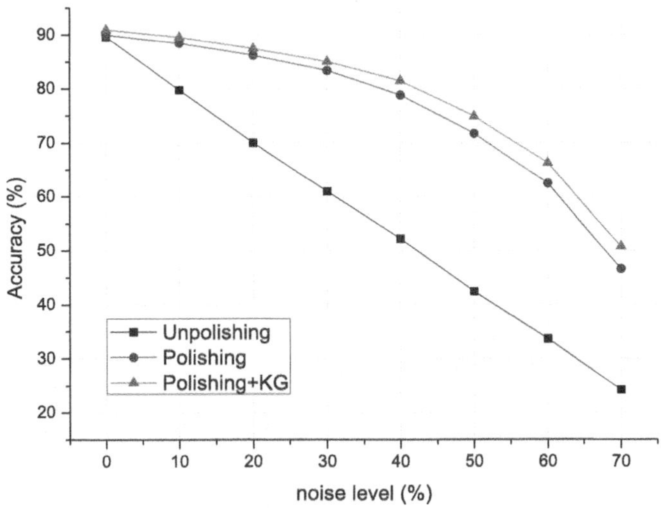

Fig. 2. A comparison accuracy on data by *Unpolishing*, *Polishing* and *Polishing* + *KG* on the medical Q&A data set

used for training data to test the accuracy of the rest fold. The final accuracy is the average accuracy of 10 trials. Here we use cross validation to evaluate classification accuracy, different from label correction phase where cross validation is used to pick up candidates and construct classifiers as voters. We choose cross validation to validate accuracy because it can reduce the risk of overfitting on the test set.

Figure 2 shows the comparison of three approach on classification accuracy at different noise levels. For *Unpolishing* approach, accuracy declines almost linearly with the noise level increase. At most cases, the improvement of *Polishing* and *Polishing*+*KG* on *Unpolishing* is quite significant, the performance of *Polishing* is 10% - 30% higher than *Unpolishing*, while our approach *Polishing* + *KG* acquires accuracy usually 1% - 4% higher than the pure *Polishing*. We can see noise data cut down accuracy dramatically when no correction is conducted. *Polishing* corrects part of the error labels and provides a much higher accuracy. Furthermore, *Polishing* + *KG* approach mines the relationships between entity features and endows more weights to the more informative ones, so it achieves better accuracy score than *Polishing*. Particularly, at noise level of 0%, the improvements of *Polishing* and *Polishing* + *KG* are both not remarkable, *Polishing* is merely 0.3% higher than *Unpolishing*, and *Polish*+*KG* is 1.3% higher than *Unpolishing*, we believe *Polishing* + *KG* also has effect on improving classification accuracy even when data is nearly noise-free.

5.4 Data Quality Promotion

We compare the classification-independent metrics to test data quality promotion by *Polishing* and *Polishing* + *KG* approach. When we artificially corrupt the data, we have made a mark to every example what is the real label of it. After label correction by two approaches, we check the precision, recall and noise reduction rate depending on these marks. We use noise reduction rate as the main metric on data quality promotion, while the other two help us to understand and explain the relevant promotion.

Figure 3 shows noise reduction rate by two approaches. The noise reduction rate of *Polishing* + *KG* is approximately 1% - 4% higher than *Polishing*. It seems odd that the noise reduction is negative at noise level of 0%, which means the noises increase after label correction. However, this phenomenon can be explained. At noise level of 0%, we assume data to be noise-free, while data can't be completely noise-free in real-world. So it is reasonable that *Polishing* and *Polishing* + *KG* has modified some labels which are quite possibly error labels. Generally speaking, it is shown that *Polishing* has enormous significance in data quality promotion and *Polishing* + *KG* achieves better performance on the basis of *Polishing*.

Figure 4 shows the precision and recall. We do not considerate precision and recall at noise level of 0% because it's meaningless. At most noise levels, precision of *Polishing* + *KG* is less than *Polishing*, however the recall of *Polishing* + *KG* is much higher than *Polishing*. Usually precision and recall have a contradictory relationship that precision decreases along when recall increases. So it's reasonable that *Polishing* + *KG* has a lower overall precision. When the noise level is quite higher, the precision and recall of *Polishing* + *KG* are both higher than

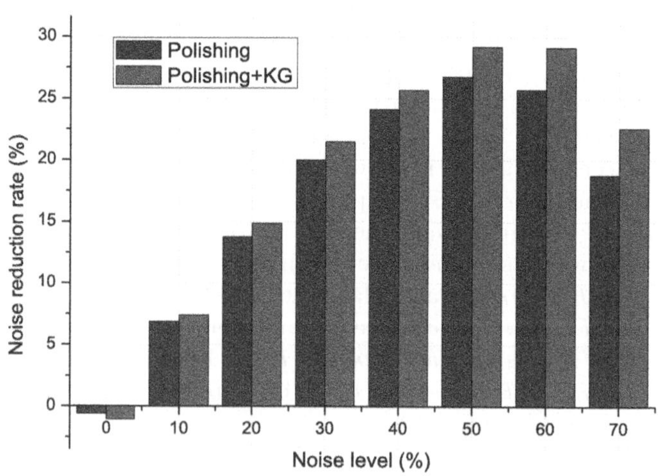

Fig. 3. A comparison of noise reduction rate by *Polishing* and *Polishing* + *KG* on the medical Q&A data set

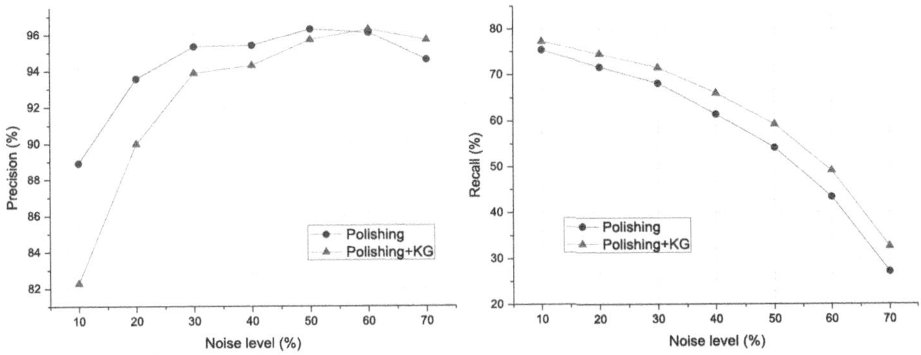

Fig. 4. A comparison of precision, recall by *Polishing* and *Polishing* + *KG* on the medical Q&A data set

Polishing. We assume this is caused by that knowledge diminishes the interference of noises, the effect is more remarkable when the noise level is higher.

5.5 Knowledge Depth Affection

We conduct an experiment of how knowledge depth affects the results. According to (3), we adjust the entity weights by computing closeness of an entity to other entities. We believe the bigger $MAXSTEP$ is, the more precise weights will be generated. This thought is driven by that we get more information about something when we recognize it more deeply. Figure 5 shows the accurate comparison of different knowledge depth from 1 to 3. The accuracy improves 0-1.3% when

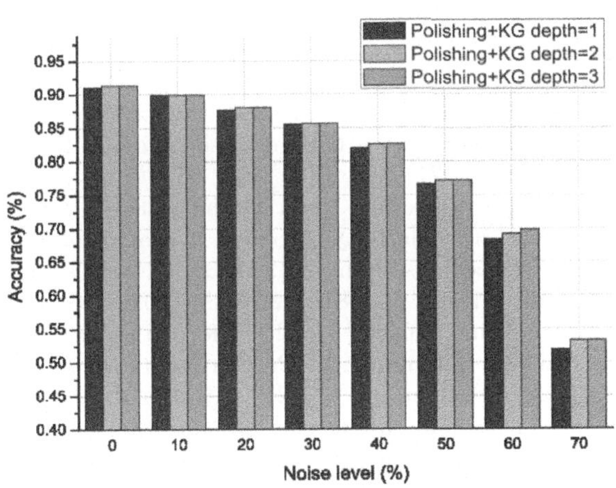

Fig. 5. Knowledge depth affection on accuracy

knowledge depth grows from 1 to 2 at different noise levels, while the accuracy improvement is insignificant when depth grows from 2 to 3. When knowledge depth grows, the amount of relationships of one entity to others grows rapidly and more weights are endowed with the more informative ones. The results show deep knowledge perception can enhance classification performance.

6 Conclusion

In this paper, we present a knowledge graph based approach combined with polishing to handle label imperfection problem. This method is distinct from previous statistical methods in that it tries to recognize the data in a way similar to the real world. Experimental results demonstrate our approach has an impact on boosting classification performance and data quality. It can effectively correct mislabeled even under the circumstance of a quite high noise level of approximately 60%. Beside handling the noise data, the knowledge graph technique we used can be applied in feature selection in classification as well.

Our future work will be focused on ameliorating the graph by establishing more types of entities and more detailed relationships in it. More researches will be conducted to recognize data noises in a more human-like rather than machine-like approach. In addition, we shall apply our approach to other fields such as social networks and business data analysis.

Acknowledgement. This work was supported by the NSFC (No. 61272099, 61261160502 and 61202025), Shanghai Excellent Academic Leaders Plan(No. 11XD1402900), the Program for Changjiang Scholars and Innovative Research Team in University of China (IRT1158, PCSIRT), the Scientific Innovation Act of STCSM(No.13511504200), Singapore NRF (CREATE E2S2), and the EU FP7 CLIMBER project (No. PIRSES-GA-2012-318939).

References

1. Zhu, X., Wu, X.: Class noise vs. attribute noise: A quantitative study. Artificial Intelligence Review 22(3), 177–210 (2004)
2. Quinlan, J.R.: Induction of decision trees. Machine Learning 1(1), 81–106 (1986)
3. Wu, W., Li, H., Wang, H., Zhu, K.Q.: Probase: A probabilistic taxonomy for text understanding. In: Proceedings of the 2012 ACM SIGMOD International Conference on Management of Data, pp. 481–492. ACM (2012)
4. Zhang, Y.: Contextualizing consumer health information searching: an analysis of questions in a social q&a community. In: Proceedings of the 1st ACM International Health Informatics Symposium, pp. 210–219. ACM (2010)
5. Kunz, H., Schaaf, T.: General and specific formalization approach for a balanced scorecard: An expert system with application in health care. Expert Systems with Applications 38(3), 1947–1955 (2011)
6. Zeng, X., Martinez, T.R.: An algorithm for correcting mislabeled data. Intelligent Data Analysis 5(6), 491–502 (2001)

7. Wilson, D.R., Martinez, T.R.: Instance pruning techniques. In: ICML, vol. 97, pp. 403–411 (1997)
8. Wilson, D.R., Martinez, T.R.: Reduction techniques for instance-based learning algorithms. Machine Learning 38(3), 257–286 (2000)
9. Wilson, D.L.: Asymptotic properties of nearest neighbor rules using edited data. IEEE Transactions on Systems, Man and Cybernetics (3), 408–421 (1972)
10. Aha, D.W., Kibler, D.F.: Noise-tolerant instance-based learning algorithms. In: IJCAI, pp. 794–799. Citeseer (1989)
11. Brodley, C.E., Friedl, M.A.: Identifying and eliminating mislabeled training instances. In: AAAI/IAAI, vol. 1, pp. 799–805. Citeseer (1996)
12. Brodley, C.E., Friedl, M.A.: Identifying mislabeled training data. arXiv preprint arXiv:1106.0219 (2011)
13. Teng, C.M.: Evaluating noise correction. In: Mizoguchi, R., Slaney, J.K. (eds.) PRICAI 2000. LNCS, vol. 1886, pp. 188–198. Springer, Heidelberg (2000)
14. Teng, C.M.: Polishing blemishes: Issues in data correction. IEEE Intelligent Systems 19(2), 34–39 (2004)
15. Teng, C.M.: A comparison of noise handling techniques. In: FLAIRS Conference, pp. 269–273 (2001)
16. Li, J., Zhang, K., et al.: Keyword extraction based on tf/idf for chinese news document. Wuhan University Journal of Natural Sciences 12(5), 917–921 (2007)
17. Yang, Y., Pedersen, J.O.: A comparative study on feature selection in text categorization. In: ICML, vol. 97, pp. 412–420 (1997)
18. Dijkstra, E.W.: A note on two problems in connexion with graphs. Numerische Mathematik 1(1), 269–271 (1959)
19. McCallum, A., Nigam, K., et al.: A comparison of event models for naive bayes text classification. In: AAAI 1998 Workshop on Learning for Text Categorization, vol. 752, pp. 41–48. Citeseer (1998)

Providing Alternative Declarative Descriptions for Entity Sets Using Parallel Concept Lattices

Thomas Gottron[1], Ansgar Scherp[2], and Stefan Scheglmann[1]

[1] WeST – Institute for Web Science and Technologies
University of Koblenz-Landau, Koblenz, Germany
{gottron,schegi}@uni-koblenz.de
[2] Kiel University, Kiel, Germany
Leibniz Information Center for Economics, Kiel, Germany
mail@ansgarscherp.net

Abstract. We propose an approach for modifying a declarative description of a set of entities (e.g., a SPARQL query) for the purpose of finding alternative declarative descriptions for the entities. Such a shift in representation can help to get new insights into the data, to discover related attributes, or to find a more concise description of the entities of interest. Allowing the alternative descriptions furthermore to be close approximations of the original entity set leads to more flexibility in finding such insights. Our approach is based on the construction of parallel formal concept lattices over different sets of attributes for the same entities. Between the formal concepts in the parallel lattices, we define mappings which constitute approximations of the extent of the concepts. In this paper, we formalise the idea of two types of mappings between parallel concept lattices, provide an implementation of these mappings and evaluate their ability to find alternative descriptions in a scenario of several real-world RDF data sets. In this scenario we use descriptions for entities based on RDF classes and seek for alternative representations based on properties associated with the entities.

Keywords: #eswc2014Gottron.

1 Introduction

Declarative descriptions of sets of entities are used in many scenarios. For instance, when querying a data backend using declarative query languages or in faceted browsing when exploring a data set. In such scenarios it is commonly assumed that a user is aware of all the declarative descriptions he may use. Quite often, however, finding an appropriate description itself is an exploratory task. This is the case in particular when dealing with data which is managed in a de-centralised manner and for which there is no fixed and pre-defined schema.

In such a case, the task of seeking a suitable declarative description for an intended data set is difficult. As the user does not know for sure what data model and vocabulary the data engineers have used to model their data, he might encounter difficulties to formulate an adequate declarative description for the data he is interested in. Even when succeeding to find an initially successful entry point for the description of the desired

V. Presutti et al. (Eds.): ESWC 2014, LNCS 8465, pp. 364–379, 2014.

set of entities, users might not be able to find the best description, i. e. a brief, concise and exhaustive description.

Existing approaches for finding alternative descriptions so far operate locally, i.e. they iteratively add or remove single declarative constraints [9]. While providing some support, these approaches cannot help in breaking out of a local optimum. Furthermore, they do not provide new inspirations to the users, which enable them to think out of the box and get new ideas for how to describe the set of data they are interested in. In traditional document search systems such problems have been encountered already and addressed with methods such as automatic result set expansion, relevance feedback and query reformulation. Similar approaches have recently been investigated for semantic web data. For example, the LOD search engine LODatio provides services to generate related, alternative SPARQL queries [9]. Other approaches aim at finding clusters of related entities [19] or refining graph-based queries [21].

In this paper, we present a generic method for finding alternative declarative descriptions for a given set of entities. It is based on building parallel formal concept lattices [22] over different sets of attributes of the data at hand and providing mappings between these lattices. These mappings allow to find alternative descriptions while preserving the set of entities as far as possible. Given the structure of formal concept lattices, we restrict ourself in this paper on conjunctive forms of declarative descriptions. However, the method is generic as the lattices can be built over arbitrary attributes of the data. A mapping between these lattices can make use of the set of described entities (i. e. the *extent* of the formal concepts) to find alternative descriptions (i. e. the *intent* of the formal concepts) for close approximations of the entity set. We present two such mappings and analyse their behaviour and quality in finding alternative descriptions of formal concepts from different lattices.

The rest of the paper is structured as follows: We provide a high level overview of the idea of suggesting alternative declarative descriptions using formal concept lattices in Section 2. In Section 3 we briefly review formal concept analysis [22] which provides the foundation for our work before we present a thorough formalisation of our idea in Section 4. In Section 5, we implement our approach and investigate its performance for a particular use case of finding alternative representations based on properties for sets of entities which are initially described on the basis of RDF type classes. We review related work in Section 6, before we conclude the paper in 7.

2 Overview to Our Approach

The idea of our approach for finding alternative declarative descriptions for a set of entities is based on two assumptions:

1. There are different sets of attributes which can be used to describe the data. In the context of RDF such different attributes can be the class types of entities, the properties used to describe them, the objects they are linked to, the vocabularies used to model them or the data sources providing information about them.
2. The user has not found an ideal declarative description in the sense that the described data set either contains too many or too few entities. Accordingly, an alternative description may extend the data set with additional entities (as long as none

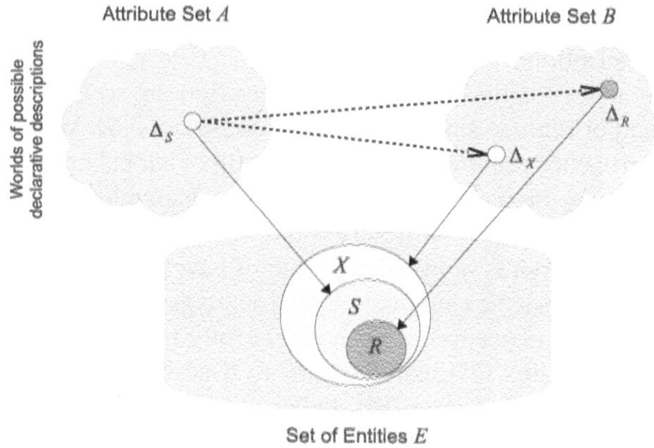

Fig. 1. Our approach is based on the idea of finding declarative descriptions Δ_X or Δ_R using an alternative set of attributes which approximates a set of entities S defined by declarative description Δ_S as close as possible

of the original entities is lost) or may restrict the data set by removing some entities (as long as no new entities are added).

Based on these assumptions, we build parallel formal concept lattices using different attribute sets. The obtained lattices structure the data set under different conjunctive combinations of the available attributes and their observed combinations. For a given node in one lattice we then define mappings which look for alternative descriptions in other lattices while trying to preserve the set of described entities as far as possible. The result is a set of entities which extends or restricts the original set as much as required to find a concise declarative description using the alternative attribute set.

Figure 1 illustrates the approach. Assume, we can alternatively use attribute sets A or B to describe entities in a set E. The two sets of attributes give rise to two worlds of possible declarative descriptions for sets of entities. Figure 1 depicts one element Δ_S of the world of descriptions using the attribute set A. This description corresponds to a subset S of entities in E. The idea is to look for alternative descriptions using the set of attributes B. Such descriptions might correspond to extensions X of S (as in the case of Δ_X) or to reductions R of S (as in the case of Δ_S).

The advantage of using a lattice structure in the world of possible declarative descriptions is that we can easily navigate in the hierarchy of sets and their subsets and supersets while having at the same time the descriptions of these sets readily available. Thus, we can efficiently explore the space of possible alternative descriptions.

3 A Review of Formal Concept Analysis

Formal concept analysis has been introduced as a mathematical framework for structuring data and deriving concepts based on the objects belonging to a concept and their common attributes [22]. Therefore, the foundation is a formal context of objects and their attributes.

Definition 1 (Formal Context, Derivative). *Let G and M be sets and $I \subseteq G \times M$ a relation. The elements in G are usually interpreted as objects, the elements in M as attributes and the reading of $(g, m) \in I$ is that object g has attribute m. Then (G, M, I) provides a* formal context.

Let $A \subseteq G$ be a set of objects in G. Then the derivative *A' of A is defined as $A' := \{m \in M : (g, m) \in I, \forall g \in A\} \subseteq M$. Likewise, for a subset B of attributes (i. e. $B \subseteq M$), the* derivative *B' is defined as $B' := \{g \in G : (g, m) \in I, \forall m \in B\} \subseteq G$.*

Thus, A' is the set of attributes which is common to all objects in A and B' corresponds to the set of all objects which exhibit all the attributes in B. The definition of formal concepts is based on formal contexts and the notion of derivatives.

Definition 2 (Formal Concept, Extent, Intent). *A* formal concept *(A, B) is defined to consist of a subset $A \subseteq G$ and a subset $B \subseteq M$, for which $A' = B$ and $B' = A$. For such a formal concept, the set of objects belonging to the concept (so A) is the* extent *and the set of attributes (so B) is the* intent *of the concept. The set of all formal concepts in a formal context is denoted with $\mathfrak{B}(G, M, I)$.*

According to this definition, we can use the derivative operator to shift between the two representations for a formal concept: its extent and its intent. Furthermore, we always have two particular formal concepts: the top concept $\top = (G, \emptyset)$ containing all objects and the bottom concept $\bot = (\emptyset, M)$ containing all attributes.

Definition 3 (Formal Concept Lattice). *A* formal concept lattice *$\underline{\mathfrak{B}}(G, M, I)$ is defined as the set of all formal concepts together with the partial order $\leq$ induced by the set inclusion, i. e. $(A_1, B_1) \leq (A_2, B_2) \Leftrightarrow A_1 \subseteq A_2$ (which is equivalent to $B_1 \supseteq B_2$).*

Corollary 1 (Top and Bottom Concepts in a Formal Concept Lattice). *From Definition 3, we can directly deduce that $C \leq \top, \forall C \in \mathfrak{B}$ and $\bot \leq C, \forall C \in \mathfrak{B}$.*

Example 1. We consider a set G of ten objects which for the sake of simplicity we simply enumerate from 1 to 10. The set M of attributes shall be $\{a, b, c\}$ and the left side in Table 1 visualises the relation I of which object has which attributes.

The tuple $(\{1, 4, 6, 9, 10\}, \{a, b\})$ constitutes a formal concept. The derivative of $\{1, 4, 6, 9, 10\}$ is $\{a, b\}$, as the objects $1, 4, 6, 9$ and 10 have the attributes a and b in common. Inversely, the derivative of $\{a, b\}$ is $\{1, 4, 6, 9, 10\}$ as these are the only objects exhibiting these properties.

When constructing a formal concept lattice over the formal context from Table 1, we obtain a structure as shown on the left hand side in Figure 2. The visualisation arranges concepts from the top concept above to the bottom concept below and connects two concepts with a line, if there is no other concept between them w.r.t $\leq$.

4 Using Parallel Lattices to Derive Alternative Descriptions

We now present our idea of building parallel concept lattices and how to exploit mappings between theses lattices for finding alternative descriptions.

Table 1. Example of two formal contexts over two different attribute sets

Object	a	b	c
1	×	×	×
2	×		
3		×	
4	×	×	
5	×		×
6	×	×	
7			×
8		×	×
9	×	×	
10	×	×	×

Object	x	y	z
1		×	×
2	×		
3		×	
4	×	×	×
5		×	
6	×	×	×
7		×	
8	×		
9		×	×
10	×	×	

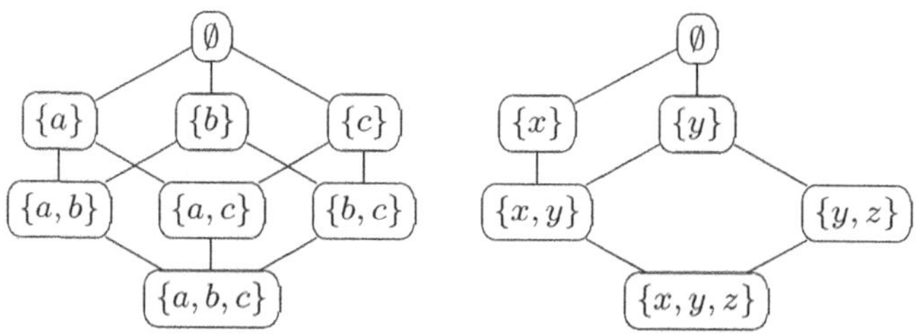

Fig. 2. Formal concept lattice structures based on the relations in Table 1. The concepts are represented by their intent—which provides a better overview.

4.1 Parallel Formal Concept Lattices

Assume we have two sets M_1 and M_2 which can serve as attributes to describe the objects in G. Accordingly, there are two relations I_1 and I_2. Then, we can construct two parallel formal concept lattices $\mathfrak{B}(G, M_1, I_1)$ and $\mathfrak{B}(G, M_2, I_2)$. Note, that while the intent of the concepts in parallel lattices is defined over two different sets of attributes, the extent of the concepts are always based on the same set G. The idea of parallel lattices can easily be extended to an arbitrary number of attribute sets.

Example 2 (Parallel Concept Lattice). In Table 1, we have listed a second relation I_2 over the set of attributes $M_2 = \{x, y, z\}$. In I_2 the same objects are related to a different set of attributes. If we construct a formal concept lattice over this relation we obtain the lattice on the right hand side in Figure 2.

4.2 Extension and Reduction Mappings between Parallel Concept Lattices

We now introduce two mappings between parallel lattices which are defined over the extent of the formal concepts in the lattices. Such mappings will allow for the approximation of the extent of a concept from a base lattice using the extent of a concept in an alternative lattice. The concept in an alternative lattice provides an alternative representation via its intent composed over a different set of attributes.

In this section, we use $\underline{\mathfrak{B}}(G, M_1, I_1)$ and $\underline{\mathfrak{B}}(G, M_2, I_2)$ as two formal concept lattices defined over the same set G and different sets M_1 and M_2. $\underline{\mathfrak{B}}(G, M_1, I_1)$ will serve as the *base lattice* for which we seek descriptions of its concepts in the *alternative lattice* $\underline{\mathfrak{B}}(G, M_2, I_2)$. For short notation we will refer to them as $\underline{\mathfrak{B}}_i := \underline{\mathfrak{B}}(G, M_i, I_i)$ and to the set of formal concepts by $\mathfrak{B}_i := \mathfrak{B}(G, M_i, I_i)$.

Definition 4 (Maximum Reduction). *Let $C_1 = (A_1, B_1)$ be a formal concept in $\mathfrak{B}_1$. We define the set of reductions of C_1 on an alternative lattice $\mathfrak{B}_2$ as* $\mathrm{red}(C_1) \in \mathcal{P}(\mathfrak{B}_2)$ *by:*

$$\mathrm{red}(C_1) := \{(A_2, B_2) \in \mathfrak{B}_2 : A_1 \supseteq A_2\} \tag{1}$$

Technically, the set $\mathrm{red}(C_1)$ *contains all formal concepts in $\mathfrak{B}_2$ where the extent is a subset of A_1. We then define the* maximum reduction *set* $\text{max-red}(C_1)$ *of a given concept C_1 as:*

$$\text{max-red}(C_1) := \{C_2 \in \mathrm{red}(C_1) : (\nexists C_2' \in \mathrm{red}(C_1) : C_2 \leq C_2')\} \tag{2}$$

In other words: the maximum reduction contains formal concepts in the alternative lattice for which the extent is an as large as possible reduced (i. e. subset) approximation of A_1. This means, there is no other formal concept which is larger (under the partial order $\leq$) and which still has an extent that is a subset of A_1. If no larger reduction is found, max-red will contain the bottom concept as trivial solution.

Theorem 1 (Perfect Approximation in max-red**).** *For a perfect approximation the maximum reduction set is of size 1, i. e. if $\exists B_2 \in M_2 : (A_1, B_2) \in \text{max-red}(A_1, B_1)$, then $|\text{max-red}(A_1, B_1)| = 1$.*

Proof: *Trivial, as the perfect approximation is a superset of all reductions. Thus, there cannot be any other concept in* max-red.

Definition 5 (Minimum Extension). *Let $C_1 = (A_1, B_1)$ be a formal concept in $\mathfrak{B}_1$. We define the set of extensions of C_1 on an alternative lattice $\mathfrak{B}_2$ as* $\mathrm{ext}(C_1) \in \mathcal{P}(\mathfrak{B}_2)$ *by:*

$$\mathrm{ext}(C_1) := \{(A_2, B_2) \in \mathfrak{B}_2 : A_1 \subseteq A_2\} \tag{3}$$

We then define the minimum extension *set* $\text{min-ext}(C_1)$ *of a given concept C_1 as:*

$$\text{min-ext}(C_1) := \{C_2 \in \mathrm{ext}(C_1) : (\nexists C_2' \in \mathrm{ext}(C_1) : C_2' \leq C_2)\} \tag{4}$$

In words again: the minimum extension set contains formal concepts in the alternative lattice for which the extent is an as small as possible extension of A_1. If no smaller extension is found, min-ext will contain the top concept as trivial solution.

Theorem 2 (Size of min-ext**).** *There is only one concept in the minimum extension, i. e. $|\text{min-ext}(C_1)| = 1$ for all C_1.*

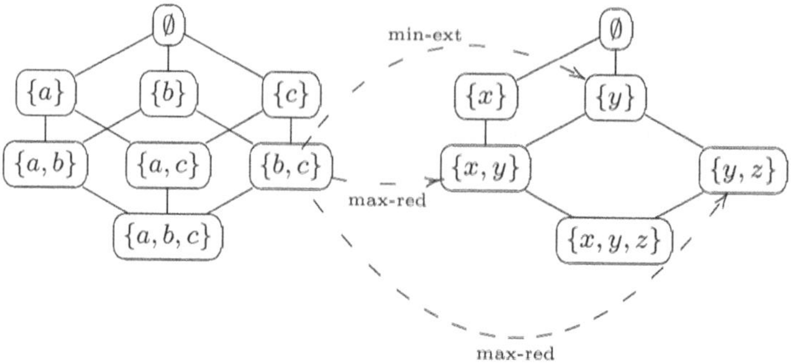

Fig. 3. max-red and min-ext mapping between two parallel formal concept lattice structures

Proof: *Assume we have* $C_2 = (A_2, B_2) \in \text{min-ext}(C_1)$ *and* $\tilde{C}_2 = (\tilde{A}_2, \tilde{B}_2) \in \text{min-ext}(C_1)$. *Now, let* $C_1 = (A_1, B_1)$, *then we have* $A_2 \cap \tilde{A}_2 \subset A_1$. *Thus, we would have a formal concept* $\hat{C}_2 = (A_2 \cap \tilde{A}_2, B_2 \cup \tilde{B}_2)$ *which is in* $\text{ext}(C_1)$ *and for which* $\hat{C}_2 \leq C_2$ *and* $\hat{C}_2 \leq \tilde{C}_2$. *This is a contradiction to the assumption that* C_2 *and* $\tilde{C}_2$ *are in* $\text{min-ext}(C_1)$. *Thus, there cannot be to two elements in* $\text{min-ext}(C_1)$.

To find alternative declarative descriptions for a given concept C_1 in the base lattice $\underline{\mathfrak{B}}_1$ we map this concept onto the sets $\text{max-red}(C_1)$ and $\text{min-ext}(C_1)$ in the alternative lattice $\underline{\mathfrak{B}}_2$.

Example 3 (Maximum Reduction and Minimum Extension). We use once more the two lattices depicted in Figure 2. Let $\mathfrak{B}_{abc} = \mathfrak{B}(G, \{a, b, c\}, I_1)$ and $\mathfrak{B}_{xyz} = \mathfrak{B}(G, \{x, y, z\}, I_2)$, where I_1 and I_2 are defined as in Table 1. We now pick the formal concept $(\{1, 4, 6, 9, 10\}, \{b, c\})$ and compute the min-ext mapping for this concept. In a first step we compute the set $\text{ext}(\{1, 4, 6, 9, 10\}, \{b, c\})$. The only two concepts in $\mathfrak{B}_{xyz}$ which satisfy that their extent is a superset of $\{1, 4, 6, 9, 10\}$ are the top concept $(G, \emptyset)$ and $(\{1, 3, 4, 5, 6, 7, 9, 10\}, \{y\})$. As the concept with intent y is smaller than the top concept, the minimum extension is:

$$\text{min-ext}(\{1, 4, 6, 9, 10\}, \{b, c\}) = \{(\{1, 3, 4, 5, 6, 7, 9, 10\}, \{y\})\}$$

This is visualised via a dashed arrow in Figure 3 labelled min-ext. The maximum reduction in this case consists of the two concepts $(\{4, 6, 10\}, \{x, y\})$ and $(\{1, 4, 6, 9\}, \{y, z\})$. The corresponding mapping is marked via dashed arrows labelled max-red.

5 Experiments

As exemplary use case and evaluation scenario we consider the task of approximating a set of Linked Data entities described through RDF type statements via a description based on properties. This task is of importance for SPARQL query recommendations in search engines [9], for deriving programmable interfaces on RDF data or when computing recommendations which vocabularies to use when modelling Linked Data [16].

Furthermore, it has been observed that sets of properties can provide good descriptors for sets of types [8]. As such the two sets of features seem promising for an approximation setting via parallel lattices.

5.1 Implementation

We used the Colibri library[1] for computing formal concept lattices [11]. The library provides a simple interface to iteratively add tuples of entities and associated attributes in order to define a formal context. These tuples can easily be extracted from RDF triples for our use case. To this end, it is sufficient to distinguish between triples using rdf:type as predicate and triples using any other URI as predicate. From the rdf:type predicate triples, we pass the subject and object, i. e. the class type URI, of the triple as entity-attribute tuple to the library for constructing a type based concept lattice. For all other triples, we pass the subject and the predicate of the triple as entity-attribute tuple to a second Colibri instance for constructing the property based lattice.

To implement the max-red and min-ext mappings, we employ a traversal of the lattices. For $\text{max-red}(C)$, we start from the bottom concept in the alternative concept lattice structure and iteratively seek upper neighbour concepts as long as they fulfil the $\text{ext}(C)$ criteria. For computing min-ext, we seek a suitable concept approximation in a similar fashion starting from the top concept and moving downwards.

5.2 Quality Metrics for the Approximations

First of all, we consider how often it is actually possible to find a non-trivial approximation in the sense that for the best match we found a concept different from top (for min-ext) and bottom (for max-red).

Furthermore, we use information retrieval metrics to evaluate how accurate are the approximative sets compared to the original set of entities. Assume, we have formal concepts $C_1 = (A_1, B_1)$ in the base lattice and a concept $C_2 = (A_2, B_2)$ in the alternative lattice. We can measure the quality of the approximation of C_1 through C_2 by means of recall (r) and precision (p) on the extent of the two concepts:

$$r(C_1, C_2) = \frac{|A_1 \cap A_2|}{|A_1|}, \quad p(C_1, C_2) = \frac{|A_1 \cap A_2|}{|A_2|}$$

Example 4 (Recall and Precision). To continue our example of the mappings from Figure 3: We approximate the concept $(\{1, 4, 6, 9, 10\}, \{b, c\})$ with a concept from the maximum reduction: $(\{1, 4, 6, 9\}, \{y, z\})$. In this case, we observe a recall of:

$$r = \frac{|\{1, 4, 6, 9\}|}{|\{1, 4, 6, 9, 10\}|} = \frac{4}{5} = 0.8$$

The precision for this approximation is $p = 1$.

Please keep in mind that for a given concept there might be multiple maximum reductions. Therefore, we select the best recall and precision values which can be achieved

[1] `https://code.google.com/p/colibri-java/`, accessed: 12 Jan, 2014.

for the approximative description in order to judge the quality of the best proposed description. This means, we compute for each concept the best recall and precision values achieved over the sets of all concepts provided as maximum reductions and select the highest score. Formally this corresponds to:

$$r\text{-}max_{\text{max-red}}(C) = \max_{C' \in \text{max-red}(C)} (r(C, C'))$$

$$p\text{-}max_{\text{max-red}}(C) = \max_{C' \in \text{max-red}(C)} (p(C, C'))$$

To assess the global quality, we aggregate the macro average of these values over all concepts in the base lattice:

$$Avg\ r\text{-}max_{\text{max-red}} = \frac{1}{|\mathfrak{B}_1|} \sum_{C \in \mathfrak{B}_1} r\text{-}max_{\text{max-red}}(C)$$

$$Avg\ p\text{-}max_{\text{max-red}} = \frac{1}{|\mathfrak{B}_1|} \sum_{C \in \mathfrak{B}_1} p\text{-}max_{\text{max-red}}(C)$$

Likewise, we define the aggregated metrics for min-ext. The only difference is that there is no need for identifying a maximum value, as there is only one candidate.

5.3 Data Sets

For our experiments, we have worked with the Billion Triple Challenge[2] (BTC) from 2012. The BTC data set was crawled from the web using a linked data spider. Thus, it represents a real-world data set of mixed quality from various application domains. While the entire BTC data set is too large to be processed with a standard implementation for formal concept analysis, the data set served as a rich resource for sampling smaller data sets. We grouped the data by the pay level domain (PLD) of the servers from which the data has been crawled originally. This lead to a total of 840 smaller data sets, each of which can be considered to be controlled by an individual data provider [4]. We selected 20 of these smaller data sets, which each contained approximately between 1 and 40 million triples. Processing data sets of this size with the Colibri implementation took between a few minutes and up to 12 hours to compute all max-red and min-ext mappings for all concepts in a pair of lattices.

For these 20 data sets, we identified the number of modelled entities, computed the base lattices using the class type definitions and the alternative lattices over the properties of the entities. Furthermore, we computed the normalised mutual information I_0 between type and property definitions. This normalised mutual information is a measure of redundancy, i. e., how well one set of attributes can explain the respective other[3]. Table 2 lists the data sets we finally used for our experiments, their size and the degree of redundancy.

[2] BTC 2012 data set: `http://km.aifb.kit.edu/projects/btc-2012/`, accessed: 12 Jan, 2014.

[3] For details we refer to [8].

Table 2. Data sets used for evaluation and their characteristics

Data set (PLD)	Triples	Entities	I_0
bbc.co.uk	1,895,817	345,087	0.717
concordia.ca	1,705,287	359,215	0.799
europa.eu	7,362,172	579,497	0.973
fao.org	1,065,538	44,095	0.954
geovocab.org	938,434	260,427	0.989
identi.ca	36,969,163	4,004,911	0.972
kasabi.com	6,170,661	974,307	0.997
legislation.gov.uk	39,200,538	4,850,236	0.897
lexvo.org	3,753,070	751,022	1.000
loc.gov	7,605,348	1,714,943	0.764
neuinfo.org	1,268,368	333,061	0.587
nytimes.com	900,892	57,072	1.000
ontologycentral.com	29,447,217	3,773,117	0.879
opera.com	44,331,144	3,547,299	0.867
ordnancesurvey.co.uk	5,765,802	589,165	0.845
oreilly.com	5,447,983	6,307	0.894
pokepedia.fr	1,043,818	25,190	0.659
rdfize.com	14,949,592	766,905	0.902
semanticweb.org	1,888,030	137,742	0.817
soton.ac.uk	2,813,256	356,701	0.690

5.4 Results and Discussion

On the base and alternative lattice structures obtained for each of the PLD data sets, we evaluated the ability of our max-red and min-ext mappings to find alternative declarative descriptions. To this end, we iterated over all the concepts in the base lattice except top and bottom and computed for each of them approximations using max-red and min-ext in the alternative lattice defined over properties. For these approximations we computed the average recall and precision and the number of concepts for which we could not find a better match than the top or bottom concept in the property lattice.

Table 3 gives an overview of how many concepts could be approximated successfully with a concept which was not the trivial match of top (for min-ext) or bottom (for max-red). We can see that for some data sets it is more difficult to find approximations than for others. The lowest performance is observed on `pokepedia.fr`, where only 2% of the concepts lead to a non-trivial approximation. This can be explained by two reasons: The number of alternative concepts is much lower than the number of concepts in the base lattice ($78 \ll 7556$). Accordingly, there is much less potential to find a good match. Moreover, as can be seen when looking at the I_0 value of this data set in Table 2, the type and property sets are not correlated very strong. Conversely, high values of I_0 and a larger number of alternative concepts are a good indicator that the mapping will find a match. Good examples for this case are `identi.ca`, `kasabi.com` and `legislation.gov.uk`. Moreover we see, that see that min-ext tendentially finds more approximations then max-red.

Table 3. Number of concepts which could be approximated by max-red and min-ext

Data set (PLD)	max-red		min-ext		Base Concepts	Alternative Concepts
bbc.co.uk	27	(38.57%)	63	(90.00%)	70	2396
concordia.ca	9	(45.00%)	15	(75.00%)	20	94
europa.eu	24	(63.16%)	35	(92.11%)	38	19046
fao.org	23	(39.66%)	45	(77.59%)	58	18007
geovocab.org	16	(64.00%)	20	(80.00%)	25	117
identi.ca	14	(93.33%)	13	(86.67%)	15	349
kasabi.com	8	(80.00%)	10	(100.00%)	10	52
legislation.gov.uk	10	(100.00%)	10	(100.00%)	10	3168
lexvo.org	6	(100.00%)	6	(100.00%)	6	327
loc.gov	49	(70.00%)	60	(85.71%)	70	1637
neuinfo.org	9	(47.37%)	9	(47.37%)	19	927
nytimes.com	4	(100.00%)	4	(100.00%)	4	69
ontologycentral.com	10	(47.62%)	10	(47.62%)	21	68739
opera.com	4	(80.00%)	4	(80.00%)	5	3073
ordnancesurvey.co.uk	27	(43.55%)	49	(79.03%)	62	171
oreilly.com	21	(80.77%)	24	(92.31%)	26	142
pokepedia.fr	152	(2.01%)	7553	(99.96%)	7556	78
rdfize.com	8	(100.00%)	8	(100.00%)	8	22
semanticweb.org	402	(39.68%)	997	(98.42%)	1013	8331
soton.ac.uk	49	(47.57%)	91	(88.35%)	103	4072

Table 4 shows the performance for successfully finding approximated declarative descriptions w.r.t. the precision and recall metrics. We can see that on average the values are quite high indicating a good capability of our approach for approximating the sets of entities. However, for a few data sets the quality of the approximations is lower than for the others. We can again point out `pokepedia.fr` which shows the lowest performance under both approximation mappings. Again, the explanation is the low correlation between the attribute sets as well as low number of alternative concepts. Also the data sets which behave good are consistent. For the data sets mentioned above (`identi.ca`, `kasabi.com`, and `legislation.gov.uk`) we get very good approximations of high quality. When comparing the two mapping methods, we see that the values for max-red are tendentially higher than the ones for min-ext. Combining this with the observation made above, we can say, that max-red might find less approximations but of higher quality, while min-ext finds more approximations which are of slightly lower average quality.

Also when looking into the obtained alternative descriptions we observed a plausible behaviour. In the `identi.ca` data set, for example, entities of type rss:Item and sioc:MicroblogPost were described as having the properties such as foaf:maker, sioc:has_ discussion, rss:link and dcterms:date, which suits the semantics of the RDF types.

To obtain deeper insights into the behaviour of our mapping functions, we compared the quality of their approximations to other indicators. Visual inspection revealed that the size of the extent of a concept seems to play an important role. In Figure 4, we see

Table 4. Results on different data sets when approximating type descriptions by properties

Data set (PLD)	max-red		min-ext	
	Avg. r	Avg. p	Avg. r	Avg. p
bbc.co.uk	0.686	1.000	1.000	0.265
concordia.ca	0.977	1.000	1.000	0.539
europa.eu	0.943	1.000	1.000	0.636
fao.org	0.808	1.000	1.000	0.510
geovocab.org	0.693	1.000	1.000	0.512
identi.ca	0.938	1.000	1.000	0.909
kasabi.com	1.000	1.000	1.000	0.807
legislation.gov.uk	0.963	1.000	1.000	0.907
lexvo.org	0.987	1.000	1.000	0.534
loc.gov	0.688	1.000	1.000	0.473
neuinfo.org	0.444	1.000	1.000	0.210
nytimes.com	1.000	1.000	1.000	1.000
ontologycentral.com	0.856	1.000	1.000	0.859
opera.com	1.000	1.000	1.000	0.500
ordnancesurvey.co.uk	0.770	1.000	1.000	0.517
oreilly.com	0.831	1.000	1.000	0.677
pokepedia.fr	0.294	1.000	1.000	0.017
rdfize.com	0.874	1.000	1.000	0.929
semanticweb.org	0.465	1.000	1.000	0.141
soton.ac.uk	0.708	1.000	1.000	0.401

a scatter plot of the size of the concepts and the quality of approximation for max-red and min-ext. The plot has been generated over the difficult pokepedia.fr data set, but demonstrates quite nicely a behaviour which we observed also for other datasets. We can see a general trend for max-red to achieve lower recall values for larger concepts. This is plausible as for higher concepts it will be difficult to get a common alternative description which does not introduce other objects. On the other hand, for min-ext we observe an increase in precision for larger concepts. Also this behaviour is plausible: if a larger concept is extended by a few additional elements, the overall precision remains quite high. Vice versa adding a few elements to a small concept drastically decreases precision.

As consequence, we propose to operate in practical applications in a mixed mode combining both methods. For small concepts it seems more fruitful to rather use minimal extension, while using for large concepts a maximal reduction. In this way, we can expect a good behaviour in general.

6 Related Work

Formal concept analysis emerged in the 80s from restructuring lattice theory in order to widen for its adoption in practice [23,22]. Various efficient algorithms have been proposed to compute formal concepts and construct a lattice from it such as [13,18]. Formal concept lattices and their creation has been successfully applied in the past in

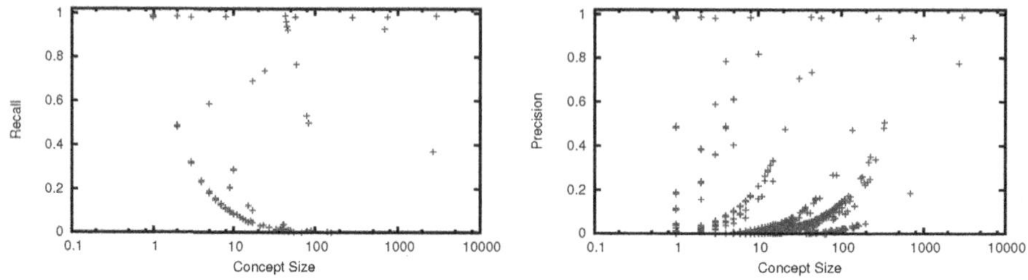

(a) max-red (b) min-ext

Fig. 4. Comparison of the size of a concept and the quality of the achieved approximations on the pokepedia.fr data set

the Semantic Web such as for analysing Linked Data [10,1] or semi-automatically constructing OWL DL ontologies [2,20]. Ferré et al. [6] describe an approach to build arbitrary relations in a formal concept lattice for the purpose of navigation. They compute a set of navigation links for a query q in order to refine the query. As concrete application scenario, they implemented a navigable UNIX file system that allows for exploring neighbouring concepts. While this allows to find *related* concepts, the approach does not aim at suggesting alternative concepts (and their attribute sets). Other works use formal concept analysis to compute mappings between the concepts of two (or more) ontologies [17,3,5]. In a first step, a lattice is constructed by analyzing a set of entities such as documents w.r.t. to the concepts defined in the ontologies. Subsequently, the lattice is used to find, e. g., class subsumption relations and class equivalence relations. Thus, the ontology alignment approaches apply a single lattice for computing the mappings between ontologies that are provided by different independent organisations. In contrast, we compute mappings between two lattices that are constructed over two kinds of intents (namely the RDF properties and the RDF types) taken from a linked data set and ontology that is curated from a single organisation and pay-level domain, respectively. Although not using formal concept analysis, we like to mention the ontology mapping work by Parundekar et al. [14,15] that computes concept mappings between two independent sources of Linked Data by considering conjunctions and disjunctions of restriction classes.

Finding alternative declarative descriptions for a set of entities can also be related to query recommendation approaches. For example, Meij et al. [12] align query logs with DBpedia concepts. They use different features for query recommendation including the history of previous queries and suggesting concepts related to the current candidate concept based on the number of concepts pointing to it (using the DBpedia property dbpprop:redirect) or concepts linked from it (count of skos:subject) [12]. Hermes [21] guides the users through the query refinement process by providing simple means such as a travel history, navigation panels, and result list panel. However, it does not proactively provide query suggestions. Based on an initial keyword query, Than et al. [19] propose a system that computes k clusters of RDF entities and presents them to the users. The clusters are computed based on their matches to the keyword query and consist of m property-value pairs. The users select relevant clusters and refine the search.

By this, the users implicitly contribute to an improved mapping of class and property combinations observed with entities that match the same keyword. Recommending related queries is also part of the LODatio system [9]. Here, Google-style modifications of SPARQL queries are provided in terms of monotonic generalisations and refinements, i. e., removing query patterns or adding new query patterns. Finally it is worth mentioning that there is also work on exact query reformulation on OWL-DL ontologies [7]. In summary, many approaches for query recommendation developed so far require the availability of a proper query log for extracting ranking information. Only a few approaches can conduct a query recommendation without such history knowledge. Among those, none have used formal concept analysis.

7 Conclusions

We presented an approach for finding alternative declarative descriptions of sets of entities which allow for a certain flexibility with respect to the entities belonging to the set. Our approach is based on using parallel formal concept lattices over the same set of objects based on different sets of descriptive attributes. We defined mappings max-red and min-ext on a base lattice, which approximate the extent of a given formal concept in an alternative concept lattice and use the intent of the approximated concept as alternative declarative description. We implemented the approach and performed experiments on 20 different data sets using formal concept lattices constructed over class types and properties of entities. The experiments showed the potential of the approach and its applicability for the presented use case.

In the future we, we plan to extend the work to implement a disjunction operator. Finally, we want to implement the approach in an application system with end users to perform a user evaluation of the alternative declarative descriptions. This will be done in the context of faceted browsing or an LOD search system.

Acknowledgements. The research leading to these results has received funding from the European Community's Seventh Framework Programme (FP7/2007-2013), REVEAL (Grant agree number 610928).

References

1. Beck, N., Scheglmann, S., Gottron, T.: LinDA: A service infrastructure for linked data analysis and provision of data statistics. In: Cimiano, P., Fernández, M., Lopez, V., Schlobach, S., Völker, J. (eds.) ESWC 2013. LNCS, vol. 7955, pp. 225–230. Springer, Heidelberg (2013)
2. Cimiano, P., Hotho, A., Stumme, G., Tane, J.: Conceptual knowledge processing with formal concept analysis and ontologies. In: Eklund, P. (ed.) ICFCA 2004. LNCS (LNAI), vol. 2961, pp. 189–207. Springer, Heidelberg (2004)
3. Curé, O., Jeansoulin, R.: An fca-based solution for ontology mediation. In: Proceedings of the 2nd International Workshop on Ontologies and Information Systems for the Semantic Web, ONISW 2008, pp. 39–46. ACM, New York (2008)

4. Ding, L., Finin, T.W.: Characterizing the Semantic Web on the Web. In: Cruz, I., Decker, S., Allemang, D., Preist, C., Schwabe, D., Mika, P., Uschold, M., Aroyo, L.M. (eds.) ISWC 2006. LNCS, vol. 4273, pp. 242–257. Springer, Heidelberg (2006)
5. Fan, L., Xiao, T.: An automatic method for ontology mapping. In: Apolloni, B., Howlett, R.J., Jain, L. (eds.) KES 2007, Part III. LNCS (LNAI), vol. 4694, pp. 661–669. Springer, Heidelberg (2007)
6. Ferré, S., Ridoux, O., Sigonneau, B.: Arbitrary relations in formal concept analysis and logical information systems. In: Dau, F., Mugnier, M.-L., Stumme, G. (eds.) ICCS 2005. LNCS (LNAI), vol. 3596, pp. 166–180. Springer, Heidelberg (2005)
7. Franconi, E., Kerhet, V., Ngo, N.: Exact query reformulation with first-order ontologies and databases. In: del Cerro, L.F., Herzig, A., Mengin, J. (eds.) JELIA 2012. LNCS, vol. 7519, pp. 202–214. Springer, Heidelberg (2012)
8. Gottron, T., Knauf, M., Scheglmann, S., Scherp, A.: A systematic investigation of explicit and implicit schema information on the linked open data cloud. In: Cimiano, P., Corcho, O., Presutti, V., Hollink, L., Rudolph, S. (eds.) ESWC 2013. LNCS, vol. 7882, pp. 228–242. Springer, Heidelberg (2013)
9. Gottron, T., Scherp, A., Krayer, B., Peters, A.: Lodatio: Using a schema-level index to support users in finding relevant sources of linked data. In: KCAP, pp. 105–108. ACM (2013)
10. Kirchberg, M., Leonardi, E., Tan, Y.S., Link, S., Ko, R.K.L., Lee, B.S.: Formal concept discovery in semantic web data. In: Domenach, F., Ignatov, D.I., Poelmans, J. (eds.) ICFCA 2012. LNCS, vol. 7278, pp. 164–179. Springer, Heidelberg (2012)
11. Lindig, C.: Mining patterns and violations using concept analysis. Tech. rep., Saarland University, Software Engineering Chair (2007)
12. Meij, E., Bron, M., Hollink, L., Huurnink, B., de Rijke, M.: Learning semantic query suggestions. In: Bernstein, A., Karger, D.R., Heath, T., Feigenbaum, L., Maynard, D., Motta, E., Thirunarayan, K. (eds.) ISWC 2009. LNCS, vol. 5823, pp. 424–440. Springer, Heidelberg (2009)
13. Nourine, L., Raynaud, O.: A fast algorithm for building lattices. Inf. Process. Lett. 71(5-6), 199–204 (1999)
14. Parundekar, R., Knoblock, C.A., Ambite, J.L.: Linking and building ontologies of linked data. In: Patel-Schneider, P.F., Pan, Y., Hitzler, P., Mika, P., Zhang, L., Pan, J.Z., Horrocks, I., Glimm, B. (eds.) ISWC 2010, Part I. LNCS, vol. 6496, pp. 598–614. Springer, Heidelberg (2010)
15. Parundekar, R., Knoblock, C.A., Ambite, J.L.: Discovering concept coverings in ontologies of linked data sources. In: Cudré-Mauroux, P., et al. (eds.) ISWC 2012, Part I. LNCS, vol. 7649, pp. 427–443. Springer, Heidelberg (2012)
16. Schaible, J., Gottron, T., Scheglmann, S., Scherp, A.: Lover: support for modeling data using linked open vocabularies. In: Guerrini, G. (ed.) EDBT/ICDT Workshops, pp. 89–92. ACM (2013)
17. Stumme, G., Maedche, A.: Fca-merge: Bottom-up merging of ontologies. In: Nebel, B. (ed.) Proceedings of the Seventeenth International Joint Conference on Artificial Intelligence, IJCAI 2001, Seattle, Washington, USA, August 4-10, pp. 225–234 (2001)
18. Stumme, G., Taouil, R., Bastide, Y., Pasquier, N., Lakhal, L.: Computing iceberg concept lattices with titanic. Data & Knowledge Engineering 42(2), 189–222 (2002)
19. Tran, T., Ma, Y., Cheng, G.: Pay-less entity consolidation: exploiting entity search user feedbacks for pay-as-you-go entity data integration. In: Web Science, pp. 317–325. ACM (2012)

20. Völker, J., Rudolph, S.: Lexico-logical acquisition of OWL DL axioms. In: Medina, R., Obiedkov, S. (eds.) ICFCA 2008. LNCS (LNAI), vol. 4933, pp. 62–77. Springer, Heidelberg (2008)
21. Wang, H., Penin, T., Xu, K., Chen, J., Sun, X., Fu, L., Liu, Q., Yu, Y., Tran, T., Haase, P., Studer, R.: Hermes: a travel through semantics on the data web. In: SIGMOD, pp. 1135–1138. ACM (2009)
22. Wille, R.: Restructuring lattice theory: An approach based on hierarchies of concepts. In: Ferré, S., Rudolph, S. (eds.) ICFCA 2009. LNCS, vol. 5548, pp. 314–339. Springer, Heidelberg (2009)
23. Wille, R.: Conceptual graphs and formal concept analysis. In: Delugach, H.S., Keeler, M.A., Searle, L., Lukose, D., Sowa, J.F. (eds.) ICCS 1997. LNCS, vol. 1257, pp. 290–303. Springer, Heidelberg (1997)

Unsupervised Link Discovery through Knowledge Base Repair

Axel-Cyrille Ngonga Ngomo, Mohamed Ahmed Sherif, and Klaus Lyko

Department of Computer Science
University of Leipzig
Augustusplatz 10, 04109 Leipzig, Germany
{ngonga,sherif,lyko}@informatik.uni-leipzig.de

Abstract. The Linked Data Web has developed into a compendium of partly very large datasets. Devising efficient approaches to compute links between these datasets is thus central to achieve the vision behind the Data Web. Unsupervised approaches to achieve this goal have emerged over the last few years. Yet, so far, none of these unsupervised approaches makes use of the replication of resources across several knowledge bases to improve the accuracy it achieves while linking. In this paper, we present COLIBRI, an iterative unsupervised approach for link discovery. COLIBRI allows the discovery of links between n datasets ($n \geq 2$) while improving the quality of the instance data in these datasets. To this end, COLIBRI combines error detection and correction with unsupervised link discovery. We evaluate our approach on five benchmark datasets with respect to the F-score it achieves. Our results suggest that COLIBRI can significantly improve the results of unsupervised machine-learning approaches for link discovery while correctly detecting erroneous resources.

Keywords: #eswc2014Ngonga.

1 Introduction

Over the last years, the Linked Open Data cloud has evolved from a mere 12 to more than 300 knowledge bases [1]. The basic architectural principles behind this data compendium are akin to those of the document Web and thus decentralized in nature.[1] This architectural choice has led to knowledge pertaining to the same domain being published by independent entities in the Linked Open Data cloud. For example, information on drugs can be found in Diseasome[2] as well as DBpedia[3] and Drugbank.[4] Moreover, certain datasets such as DBLP have been published by several bodies,[5] leading to duplicated content in the Data Web. With the growth of the number of independent data providers, the concurrent publication of datasets containing related information promises to become a phenomenon of increasing importance. Enabling the

[1] See `http://www.w3.org/DesignIssues/LinkedData.html`.
[2] `http://wifo5-03.informatik.uni-mannheim.de/diseasome/`
[3] `http://dbpedia.org`
[4] `http://wifo5-03.informatik.uni-mannheim.de/drugbank/`
[5] `http://dblp.l3s.de/`, `http://datahub.io/dataset/fu-berlin-dblp` and `http://dblp.rkbexplorer.com/`

V. Presutti et al. (Eds.): ESWC 2014, LNCS 8465, pp. 380–394, 2014.

joint use of these datasets for tasks such as federated queries, cross-ontology question answering and data integration is most commonly tackled by creating links between the resources described in the datasets. Devising accurate link specifications (also called linkage rules [11]) to compute these links has yet been shown to be a difficult and time-consuming problem in previous works [11,10,19,21].

The insight behind this work is that declarative link specifications (e.g., SILK and LIMES specifications) compare the property values of resources by using similarity functions to determine whether they should be linked. For example, imagine being given three knowledge bases K_1 that contains cities, K_2 that contains provinces and K_3 that contains countries as well as the `dbo:locatedIn` predicate[6] as relation. The specification that links K_1 to K_2 might compare province labels while the specifications that link K_1 and K_2 to K_3 might compare country labels. Imagine the city `Leipzig` in K_1 were linked to `Saxony` in K_2 and to `Germany` in K_3. In addition, imagine that `Saxony` were erroneously linked to `Prussia`. If we assume the first Linked Data principle (i.e., "Use URIs as names for things")[7], then the following holds: By virtue of the transitivity of `dbo:locatedIn` and of knowing that it is a many-to-1 relation,[8] we can deduce that one of the links in this constellation must be wrong. Note that this inference would hold both under open- and closed-world assumptions. Thus, if we knew the links between `Leipzig` and `Germany` as well as `Leipzig` and `Saxony` to be right, we could then repair the value of the properties of `Saxony` that led it to be linked to `Prussia` instead of `Germany` and therewith ensure that is linked correctly in subsequent link discovery processes.

We implement this intuition by presenting COLIBRI, a novel iterative and unsupervised approach for LD. COLIBRI uses link discovery results for *transitive many-to-1 relations* (e.g., `locatedIn` and `descendantSpeciesOf`) and *transitive 1-to-1 relations* (e.g., `owl:sameAs`) between instances in knowledge bases for the sake fo attempting to repair the instance knowledge in these knowledge bases and improve the overall quality of the links. In contrast to most of the current unsupervised LD approaches, COLIBRI takes an n-set[9] of set of resources $K_1, \ldots, K_n$ with $n \geq 2$ as input. In a *first step*, our approach applies an *unsupervised machine-learning* approach to each pair (K_i, K_j) of sets of resources (with $i \neq j$). By these means, COLIBRI generates $n(n-1)$ mappings. Current unsupervised approaches for LD would terminate after this step and would not make use of the information contained in some mappings to improve other mappings. The intuition behind COLIBRI is that using such information can help improve the overall accuracy of a link discovery process if the links are *many-to-1 and transitive* or *1-to-1 and transitive*. To implement this insight, all mappings resulting from the first step are forwarded to a *voting approach* in a *second step*. The goal of the voting approach is to detect possible errors within the mappings that were computed in the previous step (e.g., missing links). This information is subsequently used in the *third*

---

[6] The prefix `dbo:` stands for `http://dbpedia.org/ontology/`

[7] `http://www.w3.org/DesignIssues/LinkedData.html`

[8] From this characteristic, we can infer that (1) a city cannot be located in two different provinces, (2) a city cannot be located in two different countries and (3) a province cannot be located in two different countries.

[9] An n-set is a set of magnitude n.

step of COLIBRI, which is the *repair step*. Here, COLIBRI first detects the sources of errors in the mappings. These sources of errors can be wrong or missing property values of the instances. Once these sources of errors have been eliminated, a new iteration is started. COLIBRI iterates until a termination condition (e.g., a fixpoint of its objective function) is met.

Overall, the main contributions of this work are as follows:

- We present the (to the best of our knowledge) the first unsupervised LD approach that attempts to repair instance data for improving the link discovery process.
- Our approach is the first unsupervised LD approach that can be applied to $n \geq 2$ knowledge bases and which makes use of the intrinsic topology of the Web of Data.
- We evaluate our approach on six datasets. Our evaluation shows that we can improve the results of state-of-the-art approaches w.r.t. the F-measure while reliably detecting and correcting errors in instance data.

We rely on EUCLID [18] as machine-learning approach and thus provide a fully deterministic approach. We chose EUCLID because it performs as well as non-deterministic approaches on the datasets used in our evaluation [18] while presenting the obvious advantage of always returning the same result for a given input and a given setting. Moreover, it is not tuned towards discovery exclusively `owl:sameAs` links [23]. Still, COLIBRI is independent of EUCLID and can be combined with any link specification learning approach. The approaches presented herein were implemented in LIMES.[10]

2 Preliminaries

In this section, we present some of the notation and concepts necessary to understand the rest of the paper. We use Figure 1 to exemplify our notation. The formalization of LD provided below is an extension of the formalization for 2 input knowledge bases presented in [17]. Given n knowledge bases $K_1 \ldots K_n$, LD aims to discover pairs $(s_i, s_j) \in K_i \times K_j$ that are such that a given relation $\mathcal{R}$ holds between s_i and s_j. The direct computation of the pairs for which $\mathcal{R}$ holds is commonly very tedious if at all possible. Thus, most frameworks for LD resort to approximating the set of pairs for which $\mathcal{R}$ holds by using *link specifications* (LS). A LS can be regarded as a classifier C_{ij} that maps each element of the Cartesian product $K_i \times K_j$ to one of the classes of $Y = \{+1, -1\}$, where K_i is called the *set of source instances* while K_j is the *set of target instances*. $(s, t) \in K_i \times K_j$ is considered by C_{ij} to be a correct link when $C_{ij}(s, t) = +1$. Otherwise, (s, t) is considered not to be a potential link. In our example, C_{12} returns +1 for $s =$ `ex1:JohnDoe` and $t =$ `ex2:JD`.

We will assume that the classifier C_{ij} relies on comparing the value of complex similarity function $\sigma_{ij} : K_i \times K_j \rightarrow [0, 1]$ with a threshold θ_{ij}. If $\sigma_{ij}(s, t) \geq \theta_{ij}$, then the classifier returns $+1$ for the pair (s, t). In all other cases, it returns -1. The complex similarity function σ_{ij} consists of a combination of atomic similarity measures π_{ij}^l : $K_i \times K_j \rightarrow [0, 1]$. These atomic measures compare the value of a particular property of $s \in K_i$ (for example its `rdfs:label`) with the value of a particular property of

[10] `http://limes.sf.net`

$t \in K_j$ (for example its `:name`) and return a similarity score between 0 and 1. In our example, σ_{12} relies on the single atomic similarity function $trigrams(\texttt{:ssn}, \texttt{:ssn})$, which compares the social security number attributed to resources of K_1 and K_2.

We call the set of all pairs $(s,t) \in K_i \times K_j$ that are considered to be valid links by C_{ij} a *mapping* . We will assume that the resources in each of the knowledge bases $K_1, \ldots, K_n$ can be ordered (e.g., by using the lexical ordering of their URI) and thus assigned an index. Then, a mapping between the knowledge bases K_i and K_j can be represented as a matrix M_{ij} of dimensions $|K_i| \times |K_j|$, where the entry in the xth row and yth column is denoted $M_{ij}(x,y)$. If the classifier maps (s,t) to -1, then $M_{ij}(x,y) = 0$ (where x is the index of s and y is the index of t). In all other cases, $M_{ij}(x,y) = \sigma(s,t)$. For the sake of understandability, we will sometimes write $M_{ij}(s_x, t_y)$ to signify $M_{ij}(x,y)$. In our example, C_{34} is a linear classifier, $\sigma_{34} = trigrams(\texttt{:id}, \texttt{:id})$ and $\theta_{34} = 1$. Thus, (`ex3:J36`, `ex4:Cat40_1`) is considered a link.

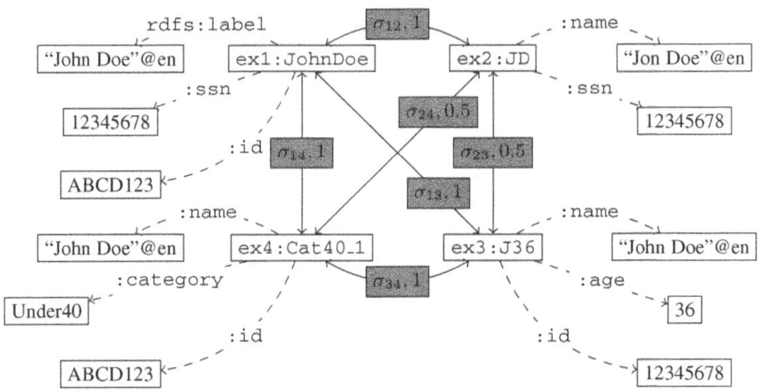

Fig. 1. Example of four linked resources from four different knowledge bases. The white nodes are resources or literals. Properties are represented by dashed labelled arrows. Links are represented by plain arrows. The grey boxes on the links show the names of the similarity measures used to link the resources they connect as well as the similarity value for each of these resource pairs. $\sigma_{12} = trigrams(\texttt{:ssn}, \texttt{:ssn})$, $\sigma_{13} = \sigma_{14} = trigrams(\texttt{:id}, \texttt{:id})$, $\sigma_{23} = \sigma_{24} = \sigma_{34} = dice(\texttt{:name}, \texttt{:name})$, $\sigma_{ij} = \sigma_{ji}$.

Supervised approaches to the computation of link specifications use labelled training data $L \subseteq K_i \times K_j \times Y$ to minimize the error rate of C_{ij}. COLIBRI relies on an unsupervised approach. The idea behind *unsupervised approaches* to learning link specifications is to refrain from using any training data (i.e., $L = \emptyset$). Instead, unsupervised approaches aim to optimize an *objective function*. The objective functions we consider herein approximate the value of the F-measure achieved by a specification and are thus dubbed pseudo-F-measures (short: PFMs) [21].

In this work, we extend the PFM definition presented in [18]. Like in [21,23,9], the basic assumption behind this PFM is that one-to-one links exist between the resources in S and T. We chose to extend this measure to ensure that it is symmetrical w.r.t. to the source and target datasets, i.e., PFM(S, T) = PFM(T, S). Our pseudo-precision $\mathcal{P}$ computes the fraction of links that stand for one-to-one links and is equivalent to the strength function presented in [9]. Let $links(K_i, M_{ij})$ be the subset of K_i whose elements are linked to at least one element of K_j. Then, $\mathcal{P}(M_{ij}) = \frac{|links(K_i,M_{ij})|+|links(K_j,M_{ij})|}{2|M_{ij}|}$. The pseudo-recall $\mathcal{R}$ computed the fraction of the total number of resources (i.e., $|K_i| + |K_j|$) from that are involved in at least one link: $\mathcal{R}(M_{ij}) = \frac{|links(K_i,M_{ij})|+|links(K_j,M_{ij})|}{|K_i|+|K_j|}$. Finally, the PFM $\mathcal{F}_\beta$, is defined as $\mathcal{F}_\beta = (1+\beta^2)\frac{\mathcal{PR}}{\beta^2\mathcal{P}+\mathcal{R}}$.

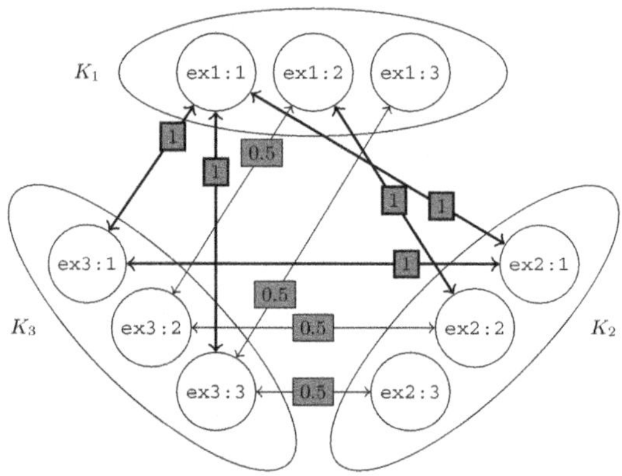

Fig. 2. Example of mappings between 3 sets of resources. K_1 has the namespace `ex1`, K_2 the namespace `ex2` and K_3 the namespace `ex3`. Thick lines stand for links with the similarity value 1 while thin lines stand for links with the similarity value 0.5.

For the example in Figure 2, $\mathcal{P}(M_{12}) = 1$, $\mathcal{R}(M_{12}) = \frac{2}{3}$ and $\mathcal{F}_1 = \frac{4}{5}$. Our PFM works best if S and T are of comparable size and one-to-one links are to be detected. For example, EUCLID achieves 99.7% F-measure on the OAEI Persons1 dataset.[11] It even reaches 97.7% F-measure on the DBLP-ACM dataset, therewith outperforming the best supervised approach (FEBRL) reported in [15]. Yet, EUCLID achieves worse results compared to FEBRL on the Amazon-Google Products dataset with an F-measure of 43% against 53.8%, where $|T| \approx 3|S|$.

3 The COLIBRI Approach

In this section, we present the COLIBRI approach and its components in detail. We begin by giving an overview of the approach. Then, for the sake of completeness, we briefly present EUCLID, the unsupervised LD approach currently underlying COLIBRI. For more information about EUCLID, please see [18]. Note that COLIBRI can be combined with any unsupervised LD approach. After the overview of EUCLID, we present the voting approach with which COLIBRI attempts to detect erroneous or missing links. In a final step, we present how COLIBRI attempts to repair these sources of error.

[11] `http://oaei.ontologymatching.org/`

3.1 Overview

Most of the state-of-the-art approaches to LD assume scenarios where two sets of resources are to be linked. COLIBRI assumes that it is given n sets of resources $K_1, \ldots, K_n$. The approach begins by computing mappings M_{ij} between resources of pairs of sets of resources (K_i, K_j). To achieve this goal, it employs the EUCLID algorithm [18] described in the subsequent section. The approach then makes use of the transitivity of $\mathcal{R}$ by computing voting matrices V_{ij} that allow detecting erroneous as well as missing links. This information is finally used to detect resources that should be repaired. An overview of COLIBRI is given in Algorithm 1. In the following sections, we explain each step of the approach.

Algorithm 1. The COLIBRI approach. $\mathcal{M}$ stands for the set of all M_{ij} while $\tilde{\mathcal{V}}$ stands for the set of all $\tilde{V}_{ij}$. The $maxIterations$ parameter ensures that the approach terminates.

```
1: F_new := 0, F_old := 0, iterations = 0
2: while F_new − F_old > 0 do
3:     F_old := F_new
4:     F_new := 0
5:     for i ∈ {1, ..., n} do
6:         for j ∈ {1, ..., n}, j ≠ i do
7:             M_ij = EUCLID (K_i, K_j)
8:             F_new := F_new + PSEUDOF(M_ij)
9:         end for
10:    end for
11:    F_new := F_new/(n(n − 1))
12:    if F_new − F_old > 0 then
13:        for i ∈ {1, ..., n} do
14:            for j ∈ {1, ..., n}, j ≠ i do
15:                V_ij = COMPUTEVOTING(M_ij, 𝓜)
16:                Ṽ_ij = POSTPROCESS(V_ij)
17:            end for
18:        end for
19:        for (a, b) ∈ GETWORSTLINKS(Ṽ) do
20:            (rs, rt) = GETREASON(a, b)
21:            REPAIR(rs,rt)
22:        end for
23:    end if
24: end while
```

3.2 EUCLID

Over the last years, non-deterministic approaches have been commonly used to detect highly accurate link specifications (see, e.g., [19,21]). EUCLID (Line 8 of Algorithm 1) is a deterministic unsupervised approach for learning link specifications. The core idea underlying the approach is that link specifications of a given type (linear, conjunctive, disjunctive) can be regarded as points in a link specification space. Finding an accurate link specification is thus equivalent to searching through portions of this specification space. In the following, we will assume that EUCLID tries to learn a conjunctive classifier, i.e., a classifier which returns $+1$ for a pair $(s,t) \in K_i \times K_j$ when $\bigwedge_{l=1}^{m} (\pi_{ij}^l(s,t) \geq \theta_{ij}^l)$ holds. The same approach can be used to detect disjunctive and linear classifiers. EUCLID assumes that it is given a set of m atomic similarity functions π^l_{ij} with which it can compare $(s,t) \in K_i \times K_j$. The atomic functions π^l_{ij} build the basis of an m-dimensional space where each of the dimensions corresponds to exactly one of the π^l_{ij}. In this space, the specification $\bigwedge\limits_{l=1}^{m} (\pi^l_{ij}(s,t) \geq \theta^l_{ij})$ has the coordinates $(\theta^1_{ij}, \ldots, \theta^m_{ij})$. The core of EUCLID consists of a hierarchical grid search approach that aims to detect a link specification within a hypercube (short: cube) which maximizes the value of a given objective function $\mathcal{F}$. The hypercubes considered by EUCLID are such that their sides are all orthogonal to the axes of the space . Note that such a hypercube can be described entirely by two points $b = (b_1, \ldots, b_m)$ and $B = (B_1, \ldots, B_m)$ with $\forall i \in \{1, \ldots, m\}(b_i \leq B_i)$.

EUCLID begins by searching through the cube defined by $b = \underbrace{(0,\ldots,0)}_{m\ times}$ and $B = \underbrace{(1,\ldots,1)}_{m\ times}$ (i.e., the whole of the similarity space). A point w with coordinates $(w_1, \ldots, w_m)$ corresponds to the classifier with the specific function $\bigwedge_{l=1}^{m} (\pi^l_{ij}(s_i, s_j) \geq w_l)$. Let $\alpha \in \mathbb{N}, \alpha \geq 2$ be the granularity parameter of EUCLID. The search is carried out by generating a grid of $(\alpha+1)^m$ points g whose coordinates $g_i = \left(b_i + k_i \frac{(B_i - b_i)}{\alpha}\right)$, where $k_i \in \{0, \ldots, \alpha\}$. We call $\Delta_i = \frac{(B_i - b_i)}{\alpha}$ the *width* of the grid in the ith dimension. EUCLID now computes the pseudo-F-measure $\mathcal{F}$ of the specification corresponding to each point on the grid. Let $g^{\max}$ be a point that maximizes $\mathcal{F}$. Then, EUCLID updates the search cube by updating the coordinates of the points b and B as follows: $b_i = (\max\{0, g^{\max}_i - \Delta_i\})$ and $B_i = (\min\{1, g^{\max}_i + \Delta_i\})$. Therewith, EUCLID defines a new and smaller search cube. The search is iterated until a stopping condition such as a given number of iterations is met.

3.3 Voting

The result of EUCLID is a set of $n(n-1)$ mappings M_{ij} which link the resource set K_i with the resource set K_j. The goal of the second step of a COLIBRI iteration is to determine the set of resources that might contain incomplete or erroneous information based on these mappings. The basic intuition behind the approach is to exploit the transitivity of the relation $\mathcal{R}$ is as follows: If the link $(s,t) \in K_i \times K_j$ is correct, then for all k with $1 \leq k \leq n$ with $k \neq i, j$, there should exist pairs of links (s,z) and (z,t) with $M_{ik}(s,z) > 0$ and $M_{kj}(z,t) > 0$. Should such pairs not exist or be weakly connected, then we can assume that some form of error was discovered.

Formally, we go about implementing this intuition as follows: We first define the voting matrices V_{ij} as $V_{ij} = \frac{1}{n}\left(M_{ij} + \sum\limits_{k=0, k\neq i,j}^{n} M_{ik}M_{kj}\right)$ (Line 15 of Algorithm 1). In the example shown in Figure 2, the mappings are

$$M_{12} = \begin{pmatrix} 1\,0\,0 \\ 0\,1\,0 \\ 0\,0\,0 \end{pmatrix}, M_{13} = \begin{pmatrix} 1 & 0 & 1 \\ 0 & 0.5 & 0 \\ 0 & 0 & 0.5 \end{pmatrix} \text{ and } M_{23} = \begin{pmatrix} 1 & 0 & 0 \\ 0 & 0.5 & 0 \\ 0 & 0 & 0.5 \end{pmatrix}.$$

The corresponding voting matrices are thus

$$V_{12} = \begin{pmatrix} 1 & 0 & 0.25 \\ 0 & 0.625 & 0 \\ 0 & 0 & 0.125 \end{pmatrix}, V_{13} = \begin{pmatrix} 1 & 0 & 0.5 \\ 0 & 0.5 & 0 \\ 0 & 0 & 0.25 \end{pmatrix} \text{ and } V_{23} = \begin{pmatrix} 1 & 0 & 0 \\ 0 & 0.5 & 0 \\ 0 & 0 & 0.25 \end{pmatrix}.$$

Each voting matrix V_{ij} encompasses the cumulative results of the linking between all pairs of resource sets with respect to the resources in (K_i, K_j). Computing V_{ij} as given above can lead to an explosion in the number of resources associated to s_i. In our example, the erroneous link between $\texttt{ex1:1}$ and $\texttt{ex3:3}$ leads to $\texttt{ex1:1}$ being linked not only to $\texttt{ex2:1}$ but also to $\texttt{ex2:3}$ in V_{12}. We thus post-process each V_{ij} by only considering the best match for each $s \in K_i$ within V_{ij}, i.e., by removing each non-maximal entry from each row of V_{ij} (Line 16 of Algorithm 1). We label the resulting matrix $\tilde{V}_{ij}$. For our example, we get the following matrices:

$$\tilde{V}_{12} = \begin{pmatrix} 1 & 0 & 0 \\ 0 & 0.625 & 0 \\ 0 & 0 & 0.125 \end{pmatrix}, \tilde{V}_{13} = \begin{pmatrix} 1 & 0 & 0 \\ 0 & 0.5 & 0 \\ 0 & 0 & 0.25 \end{pmatrix} \text{ and } \tilde{V}_{23} = \begin{pmatrix} 1 & 0 & 0 \\ 0 & 0.5 & 0 \\ 0 & 0 & 0.25 \end{pmatrix}.$$

COLIBRI now assumes that the links encoded in $\tilde{V}_{ij}$ are most probably correct. All entries of $\tilde{V}_{ij}$ being 1 are thus interpreted as all matrices agreeing on how to link the resources in (K_i, K_j). In the example in Figure 2, this is the case for $\tilde{V}_{12}(\texttt{ex1:1}, \texttt{ex2:1})$. Should this not be the case, then the disagreement between the matrices can result from the following reasons:

1. *Missing links*: This is the case in our example for the link $(\texttt{ex1:3}, \texttt{ex2:3})$ which is not contained in M_{12}. For this reason, $\tilde{V}_{12}(\texttt{ex1:3}, \texttt{ex2:3})$ is minimal.
2. *Weak links*: This is the case for the second-lowest entry in $\tilde{V}_{12}$, where the entry for $(\texttt{ex1:2}, \texttt{ex2:2})$ is due to $M_{13}(\texttt{ex1:2}, \texttt{ex3:2})$ and $M_{32}(\texttt{ex3:2}, \texttt{ex2:2})$ being 0.5.

COLIBRI now makes use of such disagreements to repair the entries in the knowledge bases with the aim of achieving a better linking. To this end, it selects a predetermined number of links (a, b) over all $\tilde{V}_{ij}$ whose weight is minimal and smaller than 1 (GETWORSTLINKS in Algorithm 1). These links are forwarded to the instance repair.

3.4 Instance Repair

For each of the links (a, b) selected by the voting approach, the instance repair routine of COLIBRI begins by computing why $\tilde{V}_{ij}(a, b) < 1$. To achieve this goal, it computes the *reason* $(rs, rt) \in \left(K_i \times \bigcup\limits_{k=1, k \neq i}^{n} K_k\right) \cup \left(\bigcup\limits_{k=1, k \neq j}^{n} K_k \times K_j\right)$ by detecting the smallest entry that went into computing $\tilde{V}_{ij}(a, b)$. Three possibilities occur:

1. $(rs, rt) \in K_i \times K_j$: In this case, the weak or missing link is due to the initial mapping M_{ij}.
2. $(rs, rt) \in K_i \times K_k$ with $k \neq i \wedge k \neq j$: In this case, the weak or missing link is due to the in-between mapping M_{ik}.
3. $(rs, rt) \in K_k \times K_j$ with $k \neq i \wedge k \neq j$: Similarly to the second case, the weak or missing link is due to the in-between mapping M_{kj}.

In all three cases, the repair approach now aims to improve the link by repairing the resource rs or rt that most probably contains erroneous or missing information. To achieve this goal, it makes use of the similarity measure σ used to generate (rs, rt). The value of this measure being low suggests that the property values p^l and q^l used across the similarity measures π^l are dissimilar. The idea of the repair is then to overwrite exclusively the values of $p^l(rs)$ with those of $q^l(rt)$ or vice-versa. The intuition behind deciding upon whether to update rs or rt is based on the *average similarity* $\bar{\sigma}(rs)$ resp. $\bar{\sigma}(rt)$ of the resources rs and rt to other resources. For a resource $s \in K_i$, this value is given by

$$\bar{\sigma}(s) = \frac{1}{n-1}\left(\sum_{k=1,k\neq i}^{n} \max_{t\in K_k} \sigma_{ik}(s,t)\right). \quad (1)$$

Here, the assumption is that the higher the value of $\bar{\sigma}$ for a given resource, the higher the probability that it does not contain erroneous information.

Let us consider anew the example given in Figure 2 and assume that the link that is to be repaired is $(\texttt{ex1:2}, \texttt{ex2:2})$. One reason for this link would be $rs = \texttt{ex1:2}$ and $rt = \texttt{ex3:2}$. Now $\bar{\sigma}(\texttt{ex1:2}) = 0.75$ while $\bar{\sigma}(\texttt{ex3:2}) = 0.5$. COLIBRI would thus choose to overwrite the values of $\texttt{ex3:2}$ with those of $\texttt{ex1:2}$.

The overwriting in itself is carried out by overwriting the values of $q^l(rt)$ with those of $p^l(rs)$ if $\bar{\sigma}(rs) \geq \bar{\sigma}(rt)$ and vice-versa. This step terminates an iteration of COLIBRI, which iterates until a termination condition is reached, such as the average value of $\mathcal{F}$ for the mappings generated by EUCLID declining or a maximal number of iterations. The overall complexity of each iteration of COLIBRI is $O(n^2 \times E)$, where E is the complexity of the unsupervised learning algorithm employed to generate the mappings. Thank to the algorithms implemented in LIMES which have a complexity close to $O(m)$ where $m = \max\{|S|, |T|\}$ for each predicate, EUCLID has a complexity of $O(pm)$, where p is the number of predicates used to compare entities. Consequently, the overall complexity of each iteration of COLIBRI is $O(pmn^2)$ when it relies on EUCLID. While we observed a quick converge of the approach on real and synthetic datasets within our evaluation (maximally 10 iterations), the convergence speed of the approach may vary on the datasets used.

4 Evaluation

The aim of our evaluation was to measure whether COLIBRI can improve the F-measure of mappings generated by unsupervised link discovery approaches. To this end, we measured the increase in F-measure achieved by COLIBRI w.r.t to the number of iterations it carried out on a synthetic dataset generated out of both synthetic and real data. To the best of our knowledge, no benchmark dataset is currently available for link discovery across $n > 2$ knowledge bases. We thus followed the benchmark generation approach for instance matching presented in [6] to generate the evaluation data for COLIBRI.

4.1 Experimental Setup

We performed controlled experiments on data generated automatically from two synthetic and three real datasets. The synthetic datasets consisted of the Persons1 and

Restaurant datasets from the OAEI2010 benchmark data sets.[12] The real datasets consisted of the ACM-DBLP, Amazon-Google and Abt-Buy datasets.[13] We ran all experiments in this section on the source dataset of each of these benchmark datasets (e.g., ACM for ACM-DBLP). We omitted OAEI2010's Person2 because its source dataset is similar to Person1's. Given the lack of benchmark data for link discovery over several sources, we generated a synthetic benchmark as follows: Given the initial source dataset K_1, we first generated $n - 1$ copies of K_1. Each copy was altered by using a subset of the operators suggested in [6]. The alteration strategy consisted of randomly choosing a property of a randomly chosen resource and altering it. We implemented three syntactic operators to alter property values, i.e., misspellings, abbreviations and word permutations. The syntactic operator used for altering a resource was chosen randomly. We call the probability of a resource being chosen for alteration the *alteration probability* (ap). The goal of this series of experiments was to quantify (1) the gain in F-measure achieved by COLIBRI over EUCLID and (2) the influence of ap and of the number n of knowledge bases on COLIBRI's F-measure.

The F-measure of EUCLID and COLIBRI was the average F-measure they achieved over all pair (K_i, K_j) with $i \neq j$. To quantify the amount of resources that were altered by COLIBRI in the knowledge bases $K_1, \ldots, K_n$, we computed the average *error rate* in the knowledge bases after each iteration as follows:

$$errorrate = 1 - \frac{1}{n(n-1)} \sum_{i=1}^{n} \sum_{j=1, j \neq i}^{n} \frac{2|K_i \cap K_j|}{|K_i| + |K_j|}. \quad (2)$$

The maximal number of COLIBRI iterations was set to 10. We present the average results but omit the standard deviations for the sake of legibility. For precision, the standard deviation was maximally 4%. The recall's standard deviation never exceeded 1% while it reached 2% for the F-measure.

4.2 Experimental Results

We varied the number of knowledge bases between 3 and 5. Moreover, we varied the alteration probability between 10% and 50% with 10% increments. We then measured the precision, recall, F-measure, runtime and number of repairs achieved by the batch version of COLIBRI over several iterations. Due to lack of space, we present portions of the results we obtained in Figure 3 and Table 1.[14] Table 1 shows an overview of the results we obtained across the different datasets. Our results show clearly that COLIBRI can improve the results of EUCLID significantly on all datasets. On the Restaurant dataset for example, COLIBRI is 6% better than EUCLID on average. On ACM, the average value lies by 4.8%. In the best case, COLIBRI improves the results of EUCLID from 0.85 to 0.99 (Amazon, $ap = 50\%$, KBs = 4). Moreover, COLIBRI never worsens the results of EUCLID. This result is of central importance as it suggests that our approach

[12] Available online at http://oaei.ontologymatching.org/2010/

[13] Available online at http://dbs.uni-leipzig.de/en/research/projects/object_matching/fever/benchmark_datasets_for_entity_resolution

[14] See http://limes.sf.net for more results.

can be used across the Linked Data Web for any combination of number of knowledge and error rates within the knowledge bases.

The results achieved on the Restaurant dataset are presented in more detail in Figure 3. Our results on this dataset (which were corroborated by the results we achieved on the other datasets) show that the results achieved by EUCLID alone depend directly on the probability of errors being introduced into the data sets. For example, EUCLID is able to achieve an F-measure of 0.94 when provided with data sets with an error rate of 30%. Yet, this F-measure sinks to 0.88 when the error rate is set to 50%. These results do suggest that EUCLID is robust against errors. This is due to the approach being able to give properties that contain a small error percentage a higher weight. Still, the COLIBRI results show clearly that COLIBRI can accurately repair the knowledge bases and thus achieve even better F-measures. On this particular data, the approach achieves an F-measure very close to 1 in most cases. Note that the number of iterations required to achieve this score depends directly on the number of knowledge bases and on the error probability.

One interesting observation is that the average F-measure achieved by EUCLID decreases with the number of knowledge bases used for linking. This is simply due to the overall larger number of errors generated by our evaluation framework when the number of knowledge bases is increased. While larger number also make the detection of errors more tedious, COLIBRI achieves significant increase of F-measure in this setting. In particular, the F-measure of EUCLID is improved upon by up to 12% absolute on the Restaurant dataset ($ap = 50\%$) as well as 7% absolute on Persons1 ($ap = 50\%$).

As expected, the runtime of our approach grows quadratically with the number of knowledge bases. This is simply due to EUCLID being run for each pair of knowledge bases.The runtimes achieved suggest that COLIBRI can be used in practical settings and on large datasets as long as the number of dimensions in EUCLID's search space remains small. In particular, one iteration of the approach on the DBLP data sets required less than 2 minutes per iteration for 3 knowledge bases, which corresponds to 3 EUCLID runs of which each checked 3125 link specifications. The worst runtimes were achieved on the Persons1 dataset, where COLIBRI required up to 11min/iteration. This was due to the large number of properties associated with each resource in the dataset, which forced EUCLID to evaluate more than 78,000 specifications per iteration.

5 Related Work

Most LD approaches for learning link specifications developed so far abide by the paradigm of supervised machine learning. One of the first approaches to target this goal was presented in [11]. While this approach achieves high F-measures, it also requires large amounts of training data. However, creating training data for link discovery is a very expensive process, especially given the size of current knowledge bases. Supervised LD approaches which try to reduce the amount training data required are most commonly based on active learning (see, e.g., [12,19]). Still, these approaches are not guaranteed to require a small amount of training data to converge. In newer works, unsupervised techniques for learning LD specifications were developed [21,18]. The main advantage of unsupervised learning techniques is that they do not require any training

Table 1. Average F-measure of EUCLID (F_E) and COLIBRI (F_C) after 10 iterations, runtime (R, in seconds) and number of repaired links L achieved across all experiments. KBs stands for the number of knowledge bases used in our experiments.

ap	10%				30%				50%			
Measures	F_E	F_C	R	L	F_E	F_C	R	L	F_E	F_C	R	L
KBs	Restaurant											
3	0.98	1.00	0.6	4	0.94	0.99	0.5	17	0.89	0.98	0.4	43
4	0.99	1.00	1.2	8	0.93	1.00	1.0	33	0.90	1.00	0.9	35
5	0.98	1.00	1.8	20	0.93	1.00	1.5	30	0.88	1.00	1.3	34
KBs	Persons1											
3	0.99	1.00	225.6	11	0.96	1.00	206.2	38	0.94	1.00	190.4	57
4	0.98	1.00	494.3	23	0.96	1.00	422.1	47	0.93	1.00	349.9	77
5	0.98	1.00	819.4	20	0.95	1.00	747.6	75	0.93	1.00	656.2	110
KBs	ACM											
3	0.95	0.96	85.7	220	0.89	0.96	69.3	301	0.84	0.95	66.5	484
4	0.94	0.94	168	12	0.88	0.88	140.4	36	0.83	0.96	131.1	261
5	0.94	0.94	271.7	30	0.87	0.94	240.9	821	0.82	0.84	202.8	348
KBs	DBLP											
3	0.94	0.98	135	220	0.85	0.97	117.2	828	0.77	0.82	111	2686
4	0.93	0.98	268.8	312	0.83	0.90	234.7	306	0.76	0.81	201.1	350
5	0.93	0.98	334.9	517	0.82	0.84	395.9	182	0.76	0.77	338.1	156
KBs	Amazon											
3	0.97	0.99	90.4	60	0.92	0.99	85.2	177	0.86	0.98	81.8	300
4	0.97	0.99	187.5	98	0.91	0.98	172.6	185	0.85	0.99	160.4	150
5	0.96	0.99	301.8	131	0.90	0.99	278.7	369	0.84	0.88	246.8	60

data to discover mappings. Moreover, the classifiers they generate can be used as initial classifiers for supervised LD approaches. In general, unsupervised approaches assume some knowledge about the type of links that are to be discovered. For example, unsupervised approaches for ontology alignment such as PARIS [23] aim to discover exclusively `owl:sameAs` links. To this end, PARIS relies on a probabilistic model and maps instances, properties and ontology elements. Similarly, the approach presented in [21] assumes that a 1-to-1 mapping is to be discovered. Here, the mappings are discovered by using a genetic programming approach whose fitness function is set to a PFM. The main inconvenient of this approach is that it is not deterministic. Thus, it provides no guarantee of finding a good specification. This problem was addressed by EUCLID [18].

While ontology-matching approaches that rely on more than 2 ontologies have existed for almost a decade [16,5], LD approaches that aim to discover between n datasets have only started to emerge in newer literature. For instance, the approach proposed by [8] suggests a composition method for link discovery between n datasets. The

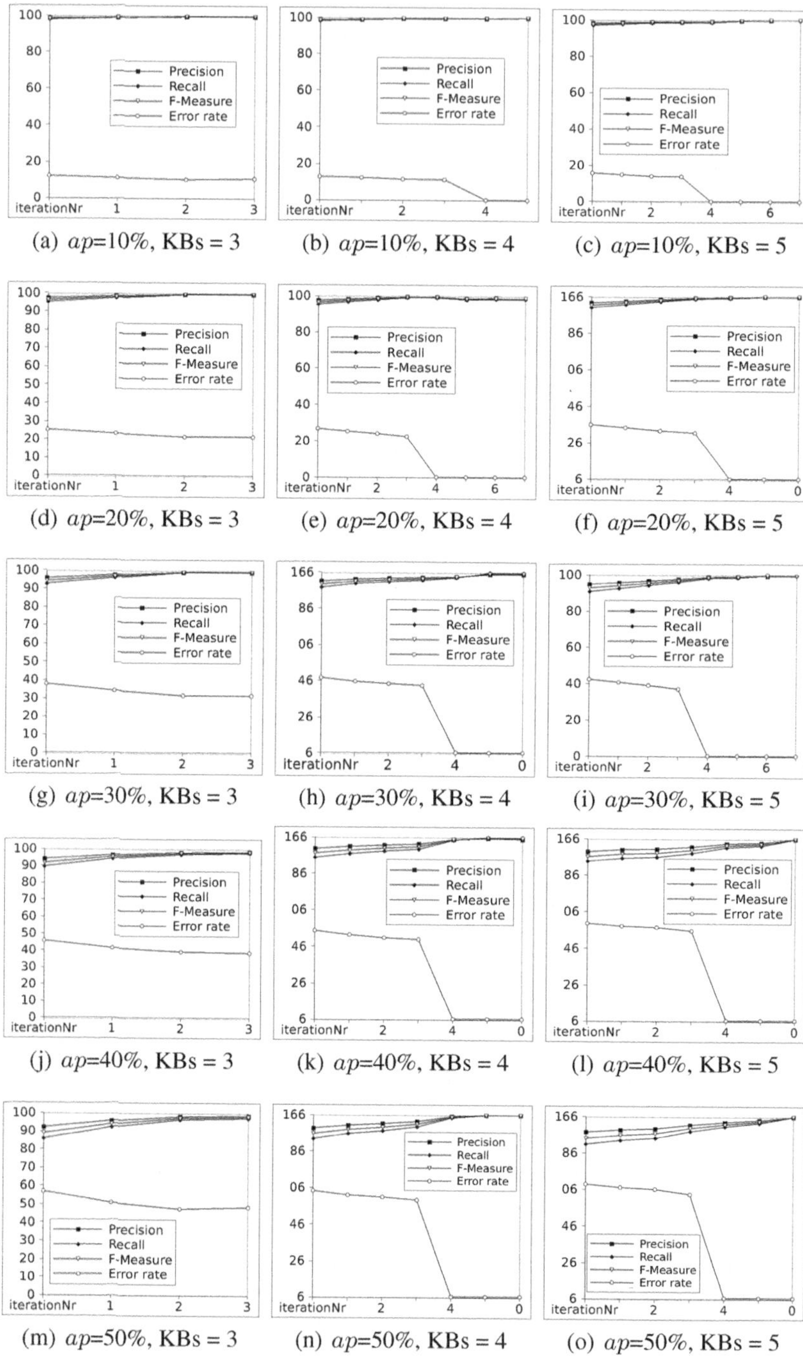

(a) ap=10%, KBs = 3 (b) ap=10%, KBs = 4 (c) ap=10%, KBs = 5

(d) ap=20%, KBs = 3 (e) ap=20%, KBs = 4 (f) ap=20%, KBs = 5

(g) ap=30%, KBs = 3 (h) ap=30%, KBs = 4 (i) ap=30%, KBs = 5

(j) ap=40%, KBs = 3 (k) ap=40%, KBs = 4 (l) ap=40%, KBs = 5

(m) ap=50%, KBs = 3 (n) ap=50%, KBs = 4 (o) ap=50%, KBs = 5

Fig. 3. Overview of the results on the Restaurants dataset approach is based on strategies for combining and filtering mappings between resources to generate links between knowledge bases. The framework introduced by [13] aims to predict links in multi-relational graph. To this end, it models the relations of the knowledge bases using set of description matrices and combines them using an additive model. The *Multi-Core Assignment Algorithm* presented by [3] automated the creation of `owl:sameAs` links across multiple knowledge bases in a globally consistent manner. The only drawback of this approach is that it requires a large amount of processing power. This problem was addressed in [3].

Approaches related to COLIBRI also include link predication approaches based on statistical relational learning (SRL). Examples of SRL approaches that can be used for predicate detection include CP and Tucker [14] as well as RESCAL [20], which all rely on tensor factorization. In general, approaches which rely on tensor factorization have a higher complexity that EUCLID. For example, CP's complexity is quadratic in the number of predicates. Related approaches that have been employed on Semantic Web data and ontologies include approaches related to Bayesian networks, inductive learning and kernel learning [4,24,2,20,22]. Due to the complexity of the models they rely on, most of these approaches are likely not to scale to very large datasets. LIMES (in which EUCLID is implemented) has yet been shown to scale well on large datasets [17]. An exact evaluation of the complexity and runtime of a combination of COLIBRI and SRL-based approaches remains future work. More details on SRL can be found in [7].

6 Conclusion and Future Work

We presented COLIBRI, the first unsupervised LD approach which attempts to repair instance knowledge in n knowledge bases ($n \geq 2$) to improve its linking accuracy. Our evaluation suggests that our approach is robust and can be used by error rates up to 50% when provided with at least 3 knowledge bases. In addition, our results show that COLIBRI can improve the results of EUCLID by up to 14% F-measure. In future work, we plan to extend our evaluation further and analyse our performance on real data as well as on knowledge bases of different size. We plan to deploy our approach in interactive scenarios within which users are consulted before the knowledge bases are updated. The voting procedure implemented by COLIBRI can be used to provide users with a measure for the degree of confidence in a predicted link and in the need for a repair within an interactive learning scenario.

Acknowledgement. The work presented in this paper was partly financed by the FP7 project GeoKnow, GA 318159 and the DFG project LinkingLOD.

References

1. Auer, S., Lehmann, J., Ngonga Ngomo, A.-C.: Introduction to linked data and its lifecycle on the web. In: Polleres, A., d'Amato, C., Arenas, M., Handschuh, S., Kroner, P., Ossowski, S., Patel-Schneider, P. (eds.) Reasoning Web 2011. LNCS, vol. 6848, pp. 1–75. Springer, Heidelberg (2011)
2. Bloehdorn, S., Sure, Y.: Kernel methods for mining instance data in ontologies. In: Aberer, K., et al. (eds.) ASWC 2007 and ISWC 2007. LNCS, vol. 4825, pp. 58–71. Springer, Heidelberg (2007)

3. Böhm, C., de Melo, G., Naumann, F., Weikum, G.: Linda: distributed web-of-data-scale entity matching. In: CIKM, pp. 2104–2108 (2012)
4. d'Amato, C., Fanizzi, N., Esposito, F.: Non-parametric statistical learning methods for inductive classifiers in semantic knowledge bases. In: ICSC, pp. 291–298 (2008)
5. Euzenat, J.: Algebras of ontology alignment relations. In: Sheth, A.P., Staab, S., Dean, M., Paolucci, M., Maynard, D., Finin, T., Thirunarayan, K. (eds.) ISWC 2008. LNCS, vol. 5318, pp. 387–402. Springer, Heidelberg (2008)
6. Ferrara, A., Montanelli, S., Noessner, J., Stuckenschmidt, H.: Benchmarking Matching Applications on the Semantic Web. In: Antoniou, G., Grobelnik, M., Simperl, E., Parsia, B., Plexousakis, D., De Leenheer, P., Pan, J. (eds.) ESWC 2011, Part II. LNCS, vol. 6644, pp. 108–122. Springer, Heidelberg (2011)
7. Getoor, L., Taskar, B.: Introduction to Statistical Relational Learning (Adaptive Computation and Machine Learning). The MIT Press (2007)
8. Hartung, M., Groß, A., Rahm, E.: Composition methods for link discovery. In: BTW, pp. 261–277 (2013)
9. Hassanzadeh, O., Pu, K.Q., Yeganeh, S.H., Miller, R.J., Popa, L., Hernández, M.A., Ho, H.: Discovering linkage points over web data. VLDB Endow. 6(6), 445–456 (2013)
10. Isele, R., Jentzsch, A., Bizer, C.: Efficient Multidimensional Blocking for Link Discovery without losing Recall. In: WebDB (2011)
11. Isele, R., Bizer, C.: Learning linkage rules using genetic programming. In: OM Workshop (2011)
12. Isele, R., Jentzsch, A., Bizer, C.: Active learning of expressive linkage rules for the web of data. In: Brambilla, M., Tokuda, T., Tolksdorf, R. (eds.) ICWE 2012. LNCS, vol. 7387, pp. 411–418. Springer, Heidelberg (2012)
13. Jiang, X., Tresp, V., Huang, Y., Nickel, M.: Link prediction in multi-relational graphs using additive models. In: SeRSy, pp. 1–12 (2012)
14. Kolda, T.G., Bader, B.W.: Tensor decompositions and applications. SIAM Rev. 51(3), 455–500 (2009)
15. Köpcke, H., Thor, A., Rahm, E.: Evaluation of entity resolution approaches on real-world match problems. VLDB Endow. 3(1-2), 484–493 (2010)
16. Madhavan, J., Halevy, A.Y.: Composing mappings among data sources. In: VLDB, pp. 572–583 (2003)
17. Ngomo, A.-C.N.: On link discovery using a hybrid approach. Journal on Data Semantics 1, 203–217 (2012)
18. Ngomo, A.-C.N., Lyko, K.: Unsupervised learning of link specifications: deterministic vs. non-deterministic. In: OM Workshop (2013)
19. Ngomo, A.-C.N., Lyko, K., Christen, V.: COALA – correlation-aware active learning of link specifications. In: Cimiano, P., Corcho, O., Presutti, V., Hollink, L., Rudolph, S. (eds.) ESWC 2013. LNCS, vol. 7882, pp. 442–456. Springer, Heidelberg (2013)
20. Nickel, M., Tresp, V., Kriegel, H.-P.: Factorizing yago: Scalable machine learning for linked data. In: WWW, pp. 271–280. ACM, New York (2012)
21. Nikolov, A., d'Aquin, M., Motta, E.: Unsupervised learning of link discovery configuration. In: Simperl, E., Cimiano, P., Polleres, A., Corcho, O., Presutti, V. (eds.) ESWC 2012. LNCS, vol. 7295, pp. 119–133. Springer, Heidelberg (2012)
22. Pérez-Solà, C., Herrera-Joancomartí, J.: Improving relational classification using link prediction techniques. In: Blockeel, H., Kersting, K., Nijssen, S., Železný, F. (eds.) ECML PKDD 2013, Part I. LNCS, vol. 8188, pp. 590–605. Springer, Heidelberg (2013)
23. Suchanek, F.M., Abiteboul, S., Senellart, P.: PARIS: Probabilistic Alignment of Relations, Instances, and Schema. PVLDB 5(3), 157–168 (2011)
24. Sutskever, I., Salakhutdinov, R., Tenenbaum, J.B.: Modelling relational data using bayesian clustered tensor factorization. In: NIPS, pp. 1821–1828 (2009)

Trusty URIs: Verifiable, Immutable, and Permanent Digital Artifacts for Linked Data

Tobias Kuhn[1] and Michel Dumontier[2]

[1] Department of Humanities, Social and Political Sciences, ETH Zurich, Switzerland
[2] Stanford Center for Biomedical Informatics Research, Stanford University, USA
tokuhn@ethz.ch, michel.dumontier@stanford.edu

Abstract. To make digital resources on the web verifiable, immutable, and permanent, we propose a technique to include cryptographic hash values in URIs. We call them *trusty URIs* and we show how they can be used for approaches like nanopublications to make not only specific resources but their entire reference trees verifiable. Digital artifacts can be identified not only on the byte level but on more abstract levels such as RDF graphs, which means that resources keep their hash values even when presented in a different format. Our approach sticks to the core principles of the web, namely openness and decentralized architecture, is fully compatible with existing standards and protocols, and can therefore be used right away. Evaluation of our reference implementations shows that these desired properties are indeed accomplished by our approach, and that it remains practical even for very large files.

Keywords: #eswc2014Kuhn.

1 Introduction

The vision of the semantic web is to make the content of the web machine-interpretable, allowing, among other things, for automated aggregation and sophisticated search procedures over large amounts of linked data. As even human users are sometimes easy to trick by spam and fraudulent content that can be found on the web, we should be even more concerned in the case of automated algorithms that autonomously analyze semantic web content. Without appropriate counter-measures, malicious actors can sabotage or manipulate such algorithms by adding just a few carefully manipulated items to large sets of input data. To solve this problem, we propose an approach to make items on the (semantic) web verifiable, immutable, and permanent. This approach includes cryptographic hash values in Uniform Resource Identifiers (URIs) and adheres to the core principles of the web, namely openness and decentralized architecture.

A cryptographic hash value (sometimes called *cryptographic digest*) is a short random-looking sequence of bytes (or, equivalently, bits) that are calculated in a complicated yet perfectly predictable manner from a digital artifact such as a file. The same input always leads to exactly the same hash value, whereas just a minimally modified input leads to a completely different value. While there is an

V. Presutti et al. (Eds.): ESWC 2014, LNCS 8465, pp. 395–410, 2014.

infinity of possible inputs that lead to a specific given hash value, it is impossible in practice (for strong state-of-the-art hash algorithms) to reconstruct *any* of the possible inputs just from the hash value. This means that if you are given some input and a matching hash value, you can be sure that the hash value was obtained from exactly that input. On this basis, our proposed approach boils down to the idea that references can be made completely unambiguous and verifiable if they contain a hash value of the referenced digital artifact. Our method does not apply to all URIs, of course, but only to those that are meant to represent a specific and immutable digital artifact.

Let us have a look at a concrete example: Nanopublications have been proposed as a new way of scientific publishing [10]. The underlying idea is that scientific results should be published not just as narrative articles but in terms of minimal pieces of computer-interpretable results in a formal semantic notation (i.e. RDF). Nanopublications can cite other nanopublications via their URIs, thereby creating complex citation networks. Published nanopublications are supposed to be immutable, but the current web has no mechanism to enforce this: It is well-known that even artifacts that are supposed to be immutable tend to change over time, while often keeping the same URI reference. For approaches like nanopublications, however, it is important to specify exactly what version of what resource they are based on, and nobody should be given the opportunity to silently modify his or her already published contributions.

With the approach outlined below, nanopublications can be identified with *trusty URIs* that include cryptographic hash values calculated on the RDF content. For example, let us assume that you have a nanopublication with identifier I_1 that cites another nanopublication with identifier I_2. If you want to find the content of I_2, you can simply search for it on the web, not worrying whether the source is trustworthy or not, and once you have found an artifact that claims to be I_2, you only have to check whether the hash value actually matches the content. If it does, you got the right nanopublication, and if not you have to keep searching (this can of course be automated). A trusty URI like I_1 does not only allow you to retrieve its nanopublication in a verifiable way, but in the next step also all nanopublications it cites (such as I_2) and all nanopublications they cite and so on. Any trusty URI in a way "contains" the complete backwards history. In this sense, the "range of verifiability" of a resource with a trusty URI is not just the resource itself, but the complete reference tree obtained by recursively following all contained trusty URIs. This is illustrated in Figure 1.

Another important property of nanopublications is that they are self-contained in the sense that they consist not only of the actual scientific assertions but also of their provenance information and meta-data. This means that nanopublications contain self-references in the form of their own identifying URIs. The calculation of a trusty URI must therefore allow for the resulting URI to be part of the digital artifact it is calculated on (this might sound impossible at first, but we show below how it can be achieved). This leads us to the formulation of the following requirements for our approach:

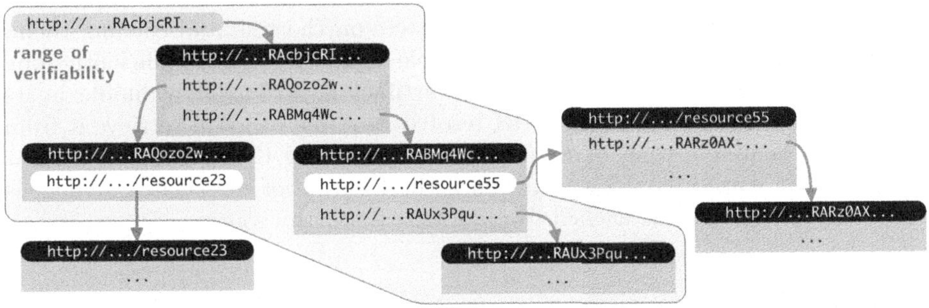

Fig. 1. Schematic illustration of the range of verifiability for the trusty URI on the top left. The green area shows its range of verifiability that covers all artifacts that can be reached by following trusty URI links (green arrows).

1. To allow for verification of not only the given digital artifact but its entire reference tree, the hash should be part of the URI of the artifact.
2. To allow for the inclusion of meta-data, digital artifacts should be allowed to contain self-references (i.e. their own URIs).
3. The verification should be performed on a more abstract level than just the bytes of a file, with modules for different types of content. It should be possible to verify a digital artifact even if it is presented in a different format.
4. The complete approach should be decentralized and open: Everybody should be allowed to make verifiable URIs without a central authority.
5. The approach should be based on current established standards and be compatible with current tools and formats, so that it can be used right away.

Though there are a number of related approaches, we are not aware of any general approach that complies with all these requirements. In particular, requirements 2 and 3 are not addressed by existing approaches. The main benefits of artifacts with a trusty URI are that they are (1) verifiable, (2) immutable, and (3) permanent. Let us briefly explain what we mean by these properties.

Trusty URI artifacts are *verifiable* in the sense that a retrieved artifact for a given URI can be checked to contain the content the URI is supposed to represent. It can be detected if the artifact got corrupted or manipulated on the way, assuming that the trusty URI for the required artifact is known, e.g. because another artifact contains it as a link. (Of course, somebody can give you a manipulated artifact with a *different* trusty URI.)

It directly follows that trusty URI artifacts are *immutable*, as any change in the content also changes its URI, thereby making it a *new* artifact. Again, you can of course change your artifact *and* its URI and claim that it has always been like this. You can get away with that if the trusty URI has not yet been picked up by third parties, i.e. linked by other resources. Once this is the case, you cannot change it anymore, because all these links will still point to the old trusty URI and everybody will notice that your new artifact is a different one.

Third, trusty URI artifacts are *permanent* if we assume that there are search engines and web archives crawling the artifacts on the web and caching them. In this situation, any artifact that is available on the web for a sufficiently long time will remain available forever. If an artifact is no longer available in its original location (e.g. the one its URI resolves to), one can still retrieve it from the cache of search engines or web archives. The trusty URI guarantees that it is the artifact you are looking for, even if the location of the cached artifact is not trustworthy or it was cached from an untrustworthy source.

2 Background

There are a number of related approaches based on cryptographic hash values. The Git version control system (`git-scm.com`), for example, uses hash values to identify commits of distributed repositories. An important difference to our approach is that hash values (called *checksums* in Git) are used to identify the respective artifacts (*commits* in Git) only within a given repository and not on the web scale. A second important difference is that the hash represents the byte content of files, whereas our approach allows for digital content at different levels of abstraction. On the technical side, Git uses the SHA-1 algorithm, which is no longer considered secure (which is not a serious problem for Git, because typically only trusted parties have write access to a repository).

The proposed standard for Named Information (ni) URIs [9] is another important related approach. It introduces a new URI protocol `ni` to refer to digital artifacts with hash values in a uniform way. These are two examples of ni-URIs:

```
ni:///sha-256;UyaQV-Ev4rdLoHyJJWCi11OHfrYv9E1aGQAlMO2X_-Q
ni://example.org/sha-256;5AbXdpz5DcaYXCh9l3eI9ruBosiL5XDU3rxBbBaUO70
```

The ni-URI approach allows for different hash algorithms, such as SHA-256 (which is, in contrast to SHA-1, considered secure) and optional specification of an authority, such as `example.org`, where the artifact can be found. It misses, however, some of the features of our requirements list. As with Git, ni-URIs do not define how digital artifacts can be represented at a more abstract level than their sequence of bytes, and self-references are not supported. Furthermore, current browsers do not recognize the `ni` protocol, and administrator access to a server is needed to make these URIs resolvable. The latter two points are not a real problem in the long run, but they might hinder the adoption of the standard in the first place. The approach presented in this paper is complementary and compatible. We propose trusty URIs, which can be mapped to ni-URIs but are more flexible and provide additional features.

There are a number of existing approaches to include hash values in URIs for verifiability purposes, e.g. for legal documents [11]. The downside of such custom-made solutions is that custom-made software is required to generate, resolve, and check the hash references. Standards have been proposed for the verification of quantitative datasets [1] and XML documents [2], but they are not general enough to cover RDF content (at least not in a convenient way) and keep the hash value separate from the URI reference, which means that the range of verifiability does not directly extend to referenced artifacts.

To calculate hash values on content that is more abstract than just a fixed sequence of bytes, common approaches require the normalization (also called *canonicalization*) of the respective data structures such as RDF graphs. In the general case, RDF graph normalization is known to be a very hard problem, possibly unsolvable in polynomial time [8]. This stems from the difficulty of handling blank nodes, i.e. identifiers that are only unique in a local scope and can be locally renamed without effects on semantics. Without blank nodes, normalization boils down to sorting of RDF triples, which can be performed in $O(n \log n)$. The need for sorting can even be eliminated by using incremental cryptography [3], which allows for calculating digests for RDF graphs without blank nodes in linear time [17]. Such incremental approaches, however, are not as well-studied as mainstream cryptography methods, and open the possibility of new kinds of attacks [16]. Efficient normalization algorithms that support blank nodes put restrictions on the graph structure and require additional (semantically neutral) triples to be added to some graphs before they can be processed [8,17].

Similar methods to the ones presented in this paper, i.e. calculating hash values in a format-independent manner, have been proposed to track the provenance of data sets [14]. This has been used to define a conceptualization of multi-level identities for digital works based on cryptographic digests and formal semantics, covering different conceptual levels from single HTTP transactions to high-level content identifiers [15].

3 Approach

We propose here a modular approach, where different modules handle different kinds of content on different conceptual levels of abstraction, from byte level to high-level formalisms. Besides that, the most important features of our approach are self-references, the handling of blank nodes, and the mapping to ni-URIs.

General Structure. Trusty URIs end with a hash value in Base64 notation (i.e. `A`–`Z`, `a`–`z`, `0`–`9`, `-`, and `_` representing the numbers from 0 to 63) that is preceded by a module identifier. This is an example:

```
http://example.org/r1.RA5AbXdpz5DcaYXCh9l3eI9ruBosiL5XDU3rxBbBaUO70
```

Everything that comes after `r1.` is the part that is specific to trusty URIs, which we call *artifact code*. Its first two characters `RA` identify the module specifying its type (first character) and version (second character). The remaining 43 characters represent the actual hash value. The modules defined so far use SHA-256 hashes, but future modules might use other hash functions. For convenience reasons, a file extension like `.nq` can be added to the end of such URIs:

```
http://example.org/r1.RA5AbXdpz5DcaYXCh9l3eI9ruBosiL5XDU3rxBbBaUO70.nq
```

This is technically not a trusty URI anymore, but it is easy to strip the extension and get the respective trusty URI from it. As the hash is located in the final part of the URI, it is straightforward to store it in file names and to deal with it in a local file system without worrying about the first part of the URI:

```
r1.RA5AbXdpz5DcaYXCh9l3eI9ruBosiL5XDU3rxBbBaUO70.nq
```

We call these *trusty files*. The precise specification of trusty URIs can be found online.[1] As a general side remark, it is noteworthy that our approach entails a certain shift of authority: Once a trusty URI is established, its artifact code defines what object it refers to, and the issuing authority has no longer the power to change its meaning.

Self-References. To support self-references, i.e. resources that contain their own trusty URI, the generation process involves not just to compute the hash from a given artifact but to actually transform the artifact into a new version that contains the newly generated trusty URI. For example, a resource like `http://example.org/r2` might have the following RDF content with a self-reference:

```
<http://example.org/r2> dc:description "something" .
```

To transform such a resource, we first define the structure of the new trusty URI by adding a placeholder [C] where the artifact code should eventually appear. In the given example, the content would then look like this:

```
<http://example.org/r2.[C]> dc:description "something" .
```

Note that it is necessary to add a non-Base64 character (in this case a dot ".") as a delimiter in front of [C] if it would otherwise be preceded by a Base64 character. On such content, we can calculate a hash value by interpreting the placeholder [C] as a blank space (the result is unambiguous as URIs are not allowed to otherwise contain blank spaces). Then we can replace the placeholder by the calculated artifact code and we end up with a trusty URI like this:

```
http://example.org/r2.RAi7LA7Zlew99hdp0joN0APT4_uB3XDFwduiKXnNBja5E
```

For strong hashing algorithms, it is impossible in practice that this calculated sequence of bytes was already part of the original content before the transformation. This entails that the replacing of the placeholder is reversible.

This reversibility is needed once an existing trusty URI resource containing self-references should be verified. We can revert the transformation described above by replacing all occurrences of the artifact code with a blank space, and then calculate the hash in the same way as when a resource is transformed. The content is successfully verified if and only if the resulting hash matches the one from the trusty URI.

[1] `https://github.com/trustyuri/trustyuri-spec`

Blank Nodes. The support for self-references requires us to transform the preliminary content of a trusty URI artifact into its final version, and we can make use of this transformation to also solve the problem of blank nodes in RDF. Our approach is to eliminate blank nodes during the transformation process by converting them into URIs. Blank nodes can be seen as existentially quantified variables, which we can turn into constants by Skolemization, i.e. by introducing URIs that have not been used anywhere before. Using the trusty URI with a suffix enumerating the blank nodes, we can create such URIs guaranteed to have never been used before (the artifact code being just a placeholder at first, as above):

```
http://example.org/r3.RACjKTA5d123ed7JIpgPmSOEOdcU-XmWIBnGn6Iyk8B-U..1
http://example.org/r3.RACjKTA5d123ed7JIpgPmSOEOdcU-XmWIBnGn6Iyk8B-U..2
```

The two dots "`..`" indicate that these were derived from blank nodes, but they are now immutable URIs. This approach solves the problem of blank nodes for normalization, is completely general (i.e. works on any possible input graph), fully respects RDF semantics, and does not require auxiliary triples to be added.

ni-URIs. Our approach is compatible with ni-URIs (see above), and all trusty URIs can be transformed into ni-URIs, with or without explicitly specifying an authority:

```
ni:///sha-256;5AbXdpz5DcaYXCh9l3eI9ruBosiL5XDU3rxBbBaUO70
ni://example.org/sha-256;5AbXdpz5DcaYXCh9l3eI9ruBosiL5XDU3rxBbBaUO70
```

The fact that the module identifier is lost does not affect the uniqueness of the hash, but to verify a resource all available modules have to be tried in the worst case. To avoid this, we propose to use an optional argument `module`:

```
ni:///sha-256;5AbXdpz5DcaYXCh9l3eI9ruBosiL5XDU3rxBbBaUO70?module=RA
```

Modules. There are currently two module types available: `F` for representing byte-level file content and `R` for RDF graphs. For both types, version `A` is the only version available as of now, leading to the module identifiers `FA` and `RA`. For module `FA`, a hash value is calculated using SHA-256 on the content of a file in byte representation. The hash value is transformed to Base64 notation (after appending two zero-bits), and the resulting 43 characters make up the hash part of the trusty URI. Module `RA` works on RDF content and can cover multiple named graphs. It supports self-references and handles blank nodes as described above. To calculate the hash, the RDF statements are sorted, then they are serialized in a given way (interpreting the artifact's hash as a blank space), and finally SHA-256 is applied in the same way as for `FA`.

Note that for an RDF document, either of the modules `FA` and `RA` could be used. The right choice depends on what the URI should identify. If it should identify a *file* in a particular format and containing a fixed number of bytes, then `FA` should be used. If it should, however, identify *RDF content* independently of its serialization in a particular file, then `RA` should be used. For modules such as `RA` that operate not just on the byte level, *content negotiation* can be used to return the same content in different formats (depending on the requested content type in the HTTP request) when a trusty URI is accessed.

Even though we focus on RDF in this paper, the approach and architecture of trusty URIs are general and we plan to provide modules for additional kinds of content in the future. This could include tabular or matrix content (e.g. CSV or Excel files), content with tree structure (e.g. XML), hypertext (e.g. HTML or Markdown), bitmaps (e.g. PNG or JPEG), and vector graphics (e.g. SVG). New modules might also become necessary if the used hash algorithms should become vulnerable to attacks in the future.

4 Implementation

There are currently three trusty URI implementations in the form of code libraries in Java, Perl, and Python.[2] The Java implementation uses the *Sesame* library [5] for RDF processing and the *nanopub-java* library[3] for dealing with nanopublications. The Perl implementation makes use of the *Trine* package for processing RDF, and the Python implementation uses the *RDFLib* package.[4]

These implementations provide a number of common functions for the different modules and formats. Currently, the following functions are available:

CheckFile takes a file and validates its hash by applying the respective module.
ProcessFile takes a file, calculates its hash using module `FA`, and renames it to make it a trusty file.
TransformRdf takes an RDF file and a base URI, and transforms the file into a trusty file using module `RA`.
TransformLargeRdf is the same as above but using temporary files instead of loading the entire content into memory.
TransformNanopub takes a nanopublication file and calls TransformRdf to transform it.
CheckLargeRdf checks an RDF file using module `RA` without loading the whole content into memory but using temporary files instead.
CheckSortedRdf checks an RDF file assuming that it is already sorted (and raises an error otherwise). The current implementations generate such sorted files by default, but this is not required by the specification.
CheckNanopubViaSparql takes a SPARQL endpoint URL and a trusty URI representing a nanopublication, retrieves the nanopublication from the repository, and tries to validate it.
RunBatch reads commands (any of the above) from a file and executes them one after the other.

---

[2] `https://github.com/trustyuri/trustyuri-java`, `https://github.com/trustyuri/trustyuri-perl`, `https://github.com/trustyuri/trustyuri-python`
[3] `https://github.com/Nanopublication/nanopub-java`
[4] `http://search.cpan.org/dist/RDF-Trine/`, `https://github.com/RDFLib/rdflib`

Table 1. Comparison of the different trusty URI libraries ('✓' = implemented features; '–' = cases where the necessary features are not available in the used RDF libraries)

module	function	format	Java	Perl	Python
(general)	RunBatch		✓	✓	✓
File	CheckFile		✓	✓	✓
	ProcessFile		✓	✓	✓
RDF	CheckFile	RDF/XML	✓	✓	✓
		Turtle	✓	✓	✓
		N-Triples	✓	✓	✓
		TriX	✓	–	✓
		TriG	✓	✓	–
		N-Quads	✓	✓	✓
	CheckLargeRdf	*(all of the above)*	✓		
	CheckSortedRdf	*(all of the above)*	✓		
	TransformRdf	RDF/XML	✓		✓
		Turtle	✓		✓
		N-Triples	✓		✓
		TriX	✓	–	✓
		TriG	✓	–	–
		N-Quads	✓		✓
	TransformLargeRdf	*(all of the above)*	✓		
	TransformNanopub	TriX	✓	–	
		TriG	✓	–	–
		N-Quads	✓		
	CheckNanopubViaSparql		✓		

Not all these functions are currently supported by all implementations, as shown in Table 1.

5 Application

Below, we describe two applications of the trusty URI approach: one involving nanopublications (nanobrowser) and one involving a dataset in RDF format with a large variation in file size (Bio2RDF).

5.1 Nanobrowser

Nanobrowser [13] is a prototype of a web application via which nanopublications can be searched, browsed, published, and commented. Figure 2 shows a screenshot. Nanobrowser applies a number of extensions to the nanopublication approach, such as support for semi-formal and informal statements (represented by atomic and independent English sentences, i.e. a kind of controlled natural language [12]) and support for meta-nanopublications, e.g. nanopublications containing opinions on other nanopublications.

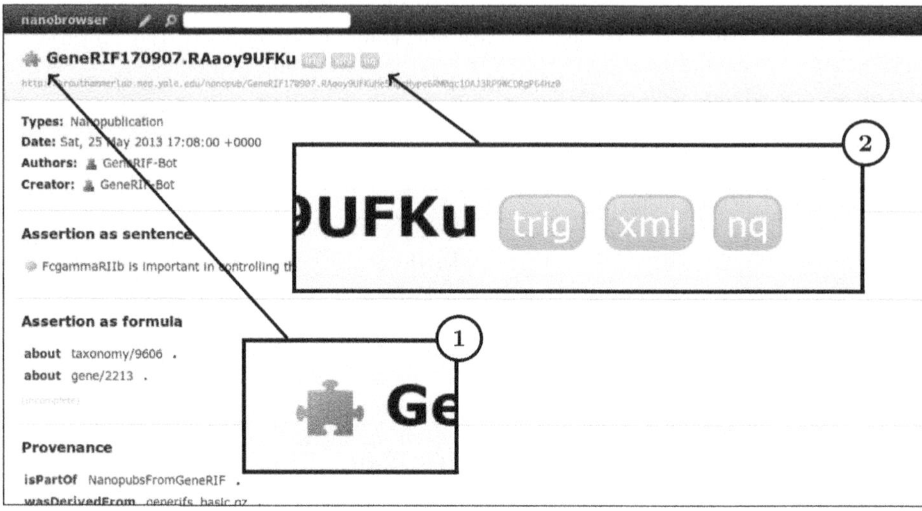

Fig. 2. Screenshot of the nanobrowser interface. A green jigsaw puzzle icon (1) indicates successful verification of nanopublications, which can be downloaded (and verified locally) in different formats (2).

All nanopublications created via the nanobrowser interface are identified by trusty URIs. If a user requests a nanopublication with a given trusty URI, it is retrieved from the internal triple store and verified before it is shown to the user. A green jigsaw puzzle icon indicates that the verification was successful (see Figure 2). A particular nanopublication can be downloaded in different formats and its trusty URI can be checked locally and independently of the format.

5.2 Bio2RDF

Bio2RDF (`bio2rdf.org`) is an open-source project focused on the provision of linked data for the life sciences [6,4]. Bio2RDF scripts convert heterogeneously formatted data (e.g. flat files, tab-delimited files, dataset-specific formats, SQL, and XML) into a common format — RDF. Bio2RDF entities are identified using URIs that are resolvable using the Bio2RDF Web Application, a servlet that answers HTTP requests by formulating SPARQL queries against the appropriate SPARQL endpoints. Over 1 billion triples for 19 resources were made available in the second coordinated release of Bio2RDF [6], and mappings to the Semanticscience Integrated Ontology [7] have been established. Together, these serve to provide ontology-based access to data on the emerging semantic web.

The release numbers of Bio2RDF provide a way to refer to a specific version of a dataset, e.g. for citing it in a scientific article or a nanopublication. However this assumes trust in the Bio2RDF developers that they do not silently change the data of a particular release. Furthermore, an intruder might be able to change parts of the data without being noticed, the data might get corrupted or manipulated when transferred or downloaded, and there might be no other trusted parties providing the dataset if the Bio2RDF website should become temporarily or permanently inaccessible. The use of trusty URIs would solve all these problems. Below we show an evaluation on release 2 of Bio2RDF, and we plan to provide trusty URIs for the datasets of its upcoming next release.

6 Evaluation

Below we present some experiments on the trusty URI concept and its implementations, based on two collections of RDF files.

6.1 Hash Generation and Checking on Nanopublications

To test our approach and to evaluate its implementations, we first took a collection of 156,026 nanopublications in TriG format that we had produced in previous work [13]. We transformed these nanopublications into the formats N-Quads and TriX using existing off-the-shelf converters. Then, we transformed these into trusty URI nanopublications using the function TransformNanopub of the Java implementation. To be able to check not only positive cases (where checking succeeds) but also negative ones (where checking fails), we made copies of the resulting files where we changed a random single byte in each of them (only considering letters and numbers, and never replacing an upper-case letter by its lower-case version or vice versa, as some keywords are not case-sensitive). The resulting six sets of 156,026 files each (three formats, each in two versions: valid and corrupted) were the basis for our evaluation.

The first important result is that all original nanopublications ended up with the same trusty URI, no matter which format was used. This shows that our implementations are successful in handling the content on a more abstract level (i.e. RDF graphs in this case) leading to identical hash values for files that contain the same content but are quite different on the byte level.

Next, we checked the trusty URI of each nanopublication file with the function CheckFile of all implementations that support the respective format. The three right-most columns of Table 2 show the results. For all valid files (i.e. those we did not corrupt), all implementations correctly verified their trusty URIs. For the corrupted ones, where we randomly changed one byte, the checks almost always failed (by either calculating a different hash value than the one of the trusty URI, or by raising an error that the respective file was not well-formed).

The only corrupted files that were successfully validated were 1,290 TriX files (0.83%) when running the Java implementation and 181 TriX files (0.12%) when running the Python implementation. Looking at these concrete cases reveals that they are all harmless. In these cases, the randomly changed byte was not part of the RDF content, but of the meta-information. Due to minor bugs in the used RDF libraries, this meta-information is not sufficiently checked, which leads to accepting the valid content instead of failing because of violated well-formedness. All our TriX files start with the following two lines:

Table 2. Performance and results of the different implementations for checking trusty URI nanopublications in normal mode (top) and batch mode (bottom) on valid and corrupted files

NORMAL MODE

	method		time in seconds					result		
	impl.	format	mean	stdev	min	max	histogram	valid	invalid	error
valid files	Java	N-Quads	0.5229	0.0591	0.3750	5.5420		100%	0%	0%
	Java	TriG	0.5113	0.0569	0.3650	5.5340		100%	0%	0%
	Java	TriX	0.5383	0.0648	0.3900	5.5240		100%	0%	0%
	Perl	N-Quads	0.7843	0.1713	0.5990	5.7960		100%	0%	0%
	Perl	TriG	0.7901	0.1734	0.6030	5.7840		100%	0%	0%
	Python	N-Quads	0.1935	0.0164	0.1150	0.3050		100%	0%	0%
	Python	TriX	0.1912	0.0162	0.1190	0.3460		100%	0%	0%
corrupted files	Java	N-Quads	0.5227	0.0591	0.3450	5.5420		0%	99.72%	0.28%
	Java	TriG	0.5003	0.0621	0.3200	5.4250		0%	83.37%	16.63%
	Java	TriX	0.5322	0.0655	0.3360	5.5230		0.83%	84.15%	15.03%
	Perl	N-Quads	0.7842	0.1712	0.6000	5.8880		0%	100%	0%
	Perl	TriG	0.7872	0.1727	0.5700	5.8230		0%	84.49%	15.51%
	Python	N-Quads	0.1934	0.0165	0.1200	0.3080		0%	100%	0%
	Python	TriX	0.1884	0.0176	0.1070	0.2760		0.12%	84.46%	15.42%
							0 0.5 1 1.5			

BATCH MODE

	method		time in seconds					result		
	impl.	format	mean	stdev	min	max	histogram	valid	invalid	error
valid files	Java	N-Quads	0.0019	0.0062	0.0013	1.7202		100%	0%	0%
	Java	TriG	0.0009	0.0050	0.0008	1.7412		100%	0%	0%
	Java	TriX	0.0011	0.0050	0.0009	1.5656		100%	0%	0%
	Perl	N-Quads	0.0172	0.0006	0.0171	0.0679		100%	0%	0%
	Perl	TriG	0.0214	0.0016	0.0211	0.0872		100%	0%	0%
	Python	N-Quads	0.0070	0.0011	0.0065	0.0644		100%	0%	0%
	Python	TriX	0.0070	0.0009	0.0066	0.0578		100%	0%	0%
corrupted files	Java	N-Quads	0.0012	0.0062	0.0006	1.6559		0%	99.72%	0.28%
	Java	TriG	0.0010	0.0049	0.0003	1.6335		0%	83.37%	16.63%
	Java	TriX	0.0011	0.0044	0.0005	1.3451		0.83%	84.15%	15.03%
	Perl	N-Quads	0.0171	0.0005	0.0169	0.0732		0%	100%	0%
	Perl	TriG	0.0195	0.0055	0.0007	0.0841		0%	84.49%	15.51%
	Python	N-Quads	0.0069	0.0011	0.0065	0.1716		0%	100%	0%
	Python	TriX	0.0063	0.0021	0.0006	0.1325		0.12%	84.46%	15.42%
							0 0.01 0.02			

```
<?xml version='1.0' encoding='UTF-8'?>
<TriX xmlns='http://www.w3.org/2004/03/trix/trix-1/'>
```

The RDF implementations in Java and Python (or the respective system utilities to load XML files) do not properly check these two lines containing meta-data. Both libraries raise no error if a file starts with something like `<?Aml` instead of `<?xml` (106 files); the Python library accepts invalid XML version numbers such as `1.a` (73 files); and the Java library does not check the TriX namespace argument, raising no error if the argument name is changed to something like `xmlnZ` (175 files) or the URI is wrong, such as `.../Prix-1/` (1007 files). In addition, both libraries correctly accept the rare cases (2 files) where the XML version was changed from `1.0` to `1.1`, which is the only other valid XML version as of now (though much less common).

6.2 Performance Tests on Nanopublications

Next, we used the same set of nanopublication files to test the performance of the different modules for checking trusty URI artifacts in different formats. There are two scenarios of how to run such checks: One can run one after the other, as when a small number of nanopublications are manually checked, or one can execute such checks in the form of a batch job in a single program run, which is the preferred procedure to run a large number of checks without supervision. The time required per file is typically much lower in batch mode, as the runtime environment has to start and finalize only once. Therefore it makes sense to have a look at both scenarios.

Table 2 shows the results of these performance checks for the normal mode (top) and batch mode (bottom). These results and the ones presented below were obtained on a Linux server (Debian) with 16 Intel Xeon CPUs of 2.27GHz and 24GB of memory. As expected, the times are much lower in batch mode, but checking is reasonably fast also in normal mode. The average values are always below 0.2 seconds. Using Java in batch mode even requires only 0.1ms per file. Apart from the runtimes, the two modes had no effect on the results.

6.3 Performance Tests on Bio2RDF

The tests above cover only very small RDF files, but our approach should also work for larger files. For that reason, we performed a second evaluation on Bio2RDF, which includes much larger files. Release 2 of this dataset contains 874 RDF files in N-Triples format, but 16 of them lead to well-formedness errors when loaded with the current version of the Sesame library. (These problems might be related to the transition to the new RDF 1.1 standard, and they will be fixed for the next release of Bio2RDF.) This leaves us with 858 files of sizes ranging from 1.4kB to 177GB.

Figure 3 shows the results of these performance tests. There is a lot of random variation on the lower end, where files are smaller than 10MB and require less than three seconds to be processed. For the upper part, time values nicely

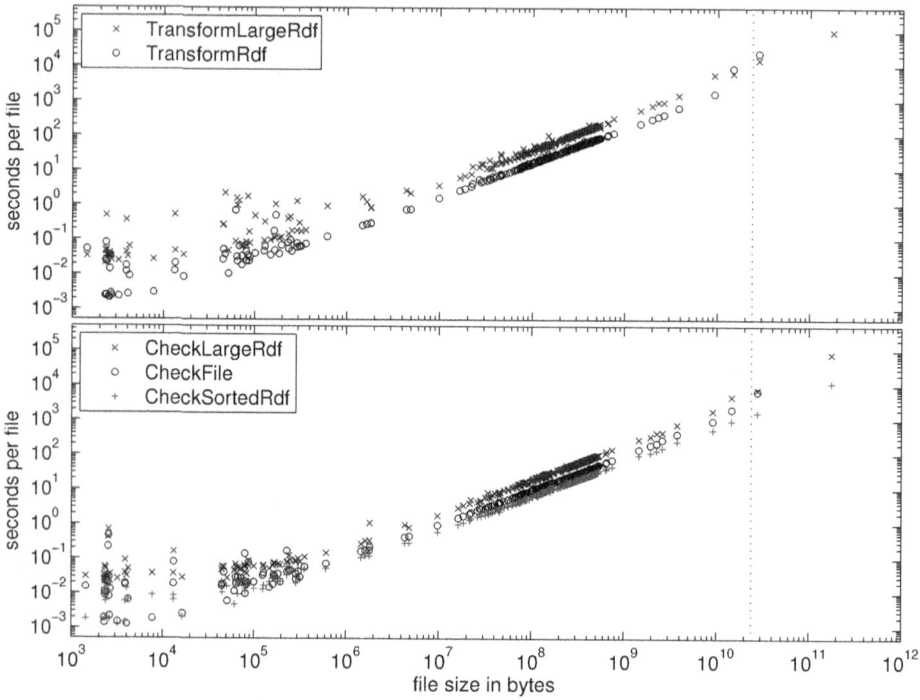

Fig. 3. Time required for transforming (top) and checking (bottom) files versus file size for the Bio2RDF dataset. The dotted line shows the available memory.

follow near-linear trajectories (for the functions that do not load the whole content into memory). When hash calculation involves statement sorting, there is a strict theoretical limit on its performance due to the computational complexity of $O(n \log n)$. TransformLargeRdf and CheckLargeRdf are superior to their counterparts only for very large files, and CheckSortedRdf is, as expected, faster than the other checking procedures. A large file of 2GB requires about five minutes to be transformed and about two minutes to be checked. Files larger than available memory take more time, but even the largest file of the dataset of 177GB was successfully transformed in 29 hours and checked in about three hours.

7 Conclusions

We have presented a proposal for unambiguous URI references to make digital artifacts on the (semantic) web verifiable, immutable, and permanent. If adopted, it could have a considerable impact on the structure and functioning of the web, could improve the efficiency and reliability of tools using web resources, and could become an important technical pillar for the semantic web, in particular for scientific data, where provenance and verifiability are crucial. To improve reproducibility, for example, scientific data analyses might be conducted in the future within "data projects" analogous to today's software projects. The dependencies in the form of datasets could be automatically fetched from the web, similar to what Apache Maven (`maven.apache.org`) does for software projects but decentralized and verifiable. In general, trusty URIs might contribute in a significant way to shape the future of publishing on the web.

References

1. Altman, M., King, G.: A proposed standard for the scholarly citation of quantitative data. D-Lib Magazine 13(3), 5 (2007)
2. Bartel, M., Boyer, J., Fox, B., LaMacchia, B., Simon, E.: XML signature syntax and processing. Recommendation, W3C (June 2008)
3. Bellare, M., Goldreich, O., Goldwasser, S.: Incremental cryptography: The case of hashing and signing. In: Desmedt, Y.G. (ed.) CRYPTO 1994. LNCS, vol. 839, pp. 216–233. Springer, Heidelberg (1994)
4. Belleau, F., Nolin, M., Tourigny, N., Rigault, P., Morissette, J.: Bio2RDF: towards a mashup to build bioinformatics knowledge systems. Journal of Biomedical Informatics 41(5), 706–716 (2008)
5. Broekstra, J., Kampman, A., Van Harmelen, F.: Sesame: A generic architecture for storing and querying RDF and RDF schema. In: Horrocks, I., Hendler, J. (eds.) ISWC 2002. LNCS, vol. 2342, pp. 54–68. Springer, Heidelberg (2002)
6. Callahan, A., Cruz-Toledo, J., Ansell, P., Dumontier, M.: Bio2RDF release 2: Improved coverage, interoperability and provenance of life science linked data. In: Cimiano, P., Corcho, O., Presutti, V., Hollink, L., Rudolph, S. (eds.) ESWC 2013. LNCS, vol. 7882, pp. 200–212. Springer, Heidelberg (2013)
7. Callahan, A., Cruz-Toledo, J., Dumontier, M.: Ontology-based querying with Bio2RDF's linked open data. Journal of Biomedical Semantics 4(suppl. 1), S1 (2013)
8. Carroll, J.J.: Signing RDF graphs. In: Fensel, D., Sycara, K., Mylopoulos, J. (eds.) ISWC 2003. LNCS, vol. 2870, pp. 369–384. Springer, Heidelberg (2003)
9. Farrell, S., Kutscher, D., Dannewitz, C., Ohlman, B., Keranen, A., Hallam-Baker, P.: Naming things with hashes. Standards Track RFC 6920, Internet Engineering Task Force (IETF) (April 2013)
10. Groth, P., Gibson, A., Velterop, J.: The anatomy of a nano-publication. Information Services and Use 30(1), 51–56 (2010)
11. Hoekstra, R.: The MetaLex document server. In: Aroyo, L., Welty, C., Alani, H., Taylor, J., Bernstein, A., Kagal, L., Noy, N., Blomqvist, E. (eds.) ISWC 2011, Part II. LNCS, vol. 7032, pp. 128–143. Springer, Heidelberg (2011)
12. Kuhn, T.: A survey and classification of controlled natural languages. Computational Linguistics 40(1), 121–170 (2014)
13. Kuhn, T., Barbano, P.E., Nagy, M.L., Krauthammer, M.: Broadening the scope of nanopublications. In: Cimiano, P., Corcho, O., Presutti, V., Hollink, L., Rudolph, S. (eds.) ESWC 2013. LNCS, vol. 7882, pp. 487–501. Springer, Heidelberg (2013)
14. McCusker, J.P., Lebo, T., Chang, C., McGuinness, D.L., da Silva, P.P.: Parallel identities for managing open government data. IEEE Intelligent Systems 27(3), 55 (2012)

15. McCusker, J.P., Lebo, T., Graves, A., Difranzo, D., Pinheiro, P., McGuinness, D.L.: Functional requirements for information resource provenance on the web. In: Groth, P., Frew, J. (eds.) IPAW 2012. LNCS, vol. 7525, pp. 52–66. Springer, Heidelberg (2012)
16. Phan, R.C.W., Wagner, D.: Security considerations for incremental hash functions based on pair block chaining. Computers & Security 25(2), 131–136 (2006)
17. Sayers, C., Karp, A.H.: Computing the digest of an RDF graph. Technical Report HPL-2003-235(R.1), Mobile and Media Systems Laboratory, HP Laboratories, Palo Alto, USA (2004)

Leveraging Distributed Human Computation and Consensus Partition for Entity Coreference

Saisai Gong, Wei Hu, and Yuzhong Qu

State Key Laboratory for Novel Software Technology, Nanjing University, Nanjing 210023, PR China
ssgong@smail.nju.edu.cn,{whu,yzqu}@nju.edu.cn

Abstract. Entity coreference is important to Linked Data integration. User involvement is considered as a valuable source of human knowledge that helps identify coreferent entities. However, the quality of user involvement is not always satisfying, which significantly diminishes the coreference accuracy. In this paper, we propose a new approach called coCoref, which leverages distributed human computation and consensus partition for entity coreference. Consensus partition is used to aggregate all distributed user-judged coreference results and resolve their disagreements. To alleviate user involvement, ensemble learning is performed on the consensus partition to automatically identify coreferent entities that users have not judged. We integrate coCoref into an online Linked Data browsing system, so that users can participate in entity coreference with their daily Web activities. Our empirical evaluation shows that coCoref largely improves the accuracy of user-judged coreference results, and reduces user involvement by automatically identifying a large number of coreferent entities.

Keywords: #eswc2014Gong.

1 Introduction

Entity coreference is to identify entities from diverse data sources that refer to the same real-world object. It is important to the reuse, integration and application of Linked Data. Many entity coreference approaches have been proposed in literature, which can be divided to two main categories: *fully-automatic* and *semi-automatic*. Although automatic methods have been continuously improved using various sophisticated algorithms, e.g., taking advantages of OWL semantics [10], computing similarities among entities [20], machine learning [11,16], they still remain far from perfect.

On the other hand, semi-automatic approaches bring user involvement into the entity coreference process and gain benefits from human knowledge. To acquire human contributions, a number of existing semi-automatic methods introduced micro-task crowdsourcing [3], some of which also dedicated to minimizing user involvement while preserving certain coreference accuracy, based on techniques like active learning [19]. In addition to use the modern crowdsourcing platform

V. Presutti et al. (Eds.): ESWC 2014, LNCS 8465, pp. 411–425, 2014.

like Amazon Mechanical Turk and CrowdFlower, there are also other *distributed human computation* systems that can be used for entity coreference, e.g., [25], which hold promises for using computers and humans together to scale up the kind of tasks that only humans do well. To this end, in this paper we try to attract users to participate in entity coreference with their daily Web browsing activities. A typical scenario is that a user identifies several coreferent entities denoting the same real-world object as the current entity that she is browsing. The behind incentives for users to do so are that they like to view more data about some real-world objects across different sources in Linked Data.

For entity coreference with distributed human computation, a central problem is the quality control of users' coreference results, which draws attentions in many works [3,12]. The quality of user-judged results is not always satisfying; mistakes and outliers frequently happen due to various reasons. For example, the ambiguity of candidate entities, caused by lacking enough domain knowledge, data evolvement and so on, may lead to incorrect user judgement. Additionally, user involvement is expensive and usually slow. A user can only complete a small number of coreference tasks with limited time and energy, leading to omissions in her coreference result. Therefore, it is important to leverage all distributed user-judged results and minimize the disagreements among them.

In this paper, we propose a new approach *coCoref* to leveraging distributed human computation and consensus partition for entity coreference. coCoref improves the quality of user-judged results by aggregating users' individual results into a more robust and comprehensive consensus partition with better accuracy [22]. Furthermore, coCoref adopts the consensus partition as labelled data and proposes an ensemble learning algorithm to alleviate user involvement by automatically identifying coreferent entities that have not been judged by users. We develop coCoref as an important component in a Linked Data browsing system called SView.[1] We also believe that coCoref is applicable to various entity coreference scenarios involving users. We empirically evaluate the performance of coCoref based on real users' browsing logs from SView. We also compare coCoref with several existing systems on an OAEI test and show that coCoref automatically identifies a large amount of coreferent entities using a small portion of consensus partition.

The rest of this paper is structured as follows. Section 2 gives an overview of our approach. Section 3 introduces consensus partition. Section 4 describes ensemble learning. Our evaluation is reported in Section 5, while related work is discussed in Section 6. We conclude this paper in Section 7.

2 Overview of the Approach

We show the overview of our approach in Figure 1, where users perform coreference on a set of entities in distributed data sources. Let $\mathbf{E} = \{e_1, e_2, \ldots, e_n\}$ be the set of all entities. In this paper, an entity $e_i \in \mathbf{E}$ is denoted by a URI

[1] `http://ws.nju.edu.cn/sview/`

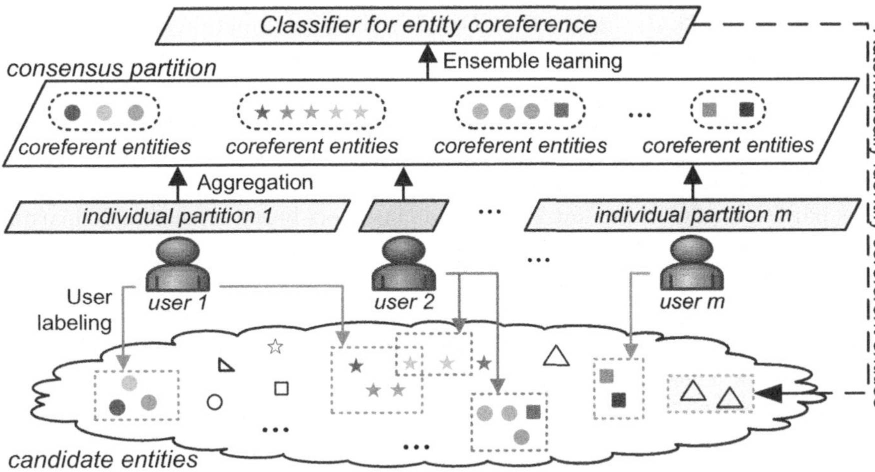

Fig. 1. Overview of coCoref

and described by a set of property-value pairs, which can be extracted by dereferencing the URI of e_i. We define the extraction of e_i's involved properties by $Prop(e_i)$, and the extraction of e_i's values w.r.t. property p_l by $Value(e_i, p_l)$.

Individual partition. Let $\mathbf{U} = \{u_1, u_2, \ldots, u_m\}$ be the set of all users participated in entity coreference on $\mathbf{E}$. For a user $u_j \in \mathbf{U}$, when she browses some entities, she may help identify some coreferent entities. However, with her limited time and energy, u_j can only view and judge a small set of entities. Let $\mathbf{X}_j \subseteq \mathbf{E}$ be the subset of entities judged by u_j. The entity coreference on $\mathbf{X}_j$ w.r.t. u_j is defined to find a partition π on $\mathbf{X}_j$, which consists of a set of pairwise disjoint nonempty subsets of $\mathbf{X}_j$. For $s_a, s_b \in \pi, a \neq b$, $s_a \cap s_b = \emptyset$, and $\bigcup_{a=1,\ldots,|\pi|} s_a = \mathbf{X}_j$. In fact, for any $s_a \in \pi$, the entities in s_a denote the same real-world object and form an *equivalence class*, where the equivalence relation holds between the entities in s_a. s_a will be updated if the user u_j links other entities to some elements in s_a (essentially, to merge two equivalence classes), or she removes some elements from s_a as she believes that they are no longer coreferent with others in s_a. Therefore, the partition π can be considered as u_j's individual partition about entity coreference on $\mathbf{X}_j$.

Consensus partition. Different users perform entity coreference on different entities and their coreference results may also have differences. For two individual partitions π_i, π_j judged by users u_i, u_j respectively, π_i, π_j can be equal, totally disjoint or have overlaps. In order to aggregate users' individual partitions and resolve their disagreements, we use consensus partition [22] to establish a more robust and comprehensive result with better overall accuracy. To formalize, let $\mathrm{T} = \{\pi_1, \pi_2, \ldots, \pi_m\}$ be a set of individual partitions. Each $\pi_j \in \mathrm{T}$ is judged by user u_j on a set of entities $\mathbf{X}_j \subseteq \mathbf{E}$. The entity coreference with distributed human computation is defined to find a partition τ on $\mathbf{X} = \bigcup_{j=1,\ldots,|\mathrm{T}|} \mathbf{X}_j$ that minimizes $\sum_{\pi_j \in \mathrm{T}} Dist(\tau, \pi_j)$, where $Dist$ is a distance function between any two partitions. We refer to the equivalence class in τ as *consensus equivalence class.*

Ensemble learning. Although many users can participate in entity coreference, there are still a large number of entities that have not been judged by any users, that is, $\mathbf{X} \subseteq \mathbf{E}$. In order to alleviate user involvement, we make use of the consensus partition as training data and build classifiers based on ensemble learning. Each base learner is trained on a random sample of consensus equivalence classes in the consensus partition; different base learners are combined to generalize a global classifier. The classifier is applied to automatically identify coreferent entities that have not been judged by enough users. For a new entity, coCoref uses the classifier to classify other coreferent entities and forms a new equivalence class. The classifier will be updated offline when more users' coreference results are collected and aggregated. Currently, coCoref does not modify users' individual partitions. The reconciliation of users' coreference results and the result from ensemble learning will be our future work.

Example 1. To help understanding, we show a running example here. Assuming that Alice browses some entity `NewYorkCity` and helps identify its coreferent entities `NY` and `TheBigApple`. She also browses another entity `Manhattan` and finds its coreferent entity `NewYorkCounty`. Therefore, Alice's individual partition is { {`NewYorkCity`, `NY`, `TheBigApple`}, {`Manhattan`, `NewYorkCounty`} }.

Similarly, Tom participates in entity coreference and delivers his individual partition { {`NewYorkCity`, `TheBigApple`, `NewYorkCounty`}, {`NY`, `Manhattan`} }. Mike forms his partition { {`NewYorkCity`, `TheBigApple`}, {`NY`, `Manhattan`} }.

coCoref aggregates the three individual partitions to build a consensus partition { {`NewYorkCity`, `TheBigApple`}, {`NY`, `Manhattan`}, {`NewYorkCounty`} }. Furthermore, coCoref trains an ensemble of classifiers on this consensus partition and uses the classifier to identify entity coreference, e.g., a new entity `Nanjing`.

3 Consensus Partition

As described in Section 2, the problem of improving the quality of user-judged coreference results is transformed to the problem of achieving a consensus partition in terms of users' individual partitions. In this section, we firstly provide a formal definition of the consensus partition problem, and then introduce an approximation algorithm for obtaining a sub-optimal solution to the problem.

3.1 Formalization

The goal of computing consensus partition is to aggregate individual partitions such that the disagreements among them are minimized. Disagreements can be caused by mistakes, omissions and so on. There are two reasons that consensus partition can improve the quality of individual partitions. Firstly, by minimizing disagreements in the consensus partition, mistakes and outliers made by a few users can be filtered out because there is no agreement on how they should be aggregated [7]. In other words, consensus partition is more robust to mistakes and outliers. Secondly, the consensus partition is naturally more comprehensive than any individuals since it comprises more coreferent entities from individual partitions to avoid omissions by individual users.

Next, we provide a formalization of consensus partition. The disagreements between two partitions can be measured with a distance function, and various distance functions have been proposed [22]. In this paper, we use the *symmetric difference distance* [9] for our purpose. Specifically, let T be a set of individual partitions, each individual partition π_j is generated from user u_j on a subset of entities $\mathbf{X}_j \subseteq \mathbf{E}$. Computing a consensus partition in our approach is to find a partition τ on $\mathbf{X} = \bigcup_{j=1,\ldots,|\mathrm{T}|} \mathbf{X}_j$ that minimizes the following distance:

$$\begin{aligned} Dist_{\mathrm{T}}(\tau) &= \sum_{\pi_j \in \mathrm{T}} Dist(\tau, \pi_j) \\ &= \sum_{\pi_j \in \mathrm{T}} \sum_{v<w} (\delta_\tau(e_v, e_w)\psi_{\pi_j}(e_v, e_w) + (1 - \delta_\tau(e_v, e_w))\delta_{\pi_j}(e_v, e_w)), \end{aligned} \quad (1)$$

where, for two entities e_v, e_w and a partition π,

$$\delta_\pi(e_v, e_w) = \begin{cases} 1, & \text{if } \exists s_l \in \pi, e_v \in s_l, e_w \in s_l \\ 0, & \text{otherwise} \end{cases}, \quad (2)$$

$$\psi_\pi(e_v, e_w) = \begin{cases} 1, & \text{if } \exists s_a, s_b \in \pi, a \neq b, e_v \in s_a, e_w \in s_b \\ 0, & \text{otherwise} \end{cases}. \quad (3)$$

Let N_{vw} be the number of partitions of which e_v, e_w are in different equivalence classes, i.e., $N_{vw} = |\{\pi \in \mathrm{T} \mid \exists s_a, s_b \in \pi, a \neq b, e_v \in s_a, e_w \in s_b\}|$, and M_{vw} be the number of partitions of which e_v, e_w are in the same equivalence class, i.e., $M_{vw} = |\{\pi \in \mathrm{T} \mid \exists s_a \in \pi, e_v \in s_a, e_w \in s_a\}|$. We rewrite Eq. (1) as:

$$\begin{aligned} Dist_{\mathrm{T}}(\tau) &= \sum_{v<w} (\delta_\tau(e_v, e_w) \sum_{\pi_j \in \mathrm{T}} \psi_{\pi_j}(e_v, e_w) + (1 - \delta_\tau(e_v, e_w)) \sum_{\pi_j \in \mathrm{T}} \delta_{\pi_j}(e_v, e_w)) \\ &= \sum_{v<w} (\delta_\tau(e_v, e_w) N_{vw} + (1 - \delta_\tau(e_v, e_w)) M_{vw}) \\ &= \sum_{v<w} M_{vw} - \sum_{v<w} \delta_\tau(e_v, e_w)(M_{vw} - N_{vw}). \end{aligned} \quad (4)$$

Note that $\sum_{v<w} M_{vw}$ is independent to τ, so minimizing $Dist_{\mathrm{T}}(\tau)$ is equivalent to maximize $\sum_{v<w} \delta_\tau(e_v, e_w)(M_{vw} - N_{vw})$. Let $Q_{vw} = M_{vw} + N_{vw}$, where $0 \leq Q_{vw} \leq |\mathrm{T}|$. We have $\sum_{v<w} \delta_\tau(e_v, e_w)(M_{vw} - N_{vw}) = 2\sum_{v<w} \delta_\tau(e_v, e_w)\phi_{vw}$, where $\phi_{vw} = M_{vw} - \frac{Q_{vw}}{2}$.

3.2 An Approximation Algorithm for Consensus Partition

Computing consensus partition to maximize $\sum_{v<w} \delta_\tau(e_v, e_w)(M_{vw} - N_{vw})$ has been proven to be a NP-complete problem [9]. Due to the hardness of the

problem, it is intractable to exactly solve it on a large scale, e.g., entity coreference in Linked Data. Various approximations or heuristics with/without performance guarantees have been proposed to give a sub-optimal solution to the problem. In our approach, we use an approximation algorithm called CC-Pivot [1], because CC-Pivot is usually more efficient and applicable for large-scale data than others [9]. The details of CC-Pivot applied in our method is shown in Algorithm 1, where ϕ'_{vw} in Line 4 is defined as follows:

$$\phi'_{vw} = \begin{cases} \phi_{vw}, & Q_{vw} \geq \theta \\ -\frac{Q_{vw}}{2}, & \text{otherwise} \end{cases}, \tag{5}$$

where Q_{vw} and ϕ_{vw} are defined in Section 3.1. θ is a threshold that is used to see whether two given entities are judged by enough users.

Algorithm 1. CC-Pivot [1]

Input: entity set $\mathbf{X}$, individual partition set T
Output: consensus partition τ on $\mathbf{X}$

1 Choose a pivot entity $e_v \in \mathbf{X}$ uniformly at random;
2 Let $C \leftarrow \{e_v\}$, $\mathbf{X}' \leftarrow \emptyset$;
3 **foreach** $e_w \in \mathbf{X}, w \neq v$ **do**
4   **if** $\phi'_{vw} > 0$ **then**
5         $C \leftarrow C \cup \{e_w\}$;
6   **else**
7         $\mathbf{X}' \leftarrow \mathbf{X}' \cup \{e_w\}$;
8 **return** $\tau \leftarrow \{C\} \cup \text{CC-Pivot}(\mathbf{X}', \mathrm{T})$;

Algorithm 1 repeatedly chooses a pivot entity e_v uniformly at random from the unpartitioned entity set. Then, the algorithm generates an equivalence class containing e_v and every entity e_w holding $\phi'_{vw} > 0$. The recursion continues on the rest entities until all entities are checked. Algorithm 1 is a 3-approximation algorithm with time complexity $\mathcal{O}(|\tau| \cdot |\mathbf{X}| \cdot |\mathrm{T}|)$ [1], where τ denotes the final consensus partition. By using this approximation algorithm, more robust and comprehensive coreference results can be achieved efficiently.

Example 2. We show the running process of Algorithm 1 on Example 1. Assume $\theta = 2$. Initially, `NewYorkCity` is chosen as the pivot entity. The algorithm finds $\phi'_{\texttt{NewYorkCity,NY}} = -0.5$, $\phi'_{\texttt{NewYorkCity,Manhattan}} = -1.5$, $\phi'_{\texttt{NewYorkCity,NewYorkCounty}} = 0$ and $\phi'_{\texttt{NewYorkCity,TheBigApple}} = 1.5$. Only $\phi'_{\texttt{NewYorkCity,TheBigApple}} > 0$, so `NewYorkCity` and `TheBigApple` are put together and form an equivalence class { `NewYorkCity`, `TheBigApple` }. Algorithm 1 continues for the remaining three entities. It selects `NY` as the pivot entity and finds $\phi'_{\texttt{NY,Manhattan}} = 0.5$ and $\phi'_{\texttt{NY,NewYorkCounty}} = -1$, so it puts `NY` and `Manhattan` together and forms a new equivalence class { `NY`, `Manhattan` }. Now, only `NewYorkCounty` is left, which forms the third equivalence class { `NewYorkCounty` }. The final consensus partition is { {`NewYorkCity`, `TheBigApple`}, {`NY`, `Manhattan`}, {`NewYorkCounty`} }.

4 Ensemble Learning

User involvement is expensive and slow. Consequently, there are still a lot of coreferent candidates that have not been judged by users. In this section, we will build classifiers based on the consensus partition using ensemble learning and use them to automatically identify coreferent entities.

4.1 Training Data

A classifier decides whether a candidate entity is coreferent with the given one. So the training examples used in our method are entity pairs. We leverage the consensus partition to generate training examples. Specifically, all entities in the same consensus equivalence class pairwise compose positive examples, while entities across different consensus equivalence classes form negative examples. We keep the sizes of positive and negative examples at the same order of magnitude.

We follow the assumption that coreferent entities often have similar descriptions [20]. Thus, we use the similarities between property-values in entity pairs as learning features. Let $\mathbf{P}$ be all properties associated with the entities in the training set. For two properties $p_i, p_j \in \mathbf{P}$ w.r.t. a pair of entities (e_v, e_w) in the training set, $VSIM_{p_i,p_j}(e_v, e_w)$ is defined as follows:

$$VSIM_{p_i,p_j}(e_v, e_w) = \max_{(o,o') \in VP_{p_i,p_j}(e_v,e_w)} sim(o, o'), \tag{6}$$

$$\begin{aligned} VP_{p_i,p_j}(e_v, e_w) = &\{(o, o') \mid o \in Value(e_v, p_i), o' \in Value(e_w, p_j)\} \\ &\bigcup \{(o, o') \mid o \in Value(e_v, p_j), o' \in Value(e_w, p_i)\}, \end{aligned} \tag{7}$$

where $0 \leq VSIM_{p_i,p_j}(\cdot, \cdot) \leq 1$ and $sim(\cdot, \cdot)$ computes the value similarities:

- If both values are entities (URIs), the similarity equals 1 if their URIs are identical or they are in the same consensus equivalence class; otherwise 0.
- If both values are numerics like `xsd:double` or `xsd:integer`, their similarity equals 1 if their difference is less than a threshold (0.1); otherwise 0.
- If both values are boolean, their similarity equals 1 iff they are equal.
- For other cases, we normalize and split the value strings, and compute their Jaccard similarity.

For a pair of entities (e_v, e_w) in the training set, its feature vector of d-dimension is denoted by $\mathbf{F} = [f_1, f_2, \ldots, f_d]'$, where $f_l = VSIM_{p_i,p_j}(e_v, e_w)$, $1 \leq l \leq d$, $p_i, p_j \in \mathbf{P}$ and $d \leq \frac{|\mathbf{P}|(|\mathbf{P}|-1)}{2}$. In our approach, we use the subset of property pairs $\{(p_i, p_j) \mid \exists (e_v, e_w) \in \mathbf{X} \times \mathbf{X}, VSIM_{p_i,p_j}(e_v, e_w) > 0\}$ to construct the feature vector. More sophisticated strategies may be developed to select a better subset of property pairs for learning, but it is out of scope of this paper.

4.2 Ensemble Learning Model

Ensemble learning is a popular learning paradigm, which employs multiple base learners and combines their predictions. The predictive performance of an ensemble is usually much better than that of base learners. As aforementioned, the size of training set is relatively small because users can only accomplish a small number of coreference tasks. The reason for using ensemble learning in our approach is that, even the training examples are insufficient or the features used for training are not strong enough, ensemble learning may still find a good classifier [4], which is very suitable to our application scenario. Various methods for constructing ensembles have been developed using different base learning algorithms, manipulating input features and so on. We choose manipulating training examples to train base learners as this kind of methods is more suitable when the number of training examples is relatively small [4]. We choose decision tree as our base learner. Bagging and Boosting are two common ways to manipulate training examples and Bagging may be more robust to noises in the training examples than Boosting [17]. Because there are still a small amount of mistakes or outliers in the consensus partition, we choose Bagging and build base learners on random samples of training data.

Certain property pairs with their values are important for identifying coreferent entities. Unfortunately, when the training set is not representative, some potentially important property pairs cannot be characterized by the training data. As a result, they may not be chosen to split nodes in the construction of decision trees. To address this problem, we combine our base learners using Random Forests [2]. Random Forests is an ensemble classifier that combines a collection of decision trees. When splitting each node of a decision tree, Random Forests firstly randomly selects a subset of variables (property pairs in our context) and then leverages the most important variable in the subset based on information gain to split the node. In this way, the potentially important pairs that are not characterized by the training data can also be used to identify coreferent entities. Furthermore, Random Forests can handle training examples with thousands or even tens of thousands of features. This is also very suitable to our approach as **P** can be very large. For implementation, we use Weka 3 to realize our algorithm and adopt the default value setting for the parameter of the number of features when splitting a tree node. We set the parameter of the number of trees to 30 in our experiments.

Example 3. In Example 1, two positive examples from the consensus partition are `(NewYorkCity, TheBigApple)` and `(NY, Manhattan)`. Other entity pairs are negative examples such as `(NewYorkCity, Manhattan)` and `(NewYorkCity, NewYorkCounty)`. Using Random Forests, an ensemble of three decision trees is learnt based on the training data. A decision tree uses different property pairs to find coreferent entities , e.g., `(homepage, homepage)` and `(geometry,geometry)`. By using the classifier, we will identify `Nanking` coreferent with `Nanjing`.

5 Evaluation

We integrated coCoref in an online Linked Data browsing system called SView. When a user browses an entity using SView, she can check candidate coreferent entities provided by SView if she wants to browse more relevant data.

The candidates are founded by SView using `owl:sameAs` links and web services like sameas.org[2]. The user just needs to accept or reject some candidates. All the accepted ones are then added into the equivalence class of the current entity being browsed in the user's individual partition, and their data will be integrated with that of the current entity immediately for browsing. In addition, the user can also remove some previous accepted entities from the equivalence class listed by SView if she believes they are no longer coreferent with others.

In this section, we will firstly present the evaluation on real users' browsing logs from SView. Then, we will report the experimental results on the OAEI New-York Times (NYT) test. All the experiments were carried out on an 2.5GHz Intel Core i5 CPU, Windows 7 and 1GB Java virtual memory.

5.1 Test on SView Dataset

Dataset. The target of this experiment is to evaluate how coCoref improves the quality of user-judged results using consensus partition. We collected 36 registered users' individual partitions in SView from Oct. 2013 to Dec. 2013 and used them in this test. This dataset contains 1,489 entities from 76 distributed data sources in terms of their URI namespaces. In average, a user viewed 41 entities. An entity was viewed by 2.6 users in average. To identify which entities are truly coreferent, we invited three master students in our group with good experience on entity coreference to manually build a reference partition for the 1,489 entities. For this reference partition, an entity is coreferent with 1.6 other entities in average (the maximal size is 51), and 40.3% (704 in 1,489) entities are coreferent with at least one other. This means that the entities in the SView dataset have diverse numbers of coreferent entities.

Experiment setup. Using the reference partition as golden standard, we evaluated the consensus partition and individual partitions generated from the 36 users in terms of the following five measures: Precision, Recall, F-measure, Rand Index and Normalized Mutual Information (NMI). These measures are well-known criteria showing how well a partition matches the golden standard. For a partition π, $S(\pi)$ counts the total number of entity pairs in the same equivalence class:

$$S(\pi) = \{(e_v, e_w) \mid \exists s_a \in \pi, e_v \in s_a, e_w \in s_a, v < w\}. \tag{8}$$

Let π_{ref} denote the golden standard partition. The Precision, Recall and F-measure for a partition π w.r.t. π_{ref} are calculated as follows:

$$\text{Precision} = \frac{S(\pi) \bigcap S(\pi_{ref})}{S(\pi)}, \quad \text{Recall} = \frac{S(\pi) \bigcap S(\pi_{ref})}{S(\pi_{ref})},$$
$$\text{F-measure} = \frac{2 * \text{Precision} * \text{Recall}}{\text{Precision} + \text{Recall}}. \tag{9}$$

Rand Index penalizes both false positive and false negative decisions in partition, while NMI can be information-theoretically interpreted. Their values are

[2] `http://sameas.org/`

Table 1. Performance comparison on the SView dataset

	Precision	Recall	F-measure	Rand Index	NMI
Baseline	0.665	0.071	0.120	0.012	0.105
Best-of-K with highest F-measure	0.773	0.201	0.319	0.021	0.208
Best-of-K with highest Rand Index	**0.863**	0.186	0.306	0.090	0.439
Best-of-K with highest NMI	0.708	0.107	0.186	0.088	0.446
coCoref	0.807	**0.297**	**0.434**	**0.997**	**0.951**

both rational numbers in range [0, 1]; a higher value indicates a better partition. Their detailed calculation methods can be found in [23].

In order to determine the threshold θ used for computing consensus partition (see Eq. (5) in Section 3.2), we evaluated different values for θ and computed a consensus partition using Algorithm 1 on each value. The Precision and Recall of the resulting partitions w.r.t. various θ are shown in Fig. 2. According to the figure, we set $\theta = 3$ for our experiment since it led to very high precision while keeping good recall (we prefer the precision larger than 0.8). This setting distinguishes whether each entity pair is judged by at least three users. We ran Algorithm 1 ten times and computed the average values of the five measures on the consensus partition, respectively. The average running time was 1.02 seconds.

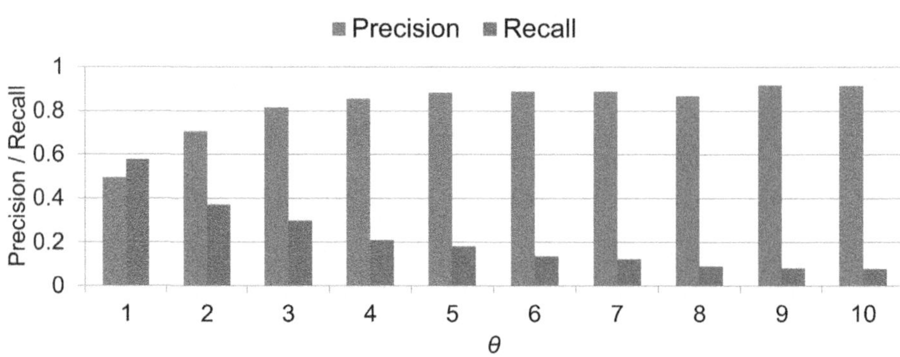

Fig. 2. Precision and Recall versus different thresholds

We used the average values of the five measures on the 36 users' individual partitions as baseline. We compared coCoref with Best-of-K [9], which is a 2-approximation algorithm to compute consensus partition. The idea of Best-of-K is to select the best individual partition as consensus partition. To this end, we selected the individual partitions with highest value of F-measure, Rand Index and NMI respectively and compared the three results of Best-of-K with that of coCoref. The comparison results are listed in Table 1.

Result analysis. From Table 1, we can observe that the consensus partition computed by coCoref has very high score of Rand Index and NMI as compared with others. Thus, coCoref's consensus partition matched the golden standard better than others. coCoref also has the highest Recall and F-measure. All of these means the coreference results from coCoref's consensus partition are more comprehensive since it aggregated more coreferent entities. From the value of Precision on baseline, we can see the average accuracy of the 36 users' coreference results is low. There were not a few mistakes and outliers in many users' coreference results. Compared with the Precision of baseline, the Precision of coCoref's consensus partition improved very largely by 21%. Furthermore, though many users' individual coreference results are noisy, coCoref's consensus partition still achieves close precision 0.807 to the best user's result (0.863). This indicates that coCoref is robust and can largely improve the accuracy of coreference results.

5.2 Test on OAEI NYT

Dataset. The target of this experiment is to evaluate the effectiveness of consensus partition and ensemble learning algorithm on a large scale. We leveraged the results of several tools participated in the OAEI NYT test to conduct this experiment. The NYT test is to rebuild the linkages between the New-York Times dataset and three external large-scale datasets: DBpedia, Freebase and Geonames on the domains of locations, organizations and people. The tools that we used were ObjectCoref [11], Zhishi.links [16] and Knofuss [15]. Zhishi.links and Knofuss offered the download links of their coreference results in their papers. We used the three tools' results to simulate the coreference results of three users, which contain 33,914 entities in all. We set $\theta = 2$ in this experiment because there are only three systems. Besides, the NYT test offers the golden standard that can be used to evaluate the performance of coreference algorithms. The golden standard is provided in random segments for cross-validation of learning systems that use training data.

Experiment setup. We firstly built a consensus partition for the total 33,914 entities based on the results of the three tools. The original coreference results of each tool are entity pairs. To form a partition, we assumed that transitivity holds on each dataset, i.e., if a tool identifies two coreferent entity pairs (e_i, e_j) and (e_j, e_k), then (e_i, e_k) is assumed to be also coreferent. Based on this assumption, we clustered coreferent entities for each tool's dataset and constructed its partition. With the partitions for the three tools' results, we applied coCoref to build consensus partition. The running time for computing consensus partition was 211.5 seconds. The F-measure of the consensus partition compared with the coreference results of ObjectCoref, Zhishi.links and Knofuss that we collected are listed in Table 2. As shown in the table, we can find that the consensus partition of coCoref generally performed better than ObjectCoref, Zhishi.links and Knofuss in terms of F-measure, which is in accordance with the results in the previous experiment.

Table 2. F-measure comparison on the OAEI NYT test

	Consensus partition	ObjectCoref	Zhishi.links	Knofuss
NYT–DBpedia loc.	**0.948**	0.859	0.910	0.891
NYT–DBpedia org.	**0.939**	0.882	0.900	0.916
NYT–DBpedia peop.	**0.985**	0.958	0.970	0.960
NYT–Freebase loc.	**0.951**	0.938	0.882	0.913
NYT–Freebase org.	**0.959**	0.901	0.870	0.889
NYT–Freebase peop.	**0.988**	0.973	0.926	0.942
NYT–Geonames loc.	0.937	**0.938**	0.910	0.878

We can obtain positive training examples from the consensus partition, which are entity pairs within the same equivalence classes. We divided these positive examples into 10 folds according to the division of the NYT golden standard. The training examples out of the golden standard, which were false positive coreference results of the consensus partition, were randomly assigned to the 10 folds as positive examples. Therefore, the number of positive examples is different from that of the golden standard. For each fold, we randomly generated a set of negative training examples holding the similar size of positives. Table 3 shows the statistical data of the training set. We adopted 10-fold cross validation, each time we learnt on each fold of training data, and validated the classifier's Precision and Recall on the combination of the remaining 9 folds. Then, we averaged the Precision and Recall, and computed the average F-Measure. The learning results compared with those of the consensus partition are shown in Fig. 3.

Table 3. Statistics of training data

	Locations	Organizations	People
Positive examples in NYT–DBpedia	1,788	1,851	4,902
Negative examples in NYT–DBpedia	2,752	2,730	1,803
Positive examples in NYT–Freebase	1,773	2,812	4,868
Negative examples in NYT–Freebase	1,986	3,937	9,864
Positive examples in NYT–Geonames	1,692		
Negative examples in NYT–Geonames	3,688		

Result analysis. From Fig. 3 and Table 2, we observe that our ensemble learning algorithm achieved higher F-measure than ObjectCoref, Zhishi.links and Knofuss, and is comparable to (sometimes better than) the consensus partition. This indicates that, by using only a small subset (10%) of training data from the consensus partition, our ensemble learning algorithm successfully found a similar size of correct coreferent entities as consensus partition. Many coreferent entities can be automatically identified by ensemble learning, therefore user involvement can be significantly reduced in real-world scenarios. Also, we can observe that the original F-measure of the consensus partition is already very good.

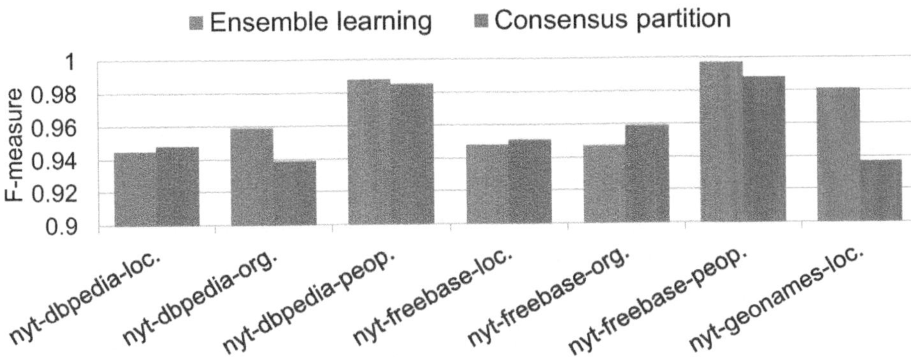

Fig. 3. Performance of ensemble learning

6 Related Work

In the Semantic Web area, traditional works address entity coreference mainly from two directions: fully-automatic and semi-automatic. One kind of automatic methods is by equivalence reasoning in terms of standard OWL semantics, e.g., `owl:sameAs` [8] and inverse functional properties [10]; the other is by similarity computation, with the assumption that instances denote the same object if they share similar property-values [14,20]. Recent works also used machine learning techniques to learn complex similarity combination rules [11,16]. We refer the reader to the report of the OAEI instance matching track for more details [6].

While the automatic methods can suggest coreferent entities, for many applications they must still be manually verified by humans. Entity coreference is recognized as the AI-complete problem, which is hard to be solved by computers but easy for humans [25]. To leverage user involvement, the works in [3,18] used crowdsourcing platforms for entity coreference, which differ from our deployment. Sig.ma [21] developed a Web-based user interface to view Linked Data, which allowed users to give judgement by filtering property-values and data sources. iamResearcher [25] addressed the scientific publication author identity coreference problem for integrating distributed bibliographic datasets. Currently they do not present any mechanism to learn from user-judged results.

To resolve disagreements among user-judged results, dedicated algorithms were proposed to estimate the quality of users, allowing for the rejection and blocking of the unreliable users [3,12]. After that, different user-judged results can be aggregated using machine learning or other customizable methods [5]. Different from them, our approach uses consensus partition to minimize the disagreements among all users, because even reliable users can make mistakes. Furthermore, various theoretical results on consensus partition are provided including the performance guarantee [9].

Some methods also focused on how to make the best use of human contributions, e.g., by machine learning to minimize user involvement while preserving certain coreference accuracy [13,24], which implicitly assumed that a user can certainly give truth about coreference result, and there is only one single right answer for each pair of coreferent entities, but both of the two assumptions do not conform to the real world. In this paper, we ground our learning algorithm on the consensus partition, which can accommodate inconsistencies and errors. Moreover, we integrate the entity coreference tasks in users' browsing activities, which gives users incentives for active participation.

7 Conclusions and Future Work

Distributed human computation for entity coreference is important to improve its accuracy, however, user involvement is often expensive, slow and error-prone. In this paper, we proposed coCoref to leverage distributed human computation and consensus partition for entity coreference. The main contributions of this paper are as follows:

- All distributed users' individual partitions are collected and aggregated to build a consensus partition, which increases the scale of coreferent entities and resolves the disagreements simultaneously.
- Ensemble learning is performed on the consensus partition to alleviate user involvement, which automatically identifies a large number of coreferent entities that users have not judged.
- We integrated coCoref with the Web browsing activities, which is different from many approaches that use crowdsourcing platforms. We also conducted experiments to demonstrate the good accuracy of consensus partition and the considerable reduction of user involvement.

In future work, we look forward to studying other sophisticated methods to consensus partition and ensemble learning with the consideration of user preference.

Acknowledgements. This work is supported in part by the National Natural Science Foundation of China under Grant Nos. 61370019 and 61170068, and in part by the Natural Science Foundation of Jiangsu Province under Grant Nos. BK2011189 and BK2012723.

References

1. Ailon, N., Charikar, M., Newman, A.: Aggregating inconsistent information: ranking and clustering. Journal of the ACM 55(5), 23 (2008)
2. Breiman, L.: Random forests. Machine Learning 45(1), 5–32 (2001)
3. Demartini, G., Difallah, D., Cudré-Mauroux, P.: ZenCrowd: Leveraging probabilistic reasoning and crowdsourcing techniques for large-scale entity linking. In: WWW, pp. 469–478 (2012)
4. Dietterich, T.G.: Ensemble methods in machine learning. In: Kittler, J., Roli, F. (eds.) MCS 2000. LNCS, vol. 1857, pp. 1–15. Springer, Heidelberg (2000)
5. Do, H.H., Rahm, E.: COMA: A system for flexible combination of schema matching approaches. In: VLDB, pp. 610–621 (2002)

6. Ferrara, A., Nikolov, A., Noessner, J., Scharffe, F.: Evaluation of instance matching tools: The experience of OAEI. Journal of Web Semantics 21, 49–60 (2013)
7. Gionis, A., Mannila, H., Tsaparas, P.: Clustering aggregation. ACM Transactions on Knowledge Discovery from Data 1(1), 4 (2007)
8. Glaser, H., Jaffri, A., Millard, I.: Managing co-reference on the semantic web. In: WWW Workshop on LDOW (2009)
9. Goder, A., Filkov, V.: Consensus clustering algorithms: Comparison and refinement. In: ALENEX, pp. 109–117 (2008)
10. Hogan, A., Zimmermann, A., Umbrich, J., Polleres, A., Decker, S.: Scalable and distributed methods for entity matching, consolidation and disambiguation over linked data corpora. Journal of Web Semantics 10, 76–110 (2012)
11. Hu, W., Chen, J., Qu, Y.: A self-training approach for resolving object coreference on the semantic web. In: WWW, pp. 87–96 (2011)
12. Ipeirotis, P., Provost, F., Wang, J.: Quality management on Amazon Mechanical Turk. In: ACM SIGKDD Workshop on Human Computation, pp. 64–67 (2010)
13. Isele, R., Bizer, C.: Active learning of expressive linkage rules using genetic programming. Journal of Web Semantics 23, 2–15 (2013)
14. Li, J., Tang, J., Li, Y., Luo, Q.: RiMOM: A dynamic multi strategy ontology alignment framework. IEEE Transactions on Knowledge and Data Engineering 21(8), 1218–1232 (2009)
15. Nikolov, A., d'Aquin, M., Motta, E.: Unsupervised learning of link discovery configuration. In: Simperl, E., Cimiano, P., Polleres, A., Corcho, O., Presutti, V. (eds.) ESWC 2012. LNCS, vol. 7295, pp. 119–133. Springer, Heidelberg (2012)
16. Niu, X., Rong, S., Wang, H., Yu, Y.: An effective rule miner for instance matching in a web of data. In: CIKM, pp. 1085–1094 (2012)
17. Rokach, L.: Pattern classification using ensemble methods. World Scientific (2010)
18. Sarasua, C., Simperl, E., Noy, N.F.: CROWDMAP: Crowdsourcing ontology alignment with microtasks. In: Cudré-Mauroux, P., et al. (eds.) ISWC 2012, Part I. LNCS, vol. 7649, pp. 525–541. Springer, Heidelberg (2012)
19. Settles, B.: Active learning literature survey. University of Wisconsin–Madison (2010)
20. Song, D., Heflin, J.: Automatically generating data linkages using a domain-independent candidate selection approach. In: Aroyo, L., Welty, C., Alani, H., Taylor, J., Bernstein, A., Kagal, L., Noy, N., Blomqvist, E. (eds.) ISWC 2011, Part I. LNCS, vol. 7031, pp. 649–664. Springer, Heidelberg (2011)
21. Tummarello, G., Cyganiak, R., Catasta, M., Danielczyk, S., Delbru, R., Decker, S.: Sig.ma: Live views on the web of data. Journal of Web Semantics 8(4), 355–364 (2010)
22. Vega-Pons, S., Ruiz-Shulcloper, J.: A survey of clustering ensemble algorithms. International Journal of Pattern Recognition and Artificial Intelligence 25(3), 337–372 (2011)
23. Wagner, S., Wagner, D.: Comparing clusterings: an overview. Universität Karlsruhe, Fakultät für Informatik (2007)
24. Wang, J., Kraska, T., Franklin, M., Feng, J.: CrowdER: Crowdsourcing entity resolution. In: VLDB, pp. 1483–1494 (2012)
25. Yang, Y., Singh, P., Yao, J., Au Yeung, C.-m., Zareian, A., Wang, X., Cai, Z., Salvadores, M., Gibbins, N., Hall, W., Shadbolt, N.: Distributed human computation framework for linked data co-reference resolution. In: Antoniou, G., Grobelnik, M., Simperl, E., Parsia, B., Plexousakis, D., De Leenheer, P., Pan, J. (eds.) ESWC 2011, Part I. LNCS, vol. 6643, pp. 32–46. Springer, Heidelberg (2011)

SPARQL Query Verbalization for Explaining Semantic Search Engine Queries

Basil Ell[1], Andreas Harth[1], and Elena Simperl[2]

[1] Karlsruhe Institute of Technology (KIT),
Karlsruhe, Germany
{basil.ell,harth}@kit.edu,
[2] University of Southampton,
Southampton, United Kingdom
E.Simperl@soton.ac.uk

Abstract. In this paper we introduce Spartiqulation, a system that translates SPARQL queries into English text. Our aim is to allow casual end users of semantic applications with limited to no expertise in the SPARQL query language to interact with these applications in a more intuitive way. The verbalization approach exploits domain-independent template-based natural language generation techniques, as well as linguistic cues in labels and URIs.

Keywords: #eswc2014Ell, SPARQL verbalization, Natural Language Generation, Natural Language Interfaces.

1 Introduction

SPARQL is the W3C Recommendation for querying and accessing RDF data [7]. While it has found broad acceptance among semantic application developers, its usage among those who possess limited to no expertise in semantic technologies remains understandably limited.

A wide variety of systems propose different means for the users to express what they are looking for: (i) keywords, as supported by systems such as SemSearch [11]; (ii) free-text questions, sometimes using a controlled language, such as ORAKEL [1] and FREyA [3], and (iii) pre-defined forms [15]. Independently of how the input is given, SPARQL queries are generated and evaluated.

The system we introduce in this paper, Spartiqulation, is complementary in functionality and purpose to these approaches. More concretely, we address the question of query verbalization, by which the meaning of a query encoded in SPARQL is conveyed to the user via English text. The verbalization allows for the user to observe a potential discrepancy between an intended question and the system-generated query. In addition, Spartiqulation offers an easy-to-use means to gain better insight into the operation of a search system.

We illustrate these aspects via an example. Assume the information need of the user is *The second highest mountain on Earth*; if the system does not know the meaning of the term *second*, it will very likely simply ignore the qualifier and

V. Presutti et al. (Eds.): ESWC 2014, LNCS 8465, pp. 426–441, 2014.

display the highest mountain. Using Spartiqulation, the meaning of the generated SPARQL query can be communicated to the users in a comprehensible way and eventually inform them that the system understood a different question.

Our main contributions are: 1) We introduce a domain-independent SPARQL query verbalization approach based on domain-independent templates. 2) We define the anatomy of a query verbalization. 3) We verbalize a query in a top-down manner by breaking a query into independently verbalizable parts. This allows for a more concise verbalization compared to a bottom-up manner where smallest part of a query are mapped to their realization and then combined.

All verbalizations presented as captions of query listings are generated using Spartiqulation. The work we present here is an extension of our previous work [6] which described the document structuring task. In this paper we provide details on the remaining four tasks that are necessary for the complete system and provide evaluation results. Additional material is available online.[1]

2 The Spartiqulation Approach

2.1 Coverage

SPARQL knows the query forms `SELECT`, `CONSTRUCT`, `ASK`, and `DESCRIBE`. Tools such as SemSearch [11], ORAKEL [1], and FREyA [3] that translate user input into SPARQL queries generate `SELECT` queries (e.g., Listing 1) and `ASK` queries (e.g., Listing 2), which are also the query forms that our approach supports. In the current form our approach verbalizes SPARQL 1.1 `SELECT` and `ASK` queries where the `WHERE` clause is a connected basic graph pattern that may contain filter expressions. The aggregation function `COUNT` and the solution modifiers `DISTINCT`, `HAVING`, `LIMIT`, `OFFSET`, and `ORDER BY` may be used. Currently not supported are unconnected basic graph patterns, variables in predicate positions, negations via the language features `EXISTS` and `MINUS`, subqueries, the language features `BIND` and `VALUES`, the solution modifier `REDUCED`, aggregation functions besides `COUNT`, graph names, and path matching.

2.2 Tasks

Our approach is inspired by the pipeline architecture for NLG systems and the tasks these systems commonly perform, as introduced by Reiter and Dale [20]:

T1. Content determination is about deciding which information will be communicated by the text to be generated – see [6] for details.

T2. Document structuring refers to the task of constructing independently verbalizable messages from the input query, and deciding upon the order and structure of these messages.

[1] `http://km.aifb.kit.edu/projects/spartiqulator/ESWC2014SPARQL`

T3. Lexicalization is the task of deciding which specific words to use for conveying the meaning of the original content in text.

T4. Referring expression generation concerns the task that specifies how to refer to an entity that is already introduced in the text.

T5. Aggregation is the task of deciding how to map structures created during content determination and document structuring onto linguistic structures, such as sentences and paragraphs.

T6. Linguistic realization is the task of converting abstract representations of sentences into actual text.

Our system is template-based. In particular, inspired by [9] and [21], we have manually collected a series of schema-independent templates, which are used in the verbalization process to generate coherent natural-language text from the different parts of a SPARQL query. These templates could be extended to capture user-, domain- or application-specific aspects to further improve the verbalization results. Our implementation supports such extensions, but already delivers meaningful results in its current generic form. The anatomy of a verbalization consists of up to four parts:

Main entity (ME): `SELECT` and `ASK` queries contain a `WHERE` clause containing a basic graph pattern. Verbalization of a graph or graph pattern requires a starting point. We refer to the node that we chose to begin with as the *main entity*. The main entity is rendered as the subject of the verbalization in singular or plural, with a definite or an indefinite article, and may be counted. Examples are: *Persons* for the `SELECT` query in Listing 1 and *a record* for the `ASK` query in Listing 2.

Constraints (CONS): `CONS` covers restrictions regarding the main entity, such as the relations with other resources and literals. Constraints are rendered in singular or plural, depending on the number of the main entity, and may contain information from the `ORDER BY` and `LIMIT` parts of the query, as well as from `FILTER` expressions. Examples are: *that have a birth place*, *that have "Dana" as an English given name*, *that have an alias that matches "Dana"*.

Requests (REQ): `REQ`, which is only created for `SELECT` queries, includes the projection variables (those that appear in the `SELECT` clause) besides the main entity of a query. Examples of requests are *these birth places* and *if available, their English labels* in Listing 1. Renderings of requests may include information from `FILTER`s and from domain/range information of properties and whether the variable is optional.

Modifiers (MOD): `MOD` is represented using the features `LIMIT`, `OFFSET`, and `ORDER BY` and apply to `SELECT` queries. `MOD` can be partially included within other parts of the verbalization, for example in the ME part (*10 persons*), within constraints (*that has the highest number of languages*), or as an own sentence (*Omit the first 10 results; show not more than 10 results.*).

```
SELECT DISTINCT ?uri ?string ?p WHERE {
  ?uri :birthPlace ?p . ?uri :surname 'Elcar' .
  ?uri rdf:type foaf:Person.
  { ?uri foaf:givenName 'Dana'@en. } UNION {
    ?uri prop:alias ?alias . FILTER regex(?alias,'Dana') .
  }
  OPTIONAL {
    ?uri rdfs:label ?string . FILTER (lang(?string) = 'en')
  }
} LIMIT 10
```

Listing 1. *Persons that have a birth place and that have the surname "Elcar" and that have "Dana" as an English given name or that have an alias that matches "Dana". Show also these birth places and, if available, their English labels.*

```
ASK WHERE {
  ?album rdf:type mo:Record.
  ?album mo:release_status mo:bootleg.
  ?album foaf:maker ?artist.
  ?artist foaf:name 'Pink Floyd'.
}
```

Listing 2. *Is it true that there is a record that has a maker that has the name "Pink Floyd" and that has the release status bootleg?*

```
SELECT ?uri ?string WHERE {
  ?uri rdf:type onto:Country .
  ?uri onto:language ?language.
  OPTIONAL {
    ?uri rdfs:label ?string.
    FILTER (lang(?string) = 'en')
  }
} ORDER BY DESC(COUNT(?language))
LIMIT 1
```

Listing 3. *The country that has the highest number of languages. Show also, if available, its English labels.*

2.3 Document Structuring

The system constructs independently verbalizable messages from the input query and determines an appropriate ordering and structure. We first identify the subject of the verbalization and then create and classify the messages.

Main Entity Selection. `SELECT` queries are a means to retrieve bindings for variables. We assume that a user is more interested in variable values than in entities used in the query. *Projection variables* are those variables that appear in the `SELECT` clause and in the `WHERE` clause, such as the variable `?title` in Listing 5. Only bindings retrieved for projection variables are returned as result of a query execution. Therefore, only projection variables are candidates for the main entity selection. Furthermore, only non-optional projection variables come into consideration. A variable is a non-optional variable if within the `WHERE` clause it does not only appear within `OPTIONAL` blocks. For example, in Listing 3 the variable `?uri` is non-optional and the variable `?string` is optional. Due to their nature of being optional and thus less relevant than non-optional variables, only non-optional projection variables come into consideration. The same holds for variables for which a `NOTBOUND` filter (e.g. `! bound(?var)`) is specified.

If a `SELECT` query has multiple non-optional projection variable, a choice is made among these candidates (see [6] for details). For example, given the query shown in Listing 5, selecting `?track` would result in *Things that have a creator that has the title "Petula Clark"*; selecting `?title` would result in *Distinct things that are titles of tracks that have a creator that have the title "Petula Clark"*.

```
SELECT DISTINCT ?uri ?book WHERE {
  ?book rdf:type onto:Book .
  ?book onto:author ?uri .
  ?book rdfs:label 'The Pillars of
    the Earth'@en .
}
```

Listing 4. Books that have the label "The Pillars of the Earth" in English and that have an author. Show also these books' authors.

```
SELECT ?track ?title
WHERE {
  ?track rdf:type mm:Track.
  ?track dc:title ?title.
  ?track dc:creator ?artist.
  ?artist dc:title 'Petula Clark'.
}
```

Listing 5. A SELECT query with two non-optional projection variables.

ASK queries are a means to assess whether a query pattern has a solution. If ASK queries contain variables then the selection procedure is the same as for projection variables in SELECT queries. Otherwise, we select the triple's subject.

Message Creation and Classification. After the main entity identification the graph is transformed so that the main entity is the root and all edges point away from the root. For details we refer to [6]. During this transformation edges may become reversed, which means that subject and object of the underlying triple are exchanged and the property is marked with a prepended `-`.

The query graph is split into independently verbalizable messages which represent paths that start at the main entity and consist of sets of triple patterns. For the query in Listing 4, where the variable `?uri` is selected as the main entity, two path messages are created. The first message represents the path `(?uri -onto:author ?book. ?book rdf:type onto:Book.)`.[2] The second message represents the path `(?uri -onto:author ?book. ?book rdfs:label 'The Pillars of the Earth'@en.)`. Further messages are created for variables and contain information about filters, as well as information related to the SPARQL features HAVING, LIMIT, OFFSET, OPTIONAL, ORDER BY, and UNION.

The messages that represent the SELECT query from Listing 1 are depicted in Fig. 1. The query is represented using 6 path-representing messages and 3 variable-representing messages. The main entity is represented with message id (MID) M6. The query contains one UNION with 2 branches. Note that the REGEX_VL filter related to the main entity is specific to branch 2 in UNION 1.

Messages that represent a path are classified as CONS. In case of a SELECT query if the path contains a projection variable besides the main entity, then the path-representing message is also classified as REQ. In Fig. 1, the path-representing messages M1 and M6 are classified as REQ messages.

2.4 Lexicalization

During lexicalization the system determines the actual wording to denominate an entity; in our case, such entities are RDF resources represented by URIs or variables. For each entity, the URI that represents the entity is dereferenced to

[2] Note that the minus symbol in `-onto:author` indicates that the property is reversed.

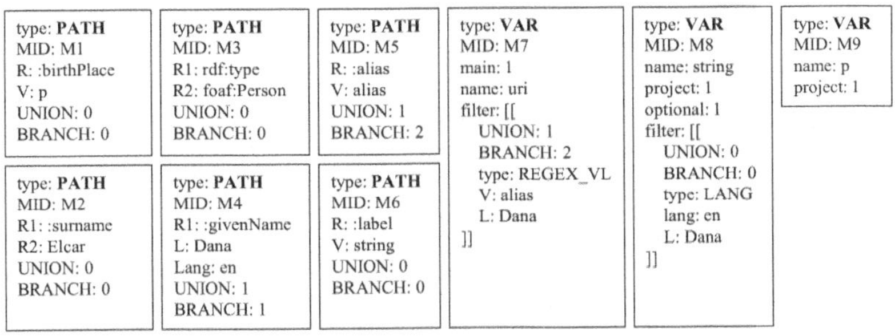

Fig. 1. Messages representing the SPARQL query in Listing 1

retrieve a label from the resulting RDF data using one of the 36 labeling properties defined in [5]. Should no label be available for a given entity, the system derives one from the local name of the URI string. For instance, the local name of the URI `http://purl.org/ontology/mo/MusicGroup` is `MusicGroup`, which can be de-camelcased and lowercased to *music group*. Variables are expressed in natural language either using their type constraints or, if absent, using the term *thing*. A variable can be explicitly constrained by its type such as the variable `?v` in `?v rdf:type ex:Actor`. In this case, we lexicalize the variable using the label of the typing class, that is *Actor*. Such typing information can also be determined taking into account the domain and range of a property. For example, in the triple pattern `?var1 dbo:capital ?var2` with domain of `dbo:capital` defined as *PopulatedPlace*, we can derive `?var1` as *populated place*.

We lexicalize properties as shown in Table 1. We use the Stanford parser [10] to identify the part of speech of a property's label or local name to chose the most appropriate lexicalization. These property patterns are based on the work by Hewlett et al. [9].

2.5 Referring Expression Generation

Referring expression generation is the task of deciding how to refer to a previously introduced entity. For example, the query in Listing 4 asks for books that have a certain label and known authors. The variable `?uri` is introduced and rendered as *authors* within the `CONS` part *have authors*. Since the `SELECT` clause contains a second variable `?uri` besides the main entity `?book`, the verbalization needs to communicate that entities that can be bound to `?uri` need to be part of the query result. This is achieved by adding the phrase *Show also these books' authors* to the verbalization, where *these books' authors* is the referring expression corresponding to the second variable `?uri`.

On the one hand, a referring expressions needs to unambiguously refer to an entity. On the other hand, a referring expression should be concise to aid the understandability of a verbalization. For example, for the `SELECT` query in Listing 1, the projection variable can be verbalized as *these birth places* or as *these persons' birth places*. Since within the query *birth place* does not occur

$A \triangleq$ The DISTINCT modifier is used
$B \triangleq$ Main entity is counted as in `SELECT(COUNT ?main)`
$C \triangleq$ Result set is limited with LIMIT as in `LIMIT 10`
$D \triangleq$ ME needs to be verbalized in singular (LIMIT = 1)
$E \triangleq$ Main entity is ordered as in `ORDER BY DESC(?main)`
$F \triangleq$ Main entity has multiple types as in
`?main rdf:type ex:A. ?main rdf:type ex:B.`

Fig. 2. The set of facts that control within the verbalization template how the main entity is verbalized as shown in Fig. 3

multiple times, it is sufficient to generate *these birth places*, which means that from the REQ message only the projection variable itself needs to be verbalized. If this leads to an ambiguity, which means that two referring expressions are identical or substring of each other, then the part of the REQ message that is actually verbalized needs to be extended step by step until the full path between that variable and the main entity is verbalized. We perform this extension until the set of all referring expressions is free of ambiguities or if the full paths have already been verbalized which means that in this case we cannot generate nonambiguous referring expressions.

2.6 Linguistic Realization

Abstract representations of sentences are translated into actual text. Verbalization of the MOD part of a query is straightforward; the verbalization of REQ messages is similar to the verbalization of CONS messages. Therefore, the remainder of this section will focus on the realization of the messages corresponding to the main entity and the CONS part.

A set of 6 boolean variables, shown in Fig. 2, is necessary to fully capture the necessary variations for the main entity template. Fig. 3 shows an excerpt of this template.[3] Besides these boolean variables the template is provided with a hash map $D that contains strings that are either literals appearing in the query or labels of resources. For example, $D{TPL} is the variable's type in plural,[4] $D{TSI} is the variable's type in singular, and $D{L} is a limit value as specified using the SPARQL `LIMIT` feature. The strings, such as `Abcdef`, indicate which of the boolean variables is true. Capital characters indicate a true value, lowercase characters indicate a false value.

CONS messages are verbalized in smaller parts, each with the help of a template, which are then joined together. Consider for example a CONS message that represents a path consisting of two triples `?main :prop1 ?v1. ?v1 rdfs:label "x"`. This path is split into the parts (i) `:prop1 ?v1`, and (ii) `rdfs:label "x"`.

[3] Given the 6 boolean variables, the template could define up to 64 different verbalizations. However, the variables are not independent. Therefore, the number of different slots that need to be filled in this template is reduced from 64 to 17.

[4] We use the Perl module Lingua::EN::Inflect in order to convert a word to plural.

`Abcdef` 'Distinct ' . \$D{TPL}
→ Distinct scientists
`aBcdef` 'Number of ' . \$D{TPL}
→ Number of scientists
`AbcdEf` 'The distinct ' . \$D{TPL}
→ The distinct scientists
`abCdef` 'Not more than ' . \$D{L}
.' '.\$D{TPL}
→ Not more than 10 scientists
`abcDEf` 'The ' . \$D{TSI}
→ The scientist

Fig. 3. Excerpt of the ME template

`abcdefghIJ` 'that has no ' . \$D{PSI}
→ that has no email
`abcdEFGHij` 'that have the highest
number of '.\$D{PPL}
→ that have the highest
number of languages
`abcDefghIj` 'that is not '.\$D{A}
.' '.\$D{PSI}.' of a thing'
→ that is not a holder
of a thing

Fig. 4. Excerpt of the CONS-RV template for properties of class 1

Table 1. Classes of properties, expansions, and expansions of the reverted properties

№	Examples	Expansions	№	Examples	Expansions
1	email, hasColor	X has an email Y X has a color Y R: Y is an email of X R: Y is a color of X	5	collaboratesWith	X collaborates with Y R: Y collaborates with X
2	knows	X knows Y R: Y is known by X	6	visiting R: Y is visited by X	X is visiting Y
3	brotherOf, isBrotherOf	X is brother of Y R: Y has a brother X	7	locatedInArea	X is located in area Y in which X is located
4	producedBy, isMadeFrom	X is produced by Y X is made from Y R: Y produces X R: Y is used to make X	8	marriedTo	X is married to Y R: Y is married to X

A ≙ the variable is the first optional variable and this variable is not NOTBOUND
B ≙ the variable has exactly one type
C ≙ the variable has more than one type
D ≙ the property is reversed
E ≙ the variable is counted
F ≙ plural form is required
G ≙ ordered by variable
H ≙ descending order
I ≙ the variable is OPTIONAL and NOTBOUND
J ≙ the property is numeric

Fig. 5. The set of facts that control how a CONS part is verbalized as shown in Fig. 4

For the first part, that consists of a resource (R) and a variable (V), a specific `RV` template is selected based on linguistic properties of that resource. For example, if the property label is a noun, then the template `CONS-RV-C1` is selected. Similar to the main entity verbalization, the specific verbalization procedure is controlled by a set of facts as shown in Fig. 5. Given these facts the template produces verbalizations as shown in Fig. 4.

2.7 Aggregation

Aggregation maps the structures created so far onto linguistic structures such as sentences and paragraphs. Verbalization consists of at least one and no more than three sentences in case of `SELECT` queries and of one sentence in case of `ASK` queries. The first sentence begins with the main entity (ME) followed by *that is* or *that are* followed by the verbalized and joined `CONS` messages. The second sentence begins with *Show also* followed by the verbalized and joined `REQ` messages. If there are no `REQ` messages then we omit the sentence. The third sentence verbalizes all `MOD` messages if they have not yet been verbalized as part of the main entity verbalization. Verbalizations of `ASK` queries consist of exactly one sentence which verbalizes the main entity and the `CONS` messages. They begin with *Is it true that* followed by *there is* or *there are* followed by the verbalized and joined `CONS` messages.

`UNION`s are dealt with in the aggregation step as follows. For the set of `CONS` messages that do not belong to any `UNION`, their verbalizations are joined with and. For the query in Listing 1, verbalization of the `CONS` messages M1 and M2 results in the string *that have a birth place and that have the surname "Elcar"*. For a set of `CONS` messages that belong to the same branch of a `UNION`, the `CONS` verbalizations are joined by *and* to create the branch verbalization. Each `UNION` is verbalized by joining the branch verbalizations by *or* to create the `UNION` verbalization, for example resulting in *that have "Dana" as an English given name or that have an alias that matches "Dana"*.

Another aspect of the aggregation is the inclusion of the `LIMIT`, `OFFSET` and `ORDER BY` modifiers into the main entity verbalization, as shown in Section 2.4. This form of aggregation allows for more concise verbalizations compared to the more wordy alternative where a dedicated sentence is created.

3 Evaluation

3.1 Overview

According to Mellish and Dale [14], evaluation in the context of an NLG system can be carried out for the purpose of assessing (i) the properties of a theory; (ii) the properties of a system; and (iii) the application potential. We focused on the second aspect: on the quality of our system in terms of a set of specific dimensions. We performed (i) a comparative evaluation where we compared Spartiqulation against the (to the best of our knowledge) only other available alternative, SPARQL2NL [18]; and (ii) assessed the performance of our system according to these dimensions.

3.2 Dimensions

The evaluation dimensions, inspired by [12,14,19], are defined as follows:

Coverage: the ratio of SPARQL `SELECT` queries the system accepts. This dimension can be measured automatically.

Accuracy: the degree to which the verbalization conveys the meaning of the SPARQL query. This quality is measured through human judgement using a 4-point scale adapted from [17]: (1) The meaning of the verbalization does neither leave out any aspect of the query, nor does it add something. (2) The meaning of the query is not adequately conveyed to the verbalization.

Some aspects are missing. (3) The meaning of the query is not adequately conveyed to the verbalization. Most aspects are missing. (4) The meaning of the query is not conveyed to the verbalization.

Syntactic correctness: the degree to which the verbalization is syntactically correct, in particular whether it adheres to English grammar: (1) The verbalization is completely syntactically correct. (2) The verbalization is almost syntactically correct. (3) The verbalization presents some syntactical errors. (4) The verbalization is strongly syntactically incorrect.

Understandability: The level of understandability of the verbalization, adapted from [17]: (1) The meaning of the verbalization is clear. (2) The meaning of the verbalization is clear, but there are some problems in word usage, and/or style. (3) The basic thrust of the verbalization is clear, but the evaluator is not sure of some detailed parts because of word usage problems. (4) The verbalization contains many word usage problems, and the evaluator can only guess at the meaning. (5) The verbalization cannot be understood at all.

Adequacy and Efficiency: According to Dale [2], criteria relevant for referring expressions are *adequacy* and *efficiency*. A referring expression is adequate if it allows to unambiguously identify the referent. It can be measured as the ratio of expressions for variables within the REQ part that unambiguously identify a variable. In addition, a referring expression is said to be efficient if it is perceived to not contain more information than necessary. Since these criteria are clearly defined, they are manually evaluated by the authors.

3.3 Data Set

We created a corpus of SPARQL queries using data from the QALD-1[5] and the ILD2012 challenges.[6] The aim of these challenges was to answer natural language questions against data from DBpedia and MusicBrainz. The organizers provide a training set encompassing questions and the corresponding SPARQL queries. Our corpus refers to 291 of a total of 300 queries, more concretely `SELECT` and `ASK` queries. Nine of the questions in the original data set were eliminated since no SPARQL equivalent was specified. We randomly split the data into a training set (251 queries) and an evaluation set (40 queries) as follows:

Training data set: 44 queries from *2011-dbpedia-train*, 44 queries from *2011-musicbrainz-train*, 79 queries from *2012-dbpedia-train*, and 84 queries from *2012-musicbrainz-train*. The set contained 251 queries (228 SELECT queries, 23 ASK queries) which is about 86% of the full corpus.

Evaluation data set: 6 queries from *2011-dbpedia-train*, 6 queries from *2011-musicbrainz-train*, 14 queries from *2012-dbpedia-train*, and 14 queries from *2012-musicbrainz-train*. The set contained 40 queries (35 SELECT queries and 5 ASK queries) which is about 14% of the full corpus.

[5] `http://www.sc.cit-ec.uni-bielefeld.de/qald-1`

[6] `http://greententacle.techfak.uni-bielefeld.de/~cunger/qald/`

3.4 Comparative Evaluation

We compared our work with SPARQL2NL in a blind setting with the help of six evaluators who had experiences with writing SPARQL queries. The evaluators were not aware of the fact that the verbalizations were generated by different systems. In cases where both systems successfully verbalized a query (38/40 queries), their task was, given a query and two verbalizations, to compare the first verbalization with the second regarding accuracy, syntactic correctness, and understandability. For example, we asked *Compare the two verbalizations regarding accuracy* where we provided the options (i) *The first one is more accurate,* (ii) *They are equally accurate,* (iii) *The first one is less accurate,* and (iv) *Not applicable (Please explain).*

3.5 Non-comparative Evaluation

After the comparative evaluation we asked the same group to evaluate the *accuracy*, *syntactical correctness*, and *intelligibility* of Spartiqulation. Given the set of 40 successfully verbalized queries, we asked the evaluators to assess the verbalizations along these three criteria.

Coverage was measured as – per definition – the ratio of queries accepted by our system both in the training and the evaluation data set. Adequacy and efficiency of referring expressions were evaluated manually by the authors. Since these criteria, unlike accuracy, syntactic correctness, and understandability, are unambiguously defined in the literature, we evaluated them ourselves without diminishing the objectivity of the remaining findings.

3.6 Results

Comparative Evaluation. Fig. 6 shows the results of the comparative evaluation. 38 verbalizations were assessed by the 6 evaluators, leading to a total number of 114 assessments. Higher accuracy was reported in 43 cases (37.72%), equal accuracy was reported in 66 cases (57.89%), higher syntactical correctness was reported in 52 cases (45.61%), equal syntactical correctness was reported in 45 cases (39.47%), higher understandability was reported in 74 cases (64.91%), and equal understandability was reported in 16 cases (14.04%). We used Krippendorff's alpha [8] to measure inter-rater agreement regarding whether our results are comparable or. The results are $\alpha = 0.56$ for accuracy, $\alpha = 0.726$ for syntactical correctness and $\alpha = 0.676$ for understandability.

Non-comparative Evaluation. Coverage: We counted how many queries contain features that our system does not support using the data set described in Section 3.3. Within the evaluation set of 40 queries, every query was verbalizable. Within the training set of 251 queries, four queries did not meet the limitations described in Section 2.1. Each of these queries contained two disconnected basic graph patterns that were only connected via FILTER expressions, such as `FILTER (?large = ?capital)`. This means a total coverage of 287/291 (98.6%).

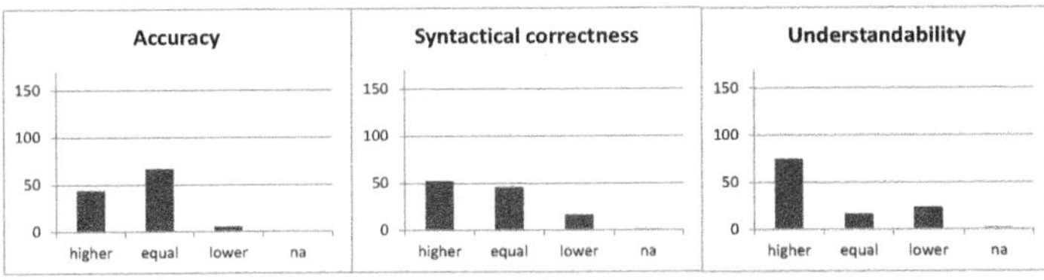

Fig. 6. Results regarding accuracy, syntactical correctness, and understandability from the comparative evaluation

Accuracy, Syntactical Correctness, and Understandability: Fig. 7 shows the results regarding the 40 evaluation queries that were were assessed by the 6 evaluators, leading to a total number of 120 assessments. The numbers on the x-axis correlate with the scales introduced in Section 3.2. Verbalizations show a high accuracy, high syntactical correctness, and good understandability. 106 out of 120 times the evaluators attested the best accuracy score (88.33%). Regarding syntactical correctness, and understandability there is room for improvement. 70 out of 120 times the evaluators attested the best accuracy score (58.33%), 47 out of 120 times the evaluators attested the best understandability score (39.16%).

Adequacy and Minimality of Referring Expressions: Among the 40 queries in the evaluation set, for 25 queries referring expressions (RE) had to be generated. In 24 cases the RE were nonambiguous which means an adequacy of 96%. In 3 out of 25 cases the RE was not efficient. For example, a query was verbalized as *Distinct things that are presidents of the united states or that are presidents that have President of the United States as a title. Show also, if available, these things' (that are presidents of the united states or presidents) English labels.* Here, the RE *these things' (that are presidents of the united states or presidents) English labels* could by reduced to *these things' English labels.*

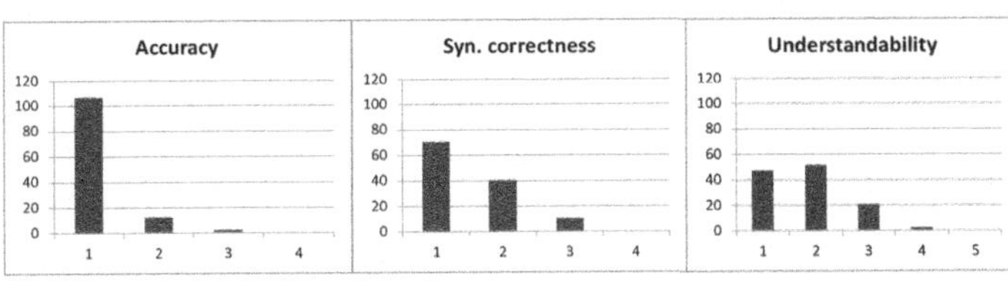

Fig. 7. Results regarding accuracy, syntactical correctness, and understandability from the non-comparative evaluation

3.7 Discussion

What makes the verbalization generated by the SPARQL2NL system less understandable for complex queries is the fact that variable names are included in the verbalization such as in *"This query retrieves distinct countries ?uri and distinct values ?string such that ?string is in English. Moreover, it returns exclusively results that the number of ?uri's official languages is greater than 2.*" In comparison, our system verbalizes the same query as *"Distinct countries that have more than 2 official languages. Show also, if available, these countries' English labels.*" In some cases experts tended to prefer the variant with variable names since this seems to be more natural to them. However, the experts pointed out their belief that verbalizations containing variables will be hard to understand by non-experts. We claim that as long as experts are not the only intended users of semantic search engines this verbalization style is inappropriate. Especially, variable names in automatically generated queries may carry little information. An interesting feature is that datatypes are utilized as in the verbalization of the literal `?date <= '2010-12-31'^^xsd:date` to *?date is greater than or equal to January 31, 2010.* SPARQL2NL was capable of verbalizing the 4 queries that were rejected by our system.

Problems both systems were facing arise from four areas: 1) Missing labels for entities. Relying on local names leads to results such as *that have the release type type soundtrack* for the triple pattern `?album mm:releaseType mm:TypeSoundtrack`. 2) The way the data is modeled complicates the verbalization as in *Things that are begin dates of things that have to artists that have the title "Slayer"*. Here, the verbalization of the property in `?bandinstance ar:toArtist ?band` as *to artist* is currently the best guess the system can make. 3) Missing linguistic information about properties. The property `dbo:crosses` in the triple pattern `res:Brooklyn_Bridge dbo:crosses ?uri` can be interpreted as the plural of the noun cross or an inflected form of the verb to cross. Here, verbalization could be improved if linguistic information was attached to the vocabulary, for example using the *lemon model* [13]. 4) Problems with pluralization and capitalization exist and could also be fixed given a lexicon.

4 Related Work

To the best of our knowledge SPARQL2NL [18] is the only approach which is similar to ours in scope and functionality. One part of our evaluation was dedicated to the comparison along a number of quality dimensions established in the field of Natural Language Generation. The evaluation revealed that both approaches have advantages and disadvantages, whereas Spartiqulation seems to perform better for cases dealing with complex queries with multiple variables.

Both approaches are geared towards a similar subset of SPARQL. How a triple is verbalized depends on linguistic cues found in property labels and type information extracted from the queries. The main differences are two-fold: 1) SPARQL2NL maps each atom (variable, property, resource, literal) to their realization, stores these realizations as dependency trees and aggregate these trees in a later step. In our approach, we fragment the query graph into independently verbalizable parts (messages). This higher level of granularity has positive influences on conciseness of the resulting verbalization. 2) SPARQL2NL does not map variables to realizations, which means that names of variables appear in verbalizations as they are in the query. Even in a scenario where variable names are meaningful this is expected to have a negative impact on the understandability of the verbalization for non-experts. Moreover, meaningful variable names cannot be guaranteed if queries are generated by a natural language interface. In cases where variables have been introduced due to filters, SPARQL2NL is capable of removing those variable names from the verbalizations using aggregation.

Further related work comes from three areas: verbalization of RDF data [21], verbalization of OWL ontologies [22], and verbalization of SQL queries. The first two fields provide techniques that we can apply to improve the lexicalization and aggregation tasks, such as the template-based approach presented in [4]. The main difference between Spartiqulation and the work by Minock [16], which focuses on relational queries over tuples, is that our approach is schema-agnostic. Besides some dependencies to RDF(S) and OWL, our system does not require any information about the domain of the application scenario, and about the vocabularies used to encode knowledge about this domain. By contrast, the verbalizer by Minock foresees manually created patterns covering all possible combinations of relations in the schema.

5 Conclusions

In this paper we presented our approach to SPARQL query verbalization. Our aim is to create natural-language descriptions of queries to communicate the meaning of these queries to users who are not familiar with the intricacies of the query language. To do so, we realized a system which implements an established natural language generation pipeline complemented by templates manually derived through the analysis of a representative set of SPARQL queries used by the community in related research challenges.

The results of our work could be beneficial for a variety of Linked-Data-related scenarios in which SPARQL cannot be assumed as the most appropriate form of interaction between an application and its users. In particular, verbalization could complement the functionality of information retrieval systems, which transform unstructured or semi-structured user queries into SPARQL, as the availability of human-readable renderings of SPARQL queries allows users to gain a better understanding of the way the information retrieval system matches their information needs to sources, and of the reasons why certain sources are included in the result set.

Acknowledgements. The authors acknowledge the support of the European Commission's Seventh Framework Programme FP7/2007-2013 (PlanetData, Grant 257641) and FP7-ICT-2011-7 (XLike, Grant 288342).

References

1. Cimiano, P., Haase, P., Heizmann, J., Mantel, M., Studer, R.: Towards portable natural language interfaces to knowledge bases–The case of the ORAKEL system. Data & Knowledge Engineering 65(2), 325–354 (2008)

2. Dale, R.: Cooking up referring expressions. In: Proceedings of the 27th Annual Meeting on Association for Computational Linguistics, ACL 1989, pp. 68–75. Association for Computational Linguistics, Stroudsburg (1989)
3. Damljanovic, D., Agatonovic, M., Cunningham, H.: FREyA: An interactive way of querying Linked Data using natural language. In: García-Castro, R., Fensel, D., Antoniou, G. (eds.) ESWC 2011. LNCS, vol. 7117, pp. 125–138. Springer, Heidelberg (2012)
4. Davis, B., Iqbal, A., Funk, A., Tablan, V., Bontcheva, K., Cunningham, H., Handschuh, S.: RoundTrip Ontology Authoring. In: Sheth, A.P., Staab, S., Dean, M., Paolucci, M., Maynard, D., Finin, T., Thirunarayan, K. (eds.) ISWC 2008. LNCS, vol. 5318, pp. 50–65. Springer, Heidelberg (2008)
5. Ell, B., Vrandečić, D., Simperl, E.: Labels in the Web of Data. In: Aroyo, L., Welty, C., Alani, H., Taylor, J., Bernstein, A., Kagal, L., Noy, N., Blomqvist, E. (eds.) ISWC 2011, Part I. LNCS, vol. 7031, pp. 162–176. Springer, Heidelberg (2011)
6. Ell, B., Vrandečić, D., Simperl, E.: SPARTIQULATION: Verbalizing SPARQL queries. In: Proceedings of the Interacting with Linked Data (ILD) Workshop at ESWC 2012, p. 5 (2012)
7. Harris, S., Seaborne, A.: SPARQL 1.1 Query Language. W3C Recommendation (2010), http://www.w3.org/TR/sparql11-query/ (last accessed October 19, 2013)
8. Hayes, A.F., Krippendorff, K.: Answering the call for a standard reliability measure for coding data. Communication Methods and Measures 1(1), 77–89 (2007)
9. Hewlett, D., Kalyanpur, A., Kolovski, V., Halaschek-Wiener, C.: Effective NL Paraphrasing of Ontologies on the Semantic Web. In: End User Semantic Web Interaction Workshop at ESWC 2005 (2005)
10. Klein, D., Manning, C.D.: Accurate Unlexicalized Parsing. In: Hinrichs, E., Roth, D. (eds.) Proceedings of the 41st Annual Meeting of the Association for Computational Linguistics (2003)
11. Lei, Y., Uren, V.S., Motta, E.: SemSearch: A search engine for the semantic web. In: Staab, S., Svátek, V. (eds.) EKAW 2006. LNCS (LNAI), vol. 4248, pp. 238–245. Springer, Heidelberg (2006)
12. Lester, J., Porter, B.: Developing and empirically evaluating robust explanation generators: The KNIGHT experiments. Comp. Linguistics 23(1), 65–101 (1997)
13. McCrae, J., Spohr, D., Cimiano, P.: Linking Lexical Resources and Ontologies on the Semantic Web with Lemon. In: Antoniou, G., Grobelnik, M., Simperl, E., Parsia, B., Plexousakis, D., De Leenheer, P., Pan, J. (eds.) ESWC 2011, Part I. LNCS, vol. 6643, pp. 245–259. Springer, Heidelberg (2011)
14. Mellish, C., Dale, R.: Evaluation in the conext of natural language generation. Computer Speech and Language 12(4), 349–374 (1998)
15. Mendes, P., McKnight, B., Sheth, A., Kissinger, J.: TcruziKB: Enabling Complex Queries for Genomic Data Exploration. In: Semantic Computing, pp. 432–439 (2008)
16. Minock, M.: C-Phrase: A system for building robust natural language interfaces to databases. Data Knowl. Eng. 69(3), 290–302 (2010)
17. Nagao, M., Tsujii, J.-I., Nakamura, J.-I.: The Japanese government project for machine translation. Comput. Linguist. 11(2-3), 91–110 (1985)
18. Ngonga Ngomo, A.-C., Bühmann, L., Unger, C., Lehmann, J., Gerber, D.: SPARQL2NL: Verbalizing Sparql Queries. In: International World Wide Web Conferences Steering Committee, pp. 329–332 (2013)

19. Reiter, E., Belz, A.: An investigation into the validity of some metrics for automatically evaluating natural language generation systems. Computational Linguistics 35(4), 529–558 (2009)
20. Reiter, E., Dale, R.: Building Natural Language Generation Systems. In: Natural Language Processing. Cambridge University Press (2000)
21. Sun, X., Mellish, C.: An experiment on "free generation" from single RDF triples. In: ENLG 2007, pp. 105–108. Association for Computational Linguistics, Stroudsburg (2007)
22. Third, A., Williams, S., Power, R.: OWL to English: a tool for generating organised easily-navigated hypertexts from ontologies. In: ISWC 2011 (2011)

Optimising Linked Data Queries in the Presence of Co-reference

Xin Wang, Thanassis Tiropanis, and Hugh C. Davis

Electronics and Computer Science
University of Southampton, UK
{xw4g08,tt2,hcd}@ecs.soton.ac.uk
http://www.ecs.soton.ac.uk/

Abstract. Due to the distributed nature of Linked Data, many resources are referred to by more than one URI. This phenomenon, known as co-reference, increases the probability of leaving out implicit semantically related results when querying Linked Data. The probability of co-reference increases further when considering distributed SPARQL queries over a larger set of distributed datasets. Addressing co-reference in Linked Data queries, on one hand, increases complexity of query processing. On the other hand, it requires changes in how statistics of datasets are taken into consideration. We investigate these two challenges of addressing co-reference in distributed SPARQL queries, and propose two methods to improve query efficiency: 1) a model named Virtual Graph, that transforms a query with co-reference into a normal query with pre-existing bindings; 2) an algorithm named Ψ, that intensively exploits parallelism, and dynamically optimises queries using runtime statistics. We deploy both methods in an distributed engine called LHD-d. To evaluate LHD-d, we investigate the distribution of co-reference in the real world, based on which we simulate an experimental RDF network. In this environment we demonstrate the advantages of LHD-d for distributed SPARQL queries in environments with co-reference.

Keywords: #eswc2014Wang, SPARQL, Linked Data, distributed query, dynamic optimisation, co-reference.

1 Introduction

Over years a large amount of Linked Data have been published by numerous independent individuals and organisations. When referring to resources, it is desirable to reuse existing URIs [10]. However, it is impractical to guarantee that one resource is only bound to a single URI due to the distributed nature of Linked Data. On class level, common vocabularies, such as Friend of a Friend (FOAF)[1], and Dublin Core Metadata Initiative (DCMI)[2], are shared in many RDF datasets. On instance level, poor agreement is made [7]. For example, 23

[1] http://www.foaf-project.org/
[2] http://www.dublincore.org/documents/dcmi-terms/

V. Presutti et al. (Eds.): ESWC 2014, LNCS 8465, pp. 442–456, 2014.

different URIs are found referring to the person Tim Berners-Lee out of 1.118 billion triples [8]. This phenomenon, that multiple URIs referring to the same resource, is known as co-reference. Co-referent URIs are semantically equal[3] from the perspective of Linked Data queries. Without taking co-reference into account, Linked Data queries may leave out valid results that are not explicitly available.

A variety of work has been done to identify co-reference in Linked Data (i.e. co-reference resolution) [7,4]. Once resolved, a pair of co-referential URIs is expressed as an *owl:sameAs* [3] assertion, which states that two URIs are semantically equivalent. By examining existing *owl:sameAs* statements, it is possible to retrieve additional semantically valid results when querying Linked Data. However, the following issues persist in the above process:

1. A naïve approach to query Linked Data with co-reference requires three steps. First, retrieving co-reference for every concrete URI in a given query by consulting *owl:sameAs* statements. Second, executing the original query, as well as its co-referential queries that are obtained by replacing one or more original URIs with their co-reference. Third, combining results of all previously executed queries. This approach results in significant query overheads, and each co-referential query can only be optimised on its own (i.e. the total costs of all co-referential queries are not necessarily minimised).
2. A small amount of co-reference can potentially lead to a large amount of additional results. Thus, query processing with enhanced performance is desirable.
3. Query efficiency is closely related to the statistics of datasets. On a large scale, it is unlikely to have pre-computed statistics taking co-reference into account.

Regarding the above issues, we propose two methods to improve the performance of Linked Data queries in the presence of co-reference:

- A model named Virtual Graph (VrG), that merges all co-referential queries into a normal query with pre-existing bindings. VrG saves the overheads of sending many queries, and especially, enables optimisation regarding all co-referential queries.
- An algorithm named Ψ, that identifies independent sub-queries, which can be optimised and executed independently in parallel, without increasing communication traffic. It is worth mentioning that Ψ helps increase degree of parallelism, and can be as well used in engines that do not take co-reference into account.

Furthermore, sub-queries identified by the Ψ algorithm are optimised at runtime (i.e. dynamic optimisation [11]), using runtime statistics instead of pre-computed statistics. Based on the aforementioned methods, we implement a

[3] In practice, co-referential URIs usually refer to closely related resources rather than the exact same resource. However, this issue is not essential in this paper.

distributed SPARQL engine, named LHD-d[4] that is able to process co-referential queries with improved efficiency.

To evaluate our approach, we investigate co-reference in the real world. Based on the distribution of real-world co-reference, we propose a method to simulate co-reference for arbitrary datasets. We set up a RDF network containing co-reference using an evaluation framework [15,16] that extends the Berlin SPARQL Benchmark (BSBM) [2].

The remainder of this paper is organised around presenting and demonstrating the effectiveness of VrG and Ψ through the evaluation of LHD-d. In section 2 we provide the background of this work and review related approaches that LHD-d is compared to. The core techniques of LHD-d, VrG and Ψ, are described in section 3 and 4 respectively. In section 5 we describe how VrG and Ψ are deployed alongside dynamic optimisation in LHD-d. After that, in section 6, we investigate the distribution of co-reference in the real world, based on which we propose a method to simulate RDF networks having co-reference. We also describe the environment in which LHD-d is evaluated and compared with related approaches. The performance of LHD-d is thoroughly examined in two situations, respectively with or without the presence of co-reference. In section 7 we evaluate LHD-d without taking co-reference into account (by disabling VrG) and compare it with existing engines. This evaluation primarily demonstrate the effectiveness of using Ψ and runtime-statistic-based optimisation. In section 8 we assess LHD-d with the presence of co-reference and compare it with the aforementioned naïve approach. This evaluation focuses on demonstrating the effectiveness of VrG. Finally we give our conclusions and future plans in section 9.

2 Related Work

In this section we discuss the current state and issues of co-reference in Linked Data, and review relevant approaches of Linked Data query processing.

2.1 Co-reference in the Linked Data Cloud

The ubiquity of co-reference in Linked Data motivates many researchers to investigate the similarity between URIs and to infer co-reference relationships [7,14]; to study the semantic and structure of co-referential identifiers [9], and to develop efficient methods for co-reference representation and management [4].

Co-reference can be explicitly presented by *owl:sameAs*. However, many co-referential URIs are inexplicit in reality. To determine equivalent URIs, or co-reference resolution, it requires to investigate the semantic and relationship of relevant URIs. Taking [7] as an example, the authors proposed a method that uses inverse-functional property, *owl:InverseFunctionalProperty*[5], to infer the

[4] LHD stands for **L**arge scale, **H**igh performance and **D**istributed. “d” stands for **d**ynamic optimisation.

[5] The value of an inverse-functional property uniquely identifies the subject of this property.

equivalence of URIs. Similarly, *owl:FunctionalProperty*, *owl:maxCardinality*, and *owl:cardinality* have also been examined to infer *owl:sameAs* statements [6]. Furthermore, a scalable candidate selection algorithm is proposed by Song et al. [14]. This algorithm firstly identifies properties that have discriminability and coverage larger than a certain threshold, as keys. These keys are used to disclose additional co-referential URIs closely related in semantics. In practice, co-reference resolution services, such as *sameas.org*[6] [4], have been established.

It is realistic to assume that there are a large number of existing *owl:sameAs* statements provided either by datasets themselves or third-party services. In this work we do not deal with co-reference resolution. We focus on improving the efficiency of Linked Data queries taking existing *owl:sameAs* statements into account. It is straightforward to add co-reference resolution as an extra layer on top of LHD-d.

2.2 Distributed Query Processing over Linked Data

Query processing over Linked Data has attracted much attention in recent years. As a result, many distributed SPARQL engines, such as DARQ [12], DSP [15], FedX [13], SPLENDID [5] and LHD [16], have been proposed to address various issues of Linked Data queries. However, none of these engines investigate the possibility of taking co-reference into Linked Data queries[7]. Since LHD-d will be evaluated without co-reference as well, it is worth providing details of representatives of existing engines. Evaluation results of [15,5,13,16] suggests that FedX and LHD have certain advantages over other approaches. We provide their details here and will compare LHD-d to these two engines in section 7.

FedX does not require statistics of datasets. Given a query, FedX sends *ASK* queries to all known datasets to identify those relevant to a certain triple pattern. This selection is accurate but introduce additional network overheads. The optimisation of FedX adopts a greedy algorithm that picks the minimum from triple patterns that are not executed. Triple patterns are ranked using heuristics, according to the number and position of variables in those triple patterns. As a result, it does not distinguish arbitrary two triple patterns having variables at the same positions. FedX adopts an novel method that executes triple patterns using multiple threads, which significantly improves query efficiency.

LHD follows almost an opposite direction of FedX. It requires detailed statistics that are retrieved from VoID [1] files. However, as admitted by the authors, detailed VoID files are unlikely to be available on a large scale. Relevant datasets are selected using the predicate-matching method, that a triple pattern is assigned to datasets that contains its predicate. This method is less accurate than the ASKing approach of FedX, but causes no extra network overhead. LHD adopts dynamic programming that exhaustively searches for the optimal plans,

---

[6] `www.sameas.org`

[7] To the best of our knowledge, the OpenLink Virtuoso is the only distributed engine that provides support of co-reference in a recent release. However, Virtuoso focus on resolving co-reference rather than improving query efficiency.

and the quality of query plans only depends on the accuracy of VoID statistics. A sophisticated parallel query execution is used in LHD to maximumly exploit bandwidth of connections to remote datasets.

3 Virtual Graph: Merging Co-reference into SPARQL Queries

Assuming there is a query {?x foaf:knows p_0} and a co-reference statement {p_0 owl:sameAs p_1}, results of both {?x foaf:knows p_0} and {?x foaf:knows p_1} are semantically valid for the original query. For convenience, we say two queries are co-referential if there is a mapping between these two queries that maps a concrete URI to either itself or its co-reference. Also, we refer to the result set extended by co-reference (including original results) as co-referential results. Using existing *owl:sameAs* statements in the Linked Data cloud, it is straightforward to gather co-referential results by executing a given query and all co-referential ones. However, this method is not practical to handle complex queries, since we have to execute the Cartesian product of the co-reference of all triple patterns. To address this issue, we propose a model called Virtual Graph (VrG) that enables simultaneous optimisation and execution of all co-referential queries.

During query execution, variables are gradually bound to values. Following the same idea, VrG regards a concrete node as a variable that is bound to one value. When taking co-reference into account, a concrete node is regarded as a variable whose values are the union of its original URI and all co-reference. An example of Virtual Graph is shown in Figure 1.

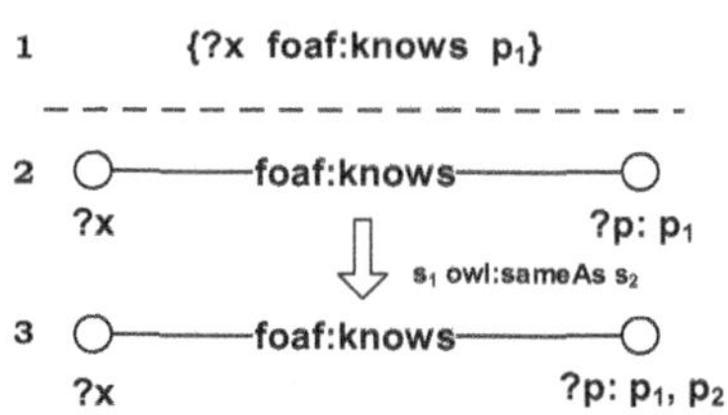

Fig. 1. ① shows a triple pattern of a SPARQL query. The corresponding VrG is shown in ②. ③ is the VrG after taking an *owl:sameAs* statement into account.

In LHD-d, the transformation of VrG is applied at the beginning of query processing. For each concrete URI denoted by v in a given query, our engine firstly generates a query {v owl:sameAs ?coref} to all datasets that may contain co-referential URIs of v. Then v is replaced by a variable node ?v, whose values are the union of v and its co-reference. The whole transformation is analogous to the process shown in Figure 1. The essential of VrG is to enable query optimisation algorithms to produce optimal plans w.r.t all co-referential queries. Also it enables query engines to better exploit parallelism.

4 Ψ: Parallel Sub-query Identification

SPARQL queries are composed by Basic Graph Patterns (BGPs), which are a set of conjunctive triple patterns. A BGP can be regarded as a connected graph whose nodes (or vertices) are subjects and objects and whose triple patterns are edges. We observed that given two edges (triple patterns) whose shared node is concrete (e.g. {s p_1 ?x. s p_2 ?y}), they can be processed as two independent sub-queries without increasing network traffic. This is because the number of values of the shared node (which is concrete) is not affected by any edge that connects to it. This observation also holds for variables whose number of values does not change during execution.

We generalise the above observation as follows. We say a node has a *fixed cardinality* if, during the execution of edges connecting to it, its number of values does not change more than a certain percentage. If "removing" all fixed-cardinality nodes results in disconnected sub-graphs, these sub-graphs can be optimised and executed independently and in parallel. For example, in the graph shown in Figure 2, if both node B and C are fixed-cardinality nodes, then we have three independent sub-graphs $\{AC, AB\}, \{BC\}, \{CD, BD\}$. If only B has fixed cardinality, then the given graph cannot be further broken down[8].

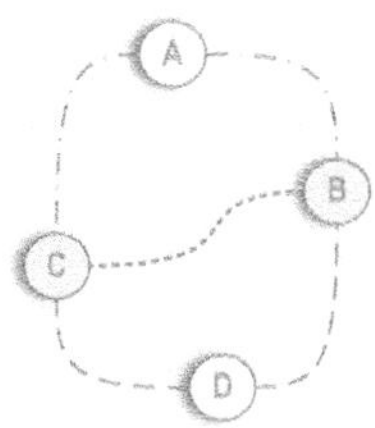

Fig. 2. If B and C are fixed-cardinality nodes, there are three independent components shown by three different types of dash lines

Utilising the aforementioned idea, we propose the algorithm Ψ[9] (shown in Algorithm 1) that quickly breaks a connected graph into independent components. At the beginning the algorithm creates a sub-graph for each edge (the loop at line 1). Then all nodes are scanned and sub-graphs that share a none-fixed-cardinality node are merged (the loop at line 4). At the end of this algorithm, all remaining sub-graphs can be processed in parallel. The time complexity of

[8] A more subtle case is that cardinality of both B and C are only changed by AB and AC respectively, while BC and BD have comparable cardinality at B, and BC and CD have comparable cardinality at C. That is, B and C are not fixed-cardinality nodes w.r.t all connecting edges, but they are w.r.t some edges. In this case $\{CB\}, \{CD, BD\}$ can still be executed in parallel, and we say this two components form a partial parallel group. However, identifying all partial parallel group can be costly and not worthy in practice.

[9] Ψ=PSI=**P**arallel **S**ub-query **I**dentification.

Algorithm 1. Ψ(V,E)

input : A connected graph (V, E)
output: Independent sub-graphs

foreach $e \in E$ **do**
  $sg_{\{e\}} \leftarrow e$;
end
foreach $v \in V \wedge \neg$ `fixCard(`v`)` **do**
  merge sub-graphs containing v;
end

the first loop is linear to the number of edges $|E|$. The merge operation in the second loop can be done in constant time by maintaining a hash table that maps a node to the set of sub-graphs connected to it. Therefore, the complexity of the second loop is linear to the number of vertices $|V|$. The complexity of Ψ (upper bound) is $O(\max(|E|, |V|))$.

In practice, concrete nodes always have fixed-cardinality. Besides, if we can know in advance that the cardinality of a variable node will probably remain the same, that node can be regarded as a fixed-cardinality node as well. For example, in {?person foaf:firstName ?frstN. ?person foaf:familyName ?fmName}, the cardinality of *?person* is probably fixed during execution, since a dataset usually contains both the first name and family name of a person[10]. Besides, heuristics can be used to identify fixed-cardinality nodes. For example, if the estimations of the cardinality of a variable $?v$ w.r.t all its connected triple patterns are close[11], the number of bindings of $?v$ probably will not change. Also, if the number of existing bindings of $?v$ is very small[12], it probably will not change. The effectiveness of the above two heuristics depends on the accuracy of cardinality estimation. We enable these heuristics in LHD-d since runtime statistics are used (described as below).

5 Dynamic Optimisation Using Runtime Statistics

The effectiveness of query optimisation is closely related to the accuracy of cost estimation [11]. On a large scale, the most promising way of obtaining statistics is from VoID [1] files provided by RDF datasets. However, these statistics are unlikely to take co-reference into account. To this end, LHD-d exploits statistics that become available at runtime, and interleaves query optimisation and execution. Each time a triple pattern is executed, its result size is used to estimate cost of remaining triple patterns.

[10] Property schemas are required to accurately predict the invariance of a node's cardinality. For instance, in this example we need to know that both properties have the same domain, have close numbers of distinct subjects, and are closely relevant.

[11] $90\% < \frac{card(T_i,?v)}{card(T_j,?v)} < 110\%$, that T_i, T_j are triple patterns connecting to $?v$.

[12] $|?v| < \min(card(T,?v))/10$, that T connects to $?v$.

Cost Estimation

We denote by $sel(t, n)$ the selectivity of a node (either a subject or an object) w.r.t a triple pattern t, and by $|p|$ the number of triples having p as predicate in relevant datasets. $sel(t, n)$ and $|p|$ are obtained from available statistics such as VoID files. For more details of these values please refer to SPLENDID [5] and LHD [16]. The cardinality $card(t)$ of a triple pattern $t : \{s\ p\ o\}$ is estimated as:

$$card(t) = |s| \cdot sel(t, s) \cdot |p| \cdot |o| \cdot sel(t, o) \tag{1}$$

where $|s| = 1/sel(t, s)$ if s is a variable having no bindings (i.e. an unbound variable does affect the cardinality), otherwise $|s|$ is the number of values of s. $|o|$ is determined in the same manner. During query execution, $|s|$ and $|o|$ are updated as new bindings becoming available.

The cost of a triple pattern depends on the execution method. If it is evaluated over relevant datasets without attaching existing bindings, the cost is estimated as $card(t) \cdot c$, where c is a constant. If existing bindings, presumably from s, are attached, the cost is estimated as $|s| \cdot c + 1 \cdot sel(t, s) \cdot |p| \cdot |o| \cdot sel(t, o) \cdot c$.

Query Optimisation

Given a (sub-)graph, we use a minimum-spanning-tree-based algorithm, shown in Algorithm 2, to find the order of triple pattern execution in real time. Each time the algorithm is called, it maintains a list of remaining edges ordered by their costs from low to high. If an edge has two possible costs, the smaller one is chosen. Then the algorithm returns and removes the minimum edge (i.e. an edge belongs to the MST), which is going to be executed. It also returns edges whose subjects and objects are all bound (i.e. edges that do not belong to the MST), which are used to prune existing bindings.

Algorithm 2. NextEdges(V,E)

input : A connected (sub-)graph (V, E)
output: *next* a set of edges to be executed

$edges \leftarrow sort(E)$;
$next \leftarrow edges[0]$;
$next \leftarrow next \cup findBoundEdges(edges)$;
$E \leftarrow edges - next$;

The overview of query execution of LHD-d is shown as Algorithm 3. Firstly a given query is broken into sub-graphs. For each sub-graph a new thread is created. At each step, minimum-cost triple patterns are selected (lines 6) and executed (line 7 to 8). Then cost of remaining edges (executed edges are removed at the end of algorithm $NextEdges(V, E)$) are updated using runtime statistics and $Execute(V, E)$ is called recursively. It should be noticed that a sub-graph can be further divided in future call of $Execute(V, E)$ w.r.t updated edge cost.

Algorithm 3. Execute(V,E)

input : A connected (sub-)graph (V, E)

if *E is empty* **then**
    return;
end
$components \leftarrow \Psi(V, E)$;
foreach *sub-graph* $(V', E') \in$ *components create a new thread* **do**
    $next \leftarrow NextEdges(V', E')$;
    evaluate $next[0]$;
    use remaining edges of *next* to prune bindings;
    update costs of edges in E';
    $Execute(V', E')$;
end

6 Experimental Environment

We use an evaluation framework that extends BSBM [2] to set up the experiment environment. For more details of the evaluation framework please refer to [15,16]. In this section we further study the distribution of co-reference in Linked Data to set up an environment in which LHD-d is evaluated.

6.1 Distribution of Co-reference in Linked Data

Some research implies that co-reference follows a power law distribution [9], without giving explicit evidence. We analyse the data of Billion Triple Challenge (BTC) 2011[13], which can be regarded as a snapshot of real world Linked Data. We counted the number of resources involved in 1, 2, 3 ... *owl:sameAs* statements respectively, and produce the diagram shown in Figure 3. We find that points in Figure 3 approximate a power law distribution $p(x) = \alpha x^{-\beta}$ where $\beta = 2.528$. The scale-free property of power law distribution allows us to replicate the real-world co-reference distribution on a smaller scale.

Generation of co-reference is achieved by linking resources using *owl:sameAs*. To reproduce the distribution of real-world co-reference, we use a power law random number generator that accepts two parameters which are the power law exponent $\beta = 2.528$ and the number of elements (i.e. distinct resources that have co-reference). For a given resource, we use this generator to decide the number of *owl:sameAs* statements that link this resource with other randomly chosen resources. We also take into account that resources of BSBM data fall into different classes. We generate co-reference for each class separately to make sure that resources are only equivalent to those of the same class. Furthermore, numbers that are larger than the total number of instances of a class are discarded, since the maximum number of co-references a resource can have is the cardinality of the class to which it belongs.

[13] `http://challenge.semanticweb.org/`

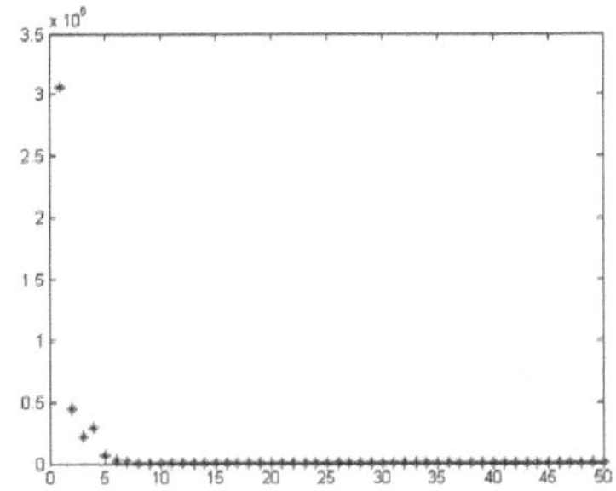

Fig. 3. The horizontal axis presents categories of resources having 5, 10, 15 ... co-reference respectively, while the vertical axis presents the number of resources falling in each category.

6.2 Experimental Settings

We generate about 70 million triples using the BSBM generator, and 0.18 million *owl:sameAs* statements following the aforementioned method. All the triples (including the *owl:sameAs* statements) are distributed over 20 SPARQL endpoints which are deployed on 10 remote virtual machines having 2GB memory each. All SPARQL endpoints are set up using Sesame 2.4.0 and Apache Tomcat 6 with default settings. Engines to be evaluated are run on a machine having an Intel Xeon W3520 2.67 GHz processor and 12 GB memory.

In the following sections we will provide details of LHD-d, and evaluate it afterwards in the above environment.

7 Evaluating LHD-d in the Absence of Co-reference

In this section we evaluate LHD-d without co-reference, and compare it with up-to-date engines, namely FedX and LHD. In this evaluation VrG is disabled in LHD-d, and we focus on demonstrating the effectiveness of using Ψ with the runtime-statistic-based query optimisation.

7.1 Evaluation Results and Analysis

The QPS, incoming traffic, outgoing traffic, and transmission rate of FedX, LHD and LHD-d are shown in Figure 4a, 4b, 4c and 4d. "0" and "NA" stand for failures of execution.

It is shown in Figure 4a that LHD-d has an higher QPS over LHD on most queries. Especially, significant performance boost is shown on Q2, Q3, Q4 and Q7. The boost on Q2 and Q4 is primarily due to increased transmission rate (Figure 4d), on Q3 is due to decreased network traffic (Figure 4b and 4c), and on Q7 is due to both factors. LHD-d is slower than LHD on Q8 (but still two times faster than FedX), which is due to its relatively slow transmission rate. On Q10 LHD-d shows slight improvement, but FedX is still the one with highest QPS.

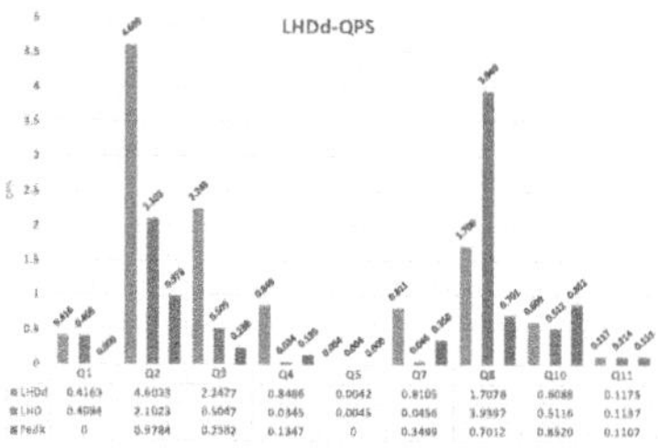

(a) QPS

(b) Incoming traffic

(c) Outgoing traffic

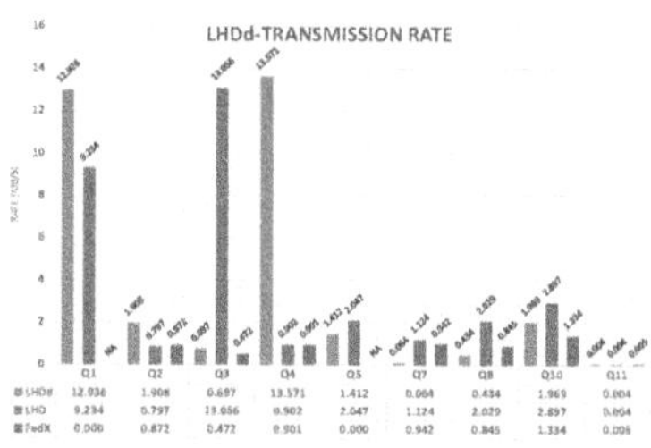

(d) Average transmission rate

Fig. 4. Evaluation without co-reference

LHD-d produces the smallest amount of network traffic on most queries (Figure 4b and 4c). It is worthy noticing that in LHD-d parallelisation is determined by the Ψ algorithm without increasing network traffic, and each sub-query is optimised with an aim of minimum traffic. Compared to the network traffic of FedX and SPLENDID (recalling that SPLENDID produces more traffic than FedX), we conclude that using runtime statistics yields more accurate estimations and leads to query plans that are closer to optimal. The results further reinforce the previous discussion that the existing cost models or VoID statistics are not sufficiently accurate.

The transmission rate of LHD-d varies on different queries. On Q1, Q2 and Q4 LHD-d has even higher transmission rate than LHD, while on Q3, Q7 and Q8 its transmission rate is relatively low. A closer look reveals that LHD-d produces a small amount of network traffic on Q3, Q7 and Q8, and still has highest QPS on these queries.

In summary, LHD-d better balances between reducing network traffic and increasing average transmission rate, and thus shows a higher overall efficiency. The primary advantage of LHD-d results from the Ψ algorithm and the usage of runtime statistics. It also demonstrates that dynamic optimisation is promising for large scale Linked Data queries, in which cases detailed statistics are difficult to obtain.

8 Evaluating LHD-d in the Presence of Co-reference

In this section we evaluate the efficiency of LHD-d with co-reference taken into account (thus VrG is enabled), and compare it with the naïve approach of processing co-referential queries described in section 1. In the naïve approach, each co-referential query is executed individually using LHD-d without enabling VrG. It still benefits from Ψ and runtime optimisation. This evaluation focuses on demonstrating the effectiveness of VrG. To demonstrate the consequence of taking co-reference into account, we compare the performance of LHD-d with or without co-reference. In the remainder of this section we use LHD-d* to represent the evaluation results obtained in the presence of co-reference, and LHD-d to represent the results obtained without co-reference.

8.1 Evaluation Results and Analysis

We show in Table 1 that both LHD-d and the naïve approach produce the same sizes of results with co-reference taken into account. This confirms the ability of VrG to fully retrieve additional results due to co-reference. Meanwhile, the result sizes are raised many times (even orders of magnitude on specific queries) by the small proportion of additional co-reference statements. The result sizes of Q5 and Q11 remain the same for different reasons. Q5 selects for products that share the same feature with a given product. There are 14499 distinct products in our dataset, all of which are already contained in the result of Q5 without co-reference. By turning on co-reference, many more intermediate results are generated (demonstrated by the network traffic of Q5 in Figure 5b), but the final result does not change. Q11 does not have concrete subjects or objects, so its result size remains the same.

Three factors are relevant to the significant amount of additional results. First, the same vocabulary is shared by all endpoints. Second, in our datasets co-reference exists between instances of all classes. Consequently, Cartesian product is likely to be produced by the co-reference of the concrete subjects and objects in a query. Finally, instances of the same class have similar relationships with instances of other classes. Therefore, each co-referential URI may well lead to a valid result.

Table 1. Result sizes of co-reference

	Q1	Q2	Q3	Q4	Q5	Q7	Q8	Q10	Q11
LHD-d*	7397	103	23	65510	14499	1579	101	32	10
Naïve	7397	103	23	NA	NA	NA	101	32	10
LHD-d	53	29	8	29	14499	63	21	12	10

We present the QPS, the incoming and outgoing traffic, and the transmission rate of LHD-d*, LHD-d, and the naïve approach respectively in Figure 5a, 5b, 5c and 5d. "0" and "NA" stand for time out.

It is shown in Figure 5a that the efficiency of query processing decreases multifold times after introducing co-reference, especially for the naïve approach. Moreover, the naïve approach runs out of time on several queries (Q4, Q5 and Q7) that have a large result size. Though having low QPS on a few queries, LHD-d*, or VrG, substantially increase the efficiency of co-reference query processing. Furthermore, on Q10 LHD-d* has an even higher QPS than LHD-d, indicating a query plan that overcomes the negative impact of co-reference, is generated. Q11 has no co-reference, and the three approaches show close QPS.

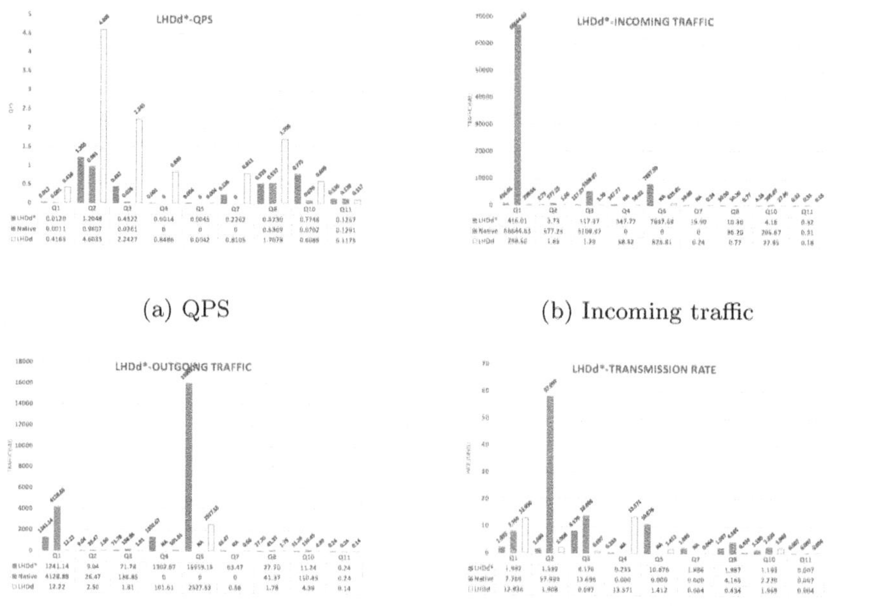

(a) QPS (b) Incoming traffic

(c) Outgoing traffic (d) Average transmission rate

Fig. 5. Evaluation with co-reference

From the network traffic of both LHD-d* and the naïve approach (Figure 5b and 5c), it is shown that co-reference significantly increase the sizes of intermediate results. Recalling that the usage of VrG is the only difference between LHD-d* and the naïve approach, we conclude that optimising co-reference queries w.r.t all co-reference yields better query plans. On the contrary, although the naïve approach produces optimal plans for each co-referential query, the total query time is not well controlled. In the meantime, LHD-d* shows much smaller network traffic over the naïve approach. LHD-d* and the naïve approach have the same amount of traffic on Q11, which is slightly larger than that of LHD-d. The extra traffic over LHD-d is due to searching for co-reference of Q11.

The transmission rate of LHD-d* are not always larger than that of LHD-d. This is further confirms that VrG enables LHD-d* to generate query plans that are tailored for co-reference. If the same LHD-d's query plans are used, the transmission rate of LHD-d* would always be no less than LHD-d, since more traffic is generated in the case of LHD-d*.

9 Conclusion and Future Plan

In this paper we investigate efficiency issues of Linked Data queries in the presence of co-reference. For addressing these issues we propose two techniques called Virtual Graph and Ψ. VrG is able to merge all co-referential queries into a single query with pre-existing bindings. Thus, VrG enables query optimisation algorithms to produce optimal plans w.r.t all co-referential queries. Ψ breaks a query into sub-queries that can be optimised and executed in parallel. We combine Ψ with runtime optimisation to improve query efficiency without relying on detailed pre-computed statistics.

The aforementioned techniques are deployed in LHD-d. We compare LHD-d with representative engines, LHD and FedX, without co-reference, and demonstrate the advantage of using Ψ with runtime optimisation. We also evaluate LHD-d in the presence of co-reference, and demonstrate that VrG significantly improves query optimisation and thus reduces query response time.

In the future we plan to integrate co-reference resolution into our optimisation techniques, which will significantly expand the ability of Linked Data queries. In addition, it is worth further investigating optimisation techniques that consume runtime statistics, since reliable statistics are unlikely to be available in large scale Linked Data.

References

1. Alexander, K., Cyganiak, R., Hausenblas, M., Zhao, J.: Describing linked datasets on the design and usage of VoID, the "Vocabulary of Interlinked Datasets". In: Proceedings of the Linked Data on the Web Workshop (LDOW), at the International World Wide Web Conference, WWW (2009)
2. Bizer, C., Schultz, A.: The Berlin SPARQL benchmark. International Journal On Semantic Web and Information Systems (IJSWIS) - Special Issue on Scalability and Performance of Semantic Web Systems 5(2), 1–24 (2009)
3. Carroll, J., Herman, I., Patel-Schneider, P.F.: OWL 2 Web Ontology Language RDF-Based Semantics, 2nd edn (2012), `http://www.w3.org/TR/2012/REC-owl2-rdf-based-semantics-20121211/`
4. Glaser, H., Jaffri, A., Millard, I.: Managing Co-reference on the Semantic web. In: Proceedings of the Linked Data on the Web Workshop (LDOW), at the International World Wide Web Conference, WWW (2009)
5. Görlitz, O., Staab, S.: SPLENDID: SPARQL Endpoint Federation Exploiting VOID Descriptions. In: Proceedings of the Consuming Linked Data Workshop(COLD) (2011)

6. Hogan, A.: Exploiting RDFS and OWL for Integrating Heterogeneous, Large-Scale, Linked Data Corpora (2011)
7. Hogan, A., Harth, A., Decker, S.: Performing object consolidation on the semantic web data graph. In: Proceedings of 1st I3: Identity, Identifiers, Identification Workshop (2007)
8. Hogan, A., Harth, A., Umbrich, J., Kinsella, S., Polleres, A., Decker, S.: Searching and browsing Linked Data with SWSE: the Semantic Web search engine. Semantic Search Over the Web, 361–414 (2012)
9. Hu, W., Chen, J., Zhang, H., Qu, Y.: How matchable are four thousand ontologies on the semantic Web. The Semantic Web: Research and Applications 6643, 290–304 (2011)
10. Hyland, B., Villazón-Terrazas, B., Atemezing, G.: Best practices for publishing Linked Data (W3C editor's draft 13 March 2013) (2013), `https://dvcs.w3.org/hg/gld/raw-file/default/bp/index.html`
11. Özsu, M.T., Valduriez, P.: Principles of distributed database systems (1999)
12. Quilitz, B.: Querying distributed RDF data sources with SPARQL. The Semantic Web: Research and Applications, 524–538 (2008)
13. Schwarte, A., Haase, P., Hose, K., Schenkel, R., Schmidt, M.: FedX: Optimization Techniques for Federated Query Processing on Linked Data. In: Proceedings of the International Semantic Web Conference, ISWC (2011)
14. Song, D., Heflin, J.: Automatically generating data linkages using a domain-independent candidate selection approach. In: Aroyo, L., Welty, C., Alani, H., Taylor, J., Bernstein, A., Kagal, L., Noy, N., Blomqvist, E. (eds.) ISWC 2011, Part I. LNCS, vol. 7031, pp. 649–664. Springer, Heidelberg (2011)
15. Wang, X., Tiropanis, T., Davis, H.C.: Evaluating graph traversal algorithms for distributed SPARQL query optimization. In: Pan, J.Z., Chen, H., Kim, H.-G., Li, J., Wu, Z., Horrocks, I., Mizoguchi, R., Wu, Z. (eds.) JIST 2011. LNCS, vol. 7185, pp. 210–225. Springer, Heidelberg (2012)
16. Wang, X., Tiropanis, T., Davis, H.C.: LHD: Optimising Linked Data query processing using parallelisation. In: Proceedings of the Linked Data on the Web Workshop (LDOW), at the International World Wide Web Conference, WWW (2013)

Survey on Common Strategies of Vocabulary Reuse in Linked Open Data Modeling

Johann Schaible[1], Thomas Gottron[2], and Ansgar Scherp[3]

[1] GESIS Leibniz-Institute for the Social Sciences, Cologne, Germany
johann.schaible@gesis.org
[2] Institute for Web Science and Technologies, University of Koblenz-Landau, Germany
gottron@uni-koblenz.de
[3] Kiel University and Leibniz Information Center for Economics, Kiel, Germany
mail@ansgarscherp.net

Abstract. The choice of which vocabulary to reuse when modeling and publishing Linked Open Data (LOD) is far from trivial. There is no study that investigates the different strategies of reusing vocabularies for LOD modeling and publishing. In this paper, we present the results of a survey with 79 participants that examines the most preferred vocabulary reuse strategies of LOD modeling. The participants, LOD publishers and practitioners, were asked to assess different vocabulary reuse strategies and explain their ranking decision. We found significant differences between the modeling strategies that range from reusing popular vocabularies, minimizing the number of vocabularies, and staying within one domain vocabulary. A very interesting insight is that the popularity in the meaning of how frequent a vocabulary is used in a data source is more important than how often individual classes and properties are used in the LOD cloud. Overall, the results of this survey help in better understanding the strategies how data engineers reuse vocabularies and may also be used to develop future vocabulary engineering tools.

Keywords: #eswc2014Schaible.

1 Introduction

With the increasing use of LOD, it becomes more and more important for data providers not only to publish their data as LOD, but also to model it in an easy to process way, i.e., make the data more human-readable and machine-processable. During the modeling process a data engineer has to—among many other tasks—decide with which vocabularies to express the data. Hereby, reusing vocabularies is clearly motivated by the best practices and recommendations for designing and publishing Linked Data [1]. Experienced Linked Data engineers decide which vocabularies to reuse based on their knowledge and "gut-feeling" in order to achieve several goals such as providing a clear structure of the data or making it easy to be consumed. Such goals, or aspects, lead to various vocabulary reuse strategies. For example, one might reuse only one domain specific vocabulary to provide a clear data structure, and the other might reuse popular vocabularies to make the data easier to be consumed. However, these strategies are quite

V. Presutti et al. (Eds.): ESWC 2014, LNCS 8465, pp. 457–472, 2014.

vague and not described in the literature in a formalized way. In fact, besides reusing "well-known" vocabularies, as it increases the probability that data can be consumed by applications [2], there are no established recommendations formulated on *how to choose* which vocabularies to reuse. This implies the challenge, especially for an unexperienced engineer, to decide on an appropriate mix of vocabularies optimally capturing the domain under investigation. More concrete, the Linked Data engineer needs to answer the question which vocabularies shall be used and how many shall be combined. There are various factors influencing the engineer's decision to reuse classes and properties from existing vocabularies. These factors include the popularity of a vocabulary, the match to the domain which is modeled, the maintenance of the vocabulary, the authority who has published the vocabulary, and others. Overall, deciding for which and how many vocabularies to reuse is a "non-trivial" task [3,4] and hardly addressed by today's research. Therefore, either the data engineer decides not to reuse vocabularies at all or the decision for which and how many vocabularies to reuse is solely based on the engineer's knowledge and experience. Thus, the main contribution of this paper is to condense and aggregate the knowledge and experience of Linked Data experts and practitioners regarding which reuse strategy to follow in a real-world scenario in order to achieve the previously stated goals.

Why this study? To the best of our knowledge, there is no study which empirically examines how to select vocabularies and vocabulary terms for reuse. More insights about the different factors and strategies that influence the engineers in their decision to select reusable classes and properties is needed. Such insights would provide guidance for the modeling process and aid the Linked Data engineer in deciding which vocabularies to reuse. In this study, we intend to identify these key factors and strategies.[1] To this end, we have conducted a survey among Linked Data practitioners and experts. The aim of the survey is to aggregate the knowledge and experience of these practitioners and experts to condense best practices and established approaches on how to select vocabularies for reuse.

We have asked the participants of the survey to rank several data models, which exemplify different vocabulary reuse strategies, from *most preferred* to *least preferred* with respect to the reuse of vocabularies. Such reuse strategies are "reuse mainly popular vocabularies", "reuse only domain specific vocabularies", or other. In addition, the participants had to answer different questions regarding their preferences when reusing vocabularies (cf. Section 2). We have obtained feedback from 79 participants acquired through public mailing lists (cf. Section 3). The main findings of our work are that reusing vocabularies directly is considered significantly better than defining proprietary terms and establishing links on a schema-level to other vocabulary terms. In addition, a trade-off should be made between reusing popular and domain specific vocabularies. Furthermore, additional meta-information on the domain of a vocabulary and on the number of LOD datasets using a vocabulary are considered the most helpful information for deciding which vocabulary to reuse (cf. Section 4 and Section 5). Overall, the results provide very valuable insights in how data engineers decide which vocabularies to reuse when modeling Linked Open Data (cf. Section 6). This may also lead to the

[1] An extended description of this study and a more detailed statistical analysis of its results is available as technical report in [5].

development of novel recommendation services for future vocabulary engineering tools (cf. Section 8).

2 The Survey

The survey consists of ranking tasks, where the participants have to decide which of the provided data models reuses vocabularies the best way, and explanations, where the participants have to rate different aspects why they have ranked the models the way they did. [2] Hereby, each data model represents a specific vocabulary reuse strategy such as reusing only popular or domain specific vocabularies. In Section 2.1, we define a set of features, which describes the data models and their underlying vocabulary reuse strategy, provide a detailed description of the survey design (Section 2.2), and finally illustrate and explain each of the data models in Section 2.3.

2.1 Features for LOD Modeling

To describe the differences of the data models that express the same example instance with different vocabularies and vocabulary terms, we make use of features such as the number of datasets using a vocabulary or the total occurrence of a vocabulary term. In general, such a set of features is based on datasets and vocabularies used in some LOD collection, e.g., a huge collection of RDF graphs that was crawled by a Linked Data crawler like the Billion Triple Challenge dataset.

Let $W = \{V_1, V_2, ..., V_n\}$ with $n \in \mathbb{N}$ be the set of all vocabularies used in the LOD cloud. Each vocabulary $V \in W$ consists of properties and type classes such that $V = P_V \cup T_V$. P_V is the set of all properties and T_V is the set of all classes in vocabulary V. Furthermore, let $\mathbb{DS} = \{DS_1, DS_2, ..., DS_m\}$ with $m \in \mathbb{N}$ be the set of all datasets in the LOD cloud. Each $DS \in \mathbb{DS}$ is a tuple $DS = (G, c)$ consisting of a context URI c of DS, where an RDF graph G can be found. G is a set of triples with

$$G = \{(s,p,o)|p \in URI, s \in URI, o \in (URI \cup LIT)\} \quad (1)$$

where URI is a set of URI's and LIT a set of literals. We define the function $\phi : \mathbb{DS} \rightarrow \mathcal{P}(W)$ that maps each dataset to the set of vocabularies used by the dataset

$$\phi((G,c)) = \{V \mid (\exists\, (s,p,o) \in G : p \in V) \vee (\exists\, (s,\text{rdf:type},o) \in G : o \in V)\} \quad (2)$$

Hereby, $|\phi((G,c))|$ is the number of all used vocabularies in dataset DS. Accordingly, the function $\Phi : W \rightarrow \mathcal{P}(\mathbb{DS})$ specifies which datasets in the LOD cloud use a vocabulary $V \in W$

$$\Phi(V) = \{(G,c) \mid (\exists\, (s,p,o) \in G : p \in V) \vee (\exists\, (s,\text{rdf:type},o) \in G : o \in V)\} \quad (3)$$

Therefore, $|\Phi(V)|$ is the number of datasets in the LOD cloud that use vocabulary V. To identify how often a vocabulary term $v \in V$ has occurred in the LOD cloud, we first

[2] The survey was designed with the online survey software *QuestBack Unipark* (`http://www.unipark.com/`) and is archived at the GESIS data repository service *datorium* (`http://dx.doi.org/10.7802/64`) including the raw result data in SPSS format.

define an auxiliary function $\psi : (V, \mathbb{DS}) \rightarrow \mathbb{N}$ that calculates the cardinality of the set of all triples $(s, p, o) \in G$ that include a vocabulary term $v \in V$ with

$$\psi(v, (G, c)) = |\{(s, p, o) \in G | v = p \vee (v = o \wedge p = \text{rdf:type})\}| \tag{4}$$

To finally calculate the overall occurrences of a vocabulary term $v \in V$ in the LOD cloud, we simply sum up the values $\psi(v, (G, c))$ over all $DS \in \mathbb{DS}$ with $\Psi : V \rightarrow \mathbb{N}$ that is defined as

$$\Psi(v) = \sum_{(G,c) \in \mathbb{DS}} \psi(v, (G, c)) \tag{5}$$

For the survey, we have retrieved metrics from LODStats [6] and the Linked Open Vocabulary index (LOV) [7] regarding the number of datasets using a specific vocabulary and vocab.cc [8] regarding the total occurrence of a vocabulary term.

2.2 Survey Design and Measurements

As mentioned, the survey consists of several ranking tasks and rating preferences regarding how much it influenced the ranking decision. For the ranking tasks, we provided several alternative data models, which exemplify different vocabulary reuse strategies, that had to be ranked from *most preferred* to *least preferred*. We let the participants rank such modeling examples instead of the reuse strategies directly in order to elude answers that are simply influenced by the theory of vocabulary reuse [1,2].

To illustrate the differences of the strategies, we use the previously defined features $\phi((G, c))$, $|\phi((G, c))|$, $|\Phi(V)|$, and $\Psi(v)$. The vocabularies in $\phi((G, c))$ provide information on which vocabularies have been used, e.g., some domain specific vocabularies, whereas the values of $|\Phi(V)|$ and $\Psi(v)$ provide information on the popularity of a vocabulary V and a vocabulary term v, respectively.

We consider the modeling examples and thus the underlying reuse strategies as different, if there is a difference in their features. For example, strategies like *minimize number of vocabularies* or *maximize number of vocabularies* are reflected by $|\phi((G, c))|$ that states the number of reused vocabularies. Listing 1.1 and Listing 1.2 provide two data models that describe the same example instance with different sets of vocabularies and different vocabulary terms.

```
<http://ex1.org/publ/01>
    rdf:type swrc:Publication;
    swrc:title "Title";
    swrc:author <http://ex1.org/pers/xyz>.
<http://ex1.org/pers/xyz>
    rdf:type swrc:Person;
    swrc:name "xyz".
```

Listing 1.1. Example data model M_a

- $\phi(M_a) = \{\text{swrc}\}$
- $|\phi(M_a)| = 1$
- $|\Phi(\text{swrc})| = 6$
- $\Psi(\text{swrc:Publication}) = 30$
- $\Psi(\text{swrc:title}) = 10,487$
- $\Psi(\text{swrc:author}) = 26,478$
- $\Psi(\text{swrc:Person}) = 30,510$
- $\Psi(\text{swrc:name}) = 35,756$

```
<http://ex1.org/pub/001>
    rdf:type swrc:Publication;
    dc:title "Title";
    dc:creator <http://ex1.org/pers/xyz>.
<http://ex1.org/pers/xyz>
    rdf:type foaf:Person;
    foaf:name "xyz".
```

Listing 1.2. Example data model M_b

- $\phi(M_b) = \{\text{swrc, dc, foaf}\}$
- $|\phi(M_b)| = 3$
- $|\Phi(\text{swrc})| = 6$
- $|\Phi(\text{dc})| = 287$
- $|\Phi(\text{foaf})| = 232$
- $\Psi(\text{swrc:Publication}) = 30$
- $\Psi(\text{dc:title}) = 3,605,629$
- $\Psi(\text{dc:creator}) = 1,653,155$
- $\Psi(\text{foaf:Person}) = 18,477,533$
- $\Psi(\text{foaf:name}) = 9,235,251$

Model M_a in Listing 1.1 follows the strategy to reuse only one domain specific vocabulary, namely the Semantic Web for Research Communities (SWRC[3]) vocabulary, and model M_b in Listing 1.2 follows the strategy to reuse popular vocabularies such as FOAF[4] and Dublin Core. [5] According to the features from Section 2.1, the FOAF and Dublin Core vocabularies are more popular than SWRC ($|\Phi(\text{foaf})| = 232 > 6 = |\Phi(\text{swrc})|$ and $|\Phi(\text{dc})| = 287 > 6 = |\Phi(\text{swrc})|$), which also applies to their classes and properties as indicated by the various values of Ψ. Nonetheless, the entire data model can be expressed with the SWRC vocabulary, and with $\Psi(\text{swrc:title}) = 10,487$ for example, SWRC is used in a few but quite large data sets. The central research question is to find out which vocabulary reuse strategies as the ones in M_a and M_b are considered better in a real-world scenario.

The different models and their strategies are based on several aspects of *preference* that we have identified from the state of the art about how to publish Linked Data [1,2]. In detail, they are: (A1) providing a clear structure of the data, (A2) making the data easier to be consumed, and (A3) establishing an ontological agreement in data representation. As part of our questionnaire, we asked the participants to rate these aspects on a 5-point-Likert scale at the beginning and after the first two ranking tasks, to investigate whether they have influenced the participant's ranking decision or not. Besides insights on the participant's answers, it allows us to make a qualitative correlation between the ratings and the rankings of the data models. For example, if aspect (A1) is considered the most important aspect and the ranking of the strategy which reuses only a minimum number of vocabularies is significantly the best, then this would suggest that in order to provide a clear data structure, one has to minimize the number of reused vocabularies instead of reusing popular vocabularies.

2.3 Ranking Tasks

The survey contains three ranking tasks, each covering a different aspect of the engineer's decision making process [3,9]. In the following, we will describe the different tasks, their motivation, and the used schema models (including the most decisive features). The models are fictive and prototypical for the different strategies. They are not real world schemas to prevent biased rankings as real-world schemas might be known

[3] `http://www.ontoware.org/index.html`, access 12/19/2013.

[4] `http://xmlns.com/foaf/spec/`, access 1/9/2014.

[5] `http://dublincore.org/documents/dcmi-terms/`, access 1/9/2014.

to some participants. The underlying strategies for the schemas are as follows: reuse popular vocabularies (*pop*), interlink proprietary terms with existing ones (*link*), minimize total number of vocabularies (*minV*), minimize number of vocabularies per concept (*minC*), confine to domain specific vocabularies (*minD*), and maximize number of vocabularies (*max*). Tables 1 to 3 illustrate for each ranking task the key features of the models and their underlying strategies. The upper section of the tables displays the reused vocabularies, and the lower section displays the most decisive vocabulary terms in the meaning of their total occurrence as in $\Psi(v)$. A "✓" in the table cells indicates whether the specific vocabulary V or vocabulary term v is used in the schema model, whereas a "–" indicates that the specific V or v is not used in the schema. The values in the last two columns show the features of the vocabularies ($|\Phi(V)|$) and their terms ($\Psi(v)$). Please note, meta-information such as $|\Phi(V)|$ and $\Psi(v)$ were provided to the participants only in the third ranking tasks for two reasons: (i) for the first two ranking tasks the goal was to aggregate and condense the participant's experience and "gut-feeling" without having these numbers at hand, and (ii) the third ranking task investigates how such meta-information influences the participant's ranking decision.

Furthermore, all data models within a ranking task describe data from the same domain (important for comparability). Between the ranking tasks, the models are from different domains (important to avoid domain-specific bias).

Ranking Task T_1: Reuse vs. Interlink. The first ranking task is about reusing vocabularies vs. establishing links on schema-level. We provided the participants with three schema models (displayed in Table 1). Each model expresses the same example instance, which represents an *Actor* who played in a certain *Movie*, with a different vocabulary reuse strategy. Model M_{1a} reuses vocabulary terms from the FOAF and Dublin Core vocabularies directly, which is considered very popular as indicated by the values $|\Phi(V)|$ and $\Psi(v)$, i.e., it follows the *pop* strategy. On the other hand, model M_{1b}, uses a self-defined vocabulary but links its classes and properties to the FOAF and Dublin Core vocabularies via rdfs:subClassOf and owl:equivalentProperty. It is arguable whether M_{1a} or M_{1b} is more likely to achieve such goals as provided in the aspects (A1), (A2), and (A3). Whereas M_{1a} reuses vocabulary terms directly and makes the data easier to read for humans, M_{1b} might be easier to be processed by Linked Data applications. Strategy *max*, exemplified by M_{1c}, pursues the same principle as M_{1a}, but maximizes the number of different vocabularies within one dataset by also using the MOVIE[6] and AWOL[7] vocabulary. We have set this strategy as a *lower boundary*, indicated by $|\Phi(\text{movie})| = 0$ and $|\Phi(\text{awol})| = 0$, to investigate whether other strategies are significantly different with respect to the quality of modeling and publishing LOD.

Ranking Task T_2: Appropriate Mix of Vocabularies. The second ranking task covers the topic of mixing an appropriate amount of different vocabularies. We provided the participants with four schema models $M_{2a} - M_{2d}$ described in Table 2. They all express the same example instance with different strategies about a *Publication* including a title, creation and publication date, as well as its *Author*, who has a name and a working place as properties. Model M_{2a} reuses only one vocabulary (strategy *minV*), which

[6] `http://data.linkedmdb.org/all`, access 1/12/2014.
[7] `http://bblfish.net/work/atom-owl/2006-06-06/`, access 1/12/2014.

Table 1. Ranking Task T_1: The models $M_{1a} - M_{1c}$, their reuse strategy, and features

	M_{1a}	M_{1b}	M_{1c}	$\|\Phi(V)\|$	$\Psi(v)$
Reuse Strategy	*(pop)*	*(link)*	*(max)*		
$\|\phi(M)\|$	2	4	3	/	/
$V =$ foaf	✓	✓	✓	232	/
$V =$ dc	✓	✓	–	287	/
$V =$ owl	–	✓	–	277	/
$V =$ rdfs	–	✓	–	533	/
$V =$ awol	–	–	✓	0	/
$V =$ movie	–	–	✓	0	/
$v =$ foaf:Person	✓	✓	✓	/	$18,477,53$
$v =$ dc:title	✓	✓	–	/	$3,605,629$
$v =$ foaf:made	✓	✓	–	/	$57,791$
$v =$ rdfs:subClassOf	–	✓	–	/	$12,207$
$v =$ owl:equivalentProperty	–	✓	–	/	127
$v =$ movie:performance	–	–	✓	/	0
$v =$ awol:title	–	–	✓	/	0

is neither used in very many dataset ($|\Phi(\text{swrc})| = 10$) nor are its vocabulary terms occurring frequently. However, it is highly domain specific and the entire data can be described by using terms from this vocabulary. Model M_{2b}reuses a maximum set of different vocabularies (strategy *max*) and is again the *lower boundary* in this ranking task. Most vocabularies are not used by many data sets, and with the exception of foaf:name and dcterms:title, the total occurrences of the remaining vocabulary terms is also quite low. Strategy *pop*, exemplified by M_{2c}, on the other hand reuses only the most popular vocabulary terms and vocabularies. The strategy *minC*, exemplified by M_{2d}, reuses one vocabulary per concept, i.e., the entity *Publication* is described via the popular Dublin Core vocabulary and the entity *Person* is described via the domain-specific SWRC vocabulary. Apart from M_{2b}, every other model and their underlying vocabulary reuse strategies in this ranking task is likely to comply with aspects (A1) to (A3). Reusing a minimum amount of vocabularies might provide a clear data structure, but it might also fail to capture the entire semantics of the data. Reusing mainly popular vocabularies might also fail to capture some domain specific semantics, but it is easy to understand by humans. In such case, M_{2d} might provide a well defined trade-off between M_{2a} and M_{2c}.

Ranking Task T_3: Vocabulary Reuse with Additional Meta-Information. This ranking task is different from the previous ones, as we wanted to investigate the influencing factors for vocabulary reuse by providing additional information about the vocabularies and vocabulary terms. Furthermore, by letting the respondents rank the given meta-information, we can also conclude whether it is helpful to provide additional information such as documentation on the semantics of a vocabulary term or pattern-based vocabulary term information. First, the participants were given an initial data model (IM), which represents an example instance of a *Music Artist*, who has a specific name and has published an *Album* having a title. The initial data model uses three vocabularies

Table 2. Ranking Task T_2: The models $M_{2a} - M_{2d}$, their reuse strategy, and features

	M_{2a}	M_{2b}	M_{2c}	M_{2d}	$\|\Phi(V)\|$	$\Psi(v)$
Reuse Strategy	*minV*	*max*	*pop*	*minC*		
$\|\phi(M)\|$	1	6	3	2	/	/
$V =$ swrc	✓	✓	✓	✓	10	/
$V =$ dc	–	✓	✓	✓	287	/
$V =$ foaf	–	✓	✓	–	232	/
$V =$ npg	–	✓	–	–	5	/
$V =$ umbc	–	✓	–	–	1	/
$v =$ swrc:author	✓	✓	–	–	/	16,754
$v =$ umbc:institution	–	✓	–	–	/	0
$v =$ npg:Contributor	–	✓	–	–	/	0
$v =$ foaf:name	–	✓	✓	–	/	3,287,920
$v =$ dc:title	–	✓	✓	✓	/	17,120,348
$v =$ foaf:Person	–	–	✓	–	/	2,333,589
$v =$ dc:creator	–	–	✓	✓	/	7,372,111

$\phi(DS) = \{\text{foaf, mo, rdfs}\}$, of which the MO[8] vocabulary is very specific for the domain of musical artists. Subsequently, the participants were provided the three schema models described in Table 3, each extending the IM with further properties such as the artist's homepage, the record's image, and others. Hereby, some vocabulary terms used in IM were updated with other vocabulary terms. Model M_{3a} extends the schema in IM with further properties from the MO ontology, but also replaces the other terms such as foaf:Agent with mo:MusicArtist or foaf:name with rdfs:label. Hereby, the *minD* strategy tries to express the data with (as few as possible) domain-specific vocabularies. The strategy *minV*, exemplified by M_{3b}, uses only one vocabulary, but the schema.org[9] vocabulary covers a broad range of different domains, including music artists. Thus, it is possible to express the entire dataset with this one vocabulary, although it is not quite popular as indicated by the features $|\phi|$ and Ψ. Model (M_{3c}) again follows the strategy to reuse popular vocabularies (*pop*). Their terms are very broad and not domain specific, but the popularity of the vocabularies and their terms is very high.

The additional meta-information, to which we will also refer to as "support type", on the provided data models contain the following information: ST_1- *Domain of a vocabulary:* domain of FOAF is people and relationships; domain of MO is musical work and artists; ST_2- *Statistics about vocabulary usage:* number of data providers in LOD cloud using FOAF: 500; number of data providers using MO: 50; ST_3- *Statistics about vocabulary term usage:* number of uses of foaf:homepage: 800; number of uses of mo:homepage: 200; ST_4- *Semantic information on vocabulary term:* foaf:homepage is used for the web page of a person, while mo:homepage is used for a fan/band page of an artist; and ST_5- *Statistics about vocabulary terms in triple context:* Most common object property between mo:MusicArtist and mo:Record is mo:published. Hereby, the data for ST_2, ST_3, and ST_5 is *fictive* and not retrieved from some web service.

[8] `http://purl.org/ontology/mo/`, access 1/4/2014.

[9] `http://schema.org/`, access 1/4/2014.

Table 3. Ranking Task T_3: The models $M_{3a} - M_{3c}$, their reuse strategy, and features

Model	M_{3a}	M_{3b}	M_{3c}	$\vert\Phi(V)\vert$	$\Psi(v)$
Reuse Strategy	*minD*	*minV*	*pop*		
$\vert\phi(M)\vert$	3	1	3	/	/
V = foaf	✓	–	✓	232	/
V = mo	✓	–	✓	4	/
V = rdfs	✓	–	–	533	/
V = schema	–	✓	–	3	/
V = dc	–	–	✓	287	/
v = foaf:Agent	✓	–	–	/	2,818,352
v = mo:homepage	✓	–	–	/	0
v = mo:MusicArtist	✓	–	✓	/	1,713,860
v = schema:name	–	✓	–	/	0
v = schema:Person	–	✓	–	/	375,277
v = schema:MusicAlbum	–	✓	–	/	59,248
v = dc:title	–	–	✓	/	3,605,629
v = foaf:name	–	–	✓	/	9,235,251
v = foaf:homepage	–	–	✓	/	8,244,952

3 Participants

Overall, $N = 79$ participants (16 female) took part in the survey. However, it was not mandatory to answer every question resulting in a participation range from minimum $N = 59$ to maximum $N = 79$. $N = 67$ finished the entire survey including demographic information. About 67% of these 67 participants work in academia, 23% work in industry, and 10% in both. The variety of the participants ranges from research associates (22) over post doctoral researchers (14) to professors (8) with an average age of $M = 34.6$ ($SD = 8.6$). On average the participants have worked for 4 years with Linked Open Data ($M = 4.07, SD = 2.64$), and rated their own expertise consuming and publishing LOD quite high ($M = 3.64, SD = 1$) on a 5-point-Likert scale from 1 (*none at all experienced*) to 5 (*expert*). Hereby, about 59, 7% of the participants consider themselves to be high experienced or above (4 or 5 on the Likert-scale) and 40, 3% consider themselves to have moderate knowledge or less. In total, we can say that our participants are quite experienced in the field of Linked Data. This makes the results of the survey very promising with respect to their validity for identifying the best strategy to choose appropriate vocabulary terms.

The participants were acquired using the following mailing lists: (a) public LOD mailing list,[10] (b) public Semantic Web mailing list,[11] and (c) EuropeanaTech-Community.[12] In addition, we contacted various authors and data maintainers of LOD datasets

[10] `http://lists.w3.org/Archives/Public/public-lod/`, access: 1/4/2014.
[11] `http://lists.w3.org/Archives/Public/semantic-web/`, access 1/4/2014.
[12] `http://pro.europeana.eu/web/network/europeana-tech`, access 1/4/2014.

Table 4. Results of the three ranking tasks $T_1 - T_3$

Ranking Task	Model	Strategy	Median Rank (Mdn)	Friedman test
T_1	M_{1a}	*pop*	1	$\chi^2(2,78) = 11.521, p = .003$
	M_{1b}	*link*	2	
	M_{1c}	*max*	2	
T_2	M_{2a}	*minV*	3	$\chi^2(3,63) = 40.536, p < .001$
	M_{2b}	*max*	4	
	M_{2c}	*pop*	1	
	M_{2d}	*minC*	2	
T_3	M_{3a}	*minD*	2	$\chi^2(2,61) = 3.1,$ **n.s.**$, p = .211$
	M_{3b}	*minV*	2	
	M_{3c}	*pop*	2	

on CKAN[13] as well as participants and lecturers from the Summer School for Ontological Engineering and Sematic Web (SSSW[14]) in person and asked them to participate in the survey and share their expertise.

4 Results of Ranking Tasks

We encode the obtained ranking position for the data models with numbers starting at 1, 2, and so on, i.e., the lower the ranking number the better rank position of a response option. For each ranking task, we performed a Friedman test to detect significant differences between the strategies (with $\alpha = .05$), as the answers are provided on an ordinal scale. Subsequently, we applied pairwise Wilcoxon signed-rank tests with Bonferroni correction, if significant differences have been found.

Table 4 summarizes the results of all three ranking tasks and gives a first insight into how the schema models and its underlying vocabulary reuse strategy have been ranked (including the significant differences between the rankings which are provided in the last column).

Ranking Task T_1. Regarding the task T_1, which was completed by $N = 78$ respondents, a significant difference of the three data models with respect to an appropriate reuse of vocabularies can be observed in Table 4. The Median (*Mdn*) ranks show that M_{1a} with the underlying strategy of reusing popular vocabulary terms is ranked better (*Mdn=1*) than the other two models and their strategy (*Mdn=2*). A post hoc analysis with Wilcoxon signed-rank tests, which were conducted with a Bonferroni correction applied (now $\alpha = .017$), provide final evidence that M_{1a} is significantly better than the other two models. However, there was no significant difference between the strategy to

[13] `http://datahub.io/group/lodcloud`, access 1/4/2014.

[14] `http://sssw.org/2013/`, access 1/11/2014.

Table 5. Results of the Support Types from Ranking Task T_3

Support Type	Support	*Mdn*	Friedman test
ST_1	Information on domain of vocabulary	2	$\chi^2(2,78) = 11.521, p = .003$
ST_2	Number of LOD datasets using a vocabulary	2	
ST_3	Number of all occurrences of a vocabulary term in LOD cloud	3	
ST_4	Documentation of a vocabulary term	3	
ST_5	Information on most common use of an object property	4	

interlink self-defined vocabulary terms with external classes and properties and the *max* strategy that was merely provided as a lower boundary for vocabulary reuse.

Ranking Task T_2. The second ranking task, which was completed by $N = 63$ respondents, again shows a statistical significant difference between the four different reuse strategies and that the model with the strategy of reusing mainly popular vocabularies (M_{2c}) is ranked first (*Mdn=1*). A further post hoc analysis with Wilcoxon signed-rank tests was conducted with a Bonferroni correction applied (now $\alpha = .008$), and it proves that M_{2c} is significantly better than M_{2a} and M_{2b}, but there was no significant difference to schema model M_{2d}. Furthermore, M_{2d} was significantly better than M_{2b} but no difference to M_{2a}, and schema model M_{2a} was significantly better than M_{2b}.

Ranking Task T_3. The last ranking task had two parts, and a total of $N = 61$ respondents have completed the first part and $N = 59$ completed the second part. In the first part, as shown in Table 4, the median ranks for the three model and their strategies are the same (*Mdn=2*). The results of the Friedman test to detect significant differences show that there is no difference between the strategies whatsoever (**n.s.**). In the second part, the participants had to rank which provided support type (the additional meta-information) was most helpful for making their ranking deciding. The five support types, their median ranks and whether there was a significant difference detected is displayed in Table 5. It can be observed that ST_1 and ST_2 are considered to be more helpful for making the right choice considering vocabulary reuse, whereas ST_4 seems not to be quite as helpful. Further post hoc analysis with Wilcoxon signed-rank tests show that ST_1 is significantly different to every other support type except ST_2. Support type ST_2 is again significantly different to all remaining support types but ST_4, and ST_3, ST_4, and ST_5 have no significant differences whatsoever.

5 Results of the Aspect Questions

We asked the participants to evaluate the different aspects regarding "why reuse vocabularies?", as introduced in Section 2.2, at the beginning of the survey and after the first and second ranking task. The median rating for the three aspects *A1:* provide a clear structure of the data, *A2*: make the data easier to be consumed, and *A3*: establish an ontological agreement was in general high (*Mdn*≥*4*). Applying Friedman test to measure whether there are significant differences to the second and third rating, shows that in each case, the respondents ranked the three aspects at the beginning of the survey significantly higher than after the two ranking tests, which is also proved by the post hoc analysis with Wilcoxon signed-rank tests. Basically, the median ratings for *A1* and *A2* was first *Mdn=5* and at the second and third rating it was *Mdn=4*. The aspect *A3* was asked only twice and the post hoc analysis showed that the first rating was significantly better that the second one despite the fact that the median rating for this aspect in both rating was *Mdn=4*. Furthermore, splitting the ratings into two groups with one group having an LOD experience of <4 (moderate and below) and the other group being ≥ 4 (high to expert knowledge), shows that both groups have decreased the ratings of the aspects *A1* to *A3*.

6 Discussion

The results of analyzing the most important aspects to reuse vocabularies show that most participants have, in theory, the intention to publish Linked Open Data in an easy to process way, i. e., provide a clear structure of the data and make it as easy as possible to consume the data. However, it is very interesting to see that the theoretical intention to follow these best practices (*A1* to *A3*) seem to be higher than the intention to follow them in a real-life scenario. This is indicated by the ratings of *A1* to *A3* being high at the beginning ($Mdn = 5$) but not as high after asking the participants whether these aspects influenced the ranking decision ($Mdn = 4$). Nonetheless, each of these aspects was still rated with a median of $Mdn = 4$ on a 5-point-Likert scale, which still shows that these aspects are considered as "somewhat important". Therefore, the participant's goals to provide a clear structure and thereby increase the readability of the dataset can be considered as relatively consistent throughout the survey. Furthermore, there were no significant differences between the group of participants who have high to expert knowledge to the group with moderate LOD knowledge and below. This indicates that these goals are very genuine ones. Having these goals in mind, it is very interesting to look at the rankings of the three ranking tasks.

For **Ranking Task** T_1, the *pop* strategy is the significantly preferred choice. This is quite interesting, as theoretically, it is considered by the best practices to be important to establish links on schema level to other vocabulary terms. However, this *link* strategy was not significantly better than the *max* strategy (lower boundary). Furthermore, looking at the quite small total occurrence of properties such as owl:equivalentProperty indicates that other data providers do not follow this good practice either. In fact, looking at the total occurrence of the term owl:sameAs ($|\Phi(\text{owl:sameAs})| = 18,678,552$) indicates that for data providers it is more important to link Linked Open Data on instance level.

In **Ranking Task** T_2, the results showed that reusing widely-used vocabulary terms from widely-used vocabularies is considered better than reusing only domain specific vocabularies. This is quite interesting, as it is considered good practice to select the domain vocabulary first and use as many of its terms, if possible, as other vocabularies might not be needed. Apparently, this was not considered helpful in providing a clear data structure. In fact, correlating the ranking of the various aspects why vocabularies should be reused and the results of this ranking task, it seems that preferring widely-used vocabulary terms from widely used vocabularies serves the purpose more than reusing mainly the domain specific vocabulary. Despite this, both of these strategies were not significantly better than the strategy that uses a minimum amount of vocabularies per concept (*minC*). This *minC* strategy indeed seems to provide a good trade-off between reusing popular and domain specific vocabularies.

For **Ranking Task** T_3, no significant differences between the strategies were found in the first part of this task. The second part showed that the information on how many datasets use a specific vocabulary and the information on the domain of a vocabulary seem to be the most preferred additional meta-information. The results are interesting in a two-fold way: First, ranking task T_3 was very similar to ranking task T_2. Despite this similarity, the obtained results are very different. In detail, the information in ST_1 states that the MO vocabulary covers the domain of musical artists and their work as well as that the MO vocabulary is used by 50 data sets (fictive number; real number is $|\Phi(\text{MO})| = 3$). This might lead to believe that the MO vocabulary is a suitable candidate to express musical data, as it is used by many other data providers. Therefore, other vocabularies such as FOAF or Dublin Core are not needed, as MO is well-known and widely-used. Second, regarding the different support types, it is interesting to observe that the number of datasets using vocabulary V was considered more informative than the number of the total occurrences of vocabulary term $v \in V$. Particularly, to establish an ontological agreement in data representation, it seems to be better to reuse vocabulary terms from a vocabulary that is used by many, probably smaller datasets.

The results of our survey might have been influenced by several factors such as specific use cases, which were not considered in detail for ranking the LOD models, as well as the format in which we depicted the examples to the participants. Regarding different use cases, one might primarily use LOD for publishing the data on the web for automated consumption, but one might also define a LOD vocabulary to represent the domain knowledge for an own application. For example, the proprietary class myMov:Actor represents an actor. When modeling Linked Open Data and trying to provide a clear schema structure as well as to make the data easier to be consumed, the use of foaf:Person might be adequate. Whereas when defining an ontology, defining the proprietary vocabulary term and specifying a rdfs:subClassOf relationship might be considered better and more correct. As we did not specify the concrete application the Linked Data is created for, there are several other factors that might have influenced the results in a similar way. However, we did not focus on these factors as they are very difficult to grasp in a structured way and to simplify the study. The survey is addressing Linked Data practitioners, who work with Linked Open Data on a regular basis. Therefore, we showed the modeling examples in N3/Turtle syntax as this is the most common way of representing data in a good human readable way. We might have excluded some participants, who might not be comfortable with N3/Turtle syntax.

7 Related Work

Previous studies regarding the datasets contained in the LOD cloud are mainly focused on investigating the compliance of LOD sources to different characteristics or best practices. Hogan et al. [3] performed an empirical analysis examining 4 million RDF/XML documents on their conformance to several best practices that were elaborated in [1], and in [9], the authors analyze LOD datasets and discuss common errors in the modeling and publishing process. In addition, Poveda Villalón et al. [10] performed a similar analysis of ontology reuse in the LOD context. As a result, reusing and mixing vocabularies is identified as an issue that is more difficult to resolve.

A study in the field of reusing *ontologies* was done by Simperl [4]. The author performs a feasibility study on reusing ontologies, where most prominent case studies on ontology reuse as well as methods and tools are enumerated. It is demonstrated that different methods for reusing ontologies are perfectly suitable to for a development of a new ontology, but in all case studies each reused ontology has to be found, evaluated, and chosen manually, which results in making the decision on which ontology to reuse based on personal experience.

There are also a couple of different methods that help the data engineer in deciding which vocabulary to reuse. However, these are focused on specific domains such as cultural heritage [11], governmental data,[15] bibliographic data,[16] and human resources [4]. These domain-specific methods provide valuable information on how to model and publish data as LOD in these domains, but may be too specific in order to apply it to the general case. The most recent work on the best practices about how to generally publish Linked Data is a tech report by the W3C [12]. It includes a basic checklist about what appropriate vocabularies must or should have, but besides the factor that one should reuse a vocabulary that is used by many other datasets, the other items on that checklist rather suggest to check whether a vocabulary is documented, self-descriptive, or is accessible for a long period. These aspects are not considered in our survey, but might be an interesting factor for future vocabulary recommendation tools.

The Linked Open Vocabulary index (LOV) [7] is an inspirational service to aid the Linked Data engineer in finding appropriate vocabulary terms for reuse. It provides the engineer with the most common and popular vocabularies as well as a lot of meta-information about each vocabulary and vocabulary term. This makes it possible to find the most suitable classes and properties to express data as LOD. However, it is solely based on a best string-match search and each vocabulary term has to be implemented in the engineering process manually. To alleviate this, a first implementation of a recommendation service for reusing ontologies is the Watson [13] plugin for the NeOn ontology engineering toolkit [14]. It uses semantic information from a number of ontologies and

[15] `http://www.w3.org/2011/gld/wiki/Linked_Data_Cookbook#Step_3_Re-use_Vocabularies_Whenever_Possible`, access: 5/16/2013.

[16] `http://aims.fao.org/lode/bd`, access: 5/16/2013.

other semantic documents published on the Web to recommend appropriate vocabulary terms, but it does consider the typical strategies for modeling Linked Data.

8 Conclusion

We presented a study that investigates which vocabulary reuse strategy is followed by Linked Data experts and practitioners in various real-life scenarios. It was examined via a survey consisting of ranking tasks, where the participants were asked to rank various modeling examples according to their understanding of good reuse of vocabularies, and rating assignments to explain which aspects most influenced the ranking decisions. The results of the ranking tasks illustrate that reusing vocabulary terms from widely-used as well as domain specific vocabularies directly is considered a better approach than defining proprietary terms and interlink them with external classes and properties. Furthermore, reusing popular vocabulary terms from frequently used vocabularies is more important than frequently used vocabulary terms from vocabularies that are not used by many data providers. To balance vocabulary terms from popular and domain specific vocabularies, it is considered to be important to maintain an appropriate mix, in order to provide a clear structure of the data and make it easier to be consumed. These findings of our survey can also be used for future vocabulary recommendation systems such as the LOVER approach [15] or implemented in existing tools such as Watson [13] for the NeOn ontology engineering toolkit [14].

Acknowledgement. We thank the participants for their time and effort. We additionally thank Natasha Noy, Asunción Gómez-Pérez, Laura Hollink, Jérôme Euzenat, and Richard Cyganiak for their valuable feedback on the survey and the modeling examples. The research leading to these results has received funding from the European Community's Seventh Framework Programme (FP7/2007-2013), REVEAL (Grant agree no. 610928).

References

1. Bizer, C., Cyganiak, R., Heath, T.: How to publish linked data on the web. Web page (2007) (revised 2008) (access January 03, 2014)
2. Heath, T., Bizer, C.: Linked Data: Evolving the Web into a Global Data Space. Synthesis Lectures on the Semantic Web. Morgan Kaufmann (2011)
3. Hogan, A., Umbrich, J., Harth, A., Cyganiak, R., Polleres, A., Decker, S.: An empirical survey of linked data conformance. Web Semantics: Science, Services and Agents on the World Wide Web, 14–44 (2012)
4. Simperl, E.: Reusing ontologies on the semantic web: A feasibility study. Data Knowledge Engineering 68, 905–925 (2009)
5. Schaible, J., Gottron, T., Scherp, A.: Extended description of the survey on common strategies of vocabulary reuse in linked open data modeling. Technical Report 01/2014, Institute for Web Science and Technologies, Universität Koblenz-Landau (2014) http://www.uni-koblenz.de/~fb4reports/2014/2014_01_Arbeitsberichte.pdf

6. Auer, S., Demter, J., Martin, M., Lehmann, J.: LODStats – an extensible framework for high-performance dataset analytics. In: ten Teije, A., Völker, J., Handschuh, S., Stuckenschmidt, H., d'Acquin, M., Nikolov, A., Aussenac-Gilles, N., Hernandez, N. (eds.) EKAW 2012. LNCS, vol. 7603, pp. 353–362. Springer, Heidelberg (2012), http://dblp.uni-trier.de/db/conf/ekaw/ekaw2012.html#AuerDML12
7. Vandenbussche, P.Y., Vatant, B., Rozat, L.: Linked open vocabularies: an initiative for the web of data. In: QetR Workshop, Chambery, France (2011)
8. Stadtmüller, S., Harth, A., Grobelnik, M.: Accessing information about linked data vocabularies with vocab.cc. In: Semantic Web and Web Science, 391–396 (2013)
9. Hogan, A., Harth, A., Passant, A., Decker, S., Polleres, A.: Weaving the pedantic web. In: Proceedings of the Linked Data on the Web Workshop, LDOW 2010 (2010)
10. Poveda Villalón, M., Suárez-Figueroa, M.C., Gómez-Pérez, A.: The landscape of ontology reuse in linked data. In: Proceedings Ontology Engineering in a Data-driven World, OEDW 2012 (2012)
11. Hyvönen, E.: Publishing and using cultural heritage linked data on the semantic web. Synthesis Lectures on The Semantic Web: Theory and Technology (2012)
12. Atemezing, G.A., Villazón-Terrazas, B., Hyland, B.: Best practices for publishing linked data. W3C note, W3C (2014), http://www.w3.org/TR/2014/NOTE-ld-bp-20140109/ (access January 03, 2014)
13. d'Aquin, M., Baldassarre, C., Gridinoc, L., Sabou, M., Angeletou, S., Motta, E.: Watson: Supporting next generation semantic web applications. In: Proceedings of the IADIS International Conference WWW/Internet 2007, pp. 363–371 (2007)
14. Haase, P., Lewen, H., Studer, R., Tran, D.T., Erdmann, M., d'Aquin, M., Motta, E.: The neon ontology engineering toolkit. In: Korn, J. (ed.) WWW 2008 Developers Track (2008)
15. Schaible, J., Gottron, T., Scheglmann, S., Scherp, A.: Lover: support for modeling data using linked open vocabularies. In: Proceedings of the Joint EDBT/ICDT 2013 Workshops (2013)

Generating and Summarizing Explanations for Linked Data

Rakebul Hasan

INRIA Sophia Antipolis, Wimmics, 2004 route des Lucioles - B.P. 93, 06902 Sophia-Antipolis Cedex, France
hasan.rakebul@inria.fr

Abstract. Linked Data consumers may need explanations for debugging or understanding the reasoning behind producing the data. They may need the possibility to transform long explanations into more understandable short explanations. In this paper, we discuss an approach to explain reasoning over Linked Data. We introduce a vocabulary to describe explanation related metadata and we discuss how publishing these metadata as Linked Data enables explaining reasoning over Linked Data. Finally, we present an approach to summarize these explanations taking into account user specified explanation filtering criteria.

Keywords: #eswc2014Hasan, explanation, summarization, Linked Data.

1 Introduction

In the recent years, we have seen a growth of publishing Linked Data from community driven efforts, governmental bodies, social networking sites, scientific communities, and corporate bodies [7]. These data publishers from various domains publish their data in an interlinked fashion[1] using vocabularies defined in RDFS/OWL. This presents opportunities for large-scale data integration and reasoning over cross-domain data. In such a distributed scenario, consumers of these data may need explanations for debugging or understanding the reasoning behind producing the data; they may need the possibility to transform long explanations into more understandable short explanations [19]. Much of the previous work on explanations for the Semantic Web does not address explanation in a distributed environment [12]. The Inference Web [19] approach proposes a centralized registry based solution for publishing explanation metadata from distributed reasoners. We propose a decentralized solution to this problem. In essence, we discuss how to explain Linked Data in a decentralized fashion and how to summarize the explanations.

To explain Linked Data in a decentralized fashion, we publish explanation related metadata as Linked Data. In this approach, there is no constrain to publish the explanation metadata in a centralized location like in the Inference

[1] See `http://richard.cyganiak.de/2007/10/lod/` for a graph linking these datasets.

V. Presutti et al. (Eds.): ESWC 2014, LNCS 8465, pp. 473–487, 2014.

Web approach. To generate explanations, we retrieve the metatada by following their dereferenceable URIs and present them in a human understandable form. For publishing explanation related metadata, we present a vocabulary to describe explanation metadata and guidelines to publish these metadata as Linked Data. To provide short explanations, we summarize the explanations by centrality, coherence, abstractness, and concept filtering.

The structure of the rest of this paper is as follows: in section 2, we present the related work. In section 3, we discuss how to represent and generate explanations for Linked Data. In section 4, we present our approach to summarize explanations. In section 5, we evaluate our summarization approach. Finally, we conclude and discuss the future work in section 6.

2 Related Work

Inference Web [19–21] is an explanation infrastructure which addresses explanation requirements of web services discovery, policy engines, first order logic theorem provers, task execution, and text analytics. Information manipulation traces of these various kinds of systems are encoded using Proof Markup Language (PML) [25]. Inference Web provides a set of software tools and services for building, presenting, maintaining, and manipulating PML proofs. PML is an explanation interlingua consisting of three OWL ontologies: PML provenance ontology (PML-P), PML justification ontology (PML-J), and PML trust ontology (PML-T). Inference Web authors define justification as a logical reasoning step, or any kind of computation process, or a factual assertion or assumption. Inference Web proposes a centralized registry based solution for publishing explanation metadata from distributed reasoners. In contrast, we propose a decentralized solution to address explanations in the distributed setting of Linked Data. The WIQA (Web Information Quality Assessment) framework [6] provides explanations of information filtering process for supporting information consumers in their trust decisions. WIQA exposes its explanations in RDF using the Explanation (EXPL) Vocabulary[2]. Forcher *et al.* [11] present the explanation-aware semantic search engine called KOIOS. The keyword search result explanations include information on how keywords are mapped to concepts and how concepts are connected. KOIOS uses a set of ontologies to formally describe the content of explanations in RDF. Both WIQA and KOIOS provide application specific explanations which include process descriptions of specific algorithms. In contrast, our explanations are suitable for generic Linked Data scenarios. Horridge *et al.* [14] present justification based explanation techniques. The authors define a justification for an entailment in an ontology as "a minimal subset of the ontology that is sufficient for the entailment to hold". The authors present laconic and precise justifications which are fine-grained justifications consisting of axioms with no superfluous part. The authors present an optimized algorithm to compute laconic justifications showing the feasibility of computing laconic justifications and precise justifications in practice. We do not focus on the theoretical

[2] `http://www4.wiwiss.fu-berlin.de/bizer/triqlp/`

aspects of the justifications such as the minimal parts of axioms in a justification which are required to hold an entailment. Rather, we focus on the aspects related to publishing and consuming explanation metadata in a distributed environment. Other notable works on explanations in the Semantic Web literature include OntoNova [3] and Knowledge in a Wiki (KiWi) [17]. OntoNova and KiWi provide explanations of their reasoning. However, they do not represent their explanation metadata using standard data formats. This is an undesirable situation for Linked Data scenarios because data consumers would not be able to process such non standard explanation metadata.

To the best of our knowledge, there is no comparable published work on summarizing explanations in the Semantic Web literature. But researchers have studied ontology summarization. RDF Sentence graph based summarization [27] extracts RDF sentences based on centrality measures. Our work has a similar approach to sentence graph summarization approach. However, we define new measures for summarizing explanations. Peroni *et al.* [23] discuss how to identify key concepts in an ontology. They draw summarization criteria from cognitive science (natural categories), network topology (density and coverage), and lexical statistics (term popularity). Alani *et al.* [2] discuss shrinking an ontology by analyzing the usage of the ontology. Alani *et al.* analyze the query log against an ontology to understand the important parts of the ontology. Peroni *et al.* and Alani *et al.* focus on a concept level summarization of ontologies. In contrast, our focus is on statement level summarization.

3 Explaining Linked Data

We follow the Linked Data principles [5] to publish our explanation metadata. We describe these metadata using our proposed vocabulary *Ratio4TA*[3]. We generate explanations by retrieving the explanation metatada by following their dereferenceable URIs and presenting them in a human understandable form.

3.1 Representing and Publishing Explanation Metadata

Ratio4TA (inter*r*linked explan*ations for t*riple *a*ssertions) is an OWL ontology for describing explanation metadata. *Ratio4TA* extends the W3C PROV Ontology[4]. This promotes interoperability by enabling data consumers process explanation metadata according to W3C PROV standards. Consumers of these explanation metadata can use their preferred tools to present and visualize explanations. Figure 1 shows the core concepts and relations of *Ratio4TA*. They allow describing data, reasoning processes, results, data derivations, rules, and software applications. The *ExplanationBundle* concept allows to define named graph containers for RDF statements representing explanation metadata.

We publish the explanation metadata as Linked Data. This means that all the resources in our explanation metadata have dereferenceable HTTP URIs.

[3] `http://ns.inria.fr/ratio4ta/`

[4] `http://www.w3.org/TR/prov-o/`

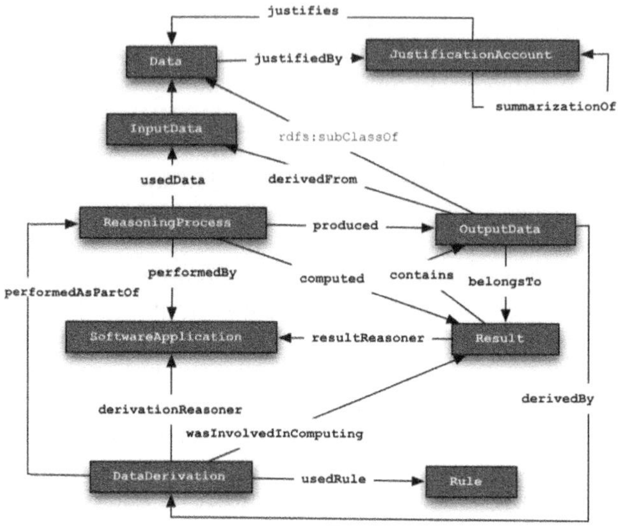

Fig. 1. The core classes and properties of *Ratio4TA*

We avoid using blank nodes to keep the resources globally dereferenceable. We use the named graph mechanism [8] to make statements about RDF triples. Using named graph allows us to associate explanation metadata for data with different level of granularity – explanation metadata for a triple or a graph containing more than one triple. Furthermore, we use named graphs to group together explanation metadata and make the metadata for an explanation referenceable by a single URI. Listing 1.1 shows an extract of an explanation described using *Ratio4TA* in TriG [8] notation. The example in this listing shows the explanation metadata for the derived triple *lodapp:data1*. The named graph *lodapp:explanation1* contains the explanation metadata. The metadata include links to the reasoning process, the input data, the rule, the software application, and the result to which the derivation contributes.

Listing 1.1. Extract from the explanation metadata for a derivation

```
# Explanation Metadata
lodapp:explanation1 {
  lodapp:explanation1 r4ta:explains lodapp:data1.
  # Type declarations
  lodapp:explanation1 rdf:type r4ta:ExplanationBundle.
  lodapp:corese rdf:type r4ta:SoftwareApplication.
  ....
  ....
  # Reasoning process
  lodapp:reasoningProcess1 r4ta:performedBy lodapp:corese;
      r4ta:usedData lodapp:inputData1;
      r4ta:usedData lodapp:inputData2;
      r4ta:computed lodapp:result1;
      r4ta:produced lodapp:data1.
  # Computed result
  lodapp:result1 r4ta:resultReasoner lodapp:corese .
  # Output data
  lodapp:data1 r4ta:derivedFrom lodapp:inputData1;
      r4ta:derivedFrom lodapp:inputData2;
      r4ta:belongsTo lodapp:result1;
      r4ta:derivedBy lodapp:derivation1.
  # Data derivation
  lodapp:derivation1 r4ta:usedRule lodapp:geoFeatureRule;
      r4ta:wasInvolvedInComputing lodapp:result1;
      r4ta:derivationReasoner lodapp:corese;
      r4ta:performedAsPartOf lodapp:reasoningProcess1.
}
# Derived data
lodapp:data1 {
  dbpedia:Philadelphia gn:parentFeature geonames:5205788.
}
# Dbpedia data
lodapp:inputData1 {
  dbpedia:Philadelphia owl:sameAs geonames:4560349 .
}
# GeoNames data
lodapp:inputData2 {
  geonames:4560349 gn:parentFeature geonames:5205788.
}
```

Why a New Ontology? Proof Markup Language (PML) [25] and the AIR Justification Ontology (AIRJ) [16] are important previous works on representing explanation metadata. PML allows describing provenance metadata, justifications for derivations of conclusions, and trust related metadata. Additionally, a light weight variant of PML known as PML-Lite [24] presents a simple subset of PML. AIRJ extends PML-Lite and provides primitives to represent the different events and the operations performed by reasoners. PML and AIRJ use RDF container concepts. RDF containers use blank nodes to connect a sequence of items [1]. However, as a common practice, blank nodes are avoided while publishing Linked Data [13]. It is not possible to make statements about blank nodes as they do not have identifiers. Therefore, blank nodes make data integration harder in the global dataspace of Linked Data. Additionally, the existing ontologies do not use any common data interchanging standard such as W3C PROV-O. This makes it hard for applications across the web to make sense of the explanation metadata.

3.2 Generating Explanation

We generate explanations from the published explanation metadata by recursively following the links between the involved explanation metadata and the data they describe. For a derived RDF statement *dst*, we crawl through the related metadata with a maximum depth limit and collect the set of explanation meta statements, and the set of RDF statements from which the derived RDF statement *dst* is derived. In the remaining for this paper, we refer to the derived RDF statement (the initial *dst*) that we are explaining as the root statement rs. We refer to the set of RDF statements from which rs is derived as knowledge statements KST. The RDF knowledge graph KG is the graph formed by union of KST and the root statement: $KG = RDFGraph(KST \cup rs)$. We generate natural language descriptions from the RDF statements in KG (using *rdfs:label* property values) and present them as explanations for human end-users. Figure 2 shows an example of our explanation for a derived statement that "Bob is

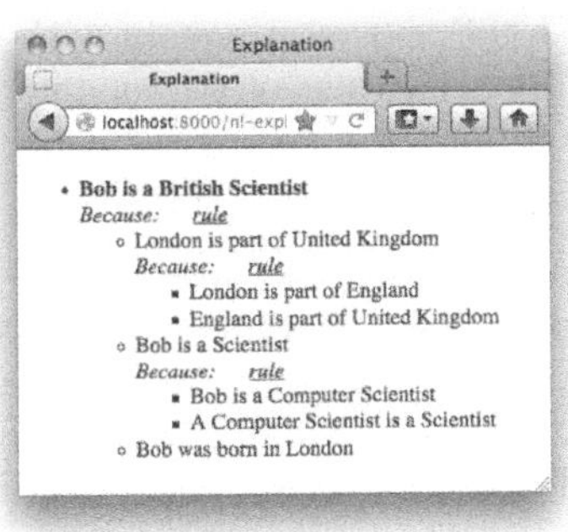

Fig. 2. Full explanation

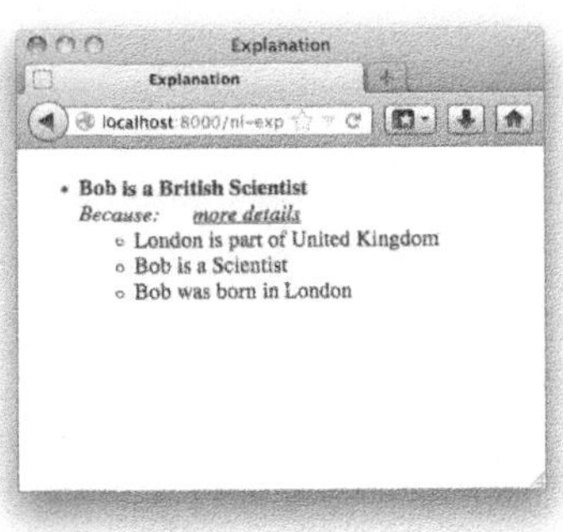

Fig. 3. Summarized explanation

a British Scientist". Each derivation contains a link to the natural language representation of the used rule. Although this kind of explanations with the details of all the steps may be useful for expert users, they may overwhelm non-expert users with too much information [3, 12, 21]. We provide summarized explanations to address this problem. Figure 3 shows an example of a summarized explanation for "Bob is a British Scientist". Users can switch to the full explanation by clicking on the "more details" link. In the next section, we discuss our approach to summarizing explanations.

4 Summarizing Explanations

In [3, 12, 21], researchers discuss the importance of providing short explanations rather than overwhelming the end-users with too much information. The authors of [3] also discuss filtering information in explanations in order to provide more relevant explanations. We propose an approach to summarizing explanations taking into account user specified filtering criteria. More formally, let $KG = (R, T)$ be an RDF knowledge graph, where R is the set of resources and literals and T is the set of RDF statements. Let rs be the root statement (therefore the knowledge statements $KST = T \setminus rs$). We provide summarized explanations by summarizing RDF statements from KST. We use the term "oriented graph" to refer to KG throughout the paper. Our summarization approach includes first a ranking step and then a re-ranking step. It is important to note that our summarized explanations may not always conform to the correctness of deductions from a logical point of view. Our summarized explanations are not aimed at explaining the correct deduction steps. Rather the aim is to provide a short overview of the background information used in a deduction. We describe below the measures we use for summarizing explanations.

4.1 Measures for Ranking

We rank the statements in KST based on their scores we compute using our summarization measures. The scores are normalized and range from 0.0 to 1.0. A higher score for a statement means that the statement is more suitable for a summary. Taking n statements, where $n <\mid KST \mid$, or statements with scores greater than a threshold value will give a summarized list of statements which can explain rs. For the ranking step, we compute the scores by using three measures: salience (S_{SL}), similarity (S_{SM}), and abstractness (S_{AB}).

Salient RDF Statements. The salience of an RDF statement indicates the importance of the RDF statement in the oriented graph. We use normalized degree centrality, $C_{DN}(v)$, to compute salience of RDF statements. Degree centrality of a vertex in a graph is the number of links the vertex has. We compute the salience $S_{SL}(i)$ of an RDF statement i using (1).

$$S_{SL}(i) = \theta_1 \times C_{DN}(subjectOf(i)) + \theta_2 \times C_{DN}(objectOf(i)) \tag{1}$$

In (1), $\sum_i \theta_i = 1$ and $\forall_i : \theta_i \geq 0$ *i.e.* we take the weighted average of the normalized degree centrality of the subject and the object of the RDF statement i. The $subjectOf(i)$ and the $objectOf(i)$ functions return respectively the subject resource and the object resource of the RDF statement i. We did not use the centrality of the predicate of statement while computing S_{SL} because we wanted an importance score representing the importance of the information in a statement but not the importance of the relation between the information. The centrality values of predicates in a RDF graph often do not change as they are directly used from the schemata. In contrast, every new RDF statement changes the centrality values of its subject and object.

Similar RDF Statements. The consumers of our explanations can specify a set of classes, FL, as their filtering criteria, where $FL \subseteq SC$ and SC is the set of all classes in the schemata used to describe KG. We rank the more similar statements to the concepts given in filtering criteria higher. We use the approximate query solving feature [9] of Corese[5] to compute similarity. The approximate query solving feature is a semantic distance-based similarity feature to compute conceptual similarity between two classes in a schema. For a statement i and a set of classes as filtering criteria FL, we compute similarity $S_{SM}(i, FL)$ using (2).

$$\begin{aligned} S_{SM}(i, FL) = {} & \theta_1 \times similarity_{node}(subjectOf(i), FL) \\ & + \theta_2 \times similarity_{node}(predicateOf(i), FL) \\ & + \theta_3 \times similarity_{node}(objectOf(i), FL) \end{aligned} \tag{2}$$

The function $predicateOf(i)$ returns the predicate of the statement i. We compute $similarity_{node}(j, FL)$ where $j \in R \cup SC$ as following:

$$similarity_{node}(j, FL) = \begin{cases} similarity_{type}(\{j\}, FL) & \text{if } j \in SC \\ similarity_{type}(typesOf(j), FL) & \text{if } j \notin SC \end{cases} \tag{3}$$

In (3), for the case $j \in SC$, we compute the similarity between the class j and the set of classes in FL. For the case $j \notin SC$, we compute the similarity between the set of classes of which j is an instance and the set of classes in FL. The $similarity_{type}$ function takes as arguments a set of classes $TP \in SC$ and the set of filtering criteria FL, and returns the similarity value between them. The $typesOf(j)$ function for a resource $j \in R$ returns the set of classes of which j is an instance. The $similarity_{type}$ function in (4a) computes its value by taking the average of all the values of $maxSimilarity_{type}(m, TP)$ where $m \in FL$ and $TP \in SC$. The $maxSimilarity_{type}$ function in (4b) returns the maximum similarity value between a class m and all the classes in TP. This is to ensure that when a resource is an instance of multiple classes, we filter it by the class which is more similar to the filtering criteria. The $similarity_{type}$ function calculates a combined similarity score of TP with respect to all the classes in FL. Again, we consider the weighted average, and therefore $\sum_i \theta_i = 1$ and $\forall_i : \theta_i \geq 0$ in (2).

[5] `http://wimmics.inria.fr/corese`

$$similarity_{type}(TP, FL) = \frac{\sum\limits_{m \in FL} maxSimilarity_{type}(m, TP)}{| FL |} \quad (4a)$$

$$maxSimilarity_{type}(m, TP) = \max_{n \in TP} (similarity_{corese}(m, n)) : \quad (4b)$$

For a class $m \in FL$ and a class $n \in TP$, $similarity_{corese}(m, n)$ computes the similarity score between class m and n ranging from 0.0 to 1.0 using SPARQL similarity extension of Corese. A value of 1.0 represent exact match and a value of 0.0 represents completely not similar. The S_{SM} score for a statement indicates the similarity of the information in the statement to the information specified in FL.

Abstract Statements. We consider a statement that is close to the root, rs, in corresponding proof tree is more abstract than a statement that is far from the root rs. We define the distance of a node in the proof tree from the root node as the level of the tree to which the node belongs. The root node belongs to level one in the proof tree. The root node is derived from the nodes in level two. A node in level two is derived from the nodes in level three, and so on. For a statement $i \in KST$, we compute the abstraction score $S_{AB}(i)$ using (5).

$$S_{AB}(i) = \frac{1}{level(i)} \quad (5)$$

The function $level(i)$ returns the proof tree level to which the statement i belongs. The $S_{AB}(i)$ measure gives a value greater than 0.0 and less than or equal to 1.0, where a smaller value means less abstract and a larger value means more abstract.

4.2 Measures for Re-ranking

We use two more measures to improve the rankings produced by the combinations of three measures we presented so far.

Subtree Weight in Proof Tree. For a subtree of the proof tree with root i, we compute the subtree weight of the statement i by taking the average score of all the statements in that subtree.

$$score_{ST}(i) = \frac{\sum\limits_{j \in subtree(i)} score(j)}{| subtree(i) |} \quad (6)$$

The $subtree(i)$ function returns the RDF statements from the subtree of proof tree with root i. The $score(j)$ for a statement j here can be computed by combinations of the measures we present in section 4.1. We discuss more about how to combine the different measures in section 5.

Coherence. Previous works in text summarization [10] and ontology summarization [27] have shown that coherent information are desirable in summaries. We consider an RDF statement x to be coherent to an RDF statement y if x is directly derived from y. Let RL be a ranked list of RDF statements; S be a list of already selected RDF statements in the summary; i be the next RDF statement to be selected in S. We re-rank RL by repeatedly selecting next i with $\mid RL \mid$ repetitions using (7).

$$i = \operatorname*{arg\,max}_{j \in RL \setminus S} (\lambda_1 \times score(j) + \lambda_2 \times reward(j, S)) \tag{7}$$

Again, the $score(j)$ for a statement j here can be computed by combinations of the measures we presented before. We take the weighted average of $score(j)$ and $reward(j, S)$ in (7), therefore $\sum_i \lambda_i = 1$ and $\forall_i : \lambda_i \geq 0$.

$$reward(j, S) = 1 - \frac{coherent(S)}{coherent(S \cup j)} \tag{8}$$

As (8) shows, the $reward$ score of a statement j is the amount of potential contribution value – ranging from 0.0 to 1.0 – to the total coherence of the summary if j is added to S. The function $coherent(S)$ in (8) returns the number of coherent statements in the summary S.

5 Evaluation

Ontology summarization [18] and text summarization [10, 26] technologies are evaluated by measuring agreements between human-generated summaries – known as "ground truths" – and automatically generated summaries. We obtained our ground truths by surveying 24 people: 17 computer scientists, 1 chemist, 1 social scientist, 1 mathematician, 1 journalist, 1 psychologist, 1 biologist, and 1 business administrator. 18 participants in our survey had knowledge of RDF and 6 participants did not have any knowledge of RDF. The ages of the participants range from 22 to 59. 20 participants were male and 4 were female. The explanations, the questionnaires, the responses, and the results of the evaluation are publicly available online[6]. We selected a subset of geographical locations from GeoNames[7] and a subset of artists, events, and places from DBPedia[8], then derived new information from these selected subsets. Our ad-hoc reasoner infers new RDF statements with respect to RDFS type propagation; and owl:sameAs and transitivity of the parentFeature property of GeoNames schema. In addition, the reasoner generates explanations for each derivation it performs. We used three test cases – three queries with their results along with the explanations for the results. Each query result is an inferred statement by our reasoner. Each test case has two scenarios: without filtering criteria FL, and

[6] http://ns.inria.fr/ratio4ta/sm/

[7] http://www.geonames.org/

[8] http://dbpedia.org/

with filtering criteria FL. Each participant answered questions for one test case. We randomly assigned a test case to a participant. We ask the participants to rate, from a scale of 1 to 5, the need for each of the statements in the explanation. For, the scenario with filtering criteria FL, we give the query, the answer, and the explanation but with a user's filtering criteria class taken from the schemata used in the reasoning process. The ratings of the explanation statements are our ground truths. We compute the ground truth rankings of explanation statements by ordering them by their rating values.

5.1 Comparing Summarization Measures

We evaluate different combinations of the summarization measures we define. In equation (9), we compute $score_{S_{SL}}(i)$ for a statement i considering salience of the statement. We always include S_{SL} in our measure combinations. The motivation is to first include the salient statements in a summary and then find the statements with other measure combination scores (*e.g.* S_{AB} or S_{SM} or $S_{AB}+S_{SM}$) in those salient statements. Equations (10), (11), and (12) show three more combinations of measures that we consider for our evaluation. In (10), we compute $score_{SL+AB}(i)$ for a statement i considering salience and abstractness of the statement. In (11), we compute the $score_{SL+SM}(i)$ for a statement i considering the salience (S_{SL}), and the similarity (S_{SM}) with respect to user's filtering criteria FL. In (12), we compute $score_{SL+AB+SM}(i)$ for a statement i considering the salience (S_{SL}), the abstractness (S_{AB}), and the similarity (S_{SM}) with respect to user's filtering criteria FL.

$$score_{SL}(i) = S_{SL}(i) \tag{9}$$

$$score_{SL+AB}(i) = \lambda_1 \times S_{SL}(i) + \lambda_2 \times S_{AB}(i) \tag{10}$$

$$score_{SL+SM}(i) = \lambda_1 \times S_{SL}(i) + \lambda_2 \times S_{SM}(i, FL) \tag{11}$$

$$\begin{aligned} score_{SL+AB+SM}(i) = {} & \lambda_1 \times S_{SL}(i) + \lambda_2 \times S_{AB}(i) \\ & + \lambda_3 \times S_{SM}(i, FL) \end{aligned} \tag{12}$$

These combinations are combinations of ranking measures we present in section 4.1. For re-ranking, we first compute the score using any of (9), (10), (11), and (12), then we re-rank using (6), or (7). In remaining of this paper, we denote subtree weight measure as S_{ST}, and coherence measure as S_{CO}. For the scenario without FL, we compare our summaries to sentence graph summarization [27] – denoted as S_{SG}. As the authors of sentence graph summarization approach suggest, we use 0.8 as the navigational preference p parameter value. We implemented sentence graph summarization using degree centrality as the authors found degree centrality performs better than other centrality measures in general, and for its simplicity. We do not consider sentence graph summarization for the scenarios with FL because sentence graph summarization does not have a feature for filtering information using ontology concepts as filtering criteria.

In (10), (11), and (12), $\sum_i \lambda_i = 1$ and $\forall_i : \lambda_i \geq 0$. Thus we take the weighted averages of the measure combinations. For this evaluation, we use equal weights in (10), (11), (12), (1), (2), and (7). Therefore, we set $\forall_i : \lambda_i = \frac{1}{N_\lambda}$ in (10), (11), (12), and (7) where N_λ = number of λ parameters in the corresponding equations; and $\forall_i : \theta_i = \frac{1}{N_\theta}$ in (1), and (2) where N_θ = number of θ parameters in the corresponding equations. However, one can use parameter estimation techniques for finding the optimal parameter values.

5.2 Analysis of Ground Truths

We use cosine similarity to measure the agreements between rating vectors. Cosine similarity values in positive space are in the interval 0 to 1. Table 1 shows the total average agreement measured by cosine similarity and standard deviations for two scenarios – without filtering criteria FL and with filtering criteria FL. The average agreements for both the scenarios are more than 0.8

Table 1. Average agreements between ratings measured by cosine similarity

	avg.	std. dev.
Without FL	0.836	0.048
With FL	0.835	0.065

which is considerably high. However, the standard deviation is higher for the scenario with FL. The reason for this higher standard deviation is that the participants had to consider the highly subjective [4] factor of similarity and therefore their ratings had more variance for the scenario with FL.

5.3 Evaluating the Rankings

We use normalized discounted cumulative gain to evaluate ranking quality. Discounted cumulative gain (DCG) [15, 22] measures the quality of results of an information retrieval system in a ranked list. DCG assumes that judges have graded each item in a list of results. Using these grades, DCG measures the usefulness, or gain, of a ranked list of results. DCG penalizes high quality results appearing lower in a ranked list of results. Normalized discounted cumulative Gain ($nDCG$) allows to calculate and compare this measure across multiple lists of results where each of the lists might have different length. $nDCG$ values are in the interval 0.0 to 1.0. An $nDCG_p$ value of 1.0 means that the ranking is perfect at position p with respect to the ideal ranking – ranking based on grades. The $nDCG_p$ value 0.0 means that the ranking is completely imperfect at position p with respect to the ideal ranking. In our study, the average of ratings by all the survey participants for a statement s is the grade for the statement s. Figure 4 shows the average $nDCG$ values of the three test cases for different rankings by different measure combinations. The *x-axis* represents ranks and the *y-axis* represents $nDCG$. We plot 21 ranks in the *x-axis* because the shortest explanation among the three test cases had 21 statements. For the scenario without FL (the figure on the left), the measure combinations $S_{SL}+S_{AB}+S_{CO}$, $S_{SL}+S_{AB}+S_{ST}$, and $S_{SL}+S_{AB}+S_{ST}+S_{CO}$ produce more closer rankings to the ground truth rankings. For the scenario with FL (the figure on the right), the same three measure combinations with added S_{SM} measure have the best $nDCG$ values. This means that the participants consider central (with respect to the oriented graph and the proof tree), abstract, and coherent information as necessary information in explanation summaries for the scenario without FL. This also holds for the scenario with FL with the added observation that the participants also consider similar information as necessary information. The $nDCG$ values for these measure combinations are higher than 0.9 for all ranks. This means that the rankings by these measure combinations are highly similar to the ground truth rankings. In contrast, the sentence graph summarization ranking has low $nDCG$ values compared to all the other rankings for the scenario without FL. This shows that our explanation summarization algorithms produce much higher quality rankings than sentence graph summarization algorithm.

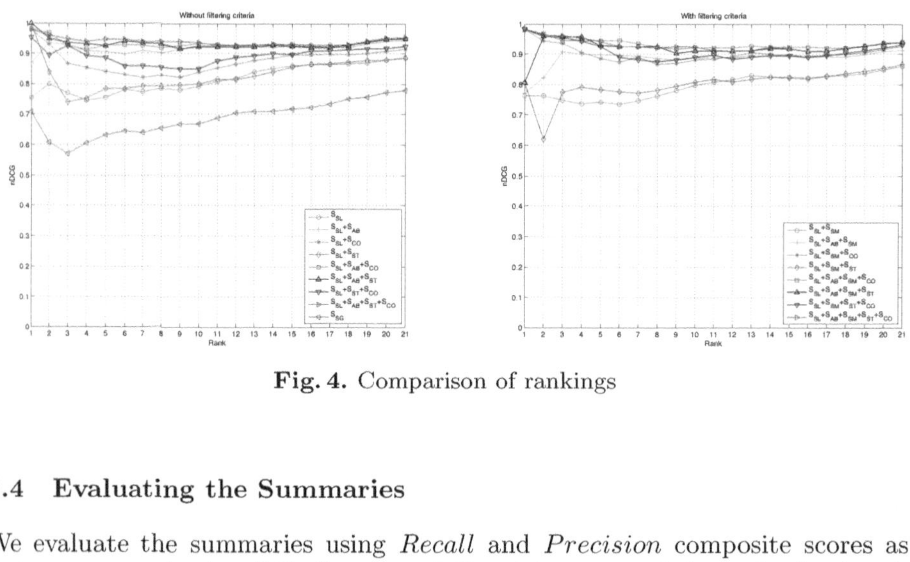

Fig. 4. Comparison of rankings

5.4 Evaluating the Summaries

We evaluate the summaries using *Recall* and *Precision* composite scores as in text summarization [10]. *Recall* and *Precision* quantify how closely the algorithm generated summaries correspond to the human produced summaries. *Recall* reflects how many good statements the algorithm missed, and *Precision* reflects how many of the algorithm's selected statements are good. *F-score* is the composite measure of *Recall* and *Precision*. We use the basic *F-score* as in [26]: $F\text{-}score = \frac{2 \times Precision \times Recall}{Precision + Recall}$. We measure *F-score* for summarized explanations with different compression ratios, CR, to evaluate summaries of different sizes. Compression ratio CR is the ratio of the size of the summarized explanation to the size of original explanation. We evaluate the summarized explanations produced by different measure combinations by comparing them to human generated summarized explanations (*i.e.* ground truth summarized explanations)

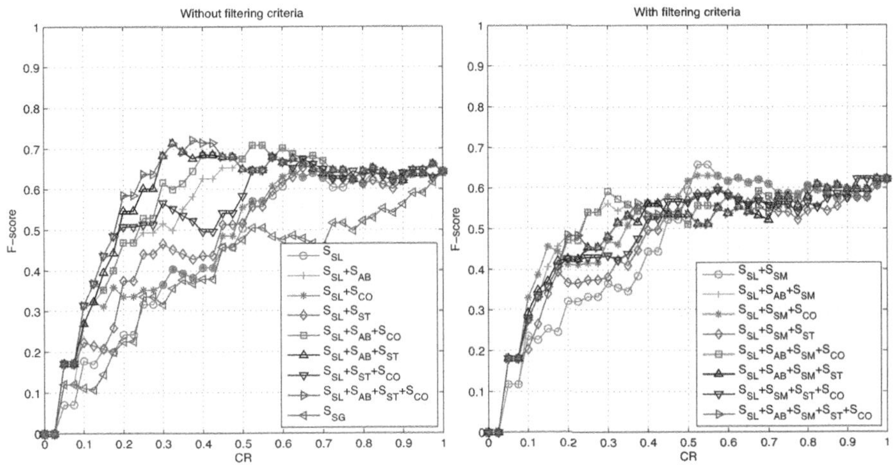

Fig. 5. Compression ratio (CR) vs *F-score*

using *F-score*. To generate the ground truth summarized explanation for an explanation, we include a statement in the ground truth summarized explanation if its rating is greater than or equal to the average rating of all the statements in the original explanation. *F-scores* reflects the accuracy of automatically generated summaries with respect to the ground truth summary. A desirable situation would be a summarized explanation with high *F-score* and low CR. Figure 5 shows the average *F-scores* for different measure combinations for summaries with different sizes for the three test cases. The *x-axis* represents compression ratio CR. The *y-axis* represents *F-scores*. For the scenario without FL (the figure on the left), the best *F-score* is 0.72 when CR value is 0.33 by the measure combinations $S_{SL} + S_{AB} + S_{ST}$ and $S_{SL} + S_{AB} + S_{ST} + S_{CO}$. This is a desirable situation with a high *F-score* and low CR. The sentence graph summarization performs poorly with a best *F-score* value of 0.34 in the CR interval 0.05 to 0.3. This shows that our summarized explanations are more accurate than the summarized explanations generated by sentence graph summarization algorithm. For the scenario with FL (the figure on the right), the best *F-score* is 0.66 at CR values 0.53 and 0.55 by the measure combination$S_{SL} + S_{SM}$. However, the *F-score* 0.6 at CR value 0.3 by the measure combination $S_{SL} + S_{AB} + S_{SM} + S_{CO}$ is more desirable because the size of the summary is smaller. As expected, our summarization approach perform worse in the scenario with FL where we use S_{SM}. This is due to the fact that the survey participants had to consider the highly subjective factor of similarity.

6 Conclusion and Future Work

In this paper, we discuss how to generate and summarize explanations for Linked Data. We present an ontology to describe explanation metadata and discuss publishing explanation metadata as Linked Data. In addition, we presented five summarization measures to summarize explanations. We evaluate different combinations of these measures. The evaluation shows that our approach produces high quality rankings for summarizing explanation statements. Our summarized explanations are also highly accurate with *F-score* values ranging from 0.6 to 0.72 for small summaries. Our approach outperforms the sentence graph based ontology summarization approach.

In the future work, we would like to explore how we can effectively present explanations and summarized explanations using different kinds of user interfaces and user interactions. We would like to explore how we can effectively use the summarization rankings while presenting information in personalized scenarios. Finally, we are going to evaluate the impact of explanations and summarized explanations on end-users.

Acknowledgments. This work is supported by the ANR CONTINT program under the Kolflow project (ANR-2010-CORD-021-02).

References

1. RDF semantics. W3C recommendation (2004)
2. Alani, H., Harris, S., O'Neil, B.: Winnowing ontologies based on application use. In: Sure, Y., Domingue, J. (eds.) ESWC 2006. LNCS, vol. 4011, pp. 185–199. Springer, Heidelberg (2006)
3. Angele, J., Moench, E., Oppermann, H., Staab, S., Wenke, D.: Ontology-based query and answering in chemistry: Ontonova project halo. In: Fensel, D., Sycara, K., Mylopoulos, J. (eds.) ISWC 2003. LNCS, vol. 2870, pp. 913–928. Springer, Heidelberg (2003)
4. Araújo, R., Pinto, H.S.: Towards semantics-based ontology similarity. In: Shvaiko, P., Euzenat, J., Giunchiglia, F., He, B. (eds.) Proceedings of the 2nd International Workshop on Ontology Matching (OM-2007) at ISWC-2007/ASWC-2007 (2007)
5. Berners-Lee, T.: Linked Data. W3C Design Issues (2006), `http://www.w3.org/DesignIssues/LinkedData.html`
6. Bizer, C.: Quality-Driven Information Filtering in the Context of Web-Based Information Systems. Ph.D. thesis, Freie Universität Berlin (2007)
7. Bonatti, P., Hogan, A., Polleres, A., Sauro, L.: Robust and scalable linked data reasoning incorporating provenance and trust annotations. Web Semantics: Science, Services and Agents on the World Wide Web 9(2), 165–201 (2011)
8. Carroll, J.J., Bizer, C., Hayes, P., Stickler, P.: Named graphs, provenance and trust. In: Proceedings of the 14th International Conference on World Wide Web, WWW 2005, pp. 613–622. ACM, New York (2005)
9. Corby, O., Dieng-Kuntz, R., Gandon, F., Faron-Zucker, C.: Searching the Semantic Web: approximate query processing based on ontologies. IEEE Intelligent Systems 21(1), 20–27 (2006)
10. Eduard, H.: Text summarization. In: Mitkov, R. (ed.) The Oxford Handbook of Computational Linguistics. Oxford University Press (2005)
11. Forcher, B., Sintek, M., Roth-Berghofer, T., Dengel, A.: Explanation-aware system design of the semantic search engine koios. In: Proc. of the the 5th Int'l. Workshop on Explanation-Aware Computing (2010)

12. Hasan, R., Gandon, F.: A Brief Review of Explanation in the Semantic Web. In: Workshop on Explanation-aware Computing (ExaCt 2012), European Conference on Artificial Intelligence (ECAI 2012) (2012)
13. Heath, T., Bizer, C.: Linked Data: Evolving the Web into a Global Data Space, 1st edn. Morgan & Claypool (2011), http://linkeddatabook.com/
14. Horridge, M., Parsia, B., Sattler, U.: Laconic and precise justifications in OWL. In: Sheth, A.P., Staab, S., Dean, M., Paolucci, M., Maynard, D., Finin, T., Thirunarayan, K. (eds.) ISWC 2008. LNCS, vol. 5318, pp. 323–338. Springer, Heidelberg (2008)
15. Järvelin, K., Kekäläinen, J.: Cumulated gain-based evaluation of IR techniques. ACM Trans. Inf. Syst. 20(4), 422–446 (2002)
16. Kagal, L., Jacobi, I., Khandelwal, A.: Gasping for AIR – why we need linked rules and justifications on the semantic web. Tech. Rep. MIT-CSAIL-TR-2011-023, MIT (2011)
17. Kotowski, J., Bry, F.: A perfect match for reasoning, explanation and reason maintenance: OWL 2 RL and semantic wikis. In: Proc. of 5th Semantic Wiki Workshop (2010)
18. Li, N., Motta, E.: Evaluations of user-driven ontology summarization. In: Cimiano, P., Pinto, H.S. (eds.) EKAW 2010. LNCS, vol. 6317, pp. 544–553. Springer, Heidelberg (2010)
19. McGuinness, D.L., da Silva, P.P.: Infrastructure for web explanations. In: Fensel, D., Sycara, K., Mylopoulos, J. (eds.) ISWC 2003. LNCS, vol. 2870, pp. 113–129. Springer, Heidelberg (2003)
20. McGuinness, D., Furtado, V., Pinheiro da Silva, P., Ding, L., Glass, A., Chang, C.: Explaining semantic web applications. In: Semantic Web Engineering in the Knowledge Society (2008)
21. McGuinness, D., Pinheiro da Silva, P.: Explaining answers from the semantic web: the inference web approach. Web Semantics: Science, Services and Agents on the World Wide Web 1(4), 397–413 (2004)
22. McSherry, F., Najork, M.: Computing information retrieval performance measures efficiently in the presence of tied scores. In: Macdonald, C., Ounis, I., Plachouras, V., Ruthven, I., White, R.W. (eds.) ECIR 2008. LNCS, vol. 4956, pp. 414–421. Springer, Heidelberg (2008)
23. Peroni, S., Motta, E., d'Aquin, M.: Identifying key concepts in an ontology, through the integration of cognitive principles with statistical and topological measures. In: Domingue, J., Anutariya, C. (eds.) ASWC 2008. LNCS, vol. 5367, pp. 242–256. Springer, Heidelberg (2008)
24. Pinheiro da Silva, P., McGuinness, D., Del Rio, N., Ding, L.: Inference web in action: Lightweight use of the proof markup language. In: Sheth, A.P., Staab, S., Dean, M., Paolucci, M., Maynard, D., Finin, T., Thirunarayan, K. (eds.) ISWC 2008. LNCS, vol. 5318, pp. 847–860. Springer, Heidelberg (2008)
25. Pinheiro da Silva, P., McGuinness, D., Fikes, R.: A proof markup language for semantic web services. Information Systems 31(4-5), 381–395 (2006)
26. Steinberger, J., Jezek, K.: Evaluation measures for text summarization. Computing and Informatics 28(2), 251–275 (2009)
27. Zhang, X., Cheng, G., Qu, Y.: Ontology summarization based on RDF sentence graph. In: Proceedings of the 16th International Conference on World Wide Web, WWW 2007, pp. 707–716. ACM, New York (2007)

Hybrid Acquisition of Temporal Scopes for RDF Data

Anisa Rula[1], Matteo Palmonari[1], Axel-Cyrille Ngonga Ngomo[2], Daniel Gerber[2], Jens Lehmann[2], and Lorenz Bühmann[2]

[1] University of Milano-Bicocca, Italy
{anisa.rula,palmonari}@disco.unimib.it
[2] Universität Leipzig, Institut für Informatik, AKSW, Germany
{ngonga,dgerber,lehmann,buehmann}@informatik.uni-leipzig.de

Abstract. Information on the temporal interval of validity for facts described by RDF triples plays an important role in a large number of applications. Yet, most of the knowledge bases available on the Web of Data do not provide such information in an explicit manner. In this paper, we present a generic approach which addresses this drawback by inserting temporal information into knowledge bases. Our approach combines two types of information to associate RDF triples with time intervals. First, it relies on temporal information gathered from the document Web by an extension of the fact validation framework DeFacto. Second, it harnesses the time information contained in knowledge bases. This knowledge is combined within a three-step approach which comprises the steps matching, selection and merging. We evaluate our approach against a corpus of facts gathered from Yago2 by using DBpedia and Freebase as input and different parameter settings for the underlying algorithms. Our results suggest that we can detect temporal information for facts from DBpedia with an F-measure of up to 70%.

Keywords: #eswc2014Rula, Temporal Information Extraction, Temporal Semantic Web, Temporal Scoping, Fact Checking.

1 Introduction

Over the last few years, the Linked Open Data (LOD) Cloud has developed into a large amalgamation of diverse data sets from several domains [2]. Some of these data sets provide encyclopedic knowledge on the real world. For example, DBpedia [12] contains RDF extracted from the infoboxes of Wikipedia.[1] While some of the statements contained in the LOD Cloud are universally valid (e.g., the fact that the birth place of Mario Balotelli is Palermo), a large portion of the facts which are referred to by the triples in the LOD Cloud are only valid within a certain time interval, which we call their *time scope*. For example, DBpedia states that Mario Balotelli plays for the teams Inter Milan and Manchester City.

[1] http://wikipedia.org

V. Presutti et al. (Eds.): ESWC 2014, LNCS 8465, pp. 488–503, 2014.

While the semantics of the predicate `dbo:team`[2] remains a matter of discussion, manifold applications such as question answering [20], temporal reasoning and temporal information retrieval [9] require having the temporal scope of facts such as "Mario Balotelli plays for the team Inter Milan from 2007 to 2010".

In this paper, we introduce an approach for detecting the temporal scope of facts referred to by triples (short: the temporal scope of the triples). Given a fact (i.e., an RDF triple), our approach aims to detect the time points at which the temporal scope of the triple begins and ends. Two sources can be envisaged for gathering such information: the document Web and the Linked Data Web. Our approach is able to take advantage of both: the document Web is made use of by extending upon a fact validation approach [11], which allows detecting Web documents which corroborate a triple. In contrast to typical search engines, the system does not just search for textual occurrences of parts of the statement, but tries to find webpages which contain the actual statement phrased in natural language. The second source of information for time scopes is the Web of Data itself. Here, we use the RDF data sets that contain the facts, e.g., DBpedia and Freebase, for possible time scopes and devise an algorithm for combining the results extracted from Web documents with those fetched from RDF sources. The algorithm consists of three main steps. First, the evidence extracted from Web documents is *matched* against a set of relevant time intervals to obtain a significance score for each interval. Second, a small set of more significant intervals is *selected*. Finally, the selected intervals are *merged*, when possible, by considering their mutual temporal relations. The set of disconnected intervals [1] returned by the algorithm defines the temporal scope of the fact. We also propose two *normalization* strategies that can be applied to the data extracted from Web documents before running the algorithm, to account for the significance of dates appearing in the documents corroborating the input fact.

The main contributions of this paper are:

- We introduce a temporal extension of the DeFacto framework based on a sliding window approach on fact-confirming documents.
- We present an approach for modeling a space of relevant time intervals for a fact starting from dates extracted from RDF triples.
- We devise a three-phase algorithm for temporal scoping, i.e. for mapping facts to sets of time intervals, which integrates the previous steps via matching, selection and merging.
- Finally, we evaluate the integrated algorithm on facts extracted from DBpedia and Freebase against the Yago2 knowledge base.

The rest of this paper is structured as follows: Section 2 describes our general approach and the system infrastructure. In Section 3, we describe how temporal information is extracted from web pages using a temporal extension of the DeFacto algorithm [11]. Section 4 shows how this information can be mapped to a set of time intervals specifying its temporal scope. We then evaluate the approach by using temporal scopes from Yago2 as gold standard and facts from

[2] `dbo` stands for `http://dbpedia.org/ontology/`

DBpedia and Freebase as input in Section 5. We give an overview of related work in Section 6. Finally, we conclude and give pointers to future work.

2 Problem Definition and Approach Overview

Linked Open Data describes resources identified by HTTP URIs by representing their properties and links to other resources using the RDF language. Given an infinite set $\mathcal{U}$ of URIs, an infinite set $\mathcal{B}$ of blank nodes, and an infinite set $\mathcal{L}$ of literals, a statement $< s, p, o > \in (\mathcal{U} \cup \mathcal{B}) \times \mathcal{U} \times (\mathcal{U} \cup \mathcal{B} \cup \mathcal{L})$ is called an *RDF triple*. As the use of blank nodes is discouraged for LOD [3], we will assume that the subject and the property are URIs, while the object can be either a URI or a literal.

Most of the resources described in the LOD Cloud represent real-world objects (e.g., soccer players, places or teams); we use the term *entities* as a short form for *named individuals* as defined in the OWL 2 specification. According to the LOD principles [3], we assume that each entity e can be dereferenced. The result of the dereferencing is an RDF document denoted d^e which represents a *description* of the entity e. We say that d^e *describes* e and d^e is an *entity document* [8]. As an example, an entity document d^e returned by DBpedia in NTriples [6] format contains all the RDF triples where e occurs as a subject. In this work, RDF triples occurring in entity documents are called *facts*.

A *fact* represents a relation between the subject and the object of the triple and, intuitively, it is considered true when the relation is acknowledged to hold. We use the term *volatile facts* to refer to facts that change over time, and are represented by triples whose validity can be associated with a temporal context (e.g., <Balotelli, team, Inter_Milan> refers to a fact occurring from 2007 to 2010). Adopting a terminology used in previous work on temporal information extraction, we call *temporal scope* of facts the specification of the time during which facts occured [19].

Despite several models to represent time into RDF having been suggested, only a small amount of RDF data sets annotate triples with their temporal scope. This is partly due to the sophisticated meta-modeling strategies needed to represent temporal annotations in RDF [18]. As a consequence, several knowledge bases contain *volatile facts* without explicitly annotating the triples with information about their temporal scope. We define a *temporal annotation* of a fact a couple $< f, [t_i, t_j] >$, where f is a fact and $[t_i, t_j]$ is a time interval delimited by a starting time point t_i and an ending time point t_j. In this paper we regard time as a discrete, linearly ordered domain, as proposed in [7]. In our discrete time model, two intervals $[t_i, t_j]$ and $[t_h, t_k]$ are *disconnected* iff $t_j < t_h$, or $t_k < t_i$, and *connected* otherwise. The *temporal scope* of a fact f is defined as a set of - possibly many - temporal annotations of f with *disconnected* time intervals.

The problem addressed in this paper can be defined as follows: for each volatile fact $f \in F$ extracted from a data set Δ, we map f to a set $TS^f = \{[t_{i_1}, t_{j_1}], ..., [t_{i_n}, t_{j_n}]\}$ where TS^f defines the temporal scopes of f and each element represents a time interval when the fact is true. Figure 1 gives an overview

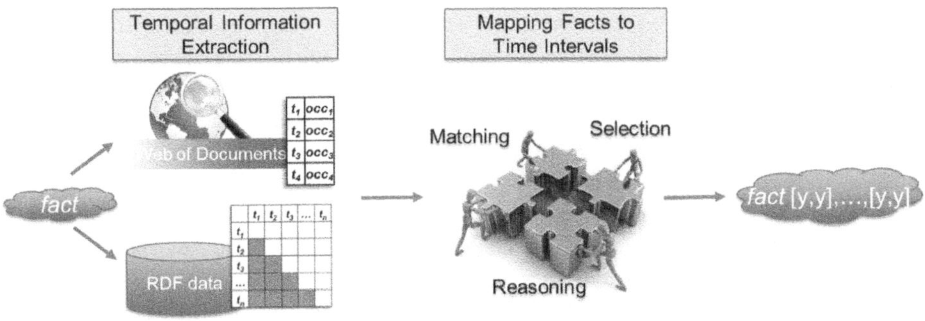

Fig. 1. Approach Overview

of our solution. Evidence is extracted from Web and RDF documents and a space of possible time intervals relevant to the fact is built; the evidence extracted from Web documents is matched against the space of relevant time intervals and a final set of temporal scopes are associated with the input fact.

3 Temporal Information Extraction

In this section we describe the methods we adopted to extract temporal information from two sources: the Web of documents and the Web of Data. The latter source contains the facts to be assigned with a temporal scope.

3.1 Extraction of Temporal Information from the Web

Temporal DeFacto is an extension to the DeFacto framework presented in [11]. The system takes an RDF triple as input and returns a confidence value for this triple as well as possible evidence for the fact. The evidence consists of a set of webpages, textual excerpts from those pages and meta-information on the pages. The first task of DeFacto is to retrieve webpages which are relevant for the given task. The retrieval is carried out by issuing several queries to a search engine. These queries are computed by verbalizing the RDF triple using natural-language patterns extracted by the BOA framework [5]. As a next step, the highest ranked webpages for each query are retrieved, which are candidates for being sources for the input fact. Both the search engine queries as well as the retrieval of webpages are executed in parallel to keep the response time for users within a reasonable limit. Once a webpage has been retrieved, we extract plain text by removing HTML markup and apply our fact confirmation approach on this text. In essence, the algorithm decides whether the web page contains natural language formulations of the input fact. If no webpage confirms a fact according to DeFacto, then the system falls back on light-weight NLP techniques and computes whether the webpage does at least provide useful evidence. In addition to fact confirmation, the system computes different indicators for the trustworthiness of a webpage as presented in [15]. These indicators are of central importance because a single trustworthy webpage confirming a fact may be a more useful source than several webpages with low trustworthiness. In addition to finding and displaying useful sources, DeFacto also outputs a general confidence value for the input fact. This confidence value ranges between [0, 1] and serves as an indicator for the user: Higher values indicate that the found sources appear to confirm the fact and can be trusted. Low values mean that not much evidence for the fact could be found on the Web and that the websites that do confirm the fact (if such exist) only display low trustworthiness. The generated provenance output can also be saved directly as RDF and abides by the PROV Ontology[3]. The source code of the DeFacto algorithms and DeFacto's user interface are open-source[4].

Temporal Extension of DeFacto. To also incorporate time information into the fact validation process we extended DeFacto as follows. On all retrieved webpages we apply the Stanford Named Entity Tagger[5] and extract all entities of the *Date* class. We then examine all occurrences $occ_{so} \in Occ_{so}$ of the subject and object label of the input fact (or their surface forms, e.g. "Manchester United F.C." might also be called "ManU") in a proximity of less than 20 tokens. We then build a local context window of n characters before and after occ_{so} and analyze all contained *Date* entities. Finally we return a distribution of all dates and their number of occurrences in a given context. Hence, the output of temporal DeFacto for a fact f $<s, p, o>$ can be regarded as a vector DFV over all possible time points t_i whose i^{th} entry is the number of co-occurrences of s or o with t_i. We will use the function $dfv_i(f, t_i)$ to denote the value of DFV_i for the fact f.

3.2 Extraction of Temporal Information from RDF Documents

Given a set F of facts to map to time intervals, we first identify the set of entities E that occur as subjects for the set of facts in F. Given the entity e subject of the fact, we use the HTTP content negotiation mechanism to retrieve the entity document d^e. As an example, given the fact *<Cristiano Ronaldo, team, Real Madrid>*, we extract the RDF document describing *Cristiano Ronaldo*. Once an entity document has been retrieved, we extract time points from the temporal triples that are contained in the entity document. We define a *temporal triple* a triple of the form $< s, p, t >$, where the object t is a time point. As an example, although DBpedia does not provide temporal annotations for the fact *<Cristiano Ronaldo, team, Manchester United>*, it has the temporal triples *<Cristiano Ronaldo, years, 2009>* and *<Cristiano Ronaldo, youthYears, 1995>*. Some of these dates refer to other facts of the same entity; however, the link between the facts containing the dates and the facts these dates were related to has been lost. We use temporal triples available in the knowledge base under the assumption that this information can be *relevant* to define the scope of facts.

[3] `http://www.w3.org/2011/prov/`

[4] `https://github.com/AKSW/DeFacto`

[5] `http://www-nlp.stanford.edu/software/CRF-NER.shtml`

Given an entity e subject of a fact, we identify temporal triples in the entity document d^e and extract dates by using regular expressions, which identify standard date formats and variations. In this step we adopt an approach that was used in previous work [18]. We add to this set of extracted dates a date representing the *current time*. As a result of this step, each fact $f \in F$ is associated with a set of *relevant time points* T^e extracted from the RDF document describing the subject of the fact. In principle, our approach can consider dates represented at any granularity level; in the following examples and in the experiments, time is represented at the year level similarly as in other related work [13, 19].

Intuitively, we want to use the relevant time points T^e associated with an entity e to identify a set of most *relevant time intervals* for scoping facts having e as subject; in this way, we can reduce the space of all possible time intervals considered for an individual fact. The set of time intervals relevant to an entity e is defined as the set of all time intervals whose starting and ending points are members of T^e. Relevant time intervals are represented using an upper triangular matrix, i.e., a square matrix where all entries below the diagonal are 0.

Given a set T^e of relevant time points for an entity e, a relevant time interval matrix (*Relevant Interval Matrix* for short) RIM^e is an upper triangular matrix of size $|T^e| \times |T^e|$ defined as follows:

$$RIM^e = \begin{bmatrix} rim^e_{t_1,t_1} & \cdots & \cdots & rim^e_{t_1,t_n} \\ 0 & \ddots & & \\ 0 & 0 & \ddots & \\ 0 & 0 & 0 & rim^e_{t_n,t_n} \end{bmatrix} \quad (1)$$

Columns and rows of a relevant interval matrix RIM^e for an entity e are indexed by ordered time points in T^e; each cell $rim^e_{t_i,t_j}$ with $i, j > 0$ represents the time interval $[t_i, t_j]$, where $t_i, t_j \in T^e$. At the moment we assign a placeholder value `null` to each cell $rim^e_{i,j}$ such that $i \leq j$. In the matching phase, we will use entity-level RIMs as schemes for fact-level matrices; in these fact-level matrices `null` values will be replaced by scores that represent the significance of intervals for individual facts. Observe that the use of an upper triangular matrix is suitable for representing time intervals since the time intervals represented in the cells in the lower part of the matrix $(i > j)$ are not valid by definition. Also note that, the cells in the diagonal of the RIM^e matrix represent time intervals whose start and end points coincide.

4 Mapping Facts to Time Intervals

The process used to provide a final mapping between a volatile fact and a set of time intervals defining its temporal scope consists of three phases: 1) Temporal Distribution-to-Time Intervals Matching, 2) Time Intervals Selection 3) Time Interval Merging. Figure 2 shows an overview of the application of the three phases to a fact f, with a RIM built from a set of four relevant time points

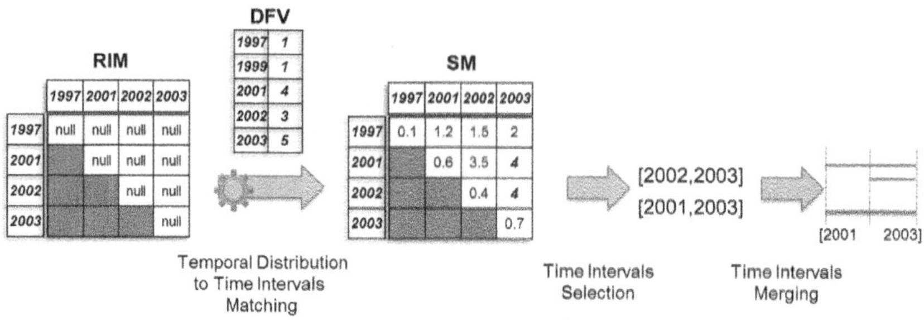

Fig. 2. Time Interval Mapping Overview

extracted from the entity document. The algorithm can take as input the vectors returned by Temporal DeFacto, i.e., DFVs, as well vectors normalized using two functions defined in Section 4.2.

4.1 Matching, Selection and Reasoning

Temporal Distribution to Time Intervals Matching. The inputs of the matching phase for a fact f that has an entity e as subject are the following: a relevant interval matrix RIM^e extracted the entity document d^e and a time distribution vector $DFV^{e,f}$. Probabilistic time distribution vectors obtained by normalization (see Section 4.2) can be also used as input instead of DFVs. The matching phase returns an *interval-to-fact significance matrix*, Significance Matrix (SM) for short, $SM^{e,f}$ associated with the fact f. An $SM^{e,f}$ is a triangular square matrix having the same size and structure of the input RIM^e. As a next step, `null` values of a RIM^e are replaced with significance scores returned by a matching function.

In practice, to build an $SM^{e,f}$ of a fact f with subject e, we match a fact-level DFV^f associated to the fact f against an entity-level RIM^e, i.e. the matching aims to inject a time distribution vector into RIM^e by producing a significance matrix $SM^{e,f}$. The matching function $match(DFV^f, RIM^e) = SM^{e,f}$, where e is an entity and f is a fact, is given as follows:

$$sm_{i,j} = \begin{cases} 0 & \text{if } rim_{i,j} = 0 \\ \frac{\sum_{k=i}^{j} dfv(f,k)}{(j-i)+1} & \text{if } rim_{i,j} = null \wedge i < j \\ dfv(f,i) * w_{i,j} & \text{if } rim_{i,j} = null \wedge i = j \end{cases} \tag{2}$$

Since the denominator $(j-i)+1$ in the formula used in case two represents the number of time points included in the interval $[i,j]$, the formula is equal to the average of DFVs for the time points contained in the interval. As an example, the score for a cell $sm_{1995,2000}$ is defined as the average value of DFV for the time points between 1995 and 2000 (including the starting and ending points). Since the elements in the diagonal have length equal to 1, the formula used in case three is equivalent to multiplying the score computed with the formula used in case two for a weight $w_{i,j}$; we use this weight to penalize the scores in the diagonal as we discovered that formula in case two would assign high scores to the element in the diagonal, thus favoring time intervals with length equal to 1 in the selection phase. Intuitively we want to penalize elements in the diagonal unless they are the only significant values selectable in the SM matrix. The weight is defined as inversely proportional to the difference between the length of the considered interval (equal to 1) and $length(DFV^f)$ the length of the DFV vector as follows:

$$w_{i,j} = \frac{1}{c * length(DFV^f)} \tag{3}$$

where c is a constant used to control the score reduction ratio applied to the elements in the diagonal of the SM matrices.

Mapping Selection. Once we have a set of significance matrices $SM^{e,f_1}, ...,$ SM^{e,f_n}, each one associated with a fact f_i referred to e, we then select the time intervals that might be mapped to the considered facts. We propose two basic selection functions that use SMs; both functions can select more than one interval to associate with a fact f. The *top-k* function selects the k intervals that have best scores in the SM matrix. The *neighbor-x* selects a set of intervals whose significance score is close to the maximum significance score in the SM matrix, up to a certain threshold. In other terms, we define the *neighborhood of the time interval with maximum significance score* as the set of intervals whose significance scores fall in the range defined by the maximum score as upper bound and by a threshold based on a parameter x as lower bound. The threshold is linearly proportional to the maximum significance score, so that the threshold is higher when the maximum significance is higher (e.g., 0.9) and lower when the maximum significance is lower. The parametric function *neighbor-x* with an SM and a parameter x given as input is defined as follows:

$$neighbor(SM, x) = \left\{ [i,j] \mid sm_{i,j} \geq maxScore - \frac{x * maxScore}{100} \right\} \tag{4}$$

The two basic functions *top-k* and *neighbor-x* can be combined into a function *neighbor-k-x* that selects the top-k intervals in the neighborhood of the interval with higher significance score. Observe that neighbor-0 is equal to top-1 for every value of the parameter x. The neighbor-k function behaves as a filter on the results of the top-k function, by selecting only intervals whose significance is close enough to the most significant interval.

Interval Merging via Reasoning. Finally, we use rules based on Allen's interval algebra to merge the selected time intervals and map each fact to a set of disconnected intervals. Let a and b be two time intervals associated with a fact f and defined respectively by $[t_i, t_j]$ and $[t_h, t_k]$; we merge a and b into an interval defined by $[min(t_i, t_h), max(t_j, t_k)]$ whenever one of the following conditions, each one based on Allen's algebra relations [1], is verified:

- a overlap b or a is-overlapped-by b
- a meets b or a is-met-by b
- a during b or b during a
- a starts b or b starts a
- a finishes b or b finishes a

The temporal scope of a fact is defined by the set of disconnected time intervals mapped to it after the interval merging phase.

4.2 Temporal Distribution Normalization

Two types of normalization functions can be envisaged: *local normalization* and *global normalization*. These functions aim to transform the output vector of temporal DeFacto (the DFV vector) into a probabilistic time distribution (PTD) vector. Here, the main idea of the local normalization is that the PTD contains the probability that the fact $<s,\ p,\ o'>$ should be mapped to a given time point t_i. The main drawback of such a normalization is that it does not take the PTD vector for other facts $<s,\ p,\ o'>$ into consideration. We thus defined global normalization functions that allow transforming the output of temporal DeFacto for all triples with subject s and predicate p. When normalization strategies are adopted, the PTDs are used instead of DFVs in Equation 2.

Local Normalization. Several approaches can be used to generate a PTD. The approach we follow is based on the frequency-based interpretation of the output of Temporal DeFacto: The ith entry in DFV basically states the number of times f co-occurred with the time point t_i in a relevant document. Thus, the probability that f co-occurs with the time point t_i is:

$$PTD_i = \frac{DFV_i}{\sum_{j=1}^{|T^e|} DFV_j}. \tag{5}$$

Global Normalization. Our approach to the computation of a global normalization was based on χ^2 statistics. Given a resource s, a predicate p and a point t_i in time, the aim of the normalization was to compute the significance of the value of DFV_i. Let E_i be the expected value of DFV_i for the time t_i, computed as average value of all DFV_i entries for the resource s over all objects of p. The significance of the time t_i for the triple $<s,\ p,\ o_j>$ with vector DFV is then

$$\frac{(DFV_i - E_i)^2}{E_i}. \tag{6}$$

5 Experimental Evaluation

5.1 Experimental Setup

Methodology and Gold Standard. To evaluate our approach we acquire the temporal scopes of a population of volatile facts from three different domains and compare the results of our method against a gold standard. We use manually curated data from Yago2[6] as gold standard. We omitted all facts with `null` values, i.e. missing starting or end time. We choose Yago2 because it is one of the few large open-source knowledge bases that provides temporal annotations for a significant number of facts (714,925 time points associated with facts).

Significant parts of DBpedia[7], Freebase[8] and Yago2 are extracted from the same source which makes it possible to automatically map some facts in DBpedia or Freebase to facts in Yago2. We therefore use facts in DBpedia, and Freebase in our experiments and we extract RDF data from these sources. We additionally consider the case where RIMs (see Section 3.2) are created with the time points returned by Temporal DeFacto, to simulate the case when temporal information from RDF data is not available.

Properties of Interests. The facts considered in our experiments are defined using the top three properties having the largest number of occurrences in Yago2. Table 1 shows the properties and the number of facts for each property.

Table 1. Properties of interest and the number of facts for each property

Property	Number of facts
<ismarriedTo>	3,501
<holdsPoliticalPosition>	5,610
<playsFor>	114,367

Because we have a limit of queries sent through temporal DeFacto, which is imposed by traffic limitations of its underlying search engine, we perform the experiment on a subset of all available facts by applying some selection rules: the top 1000 facts on the most important soccer players who are born after 1983 ($\leq$30 years old), the top 1000 facts on politicians born after 1940, and the top 500 facts on celebrities born after 1930.

Measures. In order to evaluate the accuracy of our method, we measured the degree to which the temporal scope we retrieved is correct w.r.t. the gold standard. Therefore, for each fact, we consider the degree of overlap between the retrieved intervals and the interval in the gold standard. This degree of overlap can be computed by adapting the well-known metrics of precision, recall and F_1-measure to this problem leveraging the discrete time model. Intuitively, the precision of a temporal scope can be measured by the number of time points in the temporal scope generated by our solution that fall into the time interval in the gold standard. The recall of our solution can be measured by the number of time points in the gold standard that are covered by the temporal scope.

6 `http://www.mpi-inf.mpg.de/yago-naga/yago/`
7 `http://dbpedia.org/`
8 `http://freebase.com/`

Let $R(f)$ be the set of time points in the temporal scopes retrieved for a fact f and Ref(f) be the set of time points included in the reference temporal scopes for f; the following formulas capture the intuitions described above:

$$precision(f) = \frac{|R(f) \cap Ref(f)|}{|R(f)|}, \quad recall(f) = \frac{|R(f) \cap Ref(f)|}{|Ref(f)|}. \tag{7}$$

Precision and recall for a fact f can be combined as usual in F_1-measure defined as the harmonic mean of precision and recall. Note that: when $precision(f) = 1$, each interval in the retrieved temporal scope is included in the interval of the gold standard; when $recall(f) = 1$, all the time points in the interval of the gold standard are covered by the retrieved temporal scopes; when $F_1(f) = 1$ the temporal scope contains exactly the same time points as the gold standard.

Baseline. Given that no prior algorithm aims to tackle exactly the task at hand, we computed the precision, recall and F-measure that a random approach would achieve. To this end, we assumed that given the restrictions we set on the intervals within which our solutions must lie (e.g., 1983-2014 for soccer players), a random solution would simply guess for each date whether it should be part of the final solution. This serves as a lower bound for the score a temporal scoping algorithm should achieve.

5.2 Results and Discussion

In order to evaluate the overall accuracy of scoping facts with temporal intervals we need to set up different configurations for each component of each phase. Hence, we approximate the best configurations for some key components of the proposed approach by using genetic programming[9] based on opt4j[10], an open-source framework comprising a set of optimization algorithms. Genetic programming allows to determine an appropriate configuration of our approach. In the configuration setup we consider the interval selection functions and the merging process of the selected intervals through reasoning (see Section 4.1) as well as the normalizations strategies applied to the Temporal DeFacto Vectors to obtain Probabilistic Temporal Distributions (PTDs) (see Section 4.2).

In the first experiment, we compare the best configurations for properties of interests, i.e., (1) `isMarriedTo`, (2) `holdsPoliticalPosition` and (3) `playsFor`. The space of relevant time intervals (RIM) is built from time points collected from three different sources, i.e., Temporal DeFacto, Freebase and DBpedia. Table 2 reports for each property and for each source the best F-measure achieved by our approach. In one case, the RIM and the scores are defined with evidence retrieved only from the web of documents (TempDeFacto for short). In other two cases, the RIM is build with dates extracted from the web of data (Freebase or DBpedia) and the scores are computed by injecting evidence from the web of documents into this matrix. We observe that our approach perform much better

[9] `http://goo.gl/2ve3xP`
[10] `http://opt4j.sourceforge.net/`

Table 2. Results of best configurations for all property of interests

Property	Baseline		Temp DeFacto			Freebase			DBpedia		
	#facts	F_1	Config	#facts	F_1	Config	#facts	F_1	Config	#facts	F_1
1	500	0.163	top-3	311	**0.511**	top-1 loc	213	0.477	top-1 loc	264	0.505
2	1000	0.263	top-3	709	0.586	neigh-10-2	242	0.549	neigh-10	702	**0.699**
3	1000	0.207	top-3	709	0.545	neigh-10	524	0.547	neigh-10	705	**0.600**

than the baseline, which does not use a prior algorithm, for every property and for every source used to construct the RIMs. The best configurations is obtained for the property `holdsPoliticalPosition` with time points extracted from DBpedia and with selection function neighbor-k with $x = 10$. The configuration that extracts time points from DBpedia outperforms Freebase and Temporal DeFacto results except for the property `isMarriedTo`. The reason for this major gain can be explained with the quantity and quality of relevant time points extracted from the three sources. The problem is that Freebase and Temporal DeFacto do not provide enough time points which can prevent the effective identification of intervals. We notice that, while local normalization improves the results in one experiment (for the property `isMarriedTo`), the global normalization strategy is never optimal in any experiment. We will now compare the reasoning and selection functions.

Different Components. Table 3 shows the contribution of reasoning for the best configurations identified in the previous experiment. We use the full approach with and without reasoning and apply it on the three properties. We observe that enabling reasoning improves the performance of the temporal scoping of facts. This validates our motivation behind using Allen's Algebra, as it can get rid of incomplete intervals.

Table 3. Effect of using reasoning during temporal scoping from the three best configurations

Property	Source	Config	With reasoning		Without reasoning	
			# facts	F_1	# facts	F_1
1	Temp DeFacto	top-3	311	0.511	505	0.467
2	DBpedia	neigh-10	702	0.699	822	0.667
3	DBpedia	neigh-10	705	0.60	977	0.563

Based on these results, we can evaluate the effect of selection functions and their application in DBpedia for the property `holdsPoliticalPosition`. Figure 3 compares four configurations. We observe that recall is improved when k is increased but on the other side precision decreases as the approach returns larger intervals including the correct interval and additional incorrect time points. The best precision-recall is given with the combined selection function, neighbor-k with $x = 10$.

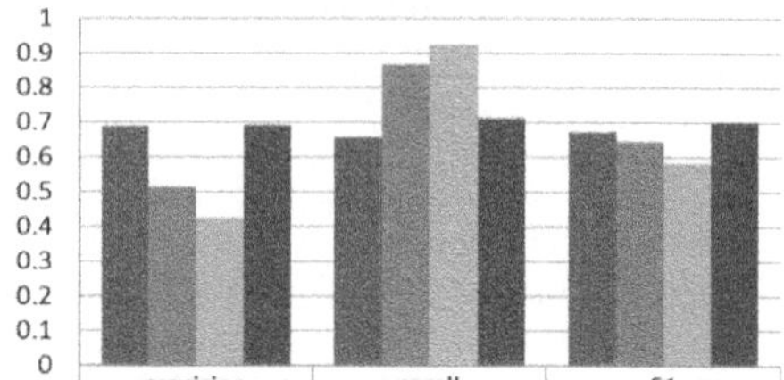

	precision	recall	F1
top-k, k = 1	0.686	0.654	0.67
top-k, k = 2	0.515	0.865	0.645
top-k, k = 3	0.426	0.924	0.583
neighbor x = 10	0.689	0.709	0.699

Fig. 3. Effect of using selection function during temporal scoping of `holdsPoliticalPosition` from DBpedia source

6 Related Work

The work presented in this paper relies on two areas of research: the extraction of time information and fact checking. **Extraction of Time Intervals.** Several machine learning approaches have been developed to discover links between events and temporal information (e.g., dates) into one or more sentences of a document where the event is mentioned [21]. In alternative, the work in [10] presents a method to link events or facts with timestamps according to a classification approach. In contrast to these approaches, our approach is completely unsupervised and it does not need training data. Temporal Information Extraction (TIE) [13] is a more recent system that finds a maximal set of temporal annotations for events mentioned in a given sentence. Therewith, it can infer relations between these events using the temporal annotations. Instead of Allen-style intervals [1], TIE uses time points. However, this approach is not sufficient to extrapolate the temporal scope of facts because it focuses on the micro-reading of temporal annotations in single documents or sentences. Although the aim of temporal bounding [4] and our approach is the same since both retrieve temporal constraints given a fact, there are fundamental differences. NLP techniques employed in temporal bounding are more sophisticated but at the same time more expensive and extract evidence from the text on a limited corpus. Our approach uses softer, but more efficient, NLP techniques to extract evidence from the whole web. Moreover, our approach investigates how to complement evidence retrieve from texts with evidence from the web of data.

Timely Yago2 [9] has the objective of enriching facts with temporal scopes. Instead of using the original data source (i.e, Wikipedia) where the link between facts and time intervals is explicitly made available, our approach exploit the evidence from the web of data where facts are not associated with time intervals and the web of documents, i.e., free text evidence. Yago2 identify the time of a fact if the time of the entities occurring in the fact is known and the property occurring in the fact belongs to a predefined category. PRAVDA [22] is a recently proposed method to harvest basic and temporal facts from free text. The approach is based on a semi-supervised label propagation algorithm that determines the similarity between structured facts and textual facts. Yet, it does not use the verbalization of RDF triples to check for RDF triples in text like DeFacto does. The system CoTS provided in [19] is similar to our system since it also detects temporal scopes for facts. In contrast to our approach, CoTS relies on document meta-data such as its creation data to assign temporal scopes to facts. To ensure that it gathers enough information, CoTS aggregates evidences from a large number of documents to temporally scope a set of facts. This approach is complementary to our current approach and can easily be combined with it.

Fact Checking. Regarding the fact checking part of our approach, a very recent algorithm was developed in [14]. It describes an approach, which allows to evaluate the truth value of statements by querying the web and processing unstructured web pages. It is based on training a supervised classifier with features extracted from web pages. A difference to our own previous work on DeFacto [11] is that we optimised the extraction by considering a larger variety of features related to patterns found on websites and also combined those features with an analysis of the trustworthiness of web pages. In another line of research on fact checking in [16, 17], trustworthy is also a central element. The authors rely on a model based on hubs and authorities. This model allows to compute the trustworthiness of facts and websites by generating a k-partite network of pages and facts and propagating trustworthiness information across it. The approach returns a score for the trustworthiness of each fact. An older yet similar approach is that presented in [23]. Here, the idea is to use a 3-partite network of webpages, facts and objects and apply a propagation algorithm to compute weights for facts and webpages.

7 Conclusion and Future Work

In this paper, we presented an approach for mapping volatile facts to time intervals. Our approach is hybrid and combines information from the document Web and temporal statements included in knowledge bases. We evaluated our approach on volatile facts extracted from DBpedia and Freebase by using cleaned-up temporal scopes extracted from Yago2. The cleaning was made necessary by approximately 50% of the information in that knowledge base being either incomplete or inconsistent (begin after end). This underlines the *difficulty of the task at hand.* Our approach achieved promising results, delivering approximately 70% F-measure on the facts at hand. In future work, we will create a larger gold standard for evaluating temporal scopes. Finally, we will develop applications that use temporal information. For example, we plan to develop a temporal extension of the TBSL question answering framework that can answer questions such as "When did Balotelli play for Inter Milan?".

Acknowledgements. This research has been supported in part by FP7/2013-2015 COMSODE (under contract number FP7-ICT-611358).

References

[1] Allen, J.F.: Maintaining knowledge about temporal intervals. Communications of the ACM 26(11), 832–843 (1983)
[2] Auer, S., Lehmann, J., Ngonga Ngomo, A.-C.: Introduction to linked data and its lifecycle on the web. In: Polleres, A., d'Amato, C., Arenas, M., Handschuh, S., Kroner, P., Ossowski, S., Patel-Schneider, P. (eds.) Reasoning Web 2011. LNCS, vol. 6848, pp. 1–75. Springer, Heidelberg (2011)
[3] Bizer, C., Heath, T., Berners-Lee, T.: Linked Data - The Story So Far. In: IJSWIS, pp. 1–22 (2009)
[4] Derczynski, L., Gaizauskas, R.: Information retrieval for temporal bounding. In: 4th ICTIR, pp. 29:129–29:130. ACM (2013)
[5] Gerber, D., Ngomo, A.-C.N.: Extracting Multilingual Natural-Language Patterns for RDF Predicates. In: ten Teije, A., Völker, J., Handschuh, S., Stuckenschmidt, H., d'Acquin, M., Nikolov, A., Aussenac-Gilles, N., Hernandez, N. (eds.) EKAW 2012. LNCS, vol. 7603, pp. 87–96. Springer, Heidelberg (2012)
[6] Grant, J., Becket, D.: Rdf test cases - N-Triples. Technical report, W3C Recommendation (2004)
[7] Gutierrez, C., Hurtado, C.A., Vaisman, A.A.: Temporal RDF. In: Gómez-Pérez, A., Euzenat, J. (eds.) ESWC 2005. LNCS, vol. 3532, pp. 93–107. Springer, Heidelberg (2005)
[8] Heath, T., Bizer, C.: Linked Data: Evolving the Web into a Global Data Space. Synthesis Lectures on the Semantic Web. Morgan & Claypool Publishers (2011)
[9] Hoffart, J., Suchanek, F.M., Berberich, K., Weikum, G.: Yago2: A spatially and temporally enhanced knowledge base from wikipedia. Artificial Intelligence 194, 28–61 (2013)
[10] Hovy, D., Fan, J., Gliozzo, A., Patwardhan, S., Welty, C.: When did that happen?: linking events and relations to timestamps. In: 13th EACL (2012)
[11] Lehmann, J., Gerber, D., Morsey, M., Ngonga Ngomo, A.-C.: DeFacto - deep fact validation. In: Cudré-Mauroux, P., et al. (eds.) ISWC 2012, Part I. LNCS, vol. 7649, pp. 312–327. Springer, Heidelberg (2012)
[12] Lehmann, J., Isele, R., Jakob, M., Jentzsch, A., Kontokostas, D., Mendes, P.N., Hellmann, S., Morsey, M., van Kleef, P., Auer, S., Bizer, C.: DBpedia - a large-scale, multilingual knowledge base extracted from wikipedia. In: SWJ (2014)
[13] Ling, X., Weld, D.S.: Temporal information extraction. In: 25th AAAI (2010)
[14] Mehdi Samadi, M.B.: Manuela Veloso. OpenEval: Web information query evaluation. In: 27th AAAI (2013)
[15] Nakamura, S., Konishi, S., Jatowt, A., Ohshima, H., Kondo, H., Tezuka, T., Oyama, S., Tanaka, K.: Trustworthiness analysis of web search results. In: Kovács, L., Fuhr, N., Meghini, C. (eds.) ECDL 2007. LNCS, vol. 4675, pp. 38–49. Springer, Heidelberg (2007)
[16] Pasternack, J., Roth, D.: Generalized fact-finding. In: 20th WWW (2011)
[17] Pasternack, J., Roth, D.: Making better informed trust decisions with generalized fact-finding. In: 20th IJCAI (2011)
[18] Rula, A., Palmonari, M., Harth, A., Stadtmüller, S., Maurino, A.: On the diversity and availability of temporal information in linked open data. In: Cudré-Mauroux, P., et al. (eds.) ISWC 2012, Part I. LNCS, vol. 7649, pp. 492–507. Springer, Heidelberg (2012)

[19] Talukdar, P.P., Wijaya, D.T., Mitchell, T.: Coupled temporal scoping of relational facts. In: 5th WSDM, pp. 73–82 (2012)
[20] Unger, C., Bühmann, L., Lehmann, J., Ngomo, A.-C.N., Gerber, D., Cimiano, P.: Sparql template-based question answering. In: 21st WWW (2012)
[21] UzZaman, N., Allen, J.F.: Trips and trios system for tempeval-2: Extracting temporal information from text. In: SemEval, pp. 276–283. ACL (2010)
[22] Wang, Y., Dylla, M., Ren, Z., Spaniol, M., Weikum, G.: Pravda-live: interactive knowledge harvesting. In: 21st CIKM, pp. 2674–2676. ACM (2012)
[23] Yin, X., Han, J., Yu, P.S.: Truth discovery with multiple conflicting information providers on the web. IEEE Trans. Knowl. Data Eng. 20(6), 796–808 (2008)

Detecting Incorrect Numerical Data in DBpedia

Dominik Wienand[1] and Heiko Paulheim[2]

[1] Technische Universität Darmstadt, Germany
Knowledge Engineering Group
dominik.wienand@online.de

[2] University of Mannheim, Germany
Research Group Data and Web Science
heiko@informatik.uni-mannheim.de

Abstract. DBpedia is a central hub of Linked Open Data (LOD). Being based on crowd-sourced contents and heuristic extraction methods, it is not free of errors. In this paper, we study the application of unsupervised numerical outlier detection methods to DBpedia, using Interquantile Range (IQR), Kernel Density Estimation (KDE), and various dispersion estimators, combined with different semantic grouping methods. Our approach reaches 87% precision, and has lead to the identification of 11 systematic errors in the DBpedia extraction framework.

Keywords: #eswc2014Wienand, Linked Open Data, DBpedia, Data Quality, Error Detection, Outlier Detection, Clustering.

1 Introduction

DBpedia [10] is a central hub of the Linked Open Data Cloud [2]. Its goal is to make structured data from Wikipedia available to the Semantic Web. In its current version,[1] DBpedia[2] contains information about more than 4.0 million things, including 832,000 persons, 639,000 places, 372,000 creative works, 209,000 organizations, and 226,000 species.[3]

Given its approach of heuristic information extraction from a crowd-sourced web site, DBpedia contains various kinds of errors [18]. Data is entered and maintained manually in Wikipedia, and the input is neither restricted nor validated automatically. This makes it prone to both factual errors and problems during parsing, e.g., if number formats or units of measurement are used which are not expected by the DBpedia extraction code.

While DBpedia deals with various kinds of information, given as classes, instances, and relationships, this paper focuses on the detection of errors in the

[1] DBpedia version 3.9, which has been released on September 17th, 2013.

[2] Unless otherwise indicated, all statements about the DBpedia knowledge base refer to version 3.8. Many of the errors reported in this paper have been fixed for the 3.9 release due to the fact that we were able to identify them with methods discussed in this paper.

[3] http://dbpedia.org/About

V. Presutti et al. (Eds.): ESWC 2014, LNCS 8465, pp. 504–518, 2014.

primitive numerical attributes, using outlier detection and clustering. That is, given one property, such as `dbpedia-owl:populationTotal`,[4] representing the population of a place, we want to detect wrong values that are used as literal objects of that property. We focus on *unsupervised* methods, i.e., methods that do not use domain knowledge such as typical ranges of attributes.

Outlier detection is the method of finding an observation "that appears to deviate markedly from other members of the sample in which it occurs." [4] An outlier may be caused by an error in the data, as well as represent an unusual, but correct value. For example, in a series of country populations in the order of magnitude of millions, a value larger than a billion may be wrong, or refer to unusually large countries, such as China or India. However, in many cases, outliers are caused by wrong data points. Therefore, outlier detection can be used as a means to detect errors in data.

The rest of this paper is structured as follows. Our approach, as well as the methods used for clustering and outlier detection, is sketched in section 2. We show the evaluation of our approach in both a pre-study with a selection of prominent attributes from DBpedia, as well as on a random sample of resources in section 3, and we discuss systematic sources of errors identified in DBpedia in section 4. We wrap up with a review of related approaches in section 5, and an outlook on future work in section 6.

2 Approach

As discussed above, simple outlier detection approaches are limited by the existence of natural outliers. Consider a property such as `dbpedia-owl:populationTotal`, which represents the total population of a `dbpedia-owl:PopulatedPlace`. This includes villages, towns, cities, states, countries, continents and – contrary to the label – also some unpopulated places such as ghost towns and uninhabited islands. That means that most countries and continents will appear to be outliers by most metrics because they are only few in number, but exceed the population of the villages, towns and cities, that make up the majority of the entries, by far.

To cope with that problem, we propose a two-step approach: first, we group the subjects by their types – in the example, separating villages, cities, countries, etc. – and then apply outlier detection to those groups in isolation in order to obtain a more robust error detection.

2.1 Grouping Subjects

Many resources in DBpedia have one or more types, which we can utilize to separate subjects. The most basic way of doing that is to group the subjects of

[4] The following namespace conventions are used in this document:
`dbpedia=http://dbpedia.org/resource/`,
`dbpedia-owl= http://dbpedia.org/ontology/`,
`dbpprop=http://dbpedia.org/property/`, `owl=http://www.w3.org/2002/07/owl`

each property based on each RDF type found in the set of subjects. However, not all types are actually useful for the outlier detection process and some are actually detrimental.

Since in OWL everything is an instance of `owl:Thing`, the subset containing all subjects of type `owl:Thing` will generally contain all subjects of the original set and therefore not provide any further insight. The same can be true for other types (e.g., `dbpedia-owl:PopulatedPlace` for `dbpedia-owl:populationTotal`), so when grouping by single types, it is advisable to first check if the group represents a significantly smaller subset before applying any further outlier detection methods.

Another problem to cope with is the presence of faulty types. Sometimes, types are missing in DBpedia, in other cases, types are wrongly assigned. [12] A typical example are the types `dbpedia-owl:Village` and `dbpedia-owl:City`, which are not uniformly used: there are instances of `dbpedia-owl:Village` with a population over 100,000 inhabitants, as well as instances of `dbpedia-owl:City` with less than 10 inhabitants. Therefore, relying on single types for grouping the subjects of examination can lead to problems.

Since the missing and wrongly assigned types are not equally distributed across all schemas used in DBpedia (e.g., DBpedia, UMBEL, and YAGO), we consider another preprocessing strategy, i.e., clustering by type vectors. For this approach, we consider all types of a subject as a vector of boolean values, representing whether or not the subject is of a certain type, and then apply traditional clustering techniques to subjects stored in this vector representation. To create these vectors, we use the *FeGeLOD* framework [13], which is designed to automatically enrich resources with information gathered from Linked Open Data. FeGeLOD first collects the information for all subjects, creating a binary feature for each type. Then, we apply a threshold p to filter out features that are either too generic, appearing in over $p\%$ of all cases, or too specific, appearing in less than $1 - p\%$ of all cases. The actual clustering is done with the Estimation Maximization (EM) algorithm [3], using the implementation in *WEKA* [5].

2.2 Outlier Detection Approaches

Classical outlier detection approaches assume an underlying distribution (usually a normal distribution). The basic method of those classical approaches is that values that do not fall into the assumed distribution are outliers.

However, those approaches are unsuitable for our purposes, because the data we are dealing with often does not meet those assumptions. Most importantly, the assumption of a normal distribution is not suitable for the vast range of different datasets found in DBpedia. For example, the population sizes of cities follow a log-normal rather than a normal distribution, i.e., there are many more small cities than there are very large cities. Further problems arise with regards to methods being designed for small sample sizes, or only being able to detect one or a few outliers at a time.

More recent outlier detection approaches, which are not that dependent on the assumption of a normal distribution, are based on robust statistics. One simple such approach is based on the Interquartile Range (IQR). For this method, three points are defined: the median of all values is the 2-quartile (Q_2), the median of those values smaller than Q_2 is Q_1, and the median of those values larger than Q_2 is Q_3. The interquartile range IQR is then defined as the distance between Q_3 and Q_1. Traditionally, every data point smaller than $Q_1 - 1.5 \cdot IQR$ and every point larger than $Q_3 + 1.5 \cdot IQR$ would be considered an outlier, as this roughly corresponds to three standard deviations from the mean for a normal distribution. This approach can be generalized to use the distance between arbitrary subdivisions of the data set, such as $P_{95} - P5$ for percentiles. Also, for our purposes, we will need to use much larger factors than 1.5 due to the heterogeneous nature of the data in DBpedia. The two main parameters of IQR are thus the factor used, and the number of percentiles.

Other approaches are based on estimating the center of the distribution and a range of assumed to be valid values. The median is the most common way of estimating the center of the population. The range of valid values can be estimated in various ways. The classic approach to estimating the dispersion of a population in a robust way is the Median absolute deviation (MAD), defined as $MAD = median_i(|X_i - median_j(X_j)|)$. That is, we first calculate the distance from each point to the median of the dataset and then take the median of those values as the measure of dispersion. As for IQR, a constant factor determining the allowed distance from the median for values considered as non-outliers is the main parameter.

An approach to outlier detection that is not based on robust statistics utilizes Kernel Density Estimation (KDE) [11]. Let $x_1, x_2, ...x_n$ be independent and identically distributed (iid) random variables, drawn from a distribution with an unknown density function f, then

$$f_h(x) := \frac{1}{nh}\sum_{i=1}^{n} K(\frac{x - x_i}{h}) \tag{1}$$

is the kernel density estimator of f, where h is a smoothing factor called *bandwidth*, and K is a so-called Kernel, a symmetric, non-negative function that integrates to 1. For our purposes, we will use the Gaussian normal distribution, $\frac{1}{\sigma\sqrt{2\pi}}e^{\frac{-(x-\mu)^2}{2\sigma^2}}$, using the data sample's mean (μ) and standard deviation (σ), which satisfies all requirements of a kernel. The bandwidth h can be chosen according to "Silverman's rule of thumb" [14] as $(\frac{4\hat{\sigma}^5}{3n})^{\frac{1}{5}}$, where $\hat{\sigma}$ is the sample standard deviation. This bandwidth has been shown to yield optimal results for cases where the underlying distribution is actually normal and reasonable results for unimodal, symmetric distributions. [6].

To calculate outlier scores for a given dataset, we first create a KDE from the data and then calculate the resulting probability at each point. To put this probability into relation we compare it to the mean probability over all points, $mp = \frac{1}{n}\sum_{i=1}^{n} \hat{f}_h(x_i)$. The relative probability of one data point being normal is then $rp(x) = \frac{\hat{f}_h(x)}{mp}$, where $rp(x) > 1$ indicates an above average probability, $rp(x) < 1$ indicates a below average probability. To obtain a binary classification, a threshold is applied, e.g., all x with $rp(x) < 0.1$ are considered as outliers.

As naïve implementations that evaluate the KDE at every input point individually can be inefficient on large datasets, implementations based on Fast Fourier Transformation (FFT) have been proposed. [15] Those implementations allow sampling the function only at equidistant points, but offer a performance that is orders of magnitudes faster than naïve implementations. A million samples can be evaluated in about one second, while evaluating the same number of data points individually would take hours. However, rounding to the nearest available sample usually leads to a loss in precision.

Furthermore, since KDE is not an inherently robust method, outliers can affect the outcome. Thus, an *iterative application* of the approach, i.e., detecting outliers with KDE, removing the outliers, and re-running the process on the remaining data, often improves the results. [7].

3 Evaluation

We perform a two-fold evaluation. First, we conduct a pre-study with three selected attributes. Then, we evaluate the performance of the best performing methods on a random sample of DBpedia.

3.1 Pre-study

We conduct a pre-study on three properties, `dbpedia-owl:populationTotal`, `dbpedia-owl:height`, and `dbpedia-owl:elevation`, to assess their usefulness with regard to typical data provided by DBpedia. These predicates were selected due to their high coverage, as well as their diverse use (for example, height is used for vehicles as well as for persons, which mixes two different distributions).

To conduct the study, we collected all triples that use the three properties as predicates. The three datasets encompass 52,522 (`dbpedia-owl:height`), 206,997 (`dbpedia-owl:elevation`), and 237,700 (`dbpedia-owl:populationTotal`) triples. While it would be too expensive to build a complete gold standard for those datatsets, we only check whether the outliers identified by the different approaches are true or false errors.

We evaluate according to two dimensions: the outlier detection method itself (IQR, dispersion mode, KDE, iterative KDE, and KDE with FFT), as well as the preprocessing technique (*default*, i.e., no preprocessing, grouping by *single type*, as well as *clustering* by type vectors). For grouping by single types, we use only classes from the DBpedia ontology that represent leaves of the class hierarchy. Clustering by type vectors was done using the *FeGeLOD* framework with a threshold of 0.95 to create the type vectors, which are then clustered using the EM algorithm with a maximum of 100 iterations, no fixed number of clusters to create, and a minimum allowable standard deviation of 10^{-6} for normal density calculation. The reported results show the averages over all three predicates. For each of the algorithms, a large number of parameter settings was tested systematically.

The runtime for one analysis run in default mode on the three datasets were 1,832ms for IQR, 2,297ms for dispersion, 6,922ms for KDE-FFT, and

2,469,011ms (i.e., more than 40 minutes) for KDE. These runtimes include analysis overhead one the one hand and some caching on the other hand so they should only be viewed in comparison to each other, not as absolute values. In single type mode, IQR takes 41,538ms, KDE-FFT 31,336ms and dispersion 72,852ms for one sample run.

The clustering mode suffers from extremely high runtimes of around one hour for the height dataset, and over 24 hours for the larger `dbpedia-owl:elevation` and `dbpedia-owl:populationTotal` datasets. For those, about an hour is spent creating the vectors, using the public DBpedia SPARQL endpoint for retrieving the types, and the rest of the time running the actual clustering, which is the bottleneck of this approach.

The results of the pre-study are depicted in Fig. 1. As we are interested in methods for automatically detecting outliers, we were aiming at finding methods with high precision. Thus, we chose a set of parameters for each approach which optimizes the trade-off of precision and total number of outliers in a way that clearly prefers precision, such that if applied in an automatic setting, the probability of removing correct information is low. To that end, we use those parameters that optimize the trade-off between precision and absolute number of outliers. It can be observed that the precision for both dispersion and KDE FFT is much too low for the methods to be of actual use, since the loss induced by rounding to the next available example is very high on the dataset at hand.

Grouping is obviously useful as no method is able to achieve more than 30% precision in the baseline default mode. On the other hand, both IQR and KDE can yield precision scores of over 80%, if combined with some method of grouping. The results of grouping by single types and clustering by type vectors are comparable, which makes grouping by single type more preferable, considering the high runtime of the clustering approach. Furthermore, we find some improvement in precision for KDE by applying it iteratively to the same dataset.

Looking at the total number of outliers that each method can detect, we find that while IQR and KDE are able to achieve similar precision scores, KDE is able to detect much more outliers than IQR. Indeed, KDE iterative default detects 1622 incorrect values, most of which are incorrectly truncated values of 1.52 meters in the `dbpedia-owl:height` dataset (see Fig. 3, albeit at a low precision of 18%, as those values are too close to the valid range of body heights. However, such frequent anomalies can be used to detect errors in the DBpedia extraction code (see section 4).

3.2 Evaluation on Random Resources

Since the combination of IQR and grouping by single type provided some of the highest precision scores (88%) as well as runtimes that seemed suitable for large scale analysis, we chose to evaluate this combination further on a representative sample from DBpedia. To construct that sample, we used 50 random resources as a seed set, and collected all the data properties that have these resources as their subject. For those properties, we selected all triples that have these properties as their predicate, and used those for which more than 50% of all triples, and at

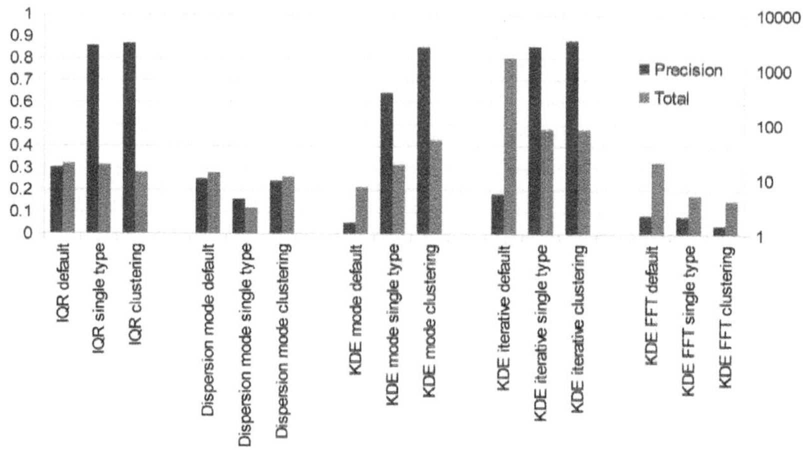

Fig. 1. Results of the pre-study on three selected properties. The x-axis shows the different approaches. Precision is shown on the left y-axis, the total number of outliers identified (true and false) is shown on the right y-axis.

least 100 in total, could be parsed to numeric values. This lead us to a random sample of 12,054,727 triples with literal, mostly numerical values.

As a first account, we used the parameters that had shown the highest precision in the pre-study (percentile=1.1, constant multiplier=50), and from that starting point, we systematically evaluated different parameter settings. The initial parameter setting yielded 1,703 suspicious triples, which we then evaluated manually. Manual verification was made feasible by using some shortcuts: The outliers did not occur at random but in clusters. For example, we found 122 area codes with eight or more digits. Since US area codes are all three digits in length, all triples with subjects of the form `[place],_[US state]` (which made up the vast majority) could be discarded at a glance. In some cases, however, we were not able to confidently determine what a certain property is supposed to represent and thus what values its objects should have. For example, the objects of the property `dbpprop:map` are so diverse that it is hard to tell what exactly they are supposed to represent. Thus, we labeled outliers for those properties as "unknown". Even if we pessimistically assume that all the outliers of unknown status are actually correct, IQR achieved a precision of 81% on our random sample. After removing the unclear data points, the highest precision is achieved at 88% with 859 true positives and 108 false positives, using a constant multiplier of 90 and 0.7 percentiles.

We also applied the methods in default mode to the sample data, which yielded nominally impressing results of thousands of outliers. The reason that we can find so many more outliers in general is that in order for an outlier to be found using the *single type* mode, its subject has to have a useful type, which is by far not given for all resources in DBpedia [12]. In our random sample, only two thirds of the subjects had at least one type.

Overall, three predicates, `dbpprop:date`, `dbpprop:years`, and `dbpprop:postalCode`, were responsible for the vast majority of those outliers. For those predicates, identifying true positives is easy because years and dates with more than four digits do not make sense, and the same holds for postcodes with more than ten digits.

By merely counting the corresponding objects for those three predicates, we would achieve true positive to unknown/false positive ratios of 7838:8751 (89%) with dispersion (MAD, constant factor = 300,000) and 5917:7216 (82%) with IQR (percentile = 1, constant multiplier = 41).

To verify that these results are not an effect of only a few low quality predicates, we chose to evaluate on the higher quality `dbpedia-owl` namespace only as well, which left us with 3,162,059 triples (26.2%) in 38 properties (22.6%) to analyze. Since we are dealing with a subset, the number of true and false positives cannot increase. With the same set of parameters, we find fewer outliers, but the overall trend remains, with 406 true positives (i.e., one wrong statement is identified in a thousand statements), and a precision of 87%.

4 Error Analysis

Based on the results obtained in our quality evaluations, we further examined common patterns in the errors we found to identify their causes. There are two basic classes of errors: those that exist as factual errors in Wikipedia, and those that occur while parsing the data from Wikipedia to DBpedia. Figure 2 shows the distribution of the error sources we identified.

In the following, we provide examples and explanations for errors found with our approach,[5] roughly classified into errors in Wikipedia, problems parsing primitive values, problems parsing non-primitive values, and problems interpreting and converting units.

4.1 Errors in Wikipedia

In some cases, the data is already wrong at the source, i.e. the Wikipedia page. For example, the page `http://en.wikipedia.org/wiki/Lerma,_State_of_Mexico` gives the elevation of a town in Mexico as *25,700m 84,300ft*, which is clearly a wrong elevation, as it would be roughly three times higher than

[5] Note that since our study was performed on DBpedia 3.8, all examples shown refer to that version. Since, as a result of the research reported in this paper, we reported these errors to the DBpedia development team during our investigation, some of those have already been fixed for the latest DBpedia release, so not all of those errors can be reproduced with the latest version of DBpedia. Likewise, some of the examples for wrong data in Wikipedia used in this paper may have been fixed since this paper has been written.

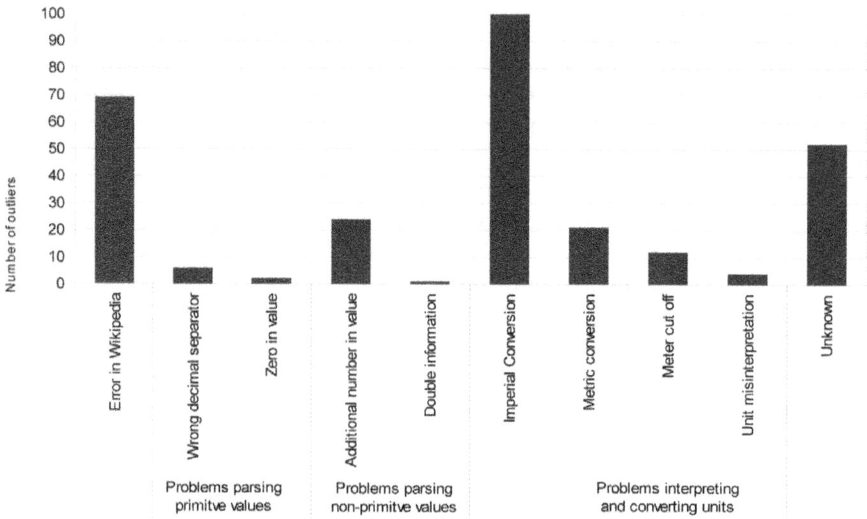

Fig. 2. Distribution of error sources. The value for *Imperial Conversion* is 1,506; the y-axis has been cut off at 100 for providing a better visualization.

Mount Everest. These errors are hard to quantify, as they do not seem to follow a specific pattern.

In other cases, the correct data exists at Wikipedia along with another incorrect value, and the wrong value is selected during the extraction of DBpedia. For example, the page `http://en.wikipedia.org/wiki/Portland,_Michigan` gives the elevation of this town as *30,035ft (221m)*. 221 meters would be the correct value, but the DBpedia extraction code picks up the incorrect elevation in feet and converts it to the value of 9154.67 meters.

Some infobox keys in Wikipedia are used with inconsistent semantics. One example is the property `dbpprop:runtime`. Used for TV shows, it most often denotes the runtime of a single episode, while in some cases, it denotes the total time the series was aired. For example, the series *Wielie Wielie Walie*, a South African children's program, was aired for 18 years. The running time *18 years* is then transformed to a runtime of `568,036,800` seconds.

4.2 Problems Parsing Primitive Values

In this paper, we concentrate on numerical data. Such data can be obtained from primitive (simple numbers) as well as non-primitive (several numbers in one value, e.g., a population value and a year in which the population figures were collected) values. One problem in an earlier version of the DBpedia extraction code was that some characters were converted to additional zeros in numbers. For example, `dbpedia:Durg` gives the population of the city of *Durg* as *2810436*, when it really is 281,436. A similar error can be seen with regards to the city of Nantong (`dbpedia:Nantong`). DBpedia gives the population as *72828350*, while, according to Wikipedia, it is actually 7,282,835.

Another class of problems comes from misinterpretation of wrong thousands and decimal separators.[6] For example, the comet *1134 Kepler* (`dbpedia:1134_Kepler`) has an eccentricity of *0.4650*, which is given in Wikipedia as *0,4650*, and gets misinterpreted to `4650` in DBpedia. Similarly, there are cases where dots are used as a thousands separator, e.g., for the city `dbpedia:Garg%C5%BEdai`, which has a population of *16,814*, defined as *16.814* in Wikipedia, which, after rounding, becomes a population of `17` in DBpedia.

4.3 Problems Parsing Non-primitive Values

The most prominent indicator of non-primitive values is the presence of an additional number in the value. This happens, for example, with a year given for another value, such as a population. For example, the population of the village *Semaphore* (`dbpedia:Semaphore,_South_Australia`) is given as `28,322,006` (which exceeds the total population of Australia), when it is actually *2,832* – here, the year *2006* is reported next to the population, and the two numbers get concatenated during the extraction. A similar phenomenon can be observed for some runtimes, e.g., the runtime of the song *Last Christmas*, which is given as *3:02 (1946 recording)* in Wikipedia, and misinterpreted as `1,946` seconds.

A similar case is the presence of different numbers (e.g., ranges) for one property. This occurs, for example, with area codes, which are frequently given as lists or ranges, for example, Wikipedia gives the area code of *Central California* as *805, 559, 831*, which the extraction code turns into `805559831` at `dbpedia:Central_California`. Since Wikipedia entries can contain arbitrary text where a proper number may be expected by the DBpedia extraction code, entries such as *Mid-90s* may also be misinterpreted, leading to the starting date of `90 A.D.` for the band *Depswa* (`dbpedia:Depswa`).

In some cases, double information is extracted from more than one place. For example, the Wikipedia article for *Johnstown, Colorado* (`http://en.wikipedia.org/wiki/Johnstown,_Colorado`) gives its population as *9,887*. However, in the introduction, a population of *3,827* in 2000 is also mentioned. The two values get concatenated, so that in DBpedia (`dbpedia:Johnstown,_Colorado`), we find a combination of those two values as `38,279,887`.

4.4 Problems Interpreting and Converting Units

There are properties which use different units of measures. For example, the runtime of films (`dbpprop:runtime`) usually uses time intervals, such as hours, minutes, and seconds, and is represented in DBpedia as seconds. However, there are also films such as the 1919 movie *The Unpardonable Sin*, whose runtime is

[6] As we only look at the English language Wikipedia, these should in theory be free from regional variations.

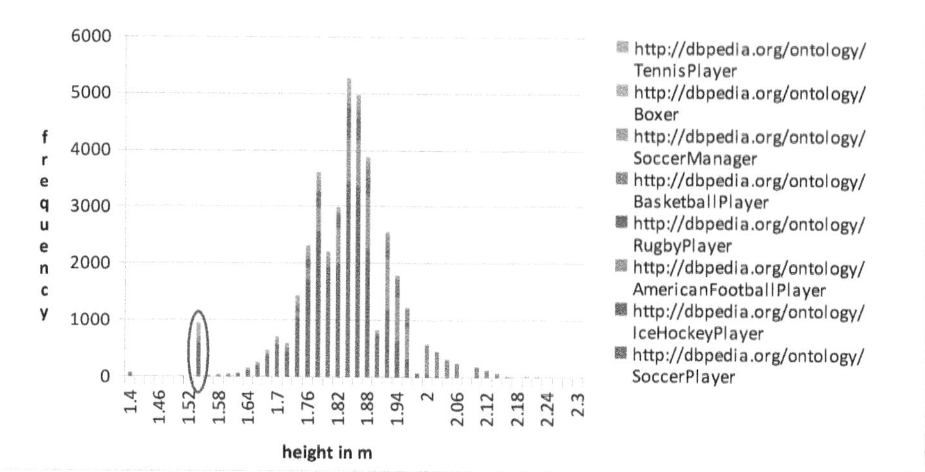

Fig. 3. Distribution of persons' heights, showing an anomaly at 1.52m

given as *9 reels (2,700 meters)*, which is converted to 9 (i.e., nine seconds) in DBpedia (`dbpedia:The_Unpardonable_Sin_ (1919_film)`).

Another typical problem can occur with height or length values that are reported in mixed notation, using the unit of measurement in the middle. This leads to the *meter cut off problem*: a set of people with actual heights of around 1.5-1.9 meters have their heights represented in DBpedia as exactly 1.0 meters. This does seem to happen most often with somewhat unclean height specifications in Wikipedia. For example, Wikipedia states the height of the footballer *Guy Poitevin* as *1 m 81, 80 kg*, which then gets interpreted as 1.0m at `dbpedia:Guy_Poitevin`.

The by far largest source of errors happens during conversion of imperial units. In many cases, the given value differs only between about 0.025 and 0.3 meters from the actual value. In most cases the given height equals a round number of feet. For persons, the most common incorrect height is 1.524 meters or 5 feet; for example, the goalkeeper *Ray Wood* (`dbpedia:Ray_Wood`) is *1.80* meters in height according to Wikipedia, but DBpedia gives his height as `1.524` meters. This indicates that this error is caused by an incorrect parsing procedure from Imperial units to metric units where only the value in feet is correctly read while the remaining inches are cut off. Such errors can be observed as frequent anomalies in the distributions, as shown in Fig. 3.

The interpretation of values in metric units is also not free of errors. In some cases, heights appear too small by a factor of one hundred. For example, the correct height for `dbpedia:Humberto_Contreras` would be *1.76 meters* according to Wikipedia, however, DBpedia gives a value of `0.0176` meters, since the extraction code expects a value in centimeters, not meters. A similar error can be observed with regards to some resources that have their height given in millimeters at Wikipedia, e.g. `http://en.wikipedia.org/wiki/FS_Class_E491/2`

states the height of this locomotive as *4,310 mm (14 ft 1.7 in)*, which is rendered as `0.004310` [meters] at DBpedia. However, in other cases, the error is already present in Wikipedia. For example, the height of athlete *Katrina Porter* (`http://en.wikipedia.org/wiki/Katrina_Porter`) is given as `1.55cm`, which DBpedia correctly converts to `0.0155` meters.

It may also occur that imperial units are interpreted as metric, or vice versa. For example, Wikipedia gives the elevation of *Shadow Mountain Lake* as *8367'* (8367 ft.), which DBpedia misinterprets as `8,367` meters, thus causing the parsed value at `dbpedia:Shadow_Mountain_Lake` to be about three times (1 meter = 3.28084 feet) higher than it actually is. The entry on the *Zapatoca* mountain (`dbpedia:Zapatoca`) features even two of those errors: Wikipedia gives the elevation as *1,720 m (4,000 ft)*, and DBpedia renders this as both `1219.200000` and `13123.000000`. The first value corresponds to converting 4,000ft to meter and the latter to converting 4,000 meter to feet.

Time values are also prone to misinterpretation. Wikipedia lists the runtime of some albums as *mm:ss:msms*, for example `http://en.wikipedia.org/wiki/ Les_Dudek_(album)`. The DBpedia extraction codes interprets this as *hh:mm:ss* and converts it to `2589.1666666666665` [minutes] at `dbpedia:Les_Dudek_(album)`.

5 Related Work

In [18], a taxonomy of errors in LOD is introduced. The taxonomy consists of four dimensions (accuracy, relevancy, representational consistency, and interlinking), seven categories, and 17 sub-categories. It encompasses plain errors, such as incorrectly extracted triples, as well as undesirable features, such as information being redundant or irrelevant. The errors found by the approach discussed in this paper mainly fall into the first category, i.e., incorrectly extracted triples.

The problem of automatically detecting errors in knowledge bases automatically has been acknowledged to be hard. In [16], an approach is evaluated of first enriching the DBpedia ontology with additional domain and range restrictions, as well as class disjointness axioms, and then using the enhanced ontology for error detection by reasoning. A similar approach is discussed in [8], but no quantitative results on DBpedia are provided. However, these two approaches target at finding wrong statements involving object properties, i.e., relations between two resources, rather than wrong numerical literals.

Other approaches use external knowledge to validate statements, either from experts or from external data sources, and with different scopes (e.g., validating both object and data type properties vs. only data type properties). [1] discuss crowd-sourcing, using platforms such as Amazon Mechanical Turk which pay users for micro-tasks, such as the validation of a statement. Furthermore, they used a custom platform which organized the validation of statements as a competition. Their evaluation concentrates on three error classes, i.e., wrong literal values, wrong literal datatypes, and wrong interlinks to other datasets. For the first, which we also address with our approach, they report a precision of 0.90, which is close to our results, which, however, does not rely on the wisdom of the crowds. [17] use games with a purpose to evaluate DBpedia and spot inconcistencies. They report that in 4,051 statements used in the game, 265 inconsistencies have been detected by users, 121 out of which were actually inconsistencies. This leads to a precision of only 0.46, which makes that approach only partially suitable for increasing data quality, at least without expert reviewing.

External knowledge is used, e.g., by DeFacto [9]. The authors have build a pattern library of lexical forms for properties frequently used in DBpedia. Using those lexical patterns, DeFacto runs search engine requests for natural language representations of DBpedia statements. While DeFacto seems to work on ObjectProperties, not DatatypeProperties, the approach is transferable to the problem of identifying errors in numerical data as well. Their approach reaches a precision of 0.88, which is comparable to our approach.

Overall, there are not too many approaches for automatically identifying wrong numerical values in Linked Open Data, in particular not without using external sources of knowledge, such as the wisdom of the crowds. Furthermore, it is interesting to see that even approaches using external knowledge sources do not reach significantly higher precision figures.

6 Conclusion and Outlook

In this paper, we have examined the possible usage of different outlier detection methods, i.e., Interquantile Range (IQR), Kernel Density Estimation (KDE), and dispersion estimators, for identifying wrong statements in DBpedia. The outlier detection methods are combined with different preprocessing strategies, i.e., grouping subjects by the single types, as well as clustering by type vectors. The simple IQR method delivers some of the best results in our tests. Combined with grouping by single type preprocessing, we achieved a precision of 87% on small high quality samples as well as on large random samples. Basic KDE shows similar results, but suffers from high runtimes. The other methods examined, i.e., dispersion and KDE-FFT, mostly fail to deliver results with sufficient precision.

The evaluation has shown that exploiting further semantics in DBpedia, i.e., the type information of the statements' subjects, leads to an improvement compared to simply applying outlier detection to all numerical values of a property at once. Clustering by type vectors does produce promising results as well but is, at least in our current implementation, not feasible runtime-wise. Iterative application of analysis methods does not improve results for most methods. Only KDE clearly benefits from using more than one iteration; with all other methods, results either do not change or, if they were bad to begin with, tend to get even worse. Overall, the combinations of IQR and iterative KDE, and grouping by single type or clustering by type vector, produce the best results.

As a result of applying our approach, we identified a number of common sources of errors in DBpedia. Large amounts of the faulty numerical values in

DBpedia are caused by only a few of those error sources. Overall, 11 different types of errors in the DBpedia extraction framework regarding properties in the `dbpedia-owl` namespace were identified and forwarded as bug reports to the developers of DBpedia, many of which have been resolved for the current DBpedia release. While we were identifying these errors by manual inspection, automatically detecting patterns for data formats that are not handled correctly would be a useful extension of the approach.

So far, we have only considered numerical data, i.e., integer or double values. Extending the approach to dates would be interesting, straight forward, and particularly useful, since dates, like numbers, are prone to being parsed wrongly.

While the clustering approach showed promising results, but had runtime problems, there is clearly room for improvement here. We evaluated one clustering approach on RDF types, which showed promising results but suffered from extremely high runtimes. However, there is an abundance of clustering algorithms, and there is much more information available for each subject beyond its type that could be used in the clustering process, e.g., vectors of relations or Wikipedia categories. Other feature vector representations, combined with different clustering algorithms, could improve the clustering results as well as runtime.

In general, outlier detection as a method of identifying errors has some fundamental limitations in that in order for an erroneous data point to be detected, it has to be "outlying" in some numerical manner. For example, if all regular ZIP codes have five digits, it should be possible to detect invalid ZIP codes with 3 or 14 digits. However, if a ZIP code is simply wrong as in *96377* instead of *94303*, it will be practically impossible to detect as an outlier without using background knowledge.

In this paper, we have restricted ourselves to applying outlier detection methods on single attributes. While the results are promising, using more than one variable at the same time seems promising, e.g., finding outliers in cities' *populations* by taking the *area* attribute into account (assuming that cities with larger population also occupy a larger area).

So far, we have only considered one particular data source, i.e., DBpedia. While the approach itself is transferable to any RDF knowledge base, exploiting links to other datasets and using information from more than one dataset at the same time could help further improving the results. By comparing suspicious values to corresponding values from other sources, e.g., other language editions of DBpedia, it could not only be possible to detect more outliers, but also to correct them automatically too. Applying the findings not only on DBpedia, but also on Wikipedia directly, e.g., in the form of editing support, would be another possible application.

In summary, we have shown that even basic outlier detection methods, combined with suitable preprocessing strategies, lead to highly effective error detection mechanisms.

References

1. Acosta, M., Zaveri, A., Simperl, E., Kontokostas, D., Auer, S., Lehmann, J.: Crowdsourcing linked data quality assessment. In: Alani, H., et al. (eds.) ISWC 2013, Part II. LNCS, vol. 8219, pp. 260–276. Springer, Heidelberg (2013)
2. Bizer, C., Heath, T., Berners-Lee, T.: Linked Data - The Story So Far. International Journal on Semantic Web and Information Systems 5(3), 1–22 (2009)
3. Dempster, A.P., Laird, N.M., Rubin, D.B.: Maximum likelihood from incomplete data via the em algorithm. Journal of the Royal Statistical Society. Series B (Methodological), 1–38 (1977)
4. Grubbs, F.E.: Procedures for detecting outlying observations in samples. Technometrics 11(1), 1–21 (1969)
5. Hall, M., Frank, E., Holmes, G., Pfahringer, B., Reutemann, P., Witten, I.H.: The WEKA data mining software: an update. SIGKDD Explor. Newsl. 11, 10–18 (2009)
6. Hardle, W.: Nonparametric and semiparametric models. Springer (2004)
7. Hodge, V.J., Austin, J.: A survey of outlier detection methodologies. Artificial Intelligence Review 22(2), 85–126 (2004)
8. Lehmann, J., Bühmann, L.: Ore-a tool for repairing and enriching knowledge bases. In: Patel-Schneider, P.F., Pan, Y., Hitzler, P., Mika, P., Zhang, L., Pan, J.Z., Horrocks, I., Glimm, B. (eds.) ISWC 2010, Part II. LNCS, vol. 6497, pp. 177–193. Springer, Heidelberg (2010)
9. Lehmann, J., Gerber, D., Morsey, M., Ngonga Ngomo, A.-C.: Defacto-deep fact validation. In: Cudré-Mauroux, P., et al. (eds.) ISWC 2012, Part I. LNCS, vol. 7649, pp. 312–327. Springer, Heidelberg (2012)
10. Lehmann, J., Isele, R., Jakob, M., Jentzsch, A., Kontokostas, D., Mendes, P.N., Hellmann, S., Morsey, M., van Kleef, P., Auer, S., Bizer, C.: DBpedia – A Large-scale, Multilingual Knowledge Base Extracted from Wikipedia. Semantic Web Journal (2013)
11. Parzen, E.: On estimation of a probability density function and mode. The Annals of Mathematical Statistics 33(3), 1065–1076 (1962)
12. Paulheim, H., Bizer, C.: Type inference on noisy RDF data. In: Alani, H., Kagal, L., Fokoue, A., Groth, P., Biemann, C., Parreira, J.X., Aroyo, L., Noy, N., Welty, C., Janowicz, K. (eds.) ISWC 2013, Part I. LNCS, vol. 8218, pp. 510–525. Springer, Heidelberg (2013)
13. Paulheim, H., Fürnkranz, J.: Unsupervised Generation of Data Mining Features from Linked Open Data. In: International Conference on Web Intelligence, Mining, and Semantics (WIMS 2012) (2012)
14. Silverman, B.W.: Density estimation for statistics and data analysis, vol. 26. CRC Press (1986)
15. Silverman, B.W.: Algorithm as 176: Kernel density estimation using the fast fourier transform. Journal of the Royal Statistical Society. Series C (Applied Statistics) 31(1), 93–99 (1982)
16. Töpper, G., Knuth, M., Sack, H.: Dbpedia ontology enrichment for inconsistency detection. In: Proceedings of the 8th International Conference on Semantic Systems, pp. 33–40. ACM (2012)
17. Waitelonis, J., Ludwig, N., Knuth, M., Sack, H.: Whoknows? evaluating linked data heuristics with a quiz that cleans up dbpedia. Interactive Technology and Smart Education 8(4), 236–248 (2011)
18. Zaveri, A., Kontokostas, D., Sherif, M.A., Bühmann, L., Morsey, M., Auer, S., Lehmann, J.: User-driven quality evaluation of dbpedia. In: 9th International Conference on Semantic Systems (I-SEMANTICS 2013) (2013)

A Scalable Approach for Efficiently Generating Structured Dataset Topic Profiles

Besnik Fetahu[1], Stefan Dietze[1], Bernardo Pereira Nunes[2], Marco Antonio Casanova[2], Davide Taibi[3], and Wolfgang Nejdl[1]

[1] L3S Research Center, Leibniz Universität Hannover, Germany
{fetahu,dietze,nejdl}@L3S.de
[2] Department of Informatics - PUC-Rio - Rio de Janeiro, RJ - Brazil
{bnunes,casanova}@inf.puc-rio.br
[3] Institute for Educational Technologies, CNR, Palermo Italy
davide.taibi@itd.cnr.it

Abstract. The increasing adoption of Linked Data principles has led to an abundance of datasets on the Web. However, take-up and reuse is hindered by the lack of descriptive information about the nature of the data, such as their topic coverage, dynamics or evolution. To address this issue, we propose an approach for creating linked dataset profiles. A profile consists of structured dataset metadata describing topics and their relevance. Profiles are generated through the configuration of techniques for resource sampling from datasets, topic extraction from reference datasets and their ranking based on graphical models. To enable a good trade-off between scalability and accuracy of generated profiles, appropriate parameters are determined experimentally. Our evaluation considers topic profiles for all accessible datasets from the Linked Open Data cloud. The results show that our approach generates accurate profiles even with comparably small sample sizes (10%) and outperforms established topic modelling approaches.

Keywords: Profiling, Metadata, Vocabulary of Links, Linked Data.

1 Introduction

The emergence of the Web of Data, in particular Linked Open Data (LOD) [3], has led to an abundance of data available on the Web. Data is shared as part of datasets and contains inter-dataset links [17], with most of these links concentrated on established reference graphs, such as DBpedia [1].

Linked datasets vary significantly with respect to represented resource types, currentness, coverage of topics and domains, size, used languages, coherence, accessibility [7] or general quality aspects [11]. The wide variety and heterogeneity of these dataset aspects pose significant challenges for data consumers when attempting to find useful datasets without prior knowledge of available datasets.

V. Presutti et al. (Eds.): ESWC 2014, LNCS 8465, pp. 519–534, 2014.

Hence, a large proportion of datasets from the LOD cloud[1] has been overlooked in favor of well-known datasets like DBpedia or YAGO [19].

To facilitate search and reuse of existing datasets, descriptive and reliable metadata is required. However, as witnessed in the popular dataset registry DataHub[2], dataset descriptions are often missing entirely, or are outdated, for instance describing unresponsive endpoints [7]. This issue is partially due to the lack of automated mechanisms for generating reliable and up-to-date dataset metadata, which hinders the retrieval, reuse or interlinking of datasets. The dynamics and frequent evolution of datasets further exacerbates this problem, calling for scalable and frequent update mechanisms of respective metadata.

In this work, we address the above described challenge of automatically describing linked datasets with the goal of facilitating dataset search and reuse. This paper proposes an approach for creating structured dataset profiles, where a profile describes the topic coverage of a particular dataset through a weighted graph of selected DBpedia categories. Our approach consists of a processing pipeline that combines tailored techniques for dataset sampling, topic extraction from reference datasets and topic relevance ranking. Topics are extracted through named entity recognition (NER) techniques which use reference datasets and then scored according to their relevance for a dataset based on graphical models like *PageRank* [6], *K-Step Markov*[20], and *HITS* [15]. Although this is a computationally expensive process, we experimentally identify the parameters which enable a suitable trade-off between representativeness of generated profiles and scalability. Finally, generated dataset profiles are exposed as part of a public structured dataset catalog based on the *Vocabulary of Interlinked Datasets* (VoID[3]) and the newly introduced vocabulary of links (VoL)[4]. During our experimental evaluation, dataset profiles were generated for all LOD cloud datasets which were responsive at the time of writing and our approach showed superior performance to established topic modelling techniques.

Our main contributions consist of (i) a scalable method for efficiently generating structured dataset profiles, combining and configuring suitable methods for NER, topic extraction and ranking as part of an experimentally optimised configuration, and (ii) the generation of structured dataset profiles for a majority of LOD cloud datasets according to established dataset description vocabularies.

The remainder of the paper is structured as follows. Section 3 describes the automated processing pipeline to create and expose datasets profiles. Section 4 shows the experimental setup, with the datasets and baselines used, along with the generation of the ground truth and Section 5 presents the results and their discussion. Section 6 reviews related literature. Finally, Section 7 presents the conclusion and future work.

[1] http://datahub.io/group/lodcloud

[2] http://www.datahub.io

[3] http://vocab.deri.ie/void

[4] http://data.linkededucation.org/vol/

2 Problem Definition

This section introduces and formalises the used notions of *dataset profiling*. Recall that an *RDF statement* is a triple of the form $\langle s, p, o \rangle$, where s is the *subject* (an RDF URI reference or a blank node), p is the *property*, and o is the *object* (a URI, a literal or a blank node) of the triple, respectively.

A *resource instance* r is a set of triples and is identified by a URI s. The resource *type* is determined by the triple $c = \langle s, \texttt{rdf:type}, o \rangle$. A literal l *describes* a resource instance r **iff** there exists a triple of the form $\langle s, p, l \rangle$. Given a set of datasets $\mathbf{D} = \{D_1, \ldots, D_n\}$, we denote the set of resource instances $R_i = \{r_1, \ldots, r_k\}$ and resource types $C_i = \{c_1, \cdots, c_k\}$ for $D_i \in \mathbf{D}$ $(i = 1, \ldots, n)$ by $\mathbf{R} = \{R_1, \ldots, R_n\}$ and $\mathbf{C} = \{C_1, \ldots, C_n\}$, respectively.

A *reference dataset* or *knowledge base* $\mathcal{R}$ represents a special case of a dataset D by providing a topic vocabulary. We distinguish two resource types in $\mathcal{R}$, $C = \{\texttt{entity}, \texttt{topic}\}$. An instance e of type `entity` has a literal l describing its *label* (e.g. $\langle e, \texttt{rdfs:label}, l \rangle$) and at least one triple that refers to an instance of type `topic` describing its topic. On the other hand, an instance t of type `topic` is described with a literal l, i.e. the topic label (e.g. $\langle t, \texttt{rdfs:label}, l \rangle$). In our work, DBpedia is used as reference dataset where DBpedia entities and categories represent entity and topic instances.

The set of entities $E_k = \{e_1, \ldots, e_m\}$ of a specific resource $r_k \in R_i$ of D_i (for $i = 1, \ldots, n$) is extracted through a named entity recognition function applied to literal values from r_k. The set of corresponding topics $T_k = \{t_1, \ldots, t_q\}$ for r_k is computed by accumulating all objects indicated by triples of the form $\langle e_j, \texttt{dcterms:subject}, t \rangle$ (for $j = 1, \ldots, m$). Consequently, $\mathbf{T} = \{t_1, \ldots, t_p\}$ corresponds to the set of topic classifications for all resource instances $\forall r \in \mathbf{R}$.

A *profile graph* is a labelled, weighted and directed bipartite graph $\mathcal{P} = (\sigma, \varphi, \Delta)$, where $\sigma = \mathbf{D} \cup \mathbf{T}$, and $\varphi = \{\langle D, t \rangle | D \in \mathbf{D} \wedge t \in \mathbf{T}\}$ is a set of edges between datasets and topic classifications, extracted from $\mathcal{R}$. Finally, Δ is a function that assigns an *edge weight* for each edge in φ. Correspondingly for a dataset D_k a *dataset profile graph* $\mathcal{P}_{D_k}$ represents a sub-graph of $\mathcal{P}$, hence, $\sigma = D_k \cup \mathbf{T}$, and $\varphi = \{\langle D_k, t \rangle | t \in \mathbf{T}\}$.

3 Profiling of Linked Datasets

In this section, we provide an overview of the processing steps for generating structured dataset profiles. The main steps shown in Figure 1 are the following: (i) dataset metadata extraction from DataHub; (ii) resource type and instance extraction; (iii) entity and topic extraction; (iv) topic filtering and ranking; and (v) dataset profile representation. Step (i) uses the CKAN API to extract dataset metadata for datasets part of the LOD-Cloud group in DataHub. Steps (ii) - (v) are explained in detail below.

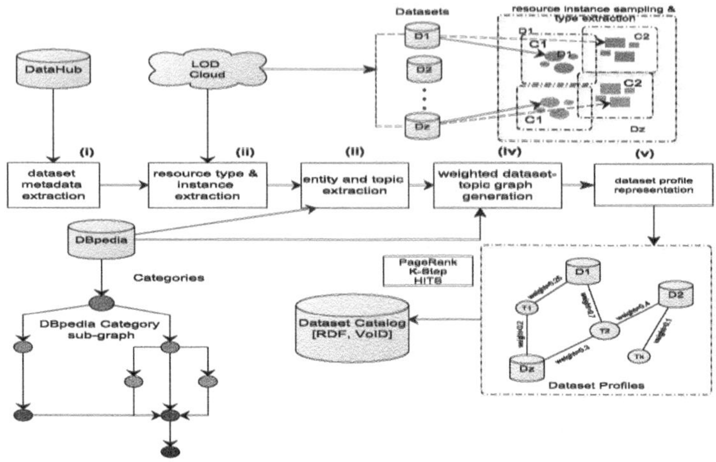

Fig. 1. Processing pipeline for generating structured profiles of Linked Data graphs

3.1 Resource Type and Instance Extraction

From the extracted dataset metadata (i.e. SPARQL endpoint) from DataHub in step (i), step (ii) extracts *resource types* and *instances* via SPARQL queries[5] that conform to the definition of *resource types* and *instances* in Section 2. Considering the large amount of resources per dataset, we investigate sample-based strategies as follows:

Random Sampling: randomly selects resource instances from R_i of D_i for further analysis in the profiling pipeline.

Weighted Sampling: weighs each resource as the ratio of the number of datatype properties used to define a resource over the maximum number of datatype properties over all resources for a specific dataset. The weight for r_k is computed by $w_k = |f(r_k)|/max\{|f(r_j)|\}$ $(r_j \in R_i | j = 1, \cdots, n)$, where $f(r_k)$ represents the datatype properties of resource r_k. An instance is included in a sample if, for a randomly generated number p from a uniform distribution, the weight w_k fulfils the condition $w_k > (1 - p)$. Such a strategy ensures that resources that carry more information (having more literal values) have higher chances of being included earlier at low cut-offs of analysed samples.

Resource Centrality Sampling: weighs each resource as the ratio of the number of resource types used to describe a particular resource ($V'_k \subset V_k$) divided by the total number of resource types in a dataset. The weight is defined by $c_k = |C'_k|/|C|$ with $C'_k = C \cap V'_k$. Similarly to 'weighted sampling', for a randomly generated number p, r_k is included in the sample if $c_k > (1 - p)$. The main motivation behind computing the centrality of a resource is that important concepts in a dataset tend to be more structured and linked to other concepts.

[5] `http://data-observatory.org/lod-profiles/profiling.htm`

3.2 Entity and Topic Extraction

Here we describe the process of entity and topic extraction from sampled resource instances in step (ii). Recall that we use DBpedia as our reference dataset due to its broad topics coverage. To extract entities, first we combine all textual literal values of a resource (in order to provide contextual information) and consequently extract named entities from the resulting textual content using the NER tool of choice, DBpedia Spotlight [16]. The topics $\mathbf{T}$ of sampled resources $\mathbf{R}$ represent DBpedia category instances assigned to extracted entities through the datatype property `dcterms:subject`. The topics in $\mathbf{T}$ are expanded with related topic instances (associated through datatype property `skos:broader`) up to two levels (l=2) (determined experimentally as the best expansion level, see Figure 3b).

3.3 Constructing a Profile Graph

An important step in generating the *profile graph* $\mathcal{P}$ is the ranking of associated topics in $\mathbf{T}$ for datasets in $\mathbf{D}$. Recall that $\mathcal{P}$ represents a bipartite graph, hence, a topic $t \in \mathbf{T}$ can have one or more edges connecting to datasets in $\mathbf{D}$. For instance, given two edges $\langle D_i, t\rangle$ and $\langle D_j, t\rangle$, where $D_i \neq D_j$ the computed weights $\Delta\langle D_i, t\rangle = w_i$ and $\Delta\langle D_j, t\rangle = w_j$ can be different depending on how well they represent, D_i and D_j, for $i, j = 1, \ldots, z$, respectively.

Furthermore, the function Δ relies on probabilistic graphical models. Such models are suitable as they measure the importance of each vertex with respect to other vertices in the corresponding profiles. Given a profile graph $\mathcal{P}$ and for datasets D_i, respectively its analysed resource instances are assumed to be prior knowledge. The computation of vertex weights with D_i as prior knowledge results in the computation of importance of the vertices which are part of the sub-graph connected to D_i. Consequently, this translates into computing the importance of topics $t_k \in \mathbf{T}$ ($k = 1, \ldots, n$) with regards to D_i. Additionally, to ensure certainty of importance for D_i, the prior probability is distributed uniformly to all analysed resources in R_i, while for resources R_j from D_j the prior probabilities are set to zero.

Finally, the assigned weight to vertex t_k, with D_i as prior knowledge, infers exactly $\Delta\langle D_i, t_k\rangle$. Hence, the relationships (edges) between topic t_k and individual datasets (given as prior knowledge) have different weights, depending on the set of resources that link t_k with D_i. One of the advantages of computing the edge weights Δ is that any new dataset, which is not part of the profiles $\mathcal{P}$, can be added incrementally to the existing ones by simply computing the edge weights with its associated topics.

To illustrate why this works, consider the following example with a profile graph $\mathcal{P}$ consisting of datasets $\mathbf{D} = \{D_1, D_2\}$ with sets of resources $R_1 = \{r_{11}, r_{12}, r_{13}, r_{14}\}$ and $R_2 = \{r_{21}, r_{22}, r_{23}, r_{24}\}$, and the set of topics $\mathbf{T} = \{t_1, t_2, t_3\}$. The individual topics are associated with the following resources: $t_1 = \{r_{11}, r_{22}\}, t_2 = \{r_{11}, r_{23}, r_{24}\}, t_3 = \{r_{11}, r_{12}, r_{13}, r_{14}, r_{24}\}$. Assume we want to compute the *edge weights* between dataset D_1 and topics in $\mathbf{T}$. First, we consider D_1 as prior knowledge. Hence, we uniformly distribute the prior probability

$(1/|R_1|)$ to its resources. For resources in R_2, the prior probabilities are set to zero. Finally, depending on the connectivity in the corresponding dataset profile, the topics would be ranked as follows: $\langle t_3, t_1, t_2 \rangle$. The computed weights would represent the edge weights by the tuples: $\Delta\langle D_1, t_3 \rangle \geq \Delta\langle D_1, t_1 \rangle \geq \Delta\langle D_1, t_2 \rangle$. Similarly, the *edge weights* are computed for dataset D_2.

3.4 Topic Ranking Approaches

Due to the large number of topics associated with the profile graph $\mathcal{P}$, ranking topics with respect to their relevance to datasets in $\mathbf{D}$ is crucial. A ranked set of topics enhances the usefulness of the generated profiles and facilitates the dataset recommendation and querying with higher accuracy.

Since topic extraction from the extracted entities is prone to noise from non-accurately disambiguated entities, we compute a *Normalised Topic Relevance (NTR)* score. *NTR* is a variant of the well-known *tf-idf* measure and is used to filter out noisy topics. In combination with other topic ranking approaches, it is used to determine the ideal topic expansion level. The topic rankings (edge weights) are computed through the *PageRank, K-Step Markov* and *HITS* [6,15] graphical models, applied to the *profile graph.* The adoption of the graphical models is discussed in what follows.

Normalised Topic Relevance (NTR): The *NTR* score is an important step for pre-filtering noisy topics as a result of non-accurate entity extraction. It is computed by taking into account (i) the number of entities $\Phi(t, D)$ assigned for a topic t within a dataset D and that of entities $\Phi(t, \cdot)$ across all datasets $\mathbf{D}$ and (ii) the number of entities $\Phi(\cdot, D)$ assigned to a dataset D and for datasets in $\mathbf{D}$ $\Phi(\cdot, \cdot)$. Topics are filtered out if they have a score below a given threshold:

$$NTR(t, D) = \frac{\Phi(\cdot, D)}{\Phi(t, D)} + \frac{\Phi(\cdot, \cdot)}{\Phi(t, \cdot)}, \quad \forall t \in \mathbf{T},\ D \in \mathbf{D} \tag{1}$$

PageRank with Priors: is a variant of the PageRank [6] algorithm (Equation 2) that, given a data graph, in this case a dataset profile $\mathcal{P}_{D_k}$ for dataset $D_k \in \mathbf{D}$, computes the importance of dataset-topic edge weights, for each $t \in \mathbf{T}$ such that there is an edge $\langle D_k, t \rangle$. The computation of edge weights $\Delta\langle D_k, t \rangle$ is biased towards the resource instances $r \in R_k$ of D_k. Hence, the importance of a topic t is highly influenced by its connectivity with resource instances in R_k. Prior knowledge is the analysed resource instance $r \in R_k$ with prior probabilities assigned as the ratio $1/|R_k|$, while for the remaining vertices a probability of zero is assigned.

$$\pi(t)^{(i+1)} = (1 - \beta) \left(\sum_{u=1}^{d_{in}(t)} p(t|u) \pi^{(i)}(u) \right) + \beta p_t \tag{2}$$

where, t is a topic such that $\langle D_k, t \rangle \neq \emptyset$, part of the dataset profile $\mathcal{P}_{D_k}$. β is the probability of jumping back to vertices that are a priori known, $r \in R_k$. $\pi(t)$ quantifies the relative importance of t w.r.t vertices in $\mathcal{P}_{D_k}$ and is biased towards the prior knowledge $r \in R_k$. The summation in the equation quantifies the importance of t relative to vertices that have incoming connections (resource instances classified with t), $d_{in}(t)$.

HITS with Priors: although similar to PageRank with Priors, it represents a slightly different approach. The flow of visiting one vertex depends on a randomly generated binary value, where in cases it is zero it visits a vertex from an in-link for an even step, while for an odd step it follows an out-link. Otherwise, it visits one of the given vertices in R_k. As we cannot distinguish between *hubs* and *authoritative* vertices from the set of topics $t \in \mathbf{T}$ (due to their equivalent importance), the process is simplified by having no *hub* or *authoritative* vertices.

$$a^{(i+1)}(t) = (1-\beta)\left(\sum_{u=1}^{d_{in}(t)} \frac{h^{(t)(u)}}{\sum_{t \in \mathbf{T}} \sum_{u=1}^{d_{in}(t)} h^{(i)}(t)}\right) + \beta p_t \quad (3)$$

$$h^{(i+1)}(t) = (1-\beta)\left(\sum_{u=1}^{d_{out}(t)} \frac{a^{(t)(u)}}{\sum_{t \in \mathbf{T}} \sum_{u=1}^{d_{out}(t)} a^{(i)}(u)}\right) + \beta p_t \quad (4)$$

K-Step Markov: the previous approaches represent *Markov Chains* in which the number of steps taken from the *random walk* is stochastic. *K-Step Markov* limits the number of steps to K. That is, the random walk starts for the given vertices of interest $t \in \mathbf{T}$ and stops after K steps. For a large enough K, the result of the ranking converges to the limit of *PageRank*. The main advantage of such an approach is scalability for large data graphs. On the other hand for step sizes not large enough the ranking lacks accuracy.

3.5 Dataset Profile Representation

The resulting profiles $\mathcal{P}$ are represented in RDF using the VoID vocabulary and are publicly available according to Linked Data principles[6]. However, VoID alone does not provide the representativeness required to capture the computed topic ranking scores. Hence, the complementary Vocabulary of Links (VoL) is introduced to complement the dataset description with a set of links to the associated dataset topics, the used ranking method and the respective score. Thus, we enable queries to select relevant datasets for a given topic. For further details, we refer the reader to the website at `http://data-observatory.org/lod-profiles/`

4 Experimental Setup

This section describes the experimental setup used for the evaluation of our approach and data. We introduce the used data, the *ground truth* and *evaluation metrics* used to measure the profiling accuracy, and the *baseline* approaches for comparison. Furthermore, the use of DBpedia in our experimental setup, for

[6] `http://data-observatory.org/lod-profiles/sparql`

extracting structured information for the dataset profiles, does not present a limitation on using other more specialised reference dataset or a combination of reference datasets.

4.1 Data and Ground Truth

In our experiments we covered all LOD Cloud datasets whose endpoints were available. This resulted in 129 datasets with approximately 260 million resource instances and billions of triples.

For the evaluation we considered a subset of datasets for which we have constructed a *ground truth*[7] in the form of dataset profiles. For this task, we have exploited crowd-sourced, topic profiles already available from existing datasets. Several datasets provide a sufficient amount of manually assigned topic indicators for their resources (not the datasets themselves). These are represented by *keywords* (in the case of bibliographic resource metadata) or *tags* (for user-generated content metadata). We exploit these topic indicators, usually assigned by domain experts, to generate dataset profiles. To link such term-based topic indicators to DBpedia categories, we manually extracted entities (and eventually categories) for each topic indicator, unless the topic indicators were already available in the form of DBpedia entities. Queries to DBpedia were used to retrieve candidate entities where matching ones were selected manually. The resulting topics were ranked according to their accumulated frequency from all resources within a dataset. This is assumed to provide a more representative dataset profile.

Table 1 shows for each dataset the number of resources and the datatype properties from which topic indicators were extracted. However, due to non-accurately extracted entities, we manually checked for correctness of the named entity recognition process.

Table 1. Entity and Category from annotated resource instances with topic indicators for the specific datatypes properties (in the form of *keywords, tags, subjects*) for the ground truth datasets

Dataset-ID	Properties	#Resources
yovisto	`skos:subject`, `dbpedia:{subject, class, discipline, kategorie, tagline}`[8]	62879
oxpoints	`dcterms:subject,dc:subject`	37258
socialsemweb-thesaurus	`skos:subject`, `tag:associatedTag`, `dcterms:subject`[9]	2243
semantic-web-dog-food	`dcterms:subject, dc:subject`	20145
lak-dataset	`dcterms:subject, dc:subject`	1691

*The datasets are accessible under: `http://datahub.io/dataset/DATASET_ID`

[7] `http://data-observatory.org/lod-profiles/ground-truth`
[8] `http://dbpedia.org/property/`
[9] `http://www.holygoat.co.uk/owl/redwood/0.1/tags/`

4.2 Evaluation Metrics

The profiling accuracy of the generated dataset profiles is measured using the NDCG metric (normalised discounted cumulative gain). It takes into account the ranking of topics generated using the methods in Section 3.4 compared to the ideal ranking indicated by the *ground truth*. The computation of NDCG is shown in Equation 5.

$$NDCG@l = \frac{DCG@l}{iDCG@l} \quad \text{where} \quad DCG@l = rel_1 + \sum_{i=2}^{l} \frac{rel_i}{log_2 i} \tag{5}$$

where $DCG@l$ represents the discounted cumulative gain at rank l, whereas $iDCG@l$ is the ideal $DCG@l$ computed from the *ground truth*.

Note that, the set of topics from the computed dataset profiles and the ones from the *ground truth* are overlapping, but not identical. Hence, for the cases where topics from the dataset profiles do not exist in the ranked set of topics in our *ground truth*, we set the ranking value to zero.

4.3 Baselines

As baselines, we chose well established approaches for topic detection. The baselines of choice generate a *profile graph* based on (i) simple *tf-idf* term weighting and (ii) *LDA* topic modelling[10] tool. In order to generate profiles consisting of DBpedia categories according to our definition from the sets of terms generated by the baselines, we followed the same approach as in Section 3.2. For the baselines, we consider the full set of resource instances for analysis. The output of each method is a set of ranked terms:

tf-idf: as the standard term frequency weighting in Information Retrieval. For *tf-idf* we assessed several initialisations of top ranked included terms (excluding stop words) $\{50, 100, 150, 200\}$, sorted based on their score. Relating to standard usage of *tf-idf*, each resource instance represents a document.

LDA: produces terms describing topics using machine learning approaches. As in the case of *tf-idf*, we use several initialisations with varying number of topics and terms defining a topic. The number of topics are $\{10, 20, 30, 40, 50\}$, with various numbers of terms per topic $\{50, 100, 150, 200\}$. The datasets are represented as single documents, since the decomposition into resource instances as documents does not influence the topic modelling tool.

The generated and ranked terms from the corresponding baseline approaches are used as seeds to generate dataset profiles. For each individual term a DBpedia entity is extracted, when there is a match from the automatic NER process. From the extracted entities, we construct the dataset profiles by taking the corresponding DBpedia categories assigned to the property `dcterms:subject` and additionally expand with equivalent broader categories. Finally, the edge weights in the profile graph $\mathcal{P}$ consist of topic scores assigned for the individual datasets and correspond to the *term weight* (computed from one of the baselines).

[10] `http://mallet.cs.umass.edu`

5 Results and Evaluation

In our experimental evaluation, we focus on two aspects: i) *profiling accuracy* which assesses the topic rankings induced by the graphical-models and baselines against those in the *ground truth*, and ii) *scalability* of the profiling approach finding the right trade-off between profiling accuracy and computation time.

5.1 Profiling Accuracy

In this section, we compare the *profile accuracy* from our profiling pipeline in different configurations with those of the baseline approaches.

The *profiling accuracy* results shown in Figure 2a are generated based on our profiling pipeline (using *PRankP*, *HITSP*, *KStepM* for topic ranking) and *tf-idf, LDA*. The results from *PRankP* and *HITSP* are generated with only 10 iterations and parameter $\beta = 0.5$, which indicates the probability of jumping back to a known vertex (in our case, an analysed resource instance of a specific dataset). For *KStepM* the number of steps was set to $K = 5$. In the case of baseline approaches we ran the experiments with several initialisations; however here we report the best performing. For *tf-idf*, the dataset profiles were generated using the top-200 terms. For the second baseline, *LDA*, we used the topic modelling tool, Mallet, with 20 topics and top-100 ranked terms. The results shown in Figure 2a correspond to an analysis conducted on the full set of resource instances. Hence, the various sampling strategies in the profiling pipeline are equal. Furthermore, the `NDCG` scores are averaged for all datasets. In the case of *PRankP, HITSP, KStepM*, the values reflect the ranking gained in combination with *NTR* as a pre-filtering step. Similarly, the results in Figure 2b show the *profiling accuracy* for the individual datasets and the best performing ranking approach, *KStepM*, where *PRankP* has comparably similar ranking with a negligible difference.

Highlighting the benefits of applying the ranking approaches in combination with *NTR*, Figure 3a shows the difference in profiling accuracy for *KStepM* approach at `NDCG@100` (averaged over all datasets) for different sample sizes. The topic scores computed by *NTR* are used to filter noisy topics, when their values are below the average from all topics in a dataset profile $\mathcal{P}_D$.

To determine the correct topic expansion level, we measure the correlation between the expansion level and *profiling accuracy* Figure 3b. The results show the impact of the expansion level on the *profiling accuracy* for the case of the topic ranking approach, *KStepM*. The intuition is that, at a certain expansion level, the dataset profiles are associated with noisy topics (when a topic is assigned to too many entities). Figure 3b shows that the highest overall ranking accuracy was achieved at the expansion level of two.

5.2 Scalability vs. Accuracy Trade-Off: Impact of Sample Size

We analyse the impact of the various sampling strategies (*random*, *weighted* and *centrality*) at different sample sizes on ranking accuracy, to identify a suitable balance between *ranking time* and *profiling accuracy*.

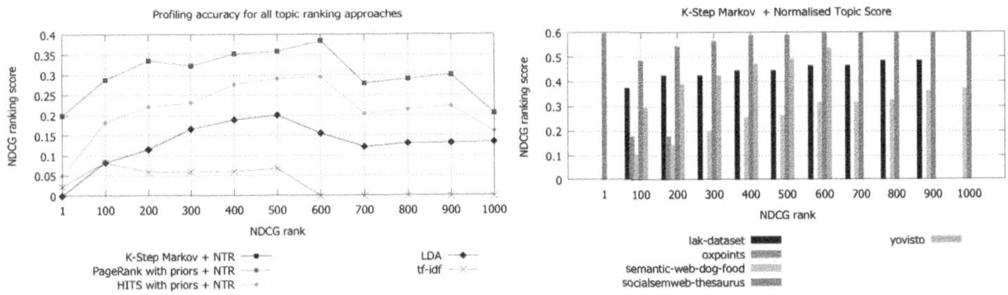

(a) (b)

Fig. 2. (a) Profiling accuracy for the different ranking approaches (in combination with NTR) using the full sample of analysed resource instances with NDCG score averaged $\forall D \in \mathbf{D}$; (b) Best performing topic ranking approach *KStepM* (in combination with NTR) for the full set of analysed resource instances

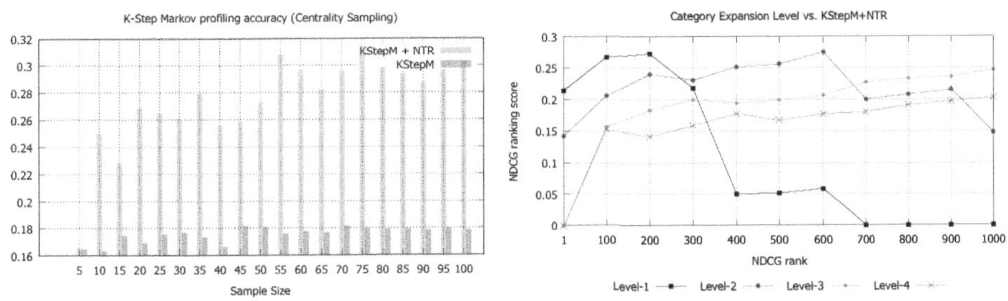

(a) (b)

Fig. 3. (a) Comparison of profiling accuracy for *KStepM+NTR* and *KStepM* at NDCG@100; (b) Category level expansion impact on profiling accuracy for *KStepM+NTR*

To find the ideal trade-off between *scalability* and *accuracy*, we analyse the behaviour of the ranking metric NDCG as follows: (i) average performance (ΔNDCG) over all datasets and computed ranks ($l = 1, \ldots, 1000$), (ii) *profiling accuracy* and *topic ranking time*, using *KStepM* ranking approach.

For (i), Figure 4 shows the results of the ΔNDCG score for *KStepM* at different sample sizes (x-axis). The plot for the individual datasets shows the *standard deviation* from the average value of ΔNDCG, indicating the stability of the profiling accuracy. While, for (ii), Figure 5 shows the correlation between profiling accuracy and ranking time. It assesses attributes such as the amount of time taken to rank topics (*KStepM, HITSP, PRankP*) and the different sample sizes. In detail, the leftmost *y-axis* shows the log-scale of the amount of time (in seconds) it takes to rank the topics at the different sample sizes. The rightmost *y-axis* shows the profiling accuracy achieved at a specific sample size.

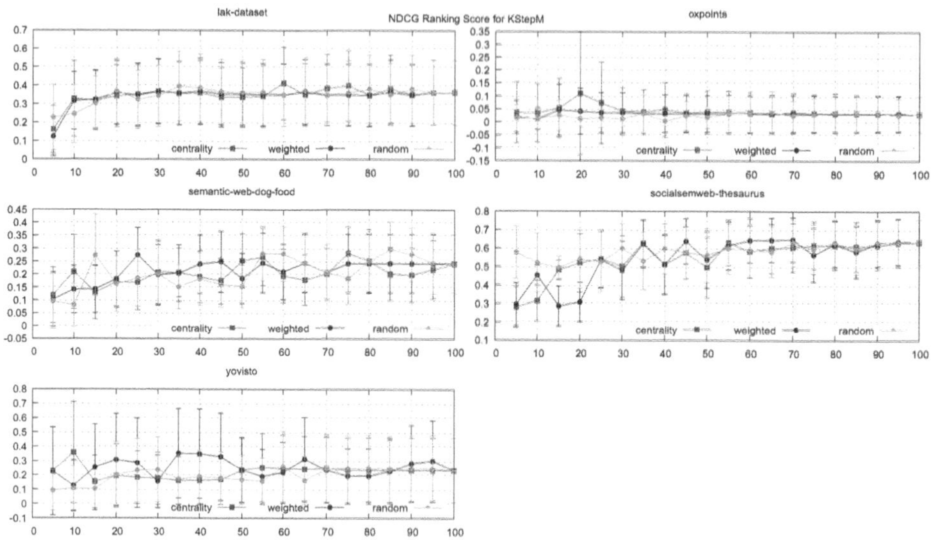

Fig. 4. Profiling accuracy averaged for all ranks $l = \{1, \ldots, 1000\}$. The graph shows the standard deviation of ΔNDCG from the expected ranking at the different sample sizes (x-axis).

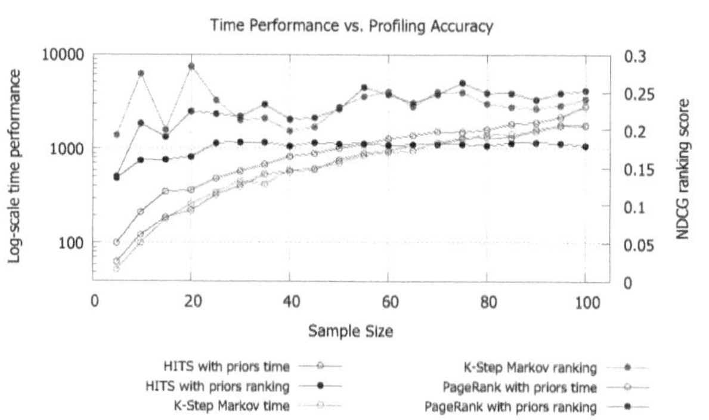

Fig. 5. The trade-off between profiling accuracy (ΔNDCG averaged over all datasets and ranks) and the topic ranking time based on the different graphical-models

5.3 Discussion and Analysis

The results shown in the previous two sections support the proposed choice of steps in the profiling pipeline and identified suitable parameters. The combination of topic ranking approaches (*PRankP, HITSP* and *KStepM*) with *NTR* significantly improves the profiling accuracy. In Figure 3a and for *KStepM*, a drastic increase in accuracy can be noted for all sample sizes. This is rather expected as the *NTR* scores serve as a pre-filtering mechanism for noisy topics. From the overall ranking comparisons in Figure 2a, *KStepM* achieves the best results (Figure 2b), with *PRankP* having comparably similar results.

By contrast, the baseline ranking approaches show that the overall performance is relatively low. The *LDA*-based baseline approach achieves comparable accuracy only at rank $l = 500$. The results for the second baseline based on *tf-idf* are uniformly very low at all ranks, with most values being well below 0.1. The results from the baselines are attained from the best performing initialisations (see Section 4.3). In the case of *LDA* we used 20 topics with top-100 terms per topic, and for *tf-idf* an increase of more than top-200 analysed terms did not benefit significantly the profiling accuracy. The difference between the best performing baseline based on *LDA* and that based on *KStepM+NTR* is Δ`NDCG@100`=+0.21 in favour of the latter.

The results in Figure 4 show that, at low sample sizes, the accuracy is already fairly stable. In other words, the average profiling accuracy for the different ranking approaches and sampling strategies increases slightly with the increase of sample size, while its standard deviation decreases. We could identify sample sizes of 5% and 10% as nearly optimal, which are also nearly optimal with regards to the balance between accuracy and scalability in Figure 5. The dataset profiling time is reduced significantly while aiming for a suitable trade-off between scalability and profile accuracy. The process of generating profiles contains three computationally intensive steps: (i) indexing resources for further analysis; (ii) performing the NER process; and (iii) topic ranking. With respect to (i), indexing 10% of resource instances takes on average, 7 minutes per dataset, in contrast to up to 3 hours on average when considering all resource instances. For (ii), since we use the online service of DBpedia Spotlight, the process is non-deterministic, as it is dependent on the network load and the number of simultaneous requests. Such process could be optimised by hosting the service locally. Finally, for (iii), the topic ranking process is optimised down to 2 minutes, for 10% resources, from 45 minutes, when considering the full set of resources (Figure 5).

Finally, the fluctuations in profiling accuracy in Figure 4 show high deviations for dataset '`oxpoints`'. This can be explained by the fact that its resources contain geo-information about the University of Oxford and as such it presents a difficult case due to the low coverage from DBpedia content.

6 Related Work

Although no approach considers specifically the problem of generating metadata about Linked Data sets profiles, our approach is closely related to a LOD Cloud dynamics of changes analysis [13]. The work in the reported paper is related to several fields ranging from VoID data generation [5,4], semantic indexing [18], graph importance measures [20,12], and topic relevance assessment [8,9] address similar problems. Thus, in this section, we briefly review the literature and compare our approach with related literature.

Generating VoID data about Linked Data sets is considered in [5], where individual triples are analysed and, based on commonly shared predicates, the corresponding datasets are clustered. In a later work, Böhm et al. [4] cluster resources based on the dataset specific ontologies used by considering the relationship between the different resource classes. In spite of using specific ontologies to create clusters, we use established reference datasets.

Recently, Hulpus et al. [12] proposed the *Canopy* framework that, for a given set of extracted topics from analysed textual resources, the matching DBpedia sub-graph is retrieved and the corresponding relationships are quantified using graph importance measures. In our case, we automatically extract entities from textual resources and further expand to the related DBpedia category sub-graphs. A different approach is presented by White et al. [20], where they measure the relative importance of a node in a data graph by incorporating knowledge about prior probability of a specific node. We follow the same strategy to measure the importance of topics in the generated dataset profiles.

Tìpalo, a framework introduced by Gangemi et al. [10], analyses heuristics for typing DBpedia entities using information extracted from Wikipedia pages mentioning a specific entity. In our work, we focus on topic assessment using DBpedia graph and the context of analysed resources of a dataset from which an entity is extracted.

Another framework is *Sindice* [18], that indexes RDF documents and uses DBpedia entities as a source to actively index resources. Additionally, Kiryakov et al. [14] index the Web of Documents and capture extracted named entities in a manually crafted ontology. Comparing to our work, we go beyond mere annotations and generate an interlinked data graph of datasets based on topics which are quantified for their importance based on the support given from the individual resource instances.

Käfer et al. [13] have crawled and analysed the LOD cloud focusing mostly on the dynamics of changes in datasets (predicates, number of instances, etc). The crawling process relies on pre-selection of prominent resources (ranked based on PageRank). We aim at generating dataset profiles and analysing the temporal aspects of topics on how they evolve during time. LODStats [2] analyses the LOD-cloud structure and provides statistical characteristics of datasets and metrics related to vocabulary usage. In spite of the insights gained through such an analysis, we focus at a content-wise analysis.

7 Conclusions

In this paper, we proposed an approach to automatically generate structured dataset profiles with the overall goal of facilitating the assessment, search and discovery of LD datasets. Aiming for a method which is scalable and efficient and yet, at the same time, provides a high level of accuracy and representativeness of the generated data, our approach uses sampling techniques together with ranking methods to provide the *profile graph*. Based on experimental evaluation, the most suitable trade-off is found between small sample sizes to cater for efficiency and representativeness of the resulting profiles.

As part of our experiments, we generated dataset profiles for all datasets in the LOD Cloud. The evaluation shows that, even with comparably small sample sizes (10%), representative profiles and rankings can be generated (i.e.

ΔNDCG=0.31 for '`socialsemweb-thesaurus`'), when applying *KStepM* combined with the *NTR*. The results demonstrate superior performance when compared to *LDA* with ΔNDCG=0.10 (with the full set of resource instance).

It has been noted that meaningfulness and comparability of topic profiles can be increased when considering topics associated with certain resource types only. As part of our current work we are developing resource type-specific dataset profiles and the tracking of topic profile evolution. These take advantage of our *profile graph* to provide more specific dataset search and browsing capabilities.

Acknowledgements. This work was partly funded by the LinkedUp (GA No:317620) and DURAARK (GA No:600908) projects under the FP7 programme of the European Commission.

References

1. Auer, S., Bizer, C., Kobilarov, G., Lehmann, J., Cyganiak, R., Ives, Z.G.: DBpedia: A nucleus for a web of open data. In: Aberer, K., et al. (eds.) ASWC 2007 and ISWC 2007. LNCS, vol. 4825, pp. 722–735. Springer, Heidelberg (2007)
2. Auer, S., Demter, J., Martin, M., Lehmann, J.: LODStats – an extensible framework for high-performance dataset analytics. In: ten Teije, A., Völker, J., Handschuh, S., Stuckenschmidt, H., d'Acquin, M., Nikolov, A., Aussenac-Gilles, N., Hernandez, N. (eds.) EKAW 2012. LNCS, vol. 7603, pp. 353–362. Springer, Heidelberg (2012)
3. Bizer, C., Heath, T., Berners-Lee, T.: Linked data - the story so far. Int. J. Semantic Web Inf. Syst. 5(3), 1–22 (2009)
4. Böhm, C., Kasneci, G., Naumann, F.: Latent topics in graph-structured data. In: 21st ACM International Conference on Information and Knowledge Management (CIKM), pp. 2663–2666 (2012)
5. Böhm, C., Lorey, J., Naumann, F.: Creating void descriptions for web-scale data. J. Web Sem. 9(3), 339–345 (2011)
6. Brin, S., Page, L.: The anatomy of a large-scale hypertextual web search engine. Computer Networks 30(1-7), 107–117 (1998)
7. Buil-Aranda, C., Hogan, A., Umbrich, J., Vandenbussche, P.-Y.: SPARQL web-querying infrastructure: Ready for action? In: Alani, H., et al. (eds.) ISWC 2013, Part II. LNCS, vol. 8219, pp. 277–293. Springer, Heidelberg (2013)
8. d'Aquin, M., Adamou, A., Dietze, S.: Assessing the educational linked data landscape. In: Web Science (WebSci), pp. 43–46 (2013)
9. Fetahu, B., Dietze, S., Pereira Nunes, B., Antonio Casanova, M.: Generating structured profiles of linked data graphs. In: Proceedings of the 12th International Semantic Web Conference (ISWC). Springer (2013)
10. Gangemi, A., Nuzzolese, A.G., Presutti, V., Draicchio, F., Musetti, A., Ciancarini, P.: Automatic typing of dBpedia entities. In: Cudré-Mauroux, P., et al. (eds.) ISWC 2012, Part I. LNCS, vol. 7649, pp. 65–81. Springer, Heidelberg (2012)
11. Guéret, C., Groth, P., Stadler, C., Lehmann, J.: Assessing linked data mappings using network measures. In: Simperl, E., Cimiano, P., Polleres, A., Corcho, O., Presutti, V. (eds.) ESWC 2012. LNCS, vol. 7295, pp. 87–102. Springer, Heidelberg (2012)

12. Hulpus, I., Hayes, C., Karnstedt, M., Greene, D.: Unsupervised graph-based topic labelling using dbpedia. In: ACM International Conference on Web Search and Data Mining (WSDM), pp. 465–474 (2013)
13. Käfer, T., Abdelrahman, A., Umbrich, J., O'Byrne, P., Hogan, A.: Observing linked data dynamics. In: Cimiano, P., Corcho, O., Presutti, V., Hollink, L., Rudolph, S. (eds.) ESWC 2013. LNCS, vol. 7882, pp. 213–227. Springer, Heidelberg (2013)
14. Kiryakov, A., Popov, B., Terziev, I., Manov, D., Ognyanoff, D.: Semantic annotation, indexing, and retrieval. J. Web Sem. 2(1), 49–79 (2004)
15. Kleinberg, J.M.: Authoritative sources in a hyperlinked environment. J. ACM 46(5), 604–632 (1999)
16. Mendes, P.N., Jakob, M., García-Silva, A., Bizer, C.: Dbpedia spotlight: shedding light on the web of documents. In: 7th International Conference on Semantic Systems (ISWC), pp. 1–8 (2011)
17. Pereira Nunes, B., Dietze, S., Casanova, M.A., Kawase, R., Fetahu, B., Nejdl, W.: Combining a co-occurrence-based and a semantic measure for entity linking. In: Cimiano, P., Corcho, O., Presutti, V., Hollink, L., Rudolph, S. (eds.) ESWC 2013. LNCS, vol. 7882, pp. 548–562. Springer, Heidelberg (2013)
18. Oren, E., Delbru, R., Catasta, M., Cyganiak, R., Stenzhorn, H., Tummarello, G.: Sindice.com: a document-oriented lookup index for open linked data. IJMSO 3(1), 37–52 (2008)
19. Suchanek, F.M., Kasneci, G., Weikum, G.: Yago: a core of semantic knowledge. In: Williamson, C.L., Zurko, M.E., Patel-Schneider, P.F., Shenoy, P.J. (eds.) WWW, pp. 697–706. ACM (2007)
20. White, S., Smyth, P.: Algorithms for estimating relative importance in networks. In: Proceedings of the 9th ACM SIGKDD International Conference on Knowledge Discovery and Data Mining (SIGKDD), pp. 266–275 (2003)

Facilitating Human Intervention in Coreference Resolution with Comparative Entity Summaries

Danyun Xu, Gong Cheng*, and Yuzhong Qu

State Key Laboratory for Novel Software Technology, Nanjing University,
Nanjing 210023, P.R. China
dyxu@smail.nju.edu.cn, {gcheng,yzqu}@nju.edu.cn

Abstract. A primary challenge to Web data integration is coreference resolution, namely identifying entity descriptions from different data sources that refer to the same real-world entity. Increasingly, solutions to coreference resolution have humans in the loop. For instance, many active learning, crowdsourcing, and pay-as-you-go approaches solicit user feedback for verifying candidate coreferent entities computed by automatic methods. Whereas reducing the number of verification tasks is a major consideration for these approaches, very little attention has been paid to the efficiency of performing each single verification task. To address this issue, in this paper, instead of showing the entire descriptions of two entities for verification which are possibly lengthy, we propose to extract and present a compact summary of them, and expect that such length-limited comparative entity summaries can help human users verify more efficiently without significantly hurting the accuracy of their verification. Our approach exploits the common and different features of two entities that best help indicate (non-)coreference, and also considers the diverse information on their identities. Experimental results show that verification is 2.7–2.9 times faster when using our comparative entity summaries, and its accuracy is not notably affected.

Keywords: #eswc2014Xu, comparative entity summary, coreference resolution, entity consolidation, entity summarization.

1 Introduction

The heterogeneous nature of the Web further motivates the research on data integration, where a primary challenge is how to identify entity descriptions from different data sources that refer to the same real-world entity, which is called coreference resolution, entity consolidation, etc. For instance, DBpedia and GeoNames provide descriptions of many common places but with different identifiers (i.e. URIs); DBpedia and LinkedMDB describe overlapping films.

Apart from a wide variety of automatic methods for solving this problem, recent studies have started to involve human users in this process and, in particular, they solicit user feedback for verifying candidate coreferent entities computed by

* Corresponding author.

V. Presutti et al. (Eds.): ESWC 2014, LNCS 8465, pp. 535–549, 2014.

automatic methods. Among others, active learning [7] seeks to improve the underlying learning-based approach with a minimized amount of user interaction, e.g. a minimum number of verification tasks; crowdsourcing approaches [13] focus on the assignment of verification tasks to a group of paid users and aim to reduce cost while providing high-quality results; pay-as-you-go approaches [6] promise to provide better information to meet a user's need if, for example, the user helps carry out some verification tasks. Along with these solutions, an equally important issue is how to *improve the efficiency of performing each single verification task*, which has received very little attention. Existing efforts mainly enhance the visualization of entity descriptions [1,4], but problems arise when entity descriptions are lengthy, e.g. comprising several hundred property-value pairs as in DBpedia, which overload users with too much information and bring about inefficient verification.

To meet the challenge, in this paper, we propose to automatically generate a compact summary of two entity descriptions for verification. Such length-limited *comparative entity summaries* are expected to help users verify more efficiently due to the reduction in length. Meanwhile, if summaries are generated appropriately, the accuracy of verification is expected to be maintained at a high level. To achieve these, our approach extracts, from entity descriptions, the property-value pairs that best reflect the commonality and difference between the two entities, and also carry the largest amount of diverse information on their identities. We will confirm the above two expectations based on real-world verification tasks and, in particular, show that the comparative entity summaries generated by our approach outperform the entity summaries generated for generic use [3].

Our contribution is threefold.

- We propose to help human users more efficiently verify candidate coreferent entities by using comparative entity summaries.
- We analyze and formalize the goodness of a comparative entity summary to optimize from four angles, and transform these objectives into a binary quadratic knapsack problem to solve.
- We implement and evaluate a solution based on real-world verification tasks.

The remainder of this paper is structured as follows. Section 2 gives the problem statement. Section 3 defines the goodness of a summary. Section 4 describes how to generate a good summary. Section 5 presents the experiments. Section 6 discusses related work. Section 7 concludes the paper with future work.

2 Problem Statement

Let $\Sigma_E, \Sigma_C, \Sigma_P, \Sigma_L$ be the sets of all entities, classes, properties, and literals, respectively; and let $\Sigma_V = \Sigma_E \cup \Sigma_C \cup \Sigma_L$, i.e. the set of all possible property values. The description of an entity e, denoted by $d(e) \subseteq (\Sigma_P \times \Sigma_V)$, comprises a set of property-value pairs (a.k.a. features [3]) extracted from RDF data; in fact, an entity and a feature together correspond to an RDF triple. For convenience, given a feature $f \in d(e)$, let $p(f)$ and $v(f)$ return the property and the value of

Table 1. Three Entity Descriptions as a Running Example

TimBL	TBL	Wendy
⟨givenName, "Tim"⟩	⟨name, "Tim Berners-Lee"⟩	⟨fullName, "Wendy Hall"⟩
⟨surname, "Berners-Lee"⟩	⟨type, ComputerScientist⟩	⟨type, ComputerScientist⟩
⟨altName, "Tim BL"⟩	⟨type, RoyalSocietyFellow⟩	⟨type, RoyalSocietyFellow⟩
⟨type, Scientist⟩	⟨sex, "Male"⟩	⟨sex, "Female"⟩
⟨gender, "male"⟩	⟨invented, WWW⟩	⟨birthplace, London⟩
⟨isDirectorOf, W3C⟩	⟨founded, WSRI⟩	⟨founded, WSRI⟩

this feature, respectively. It is worth noting that, in this paper, only the outgoing arcs of an entity in RDF graph are considered as its description for simplicity. However, the extension to both outgoing and incoming arcs is straightforward. As a running example in this paper, Table 1 presents the descriptions of three entities, where TimBL and TBL refer to the same person in the real world, whereas Wendy refers to a different one.

Each entity, class, and property is assumed to have a human-readable name, which could be given by properties like rdfs:label, foaf:name, and dc:title, or otherwise its local name. When presenting a feature to human users, for entities, classes, and properties, we show their names; and for literals, we show their lexical forms. Both names and lexical forms are strings, or in other words, character sequences. The length of a feature f, denoted by $l(f)$, is then naturally defined as the sum of the length of the name of $p(f)$ and the length of the name or lexical form of $v(f)$. For instance, $l(\langle$gender, "male"$\rangle) = 6 + 4 = 10$.

Given the descriptions of two entities e_i and e_j, we define a *comparative entity summary*, or a summary for short, as $\langle S_i, S_j \rangle$ subject to $S_i \subseteq d(e_i)$ and $S_j \subseteq d(e_j)$. That is, a summary consists of a subset of features extracted from each of the two entity descriptions. A summary $\langle S_i, S_j \rangle$ is *feasible* if

$$\sum_{f_m \in S_i} l(f_m) + \sum_{f_n \in S_j} l(f_n) \leq C\,, \tag{1}$$

where C is a character limit defined by the specific application.

Among all feasible summaries, we aim to find the optimum one in terms of some criterion, i.e. one that maximizes some objective function called *Goodness*, which will be discussed in the next section.

3 Goodness of a Summary: A High-Level Analysis

In this section, we discuss, at a high level and from four angles, what kinds of features constitute a good summary. We will illustrate our ideas with the three entity descriptions presented in Table 1. Our approach to the generation of such good summaries and a detailed implementation of those low-level measures that are used will be introduced in the next section.

3.1 Commonality

In general, human users identify coreferent entity descriptions based on their common features. So a good summary here should include those features that can be found in both of the two entity descriptions $d(e_i)$ and $d(e_j)$ to compare. For instance, in Table 1, `TimBL` and `TBL` have the same name and gender, indicating that they probably have the same referent. However, as illustrated by this case, there are three challenges to be met.

Comparability between Properties. Due to the heterogeneous nature of the Web, it is more practical to seek and exploit semantically (rather than syntactically) equivalent features. In particular, entities may be described using different properties. These properties may have the same meaning but different names, e.g. `gender` and `sex`; they may also describe not exactly the same but overlapping aspects of an entity, e.g. `givenName` and `name`. In light of these, to find semantically equivalent features, we need to firstly identify which properties are comparable and to what extent. Given two properties p_i and p_j, we use $comp(p_i, p_j) \in [0, 1]$ to denote their *comparability*. Intuitively, $comp$(`gender`,`sex`) should be as high as 1; $comp$(`givenName`,`name`) should also be considerably high; for many other pairs of properties such as `sex` and `givenName`, their comparability should be very low, if not 0.

Similarity between Values. For the same reason, we need to measure the *similarity* between two property values v_i and v_j, denoted by $sim(v_i, v_j) \in [-1, 1]$, where 1 indicates they are exactly the same and -1 indicates completely different. For instance, the similarity between "male" and "Male" should be as high as 1; "Berners-Lee" and "Tim Berners-Lee" should also be similar to each other; however, "male" and "Berners-Lee" should be dissimilar. In particular, those pairs of values having positive similarity are of interest to us here.

Likeness to an IFP. Not all the properties are equally useful in indicating coreference. For instance, sharing a common gender is a much weaker indicator than sharing a common name. One extreme is inverse functional properties (IFP) in OWL such as the mailbox of a person, which is one of the strongest properties in indicating coreference because two people sharing a common mailbox must be coreferent according to the semantics of IFP defined in OWL. However, most properties are not defined as IFP, but they indeed exhibit different abilities to indicate coreference, e.g. name being stronger than gender. So for each property p, we use $ifp(p) \in [0, 1]$ to denote its *likeness to an IFP*. Intuitively, $ifp(p) = 1$ if p is exactly an IFP; ifp(`name`) should also be considerably high and, in particular, much higher than ifp(`gender`).

With these three measures, given a pair of features f_m and f_n satisfying $sim(v(f_m), v(f_n)) > 0$, we define their *strength of indicating coreference* as

$$ind_C(f_m, f_n) = comp(p(f_m), p(f_n)) \cdot sim(v(f_m), v(f_n)) \cdot \frac{2 \cdot ifp(p(f_m)) \cdot ifp(p(f_n))}{ifp(p(f_m)) + ifp(p(f_n))}, \tag{2}$$

where in case f_m and f_n have different properties, the harmonic mean of their likeness to an IFP is used.

Finally, we aim to find a feasible summary $\langle S_i, S_j \rangle$ that reflects the most *commonality*:

$$COMM(\langle S_i, S_j \rangle) = \sum_{\substack{\langle f_m, f_n \rangle \in (S_i \times S_j) \\ sim(v(f_m), v(f_n)) > 0}} ind_C(f_m, f_n) \,. \tag{3}$$

3.2 Difference

A summary only reflecting commonality may be one-sided. For instance, for `TBL` and `Wendy` in Table 1, a "commonality-only" summary probably only includes the three common features shared by them. As a result, a human user is likely to be misled and judge them as coreferent. The problem resides in the fact that such a summary fails to show the difference between them. To fix it, we propose to also choose dissimilar features that can help human users identify non-coreferent entity descriptions. To achieve this, similar to the discussion of commonality, we also consider three factors.

Comparability between Properties. Dissimilar features make sense only when they have comparable properties. Here we reuse the measure *comp* introduced previously.

Dissimilarity between Values. To show the difference between entity descriptions, we need to choose dissimilar values (of comparable properties). Since the measure *sim* previously introduced is in the range $[-1, 1]$ and negative values indicate dissimilarity, here we only consider those pairs of values having negative similarity, and more dissimilar ones are with larger absolute values of *sim*.

Likeness to a FP. Not all the properties are equally effective in indicating non-coreference. For instance, in Table 1, although `TBL`'s `ComputerScientist` and `Wendy`'s `RoyalSocietyFellow` are dissimilar `type`s, it should not be regarded as an indicator of non-coreference; in fact, their `type` properties take exactly the same values. The problem is caused by the multiple values of a property. Actually, the fewer values a property can take, the stronger indicator it is. One extreme is functional properties (FP) in OWL such as the gender of a person, which is one of the most effective properties in indicating non-coreference because one person can have only one gender according to the semantics of FP defined in OWL so that two people sharing different genders must be non-coreferent. Since most properties are not defined as FP, for each property p, we use $fp(p) \in [0, 1]$ to quantify its *likeness to a FP* and characterize its ability to indicate non-coreference. Intuitively, $fp(p) = 1$ if p is exactly a FP; $fp($`type`$)$ should not be very high because an entity often has several types.

Then, given a pair of features f_m and f_n satisfying $sim(v(f_m), v(f_n)) < 0$, similar to Eq. (2), we define their *strength of indicating non-coreference* as

$$ind_{NC}(f_m, f_n) = comp(p(f_m), p(f_n)) \cdot |sim(v(f_m), v(f_n))| \cdot \frac{2 \cdot fp(p(f_m)) \cdot fp(p(f_n))}{fp(p(f_m)) + fp(p(f_n))} \,, \tag{4}$$

where in case f_m and f_n have different properties, the harmonic mean of their likeness to a FP is used.

Finally, we aim to find a feasible summary $\langle S_i, S_j \rangle$ that reflects the most *difference*:

$$DIFF(\langle S_i, S_j \rangle) = \sum_{\substack{\langle f_m, f_n \rangle \in (S_i \times S_j) \\ sim(v(f_m), v(f_n)) < 0}} ind_{NC}(f_m, f_n) . \tag{5}$$

3.3 Information on Identity

Sometimes two features not explicitly related to each other may also help human users identify coreferent entity descriptions. For instance, in Table 1, ⟨`isDirectorOf`, `W3C`⟩ in `TimBL`'s description and ⟨`invented`, `WWW`⟩ in `TBL`'s description are weak in indicating both coreference and non-coreference according to Eq. (2) and (4), respectively, because their properties, `isDirectorOf` and `invented`, are not comparable. However, if a human user has some knowledge of the World Wide Web, from these two features she can infer that `TimBL` and `TBL` should both refer to Tim Berners-Lee, thereby being coreferent. The inference actually hinges on the fact that these two features can both precisely reflect the identities of these two entities. In other words, both of them carry a sufficiently large amount of information on the identity of an entity.

More generally, we use $inf(f) \in [0, 1]$ to denote the *amount of information on identity* carried by f. Intuitively, $inf(f) = 1$ if f uniquely indicates the identity of an entity; for instance, the director of W3C must be Tim Berners-Lee. By contrast, ⟨`type`, `ComputerScientist`⟩ carries a relatively small amount of information on identity because many people are computer scientists; and ⟨`gender`, "male"⟩ provides very little information. Finally, we aim to find a feasible summary $\langle S_i, S_j \rangle$ that carries the largest *amount of information on identity*:

$$INF(\langle S_i, S_j \rangle) = \sum_{f_m \in S_i} inf(f_m) + \sum_{f_n \in S_j} inf(f_n) . \tag{6}$$

3.4 Diversity of Information

Features in an entity description may share overlapping aspects, e.g. the `givenName` and `altName` of `TimBL` in Table 1. Selecting such overlapping features into a summary will lead to information redundancy. To fully exploit the capacity of a feasible summary, we expect it to provide information that is as diverse as possible. To achieve this, we use $ovlp(f_m, f_n) \in [0, 1]$ to denote the *overlap* between two features f_m and f_n. For instance, the overlap between ⟨`givenName`, "Tim"⟩ and ⟨`altName`, "Tim BL"⟩ is considerably large, whereas ⟨`type`, `Scientist`⟩ and ⟨`gender`, "male"⟩ appear to share no overlap in information. A diverse summary is one containing features sharing small overlap. Therefore, we aim to find a feasible summary $\langle S_i, S_j \rangle$ that maximizes the *diversity of information* it carries:

$$DIV(\langle S_i, S_j \rangle) = \sum_{f_m, f_{m'} \in S_i} -ovlp(f_m, f_{m'}) + \sum_{f_n, f_{n'} \in S_j} -ovlp(f_n, f_{n'}) . \tag{7}$$

3.5 Goodness

In general, the four objective functions, namely $COMM$, $DIFF$, INF, and DIV, can be conflicting, i.e., sometimes no single feasible summary can simultaneously optimize each objective. To solve this multi-objective optimization problem, one common way of quantifying the trade-offs in satisfying different objectives is to maximize a linear scalarization:

$$\begin{aligned} Goodness(\langle S_i, S_j \rangle) =& \alpha \cdot COMM(\langle S_i, S_j \rangle) + \beta \cdot DIFF(\langle S_i, S_j \rangle) \\ &+ \gamma \cdot INF(\langle S_i, S_j \rangle) + \delta \cdot DIV(\langle S_i, S_j \rangle) \,, \end{aligned} \tag{8}$$

where $\alpha, \beta, \gamma, \delta > 0$ are weights to be tuned in the specific application. We will solve this scalarization in the next section.

4 Generation of a Good Summary

In this section, firstly we introduce how we find a feasible summary that can maximize the scalarization in Eq. (8) by using the binary quadratic knapsack model. Then, we describe our implementation of those low-level measures invoked in the four objective functions.

4.1 Problem Transformation and Solution

The scalarization in Eq. (8) exactly fits the binary quadratic knapsack problem (QKP) [8]. Specifically, given two entities e_i and e_j, we number the features in $d(e_i)$ and $d(e_j)$ from 1 to $|d(e_i)|$ and from $|d(e_i)| + 1$ to $N = |d(e_i)| + |d(e_j)|$, respectively. By introducing a series of binary variables x_m to indicate whether feature f_m is selected into the optimum summary, the problem is formulated as:

$$\begin{aligned} \text{maximize} & \sum_{m=1}^{N} \sum_{n=m}^{N} p_{mn} x_m x_n \\ \text{subject to} & \sum_{m=1}^{N} l(f_m) x_m \leq C \,, \\ & x_m \in \{0, 1\},\, m = 1, \ldots, N \,, \end{aligned} \tag{9}$$

where $l(f_m)$ and C (cf. Eq. (1)) are regarded as the "weight" of feature f_m and the "capacity" of the knapsack, respectively, and "profit" p_{mn} is defined as:

$$p_{mn} = \begin{cases} \alpha \cdot ind_C(f_m, f_n) & \text{if } f_m \in d(e_i), f_n \in d(e_j), sim(v(f_m), v(f_n)) > 0, \\ 0 & \text{if } f_m \in d(e_i), f_n \in d(e_j), sim(v(f_m), v(f_n)) = 0, \\ \beta \cdot ind_{NC}(f_m, f_n) & \text{if } f_m \in d(e_i), f_n \in d(e_j), sim(v(f_m), v(f_n)) < 0, \\ \gamma \cdot inf(f_m) & \text{if } m = n, \\ -\delta \cdot ovlp(f_m, f_n) & \text{otherwise.} \end{cases} \tag{10}$$

Since QKP is strongly NP-hard, we cannot expect to find a fully polynomial-time approximation scheme (FPTAS) unless P=NP. Among heuristic methods that are of interest to practical applications, to the best of our knowledge, a GRASP-based implementation presented in [14] performs the best both in the quality of solutions and in running time. In our experiments, we use this implementation to find near-optimum summaries.

4.2 Implementation of Low-Level Measures

Six low-level measures, namely *comp*, *sim*, ifp, fp, inf, and *ovlp*, are invoked in the four objective functions. In the following, we present just one way of implementing them, which is not the core contribution of this paper and can certainly be substituted with others.

ISub [10] returns the similarity between two strings, which is in the range $[-1, 1]$, where 1 and -1 indicate completely similar and dissimilar, respectively. Given two properties or two property values, let *isub* return the ISub similarity between their names or lexical forms. The similarity between property values v_i and v_j is then simply given by

$$sim(v_i, v_j) = isub(v_i, v_j) .$$

Analogously, the overlap between features f_m and f_n is defined as

$$ovlp(f_m, f_n) = \max(isub(p(f_m), p(f_n)), isub(v(f_m), v(f_n)), 0) .$$

To measure the comparability between two properties, we compute their similarity as a surrogate, which has been extensively studied in the field of ontology matching [9]. We use a learning-based method to measure *comp*, which assumes the existence of some pairs of coreferent entities, denoted by $M \subseteq (\Sigma_E \times \Sigma_E)$. For two properties p_i and p_j, we use the subset of M that are relevant to them:

$$M(p_i, p_j) = \{\langle e_s, e_t \rangle \in M : \exists f_m \in d(e_s), f_n \in d(e_t), (p(f_m) = p_i, p(f_n) = p_j)\} .$$

Then, we look at, within these coreferent entity descriptions, to what extent the values of p_i and p_j can find good matches in each other:

$$comp_L(p_i, p_j) = \frac{1}{|M(p_i, p_j)|} \cdot \sum_{\langle e_s, e_t \rangle \in M(p_i, p_j)} \frac{1}{2}(as(p_i, p_j, e_s, e_t) + as(p_j, p_i, e_t, e_s))$$

$$as(p_i, p_j, e_s, e_t) = \frac{1}{|V(p_i, e_s)|} \cdot \sum_{v_k \in V(p_i, e_s)} \max_{v_l \in V(p_j, e_t)} isub(v_k, v_l) ,$$

where $V(p_i, e_s)$ returns all the values of p_i in $d(e_s)$. Finally, we define

$$comp(p_i, p_j) = \begin{cases} max(comp_L(p_i, p_j), 0) & \text{if } M(p_i, p_j) \neq \emptyset, \\ max(isub(p_i, p_j), 0) & \text{otherwise.} \end{cases}$$

That is, given no training data for p_i and p_j, their ISub similarity will be used.

Given a property p, inspired by [5], we estimate $ifp(p)$ and $fp(p)$ based on a corpus. Specifically, given a corpus of entity descriptions denoted by D, we have

$$ifp(p) = \frac{|\bigcup_{d(e)\in D}\{v(f) : \exists f \in d(e), (p(f) = p)\}|}{\sum_{d(e)\in D}|\{f \in d(e) : p(f) = p\}|}$$
$$fp(p) = \frac{|\{d(e) \in D : \exists f \in d(e), (p(f) = p)\}|}{\sum_{d(e)\in D}|\{f \in d(e) : p(f) = p\}|}.$$

The amount of information on identity carried by feature f is also estimated based on D. According to information theory, we have

$$inf(f) = 1 - \frac{\log|\{d(e) \in D : f \in d(e)\}|}{\log|D|}.$$

5 Experiments

To evaluate the proposed approach, we invited human users to verify candidate coreferent entities found between real-world data sets by using entity summaries generated by different approaches, and examined the accuracy of their verification and the time used, to test the following hypotheses.

1. Length-limited entity summaries that are appropriately generated help human users verify candidate coreferent entities more efficiently than their entire descriptions, without significantly hurting the accuracy of verification.
2. Comparative entity summaries that consider commonality and difference produce more accurate verification than traditional generic entity summaries.
3. Comparative entity summaries will produce less accurate verification on non-coreferent entities if their difference is not considered.

5.1 Data Sets and Test Cases

The data sets used were DBpedia (3.9-en), GeoNames (2013-08-27), and LinkedMDB (2010-01-29). In particular, for DBpedia, we imported Mapping-based Types, Mapping-based Properties, Titles, Geographic Coordinates, Homepages, Persondata, PND, and YAGO types. We removed RDF triples containing non-English characters. From GeoNames and LinkedMDB, we removed `rdfs:seeAlso` and `owl:sameAs` links, respectively, because they reveal the expected answers.

From DBpedia and GeoNames (places), and from DBpedia and LinkedMDB (films), we obtained both pairs of coreferent entities (based on `owl:sameAs` links in DBpedia) and pairs of non-coreferent entities, called *positive* and *negative* test cases to be verified, respectively. To generate challenging negative cases, we leveraged the Disambiguation links in DBpedia to find the entities in DBpedia that have a common name. For instance, "Paris" may refer to 103 entities in DBpedia, 24 of which have `owl:sameAs` links to GeoNames. From these links we can reliably obtain 24 positive cases and the remaining $24^2 - 24 = 552$ combinations as negative cases. In this way, 113,587 positive and 743,504 negative cases were generated between DBpedia and GeoNames, and 2,915 positive and 580 negative cases were generated between DBpedia and LinkedMDB.

5.2 Participant Approaches

To test the three hypotheses, we designed four approaches to compare in the experiments: **NOSUMM** which simply returns the entire descriptions of two entities without summarization, and three variants of the proposed approach.

- **GENERIC** fixes $\alpha = \beta = 0$ in Eq. (8) so that only the information on identity and the diversity of information are considered. It actually includes and goes beyond the core of RELIN [3], a state-of-the-art approach to generating generic entity summaries that mainly leverages the information on identity carried by each feature.
- **COMPSUMM** considers all the four terms in Eq. (8) and generates comparative entity summaries.
- **COMPSUMM-C** fixes $\beta = 0$ in Eq. (8) so that, compared with COMPSUMM, it also generates comparative entity summaries but ignores the difference between entities.

In these approaches, when calculating $comp_L$, we used 1,000 positive cases randomly selected from each pair of data sets as training data (i.e. M). When estimating ifp, fp, and inf, we used all the entity descriptions in each corresponding data set as the corpus (i.e. D).

Tuning the weights $\alpha, \beta, \gamma, \delta$ is a challenge and may depend on the specific data sets. In our experiments, from each pair of data sets, we randomly selected five positive and five negative cases (which were then kept separate from those to be verified in subsequent experiments), and then tuned the weights based on our subjective assessment of the quality of their summaries generated using different weight settings. The weights were tuned one after another. Firstly, γ was fixed to 1, and δ was tuned to obtain GENERIC. Then, α was tuned to obtain COMPSUMM-C. Finally, β was tuned to obtain COMPSUMM. In this way, for DBpedia and GeoNames, we set $\alpha = 6$, $\beta = 4$, $\gamma = 1$, and $\delta = 4$, and for DBpedia and LinkedMDB, we set $\alpha = 8$, $\beta = 4$, $\gamma = 1$, and $\delta = 6$.

5.3 Experimental Design and Evaluation Metrics

We invited 20 students majoring in computer science and technology to the experiments. For each subject, between DBpedia and GeoNames, as a warmup at the beginning, 1 positive and 1 negative case were randomly selected whose entire descriptions were presented to be verified. Then, using each of the four approaches, 3 positive and 3 negative cases were randomly selected and their summaries were generated; all these 24 cases were sorted in random order to be blindly verified by the subject. The character limit for GENERIC, COMPSUMM, and COMPSUMM-C was set to 140, which is around the (estimated) limit of a common snippet in Google search. After verifying each case, the subject's decision could be "coreferent", "non-coreferent", or "not sure". For DBpedia and LinkedMDB, the process was similar.

In a positive case, a "coreferent" and a "non-coreferent" decision are called *accurate* and *erroneous*, respectively. Negative cases are similarly defined. A "not

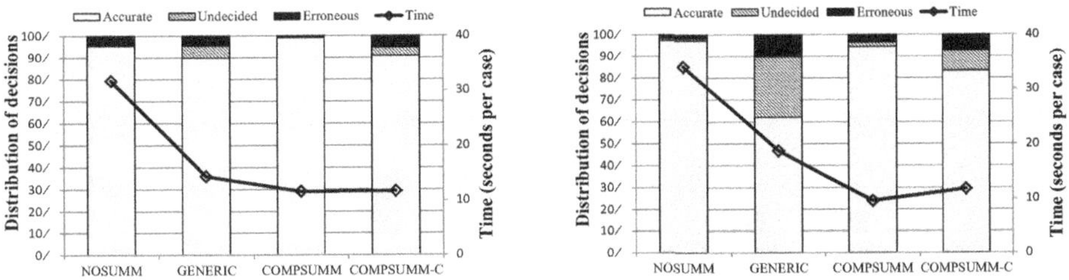

(a) DBpedia—GeoNames. (b) DBpedia—LinkedMDB.

Fig. 1. Distribution of decisions and the average time used for verification

sure" decision is called *undecided*. Then we evaluated the accuracy of verification based on the distribution of decisions. We also measured the efficiency of verification by the average time used for verification.

5.4 Results

All the decisions made by two subjects were excluded from the results because they unusually made two or more erroneous decisions when using NOSUMM (i.e. entire entity descriptions) so that we were not very confident about the quality of their decisions and thus excluded all of them.

Figure 1 shows the distribution of the remaining 864 decisions made by 18 subjects and the average time used for verifying a case. Between DBpedia and GeoNames, when using NOSUMM, more than 95% of the decisions were accurate, and when using other approaches that perform summarization, the accuracy rates were all above 90%. Between DBpedia and LinkedMDB, the accuracy rates were also very high when using NOSUMM and COMPSUMM. However, it decreased notably to 83% when using COMPSUMM-C and largely to 62% when using GENERIC. As to the time used, between DBpedia and GeoNames, more than 30 seconds were needed for verifying a case when using NOSUMM, but only less than 15 seconds (i.e. reduced by half or more) were needed when using other approaches that perform summarization. Between DBpedia and LinkedMDB, the results were similar. These results support our first hypothesis, that is, *length-limited entity summaries generated by COMPSUMM help human users verify more efficiently than entire entity descriptions, without notably affecting the accuracy of verification.*

The error rate of using GENERIC was 2.7–5 times higher than using COMPSUMM, depending on the data sets, and the number of undecided decisions was also much larger. These results support our second hypothesis, that is, *comparative entity summaries generated by COMPSUMM produce more accurate verification than generic entity summaries generated by GENERIC.* Besides, using COMPSUMM took even less time than using GENERIC.

Figure 2 shows the total number of undecided and erroneous decisions, divided into positive and negative cases. Between DBpedia and GeoNames, in positive

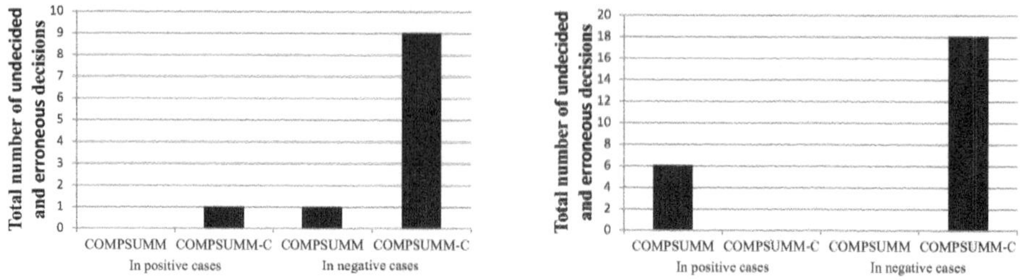

(a) DBpedia—GeoNames. (b) DBpedia—LinkedMDB.

Fig. 2. Total number of undecided and erroneous decisions

cases, there were very few undecided or erroneous decisions when using COMPSUMM and COMPSUMM-C, whereas in negative cases, 9 ones were made when using COMPSUMM-C, much more than using COMPSUMM. Between DBpedia and LinkedMDB, there was no undecided or erroneous decision when using COMPSUMM in negative cases, whereas using COMPSUMM-C made 18 ones. These results support our third hypothesis, that is, *comparative entity summaries generated by COMPSUMM-C which ignore the difference between entities produce less accurate verification on non-coreferent entities.* However, using COMPSUMM made 6 undecided or erroneous decisions in positive cases between DBpedia and LinkedMDB, which is unexpected and will be discussed later.

To sum up, all the three hypotheses have been confirmed. In particular, verification using comparative entity summaries generated by our approach (i.e. COMPSUMM) is 2.7–2.9 times faster than using entire entity descriptions (i.e. NOSUMM), when their accuracy rates differ insignificantly (-2.8% to 3.7%).

5.5 Discussion

A closer analysis of the undecided and erroneous decisions provided the following insights into the problem and the participant approaches.

Firstly, even using entire entity descriptions (i.e. NOSUMM), human users still occasionally made erroneous decisions. Actually, sometimes it is really difficult to make a decision. For instance, a place may have slightly different longitudes and latitudes in DBpedia and GeoNames; two different places may be very close in name and location. These greatly challenge coreference resolution.

Secondly, generic entity summaries (i.e. GENERIC) led to a large number of undecided decisions between DBpedia and LinkedMDB. A major reason is that the features selected into such a summary are often not comparable even though they are highly informative. For instance, a film may be with its writer and an actor on one side, but with its producer and another actor on the other side. The proposed comparative summaries exactly target this issue.

Thirdly, using comparative summaries that ignore the difference between entities (i.e. COMPSUMM-C) was prone to inaccurate decisions in negative cases. It is because non-coreferent entity descriptions may share common features, which make commonality-only summaries misleading. For instance, given two different films having a common producer, a common director, but different editors, if ignoring the difference between them, their common producer and director will be selected into a comparative summary, which seems to indicate coreference. The proposed approach considers both commonality and difference, which exactly target this issue.

Last but not least, considering both commonality and difference (i.e. COMP-SUMM) led to several inaccurate decisions in positive cases between DBpedia and LinkedMDB. It is because in coreferent entity descriptions, a property of high likeness to FP may occasionally have more than one value, and different values of this property may be selected on different sides due to their dissimilarity, which is misleading. For instance, a film having two editors (which is not often the case) may be misleadingly with one editor on one side, but with the other editor on the other side. This motivates us to improve our measure of difference between entities in future work.

5.6 Performance Testing

We tested the performance of our implementation on an Intel Xeon E3-1225 v2 with 512MB memory for JVM. Prior to testing, $comp_L$, ifp, fp, and inf were precomputed, and all the relevant data was loaded into memory. From DBpedia and GeoNames, 1,000 test cases were randomly selected, on which the average running time of COMPSUMM was 24 ms per case. Similarly, for DBpedia and LinkedMDB, the average running time was 35 ms per case.

6 Related Work

6.1 Coreference Resolution

More and more solutions to coreference resolution solicit user feedback for verifying candidate coreferent entities. Active learning [7] seeks to pick a set of candidate coreferent entities that, when verified, will provide the most benefit to the learner. Further, pay-as-you-go data integration [6] considers the benefit not only to the overall quality of data integration but also to the user's current task (e.g. a search). Crowdsourcing approaches [13] pay a group of users to verify candidate coreferent entities, and intend to achieve both high-quality results and a low cost. In all these approaches, the verification of candidate coreferent entities requires tool support. However, to the best of our knowledge, very little attention has been paid to it. D-Dupe [1] exactly addresses this issue with a layout highlighting the common features shared by the entities. In the field of ontology matching, tools like COGZ [4] primarily focus on the various layouts of class hierarchies to help human users verify candidate mappings between classes. *All these tools mainly concern the visualization of descriptions, whereas what we study is summarization or extraction, which complements existing tools well.*

Some low-level measures used in our approach are borrowed from automatic methods for coreference resolution, e.g. [5,10]. Not surprisingly, both resolving entity coreference and generating comparative entity summaries involve similarity measurement. However, *they address different, though related, research problems and, in particular, our approach is designed to help human users make a decision rather than to make a decision by itself*, and thus pays attention to human factors, e.g. to consider a length limit so as to not overload human users with too much information.

6.2 Entity Summarization

Entity summaries have proven to be useful as snippets in search engine results pages [2,15], where they indicate the relevance of an entity to a keyword query. Recent studies mainly focus on the more general problem of entity summarization and generate a summary of an entity description for generic use. Among others, RELIN [3] employs a random surfer model to rank features mainly based on their informativeness but also based on the relatedness between them. DIVERSUM [11] proposes to improve the diversity of an entity summary by choosing features having different properties. Thalhammer et al. [12] prefer the features of an entity that are shared with its nearest neighbors, where the distance between entities is derived from usage data. The generic entity summaries generated by these approaches can of course be used in the verification of candidate coreferent entities. However, as demonstrated by our experimental results, *verification will be more accurate if using our comparative entity summaries that are specifically designed for this task.*

7 Conclusion

In consideration of the growing trend toward human intervention in coreference resolution through verifying candidate coreferent entities, we have addressed the improvement of the efficiency of such a verification task. Our solution extracts and presents a compact summary of entire entity descriptions in order to help human users spend less time verifying. We have defined the goodness of such a comparative entity summary from four angles. These four objectives exactly fit the binary quadratic knapsack problem, which can be efficiently solved by an effective heuristic method. We have presented an implementation of our approach, and demonstrated its effectiveness based on real-world verification tasks. The experimental results show that the comparative entity summaries generated by our approach can, as expected, help human users verify more efficiently without notably affecting the accuracy of their verification. In particular, they outperform non-comparative entity summaries generated for generic use.

To improve our approach, in the future, we will particularly explore how to automatically (or more systematically) configure the weights of different objectives. We will also extend the experiments. Specifically, we will examine how the length of a summary will influence the accuracy and efficiency of verification, and will experiment with more challenging verification tasks in different domains.

Acknowledgments. We thank all the participants and reviewers. This work was supported in part by the NSFC under Grant 61100040, 61170068, and 61223003, and in part by the JSNSF under Grant BK2012723 and BK2011189.

References

1. Bilgic, M., Licamele, L., Getoor, L., Shneiderman, B.: D-Dupe: An Interactive Tool for Entity Resolution in Social Networks. In: 2006 IEEE Symposium on Visual Analytics Science and Technology, pp. 43–50. IEEE, Washington, DC (2006)
2. Cheng, G., Qu, Y.: Searching Linked Objects with Falcons: Approach, Implementation and Evaluation. Int'l J. Semant. Web Inf. Syst. 5(3), 49–70 (2009)
3. Cheng, G., Tran, T., Qu, Y.: RELIN: Relatedness and Informativeness-based Centrality for Entity Summarization. In: Aroyo, L., Welty, C., Alani, H., Taylor, J., Bernstein, A., Kagal, L., Noy, N., Blomqvist, E. (eds.) ISWC 2011, Part I. LNCS, vol. 7031, pp. 114–129. Springer, Heidelberg (2011)
4. Falconer, S.M., Storey, M.-A.: A Cognitive Support Framework for Ontology Mapping. In: Aberer, K., et al. (eds.) ISWC/ASWC 2007. LNCS, vol. 4825, pp. 114–127. Springer, Heidelberg (2007)
5. Hogan, A., Zimmermann, A., Umbrich, J., Polleres, A., Decker, S.: Scalable and Distributed Methods for Entity Matching, Consolidation and Disambiguation over Linked Data Corpora. J. Web Semant. 10, 76–110 (2012)
6. Madhavan, J., Jeffery, S.R., Cohen, S., Dong, X., Ko, D., Yu, C., Halevy, A.: Web-scale Data Integration: You Can Only Afford to Pay As You Go. In: 3rd Biennial Conference on Innovative Data Systems Research, pp. 342–350. Cidrdb.org (2007)
7. Ngonga Ngomo, A.-C., Lehmann, J., Auer, S., Höffner, K.: RAVEN - Active Learning of Link Specifications. In: 6th International Workshop on Ontology Matching, pp. 25–36. CEUR-WS.org (2011)
8. Pisinger, D.: The Quadratic Knapsack Problem - A Survey. Discrete Appl. Math. 155(15), 623–648 (2007)
9. Shvaiko, P., Euzenat, J.: Ontology Matching: State of the Art and Future Challenges. IEEE Trans. Knowl. Data Eng. 25(1), 158–176 (2013)
10. Stoilos, G., Stamou, G., Kollias, S.: A String Metric for Ontology Alignment. In: Gil, Y., Motta, E., Benjamins, V.R., Musen, M.A. (eds.) ISWC 2005. LNCS, vol. 3729, pp. 624–637. Springer, Heidelberg (2005)
11. Sydow, M., Pikuła, M., Schenkel, R.: The Notion of Diversity in Graphical Entity Summarisation on Semantic Knowledge Graphs. J. Intell. Inf. Syst. 41(2), 109–149 (2013)
12. Thalhammer, A., Toma, I., Roa-Valverde, A.J., Fensel, D.: Leveraging Usage Data for Linked Data Movie Entity Summarization. In: 2nd International Workshop on Usage Analysis and the Web of Data (2012)
13. Wang, J., Kraska, T., Franklin, M.J., Feng, J.: CrowdER: Crowdsourcing Entity Resolution. Proc. VLDB Endowment 5(11), 1483–1494 (2012)
14. Yang, Z., Wang, G., Chu, F.: An Effective GRASP and Tabu Search for the 0-1 Quadratic Knapsack Problem. Comput. Oper. Res. 40(5), 1176–1185 (2013)
15. Zhang, L., Zhang, Y., Chen, Y.: Summarizing Highly Structured Documents for Effective Search Interaction. In: 35th International ACM SIGIR Conference on Research and Development in Information Retrieval, pp. 145–154. ACM, New York (2012)

The Usability of Description Logics

Understanding the Cognitive Difficulties Presented by Description Logics

Paul Warren, Paul Mulholland, Trevor Collins, and Enrico Motta

Knowledge Media Institute, The Open University
Milton Keynes, Buckinghamshire, MK7 6AA, U.K.
paul.warren@cantab.net,
{paul.mulholland,trevor.collins,enrico.motta}@open.ac.uk

Abstract. Description Logics have been extensively studied from the viewpoint of decidability and computational tractability. Less attention has been given to their usability and the cognitive difficulties they present, in particular for those who are not specialists in logic. This paper reports on a study into the difficulties associated with the most commonly used Description Logic features. Psychological theories are used to take account of these. Whilst most of the features presented no difficulty to participants, the comprehension of some was affected by commonly occurring misconceptions. The paper proposes explanations and remedies for some of these difficulties. In addition, the time to confirm stated inferences was found to depend both on the maximum complexity of the relations involved and the number of steps in the argument.

Keywords: #eswc2014Warren.

1 Introduction

During the past few decades the decidability and computational tractability of Description Logics (DLs) have been extensively studied. Baader et al. (2010) provide a comprehensive overview of the theory of DLs and also describe a number of applications. In particular, the properties of the various profiles of OWL, the Web Ontology Language, are well understood; see Motik et al. (2012). The usability of DLs has been much less investigated. This paper describes an experiment to understand the comprehensibility of the most commonly used features of DLs, as implemented in OWL. The study has revealed a number of misconceptions and the paper makes suggestions as to how these can be overcome. A particular goal of the study was to determine whether any of the psychological theories of reasoning could be used to explain the accuracy of human reasoning with DL statements and the time taken to undertake such reasoning. This theoretical approach has helped to explain the most significant of the misconceptions and also explained the time to confirm inferences.

Section 2 describes related work. This falls into two categories: work undertaken by computer scientists to understand the comprehensibility of DLs; and the work of

V. Presutti et al. (Eds.): ESWC 2014, LNCS 8465, pp. 550–564, 2014.

cognitive psychologists to understand the nature of reasoning in general. Section 3 then describes how the most commonly used DL features were identified. The study focuses on the features that are commonly used, rather than those features which, whilst useful in particular domains, are not extensively used. Section 4 explains how the study was designed and conducted. Section 5 presents the study questions and discusses the five which were found most difficult by participants. Where applicable we have used theories from cognitive science to help explain these difficulties. Some potential remedies for these problems are also suggested. The section also discusses participants' feedback, which confirm the usefulness of some of the suggestions. Section 6 provides a more detailed analysis, including some results relating the time taken to answer questions to psychological theories of reasoning. Finally, section 7 draws some conclusions and outlines areas for future study.

2 Related Work

2.1 Comprehensibility of Description Logics

There have been few studies of the comprehensibility of Description Logics. Rector et al. (2004) describe the difficulties experienced by newcomers to OWL, based on their experience in teaching the language. They provide a set of guidelines and also English paraphrases of some OWL expressions. Horridge et al. (2011) were interested in supporting the ontology developer during the debugging process. One way to offer such support is to display the minimal subset of the ontology that generates a particular entailment. Such a subset is termed a justification. Horridge et al. investigated the cognitive complexity of justifications for entailments of OWL ontologies. They developed a complexity model and compared the predictions of this model with the difficulty experienced by computer scientists in identifying correct entailments. Their model, which was not grounded in any psychological theory, "fared reasonably well". Commenting on a study by Newstead et al. (2006), Horridge et al. identified a strong advantage of studies within the psychological literature, i.e. that the problems considered "are very constrained and comparatively easy to analyse". The difficulty in studying DLs is the need to consider a wide range of commonly occurring constructs.

Nguyen et al. (2012) had a similar interest in assisting developers to debug ontologies. Their goal was to explain, in English, why an entailment follows from an ontology. In particular, they wished to predict the comprehensibility of alternative proof trees, when expressed in English. To do this they needed to first understand the comprehensibility of the individual deduction rules comprising a proof tree. They took 51 such deduction rules, expressed in English, and tested their comprehensibility on participants obtained through a crowdsourcing service. This enabled them to generate a facility index representing the ease of comprehensibility of each deduction rule, calculated as the proportion of participants who identified the deduction rule as being correct. Since their interest was in calculating these facility indices for future use, they did not attempt to create a model to predict and explain the indices.

2.2 Theories of Human Reasoning

There is a considerable psychological literature on human reasoning. One distinction is between rule-based and model-based theories. The rule-based approach is represented by the work of Rips, e.g. Rips (1983). The assumption is that the processes of human reasoning are akin to the steps executed by a logician in carrying out a proof. The model-based approach is represented by Johnson-Laird, e.g. Johnson-Laird and Byrne (1991), for whom mental models "have the same structure as human conceptions of the situations they represent". Johnson-Laird and his collaborators have built an extensive body of experimental evidence to support the view that at least 'naïve reasoners' (i.e. people not trained in logic), do use mental models in reasoning. It may be, though, that some people use a mixture of mental models and rules-based reasoning, depending upon the particular situation and their degree of training in logic. Our hypothesis is that when logicians are constructing a proof in a rule-based way, they use mental models at some or all of the deduction steps.

The mental model theorists propose that difficulties in reasoning often occur when several models need to be maintained in working memory. It is suggested that in certain situations people may ignore some of the possible models, thereby leading to errors. This may happen, for example, when a disjunction occurs. Moreover, mental model theory suggests that an inclusive disjunction will give rise to more errors than an exclusive disjunction, since the former requires three models to be held in working memory whilst the latter requires only two. This is borne out by experiment, e.g. see Johnson-Laird et al. (1992).

Relational complexity (RC) theory offers another approach to understanding performance in reasoning. Here complexity is defined "as a function … of the number of variables that can be related in a single cognitive representation", i.e. the number of arguments of a relation (Halford & Andrews, 2004). The theory proposes that it is the maximum relational complexity in a given process of reasoning which determines the difficulty of that reasoning. RC theory could be seen as compatible with either the rule-based or the model-based approach. Zielinski et al. (2010) have attempted to reconcile the mental model and RC theories for categorical syllogisms. Goodwin and Johnson-Laird (2005) have combined mental model theory and RC theory in their study of reasoning about relations. Apart from the number of arguments, they see depth of the relation as contributing to complexity. Relations between individuals are regarded as of first-order depth; relations between relations of second-order depth; relations between relations between relations of third-order depth.

It seems likely that the experimental success of the mental model theory, e.g. as described in Johnson-Laird and Byrne (1991) and Johnson-Laird et al. (1992), arises because the individual models were of broadly equal complexity. As a consequence, situations requiring two models created more difficulty than those requiring one, and situations requiring three models were even more difficult.

3 Identifying the Commonly Used Features

To identify the most commonly used features we drew on four sources. Power and Third (2010) provide a list of the most commonly used OWL functors based on an analysis of ontologies in the TONES Ontology Repository[1]. Power (2010) also used TONES to identify common axiom patterns. This identified the frequency of use of Boolean operators such as intersection, and also of the existential and universal restrictions. Khan and Blomqvist (2010) searched 682 online ontologies to determine the frequency of occurrence of content patterns from the ODP (ontology design pattern) portal[2]. This portal provides information on a variety of patterns, including around 100 content patterns. These are essentially small autonomous solutions to particular design problems. We then analyzed the 20 most frequent patterns that they detected, to determine the commonly occurring OWL features. In addition, Warren (2013) undertook a survey of ontology users which included a question about the usage of OWL features. Based on 47 responses to this question, these features were ranked by frequency of reported use.

The resultant lists were then compared. They identified broadly the same set of commonly occurring features. There were a few differences, e.g. Power and Third found class equivalence to be the second most commonly used functor; analysis of the common content patterns from Khan and Blomqvist identified class equivalence as the thirteenth most commonly used OWL feature, whilst it was not included in the survey by Warren. The set of features used in this study consisted of all those features which were relatively common in at least one of these lists, with two exceptions. The reason for these exceptions was that the study participants would not necessarily be familiar with OWL and they would need to be given information about the language which should be kept brief. Firstly, all features relating to datatype properties were ignored. It was felt that datatype properties would present no cognitive challenges that could not be represented with object properties. This is not to say that there might not be challenges arising from datatype properties during the learning process, but rather that subsequently, when working with ontologies, they do not give rise to any specific problems of cognition. Secondly, cardinality restrictions were not included. In fact, these did not occur in the list of most commonly used patterns in Power and were ranked relatively low in the survey by Warren. The 'min 1' cardinality restriction did occur moderately frequently in the patterns identified by Khan and Blomqvist. This states that a particular individual is the subject of at least one instance of a particular property. It is equivalent to an existential restriction, which was included in the study.

Table 1 shows the set of OWL features chosen for the study. In each case the Manchester OWL Syntax (MOS) representation of the language feature is also shown (Horridge et al., 2006). The features are grouped into those relevant to classes, those relevant to properties and the existential and universal restrictions. In each of these groupings, they are listed broadly in order of occurrence (i.e. with most commonly occurring at the top), although, as already noted, rankings differed across the various sources.

[1] `http://rpc295.cs.man.ac.uk:8080/repository/`

[2] `http://ontologydesignpatterns.org/wiki/Main_Page`

Table 1. Commonly used OWL features investigated in the study

Class features

language feature	MOS
subsumption	SubClassOf
class equivalence	EquivalentTo
disjoint classes	DisjointWith
class assertion	Type
conjunction	and
disjunction	or
complement	not

Property features

language feature	MOS
property range	Range
property domain	Domain
property hierarchy	SubPropertyOf
inverse object properties	InverseOf
transitive object property	Characteristics: Transitive
functional object property	Characteristics: Functional
symmetric object property	Characteristics: Symmetric

Restrictions

language feature	MOS
qualified existential restriction	some
universal restriction	only

4 The Study

In order to test comprehension of these OWL features, they were incorporated into a set of twenty-one questions based on three patterns from the the ODP portal (see beginning of previous section). The three patterns used were: Componency, Coparticipation, and Types of Entities; the second and third were modified to enable all the features in table 1 to be tested, with some simplification of the second to remove unnecessary statements. The three modified patterns were associated with ten, six and five questions. Each of the questions consisted of a set of statements and a proposed inference. The participant was required to indicate, by clicking on a button, whether the inference was or was not valid. In all there were thirteen questions with valid inferences and eight where the inference was not valid. The patterns and question statements were expressed in a simplified form of the Manchester OWL Syntax. Classes and properties were defined in the patterns and had intuitive names. Individuals were defined in the questions and were named A, B, C, D.

These patterns and questions were incorporated in a test, using the tool *SurveyExpression*[3]. The three patterns were ordered in all six permutations; each of these permutations existed in a form with the 'yes' option first and with the 'no' option first, to safeguard against any bias from the order of the possible answers. Thus there were twelve variants of the test. There were also twelve participants, i.e. one participant per variant. All the participants, of whom three were female, were researchers at the Centre for Research in Computing or the Knowledge Media Institute at the Open University, U.K. Screen capture software was used to record the participant's behaviour and in particular to provide the precise times spent in each question. The participants were observed as they took part in the study and any comments they made were noted.

The study was organized into five sections. In the first section participants were asked to rate their knowledge of logic and of OWL. The wording and the percentage of responses in each category for logic and OWL respectively were: no knowledge at all (0%,0%); a little knowledge, e.g. from an introductory course in formal logic (17%,25%); some knowledge, e.g. from a university course in formal logic

[3] http://www.surveyexpression.com/

(67%,42%); expert knowledge (17%,33%). The next three sections contained the three patterns and the questions. Each section began with a webpage displaying the pattern and then a series of pages, with each page repeating the pattern and containing one question. Participants were able to move through the pages at their own speed. The final section was an opportunity for the participants to provide feedback. Participants were provided with a handout containing all the necessary information about the OWL features and notation used. They were asked to read this at the beginning and it was available to them for reference during the session.

5 Study Results

5.1 The Difficult Questions

Of the 21 questions, eight were answered correctly by all of the participants, four were answered correctly by all but one of the participants, and a further four were answered correctly by all but two of the participants. The remaining five are discussed here in decreasing order of difficulty. Tables 2, 3 and 4 show the three patterns and the associated questions. The columns headed 'yes/no', 'MM' and 'RC' represent the correct answer, the maximum number of mental models and the maximum relational complexity associated with the question. The column headed 'num steps' shows the number of steps to arrive at a correct deduction for questions with answer 'yes'. The remaining two columns show the percentage of correct responses and the average time for each question.

Table 2. Questions based on the modified entity types pattern

Class Entity	EquivalentTo Event or Abstract or Quality or Object
Class Event	SubClassOf Entity DisjointWith Abstract, Quality, Object
Class Abstract	SubClassOf Entity DisjointWith Event, Quality, Object
Class Quality	SubClassOf Entity DisjointWith Event, Abstract, Object
Class Object	SubClassOf Entity DisjointWith Event, Abstract, Quality
Class Nonconceptual	EquivalentTo Event or Object
Class Nontemporal	EquivalentTo Abstract or Quality or Object
Property represents	Characteristic Functional

	Question	yes/no	MM	RC	num steps	%age corr	av. time (secs)
1	A represents B; C represents D => A DifferentFrom C	no	1	2	n/a	83%	91.5
2	A Type Entity; A Type not (Event and Quality) => A Type (Abstract or Object)	no	4	3	n/a	25%	75.1
3	A represents B; C represent D; B Type Object; D Type Event => A DifferentFrom C	yes	1	4	2	50%	75.8
4	A Type Entity; A Type not (Event or Quality) => A Type (Abstract or Object)	yes	4	4	2	92%	44.0
5	A Type (Nonconceptual and Nontemporal) => A Type Object	yes	3	3	3	75%	63.1

Table 2: Q2 - Complementing the *and* operation (ans: no; 25% correct responses) The most direct way of arriving at a 'no' conclusion for this question is to note that, since Event and Quality are disjoint classes, then *Event and Quality* must be Nothing (⊥). Hence *not (Event and Quality)* is Thing (⊤) and the statement *A Type not (Event and Quality)* is tautological.

The question should be contrasted with question Q4 in table 2, which is identical in form except for the replacement of the *and* with *or*, and has correct answer 'yes'. Q4 had 92% correct responses and was answered much more quickly; the average response time was 44 seconds for Q4 and 75 seconds for Q2. It is interesting to compare these results with those of Khemlani et al. (2012a), reporting on an experiment with 'naïve reasoners'. They investigated the comprehension of compound sentences of the form *not (A and B)* and *not (A or B)* and found a similar wide gap in accuracy of answering questions: 18% correct for the negated conjunction and 89% correct for the negated disjunction. They interpret these results in terms of the mental model theory. *not (A or B)* consists of only one mental model, i.e. *not A and not B*. However, *not (A and B)* consists of three mental models: *not A and not B*; *A and not B*; *not A and B*. They suggest that many people do not go beyond constructing the first of these, leading to erroneous reasoning. They elaborate this theory of negation in (Khemlani, Orenes, & Johnson-Laird, 2012b). In fact, in both Q2 and Q4, arguably four mental models are required, representing the decomposition of Entity (*Event or Abstract or Quality or Object*). The problem is not simply one of managing a number of different models, but of the difficulty of creating the full set of models in the negation process. In Q4 all the participant has to do is to erase Event and Quality from the decomposition of Entity, leaving Abstract and Object. In Q2, rather than evaluate *Event and Quality* and then *not (Event and Quality)* as proposed in the paragraph above, many participants may attempt to expand *not (Event and Quality)* and may arrive at a single mental model corresponding to the term *not Event and not Quality*.

Apart from emphasis during training, potential solutions to this problem are:

- automatic expansion of *not (A and B)* into its three atomic constituents;
- an automatically generated graphical representation.

There is also the additional possibility of confusion between the everyday use of *and* and its logical use. It may be that, when faced with the difficulty of negating a conjunction, participants take the easy option by interpreting *and* as equivalent to *or* (e.g. as in the English statement "the car is available in blue and silver"). The use of an alternative keyword to *and*, e.g. *intersection* or *int*, could avoid this linguistic confusion.

Whatever the reason for the erroneous treatment of Q2, it is striking that the results for naïve reasoners were so similar to those found amongst our participants. This suggests that both groups were using the same mental processes.

The complement operation was used by 22 of the 47 respondents to the question on DL feature usage in the survey by Warren (2013). However, it was not identified by Power (2010) as being commonly used and was not in the commonly used patterns identified by Khan and Blomqvist (2010). This relatively low usage may account for the low proportion of correct responses, since some participants may not have been familiar with the use of the complement operation.

Table 3. Questions based on the compponency pattern

Class Object	SubClassOf has_component only Object SubClassOf is_component_of only Object
Property has_part Property is_part_of	Characteristic Transitive Characteristic Transitive InverseOf has_part
Property has_component Property is_component_of	SubPropertyOf has_part SubPropertyOf is_part_of InverseOf has_component

	Question	yes/ no	MM	RC	num steps	%age corr	av. time (secs)
1	A is_part_of B; C is_part_of B => A is_part_of C	no	1	2	n/a	100%	62.3
2	A is_part_of B; B is_part_of C => A is_part_of C	yes	1	2	1	100%	20.3
3	B is_part_of C; A is_part_of B => A is_part_of C	yes	1	3	1	100%	30.7
4	A has_component B; B has_component C => A has_component C	no	1	2	n/a	33%	62.8
5	A has_component B; B has_component C => A has part C	yes	1	2	3	83%	29.0
6	A has_component B; B is_part_of C => A has_part C	no	1	2	n/a	83%	57.9
7	A has_component B; C is_part_of B => A has_part C	yes	1	4	3	100%	37.4
8	A Type Object; A has_component B; C Type not Object => B DifferentFrom C	yes	1	3	2	100%	49.9
9	A Type Object; A has_part B; C Type Not Object => B DifferentFrom C	no	1	2	n/a	83%	47.5
10	A has_component B; C is_component_of B => C is_part_of A	yes	1	4	4	100%	54.2

Table 3: Q4 - Non-inheritance of transitivity (ans: no; 33% correct responses) In the pattern, *has_component* is defined as a subproperty of *has_part*, which is defined to be transitive. For the deduction to be true it would be necessary for *has_component* to also be transitive. There are a number of reasons why this question might be answered incorrectly. It may be that participants forget which is the parent, transitive property, and which is the subproperty, i.e. that they confuse the two names. It might also be that the name *has_component* suggests transitivity. Alternatively, people may assume that property characteristics are necessarily inherited by subproperties. This would be natural for people coming from an object oriented background, or those chiefly used to thinking about class subsumption relations in ontologies. That this is not the case for transitivity was noted in the handout, which cited the example of the property *is_descendant_*of and its subproperty *is_child_of*[4]. In fact, a different choice of property name might guard against all these problems; *has_direct_part*, in place of *has_component*, could better convey the required meaning. Subproperties appear to be relatively frequently used, and the transitive characteristic is one of the most commonly used characteristics. When training ontology users, attention needs to be drawn to the fact that not all characteristics are inherited, perhaps spelling out those which are and those which are not.

[4] Similarly, the characteristic of symmetry is not inherited, as can be seen from the property *is_sibling_of* and its subproperty *is_brother_of*. On the other hand, functionality is inherited, since if a subproperty has two values for the same subject, then so will its superproperty.

Table 2: Q3 - The functional characteristic (ans: yes; 50% correct responses)
Since Object and Event are disjoint, B and D must be different. The functionality of *represents* then ensures that A and C are different. It may be that those who answered this question incorrectly did not fully understand the nature of a functional characteristic, despite it being explained in the handout. It may also be that the high relational complexity (i.e. RC = 4) of the question contributed to its difficulty. Here again, a diagrammatic representation would aid comprehension.

Table 4. Questions based on the modified coparticipation pattern

Class Event	EquivalentTo has_participant some Object DisjointWith Object
Class Object	DisjointWith Event
Class Player	SubClassOf Object
Class Game	SubClassOf has_participant some Player
Property coparticipates_with	Domain Object, Range Object Characteristics Symmetric, Transitive
Property has_participant	Domain Event, Range Object InverseOf is_participant_in

	Question	yes/no	MM	RC	num steps	%age corr	av. time (secs)
1	A coparticipates_with B => A Type not Event	yes	1	2	2	92%	54.9
2	A is_participant_in B; C coparticipates_with D => A DifferentFrom C	no	1	2	n/a	92%	68.8
3	A is_participant_in B; C is_participant_in B => A is participant in C	no	1	2	n/a	100%	43.6
4	A has_participant B; C is_particpant_in D => B DifferentFrom D	yes	1	2	3	92%	44.6
5	B coparticipates_with A; B coparticipates_with C => C coparticipates_with A	yes	1	3	2	100%	34.8
6	A Type Game => A Type Event	yes	1	3	3	67%	47.6

Table 4: Q6 - The existential quantifier (ans: yes; 67% correct responses)
Each member of the class Game *has_participant some Player*; hence this is true of A. Since Player is a subclass of Object, *A has_participant some Object.* Since Event is defined as the set of individuals that *has_participant some Object*, A is in Event. The fact that a relatively large number of participants got this question right, despite its apparent complexity, may be due to the frequency of use of the existential quantifier, e.g. see Khan and Blomqvist (2010), Power (2010) and Warren (2013).

Table 2: Q5 - Superclasses (ans: yes; 75% correct responses)
Participants did relatively well on the question, only two providing incorrect answers and one not responding. In all the analyses the non-response is treated as an incorrect answer. The question is discussed here in part because it provides an example of a different approach to the use of mental models. Entity is composed of four disjoint subclasses. Nonconceptual and Nontemporal comprise two and three of these disjoint subclasses respectively. The only one they have in common is Object; hence their conjunction is equivalent to Object. A straightforward application of the mental model approach suggests that the maximum number of mental models is three, since Nontemporal is comprised of three disjoint classes. There is, however, little difficulty in formulating these models, unlike in the case of negation of a conjunction in

table 2, Q2. In fact, a quite natural way to think about this is as two overlapping superclasses, with Object constituting the overlapping portion. This also lends itself naturally to a graphical representation; some participants might even have visualized it. This only requires that two models be held in working memory, one representing Nonconceptual, and the other Nontemporal.

5.2 Participants' Feedback

After completing the questions, participants were able to provide written feedback about what they found difficult and what they found easy, and to make general comments. Some participants also made comments verbally. The most common theme was the use of intuition, in particular relating to names. There were conflicting views. One participant (p1) commented that "using named individuals instead of capital letters would have been easier" whilst another (p2) held the opinion that it was "easy to reason with anonymous things", since this safeguarded against the danger of using intuition rather than relying on the formal axioms. The contrasting views were also present when considering class and property names. One participant (p3) commented that because the class and property names were familiar it was necessary to check whether the meaning in the OWL expression was similar to the normal English usage; another (p4) stated that "the axioms were realistic so one could rely to some extent on common sense". Participant p1 also commented favourably on the lack of use of formal logic symbols, which is a feature of the Manchester OWL syntax.

Four participants commented on the value of diagrams. Here there were no conflicting views but a consensus that diagrams are useful, e.g. participant p3 stated: "perhaps I would have done better if I'd drawn diagrams on paper" and another participant (p5) commented: "a pictorial representation of the relationships would have been easier to use". Indeed, the automatic generation of diagrams is likely to have helped comprehension in all the questions discussed above. One participant (p6) expressed a related view that colour-coding for OWL entity types and font weights and styles for keywords would be useful.

There were some interesting comments about OWL features, including the difficulty of using the existential and universal quantifiers (participant p1); confusion between *and* and *or* (participant p3, see Q2 from table 1 discussed in subsection 5.1); and (participant p7) the effect of users' legacy, e.g. that of a database background. Each of these comments is relevant to one of the questions discussed in section 5.1.

6 Statistical Analysis

6.1 The Participants

The majority of participants achieved high scores; two achieved twenty out of twenty-one, whilst the lowest score was thirteen. Ranking on knowledge of logic and OWL significantly correlates with ranking on accuracy. The Spearman rank correlation coefficient between knowledge of logic and accuracy was 0.53, corresponding to $p = 0.038$ on a one-tailed t test. For the correlation between knowledge of OWL and accuracy, the coefficient was 0.54, corresponding to p = 0.036 on a one-tailed t test. The effect was greater when we consider just the questions with correct answer 'yes'. For these questions, the correlation factor was 0.57 (p = 0.027) for knowledge of logic and 0.60 (p = 0.019) for knowledge of OWL. For the 'no' questions the rank correlation with knowledge of logic and knowledge of OWL were no longer significant (p = 0.052 and p = 0.102 respectively). The number of participants did not permit a statistical analysis on a per-question basis. None of the participants classifying themselves as having a little knowledge of either logic or OWL answered correctly the first two questions discussed in section 5.1, i.e. the two questions with fewest accurate responses. However, there were also some experts who got these questions wrong.

There was considerable variation in the total time taken to answer the questions, ranging from around thirteen minutes to around forty-two minutes. For our participants, knowledge of OWL had a much greater effect on the total time taken than did knowledge of logic. For knowledge of OWL the Spearman rank correlation coefficient was -0.65, with p = 0.011 on a one-tailed t test; for knowledge of logic the coefficient was -0.29, with p = 0.178. The low correlation in the case of knowledge of logic may have occurred because the majority (67%) of our participants ranked themselves in the same category ('some knowledge').

6.2 The Questions

Most of the questions were answered correctly by all or most of the participants, with an apparent tendency to achieve greater accuracy on the questions with correct answer 'yes'. Table 5 provides a breakdown of the responses showing how many were correct and incorrect for the two categories of questions; it also shows the average times for each combination. A Pearson χ^2 test confirmed the greater accuracy on the 'yes' questions (p = 0.005). The greater accuracy for the 'yes' questions occurs despite the fact that the average maximum relational complexity for these questions is greater than that for the 'no' questions, i.e. they appear on average to be harder.

Table 5. Breakdown of responses, also showing average times in each category

	Yes	No
Correct	138; 43.4 secs	72; 59.5 secs
Incorrect	18; 58.4 secs	24; 76.3 secs

The time spent by any participant answering a single question varied from 9 seconds to 208 seconds, the average time across all participants for each of the twenty-two question varied from 20.3 seconds to 91.5 seconds. A two sample one-sided unpaired t test indicated that the 'yes' questions were answered on average significantly more quickly than the 'no' questions (p < 0.001). This may represent a tendency to initially attempt to prove the validity of the deduction. After first such attempts fail, the participant then has two possible strategies: either to continue such attempts until convinced that a proof is not possible or to attempt to prove explicitly that the deduction does not hold. The strategy adopted is likely to depend upon the person and the particular question. A one-sided unpaired t test also indicated that the correct responses were arrived at significantly more quickly than the incorrect responses ($p < 0.001$). Thus there was no trade-off between accuracy and speed of response. A two-way ANOVA indicated that the two factors did not interact ($p = 0.884$). Hence the correct responses to the 'yes' questions averaged the least time (43.4 seconds) whilst the incorrect responses to the 'no' questions averaged the greatest time (76.3 seconds).

A simple linear regression showed that, overall, questions with a large number of correct responses were answered more quickly than questions with fewer correct responses ($p < 0.001$). This was also true when analysis was restricted to those questions with correct answer 'yes' ($p < 0.001$) and also to all those questions correctly answered ($p = 0.001$). However, there was no significant relationship between time and number of correct responses for those questions where the correct answer was 'no' ($p = 0.349$), nor for the incorrectly answered questions ($p = 0.947$).

6.3 Theories of Reasoning

As already noted, an objective was to determine whether any of the psychological theories could be used to predict, in terms of accuracy and time, the behaviour of our participants, and thus whether any of these theories would be useful in understanding how people reason about DLs. Each question was analyzed to determine the maximum number of mental models and maximum relational complexity which it would entail; as shown in tables 2, 3 and 4. For the questions with correct answer 'yes', this was done by constructing the proof of the deduction, and determining the number of mental models and the relational complexity at each stage. The questions with correct answer 'no' were examined to determine the maximum number of mental models and maximum relational complexity which would be met in thinking about them.

Only three questions required more than one mental model, making any statistical analysis impossible. One (table 2, Q2) was a 'no' question requiring four mental models and was the least well answered, with only three correct responses; this question is discussed at the beginning of subsection 5.1. The other two were 'yes' questions requiring four (table 2, Q4) and three mental models (table 2, Q5) and with 11 and 9 correct responses; the second of these is also discussed in subsection 5.1. Moreover, whilst these three questions might be regarded as requiring more than one mental model, a participant with some knowledge of logic might well have used an alternative approach. The prevalence of questions requiring only one mental model seems to arise from the way in which Description Logics are used. The complexity is often in the relations, rather than in the existence of numerous possibilities.

This last statement might lead one to expect that relational complexity would be a better predictor of performance. However, a logistic regression of accuracy against maximum relational complexity did not provide a significant result ($p = 0.665$). This was also the case for a linear regression of time to answer each question versus maximum relational complexity ($p = 0.861$). When the latter regression was limited to the 'yes' questions, then there was a significant result ($p = 0.009$). The difference between 'yes' and 'no' questions may be a feature of the way people approach 'no' questions, or it may arise from the design of questions; all but one 'no' question had relational complexity of 2.

The rule-based theory leads one to expect that, for the 'yes' questions, performance might be predicted by the number of steps in the reasoning chain. Whatever the validity of this theory is for naïve reasoners in everyday life, it could have some relevance to our participants, all of whom had at least a little knowledge of logic. This was investigated by looking at the 13 'yes' questions. It might be expected that, as the number of steps in the reasoning chain increases, the accuracy of answering will decline, as the possibility of error multiplies and fatigue sets in. A logistic regression of accuracy against number of steps did not provide a significant result ($p = 0.355$). However, all questions had one, two or three steps, with the exception of Q10 of table 3 which had four steps and was correctly answered by all participants. When this question is removed from the analysis, a significant result is achieved ($p = 0.046$).

A linear regression of time for each response against number of steps also provided a significant result ($p = 0.036$). This was slightly more significant when only the correct responses were analyzed ($p = 0.028$), but not significant for the incorrect responses ($p = 0.360$). The mean times for one, two, three and four step questions were 25.5, 51.9, 44.3 and 54.2 seconds respectively. A Tukey range test at the 95% level indicated a significant difference between the means of only the first two groups.

7 Conclusions and Future Work

This study represents an attempt to understand the cognitive difficulties of using Description Logics. A key message is that, despite training, users are prone to certain misconceptions. These include confusion about the combined use of *not* and *and*; about the inheritance of property characteristics; and to a lesser extent about the functional characteristic and also the existential quantifier. Confusion may also arise through choice of names, a point taken up in the comments made by participants. The use of realistic names can lead to erroneous intuitions; however the mnemonic advantage is likely to outweigh this disadvantage. The important thing is to use names which are not likely to create incorrect intuitions.

In the study, maximal relational complexity did not significantly affect accuracy but did significantly affect the time to confirm an inference. The number of steps in a reasoning chain affected the time to reason and also, when one question was removed from the analysis, affected the accuracy of reasoning. Given the participants' background and the nature of the questions, it seems likely that they did at the conscious level adopt a rule-based approach, as evidenced by the effect of number of steps on accuracy and time. The fact that one-third of the respondents commented on the value of drawing a diagram indicates that they were also thinking in terms of models.

There are a number of different areas for further investigation. The effect of alternative linguistic usages is a valuable area for study. This applies to keywords, entity names and the structure of logical statements. For the non-logician the Manchester

OWL Syntax appears to offer a considerable improvement over formal logical notation, as evidenced by one of the participants' comments. However, the choice of linguistic terms can have a significant effect on cognition, e.g. see Johnson-Laird and Byrne (1989); this has not been systematically studied in the context of Description Logics. Allied to this is the effect of the way the linguistic terms are displayed, e.g. with the use of colour coding.

The value of diagrams in reasoning has been noted by other researchers. Larkin and Simon (1987) have analysed the benefits of diagrams in terms of support for search, recognition and inference. The importance of the design of diagrams has been pointed out by Bauer and Johnson-Laird (1993) who noted the need to avoid arbitrary symbols and make explicit alternative states of affairs. In the context of DLs, diagrams offer a strategy to overcome misconceptions and generally support reasoning. In fact, a large number of tools have been created to display ontological structures, e.g. see Katifori et al. (2007). These are chiefly aimed at viewing the structure of the overall ontology or parts of the ontology, i.e. at the subsumption relations, rather than the more cognitively difficult features of Description Logics. An exception to this is the work of Howse et al. (2011) who use concept diagrams not only to view subsumption relations but also to view and reason about role restrictions. The most successful such representations may mirror the mental models we construct when reasoning, so this work should also draw on what is known about such mental models and what is known about the role of diagrams in complementing reasoning.

A valuable experimental strategy would be to compare the current approach with a modified linguistic approach and with a diagrammatic approach, and possibly with a combination of the last two.

Finally, a better understanding of the effect of complexity would require a controlled study in which questions of varying complexity are posed with a limited subset of OWL features which are known to be well understood, to avoid any confounding of complexity with differences in comprehension of different logical features.

In each case a better understanding of the participant's thought processes is needed. Follow-up questions to specifically elucidate this would be valuable.

References

1. Baader, F., Calvanese, D., McGuiness, D., Nardi, D., Patel-Schneider, P.F.: The Description Logic Handbook: Theory, Implementation and Applications. In: CUP (2010)
2. Bauer, M.I., Johnson-Laird, P.N.: How diagrams can improve reasoning. Psychological Science 4(6), 372–378 (1993)
3. Goodwin, G.P., Johnson-Laird, P.N.: Reasoning about relations. Psychological Review 112(2), 468 (2005)
4. Halford, G.S., Andrews, G.: The development of deductive reasoning: How important is complexity? Thinking & Reasoning 10(2), 123–145 (2004)
5. Horridge, M., Bail, S., Parsia, B., Sattler, U.: The cognitive complexity of OWL justifications. In: Aroyo, L., Welty, C., Alani, H., Taylor, J., Bernstein, A., Kagal, L., Noy, N., Blomqvist, E. (eds.) ISWC 2011, Part I. LNCS, vol. 7031, pp. 241–256. Springer, Heidelberg (2011)
6. Horridge, M., Drummond, N., Goodwin, J., Rector, A., Stevens, R., Wang, H.H.: The manchester owl syntax. OWL: Experiences and Directions, 10–11 (2006)

7. Howse, J., Stapleton, G., Taylor, K., Chapman, P.: Visualizing ontologies: A case study. In: Aroyo, L., Welty, C., Alani, H., Taylor, J., Bernstein, A., Kagal, L., Noy, N., Blomqvist, E. (eds.) ISWC 2011, Part I. LNCS, vol. 7031, pp. 257–272. Springer, Heidelberg (2011)
8. Johnson-Laird, P.N., Byrne, R.M.: Only Reasoning. Journal of Memory and Language 28(3), 313–330 (1989)
9. Johnson-Laird, P.N., Byrne, R.M.: Deduction. Lawrence Erlbaum Associates, Inc. (1991), http://psycnet.apa.org/psycinfo/1991-97828-000 (retrieved)
10. Johnson-Laird, P.N., Byrne, R.M., Schaeken, W.: Propositional reasoning by model. Psychological Review 99(3), 418 (1992)
11. Katifori, A., Halatsis, C., Lepouras, G., Vassilakis, C., Giannopoulou, E.: Ontology visualization methods—a survey. ACM Computing Surveys (CSUR) 39(4), 10 (2007)
12. Khan, M.T., Blomqvist, E.: Ontology design pattern detection-initial method and usage scenarios. In: SEMAPRO 2010, The Fourth International Conference on Advances in Semantic Processing, pp. 19–24 (2010), http://www.thinkmind.org/index.php?view=article&articleid=semapro_2010_1_40_50071 (retrieved)
13. Khemlani, S., Orenes, I., Johnson-Laird, P.N.: Negating compound sentences. Naval Research Lab Washington DC Navy Center for Applied Research in Artificial inTeLLigence (2012a), http://mindmodeling.org/cogsci2012/papers/0110/paper0110.pdf (retrieved)
14. Khemlani, S., Orenes, I., Johnson-Laird, P.N.: Negation: A theory of its meaning, representation, and use. Journal of Cognitive Psychology 24(5), 541–559 (2012b)
15. Larkin, J.H., Simon, H.A.: Why a diagram is (sometimes) worth ten thousand words. Cognitive Science 11(1), 65–100 (1987)
16. Motik, B., Grau, B., Horrocks, I., Wu, Z., Fokoue, A., Carsten, L.: OWL 2 Web Ontology Language Profiles, 2nd edn. W3C (2012), http://www.w3.org/TR/2012/REC-owl2-profiles-20121211/ (retrieved)
17. Newstead, S.E., Bradon, P., Handley, S.J., Dennis, I., Evans, J.S.B.: Predicting the difficulty of complex logical reasoning problems. Thinking & Reasoning 12(1), 62–90 (2006)
18. Nguyen, Power, Piwek, Williams: Measuring the understandability of deduction rules for OWL. Presented at the First International Workshop on Debugging Ontologies and Ontology Mappings, Galway, Ireland (2012), http://oro.open.ac.uk/34591/ (retrieved)
19. Power, R.: Complexity assumptions in ontology verbalisation. In: Proceedings of the ACL 2010 Conference Short Papers, pp. 132–136 (2010), http://dl.acm.org/citation.cfm?id=1858866 (retrieved)
20. Power, R., Third, A.: Expressing OWL axioms by English sentences: dubious in theory, feasible in practice. In: Proceedings of the 23rd International Conference on Computational Linguistics: Posters, pp. 1006–1013 (2010), http://dl.acm.org/citation.cfm?id=1944682 (retrieved)
21. Rector, A., Drummond, N., Horridge, M., Rogers, J., Knublauch, H., Stevens, R., Wroe, C.: OWL pizzas: Practical experience of teaching OWL-DL: Common errors & common patterns. In: Engineering Knowledge in the Age of the Semantic Web, pp. 63–81. Springer (2004), http://link.springer.com/chapter/10.1007/978-3-540-30202-5_5 (retrieved)
22. Rips, L.J.: Cognitive processes in propositional reasoning. Psychological Review 90(1), 38 (1983)
23. Warren, P.: Ontology Users' Survey - Summary of Results (KMi Tech Report No. kmi-13-01) (2013), http://kmi.open.ac.uk/publications/pdf/kmi-13-01.pdf (retrieved)
24. Zielinski, T.A., Goodwin, G.P., Halford, G.S.: Complexity of categorical syllogisms: An integration of two metrics. European Journal of Cognitive Psychology 22(3), 391–421 (2010)

NL-Graphs: A Hybrid Approach toward Interactively Querying Semantic Data

Khadija Elbedweihy, Suvodeep Mazumdar,
Stuart N. Wrigley, and Fabio Ciravegna

Department of Computer Science, University of Sheffield, UK
{k.elbedweihy,s.mazumdar,s.wrigley,f.ciravegna}@dcs.shef.ac.uk

Abstract. A variety of query approaches have been proposed by the semantic web community to explore and query semantic data. Each was developed for a specific task and employed its own interaction mechanism; each query mechanism has its own set of advantages and drawbacks. Most semantic web search systems employ only one approach, thus being unable to exploit the benefits of alternative approaches. Motivated by a usability and interactivity perspective, we propose to combine two query approaches (graph-based and natural language) as a hybrid query approach. In this paper, we present NL-Graphs which aims to exploit the strengths of both approaches, while ameliorating their weaknesses. NL-Graphs was conceptualised and developed from observations, and lessons learned, in several evaluations with expert and casual users. The results of evaluating our approach with expert and casual users on a large semantic dataset are very encouraging; both types of users were highly satisfied and could effortlessly use the hybrid approach to formulate and answer queries. Indeed, success rates showed they were able to successfully answer all the evaluation questions.

Keywords: #eswc2014Elbedweihy.

1 Introduction and Related Work

The overall goal of a (semantic) search system is to assist users in fulfilling their information needs. Users' experience and satisfaction with this information seeking process is influenced by many aspects including the query format, the performance of the search system and the presentation of the results. Most of the work done to date has focused on the second aspect: improving the effectiveness and retrieval performance of semantic search systems. Several query approaches have also been proposed over the years, with varying levels of interactivity and user involvement. While the progress in these areas has been encouraging, the third aspect (usability) has been largely ignored by the Semantic Web community[1].

[1] A significant lack of attention to usability and user experience has been a concern to the community. Indeed, David R. Karger's keynote talk (http://videolectures.net/eswc2013_karger_semantic/) stressing the need for designing Semantic Web solutions with explicit attention to users bears testimony to the need for such solutions.

V. Presutti et al. (Eds.): ESWC 2014, LNCS 8465, pp. 565–579, 2014.

In our previous work [7], we conducted a user-based study to evaluate the usability of different query approaches with expert and casual users. The results showed that, on one hand, both types of users liked the support given by view-based (graph- and form-based) approaches in constructing queries through visualising the search space. On the other hand, the main drawback of these approaches was the amount of effort and time required to formulate queries. Therefore, in [17], we presented the results of a learnability study which investigated whether the effects of the latter could be alleviated by practice and frequency of use of a graph-based tool (Affective Graphs). The results revealed an improvement in users' performance as well as satisfaction over time, while the effort and time involved in query formulation for frequent tasks needed much improvement, even after three practice sessions. Additionally, observations during the evaluations noted that users heavily used a (text-based) concept-search feature in addition to manual visual lookups while performing either task. This was highly interesting, as users were observed to be combining different mechanisms to perform their tasks. This finding motivated the next stage of our work and seeded ideas for a more integrated hybrid approach that can harmoniously combine differing query approaches.

In broad terms, a *hybrid query approach* uses a combination of approaches (natural language (NL)-based, keyword-based, graph-based or form-based) as the query format. However, the term *hybrid approach* has been used interchangeably in literature with *hybrid search* and *hybrid web search* to refer to different concepts. [8] and [16] use one or more of these terms to describe their application of semantic web techniques (such as using ontologies to find concepts related to the input query terms) to improve the precision of traditional keyword-based search. In a different way, [3] used two query formats: keywords and forms to perform both keyword-based traditional search and semantic search, respectively, and combine the results of both. The two query approaches are separated and linked to two different underlying data indexes. The keyword-based approach is used to search traditional documents while the form-based approach is used to visualise semantic data and ontologies. [10] combined keyword search and view-based search to support users in formulating their search queries and offer them flexibility in expressing their information needs. Their methodology is based on mapping the underlying domain ontologies into views, which facilitates view-based search.

Based on the findings from our evaluations, we propose a hybrid approach that benefits from the strength of the graph-based approach in visualising the search space, while attempting to balance the time and effort required during query formulation using a NL input feature. We hypothesise that this would provide a high level of support and satisfaction for users during query formulation. To evaluate this hypothesis, we developed our approach – NL-Graphs – as a proof of concept and conducted a third user-based study with expert and casual users to assess its usability and user satisfaction. However, it is important to note that the NL- and the graph-based components were evaluated separately in recent work [6, 17] and thus, the evaluation described here focuses on the usability of the hybrid approach as a new query mechanism. Our contribution in this paper is three-fold:

- Propose a hybrid query approach combining the benefits of NL and view-based approaches.
- Validate our approach with a user-based evaluation involving 24 participants.
- Compare how casual and expert users interact with the query approach.

The remainder of the paper is structured as follows: the architecture of NL-Graphs (implementing the hybrid approach) is described in Section 2, together with illustrative scenarios showing the querying experience. Then, in Section 3, the usability study conducted to assess the usability of the approach and its usefulness in supporting users during query formulation is presented. Finally, conclusions and future work are discussed in Section 4.

2 NL-Graphs: A Hybrid Approach toward Querying Semantic Data

As discussed previously, the hybrid approach presented here combines two different query approaches (NL- and graph-based) to support users during query formulation. *NL-Graphs* is implemented as a proof-of-concept for realising this hybrid approach. It combines the NL-approach, presented in details in [6], and Affective Graphs, similarly presented in [17]. Therefore, we limit our description to the core functionalities of each constituent approach and the interaction between them in NL-Graphs as shown in Figure 1.

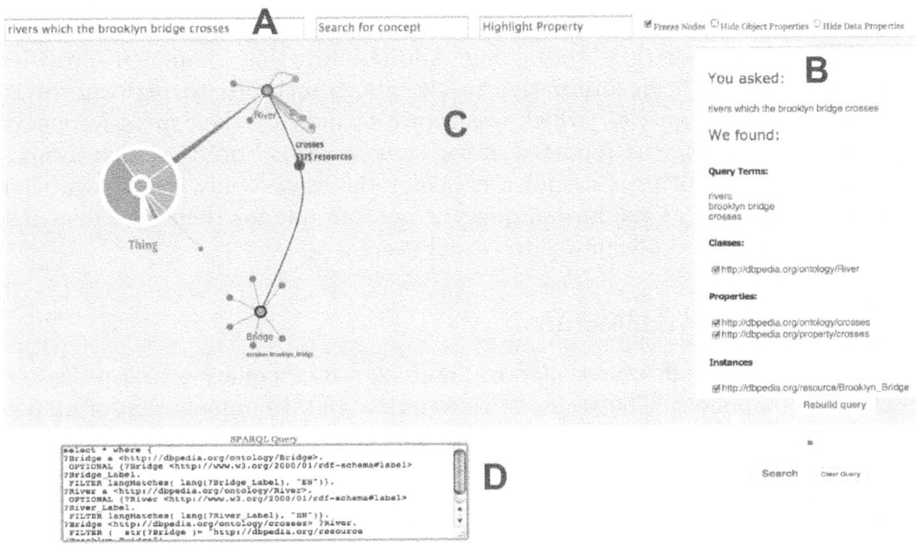

Fig. 1. NL-Graphs interface for the query *"rivers which the brooklyn bridge crosses"*

- Text Entry for NL Query (A): This allows the user to enter a NL query. Since the main drawback of the graph-based approach – when used separately – was the amount of effort and time required to formulate queries, this component provides the means for an easy-and-fast starting point for query construction. Users are free to enter keywords, phrases or full questions.
- Input Interpretation and Query Validation (B): One of the main difficulties for NL-based query approaches is mapping users' query terms onto the correct ontological concepts and properties and Linked Data entities. This is necessary to understand the correct query intent and, in turn, provide accurate answers. The employed NL-approach – similar to state-of-the-art NL-approaches – does not yet experience very high performance in this aspect and hence some query terms can be incorrectly mapped to concepts, properties or instances. As such, this component is intended to provide users with the ability to verify the interpretation of the system for their input query and perform corrections if needed.
- Visual Approach (C): As stated above, the output of the NL-component might contain incorrect interpretations of the user's query, or could be incomplete when no suitable mappings are found for one or more query term. Therefore, the visual approach provides the means for users to 1) verify the interpretation of the system for their input query; 2) correct or complete the visual query which is automatically built using the NL-component's output – as will be explained later; 3) understand the structure of the underlying data; and finally 4) explore the context surrounding their query (related concepts and properties).
- Formal Query (D): Having the formal query presented for users in the interface is motivated by the results of the usability study discussed in [7]. These showed that the formal representation of the constructed queries provided experts with the means to verify the queries and, therefore, increased their confidence in what they were doing. Additionally, this component provides expert users with an alternative to the above methods to perform direct changes to their queries (which was shown to increase the expressiveness of the query language as reported in the same study). Note that this component can be hidden for casual users since the same study has shown that the presentation of the formal query is not suitable for them and does not provide any added advantage to casual users.

2.1 NL-Graphs Architecture

As shown in the workflow presented in Figure 2, a user's query is first processed by the NL-component. The steps: 1) recognition and disambiguation of named entities; 2) parsing the NL query; 3) matching query terms with ontology concepts and properties; and finally 4) generation of candidate triples, explained in details in [6], are applied in order. In these steps, firstly, named entities are recognised using AlchemyAPI and disambiguated using a word sense disambiguation (WSD) approach as described in [6]. Then, the Stanford parser is used to generate the lemma and part of speech (POS) tag of each query term and store

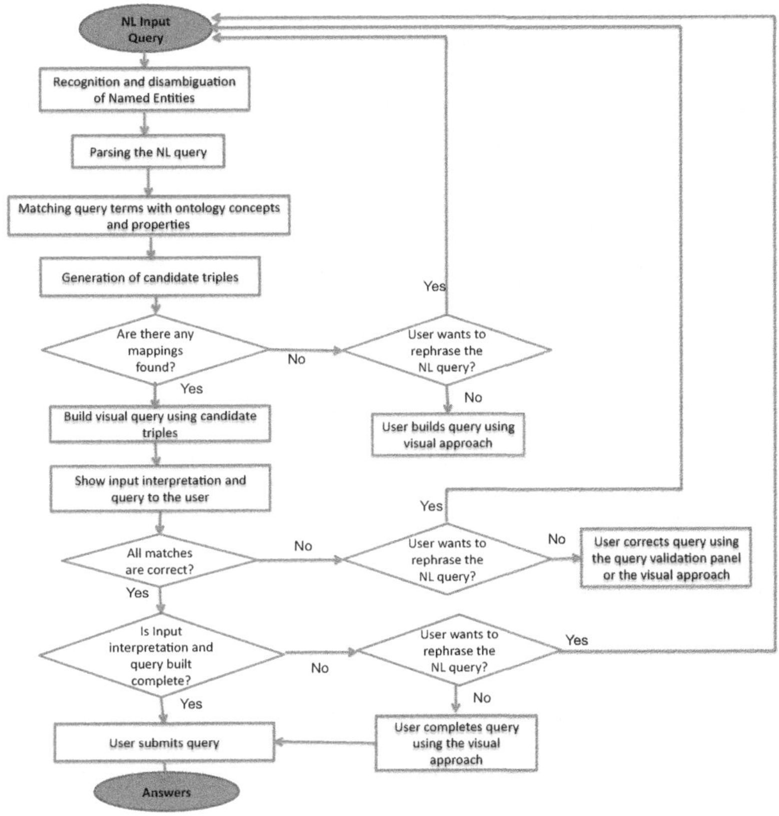

Fig. 2. NL-Graphs workflow

them with the term's position with respect to the rest of the query. These terms are then matched to concepts and properties in the underlying ontologies. Noun phrases, nouns and adjectives are matched with both concepts and properties, while verbs are only matched with properties. The structure of the ontology (taxonomy of classes and domain and range information of properties) is then used to link the identified matches (concepts, properties and instances) to generate candidate triples. An example of these triples is shown below:[2]:

```
<res:Brooklyn_Bridge> <dbo:crosses> ?river.
?river a <dbo:River>.
```

These triples are then passed to the graph-based component. Even if no complete triples are generated (for instance, if only one query term was matched with an ontology concept or with an instance) these mappings are similarly passed

[2] The prefix `res` refers to: `<http://dbpedia.org/resource/>`, `dbp` refers to: `<http://dbpedia.org/property/>` and `dbo` refers to: `<http://dbpedia.org/ontology/>`

to the graph-based component to be visualised in the graphical panel (Figure 1: C). This is performed within the next step in the workflow: "*Build visual query using candidate triples*".

In the graph-based component, any concepts found in the list of terms received from the NL-component are analysed first. Each concept is loaded, along with all its respective data and object properties[3]. Then, the instances are analysed where each instance type is added into the existing query, and a restriction (constraint) value of the instance is applied on the concept. For example, the concept *River* is loaded first and then, the constraint `res:Brooklyn_Bridge` is then applied on the concept as a text filter. The properties are finally analysed, the concepts which are domains or ranges for a property are loaded (if not previously loaded). When the analysis of all terms is complete, the final step includes loading the visual query, inspecting the query variables and completing the formal query.

Next in the workflow, the interpretation of the NL query – all matches for concepts, properties or instances – is shown in the query validation panel on the middle right side of the user interface (Figure 1: B). Additionally, the output of the graph-based component – either mappings or visual query – is displayed in the graphical panel on the middle left side of the user interface (Figure 1: C). If the system's interpretation for the user's query contains incorrect mappings, then the user can correct them using either of these panels according to their preference. Otherwise, the user can continue to submit the query if the system's interpretation and the query built were complete – entities, concepts and relations connecting them were identified. If any of the latter was missing, then the user can complete the query using the visual approach as will be explained in the next section.

2.2 Querying in NL-Graphs: – The User Experience

In order to begin the querying process with NL-Graphs, the user enters a NL query into the search box as shown in Figure 1:(A). In this example, the user enters the phrase "*rivers which the brooklyn bridge crosses*". Similar output would be generated for the complete question "*Give me all rivers which the brooklyn bridge crosses.*" or the keywords "*river brooklyn bridge crosses*". When the query is submitted, three pieces of information are shown to the user: input interpretation (B), visualised query (C) and formal query (D). The user understands from the input interpretation that the system identifies the three query terms *rivers*, *brooklyn bridge* and *crosses* and matches them to the class `dbo:River`, the instance `res:Brooklyn_Bridge` and the properties `dbo:crosses` and `dbp:crosses`, respectively. The visualised query presents the same information where the *River* and *Bridge* concepts are shown to the user and linked

[3] Loading or exploring a concept refers to the way *Affective Graphs* creates and renders a node (as a circular visual object, with a pie chart illustrating the distribution of instances across its sub-classes). In addition, the relevant data and object properties are also visualised as bezier curves and lines. The visual representation of various semantic elements are discussed in [17].

together with the property *crosses* to formulate the required query. Moreover, as shown in the figure, the instance *Brooklyn_Bridge* causes a filter (shown in orange) to be added on the concept *Bridge*. Finally, the expert user – with knowledge of formal queries – can validate or directly perform changes on the query shown at the bottom of the interface (D). In this example, the user would find the correct interpretation and complete query built and therefore, continues to submit the query to retrieve answers as shown in Figure 3.

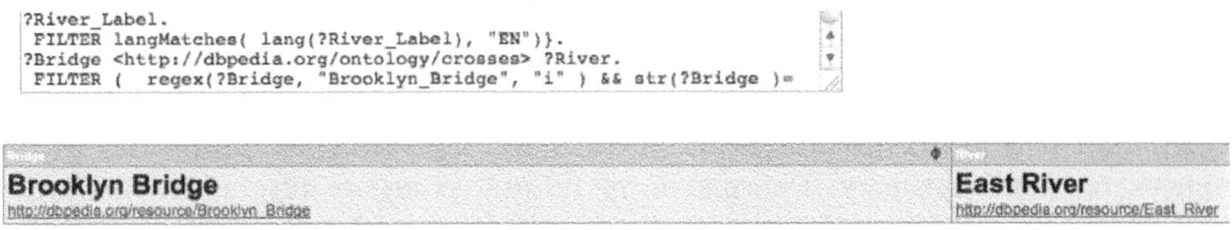

Fig. 3. NL-Graphs results for the query *"rivers which the brooklyn bridge crosses"*

Presentation of results is a challenging research problem which can have different solutions and styles. Indeed, both the content (what) and the presentation style (how) of the results affect the usability of a search system and users' satisfaction. However, since this is not the focus of this work, we decided to present results in a simple format (as a list of NL answers associated with URIs) for both casual and expert users to understand and be able to evaluate the system.

Validating and Correcting Input Interpretation. As discussed earlier, for some queries, the system's interpretation and resulting mappings might not be satisfying for a user. For instance, consider the query *"who founded microsoft?"*. Since no exact match is identified for the query term *founded*, then the algorithm returns all matches whose similarity exceeds a predefined threshold. Therefore, the properties `dbo:foundedBy`, `dbp:founder`, `dbo:foundingYear`, `dbp:foundation` and `dbo:foundingDate` are generated as candidate mappings and presented in the validation panel, as shown in Figure 4 (Left). Additionally, the data properties `dbp:foundation`, `dbo:foundingYear` and

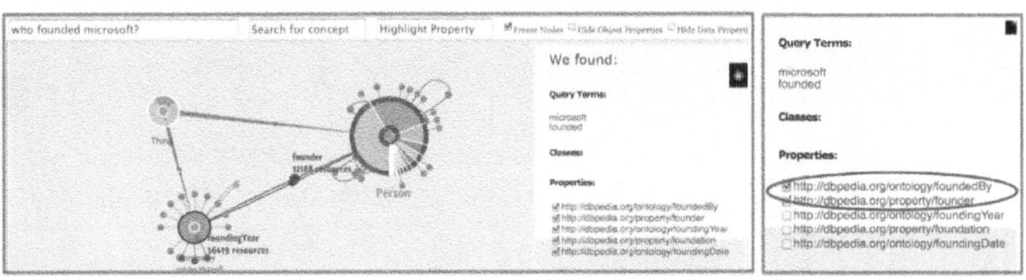

Fig. 4. Left–NL-Graphs input interpretation for the query *"who founded microsoft?"*. Right – A user validates and corrects the input interpretation of NL-Graphs for the query.

`dbo:foundingDate` associated with the concept *Company* are highlighted in the graphical panel, while the object properties `dbo:foundedBy` and `dbp:founder` linking the concepts *Company* and *Person* cause the latter to be added to the panel.

Since the user is only interested in knowing the founding person, then they will deselect the other properties and choose to *Rebuild Query*. Both panels are then updated to reflect these changes, as shown in Figure 4 (Right). As noted previously, the user can similarly perform these changes from the graphical panel.

Completing a Query. In some scenarios, the NL-component might not be able to successfully interpret and understand all key terms found in users' queries. This could be due to difficulties in either matching concepts, properties or instances to their ontological terms or in adding complex filters, for instance, featuring numerical or date ranges. To illustrate, consider the query "*brooklyn bridge traverse which river*" in which the algorithm failed to find matches for the term *traverse* in the ontology. However, to still support the user in constructing their query, Figure 5 shows the output of the system which contains mappings found for the other terms: *River* and *Brooklyn Bridge* and their datatype properties as well as object properties connecting them. The user can then directly construct the query by choosing the property *crosses* linking both concepts.

3 Evaluation

It is important to note that the NL-component and Affective Graphs were evaluated separately in terms of their performance; and usability and learnability, respectively [6, 17]. Therefore, the rest of this section is focused on the evaluation of the hybrid approach as a new query mechanism. To accomplish this, a user-based study was conducted with both expert and casual users to assess the usability of the hybrid approach and the level of support it provides for users and their resulting experience and satisfaction.

Furthermore, as a first evaluation with real users, we note that our key interest is in understanding the benefit and usefulness of the hybrid approach in itself and

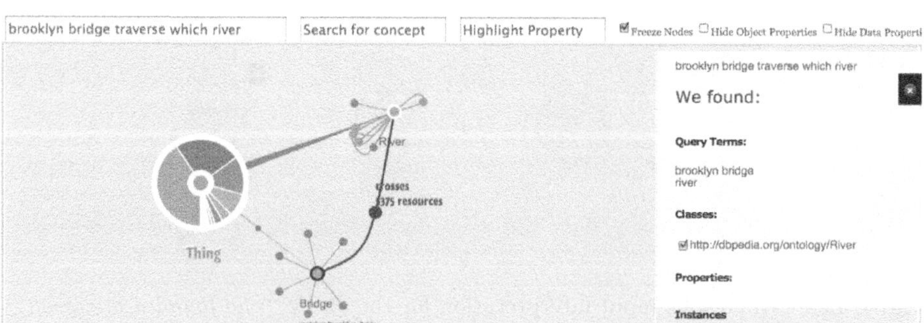

Fig. 5. NL-Graphs interpretation for the query "*brooklyn bridge traverse which river*"

identify interaction issues that can arise out of a novel query approach. A larger evaluation, in a comparative setting, would indeed be beneficial in a later stage. Our work stresses the need to engage users from an early stage of development, and this evaluation is a part of this effort which is currently receiving little attention in the SW community.

3.1 Dataset and Questions

To allow assessing the usefulness of the hybrid approach, we attempted to find a set of queries which would be problematic for NL-based approaches. These problems would, for instance, result from the difficulty of mapping user query terms to ontological ones or understanding complex questions such as those containing superlatives or advanced constraints. Therefore, five queries were selected from the DBpedia training and test data provided by the 2nd Open Challenge on Question Answering over Linked Data [13]. These queries are listed below:

1. When was Capcom founded?
2. What did Bruce Carver die from?
3. Who was the wife of U.S. president Lincoln?
4. Give me all cities in Alaska with more than 10000 inhabitants.
5. Show me all songs from Bruce Springsteen released between 1980 and 1990.

As noticed, the queries feature different levels of complexity and difficulty. For instance, the query term *founded* could be mapped to a large number of properties in the ontology including `dbo:foundingYear`, `dbp:foundation`, `dbo:foundedBy` and `dbp:founder`. However, selecting the right property depends on understanding the question and identifying the answer type – date. Also, some approaches would face difficulty mapping the expression *die from* to the object property `dbo:deathCause` linking `dbo:Person` and `dbo:Disease` concepts. Finally, the most complex query *Show me all songs from Bruce Springsteen released between 1980 and 1990* contains a date range constraint and was found too hard to answer by all systems evaluated in the QALD evaluation [5].

Note that although the current version of NL-Graphs has been tested with DBpedia, it can be easily configured to query other datasets. The NL-component requires building an index for the ontology while the graph-based component is configured to query either local or remote SPARQL endpoints.

3.2 Evaluation Setup

For this study, 24 subjects (12 expert users and 12 casual users), aged between 18 and 53 with a mean of 31 years, were recruited for the experiment which took place in a controlled laboratory setting. Subjects were compensated for their time. The casual users were drawn from the staff and student population of the University of Sheffield, while the expert users were drawn from the Organisations, Information and Knowledge (OAK) Group[4] within the Department of

[4] `http://oak.dcs.shef.ac.uk/`

Computer Science at the University of Sheffield and from K-Now[5] – a software development firm, working on semantic technologies. At the beginning, subjects were introduced to the experiment and its goal and any instructions required to be able to complete the experiment. They were given a short demo session explaining the query language adopted by the system (hybrid approach) and – through an example – how to use it to formulate a sample query. After this, subjects were asked to formulate each of the five questions in turn using the system's interface. After finishing all questions, subjects were asked to fill in two questionnaires to capture their experience and level of satisfaction. Finally, they were presented with a third questionnaire to collect demographics data such as age, profession and knowledge of formal query languages and visual interfaces, among others. Each full experiment with one subject lasted 30–40 minutes.

Similar to other usability studies (e.g., [9, 11, 12, 14]) and to allow for deeper analysis, both objective and subjective data covering the experiment results were collected. To measure efficiency, the *input time* required by users to formulate their queries as well as the *number of attempts* showing how many times on average users reformulated their query, were recorded. Additionally, *success rate*, capturing the percentage of tasks successfully completed, was used to measure effectiveness. This data was collected using custom-written software which allowed each experiment to be orchestrated. The subjective data was collected using two post-search questionnaires. The first is the *System Usability Scale (SUS) questionnaire* [4], a standardised usability test comprising ten normalised questions covering usability aspects such as the need for support, training, and complexity and has proven to be very useful when investigating interface usability [1]. The second questionnaire (*Extended Questionnaire*) is one which was designed to include a further question focused on the ease of use of the hybrid approach in addition to two open-ended questions to gather additional feedback regarding users' experience. These questions are listed below:

1. The query construction process was X. This question was answered on a 5-point Likert scale, ranging from *Laborious* to *Effortless.*
2. What did you like about the hybrid approach as a mechanism for expressing your query? and why?
3. What things you didn't like about the hybrid approach as a mechanism for expressing your query? and why?

3.3 Results and Discussion

According to the adjective ratings introduced by [2] and the resulting SUS scores, NL-Graphs is classified as *Excellent* by expert users (median: '73.75') and *Good* by casual users (median: '61.25'). These encouraging results are also supported by the success rate, informing effectiveness, and reported as 100%, showing that all users were able to successfully answer all the questions given in the study. Additionally, the median score given to the question regarding the *query construction process* is '4' (for both types of users), showing that most users could

[5] `http://www.k-now.co.uk/k-now/`

effortlessly use the hybrid approach (as a query mechanism) to formulate and answer questions. Moreover, these results are supported by the users' feedback in the open-ended questions: 19 of the positive (liked) comments – 10 from expert users and 9 from casual users – were directly focused on the usability and support provided by the hybrid approach during query construction. On the other hand, only one expert user and three casual users provided negative feedback regarding the approach; one casual user directly stated that she found the approach to be "*complicated and not intuitive*", while the others commented on the longer time or more steps required to build queries than with text-based search engines such as Google.

The second finding observed from these numbers is that, expert users were more satisfied with the usability of NL-Graphs. Our explanation for this finding is that, firstly, since NL-graphs features a graph-based component, this caused it to be more complicated for casual users than for expert users as was concluded in [7]. Indeed, expert users are more familiar with Semantic Web and graph data – underlying data seen as a graph of concepts with properties and relations linking them. Additionally, some of the casual users expected – and were thus comparing NL-Graphs with – a Google-like interface where they only need to type in a question. Therefore, they were more reluctant to do the extra step – if required – to complete their queries using the visual approach. For instance, some of their feedback regarding this aspect is as follows:

- *It seemed an extra step to get to your answer rather than just typing in a search and it appearing in results.*
- *May take longer than other ways especially if the query is overly complex.*

Although the experience (and thus the SUS score) of these few users might have affected the average SUS score of casual users, feedback of the other users showed that they liked the hybrid approach and found it to be very helpful in finding answers for their questions. It was interesting to find out that most of the casual users felt an appreciation for – and thus commented on – having the visual approach as part of NL-Graphs since it was useful in several ways as shown from their feedback given below:

- *Graphical representation of the relationships between the different concepts was helpful and interesting.*
- *Visualising the query helped me to understand exactly what I was searching for, it is also interactive and I could quickly change my query if necessary.*
- *It increases the chances to find viable answers, also, it is more interactive and shows options that you might not have considered exploring before.*

Indeed, we believe that the casual users' satisfaction and, in turn, the resulting SUS scores could have been much higher if users were given more training and time to practice using the new query approach. As stated in [15, p. 41], a system that is initially hard to learn could be eventually efficient. This was also confirmed from both casual and expert users' feedback, shown below:

- *I might need more assistance and guidance when using the query mechanism at the start.*
- *You may need a more specialised person to use it. However, after training, I think anyone would be able to use it.*
- *I was unfamiliar with the system and I think it would become easier with regular use.*

On the contrary, expert users who are familiar with graph-based approaches appreciated the support provided by the NL-component which led to a faster approach for constructing their queries – compared to visually doing the same process. This is supported by their feedback, as follows:

- *I thought the NL part was very straightforward to use and made a good starting point for constructing queries.*
- *Providing the NL first was user friendly, made it fast to formulate queries.*
- *I liked that the system automatically identified the main concepts from the query so the exploration process was faster.*

Another output to report from this evaluation is with regards to the efficiency of the hybrid approach, assessed using effort-based measures. On average, expert users needed 94.48 seconds to construct a query, while casual users needed 76.88 seconds. Both types of users needed only one attempt on average to construct

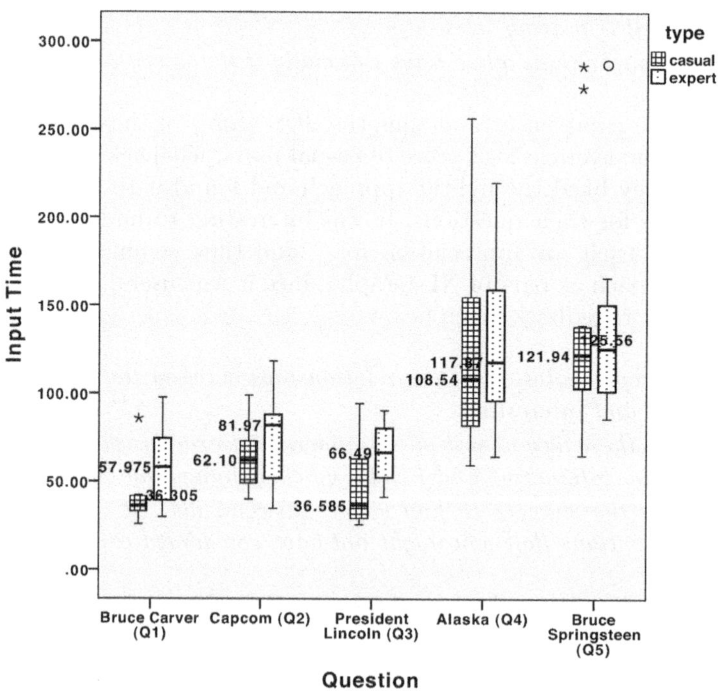

Fig. 6. Average time required to formulate each question

a query. Although direct comparison cannot be performed with the results of the usability study presented in [7] since the data used in the evaluation is different, from a broader view, one could observe that, on average, both types of users seemed to require less amount of effort to formulate queries using NL-Graphs (employing a hybrid approach) than with Affective Graphs (employing a graph-based approach). In the usability study, with the latter, casual users needed 72.8 seconds and 1.5 attempts, expert users needed 88.86 seconds and 1.7 attempts. This view is supported by our observations and users' feedback from both studies: the graph-based approach was judged as laborious and time consuming in the first study, while in the current evaluation, only three users commented on the effort required to build queries since they were comparing it with purely text-based search engines. Indeed, the rest of the users appreciated the hybrid approach for supporting them in building queries in a fast and interactive manner. Additionally, figure 6 shows that the average time for all questions is negatively affected by the time required to answer the questions *Alaska* and *Bruce Springsteen*. Our observations showed the following reasons as the cause for the increase in the amount of time required:

- Give me all cities in Alaska with more than 10000 inhabitants: Firstly, a few subjects attempted to use the query term *alaskan*, which was not recognized by Alchemy API and in-turn by the NL-component, resulting in these users trying to set a constraint to the concept itself, a step which required an additional amount of time. Secondly, the property `dbo:isPartOf`, connecting *Alaska* and the *cities* found in it, was confusing and not self-explainable for users – even expert users – and they needed more time to check all the other alternatives shown to them (such as `capital` or `largest`) before completing their query. Finally, numerical constraints were not automatically identified and added by the NL-component to the query and thus, users needed to add the constraint '*more than 10000*' to the property `populationTotal` using the visual approach, which required three additional steps.
- Show me all songs from Bruce Springsteen released between 1980 and 1990: For this query, most of the additional time was spent by users to add the date range constraint 'between 1980 and 1990' to the property `releaseDate`. This task required five steps: 1) Add property to the query, 2) Add constraint to the property, 3) Use date picker to specify the date required (as shown in Figure 7). Steps 2 and 3 are then repeated to add the second date constraint. Additionally, some users took more time while attempting to input the constraint in one step and searching for the feature to do this, for instance, like '1980 <date <1990', an implementation detail which was not available.

Moreover, Figure 6 shows that, on average, expert users took more time to build their queries than casual users. Again, we observed two reasons that could explain this behavior: 1) expert users followed logic and their understanding of the Semantic Web concepts to plan, formulate and validate their queries, which resulted in higher query input time; and 2) some of them took more time to validate their queries using the formal (SPARQL) query presented in the interface and, in few cases, to perform direct changes to their queries.

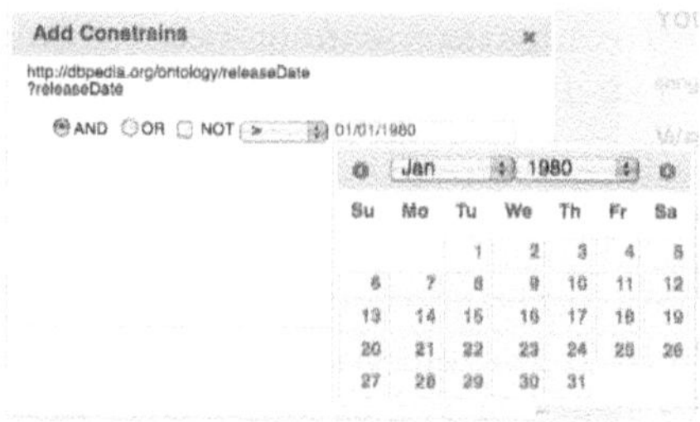

Fig. 7. The date picker used to add the constraint found in the query '*Show me all songs from Bruce Springsteen released between 1980 and 1990*'

Query Validation. As illustrated in Section 2.2, the query validation feature is provided to give users the ability to understand the interpretation of the NL-component to their query and correct it if possible. This was motivated by our observation in earlier evaluations: in many scenarios, the results returned by a search system might not be satisfying for users due to a misinterpretation of their query terms. The difficulty then occurs when users are only presented with the results, with no reference or explanation for them. Then, they would usually try different query terms in order to find the required answers. Interestingly, the evaluation showed how this feature proved to be very useful and helpful for users while constructing their queries. Indeed, we found that almost all users used this feature in the query "*when was capcom founded?*" to correct the interpreted input and only select the properties `foundingDate` and `foundingYear`, which they found to be the most suitable for the query (among other properties such as `dbo:foundedBy` or `dbp:founder`). Additionally, users' positive (liked) feedback included the following comments, focused on the query validation feature:

- *I liked that there was an information box on the right hand side which showed the identified matches to my terms so that I didn't need to click on them a lot in the visual interface to do changes.*
- *The options to validate and refine searches were obvious and well set out.*

4 Conclusions

In this paper, we have presented a hybrid query approach intended to improve users' experience and satisfaction with the search process. It takes advantage of visualising the search space offered by a graph-based query approach and the ease of use and speed of query formulation offered by a NL-component. A user-based study, conducted with expert and casual users to assess the usability of the approach and its usefulness in supporting users during query formulation, was presented. The results are very encouraging: both types of users provided high SUS scores for NL-Graphs – with expert users being more satisfied. Success rates also showed that all users were able to successfully answer all the evaluation questions. Additionally, feedback showed that most users could *effortlessly* use the hybrid approach to formulate and answer queries. We believe these encouraging results provide a good basis and motivation for a deeper investigation into hybridising semantic search systems and their resulting performance.

References

1. Bangor, A., Kortum, P.T., Miller, J.T.: An Empirical Evaluation of the System Usability Scale. Int. J. Hum-Comput. Int. 24, 574–594 (2008)
2. Bangor, A., Kortum, P.T., Miller, J.T.: Determining what individual SUS scores mean: Adding an adjective rating scale. JUS 4, 114–123 (2009)
3. Bhagdev, R., Chapman, S., Ciravegna, F., Lanfranchi, V., Petrelli, D.: Hybrid Search: Effectively Combining Keywords and Semantic Searches. In: Bechhofer, S., Hauswirth, M., Hoffmann, J., Koubarakis, M. (eds.) ESWC 2008. LNCS, vol. 5021, pp. 554–568. Springer, Heidelberg (2008)
4. Brooke, J.: SUS: a quick and dirty usability scale. In: Usability Evaluation in Industry, pp. 189–194. Taylor and Francis (1996)
5. Cimiano, P., Lopez, V., Unger, C., Cabrio, E., Ngonga Ngomo, A.-C., Walter, S.: Multilingual question answering over linked data (QALD-3): Lab overview. In: Forner, P., Müller, H., Paredes, R., Rosso, P., Stein, B. (eds.) CLEF 2013. LNCS, vol. 8138, pp. 321–332. Springer, Heidelberg (2013)
6. Elbedweihy, K., Wrigley, S., Ciravegna, F., Zhang, Z.: Using BabelNet in Bridging the Gap Between Natural Language Queries and Linked Data Concepts. In: Proceedings of 1st International Workshop on NLP and DBpedia, ISWC (2013)
7. Elbedweihy, K., Wrigley, S.N., Ciravegna, F.: Evaluating Semantic Search Query Approaches with Expert and Casual Users. In: Cudré-Mauroux, P., et al. (eds.) ISWC 2012, Part II. LNCS, vol. 7650, pp. 274–286. Springer, Heidelberg (2012)
8. Han, L., Chen, G.: The HWS hybrid web search. Information and Software Technology 48, 687–695 (2006)
9. Hix, D., Hartson, H.R.: Developing User Interfaces: Ensuring Usability Through Product and Process. J. Wiley (1993)
10. Hyvnen, E., Viljanen, K.: Ontogator: combining view- and ontology-based search with semantic browsing. In: Proceedings of XML (2003)
11. Kaufmann, E., Bernstein, A.: How Useful are Natural Language Interfaces to the Semantic Web for Casual End-users? In: Aberer, K., et al. (eds.) ASWC 2007 and ISWC 2007. LNCS, vol. 4825, pp. 281–294. Springer, Heidelberg (2007)
12. Kelly, D.: Methods for Evaluating Interactive Information Retrieval Systems with Users. Found. Trends Inf. Retr. 3, 1–224 (2009)
13. López, V., Unger, C., Cimiano, P., Motta, E.: Evaluating question answering over linked data. In: Web Semantics: Science, Services and Agents on the World Wide Web (2013)
14. Miller, R.: Human Ease of Use Criteria and Their Tradeoffs. IBM, Systems Development Division (1971)
15. Nielsen, J.: Usability Engineering. Morgan Kaufmann Publishers Inc. (1993)
16. Rocha, C., Schwabe, D., Aragao, M.P.: A hybrid approach for searching in the semantic web. In: Proceedings of WWW (2004)
17. Mazumdar, S., Petrelli, D., Elbedweihy, K., Lanfranchi, V., Ciravegna, F.: Affective graphs: The visual appeal of linked data. In: Semantic Web: Interoperability, Usability, Applicability (2013) (in press)

Evaluating Citation Functions in CiTO: Cognitive Issues

Paolo Ciancarini[1,2], Angelo Di Iorio[1], Andrea Giovanni Nuzzolese[1,2], Silvio Peroni[1,2], and Fabio Vitali[1]

[1] Department of Computer Science and Engineering, University of Bologna, Italy
[2] STLab-ISTC, Consiglio Nazionale delle Ricerche, Italy
{ciancarini,diiorio,nuzzoles,fabio}@cs.unibo.it,
silvio.peroni@unibo.it

Abstract. Networks of citations are a key tool for referencing, disseminating and evaluating research results. The task of characterising the functional role of citations in scientific literature is very difficult, not only for software agents but for humans, too. The main problem is that the mental models of different annotators hardly ever converge to a single shared opinion. The goal of this paper is to investigate how an existing reference model for classifying citations, namely *CiTO* (*Citation Typing Ontology*), is interpreted and used by annotators of scientific literature. We present an experiment capturing the cognitive processes behind subjects' decisions in annotating papers with CiTO, and we provide initial ideas to refine future releases of CiTO.

Keywords: #eswc2014Ciancarini, CiTO, citation functions, human inter-rater agreement, mental models, usability, user testing session.

1 Introduction

The interest in alternative ways for publishing scientific results is rapidly increasing, especially for the Semantic Web community that is producing a lot of scientific data as linked datasets which can be browsed and reasoned on [15] [11]. On the other hand, most of the current scientific production is still disseminated by "traditional" papers, and citations remain the key *tools* to connect, explore and evaluate research works.

Citations are not all equal, as discussed by [31]. The frequency a work is cited is a partial indicator of its relevance for a community. More effective results can be obtained by looking for the *citation functions*, i.e. "the author's reasons for citing a given paper" [30]. Yet, it is extremely difficult to characterise the nature of a citation univocally.

A fairly successful classification model is *CiTO* (*Citation Typing Ontology*)[1] [22], an OWL ontology for describing factual as well as rhetorical functions of citations in scientific articles and other scholarly works. CiTO defines forty-one

[1] CiTO: http://purl.org/spar/cito

V. Presutti et al. (Eds.): ESWC 2014, LNCS 8465, pp. 580–594, 2014.

properties that allow users to characterise precisely the semantics of a citation act. CiTO has been successfully used in large projects like *CiteULike*[2] and *Data.open.ac.uk*[3], and several tools have been developed to annotate citations with CiTO properties directly via browser[4] or CMS plugins[5].

Despite (or possibly because of) the richness and variety of CiTO properties, most users actually employ a sub-set of these properties: a smaller set of properties is easier to memorise and handle, some properties are not perceived as precise in specific domains, some others are considered too similar to each others, and so on. For instance, Pensoft Publishers[6] (to our knowledge, the first commercial user of CiTO) are going to enable authors to annotate their citations according to six CiTO properties only. The *Link to Link Wordpress* plugin supports about ten properties.

This paper introduces an experimental analysis on how the CiTO model is accepted, understood, and adopted by humans. In particular, it presents an experiement with two conditions, i.e., the use of the full set of CiTO properties and the use of a specific subset of them. In addition, the paper discusses the outcomes of the experiment along with the feedback provided by the subjects. The goal is to validate and assess the usability of CiTO and to distill guidelines for a more effective use of the current ontology and for improvements to the future releases. Also, we want to study human's behaviour in order to simulate it within CiTalO[7] [10], a chain of tools for identifying automatically the nature of citations. The most critical aspect identified by our experiment is that opinions about the most appropriate CiTO properties are often misaligned. Unsurprisingly, each reader relies on a different *mental model*, and the reader's model can be and often is different from the one of the authors of the CiTO annotation, which in turn can be and often is different from the one of the authors of the citation in the paper.

This paper is structured as follows: in Section 2 we review previous works on classification of citations. In Section 3 we present CiTO and relate it with humans' mental models. In Section 4 and Section 5 we introduce our experimental setting and findings. In Section 6 we discuss the lesson learnt and sketch out some possible developments of CiTO and CiTalO.

2 Related Works

The analysis of networks of citations is gaining more and more attention. Copestake *et al.* [7] present an infrastructure, called SciBorg, based on NLP techniques

[2] CiteULike homepage: `http://www.citeulike.org`
[3] Open Linked Data from The Open University: `http://data.open.ac.uk`
[4] CiTO Reference Annotation Tools for Google Chrome: `https://chrome.google.com/webstore/detail/annotate-journal-citation/geajighoohelnjnhfmhbcaddbcgcbphn`
[5] Link to Link Wordpress plugin: `http://wordpress.org/plugins/link-to-link/`
[6] PenSoft Publishers homepage: `http://www.pensoft.net/`
[7] CiTalO homepage: `http://wit.istc.cnr.it:8080/tools/citalo`

that allows one to automatically extract semantic characterisations of scientific texts. In particular, they developed a module for discourse and citation analysis based on the approach proposed by Teufel *et al.* [28] called *Argumentative Zoning (AZ)*. AZ provides a procedural mechanism to annotate sentences of an article according to one out of seven classes of a given annotation scheme (i.e. *background*, *own*, *aim*, *textual*, *contrast*, *basis* and *other*), thus interpreting the intended authors' motivation behind scientific content and citations.

Teufel *et al.* [29] [30] study the *function* of citations – that they define as "author's reason for citing a given paper" – and provide a categorisation of possible citation functions organised in twelve classes, in turn clustered in *Negative*, *Neutral* and *Positive* rhetorical functions. In addition, they performed some tests involving hundreds of articles in computational linguistics (stored as XML files), several human annotators and a machine learning approach for the automatic annotation of citation functions. The results were quite promising; however the agreement between human annotators (i.e. K = 0.72) is still higher than the one between the human annotators and the machine learning approach (i.e. K = 0.57).

Jorg [14] analysed the ACL Anthology Networks[8] and found one hundred fifty *cue verbs*, i.e. verbs usually used to carry important information about the nature of citations: *based on*, *outperform*, *focus on*, *extend*, etc. She maps cue verbs to classes of citation functions according to the classification provided by Moravcsik *et al.* [19] and makes the bases to the development of a formal citation ontology. This works actually represent one of the sources of inspiration of *CiTO* (the *Citation Typing Ontology*) developed by Peroni *et al.* [22], which is an ontology that permits the motivations of an author when referring to another document to be captured and described by using Semantic Web technologies such as RDF and OWL.

Closely related to the annotation of citation functions, Athar [1] proposes a sentiment-analysis approach to citations, so as to identify whether a particular act of citing was done with positive (e.g. praising a previous work on a certain topic) or negative intentions (e.g. criticising the results obtained through a particular method). Starting from empirical results Athar *et al.* [2] expand the above study and show how the correct sentiment (in particular, a negative sentiment) of a particular citation usually does not emerge from the citation sentence – i.e. the sentence that contains the actual pointer to the bibliographic reference of the cited paper. Rather, it actually becomes evident in the last part of the considered *context window*[9] [23].

Hou *et al.* [13] use an alternative approach to understand the relevance (seen as a form of positive connotation/sentiment) of citations: the citation counting in a text. Paraphrasing the authors, the idea is that the more a paper is cited within a text, the more its scientific contribution is significative.

[8] ACL Anthology Network: `http://clair.eecs.umich.edu/aan/index.php`

[9] The *context window* [23] of a citation is a chain of sentences implicitly referring to the citation itself, which usually starts from the citation sentence and involves few more subsequent sentences where that citation is still implicit [3].

3 Users' Adoption of CiTO

There are several reference models to characterise citations, as presented in the previous section. One of the most used within the Semantic Web domain is CiTO [22]. The ontology basically defines a property *cites* (and its inverse *isCitedBy*) and 41 sub-properties (each of which has its own inverse) that describe the semantics of a citation act.

The richness of properties is a key feature of CiTO. To the best of our knowledge, there is no other OWL ontology that provides a set of properties for annotating citation types as rich as CiTO. This aspect has contributed to the adoption of the ontology by the Semantic Publishing [25] community, which is currently exploiting CiTO in projects like *CiteULike*, *Data.open.ac.uk*, and the *Open Citation Corpus* [26].

On the other hand, the richness of CiTO is perceived as a hindrance by some annotators. We studied the actual adoption of the model within these projects and discovered that most tools actually employ a sub-set of the CiTO properties (CiTO-Ps on the rest of the text). For instance, Pensoft Publishers are going to enable authors to annotate their citations according to only six CiTO-Ps – i.e., *citesAsDataSource*, *related*, *critiques*, *supports*, *reviews* and *discusses* – while the *Link to Link Wordpress plugin* allows users to specify the generic function *cites* and some of its sub-properties: *citesAsSourceDocument*, *confirms*, *extends*, *obtainsBackgroundFrom*, *reviews*, *supports*, *usesDataFrom*, *usesMethodIn*, and *disagreesWith.*

We believe that one of the reasons for this fragmented adoption is that CiTO was developed with a *top-down* approach: the authors of the ontology, supported by a group of experts and end-users, and with the help of previous works on this topic, studied collections of scientific papers and citation patterns and came up with a set of properties that was incrementally refined.

The goal of this work is to assess and validate the CiTO-Ps from a *bottom-up* perspective. This approach is complementary to the current CiTO development process and allows us to study how CiTO-Ps are actually perceived by humans in the task of annotating citations.

3.1 CiTO Annotations and Mental Models

One of the most relevant issues we found is that multiple views coexist **and often conflict** when performing an annotation task with CiTO. We can see three steps in this process: (i) the interpretation of the text so as to guess the citation function as it was originally conceived by the author, (ii) the understanding of the CiTO-Ps and (iii) the creation of a mapping between the supposed function of a citation and the most appropriate CiTO property.

For each step, each annotator creates her/his own *mental model*. Mental models were introduced in 1943 by Craik [8] as *small-scale models* of reality that the humans' mind uses to anticipate events. For most cognitive scientists today, a mental model is an internal scale-model representation of an external reality. It is built on-the-fly, from knowledge of prior experience, schema segments, perception, and problem-solving strategies [9]. In Human-Computer Interaction (HCI) mental models are detected for improving the usability of a system. It is commonly accepted that humans interact with systems based on a set of beliefs[10] about how a system works [20].

This also applies to CiTO processes: humans annotate a citation based on a set of beliefs that they obtain by only interpreting the citation's context and finding an appropriate property in CiTO according to their interpretation of the ontology. Our goal is to study these beliefs and the mental models built by the humans. The work is based on the hypothesis that usability is tied strongly to the extent to which these models match and predicts the action of a system, as suggested by [9]. The overall objective is to reduce the gap between the System Model, the mental model constructed by the ontology engineer while modelling CiTO-Ps, and the User Model, the mental model constructed by a user for understanding how to use CiTO-Ps.

4 Experimental Analysis of CiTO Use

In order to assess how CiTO is used to annotate scholarly articles, we compared the classifications performed by humans on a set of citations. The experiment involved twenty subjects with different background and skills. We meant to collect a set of quantitative indicators to answer the following numbered research questions (RQn) on CiTO:

1. Which properties have been used by subjects during the experiment?
2. Which were the most used properties?
3. What was the global inter-rater agreement of the subjects?
4. Did the number of available choices bias the global inter-rater agreement?
5. Which properties showed an acceptable positive agreement among subjects?
6. Could properties be clustered according to their similarity in subjects' annotations?
7. What was the perceived usability of the CiTO-Ps?
8. Which were the features of CiTO-Ps that subjects perceived as most useful or problematic?

After the completion of the annotation task, we asked each subject to fill two questionnaires: a multiple-choice questionnaire aimed at measuring the System Usability Scale (SUS) [5], and a second questionnaire with free-text answers to capture the users' satisfaction in using CiTO-Ps for annotating citations.

In order to simplify the task of annotating citations, we prepared and normalised how the citations were presented to the subjects. Identifying the boundaries of a citation, or better which boundaries are needed to capture the nature of that citation, is not a trivial task: the citation sentence, i.e. the sentence containing directly the citation, often is not enough. As confirmed by Athar *et al.* [2], the actual intended sentiment and motivation of a citation might be explicated in other sentences close to the citation and can refer implicitly (i.e.

[10] This set of beliefs corresponds to the a human's mental model.

by means of *implicit citations* [3]) to the cited work (through authors' names, project's name, pronouns, etc.). This issue is known as the *identification of context window* [23]. Even if there are multiple techniques for automatic extraction of the context window, taking care also of implicit citations, in this experiment we identified them manually: we read the text and tried to understand which sequence of sentences around a particular citation conveyed its citation function at the best. Hence, the size of context windows varies from case to case.

4.1 Experimental Setting

The test bed includes some scientific papers encoded in XML DocBook chosen among the seventh volume of the proceedings Balisage Conference Series[11]. We automatically extracted citation sentences, through an XSLT transform (available at `http://www.essepuntato.it/2013/citalo/xslt`). We took into account only those papers for which the XSLT transform retrieved at least one citation (i.e. 18 papers written by different authors). The total number of citations retrieved was 377, for a mean of 20.94 citations per paper.

We then filtered all the citation sentences that contain verbs (extends, discusses, etc.) and/or other grammatical structures (uses method in, uses data from, etc.) that carry explicitly a citation function. We considered that rule as a strict guideline as also suggested by Teufel *et al.* [29]. We obtained 105 citations out of 377, obtaining at least one citation for each of the 18 paper used (a mean of 5.83 citations per paper). These citations are very heterogeneous and provide us a significative sample for our experiment. Finally, we manually expanded each citation sentence (i.e. the sentence containing the reference to a bibliographic entity) selecting a context window that we think is useful to classify that citation, as explained above.

The experiment had one independent variable, i.e., the number of CiTO-Ps available to subjects for the annotation. The experiment involved two groups[12], each one composed by ten subjects. The first group used properties out of the full list of 41 CiTO-Ps (condition *T41* from now on). Instead, the second one performed the same task by only using 10 CiTO-Ps[13] (condition *T10*). This reduced set of properties comes from a preliminary experiment we undertook in [6] that showed that only these properties had a moderate inter-rater agreement (Fleiss' $k > 0.33$). The goal in fact is to answer RQ4.

Both groups were composed mainly by computer scientists (the main area of the Balisage Conference), none an expert user of CiTO. Each subject read each citation sentence separately, with its full context window, and had to select one CiTO-Ps for that sentence. Subjects could also revise their choices and perform the experiment off-line. There was no time constraint and subjects could freely access the CiTO documentation.

[11] Proceedings of Balisage 2011: `http://balisage.net/Proceedings/vol7/cover.html`

[12] By means of a Web interface:
`http://www.cs.unibo.it/\char'~nuzzoles/cito_1/?user=r`

[13] Available at
`http://www.cs.unibo.it/\char'~nuzzoles/cito_2/materials/cito_props.html`

All the data collected were stored in RDF and we used R[14] to load the data and elaborate the results[15].

4.2 Results

The experiment confirmed some of our hypotheses and highlighted some unexpected issues too. The first point to notice is that our subjects have selected 37 different CiTO properties over 41 in T41, with an average of 21.7 properties per subject, while they have selected all the 10 properties in T10 (the mean by subject is 10) (RQ1). Moreover, in T41 a few of these properties have been used many times, while most of them have been selected in a small number of cases, as shown in Table 1 – this table answers to RQ2.

Table 1. The CiTO-Ps selected by the subjects on the experimental dataset

CiTO property in T41	# in T41	CiTO property in T10	# in T10
citesForInformation	151	citesForInformation	190
citesAsRelated	122	obtainsBackgroundFrom	152
citesAsAuthority	85	citesAsRelated	137
citesAsRecommendedReading	72	citesAsDataSource	126
usesMethodIn, citesAsSourceDocument, citesAsPotentialSolution, credits, citesAsDataSource, citesAsEvidence,	< 72	citesAsRecommendedReading	116
describes, obtainsSupportFrom, extends, obtainsBackgroundFrom, usesDataFrom, agreesWith, critiques	< 40	credits	86
discusses, usesConclusionsFrom, confirms, containsAssertionFrom, includesQuotationFrom, supports, citesAsMetadataDocument, reviews, documents	< 18	citesAsPotentialSolution, usesMethodIn	80
updates, disputes, compiles, corrects, qualifies, disagreesWith, includesExcerptFrom, refutes, speculatesOn, derides, retracts	< 6	critiques, includesQuotationFrom	< 80

In T41, there were 4 properties not selected by any subject: *parodies*, *plagiarizes*, *repliesTo* and *ridicules*. This is not surprising considering the meaning of these properties.

These data show that there is a great variety in the choices of humans. In fact, only 18 citations in T41 and 24 citations in T10 (out of 105) have been classified with exactly the same CiTO property by at least 6 subjects. These results are summarised in Table 2, together with the list of selected properties for both T41 and T10. We indicate how many citations of the dataset subjects agreed on, and the number of properties selected by the subjects.

[14] R project for statistical computing: `http://www.r-project.org/`

[15] All the data collected and related material are available online at `http://www.essepuntato.it/2014/eswc/test`

Table 2. The distribution of citations and CiTO properties on which subjects agreed

Condition	# citations	CiTO properties
T41	18	citesForInformation (28), citesAsRelated (26), citesAsPotentialSolution (21), citesAsDataSource (19), citesAsRecommendedReading (17), citesAsAuthority (16), usesDataFrom (7), agreesWith (6), citesAsSourceDocument (6), usesMethodIn (6), confirms (5), credits (5), obtainsSupportFrom (5), supports (4), citesAsEvidence (3), compiles (2), describes (2), obtainsBackgroundFrom (2)
T10	24	citesAsDataSource (56), citesAsRecommendedReading (43), citesForInformation (35), obtainsBackgroundFrom (30), citesAsRelated (26), includesQuotationFrom (16), critiques (15), citesAsPotentialSolution (11), credits (5), usesMethodIn (3)

4.3 Data Evaluation

Considering all the 105 citations, the agreement among humans was very poor in both T41 and T10. In fact we measured the Fleiss' k (that assesses the reliability of agreement between a fixed number of raters classifying item) for the 10 raters over all 105 subjects and obtained $k = 0.13$ in T41 and $k = 0.15$ in T10, meaning that there exists a positive agreement between subjects but it is very low – this answers to RQ3. In addition, the use of a larger number of CiTO-Ps (in T41 compared to T10) does not seem to affect the agreement among subjects (RQ4).

Another very interesting finding is that subjects eventually agree only on one property per condition. Even considering the whole dataset whose k value was very low, we found a moderate positive local agreement (i.e. $0.33 < k < 0.66$) on *citesAsPotentialSolution* in T41 and on *includesQuotationFrom* in T10 – this answers to RQ5.

In order to identify other properties that showed a partial positive local agreement among subjects, we filtered only the 18 (in T41) and 24 (in T10) citations on which at least 6 subjects used the same property, as mentioned earlier in Table 2. The k value on that subset showed a moderate positive agreement: $k = 0.39$ in T41 and $k = 0.43$ in T10. In addition, we had $k > 0.5$ for 5 CiTO-Ps in T41 – i.e., *agreesWith* ($k = 0.54$), *citesAsDataSource* ($k = 0.52$), *citesAsPotentialSolution* ($k = 0.66$), *citesAsRecommendedReading* ($k = 0.6$), *usesMethodIn* ($k = 0.54$) – and for 4 CiTO-Ps in T10 – *citesAsDataSource* ($k = 0.63$), *citesAsPotentialSolution* ($k = 0.71$), *citesAsRecommendedReading* ($k = 0.52$, *includesQuotationFrom* ($k = 0.69$).

Given this heterogeneity, we tried to identify clusters of properties and to understand whether the subjects selected the same properties together. The goal is to found which properties have similar meaning according to subjects' annotation. To do so, we applied the Chinese Whispers clustering algorithm [4] to the graphs of collocates obtained by looking at the annotations provided by each subject for each citation in T41. The graphs were built as follows. For each citation, we considered all the combinations of pairs of different CiTO-Ps as annotated by subjects, considering repetitions in the graph *Gr* and without repetitions in the graph *Gn* – it means that, for instance, having three annotations of a citation, e.g., *extends*, *extends*, and *updates*, we generated two pairs in Gr, i.e., *(extends,updates)* and *(extends,updates)*, and one pair in Gn, i.e., *(extends,updates)*. In fact we were interested in highlighting recurrent collocates when CiTO-Ps were used at local level (Gr) or at a global level (Gn). Then, we created an edge linking two nodes (i.e., two different CiTO-Ps) for each collocate and we weighted it according to how many times that collocate is repeated in the dataset. We run the Chinese Whisper algorithm for 20 iterations on each graph and we observed that:

- in Gr, considering only those arcs having weight at least 3, the algorithm returned a small cluster composed by the CiTO-Ps *disputes*, *critics*, *derides* and *refutes*;
- in Gn, considering only those arcs having weight at least 5, the algorithm returned another small cluster composed by the CiTO-Ps *credits*, *confirms* and *obtainsSupportFrom*.

The algorithm results seem to indicate that there exist some sort of relations (e.g., taxonomical, equivalence) among the CiTO-Ps of each cluster and, to some extent, they can be used in an interchangeable way when annotating the citations – this answer to RQ6.

5 SUS and Grounded Analysis

At the end of the experiment, both groups of subjects were asked to answer to a SUS questionnaire including some free-text answering fields – in order to get some feedback on CiTO. The usability score for CiTO-Ps was computed using the *System Usability Scale* (*SUS*) [5], a well-known metrics used for the perception of the usability of a system. It has the advantage of being technology independent and it is reliable even with a very small sample size [24]. In addition to the main SUS scale, we also were interested in examining the sub-scales of pure *Usability* and pure *Learnability* of the system, as proposed recently by Lewis and Sauro [16]. As shown in Table 3, the mean SUS score for CiTO-Ps in T41 was 53.5 while in T10 was 62.5 (in a 0 to 100 range). The mean values for the SUS sub-scales Usability and Learnability were, respectively, 50.94 and 63.7 in T41 and 60.94 and 68.7 in T10. However, the only difference approaching the statistical significance (i.e., $0.05 < p < 0.1$) was found between the Usability measures (i.e., $p = 0.06$), suggesting that the perceived usability of CiTO-Ps in T10 is better than that of CiTO-Ps in T41 – this answer to RQ7.

The final text questionnaire contained a few questions, two asking for positive aspects, and two for negative aspects of CITO, and orthogonally two asking for

Table 3. SUS values and related sub-measures (*s.d.* stands for *standard deviation*)

CiTO-Ps	SUS mean	Usability mean	Learnability mean
CiTO-Ps in T41	53.5 (s.d. 14.5)	50.94 (s.d. 12.42)	63.7 (s.d. 25.99)
CiTO-Ps in T10	62.5 (s.d. 11.79)	60.94 (s.d. 10.13)	68.7 (s.d. 25.85)

qualifications (i.e., adjectives), and two for features (i.e., substantives) of the tool:

- *How effectively did CiTO properties support you in answering to the previous tasks?*
- *What were the most useful features (labels, descriptions, examples, etc.) of CiTO properties to help you realise your tasks?*
- *What were the main weaknesses that CiTO properties exhibited in supporting your tasks?*
- *Can you think of any additional features that would have helped you to accomplish your tasks?*

A fifth question was added to propose a discussion about the sheer size of the list of CITO properties:

- *Considering the experiment you have just completed, do you think that the number of CiTO properties was:*

All 20 (10 in T41 and 10 in T10) subjects produced relevant content for the questions. In order to obtain some meaningful results, we subjected the text answers to a *grounded theory* analysis. Grounded theory [27] is a method often used in Social Science to extract relevant concepts from unstructured corpora of natural language resources (e.g., texts, interviews, or questionnaires). In opposition to traditional methods aiming at fitting (and sometimes forcing) the content of the resources into a prefabricated model, grounded theory aims at having the underlying model emerge "naturally" from the systematic collection, rephrasing, reorganisation and interpretations of the actual sentences and terms of the resources. We thus believe it is a reasonable tool to examine our questionnaires in order to let relevant concepts emerge from the analysis. We proceeded first with *open coding*, with the purpose of extracting actual relevant sentences – called *codes* – from the texts, and subsequently performed the so-called *axial coding*, which is the rephrasing of the original codes so as to have semantic connections emerge from them and generate concepts. We finally analysed the respective frequency of each emerged concept (defined as the number of codes which contributed to the concept's existence) so as to consider the most important issues arising from the answers. Coding was performed separately in T41 and T10, but a later effort to homogenise the concepts drawn from the two groups was performed, so that results from the two experimental conditions could be compared. Fig. 1 shows the results of those codes that were mentioned at least twice. Some interesting suggestions came up from these data – this answers to RQ8.

Need to Improve Labels. The first question basically asked to identify the best between property label, property description and example, in conveying the best use of the property. Subjects massively preferred examples, with descriptions in the middle and labels last. This clearly indicates that CiTO labels should be improved to capture the nuances in the semantics of the CITO-Ps.

Need for a Structure in the Properties. It was evident the perception that many properties, for good or worse, overlapped semantically, often forcing a

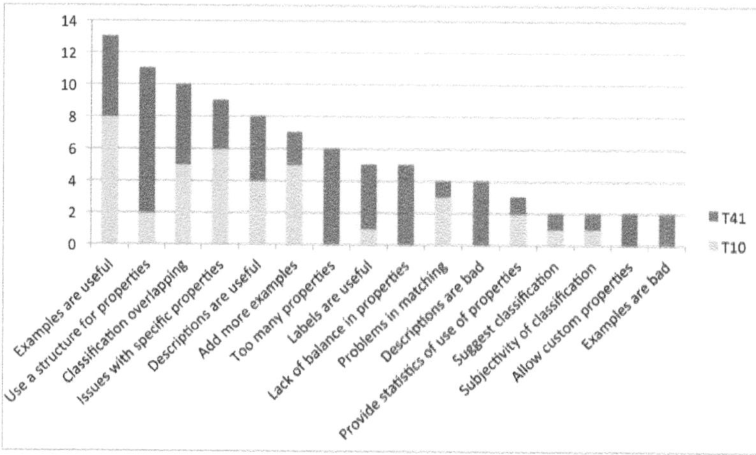

Fig. 1. A chart of the most mentioned pros and cons in the questionnaires

choice between similar properties rather than offering a clear and natural candidate. The issue of the hierarchy was particularly felt by the subjects in T41, working with a flat list of 41 items: nine people (i.e., all but one) complained about this fact and asked for structured guidance. Another difference between the two experimental conditions (probably obvious in hindsight), is that subjects in T41 had issues with the sheer number of properties (six individuals discussed about this) and with a feeling of imbalance in how they addressed the semantic scope of the citations. This suggests that the structuring of the properties loudly asked by the subjects should also consider an adequate balancing of the properties, without exaggerating with negative ones, with sentiment-loaded ones, or with relationships.

Need for Uniformity and Bi-directional Properties. A final mention should be given, in our view, to specific ideas and suggestions that, although provided by one subject each, are nonetheless interesting and worth further exploration: making all properties bi-directional (so that we could have both "gives support to" and "receives support from"), providing a decision tree for properties (so as to simplify the task of choosing the right one), or helping with the use of statistics (e.g., 30% of citations are request for information, 6% are credits, etc.) which also could provide guidance, if not for the best candidate property, at least for uniformity in choices between different annotators.

6 Lessons Learnt and Conclusions

The starting point of this paper was that the characterisation of citations is an extremely difficult task also for humans. We presented an experiment to investigate which are the main difficulties behind this characterisation and, in particular, how the humans understand and adopt CiTO based on the mental models they construct for addressing the annotations task. Our analysis – both experimental data and subjects' feedback – gave us some indications to improve CiTO and to increase its effectiveness, that we would summarise as follows.

Reduce the Number of Less-Used Properties. One of our findings was that some of the CiTO-Ps in T41 were used only few times or not used at all. This result can depend on a variety of factors. First, the authors of the articles in our dataset, which are researchers on markup languages, use a quite specific jargon so the context windows resulted not easy to interpret with respect to citations. Second, the positive or negative connotation of the properties was difficult to appreciate. For instance, the fact that the properties carrying negative judgements (*disagreesWith*, *disputes*, *parodies*, *plagiarizes*, *refutes*, *repliesTo*, *ridicules*, etc.) are less frequent than neutral and positive ones supports the findings of Teufel *et al.* [29] on this topic. Notice also that, as highlighted by [12], a criticism can be postponed far from the sentence containing the citation and can be prefaced with positive feedback; where ever the criticism occur, it can be "toned down, disguised, or redirected away from important people" [17].

Identify the Most-Used Neutral Properties. Although we think the intended audience of the research articles one choose for such an experiment may bias the use of some properties, we also believe that some properties are actually shared among different scholarly domains. The property *citesForInformation* and *citesAsRelated* are a clear example. As expected, they were the most used properties, being the most neutral ones of CiTO. This is in line with the findings of Teufel *et al.* [30], on the analysis of citations within Linguistics scholarly literature. In that paper, the neutral category *Neut* was used for the majority of annotations by humans. Although their large adoption, *citesForInformation* and *citesAsRelated* had a very low positive local agreement (k = 0.07 and k = 0.2 respectively). This is not surprising since the properties were used many times, often as neutral classification on citations that were classified in a more precise way by other subjects. Note that one particular subject in T41 identified *credits* as the most used (and, thus, neutral) property, which is also confirmed by running the Chinese Whispers algorithm on Gr, considering only those arcs having weight at least 5, that showed how *credits* formed a cluster of one element only and was linked to other more specific properties such as *citesAsAuthority*, *citesAsDataSource*, *discusses*, etc.

Investigate Motivations for Low Inter-rater Agreement. The reason for having two experimental conditions T41 and T10 was to investigate whether the high number (i.e., 41) of CiTO-Ps could be a justification for obtaining a so low positive agreement in total (i.e., k = 0.13), due to the cognitive effort subjects spent to choose among such huge set of properties for annotating citations. Intuitively, a reduced number of properties should reduce the cognitive effort required by the subjects in building their mental models for understanding CiTO-Ps for annotating a given set of citations. Although the comparison of the SUS values obtained for T41 (which involved 41 CiTO-Ps) and T10 (where we asked to use only 10 CiTO-Ps) was in favour of the latter, i.e., the subjects perceived the small set of properties as more usable of the full set for annotating citations, the inter-rater agreements obtained in T41 (i.e., k = 0.13) and T10 (i.e., $k = 0.15$) show how the number of available CiTO-Ps did not actually impact too much. We have also tried to consider the results obtained in the two conditions if only expert users of citations (i.e., professors, academic researchers, postdoc and PhD students, representing half of the subjects in each condition) were involved, and we noticed that the inter-rater agreements do not change at all for both conditions. It seems that the number of CiTO-Ps and the kinds of users are not the main factors to take into account for that low agreement.

Define Explicit Relations between CiTO Properties. Since there is no hierarchical structure[16], each subject followed its own mapping determined by the mental model built and ended up selecting very different values – probably because subjects' mental models differed largely between subjects. Our opinion is that a further investigation is needed on the structure of CiTO properties. To this end, the identification of clusters of properties, such as those introduced in the previous section, could be a possible way to follow, as well as the use of other approaches, i.e., pure statistical techniques for assessing collocates of CiTO-Ps (e.g., the use of chi-square test to analyse bigrams of collocates [18]) and empirical algorithms used for identifying relations (taxonomical, equivalence, meronomy, etc.) among keywords (e.g., Klink [21]). These approaches could be useful, for instance, to suggest ways to separate general properties form more specific ones or to build one or multiple hierarchies over the list of properties.

Add Support for Customised Properties. One of the aspects of CiTO that subjects suggested to improve is its support for customisation. In some cases subjects could not find a property that perfectly fit their needs: they selected the one apparently closest to their mental model but they perceived this as a limitation of the model. To solve this issue, the latest release of CiTO – supported by our findings – includes an extension mechanism that allow users to use their own citation function. The syntax is briefly shown below:

```
@prefix cito: <http://purl.org/spar/cito/> .
@prefix oa: <http://www.w3.org/ns/oa#> .
@prefix dcterms: <http://purl.org/dc/terms/> .
[] a oa:Annotation ; oa:hasBody [
  dcterms:description "The cited paper initiated a whole field of research"];
  oa:hasTarget [ a cito:CitationAct ; cito:hasCitingEntity <citing-paper>;
    cito:hasCitationEvent cito:cites ; cito:hasCitedEntity <cited-paper> ].
```

The interesting aspect is that the overall organisation of the ontology (i.e., the TBox) does not change, while users are free to express precisely their characterisation capturing details and tones.

Extend Examples, Labels and Explanations. The fact that some properties were misunderstood by the subjects – or the same property interpreted in different ways – is an indicator of the need for improvements in examples shown in our experiment. One possible way of improving them will be to use the citations with the highest agreement and create additional samples from them.

These findings will also provide a basis for improving CiTalO [10], a tool for identifying automatically the nature of citations. In particular, we plan to in our

[16] The authors of CiTO decided on purpose to avoid a taxonomical organisation, since they thought it could be difficult to reach a global agreement.

ongoing work to investigate cognitive architecture in order to extend CiTalO to simulate humans' behaviour determined by mental models.

Acknowledgements. We would like to thank all the people who participated to our (intensive and stressing) evaluation. A particular thank goes to David Shotton for his precious comments.

References

1. Athar, A.: Sentiment Analysis of Citations using Sentence Structure-Based Features. In: Proceedings of the 49th Annual Meeting of the Association for Computational Linguistics: Human Language Technologies, pp. 81–87 (2011)
2. Athar, A., Teufel, S.: Context-Enhanced Citation Sentiment Detection. In: Proceedings of Human Language Technologies: Conference of the North American Chapter of the Association of Computational Linguistics 2012, pp. 597–601 (2012)
3. Athar, A., Teufel, S.: Detection of implicit citations for sentiment detection. In: Proceedings of the 50th Annual Meeting of the Association for Computational Linguistics, pp. 18–26 (2012)
4. Biemann, C.: Chinese whispers: an efficient graph clustering algorithm and its application to natural language processing problems. In: Proceedings of the 1st Workshop on Graph Based Methods for Natural Language Processing (TextGraph 2006), pp. 73–80 (2006)
5. Brooke, J.: SUS: a "quick and dirty" usability scale. In: Usability Evaluation in Industry, pp. 189–194 (1996)
6. Ciancarini, P., Di Iorio, A., Nuzzolese, A.G., Peroni, S., Vitali, F.: Characterising citations in scholarly articles: an experiment. In: Proceedings of 1st International Workshop on Artificial Intelligence and Cognition (AIC 2013), pp. 124–129 (2013), `http://ceur-ws.org/Vol-1100/paper13.pdf` (last visited March 10, 2014) (retrieved)
7. Copestake, A., Corbett, P., Murray-Rust, P., Rupp, C.J., Siddharthan, A., Teufel, S., Waldron, B.: An architecture for language processing for scientific text. In: Proceedings of the UK e-Science All Hands Meeting 2006 (2006)
8. Craik, K.J.W.: The nature of explanation. Cambridge University Press (1967) ISBN: 0521094453
9. Davidson, M.J., Dove, L., Weltz, J.: Mental models and usability. Depaul University, Chicago (1999), `http://www.lauradove.info/reports/mental%20models.htm` (last visited March 10, 2014) (retrieved)
10. Di Iorio, A., Nuzzolese, A.G., Peroni, S.: Towards the automatic identification of the nature of citations. In: Proceedings of 3rd Workshop on Semantic Publishing (SePublica 2013), pp. 63–74 (2013), `http://ceur-ws.org/Vol-994/paper-06.pdf` (last visited March 10, 2014) (retrieved)
11. Gil, Y., Ratnakar, V., Hanson, P.C.: Organic data publishing: a novel approach to scientific data sharing. In: Proceedings of the 2nd International Workshop on Linked Science, LISC 2012 (2012), `http://ceur-ws.org/Vol-951/paper1.pdf` (last visited March 10, 2014)
12. Hornsey, M.J., Robson, E., Smith, J., Esposo, S., Sutton, R.M.: Sugaring the Pill: Assessing Rhetorical Strategies Designed to Minimize Defensive Reactions to Group Criticism: Strategies to Soften Criticism. Human Communication Research 34(1), 70–98 (2008), doi:10.1111/j.1468-2958.2007.00314.x

13. Hou, W., Li, M., Niu, D.: Counting citations in texts rather than reference lists to improve the accuracy of assessing scientific contribution. BioEssays 33(10), 724–727 (2011), doi:10.1002/bies.201100067
14. Jorg, B.: Towards the Nature of Citations. In: Poster Proceedings of the 5th International Conference on Formal Ontology in Information Systems (2008)
15. Kauppinen, T., Baglatzi, A., Keuler, C.: Linked Science: interconnecting scientific assets. In: Data Intensive Science, CRC Press (2013)
16. Lewis, J.R., Sauro, J.: The Factor Structure of the System Usability Scale. In: Kurosu, M. (ed.) HCD 2009. LNCS, vol. 5619, pp. 94–103. Springer, Heidelberg (2009)
17. MacRoberts, M.H., MacRoberts, B.R.: The Negational Reference: Or the Art of Dissembling. Social Studies of Science 14(1), 91–94 (1984)
18. Manning, C.D., Schütze, H.: Foundations of statistical natural language processing. MIT Press (1999) ISBN: 0262133601
19. Moravcsik, M.J., Murugesan, P.: Some Results on the Function and Quality of Citations. Social Studies of Science 5(1), 86–92 (1975)
20. Norman, D.A.: The psychology of everyday things. Basic Books (1988) ISBN: 0465067093
21. Osborne, F., Motta, E.: Mining Semantic Relations between Research Areas. In: Cudré-Mauroux, P., et al. (eds.) ISWC 2012, Part I. LNCS, vol. 7649, pp. 410–426. Springer, Heidelberg (2012)
22. Peroni, S., Shotton, D.: FaBiO and CiTO: ontologies for describing bibliographic resources and citations. Journal of Web Semantics 17, 33–43 (2012), doi:10.1016/j.websem.2012.08.001
23. Qazvinian, V., Radev, D.R.: Identifying non-explicit citing sentences for citation-based summarization. In: Proceedings of the 48th Annual Meeting of the Association for Computational Linguistics, pp. 555–564 (2010)
24. Sauro, J.: A Practical Guide to the System Usability Scale: Background, Benchmarks & Best Practices. CreateSpace (2011) ISBN: 1461062707
25. Shotton, D.: Semantic publishing: the coming revolution in scientific journal publishing. Learned Publishing 22(2), 85–94 (2009), doi:10.1087/2009202
26. Shotton, D.: Publishing: Open citations. Nature 502(7471), 295–297 (2013), doi:10.1038/502295a
27. Strauss, A., Corbin, J.: Basics of Qualitative Research Techniques and Procedures for Developing Grounded Theory, 2nd edn. Sage Publications (1998) ISBN: 0803959408
28. Teufel, S., Carletta, J., Moens, M.: An annotation scheme for discourse-level argumentation in research articles. In: Proceedings of the 9th Conference of the European Chapter of the Association for Computational Linguistics, pp. 110–117 (1999)
29. Teufel, S., Siddharthan, A., Tidhar, D.: Automatic classification of citation function. In: Proceedings of the 2006 Conference on Empirical Methods in Natural Language Processing, pp. 103–110 (2006)
30. Teufel, S., Siddharthan, A., Tidhar, D.: An annotation scheme for citation function. In: Proceedings of the 7th SIGdial Workshop on Discourse and Dialogue, pp. 80–87 (2009)
31. Zhu, X., Turney, P., Lemire, D., Vellino, A.: Measuring academic influence: Not all citations are equal. To appear in Journal of the American Society for Information Science and Technology (2014), Preprint available at `http://lemire.me/fr/documents/publications/citationjasist2013.pdf` (last visited March 10, 2014)

Accepting the XBRL Challenge with Linked Data for Financial Data Integration

Benedikt Kämpgen[1], Tobias Weller[1], Sean O'Riain[2], Craig Weber[3], and Andreas Harth[1]

[1] Institute AIFB, Karlsruhe Institute of Technology, Karlsruhe, Germany
{kaempgen,harth}@kit.edu, tobias.weller@student.kit.edu

[2] Digital Enterprise Research Institute, National University of Ireland, Galway, Ireland
sean.oriain@deri.org

[3] Financial Intelligence, LLC, Los Altos, CA, USA
cpatax@sbcglobal.net

Abstract. Analysts spend a disproportionate amount of time with financial data curation before they are able to compare company performances in an analysis. The Extensible Business Reporting Language (XBRL) for annotating financial facts is suited for automatic processing to increase information quality in financial analytics. Still, XBRL does not solve the problem of data integration as required for a holistic view on companies. Semantic Web technologies promise benefits for financial data integration, yet, existing literature lacks concrete case studies. In this paper, we present the Financial Information Observation System (FIOS) that uses Linked Data and multidimensional modelling based on the RDF Data Cube Vocabulary for accessing and representing relevant financial data. FIOS fulfils the information seeking mantra of "overview first, zoom and filter, then details on demand", integrates yearly and quarterly balance sheets, daily stock quotes as well as company and industry background information and helps analysts creating their own analyses with Excel-like functionality.

Keywords: #eswc2014Kampgen.

1 Introduction

Analysts play a crucial role in the functioning of equity markets. Besides the actual analysis, e.g., comparing key performance indicators (KPIs) such as the Gross Profit Margin between companies, analysts spend a disproportionate amount of time with data curation, i.e., identifying, gathering and preparing data [4] and pursue to minimise time spent on tedious curation tasks. The Extensible Business Reporting Language (XBRL)[1] is an XML format for financial information that is more amenable to automatic processing than traditional financial information representations such as PDF, HTML and text documents.

[1] http://www.xbrl.org/Specification/XBRL-2.1/REC-2003-12-31/XBRL-2.1-REC-2003-12-31+corrected-errata-2013-02-20.html

V. Presutti et al. (Eds.): ESWC 2014, LNCS 8465, pp. 595–610, 2014.

Still, XBRL does not solve the problem of data integration – e.g., of company background information, balance sheets, stock quotes – for a holistic view on companies [8]:

- XBRL uses XML that is difficult to understand and process, e.g., due to an extension with link bases for referencing across documents [3].
- Automatically deriving information from XBRL is difficult since formal semantics are limited [12,10]. Relationships between financial concepts, such as "SalesRevenueNet" and "Revenues" in the U.S. Generally Accepted Accounting Principles (US-GAAP), are only textually described.
- Financial information from different XBRL documents often cannot be compared since accounting and regulatory organisations do not align their taxonomies of financial concepts; new versions, e.g., of US-GAAP, lack backward compatibility; and XBRL allows publishers to define their own concepts.
- Gathering information about a company is difficult since there are no unique company identifiers across different reporting sources[2] and relationships between companies are obscure.
- Other finance-related Open Data such as stock quotes and background information are published using different data models.

Literature has proposed the use of Semantic Web technologies, but has not evaluated the benefit in financial case studies [12,5,1]. In this In-Use paper, after we describe a concrete XBRL scenario (Section 2), we present the Financial Information Observation System (FIOS) with the following contributions (Section 3):

1. For standardised data access, FIOS models XBRL and non-XBRL as Linked Data using the RDF Data Cube Vocabulary and other standard vocabularies.
2. FIOS integrates financial data using entity consolidation for background information, multi-company KPI, and cross-data-sources KPI analysis.
3. For intuitive and explorative analyses, FIOS provides SPARQL templates with visualisations, a Linked Data browser and a self-serve OLAP interface on top of a triple store.

For evaluation, we describe a case study implementing and applying FIOS for financial analysis (Section 4) and derive lessons learned (Section 5). We describe related work in Section 6 and conclude in Section 7.

2 Scenario: Integrating XBRL Data for Company Performance Analysis

In this section, we present a financial data analysis scenario inspired by the Annual XBRL Challenge organised by XBRL US: an investor wants to assess companies based on corporate XBRL data from the U.S. Securities and Exchange Commission (SEC) that since 2009 requires more than 8,000 U.S. companies

[2] `http://sunlightfoundation.com/sixdegrees/`

traded on the stock market to provide financial statement information such as quarterly and yearly balance sheets in the XBRL format to the SEC Edgar Database. The investor would find useful several analyses:

Background information analysis, e.g., looking at company information from different sources such as the address, the founding date and the industry.

Multi-company KPI analysis, e.g., comparing KPIs over time for several companies such as the stock market price for companies from the same industry.

Cross-data-sources KPI analysis, e.g., comparing values from heterogeneous datasets such as the Earnings per Share from yearly balance sheets with prices per share from electronic stock quotes as well as Total Assets published using the US-GAAP version 2009 and version 2011.

We can derive the following requirements: Answering above queries requires integration of different entities such as yearly and quarterly balance sheets using different taxonomy versions of US-GAAP, company and industry background information from Wikipedia/DBpedia and daily stock quotes. Since there is no standard way to model and publish finance data, data from the the SEC Edgar Database, from Wikipedia/DBpedia and from the Yahoo! Finance Web API need to be published as Linked (Open) Data and continuously extracted and stored (**Requirement 1**). To make the analyst understand and trust data that the system presents, the query interface needs to fulfil Shneiderman's information seeking mantra "overview first, zoom-in, details on demand" (**Requirement 2**). Also, since analysts can not use complex query languages, the analysis system needs to help them creating their own analyses, if possible with Excel-like functionality (**Requirement 3**).

3 Financial Information Observation System (FIOS)

We now describe our approach using Linked Data. As illustrated in Figure 1, FIOS' architecture is separated into two types of components, the *offline ETL components* and *online analysis components*, described in the following.

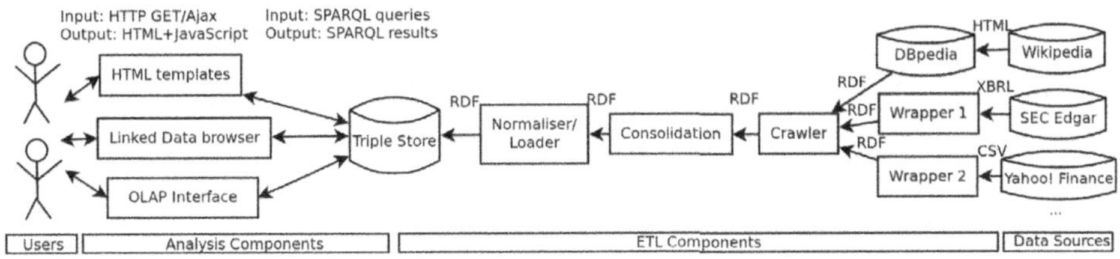

Fig. 1. Flow diagram illustrating architecture of Financial Information Observation System (FIOS)

3.1 Identification and Acquisition of Distributed Data

FIOS uses the Linked Data principles to identify and retrieve relevant information spread across different web servers.

Identification: We uniquely name things/entities with URIs: XBRL balance sheets from the SEC Edgar Database, including their taxonomies, and daily stock quotes from the Yahoo! Finance Web API; companies and industries listed by the SEC, Yahoo! Finance and Wikipedia/DBpedia. The SEC uniquely identifies the companies using a Central Index Key (CIK, e.g., Mastercard has "1141391"), Yahoo! Finance uses Ticker symbols (e.g., "MA" for Mastercard). Wikipedia uses their own non-standardised identifiers that are typically based on the name of the company, e.g., "Mastercard".

If looked up, URIs provide useful information in RDF either by originating from Linked Data providers or created by wrappers around data sources not publishing Linked Data. Wrappers mint new URIs and internally transform available information about such entities in the data source to RDF. Since the actual URIs are application-specific, in the following, we simply abbreviate URIs from our selected data sources using intuitive namespaces (abusing CURIE syntax): `edgar` for entities from the SEC Edgar Database, `yahoo` for Yahoo! Finance Web API and `dbpedia` for Wikipedia. Table 1 shows example mappings between things/entities, data sources with useful information about these entities and URI identifying those entities in Linked Data.

Table 1. Example mappings between things/entities, data sources and URIs

Entity	Original data source	URI
Company Mastercard	Mastercard from DBpedia	`dbpedia:Mastercard`
Company Mastercard	SEC Edgar company Mastercard with CIK 1141391	`edgar:cik/1141391#id`
Company Mastercard	Yahoo! Finance company Mastercard with Ticker MA	`yahoo:ticker/MA#id`
Balance sheet	XBRL document from SEC Edgar[3]	`edgar:archive/1141391/0001193125-11-207804#ds`
Stock Quotes table	Stock Quotes table from Yahoo! Finance Web API[4]	`yahoo:archive/MA/2010-12-01#ds`

Acquisition: For a holistic view on selected companies from the SEC Edgar Database, FIOS regularly looks up their URIs and checks the RDF (as well as the RDF of linked entities) for new data.

---

[3] `http://www.sec.gov/Archives/edgar/data/1141391/000119312511207804/0001193125-11-207804-xbrl.zip`

[4] `http://ichart.yahoo.com/table.csv?s=MA&a=11&b=01&c=2010&d=11&e=01&f=2010&g=d&ignore=.csv`

3.2 Modelling and Linking of Finance Data

To allow FIOS to use the retrieved information, we model financial data reusing existing Linked Data vocabularies and link entities from different sources.

Modelling: Whereas there are well-adopted vocabularies for all kinds of metadata, e.g., SKOS, FOAF and the DBpedia ontology, there is no standard way to represent XBRL data as Linked Data [5,1,12]. XBRL distinguishes instance and taxonomy documents. An *XBRL instance document* (also called "filing") contains financial facts with a numeric value and a unit such as USD. A fact has a context, e.g., describing the issuing company such as Mastercard, the time period of a financial fact (often, a quarter of a year or full fiscal year) and so-called segment information, e.g., allowing to specify subgroups of financial facts, e.g., that facts are published for subsidiary members. Most importantly, a fact specifies a certain disclosed financial concept such as "Total Assets". Financial concepts are taken from *XBRL taxonomy documents.* XBRL taxonomies can be standardised, e.g., the US-GAAP, and their concepts used across many instance documents. Also, companies may create their own taxonomies and financial concepts. Within taxonomies, concepts may be given additional information, e.g., labels, and may have relations to other concepts, e.g., "part of" relationships.

We model every XBRL instance and taxonomy as a multidimensional dataset, i.e., collection of facts with independent dimension variables and dependent measure variables, using a well-adopted Linked Data vocabulary, the RDF Data Cube Vocabulary (QB)[5] as follows: for any XBRL instance with taxonomy a multidimensional dataset (`qb:DataSet`) and data structure definition (`qb:DataStructureDefinition`) are created. For any single financial fact within an XBRL instance an observation (`qb:Observation`) is created with dimensions issuer, time period (`edgar:dtstart`, `edgar:dtend`), the financial concept (`edgar:subject`), segment and one decimal measure with a unit.

Similarly, stock quotes from Yahoo! Finance can be modelled using QB: every daily collection of values is a dataset, every stock quote contains as dimensions the company (`yahoo:issuer`), the date the value is valid and the stock quote type such as price at stock market opening (Open).

Linking: We use QB for the following reason: Given datasets contains observations with certain companies, certain financial concepts and certain periods in time, financial data integration boils down to identifying and consolidating equivalent dimensions and dimension values in multidimensional datasets.

See Figure 2 for an illustration of the linking between different entities or properties. Here, the fact of an XBRL instance document disclosing Total Assets (`edgar:vocab/us-gapp-2009-01-31#Assets`) and a Opening stock quote are linked via equivalent dimensions, e.g., `dcterms:date` / `ical:dtstart` and `edgar:issuer` / `yahoo:issuer`, and via equivalent dimension members, e.g., Mastercard `edgar:cik/1141391#id` / `yahoo:ticker/MA#id`.

Whereas time periods can easily be matched by comparing canonical representations of time, for linking between different URI for companies and

[5] `http://www.w3.org/TR/vocab-data-cube/`

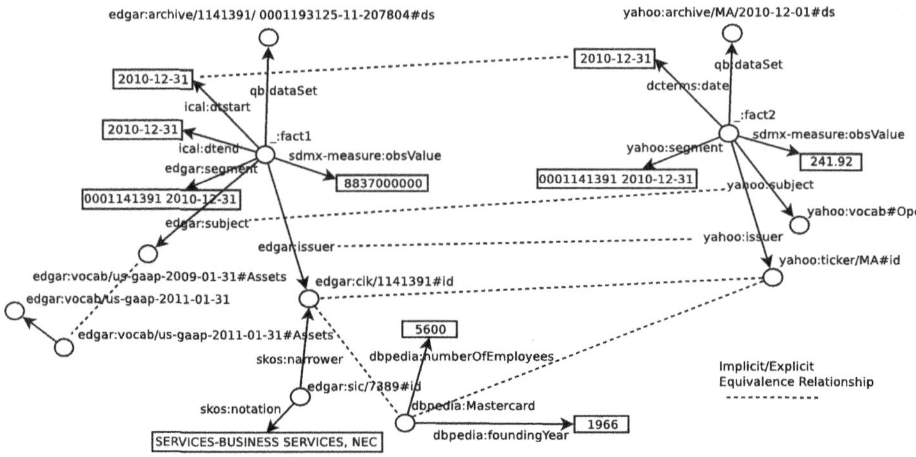

Fig. 2. Illustration of linking between Total Asset fact (top left), opening stock quote (top right), Mastercard in DBpedia (bottom center) in FIOS

financial concepts across data sources mappings need to be available. Entities or properties in RDF can explicitly be stated as equivalent via `owl:sameAs` or `owl:equivalentProperty` relationships between their URIs.

To model finance related metadata, e.g., about companies and industries, we use widely-adopted Linked Data vocabularies, e.g., FOAF and the DBpedia ontology. The industry of a company can be represented using SKOS classification hierarchies, e.g., the SEC provides for companies the Standard Industrial Classification (SIC) hierarchy, e.g., SIC concept "SERVICES-BUSINESS SERVICES, NEC" `skos:narrower` "MASTERCARD INC".

3.3 Consolidation, Normalisation, Loading and Validation of Data

FIOS allows to pre-process and store acquired data for fast access as well as to check its quality.

Consolidation: Entity consolidation in FIOS – making explicit and merging all available information about an entity, so as access to that information is available independently from a specific distribution across sources – results in simpler queries and is only different from Hogan et al. [6] in that we also consider equivalent relationships between predicates such as dimensions of datasets.

Normalisation: Queries on our consolidated data are complicated by the fact that all entities described by FIOS use distributed namespaces. Resources from FIOS thus link to external servers with non-preprocessed data, confusing the user or complicating the application. Therefore, we mint dereferenceable URIs for all entities, including URIs in the predicate position, in an own FIOS namespace `fios`. For provenance reasons, we create `owl:sameAs` and `owl:equivalentProperty` links from FIOS entities to the original entities.

Loading: After pre-processing, data is loaded into a triple store that supports SPARQL 1.1 for analytical aggregate queries and is indexed for performance.

Validation: We use SPARQL queries for quality checks, e.g., validating QB integrity constraints (as described in the specification) or XBRL-specific integrity constraints such as defined between financial concepts in XBRL calculation relationships.

3.4 Analysis of Integrated Financial Linked Data

Semantic Search engines (e.g., [6]) are too general for financial analysis and data analysis tools such as van Hage's and Kauppinen's SPARQL Package for R are too complicated for domain experts. FIOS uses three different kinds of interfaces for views on financial Linked Data.

SPARQL Templates with Visualisations, i.e., webpages that show results of SPARQL 1.1 queries on the triple store in visualisations, give a general overview of data in FIOS, e.g., number of datasets. Also, we create domain-specific reports about companies that require data integration. Templates can be parameterised with input by the analyst, e.g., a company identifier.

A **Linked Data Browser**, i.e., webpages of things/entities in RDF that show all ingoing and outgoing triples of a resource and allow follow-your-nose browsing from resource to resource, provides a more detailed view on any RDF data in FIOS.

An **OLAP Interface**, i.e., an intuitive and explorative data analysis method allows analysts to create own visualisations on multidimensional datasets. Since (parameterised) SPARQL templates have a fixed structure and Linked Data browsing does not aggregate triples, we use our approach [7] to evaluate OLAP operations using SPARQL on RDF reusing QB.

4 Implementing and Applying FIOS in a Case Study

We successfully submitted implementations of FIOS to the XBRL Challenge 2012[6] and 2013[7]. For evaluation, we now first describe the most current implementation of FIOS, then a case study applying FIOS to our scenario.

From the FIOS start page[8], we give information about the ETL process and an overview of available entities: publishing companies (`fios:issuer`/64 different values), valid time periods (`ical:dtstart`/234, `ical:dtend`/223, and `dcterms:date`/5,937) financial concepts (`subject`/3,781) and specific information (`segment`/58,395). From linked histograms, we see that most observations are from the time period between 2008 and 2013. Also, we see that we have quite evenly spread a number of observations for each company. Also, we get a good understanding of what financial concepts are published very often, e.g., `us-gaap-2009:Revenues`. Both FIOS ETL and analysis components run on a

[6] `http://xbrl.us/research/appdev/Pages/275.aspx`

[7] `http://xbrl.us/research/appdev/Pages/423.aspx`

[8] `http://fios.linked-data-cubes.org/FIOS_2_0/Queries/`

Virtual Machine with QEMU Virtual CPU version 0.12.3 with 2673.330 CPU MHz and 1GB memory and are described in the following:

ETL Components: For the `edgar` and `yahoo` namespaces, we have developed the SEC Edgar Wrapper[9] and the Yahoo! Finance Wrapper[10] using Google App Engines. Some information, e.g., XBRL calculation linkbases and footnotes currently are not considered, however, could be extracted and published as Linked Data to provide additional interesting information [9,2].

Yahoo companies link to Edgar companies using a Ticker-to-CIK mapping provided by the Yahoo! Finance API. Edgar companies link to DBpedia companies via Freebase. Datasets from SEC and Yahoo! Finance are linked by manually stating the equivalence of dimensions, such as the company, the valid time period and the financial concept. In cases where structures of datasets are less similar, approaches for data warehouse integration could be applied [11].

We created a Java program fios-etl[11] containing separate components for crawling data, applying consolidation and normalisation algorithms to the collected data and loading the data into a triple store. As crawler, we used the Open Source software LDSpider (Stable Version 1.1e).

For each run, fios-etl automatically fills a seed list with selected companies and new balance sheets from where LDSpider starts to crawl. We selected company URIs from several industries, e.g., "finance, insurance and real estate" companies such as Visa and Mastercard. New balance sheet URIs are taken from an SEC RSS feed. For example, LDSpider would start crawling at the URI of Mastercard in Yahoo! Finance Wrapper that provides links to stock quote datasets from 1990-01-01 to today and `owl:sameAs` links to Mastercard in the Edgar Linked Data Wrapper. From Edgar Linked Data Wrapper, further `owl:sameAs` links to Mastercard in DBpedia and links to SEC balance sheets would be followed. We setup LDSpider to crawl with breadth-first strategy and a depth of the traversal of 3, with a maximum number of 10 URIs crawled per round per pay-level domain. Consolidation and normalisation algorithms we implemented as described for FIOS. Experiments with differently-sized datasets show that consolidation time increases exponentially with the number of equivalence statements, normalisation time increases linearly with the number of triples. Data was then bulk-loaded to an OpenLink Virtuoso Server v06.01.3127 running in Apache/2.2.14. For our case study, we run fios-etl daily during the XBRL Challenge 2013 submission time from 15 Feb 2013 to 27 Feb 2013 GMT. On average crawling, pre-processing and loading took 25min; loading can be done offline and could further be accelerated using differential loading. In total, we crawled 1,238,041 triples.

We created integrity constraints using SPARQL ASK queries that can be manually run, e.g., evaluating whether Earnings per Share for a company in fact is computed by the ratio of net income and outstanding shares. Since we have

---

[9] `http://edgarwrap.ontologycentral.com/`

[10] `http://yahoofinancewrap.appspot.com/`

[11] `https://code.google.com/p/fios-etl/`

not found an automatic way of retrieving and validating integrity constraints, we have only implemented few checks.

Analysis Components: The SPARQL Templates with Visualisations for overviews and domain-specific reports we implemented using the JavaScript library SPARK[12]. For some templates, especially the company template, users may need to wait several minutes before all results are displayed, due to large number of separately issued SPARQL queries. As Linked Data Browser we deployed the Open Source software Pubby. For the OLAP Interface we use the Open Source OLAP client Saiku and OLAP engine olap4ld[13]. The OLAP Interface shows long loading times due to large number of multidimensional elements such as financial concepts (3781) that need to be loaded in memory. In the remainder of this section, we show how FIOS fulfills the three requirements of our scenario.

4.1 Integrating Data Across Sources (Requirement 1)

We now describe four exemplary analyses integrating entities across data sources.

1) Background information analysis: The FIOS start page provides a link to analyse companies in a *SPARK company template*. After inserting the CIK for a company in the parameterised template, e.g., "1141391" for MASTERCARD INC, the user is presented with information from various sources, e.g., address and number of employees from Wikipedia, and various overviews of available KPIs from SEC Edgar Database and Yahoo! Finance Web API. Note, since companies from SEC, Yahoo! Finance and DBpedia are explicitly stated as equivalent in RDF and consolidated, we have one identifier for MASTERCARD INC that summarises all information from those data sources; queries do not need to consider equivalent links and thus are easier to write.

2) Multi-company KPI analysis: On the SPARK company template for a company, an overview of "Adjusted Closing Price" over time is given that interactively can be extended with companies from the same industry via the SIC classification as provided by SEC Edgar.

See Figure 3 for adjusted closing price for MASTERCARD INC and other companies in SERVICES-BUSINESS SERVICES, NEC (SIC) industry. We see that MASTERCARD INC stock quotes always have been higher than VISA INC and COMSCORE INC stock quotes and at the beginning of 2013 were at an all-time-high with over 500 USD per share.

3) Cross-data-sources KPI analysis: On the SPARK company template we also show an analysis taking into account "Earnings per Share" from SEC balance sheet and the "Opening Price per Share" from Yahoo! Finance stock market data. Earnings per Share is considered the single most important variable in determining a share's price, thus an analyst may be interested to check for an obvious correlation for a company.

In Figure 4, we return for each reporting end date the maximum Earnings per Share as published in quarterly or yearly balance sheets together with the

---

[12] `http://km.aifb.kit.edu/sites/spark/`

[13] `http://olap4ld.googlecode.com/`

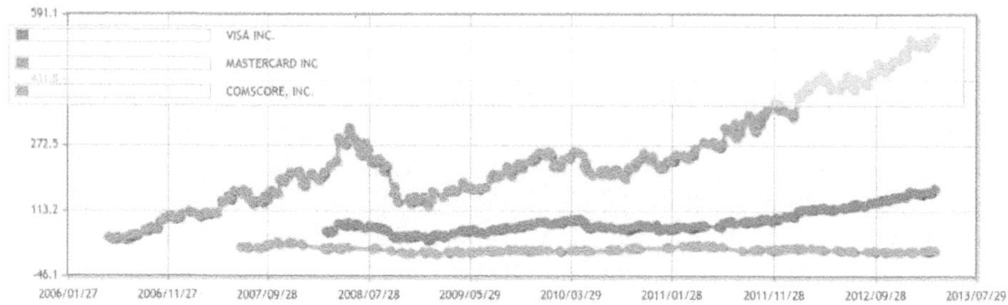

Fig. 3. Example multi-company KPI analysis of adjusted closing price for companies in industry SERVICES-BUSINESS SERVICES, NEC (SIC)

maximum opening stock market price of values between the valid start and end data of the Earnings per Share financial ratio for MASTERCARD INC. Since numbers are not normalised and SPARK visualisations would not allow several separate y-axes, it is difficult to see correlations in the figure. Another interesting analysis is the % rate of increase (decrease) for comparable periods, however, that was not easily doable since Edgar did not explicitly represent the sequence of balance sheets.

Note, since balance sheets and stock quote tables are integrated, it suffices to ask for specific values for the financial concept dimension `fios:subject` to query for financial concepts across the SEC Edgar Database and Yahoo! Finance.

As illustrated in Figure 5 for MASTERCARD INC, we can also query across different taxonomy versions: If we browse from the SPARK company template to a "Balance Sheet" template and click on "Total Assets", the company's Total Assets KPI over time is shown in a diagram from 2009 to 2012 although balance sheets from 2011 use a different US-GAAP taxonomy version. For that, Total Assets from US-GAAP-2009 and US-GAAP-2011 are stated as equivalent (either by consolidation or by adding UNION graph patterns to SPARQL queries). We see that MASTERCARD INC only twice has reduced its number of assets, at

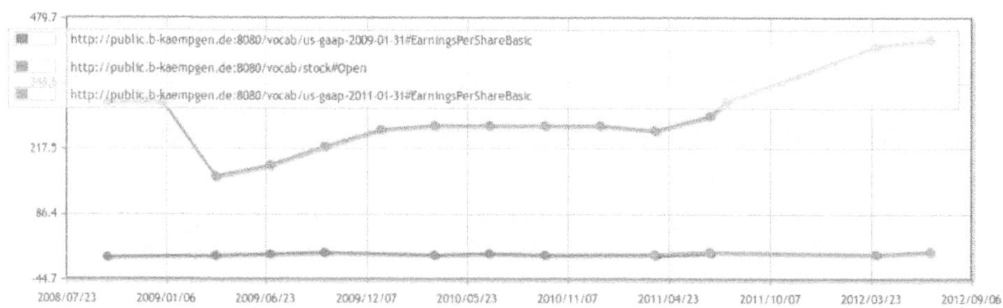

Fig. 4. Example cross-data-sources KPI analysis of Earnings per Share versus price per share for MASTERCARD INC

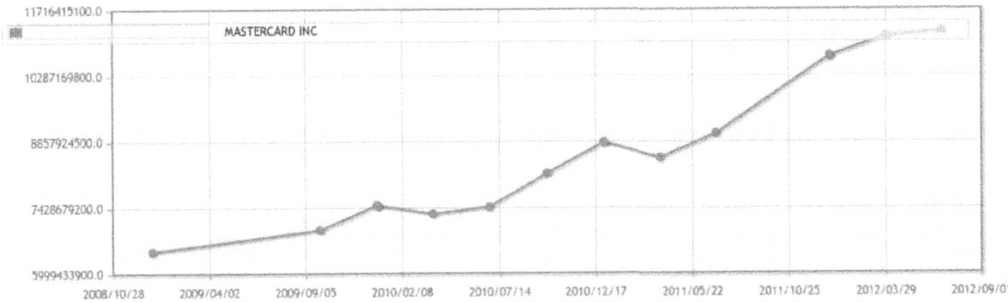

Fig. 5. Example cross-taxonomy analysis of Total Assets for MASTERCARD INC

the end of 2009 (from 7.4B USD to 7.3B USD) and the end of 2010 (from 8.8B USD to 8.5B USD), for instance indicating reduced profits and a re-organisation.

4.2 Overview First, Zoom, Details on Demand (Requirement 2)

We now demonstrate the capability of FIOS to show the same data using our three different interfaces. As an example, we again visit from the SPARK company template the assets over time for MASTERCARD INC as displayed in Figure 5.

From the top of the SPARK company template, via "Pubby Link to Data", we can then start browsing all information related to MASTERCARD INC in the Linked Data Browser Pubby. For instance, we can browse to the balance sheets and there find the single observations visualised in the line chart. For instance, see Figure 6 for a screenshot of an observation found in Pubby describing the total asset on 2011-12-31.

Anonymous Resource #1

Property	**Value**
qb:dataSet	▪ <http://public.b-kaempgen.de:8080/pubby/archive/1141391/0001141391-12-000006%23ds>
cal:dtend	▪ 2012-03-31
cal:dtstart	▪ 2012-01-01
?:issuer	▪ <http://public.b-kaempgen.de:8080/pubby/cik/1141391%23id>
sdmx-measure:obsValue	▪ 318000000 (xsd:double)
is rdfs:seeAlso of	▪ <http://public.b-kaempgen.de:8080/pubby/archive/1141391/0001141391-12-000006%23ds>
?:segment	▪ 0001141391 2012-01-01 2012-03-31
?:subject	▪ <http://public.b-kaempgen.de:8080/pubby/vocab/us-gaap-2011-01-31%23IncomeTaxExpenseBenefit>
rdf:type	▪ qb:Observation

Fig. 6. Example Linked Data browser view on total asset in 2011 for MASTERCARD INC

From the SPARK company template, we can also visit the OLAP Interface, Saiku, to create the same report as shown in the total asset line chart. For that, we create a pivot table with the issuer dimension filtered by Mastercard on columns, date dimension on rows and filtered on subject dimension with `us-gaap-2009:Assets` and `us-gaap-2011:Assets` on columns, as can be seen in Figure 7.

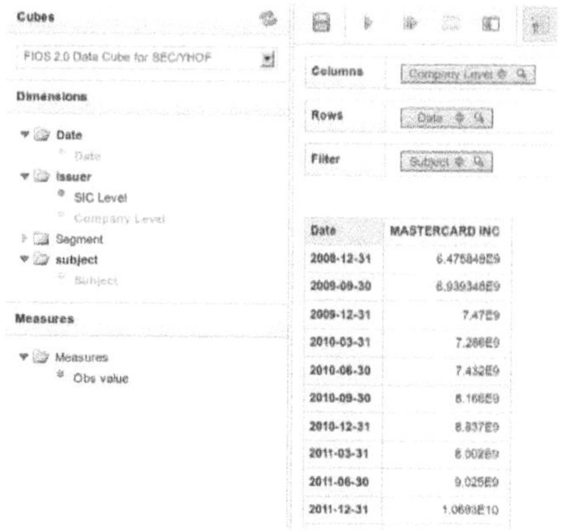

Fig. 7. Example OLAP Interface query on Total Assets over time for MASTERCARD INC

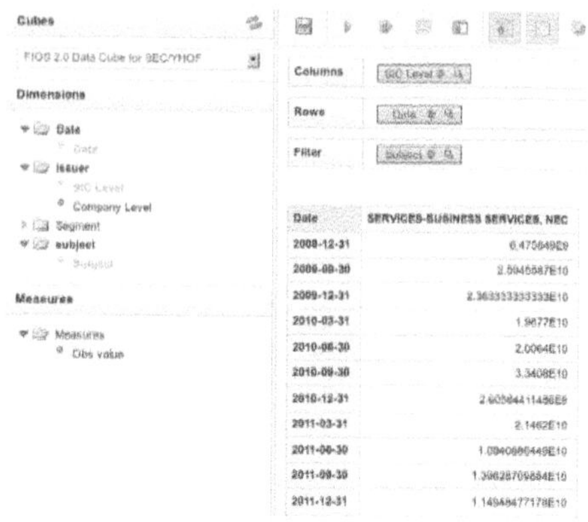

Fig. 8. Example OLAP Interface query on Total Assets over time for SERVICES-BUSINESS SERVICES (SIC)

Note, though connected through their underlying data, a better interlinking between the three provided interfaces was difficult due to technical problems: SPARK tables did not allow to show browseable links; SPARK diagrams often contained aggregated or densely-displayed facts that are difficult to select for browsing; single facts often were modelled as blank nodes in QB and thus are not directly referenceable; and to browse a URI from FIOS, Pubby required adding "pubby" and converting "#" to "%23".

4.3 Intuitively Create Own Reports and Analyses (Requirement 3)

We now show that a user can create a typical report on our integrated financial data with intuitive OLAP operations: requesting a pivot table showing the Total Assets over time, similarly as for the total asset line and pivot charts, but this time aggregated to the industry level of Mastercard as visible in Figure 8.

Projection: By drag & drop of a measure to Columns, Rows or Filter fields in the pivot table, a user can select a certain measure. Since our data cube only contains one measure, projection is not necessary.

Dice: A user can filter for certain facts by clicking on the magnifier symbol of a dimension on the Columns or Rows fields. In our case, the user filters for certain subjects (`us-gaap-2009:Assets` and `us-gaap-2011:Assets`) as well as certain companies (Mastercard).

Slice: Any dimension that a user does not drag & drop to either Columns or Row fields gets sliced, i.e., removed and aggregated over. Since QB does not provide means to describe aggregation, FIOS uses the AVERAGE function as default; for numeric values the average returns an easy-to-understand measurement.

Roll-up: Any dimension listed on the left side can exhibit a hierarchy of several levels. For instance, for the issuer dimension, either Company or SIC Level can be selected. SIC Level groups companies by their SIC industry classification. In our example, we rolled-up to SIC Level and filtered for the SIC of Mastercard, "SERVICES-BUSINESS SERVICES, NEC".

Drill-across: Although not required in our example, an analyst may request a pivot table containing both observations from balance sheets and stock quote tables. Since the Saiku interface only allows to select one dataset per pivot table, we extend the ETL components with one extra SPARQL CONSTRUCT query linking observations from several integrated datasets (datasets with the same structure) to a new integrated multidimensional dataset "FIOS 2.0 Data Cube for SEC/YHOF".

5 Discussions and Lessons Learned

FIOS benefits from Semantic Web technologies, e.g., in modelling and integrating balance sheets from the SEC Edgar Database, stock quotes from the Yahoo! Finance Web API as well as company metadata from Wikipedia/DBpedia using existing vocabularies; the Linked Data principles ensure access to data in a standard and modular way. Since the schema of RDF is flexible, new data can easily be added by allowing the crawler to reach further entities. SPARQL allows quality checks and is sufficiently expressive to implement background information, multi-company and cross-data-sources analyses. Formal semantics such as explicit equivalent statements simplify access via entity consolidation. Three interfaces with different purposes use the same backend: any data that is added to the triple store can directly be visualised in SPARQL templates, browsed using the Linked Data Browser and queried using the OLAP Interface. Consequently, we argue that Semantic Web technologies allow a continuous integration of new data. With more heterogeneous datasets and frequent addition and updates of data sources, FIOS will develop its full potential if research resolves the following challenges:

Develop interfaces and visualisations sufficiently specific to provide added value and generic to have new data immediately considered. If new information such as from text or structured databases, e.g., subsidiary relationships, product classifications or organisational structures, are continuously added to FIOS, specialists are needed to adapt or create new SPARQL templates; the Linked Data Browser provides data only on the triple level; and the OLAP Interface requires integrated QB datasets. Ideally, new data sources seamlessly and without much effort will result in extended visualisations, e.g., providing more detailed provenance information, adding new data points or allowing additional interaction capabilities such as roll-up and drill-across.

Increase coverage and quality of information by continuously integrating data sources. Integrity constraint checks need to be manually extracted and run. There may still be errors in the data, e.g., companies that share CIKs or ticker symbols because of a merger. Debreceny et al. [4] have shown that some information may be derived only in a best-guess fashion. New data sources promise to reduce data quality issues if integrated to one well-interlinked model.

Then, the same KPIs can be calculated in different ways to identify differences between data sources, e.g., DBpedia "Operating Income" and the last yearly balance sheet net income loss. FIOS would need to consider uncertainty, to draw declarative knowledge from experts or other data sources, and to describe both static and dynamic relationships between financial data.

Improve query processing performance. Although currently no issue in FIOS, pre-processing and integration will take too long for continuously updated and larger data sources. FIOS' current performance bottlenecks are large numbers of separately issued SPARQL queries and large numbers of multidimensional elements to load into the OLAP user interface. In more complex data integration and analysis scenarios optimisations such as parallelisation will be required, e.g., analytical queries that scan a large number of observations, contain filters of varying selectivity and compute aggregation functions on schema-flexible and heterogeneous data require specific data processing optimisations [7].

6 Related Work

We distinguish other financial data integration and analysis applications and related work about modelling XBRL data using Semantic Web technologies.

The Rhizomik Semantic XBRL demo [5] ties RDF representations of XBRL close to the original XML data which make mixing with other data sources difficult. The Business Intelligence Cross-lingual XBRL (BIXL) demonstrator [9] focuses on retrieving facts from unstructured text in filings as well as a multilingual interface, however does not consider data integration of XBRL balance sheets with stock quotes. Midas [2] implements a pipeline similar to FIOS without using Semantic Web technologies. Their main focus lies in extracting and linking of information about entities such as company and key people from semi-structured XML documents. However, it is unclear to what extend information from SEC and FDIC sources were integrated and what efforts would be needed to add new data sources such as Wikipedia.

Although judges saw potential, FIOS did not win the XBRL Challenge. Other submissions, in particular the winners – Calcbench and Sector3 – were more robust (e.g., FIOS still is limited to certain browsers), provide keyword search or filtering for companies (e.g., "revenue higher than"), include a larger number of companies and filings (also non-balance-sheets), exhibit short update intervals with new filings (10-15min) and often provide MS Excel exports for further processing and analysis (Saiku also provides that).

In summary, although important for a holistic view on companies, current systems do not focus on integration of different data sources: whereas multi-company KPI analysis with an Excel export often is possible, background information, such as from Wikipedia, rarely is embedded in the interfaces. Calcbench shows the actual stock quote of a company, yet, no other system allows for comparison of balance sheet KPIs with other numbers such as stock quotes over time. If systems find correspondences between companies or financial concepts, it is unclear whether the matching is hard-coded or flexibly represented with a formalism such as equivalence statements.

Several recent papers have proposed Semantic Web technologies as a suitable way to manage and model XBRL data. Wenger et al. [12] consider the interoperability problems of different taxonomy versions, but apart from proposing the criteria they do not evaluate their approach. Bao et al. [1] tries to fully keep the semantics of XBRL in an RDF/OWL representation; however, the authors do not describe the benefits of their representation in case studies. In comparison, we show that XBRL filings and taxonomies can be efficiently represented as multidimensional datasets using the RDF Data Cube vocabulary.

7 Conclusions

In this In-Use paper, we have described the Financial Information Observation System (FIOS) that models XBRL data using the RDF Data Cube Vocabulary; consolidates financial data for background, multi-company, and cross-data-sources KPI analysis; and provides intuitive and explorative analysis interfaces. The benefit of Semantic Web technologies are a flexible schema, standard access, expressive queries and formal semantics. Main challenges to scaling-up those benefits in continuous integration scenarios are interfaces sufficiently specific to provide added value and generic to have new data immediately considered; to increase coverage and data quality with added data sources; and to optimise analytical operations on flexible schemas and heterogeneous data. In future work we intend to evaluate and extend the FIOS approach to other domains.

Acknowledgements. This work was carried out with the support of the German Research Foundation (DFG) within project I01, SFB/TRR 125 "Cognition-Guided Surgery" and the German Federal Ministry of Education and Research (BMBF) within Software-Campus project "LD-Cubes" (01IS12051).

References

1. Bao, J., Rong, G., Li, X., Ding, L.: Representing Financial Reports on the Semantic Web: a Faithful Translation from XBRL to OWL. In: Dean, M., Hall, J., Rotolo, A., Tabet, S. (eds.) RuleML 2010. LNCS, vol. 6403, pp. 144–152. Springer, Heidelberg (2010)
2. Burdick, D., Hernández, M.A., Ho, H., Koutrika, G., Krishnamurthy, R., Popa, L., Stanoi, I., Vaithyanathan, S., Das, S.R.: Extracting, Linking and Integrating Data from Public Sources: A Financial Case Study. IEEE Data Eng. Bull. (2011)
3. Carretié, H., Torvisco, B., García, R.: Using Semantic Web Technologies to Facilitate XBRL-based Financial Data Comparability. In: International Workshop on Finance and Economics on the Semantic Web (2012)
4. Debreceny, R.: Feeding the information value chain: Deriving analytical ratios from XBRL filings to the SEC. Tech. rep. (2010)
5. García, R., Gil, R.: Triplificating and linking XBRL financial data. Information Storage and Retrieval (2010)
6. Hogan, A., Harth, A., Umbrich, J., Kinsella, S., Polleres, A., Decker, S.: Searching and browsing Linked Data with SWSE: The Semantic Web Search Engine. Web Semantics: Science, Services and Agents on the World Wide Web 9, 365–401 (2011)

7. Kämpgen, B., Harth, A.: No Size Fits All – Running the Star Schema Benchmark with SPARQL and RDF Aggregate Views. In: Cimiano, P., Corcho, O., Presutti, V., Hollink, L., Rudolph, S. (eds.) ESWC 2013. LNCS, vol. 7882, pp. 290–304. Springer, Heidelberg (2013)
8. O'Riain, S., Curry, E., Harth, A.: XBRL and open data for global financial ecosystems: A linked data approach. Int. J. of Accounting Information Systems 13 (2012)
9. O'Riain, S., Coughlan, B., Buitelaar, P., Declerk, T., Krieger, U., Marie-Thomas, S.: Cross-Lingual Querying and Comparison of Linked Financial and Business Data. In: Cimiano, P., Fernández, M., Lopez, V., Schlobach, S., Völker, J. (eds.) ESWC 2013. LNCS, vol. 7955, pp. 242–247. Springer, Heidelberg (2013)
10. Spies, M.: An ontology modelling perspective on business reporting. Information Systems 35 (2010)
11. Tseng, F.S.: Integrating heterogeneous data warehouses using XML technologies. Journal of Information Science 31 (2005)
12. Wenger, M., Thomas, M.A., Babb Jr., J.S.: An Ontological Approach to XBRL Financial Statement Reporting An Ontological Approach to XBRL Financial Statement Reporting. In: AMCIS 2011 Proceedings (2011)

Predicting Severity of Road Traffic Congestion Using Semantic Web Technologies*

Freddy Lécué, Robert Tucker, Veli Bicer, Pierpaolo Tommasi, Simone Tallevi-Diotallevi, and Marco Sbodio

IBM Research, Smarter Cities Technology Centre
Damastown Industrial Estate, Dublin, Ireland
{firstname.lastname}@ie.ibm.com

Abstract. Predictive reasoning, or the problem of estimating future observations given some historical information, is an important inference task for obtaining insight on cities and supporting efficient urban planning. This paper, focusing on transportation, presents how severity of road traffic congestion can be predicted using semantic Web technologies. In particular we present a system which integrates numerous sensors (exposing heterogenous, exogenous and raw data streams such as weather information, road works, city events or incidents) to improve accuracy and consistency of traffic congestion prediction. Our prototype of semantics-aware prediction, being used and experimented currently by traffic controllers in Dublin City Ireland, works efficiently with real, live and heterogeneous stream data. The experiments have shown accurate and consistent prediction of road traffic conditions, main benefits of the semantic encoding.

Keywords: #eswc2014Lecue.

1 Introduction

As the number of vehicles on the road steadily increases and the expansion of roadways is remained static, congestion in cities became one of the major transportation issues in most industrial countries [1]. Urban traffic costs 5.5 billion hours of travel delay and 2.9 billion gallons of wasted fuel in the USA alone, all at the price of $121 billion. Even worse, the costs of extra time and wasted fuel has quintupled over the past 30 years.

Three ways can be considered to reduce congestion [2]; one is to improve the infrastructure e.g., by increasing the road capacity, but this requires enormous expenditure which is often not viable. Promoting public transport in large cities is another way but it is not always convenient. Another solution is to determine the future states of roads segments, which will support transportation departments and their managers to proactively manage the traffic before congestion is reached e.g., changing traffic light strategy.

Prediction, or the problem of estimating future observations given some historical information, spans many research fields, from Statistics, Signal Processing to Database

* The research leading to these results has received funding from the European Union's Seventh Framework Programme (FP7/2007-2013) under grant agreement ID 318201 (SIMPLI-CITY).

V. Presutti et al. (Eds.): ESWC 2014, LNCS 8465, pp. 611–627, 2014.

and Artificial Intelligence. Depending on the level of data representation considered, a prediction problem [3] can be formulated as a standard machine learning classification (for symbolic values) or regression (for numeric values) model [4]. In most of data stream mining applications, prediction is estimated by (i) correlating current and past data (e.g., travel times for traffic application), (ii) identifying patterns using different distance metrics [5], and (iii) selecting rules that are used for predicting future conditions [6]. These approaches are designed for very fast processing and mining of (syntactic and numerical) raw data from sensors [7]. They rarely utilize exogenous sources of information for adjusting estimated prediction. Inclement weather condition, a concert event, a car accident, peak hours are examples of external factors that strongly impact traffic flow and congestion [8]. They also all fail in using and interpreting underlying semantics of data, making prediction not as accurate and consistent as it could be, specially when data streams are characterized by texts or sudden changes over time.

We show that the integration of numerous sensors, which expose heterogenous, exogenous, raw data streams such as weather information, road works, city events is a way forward to improve accuracy and consistency of traffic congestion prediction. To this end, we exploit semantic Web technologies and adapt recent research work in semantic predictive reasoning [9] as a way to annotate and interpret semantics of stream data. We extend the latter work by (i) presenting the prediction system[1] and architecture, (ii) focusing on the traffic congestion application, (iii) presenting various technical challenges such as semantic data stream conversion, cross-stream reasoning, consistent prediction, (iv) describing in details all data. As a system-based presentation, this work improves [9] by focusing on InUse criteria i.e., (i) providing technical details of the architecture and implementation, (ii) clearly defining their limitations for further deployments, (iii) drawing new lessons learnt from a more advanced, systemized and inUse prototype, (iv) describing the current interface of the system (Fig.10), (v) reporting new experimental results (Fig.11, Fig.12) against traditional data mining techniques [5]. This work complements [10], which explains traffic congestion in quasi-real-time. In both works data is lifted at semantic level but the diagnosis and predictive approaches are different techniques. Diagnosis is based on semantic matching of events and a probabilistic model while prediction is based on stream auto-correlation, association mining.

This paper is organized as follows: Section 2 presents the Dublin city context and highlights the main challenges we faced to predict the severity of its road traffic congestion. Section 3 describes the system architecture while detailing its limitations. Section 4 reports some experimental results regarding its scalability and accuracy. Section 5 draws some conclusions and talks about future directions.

2 Context: Transportation in Dublin City

2.1 Open Data Sources

All data sources in Table 1 are classified with respect to their velocity i.e., static, quasi stream, stream. They report various types of information coming from static or dynamic sensors, exposed as open, public data and described along heterogenous formats.

[1] Prediction part of the live IBM STAR-CITY system (`http://dublinked.ie/sandbox/star-city/`).

Quasi stream refers to low throughput sensors. Static sensing refers to stationary platform while dynamic sensing refers to moving objects. The *journey times* data stream is used for (i) monitoring road traffic flow (i.e., free, moderate, heavy, stopped) between static sensors, and (ii) deriving congestion and its severity (i.e., spatial and temporal representation of traffic queues) across 47 routes and its 732 points in Dublin city, all in real-time. Predicting the characteristics of this stream, which we called *main stream* (i.e., stream to be predicted), consists in interpreting, contextualizing and correlating its content with these six exogenous data sources: (1) *road weather condition* which captures specific features of roads conditions e.g., road temperature along 11 static stations, (2) *weather information* e.g., general condition, temperature, precipitation along 19 static stations, (3) *Dublin bus stream* which senses location, speed, delay of 1000 buses every 20 seconds, (4) *social media feeds* which relate traffic-related information e.g., accident, delays, last minute road closure from reputable sources, (5) *road works and maintenance* which plan roads disruptions, their type, duration and (potential) impact on traffic, all updated on a weekly basis, (6) *city events* which characterize social events of various type e.g., music, sport, politics, family, with an average of 187 events per day, all updated on a daily basis.

These data sets have been selected based on their (i) openness, (ii) positive spatial correlation with the *journey times* data stream (i.e., data within a boundary box: max / min latitude: 53.418536 / 53.274247; max / min longitude: -6.095459 / -6.394258), and (iii) factual (positive or negative) impact on traffic flow conditions [8]. Fig.1 spatially represents the static sensors: journey times, road condition, weather stations. The ESRI SHAPE file of Dublin city, spatially describing map-related elements, is used for (i) capturing the shape of roads, and more importantly (ii) identifying nearby roads and their spatial-based segment representation.

2.2 Semantic Predictive Reasoning: Research and in Use Challenges

Semantic predictive reasoning [9] is the inference task of *interpreting* and *mining* all *relevant* exogenous streams and their *evolution* through their *temporal changes* and *correlation*. Applied and interpreted in our transportation context, predicting severity of road traffic congestion consists of three high level challenges:

(C_1) **Handling data variety (csv, xml, tweets, pdf) and velocity (static, stream):**
Once exogenous heterogenous data streams are identified as relevant sources for prediction [8], how to represent them in a unified and common model? Which level of expressivity is required? How to automatically extract knowledge from any unstructured data sources, especially streams and social media feeds? How to capture temporal evolution of streams and its underlying knowledge? How to discretize numerical values from streams? For example, how traffic-related social media feeds can be classified around key concepts such as *incident*, *truck accident*, *car delay*, and then spatially and temporally linked with discretized road weather condition, all in real-time?

(C_2) **Reasoning on the evolution of multiple data streams:**
How to understand knowledge evolution and changes of multiple streams on a time basis? How to detect spatial, temporal, semantic correlation in a stream? How to identify

Table 1. (Raw) Data Sources for Dublin City Traffic Prediction Scenario

Type	Sensing	Data Source	Description	Format	Temporal Frequency (s)	Size per day (GBytes)	Data Provider (all open data)
Stream Data	Static	Journey times across Dublin City (47 routes)	Dublin Traffic Department's TRIPS system[a]	CSV	60	0.1	Dublin City Council via dublinked.ie[b]
Stream Data	Static	Road Weather Condition (11 stations)		CSV	600	0.1	NRA[c]
Stream Data	Static	Real-time Weather Information (19 stations)		CSV	[5, 600] (depending on stations)	[0.050, 1.5] (depending on stations)	Wunderground[d]
Stream Data	Dynamic	Dublin Bus Stream	Vehicle activity (GPS location, line number, delay, stop flag)	SIRI: XML-based[e]	20	4-6	Dublin City Council via dublinked.ie[f]
Stream Data	Dynamic	Social-Media Related Feeds	Reputable sources of road traffic conditions in Dublin City	Tweets	600	0.001 (approx. 150 tweets per day)	LiveDrive[g] Aaroadwatch[g] GardaTraffic[g]
Quasi Stream	Dynamic	Road Works and Maintenance		PDF	Updated once a week	0.001	Dublin City Council[h]
Quasi Stream	Dynamic	Events in Dublin City	Planned events with small attendance	XML	Updated once a day	0.001	Eventbrite[i]
Quasi Stream	Dynamic	Events in Dublin City	Planned events with large attendance	XML	Updated once a day	0.05	Eventful[i]
Static	Static	Dublin City Map (listing of type, junctions, GPS coordinate)		ESRI SHAPE	No	0.1	Open StreetMap[j]

[a] Travel-time Reporting Integrated Performance System - http://www.advantechdesign.com.au/trips
[b] http://dublinked.ie/datastore/datasets/dataset-215.php
[c] NRA - National Roads Authority - http://www.nratraffic.ie/weather
[d] http://www.wunderground.com/weather/api/
[e] Service Interface for Real Time Information - http://siri.org.uk
[f] http://dublinked.com/datastore/datasets/dataset-289.php
[g] https://twitter.com/LiveDrive - https://twitter.com/aaroadwatch - https://twitter.com/GardaTraffic
[h] http://www.dublincity.ie/RoadsandTraffic/ScheduledDisruptions/Documents/TrafficNews.pdf
[i] https://www.eventbrite.com/api - http://api.eventful.com
[j] http://download.geofabrik.de/europe/ireland-and-northern-ireland.html

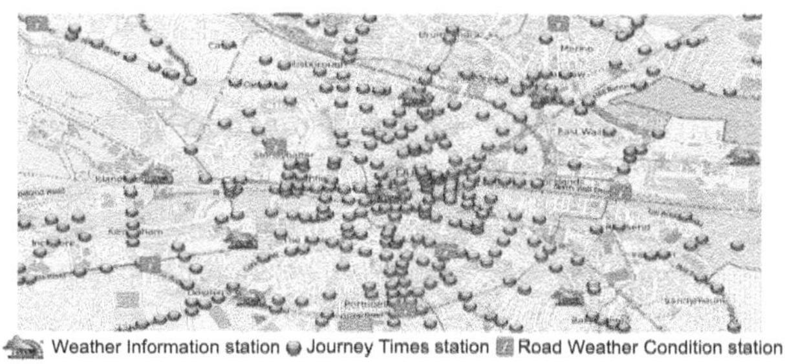

Fig. 1. Spatial Visualization of Static Dublin City Traffic-related Sensors (color print)

associations of streams? E.g., how weather condition is evolving? What were the past time slots with similar conditions? How an *incident-weather* context can be evaluated against historical and real-time traffic flow? Is there any road where a *truck accident* and an *inclement weather condition* could be associated to derive a heavy traffic flow?

(C_3) **Scalable and consistent prediction:**
How to rank and select relevant associations of streams in a scalable way? How to use them for achieving consistent prediction? E.g., are there many roads where *truck accident* and inclement weather condition are associated with a heavy traffic flow? Is

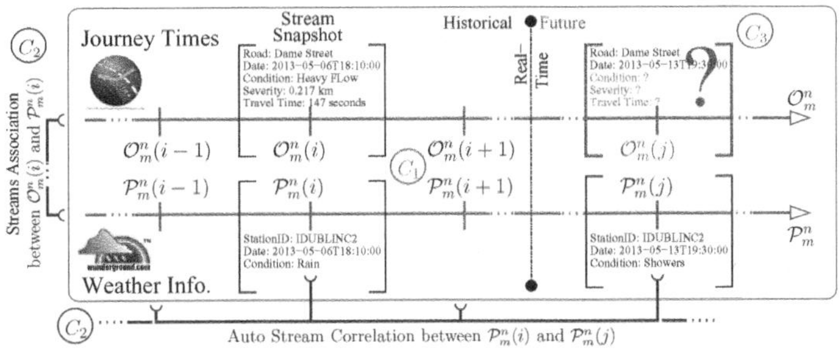

Fig. 2. Articulation of Challenges $C_{i,1\leq i\leq 3}$ in Traffic-related Predictive Reasoning (color print)

there more evidence of the latter association when a *car accident* occurred? Will the prediction be consistent with the traffic flow of connected roads?

On the one hand (C_1), intensively investigated by the semantic Web [11,12] community to represent and interpret data, can be addressed by mature technologies but still requires some technical adaptations, specially in our streams-based context. On the other hand (C_2) and (C_3) are more recent research challenges which are critical for associating and predicting [9] streams of semantic data. Fig.2 articulates and illustrates these challenges in a simple context of *"predicting the journey times $\mathcal{O}_m^n$ stream, given the exogenous weather information stream $\mathcal{P}_m^n$, where both are evolving on a time basis i.e., from time m to n"*. $\mathcal{O}_m^n(i)$ is called a snapshot of stream $\mathcal{O}_m^n$ at time $i \in [m, n]$. This illustration captures (i) records along one weather station (or stream), (ii) travel condition between two sensors on *Dame Street* at times i, j. We will consider *journey times* as the main stream to be predicted, while the remaining streams from Table 1 are exogenous streams, all used for contextualization (C_1), correlation (C_2) and prediction (C_3). This work focused on addressing these challenges by applying semantic Web related technologies in the context of road traffic congestion prediction.

3 System Architecture for Traffic-Related Predictive Reasoning

We report the system architecture (Fig.3) and provide (i) details of all components, (ii) justification of their conceptual and technical specification (if relevant), (iii) limitations and (iv) scalability i.e., applicability to other domains.

3.1 High-Level System Architecture

In addition to the components that address all challenges $C_{i,1\leq i\leq 3}$ in Section 2.2 (described in details in the remaining sections), the system architecture consists of:

• **A spatial interpreter**, required for (i) geocoding some data sources e.g., social media feeds and road works (which only give road identification), (ii) evaluating distance between spatial data but most importantly (iii) retrieving connected roads in Dublin city. IBM DB2 Spatial Extender[2] is used and configured with Ireland SHAPE file[m] in

[2] http://www-03.ibm.com/software/products/us/en/db2spaext/

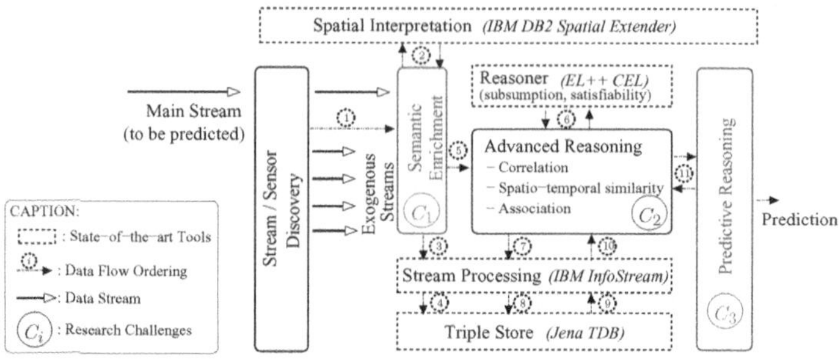

Fig. 3. High-Level System Architecture for Predictive Reasoning (color print)

Table 1, and DB2SE_IRELAND_GEOCODER geocoder. One of its main strength is its spatial grid index which ensures good query performance i.e., on average 325 ms per request.

• **A stream processing engine**, required for processing data streams e.g., serving real-time semantic streams, materializing knowledge over multiple semantic streams in real-time. IBM InfoSphere Streams[3] is coupled with the *semantic enrichment* and *reasoner*.

• **A reasoner**, required for interpreting semantic streams e.g., checking consistency of one or multiple stream(s) at a specific point of time, evaluating subsumption and satisfiability, identifying ABox entailments (i.e., assignment of data instances to concept description based on their representation). CEL DL (Description Logic) reasoner[4] [13] is used as it provides core inference tasks over DL $\mathcal{EL}^{++}$ representations (see justification of this DL family in Section 3.2), implementing a polynomial-time algorithm.

• **A triple store**, for storing the semantic representation of raw data and easily retrieving historical triples. The current prototype uses Jena TDB[5] as RDF store. We preferred the B+ Trees indexing structures which scale better in our context of many (stream) updates.

3.2 Handling Data Variety and Velocity (C_1)

Relevance: On the one hand all of our data is exposed through different formats, which limits not only their integration and semantic interpretation but also any kind of basic inference across data sources. How to measure the similarity of events or road condition? How to classify impact of weather condition on road traffic flow? These are examples of inference problems that need answers for predicting knowledge. By deriving similarity, correlation, association rules we aim at deriving knowledge facts that can be used at prediction time. Such problem cannot be achieved without a minimum of semantic representation. On the other hand data is exposed through (human or device-based) sensors, it is then crucial that real-time semantic conversion can be supported.

Conceptual and Technical Specification: The model we consider to represent static background knowledge and semantics of data stream is provided by an ontology,

[3] http://www-01.ibm.com/software/data/infosphere/streams/

[4] http://lat.inf.tu-dresden.de/systems/cel

[5] http://jena.apache.org/documentation/tdb/index.html

encoded in OWL 2 EL[6]. The selection of the W3C standard OWL 2 EL profile has been guided by (i) the expressivity which was required to model semantics of data in Table 1, (ii) the scalability of the underlying basic reasoning mechanisms we needed e.g., subsumption in OWL 2 EL is in PTIME [13]. The DL $\mathcal{EL}^{++}$ [14] is the logic underpinning OWL 2 EL and the basis of many more expressive DL. For the sake of readability we illustrate semantic representations using the DL formalism. Fig.4 illustrates a DL sample of the static background knowledge for modeling *journey times* data.

$$Road \sqcap \exists hasTravelTimeStatus.HeavyTrafficFlow \sqsubseteq CongestedRoad \quad (1)$$
$$Road \sqcap \exists hasTravelTimeStatus.StoppedTrafficFlow \sqsubseteq CongestedRoad \quad (2)$$
$$Road \sqcap \exists hasTravelTimeStatus.LightTrafficFlow \sqsubseteq FreeRoad \quad (3)$$
$$CongestedRoad \sqcap FreeRoad \sqsubseteq \bot \text{ \% Incompatibility} \quad (4)$$
$$\{r_1\} \sqsubseteq Road \text{ \% Individual Definition of a road } r_1 \quad (5)$$

Fig. 4. (Sample) Static Background Knowledge $\mathcal{T}$ for *Journey Times* Data Stream

$$\mathcal{O}^n_m(t_1) : TravelTimeReport \sqcap \quad (6)$$
$$\exists createdAt.(TemporalEntity \sqcap (\exists inXSDDateTime.\{\textit{2013-04-22T23:01:00}\})) \sqcap \quad (7)$$
$$\exists reportsForTimeInterval.(\exists hasDurationDescription.(\exists minutes.\{\textit{1}\})) \sqcap \quad (8)$$
$$\exists hasSourceFrom.\{\textit{TRIPS-DCC-44}\} \sqcap \exists hasSourceTo.\{\textit{TRIPS-DCC-351}\} \sqcap \quad (9)$$
$$\exists reportsObservation.(\{r_1\} \sqcap \exists hasTravelTimeStatus.HeavyTrafficFlow) \quad (10)$$

Fig. 5. (Sample) *Journey Times* Ontology Stream $\mathcal{O}^n_m$ at time *2013-04-22T23:01:00*

We represent knowledge evolution by dynamic and evolutive versions of ontologies i.e., ontology stream [15]. We considered an ontology stream as a sequence of ontologies where each ontology captures a snapshot of a stream at a given point of time t. Fig.5 illustrates a stream snapshot $\mathcal{O}^n_m(t_1)$ i.e., the travel flow severity of a road r_1 from sensor *TRIPS-DCC-44* to *TRIPS-DCC-351*, updated every 1 minute through the *journey times* data stream $\mathcal{O}^n_m$ at date and time t_1 : *2013-04-22T23:01:00*. The ontological representation is important to (i) capture the temporal evolution of its knowledge, (ii) reason across data streams, while the (basic) temporal representation is used to aggregate multiple data sources on a time basis.

Description: Fig.6 describes the architecture for generating OWL EL ontology streams from raw CSV, tweets, XML, PDF data, all accessed through different mechanisms. All the ontology streams have the same static background knowledge to capture time (W3C Time Ontology[7] are used for representing (7), (8)), space (W3C Geo Ontology[8] for encoding location of (9)) but differ only in some domain-related vocabularies e.g., traffic flow type, weather phenomenon, event type. These ontologies have been mainly used for enriching raw data, facilitating its integration, comparison, and matching. The

[6] http://www.w3.org/TR/owl2-profiles/
[7] http://www.w3.org/TR/owl-time/
[8] http://www.w3.org/2003/01/geo/

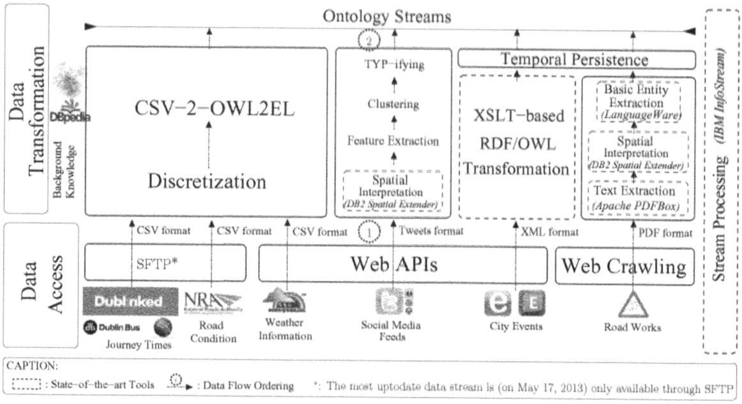

Fig. 6. Semantic Stream Enrichment (color print)

DBpedia vocabulary has been used for cross-referencing entities (not described here). We did not make use of the Semantic Sensor Network ontology[9] as it is mainly designed for reasoning over sensor-related descriptions rather than its data and associated phenomenons. In all cases [a,b,c,d], we serve real-time ontology streams by using IBM InfoSphere Streams, where different mapping techniques[15] are used depending on the data format. The main benefits of packaging our approach using stream processing are: (i) easy synchronization of streams (with different frequency updates) and their OWL2 EL transformation, (ii) flexible and scalable composition of stream operations (e.g., transformation, aggregation, filtering) by adjusting its processing units, (iii) identification of patterns and rules over different time windows (Section 3.4), (iv) possible extension to higher throughput sensors. All points are all natively supported by stream processing engines. The following refers to the four types of raw data we consider:

(a) CSV: A large portion of CSV raw data, exposed by our city sensors, refers to continuous values (e.g., *journey times*). A first step of discretization was required e.g., *Free*, *Moderate*, *Heavy*, *Stopped* traffic flow to conceptualize *journey times*. To this end we evaluated historical data over a period of 6 months to estimate the relevant intervals of values and then associate its concepts. We also adapt existing domain ontologies (e.g., SWEET[10] for (road) weather phenomenon, SIRI-BUS [10] for bus data) and design new vocabularies (e.g., journey times) to cover unsupported descriptions (e.g., travelTimeStatus from/to sensors). Each CSV row is interpreted by a mapping process, handled by our stream processing engine. Fig.7 illustrates the mapping file used for enriching a raw *journey times* data record *[Route: 6, Link: 5, STT: 32, TCS1:44, TCS2: 351]* (collected at timestamp: 1366671660, updated every minute) in its semantic representation (Fig.5) using the static background knowledge. We encoded static city sensors (e.g., *TCS1: 44*) as OWL individual (e.g., *TRIPS-DCC-44*) to reduce the size of the stream description.

[9] `http://www.w3.org/2005/Incubator/ssn/`
[10] Semantic Web for Earth, Environmental Terminology - `http://sweet.jpl.nasa.gov/`

```
@prefix owl: <http://www.w3.org/2002/07/owl#> .
@prefix rdf: <http://www.w3.org/1999/02/22-rdf-syntax-ns#> .
@prefix ttr: <http://www.ibm.com/SCTC/ontology/TravelTimeOntology#> .

_:{$uuid}_0 rdf#type ttr#TravelTimeReport .  # $uuid: URI for new travel time report
_:{$uuid}_0 owl#intersectionOf _:{$uuid}_1 . # Each report: intersection of concepts (Fig.5)
_:{$uuid}_1 rdf#first _:{$uuid}_2 .          # Join to the first existential restriction in (9)
_:{$uuid}_2 rdf#type owl#Restriction .       # Existential restriction in (9)
_:{$uuid}_2 owl#onProperty ttr#hasSourceFrom # hasSourceFrom property in (9)
_:{$uuid}_2 owl#hasValue ttr#{$sourceFom} .  # Capture of $sourceFom variable in CSV
_:{$uuid}_1 rdf#rest _:{$uuid}_3 .           # Right part of the Intersection in (9)
_:{$uuid}_3 rdf#first _:{$uuid}_4 .          # Join to the second existential restriction in (9
_:{$uuid}_4 rdf#type owl#Restriction .       # Another existential restriction in (9)
_:{$uuid}_4 owl#onProperty ttr#hasSourceTo   # hasSourceTo property in (9)
_:{$uuid}_4 owl#hasValue ttr#{$sourceTo} .   # Capture of $sourceTo variable in CSV
_:{$uuid}_3 rdf#rest _:{$uuid}_5 .           # Remaining parts of the Intersection for (7-10)
```

Fig. 7. (Sample) CSV-2-OWL2EL Mapping File for Enriching a *Journey Times* CSV Row

(b) XML: XML based city events are converted in RDF through an XSL Transformation[11]. Besides updating their representations, it also upgrades their descriptions following [10]. Existing vocabularies such as DBpedia have been used for (i) annotating predefined types of events e.g., capacity, category and (ii) handling basic comparison of events through generalization/specialization. All events are updated only on a daily basis but persist or repeat over time. We simulate these temporal persistence and repetition in the ontology stream by defining their time interval through the *ProperInterval* concept in the W3C Time ontology (by adapting (8)).

(c) PDF: The extraction of the PDF-based road works together with their location, time interval, description and traffic impact is achieved through state-of-the-art tools i.e., (i) PDFBox[12] for extracting text from PDF, (ii) DB2 Spatial extender for geocoding and (iii) LanguageWare[13] for entity extraction through semantic understanding of content. External vocabulary such as DBPedia has been used for type-ing events e.g., road works (e.g., http://dbpedia.org/resource/Roadworks), which ensures potential reuse in the LOD context. The temporal persistence is achieved similarly as city events.

(d) Tweets: Contrary to city events and road works, the semantic enrichment of social media feeds needs a more advanced learning phase. We identify the missing semantics by using an unsupervised learning technique, called Typifier [16], which consists of two major steps, namely *feature extraction* and *clustering*. As a first step, it represents each element (e.g. tweet, event, delay etc.) in the data by a set of features obtained from the attributes i.e., text. E.g., the words such as slow, collision, and delay in the social media feeds can be important features to distinguish its type of *delay*. Once those features are extracted, as a second step, it employs a hierarchical clustering algorithm which aims to maximize intra-cluster homogeneity and inter-cluster separation such that the elements in the same cluster represent the entities of the same type. The clustering method is done automatically. Finally, those clusters are mapped to particular concepts in the

[11] http://www.w3.org/TR/xslt
[12] http://pdfbox.apache.org/
[13] http://www-01.ibm.com/software/globalization/languageware/

background knowledge (DBpedia concepts e.g., Delay, Incident, Accident, Breakdown, Event) in order to enable the semantic lifting of tweets.

Scalability: Our approach can be applicable to any city, and generalized with any other (i) semantic representation e.g., OWL 2 DL, (ii) open (e.g., JSON) or proprietary data format, and (iii) application domains (not only city data) as far as data streams are required (e.g., through sensors). The ontology stream conceptualization also gives the advantage to support real-time querying [17] and reasoning [15] e.g., "*retrieving all roads in Dublin 15 with a heavy traffic flow impacted by inclement weather condition*".

Limitations: The generalization to other domains/cities may require extra manual work to identify, define or extend ontologies. New description of mapping files (e.g., a la CSV-2-OWL2EL or XSLT) would be then required. The entity extraction from natural language (i.e., PDF and tweets) requires some training phases, hence the requirement of some historical data and their pre-processing phases.

3.3 Reasoning on the Evolution of Multiple Data Streams (C_2)

Relevance: Once all data in Table 1 is semantically exposed, advanced reasoning techniques are required to capture (i) changes between ontology stream snapshots, and (ii) associations of knowledge at cross-stream level, all on a time basis. The detection of changes supports the understanding of stream evolution, and then provides the basics to compute knowledge auto-correlation along a stream over time. Auto-correlation and association are core reasoning for evaluating potential patterns at one or multi-stream level(s), which are required for predicting severity of congestion. Auto-correlation evaluates semantic similarity of stream snapshots while association aims at deriving rules across streams. E.g., identifying that "*the traffic flow is never stopped on week nights in Dublin 15*" or "*a concert event is always associated with a heavy traffic flow*" are useful facts for prediction purposes.

Conceptual and Technical Specification: On the one hand the TBox (i.e., terminological box containing concepts and their relations) of our static background knowledge, which does not change over time, is classified once using $\mathcal{EL}^{++}$ completion rules [14]. On the other hand the ABox axioms (i.e., relations between individuals and concepts), which are generated by the ontology stream conversion (Fig.6), are internalized into TBox axioms so (i) completion rules can be applied on both axioms, (ii) TBox reasoning (e.g., subsumption, satifiablility) can be performed on internalized ABox axioms. Axiom (11) illustrates some dynamic knowledge at time t_1, as an ABox entailment, derived from axioms (1), (5) in $\mathcal{T}$ (Fig.4) and (10) (Fig.5) using completion rules.

$$\mathcal{T} \cup \mathcal{O}_m^n(t_1) \models^{\text{using axioms (1),(5),(10)}}_{\text{using completion rules in [14]}} \{r_1\} \sqsubseteq \mathit{CongestedRoad} \qquad (11)$$

Cross stream association is modeled through DL $\mathcal{EL}^{++}$ rules [18], which extends the DL $\mathcal{EL}^{++}$ expressivity while preserving its polynomial complexity. Intuitively, DL

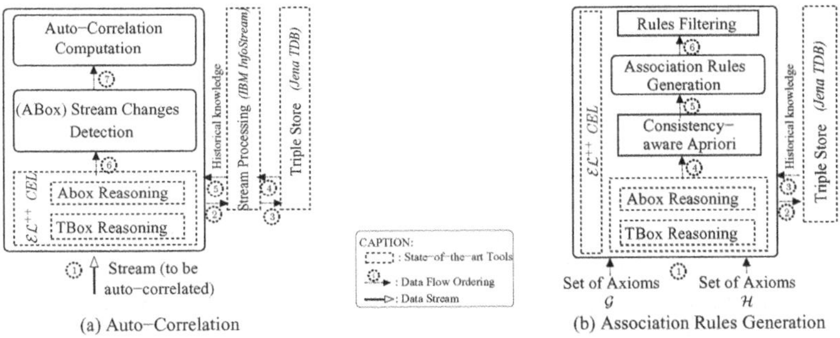

Fig. 8. Stream Auto-Correlation and Association Rules for Prediction

rules are encoded using SWRL rules[14], which is largely based on RuleML. One could, for example, formulate the timeless rule (12) "*the traffic flow of road r_1 is heavy if r_1 is adjacent to a road r_2 where an accident occurs and the humidity is optimum*". This rule connects the *journey times*, *social media* and *weather information* streams.

$$\begin{aligned} HeavyTrafficFlow(s) \leftarrow & Road(r_1) \wedge Road(r_2) \wedge isAdjacentTo(r_1, r_2) \wedge \\ & hasTravelTimeStatus(r_1, s) \wedge hasWeatherPhenomenon(r_1, w) \wedge \\ & OptimunHumidity(w) \wedge hasTrafficPhenomenon(r_2, a) \wedge \\ & RoadTrafficAccident(a) \end{aligned} \quad (12)$$

Description: The auto-correlation of snapshots along an ontology stream is illustrated by (C_2) in Fig.2 and systematized in Fig.8a. We established it by comparing the number of changes i.e., *new*, *obsolete*, *invariant* ABox entailments between snapshots. The number of invariants has a strong and positive influence on auto-correlation. On the contrary, the number of new and obsolete ABox entailments, capturing some differentiators in knowledge evolution, has a negative impact and favors negative auto-correlation. Inconsistencies e.g., (4) are mainly used for capturing incompatible road status at different times e.g., i and j. If captured, they are used to negatively weight the correlation of snapshots $\mathcal{O}^n_m(i)$, $\mathcal{O}^n_m(j)$. i is not an appropriate time to compute the prediction in j. The generation of association rules (Fig.8b) between streams (and their snapshots) such as (12) is based on a DL extension of Apriori [19], aiming at supporting subsumption for determining association rules. Contrary to the initial version of Apriori, the association is achieved between any ABox elements together with their entailments (e.g., all congested roads, weather, works, incidents, city events delayed buses). The association is possible only in the case their elements appear in at least one point of time of the streams. As the number of rules grows exponentially with the number of ABox elements and entailments in streams, we do not mine all potential rules, but filter them by adapting the definition of *support* (i.e., number of occurrences that support the elements of the rule) and *confidence* (i.e., probability of finding the consequent of the rule in the streams given the antecedents of the rule) [19] for ontology stream. In addition

[14] http://www.w3.org/Submission/SWRL/

only consistent associations are considered. For instance $HeavyTrafficFlow(s) \wedge LightTrafficFlow(s)$, which is not consistent with respect to (1), (3), (4), aims at limiting the number of rules to be generated.

Scalability: The approach, systematized from [9] (algorithmic details provided), is generic enough to reason, auto-correlate and cross-associate any ontology streams. Even in the presence of support, confidence and consistency filters, the number of potential rules grows very quickly with the (i) the number of exogenous streams, and (ii) the size of their snapshot. Further investigations along with other metrics are required to reduce this number, that would ensure a better scalability.

Limitations: Jena TDB failed to correctly handle simultaneous updates (coming from various streams). Thus the ontology stream needs to be slightly desynchronized from each other to ensure that Jena TDB handles correctly its transaction model. To this end we simply delayed some of the streams to obtain a sequence of updates instead. We ensure such a desynchronization through our stream processing platform. The B+Trees indexing structure of TDB scales the best in our stream context where large amounts of updates are performed i.e., the transaction model is much better handled in this structure. However there were some scalability issues to handle historical data over more than approximately 110 days. If we do not limit in space and time, and if we do not apply some heuristics (e.g., by restricting to a few days of historic) we could end-up dealing with $1,900,000$+ events (in a - not worst case - context of 458 days of data, where data is updated every 40 seconds). If we consider bus status that is multiplied by $1,000$ i.e., the number of buses. Some challenges such as data / knowledge summarization, stream synchronization are important challenges that need to be tackled, as they both limit the scalability of the approach to some extent.

3.4 Scalable and Consistent Prediction (C_3)

Relevance: Even if the association rules are filtered by significance (support, confidence) for scalability purpose in Section 3.3, they do not all ensure consistent prediction i.e., prediction which does not contradict other future knowledge facts. Indeed, some rules are specific and may deliver inconsistent prediction. For instance elaborating a prediction with a rule that requires *inclement weather condition* will not be necessarily consistent in a context where the *weather condition is mild*. Towards this issue, rules can be selected based on their applicability in auto-correlated past snapshots, hence reducing the number of rules and ensuring the consistency of their prediction. This motivates why combining auto-correlation and cross-stream association is important.

Description: Fig.9 presents how auto-correlation is combined with association rule generation for deriving the most relevant rules among streams.

We first identify the context (e.g., *mild weather*, *road closure*) where the prediction is required, and then perform its auto-correlation with historical contexts. Then, we identify and select rules based on their support, confidence and consistency, but

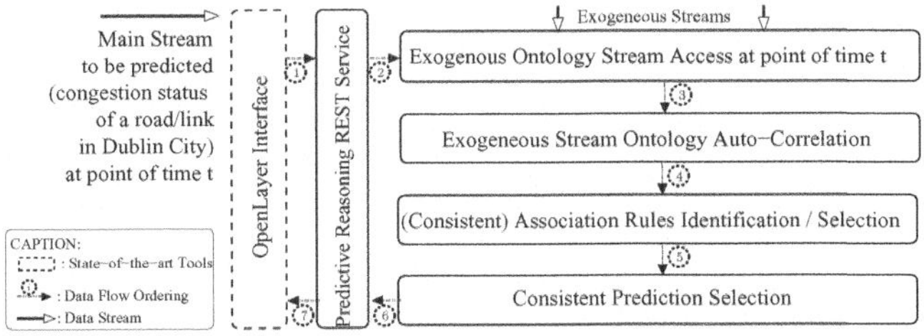

Fig. 9. Scalable and Consistent Prediction

only if the consequent of the rule is consistent with the knowledge captured by the exogenous stream. The significance of rules is contextualized and evaluated against only auto-correlated stream snapshots. Thus, the selection of rules [9] is driven by auto-correlation, making the selection knowledge evolution-aware. This ensures to learn rules that could be applied in similar contexts i.e., where knowledge does not drastically change. The prediction can be requested globally to all links of all of the 47 roads (red points in Fig.1). Fig.10 reports a 180-minutes ahead prediction of the severity of traffic congestion in Dublin city. The bottom part reports the proportion of free (green), stopped (brown) flow roads of the selected area (top part).

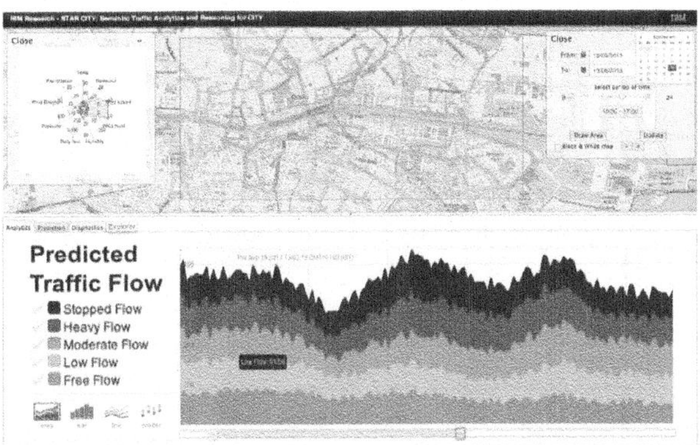

Fig. 10. Traffic Congestion Severity Prediction User Interface (color print)

Scalability and Limitations (cf detailed experimentation in Section 4): Interchanging SWRL rules with SPARQL would benefit the scalability of the approach only when prediction is requested simultaneously. However it would also reduce the expressivity, the number of interesting association rules and the accuracy of prediction.

4 Experimental Results

We focus on the scalability of our approach and its accuracy by (i) comparing its results with a (non semantics) state-of-the-art approach [5] in stream prediction, (ii) analyzing how our approach reacts to the number of stream sources, (iii) reporting the computation time of the various components in Fig.3. Requested by traffic controllers, scalability and accuracy of the system have been extensively tested. The experiments have been conducted on a server of 6 Intel(R) Xeon(R) X5650, 3.46GHz cores, and 6GB RAM.

4.1 Context

Live stream data (Table 1), transformed in OWL/RDF (Table 2) using a static background knowledge (Table 3), are used for experimentation.

Table 2. Stream Datasets Details in No Particular Order (average figures)

Data Stream	Frequency of Update (s)	Raw Update Size (KB)	Semantic Update Size (KB)	Semantic Update #RDF Triples	Semantic Conversion Computation Time (ms)
[a] Journey Times	60	20.2	6,102	63,000	0.61
[b] Bus	40	66.8	1,766	11,000	0.415
[c] Weather	300	2.2	267	1,140	0.189
[d] Road Works	once a week	146.6	77.9	820	3.988
[e] City Events	once a day	240.7	297	612	1.018
[f] Road Weather	600	715.7	181	660	0.068
[g] Incident	600	0.2	1.0	7	0.002

The objective is to predict the severity of congestion (i.e., *journey times* stream data) on some Dublin roads in the next hour using exogenous streams. We fixed the size of the stream window to 60 days, which is used for detecting auto-correlation and learning association rules. The impact of the window on predictive reasoning is reported in [9]. Adding more days will slightly increase the accuracy but strongly decrease scalability (because of auto-correlation and rules association generation). The evaluation is achieved on a different streams combinations i.e., [a], [a,b], [a,b,c], [a,b,c,d], [a,b,c,d,e], [a,b,c,d,e,f], [a,b,c,d,e,f,g] in Table 2, to evaluate their impacts on scalability, accuracy.

Table 3. Static Background Knowledge for Semantic Encoding

Ontology	Size (KB)	#Concepts	#Object Properties	#Data Properties	#Individuals	Imported Ontologies	Data Sets Covered
NASA SWEET[12] (IBM adaptation)	158.8	90	40	34	63	W3C Time, Geo	[b,c]
IBM Travel Time	4,194	41	49	22	1,429		[a]
IBM SIRI-BUS	41.9	21	17	18	-		[d]
W3C Time[9]	25.2	12	24	17	14	-	[a-g]
W3C Geo[10]	7.8	2	4	-	-	-	[a-g]
DBpedia	Only a subset is used for annotation i.e., 28 concepts, 9 data properties						[e-g]

4.2 Scalability Experimentation and Results

Fig.11 reports the scalability of our approach, noted [L14] and compares its computation time with a state-of-the-art approach [5] in stream prediction. Contrary to our approach, stream correlation is detected at raw data level using (i) statistics-based data analysis and (ii) mathematical properties of the signal (here streams).

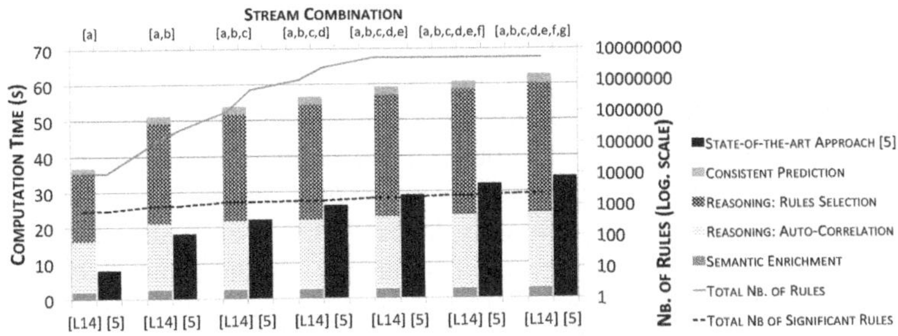

Fig. 11. Scalability of Prediction Computation

[5] scales much better than our approach in all configurations. Our approach requires some non-negligible computation time for reasoning on top of the semantics-enriched stream data. The identification of significant rules is strongly impacted by the number of potential rules, which grows exponentially with the number of elements/entailments in streams (secondary vertical axis). Once all rules are identified, consistent prediction is delivered from $1.5s$ to $2.7s$.

4.3 Accuracy Experimentation and Results

Figure 12 reports the prediction accuracy of both approaches. The accuracy is measured by comparing predictions (severity of congestion) with real-time situations in Dublin City, where results can be easily extracted and compared from the raw and semantic data in respectively [5] and our approach. The more the number of streams the better the accuracy of prediction for both approaches. However our approach reaches a better accuracy when text-related streams [d,e,g] are interpreted while the state-of-the-art approach cannot take any benefit of the semantics of such streams. Overall, our approach obtains a better accuracy, mainly because all the rules are pruned based on the consistency of their consequent. By enforcing their consistency, we ensure that rules are selected based on the surrounding context, here exogenous data streams. The semantic enrichment of data stream is then beneficial for correlating, cross-associating and then predicting streams on a common basis.

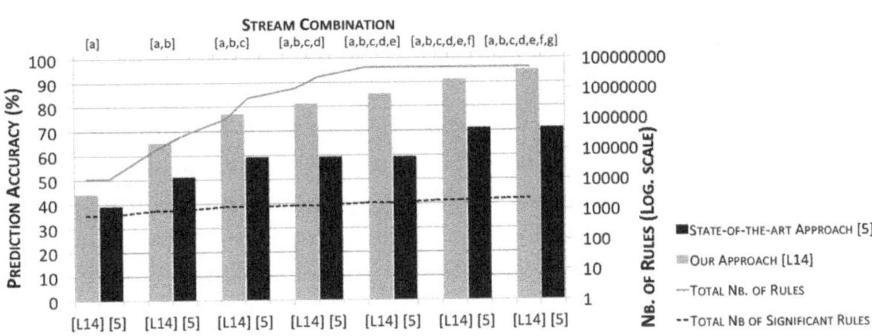

Fig. 12. Accuracy of Prediction

4.4 Lessons Learned

Our experimental results emphasize the advantage of using semantic Web technologies for predicting knowledge in streams i.e., accuracy, but also point out the scalability limitation, especially compared to pure statistical approaches. The more streams the more rules which positively (resp. negatively) impacts accuracy (resp. scalability). Since state-of-the-art approaches fail to encode text-based streams in pure value-based time series, they simply fail to interpret their semantics. On the contrary, our approach interpret their semantics to enrich the prediction model, ensuring better accuracy.

The reasoning mechanisms in Fig.8 are highly coupled with the polynomial-time CEL reasoner for determining subsumption and consistency, which fits OWL 2 EL. Considering more expressive semantics could have triggered stronger rules while reducing its number, hence improving the scalability (to some extent) and accuracy of prediction. It would also be interesting to evaluate the impact of using a subset of OWL 2 EL on the computation performance and the prediction results. Further experiments are required to provide the most appropriate context and trade-off complexity/expressivity.

In the real world, sensors exhibit noise i.e., they do not observe the world perfectly. The causes range from malfunctioning, mis-calibration, to network issues and attrition breakdown. Noisy data needs to be detected early to avoid a useless semantic enrichment, which could raise to more important problems at reasoning time, reaching to completely inaccurate prediction (due to alteration of rules support and confidence). We partially addressed this problem by integrating some *custom filter operators* at stream processing level to check validity of data e.g., data range checking, exceptions. The integration of new data stream needs a careful analysis of historical data in order to identify the most appropriate filters, avoiding as much noise as possible.

Data streams evolve over time, and release new snapshots at various point of time, making the data stream integration complex. We considered the W3C Time ontology to represent the starting date/time and the duration of each snapshot, but other more complex time feature could have been used e.g., temporal intervals. This would support more complex reasoning to reason over time intervals. For scalability reasons we use basic methods to evaluate loose temporal similarity and then integrate data stream at time level. However research challenges, already tackled by [20], would need to be considered for more accurate temporal joints.

5 Conclusion and Future Work

This work, focusing on transportation, presents how severity of road traffic congestions can be predicted. We (i) presented its challenges, (ii) motivated the use of semantic Web technologies, and (iii) exposed its scalability together with its limitation. We illustrated how recent research work in semantic predictive reasoning, using and interpreting semantics of data, can be exploited, adapted and systematized to ensure accurate and consistent prediction. Our prototype of semantics-aware prediction, experimented in Dublin City, works efficiently with real, live and heterogeneous data stream. The experiments have shown accurate and consistent prediction of road traffic conditions, main benefit of the semantic encoding of information.

As emphasized in Section 4.4, handling (i) noisy data stream, (ii) time reasoning, (iii) flexible stream integration are future domains of investigation. More end-users related evaluations are also planned e.g., user interface, interaction scenarios.

References

1. Schrank, D., Eisele, B.: 2012 urban mobility report (2012), `http://goo.gl/Ke2xU`
2. Bando, M., Hasebe, K., Nakayama, A., Shibata, A., Sugiyama, Y.: Dynamical model of traffic congestion and numerical simulation. Physical Review E 51, 1035–1042 (1995)
3. Han, J., Kamber, M.: Data mining: concepts and techniques. Morgan Kaufmann (2006)
4. Wang, H., Fan, W., Yu, P.S., Han, J.: Mining concept-drifting data streams using ensemble classifiers. In: KDD, pp. 226–235 (2003)
5. Papadimitriou, S., Sun, J., Faloutsos, C.: Streaming pattern discovery in multiple time-series. In: VLDB, pp. 697–708 (2005)
6. Schrader, C.C., Kornhauser, A.L., Friese, L.M.: Using historical information in forecasting travel times. Transportation Research Board 51, 1035–1042 (2004)
7. Min, W., Wynter, L.: Real-time road traffic prediction with spatio-temporal correlations. Transportation Research Part C: Emerging Technologies 19(4), 606–616 (2011)
8. Cairns, S., Hass-Klau, C., Goodwin, P.: Traffic impact of highway capacity reductions: Assessment of the evidence. Landor Publishing (1998)
9. Lécué, F., Pan, J.Z.: Predicting knowledge in an ontology stream. In: IJCAI (2013)
10. Lécué, F., Schumann, A., Sbodio, M.L.: Applying semantic web technologies for diagnosing road traffic congestions. In: Cudré-Mauroux, P., et al. (eds.) ISWC 2012, Part II. LNCS, vol. 7650, pp. 114–130. Springer, Heidelberg (2012)
11. Han, L., Finin, T.W., Parr, C.S., Sachs, J., Joshi, A.: RDF123: From spreadsheets to RDF. In: Sheth, A.P., Staab, S., Dean, M., Paolucci, M., Maynard, D., Finin, T., Thirunarayan, K. (eds.) ISWC 2008. LNCS, vol. 5318, pp. 451–466. Springer, Heidelberg (2008)
12. Abel, F., Gao, Q., Houben, G.-J., Tao, K.: Semantic enrichment of twitter posts for user profile construction on the social web. In: Antoniou, G., Grobelnik, M., Simperl, E., Parsia, B., Plexousakis, D., De Leenheer, P., Pan, J. (eds.) ESWC 2011, Part II. LNCS, vol. 6644, pp. 375–389. Springer, Heidelberg (2011)
13. Baader, F., Lutz, C., Suntisrivaraporn, B.: CEL — A polynomial-time reasoner for life science ontologies. In: Furbach, U., Shankar, N. (eds.) IJCAR 2006. LNCS (LNAI), vol. 4130, pp. 287–291. Springer, Heidelberg (2006)
14. Baader, F., Brandt, S., Lutz, C.: Pushing the el envelope. In: IJCAI, pp. 364–369 (2005)
15. Ren, Y., Pan, J.Z.: Optimising ontology stream reasoning with truth maintenance system. In: CIKM, pp. 831–836 (2011)
16. Ma, Y., Tran, T., Bicer, V.: Typifier: Inferring the type semantics of structured data. In: International Conference on Data Engineering (ICDE), pp. 206–217 (2013)
17. Calbimonte, J.-P., Corcho, O., Gray, A.J.G.: Enabling ontology-based access to streaming data sources. In: Patel-Schneider, P.F., Pan, Y., Hitzler, P., Mika, P., Zhang, L., Pan, J.Z., Horrocks, I., Glimm, B. (eds.) ISWC 2010, Part I. LNCS, vol. 6496, pp. 96–111. Springer, Heidelberg (2010)
18. Krötzsch, M., Rudolph, S., Hitzler, P.: Description logic rules. In: ECAI, pp. 80–84 (2008)
19. Agrawal, R., Srikant, R.: Fast algorithms for mining association rules in large databases. In: VLDB, pp. 487–499 (1994)
20. Lutz, C.: Interval-based temporal reasoning with general tboxes. In: IJCAI, pp. 89–96 (2001)

conTEXT – Lightweight Text Analytics Using Linked Data

Ali Khalili[1], Sören Auer[2], and Axel-Cyrille Ngonga Ngomo[1]

[1] AKSW, Institute of Computer Science, University of Leipzig, Leipzig, Germany
{khalili,ngonga}@informatik.uni-leipzig.de
[2] Institute of Computer Science,
University of Bonn and Fraunhofer IAIS, Bonn, Germany
auer@cs.uni-bonn.de

Abstract. The Web democratized publishing – everybody can easily publish information on a Website, Blog, in social networks or microblogging systems. The more the amount of published information grows, the more important are technologies for accessing, analysing, summarising and visualising information. While substantial progress has been made in the last years in each of these areas individually, we argue, that only the intelligent combination of approaches will make this progress truly useful and leverage further synergies between techniques. In this paper we develop a text analytics architecture of participation, which allows ordinary people to use sophisticated NLP techniques for analysing and visualizing their content, be it a Blog, Twitter feed, Website or article collection. The architecture comprises interfaces for information access, natural language processing and visualization. Different exchangeable components can be plugged into this architecture, making it easy to tailor for individual needs. We evaluate the usefulness of our approach by comparing both the effectiveness and efficiency of end users within a task-solving setting. Moreover, we evaluate the usability of our approach using a questionnaire-driven approach. Both evaluations suggest that ordinary Web users are empowered to analyse their data and perform tasks, which were previously out of reach.

Keywords: :#eswc2014Khalili.

1 Introduction

The Web democratized publishing – everybody can easily publish information on a website, blog, in social networks or microblogging systems. The more the amount of published information grows, the more important are technologies for accessing, analysing, summarising and visualizing information. While substantial progress has been made in the last years in each of these areas individually, we argue, that only the intelligent combination of approaches will make this progress truly useful and leverage further synergies between techniques. Natural Language Processing (NLP) technologies, for example, were developed for text analysis, but are often cumbersome and difficult to use for ordinary people and it is even

V. Presutti et al. (Eds.): ESWC 2014, LNCS 8465, pp. 628–643, 2014.

more difficult to make sense of the results produced by these tools. Information visualization techniques, such as data-driven documents [3], on the other hand can provide intuitive visualizations of complex relationships.

We showcase *conTEXT*[1] – a text analytics architecture of participation, which allows end-users to use sophisticated NLP techniques for analysing and visualizing their content, be it a weblog, Twitter feed, website or article collection. The architecture comprises interfaces for information access, natural language processing (currently mainly Named Entity Recognition) and visualization. Different exchangeable components can be plugged into this architecture. Users are empowered to provide manual corrections and feedback on the automatic text processing results, which directly increase the semantic annotation quality and are used as input for attaining further automatic improvements. An online demo of the conTEXT is available at `http://context.aksw.org`.

Motivation. Currently, there seems to be an imbalance on the Web. Hundreds of millions of users continuously share stories about their life on social networking platforms such as *Facebook*, *Twitter* and *Google Plus*. However, the conclusions which can be drawn from analysing the shared content are rarely shared back with the users of these platforms. The social networking platforms on the other hand exploit the results of analysing user-generated content for targeted placement of advertisements, promotions, customer studies etc. One basic principle of data privacy is, that every person should be able to know what personal information is stored about herself in a database (cf. OECD privacy principles[2]). We argue, that this principle does *not* suffice anymore and that there is an *analytical information imbalance*. People should be able to find out what patterns can be discovered and what conclusions can be drawn from the information they share.

Let us look at the case of a typical social network user Judy. When Judy updates her social networking page regularly over years, she should be able to discover what the main topics were she shared with her friends, what places, products or organizations are related to her posts and how these things she wrote about are interrelated. Currently, the social network Judy uses analyses her and other users data in a big data warehouse. Advertisement customers of the social networking platform, can place targeted adds to users being interested in certain topics. Judy, for example, is sneaker aficionado. She likes to wear colorful sports shoes with interesting designs, follows the latest trends and regularly shares her current favorites with her friends on the social network. Increasingly, advertisements for sportswear are placed within her posts. Being able to understand what conclusions can be drawn by analysing her posts will give Judy at least some of the power back into her hands she lost during the last years to Web giants analysing big user data.

conTEXT empowers users to answer a number of questions, which were previously impossible or very tedious to answer. Examples include:

[1] We choose the name conTEXT, since our approach performs analyzes *with* (Latin 'con') text and provides contextual visualizations for discovered entities in text.

[2] `http://oecdprivacy.org/#participation`

- Finding all articles or posts related to a specific person, location or organization.
- Identifying the most frequently mentioned terms, concepts, people, locations or organizations in a corpus.
- Showing the temporal relations between people or events mentioned in the corpus.
- Discovering typical relationships between entities.
- Identifying trending concepts or entities over time.
- Find posts where certain entities or concepts co-occur.

The text analytics architecture and implementation we present in this article helps to mitigate the analytical information imbalance. With almost no effort, users can analyse the information they share and obtain similar insights as social networking sites.

Approach. conTEXT lowers the barrier to text analytics by providing the following key features:

- No installation and configuration required.
- Access content from a variety of sources.
- Instantly show the results of analysis to users in a variety of visualizations.
- Allow refinement of automatic annotations and take feedback into account.
- Provide a generic architecture where different modules for content acquisition, natural language processing and visualization can be plugged together.

Semantic Web and Linked Data is used in conTEXT in particular in the following ways:

- The linked-data aware *Natural Language Interchange format* (NIF) is used for integrating various NLP tools.
- The FOX and Spotlight Linked Data based disambiguation ensures that we work with real-world entities instead of surface forms.
- Linked Data background knowledge is used to enrich the result of the analysis and provide upper-level ontological knowledge for facilitating the exploration.
- Semantic annotations are encoded in RDFa and can be re-integrated back into the original data sources.

The article is structured as follows: We show that conTEXT fills a gap in the space of related approaches in Section 2. The general workflow and interface design is presented in Section 3. The different visualizations and views supported by conTEXT are discussed in Section 4. We show the results of a qualitative and quantitative user evaluation in Section 5 and discuss some more general aspects in Section 6 before we conclude in Section 7.

2 Related Work

Analytics (i.e. the discovery and communication of meaningful patterns in data) is a broad area of research and technology. Involving research ranging from *NLP* and *Machine Learning* to *Semantic Web*, this area has been very vibrant in recent years. Related work in the domain of analytics can be roughly categorized according to the following dimensions:

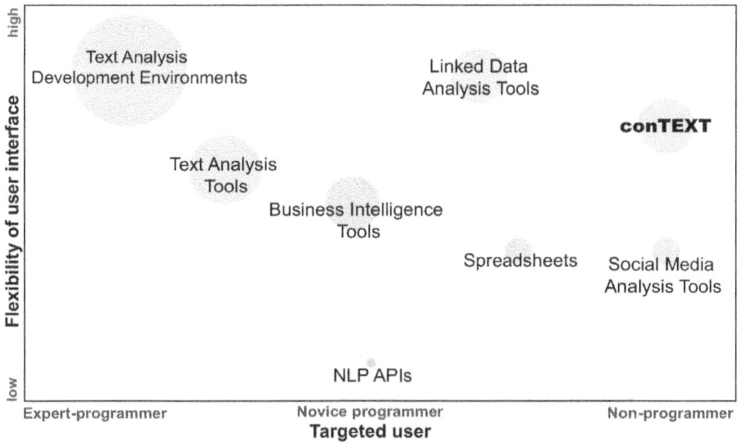

Fig. 1. Flexibility of user interfaces and targeted user groups as well as genericity (circle size) and degree of structure (circle color) for various analytics platforms

- *Degree of structure.* Typically, an analytics system extracts patterns from a certain type of input data. The type of input data can vary between *unstructured* (e.g. text, audio, videos), *semi-structured* (e.g. text formats, shallow XML, CSV) and *structured* data (e.g. databases, RDF, richly structured XML).
- *Flexibility of user interface.* Analytics systems provide different types of interfaces to communicate the found patterns to users. A flexible UI should support techniques for *exploration*, *visualization* as well as even *feedback and refinemment* of the discovered patterns. This dimension also evaluates the *interactivity* of UIs, *diversity* of analytical views as well as the capability to *mix* results.
- *Targeted user.* An analytics system might be used by different types of users including *non-programmer*, *novice-programmer* and *expert-programmer*.
- *Genericity.* This dimension assesses an analytics system in terms of *genericity of architecture* and *scalability*. These features enable reuse of components as well as adding new functionality and data at minimal effort.

Figure 1 provides an abstract view of the state-of-the-art in analytics according to these dimensions.

Text analysis development environments usually provide comprehensive support for developing customized text analytics workflows for extracting, transforming and visualizing data. Typically they provide a high degree of genericity and interface flexibility, but require users to be expert-programmers. Examples include the *IBM Content Analytics platform* [1], *GATE* [4], *Apache UIMA* [7].

Text analysis tools provide a higher level of abstraction (thus catering more novice users) at the cost of genericity. Yang et al. [20] recently published an extensive text analytics survey from the viewpoint of the targeted user and introduced a tool called *WizIE* which enables novice programmers to perform different tasks of text analysis. Examples include *Attensity*[3], *Thomson Data Analyzer*[4] *Trendminer* [19] and *MashMaker* [6].

Business intelligence (BI) tools are applications designed to retrieve, analyse and report mainly highly-structured data for facilitating business decision making. BI tools usually require some form of programming or at least proficiency in query construction and report designing. Examples include *Zoho Reports*[5], *SAP NetWeaver*[6], *Jackbe*[7], and *RapidMiner* [12].

Spreadsheet-based tools are interactive applications for organization and analysis of data in tabular form. They can be used without much programming skills, are relatively generically applicable and provide flexible visualizations. However, spreadsheet-based tools are limited to structured tabular, data and can not be applied to semi-structured or text data. Examples include *Excel*, *DataWrangler* [13], *Google Docs Spreadsheets* and *Google Refine*.

NLP APIs are web services providing natural language processing (e.g. named entity recognition and relation extraction) for analysing web pages and documents. The use of these APIs requires some form of programming and flexible interfaces are usually not provided. Examples include *Alchemy*, *OpenCalais*, *Apache OpenNLP*.[8]

Linked Data analysis tools support the exploration and visualization of Linked Data. Examples include *Facete*[9] for spatial and *CubeViz*[10] for statistical data. Dadzie and Rowe [5] present a comprehensive survey of approaches for visualising and exploring Linked Data. They conclude that most of the tools are designed only for tech-users and do not provide overviews on the data.

Social Media analysis tools such as *SRSR*, *TweetDeck*[11], *Topsy*[12], *Flumes*[13], and *Trendsmap*[14] focus in comparison to conTEXT primarily on the content aggregation across large repositories (e.g. Twitter as a whole) and perform popularity and trend analysis. conTEXT on the other hand aims at providing different exploration and visualization means for more specific types of content exploiting the extracted semantics.

When comparing these different analytics tool categories according to the dimensions genericity, UI flexibility, target users and degree of structure we discovered a lack of tools dealing with unstructured content, catering non-expert

[3] http://www.attensity.com
[4] http://thomsonreuters.com/thomson-data-analyzer/
[5] http://www.zoho.com/reports/
[6] http://sap.com/netweaver
[7] http://jackbe.com/
[8] A complete list of NLP APIs is available at http://nerd.eurecom.fr/
[9] http://aksw.org/Projects/Facete
[10] http://aksw.org/Projects/CubeViz
[11] http://tweetdeck.com/
[12] http://topsy.com/
[13] http://www.flumes.com/
[14] http://trendsmap.com/

users and providing flexible analytics interfaces. The aim of developing the text analytics tool conTEXT is to fill this gap.

3 Workflow and Interface Design

Workflow. Figure 2 shows the process of text analytics in conTEXT. The process starts by collecting information from the web or social web. conTEXT utilizes standard information access methods and protocols such as RSS/ATOM feeds, SPARQL endpoints and REST APIs as well as customized crawlers for SlideWiki, WordPress, Blogger and Twitter to build a corpus of information relevant for a certain user.

The assembled text corpus is then processed by NLP services. While conTEXT can integrate virtually any NLP services, it currently implements interfaces for *DBpedia Spotlight* [17] and the *Federated knOwledge eXtraction Framework* (FOX) [18] for discovering and annotating named entities in the text. DBpedia Spotlight annotates mentions of *DBpedia* resources in text thereby links unstructured information sources to the Linked Open Data cloud through DBpedia. FOX is a knowledge extraction framework that utilizes a variety of different NLP algorithms to extract RDF triples of high accuracy from text. Unlike DBpedia Spotlight, which supports all the DBpedia resource types, FOX is limited to `Person`, `Location` and `Organization` types. On the other hand, since FOX uses ensemble learning to merge different NLP algorithms, leads to a higher precision and recall (see [18] for details).

The processed corpus is then further enriched by two mechanisms:

- DBpedia URIs of the found entities are de-referenced in order to add more specific information to the discovered named entities (e.g. longitude and latitudes for locations, birth and death dates for people etc.).
- Entity co-occurrences are matched with pre-defined natural-language patterns for DBpedia predicates provided by *BOA* (BOotstrapping linked datA) [8] in order to extract possible relationships between the entities.

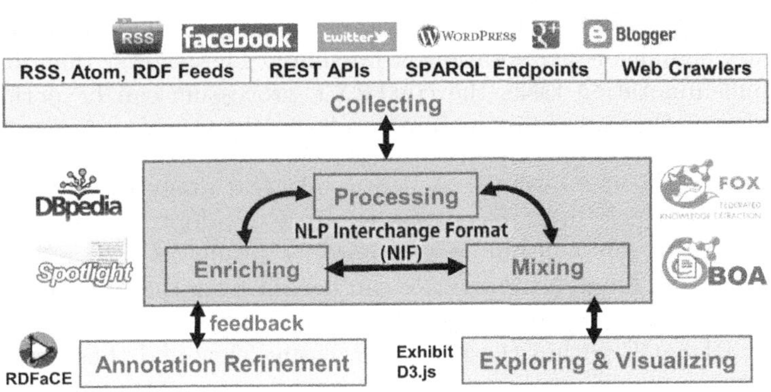

Fig. 2. Text analytics workflow in conTEXT

The processed data can also be joined with other existing corpora in a *text analytics mashup*. Such a mashup of different annotated corpora combines information from more than one corpus in order to provide users an integrated view. Analytics mashups help to provide more context for the text corpus under analysis and also enable users to mix diverse text corpora for performing a comparative analysis. For example, a user's Wordpress blog corpus can be integrated with corpora obtained from her Twitter and Facebook accounts. The creation of analytics mashups requires dealing with the heterogeneity of different corpora as well as the heterogeneity of different NLP services utilized for annotation. conTEXT employs *NIF* (NLP Interchange Format) [10] to deal with this heterogeneity. The use of NIF allows us to quickly integrate additional NLP services into conTEXT.

The processed, enriched and possibly mixed results are presented to users using different views for exploration and visualization of the data. *Exhibit* [11][15] (structured data publishing) and *D3.js* [3][16] (data-driven documents) are employed for realizing a dynamic exploration and visualization experience. Additionally, conTEXT provides an annotation refinement user interface based on the *RDFa Content Editor* (RDFaCE) [15] to enable users to revise the annotated results. User-refined annotations are sent back to the NLP services as feedback for the purpose of learning in the system.

Progressive crawling and annotation. The process of collecting and annotating a large text corpus can be time-consuming. Therefore it is very important to provide users with immediate results and inform them about the progress of the crawling and annotation task. For this purpose, we have designed special user interface elements to keep users informed until the complete results are available. The first indicator interface is an animated progress bar which shows the percentage of the collected/annotated results as well as the currently downloaded and processed item (e.g. the title of the blog post). The second indicator interface is a real-time tag cloud which is updated while the annotation is in progress. We logged all crawling and processing timings during our evaluation period. Based on these records, the processing of a Twitter feed with 300 tweets takes on average 30 seconds and the processing of 100 blog posts approx. 3-4 minutes on standard server with i7 Intel CPU (with parallelization and hardware optimizations further significant acceleration is possible). This shows, that for typical crawling and annotation tasks the conTEXT processing can be performed in almost real-time thus providing instant results to the users.

Annotation refinement interfaces. A lightweight text analytics as implemented by conTEXT provides direct incentives to users to adopt and revise semantic text annotations. Users will obtain more precise results as they refine annotations. On the other hand, NLP services can benefit from these manually-revised annotations to learn the right annotations. conTEXT employs the RDFa Content Editor RDFaCE within the faceted browsing view and thus enables users

[15] `http://simile-widgets.org/exhibit3/`
[16] `http://d3js.org/`

Table 1. NLP Feedback parameters

Parameter	Description
text	annotated text.
entityUri	the identifier of the annotated entity.
surfaceForm	the name of the annotated entity.
offset	position of the first letter of the entity.
feedback	indicates whether the annotation is correct or incorrect.
context	indicates the context of the annotated corpus.
isManual	indicates whether the feedback is sent by user or by other NLP services.
senderIDs	identifier(s) of the feedback sender.

to edit existing annotations while browsing the data. The WYSIWYM (What-You-See-Is-What-You-Mean) interface [14] provided by RDFaCE enables integrated visualization and authoring of unstructured and semantic content (i.e. annotations encoded in RDFa). The manual annotations are collected and sent as feedback to the corresponding NLP service. The feedback encompasses the parameters specified in Table 1.

Exploration and visualization interfaces. The dynamic exploration of content indexed by the annotated entities facilitates faster and easier comprehension of the content and provide new insights. conTEXT creates a novel entity-based search and browsing interface for end-users to review and explore their content. On the other hand, conTEXT provides different visualization interfaces which present, transform, and convert semantically enriched data into a visual representation, so that, users can explore and query the data efficiently. Visualization UIs are supported by noise-removal algorithms which will tune the results for better representation and will highlight the picks and trends in the visualizations. For example, we use a frequency threshold when displaying single resources in interfaces. In addition, a threshold based on the Dice similarity is used in interfaces which display co-occurrences. By these means, we ensure that the information overload is reduced and that information shown to the user is the most relevant. Note that the user can chose to deactivate or alter any of these thresholds.

Linked Data interface for search engine optimization (SEO). The `Schema.org` initiative provides a collection of shared schemas that Web authors can use to markup their content in order to enable enhanced search and browsing features offered by major search engines. *RDFa*, *Microdata* and *JSON-LD* are currently approved formats to markup web documents based on Schema.org. There are already tools like *Google Structured Data Markup Helper*[17] which help users to generate and embed such markup into their web content. A direct feature of the Linked Data based text analytics with conTEXT is the provisioning of a *SEO* interface. conTEXT encodes the results of the content annotation (automatic

[17] `https://www.google.com/webmasters/markup-helper/`

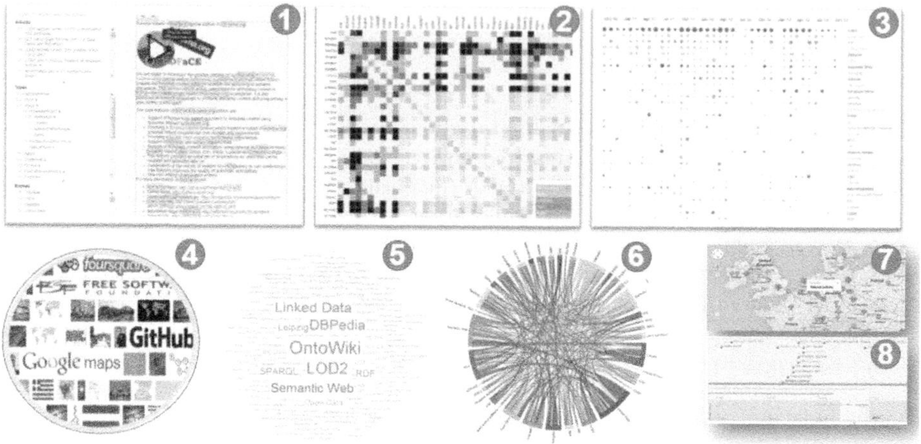

Fig. 3. Different views for exploration and visualization of an analysed corpus: 1) faceted browser, 2) matrix view, 3) trend view, 4) image view, 5) tag cloud, 6) chordal graph view, 7) map view, 8) timeline.

and revisions by the user) in the *JSON-LD*[18] format which can be directly exposed to schema.org aware search engines. This component employs the current mapping from the DBpedia ontology to the Schema.org vocabularies[19]. Thus the conTEXT SEO interface enables end-users to benefit from better exposure in search engines (e.g. through Google's *Rich Text Snippets*) with very little effort.

4 Views

A key aspect of conTEXT is to provide intuitive exploration and visualization options for the annotated corpora. For that purpose, conTEXT allows to plugin a variety of different exploration and visualization modules, which operate on the conTEXT data model capturing the annotated corpora. By default, conTEXT provides the following views for exploring and visualizing the annotated corpora:

- *Faceted browsing* allows users to quickly and efficiently explore the corpus along multiple dimensions (i.e. articles, entity types, temporal data) using the DBpedia ontology. The faceted view enables users to drill a large set of articles down to a set adhering to certain constraints.
- *Matrix view* shows the entity co-occurrence matrix. Each cell in the matrix reflects the entity co-occurrence by entity types (color of the cell) and by the frequency of co-occurrence (color intensity).
- *Trend view* shows the occurrence frequency of entities in the corpus over the times. The trend view requires a corpus with articles having a timestamp (such as blogposts or tweets).

[18] JSON for Linked Data `http://json-ld.org/`

[19] `http://schema.org/mappings.html`

- *Image view* shows a picture collage created from the entities Wikipedia images. This is an alternative for tag cloud which reflects the frequent entities in the corpora by using different image sizes.
- *Tag cloud* shows entities found in the corpus in different sizes depending on their prevalence. The tag cloud helps to quickly identify the most prominent entities in the corpora.
- *Chordal graph view* shows the relationships among the different entities in a corpus. The relationships are extracted based on the co-occurrence of the entities and their matching to a set of predefined natural language patterns.
- *Places map* shows the locations and the corresponding articles in the corpus. This view allows users to quickly identify the spatial distribution of locations refereed to in the corpus.
- *People timeline* shows the temporal relations between people mentioned in the corpus. For that purpose, references to people found in the corpus are enriched with birth and death days found in DBpedia.

Modularity and extensibility is not only limited to views in conTEXT. For example, additional NLP APIs and data collection interfaces can be registered as well.

5 Evaluation

The goal of our evaluation was two-fold. First, we wanted to provide quantitative insights in the usefulness of conTEXT. To this end, we carried out a task-driven usefulness study where we measured the improvement in efficiency and effectiveness that results from using conTEXT. Second, we aim to evaluate the usability of our approach.

5.1 Usefulness Study

Experimental Setup. To achieve the first goal of our evaluation, we carried out controlled experiments with **25** users (20 PhD students having different backgrounds from computer software to life sciences, 2 MSc students and 3 BSc students with good command of English) on a set of 10 questions pertaining to knowledge discovery in corpora of unstructured data. For example, we asked users the following question: "What are the five most mentioned countries by Bill Gates tweets?". The 10 questions were determined as follows: We collected a set of 61 questions from 12 researchers of the University of Leipzig. These questions were regarded as a corpus and analysed using conTEXT. After removing questions that were quasi-duplicates manually, we chose 10 questions that we subdivided into 2 sets of 5 questions. Each of users involved in the evaluation was then asked to solve one set of questions with conTEXT and the other one without the tool. In all cases, the users were given access to the corpus from which the question was extracted. While answering the questions with conTEXT, the users used the analysis abilities of conTEXT. Else, they were allowed to use all digital search media of their choice except conTEXT. To ensure that we did not introduce any bias in the results due to distribution of hard questions across the two sets, one half of the users was asked to solve the first set of questions with conTEXT while the others did the same with the second set and vice-versa. We evaluated the users' efficiency by measuring the time that they required to answer the questions. Note that the users were asked to terminate any task that required more than 5 minutes to solve. In addition, we measured the users' effectiveness by comparing the answers of each user to a gold standard which was created manually by the authors. Given that the answers to the questions were sets, we measured the similarity of the answers A provided by the each user and the gold standard G by using the *Jaccard* similarity of the two sets, i.e., $\frac{|A \cap G|}{|A \cup G|}$. The platform[20] provided users with a short tutorial on how to perform the tasks using conTEXT and how to add their responses for the questions.

Results. The results of our first series of evaluations are shown in Figures 4 and 5. On average, the users required 136.4% more time without conTEXT than when using the tool. A fine-grained inspection of the results suggests that our approach clearly enables users to perform tasks akin to the ones provided in the evaluation in less time. Especially complex tasks such as "Name a middle-eastern country that has never been spoken of in the AKSW blog" are carried out more than three times faster using conTEXT. In some cases, conTEXT even enables users to carry out tasks that seemed out of reach before. For example, the question "What are the five most mentioned countries by Bill Gates' tweets?" (Q10) was deemed impossible to answer in reasonable time by using normal search tools by several users. A look at the effectiveness results suggests that those users who tried to carry out these task without conTEXT failed as they achieve an average Jaccard score of 0.17 on this particular task while users relying on conTEXT achieve 0.65. The overall Jaccard score with conTEXT lies around 0.57, which suggests that the tasks in our evaluation were non-trivial. This is confirmed by the overall score of 0.19 without conTEXT. Interestingly, the average effectiveness results achieve by users with conTEXT are always superior to those achieved without conTEXT, especially on task Q8, where users without conTEXT never found the right answer. Moreover, in all cases, the users are more time-efficient when using conTEXT than without the tool.

5.2 Usability Study

Experimental Setup. The goal of the second part of our evaluation was to assess the usability of conTEXT. To achieve this objective, we used the standardized, ten-item Likert scale-based *System Usability Scale* (SUS) [16] questionnaire and asked each person who partook in our usefulness evaluation to partake in the usability evaluation. The questions were part of a Google questionnaire and can be found at `http://goo.gl/JKzgdK`.

[20] available at `http://context.aksw.org/app/evaluation`

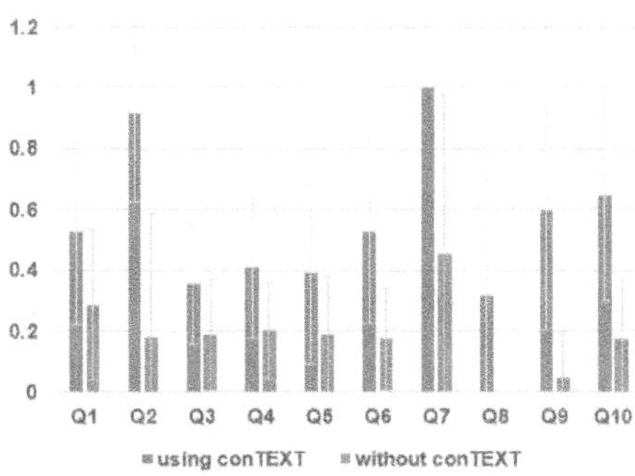

Fig. 4. Avg. Jaccard similarity index for answers using & without the conTEXT

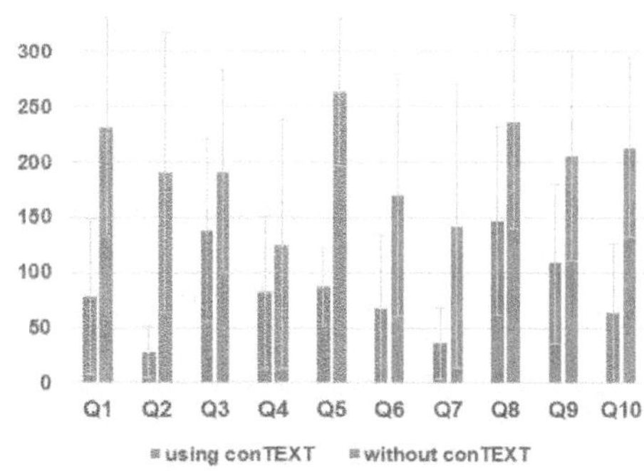

Fig. 5. Avg. time spent (in second) for finding answers using & without the conTEXT

Results. The results of our study (cf. Figure 6) showed a mean usability score of **82** indicating a high level of usability according to the SUS score. The responses to question 1 suggests that our system is adequate for frequent use (average score to question 1 = 4.23 ± 0.83) by users all of type (4.29 ± 0.68 average score for question 7). While a small fraction of the functionality is deemed unnecessary by some users (average score of 1.7± 0.92 to question 2, 1.88±1.05 to question 6 and 1.76±1.09 to question 8), the users deem the system easy to use (average score of 4.3± 0.59 to question 3). Only one user suggested that he/she would need a

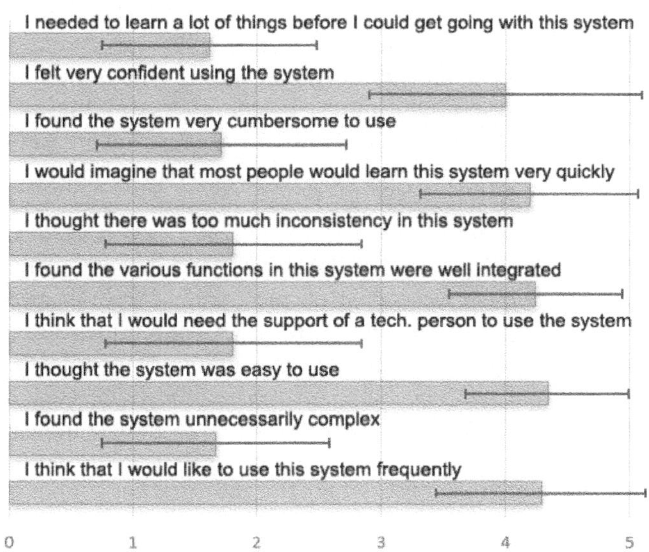

Fig. 6. Result of usability evaluation using SUS questionnaire

technical person to use the system, while all other users were fine without one. The modules of the system in itself were deemed to be well integrated (4.23 ± 0.66 average score to question 5). Overall, the output of the system seems to be easy to understand (4.11 ± 1.05 score to question 9) while users even without training assume themselves capable of using the system (1.52 ± 0.72 to question 10). These results corroborate the results of the first part of our evaluation as they suggest that conTEXT is not only easy to use but provides also useful functionality.

6 Discussion

The incentive for each author to use conTEXT is the ease of analysing unstructured and semi-structured data and the resulting sophisticated user interfaces. While this motivation is personal and the immediately perceptible benefit is local, there are far reaching effects as a result of the semantically annotated information being entirely publicly accessible in structured form. We now discuss how conTEXT, by design, is helping to democratize the use of NLP technology, helps alleviating the Semantic Web's chicken-and-egg problem and harnesses the power of feedback loops.

Democratizing the NLP usage. With conTEXT natural language processing technology is made more accessible, so that sophisticated text analytics can be used with just a few clicks by ordinary users. This was achieved by abstracting from a particular technology (e.g. by using the NIF format) and by supporting a) typical input formats for corpus generation (such as social networking feeds) and b) sophisticated visualizations employing the data-driven document metaphor. As a result, ordinary users can observe the power of natural language processing and semantic technologies with minimal effort. By directly showing the effect of semantic annotations and demonstrating the benefits for improved navigation, exploration and search, users will gain a better understanding of recent technology advances. On the other hand, users will regain control and command of their information, since they are empowered to perform similar analyses as major social and advertising networks do. If users discover using conTEXT, that the patterns of their communication habits do not correspond to what they would like others to observe, they can delete certain information and alter their blogging habits (e.g. publish more post on professional than leisure activities).

In addition to gaining insights into their own communication habits, users can also more easily discover communication habits of people in charge (e.g. politicians) or do quicker fact checking. Answering questions, such as 'What has Angela Merkel said about the Syria conflict?' or 'What are commercial property development areas discussed in the last two years by the city council?' become dramatically easier to answer, even when the information source is a large unstructured text corpus.

Alleviating the Semantic Web's chicken-and-egg problem. Recently we could observe a significant increase of the amount of structured data publishing on the Web. However, this increase can be attributed primarily to article metadata being made available and already to a much lesser extend to just a few entity types (people, organizations, products) being prevalent [2]. As a consequence, we still face the chicken-and-egg problem to truly realize the vision of a Web, where large parts of the information are available in structured formats and semantically annotated. Before no substantial amount of content is available in semantic representations, search engines will not pick up this information and without better search capabilities publishers are not inclined to make additional effort to provide semantic annotations for their content. The latter is particularly true for unstructured and semi-structured content, which is much more difficult to annotate than structured content from relational databases (where merely some templates have to be adopted in order to provide e.g. RDFa).

conTEXT can help to overcome this problem, since it provides instant benefits to users for creating comprehensive semantic annotations. The result of an annotation with conTEXT can easily be exported, re-integrated or published along the original content. Also, we plan to provide conTEXT as a service, where a user's content is continuously ingested and processed, the user is informed about updates and thus the semantic representations of the content evolve along with the content itself.

Harnessing the power of feedback loops. Thomas Goetz states in his influential WIRED Magazin article [9]: 'Provide people with information about their actions in real time, then give them a chance to change those actions, pushing them toward better behaviors.' With conTEXT, we want to give users direct feedback on what information can be extracted from their works. At the same time we want to incorporate their feedback and revisions of the semantic annotations back in the NLP processing loop. Incorporating user feedback was so far not much in the focus of the NLP community. With conTEXT, we aim to contribute to changing this. We argue, that NLP technology achieving, for example, 90% precision, recall or f-measure, might not fulfill the requirements of a number of potential use cases. When we can increase the quality of the NLP through user feedback, we might be able to substantially extend the range of potential NLP applications. The user feedback here serves two purposes: One the one hand, it directly increases the quality of the semantic annotation. On the other hand, it can serve as input for active learning techniques, which can further boost precision and recall of the semantic annotation.

7 Conclusion

With conTEXT, we showcased an innovative text analytics application for end-users, which integrates a number of previously disconnected technologies. In this way, conTEXT is making NLP technologies more accessible, so they can be easily and beneficially used by arbitrary end-users. conTEXT provides instant benefits for annotation and empowers users to gain novel insights and complete tasks, which previously required substantial development.

In future, we plan extend work on conTEXT along several directions. We aim to investigate, how user feedback can be used across different corpora. We consider the harnessing of user feedback by NLP services an area with great potential to attain further boosts in annotation quality. On a related angle, we plan to integrate revisioning functionality, where users can manipulate complete sets of semantic annotations instead of just individual ones. In that regard, we envision that conTEXT can assume a similar position for text corpora as have data cleansing tools such as OpenRefine for structure data. Finally, we aim to extend conTEXT with REST interfaces to ease its integration into other applications such as content management systems.

References

1. Solution brief: Ibm content analytics with enterprise search, version 3.0, `http://www-03.ibm.com/software/products/us/en/contentanalyticssearch`
2. Bizer, C., Eckert, K., Meusel, R., Mühleisen, H., Schuhmacher, M., Völker, J.: Deployment of rDFa, microdata, and microformats on the web – A quantitative analysis. In: Alani, H., et al. (eds.) ISWC 2013, Part II. LNCS, vol. 8219, pp. 17–32. Springer, Heidelberg (2013)
3. Bostock, M., Ogievetsky, V., Heer, J.: D3 data-driven documents. IEEE Transactions on Visualization and Computer Graphics 17(12), 2301–2309 (2011)
4. Cunningham, H., Maynard, D., Bontcheva, K., Tablan, V., Aswani, N., Roberts, I., Gorrell, G., Funk, A., Roberts, A., Damljanovic, D., Heitz, T., Greenwood, M.A., Saggion, H., Petrak, J., Li, Y., Peters, W.: Text Processing with GATE (Version 6) (2011), `http://tinyurl.com/gatebook`
5. Dadzie, A.S., Rowe, M.: Approaches to visualising linked data. Semantic Web 2(2), 89–124 (2011)
6. Ennals, R., Brewer, E.A., Garofalakis, M.N., Shadle, M., Gandhi, P.: Intel mash maker: join the web. SIGMOD Record 36(4), 27–33 (2007)
7. Ferrucci, D., Lally, A.: Uima: an architectural approach to unstructured information processing in the corporate research environment. Nat. Lang. Eng. 10(3-4), 327–348 (2004), `http://dx.doi.org/10.1017/S1351324904003523`
8. Gerber, D., Ngonga Ngomo, A.C.: Bootstrapping the linked data web. In: 1st Workshop on Web Scale Knowledge Extraction @ ISWC 2011 (2011)
9. Goetz, T.: Harnessing the power of feedback loops. WIRED Magazine (2011), `http://www.wired.com/magazine/2011/06/ff_feedbackloop/`
10. Hellmann, S., Lehmann, J., Auer, S., Brümmer, M.: Integrating NLP using linked data. In: Alani, H., et al. (eds.) ISWC 2013, Part II. LNCS, vol. 8219, pp. 98–113. Springer, Heidelberg (2013)
11. Huynh, D.F., Karger, D.R., Miller, R.C.: Exhibit: lightweight structured data publishing. In: WWW 2007, pp. 737–746. ACM, New York (2007)
12. Jungermann, F.: Information Extraction with RapidMiner, `http://citeseerx.ist.psu.edu/viewdoc/summary?doi=10.1.1.151.5586`
13. Kandel, S., Paepcke, A., Hellerstein, J., Heer, J.: Wrangler: interactive visual specification of data transformation scripts. In: Proceedings of the SIGCHI Conference on Human Factors in Computing Systems, CHI 2011, pp. 3363–3372. ACM (2011)
14. Khalili, A., Auer, S.: Wysiwym authoring of structured content based on schema.org. In: Lin, X., Manolopoulos, Y., Srivastava, D., Huang, G. (eds.) WISE 2013, Part II. LNCS, vol. 8181, pp. 425–438. Springer, Heidelberg (2013)

15. Khalili, A., Auer, S., Hladky, D.: The rdfa content editor. In: IEEE COMPSAC 2012, pp. 531–540. IEEE Computer Society (2012)
16. Lewis, J., Sauro, J.: The Factor Structure of the System Usability Scale. In: Kurosu, M. (ed.) HCD 2009. LNCS, vol. 5619, pp. 94–103. Springer, Heidelberg (2009)
17. Mendes, P.N., Jakob, M., García-Silva, A., Bizer, C.: Dbpedia spotlight: shedding light on the web of documents. In: Proceedings of the 7th International Conference on Semantic Systems, I-Semantics 2011, pp. 1–8. ACM, New York (2011)
18. Ngonga Ngomo, A.-C., Heino, N., Lyko, K., Speck, R., Kaltenböck, M.: SCMS – semantifying content management systems. In: Aroyo, L., Welty, C., Alani, H., Taylor, J., Bernstein, A., Kagal, L., Noy, N., Blomqvist, E. (eds.) ISWC 2011, Part II. LNCS, vol. 7032, pp. 189–204. Springer, Heidelberg (2011)
19. Preotiuc-Pietro, D., Samangooei, S., Cohn, T., Gibbins, N., Niranjan, M.: Trendminer: an architecture for real time analysis of social media text (June 2012)
20. Yang, H., Pupons-Wickham, D., Chiticariu, L., Li, Y., Nguyen, B., Carreno-Fuentes, A.: I can do text analytics!: designing development tools for novice developers. In: CHI 2013, pp. 1599–1608. ACM, New York (2013)

PCS2OWL: A Generic Approach for Deriving Web Ontologies from Product Classification Systems

Alex Stolz[1], Bene Rodriguez-Castro[2], Andreas Radinger[1], and Martin Hepp[1]

[1] Universitaet der Bundeswehr Munich, 85579 Neubiberg, Germany
{alex.stolz,andreas.radinger,martin.hepp}@ebusiness-unibw.org
[2] Technical University Munich, 81675 Munich, Germany
bene.rodriguez@tum.de

Abstract. The classification of products and services enables reliable and efficient electronic exchanges of product data across organizations. Many companies classify products (a) according to generic or industry-specific product classification standards, or (b) by using proprietary category systems. Such classification systems often contain thousands of product classes that are updated over time. This implies a large quantity of useful product category information for e-commerce applications on the Web of Data. Thus, instead of building up product ontologies from scratch, which is costly, tedious, error-prone, and high-maintenance, it is generally easier to derive them from existing classifications. In this paper, we (1) describe a generic, semi-automated method for deriving OWL ontologies from product classification standards and proprietary category systems. Moreover, we (2) show that our approach generates logically and semantically correct vocabularies, and (3) present the practical benefit of our approach. The resulting product ontologies are compatible with the GoodRelations vocabulary for e-commerce and with schema.org and can be used to enrich product and offer descriptions on the Semantic Web with granular product type information from existing data sources.

Keywords: #eswc2014Stolz.

1 Introduction

The classification of products and services plays a crucial role for many businesses and business applications [1]. It enables reliable and efficient electronic transactions on product data across organizations in a dynamic domain, characterized by innovation and a high degree of product specificity. Product classes generally allow for intelligent decision-making and operations over aggregated data. More specifically, the ability to operate on groups of products is generally superior to applying heuristics on unstructured product descriptions, especially at tasks for generalizing or discerning products. For instance, a search for a personal computer relying on textual matches not only returns personal computers but likely also related accessories or books that discuss the topic *personal*

V. Presutti et al. (Eds.): ESWC 2014, LNCS 8465, pp. 644–658, 2014.

computers. Class membership information helps to reliably distinguish between personal computers and related, but not necessarily relevant, products. Moreover, it adds a mechanism to query for all existing personal computers, which otherwise, with heuristics, is difficult and expensive.

In practice, organizations often arrange products and services according to product classification systems. At the same time, the number of quality, practically relevant product ontologies on the Web is still limited [2], because most ontology engineering work is done in the context of academic research projects where efforts rarely go beyond *toy* status. Thus, a cost-efficient solution able to accommodate business needs on the Web of Data would be greatly appreciated.

Product classification systems are suitable candidates for creating high-quality and low-cost product ontologies for the Web [3]. In many fields of e-commerce for example, where a domain is typically composed of thousands of classes and properties, it is difficult to engineer domain ontologies manually, because that would imply to get hold of a large number of concepts. Moreover, the conceptual dynamics [2] underlying the domain of products and services, determined by a continuous innovation progress and the high degree of specificity, make the manual creation of product ontologies even more problematic. Let us exemplify the situation by comparing the release sizes [4] of different versions of eCl@ss [5], a comprehensive industry standard for the classification and description of products and services: eCl@ss 5.1.4 had defined 30,329 classes in 2007, whereas eCl@ss 6.1, only announced two years later, was already counting 32,795 classes. The changes become even more evident for eCl@ss 6.1 and eCl@ss 8.0 BASIC with an increase of 20%, reaching 39,041 concepts within only three years. Thus, instead of engineering new ontologies, it is often more practical to derive product ontologies from works already in place, i.e. to reuse existing industrial taxonomies, as argued in [3]. This has several benefits: (1) the product classifications provide a comprehensive coverage of the conceptual domains, and that often in multiple languages; (2) there is no significant overhead involved for maintaining derived product ontologies; on the contrary, they are automatically kept up-to-date with amendments to the classifications conducted by domain experts in response to changes in the real-world; (3) existing industrial standards are popular and thus already in wide use to classify product instance data. In other words, a large amount of products in relational databases are already classified according to product categorization standards. Also numerous Web shops create and maintain proprietary category systems together with their product catalogs. Hence, instead of manually crafting complex domain ontologies and thereby in a sense reinventing the wheel, it is often sensible to unlock the potential of existing, well-maintained hierarchical structures and classify products on the Semantic Web according to them.

In this paper, we present a generic approach and a fully-fledged, modular, and largely automated tool for deriving Web ontologies from product classification systems. We show that our approach generates logically and semantically correct ontologies that (1) establish canonical URIs for every conceptual element in the original schema; (2) preserve the taxonomic structure of the original classification while making its categories usable in multiple contexts; (3) comply with the GoodRelations vocabulary for e-commerce [6] and schema.org; and (4) can be readily deployed on the Web of Data. The results of our transformation unlocks additional semantics that enable novel Web applications. Thanks to the enrichment of product master data and a more granular description of offers by virtue of product ontologies, search engines and other consumers of structured data, can take advantage of product type information for product search, comparison and matchmaking.

2 Product Classification Systems

For the scope of this research, we distinguish two groups of classification schemes relevant to the domain of commercial products and services. These are *product classification standards* and *proprietary product category systems* (or structures). We use the broader term *product classification system* (or PCS for short) to refer to any artifact from any of the two groups. The main aspects of both groups are discussed in this section. Additionally, there is further relevant information that cannot be included here due to space limitations, but is available online[1]. This supplementary material gathers a series of key attributes for every classification system comprising version, organization(s) authoring and managing the classification, available data sources, official report, target usage domain, intended regional use, and level of multilingual support.

2.1 Product Classification Standards

Product classification standards (or product categorization standards) are widely accepted knowledge structures often consisting of thousands of categories. They typically comprise: (a) hierarchical structures for the aggregation of products, which allow for example spend analysis or reasoning over hierarchical relations; (b) common features and values related to product categories; and (c) multilingual descriptions of the elements that conform the standard.

The product classification standards that we considered at the time of this research are: Classification of Products by Activity (CPA) [7], Central Product Classification (CPC) [8], Common Procurement Vocabulary (CPV) [9], eCl@ss [5], *ElektroTechnisches InformationsModell*[2] (ETIM) [10], FreeClass [11], Global Product Classification (GPC) [12], proficl@ss [13], and *Klassifikation der Wirtschaftszweige*[3] (WZ) [14]. The featured standards are grounded on industry consensus and exist for various business fields, be it horizontal or vertical industries. eCl@ss, proficl@ss, and GPC, for example, describe a wide range of products from multiple industrial sectors. By contrast, CPV is intended for the procurement domain, whereas ETIM is focused on the field of electronics. Two standards, CPA and WZ, put forward classifications of comprehensive economic

[1] `http://www.ebusiness-unibw.org/ontologies/pcs2owl/`
[2] Engl.: ElectroTechnical Information Model.
[3] Engl.: Classification of Economic Activities.

activities instead of products *per se*. Nonetheless, commercial products can be classified against them and their use is common among governmental publishers of statistical data. To solve potential ambiguity problems of product names, standards such as eCl@ss, ETIM, and proficl@ss, include synonyms to provide discriminatory features [15] and to retain higher recall in product search scenarios. Furthermore, many standards (CPA, CPV, FreeClass, and WZ) contain translations into various languages.

2.2 Proprietary Product Category Systems

Proprietary product category systems (or catalog group systems, category structures) are also suited for organizing products and services. Unlike product classification standards, catalog group systems are generally characterized by less community agreement. Single organizations or small interest groups instead of communities or standardization bodies are taking the lead for the development of such category structures. Thus, they are accepted only by a relatively small number of stakeholders, and their usage is limited to a narrow context, e.g. to represent a navigation structure in a Web shop. Some examples of catalog group hierarchies considered in the context of this paper are proprietary product taxonomies like the Google product taxonomy [16] and the productpilot category system [17] (the proprietary category structure of a subsidiary of Messe Frankfurt), as well as product categories transmitted via catalog exchange formats like BMEcat[4] [18]. The latter can take advantage of both product categorization standards and catalog group structures in order to organize types of products and services and to contribute additional granularity in terms of semantic descriptions [19].

3 Deriving Product Ontologies from Hierarchical Systems

In this section, we present a generic, semi-automated approach to turn standards and proprietary product classification systems (PCS) into respective product ontologies. Subsequently we outline the conceptual architecture of our proposal, followed by a description of the conceptual transformation.

3.1 Conceptual Architecture

Fig. 1 depicts the conceptual approach of PCS2OWL[5]. The tool consists of a modular architecture that builds upon three layers, namely *parser*, *transformation* process, and *serializer*. It only requires a moderate amount of initial human labor, mainly to prepare the import modules (parsers) for the respective classification systems, as indicated by the dashed rectangle in Fig. 1. This task includes

[4] Developed by *Bundesverband Materialwirtschaft, Einkauf und Logistik (BME)*, Engl.: Federal Association of Materials Management, Purchasing and Logistics.

[5] Short for "product classification systems to OWL", available online at `http://wiki.goodrelations-vocabulary.org/Tools/PCS2OWL`

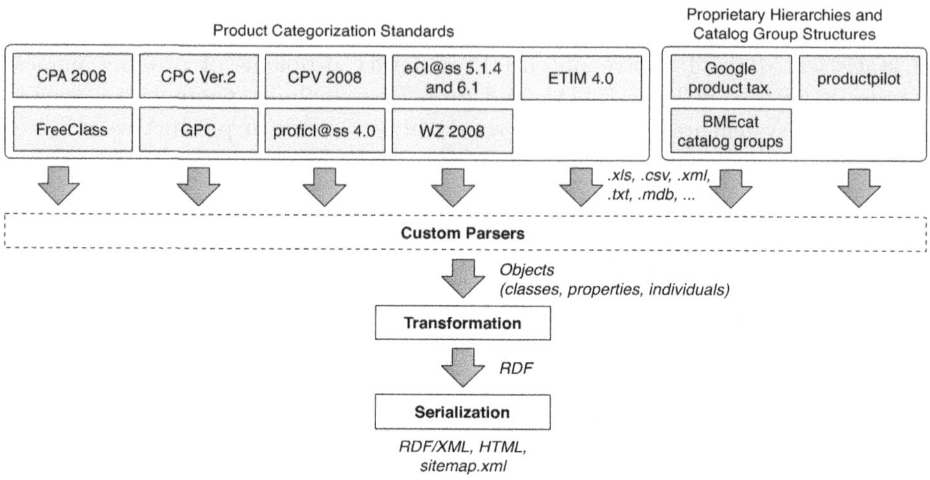

Fig. 1. Conceptual architecture of PCS2OWL

the logic for mapping the taxonomy and setting up the discerning capabilities of property types. The parsers' purpose is to load categories, features, and values of product classification systems into an internal model, which specifies ontology classes, properties, and individuals. The transformation and serialization processes are then fully automated. In the transformation step, the internal model, consisting of entities for classes, properties, and individuals, is turned into an RDF model that describes the final ontology. At this stage, also the logical rules from the parsers are applied to the internal model. Finally, the RDF model is serialized as RDF/XML, and all other files required for the on-line deployment of the product ontologies are created accordingly.

In the context of this paper, we developed custom parsers for a number of popular categorization standards and proprietary taxonomies for products and services, previously introduced in Section 2 and outlined in Fig. 1. Since the parsers have to be hand-crafted, the input formats of the source files of the classification systems do not matter much. For our conversions e.g., we had to deal with Excel spreadsheets (.xls), comma-separated value files (.csv), extensible markup language files (.xml), database tables (.mdb), and plain text files (.txt).

The effort required to develop a parser module is negligible compared to hand-crafting a product ontology from scratch. For simple classification systems with only classes and no properties such as GPC or Google, we extended the empty parser template with only twenty lines of custom code. Even the most complex parser module that we have created so far (FreeClass) required less than 200 lines of code, including sophisticated rules for raising the data quality of the resulting product ontology.

3.2 Transformation of a Product Classification System

A core aspect of the transformation step is the creation of the classes in the resulting ontology based on the source PCS being processed. To create the ontology classes, the PCS2OWL tool relies on the GenTax approach introduced in [20], whereby it is possible to generate a consistent OWL ontology while preserving the taxonomic structure of the original categories in the PCS. In order to do so, the GenTax method creates *two* OWL classes in the target ontology from each category in the PCS. The first is a broader taxonomic class that represents the category from the PCS in the target ontology. The second is a context-specific class, in our case in the domain of products and services. For a given category on the original PCS identified as *"ID"*, let us refer to the *pair* of OWL classes that GenTax creates as *C_ID-gen* and *C_ID-tax*, following the naming convention of the original GenTax specification [20].

There are additional design decisions that are applied in the conversion process to create the classes and the class structure of the resulting ontology: (1) all *C_ID-tax* taxonomic classes are arranged in a subsumption class hierarchy via the *rdfs:subClassOf* relation to preserve the hierarchical structure of the corresponding categories in the original PCS; (2) every *C_ID-gen* context-specific class is defined as a subclass of *gr:ProductOrService* of the GoodRelations ontology [6] via the *rdfs:subClassOf* property to state that it represents all instances of a certain product or service in the real world; (3) every *C_ID-gen* context-specific class is at the same moment also a subclass of the corresponding *C_ID-tax* taxonomic class, to preserve its traceability to the category in the original PCS that it was derived from; and (4) no subsumption relations exist between *C_ID-gen* context-specific classes given that as a class of an actual product or service, it is not possible to know in an automated fashion whether a subsumption relation between two *C_ID-gen* classes is applicable and valid in the real world.

Fig. 2 illustrates an example that results from the conversion of the following fragment of the English version of the Google product taxonomy [16]:

```
Cameras & Optics > Cameras > Digital Cameras
Cameras & Optics > Cameras > Disposable Cameras
```

Fig. 2 exhibits all *four* design decisions of the GenTax algorithm outlined previously. The right side shows the taxonomic class hierarchy, whereas the left part describes the context-specific class hierarchy. The black solid arrows stand for the *rdfs:subClassOf* relation. As indicated, (1) the taxonomic classes represent the categories in the Google taxonomy and preserve the same hierarchical structure; (2) the context-specific classes represent actual products and services and hence, are subsumed by *gr:ProductOrService*; (3) all context-specific classes are at the same time subclasses of their respective taxonomic class, e.g. the context-specific class *C_Cameras-gen* is a subclass of the taxonomic class *C_Cameras-tax*; and (4) no subsumption relation is imposed upfront between the context-specific classes, thus in visual terms they are arranged as mutual pair-wise siblings.

The adoption of the GenTax approach provides several features to the resulting ontologies produced by the PCS2OWL tool. GenTax creates meaningful,

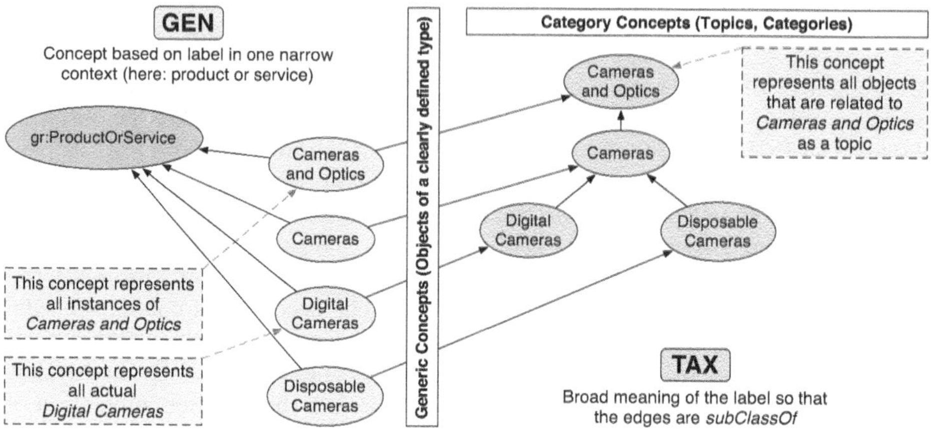

Fig. 2. GenTax applied on an extract of Google product taxonomy (cf. [20])

practically useful product classes (i.e. *"-gen"* classes on the left side of Fig. 2) by defining these as subclasses of *gr:ProductOrService*, which at the same time, renders the resulting ontology compatible with GoodRelations and schema.org. By preserving the hierarchical structure of the PCS (i.e. *"-tax"* classes on the right side of Fig. 2), GenTax allows the execution of generalization/specialization queries based on the original PCS. For example, searching for the common category *C_Cameras-tax* in order to get the union of all instances of the classes *C_DigitalCameras-gen* and *C_DisposableCameras-gen*. The use of the *rdfs:subClassOf* relation in the taxonomic classes, means that no reasoning capabilities beyond the widely supported RDFS reasoning are required to *navigate* through the taxonomic structure of the original PCS in the generated ontology. Additionally, for traceability and provenance purposes, every class indicates the ontology that describes it by taking advantage of the *rdfs:isDefinedBy* property; and moreover, every taxonomic class specifies a hierarchy code annotation property (*:hierarchyCode*) to link it to the corresponding category code used in the source classification system.

3.3 Converting Property Types and Related Values

In addition to the extraction of OWL classes from hierarchical classifications, PCS2OWL converts features and feature values of PCS, thus contributing additional semantics to categories. The different types of properties that are supported by the tool are in line with the GoodRelations ontology and consist of qualitative properties (*gr:qualitativeProductOrServiceProperty*), quantitative properties (*gr:quantitativeProductOrServiceProperty*), and datatype properties (*gr:datatypeProductOrServiceProperty*). Similarly, our tool distinguishes two enumeration types, namely qualitative values (*gr:QualitativeValue*) and quantitative values (*gr:QuantitativeValue* of type *xsd:float* or *xsd:integer*, e.g. values that indicate ranges), plus literal values with datatypes (*xsd:float*, *xsd:integer*, *xsd:boolean*, or *xsd:string*).

Custom rules and heuristics guide the distinction of the property types and related values. They have to be provided as part of the parser modules in order they can be applied in the subsequent transformation step where respective OWL properties are generated automatically. Thus, the quality of the conversion strongly depends on the correctness of these logics: As a general rule of thumb, a numerical value accompanied by a unit code in the classification system yields a quantitative value in the resulting product ontology, and not a qualitative value or a datatype literal. Some classification standards even make the intended type of features and values explicit, e.g. ETIM indicates logical values with an "L" metadata flag, hence best mapped as boolean literals in RDF.

3.4 Serialization and Deployment

In this section, we describe the serialization and deployment of the resulting product ontologies. This includes deciding on a canonical URI pattern for publishing the entities on the Web, and providing alternative ways to support standards-compliant Web ontology deployments.

The product classes and related entities in the ontologies obey a common URI pattern, which is comprised of (1) the base URI of the ontology; (2) a prefix to help humans distinguish URIs of different entity types, namely *C_* for classes, *P_* for properties, and *V_* for values; (3) an identifier unique in the context of the category system, that for categories is typically the hierarchy code; and, for classes, (4) a suffix to distinguish generic (*-gen*) from taxonomic (*-tax*) classes. Following this pattern, the URI of a context-specific class "Disposable Cameras" (hierarchy code *10001488*) in the GPC product ontology is

```
http://www.ebusiness-unibw.org/ontologies/pcs2owl/gpc/C_10001488-gen
```

PCS2OWL offers two deployment alternatives for product ontologies, namely based on *hash* and *slash* URIs. The first option generates a single comprehensive dump of the RDF graph, which is serialized as RDF/XML. The downside of this approach is the huge file size aspect that can make it infeasible for large classification systems. By contrast, the *slash*-based option generates a series of small RDF files, comprising separate files for all taxonomic and generic classes, and, if available, also for properties and individuals. This has the advantage that it allows serving smaller chunks of code for individual elements compared to its full dump counterpart. Moreover, with this option the tool creates a navigable documentation consisting of a set of interlinked HTML pages that mimic the subsumption hierarchy. The two deployment alternatives imply different URI patterns, that are

```
http://example.org/pcs#C_1234-gen -> hash-based
http://example.org/pcs/C_1234-gen -> slash-based
```

Besides the creation of RDF/XML and HTML files, PCS2OWL generates a *Semantic Sitemap*, and an *.htaccess* file for the easy deployment on an Apache Web server. Content negotiation is ensured using best practice patterns described online[6]. For *slash* URIs it means that by dereferencing an arbitrary entity URI

[6] `http://www.w3.org/TR/swbp-vocab-pub/#recipe5`

(e.g. a class URI), an HTML-preferring client is redirected to a respective HTML document using the HTTP response status code *303 See Other*. Similarly, the client retrieves RDF/XML, if the media type supplied with the HTTP *Accept*-header is `application/rdf+xml`. In this sense, our approach constitutes a full LOD-compliant deployment [21].

4 Evaluation

In the evaluation we focus on two key aspects, namely on the correctness of the conversion results, and on the amount of new product classes, properties, and enumerations obtained that are readily available for the Web.

4.1 Correctness of the Derived Product Ontologies

In this part of the evaluation, we were interested in whether the product ontologies correctly reflect the elements and the hierarchical structure provided by the product classification systems. We first did a quantitative comparison of the conceptual elements in the product classification systems and all classes, properties and individuals of the corresponding product ontologies. For that purpose we examined the number of concepts in the source files or database tables and the number of files produced for related types of concepts, e.g. the number of taxonomic classes in ontologies. If the numbers matched, it implied that the concepts were properly reflected in the product ontologies, which actually was the case for all of the ontologies that we built.

We complemented and further confirmed our previous findings by an experiment conducted on a product ontology derived from the Google product taxonomy [16]. The taxonomy file is available online[7] as plain text. It is line-based and characterized by a category tree which hierarchical structure is expressed using delimiting angle brackets as follows:

```
Food, Beverages & Tobacco > Beverages > Coffee > Coffee Pods
```

The taxonomy is read from the left starting with the most generic concept and getting more specific moving to the right. Accordingly, *Coffee* is a more specific concept than *Beverages* with respect to Google's product taxonomy. Our idea was basically to reverse-engineer the original taxonomy starting from the product ontology that we loaded into a SPARQL endpoint. A set of appropriate SPARQL queries permitted us to build up the whole hierarchy in a *top concept* → ... → *bottom concept* fashion. We then concatenated the respective RDFS labels using the exact same delimiters as advocated by the Google product taxonomy file format. And finally, the results of the concatenation were compared to the lines in the original source file. This way we were able to recreate an equivalent copy of the original file, which confirms the validity of our conversion. The single steps of our evaluation approach are described online[8] in more detail.

[7] `http://www.google.com/basepages/producttype/taxonomy.en-US.txt`

[8] `http://www.ebusiness-unibw.org/ontologies/pcs2owl/evaluation/`

4.2 Statistics on New Product Classes and Properties

In Section 1, we have argued that our approach produces a large number of readily usable product classes for the Web that to craft and maintain manually is impracticable. In order to support this claim, we report in the current section relevant statistics about the derived product ontologies[9].

As a preliminary step, we loaded all product ontologies into a SPARQL endpoint. Storing each product ontology as a different named graph (`urn:cpa`, `urn:gpc`, etc.) allowed us later to execute SPARQL queries based on their graph names. To give an example, we used the SPARQL 1.1 query of Listing 1.1 (prefix declarations omitted) to determine the number of hierarchy levels in the product ontologies. We executed the query repeatedly where in every step we incremented the property path length by one unit until we obtained no more results.

```
SELECT (COUNT(DISTINCT ?c) AS ?num_classes) WHERE {
  GRAPH <urn:gpc> {
    ?c a owl:Class .
    ?c rdfs:subClassOf{3} ?sc .
    FILTER NOT EXISTS {?c rdfs:subClassOf gr:ProductOrService}
  }
}
```

Listing 1.1. Calculating the number of hierarchy levels of PCS

Increasing the property path length from 3 to 4 in the provided example returns zero results, meaning that the hierarchy depth of the product ontology is four, i.e. the longest existing path consists of four classes linked by three consecutive *rdfs:subClassOf*-relationships. The FILTER statement of the query assures that only taxonomic classes are regarded, excluding those classes defined as products or services which would lead to otherwise incorrect results.

As reported in Section 2, our research took into account ten popular product classification standards, among them two different versions of eCl@ss, and three proprietary category structures. The common abbreviations of the PCS together with the versions that have been converted are given in the first column of Table 1. The upper part lists the numbers for the product categorization standards, whereas the lower three rows of the table represent the proprietary category systems. For BMEcat we cannot report specific numbers, since the standard permits to transmit catalog group structures of various sizes and types. Columns two to six capture the number of hierarchy levels, product classes, properties, value instances, and top-level classes for each product ontology. It is worth noting that some of the product ontologies have a fixed number of hierarchy levels (e.g. eCl@ss has four levels), while for others the numbers vary (e.g. proficl@ss, which has up to six levels). Similarly, some of them are quite shallow (e.g. ETIM with 2 levels), while others provide deep hierarchies (e.g. CPA with 6 levels) with sometimes redundant concept names at consecutive levels. The large quantity of entities (classes, properties, individuals) implies an extensive coverage of the product or services domain, which, if built up manually, would be prohibitively

[9] `http://www.ebusiness-unibw.org/ontologies/pcs2owl/`

Table 1. Statistics of product classification standards and category systems

Classification system	Number of levels	classes	properties	individuals	top-level c.	Class distr. (%)
CPC Ver.2	5	4,409	0	0	10	18
CPA 2008	6	5,429	0	0	21	53
CPV 2008	4	10,419	0	0	254	6
eCl@ss 5.1.4	4	30,329	7,136	4,720	25	18
eCl@ss 6.1	4	32,795	9,910	7,531	27	16
ETIM 4.0	2	2,213	6,346	7,001	54	8
FreeClass 2012	4	2,838	174	1,423	11	21
GPC 2012	4	3,831	1,710	9,562	37	17
proficl@ss 4.0	≤ 6	4,617	4,243	6,815	17	36
WZ 2008	5	1,835	0	0	21	33
Google prod. tax.	≤ 7	5,508	0	0	21	17
productpilot	≤ 8	7,970	0	0	20	28
BMEcat	na	na	0	0	na	na

expensive and time-consuming. Besides product classes, some product ontologies also contain properties and individuals that contribute valuable product details for the Semantic Web. Lastly, the seventh column indicates the distribution of classes within the derived product ontology (cf. Table 2 in [22]). This distribution is measured as the percentage of classes that belong to the largest top-level class with respect to the total number of classes in the ontology. This value describes the topology of the hierarchical structure and is thus an indicator for the quality of the product ontology. For example, in CPA one ("manufactured products") of the 21 top-level classes contains more than half of all the classes in the standard, while the classes in ETIM are more evenly distributed across various branches (only 8% of all classes belong to the largest class "hand tools").

Among the classification systems with multilingual support, CPA is the one with the most translations featuring class labels in 26 languages on average. Other product ontologies that also support multiple languages are CPV with an average of 22.9 languages, FreeClass with 6.9, WZ and the productpilot category system with both 2. The variety of languages supported increases the chance of finding products annotated with product classes more easily on the Web.

5 Discussion

This section presents a series of e-commerce use case examples that embody some of the novel opportunities that search engines and other consumers of structured data can exploit in areas such as product search, comparison, and matchmaking. These opportunities arise from using the now available Web product ontologies from PCS2OWL that allow to articulate more granular product descriptions across both the Web of Documents and the Web of Data.

Let us consider e.g., an online retailer interested in improving its product trading and data management processes. One enhancement consists in the adoption of the GPC classification standard instead of developing a custom scheme from scratch, leveraging the GPC Web ontology. Our retailer has published on the Web a snippet in Microdata syntax as in Listing 1.2, describing a specific disposable camera. For readability, the qualified names of the vocabulary URIs involved are used. They rely on the prefix declaration of *gr:* for GoodRelations [6], *gpc:* for the GPC product ontology[10], and *s:* for schema.org[11].

```
<div itemtype="http://schema.org/SomeProducts" itemid="#p1234" itemscope>
  <link itemprop="additionalType" href="http://www.ebusiness-unibw.org/
      ontologies/pcs2owl/gpc/C_10001488-gen" />
  <meta itemprop="name" content="Kodak 35mm Single Use Camera Flash" />
  <!-- additional features -->
</div>
```

Listing 1.2. Annotation example in Microdata syntax

Classification of Product Descriptions. Listing 1.2 specifies a disposable camera *p1234*, that is defined as an instance of the class *s:SomeProducts* (equivalent to *gr:SomeItems*) and identified by a fragment in the scope of the Web document URI. Thanks to the *additionalType* property in schema.org Microdata, *p1234* is an instance of the class *gpc:C_10001488-gen* as well. This definition, together with the existing linkage across the classes *gpc:C_10001488-gen*, *gpc:C_10001488-tax*, and the property *gpc:hierarchyCode* in the GPC Web ontology, materializes the product *p1234* on the Web as an instance of the category *10001488* labeled as "Disposable Cameras" in the original GPC classification standard.

Navigation over Product Data. The adoption of the GPC Web ontology would allow our online retailer to *navigate* along the product categories of the original GPC standard. Applied to the example in Listing 1.2, this navigation path is determined by the super- and subclasses of *gpc:C_10001488-tax*, which are defined via the *rdfs:subClassOf*-relationship. For example, the immediate parent class of *gpc:C_10001488-tax* (the category of our camera) is *gpc:C_68020100-tax*[12]. Or, in terms of the original schema, the GPC product category *68020100* "Photography" is the parent category of *10001488* "Disposable Cameras".

Web Data Format Descriptions of Product Data. The fact that product classes are published on the Web using URIs renders them applicable for use with common Web data formats, such as Microdata, RDF in attributes (RDFa), and Facebook Open Graph (OGP). Product annotations in those syntaxes can also lead to improvements on the current state of the document-based Web, namely in the form of search-engine result snippets (known as "rich snippets") and other mid-term benefits that may arise from providing more semantics.

6 Related Work

This paper partially builds upon previous works in the area of transforming classification standards into Web ontologies. The challenges in the conversion

[10] http://www.ebusiness-unibw.org/ontologies/pcs2owl/gpc/

[11] http://schema.org/

[12] http://www.ebusiness-unibw.org/ontologies/pcs2owl/gpc/C_68020100-tax

of product classification standards were already discussed in [23,3], whose findings led towards the development of the GenTax algorithm in [20], still a core component of PCS2OWL. The subsequent initial release of the GoodRelations ontology [6] motivated the first transformation of the eCl@ss standard (5.1.4)[13] relying on the GenTax methodology as a GoodRelations compliant ontology.

Alternatively, there have been previous efforts to convert other product classification schemes also supported by PCS2OWL: Most notably CPV ([24], another effort[14]), primarily used to streamline the procurement and tendering process in the public sector. On a broader scope, the research in [25] provides the most recent and comprehensive survey of methods and tools for the refactoring of most types of non-ontological resources (NORs) into ontological resources (ORs), i.e. Web ontologies. A comprehensive qualitative framework is put forward to categorize NORs based on their characteristics. One of the types of NORs acknowledged in the work are actually the general classification schemes for any given domain, such as those considered in this paper for products. In fact, two methods [26], again GenTax, and a tool, SKOS2OWL[15], are identified to focus on the conversion of classification scheme NORs specifically into Web ontologies.

Yet, in summary, to the best of our knowledge, PCS2OWL remains as the only methodology readily supplied with tool support, that extends the features and capabilities of all the conversion efforts previously mentioned, on at least one, if not several of the following fronts: (1) the level of automation; (2) modular architecture supporting the conversion of an arbitrary number of classification systems; (3) the application to a broad set of non-ontological resources, i.e. almost all relevant classification schemas; (4) traceability including preservation of the taxonomic structure between the elements in the original classification scheme and those in the derived Web ontology; (5) improved support for properties and enumerations; (6) high degree of configuration options aimed at deployment on the Web of Linked Open Data (LOD); and, lastly, (7) compliance to the GoodRelations and schema.org ontologies, which currently allows for the publishing on various Web data formats.

7 Conclusions

The ontology engineering task in the domain of products and services is typically tedious, costly, and time-consuming. To master this problem, we presented a generic method and a toolset for deriving product ontologies from existing product classification standards and proprietary category systems in a semi-automatic way, which is usually superior to building them up manually in several aspects. For example, it successfully addresses the generally large number of concepts in product categorization standards and the conceptual dynamics inherent to the domain of products and services. We have supported our contribution by converting 13 product classification systems of different scopes, sizes,

[13] http://www.heppnetz.de/projects/eclassowl/

[14] http://linked.opendata.cz/resource/dataset/cpv-2008

[15] http://www.heppnetz.de/projects/skos2owl/

and structures, and have shown that we can generate practically relevant product ontologies while effectively preserving the original taxonomic relationships. These ontologies are ready for deployment on the Web of Linked Open Data. Furthermore, we exemplified how products can be annotated using the derived product ontologies, rendering them more visible and discernible on the Web. In particular, employing product classes to semantically annotate product instances empowers product data consumers to find and aggregate products and respective offers with less effort. For example, they could be readily used for assisting faceted search over semantic e-commerce data.

As future work, we are planning to extend the set of available parsers by additional product classification systems, and to publish already converted product ontologies which, at the time of writing this paper, we were not yet granted permission due to lack of copyright clearance. Moreover, we think that our product ontologies could attract related research fields, such as finding correspondences across product classification systems by means of ontology matching. Similarly, we should point out that our generic toolset could be easily adapted to convert classification systems even outside the product domain.

Acknowledgments. The work on this paper has been supported by the German Federal Ministry of Education and Research (BMBF) by a grant under the KMU Innovativ program as part of the Intelligent Match project (FKZ 01IS10022B), and by the Eurostars program (EU 7th Framework Program) of the European Commission in the context of the OPDM project (FKZ 01QE1113D).

References

1. Fensel, D., Ding, Y., Omelayenko, B., Schulten, E., Botquin, G., Brown, M., Flett, A.: Product Data Integration in B2B E-Commerce. IEEE Intelligent Systems 16(4), 54–59 (2001)
2. Hepp, M.: Possible Ontologies: How Reality Constrains the Development of Relevant Ontologies. IEEE Internet Computing 11(1), 90–96 (2007)
3. Hepp, M.: Products and Services Ontologies: A Methodology for Deriving OWL Ontologies from Industrial Categorization Standards. International Journal on Semantic Web and Information Systems (IJSWIS) 2(1), 72–99 (2006)
4. eCl@ss: Category:Products - wiki.eclass.eu., `http://wiki.eclass.eu/wiki/Category:Products#Release_Sizes`
5. eCl@ss: eCl@ss Classification and Product Description, `http://www.eclass.de/`
6. Hepp, M.: GoodRelations: An Ontology for Describing Products and Services Offers on the Web. In: Gangemi, A., Euzenat, J. (eds.) EKAW 2008. LNCS (LNAI), vol. 5268, pp. 329–346. Springer, Heidelberg (2008)
7. European Commission: Regulation (EC) No 451/2008 of the European Parliament and of the Council of 23 April 2008 establishing a new statistical classification of products by activity (CPA) and repealing Council Regulation (EEC) No 3696/93. Official Journal of the European Union L145/51 (June 2008)
8. United Nations Statistics Division: The Central Product Classification (CPC) Version 2.0, `http://unstats.un.org/unsd/cr/registry/cpc-2.asp`

9. European Commission: Commission Regulation (EC) No 213/2008 of 28 November 2007. Official Journal of the European Union L074/51 (March 2008)
10. ETIM Deutschland: ETIM 4.0 – Das Klassifizierungsmodell der Elektrobranche, http://www.etim.de/
11. Handle, O.: Konzeption und Realisierung eines branchenübergreifenden Produktklassifikationssystems für das Bauwesen unter Nutzung der produktspezifischen Fachkompetenz der Baustoffindustrie. Master's thesis, MCI Management Center Innsbruck (2007)
12. GS1: Global Product Classification (GPC): The Global Language for Classifying Goods, 3rd edn. GS1 (April 2005)
13. proficl@ss International: proficl@ss - der Branchenstandard, http://www.proficlass.de/
14. Statistisches Bundesamt: Klassifikation der Wirtschaftszweige (WZ 2008). Wiesbaden: Statistisches Bundesamt (2008)
15. Navigli, R.: Word Sense Disambiguation: A Survey. ACM Comput. Surv. 41(2), 10:1–10:69 (2009)
16. Google Merchant Center: The Google product taxonomy, http://support.google.com/merchants/bin/answer.py?hl=en&answer=1705911
17. Messe Frankfurt: productpilot, http://www.productpilot.com/
18. Schmitz, V., Leukel, J., Kelkar, O.: Specification BMEcat 2005. Bundesverband Materialwirtschaft, Einkauf und Logistik e. V. (2005)
19. Stolz, A., Rodriguez-Castro, B., Hepp, M.: Using BMEcat Catalogs as a Lever for Product Master Data on the Semantic Web. In: Cimiano, P., Corcho, O., Presutti, V., Hollink, L., Rudolph, S. (eds.) ESWC 2013. LNCS, vol. 7882, pp. 623–638. Springer, Heidelberg (2013)
20. Hepp, M., de Bruijn, J.: GenTax: A Generic Methodology for Deriving OWL and RDF-S Ontologies from Hierarchical Classifications, Thesauri, and Inconsistent Taxonomies. In: Franconi, E., Kifer, M., May, W. (eds.) ESWC 2007. LNCS, vol. 4519, pp. 129–144. Springer, Heidelberg (2007)
21. Heath, T., Bizer, C.: Linked Data: Evolving the Web into a Global Data Space, 1st edn. Morgan & Claypool (2011)
22. Hepp, M., Leukel, J., Schmitz, V.: A Quantitative Analysis of Product Categorization Standards: Content, Coverage, and Maintenance of eCl@ss, UNSPSC, eOTD, and the RosettaNet Technical Dictionary. Knowledge and Information Systems 13(1), 77–114 (2007)
23. Hepp, M.: A Methodology for Deriving OWL Ontologies from Products and Services Categorization Standards. In: Proceedings of the 13th European Conference on Information Systems (ECIS 2005), Regensburg, Germany, pp. 1–12 (2005)
24. Polo Paredes, L., Álvarez Rodríguez, J.M., Azcona, E.R.: Promoting Government Controlled Vocabularies for the Semantic Web: the EUROVOC Thesaurus and the CPV Product Classification System. In: Proceedings of the Semantic Interoperability in the European Digital Library Workshop (SIEDL 2008), co-located with 5th European Semantic Web Conference, Tenerife, Spain, pp. 111–122 (2008)
25. Villazón Terrazas, B.: A Method for Reusing and Re-engineering Non-ontological Resources for Building Ontologies. PhD thesis, Univ. Politécnica de Madrid (2011)
26. Hakkarainen, S.E., Hella, L., Strasunskas, D., Tuxen, S.: A Semantic Transformation Approach for ISO 15926. In: Roddick, J., et al. (eds.) ER Workshops 2006. LNCS, vol. 4231, pp. 281–290. Springer, Heidelberg (2006)

Seeding Structured Data by Default via Open Source Library Systems

Dan Scott

Laurentian University,
Sudbury, Ontario, Canada
dscott@laurentian.ca
https://coffeecode.net

Abstract. Most libraries use the machine-readable cataloguing (MARC) format to encode and exchange metadata about the items they make available to their patrons. Traditional library systems have not published this data on the Semantic Web. However, some agile open source library systems have begun closing this gap by publishing structured data that uses the schema.org vocabulary to describe the bibliographic data, make offers for items available for loan, and link the items to their owning libraries. This article distills the lessons learned from implementing structured data in Evergreen, Koha, and VuFind; highlights emerging design patterns for publishing structured data in other library systems; and traces the influence these implementation experiences have had on the evolution of the schema.org vocabulary. Finally, we discuss the impact that "the power of the default" publishing of structured data could have on discoverability of library offerings on the Semantic Web.

Keywords: #eswc2014Scott, Libraries, Structured data, MARC formats, schema.org, Open source.

1 Introduction

A pragmatic incentive for publishing structured data on the Semantic Web is the promise that elevating web pages beyond mere bags of words will enable search engines to provide better responses to queries through strategies such as disambiguating terms. Search engines have assumed the most visible role of the intelligent agents described in Berners-Lee's seminal vision of the Semantic Web [1]. The goals of many search engine users parallel the information seeking goals Nardi originally classified for users of libraries, such as monitoring, planned, or exploratory searches [2]. As non-commercial repositories of resources that can satisfy these classes of queries, libraries have continually designed and evolved organizational systems for indexing and efficiently locating their resources (*traditional library systems*, as used in almost every public, academic, and special library in many parts of the world). This paper explores the results of enabling open source instances of these systems to participate in the Semantic Web by adopting structured data conventions and the generalist schema.org vocabulary,

V. Presutti et al. (Eds.): ESWC 2014, LNCS 8465, pp. 659–674, 2014.

as encouraged by major search engines, in what is commonly thought to be a highly specialized domain.

To facilitate remote queries to traditional library systems, libraries were early adopters of technology such as direct dial-up connections, TELNET, and web catalogues [3]. Since the 1960s, most traditional library systems have used the Machine Readable Cataloguing (MARC) record format to describe and exchange metadata about their resources. Traditional library systems were therefore well-positioned to be early participants in the Semantic Web.

However, cataloguing practices as encoded by MARC records have focused on strings, not things; and the strings themselves often described more than a single property. For example, until 2013, the MARC 21 format used by North American libraries combined ISBNs and a description of the physical format for the book holding that ISBN in a single descriptive field without standardized delimiters [4]. In the field of linked data, most traditional library systems offer rudimentary support for creating and maintaining links between entities such as author names by relying on *authority records* that are maintained within the same system, but those inward-facing links have not been exposed as structured data on the web.

2 Libraries at an Impasse

Where libraries have made efforts to expose the raw metadata of their traditional library systems in a more machine-readable way, adoption has been uneven and these approaches are not well-known outside of library or bibliographic contexts. For example, the COinS microformat [5] encodes NISO Z39.88 metadata in an OpenURL ContextObject that can be used to cite and locate a copy of the work. The unAPI microformat [6] enables client applications to retrieve raw metadata records in different formats such as MARCXML, MODS, and RIS. However, while these methods of surfacing machine-readable metadata are consumed by client applications such as Zotero and Mendeley, they solve specific bibliographic problems rather than broader Semantic Web problems.

By late 2011 it was clear that most traditional library systems were being left out of the emerging Semantic Web. Google continued to push for the adoption of structured data [7], and then joined Yahoo! and Bing in unveiling the schema.org vocabulary [8] with promises that web pages using schema.org could receive special treatment from search engines when it came to display ("rich snippets") and relevance. Summers succintly summarized the problem faced and caused by libraries, stating "the use of HTML5 Microdata and schema.org by Google, Bing and Yahoo, and the use of RDFa by Facebook are [...] good reminders that the library software development community is best served by paying attention to mainstream solutions, as they become available, even if they eclipse homegrown stopgap solutions" [9].

While thought leaders such as the Swedish Union Catalogue (LIBRIS) [10], the Deutsche National Bibliothek[11], the Bibliothèque nationale de France [12], and OCLC have all implemented linked data patterns, those initiatives occurred in highly centralized organizations and their results are not easily replicated by libraries with less concentrated development resources. Ronallo's analysis of the August 2012 Common Crawl corpus found that American academic library sites had failed to respond to Summers' challenge, as those sites contained very few schema.org instances: a mere 8,351 instances of Article, 1,275 instances of CollectionPage, and 298 instances of ScholarlyArticle represented the most common academic types [13].

Unfortunately, those smaller libraries that would be willing to contribute their data to the Semantic Web [1] generally lack the resources necessary to customize their existing systems, pressure or incentive vendors to enhance their software, or invest in difficult transitions to new systems. Budget challenges in particular force administrators to focus on more mundane efforts such as collection development and hinder efforts that are not perceived as offering immediate results for their users.

3 Open Source Library Systems

In a risk-averse, static domain, open source library systems offer hope for regular libraries. Many proprietary systems allow client libraries to suggest and vote on the prioritization of development efforts, but those results are not binding, and the pool of available development resource is limited to a single vendor. In comparison, the communal development effort for open source software means that a given enhancement needs to only be developed once, then shared with all other users of the same system; and "[d]istribution of source code can lead to efficiency gains by making it possible for the modifications to be done by those actors who have the best information about their value [and] are best equipped to carry them out" [14].

Accordingly, we hypothesized the simplest and most effective solution to increasing the amount of structured data published by libraries was to enhance open source library systems so that they would publish structured data by default. Just as "getting the default "right" could have a tremendous impact on the distribution of retirement savings available to individuals" [15], we felt it was important that library systems should start publishing structured data as soon as they were installed or upgraded. If libraries had to opt in to publishing their data through a configuration setting, or had to make minimal customizations to the web layer of their systems, then a significant portion of libraries would *not* choose to opt in; even if the option was found, the decision to change the default would be complex for those who are not experts with the Semantic web. Per Madrian, "the default will assume an asymmetric position in the decision-making process relative to other outcomes, and consequently, will be more likely to be picked as the chosen alternative" [15].

When working towards implementing linked data principles [16] in open source library systems, we have the advantage that all of these systems are native to the web and did not evolve from pre-web networks. For example, while many proprietary systems still use session parameters as part of their URL scheme and thus break basic functionality like bookmarking or sharing URLs, open source library systems such as Koha, Evergreen, and VuFind all use persistent URIs to offer access to individual records. This satisfies the linked data requirements to use URIs to name things (at least at the level of individual record) and to use dereferenceable HTTP URIs.

Our efforts to enable library systems to publish structured data by default focused on two mature open source library systems (Koha and Evergreen), and one mature open source discovery system: VuFind.

3.1 Evergreen

In 2004, the Georgia Public Library Service (GPLS) decided to fund the development of the Evergreen library system because "[t]he limit reached [by the existing software] was a hard one, and there was no solution using that software. Meanwhile, more libraries wanted to join PINES [the consortial resource sharing library system]" [17]. In 2006, the first version of Evergreen was released under the GPL version 2 licence and GPLS PINES launched with 252 libraries running under a single Evergreen instance. Evergreen is now used by at least 1,388 libraries worldwide [18]. We included Evergreen due to its broad reach and its familiarity to the author of this paper, who has been an Evergreen developer since 2007.

3.2 Koha

Koha was developed in 1999 to replace a proprietary system that suffered from severe Y2K-compliance problems and for which the company no longer existed. Development of the initial version of Koha was funded by a single library, the Horowhenua Library Trust (HLT), who opted to release the software under an open source license as a "gift given freely" (the meaning of the Maori word "Koha") [19]. From that single library in 2000, Koha is now being used by at least 2,500 libraries worldwide [20]. As the most widely adopted open source library system with the most mature development team and process, we felt that including Koha in our implementation efforts would have a significant impact.

3.3 VuFind

Rather than replacing its proprietary library system entirely, Villanova University opted to instead build a new discovery layer that could blend the results of both the library system catalogue and other sources such as article databases and an institutional repository of theses and dissertations. The resulting software, VuFind, began development in 2007, reached a 1.0 release in 2010 [21], and has continued to iterate with a small but robust development team. There are 135 self-reported installations [22], including York University, who listed seven key criteria in their decision to implement VuFind [23]. York's criteria did not include Semantic Web considerations, but we included VuFind in our implementation efforts because their small but stable community is growing, their development team was amenable to the addition of structured data, and we looked forward to the challenge of working with data from disparate systems.

4 Mapping Library System Records to the schema.org Vocabulary

For the purposes of this paper, publishing library system records on the web using schema.org structured data required three steps:

1. Determining the schema.org type of the bibliographic record
2. Mapping the record elements to the type's properties
3. Linking physical or electronic resources to the described object

4.1 Determining the schema.org Type of the Bibliographic Record

Koha and Evergreen expose raw MARC records to their display templates, so to properly determine their schema.org types we need to analyze both the MARC leaders and the fixed fields to discern the type of the described bibliographic data. To complicate matters, Koha can support both the MARC 21 and UNIMARC formats, each of which features their own rules for encoding bibliographic information. For example, determining that a given MARC 21 record describes a motion picture requires us to check the 6th character of the record leader, then check the 33rd character of the 008 field. As Evergreen supports only MARC 21, we narrowed the scope of our efforts by focusing only on mapping MARC 21 records, and due to the complexity of MARC 21 format, only map `schema:Book`, `schema:Map`, and `schema:MusicAlbum`, with a fallback to `schema:CreativeWork`, for this initial effort.

In contrast, VuFind supports the creation of a single index sourced from heterogeneous sets of records including, but not limited to, MARC 21 records, by normalizing the source records to a common, simplified schema. While the simplified schema inhibits us in some cases from publishing structured data properties as granular as when we have access to the raw MARC 21 records, its strictures liberate us from having to craft intricate mappings of the raw data. Therefore, in addition to the mappings available to us in Evergreen and Koha, in VuFind we were easily able to also map records to `schema:Movie` and `schema:Photograph`.

The following table lists the schema.org types that we mapped, using the sixth character of the MARC 21 leader as a guide:

Table 1. MARC 21 leader[06] values to schema.org types

Schema.org type	MARC 21 leader[06] value
Book	a
Map	e
MusicAlbum	j
CreativeWork	All other LDR values

Articles (which would map to `schema:Article`) fall under the "Language material" designation used by books, and individual music tracks (which would map to `schema:MusicRecording`), fall under the "Musical sound recordings" designation used by albums. However, neither articles nor individual tracks are typically described in these library systems and were excluded from this research.

4.2 Mapping the Record Elements to the Type's Properties

Once we have mapped the record to a schema.org type, we can map the record elements to the properties for the type. As the base types all inherit from `schema:CreativeWork`, common properties such as `schema:author`, `schema:contributor`, `schema:name`, `schema:datePublished`, and `schema:publisher` can be mapped once and reused for all types. Following this approach, special handling is required only for the extended properties for types such as `schema:MusicAlbum` which, rather than `schema:author` or `schema:contributor`, prefers a `schema:byArtist` property with a range of `schema:MusicGroup`.

The following table describes the mappings to schema.org properties from combinations of MARC 21 fields and their subfields. Unless otherwise indicated, the values of all subfields for a given occurrence of a field were concatenated to provide the value for a single occurrence of a schema.org property. "CreativeWork" implies all schema.org children, such as Book, Map, and MusicAlbum. *Note*: `schema:birthDate` and `schema:deathDate` are derived from the same subfield using the supplied regular expression.

Table 2. MARC 21 field/subfield values to schema.org properties

Schema.org property	**MARC 21 field/subfield**
CreativeWork/name	`245/All subfields except w, 0, 4, 5, 6, 8, 9`
Book/isbn	`022/a`
CreativeWork/publisher/Organization/location	`(260/a or 264[indicator 2="1"])/a`
CreativeWork/publisher/Organization/name	`(260/b or 264[indicator 2="1"])/b`
CreativeWork/datePublished	`(260/c or 264[indicator 2="1"])/c`
CreativeWork/keywords	`(600, 610, 611, 630, 650, 651, 655, 659, 690, 692, 693, 698, 699)/a-z`
MusicRecording/byArtist/MusicGroup/name	`110/a-z`
CreativeWork/author/Person/name	`100/a-z`

Table 2. (*continued*)

CreativeWork/author/Organization/name	(110, 111)/a-z
CreativeWork/contributor/Person/name	700/a-z
CreativeWork/contributor/Organization/name	(710, 711)/a-z
CreativeWork/author/Person/birthDate	100/d '^\s*(\d{4}).*$'
CreativeWork/author/Person/deathDate	100/d '^\s*.{4}-(\d{4}).*$'

4.3 Linking Physical or Electronic Resources to the Described Object

Libraries make specific resources available for use, so simply describing the general resource is not sufficient. Semantic Web agents need to be able to determine which library holds the resource, where the resource is located within the library, and whether it is available. We discuss this in detail as one of the emerging design patterns in the following section.

5 Emerging Design Patterns

Following a tactic of first marking up the text as it already exists on the web page, our initial implementation efforts simply published the personal and corporate names, as given in the source data, as literal values for the `schema:contributor` property. While for schema.org it "is not a requirement [to satisfy the expected range of a given property]–it's fine to include just regular text or a URL" [24], as libraries we strive to publish high quality structured data. Several notable design patterns emerged through our efforts to enable library systems to publish rich schema.org structured data.

Providing Better Granularity for Personal and Corporate Names: To distinguish common personal names from one another, MARC 21 records may include the birth date and death date (if applicable) in a single undifferentiated subfield. Regular expressions enable us to disambiguate that data into separate `schema:birthDate` and `schema:deathDate` properties, thus enriching the structured data that we publish beyond what the source record explicitly encoded. We were also able to differentiate between corporate authors, individual authors, and contributors to works, as well as provide special handling for music groups, rather than indiscriminately adding `schema:author` properties to works.

Linking Resources to the Described Object: One of the core functions of library systems is to serve as a catalogue that enables users to locate items and determine the current status of those items; it effectively serves as a highly localized search engine. A previous iteration of schema.org structured data in Evergreen resulted [25] in only 3,275 `schema:Book` instances being reported by Google's Webmaster Tools out of what should have been hundreds of thousands, and had no discernible impact on searches in Google or Bing in informal testing of the catalogue. Based on these results, we hypothesized that search engines want to connect searchers directly to the items that they are seeking; therefore, when we publish structured data, we now use the `schema:Offer` type to expose copies of resources. As the defined range of the `schema:itemOffered` property is `schema:Product`, we use multiple types in the RDFa `@typeof` property to express both `schema:Product` and the appropriate `schema:CreativeWork` (or child type such as `schema:Book`). This enables us to use properties from both types to describe both the generic object and the offer-specific attributes, as follows:

Table 3. Mapping available resources to the described object

Schema.org type or property	**Library entity**	**Notes**
CreativeWork/offers/Offer	Holding, item, or copy	Repeated once per holding
Offer/businessFunction	Borrowing terms (for example, reserved for in-library use)	Available for loan = http://purl.org/goodrelations/ `v1#LeaseOut`
Offer/itemOffered	Bibliographic record	
Offer/sku	Call number or shelf mark	As a literal "stock keeping unit" number, call number shares the properties of enabling the location of a group of copies of items using a single number.
Offer/seller/Library/name	Library name	Koha and VuFind use the literal value of the library name, while a working branch in Evergreen offers a full `schema:Library` object (see below).
Offer/serialNumber	Barcode	Satisfies the need for a unique identifier for an individual copy.
Offer/gtin13	ISBN	
Offer/availableAtOrFrom	Shelving location	Currently mapped to the literal value of the name of the shelving location (for example, "Stacks"), but finer granularity could be achieved through the use of `schema:containedIn`.
Offer/description	Public copy notes	

We mapped the availability of resources from common library terminology to the `schema:ItemAvailability` enumeration as follows:

Table 4. Mapping `schema:ItemAvailability` to library resource availability

schema.org type	Type of availability
`schema:InStock`	Available on shelf or awaiting reshelving
`schema:OutOfStock`	Checked out or waiting to be picked up for a hold
`schema:PreOrder`	On order, in process, or in transit to another library
`schema:InStoreOnly`	Reserved for on-site usage

Linking Resources to the Offering Library: The "seller" property of `schema:Offer` has a formally defined RDF range of `schema:Organization` or `schema:Person`; however, in keeping with the pragmatic nature of schema.org, our initial implementations simply supplied a non-semantic literal–the name of the library–or linked to an external web page that, as it is out of our control, at this time most likely does not include any structured data.

A prototype implementation in Evergreen [26] generates one web page per library containing structured data based on the `schema:Library` type. As an RDF subclass of `schema:Organization`, `schema:Library` satisfies the range constraints of `schema:seller`, and it offers an expressive set of properties to describe the organization such as contact information and hours of operation. Most library systems must maintain a current set of library operating hours to avoid accruing fines during closed times, and manage contact information such as email addresses, phone numbers, and mailing addresses to facilitate communication with users. Our enhancement generates data-rich `schema:Library` web pages that not only support Semantic Web needs, but also offer value to users and libraries by surfacing some of the most important library information directly from the relational database underpinning Evergreen.

6 Extending the schema.org Vocabulary

The author of this paper has had the pleasure of working closely with the schema.org community directly via the W3 Web Schemas group [27] and indirectly through the W3 Schema.org Bibliographic Extensions Community Group (*SchemaBibEx*) [28]. These collaborative efforts have led to several enhancements of the schema.org vocabulary.

6.1 Decommercializing the `schema:Offer` and `schema:Product` Types

When schema.org incorporated the GoodRelations vocabulary for the `schema:Product` and `schema:Offer` types, it simplified the core type and property descriptions by deemphasizing the generic agent-promise-object model underpinning the GoodRelations ontology [29] and focused instead on commercial transactions for the primary use case in schema.org. However, the `schema:Offer` definition of "An offer to sell an itemfor example, an offer to sell a product, the DVD of a movie, or tickets to an event" [30] failed to encompass many of the services offered by libraries or other non-commercial entities. When we proposed the holdings-as-Offer pattern to SchemaBibEx, several participants raised objections due to the commercial nature of the existing Offer documentation that was thought to be unsuitable for a library context. Accordingly, we proposed changes to the definitions of three types, three properties, and 11 enumerated values such that they would also accommodate non-commercial transactions and services. The proposal was accepted with minor improvements and is scheduled to be incorporated into the next revision of both the schema.org vocabulary and the GoodRelations vocabulary [31, 32].

6.2 Establishing Clear Usage Patterns for Multiple Types

schema.org users have repeatedly expressed confusion about the appropriate usage of multiple types in microdata and RDFa [34–36]. The emerging consensus that multiple schema.org types can be expressed in a single microdata `@itemtype` or RDFa `@typeof` attribute, while additional types from outside the schema.org vocabulary should be expressed via a separate `schema:additionalType` property (for microdata) or in the same `@property` attribute (for RDFa), reflects the usage pattern we adopted for linking library resources to their described objects. Our work has served as a practical example in answers to these questions.

6.3 Extending the Vocabulary to Encompass Magazines, Journals, and Other Periodicals

Although the proposal has not yet received final approval, one of the recent SchemaBibEx efforts has been to define a set of schema.org types and properties that would enable libraries and publishers to describe periodicals at the title and issue level. Given the existence of the `schema:Article` and `schema:ScholarlyArticle` types and the `schema:citation` property, there is a strong need to be able to express the publication and issue in which an article has been collected. One could use a separate vocabulary such as the Bibliographic Ontology [33], but that runs counter to the schema.org goal of providing "a single place to go to learn about markup, instead of having to graft together a schema from different sources, each with its own rules, conventions and learning curves" [38]. Therefore, while informed by the existing Bibliographic Ontology work in this area, the current proposal [37] hews closer to the existing `schema:Series` / `schema:Season` / `schema:Episode` pattern by promoting volume (a collection of issues, typically by year) into a first-class type.

7 Discussion

7.1 Assessing schema.org for Traditional Library Systems

Although previous Semantic Web efforts for library systems adopted a mix of multiple specialized vocabularies such as FOAF, SKOS, and Dublin Core [10–12], we chose to assess the ability of the generalist schema.org vocabulary to satisfy the needs of the library domain. In theory, using a single vocabulary to express structured data should simplify the publishers' mapping effort and ease the consumers' ability to consume the data. Given that the major search engines have endorsed schema.org, use of that vocabulary is expected to increase the visibility of library resources in search engines. By limiting ourselves to the schema.org vocabulary, we are well-positioned to test these perceived advantages as libraries using Evergreen, Koha, and VuFind upgrade to the schema.org-enhanced versions of the software.

While mapping human-visible elements of web catalogues to schema.org structured data, we observed that traditional library systems *could* usefully deploy schema.org and achieve an acceptable level of metadata granularity through the previously described mapping design patterns. We also identified several cases in which the schema.org enhancement process successfully addressed gaps identified by SchemaBibEx. Current proposals such as MiniSKOS [39] promise to address the longer tail of bibliographic description needs.

Although individual libraries can customize their own web catalogues on a site-by-site basis, developers of traditional library systems hold the potential to most efficiently bring libraries to the Semantic Web by enhancing their systems to publish structured data by default. The author's experience in successfully augmenting three separate library systems to publish schema.org structured data–including all code contribution, review, and integration processes–in approximately three months suggests that the implementation cost for developers of other systems should be relatively low, particularly given that the code from the work described by this paper is open for inspection and adoption.

7.2 Potential Impacts

If Evergreen, Koha, and VuFind are only the first of many library systems to publish schema.org structured data by default, we can speculate about some potential impacts a broader adoption of this approach may have in a library context:

Improved Efficiency and Accuracy of Resource-Sharing Systems: To participate in the resource-sharing networks that support interlibrary loan services, libraries periodically deliver batch updates of their records and holdings or maintain a Z39.50 server to participate in a federated search system. Batch updates enable a central service to assemble a collection of all records held by the resource-sharing participants, but those records are outdated almost immediately as resources are added or removed on a daily basis at most libraries. Z39.50 is a complex library-specific search protocol that still suffers from the implementation inconsistencies cited by Lunau [40].

Given a set of participating libraries that publish structured data with agreed-upon schema.org mappings and sitemaps, however, a new centralized service could avoid manual batch update processes by instead periodically crawling all of the new and changed pages of its member libraries to maintain a centralized database. When a resource is requested, the availability could be checked by requesting and parsing the resource page for `schema:Offer` entities with an agreeable `schema:itemAvailability` value.

Improved Efficiency of–or Disintermediated–OCLC: OCLC has emerged as one of the centralized entities responsible for mediating library-library interactions such as collaborative cataloguing efforts and resource sharing initiatives in North America, as well as supplying search engines such as Google with the data required to connect searchers to libraries [41]. Libraries currently make their resources known to OCLC (and thus to other libraries) through cumbersome "batch loads". Given schema.org structured data that follows the holdings-as-Offer pattern, OCLC could instead follow the approach established by search engines of using sitemaps to crawl library catalogues and update their indexes accordingly. With an even broader adoption of structured data by libraries, however, regular search engines could simply parse the available structured data from known libraries and return more relevant customized results based on signals such as the searcher's geographic location, known library preferences, and participation in social networks, effectively disintermediating OCLC from its current role as a metadata supplier to Google and other search engines.

7.3 Future Work

Future possibilities for work in this area include:

Improve the Mapping from MARC 21 to schema.org, and Create a Mapping for UNIMARC: For MARC 21, mappings for the base types would benefit significantly from including the MARC 21 008 and 006 fixed fields in the analysis. The mapping of MARC 21 subfields to `schema:Person` and `schema:Organization` names should only include recognizable "name" values in the `schema:name` property, while other values can be directed to more appropriate properties or ignored.

Many Koha sites use the UNIMARC record format, which currently has no mapping for schema.org. While lossy conversions from UNIMARC to MARC 21 are available, a direct mapping from UNIMARC to schema.org may provide better structured data. Alternately, the use of a more semantic intermediary format such as the Metadata Object Description Schema (MODS) [42] may be a fruitful avenue of exploration for source formats including MARC 21 and UNIMARC. Shared documentation and implementations of these mappings would enable other library systems to benefit from a common analysis, assuming that they were available under an open source license, and would contribute to enhancing the contributions of libraries to the Semantic Web.

Broader Implementation of the Agent-Promise-Object Model: The `schema:Offer` pattern for relating resources to the libraries that hold them using `schema:Library` to fulfill the agent-promise-object model has been prototyped in Evergreen [26]. To further the goal of structured data by default, we plan to extend this implementation to Koha and other library systems that track library locations, hours of operation, and contact information.

Link to External Data: While we were able to publish structured data with persistent URIs, all links other than electronic resource URIs were siloed within the library system. For MARC-based systems, the next step is to follow the existing conventions for linking bibliographic fields such as authors and subjects to authority records, and in turn link from the authority records to external records such as the Library of Congress Linked Data Service [43] or VIAF: The Virtual Authority File [44]. However, many MARC 21 fields–such as publication information recorded in MARC 260 or 264 fields–are not allowed to include linking subfields, and thus limits the basic MARC mapping approach to a best-effort string-matching approach.

Assess the Growth of Library-Published Structured Data: The impact of these changes to three major open source library systems on the proliferation of structured data published by libraries needs to be assessed. Repeating Ronallo's Common Crawl analysis with a data set in one year's time should demonstrate the results (if any) of the "structured data by default" releases of Koha, Evergreen, and VuFind. Such a study should extend its scope beyond American academic libraries, and should annotate the results by which software published the structured data to provide insight into the impact of the subject of this paper.

Assess the Impact of Library-Published Structured Data on Users: We need to confirm the hypothesis that publishing structured data will have a tangible, positive impact for users of general search engines by running usability studies. Given Evergreen's ability to surface full Product-Offer-Library relationships, we expect that search engines should be able to tailor results to local users by directly including local library resources. To assess this hypothesis, a longitudinal usability study that compares user frustration and source of discovery (for example, library catalogue or general search engine) for a set number of known local resources at the start and end of the study may offer a fruitful approach.

8 Conclusion

In this paper we described the process and lessons learned from enabling the open source library systems Evergreen, Koha, and VuFind to publish schema.org structured data by default; highlighted several of the areas where this implementation experience affected the evolution and usage of the schema.org vocabulary; and discussed the potential impact "the power of the default" publishing of schema.org structured data can have on libraries. Our next steps are to refine and expand the implementations, to link out to external data, and to assess the impact of our efforts once libraries begin publishing structured data by default.

References

1. Berners-Lee, T., Hendler, J., Lassila, O.: The semantic web. Scientific American 284(5), 28–37 (2001)
2. Nardi, B.A., O'day, V.: Intelligent agents: what we learned at the library. Libri. 46(2), 59–88 (1996)

3. Grothkopf, U.: The Internet for Librarians. Vistas in Astronomy 39(2), 137–143 (1995)
4. 020 - International Standard Book Number, http://www.loc.gov/marc/bibliographic/bd020.html (retrieved January 12, 2014)
5. OpenURL COinS: A Convention to Embed Bibliographic Metadata in HTML, http://ocoins.info/ (retrieved January 12, 2014)
6. UNAPI: An un-API for Webapps, http://unapi.info (retrieved January 12, 2014)
7. Jordan, T.: Scalable Structured Markup. In: Google I/O 2011, http://www.google.com/events/io/2011/sessions/scalable-structured-markup.html (retrieved January 12, 2014)
8. Goel, K., Gupta, P.: Introducing schema.org: Search engines come together for a richer web, http://googlewebmastercentral.blogspot.ca/2011/06/introducing-schemaorg-search-engines.html (retrieved January 12, 2014)
9. Summers, E.: GoodReads microdata, http://inkdroid.org/journal/2011/08/02/goodreads-microdata (retrieved January 12, 2014)
10. Malmsten, M.: Making a Library Catalogue Part of the Semantic Web. In: Proceedings of the International Conference on Dublin Core and Metadata Applications, pp. 146–152 (2008)
11. Linked Data Service of the German National Library, http://www.dnb.de/EN/lds
12. Simon, A., Wenz, R., Michel, V., Di Mascio, A.: Publishing Bibliographic Records on the Web of Data: Opportunities for the BnF (French National Library). In: Cimiano, P., Corcho, O., Presutti, V., Hollink, L., Rudolph, S. (eds.) ESWC 2013. LNCS, vol. 7882, pp. 563–577. Springer, Heidelberg (2013)
13. Ronallo, J.: Embedded Semantic Markup, schema.org, the Common Crawl, and Web Data Commons: What Big Web Data Means for Libraries and Archives. Digital Library Federation Forum (2013), http://jronallo.github.io/presentations/2013-dlf/presentation_with_notes/
14. Schwarz, M., Takhteyev, Y.: Half a Century of Public Software Institutions: Open Source as a Solution to Hold Up Problem. Journal of Public Economic Theory 12(4), 609–639 (2010)
15. Madrian, B.C., Shea, D.F.: The power of suggestion: Inertia in 401 (k) participation and savings behavior. The Quarterly Journal of Economics 116(4), 1149–1187 (2001)
16. Bizer, C., Heath, T., Berners-Lee, T.: Linked data–the story so far. International Journal on Semantic Web and Information Systems 5(3), 1–22 (2009)
17. Molyneux, R.: Evergreen in Context. Bulletin of the American Society for Information Science and Technology 35(2), 26–30 (2009)
18. lib-web-cats: A directory of libraries throughout the world (Evergreen), http://www.librarytechnology.org/libraries.pl?ILS=Evergreen (retrieved January 12, 2014)
19. Cormack, C., Poulain, P.: Kohacon 2009 Keynote. In: KohaCon 2009 (2009), https://archive.org/details/Kohacon09Keynote (retrieved January 12, 2014)
20. lib-web-cats: A directory of libraries throughout the world (Koha), http://www.librarytechnology.org/libraries.pl?ILS=Koha (retrieved January 12, 2014)

21. VuFind Change Log, https://vufind.org/wiki/changelog (retrieved January 12, 2014)
22. VuFind Installations, https://vufind.org/wiki/installation_status (retrieved January 12, 2014)
23. Denton, W., Coysh, S.J.: Usability testing of VuFind at an academic library. Library Hi Tech. 29(2), 301–319 (2011)
24. schema.org: Getting started with schema.org, http://schema.org/docs/gs.html#schemaorg_expected (retrieved January 12, 2014)
25. Scott, D.: Microdata: making metadata matter. In: Evergreen International Conference (2013), http://zone.biblio.laurentian.ca/dspace/handle/10219/1993 (retrieved January 12, 2014)
26. Scott, D.: Add per-library TPAC pages with schema.org structured data support, https://bugs.launchpad.net/evergreen/+bug/1261939 (retrieved January 13, 2014)
27. W3C Web Schemas, http://www.w3.org/wiki/WebSchemas (retrieved January 12, 2014)
28. W3C Schema Bib Extend Community Group, http://www.w3.org/community/schemabibex/ (retrieved January 12, 2014)
29. Hepp, M.: Goodrelations: An ontology for describing products and services offers on the web. In: Gangemi, A., Euzenat, J. (eds.) EKAW 2008. LNCS (LNAI), vol. 5268, pp. 329–346. Springer, Heidelberg (2008)
30. schema.org: Thing / Intangible / Offer, http://schema.org/Offer (retrieved January 12, 2014)
31. Broaden Offer usage, http://www.w3.org/community/schemabibex/wiki/Broaden_Offer_usage (retrieved January 12, 2014)
32. Scott, D.: Re: Support non-commercial usage of schema.org/Offer - RDF(S) patch, http://lists.w3.org/Archives/Public/public-vocabs/2013Dec/0042.html (retrieved January 12, 2014)
33. D'Arcus, B., Giasson, F.: Bibliographic Ontology Specification, http://bibliontology.com (retrieved January 12, 2014)
34. Bang, C.: CreativeWork can't be a Product? http://lists.w3.org/Archives/Public/public-vocabs/2013Oct/0091.html (retrieved January 12, 2014)
35. Scott, D.: Re: Proposal: Audiobook, http://lists.w3.org/Archives/Public/public-vocabs/2013Sep/0205.html (retrieved January 12, 2014)
36. Deering, D.: Google+ Semantic Search Marketing community post, https://plus.google.com/107534960995428499496/posts/JeER7ugmRpf (retrieved January 12, 2014)
37. Proposal for Periodicals, Articles and Multi-volume Works, http://www.w3.org/community/schemabibex/wiki/Article (retrieved January 12, 2014)
38. schema.org: Frequently Asked Questions, http://schema.org/docs/faq.html#2 (retrieved January 12, 2014)
39. Brickley, D.: MiniSKOS proposal: add Topic, an equivalentClass to skos:Concept, and relate schema properties to it, http://lists.w3.org/Archives/Public/public-vocabs/2013Nov/0121.html (retrieved March 5, 2014)

40. Lunau, C.: The Virtual Canadian Union Catalogue Project (vCuc). Resource Sharing & Information Networks 14(2), 21–35 (1999)
41. OCLC and Google to exchange data, link digitized books to WorldCat, `http://worldcat.org/arcviewer/2/OCC/2010/05/07/H1273247173434/viewer/file327.htm` (retrieved January 12, 2014)
42. Library of Congress: Metadata Object Description Schema (MODS), `http://www.loc.gov/standards/mods/` (retrieved January 12, 2014)
43. Library of Congress: Linked Data Service, `http://id.loc.gov` (retrieved January 12, 2014)
44. VIAF: The Virtual International Authority File, `http://viaf.org` (retrieved January 12, 2014)

How to Best Find a Partner? An Evaluation of Editing Approaches to Construct R2RML Mappings*

Christoph Pinkel[1], Carsten Binnig[2], Peter Haase[1], Clemens Martin[2], Kunal Sengupta[3], and Johannes Trame[1]

[1] Fluid Operations AG, Walldorf, Germany
[2] Baden-Wuerttemberg Cooperative State University, Mannheim, Germany
[3] Wright State University, Dayton OH, USA

Abstract. R2RML defines a language to express mappings from relational data to RDF. That way, applications built on top of the W3C Semantic Technology stack can seamlessly integrate relational data. A major obstacle to using R2RML, though, is the effort for manually curating the mappings. In particular in scenarios that aim to map data from huge and complex relational schemata (e.g., [5]) to more abstract ontologies efficient ways to support the mapping creation are needed.

In previous work we presented a mapping editor that aims to reduce the human effort in mapping creation [12]. While assisting users in mapping construction the editor imposed a fixed editing approach, which turned out to be not optimal for all users and all kinds of mapping tasks. Most prominently, it is unclear on which of the two data models users should best start with the mapping construction.

In this paper, we present the results of a comprehensive user study that evaluates different alternative editing approaches for constructing R2RML mapping rules. The study measures the efficiency and quality of mapping construction to find out which approach works better for users with different background knowledge and for different types of tasks.

Keywords: #eswc2014Pinkel.

1 Introduction

Motivation: The **R**DB to **R**DF **M**apping **L**anguage (R2RML[1]) has recently become a W3C standard for creating mappings from relational databases to RDF. This enables many semantic web applications to integrate easily with relational databases. Although very useful, we observe certain problems with the adoption of R2RML: (1) creating R2RML rules manually is a time consuming process, (2) even simple rules can be syntactically heavy in terms of the R2RML vocabulary, and (3) a steep learning curve is involved in gaining expertise of this new

* This work was supported by the 7th Framework Program of the EU Commission under grant agreement 318338 and by the US NSF under award 1017225.

[1] `http://www.w3.org/TR/r2rml/`

V. Presutti et al. (Eds.): ESWC 2014, LNCS 8465, pp. 675–690, 2014.

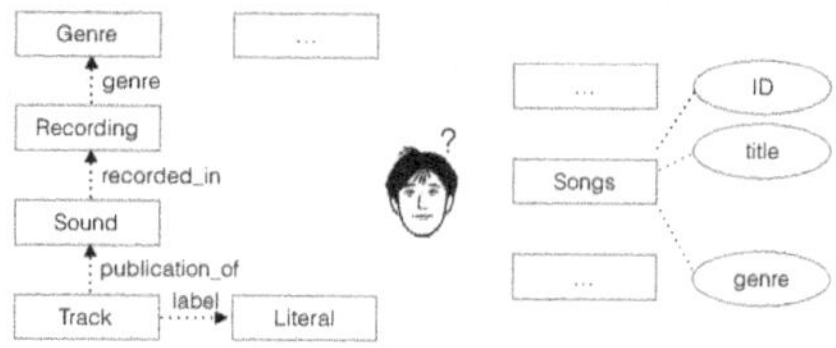

Fig. 1. Example Mapping Task (Left: Ontology, Right: Relational Schema)

language. All these issues essentially result in a high manual effort. In scenarios where data is mapped from huge and complex relational schemata to RDF, the manual effort is particularly high. In previous work [12] we demonstrated the initial version of an R2RML editor that aims to reduce the manual effort.

Problem Statement: The amount of effort that users invest for writing mapping rules depends on the mapping creation process. The usefulness of an editor therefore depends on how well it supports users in this process. Is the editing approach aligned with user expectations? Does the editor direct users in some specific direction and, if so, is this direction helpful? Or could users choose between procedural alternatives at their own discretion? Our editor initially imposed a strict editing approach, which turned out to be not optimal for many users and mapping tasks.

R2RML as a language, on the other side, leaves users a lot of of freedom about the order in which they compile different parts of a mapping rule. For example, you could start by first defining the RDF target of a mapping rule or you could start by selecting source tables from a relational database. R2RML also leaves it to the user whether to compose a separate rule for each mapping or to group many associated mappings into the same mapping rule.

Though there is a number of different approaches that a user may follow, two particular alternatives stand out: (1) the *database-driven* mapping approach where users work through the relational schema table by table and write mapping rules for all data in the tables that they find useful and (2) the *ontology-driven* mapping approach where users browse schematic aspects in an existing ontology (such as classes and properties) and then write mapping rules to add appropriate A-Box facts from the database. Essentially, these approaches start at opposite ends of a mapping. To build an efficient R2RML mapping editor we need to know which approach works better under which circumstances.

Example: Figure 1 depicts a mapping problem where instances of type *Track* should be constructed based on data in the table *Songs* of a relational database. Though both models describe the *genre* of a track, the genre is only indirectly connected to the *Track* class but directly connected to the *Songs* table.

Imagine a user trying to map the *Song* table to instances of type *Track* of the ontology, approaching the task from the database side: the user would start with exploring the table *Song*, easily identify the *ID* and the *title* attributes to construct the URIs for the *Track* instances and their labels. However, the user could have a hard time finding a mapping partner for the *genre* attribute of the table *Songs* in the ontology. In fact, what the user will have to do is (1) browse the ontology to find the corresponding partner (class *Genre*), (2) write a new R2RML rule to construct instances of class *Genre* in the ontology and (3) see how to construct triples all required triples to connect *Track* and *Genre*. This can prove to be a difficult task for a user. In this particular case, the opposite direction would appear more appealing.

Contributions: In this paper, we present the results of a comprehensive user study that evaluates different alternative editing approaches to support the construction of R2RML mapping rules in our editor. We therefore extended the mapping editor to support different approaches.

We put our main focus on the ontology-driven and database-driven approaches. Consequently, one hypothesis that we tested in our user study is that both approaches accommodate the preferences of users with a different background knowledge. For example, database experts might prefer to proceed differently than ontology experts. In another hypothesis, we assumed that either mapping approach offers different advantages and disadvantages for different mapping tasks. For example, for a mapping task where a small ontology requires only a few facts out of a huge database, the ontology-driven approach might generally appear more reasonable.

Outline: The remainder of this paper is organized as follows: Section 2 discusses different approaches implied by R2RML for constructing mapping rules. Section 3 presents the existing R2RML editor that we have extended for this study. In Section 4, we present the design of our study along a set of key questions and discuss the results of the study. Section 5 describes related work. We conclude and discuss possible future work in Section 6.

2 R2RML Editing Approaches

R2RML as a language leaves the user much freedom about how to compose mapping rules. However, logical dependencies in many cases suggest a natural order of steps for writing rules.

2.1 Implied Editing Approaches in R2RML

Figure 2 shows the basic structure of R2RML mapping rules. Mapping rules are called *triples maps*. Each triples map consists of (1) a *logical table*, which defines a view on the source database, (2) a *subject map*, which defines target instance URIs and types, and (3) any number of *predicate/object maps*, adding triples to those instances.

For example, if you wish to add a mapping for songs and their titles from a table *Songs* to an ontology class *Track*, you might write a mapping rule with the following components: (1) a logical table that builds a view on table *Songs*, (2) a subject map that constructs a unique URI for each song tuple and types it as a *Track* and (3) one predicate/object map with predicate *dc:title* and object literals constructed from the *title* attribute in table *Songs*.

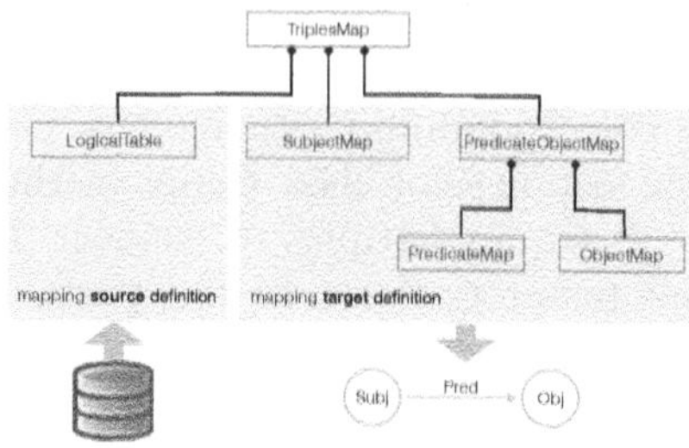

Fig. 2. Main Aspects of R2RML Mapping Rules

You may generally add those parts in any order. In the following we describe the choices a user can make based on R2RML as a language.

Mapping Direction: Most importantly, users may start by defining the logical table or by defining the subject map, i.e., they might:

1. Proceed *database-driven* by defining views over the source database.
2. Proceed *ontology-driven* by first specifying ontology classes.

Both approaches imply a different kind of thinking. Users can either think of existing database tables or of the target ontology and required information.

Subject Map Definition: Any triple depends on its subject, which is defined in a subject map. It would thus sound natural to specify the subject map before any predicate/object maps are defined. However, you may also consider the subject as implicitly given and specify it later.

Predicate/Object Map Definition: Predicate/object maps each contain a predicate map and an object map. The obvious order here is to first specify the predicate then the object but the other way around is also possible.

Predicate/Object Map Separation: The fact that each mapping rule can have only one subject map but any number of predicate/object maps suggests that as many predicate/object maps as possible should be added to the same rule. However, different properties may rely on different parts of the source database. Therefore, this assumption adds potentially heavy requirements on the source database view, i.e., on the logical table of the mapping rule. Depending on the required views this may be or may not be adequate in practice. Hence, in cases where the views would become too complex it can make sense to construct different mapping rules for each predicate/object map. Each of those rules would then reference the same subject map but a different logical table.

Incremental Rule Extensions: Finally, mapping rules may undergo many iterations, especially when working with complex data. For example, predicate/object maps may be added. Also, logical tables might be adjusted to cover a wider selection of data. The second case is particularly interesting. It basically represents the opposite strategy of predicate separation: add another rule for a new predicate or extend the logical table? Also, in some cases it may have implications on the correctness of previously added parts of a mapping.

2.2 Supported Approaches in R2RML Editors

Editors, while assisting users in various ways, may also restrict their freedom by forcing them to work with one specific approach.

In our search for the best approach we focus on mapping direction, i.e., on the choice between the database driven and ontology driven approach.

Handling subject definition is easy with editors as they can always construct a subject automatically. Users may later change these subject maps but there is no good reason to force them to edit subject maps at one specific point in time.

Predicate/object map definition plays no role in editors because a single dialog would be used to associate both. Therefore, users are always free to proceed either way. Predicate separation, i.e., the choice to construct several smaller rules instead of one single large rule may or may not be supported by editors. Similarly, incremental build-up may or may not be supported.

3 The R2RML Mapping Editor

In this paper, we use our R2RML editor [12] as a basis. For the purpose of the study we extended our editor to support different editing approaches. In the following, we first describe the original editor and then discuss our extensions.

3.1 Basic Editor (Original Version)

In terms of individual features the editor provides a user interface that hides the R2RML vocabulary details, allows an easy access to schema meta-data of the relational database for which the mappings are to be created and gives feedback at each step, such as previewing triples. The original workflow supported by the editor follows a strict step-by-step pattern which can be described as follows:

1. **Datasource & Base URI Selection:** The user chooses data sources (i.e., databases and ontologies) to work with.
2. **R2RML Rule Selection:** At this point the user may choose to edit an existing rule or add a new one.
3. **Logical Table Selection:** Logical tables in R2RML are either database tables, existing views or custom SQL queries establishing an ad-hoc view. Consequently, the user can choose an existing table or view or write a query.
4. **Subject Map Creation:** The original version of the editor requires the user to define in detail how subject URIs are generated, usually using a template. An `rdf:type` can optionally be assigned.
5. **Predicate/Object Maps Creation:** Finally, for the selected subject any number of predicates and objects can be added. The editor offers the full expressiveness of R2RML predicate/object maps including advanced options.
6. **Textual Representation:** Finally, a summary is displayed. It is still possible to step back from this point in order to modify the rule.

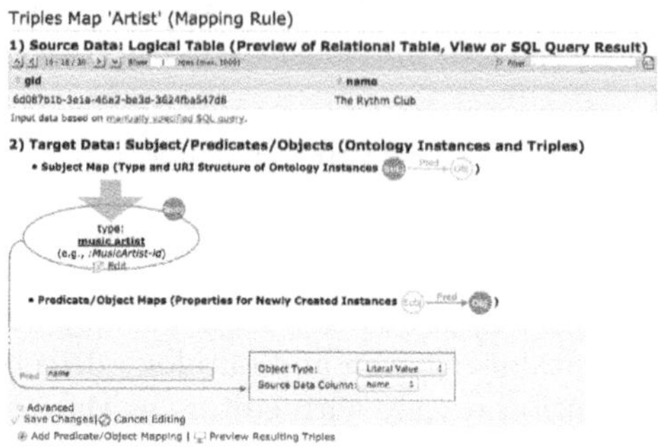

Fig. 3. A Mapping Rule in the Editor

3.2 Extensions and Modifications

While following the most obvious approach for creating mapping rules in R2RML, the original version of the editor showed little flexibility to deviate from this one approach that we required to test different hypotheses that we will explain in detail in Section 4.

To overcome those limitations, we modified the editor so that the user was free to construct mapping rules in almost any order. To this end, switching from one step to another is now possible by simply clicking the "Edit" button in the relevant part of the rule. When a user does so, a summary of all other parts of the rule still remains visible, so it is always possible to cross-check for implications of changes with those other parts at a glance. Finally, wherever possible, we also hid complex and rarely used language features behind an "Advanced" button, so that for most regular tasks the UI would not be obfuscated with a large number of extra knobs and options.

Before these changes users could not browse away from any wizard step (say, the predicate/object step) to explore relevant ontology or database aspects. It was neither possible to start exploring the ontology or database and then directly add a mapping rule for a relevant aspect just found. Instead, the users always had to get back to the editor's start page, add all mapping details in the expected order and manually enter every detail they found while exploring when requested.

Figure 3 depicts a rule in the new version of the editor where a predicate/object map is currently being edited while the summary of both the logical table and subject map are still visible.

Furthermore, we coupled the editor with ontology and database exploration: users can now add new mapping rules right from viewing the details of an ontology class, predicate, database table or column. If they do so, the rule will be initialized from the context, e.g., by automatically adding a logical table or rdf:type to the newly generated rule. This offers different entry points for adding rules and thus supports different editing approaches.

3.3 Semi Automatic Match Suggestions

Besides general UI support and preview capabilities that form the main parts of our editor, another popular method for supporting users in editing mappings are *suggestions*. Those can come, for instance, in the shape of code auto-completion while editing rules or, more specifically in form of match suggestions.

As mapping rules are logically build on matches (or correspondences) between aspects in the relational schema and the ontology, respectively, such suggestions carry high potential in reducing the amount of work that users will have to invest to identify and name the corresponding aspects while writing rules. While suggestion quality is a key factor in the usefulness during mapping creation in general, the question how matches are created is orthogonal to our work since it can be carried out in a pre-processing step.

For this reason we extend the editor with an optional semi automatic suggestion mechanism that can be turned on and off for evaluation to study its impact. In our paper, we use the IncMap system [7] to generate suggestions in both directions (i.e., from database to ontology and vice versa).

4 User Study

We have designed our user study to shed light on the following *key questions* with regard to the hypothesis mentioned in Section 1:

1. How suitable are different editing approaches when creating mapping rules in general (i.e., starting with for *browsing the ontology or the database*? *Hypothesis:* In the general case, none of the main approaches outperforms the other.
2. Is some approach more suitable for users with a *different background* (i.e., different levels of expertise, background in databases vs. semantics technologies)? *Hypothesis:* The background of the user influences results.
3. Is there a approach that works better for *different task types*? *Hypothesis:* Task characteristics will have influence on which approach works better.
4. How much can be gained when *providing mapping suggestions* resulting from using semi-automatic matching tools for the different editing approaches? Does some approach gain more than others and could thus be more suitable whenever high-quality suggestions are available? *Hypothesis:* In general mapping suggestions will help users when constructing complex mapping rules (i.e., no one-to-one mappings). Since complex mapping rules in R2RML are only supported by constructing a SQL join query, we believe that the ontology-driven approach will benefit more since then SQL queries with joins can be suggested as a logical table which maps to a prior selected class of the ontology. The other way round complex mappings are only supported by constructing multiple rules (i.e., one for each artifact of an ontology).

4.1 Task Definitions

We have built our user study around the MusicBrainz database[2] and the Music Ontology [9]. This scenario is particularly appealing because some domain knowledge can then be taken for granted with any study participant without teaching her the basic classes and properties. Moreover, a series of hand-crafted mappings provided by the EUCLID project[3] already existed. We used those mappings as a basis to define relevant and realistic mapping tasks for the user study and to make sure that our expectations towards the mapping semantics were reasonable.

For the study, we have defined three tasks around different concepts of the Music Ontology (i.e., artists, recordings, and tracks). Each task includes a similar number of rules that need be created whereas the rules cover different elements of the ontology (i.e., instances of classes and properties). Moreover, we have created the tasks such that each task comes with challenges of different complexity (e.g., defining SQL queries with and without joins for the mappings).

The high-level description of the three tasks of the user study is as follows:

1. **Artists:** We need to get some information about artists listed in the database: We need at least to be able to identify them uniquely as artists (typed) and know their names.
2. **Recordings:** We need to know about recordings listed in the database. At least, we need to have them uniquely identified and typed, and we also need to know their duration.
3. **Tracks:** We need to know about tracks listed in the database. At least, we need to have them uniquely identified and typed and we also need to know their position on the album.

We split each task in two steps: (1) The first step consisted of constructing a basic mapping between a source logical table and a target ontology class whereas the logical table had to be constructed by either choosing a plain table or writing a SQL query for joining multiple tables. (2) In the second step the user always had to add a predicate/object map in R2RML to map some attributes of a table to an appropriate ontology property. Table 1 lists all individual tasks of the user study, explains the two steps per task and discusses the associated problems that users had to solve in order to successfully complete the step.

4.2 Setup and Participants

To run the study, we extended the R2RML mapping editor [12] as described in Section 3 and provided a web front-end wrapping for the mapping editor in a specifically designed shell for the user study. Besides embedding the mapping editor and associated exploration and visualization features, the shell also implemented a questionnaire and a wizard-style series of briefing steps to prepare participants for the task. The editor implements the ontology approach as

[2] `http://musicbrainz.org/doc/MusicBrainz_Database/Schema`
[3] `http://www.euclid-project.eu`

Table 1. Study Tasks and Associated Challenges

Task	Step#	Short Description	Challenge/Non-trivial Aspects
Artists	1	Map and type instances of class *mo:MusicArtist.*	Identify the correct table in the database with more than 10 similar tables.
Artists	2	Construct *foaf:name* triples for artists	Identify the unique ID and the name attribute spread over two tables and write a SQL query for joining two tables.
Recordings	1	Map and type instances of class *mo:Recording*	Besides *mo:recording* the ontology contains other similar concepts (e.g., *recording_session*), which can be disambiguated only when carefully reading of the description.
Recordings	2	Construct *mo:duration* triples for recordings	In the relational database the *duration* property is called *length.*
Tracks	1	Map and type instances of class *mo:Track*	Identify the correct ID attribute while most attributes show purely numeric sample data.
Tracks	2	Construct *mo:track_number* triples for recordings	Task description mentions *position* on an album (like database attribute), but not *number* (as used in ontology)

ONTO mode and the database approach as *DB mode.* For providing mapping suggestions, we used the IncMap system demonstrated in [8].

Participants could openly access the web front-end from the internet. Each participant was assigned an isolated study slot. Within each slot (i.e., for each participant) the user interface was restricted to provide only the functionality required for the part of the study to which the participant has progressed.

We recruited participants different technical background (general computer science, databases, Semantic Web) and experience (professionals and computer science students). Among those asked to participate were data integration professionals, colleagues and Semantic Web experts, as well as a group of second year computer science students.

4.3 Structure of the Study

We structured the study in four parts: (1) initial questionnaire, (2) introduction and technical briefing, (3) mapping tasks (the key part of the study), and (4) a catamnestic questionnaire.

Initial Questionnaire: We asked participants to rate their technical knowledge in the relevant fields (*relational databases and SQL*, and *RDF and ontologies*) to address *key question 2* (i.e., the influence of the background knowledge). Users could rate their skills on a scale from 1 to 5 (with 1 indicating extremely low and 5 indicating very high expertise).

Study Introduction: After that, we introduced users to the study and the mapping editor in a wizard-style introduction of six subsequent web pages. Users were introduced to R2RML mappings in general (mapping from databases to ontologies), the application domain (music) and the general problems of finding correspondences without in-depth knowledge of the schema and ontology.

They were then familiarized with the mapping editor by showing and explaining an example mapping rule in screen shots.

Mapping Tasks: In the main part of the study, we asked users to perform the different mapping tasks previously described in Section 4.1. For each task, users can see the high-level description of the task's information need as well as more detailed instructions for the current step they are working on. From the task description page, users can follow a link to the editor's main page, which shows all existing mapping rules created so far as well as entry points to browse the database schema and/or the ontology.

To make sure that the users follow different exploration strategies (i.e. first browse the ontology and then the database and then the other way round), we varied the availability of entry points for browsing from task to task. This helped us to discuss *k*ey question 1, which analyzes the influence of different approaches on the mapping results. Therefore half of the users would, for their first task, only be able to browse and explore the ontology (not the database) to create associated mapping rules. Once a mapping rule was created, users could enter matching database information by using standard editor tools, i.e., lists of available database tables, data previews, as-you-type auto-completion and, possibly, automatic suggestions. For the second task, those users would then only be able to initially browse the database schema (not the ontology) to create mapping rules. Matching ontology aspects could then only be entered in the editor itself. For the other half of the users browsing and exploration went the other other way around (i.e., they could only access the database schema in the first task and only the ontology in the second). For the last task, all users were free to try either way.

Moreover, we presented the three tasks in random order to all participants in order to compensate for a potential bias introduced by the learning curve of getting familiar with the schema, ontology and mapping editor. This should help us to better analyze *k*ey question 3 (i.e., the influence of different task types).

Finally, to discuss *k*ey question 4, half of the users were provided with automated mapping suggestions, while the others were not.

While browsing, exploring or editing mapping rules, participants could always mark the current step as completed, which would advance them to the next step, again showing the task/step description with current information. Participants could as well skip a step, which would also advance them to the next step or task. We kept a record of whether user marked steps a completed or skipped in order to compare the correctness of the mappings to the participants' confidence in their correctness. Also, participants could always follow a link back to task and step instructions and double-check what to do before proceeding to edit their mapping rules.

Catamnestic Questionnaire: After all tasks were completed (or skipped) we asked for each of the tasks how the user felt about solving them. While doing so, we reminded participants of the different browsing and exploration options they had in the different tasks to draw their attention to those different strategies.

Participants could rate the options for each task on a scale from 1 to 5. This was to to inquire whether users would have a preference for one approach.

4.4 Study Results

From a total of 47 participants we considered 31 result sets for evaluation. The remaining 16 users quit the study during the briefing or during the first task and produced too little usable data. Out of all 31 participants considered, 13 ranked themselves as experts in ontologies, while 11 ranked themselves as experts in databases (skill level of 4 or 5 on a scale from 1 to 5).

General Findings: A first look mostly confirms our expectations.

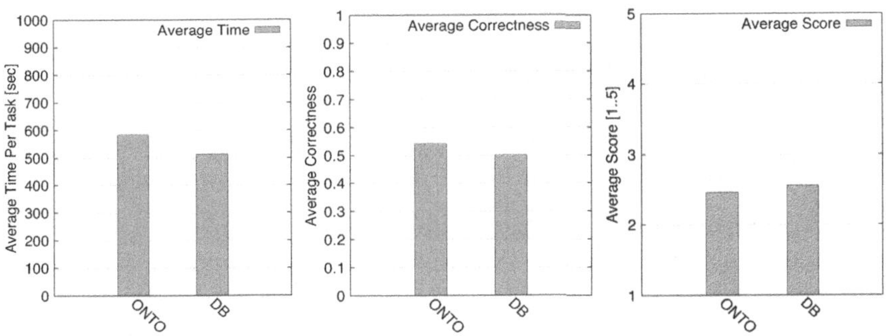

(a) Time Taken (b) Correctness (c) Average Rating

Fig. 4. Overall Per-approach Averages of Correctness, Time Taken, User Ratings

Figure 4 shows a comparison between the two main editing approaches from different angles. Neither the average time that users needed to complete a task (Fig. 4a), nor the correctness of results produced with each approach (Fig. 4b) show significant differences. Our first hypothesis, namely that in the general case no approach outperforms the other, is therefore retained.

Also, participants felt about as comfortable with the ontology approach as they did with the database approach, as the catamnestic survey reveals (Fig. 4c). This is particularly interesting, as users overwhelmingly turned to the database-driven approach when given the choice in the last task. Additionally, we observed whether users produced more and smaller or fewer and larger mapping rules under different circumstances. We found that expert users tended to produce slightly fewer rules than non-experts.

Little surprisingly, participants spent the longest time on the first task, worked faster on the second and again faster on the third (Fig. 5a). Somewhat less expected, however, the correctness of results also continuously declines with the task number (Fig. 5b). With result quality in mind this is a little unsettling because the correlation between correctness and the self-assessment of task success

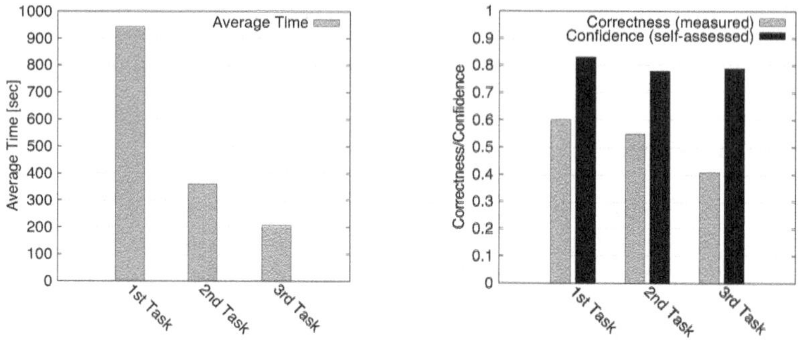

(a) Average Time (b) Correctness and User Confidence

Fig. 5. Influence of Task Number on Time Taken, Correctness, User Confidence

by the users is rather weak, as can also be seen in Figure 5b. On top of that, participants in general tend to overestimate the correctness of their mapping rules. This comes despite the fact that the editor offered preview data both for the relational source and for resulting target triples to allow for sanity checks.

Editing Approach per User Background: According to our second hypothesis, different approaches should work differently well for users with different background knowledge. As Figure 6 shows, this is in fact the case.

As was to be expected, users with a stronger background knowledge generally produce better results than those with poorer skill levels. Figure 6a shows the impact of different levels of background knowledge. Please note that, while the level of database skills was almost evenly distributed, only two users rated themselves into the middle tier of RDF and ontology skills; the drop of resulting correctness for mid-level ontology knowledge is dominated by an outlier.

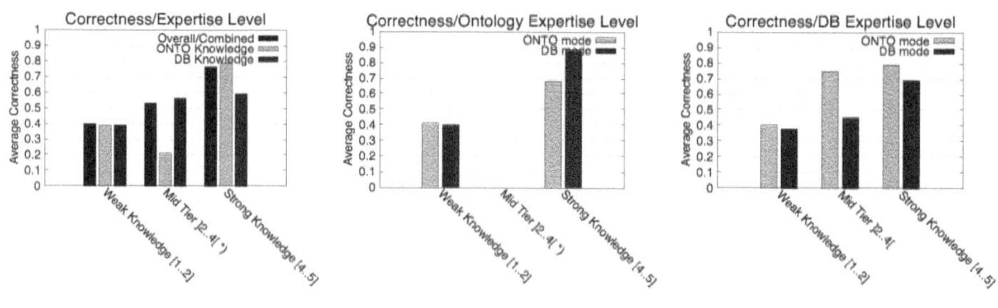

(a) By User Expertise (b) By Ontology Skills (c) By DB Skills

Fig. 6. Influence of Different Background Knowledge on Correctness

Interestingly, though, it is not the case that database experts work better with the database approach while ontology experts improve when working with the ontology approach, but the other way around. At second glance, however, this makes perfect sense: in the ontology mode, users have the opportunity to browse and explore the ontology first, then they need to identify the corresponding database table(s) in the editor, which offers less exploration and visualization possibilities (for database mode it is the other way around). Thus, users who are proficient in databases were more successful when the tougher part – finding a mapping partner – could be handled in the database world that they are familiar with, and vice-versa.

Browsing and Exploration Methodology per Task: As a third hypothesis we assumed that different approaches would work differently well on different task types and associated challenges.

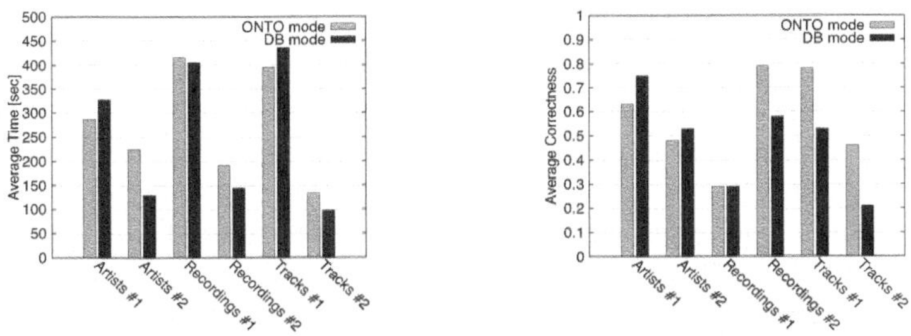

(a) Average Time (b) Average Correctness

Fig. 7. Correctness and Time Taken per Task, Step, and Editing Approach

Figure 7 clearly shows that this is the case, with each approach in the lead on correctness for some of the tasks. Observations on which approach works better for which task also largely match exceptions, when considering the specific challenges for each task and step described in Section 4.2. For instance, the second step of the Recording task (Recording#2) required to solve a lexical mismatch (i.e., duration in the ontology and task description vs. length in the database schema), which we expected to work better if users work in an ontology-driven approach since it is harder to pick an attribute in the database schema with a totally different name (i.e., length) without any context and assistance. For this task step the ontology-driven approach is on a clear lead in correctness.

Influence of Automatic Suggestions: Finally, our fourth hypothesis says that suggestions should have a stronger positive impact with the ontology approach. Figure 8 depicts the impact of automatic suggestions. We provided suggestions for logical tables in ontology mode, for ontology classes in database mode and for predicate/attribute correspondences in both cases.

Figure 8a shows that the presence of suggestions can save working time, though not in all cases. When analyzing the influence of suggestions on the correctness of R2RML mapping rules (Fig. 8b), our hypothesis is partially confirmed. As expected, the ontology-driven approach gains in most cases in correctness (i.e., in five out of six steps) when providing logical tables as mapping

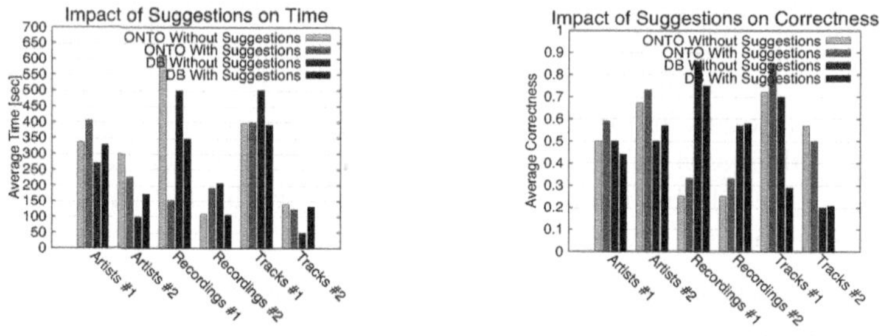

(a) Average Time (b) Average Correctness

Fig. 8. Influence of Automatic Suggestions for Different Strategies

suggestions (since this involves writing potentially complex SQL queries). In particular in the artist task, where users had to manually write a SQL join, the gain of the appropriate logical table suggestion is noticeable high and also clearly puts the ontology mode in lead before the database mode for this task. For the database-driven approach, however, mappings suggestions have a negative impact for many task steps (i.e., in three out of six steps). We cannot really explain this observation for the database-driven approach. Instead, we speculate that some users deliberately have chosen absurd suggestions at the end of the study to finish their last tasks quicker, which would also explain the general drop in correctness for the later tasks in Figure 5b.

5 Related Work

Data integration is a well studied research problem [2]. However, studying different editing approaches for mapping construction that involve user interactions for data integration tasks has gained relatively less attention so far. Most research in the field of data integration has been focusing on automatic approaches for schema alignment, record linkage, data fusion etc. We believe that with the growth of schema complexity as well as with the increasing need to integrate more and more data sources, new interactive approaches for constructing complex mappings are getting necessary.

Some RDB2RDF editors exist that offer advanced and more or less visual user interfaces, e.g., [1,10]. However, these are based on domain specific languages predating R2RML. To the best of our knowledge, no other editors to date expose R2RML semantics through a visual interface. [11] describes an Eclipse plugin that supports R2RML execution as well as mapping generation with custom algorithms. Neto et al. have demonstrated a mapping editor with a highly visual interface that eventually generates R2RML [6]. However, they not expose R2RML semantics but only simple correspondences used as assertions. Arguably, the expressiveness of these assertions is only a subset of R2RML.

Only a few recent papers exist that include user studies that analyze approaches for user-centric data integration [13,3,4]. Both [3] and [13] contain user studies that analyze the effectiveness and efficiency of existing visual tools for data integration that follow a similar cognitive support model. This cognitive support model represents a very strict approach for creating mapping rules: first, a set of mapping rules is created automatically, then these rules are applied to some data and finally users verify the individual rules by marking the results as correct or incorrect. Compared to this very strict approach, [4] introduces a new interactive data transformation language that leaves much freedom to the user which approach the user actually will apply. Basically, the user can apply a set of data transformation primitives in any order and is supported by interactive data visualization tools to preview results, histories to undo changes, etc.

Our editor is in-between these two extremes and proposes two general approaches that support users to curate mapping rules by either selecting schema elements from the source schema or the target schema that are then mapped to the other side. These approaches are analyzed in a comprehensive user study with more than 31 usable data sets of 47 participants, which is a higher number than reported in the other user studies (which range from 4-22 participants).

6 Conclusions

We presented the results of a comprehensive user study that evaluates alternative mapping editing approaches (ontology-driven vs. database-driven) to construct R2RML mapping rules in an editor. Consequently, we tested different hypotheses and measured the time and correctness for different mapping tasks.

We found out that neither approach is at a significant advantage of the other in the general case. However, we have seen that the ontology-driven approach works better for users with a background in databases and vice-versa, which was initially counter-intuitive for us. We also found a strong influence of task characteristics on the resulting mappings. Finally, it showed that automatic suggestions tend to have more impact on the ontology driven approach. It needs to be noted that, when given the choice, all users overwhelmingly tend to follow the database-driven approach, not the one that statistically works better for them.

As a result of our observations, we can make the following recommendations for building R2RML editors:

1. It is desirable to support both basic approaches, ontology-driven and database-driven, as each works better under different circumstances.
2. We cannot expect users to choose the best approach. Instead, an editor should try to learn about their background and, if possible, about the mapping tasks and then actively propose the adequate approach.
3. Prominent validation mechanisms should be offered, as users largely overestimate the quality of their mapping rules, even with data previews available.
4. When working with automatic match suggestions, the ontology-driven approach is somewhat more promising.

References

1. Bizer, C., Seaborne, A.: D2RQ-treating non-RDF databases as virtual RDF graphs. In: ISWC (2004)
2. Dong, X.L., Srivastava, D.: Big Data Integration. PVLDB 6(11), 1188–1189 (2013)
3. Falconer, S.M., Noy, N.F.: Interactive Techniques to Support Ontology Matching. In: Schema Matching and Mapping (2011)
4. Kandel, S., Paepcke, A., Hellerstein, J., Heer, J.: Wrangler: interactive visual specification of data transformation scripts. In: CHI (2011)
5. Kharlamov, E., et al.: Optique 1.0: Semantic Access to Big Data. In: ISWC (Posters & Demos) (2013)
6. Neto, L.E.T., Vidal, V.M.P., Casanova, M.A., Monteiro, J.M.: R2RML by Assertion: A Semi-automatic Tool for Generating Customised R2RML Mappings. In: Cimiano, P., Fernández, M., Lopez, V., Schlobach, S., Völker, J. (eds.) ESWC 2013. LNCS, vol. 7955, pp. 248–252. Springer, Heidelberg (2013)
7. Pinkel, C., Binnig, C., Kharlamov, E., Haase, P.: IncMap: Pay-as-you-go Matching of Relational Schemata to OWL Ontologies. In: OM (2013)
8. Pinkel, C., et al.: Pay as you go Matching of Relational Schemata to OWL Ontologies with IncMap. In: ISWC (Posters & Demos) (2013)
9. Raimond, Y., Giasson, F. (eds.): Music Ontology (2012), `http://www.musicontology.com`
10. Rodriguez-Muro, M., Calvanese, D.: -ontop- framework (2012), `http://obda.inf.unibz.it/protege-plugin/`
11. Salas, P.E., Marx, E., Mera, A., Breitman, K.K.: RDB2RDF Plugin: Relational Databases to RDF plugin for Eclipse. In: TOPI (2011)
12. Sengupta, K., Haase, P., Schmidt, M., Hitzler, P.: Editing R2RML Mappings Made Easy. In: ISWC (Posters & Demos) (2013)
13. Stuckenschmidt, H., Noessner, J., Fallahi, F.: A Study in User-centric Data Integration. In: ICEIS (3) (2012)

Towards Portable Shopping Histories: Using GoodRelations to Expose Ownership Information to E-Commerce Sites

László Török and Martin Hepp

Universität der Bundeswehr
Werner-Heisenberg-Weg 39.
85579 Neubiberg, Germany
{laszlo.toeroek,martin.hepp}@unibw.de

Abstract. Recommender systems are an important technology component for many e-commerce applications. In short, they are technical means that suggest potentially relevant products and services to the users of a Web site, typically a shop. The recommendations are computed in advance or during the actual visit and use various types of data as input, in particular past purchases and the purchasing behavior of other users with similar preferences. One major problem with recommender systems is that the quality of recommendations depends on the amount, quality, and representativeness of the information about items already owned by the visitor, e.g. from past purchases at that particular shop. For first-time visitors and customers migrating from other merchants, the amount of available information is often too small to generate good recommendations. Today, shopping history data for a single user is fragmented and spread over multiple sites, and cannot be actively exposed by the user to additional shops.

In this paper, we propose to use Semantic Web technology, namely GoodRelations and schema.org, to empower e-commerce customers to (1) collect and manage ownership information about products, (2) detect if a shop site is interested in such information in exchange for better recommendations or other incentives, and (3) expose the information to such shop sites directly from their browser. We then sketch how a shop site could use the ownership information to recommend relevant products.

Keywords: #eswc2014Torok, Semantic Web, Recommender Systems, E-Commerce, schema.org, GoodRelations, RDF, RDFa, Microdata.

1 Introduction

Recommender systems are an established part of e-commerce systems. They help prospective customers to navigate the myriad of products offered in an online shop and aid them with finding a product that best matches their needs and preferences. Many recommender systems require or benefit from data about past purchases or items ratings. This means that they perform well if the user has already a shopping history in that particular system, and perform poorly when facing a first-time user that

V. Presutti et al. (Eds.): ESWC 2014, LNCS 8465, pp. 691–705, 2014.

has not yet rated or purchased an item in a given shop. From the user's perspective, her rating and purchase history is scattered across many shop systems, which she has visited in the past. Accessing and sharing one's entire shopping history, or a subset thereof, could likely provide better personalization and better recommendations.

We also argue that purchase records are not necessarily representative when it comes to preferences. For instance, people do not always buy products for themselves. A one-time purchase of a cosmetic product for the wife does not mean that a husband has a longer-term personal interest in it. Therefore, we focus on collecting, managing and sharing **actual item ownership information**, as we believe it is a better indicator of personal preferences.

One of the key problems that prohibit a wider availability of ownership information is that parts of one's shopping history are locked up in multiple, proprietary data representations. Our goal is to develop a common data representation and exchange protocol that could improve existing recommender systems and open up new possibilities for shop systems for better understanding their customers.

1.1 Role of Item Ownership Information in Recommender Systems

Most contemporary recommender systems do not rely on actual data about items being owned by users; instead, they use past purchases, or items viewed previously, to infer likely ownership; for an overview, see e.g. [11]. In particular, Collaborative Filtering (CF) algorithms have been successfully applied to the problem of product recommendation. The numerous existing CF algorithms share two common properties: (1) they maintain a matrix of item ratings **R** or purchases where a $R_{i,j}$ entry represents that a $User_i$ rated/purchased $Item_j$ and based on this (2) calculate a ranked list of top-N items that might appeal to a given user [1]. Our focus in this paper is the use of ownership information, hence we limit our discussion to past purchases, although CF algorithms apply to item ratings and other forms of user-item interaction as well.

Let $User_c$ be the current user for whom the recommended list of items should be computed. The user-based CF algorithms employ clustering techniques over **R** to find other users that have similar preferences to $User_c$, that is, their purchase record has a significant overlap with that of $User_c$ [cf. 1, 11].

Another flavor of CF algorithms are item-based CF algorithms. The core of these algorithms is the item-similarity matrix **S**, where $S_{i,j}$ denotes a similarity between $Item_i$ and $Item_j$ [1]. The item-similarity matrix is derived from the frequency of purchasing or positively rating two particular items for each item pair [1, 11]. The output is a ranked list of items likely to be purchased by $User_c$.

Markov-chain based (a.k.a next-basket prediction) methods [6] model purchasing as a probabilistic sequential process and attempt to predict the next set of items likely to be purchased by the user. In other words, they consider the temporal relations between purchases of items. The explicit cause of the next-item relevance remain typically undefined even in semantically augmented CF approaches, such as [4], where a product taxonomy is employed in order to better capture consecutive purchases of related items, for example a camera, followed by a tripod and an additional camera lens. In other words, these advanced models may be able learn that customers who purchase a camera are likely to purchase a tripod, from training data. However, they do not reveal the fact that the reason behind the two being frequently purchased together is that the tripod is an accessory of a video camera.

More complete or more detailed ownership information could pave the way to novel product recommendation techniques that will rely on semantic relations between products. Recommender systems could e.g. utilize functional dependencies between items in certain product recommendation scenarios, for example, directing the user to a compatible toner cartridge for the laser printer that she purchased previously. Alternatively, a recommender system informed by popular preference structures could infer that someone who owns a yoga mattress is likely to be interested in organic food, because both is related to an interest in a healthy lifestyle.

1.2 Impact of Additional Item Ownership Information

As we have shown in 1.1, most personalized recommender systems are driven by past purchases. However, a Web shop only holds a fraction of a user's online purchase record, as it is only aware of items purchase there (see Figure 1).

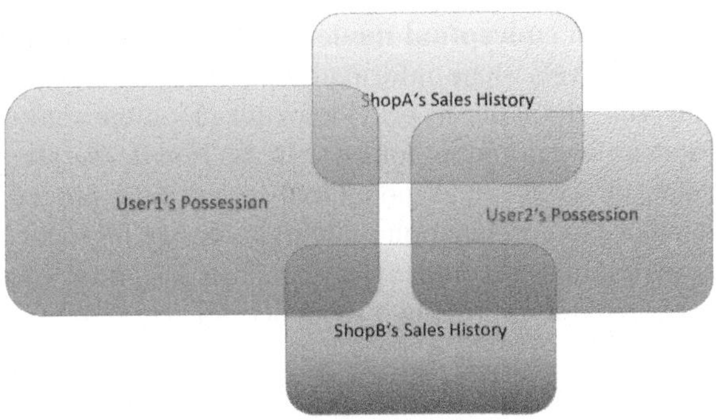

Fig. 1. Owned items versus purchase records

The ability alone to actively share purchases made at other shops could improve the performance of recommender systems. For example, they could help mitigate the cold-start problem [cf. 5] for new customers or alleviate the data sparsity problem in collaborative filtering approaches [cf. 1]. In this paper, we argue that ownership information offers additional insight into the user's preferences than pure data about past purchases. Specifically, we will develop a data model to express which items the user currently owns and which items she did own in the past. This level of detail allows one to filter out items purchased for someone else and offers hints on how long an item or a group of items were in possession of the user. Given this level of detail, someone making a one-time purchase for his spouse can be spared from constantly receiving recommendations about further products of a similar kind.

1.3 Portability Barriers on Item Ownership Information

Currently, the exchange of information about owned items between users and Web sites is hampered by the following limitations:

(1) Purchasing records as structured data are mostly available only within shop site applications but not on the machines of users. While users receive purchasing confirmation and invoices, those are typically only unstructured text[1].
(2) There is no common data model for representing and sharing ownership information.
(3) There is no common protocol for initiating and governing the exchange of item ownership information between users and Web sites.

Currently, only product model master data is exchanged between partners in value chains, mostly via XML-based product catalogs, and product models of commodities are identified via product identifiers like the standardized Global Trade Item Number[2] (GTIN). There is, however, no standard way of representing, managing, and sharing item ownership information from a user's perspective.

1.4 Our contribution

In this paper, we describe a **conceptual model, an RDF-based syntax, and a protocol** that allow users to actively share information about items owned with Web applications, thus empowering the latter to provide better recommendations even for first-time users. Our paper is structured as follows: In Section 2, we present a motivating scenario, and develop the conceptual model and its machine-processable representation based on schema.org in combination with an exchange protocol. In Section 3, we describe two relevant product recommender scenarios based on ownership information. In section 4, we provide preliminary evidence for the viability and relevance of our proposed method.

2 User-Managed Ownership Information

2.1 Our Approach

Our goal is to augment the typical interaction pattern between a user and a Web shop by the ability to share information about items owned by the user in exchange for a more personalized shopping experience or other incentives, as sketched in Figure 2. To enable this interaction pattern, both the user's Web browser and the shop system must support (1) the common data model and (2) the exchange protocol described in 2.4.

---

[1] This may improve by the availability of the support for transactions in schema.org, `http://schema.org/Order`, and schema.org markup in JSON-LD in email messages, see `https://developers.google.com/gmail/actions/`

[2] Standardized by the GS1 standards body.

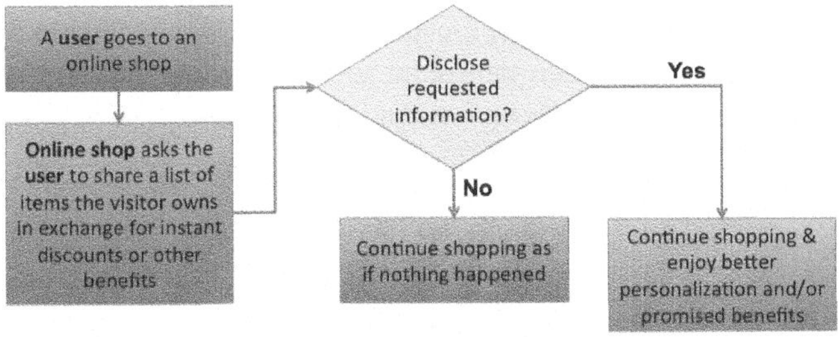

Fig. 2. High-level interaction pattern for exchanging item ownership information

2.2 Modeling Ownership Information

In the following, we first develop a conceptual model for capturing item ownership information, and then show how it can be represented in various RDF syntaxes.

Requirements. We express the requirements on the conceptual model in the form of competency questions, which is a common approach in ontology development [7]. The competency questions arose from our study of recommender system literature and novel rule-based recommendation techniques that use on granular semantic product relationships, as discussed in Section 3.

Q1: Which items does the user currently own?
Q2: Which items did the user ever own in the past?
Q3: During which period of time has a certain user owned a certain item?
Q4: Why has a user ceased to own a certain item? (e.g. sold, broken, superseded)
Q5: From whom did a user acquire a certain item?
Q6: How/for how much was the item acquired?
Q7: What class/category does the item belong to?

Conceptual Model for Item Ownership Information. We propose the following set of entity and relationship types: An ***Agent*** represents a real person or an organization that can possess arbitrary items. An ***Item*** stands for arbitrary physical or electronic goods (e.g. music) that can be owned by an *Agent*. A natural approach is to employ a binary relation "***owns***" to express basic ownership information, however, such simplistic approach has a very limited expressivity.

Following our competency questions, we extend the binary owns relation to capture more granular information of an ownership relation (see Figure 3). The attributes ***from*** and ***to*** cover the time interval during which an *Item* was owned by an *Agent*. These are particularly valuable for non-perishable goods that are intended for long-term use. In certain scenarios, it can be valuable to know from whom the *Agent* did acquire a given *Item*. This can be directly expressed via the ***acquired from*** relation. As the most common scenario for an acquisition is accepting a commercial offer of a merchant, we will reuse some of the conceptual elements of the GoodRelations and schema.org vocabulary to provide further details (e.g. purchase price) for the acquisition. In order to express the circumstances of ceasing ownership of an item, we define the relation ***disposal,*** which can point to one or more elements from a set of predefined values: ***Sell***, ***Broken***, ***Donation***, and ***Superseded***.

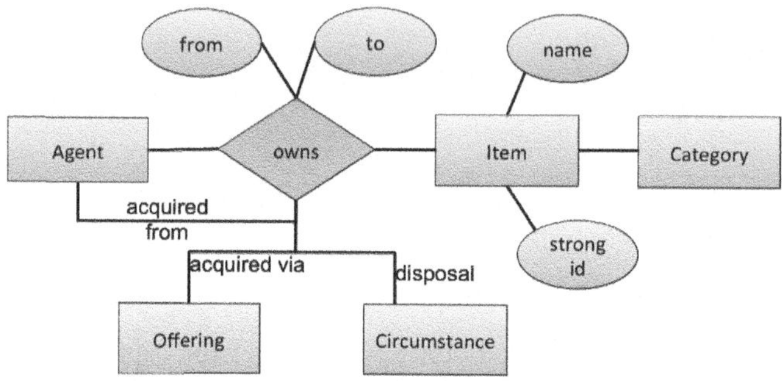

Fig. 3. Conceptual model of item ownership information

Representation Using Semantic Web Formalisms. As discussed in 2.2, we need a machine-processable representation of our conceptual model to make data adhering to our model suitable for computer-based processing. We choose RDF[3] and established Semantic Web vocabularies to implement our model. The utility of common data schemas and protocols depends on the number parties that support it. For this reason, we adopt established Semantic Web vocabularies such as **Schema.org**[4] and **GoodRelations**[5] [3]. Schema.org is a Web vocabulary covering common topics in Web publishing, such as events, news and product offers that can be used to express simple semantic structures of Web page content. The GoodRelations Web vocabulary has been designed to express fine-grained facts in the e-commerce domain and has been recently integrated into the schema.org effort, backed by major search engines. RDF's unit of information is an entity-attribute-value tuple, commonly referred to as triple. Multiple standardized concrete syntaxes have been developed for RDF that are conceptually equivalent. In this paper, we settled upon using the human-friendly, legible Turtle[6] notation.

Basic Ownership Information. Initially, GoodRelations (now part of schema.org) only allowed expressing ownership information as a binary relation between an agent and an item. For instance,

```
<http://alice.me/#i> <http://schema.org/owns>
<http://dbpedia.org/resource/Mona_Lisa>.
```

---

[3] Resource Description Framework (http://www.w3.org/standards/techs/rdf)
[4] http://schema.org/
[5] http://purl.org/goodrelations/
[6] http://www.w3.org/TeamSubmission/turtle/

encodes the statement that Alice, identified as `<http://alice.me/#i>` owns the Mona Lisa painting. The advantage of this approach is its simplicity, as it requires only a single binary attribute, yet it has very limited expressive power.

Granular Ownership Record. As RDF only allows binary relations, for N-ary relations we need to include an additional element `s:OwnershipInfo`. This element has been recently added to schema.org following a proposal by the authors of this paper, along with the attributes `s:typeOfGood` referring to the owned Product; `s:ownedFrom`, `s:ownedTo` denoting temporal bounds of ownership and the attribute `s:acquiredFrom` pointing to the source of the item.

```
@prefix s: <http://schema.org>.
<http://alice.me/#i> s:owns [
  a s:OwnershipInfo;
  s:typeOfGood <http://alice.com/mylaptop>;
  s:acquiredFrom <http://amazon.com/#company>;
  s:ownedFrom "2011-11-09T00:00:00";
  s:ownedThrough "2013-10-01T00:00:00"].
```

2.3 Data Management

One open issue with handling ownership information is that we need to make sure that the information about items owned stays in sync with the purchasing and disposal of items, and we need to organize the initial exchange, and update of previously shared, information with sites. In other words, we need to address how data is acquired, stored and edited, and shared. These are responsibilities of the client implementing the data model and the exchange protocol described in this paper. Our **prototype client**[7] currently supports manual form-based entry and the import of Amazon.de purchase history data. Other viable sources are extracting data from purchase receipts. These are usually poorly structured and manual intervention is likely necessary. As for storing the data, multiple options are available, either storing it locally or storing it remotely. Our reference implementation uses the browser's local storage, since this can be accessed from a browser extension and does not involve tackling access control, as it would be in a remote-storage scenario. Other capabilities, such as sharing ownership information selectively are also part of the client implementation, hence independent from our data model and protocol.

2.4 Protocol for Exchanging Ownership Information

We define a minimal protocol for exchanging over HTTP. Our only concern here is to support data exchange. How the recipient will actually use ownership information (OI) is not in the scope of our protocol. The protocol consists of three abstract phases:

1. **Discovery:** A Web shop advertises interest in receiving ownership info and a capable client detects this intent.

---

[7] `http://demo.portable-shopping-history.info/`

2. **Authorization:** The user decides whether item information should be shared.
3. **Sharing:** If step 2 succeeds, the browser sends ownership information to the shop.

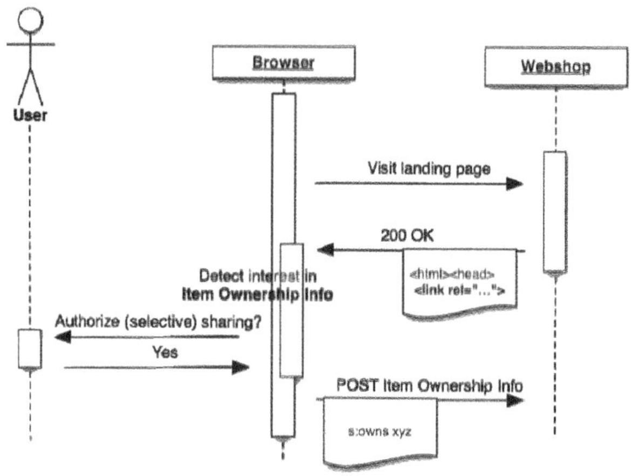

Fig. 4. Exchange of item ownership information

A Web shop may advertise its interest in OI by adding the following link element to the *<head>..</head>* of the landing page

```
<link rel="http://purl.org/xventory/sink"
media="application/json"
href="http://laptopcase.biz/personalize">
```

where `<http://purl.org/xventory/sink>` is a unique identifier which indicates that the shop is able to receive OI sent via HTTP to the URL denoted by the `href` attribute. The interaction can only take place if both parties adhere to the simple rules above. It will not break or impede the usual browsing sequence if one of the parties does not support the protocol.

3 Product Recommendation Using Item Ownership Information

In Section 1.2 we have argued that additional item information received from external sources can complement current recommender systems. The "new-user" problem and the data sparsity present in many recommender systems from a low number of past purchases can be mitigated in a straightforward way, should the user choose to share his list of belongings with the shop. Let ItemsUser denote the set of items in the user's possession and Itemsshop the items known to the shop. Taking ItemsUser Itemsshop serves as a valuable additional input for the next time the item-similarity matrix S is recomputed.

In order to provide some evidence for the further utility of item ownership information for a more personalized shopping experience, we will present two rule-based scenarios that rely on the availability of rich product data in a shop system. In the following, we will implement the recommender rules as SPARQL queries to demonstrate interesting inferences, as they are high level, declarative, yet directly executable. Depending on the problem scale, i.e. the number of items involved, real-time requirements, a real-world implementation may have to use optimizations.

Our process for obtaining useful recommendations is as follows:

1. Request product ownership information.
2. Add it to the shop's database.
3. Run recommender rules formulated as SPARQL queries over the new, integrated knowledge base.

3.1 Interpreting Transmitted Item Information

Although our data model places both the client and the shop system in a common frame of reference with respect to data schema, there is no single canonical reference to items that would serve as identity check. Product names or labels (given by `s:name`) prove rather unreliable for this purpose due to their variability and language dependence. There could be two slightly different product labels or two semantically equivalent labels in two different languages referring to the same product. These are the same issues that arise when merging data originated from two different sources.
Therefore, in our following scenarios, we only consider items received from the client for which a strong identifier is provided, such as GTIN13, which is globally unique for commodities. If such a strong identifier is available, establishing a link to a known product in the database is efficient and trivial.

Alternatively, product classification information referring to a widely deployed taxonomy, such as the Google Product Taxonomy[8] can provide valuable insights into the user's interest.

3.2 Related Product Recommendation

Due to the increasing number of specific products available in a single shop, it is not always easy for the non-expert user to choose the correct spare part or compatible product for an already owned product. High quality product catalogs typically define these relationships, so they can be used to aid the user in her search for the right product. schema.org defines `s:isConsumableFor` and `s:isAccessoryOrSparePart` attributes to denote such relationships between two products, which we use in our rule.

[8] `http://www.google.com/basepages/producttype/taxonomy.en-US.txt`

Find accessories of products owned by the user (R1)

```
PREFIX s: <http://schema.org/>
PREFIX : <http://mysemanticshop.com>
SELECT ?itemName ?relatedItemName WHERE {
# try all properties that refer to common
# globally unique ids
VALUES ?strongIdProperty { s:gtin8 s:gtin13 s:gtin14 }
# using the basic binary ownership property
 ?customer   s:owns              ?itemOwned.
 ?itemOwned  ?strongIdProperty   ?productId;
             s:name              ?itemName.
# find item in shop
 ?itemShop   ?strongIdProperty ?productId.
 ?relatedItem
   s:isAccessoryOrSparePartFor ?itemShop;
   s:name ?relatedItemName;
   :rating ?rating.
# rank by popularity, :rating is a simple
# numeric attribute
} ORDER BY DESC(?rating)
```

R1 presents a SPARQL query that retrieves all products that are suitable accessories or spare parts for any recognized item in the user's possession. For example, it will retrieve paper bags that are compatible with the user's vacuum cleaner or recommend a laptop bag for the user's 13" laptop. Ranking the result set can be performed using arbitrary criteria. In our example, we resort to ranking the results by item popularity.

3.3 Successor Product Recommendation

Recommending successor products is a common marketing tactic. In schema.org, the `s:successorOf` property denotes a successor relationship between two products. Assuming the user is in possession of a Phone123 smartphone and the shop system has the fact

```
:phone124 s:successorOf :phone123.
```

available, recommending an upgrade to Phone124 may prove valuable to the user. Collaborative filtering system will typically capture the correlation between a Phone123 and Phone124, as users interested in Phone123 may likely be interested in Phone124, too. However, a user, who has just purchased a Phone123 device is less likely to find a Phone124 recommendation useful [cf. 8].

Our semantic recommender rule is able to make a better decision based on knowing how long a given item has been in the possession of the user. Assuming that the shop system has data on the average product lifetime, that is, the average period after a product is replaced, represented as

```
:phone123 :avgProductLTMonths 24.
```

Then, the R2 rule presented below finds all successor products to the ones owned by the user and which are already past their average life-time.

Find successors of products owned by the user (R2)

```
PREFIX s: <http://schema.org/>
PREFIX : <http://myshop.com>
SELECT ?relatedItemName WHERE {
 VALUES ?strongIdProperty { s:gtin8 s:gtin13 s:gtin14 }
# use granular ownership information
 ?customer s:owns ?ownershipInfo.
 ?ownershipInfo s:typeOfGood ?itemOwned.
                s:ownedFrom ?dateOfAcq.
 ?itemOwned s:name ?itemName;
            ?strongIdProperty ?productId.

 ?itemShop ?strongIdProperty ?productId.

 ?relatedItem s:successorOf ?itemShop;
          s:name ?relatedItemName;
          :rating ?rating.
          :avgProductLTMonths ?avgPLTMonths.
# recommend a successor product if the
# currently owned is "old"
BIND (YEAR(NOW())*12+MONTH(NOW())-
 YEAR(?dateOfAcq)*12 AS ?age)
 FILTER (?avgPLTMonths < ?age) }
 ORDER BY DESC(?rating)
```

4 Evaluation and Future Work

We indicated earlier that the current recommender systems can benefit from access to ownership information in order to mitigate the cold-start problem and the data sparsity issue. For the future, we expect that precise and granular ownership information can be best leveraged by novel rule-based expert systems. These systems will capture expert-level domain-specific product recommendation knowledge and in effect act as automated sales assistants.

4.1 Expert Survey

During our initial investigation, we interviewed six e-commerce experts who possess domain knowledge in multiple product domains. The goal was to assess the relevance of information about items owned by the customer in order to improve recommendations in different product categories. For example, we wanted to know whether these human experts think they can provide more relevant recommendations for a customer in the area of consumer electronics if they knew about all the furniture owned. They were asked to rate all combinations of five item category pairs on a 5-level Likert scale. The categories were picked from the set of categories most frequently bought online [2]. Apart from three cases, our experts reached consensus, which means that the majority settled on two adjacent scores in all cases but three. The diagonal of the matrix naturally received the highest utility assessment. However, some categories can be useful to slightly improve product recommendations in other categories as well (see Table 1).

Table 1. Relevance of item ownership information for improving product recommendations (expert opinion). Likert scale scores used in the study: Helpful (4), Often helpful (3), Sometimes helpful (2), Rarely helpful (1), Not helpful (0), No consensus (X)

		Owned items				
		Furniture	*Consumer electronics*	*Apparel*	*Sportswear & gear*	*Cosmetics*
Item to recommend	*Furniture*	4	3	2	1	0
	Consumer electronics	1	4	X	1	0
	Apparel	0	1	4	2	X
	Sportswear & gear	0	1	2	3	0
	Cosmetics	0	0	X	0	4

4.2 User study

Another important factor of the viability of our approach is how willing the users are to share information about their belongings. There are situations where the perceived breach to privacy may outweigh the promised additional personalization effects and the users will be likely to refuse to reveal sensitive information. A user study described in [9] focused on personal data, e.g. name, email address, whereas we focus on revealing information about one's belongings. Also, users may be more likely to reveal certain categories of items than others. The online shop's reputation is expected to be a very important trust factor, when deciding whether to share any information with it. Online shops can encourage sharing by offering various incentives, such as discounts or free shipping. They can also explicitly declare how they intend to use the acquired information to alleviate users concerns.

In general, measuring privacy concerns of users is very difficult [see e.g. 10]. Therefore, in our work, we resorted to simulated decision making in practical scenarios. In order to provide some preliminary evidence that users are indeed willing to reveal information about their belongings in certain situations, we conducted a study, in which users were asked to complete five simulated decision-making situations in an online shopping context[9].

[9] `http://help.portable-shopping-history.info/`

Table 2. Model situations

#	Buy	Asked to reveal	Additional incentive (p=0.5)
1	Paper bag for vacuum cleaner	List of household appliances	Free shipping
2	Case for one's smartphone	Computer and smartphone	Free shipping
3	Pair of running shoes	Sportswear and gear	Free shipping
4	Belt	All clothes	10% discount
5	French cookbook	List of all book titles	10% discount and free shipping

In each situation, the user was told that she or he is looking for an item on the Web and just discovered a promising online shop that she or he decided to visit. After being taken to the site, a dialog box appeared asking the user to reveal some of her or his items of a certain category, which were related to the shopping task at hand. The standard incentive always offered in exchange for revealing the information was "reduced search time and better personalized service". Additionally, monetary incentives such as free shipping or a 10% discount on the next purchase were offered with a 0.5 probability. Table 2 contains the situations in the order of appearance, the information requested, and the additional incentive.

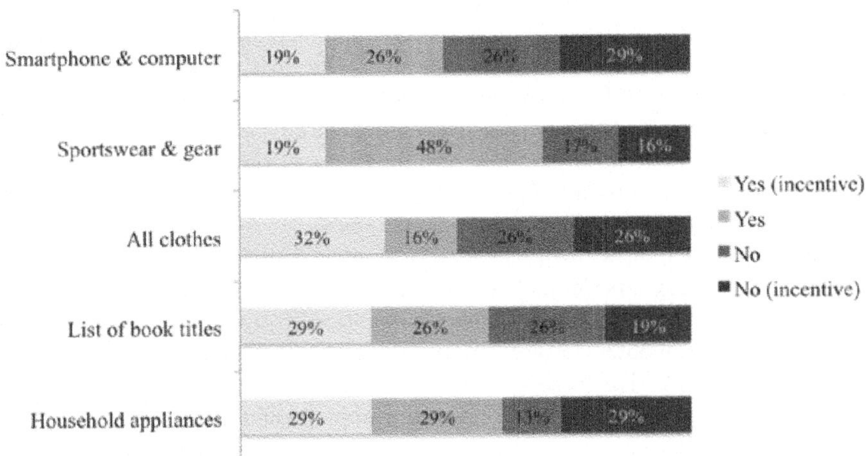

Fig. 5. Tendency to share categories of items with and without incentive

We collected responses from 31 individuals (men and women, aged 20-50) over the Web who declared themselves as knowledgeable in matters of online shopping. All respondents revealed the requested item category at least in one of the model situations (see Figure 5). In Figure 6 one can see that for almost all item categories, 50% or more of the respondents were willing to share information about owned items. It seems that in our model situations, the incentives actually had a slightly negative impact on encouraging sharing. We also see that people are happy to reveal their sportswear or sports gear, incentivized or not, however they are wary of exposing information about their cellphone and computer.

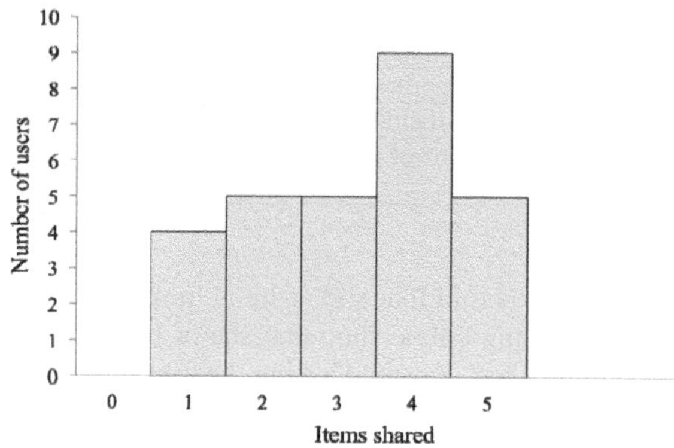

Fig. 6. User distribution per number of shared items

4.3 Conclusion and Future Work

We have presented a conceptual model (that has already been added to schema.org based on our input), a protocol, and a reference implementation for sharing item ownership information between users and Web sites. Our first evaluation provides very preliminary evidence that human experts consider such information helpful for product recommendations, and that typical users are generally willing to expose a part of their personal ownership information in turn for better recommendations or additional incentives. We plan to submit the proposed protocol to a standardization body so that it can be widely used in real-world implementations.

In our future research, we will tackle the following issues: First, we will try to understand the necessary amount and type of item information for better recommendations. Ideally, we can find a small number categories of products (e.g. car make and model, cellphone, computer, leisure activity items, the favorite pair of shoes, …) that would be already effective for better recommendations. Second, we will extend the data management part of the protocol and the implementation, e.g. how updates of information can be effectively shared between user and sites, and how the users can maintain their item information locally. Third, we will have to design and carry out more formal experiments on the effects of such information on state-of-the-art recommender systems. Another important concern is explicating incentives and designated use for the user to encourage sharing ownership information. Extensive sharing of personal data presents a privacy challenge; hence it's also worthwhile exploring. In the current state of our research we have not yet addressed these questions.

Our final goal is to have an experimental, end-to-end implementation of the presented vision deployed in real Web shops, browser extensions for all major browsers, and the broad adoption of the protocol and data model.

Acknowledgments. We would like to thank Bene Rodriguez for providing valuable feedback on our early prototypes. This research has been partially funded by the Eurostars program (within the EU 7th Framework Program) of the European Commission in the context of the Ontology-based Product Data Management (OPDM) project (FKZ 01QE1113D).

References

1. Badrul, S., George, K., Joseph, K., John, R.: Item-based Collaborative Filtering Recommendation Algorithms. In: Proceedings of the 10th International Word Wide Web Conference, Hong Kong, pp. 285–295 (2001)
2. European Commission. Bringing E-commerce Benefits to Consumers. Brussels, SEC(2011) 1640 final (2012), `http://ec.europa.eu/internal_market/e-commerce/docs/communication2012/SEC2011_1640_en.pdf`
3. Hepp, M.: GoodRelations: An Ontology for Describing Products and Services Offers on the Web. In: Gangemi, A., Euzenat, J. (eds.) EKAW 2008. LNCS (LNAI), vol. 5268, pp. 329–346. Springer, Heidelberg (2008)
4. Kanagal, B., Ahmed, A., Pandey, S., Josifovski, V., Yuan, J., Garcia-Pueyo, L.: Supercharging Recommender Systems Using Taxonomies for Learning User Purchase Behavior. Proceedings of VLDB Endow. 10, 956–967 (2012)
5. Schein, A.I., Popescul, A., Ungar, L.H., Pennock, D.M.: Methods and Metrics for Cold-start Recommendations. In: Proceedings of the 25th Annual International ACM SIGIR Conference on Research and Development in Information Retrieval, Tampere, Finland, pp. 253–260. ACM (2002)
6. Steffen, R., Christoph, F., Lars, S.-T.: Factorizing Personalized Markov Chains for Next-basket Recommendation. In: Proceedings of the 19th International World Wide Web Conference, pp. 811–820. ACM, Raleigh (2010)
7. Uschold, M., Grünninger, M.: Ontologies: Principles, Methods, and Applications. Knowledge Engineering Review 11(2), 93–155 (1996)
8. Wang, J., Sarwar, B., Sundaresan, N.: Utilizing Related Products for Post-purchase Recommendation in E-commerce. In: Proceedings of the 5th ACM Conference on Recommender Systems, Chicago, Illinois, USA, pp. 329–332. ACM (2011)
9. Ackerman, M.S., et al.: Privacy in E-commerce: Examining User Scenarios and Privacy Preferences. In: Proceedings of the 1st ACM Conference on Electronic Commerce, Denver, Colorado, USA, pp. 1–8. ACM (1999)
10. Preibusch, S.: Guide to Measuring Privacy Concern: Review of Survey and Observational Instruments. International Journal of Human-Computer Studies 71(12), 1133–1143 (2013)
11. Adomavicius, G., Tuzhilin, A.: Toward the Next Generation of Recommender Systems: A Survey of the State-of-the-Art and Possible Extensions. IEEE Trans. on Knowl. and Data Eng. 17(6), 734–749 (2005)

"Semantics Inside!" But Let's Not Tell the Data Miners: Intelligent Support for Data Mining

Jörg-Uwe Kietz[1], Floarea Serban[1], Simon Fischer[2], and Abraham Bernstein[1]

[1] DDIS, University of Zurich, Switzerland*
[2] Rapid-I, Dortmund, Germany
{serban,juk,bernstein}@ifi.uzh.ch, fischer@rapid-i.com

Abstract. Knowledge Discovery in Databases (KDD) has evolved significantly over the past years and reached a mature stage offering plenty of operators to solve complex data analysis tasks. User support for building data analysis workflows, however, has not progressed sufficiently: the large number of operators currently available in KDD systems and interactions between these operators complicates successful data analysis.

To help Data Miners we enhanced one of the most used open source data mining tools—RapidMiner—with semantic technologies. Specifically, we first annotated all elements involved in the Data Mining (DM) process—the data, the operators, models, data mining tasks, and KDD workflows—semantically using our eProPlan modelling tool that allows to describe operators and build a task/method decomposition grammar to specify the desired workflows embedded in an ontology. Second, we enhanced RapidMiner to employ these semantic annotations to actively support data analysts. Third, we built an Intelligent Discovery Assistant, eIda, that leverages the semantic annotation as well as HTN planning to automatically support KDD process generation.

We found that the use of Semantic Web approaches and technologies in the KDD domain helped us to lower the barrier to data analysis. We also found that using a generic ontology editor overwhelmed KDD-centric users. We, therefore, provided them with problem-centric extensions to Protégé. Last and most surprising, we found that our semantic modeling of the KDD domain served as a rapid prototyping approach for several hard-coded improvements of RapidMiner, namely correctness checking of workflows and quick-fixes, reinforcing the finding that even a little semantic modeling can go a long way in improving the understanding of a domain even for domain experts.

Keywords: #eswc2014Kietz.

1 Introduction

Over the last years Knowledge Discovery for Large Databases (KDD) has grown immensely and attracted more focus from both research and industry since large

* The research leading to these results has received funding from the European Union Seventh Framework Programme FP7/2007-2011 under grant agreement No 231519.

V. Presutti et al. (Eds.): ESWC 2014, LNCS 8465, pp. 706–720, 2014.

amounts of data have been generated that need to be analyzed. New algorithms and methods have been proposed and even integrated in current Data Mining (DM) tools. But KDD is a complex process transforming the raw data into actionable knowledge by applying a series of successive algorithms. Current DM tools allow users to manually build KDD workflows and select each step from a large pool of possible solutions. Yet, this is very tedious and often leads to workflows that crash after a few hours runtime. In addition, it has been shown that users and even DM experts tend to stick to a set of preferred methods and do not explore the entire design-space [13]. This often produces sub-optimal analyses. Despite the progress such tools have made during the last years, their user support is, hence, still far from perfect.

Some of the issues highlighted above have been explored by the EU funded e-Lico project.[1] An important task of this project was to *provide intelligent support for DM to simplify the data analysis process for users.* Inspired by [4] the plan was to intelligently support users by leveraging the semantic annotation of DM-operations to allow a correct composition of workflows. Hence, we annotated the main components of KDD workflows (data, algorithms, and goals) and operators available in RapidMiner [14]—one of the most used open source Data Mining tools—using ontologies. Treating the problem as a service composition problem, where algorithms are services provided by DM tools, we employed ontologies, Hierarchical Task Network (HTN) planning [7] to automatically explore the large design-space of correct workflows and recommender-system technology to help users navigate this space [20].

As KDD is a dynamic domain, we developed eProPlan—a tool that enables DM service providers to efficiently model their services and define semantics—facilitating the semantic description process and providing tools for testing and maintaining the model over time. eProPlan was used by several partners (including the RapidMiner developers) to model different operators (e.g., basic DM operators, text mining operators, etc.). As Section 5 outlines, insights from this modeling effort where included in the productive RapidMiner version to check for correctness of workflows and suggest possible fixes.We also designed an Intelligent Discovery Assistant (IDA), eIda, that enhances RapidMiner and Taverna [16] with the ability to automatically generate semantically correct workflows (i.e., exploring the design space of valid workflows) starting only from a dataset and a DM problem. Finally, we developed a recommender-component that can rank generated workflows in terms of their expected accuracy, which is able to advise a user on which of the workflows generated by eIda are expected to perform well [20] simplifying the choice significantly.

This paper's main contributions are the distillation of our experiences implementing the e-Lico tool-suite, the evaluations we undertook of the different parts, and the lessons we learned from applying semantic technologies in this increasingly important application area that is so heavily influenced by induction instead of logical reasoning. In particular, it is witness how insights from

[1] http://www.e-lico.eu/

modeling the KDD domain transcended into the actual code of one of the most used KDD-software.[2]

The discussion is structured as follows: Next, we succinctly explore related work, followed by a discussion of the three implemented systems: ePROPLAN for describing the semantics of services in Section 3, eIDA to automatically generate the KDD workflows in Section 4, and the auto-experimenting recommender in Section 4.3. The side effects of semantics are discussed in Section 5. Finally we explore the lessons learned from this project in Section 6 and we draw the main conclusions in Section 7.

2 Related Work

Researchers have been extensively looking at service composition especially in the area of web services [5,15]. The most common automation techniques for web services are either based on workflow composition [3] or AI planning [18]. Some even used a more advanced form of AI planning called Hierarchical Task Network (HTN) to find the matching web services [24]. Similarly, we use HTN planning to generate the design-space of KDD workflows. In contrast to others, we did not look for *one possible* solution but were exploring *the space of all correct solutions*. Also we did not rely on OWL-S but simple ontologies, where the conditions and effects were stored as annotations.

Other researchers looked into automating KDD [21]. Most of those tools are, however, limited to being research prototypes and did not provide explicit support for modeling their background knowledge. The Intelligent Discovery Automatic Assistant (IDEA) [4] was among the first prototypes to propose a combination of ontology-based planning, result ranking, and operator information sharing for supporting KDD. The RDM system [26] uses an OWL-DL [17] ontology for knowledge discovery. This ontology is queried using the Pellet reasoner [23] and SPARQL-DL queries [22] for retrieving the operator inputs and outputs, which are then fed into the planner. Two AI planners are used that query the ontology during the planning process.Similarly, KDDVM [6] interacts with the ontology by using the Pellet reasoner and SPARQL-DL queries. Instead of applying a standard planning algorithm it utilizes a custom algorithm that starts at the goal state and iteratively adds operators forming a directed graph until the first operator is compatible with the given dataset. Operators are added using an algorithm matching procedure, which checks the compatibility of inputs and outputs. The operator interfaces are not matched perfectly do not need to be perfectly but according to a similarity computed via their distance in the ontology graph. Finally, the produced workflows are ranked based on the similarity scores as well as other operator properties stored in the ontology (e.g. soft pre-conditions or computational complexity estimates). Finally, MLWizard,[3]

[2] According to a recent poll `http://www.kdnuggets.com/2013/06/kdnuggets-annual-software-poll-rapidminer-r-vie-for-first-place.html`

[3] `http://madm.dfki.de/rapidminer/mlwizard`

e.g., an IDA available at the RapidMiner marketplace only supports a few classification tools and no regression and clustering. It also focuses the induction step and does not consider evaluation (e.g. building a cross-validation or test-set evaluation process) and preprocessing (e.g. handling missing values, attribute type conversions, and normalization).

3 ePROPLAN: A Semantic DM Service IDE

To reason and plan about KDD operators one needs to specify the main element of the KDD domain and the capabilities of each individual operator (or service) in terms of their IOPE (Inputs, Outputs, Pre-conditions, and Effects). To facilitate these tasks we built ePROPLAN[4] [10] to be used by the DM service providers who are the DM experts. They have the knowledge about the services, how their services work, what data they can model, what they produce, and how they are implemented. ePROPLAN is a Protégé plugin that not only allows to describe semantically the services but also to improve, test, debug, and extend the service model as well as the HTN used for planning (see Figure 1a). In the following we first discuss ePROPLAN's ontology and models before discussing its features supporting editors and its usage.

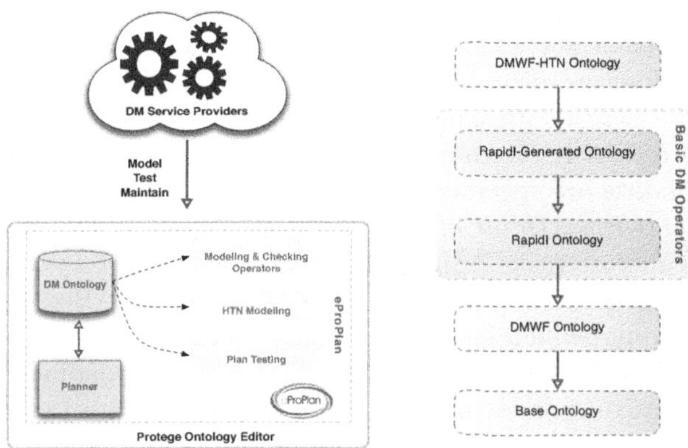

(a) ePROPLAN components (b) Ontologies

Fig. 1. ePROPLAN system and its ontologies

3.1 DM Ontology for Workflow Planning

In our case services are actual algorithms that can be organized by their capabilities and data applicability. Hence, one can use an ontology to structure and model them. We built a set of OWL-DL ontologies that are describing the DM domain. To ensure decoupling and re-use we built different ontologies organized in a stack (see Figure 1b), where each ontology imports the one directly below it (and the others below it indirectly).

[4] which is available from the e-Lico web-site.

The Base ontology (see Figs 1b and 2) contains the building blocks for modeling the services (operators). *Operators* use different inputs and produce one or several outputs—all *IO-Objects*. They also have different types: abstract (used only to organize operators in hierarchies), basic (can be executed), and dominating or loops (allowing a sequence of operators that can be repeated). Parameters are used to tune algorithms or to set mandatory values by defining *data-* or *object properties* (e.g., *parameter, simpleParameter*).

The composition of services starts by defining a *Goal* that takes as input the data that needs to be analyzed. Next, the main goal uses a *Task* that can be solved by one or more *Methods*. Each method has then a set of steps that represent the services in the composition. Such a step can either be a *Task* or an *Operator* allowing the definition of very complex workflows and even loops over the same tasks.

The main advantages of embedding the HTN-grammar into an ontology are that (1) operators are organized in an hierarchy and (2) abstract operators can be used in the HTN-grammar. The abstract HTN operator *ClassificationLearner*, e.g., has several executable sub-concepts in RapidMiner and Weka. This enabled a compact and, often, execution-system independent HTN-grammar.

The DM Workflow ontology. (DMWF in Figs 1b and 2) defines sub-classes for all the basic classes in the Base ontology. The focus of this ontology is on the composition of specific services from DM. Operators are specified for each step of the workflow from pre-processing to evaluation (e.g., *FormatData, Modeling, ModelEvaluation, etc.*). Data can be of different types as for example *DataTable, Model* or *Report*. It has nominal or ordinal columns and attributes. The characteristics of data are specified using sub-classes of the *MetaData* class (e.g., *Attribute, AttributeType, DataColumn, DataFormat*, etc.). The *MainGoal* materializes now to concrete tasks from DM like *Descriptive-* or *PredictiveModeling*.

Here we leveraged the completion of *IO-Object*'s via ABox realization and SWRL-rule reasoning, which enabled compact and understandable descriptions similar to axioms in the Planning Domain Description Language (PDDL) [25]. We, e.g., defined a concept for missing value (MV) free data tables $MVFreeDataTable \equiv DataTable \sqcap \forall inputColumn.MVFreeColumn \sqcap \forall targetColumn.MVFreeColumn$, where $MVFreeColumn$ in itself is a defined concept $MVFreeColumn \equiv DataColumn \sqcap amountOfMVs = 0$

The RapidI-Generated ontology. (see Figure 1b) specifies the RapidMiner provided algorithms (services). The ontology contains the RapidMiner operators as well as their pre-conditions and effects. These are rules that define when certain operators can be used in terms of the characteristics of the data and what they produce (either new data or changes on the input data). OWL-S [1] already provides the semantics and models for web service composition. Its support for editing in Protégé was limited when we built eProPlan and was difficult to explain to our user-base (KDD domain experts and RapidMiner developers) – experiences that were reflected by others [19]. Also, it modeled services as instances. To simplify matters we chose to describe services as OWL classes.

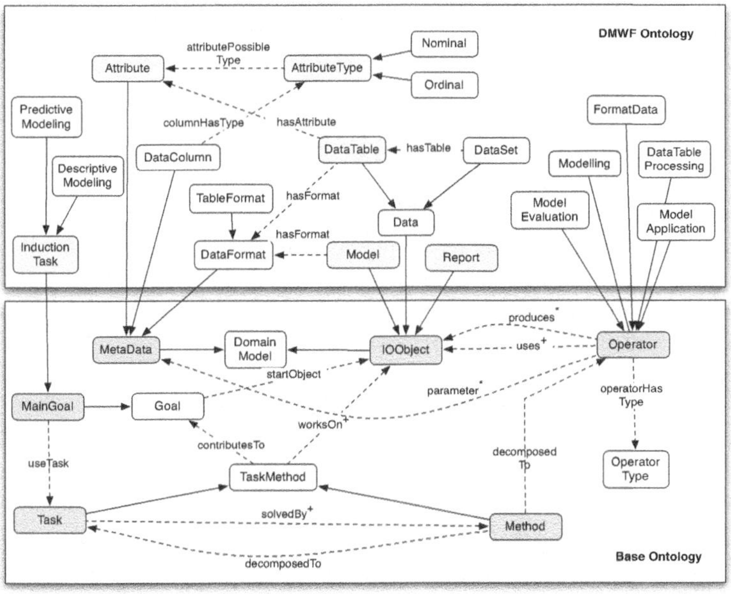

Fig. 2. Main classes from the Base and Workflow ontologies

To model the pre-conditions and effects we relied on the Protégé's SWRL plugin. Since the complexity of the rules needed was higher than it was possible to express in SWRL, we have added some new built-ins [12] and saved them as annotations in the ontology.

The operators are organized in an strict inheritance concept-hierarchy. We used the OWL-inheritance to propagate parameter restrictions from abstract to concrete, implemented operators as well as conditions/effect representations. This provided an effective way to build and maintain descriptions of over hundred different operators (see section 2.3 in[11] for an example).

The DMWF-HTN ontology. (see Figure 1b) is used to define the tasks and methods for planning. HTN planning is like a top-down grammar that specifies the skeleton or template of workflows. Each step of the workflow can be described in term of specific tasks or even sub-tasks (e.g., *DataMining, ModelingWithCrossValidation, Preprocessing, CleanMissingValues, CleanManyValuedNominals, NormalizeScalar*, etc.). Further, the planner employs the template and fills in the services that match. The planning relies on external reasoners available in Protégé for TBox reasoning and an internal ABox reasoner. Details of the operator models and of the used HTN-planning can be found in [11]

Domain Independence. The modularity of our approach would allow using our tools in another application domain by starting with the Base ontology and then adapting the upper elements. To ensure that this actually works we also modeled the Missionaries and Cannibals problem from classical planning. Hence, ePROPLAN can be used as a generic ontology editor for HTN planning for different domains.

3.2 ePROPLAN: Support for Editing, Testing, and Optimization

To allow domain experts to model operators/services for planning we developed ePROPLAN, which has several Protégé views. The *Operators tab* allows users to define conditions and effects and includes a semantic checker that highlights errors in the definition and suggests fixes. This avoids erroneous definitions of services and maintains ontology correctness.

The operator's applicability can be tested using the *Applicable operators tab*, where each operator can be applied on different types of data. Furthermore, it supports a step by step composition to ensure that correct workflows can be generated. Since standard OWL-reasoners do not support states, we built the planner in Flora2/XSB.[5] Consequently, the ontological domain needs to be compiled for planning at which stage the conditions and effects are checked again for correctness and the errors are stored as annotations to the corresponding operators. This ensures that the planning domain is defined correctly.

In the *HTN editor tab* one can create new tasks and methods and specify each step of the workflow. The editor shows the hierarchy of tasks and methods and also each independent step with their inputs and outputs. The user needs to define the matching IO-Objects from one step to another to ensure the correctness of the workflow.

3.3 Usage of ePROPLAN

ePROPLAN was used and tested by different parties as it is the main tool developed for the e-Lico project. The partners from Rapid-I were responsible for modeling the RapidMiner operators. Without prior experience in ontology modeling they successfully delivered a complex ontology that contained more than 100 modeled operators. As the number of services is relatively large (a few hundreds) they automatically generated the code by mapping their algorithm specifications to the conditions and effects in the ontology. Some additional work was then needed to check the correctness of the produced service model using ePROPLAN.

To gather feedback about the usability of ePROPLAN we designed a questionnaire based on the System Usability Scale (SUS) [2]. SUS has been used in many tests and is often described as a "quick and dirty" usability test. SUS scores can range from 0 (very little satisfaction) to 100 (very high satisfaction). Usual average satisfaction scores are reported to be between 65 and 70. For ePROPLAN we obtained SUS questionnaires from 5 users varying from 42.5 to 72.5 with a mean score of 63.5. [8] reports a SUS score for Protégé (with 15 subjects) that

[5] `http://flora.sourceforge.net/`

varies between 20 to 78 with a mean of 47.[6] We are well aware that comparing SUS scores between settings is highly problematic. We can, therefore, only infer that ePROPLAN's usability seems comparable to Protégé's.

4 eIDA – A Tool for Users

eIDA is a programming interface that provides all the functionality (in particular to the reasoner & planner) needed to build an Intelligent Discovery Assistant (IDA). It provides methods for retrieving the DM workflows starting from the dataset's meta-data and the selection of a main goal. So far it was used to build IDAs for both RapidMiner and Taverna.[7] The RapidMiner IDA Extension can be downloaded (or even auto-installed) from the Rapid-I Marketplace[8]. So far it was downloaded over 8000 times. The Taverna extension[9] can execute the workflows generated by the IDA[10] using any RapidAnalytics[11] server that provides all RapidMiner operators as web-services. Extensions for other KDD tools (e.g., KNIME, Enterprise Miner, etc.) would require two steps: first modeling their corresponding operators in the DMWF, second an implementation of the GUI and the plan-converter using the IDA-API.

We tested the IDA on 164 datasets from the UCI repository of Machine Learning datasets.[12] It produced executable plans for all 117 classification and 47 regression problems. These datasets have between 3 and 1558 attributes, being all nominal (from binary to many different values like ZIP), all scalar (normalized or not), or mixed. They also have varying degrees of missing values. We are not aware of any other Machine Learning or DM approach that is able to adapt itself to so many different and divergent datasets. The IDA also works for less well prepared datasets like the KDD Cup 1998 challenge data (370 attributes, with up to 50% missing values and nominal data), where it generates plans of around 40 operators. Generating and ranking 20 of these workflows took 400 sec. on a 3.2 GHz Quad-Core Intel Xeon.

4.1 Ease of Use

Without an IDA data mining is typically done by specialized highly-trained professionals such as DM consultants. They have to know a lot about DM methods and how they are implemented in different tools. They need to inspect the data and combine the operators into an adequate workflow. However, the large number of available algorithms is overwhelming even for specialists.

[6] That is rather a rather low score for Protégé might be the result of its comparative evaluation setting with with CLOnE, a Controlled Language Ontology Editor.

[7] http://www.taverna.org.uk/

[8] http://rapidupdate.de/UpdateServer/faces/product_details.xhtml?productId=rmx_ida

[9] http://e-lico.eu/taverna-ida.html

[10] http://e-lico.eu/taverna-rm.html

[11] http://rapid-i.com/content/view/182/196/

[12] http://archive.ics.uci.edu/ml/

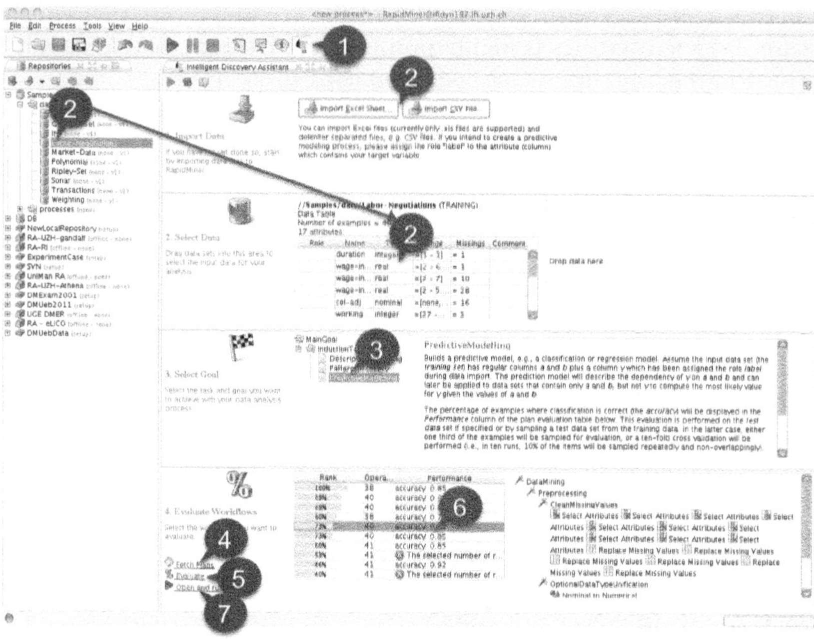

Fig. 3. IDA Interface in RapidMiner

The IDA reduces the technical burden and offers "DM with 7 clicks" (see Figure 3). (1) Show the IDA-Perspective of the tool; (2) drag the data to be analyzed from the repository to the view or import (and annotate) your data; (3) select your main goal in DM; (4) ask the IDA to generate workflows for data and goal; (5) evaluate all plans by executing them in RapidMiner; (6) select the plan you like most to see a summary of the plan (the screenshot in Figure 3 is made after this step); and finally, (7) inspect the plan and its results. Note that these steps do not require any detailed technical knowledge. Still a user should be aware of what (s)he is doing when (s)he uses DM, i.e. (s)he should know the statistical assumptions underlying DM (e.g., a user should know what it means to have a sample that is representative, relevant, and large enough to solve a problem with DM/statistics).

4.2 Speedup of Workflow Design

Besides making DM easier for inexperienced users, our main goal in building the IDA was to speed-up the design of DM workflows. To establish a possible speed-up we compared the efficiency of CS students after attending a DM class to a person using the IDA. The study comprises in total 24 students (9 in 2011 and 15 in 2012). They had to solve the following DM problems:

- Take the UCI "Communities and Crime" data-set[13] and
  a) generate a fine clustering that allows to find very similar communities
  b) generate a description of the clusters (learn a model to predict the cluster label built in task a)).
  c) generate a function to predict "ViolentCrimesPerPop" and evaluate it with 10-fold cross-validation.
- Take the UCI "Internet Advertisement" data-set[14] and generate an evaluated classification for the attribute "Ad/Non-Ad".

All data was provided already imported into RapidMiner (via a local RapidAnalytics server they could access). All students needed the full 3 hours (see Figure 10 in [11] for details on typical errors the students made and accuracy's reached by IDA and students).

As a comparison we asked a non-specialist (a member from our Group, not involved in the e-LICO project) to accomplish the same task using the IDA. It took the non-specialist 30 minutes to (IDA planning, minimal manual adaptation, and execution of the workflows) with a comparable output.

The study confirmed that standard DM problems (such as clustering and prediction tasks on complex UCI data) can be sped-up considerably (30 minutes vs. 3 hours) by using an IDA whilst maintaining a comparable quality.

The experiments also showed clearly that even students at the end of a term-long DM class were overwhelmed when confronted by two typical DM task. The IDA operated by a DM novice, with minimal guidance about which proposed workflow to use,[15] was able to provide comparable results when. Note that the students are an optimal user-group for the IDA, as they have limited DM experience but they understand the principles of DM.

4.3 Auto-Experimentation and Performance of the Generated Workflows

One of the most complex aspects of Data Analysis is to decide which KDD workflows are likely to be successful. Hence, we employed eIDA for another research task: the ranking of the generated KDD workflows. This is an important aspect since the number of valid workflows is quite large (easily over 1000 for classification problems) due to the large number of operators available in RapidMiner and modeled in our ontology. To solve this problem we combined auto-experimentation (the planing and execution of experiments) with collaborative filtering [20]. The detailed description of this approach is clearly beyond the scope of this paper. We summarize that we evaluated the ranking on 100 datasets from the UCI repository. For new datasets our approach was able to make recommendations that were at most 5% worse than the best workflow by executing only 3%-5% of the overall workflows.

[13] `http://archive.ics.uci.edu/ml/datasets/Communities+and+Crime`
[14] `http://archive.ics.uci.edu/ml/datasets/Internet+Advertisements`
[15] A problem we addressed with auto-experimentation (discussed in the next section).

This excellent result shows that *an IDA based on Semantic Technology and collaborative filtering approaches is able to automatically decide how to analyze a data-set with a result that is close to the best possible analysis.* We believe that this result clearly shows the power of Semantic Technology applied to DM problems.

5 Side Effects of Semantic Technology Usage

Besides the development of the systems described in this manuscript, several improvements were made as side effects in the core of the RapidMiner user interface. Those simple things in fact contributed a lot to the usability of RapidMiner as a data analysis workbench. They were one of the most relevant features culminating in the release of RapidMiner 5. We will briefly sketch them in this section.

RapidMiner improvements When building the DM ontology as described in Section 3.1, a lot of work went into the specification of pre-conditions and effects of operators. This information is not only useful for the DM ontology and the IDA, but also when designing processes in the traditional way. The RapidMiner-team therefore, decided to make as much information as possible also available in Java. To that end, as of RapidMiner 5.0, each operator can (and all operators in the core do) provide so-called meta-data propagation rules. They must be very quick, since they are frequently evaluated at process design time, whenever changes to the process are made. They serve three purposes.

First, they compute, given the (possibly incompletely specified) meta data delivered at the input ports, what the meta data of the output will be. Note that sometimes, this information cannot be known at design time, but only at run-time. A good example is the *Pivot* operator which transforms data values into new attributes. Since the set of all values is not necessarily known without loading the full data set, the complete set of attributes after the execution of the *Pivot* operator may not be known before execution time. Another example is loading data from dynamic sources like Web services. In such cases, the information can be marked as partially unknown.

Second, once the meta data are evaluated, these rules check pre-conditions required by the individual operators. As an example, a learning scheme like an SVM requires all input attributes to be numerical. If these pre-conditions are not satisfied, a warning is displayed in a special view (akin to errors in IDEs) and the operator is highlighted in red to signify that it cannot be executed. This saves the user the effort of test-wise executing the process for debugging.

Finally, when an operator is found to be non-applicable quick-fixes are offered to the user. Using the example above, when the user tries to apply an SVM on non-numerical data, a quick fix could be to insert an operator for dummy-coding nominal values (as shown in Figure 4).

In summary, the semantic annotation of the DM operators done for the IDA have served as a rapid-prototype that inspired the further development of RapidMiner. It significantly improved the usability of RapidMiner, which is supported

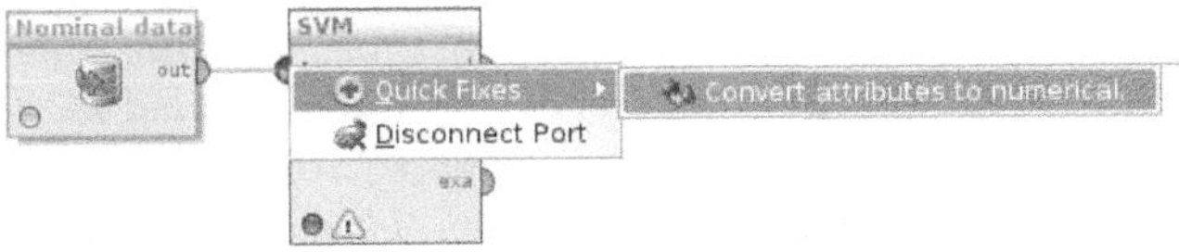

Fig. 4. A quickfix for making an SVM applicable on non-numeric data

by a significant increase of users and community activity after the release of RapidMiner 5 (including over 350'000 downloads and an increase in market-share from 21%[16] to 37.8%[17] since its launch).

Sharing scientific workflows. Designing KDD workflows is a complex task requiring both a good understanding of the problem and of the algorithms available in KDD tools. This makes sharing of such workflows a valuable feature akin to sharing program code: it allows researchers to convey their knowledge and experience to others. Imagine that people can browse through a repository of good performing workflows for a certain area and then they can test and evaluate them on their datasets. This is especially useful for novice data miners who do not know all the subtleties of the domain and do not have the required experience to avoid mistakes. But it may be beneficial even for specialists, as they may come across interesting workflows that they did not use or think about before.

Another side-effect of our modeling of the DM domain is that sharing these workflows has become easier. Within e-Lico we developed a myExperiment [9] plugin for RapidMiner. It allows scientists to have groups per research topics and share various workflows and their experience on different data. Whenever people get good workflows using the RapidMiner IDA Extension or when they manually design them, they can now share them using the myExperiment plugin. Both Taverna and RapidMiner offer this feature. Free re-usability, search, and storage of workflows is, therefore, ensured. myExperiment users can tag, write reviews, comments, and even annotate and rate workflows.

The e-Lico project participants have already shared and uploaded several dozen DM workflows on this platform, and several hundreds have been added since then by the community.

6 Lessons Learned

During the 3 year EU project we were facing the challenge of adapting and intermingling various Semantic Web techniques to build an IDA for the data analysis process. This required us to support two types of users and, therefore, provide different types of support: the DM service providers who are responsible for modeling the DM domain and the end-users who "only" want to magically get valuable knowledge out of their dataset/task at hand. An important lesson

[16] http://www.kdnuggets.com/polls/2009/data-mining-tools-used.htm

[17] http://www.kdnuggets.com/polls/2010/data-mining-analytics-tools.html

discovered in the first year is that *service providers are not ontology modeling specialists and, therefore, need debugging support for Semantic Modeling*, despite being AI specialists. In addition, *end-users are not interested in semantic technology* and the underlying details. They want to solve problems, in our case KDD analyses, with as little effort as possible. *The less we showed them about the inner workings (and semantic technology) the happier they were.*

Ontologies have become more popular and are used for modeling and structuring different domains. Ontology editors have adapted and provide different plugins to facilitate the transition to the semantic notations. From our experience with the users from the project we observed that domain specialists are extremely reluctant to climb the learning curve to use these editors. Therefore, to simplify and expedite their learning process, we found it helpful to build domain specific ontology editors (such as ePROPLAN) that hide the basic ontology constructs by replacing them with domain constructs. These facilitate bridging the application domain and semantic annotation. Reinforcing this finding we asked all e-Lico project participants what their most liked ePROPLAN feature was. The winner was the special editor for conditions and effects as well as the applicable operators' tab–both elements highly applicable to the DM operator modeling problem they had to solve. They also appreciate having any kind of validation and especially a way of finding out the problems or errors in their modeling. Consequently, it seems that *one of the biggest hurdle for wide-spread Semantic annotation is the provision of low-effort domain-specific editors with built-in validation facilities.*

One of the biggest findings of our project is that *the payoff of unexpected side-effects of using semantic technology may easily surpass the effort invested.* In the spirit of "a little semantics goes a long way"[18] we could enhance RapidMiner's interface with simple semantic functions that immensely simplified its usage. Whilst we lack proof that this is the cause of the surge of RapidMiner's popularity we gathered evidence from user testing at Rapid-I that a number of test users were able to fix problems with the quick-fix functionality that specialist data miners did not think were possible. Even if the semantic techniques where not used in this improvements, they served as a rapid-prototyping approach that influenced the further development of RapidMiner.

Last but not least, *the ability to explore the design-space of a realistic-sized DM domain and successfully propose well-performing workflows replied on semantic technology and allowed us to solve practical problems that have been pursued for decades* [21].

7 Conclusions

In this paper we presented our experiences with using semantic technologies in the KDD/DM domain. In this domain the number of available operators and resulting design space of possible DM workflows goes beyond the capability of even

[18] `http://www.cs.rpi.edu/~hendler/LittleSemanticsWeb.html`

specialists. Our solution couples HTN planning as well as auto-experimentation with recommendations with semantic web technologies to address this problem.

Specifically, we provided ePROPLAN, an editor and planning environment for services, and eIDA, an Intelligent Discovery Assistant engine that was included in both RapidMiner and Taverna. Leveraging the functionalities of these tools we were able to semantically annotate the KDD domain and use those annotations in practical usage: we found that these tools relying on semantic technologies were able to support novice users to get good results in data mining tasks. To put it to real-world tests we shipped these capabilities with RapidMiner. Furthermore, we found that when complementing these tools with advanced auto-experimentation based recommendation technology we could automatically propose good performing workflows.

We also found that the side-effects of Semantic annotation led to a series of high-impact improvements in the usability of RapidMiner indicating that "a little semantics goes a long way" – in our case helping to boost the popularity of RapidMiner. Most interestingly, *we managed to put semantic technology at work on the computers of tens of thousands and influenced the user experience of possibly hundreds of thousands users making their work simpler whilst leaving them completely oblivious about the usage of such technology* – a goal that we believe every semantic technology project should strive for.

References

1. Ankolekar, A., et al.: DAML-S: Web service description for the semantic web. In: Horrocks, I., Hendler, J. (eds.) ISWC 2002. LNCS, vol. 2342, pp. 348–363. Springer, Heidelberg (2002)
2. Bangor, A., Kortum, P., Miller, J.: Determining what individual SUS scores mean: adding an adjective rating scale. Journal of Usability Studies 4(3), 114–123 (2009)
3. Benatallah, B., Dumas, M., Fauvet, M.-C., Rabhi, F.A.: Towards patterns of web services composition. Springer (2003)
4. Bernstein, A., Provost, F.J., Hill, S.: Toward intelligent assistance for a data mining process: An ontology-based approach for cost-sensitive classification. IEEE Trans. Knowl. Data Eng. 17(4), 503–518 (2005)
5. Claro, D.B., Albers, P., Hao, J.-K.: Web services composition. In: Semantic Web Services, Processes and Applications, pp. 195–225. Springer (2006)
6. Diamantini, C., Potena, D., Storti, E.: Kddonto: An ontology for discovery and composition of kdd algorithms. In: Service-Oriented Knowledge Discovery (SoKD 2009) Workshop at ECML/PKDD 2009, pp. 13–24 (2009)
7. Erol, K.: Hierarchical task network planning: formalization, analysis, and implementation. PhD thesis, University of Maryland at College Park, College Park, MD, USA, UMI Order No. GAX96-22054 (1996)
8. Funk, A., Tablan, V., Bontcheva, K., Cunningham, H., Davis, B., Handschuh, S.: Clone: Controlled language for ontology editing. In: Aberer, K., et al. (eds.) ISWC/ASWC 2007. LNCS, vol. 4825, pp. 142–155. Springer, Heidelberg (2007)
9. Goble, C., Bhagat, J., Aleksejevs, S., Cruickshank, D., Michaelides, D., Newman, D., Borkum, M., Bechhofer, S., Roos, M., Li, P., De Roure, D.: myExperiment: a repository and social network for the sharing of bioinformatics workflows. Nucl. Acids Res. (2010)

10. Kietz, J., Serban, F., Bernstein, A.: eProPlan: A Tool to Model Automatic Generation of Data Mining Workflows. In: 3rd Planning to Learn Workshop at ECAI 2010, vol. 15 (2010)
11. Kietz, J., Serban, F., Bernstein, A.: Designing kdd-workflows via htn-planning. In: Vanschoren, J., Brazdil, P., Kietz, J.-U. (eds.) 4rd Planning to Learn Workshop at ECAI 2012. CEUR Workshop Proceedings, vol. 950 (2012)
12. Kietz, J., Serban, F., Bernstein, A., Fischer, S.: Towards cooperative planning of data mining workflows. In: Proceedings of the ECML-PKDD 2009 Workshop on Service-Oriented Knowledge Discovery, pp. 1–12 (2009)
13. Kohavi, R., Brodley, C.E., Frasca, B., Mason, L., Zheng, Z.: Kdd-cup 2000 organizers' report: peeling the onion. SIGKDD Explor. Newsl. 2, 86–93 (2000)
14. Mierswa, I., Wurst, M., Klinkenberg, R., Scholz, M., Euler, T.: Yale: Rapid prototyping for complex data mining tasks. In: Proceedings of the 12th ACM SIGKDD International Conference on Knowledge Discovery and Data Mining, pp. 935–940. ACM (2006)
15. Milanovic, N., Malek, M.: Current solutions for web service composition. IEEE Internet Computing 8(6), 51–59 (2004)
16. Oinn, T., Addis, M., Ferris, J., Marvin, D., Senger, M., Greenwood, M., Carver, T., Glover, K., Pocock, M.R., Wipat, A., et al.: Taverna: a tool for the composition and enactment of bioinformatics workflows. Bioinformatics 20(17), 3045–3054 (2004)
17. Patel-Schneider, P., Hayes, P., Horrocks, I., et al.: OWL web ontology language semantics and abstract syntax. W3C Recommendation 10 (2004)
18. Rao, J., Su, X.: A survey of automated web service composition methods. In: Cardoso, J., Sheth, A.P. (eds.) SWSWPC 2004. LNCS, vol. 3387, pp. 43–54. Springer, Heidelberg (2005)
19. Sabou, M., Richards, D., Van Splunter, S.: An experience report on using daml-s. In: The Proceedings of the Twelfth International World Wide Web Conference Workshop on E-Services and the Semantic Web (ESSW 2003), Budapest (2003)
20. Serban, F.: Towards Effective Support for Data Mining using Intelligent Discovery Assistance. PhD thesis, University of Zurich, Department of Informatics (2013)
21. Serban, F., Vanschoren, J., Kietz, J.-U., Bernstein, A.: A survey of intelligent assistants for data analysis. ACM Computing Surveys (2013) (forthcoming:Epub ahead of print)
22. Sirin, E., Parsia, B.: SPARQL-DL: SPARQL query for OWL-DL. In: Proceedings of the International Workshop on OWL Experiences and Directions (OWLED) (2007)
23. Sirin, E., Parsia, B., Grau, B., Kalyanpur, A., Katz, Y.: Pellet: A practical owl-dl reasoner. Web Semantics: Science, Services and Agents on the World Wide Web 5(2), 51–53 (2007)
24. Sirin, E., Parsia, B., Wu, D., Hendler, J., Nau, D.: Htn planning for web service composition using shop2. Web Semantics: Science, Services and Agents on the World Wide Web 1(4), 377–396 (2004)
25. Thiébaux, S., Hoffmann, J., Nebel, B.: In defense of pddl axioms. Artif. Intell. 168(1), 38–69 (2005)
26. Žáková, M., Křemen, P., Železný, F., Lavrač, N.: Automatic knowledge discovery workflow composition through ontology-based planning. IEEE Transactions on Automation Science and Engineering, online 1st, 53–264 (2010)

MatWare: Constructing and Exploiting Domain Specific Warehouses by Aggregating Semantic Data

Yannis Tzitzikas[1,2], Nikos Minadakis[1], Yannis Marketakis[1], Pavlos Fafalios[1,2], Carlo Allocca[1], Michalis Mountantonakis[1,2], and Ioanna Zidianaki[1,2]

[1] Institute of Computer Science, FORTH-ICS, Greece
[2] Computer Science Department, University of Crete, Greece
{tzitzik,minadakn,marketak,fafalios,carlo,mountant,izidian}@ics.forth.gr

Abstract. In many applications one has to fetch and assemble pieces of information coming from more than one web sources such as SPARQL endpoints. In this paper we describe the corresponding requirements and challenges, based on our experience, and then we present a process and a tool that we have developed, called *MatWare*, for constructing such semantic warehouses. We focus on domain-specific warehouses, where the focus is given on the aspects of *scope control*, *connectivity assessment*, *provenance*, and *freshness*. *MatWare* (**Mat**erialized **Ware**house) is a tool that automates the construction (and reconstruction) of such warehouses, and offers methods for tackling the aforementioned requirements. Finally we report our experiences from using it for building, maintaining and evolving an operational semantic warehouse for the marine domain, that is currently in use by several applications ranging from e-infrastructure services to smart phone applications.

Keywords: #eswc2014Tzitzikas.

1 Introduction

An increasing number of datasets are publicly available in various formats (including Linked Data and SPARQL endpoints). For exploiting this wealth of data, and for building domain specific applications, one has to fetch and assemble pieces of information coming from more than one sources. These pieces can then be used for constructing a warehouse that offers more complete browsing and query services (in comparison to those offered by the underlying sources). For instance, in the marine domain, there is not any individual source that can answer queries of the form: *"Given the scientific name of a species, find the ecosystems, water areas and countries that this species is native to, and the common names that are used for this species in each of the countries"*.

There are *domain independent* warehouses, like the Sindice RDF search engine [12], or the Semantic Web Search Engine (SWSE) [4], but also *domain specific*,

V. Presutti et al. (Eds.): ESWC 2014, LNCS 8465, pp. 721–736, 2014.

like [14,9,5]. We focus on the requirements for building domain specific warehouses. Such warehouses aim to serve particular needs, particular communities of users, consequently their "quality" requirements are higher. It is therefore worth elaborating on the process that can be used for building such warehouses, and on the related difficulties and challenges. In brief, and from our experience from running an operational semantic warehouse, the main questions and challenges include:

- How to define the objectives and the scope of such a warehouse and how to test that its contents meet the objectives?
- How to *connect* the fetched pieces of information? Common schemas, URIs or literals are not always there.
- How to measure the value of the warehouse as well as the quality of the warehouse (this is important for e-science)?
- How to keep such a warehouse fresh, i.e. how to automate its construction, and how to monitor its quality (as the underlying source change)?
- How to tackle the various issues of provenance that arise?

In this paper we present our experience on defining such a process and the tool that we have developed (*MatWare*) for realizing the process and running an operational semantic warehouse for marine resources. The rest of the paper is organized as follows: Section 2 describes the context, the main requirements, and related works. Section 3 describes the adopted integration approach for tackling the corresponding functional and non-functional requirements. Section 4 describes the tool *MatWare* and Section 5 describes how the *MatWare*-constructed warehouse is currently being used in various applications. Finally, Section 6 concludes the paper. More details are available in the web[1].

2 Context, Requirements and Related Work

2.1 Context and Requirements

Below we list the main functional and non functional requirements. The source of these requirements is the *iMarine project*[2] that offers an operational distributed infrastructure that serves hundreds of scientists from the marine domain. As regards semantic technologies, the objective is to integrate information from various marine sources, specifically from WoRMS[3], Ecoscope[4], FishBase[5], FLOD[6] and DBpedia[7].

---

[1] `http://www.ics.forth.gr/isl/MarineTLO` and `http://www.ics.forth.gr/isl/MatWare`
[2] FP7, Research Infrastructures, `http://www.i-marine.eu/`
[3] `http://www.marinespecies.org/`
[4] `http://www.ecoscopebc.ird.fr/EcoscopeKB/ShowWelcomePage.action`
[5] `http://www.fishbase.org/`
[6] `http://www.fao.org/figis/flod/`
[7] `http://dbpedia.org/`

Functional Requirements

F1 *Multiplicity of Sources.* Ability to access multiple sources (including SPARQL endpoints), get data from these sources, and ingest them to the warehouse.

F2 *Mappings, Transformations and Equivalences.* Ability to accommodate mappings, perform transformations and create `sameAs` relationships between the fetched content for connecting the corresponding schema elements and entities.

F3 *Reconstructibility.* Ability to reconstruct the warehouse periodically (from scratch or incrementally) for keeping it fresh.

Non Functional Requirements

N1 *Scope control.* Make concrete and testable the scope of the information that should be stored in the warehouse. Since we live in the same universe, everything is directly or indirectly connected, therefore without stating concrete objectives there is the risk of continuous expansion without concrete objectives regarding its contents, quality and purpose.

N2 *Connectivity assessment.* Ability to check and assess the connectivity of the information in the warehouse. Putting triples together does not guarantee that they will be connected. In general, connectivity concerns both schema and instances and it is achieved through common URIs, commons literals and `sameAs` relationships.

N3 *Provenance.* More than one levels of provenance can be identified and would be desired, e.g. provenance at triple level (from what source that triple was fetched), at URIs and values level (from what source we get a URI or value), or at query level (what sources are being used to answer a query).

N4 *Consistency and Conflicts.* Ability to specify the desired consistency, e.g. regarding the acceptance or rejection of different objects for a particular subject-predicate pair in a triple, or ability to accommodate different objects while making evident their provenance.

2.2 Related Approaches

Below we refer and discuss in brief the more related systems, namely *ODCleanStore* and *Sieve*.

ODCleanStore [11,8,7] is a tool that can download content (RDF graphs) and offers various transformations for cleaning it (deduplication, conflict resolution), and linking it to existing resources, plus assessing the quality of the outcome. It names *conflicts* the cases where two different quads (e.g. sources) have different object values for a certain subject s and predicate p. To such cases conflict resolution rules are offered that either select one or more of these conflicting values (e.g. ANY, MAX, ALL), or compute a new value (e.g. AVG). [7] describes various quality metrics (for scoring each source based on conflicts), as well for assessing the overall outcome.

Another related system is *Sieve* [10] which is part of the Linked Data Integration Framework (LDIF)[8]. That work also proposes metrics like *schema completeness* and *conciseness*. However, such metrics are not useful for the case of domain specific warehouses that have a top-level ontology, in the sense that the schema mappings and the transformation rules can tackle these problems. This is true in our warehouse (it is also assumed in the scenarios of *ODCleanStore*). Finally, [1] contains an interesting discussion about completeness in query answering.

3 The Adopted Integration Approach

This section describes how we tackled the Functional and Non-Functional Requirements, as well the entire construction process.

3.1 Tackling the Functional Requirements (F1-F3)

To tackle the need for *multiplicity of sources* (F1) and *reconstructability* (F3), we developed a tool that can automate the construction (or reconstruction) of such warehouses (it is called *MatWare* and it is described in more detail in Section 4). Regarding *Mappings, Transformations and Equivalences* (F2), it is always a good practice to have (select or define) a top-level ontology as it alleviates the schema mapping effort (avoids the combinatorial explosion of pair-wise mappings). Moreover, since the entities (instances of schemas, URIs) have to be mapped too, there is a need for approaches that can automate this as much as possible. In general there is a need for rules that can create `sameAs` relationships. For this reason, *MatWare* exploits SILK[9] which is a tool for discovering relationships between data items within different Linked Data sources.

3.2 Scope Control

As regards *scope* (N1), we use the notion of *competency queries*. A competency query is a query that is useful for the community at hand, e.g. for a human member (e.g. a scientist), or for building applications for that domain. Therefore, a list of such queries can sketch the desired scope and the desired structuring of the information. Figure 1 displays the textual description of some competency queries as they were supplied by the marine community.

These queries specify the required structuring of the ontology. It is a good practice to have a *top-level schema/ontology* not only for alleviating the schema mapping effort, but also for formulating the competency queries using that ontology (instead of using elements coming from the underlying sources, which change over time). For the iMarine project, and since there was not any ontology that allowed formulating the desired queries, we defined the top-level ontology called *MarineTLO*[10] [14].

[8] `http://www4.wiwiss.fu-berlin.de/bizer/ldif/`

[9] `http://wifo5-03.informatik.uni-mannheim.de/bizer/silk/`

[10] Documentation and examples are available in `http://www.ics.forth.gr/isl/MarineTLO`.

#Query	For a **scientific name** of a **species** (e.g. **Thunnus Albacares** or **Poromitra Crassiceps**), find/give me:
Q_1	the biological environments (e.g. **ecosystems**) in which the **species** has been **introduced** and more general descriptive information of it (such as the **country**)
Q_2	its **common names** and their complementary info (e.g. **languages** and **countries** where they are used)
Q_3	the **water areas** and their **FAO codes** in which the **species** is **native**
Q_4	the **countries** in which the **species lives**
Q_5	the **water areas** and the **FAO** portioning **code** associated with a country
Q_6	the presentation w.r.t **Country, Ecosystem, Water Area** and **Exclusive Economical Zone** (of the water area)
Q_7	the projection w.r.t. **Ecosystem** and **Competitor**, providing for each competitor the **identification information** (e.g. several codes provided by different organizations)
Q_8	a map w.r.t. **Country** and **Predator**, providing for each predator both the **identification information** and the **biological classification**
Q_9	**who** discovered it, in which **year**, the **biological classification**, the **identification information**, the **common names** - providing for each common name the **language** and the **countries** where it is **used in**.

Fig. 1. Some indicative competency queries

After deciding the schema level, the next step is to specify the contents of the underling sources that should be fetched and stored (as they are, or transformed) to the warehouse. In many cases, this requires using various access methods (SPARQL endpoints, HTTP accessible files, JDBC) and specifying what exactly to get from each source (all contents, or a specific part). For instance, and for the case of the iMarine warehouse, we fetch all triples from FLOD through its SPARQL endpoint, all triples from Ecoscope obtained by fetching OWL files from its web page, information about species (ranks, scientific names and common names) from WoRMS accessed through the Species Discovery Service of the gCube infrastructure[11], information about species only from DBpedia's SPARQL endpoint, and finally information about species, water areas, ecosystems and countries from the relational tables of FishBase.

3.3 Connectivity Assessment

Connectivity (N2) has two main aspects: *schema* connectivity and *instance* connectivity. For the first, we use the top level ontology and *schema mappings* for associating the fetched data with the schema of the top level ontology[12]. Based on these we can *transform and ingest* the fetched data. Some data can be stored as they are fetched, while others have to be transformed, i.e. apply a *format* transformation and/or a *logical* transformation for being compatible with the top-level ontology.

As regards the connectivity of instances, one has to *inspect and test the connectivity* of the "draft" warehouse, i.e. the warehouse produced by ingesting the fetched information. This is done through the competency queries as well as through a number of *connectivity metrics* that we have defined. The main metrics are: (a) the *matrix of percentages of the common URIs and/or literals* (it shows the percentage of common URIs/literals between every pair of sources),

[11] `https://i-marine.d4science.org/web/guest/about-gcube`

[12] In our case we use `rdfs:subClassOf`, `rdfs:subPropertyOf` and `owl:equivalentClass` properties.

(b) the *complementarity factor of the entities of interest* (it is the number of sources that provided unique triples for each entity of interest), (c) the table with the *increments in the average degree of each source* (it measures the increment of the graph-theoretic degree of each entity when it becomes part of the warehouse graph), and (d) the unique triple contribution of each source (the number of triples provided by a source which are not provided by any other source). The values of (a),(b),(c) allow valuating the warehouse, while (c) and (d) mainly concern each particular source. The metrics are elaborated in detail in [15], while an example is given in Figure 10. In comparison to the quality metrics introduced by other works (like those mentioned in Section 2.2) which focus more on conflicts, we focus on connectivity, which is important for a warehouse that has wide scope, rich structured conceptual model, and requirements for answering queries which contain "long" (not trivial) path expressions.

Based also on the results of the previous step, the next step is to *formulate rules for instance matching*, i.e. rules that can produce `sameAs` relationships for obtaining the desired connections. These rules are formulated by the curator by manually inspecting the contents of the sources. This is done only the first time; the formulated rules are automatically applied in the subsequent warehouse reconstructions. Specifically we *apply the instance matching rules* (SILK rules in our case) for producing (and then ingesting to the warehouse) `sameAs` relationships. Moreover we apply some transformation rules to further improve the connectivity of the warehouse, specifically for changing or enhancing the data which are fetched from different sources in order to comply to the ontology or to overcome limitations of inference.

Finally we have to test the produced repository and evaluate it. This is done again through the competency queries and the metrics. Specifically, by inspecting the proposed metric-based matrixes one can very quickly get an overview of the contribution of each source and the tangible benefits of the warehouse.

3.4 Provenance

As regards provenance (N3), we support four levels of provenance: (a) at *conceptual modeling* level, (b) at *URIs and values* level, (c) at *triple* level, and (d) at *query* level.

As regards conceptual level (level a), for the case of iMarine, part of the provenance requirements are covered by the ontology `MarineTLO`. Specifically `MarineTLO` models the provenance of species names, codes, etc. (who and when assigned them). Therefore there is no need for adopting any other conceptual model for modeling provenance (e.g. OPM[13]), also because the data fetched from the sources do not have any kind of provenance information, and the warehouse construction does not have any complex workflow that need special documentation through a provenance model.

[13] `http://openprovenance.org/`

As regards the level of *URIs and values* (level b), we adopt the namespace mechanism for reflecting the source of origin of an individual[14]. In addition, during the construction of a warehouse, there is the option of applying a uniform notation "@source" (where source can be FLOD, Ecoscope, WoRMS, FishBase or DBpedia) to literals. This notation is useful in querying for indicating how each result derived by the warehouse was produced. An example of this functionality in shown in Figure 2 for the case of the scientific name and authorship of a species. This notation allows asking source-centric queries in a relative simple way by using the SPARQL filter as follows: `FILTER(langMatches (lang(?literal), ''source''))`. The shortcoming of this approach is that it is not possible to store both the source and the language of a literal, and that before storing the data to the warehouse a data transformation step (i.e. the attachment of @source) is required. Although this approach has the above limitations and "misuses"the semantics of an RDF feature (the language tag), this level can be a reasonable choice in cases where all data should be stored in a single graph space and the storage of language is not required (e.g. if all literals are in one language). If these pre-conditions are not met, then one should use the *triple* level provenance, that is described below, since it overcomes these limitations.

scientificName	year	authority
"Thunnus albacares"@worms	"1788"@worms	"Bonnaterre"@worms
"Thunnus albacares"@dbpedia	"1788"@dbpedia	"Bonnaterre"@dbpedia

Fig. 2. Scientific Name and Authorship information of *Yellowfin Tuna*

As regards the *triple* level (level c), we store the fetched (or fetched and transformed) triples from each source in a *separate graph space*. This is useful not only for provenance reasons, but also for refreshing parts of the warehouse, as well as for computing the connectivity metrics that were described earlier. Furthermore, and compared to level b, it leaves the data intact since there is no need to add any extra information about their provenance. Finally, the separate graph spaces are also useful for the fourth level described below.

As regards the *query* level (level d), *MatWare* offers a query rewriting functionality that exploits the contents of the graph spaces for returning the sources that contributed to the query results (including those that contributed to an intermediate step). Let q be a SPARQL query that has n parameters in the select clause and contains k triple patterns of the form $(?s_i\ ?p_i\ ?o_i)$, e.g.:

[14] E.g. for the cases of Ecoscope, FLOD and DBpedia we use the namespaces, that these sources already provide, while for WoRMS we use `http://www.worms.org/entity#` as a namespace and for FishBase we use `http://www.fishbase.org/entity#`.

```
SELECT ?o_1 ?o_2 ... ?o_n
WHERE {
    ?s_1 ?p_1 ?o_1. ?s_2 ?p_2 ?o_2. ... . ?s_k ?p_k ?o_k }
```

The rewriting produces a query q' that has $n+k$ parameters in the select clause: the original n variables plus one variable for each of the k triple patterns in the query. Specifically, for each triple pattern, say $(?s_i\ ?p_i\ ?o_i)$, of the original query, we introduce a variable $?g_i$ (for getting the source of the triple) and in q' the triple pattern is replaced by the graph pattern $?g_i\{?s_i\ ?p_i\ ?o_i\}$. Eventually, the rewritten query will be:

```
SELECT ?o_1 ?o_2 ... ?o_n   ?g_1 ?g_2 ... ?g_k
WHERE {
   graph ?g_1 {?s_1 ?p_1 ?o_1}.
   graph ?g_2 {?s_2 ?p_2 ?o_2}.
   ...
   graph ?g_k {?s_k ?p_k ?o_k}}
```

A real example follows. Consider the query *"For a scientific name of a species (e.g. Thunnus Albacares) find the FAO codes of the water areas in which the species is native"*. Its evaluation will return the corresponding FAO codes, information that obviously comes from FLOD. However the fact that *Thunnus Albacares is native in a specific Water Area* comes from Fishbase, which is a fact that the end user will not be aware of, if the corresponding graph space will not be returned. The upper part of Figure 3 shows the initial SPARQL query (which has 2 triple patterns), while the lower part shows the query as it has been derived after applying the rewriting described above. The answer of the last query is shown in Figure 4(left) which shows the sources that contributed to the result.

```
SELECT ?faocode WHERE {
 ?ecoscope:thunnus_albacares     marineTLO:isNativeAt                     ?waterarea.
 ?waterarea                      marineTLO:LXrelatedIdentifierAssignment ?faocode }

SELECT ?faocode  ?waterarea_graphspace  ?faocode_graphspace WHERE {
    graph ?waterarea_graphspace
        {ecoscope:thunnus_albacares marineTLO:isNativeAt                      ?waterarea }
    graph ?faocode_graphspace
        {?waterarea                 marineTLO:LXrelatedIdentifierAssignment ?faocode } }
```

Fig. 3. Rewriting a query for keeping the provenance of the intermediate results

As another example, consider the query *"Find the Scientific Name of a Species"*. This query will return the scientific names of the species according to the various sources as shown in Figure 4(right).

Intuitively, one can conceive the query evaluation process as a pipeline defined by the triple patterns, and the values shown in the additional (due to the rewriting) columns of the answer are the names of the graph spaces (in our setting this corresponds to sources) that contributed to each step of that pipeline.

faocode	waterarea_graphspace	faocode_graphspace
41	http://www.ics.forth.gr/isl/Fishbase	http://www.ics.forth.gr/isl/FLOD
47	http://www.ics.forth.gr/isl/Fishbase	http://www.ics.forth.gr/isl/FLOD
31	http://www.ics.forth.gr/isl/Fishbase	http://www.ics.forth.gr/isl/FLOD
34	http://www.ics.forth.gr/isl/Fishbase	http://www.ics.forth.gr/isl/FLOD

scientific_name	scName_graphspace
thunnus albacares	http://www.ics.forth.gr/isl/Fishbase
Thunnus albacares	http://www.ics.forth.gr/isl/DBpedia
Thunnus albacares	http://www.ics.forth.gr/isl/Worms
Thunnus albacares	http://www.ics.forth.gr/isl/Ecoscope

Fig. 4. Left: The results of the enhanced query (of Fig. 3), Right: Scientific Names (enriched with source provenance)

3.5 Consistency and Conflicts

Instead of specifying or deciding how to cope with the different values coming from the sources (as in [8]), we instead (as shown in the provenance section) show to the user the information that is provided by each source. This is more transparent, and allows the involved authorities to spot (and hopefully fix) the various errors.

3.6 The Entire Process

Figure 5 sketches the construction process. The main effort has to be dedicated for setting up the warehouse the first time, since in that time one has to select/define the schema, the schema mappings, the instance matching rules, etc. Afterwards the warehouse is reconstructed periodically for getting refreshed content, without requiring human intervention. For *monitoring* the warehouse after reconstructing it, *MatWare* computes the connectivity metrics after each reconstruction. By comparing their values in the previous and new warehouse, one

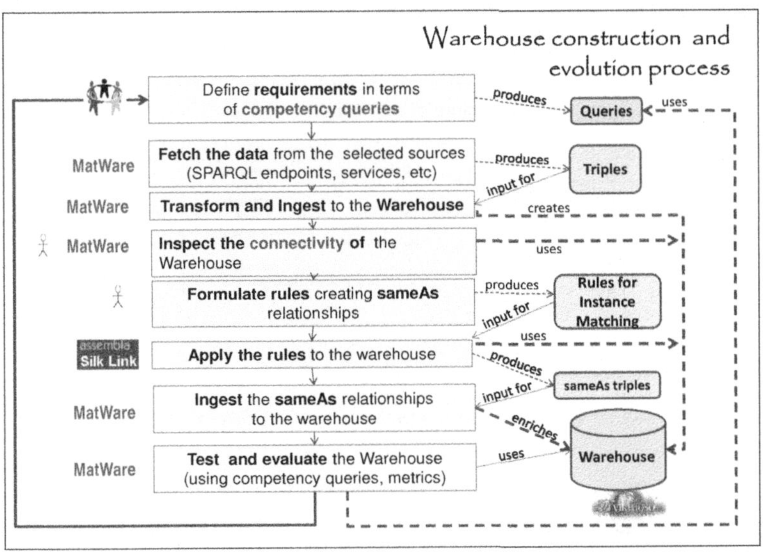

Fig. 5. The process for constructing and evolving the warehouse

can understand whether a change in the underlying sources affected negatively the quality (e.g. connectivity) of the warehouse.

For example, consider that we want to refresh the warehouse because the data coming from WoRMS have been changed and suppose that the schema of that source has not been changed. It is evident that we do not have to re-construct the warehouse from scratch since all the other sources will be the same. Instead we remove all the triples about WoRMS from the warehouse by removing them from the corresponding graph space. We also remove all same-as triples between WoRMS and any other source in the warehouse. In the sequel, we get the new contents for that source, ingest them to the warehouse and run again the steps for applying the transformation rules and the production of the same-as triples between the (new) contents of WoRMS and other sources. Finally we test and evaluate the warehouse as before. It is clear that if the schema of the source has been changed then we should also modify the mappings between that source and the top-level ontology.

4 The Warehouse Construction Tool *MatWare*

The main functionality of *MatWare* is the automatic creation and maintenance of a semantic warehouse. In brief, it is capable to: (a) download data from remote sources (e.g. FLOD, Ecoscope, WoRMS, FishBase, DBpedia), (b) create Virtuoso repositories, (c) ingest the data to the warehouse, (d) apply the necessary transformation rules to the data, (e) create **sameAs** links between the entities of the different sources, (f) create the inference ruleset, (g) refresh the repository, (h) run the competency queries, and (j) compute the connectivity metrics. It has been implemented in Java and it uses the Sesame/Virtuoso APIs. It has a modular architecture which is illustrated in Figure 6.

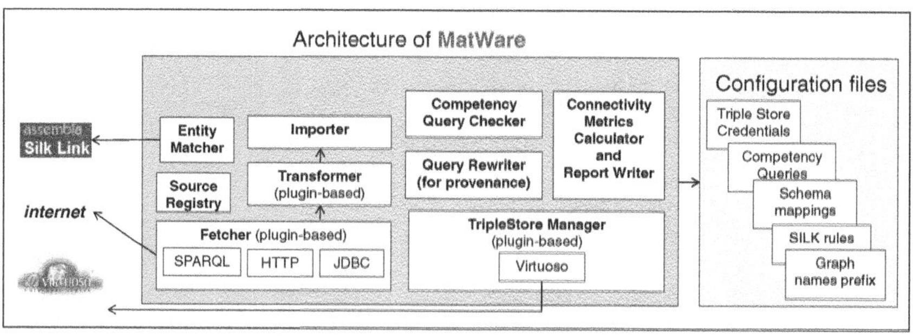

Fig. 6. The architecture of *MatWare*

Configurability is very important and in *MatWare* it is achieved by changing the context of an xml file (`config.xml`). To create a warehouse from scratch, one has to specify the type of the repository, the names of the graphs that correspond to the different sources, and the URL, username and password for connecting to the repository. These options are enough for creating the warehouse and importing the data from the sources. In addition, one can specify the next actions to be performed which include: downloading the data from each source (by providing the fetcher classes as plugins), execution of the transformation rules (by providing the transformer classes as plugins), creation of `sameAs` links between the entities of the various sources (by providing the SILK rules as xml files), calculation of the connectivity metrics, refreshing of the warehouse for the case of a source that changes, creation of the virtuoso ruleset, querying the repository, deletion of graphs. In addition one can specify the folder containing the locally stored content, and whether an existed graph should be overwritten or not.

In case one wants to add a new source, the following actions are needed: (a) include the fetcher class for the specific source as plug in, (b) provide the mapping files, (c) include the transformer class for the specific source as a plug in and (d) provide the SILK rules as xml files.

5 The Resulting Warehouse and Its Current Exploitation

5.1 The Resulted MarineTLO-Based Warehouse

Here we discuss the *MarineTLO-based warehouse*[15], which is outcome of the above process carried out using *MatWare*. Its first version is described in [14]. Now it is operational[16] and it is exploited in various applications. The objective of the warehouse is to provide a coherent set of facts about marine species. Just indicatively, Figure 7 illustrates some information about the species `Thunnus albacares` which are stored in different sources (here FLOD, Ecoscope, WoRMS, FishBase and DBpedia). These pieces of information are complementary and are assembled for enabling advanced browsing, querying and reasoning. This is also evident from Figure 8 which shows the underlying sources that contribute information regarding the main concepts of the MarineTLO ontology.

Figure 9 shows an overview of the warehouse's contents, as fetched and transformed from the various sources. As regards its evolution, a new release of the warehouse is published every two months. The current warehouse contains information for about 37,000 marine species. In total, it contains 3,772,919 triples. The current warehouse takes about 7 hours[17] to reconstruct from scratch. This process includes: downloading the sources (60 min), importing the data in the repository (230 min), applying the transformation rules (40 min), producing `sameAs` links using SILK (30 min), and computing the mertics (100 min). As regards query evaluation, the time required to answer a competency query ranges from 31 ms to 3.4 seconds. The query rewriting for provenance (which is done

[15] Complete documentation, competency queries, SILK rules and examples are available in `http://www.ics.forth.gr/isl/MatWare/#products`

[16] URL of the warehouse (restricted access): `http://virtuoso.i-marine.d4science.org:8890/sparql`

[17] Virtuoso and machine specs: OpenLink Virtuoso V6.1, Windows 8.1, 64-bit, Intel i3 dual-core, 4 GB RAM.

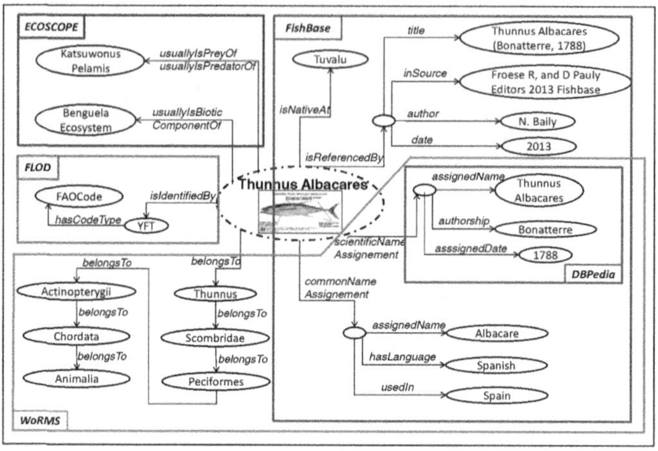

Fig. 7. Integrated information about `Thunnus albacares` from different sources

Concepts	Ecoscope	FLOD	WoRMS	DBpedia	FishBase
Species	✓	✓	✓	✓	✓
Scientific Names	✓	✓	✓	✓	✓
Authorships			✓	✓	✓
Common Names	✓	✓	✓	✓	✓
Predators	✓				✓
Ecosystems	✓				✓
Countries					✓
Water Areas		✓			✓
Vessels	✓	✓			✓
Gears	✓	✓			✓
EEZ		✓			

Fig. 8. Concept coverage by the sources in the MarineTLO-based warehouse

automatically by *MatWare*) does not increase the query evaluation time. After each reconstruction, *MatWare* computes the various connectivity metrics and exports them in the form of an HTML page, as shown in Figure 10. This not only enables monitoring the quality of the warehouse, but it is also a kind of quantitative documentation of the warehouse. For instance, and for the warehouse at hand, by considering the values of the complementarity factors and the increment of the average degrees (recall Section 3.5) we can understand that the resulting warehouse not only contains concrete information for each entity *from all* sources, but we can also see *how much* the average degree of these entities has been increased in the warehouse.

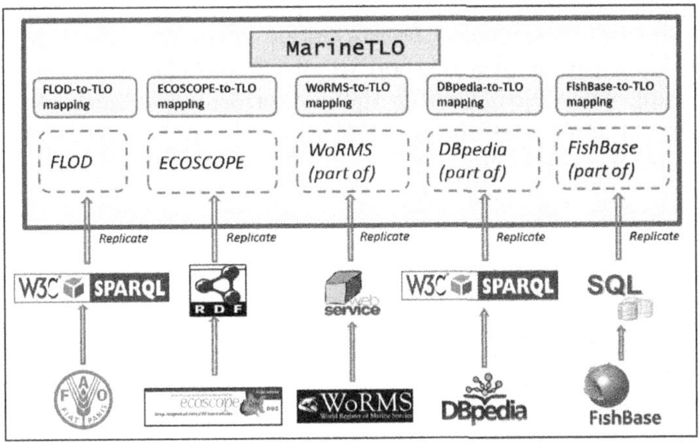

Fig. 9. Overview of the MarineTLO-based warehouse

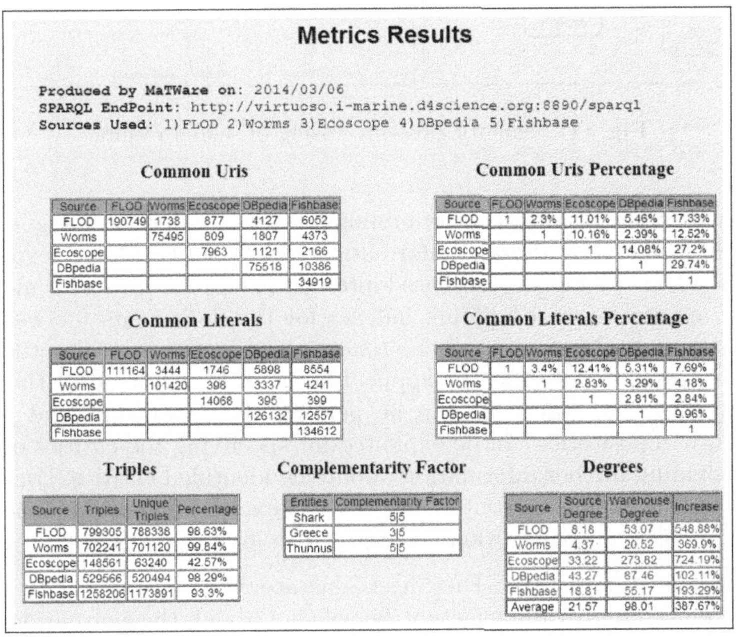

Metrics Results

Produced by MaTWare on: 2014/03/06
SPARQL EndPoint: http://virtuoso.i-marine.d4science.org:8890/sparql
Sources Used: 1)FLOD 2)Worms 3)Ecoscope 4)DBpedia 5)Fishbase

Common Uris

Source	FLOD	Worms	Ecoscope	DBpedia	Fishbase
FLOD	190749	1738	877	4127	6052
Worms		75495	809	1807	4373
Ecoscope			7963	1121	2166
DBpedia				75518	10386
Fishbase					34919

Common Uris Percentage

Source	FLOD	Worms	Ecoscope	DBpedia	Fishbase
FLOD	1	2.3%	11.01%	5.46%	17.33%
Worms		1	10.16%	2.39%	12.52%
Ecoscope			1	14.08%	27.2%
DBpedia				1	29.74%
Fishbase					1

Common Literals

Source	FLOD	Worms	Ecoscope	DBpedia	Fishbase
FLOD	111164	3444	1746	5898	8554
Worms		101420	398	3337	4241
Ecoscope			14068	395	399
DBpedia				126132	12557
Fishbase					134612

Common Literals Percentage

Source	FLOD	Worms	Ecoscope	DBpedia	Fishbase
FLOD	1	3.4%	12.41%	5.31%	7.69%
Worms		1	2.83%	3.29%	4.18%
Ecoscope			1	2.81%	2.84%
DBpedia				1	9.96%
Fishbase					1

Triples

Source	Triples	Unique Triples	Percentage
FLOD	799305	788338	98.63%
Worms	702241	701120	99.84%
Ecoscope	148561	63240	42.57%
DBpedia	529566	520494	98.29%
Fishbase	1258206	1173891	93.3%

Complementarity Factor

Entities	Complementarity Factor
Shark	5|5
Greece	3|5
Thunnus	5|5

Degrees

Source	Source Degree	Warehouse Degree	Increase
FLOD	8.16	53.07	548.88%
Worms	4.37	20.52	369.9%
Ecoscope	33.22	273.82	724.19%
DBpedia	43.27	87.46	102.11%
Fishbase	18.81	55.17	193.29%
Average	21.57	98.01	387.67%

Fig. 10. Metric's results displayed in HTML

5.2 Applications over the Warehouse

Here we describe three applications that exploit the current warehouse

A. Fusion of Structured and Unstructured Data at Search Time. One big challenge nowadays is how to integrate structured data with unstructured data (documents and text). The availability of harmonized structured knowledge about the marine domain is currently exploited for a *semantic post-processing* of the search results. Specifically the work done in the context of iMarine so far, described in [2,3], proposed a method to enrich the classical (mainly keyword based) searching with *entity mining* that is performed at *query time*. The left part of Figure 11 illustrates the process, while the right part depicts a screen shot from a prototype search system.

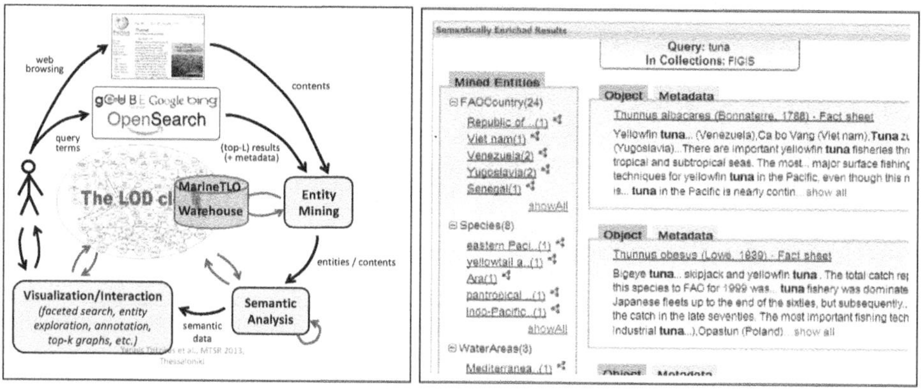

Fig. 11. Semantic post-processing of search results

In particular, the results of entity mining (entities grouped in categories) complement the query answers with information which can be further exploited by the user in a faceted and session-based interaction scheme [13]. This means that instead of annotating and building indexes for the documents (or web pages), the annotation can be done at *query time* and using the desired entities of interest. These works show that the application of entity mining over the *snippets* of the top hits of the answers can be performed at real-time, and indicated how semantic repositories can be exploited for specifying the entities of interest and for providing further information about the identified entities. For applying these methods over the full-contents it is worth exploiting multiple machines. A MapReduce-based decomposition is described in [6].

B. Fact Sheet Generator. FactSheetGenerator[18] is an application provided by IRD aiming at providing factual knowledge about the marine domain by mashing-up relevant knowledge distributed across several data sources. Figure 12(left) shows the results of the current FactSheetGenerator when searching for the species `Thunnus albacares`.

C. Android Application. We have developed (and currently improve) an Android application, called `Ichthys` that exploits the contents of the warehouse for providing to end users information about marine species in a user friendly manner. A few screens are shown in Figure 12(right).

[18] `http://www.ecoscopebc.ird.fr/`

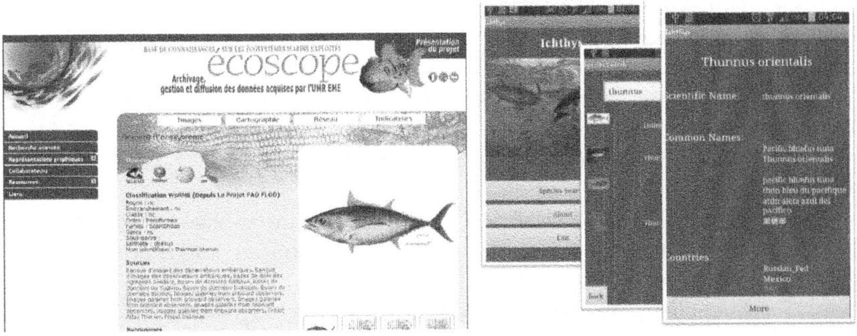

Fig. 12. Left: `Thunnus albacares` in FactSheetGenerator, Right: Screens from the `Ichthys` Android application

6 Concluding Remarks

We have described the main requirements and challenges, stemming from our experience in designing, building, maintaining and evolving an operational semantic warehouse for marine resources. We have presented the process and the tools that we have developed for supporting this process with emphasis on *scope control*, *connectivity assessment*, *provenance*, and *freshness*. To tackle these requirements and automate the warehouse construction process we have developed, *MatWare*, an extensible tool for supporting and automating the above process. In future we plan to elaborate on improving the scalability as the volume of data grows (e.g. using a single graph space that materializes all triples for offering efficient query answering, while keeping also the separate graph spaces for provenance reasons). Furthermore, we plan to further work on the evaluation of the quality of the warehouse's contents.

Acknowledgement. This work was partially supported by the ongoing project *iMarine* (FP7 Research Infrastructures, 2011-2014).

References

1. Darari, F., Nutt, W., Pirrò, G., Razniewski, S.: Completeness Statements about RDF Data Sources and Their Use for Query Answering. In: Alani, H., et al. (eds.) ISWC 2013, Part I. LNCS, vol. 8218, pp. 66–83. Springer, Heidelberg (2013)
2. Fafalios, P., Kitsos, I., Marketakis, Y., Baldassarre, C., Salampasis, M., Tzitzikas, Y.: Web Searching with Entity Mining at Query Time. In: Salampasis, M., Larsen, B. (eds.) IRFC 2012. LNCS, vol. 7356, pp. 73–88. Springer, Heidelberg (2012)
3. Fafalios, P., Tzitzikas, Y.: X-ENS: Semantic Enrichment of Web Search Results at Real-Time. In: Proceedings of the 36th International ACM SIGIR Conference on Research and Development in Information Retrieval, Dublin, Ireland, July 28 - August 01 (2013)

4. Hogan, A., Harth, A., Umbrich, J., Kinsella, S., Polleres, A., Decker, S.: Searching and Browsing Linked Data with SWSE: The Semantic Web Search Engine. Web Semantics: Science, Services and Agents on the World Wide Web 9(4) (2011)
5. Hu, Y., Janowicz, K., McKenzie, G., Sengupta, K., Hitzler, P.: A Linked-Data-Driven and Semantically-Enabled Journal Portal for Scientometrics. In: Alani, H., et al. (eds.) ISWC 2013, Part II. LNCS, vol. 8219, pp. 114–129. Springer, Heidelberg (2013)
6. Kitsos, I., Magoutis, K., Tzitzikas, Y.: Scalable Entity-based Summarization of Web Search Results Using MapReduce. In: Distributed and Parallel Databases (2013) (accepted, online first)
7. Knap, T., Michelfeit, J.: Linked Data Aggregation Algorithm: Increasing Completeness and Consistency of Data
8. Knap, T., Michelfeit, J., Daniel, J., Jerman, P., Rychnovský, D., Soukup, T., Nečaský, M.: ODCleanStore: A framework for managing and providing integrated linked data on the web. In: Wang, X.S., Cruz, I., Delis, A., Huang, G. (eds.) WISE 2012. LNCS, vol. 7651, pp. 815–816. Springer, Heidelberg (2012)
9. Makris, K., Skevakis, G., Kalokyri, V., Arapi, P., Christodoulakis, S., Stoitsis, J., Manolis, N., Rojas, S.L.: Federating Natural History Museums in Natural Europe. In: Garoufallou, E., Greenberg, J. (eds.) MTSR 2013. CCIS, vol. 390, pp. 361–372. Springer, Heidelberg (2013)
10. Mendes, P.N., Mühleisen, H., Bizer, C.: Sieve: Linked Data Quality Assessment and Fusion. In: Proceedings of the 2012 Joint EDBT/ICDT Workshops, pp. 116–123. ACM (2012)
11. Michelfeit, J., Knap, T.: Linked Data Fusion in ODCleanStore. In: International Semantic Web Conference, Posters & Demos (2012)
12. Oren, E., Delbru, R., Catasta, M., Cyganiak, R., Stenzhorn, H., Tummarello, G.: Sindice.com: a Document-Oriented Lookup Index for Open Linked Data. Int. J. Metadata Semant. Ontologies 3(1), 37–52 (2008)
13. Sacco, G., Tzitzikas, Y.: Dynamic Taxonomies and Faceted Search: Theory, Practice, and Experience, vol. 25. Springer-Verlag New York Inc. (2009)
14. Tzitzikas, Y., et al.: Integrating Heterogeneous and Distributed Information about Marine Species through a Top Level Ontology. In: Garoufallou, E., Greenberg, J. (eds.) MTSR 2013. Communications in Computer and Information Science, vol. 390, pp. 289–301. Springer, Heidelberg (2013)
15. Tzitzikas, Y., Minadakis, N., Marketakis, Y., Fafalios, P., Alloca, C., Mountantonakis, M.: Quantifying the Connectivity of a Semantic Warehouse. In: Proceedings of the 4th International Workshop on Linked Web Data Management (LWDM 2014), in Conjunction with the 17th International Conference on Extending Database Technology (EDBT 2014) (2014)

Object Property Matching Utilizing the Overlap between Imported Ontologies

Benjamin Zapilko and Brigitte Mathiak

GESIS - Leibniz Institute for the Social Sciences
Unter Sachsenhausen 6-8, 50667 Cologne, Germany
{benjamin.zapilko,brigitte.mathiak}@gesis.org

Abstract. Large scale Linked Data is often based on relational databases and thereby tends to be modeled with rich object properties, specifying the exact relationship between two objects, rather than a generic is-a or part-of relationship. We study this phenomenon on government issued statistical data, where a vested interest exists in matching such object properties for data integration. We leverage the fact that while the labeling of the properties is often heterogeneous, e.g. ex1:geo and ex2:location, they link to individuals of semantically similar code lists, e.g. country lists. State-of-the-art ontology matching tools do not use this effect and therefore tend to miss the possible correspondences. We enhance the state-of-the-art matching process by aligning the individuals of such imported ontologies separately and computing the overlap between them to improve the matching of the object properties. The matchers themselves are used as black boxes and are thus interchangeable. The new correspondences found with this method lead to an increase of recall up to 2.5 times on real world data, with only a minor loss in precision.

Keywords: #eswc2014Zapilko.

1 Introduction

The number of statistical data sets available as Linked Data has recently increased to a large degree. This is a welcome step towards governmental transparency, since professionals from many domains rely on the analysis of such data. Statistical data is periodically collected by administrative sources [30] as an attempt to describe the state of a nation in numbers, typically by collecting demographic and economic data, e.g. like population numbers and unemployment ratios but also subjective measurements like general wellbeing. One of the typical tasks for scientists using statistical data is the comparative analysis of more than one data set. Linked Open Data [13] is, in theory, a suitable source for this task as it allows the easy linking of data sets. In practice, only few links exist between these data sets and, as we will describe in Section 6, the correspondences created by matching tools have a rather low recall (0.4 on real world data). However, finding correspondences manually is much harder than dismissing wrong ones.

V. Presutti et al. (Eds.): ESWC 2014, LNCS 8465, pp. 737–751, 2014.

This systematic shortcoming is due to a high occurrence of heterogeneously labeled object properties, e.g. `ex1:geo` and `ex2:location`. The individuals linked to by object properties are not considered in full extent during ontology matching when they are part of external or separate ontologies like, e.g. code lists of country names maintained by a particular authority. Ontologies and instance data that are aligned in current benchmarks and alignment tasks of the Ontology Alignment Evaluation Initiative (OAEI) [29] do not yet address this problem. This is verified in Section 4 by comparing a large number of statistical data sets and the OAEI data sets. This critique on the current limitation on domains for ontology matching is not new. [34] suggests the consideration of new domains to reveal new challenges. Also, according to [12], domain-specific values, significant occurrences, patterns and constraints of values should also be considered.

Based on these ideas and our own findings on heterogeneous object properties, we develop a novel ontology matching method to improve the matching of object properties. The method utilizes an instance-based matcher as a core, but refines the results by matching the imported ontologies as well. The similarities between these imported ontologies are computed as an overlap score. This overlap score indicates whether a new correspondence between object properties is added to the generated correspondences between the input ontologies. This method allows us to detect additional correspondences between object properties like `ex1:geo` and `ex2:location` based on the individuals of imported ontologies. Thus, recall is increased. The approach is independent of the matching algorithm employed and may utilize any instance-based approaches or algorithms that consider extensional techniques and object similarity techniques [8].

We test different methods to calculate the overlap score: Jaccard Coefficient and three variants of it, finding that although some of the variants show clearer distinction between correct correspondences and false positive correspondences, the improvements are statistically not significant, especially not when comparing it to the influence of the matcher used.

We distinguish our method from current related work in Section 2. The problem statement of our approach is formulated in Section 3. It is supplemented by an use case and validated by a data analysis in Section 4. In Section 5, we describe our proposed algorithm in detail. Our method is evaluated in Section 6 in a benchmark scenario and a real world data scenario. In Section 7, we conclude and provide an outlook on future work.

2 Related Work

In the context of Linked Data, the matching of properties is not a trivial task as [33] argues, because the instances of two properties are typically described in ontologies that differ from those defining the properties. This observation can be adopted to ontologies when object properties are used to link to classes or individuals of another, imported ontology.

In this paper, we focus on instance-based matching of object properties. There are many established methods that perform instance-based matching and apply extensional techniques like object similarities. Both, OLA [7] and Similarity

Flooding [26], process input ontologies as graph structures and compute proximities between all elements of two graphs. These proximities are propagated throughout the graph structure. However, Similarity Flooding only detects correspondences between nodes of a graph, i.e. classes of an ontology, and does not perform property matching. COMA++ [6] contains two instance-based matchers which consider similarities and patterns of instance values. [28] presents an approach for matching RDF datatype properties based on the construction of a matrix of the property values. In [22], the domains and ranges of object properties, the property characteristics, and the cardinality restrictions are considered for computing similarities among properties. ASMOV [20] computes several similarities between properties like internal and extensional similarities. The instance values are part of an overall similarity measure consisting of four calculations. RiMOM [24] combines multiple strategies for ontology matching automatically and considers also instances for property matching. Detecting correspondences between attributes is also a traditional part in the domain of schema matching [18]. In the context of Linked Data, BLOOMS+ [19] uses contextual information from the input data for matching and a rich knowledge source. While BLOOMS+ focuses on linking classes only, ObjectCoref [15] and RAVEN [27] detect also similarities between property values. Additional prominent matching approaches are FALCON-AO [14], AgreementMaker [2], Semint [23], GLUE [4], and Dumas [1].

The above approaches have in common that only those individuals are considered for matching which are linked in the object properties of the input ontologies. In contrast, our approach identifies and considers additional individuals of an imported ontology that are not linked to in the object properties of the input ontologies. Another specific point of our approach is that we assume the imported ontologies to be sets of homogeneous entities like authority or code lists. This assumption will be verified in Section 4.

The computation of similarities between ontologies is discussed in several works. In [25], the ontology similarity is based on terminological similarity of concepts. Different similarities are combined in [5] where strings, concepts, and usage traces are considered. [35] presents a calculation between two A-Box ontologies, while also structural information out of their T-Box ontology is considered. Similar to our method is [3], where several measures are introduced for computing ontology similarity by considering available alignments. In [4], the Jaccard coefficient is introduced as a similarity measure for ontology matching. According to [17], simple similarity measures like the Jaccard coefficient perform best for instance-based matching which is why we chose it for our method.

The benchmark data set of the OAEI is an established source for evaluating ontology matching approaches. Based on an ontology describing bibliographic resources, it covers various kinds of transformations on structural and terminological levels and is used for different alignment tasks. The Islab Instance Matching Benchmark (IIMB) [11] has been created for evaluating instance matching systems. However, both benchmarks do not consider the underlying problem of our approach. Similar to the data in our use case is the RDF version [21] of the Star Schema Benchmark [31] which comprises five single data sets. However, this distributed structure is not processible by most of the current ontology matching systems.

3 Problem Statement

The problem we address in this paper is illustrated in Figure 1. We assume two ontologies O and O' that hold classes C and C' with individuals I_n and I'_n. We also assume that R and R' are ontologies with homogeneous entities RC_n and $R'C'_n$ of the same type, e.g. authority or code lists. The individuals of the ontologies O and O' contain object properties P and P' that link to entities of the ontologies R and R'. When matching ontologies O and O', correspondences between semantically similar object properties P and P' could be missed, when they are of different name and structure. This occurs although both object properties link to individuals of similar ontologies e.g. like `ex1: geo` and `ex2:location` linking to entities of country lists R and R'.

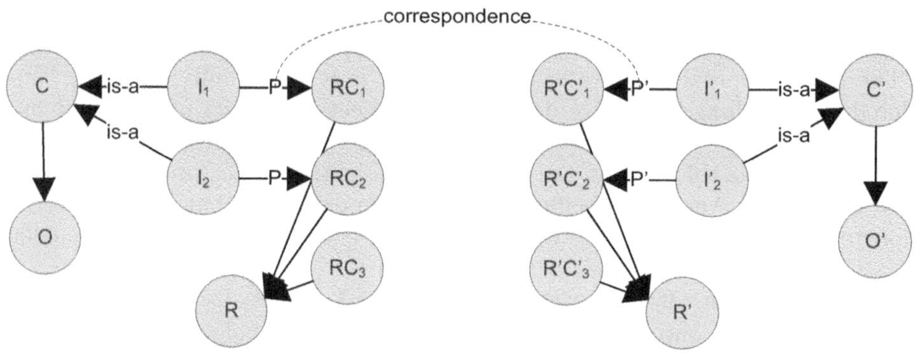

Fig. 1. Matching of object properties that link to individuals of imported ontologies

As discussed in the related work, current approaches consider the individuals linked by object properties for ontology matching like ASMOV [20], RiMOM [24] and others. However, these referenced individuals play only a subsidiary role for the computation of a correspondence between the linking properties. Also, individuals of such imported ontologies which are not linked to are not considered. Thus, correspondences between object properties can be missed.

4 Use Case: Statistical Data

The use case, which supplements our problem statement, centers on statistical data. Scientists often integrate and merge two or more of these data sets in order to conduct comparative data analysis. In theory, ontology matching is the ideal method for this task, however, in practice we show how matchers can be improved to give better results for this scenario.

Typically, statistical data is organized in a star or snowflake schema structure, which can be found in data warehouses [16] and is also reflected in the SDMX information model[1], a multidimensional standard model for describing statistical data. Represented as Linked Data, a statistical data set consists of several instances of data entries, each of which determines a particular data value, e.g. "548215". The data values are supplemented by additional objects which provide further information, e.g. in which country or at which time the data has been collected. This sets the data entries into context. Such objects are referenced in the data value instances by object properties. However, the objects themselves are classes or individuals of other external or separate data sets (typically classifications or code lists).

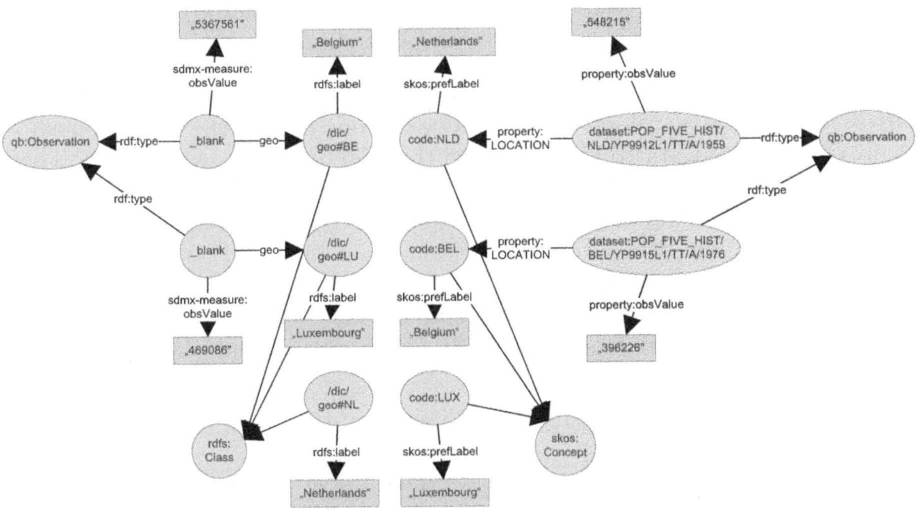

Fig. 2. Example of statistical data represented as Linked Data

In Figure 2, the problem of object property matching stated in the previous section is illustrated using real world statistical data. Excerpts of two data sets from Eurostat[2] and OECD[3] are shown. The instances of both data sets hold an object property indicating some geographical information (`geo` and `property:LOCATION`). Other object properties are omitted here. The object properties link to other individuals of code lists which is indicated by a different URI path and a different namespace. In Figure 2, the referenced data sets also contain the individuals `/dic/geo#NL` and `code:LUX`, which are not linked to

[1] `http://sdmx.org/`

[2] `http://estatwrap.ontologycentral.com/`

[3] `http://oecd.270a.info/`

by object properties. In our tests with matching systems, the object properties `geo` and `property:LOCATION` are not matched because they are labeled different and belong to different data sets. Even when matching the individuals of the referenced code lists, there is no inference on the referencing object properties.

In order to validate whether our problem statement is reasonable for the domain of statistical data by affecting a large amount of data sets, we verify our assumptions on the patterns of statistical data, which are:

1. Data entries are modeled as individuals and are accompanied by various named object properties linking to classes and individuals of external code lists or light-weight ontologies. Rather than forming a network or tree connected with homogeneous object properties, the data model is thus similar to a star schema [16].
2. Classifications and code lists[4] are often used in statistical data sets in the described way.
3. These code lists are referenced by object properties and are identifiable as additional ontologies or data sets by inspecting namespaces and URIs.

We verify our assumptions by analyzing and comparing data from three sources. Real world data sets are considered from two of the main repositories for Open Data: Data Hub[5] (DH)[6] and the wiki of Planet Data[7] (PD). They are compared to data sets used in previous campaigns of the OAEI [29] to show that this is in fact a novel problem, not one investigated before. Within this third set, we examine data sets of the instance matching (IM) tracks separately due to major differences between ontologies and data sets containing mostly instance data. Due to the diversity of the data sources, the data analysis was done manually with the help of standardized SPARQL queries and scripts.

Table 1. Comparison of statistical data and OAEI data (as of December 2013)

Criteria	**DH**	**PD**	**OAEI**	**IM**
Number of all examined data sets	49	22	54	15
Data structure	93,8 %	95,4 %	0 %	13,3 %
Presence of thesauri references	91,8 %	95,4 %	3,7 %	13,3 %
OWL/RDF data set	0 %	0 %	90,7 %	40 %
Other RDF-based data set	100 %	100 %	24,1 %	73,3 %

We investigate our data structure hypothesis by examining whether the data set is organized similar to our assumed pattern. The structure is detected by

[4] With regard to their similar function for statistical data classifications and code lists are summarized as code lists for the entire paper.

[5] `http://thedatahub.io/`

[6] Due to the amount of data sets, Data Hub has been analyzed by sampling. Data sets have been examined that are tagged with "format-rdf", "format-qb", "format-scovo" as well as "statistics", "government", "census", or "lod" and similar spellings.

[7] `http://wiki.planet-data.eu/web/datasets`

analyzing and counting the links inside a data set and out to other data sets. The results in Table 1 show that most of the examined data sets from Planet Data and Data Hub reflect this typical structure of statistical data, but almost none from the OAEI and IM challenges. Based on the identified schema structure, we then investigate whether linkes to ontologies similar to code lists can be identified. References to code lists entries could be observed in most cases of the Data Hub and the Planet Data data sets (see Table 1). The detected code lists have a list-type character, like country lists, age groups, or entries of a scale. Only in a few cases, there are hierarchies inside these code lists, e.g. in a geographical classification with different administrative levels. In the OAEI and IM challenges, only in two cases references to code lists, i.e. object properties that link to individuals of imported ontologies, could be detected.

Table 2. Analysis of the structure of statistical data (as of December 2013)

Criteria	**Percentage**
Number of all examined data sets (sample from DH and PD)	40
Different NS for input and referenced ontologies	67,5 %
URI path of linked individuals equal for particular object properties	100 %
Individuals of a referenced ontology of the same class	100 %

Finally, we examined whether the different ontologies of the detected structure can be distinguished by different namespaces and URIs. The individuals of an ontology are considered to be defined in one namespace. Moreover, the classes and individuals of an imported ontology have to be addressed by the same object property of the input ontology. The results in Table 2 show that this is indeed the case. For all studied data sets, looking at the URI path was sufficient to identify and distinguish the ontologies.

5 Computing Overlaps for Object Property Matching

Knowing the structural differences between current benchmarks and statistical data according to our problem statement, leads us to the following algorithm to improve the matching of object properties. Revisiting our use case, we complement the matching process of the two data sets by identifying those code lists that contain the referenced individuals like `/dic/geo#BE` and `code:NLD`. Then, the overlap between these code lists is computed which we conjecture to represent a semantic similarity between the object properties `geo` and `property:LOCATION`. This is used as correspondence for the overall matching between the data sets.

The algorithm is formalized as follows. Given as input are two ontologies O and O' with classes C and C', properties P and P', and individuals I and I'. The objects RC and $R'C'$ of the object property instances are classes or individuals of imported ontologies R and R'. These are ontologies with homogeneous entities of the same type, e.g. code lists. The imported ontologies are either T-Boxes or A-Boxes of their own with different namespaces. Thus, based on the data analysis conducted in Section 4 we formulate the following additional definitions.

Definition 1 (Object Property Instance and Property Object). *An instance OPI of an object property P is a tuple of the form (I,P,RC), where I is an individual of ontology O and P is the particular object property of O. A property object RC of OPI is a class or individual of a referenced ontology R.*

Definition 2 (Imported Ontology). *An imported ontology R is either a T-Box or A-Box ontology with classes or individuals RC which are objects in the object property instances OPI of the ontology O. An imported ontology R and its entities RC are held in a namespace different from the namespace of O and all its entities.*

The objective of our algorithm is to detect an alignment A as output with correspondences between all entities of O and O'. Additionally, overlaps between all R_n are used in order to generate additional correspondences between object properties P and P'. In the algorithm, we apply any given ontology matching system that generates correspondences between two input ontologies. As mentioned before, the matcher is used as a black box in our algorithm. The algorithm goes through five phases for matching two input ontologies O and O'.

1. All RC inside each ontology are grouped in order to identify the imported ontologies R_n and R'_m per each ontology O and O'.
2. The input ontologies O and O' are matched by an ontology matching tool. The resulting correspondences are included to the alignment A.
3. All pairs of R_n and R'_m are matched with each other by the same matcher. The resulting correspondences are the basis for calculating the overlap scores in the next phase.
4. Overlap scores are computed pairwise for each R_n and R'_m. Different similarity measures can be applied. We utilize the Jaccard coefficient [32,4]. However, the Jaccard coefficient is known for its unbalancy [17], especially when two sets are highly different in their size. This may complicate the choice of a suitable threshold. Hence, we introduce three additional similarity measures for addressing this problem in Definition 3. The overlap between two ontologies is computed by assuming that a correspondence between two individuals of the ontologies indicates that they are part of the intersection set of R_n and R'_m. This way, we can determine $|R_n \bigcap R'_m|$. If the overlap is higher than a specific threshold t, we assume that there is a correspondence between the object properties P and P' that hold R_n and R'_m as objects in OPI and OPI'.
5. We add the detected correspondence with the calculated overlap score between their imported ontologies R_n and R'_m as confidence value to the alignment A. If a correspondence between two object properties already exists in A, the correspondence with the higher confidence value is kept and the other one is discarded.

Definition 3 (Overlap utilizing Jaccard coefficient and variations). *The overlap between two imported ontologies R_n and R'_m is computed as*

$$JC = \frac{|R_n \bigcap R'_m|}{|R_n \bigcup R'_m|}$$

$$JC_{min} = \frac{|R_n \bigcap R'_m|}{|min(|R_n|, |R'_m|)|}$$

$$JC_{res} = \frac{|R_n \bigcap R'_m|}{|R_{n-Linked} \bigcup R'_{m-Linked}|}$$

$$JC_{min+res} = \frac{|R_n \bigcap R'_m|}{|min(|R_{n-Linked}|, |R'_{m-Linked}|)|}$$

where

- $|R_n \bigcap R'_m|$ *is the number of all correspondences between* R_n *and* R'_m,
- $|R_n \bigcup R'_m|$ *is the number of all entities in* R_n *and* R'_m *and*
- $R_{n-Linked}$ *and* $R'_{m-Linked}$ *are only those classes of* R_n *and* R'_m *that are referenced in the ontologies* O *and* O'.

Definition 4 (Correspondence between two Object Properties). *A correspondence between two object properties* P *and* P' *is described by the following 5-tuple adopted from [8].*

$$\langle id, e_1, e_2, r, n \rangle$$

where

- *id is an identifier for the particular correspondence;*
- e_1 *and* e_2 *are the object properties* P *and* P';
- r *determines the type of the relation between* P *and* P', *in our case an equivalence relationship;*
- n *represents the confidence values, which is in our case the* $overlap(R_n, R'_m)$.

This method is simple to implement with any instance-based matcher and enables us to match object properties like `geo` and `property:LOCATION` in our example. The runtime is comparable to matching the whole ontologies. The split between the different ontologies decreases the time needed for matching the particular ontologies, offsetting the need to run additional matching processes.

6 Evaluation

We evaluate our method on both artificial and real world data to show the impact of our method on object property matching. The results show a significant improvement in both scenarios, especially the sought-after improvement of recall.

6.1 Setup

The evaluation consists of two scenarios. The first scenario "Benchmark" is conducted on an artificially created benchmark for statistical data which is introduced in Section 6.2. In the second evaluation scenario "Real World Data", we apply our method on the two real world data sets from Eurostat and OECD from our use case. In each scenario, the matching systems are executed with the input ontologies at first ("State-of-the-Art"). In a second run, our method ("Object Property Matching") is applied by matching the imported ontologies additionally.

In both scenarios, the resulting correspondences are validated with their particular reference alignments. We compute precision, recall and F-measure for each alignment task, since they are standard evaluation measures for ontology matching evaluation [8]. For computing the overlap value, we utilize a threshold of 0.3 in the benchmark scenario. This has turned out to be a suitable value during pretests. Because the Jaccard coefficient can get unbalanced [17], we compare the different similarity measures defined in Section 5 in the second scenario.

We chose FALCON-AO [14] and AgreementMaker [2] as black box matcher from which we assume representative results. FALCON-AO has been chosen because of applying extensional matching techniques like object similarity, while AgreementMaker contains an instance-based matching algorithm. Our instance-based object property matching approach is compared best to those techniques. Both systems have been successful regarding their performances in previous OAEI campaigns [9,10] and are executed without any manipulation in their standard configurations.

6.2 Benchmark

It was not possible to evaluate our method on a gold standard, because unfortunately no such standard exists yet. The OAEI data sets and other data sets used for evaluations lack important characteristics we are looking for (see Sections 2 and 4). Hence, we decided to design a benchmark specific to the problem based on the principles of established benchmarks [29,11].

The benchmark reflects the assumptions made in Section 4 concerning heterogeneous object properties and their linking to classes of code lists, located in other namespaces and URI paths. The T-Box is a simplified version of a data model for statistical data: one named class representing a data entry and several object properties linking to classes of imported ontologies. These imported ontologies are included with different URI paths. We populate this seed ontology with 50 randomly generated individuals as A-Box. An example is given in Figure 3: `:Entry11` represents an observation on the satisfaction level of German young adults. The object properties link to classes of code lists from different namespaces[8].

[8] In the actual benchmark, they are differentiated by URI path not by namespace as this has the greater coverage on statistical data. This example uses namespaces for clarification. For the algorithm, there is no practical difference.

Individual of the Seed Ontology

```
:Entry11  a  STATTBOX:DataEntry ,
             owl:NamedIndividual ;
          STATTBOX:date  "1981/08/02"^^xsd:integer ;
          STATTBOX:obsValue  "886"^^xsd:integer ;
          STATTBOX:agegroup  ages:20-29 ;
          STATTBOX:gender  sex:sex-M ;
          STATTBOX:geo  countriesISO:DE ;
          STATTBOX:maritalStatus  concepts:cl_mar_total ;
          STATTBOX:occupation  indic_1:occup_value3 ;
          STATTBOX:satisfaction  indic_2:sat_value4 .
```

Classes of Referenced Ontologies

```
ages:20-29  a  owl:Class ;
rdfs:label  "From 20 to 29 years" .

sex:sex-M  a  owl:Class ;
rdfs:label  "Male" .

countriesISO:DE  a  owl:Class ;
rdfs:label  "Germany" .

concepts:cl_mar_total  a  owl:Class ;
rdfs:label  "Total" .

indic_1:occup_value3  a  owl:Class ;
rdfs:label  "Unemployed" .

indic_2:sat_value4  a  owl:Class ;
rdfs:label  "Very dissatisfied" .
```

Fig. 3. Example individual of the seed ontology

The seed ontology is used to produce variations. The namespaces of all involved code lists, i.e. imported ontologies, were changed. Additionally, specific properties were changed in accordance to what we have observed about statistical data. In the variations 010 - 011, the names of the object properties are changed on a random basis. In 020 - 024, the code lists that are referenced are changed in label name, class name, URI path, etc. This notably lowers the overlap. In 030 - 031, we test the matching without any overlap, to test how our system works on standard ontologies. Each variation forms together with the seed ontology an alignment task. The complete benchmark, the variations and the single tests are available at http://code.google.com/p/matching-statistics/.

6.3 Real World Data Sets

For the real world data scenario, we revisit the data sets from our use case. They hold many different properties that semantically overlap and are representative for statistical data. The idea is to examine many different cases in just one pair of data sets, as the preparation is quite labor-intensive. The EUROSTAT data set covers "Labour input in industry". This data set has 16783 instances and 7 object properties. The OECD data set covers "Outward activity of multinationals - Share in national total (manufacturing)". It has 5343 instances and 8 object properties. In both data sets, the object properties link to classes of particular code lists. Also, both data sets have some object properties that are not linked inside the actual instances. We manually identified five properties that match semantically.

In order to use the code lists with the matching systems, they had to be preprocessed. The changes include generic transformations of the referenced code lists from SKOS to T-Box ontologies. Similar preprocessing has been previously done in Library Tracks of OAEI, where SKOS thesauri have been transformed to OWL. The data is available at http://code.google.com/p/matching-statistics/.

6.4 Results and Discussion

The results in Table 3 indicate major improvements on matching object properties in all scenarios. The results of the tests 010 - 011, which hold differently labeled object properties, expose the strengths of our method compared to the state-of-the-art. The matchers could not find correspondences between the heterogeneous object properties, even if their referenced individuals are equal or similar like `concepts:geo#geo_DE` and `vocab:country#DE`. The information given in the labels of these classes is not considered for detecting correspondences between the referring object properties. The recall of our method is much higher for these tests. The results of the tests 020 - 024 show that the distance between our method and the state-of-the-art is decreasing depending on the matching between the imported ontologies and the resulting different overlaps. However, the results of these tests are always better or at least equal to the state-of-the-art approach when utilizing our method. This is also demonstrated with the counter check 030 - 031 (no overlap), which shows at least no worsening.

The results using real world data are similar to the benchmark tests 020 - 024, because there are not necessarily overlaps between the code lists. The object properties in both data sets are named differently, the number of classes in all code lists is unbalanced, and there may not be necessarily correspondences between all object properties. While recall improves, there is some loss of precision (see Table 3). False positives occur when the matchers find correspondences between unlike code lists, e.g. `geo` (containing country names) of Eurostat with `property:ISIC3` (containing branches of industry) of OECD. Nevertheless, the higher recall shows that by our method new correspondences have been detected that have not been identified by the state-of-the-art approach.

In order to cut off these false positives, we choose a threshold value. Since the unbalance of the simple Jaccard coefficient makes it difficult to set a suitable threshold, we have compared the similarity measures defined in Definition 3 regarding their impact on the real world data scenario.

The different overlap values computed for each detected correspondence are shown in Tables 4 and 5 and are compared to the confidence values of the

Table 3. Results for both evaluation scenarios. The best result in row is bold. For the single tasks of the variations the means have been computed. P = Precision, R = Recall, F = F-measure.

Approach	**State-of-the-Art (SotA)**						**Object Property Matching**					
System	AgreementMaker			FALCON-AO			AgreementMaker			FALCON-AO		
	P	R	F	P	R	F	P	R	F	P	R	F
Test 001	1.00	1.00	1.00	1.00	1.00	1.00	1.00	1.00	1.00	1.00	1.00	1.00
Tests 010-011	1.00	0.45	0.61	1.00	0.34	0.46	1.00	0.89	**0.94**	1.00	0.78	0.87
Tests 020-024	1.00	0.42	0.59	1.00	0.29	0.41	1.00	0.85	**0.92**	1.00	0.67	0.79
Tests 030-031	1.00	0.45	**0.61**	1.00	0.34	0.46	1.00	0.45	**0.61**	1.00	0.34	0.46
Real World Data	1.00	0.40	0.70	1.00	0.40	0.70	0.83	1.00	**0.92**	0.45	1.00	0.73

Table 4. Similarity Measures for detected Correspondences (AgreementMaker)

Found Correspondences	JC	JC_{min}	JC_{res}	$JC_{min+res}$	$SotA$
Correct Correspondences					
geo = LOCATION	0.002	**1**	0.688	**1**	0
indic_bt = VAR	0.132	0.909	**1**	**1**	0
nace_r2 = ISIC3	0.006	0.979	0.959	**1**	0
obs_status = OBS_STATUS	0.75	**1**	x	x	0.969
timeformat = TIME_FORMAT	0.571	**1**	**1**	**1**	0.872
False Positives					
geo = ISIC3	0.004	0.354	0.369	1	0

Table 5. Similarity Measures for detected Correspondences (FALCON-AO)

Found Correspondences	JC	JC_{min}	JC_{res}	$JC_{min+res}$	$SotA$
Correct Correspondences					
geo = LOCATION	0.002	0.909	0.588	**0.909**	0
indic_bt = VAR	0.012	0.090	0.083	**0.333**	0
nace_r2 = ISIC3	0.007	0.188	0.103	**0.191**	0
obs_status = OBS_STATUS	0.647	**0.917**	x	x	1
timeformat = TIME_FORMAT	0.571	**1**	**1**	**1**	1
False Positives					
geo = ISIC3	0.004	0.354	0.340	1	0
nace_r2 = VAR	0.001	0.090	0.017	0.1	0
nace_r2 = OBS_STATUS	0.012	0.938	0.306	0.306	0
freq = VAR	0.053	0.111	0.1	0.1	0
freq = OBS_STATUS	0.389	0.778	x	x	0
freq = TIME_FORMAT	0.3	0.75	1	1	0

state-of-art approach (SotA). An `x` means that no value could have been computed, because no classes of the referenced code lists have been linked in the data set (this would result in a divide by zero). Balanced values make it easier to distinguish false positives, because the difference between valid correspondences and non-valid correspondences is increased. For example, the overlap for the correspondence between `geo` and `LOCATION` is at 0.002 for JC, but much higher for the others. The best approach, in this sample, would be to use $JC_{min+res}$ and to use JC_{min}, when that fails. However, the actual effect is minimal. Only one false positive is excluded. More thorough testing might bring a clearer distinction. So far, it seems that the choice of the similarity measure to compute an overlap is much less relevant than the choice of the matcher to increase precision.

7 Conclusion and Outlook

In this paper, we have shown that object properties in statistical data are used differently than in data sets typically used for ontology matching. By leveraging this difference for object property matching, we gain an improvement of recall up to 2.5 times. Loss in precision occurs, but is relatively small in comparison. Since this loss occurs while matching the imported ontologies, adjusting the matching systems towards this problem may be helpful. For these experiments, we have used the standard parameters for both matchers, in order to keep it clearer.

While our use case has been motivated by statistical data, a lot of Linked Data sources share this data model structure, since many of them are derived from relational databases. We chose statistical data, because 1) there is clear need to integrate the data and 2) although the data sets are covering semantically similar topics, standardization usually does not cover the object properties, only the code lists themselves, if at all. This demand may increase with the number of Linked Open Data sets.

References

1. Bilke, A., Naumann, F.: Schema Matching using Duplicates. In: ICDE, pp. 69–80 (2005)
2. Cruz, I., Antonoelli, F., Stroe, C.: AgreementMaker: Effcient Matching for Large Real-World Schemas and Ontologies. In: VLDB 2009 (2009)
3. David, J., Euzenat, J., Šváb-Zamazal, O.: Ontology similarity in the alignment space. In: Proceedings of the 9th International Semantic Web Conference on The Semantic Web, pp. 129–144 (2010)
4. Doan, A., Madhavan, J., Domingos, P., Halevy, A.: Ontology Matching: A Machine Learning Approach. In: Staab, S., Studer, R. (eds.) Handbook on Ontologies in Information Systems, pp. 397–416. Springer (2003)
5. Ehrig, M., Haase, P., Stojanovic, N., Hefke, M.: Similarity for Ontologies - a Comprehensive Framework. In: European Conference on Information Systems, ECIS (2005)
6. Engmann, D., Maßmann, S.: Instance Matching with COMA++. In: BTW Workshops, pp. 28–37 (2007)
7. Euzenat, J., Valtchev, P.: Similarity-Based Ontology Alignment in OWL-Lite. In: Proceedings of the 16th Eureopean Conference on Artificial Intelligence, ECAI 2004, pp. 333–337 (2004)
8. Euzenat, J., Shvaiko, P.: Ontology matching. Springer (2007)
9. Euzenat, J., Ferrara, A., Meilicke, C., Pane, J., Scharffe, F., Shvaiko, P., Stuckenschmidt, H., Sváb-Zamazal, O., Svátek, V., dos Santos, C.T.: Results of the Ontology Alignment Evaluation Initiative (2010)
10. Euzenat, J., Ferrara, A., van Hage, W.R., Hollink, L., Meilicke, C., Nikolov, A., Ritze, D., Scharffe, F., Shvaiko, P., Stuckenschmidt, H., Sváb-Zamazal, O., dos Santos, C.T.: Results of the ontology alignment evaluation initiative (2011)
11. Ferrara, A., Lorusso, D., Montanelli, S., Varese, G.: Towards a Benchmark for Instance Matching. In: Shvaiko, P., Euzenat, J., Giunchiglia, F., Stuckenschmidt, H. (eds.) Ontology Matching (OM 2008), vol. 431, CEUR-WS.org (2008)
12. Halevy, A.: Why Your Data Won't Mix Queue, vol. 3, pp. 50–58. ACM (2005)
13. Heath, T., Bizer, C.: Linked Data: Evolving the Web into a Global Data Space. Morgan & Claypool (2011)
14. Hu, W., Qu, Y.: Falcon-AO: A practical ontology matching system. Web Semant, Elsevier 6, 237–239 (2008)
15. Hu, W., Chen, J., Cheng, G., Qu, Y.: Objectcoref and falconao: results for oaei 2010. In: Ontology Matching 2010 (2010)

16. Inmon, W.H.: Building the Data Warehouse. John Wiley & Sons, Inc. (2005)
17. Isaac, A., van der Meij, L., Schlobach, S., Wang, S.: An empirical study of instance-based ontology matching. In: Aberer, K., et al. (eds.) ASWC 2007 and ISWC 2007. LNCS, vol. 4825, pp. 253–266. Springer, Heidelberg (2007)
18. Rahm, E., Bernstein, P.A., Rahm, E., Bernstein, P.A.: A survey of approaches to automatic schema matching. The VLDB Journal 10, 334–350 (2001)
19. Jain, P., Yeh, P.Z., Verma, K., Vasquez, R.G., Damova, M., Hitzler, P., Sheth, A.P.: Contextual ontology alignment of LOD with an upper ontology: A case study with proton. In: Antoniou, G., Grobelnik, M., Simperl, E., Parsia, B., Plexousakis, D., De Leenheer, P., Pan, J. (eds.) ESWC 2011, Part I. LNCS, vol. 6643, pp. 80–92. Springer, Heidelberg (2011)
20. Jean-Mary, Y.R., Shironoshita, E.P., Kabuka, M.R.: Ontology matching with semantic verification. Web Semant, 235–251 (2009)
21. Kämpgen, B., Harth, A.: No size fits all – running the star schema benchmark with SPARQL and RDF aggregate views. In: Cimiano, P., Corcho, O., Presutti, V., Hollink, L., Rudolph, S. (eds.) ESWC 2013. LNCS, vol. 7882, pp. 290–304. Springer, Heidelberg (2013)
22. Leme, L.A.P.P., Casanova, M.A., Breitman, K.K., Furtado, A.L.: Instance-Based OWL Schema Matching. In: Filipe, J., Cordeiro, J. (eds.) Enterprise Information Systems. Lecture Notes in Business Information Processing, vol. 24, pp. 14–26. Springer, Heidelberg (2009)
23. Li, W., Clifton, C.: SEMINT: a tool for identifying attribute correspondences in heterogeneous databases using neural networks. Data Knowl. Eng. 33(1), 49–84 (2000)
24. Li, J., Tang, J., Li, Y., Luo, Q.: RiMOM: A Dynamic Multistrategy Ontology Alignment Framework. IEEE Trans. on Knowl. and Data Eng (2009)
25. Maedche, A., Staab, S.: Measuring Similarity between Ontologies. In: Proceedings of the 13th International Conference on Knowledge Engineering and Knowledge Management (EKAW), pp. 251–263 (2002)
26. Melnik, S., Garcia-Molina, H., Rahm, E.: Similarity Flooding: A Versatile Graph Matching Algorithm and Its Application to Schema Matching. In: Proceedings of the 18th International Conference on Data Engineering (2002)
27. Ngomo, A., Lehmann, J., Auer, S., Honer, K.: Raven - active learning of link specications. In: Ontology Matching (2011)
28. Pereira Nunes, B., Mera, A., Casanova, M.A., Fetahu, B., P. Paes Leme, L.A., Dietze, S.: Complex matching of RDF datatype properties. In: Decker, H., Lhotská, L., Link, S., Basl, J., Tjoa, A.M. (eds.) DEXA 2013, Part I. LNCS, vol. 8055, pp. 195–208. Springer, Heidelberg (2013)
29. Ontology Alignment Evaluation Initiative, http://oaei.ontologymatching.org/
30. OECD, IMF, ILO, Interstate Statistical Committee of the Commonwealth of Independent States: Measuring the Non-Observed Economy: A Handbook, Annex 2, Glossary (2002)
31. ONeil, P., ONeil, E., Chen, X.: Star Schema Benchmark - Revision 3. Tech. rep., UMass, Boston poneil/StarSchemaB.pdf (2009), http://www.cs.umb.edu/
32. van Rijsbergen, C.J.: Information Retrieval. Butterworth (1979)
33. Rong, S., Niu, X., Xiang, E.W., Wang, H., Yang, Q., Yu, Y.: A machine learning approach for instance matching based on similarity metrics. In: Proceedings of the 11th International Conference on The Semantic Web - Volume Part I (2012)
34. Shvaiko, P., Euzenat, J.: Ontology Matching: State of the Art and Future Challenges. IEEE Transactions on Knowledge and Data Engineering, 158–176 (2011)
35. Stuckenschmidt, H.: A semantic similarity measure for ontology-based information. In: Andreasen, T., Yager, R.R., Bulskov, H., Christiansen, H., Larsen, H.L. (eds.) FQAS 2009. LNCS, vol. 5822, pp. 406–417. Springer, Heidelberg (2009)

Towards Competency Question-Driven Ontology Authoring

Yuan Ren[1], Artemis Parvizi[1], Chris Mellish[1], Jeff Z. Pan[1],
Kees van Deemter[1], and Robert Stevens[2]

[1] Department of Computing Science, University of Aberdeen, Aberdeen, UK
[2] School of Computer Science, University of Manchester, Manchester, UK

Abstract. Ontology authoring is a non-trivial task for authors who are not proficient in logic. It is difficult to either specify the requirements for an ontology, or test their satisfaction. In this paper, we propose a novel approach to address this problem by leveraging the ideas of competency questions and test-before software development. We first analyse real-world competency questions collected from two different domains. Analysis shows that many of them can be categorised into patterns that differ along a set of features. Then we employ the linguistic notion of presupposition to describe the ontology requirements implied by competency questions, and show that these requirements can be tested automatically.

Keywords: #eswc2014Ren.

1 Introduction

In recent years, ontologies based on Description Logics [1] have been widely accepted as an important means for representing and formalising knowledge in different applications [15]. For example, the SNOMED CT (Systematized Nomenclature of Medicine-Clinical Terms) [19] ontology has been mandated for use in over thirty countries.

Ontology authoring remains a challenging task. Studies on ontology authoring such as experiences from the OWL Pizzas tutorial [18] and the NeOn project [7] suggest that ontology formalisms are often not straight-forwardly comprehensible and logical implications can be difficult to resolve. This is because ontology authors are usually domain experts but not necessarily proficient in logic. While it may be difficult for them to express their requirements for the axiomatisation of an ontology, it is also difficult to know whether the requirements are fulfilled as a result of their ontology authoring actions. Hence, ontology authoring is usually time consuming, error-prone and requires extensive training and experience [18].

As a first step towards *Competency Question-driven Ontology Authoring* (CQOA), we address the problems outlined by leveraging the ideas of *competency questions* and *testing driven software development* (where a suite of tests represents a specification for a programme and the tests are coded against). A competency question (CQ) [23] is a natural language sentence that expresses a pattern for a type of questions people expect an ontology to answer. The *answerability* of CQs hence becomes a functional requirement of the ontology. For example, in a software engineering ontology, in order to

V. Presutti et al. (Eds.): ESWC 2014, LNCS 8465, pp. 752–767, 2014.

support the answering of the question "Which process implements a given algorithm?", the ontology should contain concepts *Process* and *Algorithm*, and their instances should be able to have a relation called *Implements*. Also the ontology should (in ways we will investigate below) make it meaningful to ask the question "Which process implements algorithm X?" for any algorithm "X" in the ontology. To investigate such characteristics of ontologies, we are more interested in checking if a CQ can be meaningfully answered, instead of directly answering a CQ. Hence, our research questions are:

1. How are real-world CQs formulated?
2. How can we automatically test whether a CQ can be meaningfully answered?

In this paper, we answer question 1 through the study of real-world CQs in different domains and composed by real ontology authors/users with different levels of expertise. We categorise CQs into several frequent patterns that differ along a set of features and show that CQs collected by us and investigated in previous work can be covered by such a framework. To answer question 2, we employ the notion of presupposition from linguistics to capture the ontology requirements implied by CQs. We show that these presuppositions can be tested automatically at authoring time.

2 Competency Question-Driven Ontology Authoring

2.1 Ontological Artifacts in Description Logics

In general, when specified in a Description Logic (DL), an ontology uses classes, properties and their instances to describe the domain of discourse. Atomic classes such as $CheeseTopping$, $Pizza$ and atomic properties such as $hasTopping$ can be connected with DL constructors to compose complex classes. For example, $Pizza \sqcap \exists hasTopping.CheeseTopping$ means *pizzas that have at least one cheese topping*. The relationships between classes, properties and instances are described with ontology axioms. Considering the following typical axioms:

$$CheeseyPizza \equiv Pizza \sqcap \exists hasTopping.CheeseTopping \tag{1}$$

$$AmericanPizza \sqsubseteq Pizza \tag{2}$$

$$AmericanPizza \sqsubseteq \exists hasTopping.MozzarellaTopping \tag{3}$$

$$MozzarellaTopping \sqsubseteq CheeseTopping \tag{4}$$

Axiom (1) means that *cheesy pizzas are those pizzas that have at least one cheese topping*, in which $\equiv$ denotes an equivalence. Axiom (2) means that *American pizza is a pizza*, in which $\sqsubseteq$ denotes a subsumption relation. Axiom (3) means that *American pizza contains at least one mozzarella topping*. And axiom (4) means that *mozzarella topping is a cheese topping*.

A formal ontology consists of a set of axioms. These axioms describe the explicit knowledge in the ontology and can interact with each other to infer implicit knowledge. For example, by combining axioms (3) and (4) we can infer that $AmericanPizza \sqsubseteq \exists hasTopping.CheeseTopping$. Combining with axioms (1) and (2) we can further infer that $AmericanPizza \sqsubseteq CheeseyPizza$, i.e. *American pizza is a cheesey pizza*. Such inference can be realised by an automatic reasoner.

When a class expression C can be instantiated (i.e. it is possible for it to have instances in the domain), we say that C is *satisfiable*. Checking whether a class is satisfiable in an ontology is a reasoning task that can also be accomplished by a reasoner.

2.2 Presupposition and Cooperative Question Answering

Following on from ideas of Frege, many philosophers of language use the term *presupposition* to refer to a special condition that must be met for a linguistic expression to have a denotation [2]. For example, the question "have you stopped feeding your dog?" presupposes that the addressee has a dog and has been feeding it; it can only be successfully answered if these conditions are satisfied – otherwise the question is in some sense meaningless.

The fact that a question may have presuppositions, and that these may represent misconceptions on the part of the asker, has been exploited by researchers working on principles for cooperative question-answering from databases [9]. For instance, if a user asks "Who passed CMSC 420 in the fall semester of 1991?", the answer *nobody* is not cooperative if in fact CMSC 420 was not taught in the fall semester of 1991. In this case, the user should be alerted to the failed presupposition in their question. Such a failure can be computed in this case by detecting a subpart of the original question that produces an empty set of results (informally, *CMSC 420 in the fall semester*) [10].

In this paper we take a similar approach, identifying presuppositions of *competency questions* associated with an ontology. In this case, the aim is not to provide better answers to the questions but to help the user detect when their ontology is out of step with the kinds of questions they would like to be able to ask.

2.3 From Competency Questions To Authoring Tests

(Informal) CQs are expressions of questions that an ontology must be able to answer [23]. We consider these to be natural language sentences that express patterns for types of question people want to be able to answer with the ontology. The ability to answer questions of the type indicated by a CQ meaningfully can be regarded as a *functional requirement* that must be satisfied by the ontology.

Example 1. Below are some example CQs:

- "Which mammals eat grass?" (in an animal ontology)
- "Which processes implement an algorithm?" (in a software engineering ontology)

The first of these suggests a specific pattern, which (when the ontology is complete) could perhaps be expressed as a single SPARQL[1] query such as:

```
select ?m where
  {?m type Mammal . ?g type Grass . ?m eat ?g}
```

[1] http://www.w3.org/TR/sparql11-overview/

The second (interpreted with "an" having wide scope[2]) provides a pattern that will apply to a number of possible queries. This pattern might be thought of as a template for SPARQL queries, where certain slots will be filled in before the query is presented to the ontology. When the ontology is complete, this might look something like:

```
select ?p where
  {?p type Process . $X type Algorithm . ?p implements $X}
```

where `$X` is to be filled in (at query presentation time) with whatever algorithm (in the ontology) in which the user is interested.

The examples show that a CQ can suggest a single desired query (as in the first case) or a set of possible queries (as in the second). In the following, we will abstract away from this distinction and, for instance, talk about "answering a CQ" as a shorthand for "answering the queries implied by a CQ".[3]

Compared to more formal requirement specifications, CQs are particularly useful to ontology authors less familiar with DLs because CQs are in natural language, are about domain knowledge, and do not require understanding of DLs. Hence in ontology authoring practice, CQs help authors to determine the scope and granularity of the ontology, and to identify the most important classes, properties and their relations.

From a linguistic point of view, such questions also have presuppositions about the domain of discourse that have to be satisfied:

Example 2. In order to meaningfully answer the CQ "Which processes implement an algorithm?" it is necessary for the ontology to satisfy the following presuppositions:

1. Classes $Process$, $Algorithm$ and property $implements$ occur in the ontology;
2. The ontology allows the possibility of $Process$es implementing $Algorithm$s;
3. The ontology allows the possibility of $Process$es *not* implementing $Algorithm$s.

The last two of these perhaps need some justification. If case 2 were not satisfied, the answer to all the queries (for all `$X`) would be "none", because the ontology could never have a $Process$ implementing an $Algorithm$. This would be exactly the kind of uncooperative answer looked at by the previous work on cooperative question-answering[9]. It is hard to imagine an ontology author really wanting to retrieve this information. Rather, this can be taken as evidence of possible design problems in the ontology. If case 3 were not satisfied, the answer to all the queries (for all `$X`) would be a list of all the $Process$es. This would mean that the questions would be similarly uninteresting to the ontology author, again signalling a possible problem in the ontology.

CQs can have clear and relatively simple syntactic patterns. For example, the CQs in Example 1 are all of the following semi-formal pattern:

$$Which\ [CE1]\ [OPE]\ [CE2]?$$

[2] Alternative formulations with the same intention might be "Which processes implement a given algorithm?", "For any algorithm, what processes implement it?" or "Which processes implement this algorithm?".

[3] It is also possible to formulate the queries in a way such that the answers to the CQ are not instances of $Mammal$ or $Process$, but their sub-classes. Nevertheless, our discoveries presented later in the paper will not be affected by such a difference.

where $CE1$ and $CE2$ are class expressions (or individual expressions as a special case) and OPE is an object property expression. This pattern asks for instances or subclasses of $CE1$ that can have an OPE relation to some instance of $CE2$. With such patterns, the presuppositions shown in Example 2 can be verified automatically:

1. $CE1$, $CE2$ and OPE should occur in the ontology;
2. $CE1 \sqcap \exists OPE.CE2$ should be satisfiable in the ontology;
3. $CE1 \sqcap \neg(\exists OPE.CE2)$ should be satisfiable in the ontology. Here $\neg$ is the constructor for negation.

We call tests of this kind which can be derived from CQs *Authoring Tests* (ATs).

The idea of CQOA is to support the ontology author in the formulation of machine processable CQs for their ontology. In an implemented system, users will be allowed to either import their predefined CQs or enter new CQs in a controlled natural language. The authoring environment will identify the patterns of the inputted CQs and generate appropriate ATs. With the ATs, certain aspects of the answerability of the CQs can then be tested by the authoring environment to find places where the ontology does not yet meet the requirements. If there is a change in the status of these ATs from true to false or vice versa, the system will report the result to the users. The pattern identification, AT generation and testing procedures are all transparent to authors hence they can be utilised by novice ontology authors.

3 Related Work

Exploring competency questions (CQs) in ontology development is not a new idea in itself [23,17,21]. The NeOn methodology [20] has worked towards an ontology specification task, which results in a set of natural language CQs. A visual solution based on a goal-based methodology for capturing CQs has been presented in [8]. A formalisation of CQs into SPARQL queries [24] and CQs into DL queries [13] have also been implemented. An algorithm for checking natural language CQs has been developed by [3]. Nevertheless, these works focused on limited forms of CQs such as "What is ... ?", "How much ... ?". A wider spectrum of CQs and their usefulness in ontology authoring were not investigated. Moreover, they are more concerned with answering particularly CQs, but less with whether the answers are meaningful w.r.t. (with respect to) the presuppositions.

Testing is also widely used in different ontology authoring systems to provide feedback to authors on the quality of the ontology. The Rabbit interface [5] and the Simplified English prototype [16] offer syntactic checking such as incorrect words or disallowed input. Systems such as Protégé[4] and OntoTrack [11] use reasoners to offer basic semantic checking such as inconsistency checking. Systems such as Roo [6] intend to advise the user of the potential authoring consequences. Justification engines [11] are also used to explain why certain deductions have been made. Systems such as the OWL Unit Test Framework in Protégé, Tawny-OWL [12] and OntoStudio[5] allow users

[4] http://protege.stanford.edu
[5] http://www.semafora-systems.com/en/products/ontostudio/

to define unit tests and run them in the authoring environment. Generic tests such as consistency, input validity do not capture the requirements that are specific to the ontologies in question. The author-defined tests allow the expression of such requirements but require further knowledge and skills of ontology technologies. For novice authors, designing a test suite for an ontology is hardly easier than designing the ontology itself.

4 An Empirical Study of Competency Questions

In contrast to the existing work, we combine CQs and testing in ontology authoring, using CQs as a means for novice authors to express requirements, and derive tests from these CQs to capture their presuppositions. We aim to understand the different kinds of CQs that are asked by authors in real-world scenarios, to ensure that the ontology can respond optimally to them. We therefore address research question 1 by analysing real-world CQs.

4.1 Competency Question Collection

Due to the flexibility permitted in CQ construction, it was not feasible for us to enumerate all possible CQs. In order to cover CQs used in different domains and from authors with different levels of expertise, we collected 92 CQs from the Software Ontology Project[6] and 76 CQs from the Manchester OWL Tutorials in 2013. The software ontology project seeks to describe software such that software registries and repositories can be adequately tagged and indexed; it is also used to describe the software that used in the analysis of data. CQs in this project are proposed by the users of this ontology and hence represent requirements from a professional point of view. The OWL tutorials were events where basic ontology technologies were taught to participants, who were mostly novice authors. In the tutorials , the Pizza ontology[7] was used as a show case ontology and participants were asked to write CQs they would like to get answered with the pizza ontology working as part of an 'intelligent pizza finder' application.

After obtaining the collection of questions, we removed invalid CQs, including:

1. Redundant questions;
2. Incomplete sentences that cannot be properly understood. For example, in the software collection, one question is "What level of expertise is required?". In this question, it is not clear what the expertise is required for.
3. Sentences that are not really CQs. For example, in the pizza collection there is one question "Should we include the oven type in the pizza definition? (eg wood fired vs electric oven)". Nevertheless, "What oven type is this pizza?" can be regarded as a valid CQ.
4. Questions beyond the expressive power of a DL-based ontology language. For example, in the software collection a question asks "How can I get problems fixed?".

[6] `http://softwareontology.wordpress.com/2011/04/01/user-sourced-competency-questions-for-software/`

[7] `http://130.88.198.11/co-ode-files/ontologies/pizza.owl`

The answer to such a *How* question should be a procedure that involves conditions and actions. Whilst an ontology is mainly used for modelling of static domain knowledge instead of dynamic procedures.

With the above invalid CQs removed, we obtained 75 valid CQs in the software collection and 70 in the pizza collection.

4.2 A Framework for Patterns of Competency Questions

We analysed the collected CQs to identify the patterns to which they belong. We are more interested in the semantic meaning of the CQs than their surface form. Hence we omit the syntactic differences between variations with the same semantic meaning.

In order to represent the commonality and variability of different CQ patterns, we employed the feature-based modelling method [14] and describe different CQ patterns w.r.t. a set of features identified from our CQ collections:

1. **Question Type** determines the kinds of answer presented when answering the CQ:
   (a) *Selection question* should be answered with a set of entities or values that satisfy certain constraints. The CQs in Example 1 are all selection questions.
   (b) *Binary question* should be answered with a boolean value, i.e. *yes* or *no*, indicating the existence of any answer to a selection. For example, "Does this pizza contain halal meat?" is a binary question corresponding to a selection question "Which of these pizzas contain halal meat?".
   (c) *Counting question* should be answered with the number of different answers to a selection question. For example, "How many pizzas have either ham or chicken topping?" is a counting question. Its corresponding selection question is "Which pizzas have either ham or chicken topping?".
2. **Element Visibility** indicates whether the modelling elements, such as the class expressions and property expressions are *explicit* or *implicit* in the CQ. For example, "What are the export options for this software?" has explicit elements *Software* and *Export Option*, but also an implicit relation *hasExportOption* between softwares and export options. Note that even implicit elements should occur in the ontology to make the CQ meaningful.
3. **Question Polarity** determines if the question is asked in a *positive* or *negative* manner, e.g. "Which pizzas contain pork?" *v.s.* "Which pizza has no vegetables?".
4. **Predicate Arity** indicates the number of arguments of the main predicate:
   (a) *Unary predicate* is concerned with a single set of entities/values and its instances, e.g. "Is it thin or thick bread?".
   (b) *Binary predicate* is concerned with the relation between 2 sets of entities/values and their instances, such as the eat and $implement$ in Example 1.
   (c) *N-ary predicate* is concerned with the relation among multiple ($\geq$ 3) sets of entities/values and their instances. Given the fact that DLs can only represent unary and binary predicates, an N-ary predicate has to be represented as a concept via reification. In the next section we will show how this affects the ATs.
5. **Relation Type** indicates the kind of relation for the main relation involved in the CQ. As in DLs, CQs can have object property relations or datatype property relations. Note that a relation with more than 2 arguments or with its attributes has to be represented by an entity via reification.

6. **Modifier** is employed to impose restrictions on some entities/values:
   (a) *Quantity modifier* restricts the number of relations among entities/values.
      i. It can be a concrete value or value range. For example "If I have 3 ingredients, how many kinds of pizza I would make?" has a quantity modifier 3 on the number of pizza-ingredient relations for each pizza.
      ii. It can be a superlative value or value range. For example, "Which pizza has the most toppings?" has a quantity modifier *most* on the number of pizza-topping relations for each pizza.
      iii. It can also be a comparative value or value range. For example, "Which pizza has more meat than vegetables?" has a quantity modifier *more* on the number of pizza-meat and pizza-vegetable relations for each pizza.
   (b) *Numeric modifier* is used to restrict the value of some datatype properties. Similarly to the quantity modifier, it can be a concrete value or value/range, or a superlative value, or a comparative value. For example, "What pizza has very little ($\leq 10\%$) onion and/or leeks and/or green peppers?"
7. **Domain-independent Element** is an element that can occur across different knowledge domains. It is usually associated with some physical or cognitive measurements. Some most commonly used domain-independent elements include:
   (a) *Temporal element* in the CQ indicates that the CQ is about the time of some event, e.g. "When was the 1.0 version released?".
   (b) *Spatial element* in the CQ indicates that the CQ is about the location of some event. It does not have to be a physical location. For example "Where is the documentation?" can be answered with a file path or a URL.

We consider the *Question Type*, *Element Visibility* and *Question Polarity* as secondary features as their variabilities do not change the required modelling elements of the ontology. All other features are primary features. CQs with different primary features are distinguished into different archetypes. CQs with different secondary features in an archetype are distinguished into different sub-types. Together, they constitute a generic framework to formulate different CQ patterns. For example, the CQ pattern *Which [CE1] [OPE] [CE2]*? features a selection question with binary predicate of an object property relation and all elements are explicit.

4.3 Result of the Study

With the feature-based framework, we identify 12 archetypes of CQ patterns in our collection. They are shown in Table 1. The 1st column shows the ID of the archetype, the 2nd and 3rd columns show the pattern and 1 example from our collection. The last 4 columns are the primary features. As we mentioned above, some archetype patterns have sub-types. An example of the sub-types of archetype 1 is illustrated with Table 2, in which the last 3 columns are the secondary features.

The archetypes and sub-types of CQ patterns we have identified cover all the CQs in our collection, but we do not know directly how many CQs for other domains they will cover. Nevertheless, the feature-based framework is flexible enough to describe CQs we have not encountered. For example, a hypothetical CQ "How many pieces of software are most efficient when providing this service?" has a pattern *How many [CE1] are [NM] to [OPE] [CE2]*?, which is a counting question sub-type in archetype 6.

Table 1. CQ Archetypes (PA = Predicate Arity, RT = Relation Type, M = Modifier, DE = Domain-independent Element; obj. = object property relation, data. = datatype property relation, num. = numeric modifier, quan. = quantitative modifier, tem. = temporal element, spa. = spatial element; CE = class expression, OPE = object property expression, DP = datatype property, I = individual, NM = numeric modifier, PE = property expression, QM = quantity modifier)

ID	Pattern	Example	PA	RT	M	DE
1	Which [CE1] [OPE] [CE2]?	Which pizzas contain pork?	2	obj.		
2	How much does [CE] [DP]?	How much does Margherita Pizza weigh?	2	data.		
3	What type of [CE] is [I]?	What type of software (API, Desktop application etc.) is it?	1			
4	Is the [CE1] [CE2]?	Is the software open source development?	2			
5	What [CE] has the [NM] [DP]?	What pizza has the lowest price?	2	data.	num.	
6	What is the [NM] [CE1] to [OPE] [CE2]?	What is the best/fastest/most robust software to read/edit this data?	3	both	num.	
7	Where do I [OPE] [CE]?	Where do I get updates?	2	obj.		spa.
8	Which are [CE]?	Which are gluten free bases?	1			
9	When did/was [CE] [PE]?	When was the 1.0 version released?	2	data.		tem.
10	What [CE1] do I need to [OPE] [CE2]?	What hardware do I need to run this software?	3	obj.		
11	Which [CE1] [OPE] [QM] [CE2]?	Which pizza has the most toppings?	2	obj.	quan.	
12	Do [CE1] have [QM] values of [DP]?	Do pizzas have different values of size?	2	data.	quan.	

Table 2. CQ Sub-types of Archetype 1 (QT = Question Type, V = Visibility, QP = Question Polarity, sel. = selection question, bin. = binary question, cout. = counting question, exp. = explicit, imp. = implicit, sub. = subject, pre. = predicate, pos. = positive, neg. = negative)

ID	Pattern	Example	QT	V	QP
1a	Which [CE1] [OPE] [CE2]?	What software can read a .cel file?	sel.	exp.	pos.
1b	Find [CE1] with [CE2].	Find pizzas with peppers and olives.	sel.	imp. pre.	pos.
1c	How many [CE1] [OPE] [CE2]?	How many pizzas in the menu contains meat?	cout.	exp.	pos.
1d	Does [CE1] [OPE] [CE2]?	Does this fotware provide XML editing	bin.	exp.	pos.
1e	Be there [CE1] with [CE2]?	Are there any pizzas with chocolate?	bin.	imp. pre.	pos.
1f	Who [OPE] [CE]?	Who owns the copyright?	sel.	imp. sub.	pos.
1g	Be there [CE1] [OPE]ing [CE2]?	Are there any active forums discussing its use?	bin.	exp.	pos.
1h	Which [CE1] [OPE] no [CE2]?	Which pizza contains no mushroom?	sel.	exp.	neg.

After obtaining the competency question patterns, we analysed the distribution of each pattern in our two scenarios. The numbers of competency questions belonging to each archetype are shown in Table 3. We can see from this that among the 12 archetypes, 9 can be observed in the software collection, 9 can be observed in the pizza collection,

Table 3. Numbers of CQs in Each Archetype Pattern

Archetype	1	2	3	4	5	6	7	8	9	10	11	12
Software Collection	38	11	1	1	0	4	5	5	3	7	0	0
Pizza Collection	23	7	4	0	5	1	0	22	0	2	5	1
Total	61	18	7	1	5	5	5	27	3	9	5	1

and 6 are shared by both collections. These 6 are also the most populated archetypes, together covering 86.2% of all the collected CQs. This suggests that we might have begun to find a kind of closure in terms of the most significant CQ types and that further domains may not introduce many more important types.

We also examined the applicability of our framework to the 55 CQs mentioned in previous work [20,8,24,13,3]. Most of those CQs are covered by our framework and archetype 1 is the most populated one. The *only* CQ not definitely covered is "Why universities are organised into departments?" [24]. This can be categorised to archetype 2 if the ontology represents the answer to *why* with a textual string. However, we believe a proper modelling of such questions would require more complex formalisation.

5 Answerability of Competency Questions

In this section, we try to address research question 2 by generating ATs from CQs and showing that these ATs can be checked automatically. In contrast to previous work that attempts to find answers to concrete CQs, we investigate whether or not the CQs can be meaningfully answered.

5.1 Presuppositions in Competency Question Features

In CQOA, we are interested in whether the ontology contains the knowledge required to answer CQs meaningfully. Such knowledge requirements are closely related to the presuppositions in the CQs.

Given that our framework describes the CQs in terms of a set of features, we first analyse the presuppositions implied by different variations of each feature:

1. **Question Type:** regardless of the question type, the modelling elements mentioned in the question should **occur** in the ontology. Classes should also be **satisfiable**.
   (a) *Selection question* asks for the answers satisfying certain constraints. The ontology should allow some answers to satisfy the constraints. For example, "Which pizzas contain pork?" implies that pork is allowed to be contained in pizzas, i.e. $Pizza \sqcap \exists contains.Pork$ should be **satisfiable**. Otherwise, no pizza can contain pork at all. The ontology should also allow some entities to NOT satisfy the constraints. For example, the CQ above implies that it is possible for some pizza to contain no pork, i.e. $Pizza \sqcap \forall contains.\neg Pork$ is satisfiable. Otherwise, any pizza must contain pork and the *"contains pork"* part in the CQ becomes useless.

(b) *Binary question* asks whether there is an answer satisfying the constraint. It does not have the two satisfiability presuppositions.
(c) *Counting question* asks for the number of the answers satisfying the constraints. It assumes the possibility of some answer satisfying the constraint and also some answer not satisfying it. Hence it has the satisfiability presuppositions.

2. **Element Visibility:** regardless of the visibility of a modelling element, it should always occur in the ontology to make the CQ answerable. Nevertheless, an implicit element does not appear in the CQ hence its corresponding name in the ontology cannot be directly obtained. This name can be derived from related entities. For example, in "What are the export options for this software?" we can name the implicit relation *hasExportOption*. Otherwise it can be assigned by the author.
3. **Predicate Arity:** the arity of the predicate affects how it should occur in the ontology. Modern ontology languages support both unary (i.e. classes) and binary (i.e. properties) predicates. Hence their names can directly occur in the ontology. However, N-ary predicate has to be represented as a class via reification. This leads to the occurrence of other implicit predicates. For example, in "What is the best software to read this data?" the predicate *read* has 3 arities, namely the *software*, the *data*, and the *performance*. Hence $Reading$ should occur in the ontology as a *Class* instead of a *Property*. Moreover, there should be 3 more implicit predicates, namely the $hasSoftware$, the $hasData$ and the $hasPerformance$.
4. **Relation Type:** as the name suggests, the meta-type of a property occurring in the ontology is determined by the type of relation it represents in the CQ. In other word, if a property P is between two entities, then it is presupposed that P is an **instance** of `OWL:ObjectProperty`. If P is between an entity and a value, then it is presupposed that P is an instance of `OWL:DatatypeProperty`.
5. **Modifier:** the modifiers further impose restrictions on answers of the CQ.
   (a) **Quantity modifier** has a similar effect as *question type* on the satisfiability presupposition of certain class expressions in the ontology.
      i. If the modifier is a concrete value or range, then as for a *selection questions* it presupposes that potnetial answers are allowed to satisfy, as well as not to satisfy, this modifier. For example, "If I have 3 ingredients, how many kinds of pizza can I make?" implies that the ontology allows pizzas with 3 ingredients and ones with fewer or more than 3 ingredients, i.e. $Pizza \sqcap = 3\ hasIngredient.Ingredient$ and $Pizza \sqcap \neg(= 3\ hasIngredient.Ingredient)$ should both be satisfiable in the ontology.
      ii. If the modifier is a superlative value or value range, then the ontology should allow answers with **multiple cardinality** values on the predicate on which the modifier is imposed. For example, in "Which pizza has the most toppings?" the presupposition is that *pizzas are allowed to have different numbers of toppings* otherwise all pizzas will have exactly the same number of toppings. More formally, this means that for each number $n \geq 0$, $Pizza \sqcap \neg(= n\ hasTopping.Topping)$ should be satisfiable.
      iii. If the modifier is a comparative value or value range, then the ontology should allow an answer with the required **comparative cardinality** values on the different relations being compared, as well answers without the required comparative cardinality values. For example, "Which pizza

has more meat than vegetables?" presupposes that *pizzas are allowed to have more meat than vegetables* otherwise none of the pizza is an answer. More formally this means that for some number $n \geq 0$, $Pizza \sqcap \leq n\ has.Vegetable$ and $Pizza \sqcap \geq n+1\ has.Meat$ should both be satisfiable. It also presupposes that *pizzas are allowed to have no more meat than vegetables* otherwise all pizzas have more meat than vegetable. More formally this means that for some number $n \geq 0$, $Pizza \sqcap \leq n\ has.Meat$ and $Pizza \sqcap \geq n\ has.Vegetable$ should both be satisfiable.

(b) *Numeric modifier* has similar presuppositions to a quantity modifier. In the concrete value or value range case and comparative value case, the CQ carries the presuppositions that the ontology should allow answers satisfying the modifier and those not satisfying the modifier. In the superlative value case, the CQ carries the presupposition that the ontology should allow multiple values on the relation on which the modifier is imposed.
Furthermore, the **range** of the property on which the modifier is imposed must be a comparable datatype, such as *integer*, or *float*, otherwise the question can not be answered meaningfully.

6. **Domain-independent Element** in the CQ can also affect the meta-type and type of some modelling elements in the ontology. The temporal element is usually associated to some temporal datatypes. For example, "When was the 1.0 version released?" has presuppositions that the $wasReleasedOn$ is a datatype property, and that the range of $wasReleasedOn$ is one of the temporal datatype, such as *datatime*. It is possible to use some other datatypes, such as *integer* to denote the year of release, but this is not considered a best practice.
The *spatial element* is not necessarily representing a geographical location hence it is hard to determine the type of its corresponding element in the ontology.

5.2 Formalising the Authoring Tests

From the analysis in Sec. 5.1, we realise that the features in the CQs are related to certain categories of presuppositions. Each of these categories contains parameter(s) derived from the CQ and can be realised by some checking in the ontology. ATs formalise this idea. We summarise the ATs in Table 4. In this table the 1st column are the ATs, the 2nd column are the parameters for each AT and the 3rd column shows how each AT can be checked with ontology technologies. We omit the formalisation of some ATs, such as those associated with comparative numeric modifiers, because such features were not observed in our collection; they can be formalised in a similar manner as the ones in the table.

As one can see, all of these ATs can be checked automatically. *Occurrence* can be checked directly against the ontology. *Meta-Instance* can be checked via RDF reasoning. All the others can be checked with ontology reasoning.

In an implemented system, we offer users a controlled natural language to input CQs based on the patterns identified earlier. Hence the archetype and/or sub-type of input CQs are implicitly specified by users and automatically identified by the system: For example, CQ "What is the best software to read this data?" belongs to archetype CQ pattern 7 $What\ [CE1]\ is\ [NM]\ to\ [OPE]\ [CE2]$?

Table 4. Authoring Tests ($\sqcap$ means conjunction, $\neg$ means negation, $\exists P.E$ means having P relation to some E, $= nP.E$ ($\geq nP.E, \leq nP.E$) means having P relation(s) to exactly (at least, at most) n E(s), $\forall P.E$ means having P relation (if any) to only E, $\top$ means everything)

AT	Parameter	Checking
Occurrence	[E]	E in ontology vocabulary
Class Satisfiability	[CE]	CE is satisfiable
Relation Satisfiability	[CE1] [P] [E2]	$CE1 \sqcap \exists P.E2$ is satisfiable, $CE1 \sqcap \neg\exists P.E2$ is satisfiable
Meta-Instance	[E1] [E2]	$E1$ has `type` $E2$
Cardinality Satisfiability	[CE1] [n] [P] [E2]	$CE1 \sqcap = nP.E2$ is satisfiable, $CE1 \sqcap \neg = nP.E2$ is satisfiable
Multiple Cardinality (on superlative quantity modifier)	[CE1] [P] [E2]	$\forall n \geq 0$, $CE1 \sqcap \neg = nP.E2$ is satisfiable
Comparative Cardinality (on quantity modifier)	[CE1] [P1] [P2] [E1] [E2]	$\exists n \geq 0$, $CE1 \sqcap \leq n\ P1.E1$ and $CE1 \sqcap \geq n+1\ P2.E2$ are satisfiable, $\exists m \geq 0$, $CE1 \sqcap \leq m\ P2.E2$ and $CE2 \sqcap \geq (m+1)\ P1.E1$ are satisfiable
Multiple Value (on superlative numeric modifier)	[CE1] [P]	$\forall D \subseteq range(P)$, $CE1 \sqcap \neg\exists P.D$ is satisfiable
Range	[P] [E]	$\top \sqsubseteq \forall P.E$

From the CQ and its pattern the system can automatically extract the features and elements of the CQ: it is a selection question ("What") containing a 3-ary (among "software", "data" and some performance) predicate ("read") with a superlative numeric modifier ("best"), which should be modelled as a class and some implicit object and datatype properties, whose names can be generated from contexts or assigned by users.

Then the system can automatically generate and parameterise the following ATs:

1. Occurrence tests of $Software$, $Data$, $Read$, $hasSoftware$, $hasPerformance$ and $hasData$. The first 3 should occur as classes and the last 3 as properties. $Read$ is the class representation of the "reading" predicate in the CQ;
2. Relation Satisfiability tests of ($Read$, $hasSoftware$, $Software$), ($Read$, $hasData$, $Data$) and ($Read$, $hasPerformance$, $\top$), which guarantee that the ontology allow some $Read$ to be associated with $Software$, $Data$ and to have performance;

3. Meta-Instance test of $(hasSoftware,$ `ObjectProperty`), $(hasData,$ `ObjectProperty`) and $(hasPerformance,$ `DatatypeProperty`), which further specify the meta-types of the 3 properties;
4. Multiple Value on superlative numeric modifier test of $(Read, hasPerformance)$, which guarantees that instances of $Read$ can have *different* performance values;
5. Range test of $(hasPerformance, decimal \cup float \cup double)$, which ensures that the value of $hasPerformance$ must be a comparable numeric value, so that one can find the best performance;

As the pipeline shows, the procedure from CQs (in a controlled natural language) to ATs can be automated. Eventually, all these ATs can be automatically checked and results can be provided to users.

6 Conclusion and Future Work

We have investigated the problem of requirement description and testing in ontology authoring for novice authors. We proposed Competency Question-driven Ontology Authoring (CQOA) by leveraging the ideas of CQs and test before styles of software development. To formally describe different real-world CQs, we have collected CQs from the software and pizza domains and analysed their commonalities and varieties with a set of features. It showed that the CQ patterns we identified covered all the collected CQs. To automatically test whether a CQ can be meaningfully answered, we investigated the presuppositions implied by CQ features. All these presuppositions can be parameterised and formalised into automatic ATs. Although our research were based on CQs in English, our results are transferable to other languages.

In future, we will implement the presented pipeline both as a Protégé plug-in and as a standalone system, supported by the TrOWL reasoner [22]. We will design and conduct experiments with human participation to compare their efficiency and productivity with and without the AT assistance. We are interested in extending the current framework by investigating more CQs, features and presuppositions. For example, it is difficult to formalise the spatial element presupposition in the current framework; we plan to address it by looking into ontology design patterns or foundational ontologies [4]. We would also like to investigate presuppositions of a finer linguistic "granularity". E.g. "Which pizzas contain pork?" appears to presuppose the existence of multiple types of pizza that contain pork while "Which pizza contains pork?" does not. Finally, some ATs such as the cardinality ones (Table 4) lead to a large number of tests, and we plan to investigate optimising the testing of such ATs.

Acknowledgments. This research has been funded by the EPSRC *WhatIf* project (EP/J014176/1) and the EU IAPP K-Drive project (286348). We also thank Caroline Jay and Markel Vigo for their inspiring discussion on CQs in ontology authoring and their assistance in collecting the pizza CQs.

References

1. Baader, F., Calvanese, D., McGuinness, D.L., Nardi, D., Patel-Schneider, P.F.: The Description Logic Handbook: Theory, Implementation, and Applications. Cambridge University Press (2003)
2. Beaver, D.: Presupposition. In: van Benthem, J., ter Meulen, A. (eds.) The Handbook of Logic and Language, pp. 939–1008. Elsevier (1997)
3. Bezerra, C., Freitas, F., Santana, F.: Evaluating ontologies with competency questions. In: 2013 IEEE/WIC/ACM International Joint Conferences on Web Intelligence (WI) and Intelligent Agent Technologies (IAT), vol. 3, pp. 284–285. IEEE (2013)
4. Borgo, S., Masolo, C.: Foundational choices in dolce. In: Handbook on ontologies, pp. 361–381. Springer (2009)
5. Denaux, R., Dimitrova, V., Cohn, A.G., Dolbear, C., Hart, G.: Rabbit to OWL: Ontology authoring with a CNL-based tool. In: Fuchs, N.E. (ed.) CNL 2009. LNCS, vol. 5972, pp. 246–264. Springer, Heidelberg (2010)
6. Denaux, R., Thakker, D., Dimitrova, V., Cohn, A.G.: Interactive semantic feedback for intuitive ontology authoring. In: FOIS, pp. 160–173 (2012)
7. Dzbor, M., Motta, E., Gomez, J.M., Buil, C., Dellschaft, K., Görlitz, O., Lewen, H.: D4.1.1 analysis of user needs, behaviours & requirements wrt user interfaces for ontology engineering. Technical report (August. 2006)
8. Fernandes, P.C.B., Guizzardi, R.S., Guizzardi, G.: Using goal modeling to capture competency questions in ontology-based systems. Journal of Information and Data Management 2(3), 527 (2011)
9. Gaasterland, T., Godfrey, P., Minker, J.: An Overview of Cooperative Answering. Journal of Intelligent Information Systems 1(2), 123–157 (1992)
10. Kaplan, S.J.: Cooperative Responses from a Portable Natural Language Query System. Artificial Intelligence 19(2), 165–187 (1982)
11. Liebig, T., Noppens, O.: Ontotrack: A semantic approach for ontology authoring. Web Semantics: Science, Services and Agents on the World Wide Web 3(2), 116–131 (2005)
12. Lord, P.: The semantic web takes wing: Programming ontologies with tawny-owl. In: OWLED 2013 (2013)
13. Malheiros, Y., Freitas, F.: A method to develop description logic ontologies iteratively based on competency questions: an implementation. In: ONTOBRAS, pp. 142–153 (2013)
14. Palmer, S.R., Felsing, M.: A practical guide to feature-driven development. Pearson Education (2001)
15. Pan, J.Z., Thomas, E., Ren, Y., Taylor, S.: Tractable Fuzzy and Crisp Reasoning in Ontology Applications. In: IEEE Computational Intelligence Magazine (2012)
16. Power, R.: OWL simplified english: A finite-state language for ontology editing. In: Kuhn, T., Fuchs, N.E. (eds.) CNL 2012. LNCS, vol. 7427, pp. 44–60. Springer, Heidelberg (2012)
17. Presutti, V., Blomqvist, E., Daga, E., Gangemi, A.: Pattern-based ontology design. In: Ontology Engineering in a Networked World, pp. 35–64. Springer (2012)
18. Rector, A., Drummond, N., Horridge, M., Rogers, J., Knublauch, H., Stevens, R., Wang, H., Wroe, C.: Owl pizzas: Practical experience of teaching owl-dl: Common errors & common patterns. In: Engineering Knowledge in the Age of the Semantic Web, Springer (2004)
19. Stearns, M.Q., Price, C., Spackman, K.A., Wang, A.Y.: SNOMED Clinical Terms: Overview of the Development Process and project Status. In: Proceedings of the AMIA Symposium, p. 662. American Medical Informatics Association (2001)
20. Suárez-Figueroa, M.C., Gómez-Pérez, A., Motta, E., Gangemi, A.: Ontology engineering in a networked world. Springer (2012)

21. Suárez-Figueroa, M.C., Pradel, C., Hernandez, N.: Verifying ontology requirements with SWIP. In: EKAW 2012 (2012)
22. Thomas, E., Pan, J.Z., Ren, Y.: TrOWL: Tractable OWL 2 Reasoning Infrastructure. In: Aroyo, L., Antoniou, G., Hyvönen, E., ten Teije, A., Stuckenschmidt, H., Cabral, L., Tudorache, T. (eds.) ESWC 2010, Part II. LNCS, vol. 6089, pp. 431–435. Springer, Heidelberg (2010)
23. Uschold, M., Gruninger, M.: et al. Ontologies: Principles, methods and applications. Knowledge Engineering Review 11(2), 93–136 (1996)
24. Zemmouchi-Ghomari, L., Ghomari, A.R.: Translating natural language competency questions into SPARQL queries: A case study. In: WEB 2013, pp. 81–86 (2013)

Identifying Change Patterns of Concept Attributes in Ontology Evolution

Duy Dinh[1], Julio Cesar Dos Reis[1,2], Cédric Pruski[1], Marcos Da Silveira[1], and Chantal Reynaud-Delaître[2]

[1] CR SANTEC, Public Research Centre Henri Tudor, Luxembourg
[2] LRI, University of Paris-Sud XI, France
{duy.dinh,julio.dosreis,cedric.pruski,marcos.dasilveira}@tudor.lu,
chantal.reynaud@lri.fr

Abstract. Ontology versions are periodically released to ensure their usefulness and reliability over time. This potentially impacts dependent artefacts such as mappings and annotations. Dealing with requires to finely characterize ontology entities' changes between ontology versions. This article proposes to identify change patterns at attribute values when an ontology evolves, to track textual statements describing concepts. We empirically evaluate our approach by using biomedical ontologies, for which new ontology versions are frequently released. Our achieved results suggest the feasibility of the proposed techniques.

Keywords: ontology evolution, ontology changes, change patterns, ontology versioning, biomedical ontologies.

1 Introduction

The dynamic aspect of knowledge in various domains requires that knowledge engineers apply changes to different ontology entities by adding, removing and revising them. This periodically leads to new ontology versions, which ensures that software applications use the most up-to-date representation of the domain knowledge. Ontology changes potentially impact mappings, annotations and queries which rely on these ontologies [1,2].

Changes applied to generate new ontology versions are not always fully documented, which impedes the minimization and handling of their impact. To this end, we need methods to automatically identify ontology change operations (OCOs) in an explicit way, given two versions of the same ontology [3]. Our previous studies have underlined the need of precisely characterizing the evolution of attributes describing concepts for maintaining mappings valid over time [4,5].

When analyzing two consecutive versions of the same ontology, for instance, we found cases where textual statements which are values of attributes describing concepts are completely transferred from one concept to its siblings. This had affected the associated mappings since their definition relies on such textual information. For example, we observed this case with the concept "560.39" of the

V. Presutti et al. (Eds.): ESWC 2014, LNCS 8465, pp. 768–783, 2014.

ICD-9-CM[1] (ICD) biomedical ontology. Such concept contains three attributes and one of them has as value "Fecal impaction" (release 2009). Five mappings are defined with this concept as domain, and one of these mappings has a range called "Fecal impaction (disorder)", from SNOMED CT[2] (SCT). After evolution (*i.e.*, ICD release 2010), the attribute value "Fecal impaction" is no longer associated with the ICD concept and the previously mentioned mapping has been removed. Moreover, the concept "Fecal impaction" has been newly created in ICD (release 2010) and is reconnected to "Fecal impaction (disorder)" of SCT.

Literature has highlighted challenges related to ontology changes' management and has proposed change patterns to improve the ontology evolution process [6,7]. Although useful tools exist to identify the most traditional and frequent OCOs between two ontology versions [3,8,9], taking into account the nature of changes (*e.g.*, atomic or complex) and the type of changes (*e.g.*, addition, removal, splitting, merging of entities), these tools fail to automatically identify ontology modifications at a finer level of detail, required for supporting tasks dependent on ontology changes (*e.g.*, mapping adaptation). This remains an open issue that requires further research.

To cope with this issue, our proposal underscores a nontrivial solution to recognize the diffusion of attribute values between concepts from one version of the ontology to another. We inquire whether techniques based on linguistic characteristics of textual values, combined with similarity measure, play a role in supporting automatic change patterns identification at the level of concept attributes. In summary, we make the following contributions:

- We formally define a set of *ontology change patterns* to express different behaviours of the evolution of attributes.
- We introduce a novel linguistic-based approach implementing methods to automatically identify instances of the proposed change patterns by comparing successive ontology versions. We investigate different techniques to rank candidate attributes in the identification method. Our systematic study provides useful tools to precisely characterize ontology evolution.
- We experimentally assess our approach by using real-world biomedical ontologies as a case study. We investigate the influence of different aspects in the performance of the proposed methods and our obtained results show innovative findings.

We structure the remainder of this article as follows: Section 2 discusses related work; Section 3 reports on our approach to change patterns; Section 4 describes the techniques for identifying change patterns; Section 5 presents the evaluation while Section 6 draws conclusions and future work.

2 Ontology Change Patterns

Noy & Klein [6] have originally evoked the notion of *change patterns* (CPs) through a first simple classification of changes that may affect entities of

[1] `www.cdc.gov/nchs/icd/icd9cm.htm`

[2] `www.ihtsdo.org/snomed-ct`

ontologies at evolution time. This classification, under basic and complex changes, paved the way for new approaches addressing ontology evolution. These approaches explore CPs to characterize complex changes and evolution scenarios, simplifying the management of ontologies to control the impact of the evolution and to ensure consistency in ontology [10].

Change patterns may allow to identify complex changes between versions of the same ontology. Groner *et al.* [11] addressed the problem of refactoring recognition using reasoning to semantically compare different versions of an OWL DL ontology. They proposed a high-level categorization of ontology changes like the refactoring patterns in software engineering, and applied it to OWL ontology.

Some approaches define CPs at the level of RDF data model. Auer & Herre [12] proposed to support ontology evolution by using basic changes and aggregate them into more complex changes in RDF. Their approach consists in annotating the derived compound changes with meta-information and classifying them as ontology evolution patterns. Differently, Rieß *et al.* [13] proposed a pattern-based approach to evolving data and refactoring RDF knowledge bases. They defined basic evolution patterns that can be combined into compound ones. Their work formally specifies modular evolution patterns in a declarative manner, capturing simple evolution and refactoring operations on both data and schema levels.

Djedidi & Aufaure defined an ontology evolution methodology driven by a pattern-oriented modelling. They proposed the *Change Management Patterns* to guide the ontology evolution process by driving and controlling change application while maintaining consistency of the evolving ontology [14]. They considered four kinds of consistency concerning the OWL DL language: structural, logical, conceptual and domain modeling consistency [14]. The solution looks for invariances in change management that repeatedly appear when ontologies evolve. They proposed three types of patterns: change patterns classifying types of changes, inconsistency patterns classifying types of logical inconsistencies, and alternative patterns classifying types of inconsistency resolution alternatives.

Javed *et al.* suggested an approach to dealing with ontology evolution through a framework of compositional operators where they represent domain changes as CPs [7]. They composed this framework with different levels of change operators, and empirically studied ontology evolution to investigate the relationships between generic and domain-specific changes to determine common CPs.

This literature review clearly highlights that existing approaches exploit CPs to deal with ontology evolution, and frequently their definition relies on ontology meta-models and languages (*e.g.,* OWL or RDF). While existing change patterns seem sufficient to identify a set of inconsistencies, they remain inefficient for dealing with the impact of ontology evolution on dependent artifacts because their design fails to consider requirements for adapting mappings. We address CPs at the level of attribute values using linguistic-based features for identifying the diffusion of textual values between concepts over time. Complementary to other approaches, we refine meta-model patterns on model level to further support the ontology evolution impact, which influences the way we design the required CPs and the recognition methods.

3 Change Patterns in Attribute Values

3.1 Preliminaries and Problem Definition

We adopt a traditional definition of ontology [15]. We define a set of concepts of an ontology O_x at time j as $C(O_x{}^j) = \{c_1^j, c_2^j, ..., c_n^j\}$. Each concept $c_i^j \in C(O_x{}^j)$, described by a set of attributes, has a unique identifier. We consider the set of attributes characterizing a concept c as $A(c) = \{a_1, a_2, ..., a_n\}$ (*e.g.*, name, definition, synonym, *etc.*). For instance, an attribute a_i, of type *name*, contains the *value* "*cardio_vascular_diseases*". We use $a_i.value$ to denote the value of an attribute a_i. A relationship $r \in R$ interconnects two concepts and has a specific type, *e.g.*, "*subsumption*", "*part-of*", *etc.*

The *context of a concept* c_i in the ontology stands for a set of *super concepts* ($sup(c_i)$), *sub concepts* ($sub(c_i)$) and *sibling concepts* of c_i ($sib(c_i)$), as following:

$$CT(c_i) = sup(c_i) \cup sub(c_i) \cup sib(c_i) \quad (1)$$

where

$$\begin{aligned} sup(c_i) &= \{c_k | c_k \in C(O_x), c_i \sqsubset c_k \wedge c_i \neq c_k\} \\ sub(c_i) &= \{c_k | c_k \in C(O_x), c_k \sqsubset c_i \wedge c_i \neq c_k\} \\ sib(c_i) &= \{c_k | c_k \in C(O_x), sup(c_k) = sup(c_i) \wedge c_i \notin sup(c_k)\} \end{aligned} \quad (2)$$

where $c_i \sqsubset c_k$ means that c_i is related to c_k through a subsumption relationship.

Figure 1 depicts the investigated scenario. Given an attribute a_i from a concept c at time t_0, we investigate a way to characterize how such attribute evolves by considering the context of the concept c^1 at time t_1 (*i.e.*, in the new version of ontology O_x). Evolution of ontology entities usually remains restricted in an ontology space like the context [4]. We focus on $a_i.value$ to identify useful behaviours of evolution concerning the attributes and search for describing these behaviours as well-delineated change patterns. We face issues to determine which attribute at time t_1 represents the most adequate candidate in the recognition process to identify CPs occurrences. We apply syntactic analysis techniques to recognize textual values of attributes in different versions of the same ontology.

3.2 Proposed Change Patterns

Considering **change patterns** (CPs) as means to deal with ontology entity changes, we focus on changes related to concept's attribute values. Therefore, our defined change patterns relate to the linguistic characteristics of the attributes' value before and after their evolution. We denote O_x^0 an ontology O_x at time t_0 and $c_k^1 \in C(O_x^1)$ a concept belonging to this ontology at time t_1. A change pattern between an attribute a_p^0 of concept $c_k^0 \in C(O_x^0)$ and another attribute a_q^1 of concept $c_{cand}^1 \in CT(c_k^1)$ occurs when changes in the value of the attribute a_p^0 which shares some similarity with the attribute a_q^1 are observed. In addition, we suppose that the attribute a_q^1 is new or its value differs at time t_1 from the one at time t_0. Therefore, any change pattern must satisfy the following constraint :

$$a_q^0 \notin A(c_{cand}^0) \vee a_q^0 \neq a_q^1 \quad (3)$$

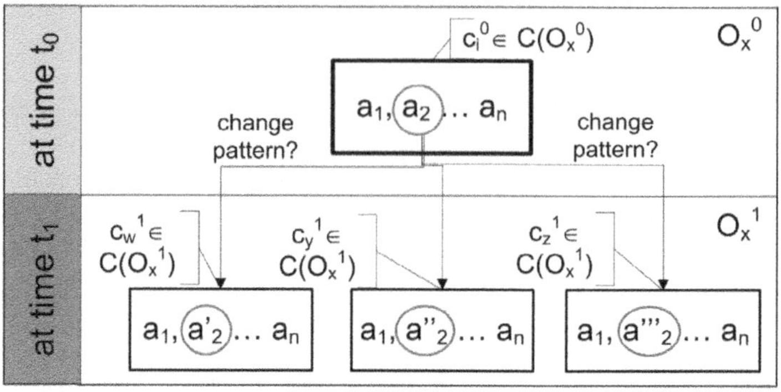

Fig. 1. Problem definition

We define the CP classes as "total copy" (TC), "total transfer" (TT), "partial copy" (PC), and "partial transfer" (PT). Table 1 illustrates the proposed change patterns and presents examples borrowed from the biomedical domain. We justify our definition of CPs through the specific needs to understand ontology changes to support mapping adaptation [5]. We assume that correctly identifying the defined CPs will support addressing the adaptation of ontology mappings [2].

Table 1. Description and examples of the proposed change patterns from attribute a_p^0 to attribute a_q^1. The symbol $\emptyset$ means that the corresponding attribute does not exist.

attribute	CP		CP type	example	
	t_0	t_1		t_0	t_1
a_p	**ABC**	ABC	total copy (TC)	*'portal systemic encephalopathy'*	'portal systemic encephalopathy'
a_q	~~ABC~~	**ABC**(D)		$\emptyset$	*'portal systemic encephalopathy'*
a_p	**ABC**	~~ABC~~	total transfer (TT)	*'fecal impaction'*	$\emptyset$
a_q	~~ABC~~	**ABC**(D)		$\emptyset$	*'fecal impaction'*
a_p	**ABC**	ABC	partial copy (PC)	'*familial* hyperchylomicronemia'	'familial hyperchylomicronemia'
a_q	~~ABC~~	**AB**(D)		$\emptyset$	'*familial* chylomicronemia'
a_p	ABC	~~ABC~~	partial transfer (PT)	'eye *swelling*'	$\emptyset$
a_q	~~ABC~~	**AB**(D)		$\emptyset$	'head *swelling*'

In what follows, we define $W(a_i^j)$ as a set of words/tokens from $a_i.value$ of an attribute a_i, and w_{ki}^j as a single word/token from an attribute value at time t_j. The $sim(a_p^0, a_q^1)$ function refers to the similarity between the value of the attributes $a_p^0 \in A(c_k^0)$ and $a_q^1 \in A(c_{cand}^1)$. The used similarity measure indicates the degree of relatedness between two given textual values. We use the γ parameter to control the overlap in terms of words between two attribute values. Since the performance of the similarity measure is not the focus of this paper, we keep it generic in our definition of CPs so that we can choose it as a parameter in our experiments. We formalize each type of CP between a_p and a_q, if any, as follows:

- **Total copy.** A total copy of content occurs between attribute a_p^0 in concept c_k and a_q^1 in concept c_{cand} if and only if a minimal degree γ of words in a_p appears in a_q and a minimal similarity value τ exists between them. Formally:

$$TC(a_p^0, a_q^1) \Leftrightarrow \begin{cases} a_p^0 \in A(c_k^0) \\ c_k^1 \in C(O_x^1) \\ a_p^1 \in A(c_k^1) \\ sim(a_p^0, a_q^1) \geq \tau \\ \|W(a_p^0) \cap W(a_q^1)\| / \|W(a_p^0)\| \geq \gamma \end{cases} \tag{4}$$

- **Total transfer.** A total transfer of content occurs between attribute a_p^0 in concept c_k and a_q^1 in concept c_{cand} if and only if a minimal degree γ of words in a_p appears in a_q and a minimal similarity value τ exists between them while the original attribute a_p^0 is removed from $c_k^1 \in O_x^1$. Note that in total copy (*cf.* Equation 4) $a_p^1 \in A(c_k^1)$ while in total transfer (*cf.* Equation 5) $a_p^1 \notin A(c_k^1)$ which states the main difference between them. Formally:

$$TT(a_p^0, a_q^1) \Leftrightarrow \begin{cases} a_p^0 \in A(c_k^0) \\ a_p^1 \notin A(c_k^1) \\ sim(a_p^0, a_q^1) \geq \tau \\ \|W(a_p^0) \cap W(a_q^1)\| / \|W(a_p^0)\| \geq \gamma \end{cases} \tag{5}$$

- **Partial copy.** A partial copy of content occurs between attribute a_p^0 in concept c_k and a_q^1 in concept c_{cand} if and only if there exists a partial overlap between words constituting attributes a_p^0 and a_q^1, while respecting a minimal similarity value τ and a degree of overlap between 0 and γ. Formally:

$$PC(a_p^0, a_q^1) \Leftrightarrow \begin{cases} a_p^0 \in A(c_k^0) \\ c_k^1 \in C(O_x^1) \\ a_p^1 \in A(c_k^1) \\ \exists w_{ip}^0 \in W(a_p^0), w_{ip}^0 \in W(a_q^1) \\ \exists w_{jp}^0 \in W(a_p^0), w_{jp}^0 \notin W(a_q^1) \\ sim(a_p^0, a_q^1) \geq \tau \\ 0 \leq \|W(a_p^0) \cap W(a_q^1)\| / \|W(a_p^0)\| \leq \gamma \end{cases} \tag{6}$$

- **Partial transfer.** A partial transfer of content occurs between attribute a_p^0 in concept c_k and a_q^1 in concept c_{cand} if and only if there exists a partial overlap between words constituting attributes a_p^0 and a_q^1 while respecting a minimal similarity value τ, a degree of overlap between 0 and γ, and the original attribute a_p^0 is removed from $c_k^0 \in O_x^0$. Formally:

$$PT(a_p^0, a_q^1) \Leftrightarrow \begin{cases} a_p^0 \in A(c_k^0) \\ a_p^1 \notin A(c_k^1) \\ \exists w_i^p \in W(a_p^0), w_i^p \in W(a_q^1) \\ \exists w_j^p \in W(a_p^0), w_j^p \notin W(a_q^1) \\ sim(a_p^0, a_q^1) \geq \tau \\ 0 \leq \|W(a_p^0) \cap W(a_q^1)\| / \|W(a_p^0)\| \leq \gamma \end{cases} \quad (7)$$

4 Recognizing Change Patterns Related to Attributes

In our approach to recognize change pattern, we first determine a candidate attribute a_q^1 in the context of a concept c_k^1 (Section 4.1). This candidate refers to a changed attribute at time t_1 related to the attribute a_p^0 in concept c_k^0 that we used to identify occurences of CPs (Section 4.2).

4.1 Candidate Attribute in the Context

We designed Algorithm 1 that explores textual attributes from a given concept at time t_0. In particular, given an attribute $a_p^0 \in A(c_k^0)$ from O_x^0, the algorithm courses the whole set of changed attributes of the context of c_k at time t_1 by calculating the similarity to retrieve candidate attributes. It aims to find the most adequate attribute in the context of the given one from $A(c_k)$, which we will use in Algorithm 2 to identify change patterns. We consider the types of comparable textual attributes as a parameter in our approach. For example, we can take only attributes of type "name" and "synonym" into consideration when comparing the attribute values (*i.e.*, strings denoting concepts). Our methods exclude all types of attributes out of the comparable set of attributes defined beforehand. The function $sim(a_i^0, a_j^1)$ computes the similarity between two given attribute values. It returns a value ranging from 0 to 1. The higher the result is, the more similar these attributes are. We explore traditional string-based similarity metrics (the *bi-gram* measure), when calculating the similarity between attribute values in Algorithm 1. We selected this metric as the default similarity because it performs well on ontology matching [16].

Algorithm 1 generates a list of candidate attributes which is denoted as $S_{cand}(a_p^0) = \{(a_{q1}, sim_{pq1}), (a_{q2}, sim_{pq2}), ..., (a_{qm}, sim_{pqm})\}$, where $a_{q_i} \in A(CT(c_k^1))$ and $sim_{pq_i} = sim(a_p^0, a_{q_i}^1)$. In fact, $S_{cand}(a_p^0)$ stores the candidate attributes along with their similarity with the attribute $a_p^0 \in A(c_k^0)$. This algorithm uses a ranking function to determine the best candidate attribute as a result.

We distinguish two ranking approaches to find the best candidate attribute: **global** and **local**. The candidate attribute may have a strong influence on the CP identification method which motivates us to investigate both rankings.

Algorithm 1. Find candidate attribute in the context

Require: $a_p^0 \in A(c_k^0); CT(c_k^1) \subset C(O_x^1)$
  $sim \leftarrow \emptyset; a_q^1 \leftarrow \emptyset; S_{cand} \leftarrow \emptyset;$
  for all $c_i^1 \in CT(c_k^1)$ **do**
    for all $a_i^1 \in A(c_i^1)$ **do**
      if $a_i^0 \notin A(c_i^0) \vee a_i^0 \neq a_i^1$ **then**
        $sim \leftarrow sim(a_p^0, a_i^1);$
        $S_{cand} \leftarrow S_{cand} \cup \{(a_i^1, c_i^1, sim)\};$
      end if
    end for
  end for
  return $S_{cand} \leftarrow rank(S_{cand}).first;$

- **Global ranking (GR).** In this ranking the best a_q^1 candidate attribute (found at time t_1) refers to the one that has the highest similarity with a given attribute $a_p^0 \in A(c_k^0)$. We denote this as the **global candidate** because the selection relies on the optimum similarity value considering the whole context. Formally:

$$candidate_{GR}(S_{cand}(a_p^0)) \leftarrow \underset{a_{q_i}^1 \in A(CT(c_k^1))}{\arg\max} \{sim(a_p^0, a_{q_i}^1)\} \tag{8}$$

- **Local ranking (LR).** Unlike the GR, this approach assumes that the best candidate attribute locates in a part of the evolving ontology where we observe most changes in attributes. LR executes two steps: (1) it analyzes which elements of the context of concept c (*i.e.*, $sup(c)$, $sub(c)$, $sib(c)$) has the highest number of changed attributes; (2) based on this result, it selects the most similar attribute. We refer to this as the **local candidate** because the selection relies on the optimum similarity value considering part of the context. We compute the distribution of the different relationship types from the context in the list of changed attributes $S_{cand}(a_p^0)$ as follows:

$$dist(S_{cand}(a_p^0), \Gamma) = \frac{\sum f(a_{q_i}^1)}{\|S_{cand}(a_p^0)\|} \tag{9}$$

- ∘ Γ is among the three types of relationships we consider in $CT(c)$ interconnecting super, sub and sibling concepts.
- ∘ $f(a_{q_i}^1)$ stands for the function counting the frequency of a particular relationship type, defined as follows:

$$f(a_{q_i}^1) = \begin{cases} 1 & \text{if } rel(a_{q_i}^1) = \Gamma \\ 0 & \text{otherwise} \end{cases}$$

where $rel(a_{q_i}^1)$ refers to the type of relationship between concepts c_k^0 denoted by attribute a_p^0 and c_{cand}^1 denoted by attribute $a_{q_i}^1$. We define the local candidate as follows:

$$candidate_{LR}(S_{cand}(a_p^0)) \leftarrow \begin{cases} best\_dist(\Gamma) \leftarrow \underset{a_{q_i}^1 \in A(CT(c_k^1))}{\arg\max} \; dist(S_{cand}(a_p^0), \Gamma) \\ \underset{a_{q_i}^1 \in best\_dist(\Gamma) \wedge rel(a_{q_i}^1) = \Gamma}{\arg\max} \; sim(a_p^0, a_{q_i}^1) \end{cases} \quad (10)$$

4.2 Identification Method

Algorithm 2 describes the designed procedure to identify CPs. The best candidate c_{cand}^1 refers to the concept denoted by attribute a_q^1, retrieved with algorithm 1. For each candidate a_q^1, the algorithm checks whether its similarity value with attribute a_p^0 is greater or equal to a threshold τ, and the conditions for applying each type of change pattern on the couple of attributes a_p^0 and a_q^1. To this end, it calculates the number of common words between a_p^0 and a_q^1 by removing stop words from the original attributes. The algorithm also explores whether attributes $a_p^0 \in A(c_k^0)$ and $a_q^1 \in A(c_{cand}^1)$ remain at time t_1 (*i.e.*, it is not removed). According to the definitions, the algorithm assigns the adequate CP. Given two versions of the same ontology, we can apply Algorithm 2 to all concepts placed in ontology regions affected by traditional change operations.

Algorithm 2. Change pattern identification

Require: $a_p^0 \in A(c_k^0); c_k^0 \in C(O_x^0); CT(c_k^1) \subset C(O_x^1)$
  $CP \leftarrow \emptyset; sim \leftarrow 0; nbEqWords \leftarrow 0$
  $a_q^1; sim \leftarrow$ Algorithm $1(a_p^0; CT(c_k^1))$;
  if $a_q^1 \neq \emptyset$ **then**
    if $0 < sim > \tau$ **then**
      $nbEqWords \leftarrow \|W(a_p^0) \cap W(a_q^1)\|$
      if $nbEqWords/\|W(a_p^0)\| \leq \gamma \wedge nbEqWords > 0 \wedge nbEqWords < \|W(a_p^0)\|$ **then**
        if $a_p^1 \in A(c_k^1)$ **then**
          $CP \leftarrow PC(a_p^0, a_q^1)$;
        else
          $CP \leftarrow PT(a_p^0, a_q^1)$;
        end if
      else
        if $nbEqWords/\|W(a_p^0)\| \geq \gamma$ **then**
          if $a_p^1 \in A(c_k^1)$ **then**
            $CP \leftarrow TC(a_p^0, a_q^1)$;
          else
            $CP \leftarrow TT(a_p^0, a_q^1)$;
          end if
        end if
      end if
    end if
  end if
  return (a_p^0, a_q^1, CP);

5 Experimental Evaluation

We present the used materials followed by the experimental procedure conducted to achieve the following objectives:

- We evaluate the effectiveness of the proposed methods for identifying change patterns based on exploiting lexical features of attributes.
- We assess the proposed ranking functions by comparing their performance.

5.1 Materials

In the conducted experiments we used various versions of three large biomedical ontologies: SNOMED-CT (SCT), MeSH and ICD-9-CM (ICD9). Table 2 presents statistics regarding the number of concepts, attributes and the number of direct subsumption relationships between concepts, since this study focused on exploiting the hierarchical structure of ontologies. SCT contains a much higher number of concepts than MeSH and ICD9. Table 2 also depicts the evolution of concepts and attributes for the three studied biomedical ontologies in a combined way over the last years. This dynamic evolution motivates us to use biomedical ontologies as a case study in this research.

Table 2. Evolution of biomedical ontologies. The numbers between parentheses represent the change rate between two releases of the same ontology.

ontology	year	#concepts	#attributes	#subsumptions
ICD-9-CM	2009	12734	34065	11619
	2011	13059 (+2.55%)	34963 (+2.64%)	11962 (+2.95 %)
SNOMED-CT	2010	386965	1531288	523958
	2012	395346 (+2.12%)	1570504 (+2.50%)	539245 (+2.83%)
MeSH	2012	50367	259565	59191
	2013	50971 (+1.18%)	264783 (+1.97%)	59844 (+1.09%)

Reference change patterns. To evaluate the effectiveness of our approach, we defined a set of reference change patterns as our standards. We needed to build our own set of reference since no available gold standard exists for the investigated context. To this end, we conducted the following steps:

- We combined the ontologies and we randomly selected a set of 1.000 couples of attributes. We defined the size of our sample in accordance with the involved experts taking into account their availability and scientific consistencies for our experiments. One attribute of a couple comes from a concept at time t_j and the other one in the same couple comes from a concept in the context of the former concept in the same ontology at time t_{j+1}. We chose these couples based on the similarity between attribute values, excluding attributes with very low similarity and unchanged attributes at time t_{j+1}.

- We invited three ontology engineering experts to evaluate all selected couples of attributes to assign their answer regarding CPs. For this purpose, we supported them with a software tool suited to present additional information regarding each attribute. This tool presents the couple of attributes along with concepts in the context, the attributes denoting concepts as well as the changes affecting them, *etc.* We gave instructions on the purpose of the different patterns, and recorded the answers for each evaluator separately.
- The evaluators performed one round of evaluation, and we merged the agreement answers. The domain experts collaborated and re-evaluated a second round only with the disagreement part of couples. We merged the final agreement couples with the respective correct answers according to the evaluators. We achieved an average agreement rate of 86%. Finally, we retained 675 pairs of attributes that had the consent from all evaluators for our experiments.

5.2 Experimental Procedure

For evaluating the effectiveness of our CP identification algorithm, we computed the standard metrics of *Precision, Recall* and *F-measure* based on the reference CPs as input. Specifically, we computed the precision as the number of CPs correctly identified by the algorithm over the total number of identified CPs. Recall was computed as the number of correctly identified CPs over the total number of relevant/expected CPs in the set of reference. F-measure was computed as the harmonic mean of precision and recall.

We investigated the influence of the similarity threshold in the CP identification algorithm. For this purpose, we analyzed the CP identification performance by varying the similarity threshold from 0 to 1 to observe the performance of our algorithm, and we set $\tau = \gamma$. Additionally, we examined the quality of the outcomes by comparing both GR and LR ranking functions proposed.

5.3 Results

Figure 2 presents the effectiveness of the CP identification algorithm in terms of precision, recall and F-measure by varying the similarity thresholds (denoted as τ). We achieved these results using the global ranking in Algorithm 1.

The performance of this algorithm varies according to the value of τ. Overall, the F-measure is greater than 0.60 for all types of CP. We observe that the similarity threshold plays a relevant role in CP identification because its performance dramatically changes when the threshold is set very low (*e.g.*, $\tau < 0.5$). Our CP identification algorithm reaches the best performance with thresholds ranging from 0.7 to 0.9, which points out the necessity of having a minimal similarity between attributes to boost the identification results.

By observing the results for each type of CP, we found that the identification of partial copy CP reaches the highest F-measure of 0.68 (precision=0.61, recall=0.77) at $\tau = 0.75$. This remains similar to the case of total copy CP, where the highest F-measure is 0.66 (precision=0.66, recall=0.66) at $\tau = 0.85$. Moreover, the recall for total copy CP tends to be higher than the precision for

$\tau < 0.85$, but we observed the contrary phenomenon for partial copy CP. We potentially explain this by the fact that for correctly identifying total copy CPs require higher similarity between attributes, while for partial copy, the higher the similarity value, the lower the number of partial copy CPs correctly identified.

Regarding total transfer CP, Algorithm 2 reaches the best F-measure at 0.78 (precision=0.90, recall=0.69) for $\tau = 0.80$. The algorithm performs better on identifying total transfer than on partial transfer. Partial transfer CP seems a particular case (not frequently found) because evaluators assigned only one case in the reference change patterns.

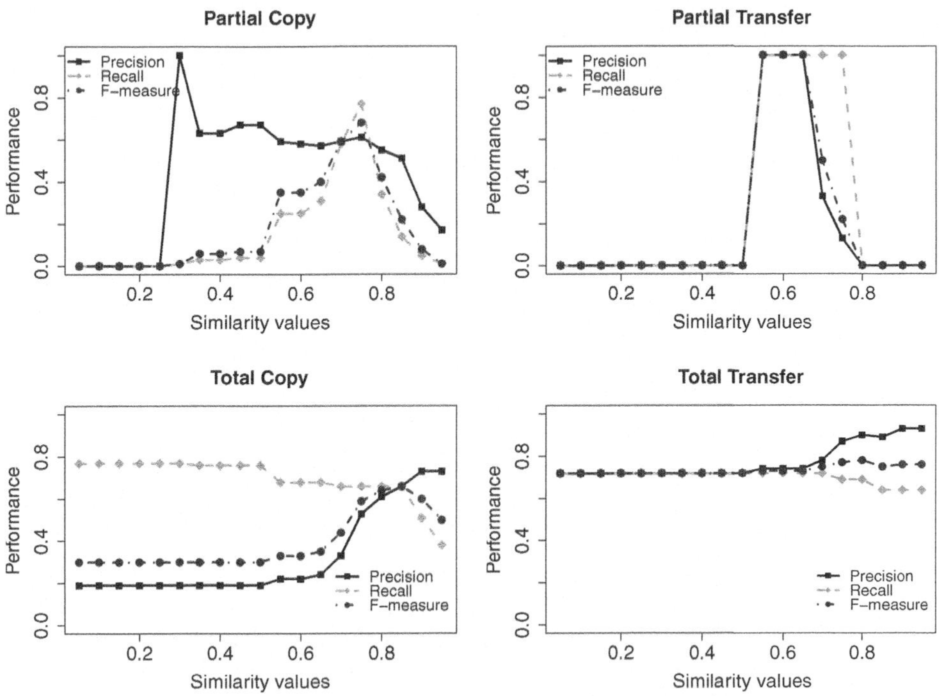

Fig. 2. Effectiveness of the CP identification method (using GR ranking) in terms of precision, recall and f-measure for the different types of change patterns

To analyze the results comparing the proposed rankings, we retain the maximum value of the similarity threshold, *i.e.*, $\tau = 0.85$, that optimizes the performance of the GR (denoted as $baseline_{MAX}$). Tables 3 and 4 present the achieved results for transfer and copy CPs by running our method using the local ranking function. We chose the similarity thresholds among the values in the set {0.2, 0.4, 0.6, 0.75, 0.8} to analyze the performance, and compare the difference in terms of precision, recall and F-measure between LR and GR.

Results in Table 3 reveal that the LR improves the performance in terms of recall for total transfer with a maximum improvement rate of +4.69%, while the performance dramatically decreases for precision and F-measure. For partial transfer CP, the LR method outperforms the baseline for values of τ in the interval $[0.6, 0.75]$. The performance of the latter is zero for either precision, recall and F-measure, probably because the similarity threshold was very high ($\tau = 0.85$). This suggests that CP identification for either partial or total transfer must use a flexible or approximate string matching with an appropriate similarity threshold that should not be very low (*e.g.*, < 0.5) nor very high (*e.g.*, > 0.8).

Regarding the performance of the local ranking for identifying copy CPs (*cf.* Table 4), we observe that for total copy CP, the precision is proportional to the similarity threshold while the recall is not. For partial copy CP, the local ranking shows a significant improvement rate of +29.41 % for precision, +378% for recall and +204% for F-measure by using $\tau = 0.75$.

Table 3. Performance of the identification method by using the LR ranking for transfer CP. Numbers in parentheses correspond to the difference between P, R, F obtained by LR comparatively to τ of the $baseline_{MAX}$ of GR.

τ \ CP	**Transfer of attributes**					
	total			**partial**		
	P (ΔP)	R (ΔR)	F (ΔF)	P (ΔP)	R (ΔR)	F (ΔF)
$baseline_{MAX}$	0.89	0.64	0.75	0.00	0.00	0.00
0.2	0.50 (-43.82%)	0.67 (**+4.69%**)	0.57 (-24.00%)	0.00 (0.00%)	0.00 (0.00%)	0.00 (0.00%)
0.4	0.50 (-43.82%)	0.67 (**+4.69%**)	0.57 (-24.00%)	0.00 (0.00%)	0.00 (0.00%)	0.00 (0.00%)
0.6	0.53 (-40.45%)	0.67 (**+4.69%**)	0.59 (-21.33%)	0.33 (INF)	1.00 (INF)	0.50 (INF)
0.75	0.79 (-11.24%)	0.67 (**+4.69%**)	0.72 (-4.00%)	0.05 (INF)	1.00 (INF)	0.10 (INF)
0.8	0.79 (-11.24%)	0.67 (**+4.69%**)	0.72 (-4.00%)	0.00 (0.00%)	0.00 (0.00%)	0.00 (0.00%)

5.4 Discussion

We found that the suggested types of CPs at the level of attributes can be observed in real cases of ontology evolution. These CPs refine the traditional ones at a finer level of granularity to characterize ontology evolution. Overall results pointed out the effectiveness of the proposed method underlaid by similarity measure and intersection of words between attribute values to recognize CPs between ontology versions. We demonstrated that the similarity threshold plays an important role in the quality of the outcomes. We explain this by the fact that our method selects the candidate attribute based on the similarity that is proportional to the degree of relatedness between the analyzed attributes.

Table 4. Performance of the identification method by using the LR ranking for copy CP. Numbers between parentheses correspond to the difference between P, R, F obtained by LR comparatively to τ of the $baseline_{MAX}$ of GR.

τ \ CP	Copy of attributes					
	total			partial		
	P (ΔP)	R (ΔR)	F (ΔF)	P (ΔP)	R (ΔR)	F (ΔF)
$baseline_{MAX}$	0.66	0.66	0.66	0.51	0.14	0.22
0.2	0.18 (-72.73%)	0.65 (-1.52%)	0.28 (-57.58%)	0.00 (-100.00%)	0.00 (-100.00%)	0.00 (-100.00%)
0.4	0.18 (-72.73%)	0.63 (-4.55%)	0.28 (-57.58%)	0.63 (**+23.53%**)	0.03 (-78.57%)	0.06 (-72.73%)
0.6	0.21 (-68.18%)	0.58 (-12.12%)	0.31 (-53.03%)	0.56 (**+9.80%**)	0.20 (**+42.86%**)	0.30 (**+36.36%**)
0.75	0.53 (-19.70%)	0.56 (-15.15%)	0.55 (-16.67%)	0.66 (**+29.41%**)	0.67 (**+378%**)	0.67 (**+204%**)
0.8	0.56 (-15.15%)	0.41 (-37.88%)	0.47 (-28.79%)	0.61 (**+19.61%**)	0.28 (**+100%**)	0.39 (**+77.27%**)

When comparing the overall performance of CP identification under the GR and LR methods, our findings demonstrated that considering both the types of context relationships as well as their distribution affect the identification results. The LR method performs better, in particular for partial copy with a significant improvement compared to the GR. However, for total copy and transfer the performance under LR remains low, probably because the nature of these CPs requires a relatively high similarity threshold. We conclude that CPs of partial type should base on the local ranking for selecting the candidate attribute in CP recognition, while for CPs of total type we recommend using the global ranking.

Our scholarly obtained findings have revealed evidences of the quality of the results that were yielded by the proposed method, relying on standard evaluation metrics. In addition, we conducted experiments using real biomedical ontologies which strengthens our results.

6 Conclusion

Ontology evolution requires further means to describe specific changes at different entities. This plays a relevant role in controlling the impact of changes on dependent artefacts. In this article, we defined change patterns of concept attributes to characterize the evolution of their textual values. We designed a novel method to recognize the change patterns between ontology versions and empirically evaluated our proposition by observing the evolution of biomedical ontologies. We studied the influence of different aspects in the change pattern identification on the quality of the outcomes. The achieved results showed evidences of the performance of the proposed method.

In addition to existing and traditional ontology change operations, our contribution in this article originally allows to characterize ontology evolution by means of change patterns at attribute level. This stands for fine-grained changes that may facilitate tasks related to the impact of ontology evolution such as mapping and annotation maintenance. As future work, we aim to study techniques to recognize the way attribute values become more or less semantically specific in ontology evolution, and to investigate to which extent the different types of change patterns may influence the way ontology mappings evolve.

Acknowledgment. The National Research Fund (FNR) of Luxembourg entirely supports this work under the *DynaMO* research project (Grant #C10/IS/786147).

References

1. Groß, A., Dos Reis, J.C., Hartung, M., Pruski, C., Rahm, E.: Semi-automatic adaptation of mappings between life science ontologies. In: Baker, C.J.O., Butler, G., Jurisica, I. (eds.) DILS 2013. LNCS, vol. 7970, pp. 90–104. Springer, Heidelberg (2013)
2. Dos Reis, J.C., Dinh, D., Pruski, C., Da Silveira, M., Reynaud-Delaitre, C.: Mapping adaptation actions for the automatic reconciliation of dynamic ontologies. In: Proc. of Conference on Information and Knowledge Management, pp. 599–608 (2013)
3. Hartung, M., Groß, A., Rahm, E.: Conto-diff – generation of complex evolution mappings for life science ontologies. Biomedical Informatics, 15–32 (2013)
4. Dos Reis, J.C., Pruski, C., Da Silveira, M., Reynaud-Delaitre, C.: Understanding semantic mapping evolution by observing changes in biomedical ontologies. Journal of Biomedical Informatics 47, 71–82
5. Dos Reis, J.C., Pruski, C., Da Silveira, M., Reynaud-Delaitre, C.: Characterizing semantic mappings adaptation via biomedical kos evolution: A case study investigating snomed ct and icd. In: Proc. of the AMIA Symposium, pp. 333–342 (2013)
6. Noy, N.F., Klein, M.: Ontology evolution: Not the same as schema evolution. Knowledge and information systems 6(4), 428–440 (2004)
7. Javed, M., Abgaz, Y., Pahl, C.: Ontology change management and identification of change patterns. Journal on Data Semantics 2(2-3), 119–143 (2013)
8. Noy, N.F., Musen, M.A.: PROMPTDIFF: A Fixed-Point Algorithm for Comparing Ontology Versions. In: Proc. of AAAI 2002, pp. 744–750 (2002)
9. Kremen, P., Smid, M., Kouba, Z.: Owldiff: A practical tool for comparison and merge of owl ontologies. In: 22nd International Workshop on Database and Expert Systems Applications (DEXA), pp. 229–233 (2011)
10. Shaban-Nejad, A., Haarslev, V.: Bio-medical ontologies maintenance and change management. In: Sidhu, A., Dillon, T. (eds.) Biomedical Data and Applications, SCI 224, pp. 143–168. Springer, Heidelberg (2009)
11. Gröner, G., Silva Parreiras, F., Staab, S.: Semantic Recognition of Ontology Refactoring. In: Patel-Schneider, P.F., Pan, Y., Hitzler, P., Mika, P., Zhang, L., Pan, J.Z., Horrocks, I., Glimm, B. (eds.) ISWC 2010, Part I. LNCS, vol. 6496, pp. 273–288. Springer, Heidelberg (2010)
12. Auer, S., Herre, H.: A Versioning and Evolution Framework for RDF Knowledge Bases. In: Virbitskaite, I., Voronkov, A. (eds.) PSI 2006. LNCS, vol. 4378, pp. 55–69. Springer, Heidelberg (2007)

13. Rieß, C., Heino, N., Tramp, S., Auer, S.: EvoPat – Pattern-Based Evolution and Refactoring of RDF Knowledge Bases. In: Patel-Schneider, P.F., Pan, Y., Hitzler, P., Mika, P., Zhang, L., Pan, J.Z., Horrocks, I., Glimm, B. (eds.) ISWC 2010, Part I. LNCS, vol. 6496, pp. 647–662. Springer, Heidelberg (2010)
14. Djedidi, R., Aufaure, M.A.: ONTO-EVOAL an Ontology Evolution Approach Guided by Pattern Modeling and Quality Evaluation. In: Proc. Foiks 2010, pp. 286–305. Springer, Heidelberg (2010)
15. Gruber, T.R.: Toward principles for the design of ontologies used for knowledge sharing? International Journal of Human-Computer Studies 43, 907–928 (1995)
16. Cheatham, M., Hitzler, P.: String similarity metrics for ontology alignment. In: Alani, H., Kagal, L., Fokoue, A., Groth, P., Biemann, C., Parreira, J.X., Aroyo, L., Noy, N., Welty, C., Janowicz, K. (eds.) ISWC 2013, Part II. LNCS, vol. 8219, pp. 294–309. Springer, Heidelberg (2013)

On the Discovery of Relational Patterns in Semantically Similar Annotated Linked Data

Guillermo Palma*

Universidad Simón Bolívar, Venezuela
gpalma@ldc.usb.ve

Abstract. A wide variety of publicly linked datasets have been annotated with domain-specific ontologies. Annotations can be naturally represented with graphs, and the knowledge encoded in these annotations can be mined to discover potential novel relationships. We propose novel mining techniques that exploit semantics represented by these graphs to discover relational patterns. Initial experimental results suggest that our approach can be effectively applied in different biomedical domains, and exhibit performance comparable to state-of-the-art solutions.

Keywords: #eswcphd2014Palma, Mining Patterns; Linking Data, Annotated Graph.

1 Introduction and Motivation

The number of highly connected datasets has exploded during the last years. The Linked Open Data (LOD) cloud has more than 50 billion facts from many different domains, e.g., media, biology, chemistry, economy and energy [1]. The LOD cloud can be naturally represented as graphs, specifically, with heterogeneous information networks. Heterogeneous information networks are graphs with multiple typed nodes and links that represent different relationships. Examples of heterogeneous information networks include social networks, the World Wide Web, research publication networks [10], biological networks, knowledge networks, among other networks. Due to the diverse meanings in heterogeneous information networks, mining patterns is difficult without considering the semantic of the typed concepts and relationships. A heterogeneous information network can be built upon highly structured data in the form of a graph, representing different types of nodes and edges. As many of these approaches rely on graph-based tasks, several efficient algorithms have been proposed not only to consume, but also to mine Linked Data. For example, Saha et al. [20] and Thor et al. [26] have defined densest subgraphs and graph summarization techniques to identify patterns between linked datasets of genes.

Furthermore, ontologies are developed by domain experts to capture knowledge specific to some domain. They have been extensively developed and widely adopted in the last decade. Simultaneously, Linked Open Data initiatives have

* **Advisor:** Maria-Esther Vidal (mvidal@ldc.usb.ve)

V. Presutti et al. (Eds.): ESWC 2014, LNCS 8465, pp. 784–794, 2014.

made available a diversity of collections that have been annotated with domain-specific ontologies. These annotations describe *properties* of these concepts. For example, the biomedical community has taken the lead in such activities; every model organism database has genes and proteins that are widely annotated using the Gene Ontology (GO). These annotated datasets have created many opportunities for large scale Linked Data mining. Annotations induce an annotated graph where nodes correspond to concepts or ontology terms, and edges represent relationships between concepts. Our research aims as defining novel methodologies to exploit and mining annotated graph datasets and the semantic knowledge captured within ontologies to discover complex patterns of semantically related concepts in the Linked Data. The methodologies are based on various mining tasks in the Linked Data, including clustering, classification, similarity metrics between concepts, relationship prediction and structural learning. We tackle these mining tasks, their principles and methodologies.

Motivating Example: We motivate our work with the link prediction problem presented by Fakhraei et al.[8]. The development of new drugs is a time-consuming and costly procedure, and one possibility is repurposing already approved drugs for new diseases. Repurposing existing drugs using computational methods has the benefits of shorter timelines to bring a drug to the market and reduce its cost. Drugs are molecules that participate in some biomolecular reaction associated with a disease target. There may be multiple relationships between drugs and targets. With the goal of predicting drug-target interactions, we can build a bipartite graph between drugs and targets, where edges are interactions known by the scientific community. We can augment the bipartite graph with drug-drug and target-target similarities. The similarities between drugs and between targets have different semantics. For example, drugs can have similarities based on chemical structure or shared side-effects, while gene targets may share sequence based or gene annotation based similarity [18]. Figure 1(a) shows a drug-target interaction network. The challenge is that the drug-target interaction graph, with multiple types of similarities, expresses a multi-relational graph structured knowledge. This drug-target graph, combined with knowledge in ontologies and additional LOD resources, will be used for discovery potentially new drug-target interaction.

2 State of the Art

Graph data mining [6] covers a broad range of methods dealing with the identification of structures and patterns in graphs. Popular techniques include graph clustering [5], community detection [9] and cliques [16]. Clustering, classification and ranking are basic mining functions for information networks. Spectral graph clustering [27] is state-of-the-art method to do clustering on homogeneous networks. For heterogeneous networks RankClus [25] is proposed and generates clusters integrated with ranking. A ranking-based classification of multiple types of objects, denoted by GNetMine, is proposed by Ming et al. [12]. Link prediction has been extensively studied in the recent years [8,26]. The problem of a

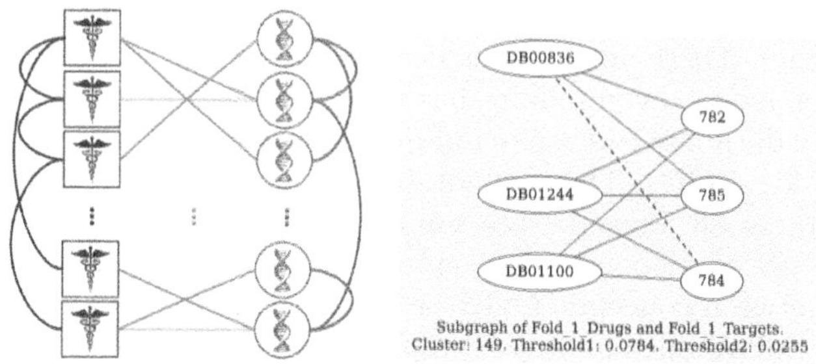

(a) Drug-Target network (b) Our approach prediction.

Fig. 1. (a) Drug-Target interaction network from [8]. Blue lines expressing drug-drug similarities, red lines target-target similarities and Green lines are known drug target interactions. (b) Cluster obtained by our approach on Dataset 1: network of drugs and targets and their interactions. The red line is a predicted interaction.

1-to-1 weighted maximal bipartite match has been applied to many problems, e.g., semantic equivalence between two sentences and measuring similarity between shapes for object recognition[22]. A key element in finding patterns is identifying related concepts and similarity metrics can be used to measure ontological relatedness. A class of metrics are path-similarity metrics based on the paths that connect the concepts in a graph. Nodes in the paths can be of the same type (e.g., PathSim [24]) or they can be heterogeneous (e.g., HeteSim [23]). Furthermore, semantic similarity metrics can be classified into two categories: *i)* structure-based metrics that exploit ontology hierarchy structure to compute the semantic similarity between terms [14,2], *ii)* information content (IC) based metrics that use IC of concepts derived from corpus statistics to measure the semantic similarity between terms [19].

Loza et al.[15] apply data mining techniques to estimate the number of bidders in public contracts represented as semantically annotated Linked Data. The proposed techniques rely on existing machine learning algorithms which are applied to a relational representation of the linked data. Our proposed approach also copes this problem but it exploits knowledge encoded in ontologies to uncover hidden relational patterns.

3 Problem Statement

How much effectively are data mining techniques to discover relational patterns in annotated Linked Data?. Our research addresses the challenge of mining large annotated graphs, and exploiting knowledge from ontologies to discover patterns that uncover hidden relationships between semantically similar data.

Our first research goal is to propose a novel similarity metric based on annotations, called *AnnSim*, that is able to measure relatedness between concepts in an annotated graph, based on the similarity of the sets of their annotations with respect to one or more ontologies. This is the necessary first step to discover complex patterns in annotated graph datasets. A practical example is identifying the relatedness or similarity of (drug, drug) pairs, based on the annotation evidence of conditions or diseases from domain-specific ontologies as the NCI Thesaurus (NCIt). NCIt Home Page: `http://ncit.nci.nih.gov/`.

Our second research goal is to discover complex relational patterns, thus we define an *annotation signature* between a pair of concepts, e.g., a pair of drugs or a pair of genes. The annotation signature builds upon the shared annotations or shared ontology terms between the pair of concepts. The signature further makes use of knowledge in the ontology to determine the ontological relatedness of the shared terms. The annotation signature is represented by N groups (clusters) of ontologically related shared terms. For example, the annotation signature for a (drug, drug) pair will be a set of N clusters, where each cluster includes a group of ontologically related disease terms from NCIt. Given a pair of concepts, and their sets of annotations, A_i and A_j from ontology O, elements $a_i \in A_i$ and $a_j \in A_j$ form the nodes of a bipartite graph (BG). Between nodes a_i and a_j there may be an edge or a path through O; an edge is the special case where a_i and a_j are identical terms from O. There may be a choice of paths between a_i and a_j depending on the the ontology structure and relationship types captured within O. One can use a variety of similarity metrics, applied to the edges and paths through the ontology O, to induce a weighted edge between a_i and a_j in BG; the weight represents the (ontologically related) similarity score in the range $[0, 1]$ between a_i and a_j. Our objective is to determine an annotation signature based on the BG. There are many alternatives to create the signature. One could partition the edges of BG with possible overlap of the nodes. Another solution is to cluster the nodes and edges of BG. One may also consider a one-to-one bipartite match. The clusters obtained may identify multiple communities (subgraphs) of ontologically related shared terms, as well as potentially overlapping communities. Our research on annotation similarity will explore such patterns that can be used for link prediction or to rank the graph concepts. Thus, we can exploit ontologically related communities identified within a data mining framework.

Our third research goal is the development of machine learning frameworks to identify interesting relational patterns involving ontologically related concepts.

4 Proposed Approach and Methodology

We can use the weight of annotation evidence, represented by a set of annotations, to define a metric to compare a pair of concepts. An annotated graph $G=(V,E)$ is a particular graph comprised of two type of nodes in V: scientific concepts and ontology terms. Given two concepts c_1 and c_2 from an annotated graph $G=(V,E)$, we define an annotation similarity metric, *AnnSim*, based on their sets of annotations, A_1 and A_2, respectively. We assume that we have a pair-wise similarity between elements of A_1 and A_2, i.e., $sim(a_1, a_2) \in [0, 1]$ for all $a_1 \in A_1$ and $a_2 \in A_2$. The value of $sim(a_1, a_2)$ is determined by the previous task of ontological similarity. These relationships between terms in A_1 and A_2 can be represented as a weighted bipartite graph $WBG=(A_1 \cup A_2,\ WE)$, see Figure 2(a). An edge between $a_1 \in A_1$ and $a_2 \in A_2$ has a weight $sim(a_1, a_2)$, where $sim(a_1, a_2)$ is computed using a distance metric. The computation of *AnnSim* first requires building a bipartite graph with the links in the Cartesian product between the set of annotations of two scientific terms, and for each of these links compute a similarity. The aim is to design the best approach to solve the *Weighted Bipartite Matching.* We first consider model *AnnSim* as a *1-to-1 maximal weighted bipartite matching* [21], see Figure 2(b). We name this annotation similarity *AnnSim*, and it is defined it as follows: Given two concepts c_1 and c_2 annotated with the set of terms A_1 and A_2 in an annotated graph, and let $MWBG$=($A_1 \cup A_2$, WEr) be *1-to-1 maximal weighted bipartite graph matching* for a WBG, where $WEr \subseteq WE$, we have $AnnSim(c_1, c_2) = \frac{2 \cdot \sum_{(a_1,a_2) \in WE_r} sim(a_1,a_2)}{|A_1|+|A_2|}$. This definition is in the style of the well-known Dice coefficient. The maximal similarity of 1.0 is achieved if and only if both annotation sets have the same cardinality ($|A_1| = |A_2|$) and all edge weights are equal to 1. This approach has limitations. We planned to obtain solutions to the many-to-many bipartite match problem to compute an enhanced metric. Initial results are reported at [17].

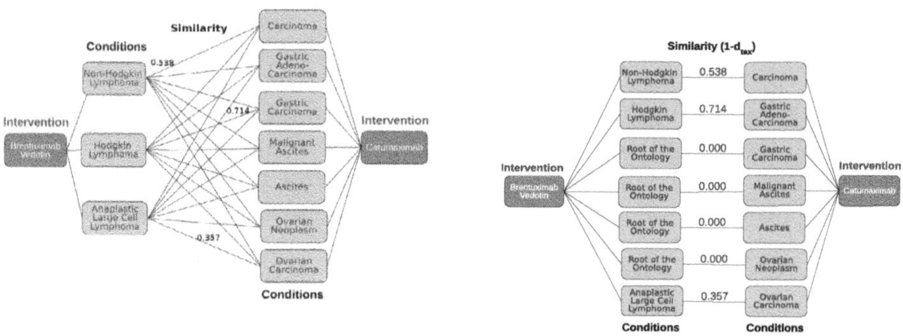

(a) Weighted Bipartite graphs for drugs Brentuximab vedotin and Catumaxomab. Shown similarity values are the highest values obtained with the metric $1 - d_{tax}$[2] on NCIt

(b) 1-to-1 Maximal Weighted Bipartite Graph Match for Brentuximab vedotin and Catumaxomab. The similarity value of *AnnSim* is 0.324

Fig. 2. Bipartite graphs for drugs Brentuximab vedotin and Catumaxomab

We define a version of the *Annotation Signature Partition* problem as the partitioning of the edges of *BG* into clusters such that the value of the aggregated cluster density is maximized. We develop *AnnSigClustering*, a clustering solution that implements a greedy iterative algorithm to cluster the edges in *BG*. We note that such a clustering will result in N clusters of the edges of *BG* with potential overlap of nodes in different clusters.

Definition 1 (Cluster Density). *Given a labeled bipartite graph $BG=(A_i \cup A_j, WE)$ with nodes A_i and A_j and edges WE, a distance metric d, and a subset p of WE, the cluster density of p $cDensity(p) = \frac{\sum_{(e=(a,b))\in p} 1-d(a,b)}{|p|}$.*

Definition 2 (Similar Nodes $\sim$). *Given two nodes a and b, a real number θ in the range $[0:1]$, and a distance metric d, nodes a and b are similar, i.e., $a \sim b$, iff $1 - d(a, b) > \theta$.*

Definition 3 (The Annotation Signature Partition Problem). *Given a labeled bipartite graph $BG=(A_i \cup A_j, WE)$, a distance metric d, and a real number θ in the range [0,1]. For each $a \in A_i$ and $b \in A_j$, if $(a \sim b)$ and $\neg((a \in A_j \wedge b \in A_i) \wedge (a \neq b))$, then there is an edge $e = (a, b) \in WE$. For each $e = (a, b) \in WE$, label(e)= 1-d(a, b). The AnnSig Partition Problem identifies a (minimal) partition P of WE such that the aggregate cluster density P $AnnSig(P) = \frac{\sum_{p\in P}(cDensity(p))}{|P|}$ is maximal.*

We model *the Annotation Signature Partition Problem* using the Vertex Coloring Graph (VCG) problem. The Vertex Coloring Graph problem assigns a color to every vertex in a graph such that adjacent vertices are colored with different colors and the number of colors is minimized; this problem has been shown to be NP-hard [13]. Each component of the shared signature of the *the Annotation Signature Partition Problem* corresponds to a color in the VCG problem. We extend a well-known approximation named the DSATUR algorithm [3] to solve the VCG to obtain a signature and compute the *AnnSigClustering* value.

AnnSigClustering is a greedy iterative algorithm, based on DSATUR algorithm [3], to solve the *Annotation Signature Partition Problem. AnnSigClustering* adds an edge to a cluster following a greedy heuristic to create clusters that maximize the cluster density. *AnnSigClustering* assigns a score to an edge e in *WE* according to the number of edges whose adjacent terms are dissimilar to the terms of e, and that have been already assigned to a cluster. Then, edges are chosen in terms of this score (descendant order). Intuitively, selecting an edge with the maximum score, allows *AnnSigClustering* to place first the edges with more restrictions; this is one for which there is a smaller set of potential clusters. The selected edge is assigned to the cluster that maximized the cluster density function. Time complexity of *AnnSigClustering* is $O(|WE|^3)$.

5 Preliminary Results

The goal of our evaluation is to validate if annotation signatures group together meaningful terms across shared annotations. Additionally, we evaluate the impact of the semantics encoded in the ontologies on the quality of the signature. We perform an evaluation of applying the *AnnSigClustering* results for link prediction. We consider two different datasets. Dataset 1 is based on a network of drugs and genetic targets and their interactions. The interactions were obtained from DrugBank [28]. The dataset has 315 drugs, 250 targets and 1306 interactions. We use 5 drug-drug similarities (Chemical-based, Ligand-based, Expression-based, Side-effect-based, and Annotation-based) and 3 target-target (Sequence-based, Protein-based and Gene Ontology-based) similarities, obtained from Perlman et al. [18]. Dataset 2 is comprised of twelve drugs within the intersection of monoclonal antibodies and antineoplastic agents; the name of the drug is followed by the abbreviation that we use in reporting results: Alemtuzumab, Bevacizumab, Brentuximab vedotin, Cetuximab, Catumaxomab, Edrecolomab, Gemtuzumab, Ipilimumab, Ofatumumab, Panitumumab, Rituximab, and Trastuzumab. The protocol to create the dataset is as follows: Each drug was used to retrieve a set of clinical trials in LinkedCT *circa* September 2011 (`linkedct.org`). Then each disease associated with each trial was linked to its corresponding term in the NCI Thesaurus version 12.05d; annotation was performed by NCIt experts. Our group of evaluators included two experts who develop databases and tools for the NCI Thesaurus, and two bioinformatics researchers with expertise on the NCIt and other biomedical ontologies.

We analyze the quality of *AnnSigClustering* predicting new iterations between drugs and targets in Dataset 1. Similarities between two drugs and two targets are considered to decide if they are or not related. We consider different thresholds between similarities drugs and targets. *AnnSigClustering* was used to compute the partition of the iterations between drugs and targets. Given a cluster, an edge between a drug and target in the cluster that was not included in the cluster was considered as a prediction. The graph density of the cluster was used as the probability that one edge was an interaction or not. We computed the Area Under the ROC Curve (AUC) to analyze the quality of our techniques. The state-of-the-art solution for this dataset is by Fakhraei et al.[8], and proposes a drug-target prediction supervised method based on PSL [4]. Table 1 shows the best result of our approach for Dataset 1. Figure 1(b) illustrates the cluster 149, the drugs DB00836 (Loperamide), DB01244 (Bepridil) and DB01100 (Pimozide) are associated with three gene targets. Predicted interactions are shown as broken edges.

Table 1. *AnnSigClustering* best result versus Fakhraei et al.[8] on the our approach prediction. Similarity drug-drug: Expression-based and target-target: Sequence-based.

Method	**AUC**	**Execution Time**
AnnSigClustering	0.9431	7 min (Intel i7 3.3 Ghz)
Fakhraei et al.[8] on this prediction	0.9269	3h + 10h of learning (Xeon 2.9 GHZ)

In Dataset 2, our challenge is to identify connectivity patterns and knowledge encoded in each component. The connectivity pattern within each cluster provides insight into the ontological relatedness of the diseases. In Figure 3(a) `Carcinoma` on the left is connected to 8 terms on the right. In Figure 3(b) is a more complex pattern, where `Sarcoma` and `Breast Neoplasm` show high betweenness centrality. `Sarcoma` on the left is connected to 9 drugs on the right, and `Breast Neoplasm` on the right is connected to 8 diseases on the left. None of the other

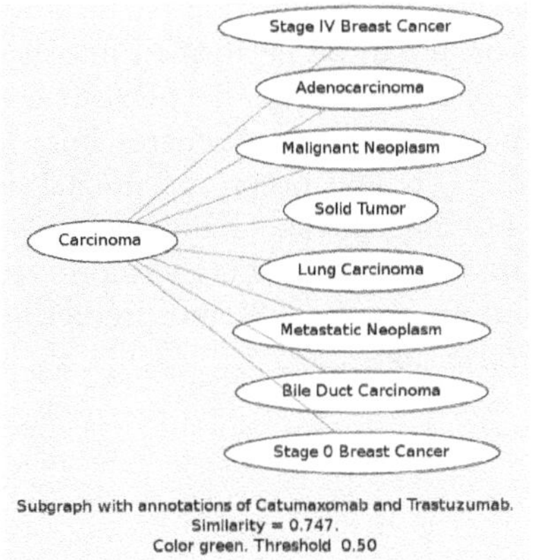

(a) Catumaxomab-Trastuzumab

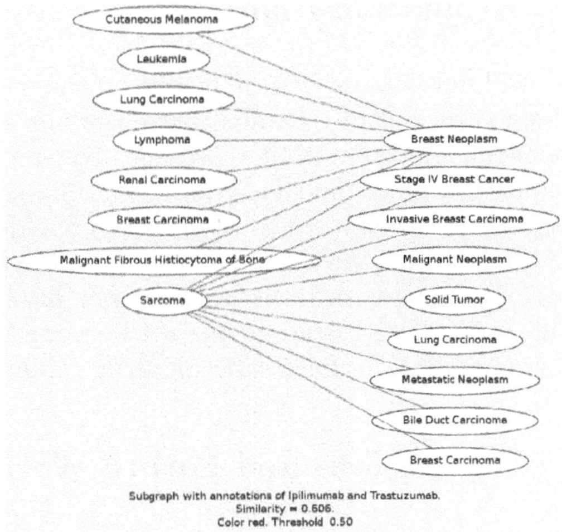

(b) Ipilimumab-Trastuzumab Red

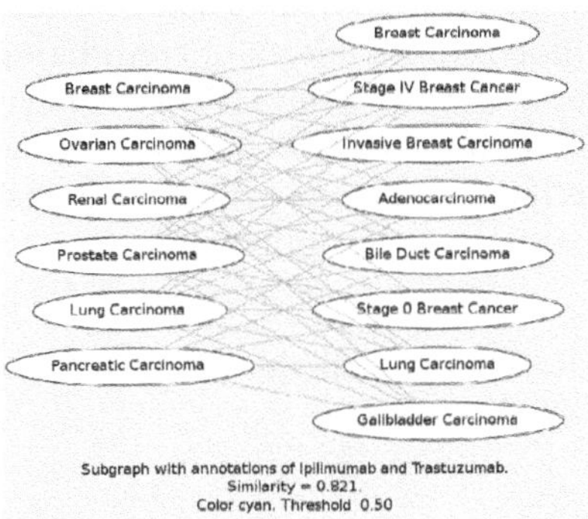

(c) Ipilimumab-Trastuzumab Cyan

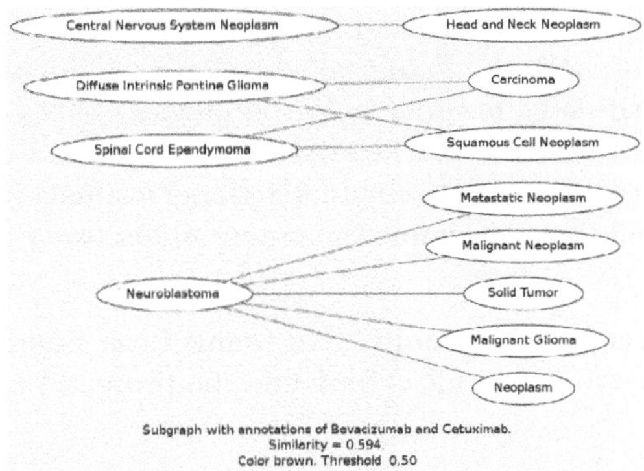

(d) Bevacizumab-Cetuximab Brown

Fig. 3. Connectivity Patterns within Each Cluster for $\theta = 0.5$

drugs has more than one adjacent drug in this subgraph. In contrast, in Figure 3(c), we see a much more general many-to-many connection pattern between the diseases on the left and right. Finally, Figure 3(d) shows a more complex connectivity pattern where the terms are ontologically related but they are placed within three disconnected graphs. The four terms `Diffuse Intrinsic Pontine Glioma`, `Spinal Cord Ependymoma`, `Carcinoma` and `Squamous Cell Neoplasm` form the most well connected cluster. Comments from the evaluators noted that while groups such as Figure 3(a) that included generic terms such as `Carcinoma` were valid, they did not convey useful information. In contrast, groups in Figures 3(c) and (d), that had more specific terms and were more densely connected, had the potential to be more meaningful.

6 Evaluation Plan

We will develop a semantic metric by the many-to-many connection pattern between two concepts. Evaluation of the our approach will be performed in other biomedical datasets that represent diverse type of relationships between drugs, diseases, targets, and enzymes. Our mining methods will use general knowledge base and ontologies as OpenCyc[1] and Yago [11] and other specialized as SNOMED CT[2]. We will develop a algorithm for learning threshold and a machine learning framework to obtain semantically related structures. Furthermore, we will compare with state-of-the-art learning-based approaches [7] and predicting system as PSL [4] for predicting drug-target interactions.

7 Conclusions and Future Work

We showed the feasibility of mining patterns semantically related in the LOD. We have defined the *Annotation Signature Partitioning Problem* and the *AnnSigClustering* algorithm to develop the components of a signature based on shared annotations and ontological relatedness. We have analyzed the effects of considering knowledge encoded in the ontologies used to annotate Linked Data. We have identified clusters can be used for link prediction and discover complex patterns. In the future we plan to conduct a deeper evaluation, as indicated in the previous section, and thus determine the potential discovery capability of the approach.

Acknowledgment. We thank Prof. Louiqa Raschid for all the insightful discussions and ideas to define the proposed approach.

References

1. Bauer, F., Kaltenbock, M.: Linked Open Data: The Essentials. edition mono/monochrom (2013)
2. Benik, J., Chang, C., Raschid, L., Vidal, M.-E., Palma, G., Thor, A.: Finding cross genome patterns in annotation graphs. In: Bodenreider, O., Rance, B. (eds.) DILS 2012. LNCS, vol. 7348, pp. 21–36. Springer, Heidelberg (2012)
3. Brélaz, D.: New methods to color vertices of a graph. Commun. ACM 22(4) (1979)
4. Broecheler, M., Mihalkova, L., Getoor, L.: Probabilistic similarity logic. In: Conference on Uncertainty in Artificial Intelligence (2010)
5. Brohee, S., van Helden, J.: Evaluation of clustering algorithms for protein-protein interaction networks. BMC Bioinformatics 7(1), 488 (2006)
6. Cook, D.J., Holder, L.B.: Mining graph data. Wiley-Blackwell (2007)
7. Ding, H., Takigawa, I., Mamitsuka, H., Zhu, S.: Similarity-based machine learning methods for predicting drug–target interactions: a brief review. Briefings in bioinformatics, bbt056 (2013)

[1] `http://www.cyc.com/platform/opencyc`

[2] `http://www.ihtsdo.org/snomed-ct/`

8. Fakhraei, S., Raschid, L., Getoor, L.: Drug-target interaction prediction for drug repurposing with probabilistic similarity logic. In: ACM SIGKDD International Workshop on Data Mining in Bioinformatics, BIOKDD (2013)
9. Fortunato, S.: Community detection in graphs. Physics Reports 486(3-5), 75–174 (2010)
10. Giles, C.L.: The future of citeSeer: CiteSeer^x. In: Fürnkranz, J., Scheffer, T., Spiliopoulou, M. (eds.) PKDD 2006. LNCS (LNAI), vol. 4213, pp. 2–2. Springer, Heidelberg (2006)
11. Hoffart, J., Suchanek, F.M., Berberich, K., Lewis-Kelham, E., De Melo, G., Weikum, G.: Yago2: exploring and querying world knowledge in time, space, context, and many languages. In: Proceedings of the 20th International Conference Companion on World Wide Web, pp. 229–232. ACM (2011)
12. Ji, M., Sun, Y., Danilevsky, M., Han, J., Gao, J.: Graph regularized transductive classification on heterogeneous information networks. In: Balcázar, J.L., Bonchi, F., Gionis, A., Sebag, M. (eds.) ECML PKDD 2010, Part I. LNCS, vol. 6321, pp. 570–586. Springer, Heidelberg (2010)
13. Karp, R.: Reducibility among combinatorial problems. In: Miller, R., Thatcher, J. (eds.) Complexity of Computer Computations, pp. 85–103. Plenum Press (1972)
14. McInnes, B., Pedersen, T., Pakhomov, S.: Umls-interface and umls-similarity: Open source software for measuring paths and semantic similarity. In: Proceedings of the AMIA Symposium, pp. 431–435 (2009)
15. Mencıa, E.L., Holthausen, S., Schulz, A., Janssen, F.: Using data mining on linked open data for analyzing e-procurement information. In: Proceedings of the International Workshop on Data Mining on Linked Data, with Linked Data Mining Challenge collocated with the European Conference on Machine Learning and Principles and Practice of Knowledge Discovery in Databases, ECMLPKDD 2013 (2013)
16. Mougel, P.-N., Plantevit, M., Rigotti, C., Gandrillon, O., Boulicaut, J.-F.: Constraint-based mining of sets of cliques sharing vertex properties. In: Workshop on Analysis of Complex NEtworks (ACNE 2010) Co-Located with ECML/PKDD. Citeseer (2010)
17. Palma, G., Vidal, M.E., Haag, E., Raschid, L., Thor, A.: Measuring relatedness between scientific entities in annotation datasets. In: Proceedings of the International Conference on Bioinformatics, Computational Biology and Biomedical Informatics, p. 367. ACM (2013)
18. Perlman, L., Gottlieb, A., Atias, N., Ruppin, E., Sharan, R.: Combining drug and gene similarity measures for drug-target elucidation. Journal of Computational Biology 18(2), 133–145 (2011)
19. Resnik, P.: Semantic similarity in a taxonomy: An information-based measure and its application to problems of ambiguity in natural language. Journal Of Artificial Intelligence Research 11, 95–130 (1999)
20. Saha, B., Hoch, A., Khuller, S., Raschid, L., Zhang, X.-N.: Dense subgraphs with restrictions and applications to gene annotation graphs. In: Berger, B. (ed.) RECOMB 2010. LNCS, vol. 6044, pp. 456–472. Springer, Heidelberg (2010)
21. Schwartz, J., Steger, A., Weißl, A.: Fast algorithms for weighted bipartite matching. In: Nikoletseas, S.E. (ed.) WEA 2005. LNCS, vol. 3503, pp. 476–487. Springer, Heidelberg (2005)
22. Shavitt, Y., Weinsberg, E., Weinsberg, U.: Estimating peer similarity using distance of shared files. In: International workshop on peer-to-peer systems (IPTPS), vol. 104 (2010)
23. Shi, C., Kong, X., Yu, P.S., Xie, S., Wu, B.: Relevance search in heterogeneous networks. In: EDBT, pp. 180–191 (2012)

24. Sun, Y., Han, J., Yan, X., Yu, P.S., Wu, T.: Pathsim: Meta path-based top-k similarity search in heterogeneous information networks. PVLDB 4(11), 992–1003 (2011)
25. Sun, Y., Han, J., Zhao, P., Yin, Z., Cheng, H., Wu, T.: Rankclus: integrating clustering with ranking for heterogeneous information network analysis. In: Proceedings of the 12th EDBT. ACM (2009)
26. Thor, A., Anderson, P., Raschid, L., Navlakha, S., Saha, B., Khuller, S., Zhang, X.-N.: Link prediction for annotation graphs using graph summarization. In: ISWC, pp. 714–729 (2011)
27. Von Luxburg, U.: A tutorial on spectral clustering. Statistics and computing 17(4), 395–416 (2007)
28. Wishart, D.S., Knox, C., Guo, A.C., Cheng, D., Shrivastava, S., Tzur, D., Gautam, B., Hassanali, M.: Drugbank: a knowledgebase for drugs, drug actions and drug targets. Nucleic acids research 36(suppl. 1), D901–D906 (2008)

Predicting SPARQL Query Performance and Explaining Linked Data*

Rakebul Hasan

INRIA Sophia Antipolis, Wimmics, 2004 route des Lucioles - B.P. 93, 06902 Sophia-Antipolis Cedex, France,
hasan.rakebul@inria.fr

Abstract. As the complexity of the Semantic Web increases, efficient ways to query the Semantic Web data is becoming increasingly important. Moreover, consumers of the Semantic Web data may need explanations for debugging or understanding the reasoning behind producing the data. In this paper, firstly we address the problem of SPARQL query performance prediction. Secondly we discuss how to explain Linked Data in a decentralized fashion. Finally we discuss how to summarize the explanations.

Keywords: #eswcphd2014Hasan, query performance, explanation, summarization.

1 Introduction

As the complexity of the Semantic Web increases, it is becoming increasingly important to develop efficient ways to query the Semantic Web data [18]. Central to this problem is knowing how a query will behave prior to executing it [15]. Moreover, data publishers publish their data in an interlinked fashion using vocabularies defined in RDFS/OWL [7]. This presents opportunities for large-scale data integration and reasoning over cross-domain data. In such a distributed scenario, consumers of these data may need explanations for debugging or understanding the reasoning behind producing the data; they may need the possibility to transform long explanations into more understandable short explanations [4,21].

In this paper, firstly we address the problem of SPARQL query performance prediction. Inspired by database research for accurate query performance prediction [2,13,14], we use machine learning techniques to predict SPARQL query execution time. Secondly we propose a decentralized solution to explanation for Linked Data. We discuss how to explain Linked Data in a decentralized fashion and how to summarize the explanations.

The structure of the rest of this paper is as follows: in section 2, we present the state of the art on related work. In section 3, we present the problems we address and our contributions. In section 4, we present our approach to the problems we

* Advisors: Fabien Gandon and Pierre-Antoine Champin.

V. Presutti et al. (Eds.): ESWC 2014, LNCS 8465, pp. 795–805, 2014.

address. In section 5 we present our preliminary results. In section 6 we present our future evaluation plan. Finally, we conclude in section 7.

2 State of the Art

Recent work on predicting database query performance [2,13,14] has argued that the analytical costs models used by the current generation query optimizers are good for comparing alternative query plans, but ineffective for predicting actual query performance metrics such as query execution time. Analytical cost models are unable to capture the complexities of modern database systems [2]. To address this, database researchers have experimented with machine learning techniques to learn query performance metrics. Ganapathi *et al.* [13] use Kernel Canonical Correlation Analysis (KCCA) to predict a set of performance metrics. For the individual query elapsed time performance metric, they were able to predict within 20% of the actual query elapsed time for 85% of the test queries. Gupta *et al.* [14] use machine learning for predicting query execution time ranges on a data warehouse and achieve an accuracy of 80%. Akdere *et al.* [2] study the effectiveness of machine learning techniques for predicting query latency of static and dynamic workload scenarios. They argue that query performance prediction using machine learning is both feasible and effective.

Related to the Semantic Web query processing, SPARQL query engines can be categorized into two categories: SQL-based and RDF native query engines [28]. SQL-based query engines rely on relational database systems storage and query optimization techniques to efficiently evaluate SPARQL queries. They suffer from the same problems mentioned above. Furthermore, due to the absence of schematic structure in RDF, cost-based approaches – successful in relational database systems – do not perform well in SPARQL query processing [28]. RDF native query engines typically use heuristics and statistics about the data for selecting efficient query execution plans [27]. Heuristics-based optimization techniques include exploiting syntactic and structural variations of triple patterns in a query [27], and rewriting a query using algebraic optimization techniques [12] and transformation rules [15]. Heuristics-based optimization techniques generally work without any knowledge of the underlying data. Stocker *et al.* [27] present optimization techniques with pre-computed statistics for reordering triple patterns in a SPARQL query for efficient query processing. However, in many use-cases involving querying Linked Data, statistics are often missing [28]. This makes these statistics-based approaches ineffective in the Linked Data scenario. Furthermore, as in the case of relation database systems, these existing approaches are unable to predict actual query performance metrics such as query execution time for a given configuration.

Related to explanations for the Semantic Web, Inference Web [20,21] explanation infrastructure addresses the explanation requirements of Semantic Web applications and exposes its explanation metadata in RDF using Proof Markup Language (PML) [26]. Inference Web provides a set of software tools for building, presenting, maintaining, and manipulating PML proofs. Inference Web provides a centralized registry based solution for publishing explanation metadata from distributed reasoners. The WIQA (Web Information Quality Assessment) framework [6] and KOIOS semantic search engine [11] provide explanations of their reasoning and expose their explanation metadata in RDF. However, they provide application specific explanations which include process descriptions of specific algorithms. Although researchers [4,21] highlighted the need for short explanations, previous work has not addressed the problem of providing short explanations. But researchers have studied ontology summarization. A notable work on ontology summarization is RDF sentence graph-based summarization [29]. This work extracts and summarizes RDF sentences based on centrality measures.

3 Problem Statement and Contributions

We address the problems of SPARQL query performance prediction and explaining reasoning over Linked Data. Our aim is to assisting users in querying and consuming Linked Data. In querying Linked Data, we provide performance related information to help understand how a query may behave. Users can use this information for query construction and refinement, workload management, and query scheduling. Also, SPARQL query optimizers can use our prediction models for query plan selection. In consuming Linked Data, we explain how a given piece of data was derived. Users can use such explanations to understand and debug Linked Data. In contrast to the previous work, we propose a decentralized solution to address explanations in the distributed setting of Linked Data. Our explanations are suitable for generic Linked Data scenarios; unlike WIQA and KOIOS. Finally, we address the problem of summarizing explanations. The main goal of summarizing explanations is twofold: (a) providing a brief overview of the background information used in the reasoning, (b) providing an entry point to the full explanation. Our approach is similar to sentence graph summarization. However, we define new measures for summarizing explanations. As an application of our research, we aim to apply our methodologies and strategies for processing and explaining distributed queries on Linked Data.

4 Research Methodology and Approach

4.1 Predicting SPARQL Query Performance

To predict query performance metrics prior to query execution, we apply machine learning techniques on the logs of executed queries. We work with query execution time as the query performance metric. We treat the SPARQL engine as a black box and learn query behaviors from the behaviors of already executed queries. This approach does not require any statistics of the underlying RDF data, which makes it ideal for the Linked Data scenario. A key challenge in applying machine learning for SPARQL query performance prediction is to represent SPARQL queries as feature vectors. We use the frequencies and the

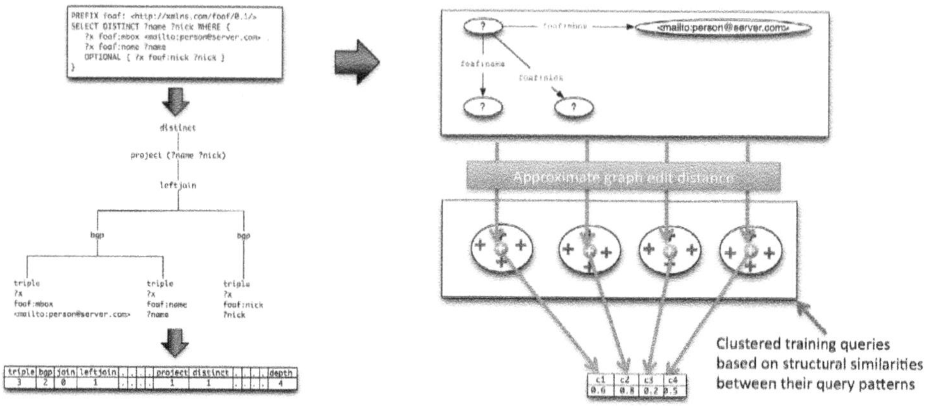

Fig. 1. Example of extracting SPARQL feature vector from a SPARQL query

cardinalities of SPARQL algebra operators[1] of a query as its features. Additionally, to represent the query patterns as features, we first cluster the training queries based on the structural similarities between the graphs constructed from the query patterns of the training queries. Each dimension of the query pattern feature vector for a query is the structural similarity score between the graph represented by the query pattern belonging to a cluster center query and the graph represented by the query pattern belonging to the query. We use a polynomial time suboptimal solution of approximate graph edit distance problem [24] to compute the structural similarities between the graphs represented by query patterns. We use the k-mediods [19] clustering algorithm with approximate graph edit distance as the distance function to cluster the training queries. Figure 1 shows an example of extracting the feature vector from a SPARQL query. We experiment on predicting query execution times using the support vector machine regression (SVR) [25] with the SPARQL algebra features, using SVR with SPARQL algebra and query pattern features, using multiple SVRs for queries with different execution time ranges with SPARQL algebra and query pattern features, and finally a single k-nearest neighbors regression (k-NN) [3] with SPARQL algebra and query pattern features. We describe the results of our experiments in section 5.1.

4.2 Generating and Summarizing Explanations

We follow the Linked Data principles [5] to publish explanation metadata. We describe these metadata using our proposed vocabulary *Ratio4TA*[2]. We generate explanations by retrieving the explanation metatada by following their

[1] `http://www.w3.org/TR/sparql11-query/#sparqlQuery`
[2] `http://ns.inria.fr/ratio4ta/`

dereferenceable URIs and presenting them in a human understandable form. We define *Ratio4TA* as an extension of the W3C PROV Ontology[3]. This promotes interoperability by enabling data consumers to process explanation metadata according to W3C PROV standards. *Ratio4TA* allows describing data, reasoning processes, results, data derivations, rules, and software applications. We use the named graph mechanism [8] to make statements about RDF triples. Using named graph allows us to associate explanation metadata for data with different levels of granularity – explanation metadata for a triple or a graph containing more than one triple. Furthermore, we use named graphs to group together explanation metadata and make the metadata for an explanation referenceable by a single URI. We opt for our own vocabulary because the prominent previous work PML has limitations with respect to Linked Data common practices. PML uses RDF container concepts. RDF containers use blank nodes to connect a sequence of items [1]. However, as a common practice, blank nodes are avoided while publishing Linked Data [17].

We define five measures to summarize explanations: salience (S_{SL}), similarity (S_{SM}), abstractness (S_{AB}), salience with respect to proof tree (S_{ST}), and coherence (S_{CO}). We compute salience of an RDF statement by combining the normalized degree centrality scores of the subject and the object of the statement. We use the measures salience, similarity, and abstractness for ranking. For the similarity measure, users can specify a set of concepts as their explanation filtering criteria. We rank the more similar statements to the concepts given in filtering criteria higher. We use the approximate query solving feature of Corese [10] for similarity computations. For abstractness, we consider a statement that is close to the root in corresponding proof tree is more abstract than a statement that is far from the root. We use salience with respect to proof tree and coherence measures to re-rank already ranked statements. We compute salience with respect to proof tree for an RDF statement by taking the average score (computed using combinations of ranking measures) of all statements of the tree that the statement roots in the corresponding proof tree. Finally we consider an RDF statement to be coherent to an RDF statement if the first statement is directly derived from the second statement. We summarize the RDF statements in an explanation using combinations of these measures.

5 Preliminary Results

5.1 Query Performance Prediction Results

We randomly select 6000 queries from DBPSB [22] DBpedia[4] query log dataset. Then we run them on a locally loaded DBpedia 3.8 into a Jena TDB triple store[5] to record their execution times. We split the 6000 queries into 60% training, 20% validation, and 20% test splits. We use R^2 (coefficient of determination)

[3] `http://www.w3.org/TR/prov-o/`

[4] `http://dbpedia.org`

[5] Jena TDB: `http://jena.apache.org/documentation/tdb`

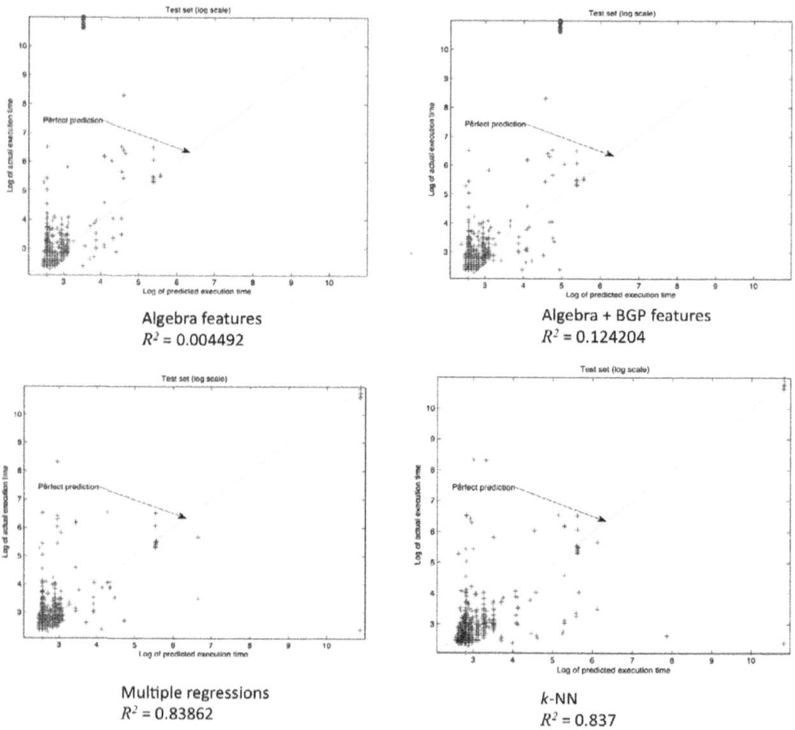

Fig. 2. Comparison of learning methods

values to evaluate our regression predictions. R^2 measures how well the regression approximates the real data points. An R^2 value of 1 means that the regression perfectly fits the data. Figure 2 shows log-log plots of the predicted and actual query execution times for the test queries for different learning methods we experimented with. Our first experiment using SVR with only SPARQL algebra features performs poorly with a low R^2 value of 0.004492. We experiment with another SVR using SPARQL algebra features and query pattern features. The R^2 value improves to 0.124204 which is still very low with outliers – highlighted in red – far from the perfect prediction line. A possible reason for this is the fact that our training dataset has queries with various different time ranges. Fitting a curve in such irregular data points is often inaccurate. To address this, we first split our training data according to execution time ranges, then we train different regressions for different time ranges. We cluster the training data into X clusters based on the execution times using x-means [23] clustering algorithm. We use x-means because it automatically chooses the number of clusters. We then train X number of SVM regressions with training queries corresponding to cluster for each regression. As features, we use SPARQL algebra and query pattern features. Then we train a Support Vector Machine (SVM) classifier [9] with a training dataset containing all the training queries and the cluster number of each query as the label for the queries. For an unseen query, we first predict the cluster for the query using the SVM classifier, then we predict the execution time using the SVM regression that corresponds to the predicted cluster for that query. The accuracy of the SVM classifier on our test dataset is 96.0833%. This means that we can accurately predict the execution time ranges of unseen queries. The overall R^2 value on our test dataset with this approach jumps to 0.83862. This is demonstrated by the long running queries moving very close to the perfect prediction line. Also more queries moved towards the perfect prediction line than before. In our final experiment, we train the regression variant of k-NN algorithm with SPARQL algebra and query pattern features. We achieve an R^2 value of 0.837 on the test dataset. The result of k-NN and multiple regressions are almost same. However, the complexity of training the k-NN regression is less. Also the concentration of the short running queries near the perfect prediction line is more for k-NN.

5.2 Explanation Summarization Results

We evaluate our summarization approach by comparing the summarized explanations generated by our approach and ground truth summarized explanations generated by humans. We obtained our ground truths by surveying 24 people from different backgrounds. We used three test cases – three queries with their results along with the explanations for the results. Each query result is an inferred statement by our reasoner. Each test case has two scenarios: without filtering criteria FL, and with filtering criteria FL. Each participant answered questions for one test case. We randomly assigned a test case to a participant. We ask the participants to rate, from a scale of 1 to 5, the need for each of the statements in the explanation. For, the scenario with filtering criteria FL, we give the query, the answer, and the explanation but with a user's filtering criteria class taken from the schemata used in the reasoning process. The explanations, the questionnaires, the responses, and the results of the evaluation are publicly available online[6]. We evaluate different combinations of the summarization measures we define. For the scenario without FL, we also compare our summaries to sentence graph summarization – denoted as S_{SG}. We evaluate evaluate summaries of different sizes by measuring *F-score* for summarized explanations with different compression ratios, CR. To generate the ground truth summarized explanation for an explanation, we include a statement in the ground truth summarized explanation if its rating is greater than or equal to the average rating of all the statements in the original explanation. *F-scores* reflects the accuracy of automatically generated summaries with respect to the ground truth summary. A desirable situation would be a summarized explanation with high *F-score* and low CR. Figure 3 shows the average *F-scores* for different measure combinations for summaries with different sizes for the three test cases. The *x-axis* represents compression ratio CR. The *y-axis* represents *F-scores*. For the scenario without FL, the best *F-score* is 0.72 when CR value is 0.33 by the measure combinations

[6] `http://ns.inria.fr/ratio4ta/sm/`

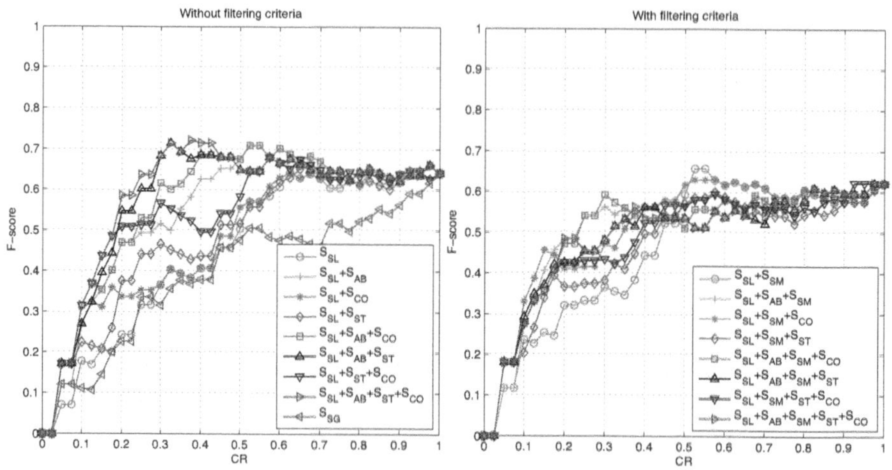

Fig. 3. Compression ratio (CR) vs *F-score*

$S_{SL} + S_{AB} + S_{ST}$ and $S_{SL} + S_{AB} + S_{ST} + S_{CO}$. This is a desirable situation with a high *F-score* and low CR. The sentence graph summarization performs poorly with a best *F-score* value of 0.34 in the CR interval 0.05 to 0.3. For the scenario with FL, the best *F-score* is 0.66 at CR values 0.53 and 0.55 by the measure combination$S_{SL} + S_{SM}$. However, the *F-score* 0.6 at CR value 0.3 by the measure combination $S_{SL} + S_{AB} + S_{SM} + S_{CO}$ is more desirable because the size of the summary is smaller. As expected, our summarization approach perform worse in the scenario with FL where we use S_{SM}. This is due to the fact that the survey participants had to consider the highly subjective factor of similarity. An overview of our work on generating and summarizing explanations for Linked Data is available in [16].

6 Evaluation Plan

Our future plan includes evaluating three more aspects. First, we would like to evaluate our prediction methods using SPARQL benchmark queries. DBPSB includes 25 query templates for evaluating SPARQL engines with DBPedia dataset. Our aim would be to generate training, validation, and test datasets from these query templates and evaluating our approach using them. Second, we would like to evaluate our prediction methods for query plan selection for SPARQL query processing over Linked Data. A possible direction for this would to use our query performance prediction approach for selecting efficient query plans in federated SPARQL query processing. Third, we will evaluate the impact of explanations and summarized explanations on end-users for a selected domain.

7 Conclusion

In this paper, firstly we study the techniques to predict SPARQL query performance. We learn query execution times from query history using machine learning techniques. This approach does not require any statistics of the underlying RDF data, which makes it ideal for the Linked Data scenario. We achieved high accuracy ($R^2 = 0.84$) for predicting query execution time.

Secondly we discuss how to generate and summarize explanations for Linked Data. We present an ontology to describe explanation metadata and discuss publishing explanation metadata as Linked Data. In addition, we presented five summarization measures to summarize explanations. We evaluate different combinations of these measures. The evaluation shows that our approach produces high quality rankings for summarizing explanation statements. Our summarized explanations are also highly accurate with *F-score* values ranging from 0.6 to 0.72 for small summaries. Our approach outperforms the sentence graph based ontology summarization approach.

Acknowledgments. This work is supported by the ANR CONTINT program under the Kolflow project (ANR-2010-CORD-021-02).

References

1. RDF semantics. W3C recommendation (2004)
2. Akdere, M., Cetintemel, U., Riondato, M., Upfal, E., Zdonik, S.: Learning-based query performance modeling and prediction. In: 2012 IEEE 28th International Conference on Data Engineering (ICDE), pp. 390–401 (2012)
3. Altman, N.: An introduction to kernel and nearest-neighbor nonparametric regression. The American Statistician 46(3), 175–185 (1992)
4. Angele, J., Moench, E., Oppermann, H., Staab, S., Wenke, D.: Ontology-based query and answering in chemistry: Ontonova project halo. In: Fensel, D., Sycara, K., Mylopoulos, J. (eds.) ISWC 2003. LNCS, vol. 2870, pp. 913–928. Springer, Heidelberg (2003)
5. Berners-Lee, T.: Linked Data. W3C Design Issues (2006), `http://www.w3.org/DesignIssues/LinkedData.html`
6. Bizer, C.: Quality-Driven Information Filtering in the Context of Web-Based Information Systems. Ph.D. thesis, Freie Universität Berlin, Universitätsbibliothek (2007)
7. Bonatti, P.A., Hogan, A., Polleres, A., Sauro, L.: Robust and scalable linked data reasoning incorporating provenance and trust annotations. Web Semantics: Science, Services and Agents on the World Wide Web 9(2), 165–201 (2011)
8. Carroll, J.J., Bizer, C., Hayes, P., Stickler, P.: Named graphs, provenance and trust. In: Proceedings of the 14th International Conference on World Wide Web, WWW 2005, pp. 613–622. ACM, New York (2005)
9. Chang, C.C., Lin, C.J.: LIBSVM: A library for support vector machines. ACM Transactions on Intelligent Systems and Technology 2, 27:1–27:27 (2011), `http://www.csie.ntu.edu.tw/~cjlin/libsvm`

10. Corby, O., Dieng-Kuntz, R., Gandon, F., Faron-Zucker, C.: Searching the Semantic Web: approximate query processing based on ontologies. IEEE Intelligent Systems 21(1), 20–27 (2006)
11. Forcher, B., Sintek, M., Roth-Berghofer, T., Dengel, A.: Explanation-aware system design of the semantic search engine koios. In: Proc. of the the 5th Int'l. Workshop on Explanation-aware Computing (2010)
12. Frasincar, F., Houben, G.J., Vdovjak, R., Barna, P.: RAL: An algebra for querying RDF. World Wide Web 7(1), 83–109 (2004)
13. Ganapathi, A., Kuno, H., Dayal, U., Wiener, J.L., Fox, A., Jordan, M., Patterson, D.: Predicting multiple metrics for queries: Better decisions enabled by machine learning. In: Proceedings of the 2009 IEEE International Conference on Data Engineering, ICDE 2009, pp. 592–603. IEEE Computer Society, Washington, DC (2009)
14. Gupta, C., Mehta, A., Dayal, U.: PQR: Predicting query execution times for autonomous workload management. In: Proceedings of the 2008 International Conference on Autonomic Computing, ICAC 2008, pp. 13–22. IEEE Computer Society, Washington, DC (2008)
15. Hartig, O., Heese, R.: The sparql query graph model for query optimization. In: Franconi, E., Kifer, M., May, W. (eds.) ESWC 2007. LNCS, vol. 4519, pp. 564–578. Springer, Heidelberg (2007)
16. Hasan, R.: Generating and summarizing explanations for linked data. In: Proc. of the 11th Extended Semantic Web Conference (to appear 2014)
17. Heath, T., Bizer, C.: Linked Data: Evolving the Web into a Global Data Space, 1st edn. Morgan & Claypool (2011), `http://linkeddatabook.com/`
18. Huang, J., Abadi, D.J., Ren, K.: Scalable SPARQL querying of large RDF graphs. Proceedings of the VLDB Endowment 4(11), 1123–1134 (2011)
19. Kaufman, L., Rousseeuw, P.: Clustering by means of medoids. In: Dodge, Y. (ed.) Statistical Data Analysis based on the L1 Norm, pp. 405–416 (1987)
20. McGuinness, D., Furtado, V., da Pinheiro Silva, P., Ding, L., Glass, A., Chang, C.: Explaining semantic web applications. In: Semantic Web Engineering in the Knowledge Society (2008)
21. McGuinness, D., da Pinheiro Silva, P.: Explaining answers from the semantic web: the inference web approach. Web Semantics: Science, Services and Agents on the World Wide Web 1(4), 397–413 (2004)
22. Morsey, M., Lehmann, J., Auer, S., Ngonga Ngomo, A.-C.: DBpedia SPARQL benchmark – performance assessment with real queries on real data. In: Aroyo, L., Welty, C., Alani, H., Taylor, J., Bernstein, A., Kagal, L., Noy, N., Blomqvist, E. (eds.) ISWC 2011, Part I. LNCS, vol. 7031, pp. 454–469. Springer, Heidelberg (2011)
23. Pelleg, D., Moore, A.W.: X-means: Extending K-means with efficient estimation of the number of clusters. In: Proceedings of the Seventeenth International Conference on Machine Learning, ICML 2000, pp. 727–734. Morgan Kaufmann, San Francisco (2000)
24. Riesen, K., Bunke, H.: Approximate graph edit distance computation by means of bipartite graph matching. Image Vision Comput. 27(7), 950–959 (2009)
25. Shevade, S.K., Keerthi, S.S., Bhattacharyya, C., Murthy, K.R.K.: Improvements to the SMO algorithm for SVM regression. IEEE Transactions on Neural Networks 11(5), 1188–1193 (2000)
26. da Pinheiro Silva, P., McGuinness, D., Fikes, R.: A proof markup language for semantic web services. Information Systems 31(4-5), 381–395 (2006)

27. Stocker, M., Seaborne, A., Bernstein, A., Kiefer, C., Reynolds, D.: SPARQL basic graph pattern optimization using selectivity estimation. In: Proceedings of the 17th International Conference on World Wide Web, WWW 2008, pp. 595–604. ACM, New York (2008)
28. Tsialiamanis, P., Sidirourgos, L., Fundulaki, I., Christophides, V., Boncz, P.: Heuristics-based query optimisation for SPARQL. In: Proceedings of the 15th International Conference on Extending Database Technology, EDBT 2012, pp. 324–335. ACM, New York (2012)
29. Zhang, X., Cheng, G., Qu, Y.: Ontology summarization based on RDF sentence graph. In: Proceedings of the 16th International Conference on World Wide Web, WWW 2007, pp. 707–716. ACM, New York (2007)

Metrics-Driven Framework for LOD Quality Assessment

Behshid Behkamal

Ferdowsi University of Mashhad, Mashhad, Iran
Behkamal@stu.um.ac.ir

Abstract. The main objective of the Linked Open Data paradigm is to crystallize knowledge through the interlinking of already existing but dispersed data. The usefulness of the developed knowledge depends strongly on the quality of the aggregated and published data. Researchers have observed many challenges with the quality of Linked Open Data; therefore, our main objective in this thesis is to propose a metric-driven framework for evaluating the inherent quality dimensions of datasets before they are published as a viable part of the linked open data cloud.

Keywords: #eswcphd2014Behkamal.

1 Introduction

Linked Open Data (LOD) provides a distributed model for the semantic Web that allows any data provider to publish its publicly available data and meaningfully link them with other information sources over the Web. The main goal of the LOD initiative is to create knowledge by interlinking dispersed data. It is undeniable that the realization of this goal depends strongly on the quality of the published data. Therefore, quality evaluation is an important issue that must be addressed with the objective of helping data providers to evaluate their data before publishing as a dataset in the LOD cloud.

In the area of data quality assessment, researchers have developed several frameworks, metrics and tools to evaluate data quality in general. For example, [1] describes subjective and objective assessments of data quality and presents three functional forms for developing objective data quality metrics. In [2], the authors have proposed a methodology for the assessment of organizational Information Quality (IQ), which consists of a questionnaire to measure IQ. In the area of the methodologies for data quality assessment, [3] provides a comparative description of existing methodologies and provides a comprehensive comparison of these methodologies. Also, the database community has developed a number of approaches such as user experience, expert judgment, sampling, parsing and cleansing techniques [4, 5] for measuring and enhancing data quality.

While data quality is an important requirement for the successful organic growth of the LOD, only a very limited number of research initiatives exist, which focus on data quality for the Semantic Web and specifically for LOD. Based on our practical experience in publishing linked data [6], we have observed that many of the published

V. Presutti et al. (Eds.): ESWC 2014, LNCS 8465, pp. 806–816, 2014.

datasets suffer from quality issues such as syntax errors, redundant instances, and incorrect/incomplete attribute values. One of the better strategies to avoid such issues is to evaluate the quality of a dataset before it is published on the LOD cloud. This will help publishers to filter out low-quality data based on the quality assessment results, which in turn enables data consumers to make better and more informed decisions when using the shared datasets.

2 State of the Art

Here we primarily focus on data quality with respect to Semantic Web and LOD, but also briefly touch upon quality assessment frameworks as relevant to our work.

2.1 Information Quality (IQ) Frameworks and Quality Models

Many attempts have been made to compile and classify information quality criteria with different goals in mind. Naumann identifies three different kinds of classifications including goal-oriented models; semantic-oriented models; and processing-oriented models [4]. Since we are going to extract inherent quality dimensions and customize them for LOD, we have systematically reviewed the semantics-oriented quality models and frameworks focusing on those models proposing inherent or intrinsic quality characteristics [7-10]. Given the models presented in [7] and [10] are proposed specifically for databases and data warehousing, they cannot be applied directly to our work. Only [9] investigates the quality dimensions in the context of our work which classifies the quality dimensions and criteria proposed by other researches in the LOD domain. Also, ISO 25012[8] is a general data quality model which defines quality dimensions from inherent and system dependent viewpoints.

2.2 Data Quality in the Context of Semantic Web and Linked Data

Despite its importance, data quality has only recently being receiving attention from the Semantic Web community. Most of related works in the context of quality assessment of LOD investigate the quality problems of the published datasets. For example, the authors of [11] have proposed a comprehensive approach that classifies quality problems of the published linked datasets and discuss common errors in RDF publishing, their consequences for applications, along with possible publisher-oriented approaches to improve the quality of machine-readable and open data on the Web. In another work, Furber and Hepp propose an approach to evaluate the quality of datasets using SPARQL queries in order to identify quality problems. Using this approach, the authors identify quality problems of already available datasets such as Geonames and DBPedia [12]. There are also a number of works focusing on the quality evaluation of ontologies [13] that we have not investigated them, because our aim is the quality evaluation of datasets.

Furthermore, some tools are developed for identifying common syntax errors in RDF documents in two groups of online validators, e.g. URIDebugger [14] and

Vapour [15], and command line validatores, such as Jena Eyeball[16] and VRP [17]. Generally, all of these works primarily focus on data quality problems in published datasets, and none of them provides a solution for identifying the quality problems before the data is published. In this paper, we argue the importance of applying a quality model for assessing the quality of a given dataset before its publications a part of the linked open data cloud.

3 Problem Statement and Contribution

Although data quality is an important issue for the successful organic growth of the Web of Data, there are only a very limited number of research initiatives that focus on data quality for the Semantic Web and specifically for the Web of Data. Based on our practical experience in publishing linked data [6], we have recognized that many of the published datasets suffer from quality deficiencies, most of which are related to inherent quality aspects of a dataset and not the context of other datasets. Thus one of the better strategies to avoid quality issues of the published datasets is to assess the quality of a dataset before release. This will help publishers to filter out low-quality data based on quality assessment results, which in turn enables data consumers to make better and more informed decisions when using shared datasets.

Therefore, the objective of our work is to propose a metrics-driven framework that enables the automatic assessment of the quality of dataset before they are publicly published. For this purpose, we will explore the structural characteristics of data published in LOD cloud as well as the quality deficiencies of dataset itself. In other words, we will try to observe and clearly formulate a set of metrics that are quantitatively measurable for a given dataset. We will then try to find meaningful statistical correlations between the proposed metrics and inherent quality dimensions (that are not directly measurable) through empirical observational studies. Based on the correlations, we will create a framework that will be able to predict the inherent quality dimensions of datasets by only observing their measurable metrics.

For this purpose, we have identified the characteristics of data published on the LOD cloud to extract the inherent quality dimensions and propose a set of metrics, which are quantitatively measurable for a given dataset. This way, we are able to assess inherent quality characteristics of datasets before publishing the data by observing the measured values of the relevant metrics. The novel contributions of our work can be summarized as follows:

- We clearly identify a set of important inherent quality characteristics for LOD datasets based on existing standard quality models and frameworks, e.g. ISO-25012.
- We systematically propose and validate a set of metrics for measuring the quality characteristics of datasets before they are published to the LOD cloud.
- We propose a quality model for LOD that considers the inherent data quality indicators of such data.
- We introduce a novel approach for the assessment of the quality of datasets on LOD, which has its roots in measurement theory and software measurement techniques.

4 Research Methodology and Approach

Our approach for data quality assessment involves the measurement of quality dimensions focusing specifically on inherent quality aspects of linked open datasets. To achieve this goal, we have applied following approach:

1. Exploratory analysis of the previous and current well-known models and frameworks on data quality and comparing dimensions and indictors of data quality presented in these models;
2. Selecting the most appropriate quality model and extracting a subset of quality dimensions that could be applied to inherent quality characteristics of LOD datasets;
3. Devising a set of metrics for assessment of selected inherent quality dimensions;
4. Theoretical validation of proposed metrics;
5. Proposing a quality models consist of selected quality dimensions and proposed metrics;
6. Implementing an automated tool for measuring the proposed metrics;
7. Empirical evaluation of the quality model by measuring the quality metrics of various dataset;
8. Developing a questionnaire for subjectively evaluation of the datasets used in the previous step;
9. Developing predictive statistical (machine learning)-based techniques to find a correlation between proposed metrics with inherent quality dimensions;
10. Applying final framework o predict the inherent quality of datasets by measuring the metrics.

According to this approach, we have undertaken an exploratory analysis of the previous and current well-known models and frameworks on data quality focusing the models and Frameworks varying in their approach and application, but sharing a number of characteristics [7, 9, 10, 18-21]. We systematically review these data quality models and Frameworks focusing on those models proposing inherent or intrinsic quality [7-10]. Comparing existing dimensions and indictors of data quality presented in these models, we tried to identify the most appropriate quality dimensions that could be applied to inherent quality characteristics of LOD datasets. These inherent quality characteristics are namely completeness, semantic accuracy, syntactic accuracy, uniqueness, consistency and interlinking.

In order to make the characteristics quantifiable, we define a set of metrics to measure the above six inherent quality characteristics. The employed approach for metric definition is Goal-Question-Metric(GQM) [22]. In GQM, the goals are gradually refined into several questions and each question is then refined into metrics. Also, one metric can be used to answer multiple questions. Considering the fact that only few studies have been conducted which define quality metrics for LOD [5, 9, 23], we had to define the required metrics from scratch and prior work could not be reused for our purpose. We propose 32 metrics as measurement references for the inherent quality of linked open dataset to address six inherent quality dimensions.

The main idea behind the design of these metrics has been comprehensiveness and simplicity. To achieve comprehensiveness, we have tried to cover as many quality deficiencies of a dataset as possible that can be identified at the time of publishing, which is the focus of our work. We have also considered as much structural characteristics of a dataset as possible. Therefore, the metrics are proposed in two main groups: quality-driven and structural. Quality-driven metric measures specific quality deficiency in a given dataset e.g. redundant instances in a dataset; while structural metrics represent a feature of any dataset presented in the RDF model, and is not related to the quality issues that might exist in those datasets, e.g. ratio of properties to classes. Furthermore, we have tried to define all of metrics in simple ratio scale. Taking into account of proposed metrics, it is understood that developing simple metrics is our secondary objective.

After defining metrics, a hierarchical data quality model focusing on the inherent viewpoint is developed as shown in Figure 1. At the first level, it consists of six inherent quality dimensions, namely interlinking, uniqueness, consistency, syntactic accuracy, semantic accuracy and completeness. The quality metrics for assessing these quality dimensions are proposed at the second level of the model, some of which are used for measuring two quality dimensions. There are 32 metrics in this model, each of which are assigned by a number and defined in Table 2.

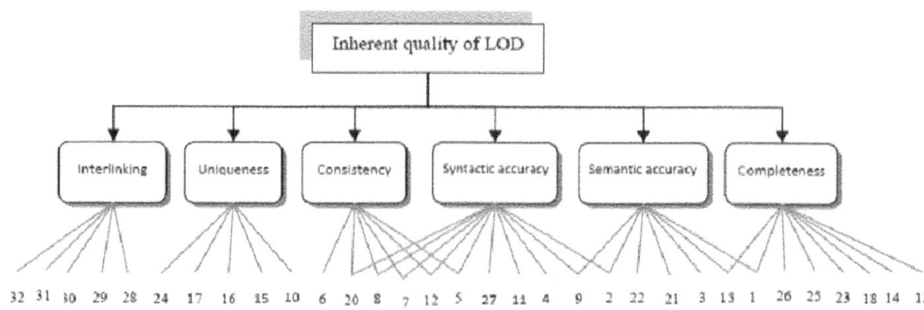

Fig. 1. The structure of LODQM

5 Intermediate Results

An important outcome of this work is the evaluation of our assumption that a dataset within LOD can be automatically processed using metrics and evaluated based on statistical predictive models for measuring its quality before release. We expect that given the metrics values for a dataset, the developed predictive models are able to estimate/predict the values of inherent quality dimensions that are not directly measurable. Generally, the main outcomes that we have achieved are the following:

- Identifying the inherent quality dimensions of LOD that can be assessed before publishing;

- Formulating a set of measurement-theoretic metrics for assessing the inherent quality of LOD;
- Developing a quality model for LOD by customizing ISO-25012;
- Achieving an innovative solution for quality assessment in the context of linked data in the early stage of publishing.

In order to put proposed metrics into practice, we have implemented a tool that is able to automatically compute the metric values for any given input dataset. The code is implemented in the Java programming language (JDK 7 Update 25 x64) using Jena 2.6.3 semantic web library. For better observation of metric behavior, different datasets from a variety of LOD domains are selected. Our codebase and selected datasets for this study are publicly accessible at [24, 25], respectively. Here, we have reported the results of our experiments over three datasets. The results of our observations over all of the datasets are reported in [26]. Table 1, presents the details of the selected datasets; and Table 2 summarizes the results of our experiments over them.

Table 1. The details of the datasets used in our experiments

Datasets	No. of triples	No. of instances	No. of classes	No. of properties
DS1- FAO Water Areas	5,365	293	7	19
DS2- Water Economic Zones	25,959	693	22	127
DS3-Large Marine Ecosystems	6,006	358	9	31

Table 2. The results of our experiments

No.	**Metrics**	DS1	DS2	DS3
1	Missing properties values (Miss_Prp_Vlu)	0.67	0.26	0.44
2	Out-of-range properties values (Out_Prp_Vlu)	0.84	0.81	0.78
3	Misspelled property values (Msspl_Prp_Vlu)	0.84	1.00	0.85
4	Undefined classes (Und_Cls)	1.00	1.00	1.00
5	Membership of disjoint classes (Dsj_Cls)	1.00	1.00	1.00
6	Inconsistent properties values (Inc_Prp_Vlu)	0.80	0.81	0.81
7	Functional properties with inconsistent values (FP)	1.00	1.00	1.00
8	Invalid usage of inverse-functional properties (IFP)	1.00	1.00	1.00
9	Improper data types for the literals (Im_DT)	1.00	1.00	1.00
10	Similar classes (Sml_Cls)	0.71	0.23	0.89
11	Undefined properties (Und_Prp)	1.00	0.72	1.00
12	Using disjoint properties (Dsj_Prp)	1.00	1.00	1.00
13	Unused classes (Unusd_Cls)	0.86	0.50	0.89
14	Unused properties (Unusd_Prp)	0.74	0.76	0.74
15	Similar properties (Sml_Prp)	1.00	0.95	1.00

Table 2. *(continued)*

No.	Metrics	DS1	DS2	DS3
16	Using similar properties (Usg_Sml_Prp)	1.00	0.95	1.00
17	Redundant triples (Rdn_Trp)	0.90	1.00	0.91
18	Heterogeneity of data types (DT)	3.00	3.00	3.00
19	Average missing properties (Avg_Miss_Prp_Vlu)	0.67	0.24	0.44
20	Misusage of properties (Msusg_Prp)	1.00	1.00	1.00
21	Misspelled classes (Msspl_Cls)	0.58	0.45	0.55
22	Misspelled properties (Msspl_Prp)	0.71	0.55	0.67
23	Ratio of properties to classes (Prp_Cls)	2.71	5.77	3.44
24	Redundant instances (Rdn_Ins)	0.00	0.00	0.00
25	Ratio of instances to classes (Ins_Cls)	41.86	31.50	39.78
26	User-defined properties (User_Def_Prp)	0.00	0.86	0.00
27	Misplaced classes/properties (Misplc_Cls_Prp)	1.00	1.00	1.00
28	Object properties (Obj_Prp)	0.13	0.21	0.13
29	Imported triples (Imp_Trp)	0.00	0.88	0.89
30	External linking (Ext_Lnk)	1.00	0.09	1.00
31	Connectivity of RDF graph (Gr_Cn)	0.02	0.01	0.02
32	Intra-linking (Int_Lnk)	0.96	0.98	0.96

In this step of our research, we are not able to address all of the research questions presented in Section 3. We can only answer RQ1 and RQ2. In response to RQ1, we have identified six inherent quality dimensions of linked open datasets that are presented in the first level of LODQM as shown in Figure 1. Regarding the second question (RQ2), a set of automatic measurable metrics is defined to measure six quality dimensions, as presented in Table 2. Currently, we are collecting the experts' subjective perception about inherent quality dimensions to find relations between the measured values of the metrics and perceived quality. Thus, the other research questions, RQ3 and RQ4, can be addressed after completion of the work.

6 Evaluation Strategy

In previous section, the results of empirical evaluation of the proposed metrics are presented. Here, we theoretically support our claim by validation of the metrics and evaluation of the quality model. Initially, the proposed metrics are validated from a measurement-theoretic perspective, and subsequently, the suitability of the proposed quality model will be discussed. Furthermore, we are going to subjectively evaluate our proposed model using expert' opinion as will be explained in the conclusion.

6.1 Theoretical Validation

Generally, any kind of measure is a homomorphism from an empirical relational system to a numerical relational system[27]; therefore, it is imperative that measures be theoretically analyzed within the framework of measurement theory. There are two main groups of frameworks for the theoretical validation of metrics in the literature. The first group consists of frameworks directly based on measurement theory principles [28]; while the second group expresses the desirable properties of the numerical relational system that need to be satisfied by the metrics [29]. In this work, we have examined the properties of our metrics according to one of the most well-known frameworks in the latter group, namely Property-based measurement framework [29]. This framework provides five types of metrics including size, length, complexity, coupling and cohesion and offers a set of desirable properties for each of these types.

Since, all of the proposed metrics are of the size type and according to [29], they are expected to exhibit three main properties, namely, non-negativity, null value and additivity. In other words, size cannot be negative (non-negativity), and it is expected to be null when a system does not contain any elements (null-value). Also, when modules of a system do not have any elements in common, we expect size to be additive (additivity).We have analyzed these three important properties for our proposed metrics and recognized that all of the metrics respect the properties required by the property-based measurement framework to form valid metric space.

6.2 Criteria Based Evaluation

In this section, we evaluate our proposed quality model, LODQM, according to criteria in two dimensions of analytical criteria and practical criteria. These meta-criteria are presented in [30] to analyzes seven well-known conceptual frameworks on information quality. The analytical criteria require clear definitions of the terms used in a framework, a positioning of the framework within existing literature, and a consistent and systematic structure. The practical dimension consists of criteria which make the framework applicable, namely conciseness and the inclusion of tools that are based on the framework. To better evaluation of the our model based on these meta-criteria, we have answer the questions corresponding to meta-criteria which is proposed in [30].

- Definitions: The exact definitions for all of the quality metrics and quality dimensions are presented in LODQM.
- Positioning: LODQM is clearly positioned within existing information quality literature in the context of LOD.
- Consistency: LODQM is divided into systematic dimensions that are collectively exhaustive. Since, our model has used GQM approach for metric development; there are common metrics for different quality dimensions.
- Conciseness: The quality model has six quality dimensions with 5-7 metrics for each of which.

- Tools: An automated tool is developed to measure the values of the proposed metrics for any input dataset in RDF format. Also, a questionnaire is developed and will be applied to capture the experts' opinion in for subjectively evaluation of our model.

According to above discussions, it is clear that the proposed quality model is a practical model for any datasets of LOD.

7 Conclusion

The goal of this research is proposing a metrics-driven framework for predicting the quality of linked open datasets from an inherent point of view. To achieve this goal, we have followed an approach which is started by analysis of the well-known IQ frameworks, resulting in selection of six quality characteristics. Then, a set of metrics for assessing each of six quality dimensions are developed including quality-driven and structural. To put the proposed metrics into practice, we have implemented an automated tool and computed the metric values for various datasets from different domains of LOD. Finally, the suitability of the LODQM metrics is discussed.

In the next phase of our work, we are going to investigate and analyze whether the proposed metrics can be good early indicators of inherent dimensions. Following our approach, we use questionnaire to receive experts' subjective perception regarding inherent quality dimensions for all of the datasets used in this experiment to find relations between the measured values for the metrics and perceived quality by collecting the opinions of the experts in LOD domain. If the proposed metrics are shown to have meaningful correlation with the quality dimensions, then we are able to predict the inherent quality dimensions of any dataset once it is integrated into the LOD, by only observing the values of proposed metrics. The results will help publishers to filter out low-quality data, which in turn enables data consumers to make better and more informed decisions when using the shared datasets.

Acknowledgement. I would like to gratefully thank Prof. Mohsen Kahani for his brilliant guidance and Dr. Ebrahim Bagheri for his great advice during my work.

References

1. Pipino, L.L., Lee, Y.W., Wang, R.Y.: Data quality assessment. Communications of the ACM 45, 211–218 (2002)
2. Lee, Y.W., Strong, D.M., Kahn, B.K., Wang, R.Y.: AIMQ: a methodology for information quality assessment. Information & Management 40, 133–146 (2002)
3. Batini, C., Cappiello, C., Francalanci, C., Maurino, A.: Methodologies for data quality assessment and improvement. ACM Computing Surveys (CSUR) 41, 16 (2009)

4. Naumann, F., Rolker, C.: Assessment methods for information quality criteria. In: 5th Conference on Information Quality, pp. 148–162 (2000)
5. Batini, C., Scannapieca, M.: Data quality: concepts, methodologies and techniques. Springer (2006)
6. Behkamal, B., Kahani, M., Paydar, S., Dadkhah, M., Sekhavaty, E.: Publishing Persian linked data; challenges and lessons learned. In: 5th International Symposium on Telecommunications (IST), pp. 732–737. IEEE (2010)
7. Helfert, M.: Managing and measuring data quality in data warehousing. In: World Multiconference on Systemics, Cybernetics and Informatics, pp. 55–65 (2001)
8. ISO: ISO/IEC 25012- Software engineering - Software product Quality Requirements and Evaluation (SQuaRE). Data quality model (2008)
9. Zaveri, A., Rula, A., Maurino, A., Pietrobon, R., Lehmann, J., Auer, S., Hitzler, P.: Quality Assessment Methodologies for Linked Open Data. Submitted to Semantic Web Journal (2013)
10. Wang, R.Y., Strong, D.M., Guarascio, L.M.: Beyond accuracy: What data quality means to data consumers. Journal of Management Information Systems 12, 5–33 (1996)
11. Hogan, A., Harth, A., Passant, A., Decker, S., Polleres, A.: Weaving the pedantic web. In: 3rd International Workshop on Linked Data on the Web, LDOW 2010 (2010)
12. Fürber, C., Hepp, M.: Using semantic web resources for data quality management. In: Cimiano, P., Pinto, H.S. (eds.) EKAW 2010. LNCS, vol. 6317, pp. 211–225. Springer, Heidelberg (2010)
13. Brank, J., Grobelnik, M., Mladenić, D.: A survey of ontology evaluation techniques (2005)
14. URI Debugger, http://linkeddata.informatik.hu-berlin.de/uridbg
15. Vapour online validator, http://validator.linkeddata.org/vapour
16. Jena Eyeball: Command line validator, http://jena.sourceforge.net/Eyeball
17. VRP: Command line validator, http://139.91.183.30:9090/RDF/VRP
18. Dedeke, A.: A Conceptual Framework for Developing Quality Measures for Information Systems. In: 5th International Conference on Information Quality, pp. 126–128 (2000)
19. Naumann, F., Rolker, C.: Do Metadata Models meet IQ Requirements? In: Iternational Conference on Information Quality (IQ), pp. 99–114 (1999)
20. Su, Y., Jin, Z.: A Methodology for Information Quality Assessment in Data Warehousing. In: IEEE International Conference on Communications, ICC 2008, pp. 5521–5525. IEEE (2008)
21. Moraga, C., Moraga, M., Caro, A., Calero, C.: Defining the intrinsic quality of web portal data. In: 8th International Conference on Web Information Systems and Technologies (WEBIST), pp. 374–379 (2012)
22. Caldiera, V.R.B.G., Rombach, H.D.: The goal question metric approach. Encyclopedia of Software Engineering 2, 528–532 (1994)
23. Hartig, O.: Trustworthiness of data on the web. In: Proceedings of the STI Berlin & CSW PhD Workshop. Citeseer (2008)
24. The code of metrics calculation tool, https://bitbucket.org/behkamal/new-metrics-codes/src
25. Networked Ontology (NeOn) project, http://www.neon-project.org
26. Behkamal, B., Kahani, M., Bagheri, E., Jeremic, Z.: A Metrics-Driven Approach for Quality Assessment of Linked Open Data. Accepted in Journal of Theoretical and Applied Electronic Commerce Research (2013)

27. Fenton, N.E., Pfleeger, S.L.: Software metrics: a rigorous and practical approach. PWS Publishing Co. (1998)
28. Poels, G., Dedene, G.: Distance-based software measurement: necessary and sufficient properties for software measures. Information and Software Technology 42, 35–46 (2000)
29. Briand, L.C., Morasca, S., Basili, V.R.: Property-based software engineering measurement. IEEE Transactions on Software Engineering 22, 68–86 (1996)
30. Eppler, M.J., Wittig, D.: Conceptualizing information quality: A Review of Information Quality Frameworks from the Last Ten Years. In: 5th International Conference on Information Quality, pp. 83–96 (2000)

Harvesting and Structuring Social Data in Music Information Retrieval

Sergio Oramas

Music Technology Group
Universitat Pompeu Fabra, Barcelona, Spain
sergio.oramas@upf.edu

Abstract. An exponentially growing amount of music and sound resources are being shared by communities of users on the Internet. Social media content can be found with different levels of structuring, and the contributing users might be experts or non-experts of the domain. Harvesting and structuring this information semantically would be very useful in context-aware Music Information Retrieval (MIR). Until now, scant research in this field has taken advantage of the use of formal knowledge representations in the process of structuring information. We propose a methodology that combines Social Media Mining, Knowledge Extraction and Natural Language Processing techniques, to extract meaningful context information from social data. By using the extracted information we aim to improve retrieval, discovery and annotation of music and sound resources. We define three different scenarios to test and develop our methodology.

Keywords: #eswcphd2014Oramas, social media mining, knowledge extraction, natural language processing, information retrieval, music.

1 Introduction

Online communities of users sharing multimedia content have become a cornerstone of the World Wide Web. Millions of users are handing out videos, photos, audios, and documents. Thus, large collections of multimedia resources have been gathered in web sites. This imposes challenges on how to deal with these data in an effective manner [1].

Music Information Retrieval (MIR) is a multidisciplinary field of research that is concerned with the extraction, analysis, and usage of information about music and audio. Traditionally, MIR has been more focused on the use of audio content, underestimating context information. However, in recent years several studies have showed the benefits of using a multimodal approach [2].

As stated by Schedl [3], factors that influence human music perception can be categorized into music content, music context, user context and user properties. According to this classification, music context, and user context seem to be a key aspect of MIR, and online communities are a very suitable place to look for this kind of information.

V. Presutti et al. (Eds.): ESWC 2014, LNCS 8465, pp. 817–826, 2014.

Sound and music related sites can be classified according to the presence or absence of music content, and the presence or absence of a community of users involved in the creation and edition of context information (Table 1).

Table 1. Categorization of sound and music related sites

User Community	Music Content	Example Sites
No	No	artist web pages, magazines
No	Yes	Internet Archive, iTunes, Spotify
Yes	No	Facebook, Twitter, MusicBrainz, Last.fm
Yes	Yes	Freesound, SoundCloud

Music context and user context information can be found in the Web in a structured or an unstructured form. On one hand, relational databases, web APIs or SPARQL endpoints are typical sources of structured content. On the other hand, unstructured content can be found in web documents, forum posts, user comments, microblogs, etc. Web content mining techniques can be applied to deal with these unstructured sources of information, harvesting relevant data from web content.

Ontologies have shown its utility to structure information in the Web, but in the creation process it is not easy to find clear agreement between different information sources. Thus, there is always the need to involve domain experts and to account for the fact that there are no single and long-lived formalizations [4]. Collaborative tagging has led to another data structure, the folksonomy. The analysis of folksonomies has demonstrated its utility [5]. However, this data structure suffers from a lack of semantic meaning.

Ontologies can also be exploited and enriched using natural language processing. Academic and industrial applications of this technique are usually called semantic technologies [6]. The combination of knowledge extraction and text mining can be addressed in two directions. First, learning ontology classes or instances in a semi-automatic way by using text mining techniques. Second, using ontologies as a guide that details what type of information to harvest, improving the process and the results of text mining [7].

In this proposal we take these ideas in order to develop a methodology to improve the process of annotation and retrieval of large audio collections. Our overall goal is to extract knowledge from structured and unstructured social data, using text mining techniques together with formal representations of the domain. For this purpose, ontologies will be created and enriched in a semi-automatic way from the analysis of context information generated by communities of experts, and they will be used to guide in the process of information extraction from user-generated content.

We will focus our research in the extraction of knowledge from music-related context information sources in the Web. To this end, we will take information from structured (Wikipedia, WordNet, MusicBrainz), semi-structured (Freesound, SoundCloud, Last.fm, Internet Archive) and unstructured sources (Facebook, Twitter).

As a first step, our intention is to take some elements from folksonomies and ontologies to improve annotation, searching and browsing in Freesound.org. Freesound is an online audio clip-sharing website with more than three million registered users and more than 200.000 user-contributed samples [8].

In addition, we plan to harvest less structured social media content from Facebook, Twitter, music-related websites, and music forums. With the obtained information we aim to improve the annotation of large collections of audio, and use this new metadata in music recommendation and artist similarity tasks.

New Music Information Systems can be created using the harvested and structured social data. Those systems would provide data in a machine-readable format, making knowledge available on the Web in a structured way. Hence, new music context information would be added to the Semantic Web.

The rest of the proposal is organized as follows. First we comment on research found in related work. Then we propose our research questions. After that we outline our plan of research and describe the methodology. Preliminary results are then reported and an evaluation plan is proposed. We conclude the proposal with an outline of future benefits derived from our research.

2 State of the Art

As this proposal is strongly related to web content mining and knowledge extraction, we will review related work on those topics in the context of MIR. Although web content mining research has been an emergent topic in the MIR community over the last years, there is scant research related to knowledge discovery. Before addressing this related research, we want to briefly summarize some relevant concepts and perspectives related to ontologies and folksonomies.

2.1 Folksonomies and Ontologies

Folksonomies are the result of a collaborative annotation process [9]. They are composed of tags, resources, users, and their three-fold relations. They are generated in websites, where users attach tags to annotate resources, usually without any restriction or predefined hierarchy. Problems associated with them are related with the linguistic and semantic limitations of tags. Synonyms, misspelt words, or semantic relations between terms are not reflected in the folksonomy [5].

An ontology represents knowledge as a set of concepts within a given domain, and the relationships between those concepts. It provides a framework to deal with structured information, making implicit knowledge explicit, describing relevant parts of a domain and making data understandable and processable by machines. To define an ontology it is required consensual agreement from community members. Therefore, creation and maintenance of ontologies are more expensive than folksonomies, which are easier to create, edit, use and reuse [1].

Ontologies are commonly created by a small set of experts, and users are not usually involved in the creation process. On the contrary, folksonomies are created by final users directly. However, they do not contain a precise representation of the relations between concepts of the domain. Hence, on one hand we have experts wisdom in ontologies, and on the other hand we have the wisdom of the crowds in folksonomies [10].

Although both ways of knowledge representations has its pros and cons, they are not absolutely opposite; they can be used in combination to create better ways of organizing information on the Internet. There are several approaches on how they can cooperate, combining the flexibility of use and cooperation of folksonomies and the structured model of knowledge of ontologies. One approach is to create an ontology that supports a folksonomy like in [9], [11] and [12]. Another approach is to use a folksonomy to create an ontology [5]. There is a third approach where tagging, taxonomy, and ontology are mixed. Here folksonomies are used to find concepts, and ontologies are used as a schema, in a way that the ontology is modified by the community, given to a socially driven ontology [10].

2.2 Web Content Mining

Early work in text mining in the context of MIR is mainly related to extraction of music artist information from artist-related web pages, using search engines to gather those pages and then parsing their DOM trees [13]. Other studies [14] [15] use weighted term profiles based on specific term sets for recommendation and classification tasks. Co-occurrence of artist names in web pages content and page count based on results provided by search engines have been used for artist similarity and recommendation tasks [16]. Another interesting application of text mining techniques is the analysis of music artist-related microblogging posts for artist similarity estimation and artist labeling [17].

Sordo et al. [18] propose a methodology for extracting semantic information from music-related forums, inferring semantic relations from the co-occurrence of musical concepts in forum posts, and using network analysis. Other application of web content mining in MIR is automatic generation of Music Information Systems [19]. Here, information about music artists and bands is automatically gathered from various sources in the Web, processed, and published.

2.3 Knowledge Extraction

The boundary between natural language processing techniques and knowledge extraction is somehow fuzzy. We address here some research related to the use of structured knowledge representations in the context of MIR. In [20] a set of semantic facets is automatically obtained and anchored upon the structure of Wikipedia, and tags from the folkosonomy of Last.fm are then categorized with respect to the obtained facets. In [21] a methodology to automatically extract semantic information and relations about musical entities from arbitrary textual sources is proposed. Although more related with music content than music context, [22] shows a method for the automatic creation of an ontology of musical instruments using formal concept analysis to build the hierarchical structure of the ontology.

3 Problem Statement and Contributions

After a concise study of the state of the art, our research questions are: Can we extract meaningful musical knowledge from social data in online communities? How can we use expert-based knowledge information and user generated content to better structure context information in audio repositories? How can we improve retrieval and discovery using the harvested and structured context information?

The creation of new methodologies to harvest and structure meaningful information from social data is a hot topic in the Big Data era. The Music Information Retrieval field has experienced an increase of related research in the last few years. However, scant studies have taken advantage of ontology-based knowledge extraction techniques. The Web is full of communities of domain experts creating meaningful knowledge in a crowd-sourced way. Therefore, it would be very valuable to extract and structure this community knowledge. By using it, we could improve structuring, browsing and annotation in music and sound repositories, and also ameliorate accuracy in some typical issues of Music Information Retrieval. This will require a combination of methodologies coming from distinct areas: Social Media Mining, Information Retrieval, Knowledge Extraction, Natural Language Processing and Semantic Multimedia Web.

4 Research Methodology and Approach

The ultimate end of this PhD work is contribute to the improvement of Music Information Systems, exploiting structured context information with semantic meaning. To obtain this domain knowledge, a two step process is defined. First, structured and unstructured social data related to the music domain is gathered from online communities using web content mining techniques. This information can be classified as expert or non-expert content. Expert generated content is considered especially suitable for knowledge extraction. However, both of them are valuable data sources for information extraction using natural language processing. User generated information can be extracted from any of the music related online-community types described above.

Second, gathered information is then structured and semantically annotated. For this purpose, it is necessary a combination of natural language processing and knowledge extraction, using ontologies as a formal knowledge representation. Ontologies play a key role in this step, working as a background for the natural language processing, and at the same time, being enriched with new extracted knowledge.

Finally, the structured and semantically annotated information can be used in a Music Information System to improve Music Information Retrieval tasks, such as music recommendation, artist similarity or the annotation of sound and music resources.

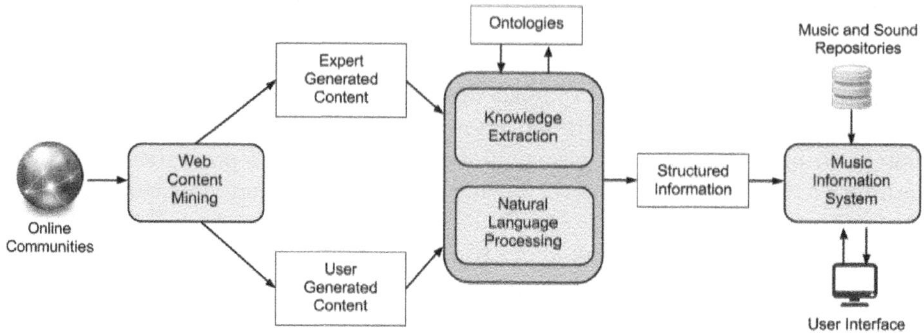

Fig. 1. Overview of the proposed methodology

We plan to apply this methodology in three different scenarios. Thus, we want to prove the importance of the use of experts knowledge in Music Information Retrieval. We plan to use structured, semi-structured and unstructured information as an input of our system, and try to use the obtained structured information to help in different tasks.

First, we plan to improve the annotation quality and the searching process of an audio-clip sharing site, Freesound.org. We will gather all the information related to resources, users and tags conforming the folksonomy. For the knowledge extraction step, we will design an ontology which is able to represent the information from the folksonomy together with domain specific semantic relations between tags and resources.

Second, we plan to improve artist similarity and genre classification tasks by using information extracted from user generated content in Facebook posts and comments. Natural language processing techniques such as sentiment analysis or topic modeling are going to be applied to this data. Expert generated content related to genre will be also gathered from Wikipedia. With the semantic information obtained we also plan to generate a new Music Information System, publishing gathered content automatically in HTML for navigation and in a machine readable way using RDF.

Third, we will use harvested user and expert generated content from different web sources to get structured information for the improvement of the annotation of the Internet Archive music collection. At this moment the context information of the collection is scant. We plan to use structured information from MusicBrainz and DBpedia, together with semi-structured and unstructured information gathered from SoundCloud, Last.fm, Twitter and Facebook.

5 Preliminary Results

The first step has been the identification of the problem for the first scenario. Members of our research group have already done some research in this area. Freesound.org has been developed at the Music Technology Group, and there are various publications analyzing its resources, folksonomy and community [23], [8], [24] and [25].

According to [25], there are 971,561 tag applications provided by 6,802 users and including 143,188 sounds, resulting in an average of 6.79 tags per resource. The folksonomy of Freesound is continuously growing, but it is quite noisy (misspelt words, synonyms, homonyms, ...). Hence, a tag recommendation system has been implemented to increase tag reuse.

As a starting point in the ontology design, we plan to reuse some concepts from the MUTO (Modular Unified Tag Ontology) ontology [11], which is, according to the literature, the most recent ontology of a folksonomy, and it suits our needs.

This ontology is only focused on the annotation process, storing all relevant information about the tripartite relations of the folksonomy. However, it does not add any semantic information about tags and resources. Therefore, our intention is to reuse some concepts of this ontology and add some domain specific semantic relations between tags and resources. For this purpose, we added a set of subclasses derived from the resource and tag classes, and some semantic properties relating them (Fig. 2).

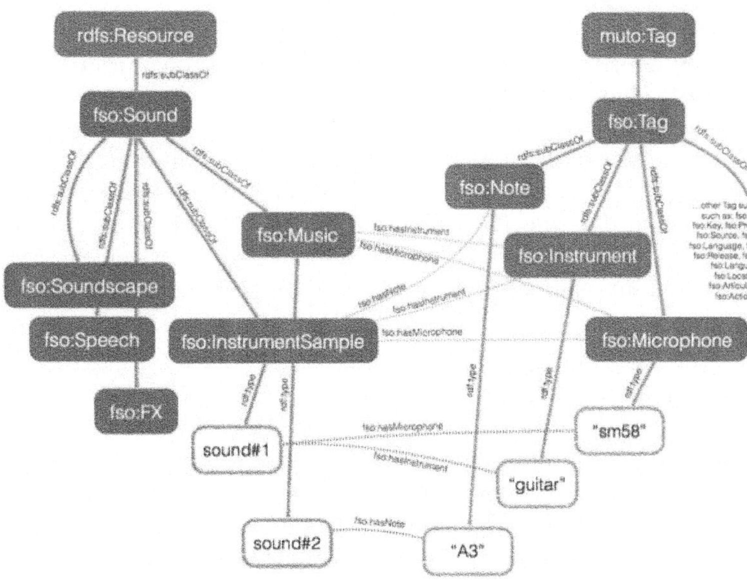

Fig. 2. Schema of the Freesound Ontology

Using this ontology, we aim to perform an automatic classification of tags. In addition, we plan to modify the web interface of Freesound, letting the user to choose the category of a tag. Thus, membership of a specific subclass of tags will be determined by the user with the use of semantically enhanced tags in the annotation process. These tags will have two members, an attribute and a value with syntax *attribute:value*, where each attribute corresponds to a specific subclass of tag.

Starting from previous studies, an initial analysis has been done to define the subclasses of resources and tags [25]. According to this we have determined five different categories of sounds and thirteen categories of tags as an starting point.

Using these categories a first version of the Freesound Ontology has been created. The ontology is already defined in OWL, and an RDF triplestore have been created to store all the information of the folksonomy following our ontology design.

6 Evaluation Plan

Our methodology implies different types of evaluation for each processing step. On one hand we need to evaluate the knowledge extraction and natural language processing step, and on the other hand, we have to measure the improvement of the Music Information System.

To evaluate a knowledge extraction system, we need to measure the quality of the inferred knowledge. The creation of gold standards based on existing ontologies, and available expert resources such as WordNet are a crucial step in our evaluation process.

To evaluate the quality of the information extracted, we may use as ground truth structured information already present in expert communities such as MusicBrainz or well annotated music repositories.

Finally, to evaluate the improvement of an MIR task, we should measure its performance with and without the use of the extracted information. Precision and recall are typical measures used for MIR evaluation. Moreover, each specific MIR task may require its specific evaluation process. User feedback is also a key value in other to evaluate Music Information Systems. User-centric evaluation experiments involving real users will be carried on to measure the performance of our systems.

7 Conclusion

Combining concepts from Information Retrieval, Social Media Mining and Knowledge Extraction in the analysis and improvement of Music Information Systems is an open field not very much explored, and with an enormous potential. We have proposed a methodology that takes advantage of this combination in order to transform social data into structured and meaningful information. With this information we plan to improve annotation in sound and music repositories, and some related MIR tasks.

Adding structured and semantic information to sound and music collections would be useful not only for users, but also for researchers. For instance, in the case of Freesound and the Internet Archive, well annotated subsets of audio files would be excellent datasets to develop and test MIR algorithms.

We expect that methodologies and prototypes created for this purpose will be applicable to other multimedia online communities, and even more, to any type of online community. Moreover, semantic technologies applied to extract structured information will be reusable in other frameworks and research fields. The Big Data era has arrived, and expert knowledge should play a key role in information retrieval tasks.

References

1. Sordo, M.: Semantic Annotation of Music Collections: A Computational Approach. PhD Thesis (2011)
2. Schedl, M., Schnitzer, D.: Location-Aware Music Artist Recommendation. In: Gurrin, C., Hopfgartner, F., Hurst, W., Johansen, H., Lee, H., O'Connor, N. (eds.) MMM 2014, Part II. LNCS, vol. 8326, pp. 205–213. Springer, Heidelberg (2014)
3. Schedl, M.: On the Use of the Web and Social Media in Multimodal Music Information Retrieval. Postdoctoral Thesis (Habilitation) (2013)
4. Serra, X.: Exploiting Domain Knowledge in Music Information Research. In: Stockholm Music Acoustics Conference 2013 and Sound and Music Computing Conference (2013)
5. Mika, P.: Ontologies are us: A unified model of social networks and semantics. Web Semantics: Science, Services and Agents on the World Wide Web 5, 5–15 (2007)
6. Gangemi, A.: A Comparison of Knowledge Extraction Tools for the Semantic Web. In: Cimiano, P., Corcho, O., Presutti, V., Hollink, L., Rudolph, S. (eds.) ESWC 2013. LNCS, vol. 7882, pp. 351–366. Springer, Heidelberg (2013)
7. Alani, H., Millard, D., Weal, M., Hall, W., Lewis, P., Shadbolt, N.: Automatic ontology-based knowledge extraction from Web documents. IEEE Intelligent Systems 18, 14–21 (2003)
8. Font, F., Roma, G., Herrera, P., Serra, X.: Characterization of the Freesound online community. In: 2012 3rd International Workshop on Cognitive Information Processing (CIP), pp. 1–6 (2012)
9. Echarte, F., Astrain, J.J., Córdoba, A., Villadangos, J.: Ontology of Folksonomy: A New Modeling Method. In: SAAKM 2007, p. 8 (2007)
10. Sharif, A.: Combining ontology and folksonomy: An Integrated Approach to Knowledge Representation. In: Emerging Trends in Technology Libraries Between Web 20 Semantic Web and Search Technology, pp. 1–13 (2007)
11. Lohmann, S., Díaz, P., Aedo, I.: MUTO: the modular unified tagging ontology. In: Proceedings of the 7th International Conference on Semantic Systems - I-Semantics 2011, pp. 95–104 (2011)
12. Angeletou, S., Sabou, M., Specia, L., Motta, E.: Bridging the Gap Between Folksonomies and the Semantic Web: An Experience Report. In: European Semantic Web Conference, pp. 30–43 (2007)
13. Cohen, W.W., Fan, W.: Web-collaborative filtering: recommending music by crawling the Web. Computer Networks 33, 685–698 (2000)

14. Ellis, D.P.W., Ellis, D.P., Whitman, B., Whitman, B., Berenzweig, A., Berenzweig, A., Lawrence, S., Lawrence, S.: The quest for ground truth in musical artist similarity. In: Proc. International Symposium on Music Information Retrieval (ISMIR 2002), pp. 170–177 (2002)
15. Whitman, B., Lawrence, S.: Inferring descriptions and similarity for music from community metadata. In: Proceedings of the 2002 International Computer Music Conference, pp. 591–598 (2002)
16. Schedl, M., Knees, P., Widmer, G.: A Web-Based Approach to Assessing Artist Similarity using Co-Occurrences. In: Proceedings of the 4th International Workshop on Content-Based Multimedia Indexing, CBMI 2005 (2005)
17. Schedl, M., Hauger, D., Urbano, J.: Harvesting microblogs for contextual music similarity estimation: a co-occurrence-based framework. Multimedia Systems (2013)
18. Sordo, M., Serrà, J., Serra, X.: A Method for Extracting Semantic Information from on-line Art Music Discussion Forums. In: 2nd CompMusic Workshop, pp. 55–60 (2012)
19. Schedl, M., Widmer, G., Knees, P., Pohle, T.: A music information system automatically generated via Web content mining techniques. Information Processing and Management: an International Journal 47 (2011)
20. Sordo, M., Gouyon, F., Sarmento, L., Celma, O., Serra, X.: Inferring Semantic Facets of a Music Folksonomy with Wikipedia. Journal of New Music Research 42, 346–363 (2013)
21. Knees, P., Schedl, M.: Towards Semantic Music Information Extraction from the Web Using Rule Patterns and Supervised Learning. In: Colocated with ACM RecSys 2011, Chicago, IL, USA, October 23, p. 18 (2011)
22. Kolozali, S., Barthet, M., Fazekas, G., Sandler, M.B.: Automatic Ontology Generation for Musical Instruments Based on Audio Analysis. IEEE Transactions on Audio, Speech, and Language Processing 21, 2207–2220 (2013)
23. Font, F., Serra, X., Gorup, M.T., Fabra, U.P.: Folksonomy-based tag recommendation for online audio clip sharing. In: Proceedings of 13th International Society for Music Information Retrieval Conference, Oporto (2012)
24. Font, F., Serra, X.: Analysis of the folksonomy of freesound. In: Proceedings of the 2nd CompMusic Workshop, pp. 48–54 (2012)
25. Font, F., Serr, J.: Audio clip classification using social tags and the effect of tag expansion. In: AES 53rd International Conference on Semantic Audio, pp. 1–9 (2014)

Route Planning Using Linked Open Data

Pieter Colpaert

Ghent University - iMinds
Department of Electronics and Information Systems, Multimedia Lab
Gaston Crommenlaan 8, Bus 201
9050 Ledeberg-Ghent, Belgium
pieter.colpaert@ugent.be

Abstract. Intermodal route planners need to be provided with a lot of data from various sources: geographical data, speed limits, road blocks, time schedules, real-time vehicle locations, etc. These datasets need to be interoperable world-wide. Today, a lot of data integration needs to be done before this data can be be reused. Route planning becomes a data problem rather than a mathematical problem. Can the Web act as a global distributed dataspace for transport data? Could introducing Linked Open Data to this field make the data quality raise?

Keywords: #eswcphd2014Colpaert, Linked Open Data, Semantic Web, intermodal route planning.

1 Introduction

Intermodal route planning is a term used for planners which can advise the end-user to use multiple modes to get from one point to another. A transport mode is a type of transport, for example a train, tram, bus, car or bicycle. The amount of data that can be used to extract information from, is infinite. For instance, trying to answer the question "how long do I have to walk from one point to another?" can take into account the geolocation of the streets, the weather conditions at that time of the day, the steepness of the road, whether or not there is a sidewalk, criminality reports to check whether it is safe to walk through these streets, the accessibility of the road for e.g., wheelchairs or blind people, whether the street is blocked by works at that time, etc. We can imagine the complexities that arise if the user does not only want to walk, but that he also wants to get advice taking different transport modes into account. Advising an end-user can use an infinite amount of data that remains relevant for the problem. An *open world* approach is needed: a certain pool of data should be queried with the assumption that there is more data outside of this pool that may be relevant to the question.

Data quality, as defined by Orr et al. [14], is the measure of the agreement between the data views presented by an information system and that same data in the real world. When there is no agreement at all, the data quality is 0%, if it complies completely, it equals 100%. Orr et al. described in 1998 how the Feedback-Control System (FCS) (cfr. Fig. 1) affects data quality. This system describes a data life cycle: data is made available for reuse (A), the reuse is stimulated and supported (B), means to provide feedback are in place (C) and the feedback is also processed (D). The data quality increases at the speed of the slowest link in this process.

V. Presutti et al. (Eds.): ESWC 2014, LNCS 8465, pp. 827–833, 2014.

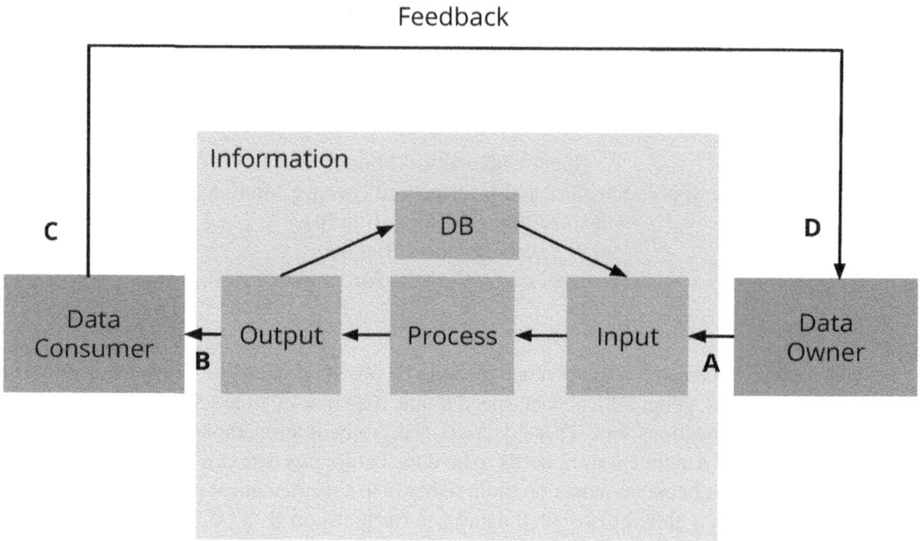

Fig. 1. The Feedback-Control System applied to data.

The trend towards Open Data is stimulating the reuse of the data. Can *Linked Open Data* indeed be used to raise the quality of transport data?

2 State of the Art

In The Netherlands in 1991, the mathematical problem of intermodal route planning has already been solved for data dumps of the Dutch railway system [16]. After that, quite a few projects came to exist, implementing intermodal route planning in their own way. The first section gives a concise overview of the state of the art of intermodal route planning systems. After discussing a couple of intermodal route planners and two algorithms for searching time tables, the state of the art of Linked Open Data is discussed. Finally, a couple of today's vocabularies used to publish or exchange transport data are discussed.

2.1 Intermodal Route Planners

Current intermodal route planners such as Open Trip Planner, Rapid Round based Routing [5] or Navitia.io use a *closed world* approach: they make the assumption that the data on the machine is complete and represents the real world perfectly. Both Open Trip Planner and Navitia.io provide a Web service to get answers to the question which routes should be followed to go from one point to another Rapid Round based Routing [5] is a C++-library which is memory efficient and has been used both from clientside as from serverside. The investment needed to add new datasets (both a new mode of transport or a new region) are high as manual intervention is needed to load the datasets in the store.

2.2 Route Planning Algorithms

For all kinds of route planning problems, Dijkstra is a popular solution. It can solve shortest path problems in a graph in $O(E + V \log V)$ with E the number of edges and V the number of vertices. It can easily be optimized by using heuristics (such as with the A* search algorithm) or the graph can be pruned while running the algorithm.

Route planning systems for public transit mostly use the RAPTOR algorithm [7]. All three route planners mentioned above are three different implementations of this algorithm. It is written to exploit the inherent structure of transport networks by operating in rounds and processing each route[1] of the network instead of popular graph based solutions based on Dijkstra.

A more recent approach is called the Connection Scan Algorithm (CSA) [8]. Just like RAPTOR, it is not graph-based. It is however not centered around routes, but around connections[2], which might be interesting as less data needs to be fetched per request. CSA is a very recent algorithm where parallel extensions, just like RAPTOR, seem promising [8].

2.3 Linked Open Data

Globally, data owners are slowly taking the decision to publish their data as Open Data. One way to go forward with Open Data is Linked Open Data (LOD), which uses RDF to structure the data and which uses the Web as a distributed dataspace. The global dataspace that comes to exist is called the LOD cloud.

There are tools available to raise the awareness of data owners. For example, "The 5 stars of Linked Open Data"[3] summarize the focus points of publishing Linked Open Data to the Web.

There are various steps to publishing Linked Open Data: data needs to be made discoverable, a suiting license need to be agreed upon, obstacles (such as privacy issues or copyright holder discussions) need to be overcome, etc. Various projects have introduced Linked Data Life Cycles [15,19,3,10]. These cycles describe the process to create and maintain Linked Open Data. More recently, also best practices to publish linked data on the web have been published by the W3C[4].

When the data is published, data is not per se discoverable. Data about the data (meta-data) needs to be published alongside the data. To make data discoverable for humans as an organisation, there is data portal software available, such as CKAN. To make data discoverable for machines, ontologies such as VoID [2] and DCAT [11] are available. There are various public Open Data Portals where datasets can be added, such as *http://datahub.io*.

While the Linked Open Data technology is available, there is however no maintained Linked Open Transport Data to be found that is published by transport agencies, at the time of writing.

---

[1] A route is a list of stop points a certain vehicle follows (e.g., a bus line).

[2] A connection in this context is a link to a next stop point.

[3] `http://5stardata.info`

[4] `http://www.w3.org/TR/2014/NOTE-ld-bp-20140109/`

2.4 Vocabularies

The General Transit Feed Specification (GTFS) for public transit[5] has been developed by Brian Ferris at Google for Google Maps. At the moment of writing, GTFS is the de facto standard for data dumps on public transit. In 2011, Ian Davis transformed this specification to an ontology, which is defined at *http://vocab.org/transit/terms/*.

Other specifications in the Open Transport field are for instance the Transmodel specification for public transport [4], SIRI for real-time public transit data exchange, Open511 for traffic events or DATEX for exchange of road transport data.

In 2009, the UK transformed 3 transport datasets towards RDF using the National Public Transport Access Network (NaPTAN) vocabulary. It is greatly inspired by Transmodel. NaPTAN defines the geographical hierarchy of the UK, defines the difference between a stop point (a place where a vehicle stops) and a stop area (a collection of stop points). It also defines different types of identification mechanisms for these stop areas and stop points and defines different types of stop points in the UK. The resulted dataset can still be queried at *http://transport.data.gov.uk/*.

3 Problem Statement and Contribution

Intermodal route planning is a data problem rather than a mathematical problem. Different datasets need to share the same identifiers (or make sure their identifiers are interoperable), need to be able to be queried nearly in real-time, need to be able to process machine readable feedback (as no dataset represents reality 100% correctly), need to track provenance, need to be made discoverable for both humans and machines, etc. These needs can all be put at a letter in Fig. 1:

- A: publishing data
- B: reusing data
- C: providing feedback
- D: processing feedback

The main contribution of this thesis is bringing together the field of intermodal route planning and Linked Open Data. The added value for data publishers researched is raising data quality. When Linked Open Data is introduced to intermodal route planning, algorithms need to be adapted to work with this technology.

4 Methodology

In order to achieve the best possible results within the available resources and timeframe, we suggest the following projects to be built: a high-level Open Transport vocabulary and an Open Transport Data Portal to make transport data discoverable and to stimulate a discussion on used vocabularies, tool chain, data reuse, etc. A third project will work together with the community at the Open Transport Data Portal to build a

[5] This thesis focuses on Open Transport, which also takes into account traffic, road signs, parking lots, taxis, bicycle routes, etc.

referential database for stop identifiers. A fourth project are various implementation of data publishing mechanisms (such as SPARQL). A last project is a proof of concept in which the Web will be used as a global distributed database for an intermodal route planning algorithm.

Future development on vocabulary will be carried out by the Open Transport community of the Open Knowledge Foundation. The methodology used for creating this vocabulary is inspired on "Process and methodology for developing semantic agreements" by the JoinUp project [1].

5 Preliminary Results

5.1 Algorithms

Dijkstra and its optimizations are to be avoided in most cases as it is hard to parallelize [7,12,13], yet it can be considered for subproblems.

For public transport, RAPTOR and CSA seem promising. Both algorithms can be considered, depending on what data each service is going to provide. For RAPTOR, starting at a certain stop, all routes are needed which leave next at that stop. For CSA, starting at a certain stop, only the next stop is needed for all next departures in that stop. Both algorithms are very promising for parallelization. Further research will show what algorithm is best in this use case.

5.2 Open Data

The 5 stars of Open Data Portals A paper has been written for the MeTTeG2013 conference [6], a conference for e-government, which summarizes five focus points for an Open Data Portal. The paper was written in a interdisciplinary setting with the communications department of Ghent University.

Open Transport. At the Open Knowledge Foundation (OKF), I have started coordinating the Open Transport Working Group[6]. The focus of this working group are three projects:

1. The Open Transport Vocabulary[7] creates a minimal representation of all concepts that are needed for intermodal route planning.
2. Stations.io[8]: a knowledge base to link identifiers for stop areas and stop points. The project links various sources together by creating owl:sameAs links, links identifiers to their concepts: stop areas or stop points and creates links between the different stop points and stop areas.
3. The Open Transport Data Portal[9] makes data discoverable, will analyze the added datasets for inconsistencies, will validate the datasets, will host conversations around transport data reuse.

[6] `http://transport.okfn.org`
[7] `http://github.com/opentransport/vocabulary`
[8] `http://stations.io`
[9] `http://transport.datahub.io`

Towards Linked Open Data The DataTank [17] is a data adapter. It takes a data source, such as a CSV file, JSON file, a web-service, a website, a database, etc. as an input and transforms it into a RESTful interface. The DataTank also supports mapping these sources towards RDF using a mapping language. The mapping language that will be supported in the next Long Term Support release of The DataTank is an extension of R2RML, called RML [9].

Using The DataTank we have create a RESTful interface to access transport data in Belgium called iRail. This interface can be found at *http://data.iRail.be/*.

Distributed Version Control for triples. R&Wbase [18] has been presented at the WWW2013 conference at the Linked Data On the Web (LDOW) workshop. It adds a version to each triple in a triple store which supports named graphs.

6 Evaluation Plan

As the thesis is still in a very early stage, the evaluation plan is still very vague. Data quality, defined as the agreement of the data with the real-world, needs to be assessed before applying Linked Open Data technologies and after. In order to get results, the FCS model will be used (see Fig. 1). Data quality will be derived from: the amount of data reuse, the amount of data feedback, the amount of data feedback that is being processed and the amount of data about a certain *real-world object* that is published. When these four factors increase, the data quality will increase [14] and the thesis will be validated.

While the data quality should increase, the intermodal route planning algorithms should remain fully functional without regressions in response time. Different architectures will be set-up which reuse the linked datasets and feed the right data in the algorithms.

7 Conclusion

This paper's contribution is to bring together the field of intermodal route planning with Linked Open Data. Linked Open Data tools are applied to data problems with intermodal route planning. Research focuses on raising the data quality. Four criteria need to be assessed – data reuse, data feedback, processing data feedback and publishing data –. Further research as part of this thesis shows whether or not the Web can then be used as a global distributed database for intermodal route planners.

Acknowledgements. This thesis is supervised by prof. Rik Van de Walle and co-supervised by dr. Erik Mannens and dr. Ruben Verborgh. The research activities described in this paper were funded by Ghent University, iMinds, the Flemish department of Economics, Science and Innovation (EWI), the Institute for the Promotion of Innovation by Science and Technology in Flanders (IWT) and the European Union.

References

1. Process and methodology for developing semantic agreements (June 2013)
2. Alexander, K., Cyganiak, R., Hausenblas, M., Zhao, J.: Describing linked datasets with the VoID vocabulary. W3C Interest Group Note (March 2011)
3. Auer, S., et al.: Managing the Life-Cycle of Linked Data with the LOD2 Stack. In: Cudré-Mauroux, P., et al. (eds.) ISWC 2012, Part II. LNCS, vol. 7650, pp. 1–16. Springer, Heidelberg (2012)
4. Bourée, K., Staub, L., van der Peet, G.: The European reference data model for public transport: Transmodel as a basis for integrated public transport information systems. In: Towards an Intelligent Transport System (1994)
5. Byrd, A., Koch, T., de Konink, S.: Rapid round-based routing (2013)
6. Colpaert, P., Joye, S., Mechant, P., Mannens, E., de Walle, R.V.: The 5 stars of open data portals. In: Conference on Methodologies, Technologies and Tools enabling e-Government 2013 Conference Proceedings (2013)
7. Delling, D., Pajor, T., Werneck, R.F.F.: Round-based public transit routing (2012)
8. Dibbelt, J., Pajor, T., Strasser, B., Wagner, D.: Intriguingly simple and fast transit routing. In: Bonifaci, V., Demetrescu, C., Marchetti-Spaccamela, A. (eds.) SEA 2013. LNCS, vol. 7933, pp. 43–54. Springer, Heidelberg (2013)
9. Dimou, A., Van der Sande, M., Colpaert, P., Mannens, E., Van de Walle, R.: Extending R2RML to a source-independent mapping language for RDF
10. Hyland, B., Wood, D.: The joy of data - a cookbook for publishing linked government data on the web. In: Wood, D. (ed.) Linking Government Data, pp. 3–26. Springer, New York (2011)
11. Maali, F., Erickson, J.: Data Catalog Vocabulary (DCAT). W3C Working Draft (August 2013)
12. Madduri, K., Bader, D.A., Berry, J.W., Crobak, J.R.: Parallel shortest path algorithms for solving large-scale instances (2006)
13. Meyer, U., Sanders, P.: δ-stepping: a parallelizable shortest path algorithm. Journal of Algorithms 49(1), 114–152 (2003)
14. Orr, K.: Data quality and systems theory. Communications of the ACM 41(2), 66–71 (1998)
15. Scharffe, F., Bihanic, L., Képéklian, G., Atemezing, G., Troncy, R., Cotton, F., Gandon, F., Villata, S., Euzenat, J., Fan, Z., Bucher, B., Hamdi, F., Vandenbussche, P.-Y., Vatant, B.: Enabling linked data publication with the datalift platform (2012)
16. Tulp, E., Siklssy, L.: Searching time-table networks. Artificial Intelligence for Engineering, Design, Analysis and Manufacturing 5, 189–198 (1991)
17. Vander Sande, M., Colpaert, P., Van Deursen, D., Mannens, E., Van de Walle, R.: The datatank: an open data adapter with semantic output
18. Vander Sande, M., Colpaert, P., Verborgh, R., Coppens, S., Mannens, E., Van de Walle, R.: R&Wbase: Git for triples. In: Proceedings of the 6th Workshop on Linked Data on the Web (2013)
19. Villazón-Terrazas, B., Vilches-Blázquez, L., Corcho, O., Gómez-Pérez, A.: Methodological guidelines for publishing government linked data. In: Wood, D. (ed.) Linking Government Data, pp. 27–49. Springer, New York (2011)

Automatic Detection and Semantic Formalisation of Business Rules

Cheikh Kacfah Emani[1,2]

[1] CSTB, 290 route des Lucioles, BP 209, 06904 Sophia Antipolis, France
[2] Université Lyon 1, LIRIS, CNRS, UMR5205, 69622, France

Abstract. Experts in construction engineering are overwhelmed by regulatory texts. It is a heavy task to go through these texts and get an unambiguous list of requirements they contain. Moreover, with regard to the number of texts and the diversity of their writers, we cannot neglect the possibility of getting inconsistencies. Finally, these requirements are to be put close to digital representation of buildings to detect potential non-conformities. This paper examines these problems and envisions solutions to help experts. We thus envisage to automate detection and extraction of business rules in regulatory texts. Next, we propose to formalise identified requirements as `SPARQL` queries. These queries will serve for conformity checking on `OWL`-representation of buildings. Moreover, we plan to leverage these queries to detect inconsistencies in regulatory texts.

Keywords: #eswcphd2014Emani.

1 Introduction

Several pieces of text govern the field of construction engineering. In addition to the literary freestyle, these texts can be understood in various ways. In the digital era, it is desirable to automate the reformulation of these Business Rules (BR) with more simple phrases. Further, these regulations have to be followed by buildings. Knowing that they are designed more and more by means of computers, we can plan an automatic verification of building mock-up's conformity. To this end, conformity requirements need to be represented in a way that allows for checking them against digital representations of buildings. Challenges proposed by this problem written in a single sentence are multiple. First we must navigate within regulatory texts and help experts in construction engineering (henceforth denoted by "building experts" or simply "experts") to detect and extract minimal phrases that act as requirements. This task requires a set of NLP functionalities, which we denote $\mathcal{F}$, like: ($\mathcal{F}_1$) identification, within a sentence containing multiple requirements, of all the words which constitute a given rule, ($\mathcal{F}_2$) detection of scope of applications and contexts of rules, ($\mathcal{F}_3$) stemming, ($\mathcal{F}_4$) paraphrases, linguistic co-references, ellipsis and mentions to other pieces of texts, ($\mathcal{F}_5$) order of premises and corresponding conclusions, ($\mathcal{F}_6$) highlighting of "implicit parameters" (e.g: "The length must be sufficient" means that the

V. Presutti et al. (Eds.): ESWC 2014, LNCS 8465, pp. 834–844, 2014.

length must be *greater than a certain value*), etc. Results of this extraction must be put in a form easily verifiable by building experts. Next these requirements must be written in a computer understandable language. Similarly the building should be represented in a vocabulary *compatible* with conformity policies. Finally, non conform elements in buildings must be signalled to building experts. With its set of standards and easy to handle tools, the Semantic Web seems to be a promising source of support for the formalisation part of our problem. Practically, many recent works have successfully taken advantage of it [6],[23]. As we will see later, many tasks described in these PhD works are manual. "Automation" (as much as possible) is therefore the leitmotiv of this work. Our goal is discussed through the following agenda. Initially, the state of the art on detecting, extracting, rephrasing and formalising of conformity requirements is introduced (Sect. 2). Next, the problem is presented through an example and we point out possible contributions and primary insights of solution (Sect. 3). Finally, we expose a plan to validate our future results (Sect. 4).

2 State of the Art

Two fields of study are the most relevant to our work: *(i)* detecting and rephrasing rules and *(ii)* automatically formalising them.

Detecting and Reformulating Business Rules. Some proposal have been made to ease writing of policies [8],[20]. In our case we assume that they have already been written and we wish to disambiguate them by cleaning them to keep only their core formulation. Indeed, a BR is supposed to be *atomic, compact, well-formed, unambiguous* and *built upon domain-vocabulary* [9]. This aim is considered to be impossible [16] or in more optimistic words complex.

Facing the necessary functionalities listed in the introduction, a good compromise for this task is to assist experts [2], [7], [15,16], [19]. In [19], a detailed but manual methodology is proposed to identify, extract and formalise rules. Such hand-done execution gives the impression that lot of functionalities (e.g ($\mathcal{F}_3$) to ($\mathcal{F}_6$)) are not implemented. More easy to delegate to machines, Breaux and Anton [7] take advantage of goal mining [1, chap. 4], to tackle security policy management. They rephrase goal statements in "restricted natural language statements" (*RNLS*). RNLS are obtained by splitting each goal into sentences with exactly one actor and action, and must contain the essence of the original goal. Although leading to an expressive and query-able model, it is applied manually. Consequently, few of the constraints listed above are broached. More complete (except ($\mathcal{F}_2$)), a deeply detailed architecture and processes to achieve extraction and refinement of rules is given in [16]. There, with the help of a terminology extraction tool, `TERMINAE` [3,4], the user builds a domain ontology from texts. Next, an "index" is output [10]. This index links each piece of text to its concepts and to its rules. Similarly to the recommendations of Bouzidi [6], these rules are written w.r.t SBVR-SE (Semantics of Business Vocabulary and

Business Rules - Structured English). The editing of these rules is done manually. During this process, the user is helped by the highlighting of domain terms in the rule [15].
A fully automatic tool for BR generation is presented in [5]. There, Bajwa et al. take as input a text written in natural language and output *rephrased* SBVR rules. Their tool has a fairly good accuracy (87.33%), however it does not handle constraints solved by ($\mathcal{F}_4$) - non appearance of business terms in regulatory texts - and ($\mathcal{F}_6$) - requirement submitted to experts' subjective appreciation.

Formalisation of Rules. The rephrasing of rules or policies in simple terms as discussed earlier paves the way for more ambitious aims. In [7], the authors use a kind of table ($Activity < actor,\ action,\ object >$) to store information. Obviously, such representation is not expressive enough for all type of requirements. It is thus languages of the Semantic Web which obtain favours when modelling become more complex [6], [21,22,23]. Indeed, they are suitable because of their expressiveness, interoperability, standardization. Yurchyshyna [23] was the first to propose to represent building requirements as `SPARQL` queries. By doing it, she intended to query the `OWL`-representation of buildings to detect non-conform elements. This successful proposition has been followed by Bouzidi [6]. But in these two theses this process is done by hand. The automation of such transformation is addressed within many papers [21,22]. These works are relative to `SPARQL`-isation of questions w.r.t an `RDF`-knowledge base. They want to find and rank possible answers to natural language questions. To address this issue, they propose a two-steps approach. First, `SPARQL`-template(s) of the question is(are) output. Secondly, each pattern is instantiated through an entity linking resolution process. Entity linking aims at identifying the most suited entity in an unambiguous knowledge base to which refers a given string. They use a domain independent lexicon to formalise recurrent terms like *who, the most, at least, etc.* A domain-dependent lexicon is also required to represent the general behaviour of terms. For instance, if they are generally *property* or *object*, their possible types, or *domain* and *range*. This domain-dependent lexicon needs to be built almost manually. Unfortunately this construction is a tedious task.

3 Problem Statement and Contributions

3.1 Use Case Description

The regulatory text taken as example here is a (non-official) translation of the second item of the second paragraph of the subsection 6.1 of the article 6 found in the first chapter of the "Arrêté" mentioned in [13]. This text is about vertical interior circulation of the common parts of residential buildings.

```
Safety in use: At the top of the stairs, flooring must allow waking
alertness at a distance of 0.50 m from the first step through a
visual and tactile contrast.
The first and last steps must be provided with a riser with
```

```
a minimum height of 0.10 m, visually contrasting with walking.
The nosings must meet the following requirements:
- Being visually contrasting with respect to other stairs;
- Be non-skid;
- Present no excessive overhang relative to the riser.
The staircase must have a lighting device that meets the
requirements set out in Article 10.
```

From this piece of text, the following "conformity" BR were extracted and validated by building experts:

Table 1. BR extracted from [13] and their SBVR rephrasing w.r.t IFC vocabulary (**Colour code**: concept - *verb* - **value** - SBVR keyword)

Fully include in the text	**Rephrased and including words from business vocabulary**
(1) At the top of the stairs, flooring must allow waking alertness at a distance of 0.50 m from the first step	*At the top* of stairs , the length *of* the slab *must be* at least **50 cm**
(2)-(3) The first/last step must be provided with a riser with a minimum height of 0.10 m	The height *of* the riser *of* the first/last step *must be* at least **0.10 m**
(4) The nosings must be visually contrasting with respect to the rest of the stairs	The contrast *between* the nosings and the steps *must be* at least **<slot>**
(5) The nosings must be non-skid	The nosings *must have* non-skid surface
(6) The nosing must present no excessive overhang relative to the riser	The nosing length *must be* at least **<slot>**

It is important to notice that, in practice, we have to resolve the co-reference implied by the phrase *"requirements set out in Article 10"*. In addition, a quick look at Tab. 1 helps us to illustrate the list of constraints given in Sect. 2.

We can now put our SBVR-written rules in processable form. As suggested in [23] we choose SPARQL language[1]:

1. Rule (1):

```
SELECT ?stair ?length
WHERE {?stair rdf:type ifc:IfcStair.
OPTIONAL{
     ?stair ifc:IfcRelAggregates ?slab.
     ?slab rdf:type ifc:IfcSlab.
     ?slab ifc:PredefinedType ifc:LANDING.
     ?slab ifc:LENGTH ?length.
     FILTER (?length >=
       "500"^^xsd:positiveInteger)}.
     FILTER (! bound (?length))}
```

2. Rules (2) and (3):

```
SELECT ?stair ?height
```

[1] Declarations of common prefixes like `owl`, `xsd`, `rdf`, `rdfs` and the prefix of our ontology `ifc` are omitted for readability purposes.

```
WHERE {?stair rdf:type ifc:IfcStair.
OPTIONAL{
     ?stair ifc:IfcRelAggregates ?stairFlight.
     ?stairFlight rdf:type ifc:IfcStairFlight.
     ?stairFlight ifc:RiserHeight ?height.
     FILTER (?height >=
       "100"^^xsd:positiveInteger)}.
     FILTER (! bound (?height))}
```

3. Rule (5):

```
SELECT ?stair ?isNonSkid
WHERE { ?stair rdf:type ifc:IfcStair.
OPTIONAL{
     ?stair ifc:HasCoverings ?buildingElement.
     ?buildingElement ifc:RelatedCoverings
      ?covering.
     ?covering ifc:PredefineType ifc:FLOORING.
     ?covering ifc:HasNonSkidSurface ?isNonSkid.
     FILTER (?isNonSkid = "true"^^xsd:boolean)}.
     FILTER (! bound (?isNonSkid))}
```

4. Rule (6):

```
SELECT ?stair ?length
WHERE { ?stair rdf:type ifc:IfcStair.
OPTIONAL{
     ?stair ifc:IfcRelAggregates ?stairFlight.
     ?stairFlight rdf:type ifc:IfcStairFlight.
     ?stairFlight ifc:NosingLength ?length.
     FILTER (?length <=
       "10"^^xsd:positiveInteger)}.
     FILTER (! bound (?length))}
```

The above queries assume that:

- Like ontoCC [23, sect. 5.2], we suppose an ontology, `ifc`, which matches IFC entities, object and data properties [17] and so on. Moreover, it is an IFC-represented "object", which therefore instantiate `ifc`, which is queried.
- In addition, as expressed in [23], we are looking for non conform characteristics of our "object". Non conformity includes a value *mismatch* or its *lack*. We thus use the function `! bound()` to check if variables we are interested in, have been bound or not.

When we look closely at these queries, we can formulate a set of challenges brought up by this problem:

- Conversion from BR to `SPARQL` is not straightforward: BR are not in a simple <*subject, verb (property), object*> form. Such a form could have made us foreseen this conversion as a mapping task: relate each element of the triple to a single element of `ifc`.
- Decoding of some recurrent words as operator has to be done (e.g: *at least* in queries 1 and 2) or in some cases, aggregation functions like `COUNT`, `MAX`, `MIN`, etc.
- Detecting implicit operands as asking. For instance in case for operand of binary operators (e.g: $isNonSkid = true$ in query 3) or in case of empty slot (e.g: minimal length (10) in query 4).
- Handling of units of measurement. In our queries, lengths are expressed in millimetres.
- Going further than *syntactic* manipulations. Indeed, some URIs in the query do not appear (even if we look at the rule through stemming, compliant editing distance, synonyms, etc.) in the original rule. It is the case of properties like `ifc:IfcRelAggregates`, `ifc:PredefinedType` and `ifc:LANDING` in query 1.

- In the current state of IFC (IFC 4), it is not always possible to express a BR as a query (e.g: rule (4)).

In practice, our set of queries are stored. They will be triggered according to user specifications. For instance a user may want to verify only accessibility (stairs, lifts, doors, etc.) or lightening, etc. It means that SPARQL queries have to be annotated. Similarly some requirements are compulsory and others are just recommendations. All such metadata have to be added to queries and taken into account during the checking process. More details are provided in [23, chap. 6]. But there the organisation of the base of conformity queries is manual.

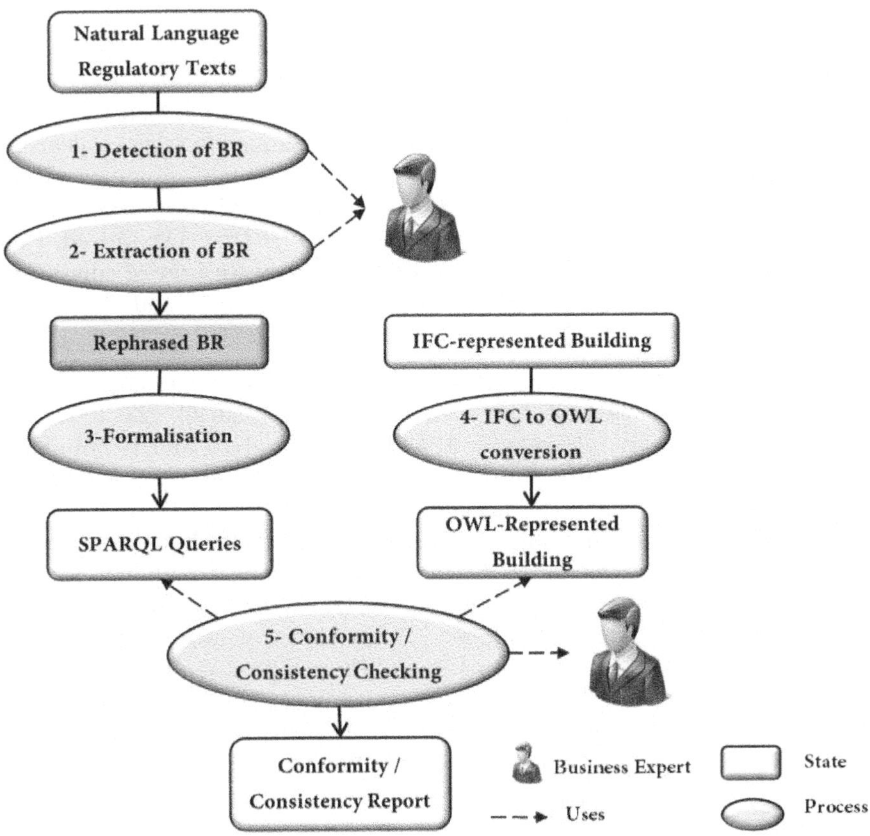

Fig. 1. The whole conformity checking process

3.2 Overview of Pursued Solutions and Approach

We have presented many sides of the problem of automation of conformity checking[2]. Some state-of-the-art methodologies and tools have been exposed. Now we present extensions, ameliorations and novel approaches.

[Steps 1 and 2] Rules Detection and Rephrasing. This is the entry point of our supply-chain (Fig. 1). As we have seen, the automation of this task is very complicated and a good trade-off is a semi-automation. First we must flatten lists and solve co-references. Here, the co-reference resolution process must disambiguate coordinators for establishing semantic relations between pieces of texts, and must handle co-reference within a paragraph (out of scope of a single sentence) as in [14]. Next, based on identification of key terms (from vocabulary or common words like minimal, at-least, etc.) and various heuristics, a proposition of possible rules should be made. These heuristics could be made on the structure (pattern) of sentences and the presence of certain words. Since it will happen to output non-sense (phrases as) rules or to have undetected rules, we intend to ask user for correction and in background seamlessly trigger a learning process. Heuristics are usually based on deep observations. Consequently, they fail due to more or less scarce exceptions. We can thus envisage a learning process designed for such context like *Ripple Down Rules (RDR)* [11]. Indeed, RDR are suitable when we want to add few exceptional cases to a set of conditional expressions and help to limit the number of conditions to be updated.

[Step 3] Automatic Formalisation of BR. Tens of languages could be used for this task. But since `SPARQL` has been successfully used [6], [23] it has our favour. But it is not the only reason. `SPARQL` is a standard and is popular in the Semantic Web community. Moreover, it is used to query `RDF` graphs and very expressive languages have been build on top of `RDF`. We principally have in mind `OWL`. It means that providing a `SPARQL` version of conformity requirements does not restrict expressiveness of digital representation of building. In addition, promising methods for full automation of translation of natural language questions to `SPARQL` have been developed [21,22]. Consequently, we can leverage methodology exposed by Unger, Lehmann and their colleagues. For our task, an extension of their domain-independent dictionary is needed (*minimal*, *maximal*, *more or less*, etc.). More we must propose an algorithm which gets around the use of the domain-dependent lexicon since it is heavy to build.
The main goal of this algorithm is to deduce triple patterns, between concept and predicate appearing in a simple phrase, by taking only the ontology of the domain (which covers this phrase) as input. We see in [21,22] that this relation is usually straight. For example in the sentence *Who produced the most films?*,

[2] We have taken here only a piece of a regulatory text to illustrate our work. For our final solution we must leverage a representative sample of regulatory texts. This representativeness is mainly about NLP challenges brought up by these texts. Moreover, the quality of the sample must be validated by the experts.

the relation between `produced` and `films` is direct. In our use case, we see in query 3 that starting at `ifc:IfcStair` and reaching `ifc:HasNonSkidSurface` leads us to pass through three intermediate properties.

Also, as mentioned earlier in this document, some operands are implicit. It is the case of the "value" *not excessive overhang* converted in *at least <slot>* in the sixth rule. This slot has been filled by the value **10**. Such value varies from one expert to another. Our job there consists to detect these cases and create slots which filling will be done at execution. This goal could be achieved using `SPIN` [12].

Let us mention that we do not focus our attention on the "step 4". It was addressed in Yurchyshyna's thesis [23].

[Step 5] Inconsistency Detection. When introducing this work, we have underlined the fact that the process described here is triggered by the volume of regulatory texts and the diversity of writers. This situation can lead to redundancies and more problematically to inconsistencies. Thus, assuming the formalisation of requirements, we could help building experts to correct texts. If requirements are represented by `SPARQL` queries, the challenge is to identify incompatible triple patterns in `SPARQL` graph patterns. Hypothetically, we have thousands or even millions of them. Therefore, we cannot plan to do pairwise comparisons. A possible method to reduce them is to index our queries. Since inconsistencies can only be found through `FILTER` clauses (excluding those about the binding), triple patterns they contain are good candidate for our keys. If we take for example `SPARQL` query number 1, the filter is applied on a *length*. When we scan the query, we see that the length is attached to *slabs*. So this requirement could be indexed by the "(length, slab)" entry. Consequently, it will be compared only with potential queries with the same entry to see if their filters are compatible. Another possible method to avoid useless comparisons is to cluster queries like in [18].

To Summarize. The whole process, from consuming raw regulatory texts to the delivering of a conformity or consistency report, is depicted by Fig. 1.

This figure clearly emphasises the five (or six) points of our work. First, with help of building experts, requirements are identified and extracted. Next we aim to automatically formalize these requirements. Simultaneously, the building is brought from IFC to `OWL`. Results of all these processes allow us to think about conformity checking. During this process we can prompt an expert for signalling non-formalised BR or to ask for implicit value as explained in Sect. 3.2. In addition, as reported on the figure, we can verify consistency of texts through their `SPARQL` representation. Unlike the conformity checking process, the consistency one does not need the building representation. In conformity report we have the concerned piece of regulation text and the precise reason of non conformity [23]. In consistency report, we present conflictual rules to the expert.

4 Evaluation Plan

Many theses have walked through the successive steps we have described. But their works have multiple manual tasks. Nevertheless, results they obtain constitute a good way to validate our work. So, our detection and extraction processes can be applied on the different corpus used by Bouzidi [6] and Yurchyshyna [23]. Since the rules they have extracted have been validated by experts, these rules will be used to evaluate the precision and the recall of our detection and extraction steps. A similar approach is planned about formalisation. Also important, we will focus on the usability of our future tool.

5 Conclusion and Perspectives

This paper presents the work envisioned for our PhD thesis. Its essence can be expressed with the word automation. At the end of our work, we plan to provide algorithms to automate detection and extraction of rules from regulatory texts. Next, we intend to re-write automatically these requirements by `SPARQL` queries (and corresponding annotations) aligned with IFC vocabulary. This task implies be able to identify all implicit functions, triple patterns and filter parameters without human help. This formalisation should be easy to apply in any domain, assuming we have its ontology. Finally we plan to propose a framework to detect incompatibility between a set of `SPARQL` queries supposed to describe coherent requirements.

References

1. Anton, A.I.: Goal Identification and Refinement in the Specification of Information Systems. Ph.D. thesis, Georgia Institute of Technology (June 1997)
2. Anton, A.I., Earp, J.B., He, Q., Stufflebeam, W., Bolchini, D., Jensen, C.: Financial privacy policies and the need for standardization. IEEE Security & Privacy 2(2), 36–45 (2004)
3. Aussenac-Gilles, N., Biebow, B., Szulman, S.: Revisiting ontology design: A methodology based on corpus analysis. In: Proceedings of the 12th European Workshop on Knowledge Acquisition, Modeling and Management, EKAW 2000, pp. 172–188. Springer, London (2000)
4. Aussenac-Gilles, N., Despres, S., Szulman, S.: The TERMINAE method and platform for ontology engineering from texts. In: Proceedings of the 2008 Conference on Ontology Learning and Population: Bridging the Gap Between Text and Knowledge, pp. 199–223. IOS Press, Amsterdam (2008)
5. Bajwa, I.S., Lee, M.G., Bordbar, B.: SBVR business rules generation from natural language specification. In: AAAI Spring Symposium: AI for Business Agility, pp. 2–8. AIII (2011)

6. Bouzidi, K.R.: Aide à la création et à l'exploitation de réglementations basée sur les modèles et techniques du Web sémantique. Ph.D. thesis, Université Nice Sophia Antipolis (September 2011)
7. Breaux, T.D., Anton, A.I.: Analyzing goal semantics for rights, permissions, and obligations. In: Proceedings of the 13th IEEE International Conference on Requirements Engineering, RE 2005, pp. 177–188. IEEE Computer Society, Washington, DC (2005)
8. Brodie, C.A., Karat, C.M., Karat, J.: An empirical study of natural language parsing of privacy policy rules using the sparcle policy workbench. In: Proceedings of the Second Symposium on Usable Privacy and Security, SOUPS 2006, pp. 8–19. ACM, New York (2006)
9. Graham, I.: Business rules management and service oriented architecture: A pattern language. John Wiley & Sons, Chichester (2006)
10. Guissé, A., Lévy, F., Nazarenko, A.: Un moteur sémantique pour explorer des textes réglementaires. In: Mille, A. (ed.) Actes des 22èmes Journées Francophones d'Ingénierie des Connaissances, pp. 451–458. Publibook (2011)
11. Kim, M.H.: Ripple-Down Rules based Open Information Extraction for the Web Documents. Ph.D. thesis, School of Computer Science and Engineering, The University of New South Wales, Australia (April 2012)
12. Knublauch, K., Idehen, K., Hendler, J.A.: SPARQL inferencing notation (SPIN), `http://spinrdf.org/`
13. Lecomte, A., Trégoat, J.: Arrêté du 1er aout 2006 fixant les dispositions prises pour l'application des articles R. 111-18 à R. 111-18-7 du code de la construction et de l'habitation relatives à l'accessibilité aux personnes handicapées des bâtiments d'habitation collectifs et des maisons individuelles lors de leur construction. Journal Officiel 195(13), 111–118 (2006)
14. Lee, H., Chang, A., Peirsman, Y., Chambers, N., Surdeanu, M., Jurafsky, D.: Deterministic coreference resolution based on entity-centric, precision-ranked rules. Computational Linguistics 39(4), 885–916 (2013)
15. Levy, F., Guisse, A., Nazarenko, A., Omrane, N., Szulman, S.: An environment for the joint management of written policies and business rules. In: Proceedings of the 2010 22nd IEEE International Conference on Tools with Artificial Intelligence, ICTAI 2010, vol. 2, pp. 142–149. IEEE Computer Society, Washington, DC (2010)
16. Lévy, F., Nazarenko, A.: Formalization of natural language regulations through SBVR structured english. In: Morgenstern, L., Stefaneas, P., Lévy, F., Wyner, A., Paschke, A. (eds.) RuleML 2013. LNCS, vol. 8035, pp. 19–33. Springer, Heidelberg (2013)
17. Liebich, T., Adachi, Y., Forester, J., Hyvarinen, J., Richter, S., Chipman, T., Weise, M., Wix, J.: IFC4 official release, `http://www.buildingsmart-tech.org/ifc/IFC4/final/html/`
18. Lorey, J., Naumann, F.: Detecting SPARQL query templates for data prefetching. In: Cimiano, P., Corcho, O., Presutti, V., Hollink, L., Rudolph, S. (eds.) ESWC 2013. LNCS, vol. 7882, pp. 124–139. Springer, Heidelberg (2013)
19. Maxwell, J.C., Anton, A.I.: Developing production rule models to aid in acquiring requirements from legal texts. In: Proceedings of the 2009 17th IEEE International Requirements Engineering Conference, RE 2009, pp. 101–110. IEEE Computer Society, Washington, DC (2009)

20. Reeder, R.W., Karat, C.-M., Karat, J., Brodie, C.: Usability challenges in security and privacy policy-authoring interfaces. In: Baranauskas, C., Abascal, J., Barbosa, S.D.J. (eds.) INTERACT 2007. LNCS, vol. 4663, pp. 141–155. Springer, Heidelberg (2007)
21. Unger, C., Bühmann, L., Lehmann, J., Ngonga Ngomo, A.C., Gerber, D., Cimiano, P.: Template-based question answering over RDF data. In: Proceedings of the 21st International Conference on World Wide Web, WWW 2012, pp. 639–648. ACM, New York (2012)
22. Unger, C., Cimiano, P.: Pythia: Compositional meaning construction for ontology-based question answering on the semantic web. In: Muñoz, R., Montoyo, A., Métais, E. (eds.) NLDB 2011. LNCS, vol. 6716, pp. 153–160. Springer, Heidelberg (2011)
23. Yurchyshyna, A.: Modélisation du contrôle de conformité: une approche ontologique. Ph.D. thesis, Université Nice Sophia Antipolis (February 2009)

Combining Linked Data and Statistical Information Retrieval

Next Generation Information Systems

Ricardo Usbeck*

University of Leipzig, Germany
usbeck@informatik.uni-leipzig.de
R & D, Unister GmbH, Leipzig, Germany

Abstract. Being a part of the *Information Age*, users are challenged with a tremendously growing amount of Web data which generates a need for more sophisticated information retrieval systems. The *Semantic Web* provides necessary procedures to augment the highly unstructured Web with suitable metadata in order to leverage search quality and user experience. In this article, we will outline an approach for creating a web-scale, precise and efficient information system capable of understanding keyword, entity and natural language queries. By using Semantic Web methods and *Linked Data* the doctoral work will present how the underlying knowledge is created and elaborated searches can be performed on top.

Keywords: #eswcphd2014Usbeck, Search, NLP, Question Answering, Ranking.

1 Introduction

In the last couple of years, the way search is perceived by end users as well as industrial agents changed dramatically. Recently, new semantic search algorithms[1] spread which account not only for keywords but for semantic entities, relations, personalized information and many more. In analogy, future developments in everyday and business search engines need to unlock the power of semantic technologies.

Linked Data is the Semantic Web methodology for publishing data based on W3C standards such as RDF [21], URI and HTTP in order to provide linkable, valuable content. Whether provided by a SPARQL [1] endpoint or embedded in a Web page via RDFa [2], Linked Data is a key technology to master the upcoming information flood. Since 2007, the Linked Open Data (LOD) Cloud gathered more than 300 datasets also known as *knowledge bases* comprising over

* Advisors: Axel-Cyrille Ngonga Ngomo, Andreas Both and Sören Auer
ngonga@informatik.uni-leipzig.de

[1] http://searchengineland.com/google-hummingbird-172816

V. Presutti et al. (Eds.): ESWC 2014, LNCS 8465, pp. 845–854, 2014.

31 billion triples[2]. Amongst others it consists of agricultural, musical, medical and geographical facts, the LOD Cloud is the largest linked encyclopaedic knowledge base known to mankind.

Using the Semantic Web is expected to drive innovation in data integration and analysis software within companies. Moreover, end users anticipate more sophisticated search engines that truly understand the underlying information need. Therefore, combining scientifically sound information retrieval methods with static and dynamic Web data as well as Linked Data will leverage information insight already in the short term. For example, fundamental scientific work has been done in the Linked Open Data [3] project. However, there is no information retrieval framework which is able to convert the scientific knowledge into a holistic Semantic Web-based search engine.

In Section 2, the state of the art in the areas of information retrieval and Linked Data-based search and ranking algorithms is presented. The problems tackled in this thesis and its contributions are described in Section 3. Section 4 presents the already available approaches *AGDISTIS* [34], which is a named entity extraction framework for unstructured Web pages, and *REX* [5], a relation extraction approach for templated websites. Furthermore, first steps towards an auto-completion functionality are pointed out and plans on further research regarding search and ranking algorithms are presented. Section 5 concludes with an outlook on the future research agenda.

2 State of the Art

(1) *Information Extraction.* This field can be considered as comprising three main sub-fields: named entity recognition (NER), named entity disambiguation (NED) and relation extraction (RE). NER is the task of identifying entities in an input text while NED is focused on pre-identified named entities and their disambiguation towards a certain knowledge base using various methods. RE is the task of finding connections between entities based on a given context. In this thesis, we restrict the identifiable entity classes to 'persons', 'locations' and 'organizations' using FOX [25] as well-known NER framework.

In the following, several NED approaches for *unstructured texts* are introduced. A framework for annotating and disambiguating Semantic Web resources in unstructured texts is DBpedia Spotlight [23]. Contrary to other tools, Spotlight is able to disambiguate against all classes of the DBpedia ontology. Another algorithm is AIDA which uses the YAGO2[3] Linked Data knowledge base using sophisticated sub-graph matching algorithms. Furthermore, the approach disambiguates w.r.t. similarity of contexts, prominence of entities and context windows. Unfortunately, the approaches presented so far are either not efficient enough (i.e. runtime lacks [7]) to handle web-scale data or do not deliver the expected extraction quality based on specific

[2] http://lod-cloud.net/state/

[3] http://www.mpi-inf.mpg.de/yago-naga/yago/

Linked Data sources [34]. Recently, Cornolti et al. [7] presented a framework for benchmarking NED approaches. The authors compared six existing approaches against five well-known datasets on different tasks and with different measures.

Information Extraction from *templated web-sites* is mainly related to the field of wrapper induction. Early approaches to learning web wrappers were mostly supervised (e.g., [17,10]). Recently, Crescenzi et al [8] described a supervised framework that is able to profit from crowd-provided training data. The learning algorithm controls the cost of the crowdsourcing campaign w.r.t. quality of the output wrapper. However, these novel approaches miss the opportunities related to existence of Linked Data, and the semantic consistency of the extracted data is out of their scope of interest.

In order to accomplish the vision of the Semantic Web, Gentile et al. [11] presents an approach for learning web wrappers that exploit Linked Data as a training data source for their wrapper induction framework. However, the process they adopt consists of a variety of manual steps and is thus very time consuming.

(2) *Search Query Support.* Auer et al. [24] describe a method to enrich search queries via a conjunctive extension based on the underlying semantic ontology. This approach is able to retrieve entities and documents provided only with a description instead of a search query. This leads to results without an overlap of keywords between query and document.

Besides keyword-based search queries, some search engines also understand natural language questions. Question answering is more difficult than keyword-based searches since retrieval algorithms need to understand complex grammatical constructs. Unger et al. [33] present a manually curated, template-based approach to match a question against a specific SPARQL query. They combine natural language processing (NLP) capabilities with Linked Data which leads to good benchmark results w.r.t. the question answering on Linked Data benchmark (QALD)[4].

(3) *Information Retrieval/Hybrid Search.* Popular search engines like Google or Yahoo! have answered search requests based on keyword queries for a long time. For a retrospective of existing information retrieval methods the interested reader may refer to standard literature [20]. However, the development of Semantic Web technologies lead to search engines being more conversational than traditional keyword-based engines [30].

Apart from those document- and keyword-centric approaches, the Linked Data movement has developed diverse strategies to leverage the advantages of semantic knowledge. Based on the underlying semantic structure of Linked Data, He et al. [13] developed an approach that transforms search queries to semantic graphs and tries to match those against the Linked Data graphs of the underlying dataset.

Furthermore, `http://swoogle.umbc.edu` represents a first prototype of a semantic search engine. Ding et al. [9] described the different search strategies to find instances via, e.g., term, document or ontology searches. Since

[4] `http://greententacle.techfak.uni-bielefeld.de/~cunger/qald`

this application was updated in 2007 for the last time and only consists of a comparably small corpus of documents and Linked Data, it cannot be considered as a web-scale approach.

`http://sindice.com/` [6] is a more recent approach that scans the Semantic Web in order to build a semantic web index that is searchable and queryable via SPARQL. Unfortunately, the underlying database does not comprise full-text information and thus cannot answer a broad range of queries.

(4) *Ranking.* The procedures and algorithms described before are capable of delivering an unordered set of search results to the user. However, the increasing number of documents available on the Web leads to a tremendous growth of search result sets. Following Smyth et al. [31], most users tend to look only at the first few results. To aid finding relevant information within the first few places, ranking algorithms need to be deployed.

Well-known representatives for Web document ranking algorithms are the Hypertext-Induced Topic Search (HITS) algorithm [19] and PageRank [4]. Both calculate the relevance of a search result based on the Web link graph and are also very scalable algorithms.

Already in 2002, Mayfield et al. [22,28] described a first approach combining information retrieval with semantic inference mechanism. Furthermore, they present an algorithm which ranks Semantic Web entities with regard to trust information.

Moreover, an extension to the PageRank algorithm using Linked Data knowledge has been described by Julia Stoyanovich [32]. Extracting semantic knowledge from a Web document and combining this with an underlying ontology has shown to improve ranking quality. Unfortunately, this version of the algorithm is not able to scale on Web data.

Furthermore, ReConRank [16] is a highly efficient algorithm based on the PageRank algorithm. It considers provenance information while ranking, leading to more trustworthy result lists. This algorithm is based on semantic sub-graphs whose size influences efficiency and precision of results.

The ranking algorithms described so far are independent of the underlying query which can steer those towards a loss of information. Gupta et al. [26] introduced an approach that enriches the query based on Linked Data in order to find, e.g., polysemes and synonyms. Afterwards, the ranking works on a context-ordered index retrieving an initial sorting of the documents, which are finally sorted according to their similarity to the query.

Moreover, xhRank [12] proves that a combination of semantic information from a Linked Data graph can lead to an improved ranking. The position, morphological features and structure of an entity within a query are used to reorder certain documents from the search result list.

Past attempts combining Linked Data and information retrieval techniques suffer from either performance leaks and high quality results with respect to Web-scale datasets or a missing holistic concept that is able to bring search technology to the next level.

3 Problem Statement and Contributions

The aim of this doctoral work is an information system/search engine framework that will address the following working domains:

(1) Initially, the proposed system needs to link crawled Web data with Semantic Web knowledge. This task can be performed by NER, NED and RE algorithms. Therefore, two types of Web pages need be distinguished: templated sites like actor pages from `http://www.imdb.com/` and unstructured Web pages like news articles from `http://www.nytimes.com/`. In this thesis, two *Information Extraction* approaches have been developed, which are described in Section 4.

(2) After the data is provided, the user has to be enabled to search it. An effective way to do so is to provide the user with a input field-like interface they are used to. As the user begins typing into the search input field the framework should present different search query suggestions. This *auto-completion* does not only speed up searching but also teaches the user which kind of queries the search engine framework understands. Moreover, this can lead to a reeducation of users' search behavior from short keyword-based searches to longer natural language queries or even real search questions. An auto-completion approach which *supports the query generation* will be developed in the next stage of the PhD work using linked knowledge.

(3) The search functionality to be developed in this thesis is going to be *hybrid*, i.e., simultaneously performing a full-text,e.g., Lucene-based[5], and an entity search. Different entity search algorithms need to be developed based on the significantly different data structures and problems arising from them. While full-text search is a well-studied field, as shown in Section 2, entity search on Linked Data has only been in the focus of research for about 10 years. A hybrid search engine is currently under development and will be evaluated against the recently published QALD-4 benchmark.

(4) Finally, when appropriate Web pages and Semantic Web entities have been found, the user wants them to be presented according to their relevance. *Ranking* algorithms aim to reorder result list with respect to one or more sorting criteria. Scientifically sound methods for classical information retrieval are already present and the most important ones can be found in Section 2. However, principles creating a combined ranking of full-text and semantic search results need to be investigated within this doctoral thesis. Therefore, we aim at creating an machine learning-based interweaving of several well-known ranking algorithms.

Combining the advantages of information retrieval methods and Linked Data technologies will overcome the information flood problem. The union of highly scalable retrieval algorithms and effective rankings is able to increase the users search experience. A formalisation of the approach is currently in progress.

[5] `http://lucene.apache.org/core/`

4 Research Approach and Initial Results

Central to this PhD work is to answer *how a search engine can benefit from the Linked Data paradigm?* Diverse technologies like RDFa, micro-data and HTML5 semantic annotations have been introduced to enrich Web data for a better user experience and machine interoperability. However, to the best of our knowledge there is no information retrieval architecture that uses the advantages of this technology holistically. Moreover, some search pipeline steps for the Web of Data need to be revised in order to perform efficient and effective searches.

To meet this obstacle, the presented thesis introduces a pipeline architecture for a Linked Data-based search engine, as depicted in Figure 1.

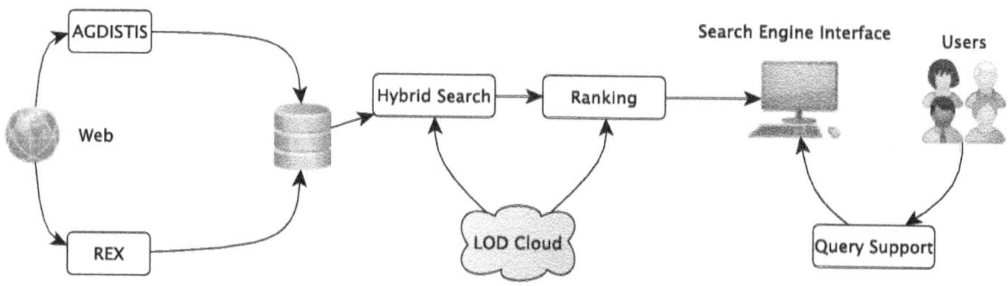

Fig. 1. Overview of the proposed information system architecture

The starting point of the proposed architecture is a two-fold data acquisition strategy based on a highly efficient, state-of-the-art industry Web crawler provided by our research partner *Unister GmbH.*

First, *unstructured Web pages* from the crawled dataset, e.g., provided texts from news portals or agencies, are annotated by a standard NER algorithm [18] followed by a novel NED approach AGDISTIS [34]. This NED approach has been developed to support arbitrary Linked Data knowledge bases to ensure future developments. Moreover, AGDISTIS uses several NLP techniques to identify a set of candidate entities and identifies the correct with the help of the graph-based HITS algorithm. To prove the quality of AGDISTIS' results several corpora have been generated, evaluated and published. These corpora, called N^3 [27], use the state-of-the-art serialization format *NIF* [14] following the "eating our own dogfood" paradigm inherent to the Semantic Web community. N^3 are expected to form a novel gold standard in the areas of semantic named entity recognition and disambiguation. Using N^3 and other well-known datasets, AGDISTIS has been proven to outperform the state-of-the-art algorithm AIDA [15] by up to 16% F-measure. In the future, AGDISTIS will be evaluated against the framework of Cornolti et al. [7] to provide a more comprehensive evaluation.

Second, *templated Web pages*, e.g., `http://www.imdb.com`, have been identified as another important source for answering user searches. Therefore, REX [5] has been developed during the early stage of this PhD work. It is a web-scale semantic relation extraction framework capable to identify known as well as novel relations on Web pages creating RDF out of them. REX combines a well-known wrapper induction technique [8] for extracting XPath expressions, AGDISTIS as its NED algorithm and a consistency checker for the extracted relations based on ad-hoc generated schemas. It has been shown that REX is able to generate new Linked Data triples with a precision of above 75% [5].

The resulting data from both pre-processing steps will serve as the underlying dataset for future research steps together with knowledge from the LOD Cloud.

Concerning the users' need for exploring the data space, the next step is to *support the formulation of queries*. A huge potential within classical search engines is contained in inexact search queries, e.g., in terms of given a description only or a question. Standard search engine methodologies fail at this point due to not being able to match keyword queries. In this thesis, we will support query formulation by providing on-the-fly recommended queries based on the real-time user input. It is planned to use Linked Data such as *BabelNet*[6] to find polysemes and synonyms within a query and thus enhancing the understanding of what the users actually mean. Furthermore, three different standard approaches as well as a Linked Data-based grammar will be compared and evaluated against each other. Another by-product of an according auto-completion approach is to teach the user which queries a search engine understands.

The research field of information retrieval/search and ranking has so far only been analysed theoretically within this doctoral work. In this thesis, a hybrid search engine is going to be implemented, i.e., an engine comprising a full-text information retrieval system enhanced by extracted Linked Data and a stake of LOD Cloud-based entity search. Especially, the keyword-based search engine *SINA* [29] will be a starting point for further research.

With respect to ranking algorithms, this PhD work focuses on two different research plans. At first, a semantic extension of graph-based authority calculating algorithms will be investigated. Therefore, a master thesis has been looked after which analysed a context-driven enhancement of Stoyanovich's work [32]. Initial results show an improvement compared to the baseline using the plain PageRank algorithm. In parallel, an ensemble learning approach of Semantic Web-based ranking algorithms will be evaluated.

To summarize, the aforementioned steps will help building an integrated information system leveraging search engine performance using Linked Data. Additionally–due to strong industry needs–this framework is going to be used in a real-life environment with web-scale amounts of users. Finally, most of the source code will be published as open source and can be downloaded via the projects homepage[7].

---

[6] `http://babelnet.org/`

[7] `http://aksw.org/RicardoUsbeck`

5 Evaluation Plan and Conclusion

This PhD work is dimensioned for three years. After intense literature reviews in the beginning of the first year the need for annotated Web data has been identified. As a logical consequence, the development of AGDISTIS and REX had been finished by the end of the first year. Alongside, a gold standard (N^3) has been created to be able to evaluate the approaches mentioned above.

The second year will be used for developing and assessing the corresponding search and ranking procedures. To measure the quality of the *auto-completion* technology, we assess different real-world query logs from our industry partner. Thereby, we analyze how much characters are need to understand the query correct. Additionally, we focus on the efficiency of the system in terms of milliseconds to react on a pressed key.

Considering the ranking evaluation, we will use standard precision, recall and f-measures as well as rank comparision measures, e.g., mean reciprocal rank. The underlying data is provided by the industry partner through human rater assessments and several comparisons to real-life search engines, e.g., Google or Wolfram Alpha.

Afterwards, the combined pipeline itself will be evaluated in a qualitative study using professionals and end users. Therefore, empirical methods like Likert-scale questionnaires and direct relevance feedback will be used.

Next to refining already submitted work and optimizing the source code to meet industrial production standards, the developed approaches and algorithms will be refined in a spiral way if unpredictable results occur. Thereby, upcoming ideas will be interweaved with the presented schedule creating a closed loop consisting of research question, development, evaluation and new research questions.

Gefördert aus Mitteln der Europäischen Union

Europa fördert Sachsen. ESF Europäischer Sozialfonds

Acknowledgements. This work has been supported by the ESF and the Free State of Saxony.

References

1. SPARQL query language for RDF. Technical report, World Wide Web Consortium (January 2008)
2. Adida, B., Birbeck, M.: RDFa primer 1.0 embedding RDF in XHTML. W3c working draft, W3C (October 2007)
3. Auer, S., et al.: Managing the life-cycle of linked data with the LOD2 stack. In: Cudré-Mauroux, P., et al. (eds.) ISWC 2012, Part II. LNCS, vol. 7650, pp. 1–16. Springer, Heidelberg (2012)
4. Brin, S., Page, L.: The anatomy of a large-scale hypertextual web search engine. In: Computer Networks and ISDN Systems, pp. 107–117. Elsevier Science Publishers B. V. (1998)
5. Bühmann, Usbeck, Ngomo Ngonga, Saleem, Crescenzi, Merialdo, Qui, Both: REX - Web-Scale Extension of RDF Knowledge Bases. Submitted to 11th Extended Semantic Web Conference, Anissaras, Crete, Greece, May 25-29 (2014)

6. Campinas, S., Ceccarelli, D., Perry, T.E., Delbru, R., Balog, K., Tummarello, G.: The sindice-2011 dataset for entity-oriented search in the web of data. In: 1st Int. Workshop on Entity-Oriented Search (EOS), pp. 26–32 (2011)
7. Cornolti, M., Ferragina, P., Ciaramita, M.: A framework for benchmarking entity-annotation systems. In: Proceedings of the 22nd International Conference on World Wide Web, WWW 2013, pp. 249–260. International World Wide Web Conferences Steering Committee, Republic and Canton of Geneva (2013)
8. Crescenzi, V., Merialdo, P., Qiu, D.: A framework for learning web wrappers from the crowd. In: Proceedings of the 22nd International Conference on World Wide Web, WWW 2013, pp. 261–272. International World Wide Web Conferences Steering Committee, Republic and Canton of Geneva (2013)
9. Ding, L., Pan, R., Finin, T., Joshi, A., Peng, Y., Kolari, P.: Finding and ranking knowledge on the semantic web. In: Gil, Y., Motta, E., Benjamins, V.R., Musen, M.A. (eds.) ISWC 2005. LNCS, vol. 3729, pp. 156–170. Springer, Heidelberg (2005)
10. Flesca, S., Manco, G., Masciari, E., Rende, E., Tagarelli, A.: Web wrapper induction: a brief survey. AI Communications 17(2), 57–61 (2004)
11. Gentile, A.L., Zhang, Z., Augenstein, I., Ciravegna, F.: Unsupervised wrapper induction using linked data. In: Proceedings of the Seventh International Conference on Knowledge Capture, K-CAP 2013, pp. 41–48. ACM, New York (2013)
12. He, X., Baker, M.: xhrank: Ranking entities on the semantic web. In: ISWC Posters & Demos 2010 (2010)
13. He, X., Baker, M.: A graph-based approach to indexing semantic web data. In: 9th International Semantic Web Conference, ISWC 2010 (November 2010)
14. Hellmann, S., Lehmann, J., Auer, S., Brümmer, M.: Integrating NLP using linked data. In: Alani, H., et al. (eds.) ISWC 2013, Part II. LNCS, vol. 8219, pp. 98–113. Springer, Heidelberg (2013)
15. Hoffart, J., Yosef, M.A., Bordino, I., Fürstenau, H., Pinkal, M., Spaniol, M., Taneva, B., Thater, S., Weikum, G.: Robust Disambiguation of Named Entities in Text. In: Conference on Empirical Methods in Natural Language Processing, EMNLP 2011, Edinburgh, Scotland, pp. 782–792 (2011)
16. Hogan, A., Harth, A., Decker, S.: Reconrank: A scalable ranking method for semantic web data with context. In: 2nd Workshop on Scalable Semantic Web Knowledge Base Systems (2006)
17. Hogue, A., Karger, D.: Thresher: automating the unwrapping of semantic content from the world wide web. In: Proceedings of the 14th International Conference on World Wide Web, WWW 2005, pp. 86–95. ACM, New York (2005)
18. Klein, D., Manning, C.D.: Fast exact inference with a factored model for natural language parsing. In: NIPS, pp. 3–10 (2002)
19. Kleinberg, J.M.: Authoritative sources in a hyperlinked environment. J. ACM 46(5), 604–632 (1999)
20. Manning, C.D., Raghavan, P., Schtze, H.: Introduction to Information Retrieval (2008)
21. Manola, F., Miller, E. (eds.): RDF Primer. W3C Recommendation. World Wide Web Consortium (February 2004)
22. Mayfield, J., Finnin, T.: Information retrieval on the Semantic Web: Integrating inference and retrieval. In: Workshop on the Semantic Web at the 26th Intl. ACM SIGIR Conf. on Research and Development in Information Retrieval, Toronto, Canada (2003)
23. Mendes, P.N., Jakob, M., Garcia-Silva, A., Bizer, C.: Dbpedia spotlight: Shedding light on the web of documents. In: Proceedings of the 7th International Conference on Semantic Systems, I-Semantics (2011)

24. Ngonga, A.: Generating conjunctive queries for keyword search on rdf data. In: Sixth ACM WSDM (Web Search and Data Mining) Conference (2013) (submitted)
25. Ngonga Ngomo, A.-C., Heino, N., Lyko, K., Speck, R., Kaltenböck, M.: SCMS – semantifying content management systems. In: Aroyo, L., Welty, C., Alani, H., Taylor, J., Bernstein, A., Kagal, L., Noy, N., Blomqvist, E. (eds.) ISWC 2011, Part II. LNCS, vol. 7032, pp. 189–204. Springer, Heidelberg (2011)
26. Sharma, A.K., Gupta, P.: Ontology driven pre and post ranking based information retrieval in web search engines (2012)
27. Röder, M., Usbeck, R., Gerber, D., Hellmann, S., Both, A.: A collection of datasets for named entity recognition and disambiguation in the nlp interchange format N^3. In: LREC. European Language Resources Association, ELRA (2014)
28. Shah, U., Finin, T., Joshi, A., Cost, R.S., Matfield, J.: Information retrieval on the semantic web. In: Proceedings of the Eleventh International Conference on Information and Knowledge Management, CIKM 2002 (2002)
29. Shekarpour, S., Marx, E., Ngomo, A.-C.N., Auer, S.: Sina: Semantic interpretation of user queries for question answering on interlinked data. Submitted to Journal of Web Semantics (2013)
30. Singhal, A.: The end of search as we know it. Presentation at Google I/O, San Francisco (2013)
31. Smyth, B., Balfe, E., Boydell, O., Bradley, K., Briggs, P., Coyle, M., Freyne, J.: A live-user evaluation of collaborative web search. In: IJCAI, pp. 1419–1424 (2005)
32. Stoyanovich, J., Bedathur, S.J., Berberich, K., Weikum, G.: Entityauthority: Semantically enriched graph-based authority propagation. In: WebDB (2007)
33. Unger, C., Bühmann, L., Lehmann, J., Ngonga Ngomo, A.-C., Gerber, D., Cimiano, P.: Template-based question answering over rdf data. In: Proceedings of the 21st International Conference on World Wide Web, pp. 639–648. ACM (2012)
34. Usbeck, Ngonga Ngomo, Roeder, Auer, Gerber, Both: AGDISTIS - Agnostic Disambiguation of Named Entities Using Linked Open Data. Submitted to 11th Extended Semantic Web Conference, Anissaras, Crete, Greece, May 25-29, 2014 (2013)

Searching Linked Data and Services with a Single Query

Mohamed Lamine Mouhoub

PSL, Université Paris-Dauphine, 75775 Paris Cedex 16, France
CNRS, LAMSADE UMR 7243
mohamed.mouhoub@dauphine.fr

Abstract. The appearance of valuable Linked Data sources as part of the LOD in the last few years and the emergence of Semantic Web services has opened new horizons for web and data research. Moreover, machine-understandability of semantics allows for efficient search and integration of data. Based on the existing standards and techniques, we address the problem of searching data and services in the LOD. Furthermore, we aim to introduce an approach that integrates data queries with data from service calls and compositions. However, many challenges and issues need to be resolved in order to achieve such a goal. In this paper we briefly discuss some of such problems and solutions.

Keywords: #eswcphd2014Mouhoub, Semantic Web, Linked Data, Semantic Web Services, Service Discovery.

1 Introduction

The appearance of valuable Linked Data sources such as DBPedia[1], YAGO[19], Freebase[2] and the advent of the Linked Open Data cloud[3] (LOD) has allowed access to terabytes of machine-understandable data. According to LODStats[4], a very recent LOD monitor[3], there are more than 61 billion triples over 2289 datasets in the LOD. However, many issues and challenges came up with the LOD such as :

- Some non-static content of the LOD can be outdated quickly unless the sources are updated frequently to provide fresh yet up-to-date information. For example, YAGO[5] which is a knowledge base extracted from Wikipedia[6] hasn't been updated since late 2012. Another example is the population of Paris in DBpedia which is not up to date even in its DBpedia Live[7] version that comes right from Wikipedia.

[1] http://www.dbpedia.org/
[2] http://www.freebase.com/
[3] http://linkeddata.org/
[4] http://stats.lod2.eu/
[5] www.mpi-inf.mpg.de/yago-naga/yago/
[6] http://www.wikipedia.com/
[7] http://live.dbpedia.org/

V. Presutti et al. (Eds.): ESWC 2014, LNCS 8465, pp. 855–863, 2014.

- Data can be incomplete and needs complementary parts of information from other sources that don't necessarily belong to the LOD[14]. For example, events, places or friends around Paris are relatively important information for a user, yet these dynamic and social information doesn't reside in the LOD and require the usage of dedicated social APIs.
- Obviously, lots of data that lies within the WWW doesn't appear yet in the LOD. Lots of modeling and publishing efforts are needed to publish data as Linked Open Data.

On the other side, there are thousands of public Web Services (WS) that provide fresh and good quality information[14]. ProgrammableWeb[8] is one example of Service repositories that indexes more than 10 000 web service. Thus, results of queries on LOD can be enriched with fresh and complementary data from web services that hide lots of exploitable data. However, finding relevant WS and integrating their provided data with LOD data is quite a hard task and requires a lifting of web services to the semantic level. Semantic Web Services (SWS) are a key raw material for such an integration that are still not abundant but lots of research has been led on their description, discovery, and composition[9].

2 State of the Art

The aforementioned motivation covers a crossing of many Semantic Web applications including Linked Data management in the LOD and SWS publishing, discovery and composition. This section presents some state-of-the art work enumerated by their application category.

2.1 Query Processing in the Linked Open Data Cloud

Lots of recent and competitive works address the processing of distributed RDF stores. They can be classified into 2 branches[7,4]:

1. Distributed approaches: that target the distributed remote LOD sources. They can be divided into :1.a) Look-up based approaches that download all the data from the remote LOD sources and run the queries locally. The lookup can be done either before execution like in [5] or on the fly during the query answering like in [6]. 1.b) Federation based approaches like [17] that send sub-queries to the remote SPARQL endpoints to be executed remotely then aggregates the returned results.
2. Parallel processing approaches like [4,8] that consider the Linked Data as Big Data and use parallelization techniques like MapReduce among others to process the large amounts of RDF triples. However, parallel processing requires bringing all the data sets to the processing cluster or cloud infrastructure, quite like in the lookup based approaches.

[8] `http://www.programmableweb.com/`

The choice of linked data processing approach depends on the usage scenario. Parallel and lookup based approaches fit best for high performance in terms of response time but require lots of bandwidth and costs to download or keep the data sets up to date. Federated approaches allow to get updated data directly from the sources without downloading as the queries are processed at their corresponding sources. However, this late advantage is also a shortcoming because delegating queries to remote sources can delay considerably the execution time if some sources are slow or busy.

2.2 Semantic Service Discovery

A lot of research has been carried out in the last decade on semantic service discovery. The survey in [10] shows some of the latest SWS discovery tools and compares them based on many criteria. There are 3 famous benchmarks for SWS discovery that allow evaluating the existing approaches : SWS challenge[9], Semantic service selection (S3) contest[10] and The Web Service Challenge (WS-Challenge)[11]. According to the surveys in [10,9], the ongoing semantic service discovery research can be categorized based on many criteria:

1) Service description : Depending on the description elements; i.e. functional elements (Inputs, Outputs, Preconditions and Effects IOPE) and non-functional elements (QoS, etc), service discovery approaches can be categorized into functional-based and non-functional-based approaches.
2) Technique : Despite description elements and language, the research on SWS discovery can be categorized into : 2.a) Logic-based approaches that reason on the semantic description elements of SWS using a semantic reasoning technique. 2.b) Non-logic based are mostly based on textual similarity of concept names. 2.c) Hybrid techniques that combine both techniques.

2.3 Data and Service Search

Aggregated Search of Data and Services[12] proposes to answer an SQL-like data query on XML datasets and RDBMS and propose relevant services to the latter. It generates a semantic graph for I/O of WSDL services using a user provided ontology and Wordnet[12]. After that it matches the query keywords with the generated service semantic graph keywords to find relevance and propose services to the user. It uses a non-logic based textual similarity to discover services. Therefore, this approach needs to be adapted to allow a search for semantic data and services as semantics allow for advanced reasoning that offers more accurate results. Moreover, many shortcomings can be considered such the error rates due to the automatic generation of semantic descriptions.

ANGIE[14] is a tool to enrich an RDF store with information from RESTful and SOAP-based services. The approach relies on mappings between the

[9] http://sws-challenge.org/wiki/index.php/Main_Page
[10] http://www-ags.dfki.uni-sb.de/~klusch/s3/
[11] http://ws-challenge.georgetown.edu/
[12] http://wordnet.princeton.edu/

concepts in the RDF store and elements of XML data provided by services. It assumes that WS are described according to a common global schema defined by a provided ontology like YAGO. The idea is to make the data provenance transparent to the user and invoke web services on-the-fly to answer queries. To answer a user query, services are composed and invoked following an execution plan generated on basis of the global schema and not on the descriptions of WS. At the execution level, services in repositories are matched with the composition requirements, then their results are mapped with the global schema. However, the global schema assumption can only be true in domain-specific WS repositories and doesn't fit to the diversity and heterogeneity nature of the LOD. Furthermore, the evolution of SW repositories (new services, new ontologies, etc) makes it difficult to maintain a global schema even for a specific domain.

Sig.ma[20] is an entity search tool that uses Sindice[11] to extract all related facts for a given entity. Sindice is a offers a platform to index, search and query documents with semantic markup in the web. It crawls the web continuously to index new documents and update the indexed ones. Both Sig.ma and Sindice are document-based and don't offer SWS discovery features or search for data using SWS.

3 Problem and Contributions

The semantic web is a fast growing research field and its standards and technologies are being more and more adopted especially by organizations and open data providers[13]. With such promising future, research can be pushed further on semantic web services and how to better involve them in the LOD[1].

As we stated in section 1, users need to search for linked data and complete the LOD answers with semantic web services. In parallel developers need an easy way to discover useful services to integrate in their mashups and applications built on Linked Data. To our knowledge, there is no existing tool that fully supports such a search over the LOD and existing similar aforementioned approaches are limited to some constraints and usages that are incompatible with the nature and the content of the LOD. Therefore, many techniques and tools can be put together and reused to achieve the determined goal. However, there are many issues that can be identified when it comes to putting all the pieces together :

- How to understand the user query and how to convert it into a service request ? How to deal with the different query templates that use UNION, OPTIONAL, FILTER, etc. The parameters of the service request must extracted from the data query, definitions of concepts must be extracted. Inputs, outputs and conditions must be distinguished.
- Is there a need for extending SPARQL 1.0 (or SPARQL 1.1) for sufficient expressivity in order to adapt the user query to the service requests. If yes, then how to define this syntax [2] and how to rewrite these no-standard queries to send them to SPARQL endpoints in the LOD.

[13] http://www.huffingtonpost.com/steve-hamby/semantic-web-technology_b_1228883.html

- How to address the heterogeneity of SWS descriptions? How to request services from multiple SWS deployed in a distributed fashion in the LOD? How to select, aggregate and rank the discovered services.
- How to compose services on the fly in order to answer the user query and integrate the results with linked data.
- How to expand the relevance criteria for service requests by entailing hierarchy and similarity between concepts ?
- How to measure the accuracy of the resulting services and verify the coherence of the resulted data ? I/O are not sufficient to find accurate services and compositions. As shown in [21], the SWS in our case are data providers and they have specific constrainsts on I/O. [15] introduces a representation method for IOPE that explicitly defines the link between I/O based on Preconditions and Effects using SPARQL.

Our goal is to provide a provide a platform that allows to combine a search of linked data and services to find both data and relevant services that can be mashed up with. Such a search often requires distinct queries : a) queries that lookup in the LOD to find data and b) service requests that discover relevant services in some SWS repositories. Our contribution is to provide a platform that allows to search for both starting from a data query, i.e. a query intended to search only for data. Starting from such a query, we automatically extract service requests and find relevant services to that data or generate service compositions that provide complementary data. Section 4 shows briefly our approach and some of what we have achieved so far.

Preliminarily, we assume that Semantic Web Services are described using any RDF based description language/ontology: OWL-S, WSMO, MSM, etc. These services are published in public repositories and are either stored in RDF stores behind SPARQL points or simply as RDF dumps. Many tools already provide that feature (iServe[13] LIDS[18]). The Inputs/Outputs are important parts of the descriptions that should reference to existing ontologies. Moreover, the links between Inputs and Outputs are essential for high accuracy service discovery and composition.

4 Proposed Approach

The goal of our approach is not to replace the existing efforts but to push the research further by building on top of them. Based on the statements in section 1, we want our approach to focus on Linked data and Semantic Web Services and we differentiate it by exploring the potential of the existing standards and techniques in Semantic Web.

When a SPARQL query is submitted by a user or an agent, it launches two disjoint processes that can be joint later by aggregation. One process is dedicated to manage the query answering in the LOD data sources. The later sources are distributed and either accessible via SPARQL endpoints or dumped in RDF files. An appropriate technique among the ones mentioned in section 2.1 must be used depending on the data source natures and the appropriate optimization and rewriting are performed at this level.

The other process is dedicated to discover and possibly compose services that are relevant to the data query. To deal with the heterogeneity of the SWS descriptions and the distributed deployments of repositories containing them, we choose to issue service requests in SPARQL queries adapted to each description language. This allows us to natively select SWS and perform logical reasoning on their descriptions to extend the search capabilities. Furthermore, this allows us deal with the heterogeneous descriptions more effectively without intermediate mapping tools.

The data query is analyzed to extract elements that can be used as I/O for a service request. Outputs are simply the selected variables of the query. Inputs are the bound values that appear in the triples of the query. The links between Inputs and Outputs can be established as Preconditions and Effects and represented using SPARQL as in [15].

SPARQL operators like OPTIONAL, UNION, FILTER, etc can reveal the preferences of the user for service discovery and composition. For instance, the I/O extracted from an Optional block probably mean that the user wants services that don't necessarily provide the optional parts.

A crucial step follows in which ontological concepts are attributed to I/O in order to make accurate service requests. Typically, and rdf:type property in the query declares the concept of a given element. However, many issues arise when this declaration is missing in the query. Moreover expanding the search of relevant concepts to sub, super or similar concepts requires finding such concepts in the corresponding ontologies or in the LOD. Among the issues is the cost of requests from the servers that store the ontologies or the services.

Once the service request elements are gathered, service discovery queries are issued in SPARQL using specific templates that correspond to each SWS description language. We retain two possible kinds of use cases for service selection. In the first, the user would like to select services that provide him the same data as in his query, as if he is looking for SWS alternatives to LOD sources. In the second the user wants to find any services that provide parts of his desired outputs or consume some of his provided inputs. The latter case is practical in assisting the user in building mashups on the go. Automatic service composition comes next to provide composite services that provide answers or complementary information to the user query.

A last aggregation step integrates both results from data sources and services in case composite services where composed and invoked. Otherwise, the relevant services to the query are ranked and ordered by their relevance.

The methodology of our research is guided by the global process described in this section. At a first stage, we need to focus on understanding the user queries and transforming them into service requests. At the same time, existing and emerging issues must be solved. Next, we can address the SWS discovery and composition and see what are the issues related to our goal that need to be resolved. On the data side, the query federation issues must be addressed, especially for SWS repositories. Caching and rewriting techniques must be conceived and tested in our particular usage scenario.

Evaluating the performance and measuring the accuracy of the established discovery and composition algorithms would allow us to partially validate our approach and confirm its feasibility. Evaluation can be made at two levels :

1. Low level : at this level, we will evaluate distinctly the performance of our query answering, service discovery and service composition using dedicated benchmarks and test collections such as FedBench[16] for data querying or OWL-S-TC[14] for service discovery.
2. High level : at this level, we will evaluate jointly all the features above put together to measure the accuracy and the performance of our search platform. A major constraint for this evaluation is to use data and service test collections that contain mutually equivalent data; i.e. common concepts, common ontologies, etc. Moreover, data and services should be deployed in a distributed fashion as in the LOD. Another challenge is to provide typical queries and typical answers in order to compare them to the platform answers and measure the accuracy.

5 Preliminary Implementation

We have already implemented a prototype that allows via a GUI to write a SPARQL query and execute the data and service queries. On the data side, we currently use FedX [17] to process the data queries on the LOD. On the service side, we have written preliminary algorithms to write service requests from data

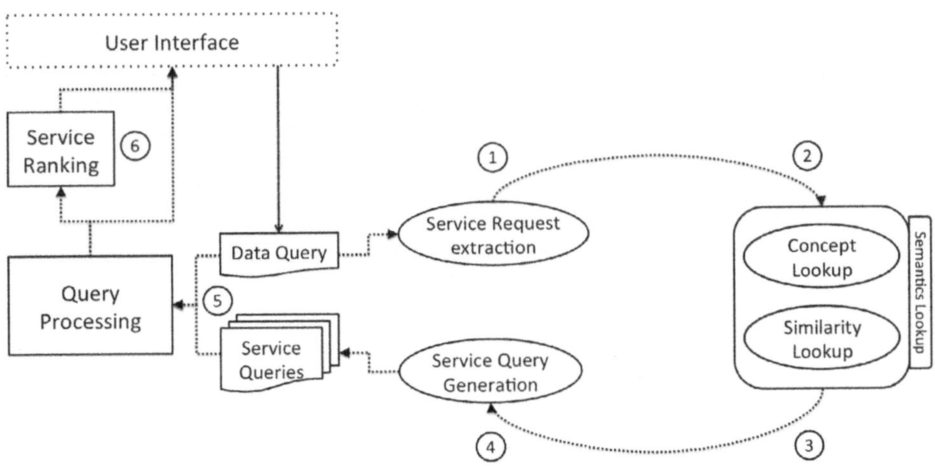

Fig. 1. Process of SWS discovery in using a data query

[14] http://projects.semwebcentral.org/projects/owls-tc/

queries and answer them from SWS repositories that have SPARQL endpoints. Figure 1 gives an overview of the service discovery process that we have made so far.

References

1. Berners-Lee, T., Hendler, J., Lassila, O.: The semantic web. Scientific American 284(5), 28–37 (2001)
2. Buil-Aranda, C., Arenas, M., Corcho, O., Polleres, A.: Federating queries in sparql 1.1: Syntax, semantics and evaluation. Web Semantics: Science, Services and Agents on the World Wide Web 18(1), 1–17 (2013)
3. Ermilov, I., Martin, M., Lehmann, J., Auer, S.: Linked open data statistics: Collection and exploitation. In: Klinov, P., Mouromtsev, D. (eds.) KESW 2013. Communications in Computer and Information Science, vol. 394, pp. 242–249. Springer, Heidelberg (2013), http://dx.doi.org/10.1007/978-3-642-41360-5_19
4. Galárraga, L., Hose, K., Schenkel, R.: Partout: A distributed engine for efficient rdf processing. CoRR abs/1212.5636 (2012)
5. Harth, A., Hose, K., Karnstedt, M., Polleres, A., Sattler, K.-U., Umbrich, J.: Data summaries for on-demand queries over linked data. In: Proceedings of the 19th International Conference on World Wide Web, pp. 411–420. ACM (2010)
6. Hartig, O., Bizer, C., Freytag, J.-C.: Executing sparql queries over the web of linked data. In: Bernstein, A., Karger, D.R., Heath, T., Feigenbaum, L., Maynard, D., Motta, E., Thirunarayan, K. (eds.) ISWC 2009. LNCS, vol. 5823, pp. 293–309. Springer, Heidelberg (2009), http://dx.doi.org/10.1007/978-3-642-04930-9_19
7. Hartig, O., Langegger, A.: A database perspective on consuming linked data on the web. Datenbank-Spektrum 10(2), 57–66 (2010)
8. Kaoudi, Z., Manolescu, I.: Triples in the clouds. In: ICDE-29th International Conference on Data Engineering (2013)
9. Klusch, M.: Service discovery. In: Alhajj, R., Rokne, J. (eds.) Encyclopedia of Social Networks and Mining (ESNAM). Springer (2014)
10. Le Duy, N., Kanagasabai, R.: Semantic web service discovery: State-of-the-art and research challenges. Personal Ubiquitous Computing 17(8), 1741–1752 (2013)
11. Oren, E., Delbru, R., Catasta, M., Cyganiak, R., Stenzhorn, H., Tummarello, G.: Sindice. com: a document-oriented lookup index for open linked data. International Journal of Metadata, Semantics and Ontologies 3(1), 37–52 (2008)
12. Palmonari, M., Sala, A., Maurino, A., Guerra, F., Pasi, G., Frisoni, G.: Aggregated search of data and services. Information Systems 36(2), 134–150 (2011)
13. Pedrinaci, C., Liu, D., Maleshkova, M., Lambert, D., Kopecky, J., Domingue, J.: iserve: a linked services publishing platform. In: CEUR workshop proceedings, vol. 596 (2010)
14. Preda, N., Suchanek, F.M., Kasneci, G., Neumann, T., Ramanath, M., Weikum, G.: Angie: Active knowledge for interactive exploration. Proceedings of the VLDB Endowment 2(2), 1570–1573 (2009)
15. Sbodio, M.L., Martin, D., Moulin, C.: Discovering semantic web services using sparql and intelligent agents. Web Semantics: Science, Services and Agents on the World Wide Web 8(4), 310–328 (2010)

16. Schmidt, M., Görlitz, O., Haase, P., Ladwig, G., Schwarte, A., Tran, T.: FedBench: A benchmark suite for federated semantic data query processing. In: Aroyo, L., Welty, C., Alani, H., Taylor, J., Bernstein, A., Kagal, L., Noy, N., Blomqvist, E. (eds.) ISWC 2011, Part I. LNCS, vol. 7031, pp. 585–600. Springer, Heidelberg (2011)
17. Schwarte, A., Haase, P., Hose, K., Schenkel, R., Schmidt, M.: FedX: Optimization techniques for federated query processing on linked data. In: Aroyo, L., Welty, C., Alani, H., Taylor, J., Bernstein, A., Kagal, L., Noy, N., Blomqvist, E. (eds.) ISWC 2011, Part I. LNCS, vol. 7031, pp. 601–616. Springer, Heidelberg (2011)
18. Speiser, S., Harth, A.: Integrating linked data and services with linked data services. In: Antoniou, G., Grobelnik, M., Simperl, E., Parsia, B., Plexousakis, D., De Leenheer, P., Pan, J. (eds.) ESWC 2011, Part I. LNCS, vol. 6643, pp. 170–184. Springer, Heidelberg (2011)
19. Suchanek, F.M., Kasneci, G., Weikum, G.: Yago: a core of semantic knowledge. In: Proceedings of the 16th International Conference on World Wide Web, pp. 697–706. ACM (2007)
20. Tummarello, G., Cyganiak, R., Catasta, M., Danielczyk, S., Delbru, R., Decker, S.: Sig.ma: Live views on the web of data. Web Semantics: Science, Services and Agents on the World Wide Web 8(4), 355–364 (2010)
21. Vaculín, R., Chen, H., Neruda, R., Sycara, K.: Modeling and discovery of data providing services. In: IEEE International Conference on Web Services, ICWS 2008, pp. 54–61. IEEE (2008)

Semantic Information Extraction on Domain Specific Data Sheets

Kai Barkschat

FH Aachen, University of Applied Science, Germany
barkschat@fh-aachen.de

Abstract. The development of information retrieval and extraction systems is still a challenging task. The occurrence of natural language limits the application of existing approaches. Therefore the approach of a new framework which combines natural language processing and semantic web technology is discussed.

This paper focuses on ontology based knowledge modelling for semantic data extraction. Therefore, semantic verification techniques which can be used to improve the extraction are introduced.

Keywords: #eswcphd2014Barkschat.

1 Introduction and Motivations

More and more modern companies in the IT sector offer their services online in the World Wide Web (WWW). As a basis for such services, i. e. online market places or product comparison portals, these companies usually depend on data aggregation of huge and steadily growing information amounts from online resources.

According to the state of the art, companies use Extract-Transform-Load (ETL)[1] processes as the basis for their data processing. ETL consists of three stages, where the first task, "Extraction", is responsible for data aggregation. In our case we focus on extraction from electronic documents in PDF format. The "Transform" task defines the mapping between extracted data and the companies' internal models (for instance database schemas). The third task, "Load", intends to populate the internal storage with the prepared data amounts.

ETL approaches require rigid structures to operate on. This requirement is not fulfilled in many cases where product documents contain free form texts. Information defined by free text forms are hardly parsable by conventional approaches because of natural language problems: Among others, high complexity and strong ambiguity have the effect that textual descriptions of product data hardly resemble each other across documents.

As a result, free form texts have to be analysed before the relevant data can be identified and extracted. Today, this task is processed by human beings, because they are able to develop a semantic understanding of the text, and they are able to interpret the content in its context.

V. Presutti et al. (Eds.): ESWC 2014, LNCS 8465, pp. 864–873, 2014.

Another problem lies in legally liability issues. For example, a special domain of the energy sector deals with pricing of energy-tariffs. Some companies act as service providers for government institutions, whose task is to uncover illegal price fixing. The government makes companies responsible for the offered services to hedge itself against accusations.

To assure high quality standards during extraction, human manpower is indispensable, although the extraction task itself contains strongly repetitive parts.

A major drawback of manual extraction results in poor scaling of the total process. In contrast to the increasing amount of electronic documents, the extraction process is limited by available human manpower. The recruitment of additional staff is not a feasible option, as this would make the process economically unviable. Therefore, the described solution approach aims to relieve employees and also can help to reduce costs.

This paper describes a solution based on an ontology-based information extraction (OBIE) framework [2]. As starting point, product data sheets containing natural language product descriptions for two highly specialized domains (life sciences area, energy sector) are processed. We used ontologies to express domain specific knowledge about semantic relations and restrictions in the given domains. The key idea is to mimic human behaviour during manual extraction using this formal representation of knowledge. This enables the development of a machine processable text understanding for improving the data extraction.

The paper is structured as follows: Section 2 gives a brief review of ongoing research on semantic information retrieval and extraction systems. Section 3 shows a general overview of the described solution approach. Further, the approach is discussed in detail in Section 4. The evaluation plan is presented in Section 5. Finally, the results are summarized in Section 6.

2 Related Work

Wimalasuriya and Dou [2] give an overview of OBIE systems and fit them into the overarching theme of general information extraction (IE) systems. IE is known as the process concerning the analysis of natural language content, the identification, and the extraction of relevant information amounts. The authors clarify the importance of OBIE approaches, as they describe such systems as a bridging technology which combines text understanding systems and IE systems.

In general, OBIE systems use ontologies to model domain knowledge for a special area of interest. They can guide the extraction process because they define the relevant pieces of information and how these information can be identified during extraction. Additionally, ontologies can be exploited to express the semantic context as a graph based structure. According to this definition, the discussed approach of this paper represents an OBIE system.

Semantator [3] is a plugin-tool for the popular Protégé framework [4]. It supports the user during the annotation process. Similar to our approach, Semantator adds semantic annotations to natural language text. The possible annotation categories and relations are retrieved from domain specific ontologies. Annotated text entities are then written back to the ontologies as class instances or properties. Reasoning capabilities are proposed for detection of inconsistencies during annotation. In contrast to our approach Semantator does not focus on natural language processing (NLP) techniques although it can be connected with a few existing tools from that domain. Semantator lacks on automatic relation extraction which is treated by this paper. Additionally input documents often contain typographic structures which are not considered by this approach, but could be helpful for semantic extraction.

SREC [5] is a mathematical computation method for automatic detection of semantic relations in the ACE-2003 corpus [6]. It combines statistical and linear algebra calculation and centers on singular value decomposition. Although promising results are shown on the given corpus, too few relations are taken into account. For our task, this approach is too general. It lacks on relation types, which are sufficient for representing natural language (NL) structures. Semantic verification of extraction results is not considered and there is no mechanism to avoid or to detect false negatives: that are entities which are mistakenly marked as relation by the system.

Sbatella and Tedesco [7] present an advanced ontology driven semantic information retrieval system which uses a tripatite domain model for information extraction from plain text. This approach is focused on the highly specialized domain of the wine business. OWL-Ontologies are used to model the domain knowledge. Classes describe the important data categories, and properties describe the relevant relation between these categories. Text entities from source documents are then mapped to the categories and saved as instances of the OWL-classes. To recognize these entities the approach uses a combination of the lexical database WordNet [8] and several stochastic computations. Because the implemented framework always extracts plain text from different source documents, it is not possible to consider semi-structured content.

In 2007 Rusu et al. [9] published two different pseudo-algorithms for semantic triple extraction from typed dependency graphs and constituency based parse trees. The extracted triples in form of subject-predicate-object are suitable for mapping to standard ontology structures as defined by RDF [10] or OWL [11]. This forms a good basis for research projects as domain knowledge is implemented with ontologies increasingly common.

3 Architecture of Information Extraction System

The central research question of this project is: how can ETL processes be improved to automate the extraction process of product documents which contain natural language?

Zhang and Sidorov [12,13] focus on statistical machine learning methods to analyse natural language content, and to identify relevant product data. Concerning liability obligations, pure statistically approaches are not sufficient to guarantee semantic cohesion. A validation mechanism is required to assure that the identified data entities are valid and do not contradict.

Therefore, it is necessary to develop semantic technologies which are able to automatically detect not only relevant data entities, but also semantic relations and the word sense within NL sentences via its context. The extraction results need to be secured from a semantic point of view.

Regarding the fact that most electronic product documents contain typographic structures and semi-structured parts close to the natural language content, investigating the influence of typographic structures for semantic IE improvement is another topic of this approach.

In the following section the overall scenario of our approach which intends to improve the existing ETL process is presented. The focus of this paper is on the OBIE task, which is highlighted in Figure 1. In the very beginning of the ETL process, data sheets are collected from multiple sources, like the web or via email communication. Given several data formats, e.g. PDF or HTML, these documents are then homogenized. The Open Document Text (ODT) format was chosen as the common data format, because it defines a large set of standardized markup elements for office applications, which are exploited to represent the structured and unstructured content of the aggregated data sheets. In addition to this, it is an open standard and can easily be expanded, if required.

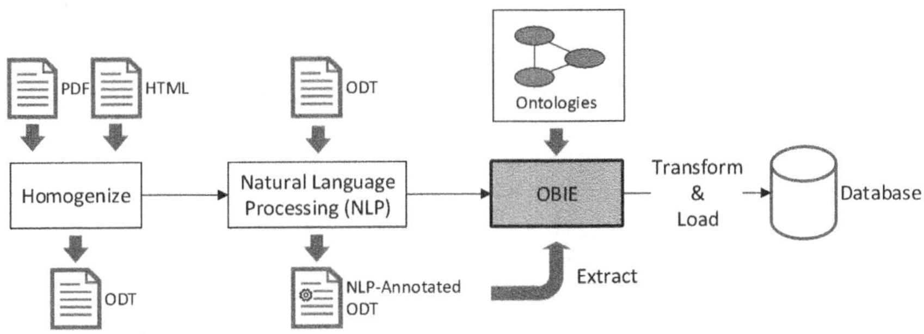

Fig. 1. The OBIE task embedded into the whole extraction process

In the second step, the ODT documents are passed to a NLP framework, which combines different tools to annotate the NL text content. Currently this framework uses implementations of OpenNLP [14] and Standford NLP [15] to generate annotations for the NLP tasks: Sentence Segmentation, Tokenization, Part-Of-Speech, Lemmatization, Named Entity Recognition (NER) and constituency based parse trees. These annotations are embedded into the ODT document and required by the third task (OBIE).

The OBIE task includes the domain knowledge in form of semantic graphs, which are defined as OWL ontologies [11]. Using this knowledge base on the one hand and the NLP annotations on the other, the OBIE process analyzes the document content, searches for relevant product data and tries to verify them.

As a note, the NLP process from the previous step already tried to mark relevant text named entities. Furthermore, we call these marked entities candidate concept (CC) and handle them purely as proposals for relevant product data. This is due to the fact applied NLP tools use neither semantic features nor context viewing for their annotation tagging.

Upon finishing, the OBIE process transforms the extracted data to a predetermined data schema and passes them to a persistent storage device like the database in Figure 1. Here it can be used by the company for building up services.

4 OBIE Approach in Detail

As already mentioned, the OBIE task takes in to account both natural language information and domain knowledge from the ontologies. Section 4.1 describes the preparation algorithm, which is used to identify triple structures in a NL sentence. These triple statements will then be matched against the domain model, which is described in Section 4.2. Section 4.3 and 4.4 explain how *semantic verification* can be done to secure and improve the extraction process.

4.1 Triple Extraction

Starting from a constituency based parse tree, we use a slightly modified version of the "triple extraction algorithm" by Rusu et al. [9] to obtain possible text entities for the grammatical roles: subject, predicate and object.

An example for such a parse-tree and the application of the algorithm can be seen in Figure 2.

The main difference between this and the original algorithm is that the predicate element in the triple structure does not exactly match to its grammatical meaning. Indeed, the algorithm looks for the deepest verb descent (excluding modal verbs) in the parse-tree and tries to connect it with the subsequent associated preposition of the object element. This is required to identify the semantic relations between subject and object in the sentences.

Figure 2 demonstrates an example: *stored at* and *stored until* imply two completely different meanings in the sentence. The first case *stored at* indicates some kind of storage condition, which in the sampled domain is equivalent to a concrete temperature value. The second case *stored until* indicates an expiration date, a special subclass of the more generic data category *date*.

The semantic relations are important, because they form the edges or properties in the ontology based domain model and they are part of the triple structure, which is matched against the domain model later.

4.2 The Different Roles of Ontologies in the OBIE Task

The ontology model of this approach is implemented in OWL and consists of four parts as seen in Figure 3. The domain ontology, the extraction ontology, the source ontology and the history ontology.

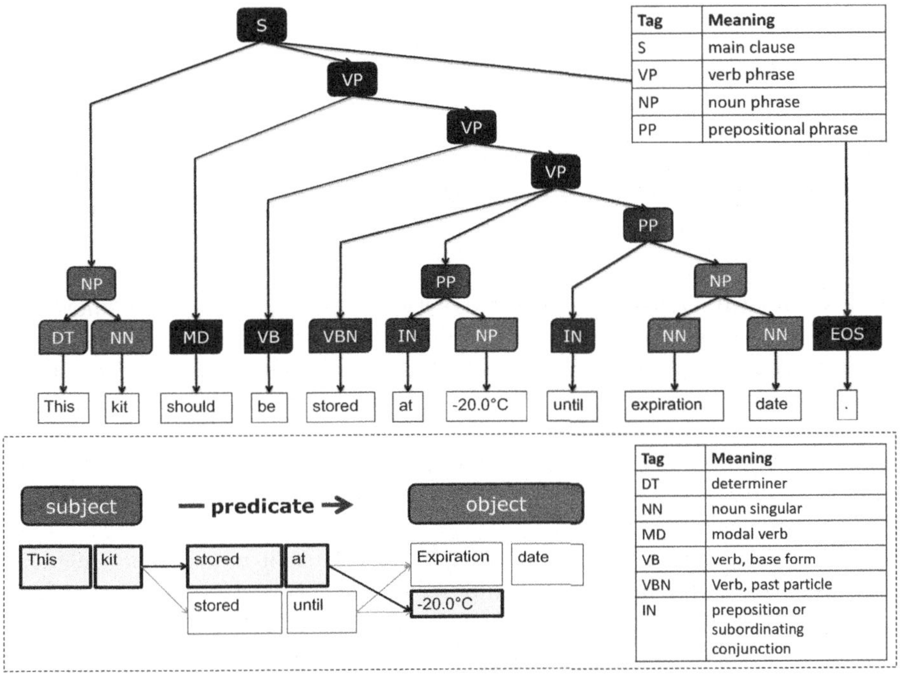

Fig. 2. triple extraction on constituency based parse-tree

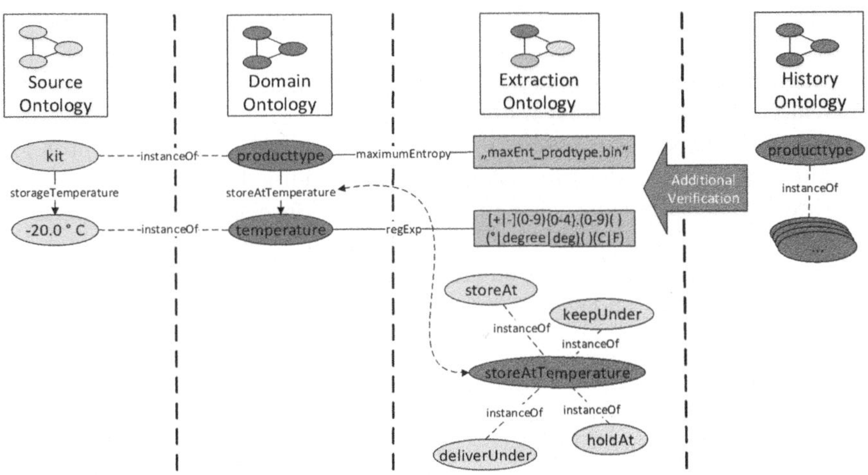

Fig. 3. Concept model for knowledge representation

The Domain Ontology. The domain ontology defines the important data categories which have to be extracted. In our setup we worked on high specific domains from the energy sector and the life sciences. Considering product descriptions from these areas, there were no existing ontologies, which could be reused to model the semantic setup of our data sheets. The domain ontology had to be created from scratch in coordination with a domain expert.

The semantic relations between the previously defined data categories are modelled as properties. There are fairly close restrictions, which can be modelled via cardinality constraints.

The Extraction Ontology. The extraction ontology defines the knowledge about how to identify concepts of the domain ontology in natural language texts. Therefore, each data category is associated with a detection method. In the first attempt, we defined three different detection methods: maximum entropy, regular expression, and closed world list. As ongoing research, it is intended to compare the results of the different detection approaches. Our hypothesis is that detection quality of the different methods greatly varies, depending on the data category to be extracted.

The detection method closed world lists (CWL) can be seen as a classical dictionary lookup. It is limited to a finite set of text forms, e.g. the different units of amount in an operating manual for an experiment. The possible text forms are saved in a normalized form, also known as lemmatized form, as instances of the corresponding data category.

Regular Expressions are defined for concepts with strong similar text forms, such as telephone numbers or postal codes. Due to the fact of missing standards in our domains, there are a lot of further concepts which have strongly varying text forms.

The last detection method describes concepts which have to be trained with a more generic approach. We used a machine learning algorithm called "Maximum Entropy Algorithm" implemented by the OpenNLP framework here. Other statistical methods are conceivable.

Relations of the domain ontology are modelled in the extraction ontology in the same way of data concepts: each relation is defined as a seperate concept class. In contrast to normal concept classes, relation classes are always associated with CWL. This is needed for linking different descriptions in the natural language which carry the same meaning in the text. We intended to expand those lists with lexical knowledge databases like WordNet in further steps.

The Source Ontology. A source ontology can be seen as the semantic representation of the associated source document. The concrete text entities from the source document are mapped to the triple structures and after semantic verification they are saved as instances to the concept classes from the domain ontology. Each source ontology contains the machine processable data content of one single source document. Instances of ontology classes can be seen on the left side in Figure 3.

The History Ontology. In our project setting, we are able to access large amounts of old product data. This is because the companies have already collected data from datasheets by their manual process. The results of the extraction by hand are stored in the companies' databases.

The history ontology defines a mapping from these already collected datasets to the OBIE process. The downside, however, is that there is no information about the source documents the data were extracted from. The history ontology will be populated using ontology-based data access (OBDA) mapping techniques as applied by Rodriguez [16].

We consider to use the history ontology as an additional knowledge source for the automated extraction process. The expectation is that it might improve the extraction as it can fulfill missing data entries via comparisons to older data.

For example, let us consider a supplier only sells products in a fixed package size. The package size could then be concluded, even if the data sheet itself does not contain any information about the size.

4.3 Semantic Verification on Natural Language

Using detection methods described in Section 4.2, we retrieve possible CC for the domain model. To verify and hedge these results a task called "semantic verification" is processed.

For each sentence it is checked if the concept candidates match the triple roles of a subject or object. If there is more than one match, the domain ontology is searched for related concepts of each concept candidate class. If the ontology contains a triple structure, whose outgoing and incoming concept node match the correct roles of the subject and object in the sentence, the relation itself has to be evaluated. Therefore, the second triple element, the predicate-preposition element, is queried against the CWL of the corresponding relation or property in the ontology. On success, we have a text based triple matching on a predefined ontology structure. This means additionally to the entity matching, we also verified the semantics of this single sentence as this semantic relation was predefined in the domain ontology. It is very likely that this step sorts out the CC which were mistakenly annotated by the NLP process. This is because in most cases, where wrong CC occur, the semantic context of the sentence contradicts that assignment.

Before such identified triples are stored in their lemmatized form in the source ontology, tools like OWL-Reasoner can be used to check if this insertion would violate any ontology constraint and would make the ontology inconsistent. In this case, the triple would be dropped.

4.4 Semantic Verification on Typographic Structures

Because the input documents of our scenario are not plain text, but sometimes also contain semi-structured parts, we are able to semantically verify content regarding to its typographic context. For this task, we extended the extraction ontology to the indicator concept. Indicators are structures like headings, tables, or footnotes. Looking at the source documents of our domain, it has been observed that specific data concepts often occur in the same typographic context. For example, the components or parts of a given product usually are listed in tables and rarely seen in free form parts of the document.

Typographic structure dependent concepts are marked in the extraction ontology as additional properties, which relate to specific structure element concept classes. Those concept classes do not occur in the domain ontology, as this is specific extraction knowledge. Whenever a data concept is proposed for a text entity by the detection methods, it is checked if this concept also has relations to specific document structures. In this case the surrounding structure is evaluated against the related structure class. On match, a corresponding triple structure of the form component–indicatedBy–table is added to the source ontology. The indicator concept is especially helpful in cases where no closed sentences occur or where only fragments of sentences are present, e.g. tables. In these cases NLP results are not viable, as their CC proposals drops drastically.

5 Evaluation Plan

The described scenario builds up on ODT documents but these are not the original source documents of the domain. Indeed, documents have data formats like PDF, HTML, XLS. ODT is used as the common data format to enable a uniform processing. At the moment a small set of nlp-annotated ODT-documents is created to define valid input documents for the OBIE process. We call this "gold standard input documents for semantic extraction". Gold standard in this term of use means that ODT documents are first checked on their typographical correctness comparing to the original sources and then enriched with proofed annotations by NLP. Finally the source ontology is populated with the correct data entries.

The evaluation of the semantic verification will be executed against this test set and compared to ETL extraction results which are generated without applying the OBIE task.

At the moment it is unclear which impact the typographic verification will have on the extraction process and how specific or general the typographic relation have to be. Possible documents might have to be clustered by producer, producttype or other criteria to retrieve the best results.

6 Conclusion

The described approach demonstrates how semantic verification can be applied to secure and validate data extraction based on entity proposals generated by state of the art tools. The inclusion of typographic elements to improve the data extraction has been barely inspected in previous research projects. Therefore, it is assumed that new insights will bring a deeper understanding for extraction of real world documents to the semantic web community.

References

1. Taniar, D., Chen, L. (eds.): Integrations of Data Warehousing, Data Mining and Database Technologies - Innovative Approaches. Information Science Reference (2011)
2. Wimalasuriya, D.C., Dou, D.: Ontology-based Information Extraction: An Introduction and a Survey of Current Approaches. Journal of Information Science 36(3), 306–323 (2010)
3. Tao, C., Song, D., Sharma, D.K., Chute, C.G.: Semantator: Semantic annotator for converting biomedical text to linked data. Journal of Biomedical Informatics 46(5), 882–893
4. Stanford Center for Biomedical Informatics Research: The Protégé Ontology Editor and Knowledge Acquisition System. `http://protege.stanford.edu/`
5. Zahedi, M.H., Kahani, M.: SREC: Discourse-level semantic relation extraction from text.. Neural Computing and Applications 23(6), 1573–1582 (2013)
6. Mitchell, A., Strassel, S., Przybocki, M., Davis, J., Doddington, G., Grishman, R., Meyers, A., Brunstein, A., Ferro, L., Sundheim, B.: Ace-2 version 1.0. Linguistic Data Consortium, Philadelphia (2003)
7. Sbattella, L., Tedesco, R.: A novel semantic information retrieval system based on a three-level domain model.. Journal of Systems and Software 86(5), 1426–1452 (2013)
8. Fellbaum, C.: WordNet: An Electronic Lexical Database. Language, Speech and Communication. MIT Press (1998)
9. Rusu, D., Dali, L., Fortuna, B., Grobelnik, M., Mladenic, D.: Triplet extraction from sentences. In: Proceedings of the 10th International Multiconference "Information Society - IS 2007", vol. A, pp. 218–222 (2007)
10. RDF Primer: W3C Recommendation (February 10, 2004), `http://www.w3.org/TR/rdf-primer/`
11. OWL Web Ontology Language Overview: W3C Recommendation (February 10, 2004), `http://www.w3.org/TR/owl-features/`
12. Zhang, S., Elhadad, N.: Unsupervised biomedical named entity recognition: Experiments with clinical and biological texts. Journal of Biomedical Informatics 46(6), 1088–1098 (2013)
13. Sidorov, G., Velasquez, F., Stamatatos, E., Gelbukh, A., Chanona-Hernández, L.: Syntactic N-grams as machine learning features for natural language processing. Expert Systems with Applications 41, 853–860 (2014)
14. The Apache Software Foundation: Apache OpenNLP, `http://opennlp.apache.org/`
15. The Stanford Natural Language Processing Group: Stanford NLP, `http://www-nlp.stanford.edu/software/index.shtml`
16. Rodriguez-muro, M., Lubyte, L., Calvanese, D.: Realizing ontology based data access: A plug-in for Protégé. In: Proceedings of the Workshop on Information Integration Methods, Architectures, and Systems (IIMAS 2008), pp. 286–289. IEEE Computer Society Press (2008)

Towards a Data Warehouse Fed with Web Services

John Samuel

LIMOS, CNRS, Blaise Pascal University, Aubière, France
samuel@isima.fr

Abstract. The role of data warehouse for business analytics cannot be undermined for any enterprise, irrespective of its size. But the growing dependence on web services has resulted in a situation where the enterprise data is managed by multiple, autonomous service providers. The goal of our work is to investigate and devise an approach to address the trade-off between scalability and adaptability in large scale integration with numerous ever-evolving web services. We present our prototype DaWeS (Data warehouse fed with Web Services) and explore how ETL using the mediation approach benefits this trade-off for enterprises with complex data warehousing requirements. The semantic web research community has proposed various standards like WSDL, WADL, hRESTS, SAWSDL for describing web service interface (API) the usage of which could have solved our requirement of automated integration. DaWeS looks to fill the current gap between the industry and research community by taking into account the key characteristics of the aforementioned description languages and using a declarative approach in order to reduce the manual effort. We also present to the semantic web research community the optimization heuristics (to reduce the API operation calls) and semantic challenges (auto-adaptability especially in the wake of an API change) devised while building DaWeS.

Keywords: #eswcphd2014Samuel.

1 Introduction

The growing dependence on the internet has influenced the rise of many small service providers offering a reduced subset of services over the internet compared to the traditional bloated computer softwares and applications. Enterprises dependent on the web services have their business data spread across multiple data centers spanning even across continents leaving them with no direct control over the web services and the associated data infrastructure and thus their own business data. Web mashups and Data as a service (DaaS) have appeared in large numbers to provide integration with some selected web services in order to provide a consolidated view of the data spread across the web services. A classical approach is to write wrappers for each such web service for extracting the relevant information. But this approach is not scalable especially if the integration is targeted towards thousands of web services.

V. Presutti et al. (Eds.): ESWC 2014, LNCS 8465, pp. 874–884, 2014.

Extracting data from web services (WS) has several constraints. The WS providers generally expose the application programming interface (API) to their services so that their clients (enterprises) can build their own internal dashboards. The APIs differ significantly among each other with respect to the resources they handle, the resource representation, the data types, the number of operations, the service level agreements or SLA (that limits the number of operations that can be made during a period of time), the authentication mechanisms (for access by enterprise and third party users), the choice of message formats and the operation request and response (or error) parameters. In addition to these, WS periodically modify their API: adding support for new resources, deprecating some operations or changing the SLA. Therefore the clients often have to deal with this volatility in the interfaces often forcing them to change their service providers or their internal applications. Therefore enterprises require a solution to be able to have an integrated view of their business data spread across multiple web services and experience a transparent continuity of their data even when they switch their service providers or when WS API undergoes a change.

Our research work looks at the problem of large scale integration with the ever-evolving web services for business analysis in providing a scalable and adaptable solution towards this end. The solution must be scalable i.e., considering the ever-increasing availability of new web service providers in the market, it must be very easy to add a new API with minimum coding effort. It must be quickly adaptable (easy update of API changes) in the wake of the versatility (or evolution) of WS. Also it must be able to manage huge and permanent storage of enterprise data coming from the WS. In addition to providing certain default performance indicators, it must be very easy to define new ad-hoc performance indicators that totally avoids hard coding. Last but not the least, it must offer a way for the enterprise to keep track of its business data, even if one of its providers is no longer available.

To address the problem previously described, we propose (and build) a *Web services fed Data Warehouse.* In section 2, we describe the current state of the art. Section 3 describes the problem and present our contributions. Section 4 describes our research approach used in our prototype DaWeS (Data Warehouse fed with Web Services). Section 5 describes the results obtained. We also discuss various scientific challenges especially in terms of dealing with reducing the number of (expensive) API operartion calls, handling incomplete information and dynamic evolution of the warehouse. Section 6 discusses how to evaluate our results. Finally in section 7, we will discuss our ongoing and future course of actions and summarize our results.

2 State of the Art

We want to offer enterprises a lightweight but powerful and online data analysis tool. So this is basically an information integration problem. Information Integration Systems [25, 5] provides a uniform query interface across multiple heterogeneous and autonomous systems.

In this field, two approaches are well studied, namely the materialized and the virtual ones. A materialized information integration system often used for the purpose of data analysis and business performance measures computation is called a data warehouse (DW). A DW contains a copy of source data structured according to a single global schema. Many ETL(extraction-transform-load) tools have been studied [23] to clean and extract data from various data sources and transform them to a format according to the data warehouse schema and loading them to the DW. A majority of the works have dealt with extracting the data from existing legacy data stores (databases, spreadsheets, web pages, textual documents) in the form of of data wrappers [20], which are ad-hoc specific pieces of software to translate from the DW to the source and vice versa. It is sensible to code such specific wrappers since DW sources are usually stable. The typical example is when a big company builds a DW to analyze data coming from its various departments. In our tool, enterprise data comes from multiple sources (services), and they must be persistent in case of a service provider failure. So it is clearly a DW issue. The problem is that services are supposed to be quite unstable in time. So it is not realistic to build a specific wrapper for each source.

The virtualized information integration approach, referred to as the mediation approach, also structures sources' data into a single global schema, but without copying data. Sources' data indeed stay at the sources. The purpose of a mediator is more query answering than data analysis. User queries are formulated over the global schema, transferred to sources, and the query answers coming from the sources are then gathered by the mediator and presented to the user. There are mainly three ways of linking the data sources to the global schema: the Global As View (GAV) [5] Local As View (LAV) [7, 22] and Global Local As View (GLAV) [10]approaches. In GAV, each relation of the global schema is defined as a query over the source relations. In LAV, each source relation is defined as a query over the global schema relation. GAV mediators are known to offer good query answering properties, while facing an evolution in the sources may be difficult (e.g., adding a new source implies to potentially updating many relation definitions in the global schema). LAV mediators are known to easily handle source changes, while query answering is algorithmically more difficult. Indeed, the user query posed to the global schema must be rewritten into queries that can be posed to the source. And rewriting algorithms have a high complexity (NP-Complete at least). In GLAV, the global and local schema relations are mapped using a set of tuple generating dependencies (TGDs). LAV is easier than GLAV with respect to an algorithmic point of view. Despite the complexity of rewriting algorithms, using a LAV approach as ETL seems to be interesting for our DW. Indeed this DW has to be easily adaptable when sources (services) evolve. And that cannot be provided by GAV approaches. Obviously, this work has to be located in the field of WS. [14, 26] deals with data integration using WS, in the context of WSs using the various standards like XML, HTTP, SOAP, WSDL, UDDI. Our proposition can be seen as an implementation addressing more specifically the content and relationship aggregation [14] issues.

Many existing tools and standards concerning WS can be used to build (parts of) a DW fed with WS. They can be divided into the syntactic and the semantic ones. The most prominent syntactic ones are WSDL [24] and hRESTS [17] (both machine and human readable). The idea is that a machine readable interface format can enable automatic code generation and then automated WS integration (discovery, composition, etc.). But industry wide adoption is currently missing: majority of the WS APIs is described in human readable format (essentially HTML web pages) and are not meant for the direct consumption by software applications. This may be due to standards that are still in their infancy, to the effort based on these standards cannot handle every real situation. [21, 1] use web service composition [9] for creating data as a service (DaaS) and WS mashups based on web service standards.

Concerning semantic web technologies and ontologies, several works [19] discuss about integrating semantic web technologies (ontologies) to the WS for easier and automated information integration. DAML-S [6], OWL-S [18], SAWSDL (Semantic Annotations for WSDL and XML Schema) [13] and hRESTS are some examples of such semantic WS description languages. These approaches already provides techniques to automate integration in constrained contexts. Indeed, thanks to their formal semantics, they're adapted to automate integration issues (e.g., automatic matchmaking of services with respect to a user query). Moreover it is now known that the underlying formalisms, especially description logics, can be used to extend query answering to ontological query answering [3, 11]. We believe the industrial acceptance will increase in the upcoming years and our proposed solution can reap the benefits of these technologies for a fully automated integration.

3 Problem Statement and Contributions

The goal of our work is to investigate and devise an approach for a scalable and adaptable solution to the problem of integrating data coming from a large number of WS using their API, that also reduces the coding effort required for data integration. Towards this direction, we brought forth the notion of the classical LAV mapping (with access patterns) to describe the WS API operations. Web service APIs are thus considered as the data sources, and viewed as relational sources with access patterns (to translate the presence of input and output parameters) [22]. "Translators" must be coded to present each API operation as a relational source with access pattern to ensure the translation between API and the global schema. Translators can be viewed as light-weight and declarative wrappers made operational by a single generic wrapper. For every domain (example: project management), a global schema is set up. Queries are then defined on the global schema to link with an API operations viewed as relational sources with access patterns. Records can be defined as queries on the global schema (records can be viewed as atomic performance indicators). Performance indicators can be defined as queries on the schema composed by record predicates.

As said before, we claim that our approach of using mediation as an ETL is interesting since mediation with LAV-approach is known to fit data integration problems when relational views are evolving, so fitting well with the scalability objective. Mediation is known to be a declarative process since it uses databases query languages like datalog and conjunctive queries which are declarative. Therefore it also fits our adaptability objective, since it allows to reduce the coding effort (e.g., defining a new performance indicator is simply an SQL query, adding a new operation implies to code the "translator" and then add a mapping) To compute a record, only a generic wrapper is needed (coded once for all). No need to code one wrapper for every new source.

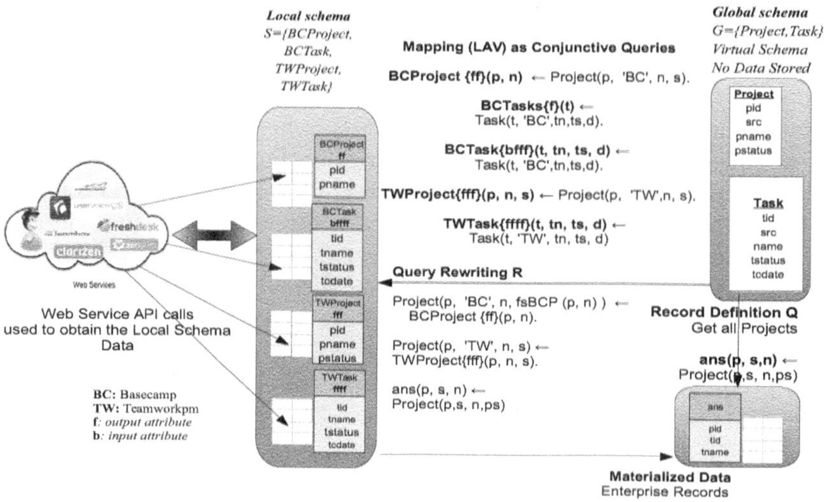

Fig. 1. Mediation approach using Local as View (LAV) Mapping

Example 1. Consider the domain *Project Management* that manages mainly two resources, Project and Task; hence two global schema relations:

$Project(pid, src, pname, pstatus)$ and $Task(tid, src, tname, tstatus, tcdate)$. and two WS: Basecamp[1] and Teamwork[2]. We consider here a simplified version of their API operations. Basecamp provides two operations related to task: the first operation provides all the task identifiers and the second requires the task identifier as input to give the complete task details. This information is captured by the access patterns. Consider LAV mapping $BCTask^{iooo}(t, tn, ts, td) \leftarrow Task(t, 'BC', tn, ts, td)$. It corresponds to the fact that the operation $BCTask$ takes as input the task identifier t and gives the details of the task (name, status and creation date. The operation has been mapped to the global schema relation $Task$ with source value as BC to signify Basecamp, its source. Now consider a

[1] http://www.basecamp.com

[2] http://www.teamworkpm.net

record definition q: *Get all Projects*, (a conjunctive query formulated over the global schema). $q(pid, src, pname) \leftarrow Project(pid, src, pname, pcdate, pstatus)$. The query rewriting generated by the inverse rules algorithm generates queries using the WS API operations that are then used for the actual calls. The mediation approach for this example is described in Fig. 1.

4 Research Methodology and Approach

Our research methodology relies on the implementation of our approach to data integration and warehousing in a prototype, that can then be validated and evaluated against the requirements expressed above. We built the first version of the data warehouse, DaWeS handling every essential aspect required to make use of the WS API to extract information. The basic underlying architecture of DaWeS is shown in Figure 2. The component *Enterprise Record Computation*, is responsible for computing the enterprise records. It takes as input the record definition (query formulated over the global schema relations) and makes use of the *answer builder* to execute the query. Answer builder consists of a (datalog) query engine, that executes the query plan obtained by rewriting the query according to the inverse rules algorithm [7, 8].

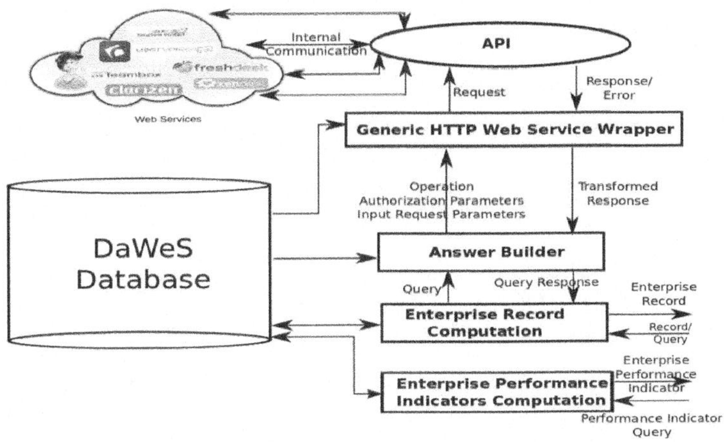

Fig. 2. DaWeS: Basic Architecture

We use the inverse rules algorithm given its capability to handle recursive datalog queries, handling access patterns in the source relations and to specify full and functional dependencies in the global schema relation (we used this capability to specify the primary keys). The *generic HTTP WS wrapper* is used to make the WS API operation calls and transform the response in a manner understood by the answer builder. The wrapper is generic since it can make any HTTP WS API operation call given the right URL, valid input and authentication parameters (in HTTP header and/or body). A response validator serves to validate the response before performing any transformation and to catch any unannounced (or unexpected) response schema changes. We also used cache with the wrapper in order to reduce the number of API operation calls so that any subsequent use of an operation call makes use of the cached response. On the completion of the datalog query evaluation, the query response is saved in the database to be later used by *Enterprise Performance Indicator Computation* component to compute interesting business measures.

During the course of the development of DaWeS, we identified various scientific locks. Reducing the number of expensive (bandwidth and cost perspective) API operation calls is important. The domain rules do not take into account any functional dependencies existing among the input attributes of an API operation. Suppose there is a functional dependency $t \rightarrow p$ between project identifiers p and task identifiers t, two input attributes for an API operation (e.g., in Figure 1, if $BCTasks$ is replaced by $BCTasks^{oo}(p, t)$ and $BCTask$ is replaced by $BCTask^{iiooo}(p, t, tn, ts, td)$. If there are 10 p and 20 t, the domain rules generated result in 200 (10×20) $BTask$ API calls (and not 20) because domain rule generate the following r.h.s $dom_p(p), dom_t(t), BCTask^{iiooo}(p, t, tn, ts, td)$, where $dom_p(p)$ and $dom_t(t)$ are the abstract domains corresponding to project identifier and task identifier respectively. Secondly, classical query rewriting algorithms [12] including inverse rules algorithm are shown not to be able to generate any rewritings for such queries. Thirdly, WS evolve and currently there are no standard mechanisms to track when an API (or an operation) is deprecated or changed. Fourthly, expecially considering the multi-domain WS environment, new global schema relations (especially when a domain of service has to be added) and LAV mappings updations occur regularly. Therefore contrary to the traditional warehouse settings, there is a dynamic evolution of the data sources, the warehouse schema, the queries formulated over the mediated schema and the performance indicators defined using these queries (for new domains).

5 Intermediate Results

DaWeS was tested with Intel(R) Pentium(R) Dual CPU @ 2.16GHz processor, system memory of 3GiB, Ubuntu 13.04 (32 bits) operating system, Oracle 11g (11.2.0.1.0) database and was developed and run using Java 1.7.0_25. We chose IRIS (Integrated Rule Inference System) [15] as the datalog engine to perform query evaluation. We configured IRIS to make use of the generic HTTP WS wrapper capable to make WS API operation calls to any web service.

We considered different domains and the associated WS APIs. For every WS API operation, we required the input and output parameters, the XSD [2] schema of the response and XSLT [16] to extract interesting information from the response. Various record definitions (mediated schema queries) were considered and the enterprise records (query responses) were stored in two tables.

We developed heuristics to deal with the scientific locks discussed before. First, in order to handle functional dependencies existing among two or more input attributes of a source relation, we implemented a static optimization heuristics by considering only valid input values (obtained from previous operations). Dynamic optimization [4] for this problem has been proposed recently. Secondly, a more recent paper [12] has shown the capability of inverse rules mechanism to handle incomplete information. We implemented this into DaWeS making use of the functional terms generated during inverse rules rewriting. Finally, we use a XML response validator to identify any unexpected API changes. We periodically compute certain records and compare the obtained response to the expected response (calibration). Response validator and calibration are our current semi-automatic error handling mechanisms to trigger a manual intervention on the event of WS evolution. DaWeS database employs two tables each for describing the mediated schema, the data sources, the mediated schema queries and the performance indicator queries, the enterprise records and performance indicator values. Advanced analytics queries like OLAP (used in conjunction with the star schema) under these settings is an open database research question.

6 Evaluation Plan

Our approach will be evaluated based on the requirements indicated previously, through measuring performance at different scales and the reduction in coding effort compared to other state of the art approach in data integration and ETL. We already performed various qualitative and quantitative experiments on DaWeS. We created 100 test organizations to simulate a multi enterprise environment. Following are the twelve different WS considered from three different domains; *Project management services*: Basecamp, Liquid Planner[3], Teamwork, Zoho Projects[4]. *email marketing services*: MailChimp[5], Campaign Monitor[6], iContact[7]. *support/ helpdesk services*: Zendesk[8], Desk[9], Zoho Support[10], Uservoice[11], FreshDesk[12]. We took into consideration 35 different operations of the 12 WS having the following characteristics: required no input arguments, required one or more input arguments or required paginated requests.

The queries formulated over the global schema consisted of a mix of (union of) conjunctive queries, and (recursive) datalog queries. We considered the following record definitions (queries), each computed on a *Daily* basis: New Projects(1), Active Projects (2), On-Hold Projects(3), On-Hold or Archived Projects(4), New Tasks(5), Open Tasks(6), Closed Tasks(7), Todo-Lists(8), Same Status Projects(9), New Forums(10), All Forums(11), New Topics(12), New Tickets(13),

[3] `http://www.liquidplanner.com`
[4] `http://www.zoho.com/projects`
[5] `http://www.mailchimp.com`
[6] `http://www.campaignmonitor.com`
[7] `http://www.icontact.com`
[8] `http://www.zendesk.com`
[9] `http://www.desk.com`
[10] `http://www.zoho.com/support`
[11] `http://www.uservoice.com`
[12] `http://www.freshdesk.com`

Open Tickets(14), Closed Tickets(15), New Campaigns(16) and Campaign Statistics(17). Twenty performance indicators were defined using SQL queries and record predicates. Example performance indicator queries include average resolution time of tickets during the last 30 days. An average (Mean) Time of *104.82 seconds* was taken to compute all the records of a single organization. Without incomplete data handling heuristics, many queries would have remained unanswered.

Figure 3 shows the time taken to compute the records using the WS API operations serially. The spikes point the situations when data is not available locally in the cache and the API operations have to be made. Use of cache and the proposed heuristics helped us to reduce the number of API operation calls, without which it takes too much time (many hours at least). Currently we are working on the precise semantics of the conjunctive query with access patterns in order to quantify (or predict) the number of API operation calls. This will help us to drive our heuristics to a complete algorithm.

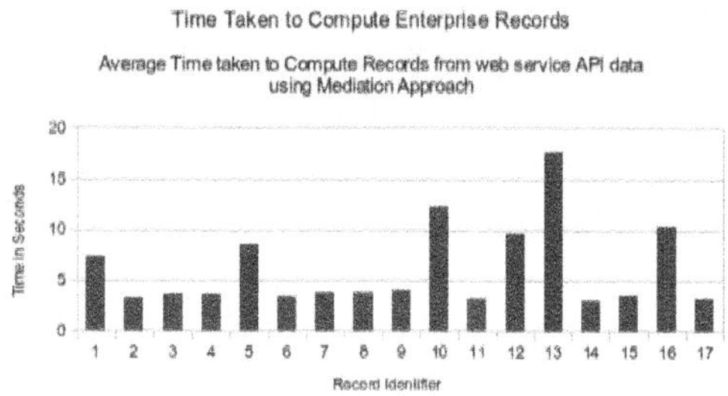

Fig. 3. DaWeS: Record Computation Time

7 Conclusion

Mediation as an ETL approach is very useful for building a WS fed data warehouse. Given its scalable and adaptable nature, it can be easily adapted by small and medium scale enterprises considering the minimum amount of coding effort while handling WS API. Inverse rules query rewriting used in conjunction with our proposed heuristics is useful to handle access patterns in the sources, data dependencies on the global schema, recursive datalog queries, incomplete information and optimize the number of expensive API operation calls.

DaWeS has been tested with real web services. Our further extensions include automatic error handling with an error ontology (e.g., to handle API changes, temporary API failures), adding more constraints in the form of TGDs to the global schema to get close to the kind of constraints used in the ontological query answering, but keeping recursive queries and defining the precise semantics of conjunctive queries with (or without) access patterns.

Given the interest of cloud computing within the industry, our current approach of storing the complete WS API enterprise data on just two big tables can be easily adapted to the cloud infrastructure. Also we want to design the system to avoid the complexity so that it may be more widely adopted than SAWSDL or other such standards.

Acknowledgement. I thank the Conseil General of the Region of Auvergne (France) and FEDER for funding our research project. I also thank Christophe Rey and Farouk Toumani of LIMOS, Blaise Pascal University, Franck Martin and Lionel Peyron of Rootsystem for their guidance and feedback for DaWeS.

References

[1] Benslimane, D., Dustdar, S., Sheth, A.P.: Services mashups: The new generation of web applications. IEEE Internet Computing 12(5), 13–15 (2008)

[2] Bray, T., Paoli, J., Sperberg-McQueen, C.M., Maler, E., Yergeau, F.: Extensible markup language (xml). World Wide Web Journal 2(4), 27–66 (1997)

[3] Calì, A., Calvanese, D., Lenzerini, M.: Data integration under integrity constraints. In: Seminal Contributions to Information Systems Engineering, pp. 335–352. Springer (2013)

[4] Calì, A., Calvanese, D., Martinenghi, D.: Dynamic query optimization under access limitations and dependencies. J. UCS 15(1), 33–62 (2009)

[5] Chawathe, S., Garcia-Molina, H., Hammer, J., Ireland, K., Papakonstantinou, Y., Ullman, J., Widom, J.: The tsimmis project: Integration of heterogeneous information sources. In: Proceedings of IPSJ Conference, pp. 7–18 (1994)

[6] Coalition, D., Ankolekar, A., Burstein, M., Hobbs, J.R., Lassila, O., Martin, D., Mcdermott, D., Narayanan, S., Mcilraith, S.A., Paolucci, M., Payne, T., Sycara, K.: Daml-s: Web service description for the semantic web (2002)

[7] Duschka, O.M., Genesereth, M.R.: Answering recursive queries using views. In: PODS, pp. 109–116 (1997)

[8] Duschka, O.M., Genesereth, M.R., Levy, A.Y.: Recursive query plans for data integration. J. Log. Program. 43(1), 49–73 (2000)

[9] Dustdar, S., Schreiner, W.: A survey on web services composition. International Journal on Web and Grid Services 1(1), 1–30 (2005)

[10] Friedman, M., Levy, A.Y., Millstein, T.D.: Navigational plans for data integration. In: AAAI/IAAI, pp. 67–73. AAAI Press / The MIT Press (1999)

[11] Gottlob, G., Schwentick, T.: Rewriting ontological queries into small nonrecursive datalog programs. In: KR. AAAI Press (2012)

[12] Grahne, G., Kiricenko, V.: Towards an algebraic theory of information integration. Inf. Comput. 194(2), 79–100 (2004)

[13] Group, S.W.: Semantic annotations for wsdl, w3c working draft. The World Wide Web Consortium, W3C (2006)

[14] Hansen, M., Madnick, S.E., Siegel, M.: Data integration using web services. In: DIWeb, pp. 3–16. University of Toronto Press (2002)

[15] IRIS: Integrated Rule Inference System - API and User Guide (2008), `http://www.iris-reasoner.org/pages/user_guide.pdf`

[16] Kay, M.: Xsl transformations (xslt) version 2.0. W3C Recommendation 23 (2007)

[17] Kopecký, J., Gomadam, K., Vitvar, T.: hrests: An html microformat for describing restful web services. In: WI-IAT 2008. IEEE Computer Society Press (2008)

[18] Martin, D., Burstein, M., Hobbs, J., Lassila, O., McDermott, D., McIlraith, S., Narayanan, S., Paolucci, M., Parsia, B., Payne, T.: Owl-s: Semantic markup for web services. W3C Member Submission 22, 2007–4 (2004)

[19] Noy, N.F.: Semantic integration: A survey of ontology-based approaches. SIGMOD Record 33 2004 (2004)

[20] Roth, M.T., Schwarz, P.M.: Don't scrap it, wrap it! a wrapper architecture for legacy data sources. In: VLDB 1997, pp. 266–275 (1997)
[21] Truong, H.L., Dustdar, S.: On analyzing and specifying concerns for data as a service. In: Kirchberg, M., Hung, P.C.K., Carminati, B., Chi, C.H., Kanagasabai, R., Valle, E.D., Lan, K.C., Chen, L.J. (eds.) APSCC, pp. 87–94. IEEE (2009)
[22] Ullman, J.D.: Information integration using logical views. Theor. Comput. Sci. 239(2), 189–210 (2000)
[23] Vassiliadis, P., Simitsis, A.: Extraction, transformation, and loading. In: Encyclopedia of Database Systems, pp. 1095–1101. Springer (2009)
[24] W3C: Web Service Description Language 1.1 (2001), `http://www.w3.org/TR/wsdl`
[25] Wiederhold, G.: Mediators in the architecture of future information systems. Computer 25(3), 38–49 (1992)
[26] Zhu, F., Turner, M., Kotsiopoulos, I.A., Bennett, K.H., Russell, M., Budgen, D., Brereton, P., Keane, J.A., Layzell, P.J., Rigby, M., Xu, J.: Dynamic data integration using web services. In: ICWS. IEEE Computer Society (2004)

Designing an Integrated Semantic Framework for Structured Opinion Summarization

Ehsan Asgarian and Mohsen Kahani

Ferdowsi University of Mashhad, Mashhad, Iran
ehsan.asgarian@stu-mail.um.ac.ir

Abstract. Knowing about people's opinions and viewpoints plays an essential role in decision-making processes involving regular customers to executive managers. Therefore, in the past decade, with the advent of Web 2.0, a new orientation of natural language processing science called opinion mining has been emerged. The main problem of exploring feature-level opinions is the complexity of feature extraction and its relations with the words containing the sentiment within unstructured texts, which reduces the accuracy of opinion mining. The purpose of the structured opinion summarization is to demonstrate the mentioned features in the reviews and express the sentiment value of users for each feature, quantitatively. The main idea of this research is to consider the semantic (knowledge) to analyze the sentiment in the review by developing the opinion ontology. Therefore, a semantic framework as an integrated method is proposed in all stages of feature-based opinion summarization.

Keywords: #eswcphd2014Asgarian, Semantic Framework, Opinion Ontology, Sentiment Analysis, feature based opinion summarization.

1 Introduction

One of the newest areas of research on natural language processing, information retrieval and text mining is opinion mining. In general, contextual information can be divided into two sets of facts (explicit information) and opinions (sentiments or implicit information). The primary aim of opinion mining is to extract, classify and summarize people's viewpoints and opinions on various features of an entity or a specific event among valid resources. Most of the work done so far in the field of opinion mining has been on the market and commercial products from the viewpoints of costumers (to select and purchase goods) or distributors (to improve business, competition in the market, effective advertising placement, benchmarking and the recognition of users' tastes and interests). Furthermore, there are applications in medical fields, social science, management and politics. Work on this research area is rapidly growing and new applications of opinion mining in different areas for optimal interactions and decision-making issues of managers or users can be defined.

In general, a sentiment analysis can be classified into three levels including the document level (review), the sentence level (semantic phrases) and feature (aspect)-based level; the feature-based level has been recently taken into consideration by

V. Presutti et al. (Eds.): ESWC 2014, LNCS 8465, pp. 885–894, 2014.

many researchers. Initial studies on opinion mining frequently attempted to classify the opinions or overall sentiments of a document into positive or negative feedbacks [1]. Afterwards, researchers tried to determine the satisfaction or dissatisfaction degree of the document (instead of a two-state classification) [2]. Often supervised methods, in which sample labels are manually marked, were used for these categories in commercial product fields where reviews are directly expressed. The main problem at this level is the assumption that the topic is the same for the entire gathered text or documents. However, different parts of a document (different reviews) may deal with various issues.

Thus, it is vital to identify the topics of different sections and study them separately before analyzing the sentiment. Therefore, opinion mining researchers continuously conducted their work on analyzing the sentiment at sentence level [3] or semantic phrase level [4]. Subjectivity analysis is generally applied to distinguish between subjective sentences and objective ones (e.g. facts such as news) at this level. In recent years most conducted researches in this field have been aimed at non-English languages [5-7]. The major problem of opinion mining at sentence level is due to the assumption that writer's opinion is the same in the entire document. In other words, there can be various opinions (more than one sentiment) on different features (topics) in a sentence. Moreover, in many cases entities (concepts) and their features are not well defined or separated by analyzing the sentiment at sentence level.

Thus, a feature-based approach to opinion mining was proposed owing to existing problems for analyzing the sentiment at document and sentence level [8, 9]. In this approach, entities (topics) and their expressed features are firstly extracted from the text and then the expressed opinions are analyzed for each feature. For example, consider this sentence "Nokia has a good call quality but it is rather expensive!"; Remarks about Nokia cell phone entity (the target) and the call quality and price features are positive and negative respectively.

Compared to simple text summarizers, structured summarization of opinions has been formed according to feature based sentiment analysis, in which useful and relevant information will be available to users. In other words, the purpose of the structured opinion summarization is to demonstrate the mentioned features in the reviews and express the sentiment value of users for each feature quantitatively. The main problem of exploring feature-level opinions is the complexities of feature extraction and their relations with the words containing the sentiment within unstructured texts, which reduces the accuracy of the opinion mining. The following figure shows an example of a summary generator based on opinion features.

In this research, a semantic framework is designed for structured summarization (based on features) of opinions. In the main phase of the proposed framework, we develop the opinion ontology for reviews by receiving opinions within various domains with different languages and, therefore, it can be used for the bulk of reviews. In other words, we can extract features of the text, analyze the sentiment, integrate and summarize opinions by the developed ontology. Using the framework of the proposed ontology, the output results of the structured summarization will be presented as semantic data (e.g. RDF).

2 State of the Art

In general, a feature-based opinions summarization comprises three main steps, extracting the features, sentiment analysis and the integration or summarization of them.

In the information retrieval area, many methods for extracting concepts and relations between them within the documents have been proposed. However, the purpose of these methods is to identify the main subject of the document and detect the words describing this subject. The relations between subjects are also identified based on their common words and by using various methods of determining the string similarity.

Different methods used to extract features in the review can be divided into five categories: 1) frequent nouns and noun phrases 2) based on relations between the feature and the opinion 3) supervised learning methods 4) topic modeling techniques and 5) hybrid methods. Most initial researches into extracting features from the document were based on nouns and relations between a feature and a sentiment expressions.

The second phase of opinions summarization aims to detect and rank the sentiment regarding each of detected features. Thus, two different approaches are employed: 1) supervised learning approaches 2) Sentiment-lexicon-based approaches.

After extracting the features and determining the sentiment of reviews, obtained results of two previous steps are combined so as to produce a summary of opinions about various features. Hence, similar features in synonymous groups should be merged together and their correspondent sentiments should be averaged. Finally, results in a structured way (quantifying the sentiment for each feature) or selection of positive and negative sentences about each feature in order of preference (time, intensity and …) are displayed.

Semantic approaches have been recently favored by the researchers of the field. This paper focuses on opinion mining methods, exclusively. A new area of semantic techniques for opinion mining with the aim of extracting the features of the main

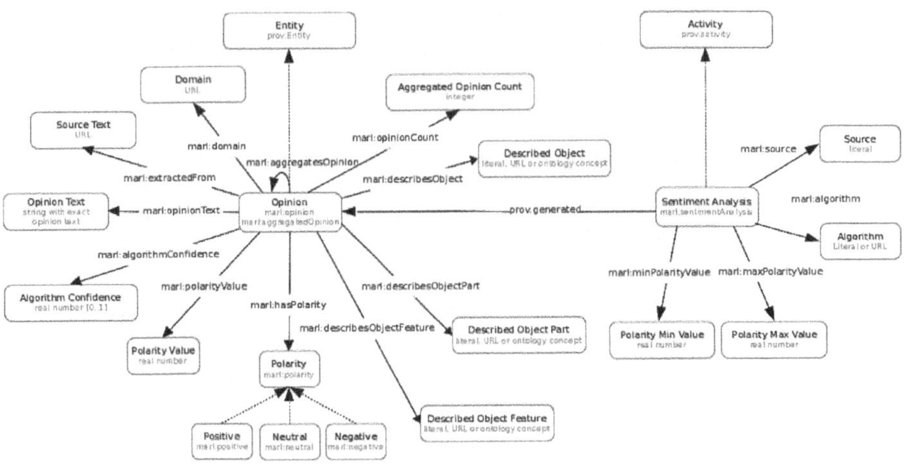

Fig. 1. Class and Properties Diagram for the Marl Ontology v1.0

entity in a hierarchical structure and determining the sentiment expressed for each feature has been recently created. However, most of these methods apply the ontology of a particular commercial product which has been manually developed by an expert so as to use the semantic in opinion mining. Generally, none of the previous studies has been worked on converting the reviews into semantic data.

The most significant part of semantic based opinion mining is to create the ontology for a group of opinions. The opinion ontology should extract features, sentiment expressions and the relations between them by receiving the basic and limited knowledge from an expert (the primary list of the sentiment words and the structural taxonomy of features within a desired domain) and applying an automatic method.

2.1 First Phase: Ontology Schema Design

To develop the opinion ontology, the first step is to design a conceptual model or ontology schema of opinions. In fact, ontology schema gives us a logical structure to keep the main entity (main subject) along with its aspects and relevant features.

In [10], a comprehensive model for keeping opinions was proposed as a quintuple (o_j, f_{jk}, so_{ijkl}, h_i, t_l). Where o_j is an object or a main entity (a target object), f_{jk} is a feature of the object, so_{ijkl} is the sentiment value, h_i is the opinion holder and t_l is the time at which the opinion is given. This definition provides a framework to transform unstructured text to structured data. The quintuple above is basically a database schema, based on which the extracted opinions can be put into a database table [11]. Accordingly, semantic data formats have been proposed to keep opinions and the sentiment value of them [12]. Figure 1 shows Marl ontology schema v1.0. However, it is not possible to express comparative opinions or conditional statements in these models. Moreover, features such as date and time (in Marl ontology), trust and data integrity have not been taken into consideration.

In Opinion-ML, a new structure based on XML Schema has been recently proposed according to the developed Emotion-ML model [13]. The main problems of this method are lack of possibility for expressing constraint of parameters, capability to express relationships between opinions and support for comparative opinions.

2.2 The Second Phase: Development of Opinion Ontology

Studies have been recently conducted into the usage of domain ontology or product ontology in opinion mining [14, 15]. However in all of them, it is assumed that this ontology is manually given to the system by an expert. In [16], a semi-automated method for developing the ontology of opinions called FDSOT for a specific product has been presented. Nevertheless, in fact, the FDSOT ontology is a bipartite graph which is simply composed of features and opinions on each one. In order to construct fuzzy domain ontology tree, features are initially identified and the hierarchy of features based on the lexical similarity and the user's knowledge are determined afterwards. However, this ontology depends on the domain, without logical schema and entirely useless for more complicated domains.

In a similar methodology in FCA (Formal Concept Analysis) system [17], some messages are reviewed by the expert and a feature/sentiment expression cross-table is executed manually. Then the ontology of word relations is semi-automatically developed by the OntoGen tool. It has some problems as follows: not using the ontology schema, limited to brief reviews on a specific domain, not considering the relations between sentiment expressions and limited to extracting one type of relation (Sub-Concept-Of).

2.3 Third Phase: Converting Reviews to the Semantic Format Using the Opinion Ontology

Various methods for using the pre-built ontology of products to extract features and their sentiment expressions have been proposed [14, 15]. However, most knowledge-based opinion mining methods use the ontology of opinions created by an expert in very few domains. Then they attempt to expand the input ontology and adapt the words within the ontology to the reviews in order to extract features and their sentiment expressions. Moreover, there is no framework of the ontology for mapping the concepts of the opinions and relation between them which is another problem of the current methods. Figure 2 shows an example of the ontology of digital camera for use in opinion mining.

Moreover, a framework for detecting a sentiment was presented using the predefined ontology of products by an expert in [18]. In Kontopoulos's article [17], a method for extracting features of various entities in twitter messages has been presented in terms of ontology, which is used to determine the interest or trends according to features of various products and rank them.

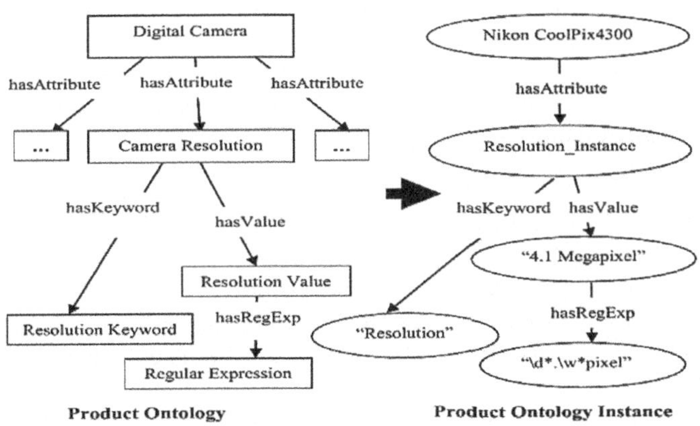

Fig. 2. Product ontology used in [15] which was created manually

3 Problem Statement and Contributions

The current feature-based opinion mining methods purely use statistical methods, machine learning technologies or syntactic relations of components for a sentence to automatically extract features and the sentiment expressions. Hence, they have many weaknesses in dealing with linguistic and conceptual complexities to identify the sentiment of opinions. Thus, considering the existing complexities of identifying the entity (the main subject), extracting the features and detecting the sentiment associated with each feature, it is vital to employ semantic methods. Employing a knowledge-based opinion mining method helps to determine various features, the relationship between them and the main entity as well as the expressed sentiment for each feature in complex domains.

Thus, in this research, a semantic framework is proposed to be applied in an integrated method in all stages of opinion summarization. The purpose of this semantic framework is to convert the bulk of opinions into the RDF format (semantic structured information) using the opinion ontology at the reasonable time and applicable to various languages and domains. However, we need to have the full knowledge of various semantic domains so as to develop a general opinion ontology, which is virtually unattainable. Thus, a semi-automatic method is presented to create the opinion ontology in a specific semantic domain. Hence, a conceptual model or ontology schema of opinions is designed to keep opinions in a structured form. Next, given the complexities of natural language to express the sentiment, the target language is determined and the opinion ontology is formed using the opinion documents on a specific domain. Then we can use it to extract features of opinions and detect sentiment expressions for each feature.

Considering the fact that there are a lot of different features, applying this ontology rather than non-semantic approaches results in accuracy improvement and time complexity reduction to extract features and recognize general or feature-specific sentiment expressions in reviews. As a further matter, it is possible to calculate semantic similarities of different features of an entity by the help of various perfectly defined relations in the ontology. As a result, synonymous features are categorized and their correspondent sentiment quantities are combined together. Sentiment quantity is calculated using quantification of sentiment expressions describing features in reviews. Moreover, taxonomic relations defined in the ontology help us determine sentiment quantity used in general and specific features, more accurately.

4 Proposed Approach

As mentioned earlier, the main objective of our research is to propose a semantic framework for using it in the all steps of feature-based opinion summarization. For this end, the opinion ontology is made using a semi-automated method and applying it on domain specific reviews corpus to analyze the sentiment in the new reviews. Therefore, a semantic framework as an integrated method is proposed in all stages of feature-based opinion summarization .

The aim of the proposed framework is to convert the bulk of unstructured reviews into the structured semantic data format in the scalable time as well as being applicable to various languages and domains. Therefore, due to the complexities of the feature-based opinion summarization, in this research, semantic methods are employed to identify the entity (main subject), extract features, detect the sentiment associated with each feature and finally show the relationships and visualize the results. Using a knowledge-based approach helps to determine various features, the relation between them and the main entity as well as the expressed sentiment for each feature in complex domains.

Before developing the opinion ontology, a conceptual model (ontology schema) of opinions independent of the language and the domain is proposed to keep them in the structured format. Next, given the complexities of natural language to express the sentiment, we select the target language and the opinion ontology is formed using the basic knowledge of the user and the domain-specific corpus of reviews. The most significant part of this research is to present an (semi)automatic method for creating the opinion ontology. The quality of obtained ontology plays an important role in accuracy of the proposed structured opinion summarization. The creation of the ontology is completed through three steps in an iterative and incremental process: 1) Extraction of features 2) Sentiment expressions detection 3) Grouping the synonymous features and the determination of the relations between features and the sentiment expressions, with an expert's feedback in an iterative process. By repeating these steps, we can make use of the obtained features and the sentiment expressions from previous iteration, for extracting new ones in the next process. In the meanwhile, the usage of an expert's knowledge (feedback) for the verification of obtained features and the sentiment expressions in each repeat prevents error propagation and improves accuracy. In order to extract the features, an iterative approach is suggested to combine the existing methods and their improved versions.

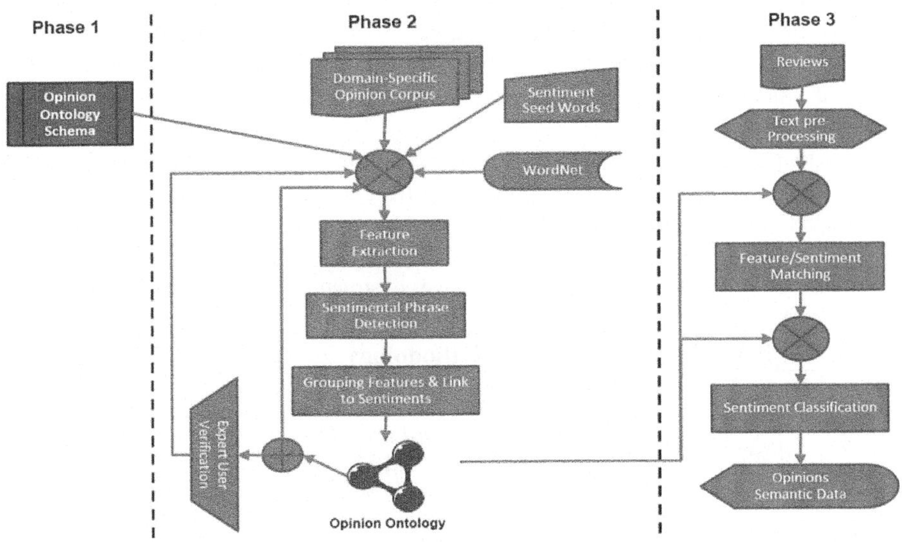

Fig. 3. Proposed semantic framework for the structured opinion mining

Then the ontology of opinions developed in the previous step will be used to detect the features and various opinions on the desired domain. Using the ontology of opinions, detected features with their sentimental expressions are classified and will be expressed in the form of semantic data (e.g. RDF format). Finally, analysis of the semantic data required to identify the sentiment of the conflicting opinions and essential inferences from comparative ones is conducted. Figure 3 shows proposed semantic framework for the structured opinion mining.

5 Evaluation Strategy

The purpose of this study is to present a semantic framework for the feature-based opinion mining. To assess the accuracy of the proposed method for opinion mining, a labeled test set should be used. However, feature labels and the sentiment values of opinions in an actual data set are not determined and these labels must be prepared by an expert In some commercial data sets the overall rating given to a product by the opinion holder (1 to 5 stars) is used as the sentiment (satisfaction) value of the whole document. In similar methodologies, two methods for measuring the accuracy of the extracted features and estimating error rate of the sentiment of each feature are employed to assess the feature-based opinion mining methods. In order to determine the accuracy of extracted features, a mapping between groups of real features and detected ones based on similarity of words of each feature set (synonyms) is established. Then metrics including the precision, recall and F1-measure are used. Moreover, in order to calculate the accuracy of the predicted sentiment value for each feature, the mean absolute error (MAE) or the mean square error (MSE) measures are used. In some papers [19, 20], the ranking loss measure is used to calculate the accuracy of the sentiment of each feature of various products. This measure demonstrates the average distance between the predicted sentiment and the main sentiment value (assigned by an expert) for each feature which is equivalent to the mean absolute error.

Given that there is no structured semantic opinion summarization system, features and challenges of comparing systems in different stages and phases have been summarized in the following table:

Table 1. Comparing systems in various stages of structured opinion summarization

Phase	Methodology	Domain
(Phase I) Ontology schema design	*Opinion Model*[10]	Domain-independent
	Marl Ontology[12]	Domain-independent
	Opinion-ML[13]	Domain-independent
(Phase II) Creating the opinion ontology	*FCA*[17]	A cell phone on twitter
	FDSOT[16]	Laptop (in Chinese)
(Phase III) Ontology-based approach for opinion mining	*OSPM*[18]	IMDB movies
	Somprasertsri's Method[15]	Cameras
	Mart'Inez's Method[14]	IMDB movies

6 Expected Results

An important outcome of this research is to provide a semantic framework for employing the semantic methods integrated in all stages of opinion summarization. Therefore, using the semantic framework, it is possible to transform the bulk of opinion documents into structured semantic data at reasonable time. Moreover, methods for conducting an analysis of the comparative and conditional opinions, drawing inference about them and combining the conflicting opinions (expressions containing the opposite sentiment) will be presented.

Another advantage of using opinion ontology is to develop relations between concepts and features of opinions and the concepts of other ontology and linked data on the Web. Furthermore, we can use visual tools of the current ontology such as protégé [21], OntoGen [22] and RDF Gravity [23] to express and demonstrate the structured summary of opinions. Thus, in order to convert the opinion documents into semantic data, we can present various categories based on the sentiment (such as the positive and negative points of the entity) or feature (monitoring the opinions on a specific feature) to the user. It is also possible to search and draw better inferences on semantic data in opinions. The ontology schema has to be designed independently of the domain and language, so that it can be used within the various domains of reviews.

References

1. Pang, B., Lee, L., Vaithyanathan, S.: Thumbs up?: sentiment classification using machine learning techniques. In: Proceedings of the ACL-02 conference on Empirical Methods in Natural Language Processing, vol. 10, pp. 79–86. Association for Computational Linguistics (2002)
2. Pang, B., Lee, L.: Seeing stars: Exploiting class relationships for sentiment categorization with respect to rating scales. In: Proceedings of the 43rd Annual Meeting on Association for Computational Linguistics, pp. 115–124. Association for Computational Linguistics (2005)
3. Riloff, E., Wiebe, J.: Learning extraction patterns for subjective expressions. In: Proceedings of the 2003 Conference on Empirical Methods in Natural Language Processing, pp. 105–112. Association for Computational Linguistics (2003)
4. Kim, S.-M., Hovy, E.: Extracting opinions, opinion holders, and topics expressed in online news media text. In: Proceedings of the Workshop on Sentiment and Subjectivity in Text, pp. 1–8. Association for Computational Linguistics (2006)
5. Alm, C.O.: Subjective natural language problems: motivations, applications, characterizations, and implications. In: Proceedings of the 49th Annual Meeting of the Association for Computational Linguistics: Human Language Technologies: short papers-, vol. 2, pp. 107–112. Association for Computational Linguistics (2011)
6. Abdul-Mageed, M., Diab, M., Korayem, M.: Subjectivity and sentiment analysis of modern standard Arabic. In: Proceedings of the 49th Annual Meeting of the Association for Computational Linguistics: Human Language Technologies, vol. 2, pp. 587–591 (2011)

7. Barbosa, L., Feng, J.: Robust sentiment detection on twitter from biased and noisy data. In: Proceedings of the 23rd International Conference on Computational Linguistics: Posters, pp. 36–44. Association for Computational Linguistics (2010)
8. Lu, B., Ott, M., Cardie, C., Tsou, B.K.: Multi-aspect sentiment analysis with topic models. In: 2011 IEEE 11th International Conference on Data Mining Workshops (ICDMW), pp. 81–88. IEEE (2011)
9. Hu, M., Liu, B.: Mining and summarizing customer reviews. In: Proceedings of the Tenth ACM SIGKDD International Conference on Knowledge Discovery and Data Mining, pp. 168–177. ACM (2004)
10. Liu, B.: Sentiment analysis and subjectivity. Handbook of Natural Language Processing 2, 568 (2010)
11. Liu, B.: Sentiment analysis and opinion mining. Synthesis Lectures on Human Language Technologies 5, 1–167 (2012)
12. Westerski, A., Iglesias Fernandez, C.A., Tapia Rico, F.: Linked opinions: Describing sentiments on the structured web of data. In: 4th International Workshop Social Data on the Web, pp. 10–21. CEUR (2011)
13. Robaldo, L., Di Caro, L.: OpinionMining-ML. Computer Standards & Interfaces 35, 454–469 (2013)
14. Peñalver-Martínez, I., Valencia-García, R., García-Sánchez, F.: Ontology-guided approach to feature-based opinion mining. In: Muñoz, R., Montoyo, A., Métais, E. (eds.) NLDB 2011. LNCS, vol. 6716, pp. 193–200. Springer, Heidelberg (2011)
15. Somprasertsri, G., Lalitrojwong, P.: Mining Feature-Opinion in Online Customer Reviews for Opinion Summarization. Journal of Universal Computer Science 16, 938–955 (2010)
16. Liu, L., Nie, X., Wang, H.: Toward a fuzzy domain sentiment ontology tree for sentiment analysis. In: 2012 5th International Congress on Image and Signal Processing (CISP), pp. 1620–1624. IEEE (2012)
17. Kontopoulos, E., Berberidis, C., Dergiades, T., Bassiliades, N.: Ontology-based sentiment analysis of twitter posts. Expert Systems with Applications 40, 4065–4074 (2013)
18. Zhou, L., Chaovalit, P.: Ontology supported polarity mining. Journal of the American Society for Information Science and technology 59, 98–110 (2008)
19. Lu, Y., Zhai, C., Sundaresan, N.: Rated aspect summarization of short comments. In: Proceedings of the 18th International Conference on World Wide Web, pp. 131–140. ACM (2009)
20. Titov, I., McDonald, R.: Modeling online reviews with multi-grain topic models. In: Proceedings of the 17th International Conference on World Wide Web, pp. 111–120. ACM (2008)
21. Noy, N.F., Sintek, M., Decker, S., Crubézy, M., Fergerson, R.W., Musen, M.A.: Creating semantic web contents with protege-2000. Intelligent Systems, IEEE 16, 60–71 (2001)
22. Fortuna, B., Grobelnik, M., Mladenic, D.: OntoGen: Semi-automatic ontology editor. In: Smith, M.J., Salvendy, G. (eds.) HCII 2007. LNCS, vol. 4558, pp. 309–318. Springer, Heidelberg (2007)
23. Goyal, S., Westenthaler, R.: Rdf gravity (rdf graph visualization tool). Salzburg Research, Austria (2004)

Erratum: Trusty URIs: Verifiable, Immutable, and Permanent Digital Artifacts for Linked Data

Tobias Kuhn[1] and Michel Dumontier[2]

[1] Department of Humanities, Social and Political Sciences, ETH Zurich, Switzerland
[2] Stanford Center for Biomedical Informatics Research, Stanford University, USA
tokuhn@ethz.ch, michel.dumontier@stanford.edu

V. Presutti et al. (Eds.): ESWC 2014, LNCS 8465, pp. 395–410, 2014.

DOI 10.1007/978-3-319-07443-6_63

The paper starting on page 395 of this volume contains two incorrect sentences. The incorrect sentences, which start on line 14 of Sect. 6.2, read as follows: "The average values are always below 0.2 seconds. Using Java in batch mode even requires only 0.1ms per file."

They should read as follows: "All average values are below 0.8s (0.03s for batch mode). Using Java in batch mode even requires only 1ms per file."

The original online version for this chapter can be found at
http://dx.doi.org/10.1007/978-3-319-07443-6_27

Author Index

The manufacturer's authorised representative in the EU is Springer Nature Customer Service Centre GmbH, Europaplatz 3, 69115 Heidelberg, Germany. If you have any concerns regarding our products, please contact ProductSafety@springernature.com

Printed and bound by CPI Group (UK) Ltd, Croydon, CR0 4YY

31/07/2026

02182821-0015